GUIDE
TO
GREAT
PLAYS

Joseph T. Shipley

Public Affairs Press, Washington, D.C.

PUBLISHER'S NOTE

With some possible exceptions the plays dealt with in this book are generally acknowledged to be the greatest ever written. For one reason or another virtually all have been considered classics of the drama by master critics and theatergoers of the past and present.

Some readers may feel that this or that play should have been excluded or included, but none can doubt that the theater would be exceedingly dismal if these plays did not exist. A few are perhaps period pieces and some may yet fall by the wayside, but most have truly enduring qualities. This is why so many of them continue to be performed today—long after they were first written.

It is pertinent to note that although this work was prepared without regard to television its possible usefulness has increased considerably in that this new medium of entertainment is now bringing into the homes of millions of people great plays which have in the past been seen by relatively few. In effect this book provides the televiewer with background notes which will, it is hoped, enhance his appreciation and enjoyment of the drama.

M. B. SCHNAPPER, *Editor*

Public Affairs Press,
Washington, D. C.

Copyright, 1956, by Joseph T. Shipley
and Public Affairs Press

Published by the Public Affairs Press
2162 Florida Avenue, Washington 8, D. C.

Printed in the United States of America
Library of Congress Catalog Card No. 56-6595

PREFATORY NOTES

What is a great play? No matter what the definition, there will be as many different lists as compilers. My choice has been based on the thought that a play should provide entertainment, enlightenment, exaltation. Without the first, the theatre would not exist; without the last, the theatre would not survive. The greatest plays give generous measure of all three; but if a play gives large measure of any one, I have deemed it a candidate for inclusion.

Some dramas aim only at emotional arousal; this, I suppose, is one aspect of entertainment. A few dramas call for inclusion because of their historical significance in the theatre. More than four times as many plays were considered as it has been possible to include; some two hundred were put aside with reluctance; and more than eighty articles were fully written that had ultimately to be withheld from the volume. Sometimes one play, among others of equal note, was chosen to be representative of a type. Some plays, as of Seneca, of Racine and Corneille, are discussed with a classical forerunner.

For each play chosen, information on the following is provided:

(1) Name of author, his country, dates, etc.

(2) A brief synopsis.

(3) Important aspects of the play's history—the first performance, when known, and other notable productions.

(4) Analysis of significant aspects of the play.

(5) Opinions of critics and reviewers.

(6) Prominent players that have acted in the play.

ACKNOWLEDGMENTS

The author's gratitude must reach out to many more than he can name in these pages. Particular acknowledgment of indebtedness must include thanks to Whittlesey House for quotations from *The Universe of G.B.S.*, by William Irvine; to George G. Harrap and Company, Ltd., for comments of Allardyce Nicoll in *Readings from British Drama*; to Harcourt, Brace & Company from *The History of Italian Literature*, by Francesco de Sanctis. For the wide range of Shakespeare's dramas, a library might be filled. The environing matter has been gathered in *The Backgrounds of Shakespeare's Plays*, by Karl J. Holzknecht, published in 1950 by the American Book Company, and the heart of the plays illuminated in *The Meaning of Shakespeare*, by Harold C. Goddard, published in 1951 by the University of Chicago Press — to whom thanks for permission to quote. Thanks also to *The Times*, London, and to Harold Hobson, for reviews from England; to my colleagues of the New York City drama pages, listed hereinafter with their papers.

In the preparation of this book the resources of various libraries have been helpful; especially of the Theatre Collection of the New York Public Library. My thanks go to its staff: to director George Freedley; Elizabeth P. Barrett; Paul Myers; William H. Matthews; and to Edith Foster, who for a sweltering summer yielded me her desk in a cool niche above Bryant Park.

Beyond and above all these, my thanks reach out to one without whom this book would not have being, whose alert mind and discriminant taste have companioned and guided me throughout: *inquietam est cor meum, donec requiescat in te.*

NEW YORK DRAMA REVIEWERS

Since quotations from New York reviews are sometimes identified only by the name of the reviewer, their papers are listed below. When no date of publication is mentioned, it may be assumed that the quotation is from the first issue after the premiere of the production under discussion. The dagger symbol (†) signifies that the reviewer is a member of the New York Drama Critics Circle.

Allen, Kelcey (Eugene Kuttner): Women's Wear, 1915-1951.

Anderson, John: Post, 1924-1928; Evening Journal, 1928 - 1937; Journal-American, 1937-1943.

Atkinson, (J.) Brooks†: Times, 1926-1942; 1946-.

Barnes, Howard†: Herald - Tribune, 1942-1951.

Benchley, Robert: Life, 1920-1929; New Yorker, 1929-1940.

Bolton, Whitney†: Telegraph, 1935-1940; 1949-.

Broun, Heywood: Tribune, 1912-1921; World, 1921-1928; Telegram, 1928-1931.

Brown, John Mason†: Post, 1929-1941; World - Telegram, 1941 - 1942; Saturday Review, 1945 -.

Chapman, John†: News, 1943-.

Colby, Ethel†: Journal of Commerce, 1939-.

Coleman, Robert†: Mirror, 1946-.

Cooke, Richard†: Wall Street Journal, 1946-.

Corbin, John: Times, 1902; Sun, 1905-1907; Times, 1917-1919.

Dale, Alan (Alfred J. Cohen): Evening World, 1887 - 1895; Evening Journal, 1895 - 1915; American, 1915-1928.

Darnton, Charles: Evening World, 1902-1931.

Dash, Thomas R.†: News Record, 1935-; Women's Wear, 1950-.

Freedley, George†: Telegraph, 1940-1949.

Gabriel, Gilbert W.: Telegram, 1924 - 1925; Sun, 1925 - 1929; American, 1929 - 1937; Theatre Arts, 1947-1949; Cue, 1948-1952.

Garland, Robert: World-Telegram, 1928 - 1937; Journal-American, 1943-1952.

Gassner, John[†]: New Theatre, 1936-1937; Forum, 1937-1952.

Gibbs, Wolcott[†]: New Yorker, 1939-.

Hammond, Percy: Tribune, 1920-1922; Herald - Tribune, 1922 - 1937.

Hawkins, William[†]: World - Telegram, 1946-.

Hewes, Henry[†]: Saturday Review, 1952-.

Keating, John[†]: Cue, 1952-.

Kerr, Walter[†]: Herald - Tribune, 1951-.

Kronenberger, Louis[†]: P.M., 1940-1949; Time, 1939-.

Littell, Robert: Post, 1927 - 1929; World, 1929-1931.

Lockridge, Richard: Sun, 1928 - 1943.

McClain, John[†]: Journal - American, 1952-.

Macgowan, Kenneth: Globe, 1919-1923; Theatre Arts, 1919-1925.

Mantle, Burns: Mail, 1910 - 1922; News, 1922-1943.

Morehouse, Ward[†]: Sun, 1943 - 1952; World - Telegram, 1952 - 1954.

Nathan, George Jean[†]: Smart Set, 1908-1923; Vanity Fair, 1930-

1933; American Mercury, 1923-1932; Journal-American, 1943-. (Quoted, with permission, from *The Theatre Book of the Year*, published by Alfred A. Knopf, 1942-1950; 1953.)

Nichols, Lewis: Times, 1942-1946.

Pollock, Arthur[†] Brooklyn Eagle, 1942-1947; Compass, 1949-1952.

Rascoe, Burton: World-Telegram, 1942-1943.

Rice, Vernon: Post, 1945-1951.

Sherwin, Louis V.: Globe, 1910-1918.

Shipley, Joseph T.[†]: Call, 1921-1924; New Leader, 1924-; Radio Station WEVD, 1940-.

Towse, J. Ranken: Post, 1873-1927.

Watts, Richard, Jr.[†]: Herald-Tribune, 1936-1942; Go, 1945; Post, 1946-.

Wenning, Thomas H.[†]: Newsweek, 1942-.

Whipple, Sidney B.: World-Telegram, 1937-1941.

Woollcott, Alexander: Times, 1914 - 1922; Herald, 1922 - 1925; World, 1925-1928.

Young, Stark[†]: Times, 1924 - 25; New Republic, 1922-1947.

MISCELLANEOUS

Dates. The date of composition of a play is not always easy to establish. Date of production or publication merely sets a limit. Shaw's *The Philanderer*, for example, was first enacted fifteen years after it was written. What used to be considered earlier plays that Shakespeare revised, are now by many thought to be pirated printings of his own first productions. Contemporary references in a play (often relied upon to establish its date) may have been added during performance or revival. The year given in this volume, unless otherwise specified, is that of publication or first known performance.

Runs. The number of performances of a play on its first presentation gives no indication of its comparative popularity. Until about a century ago, a new play might have been presented for three consecutive nights, then been given its appropriate place in repertoire. Recently (one major shift occurring in the 1890's and one in the 1940's) high costs and expectations have changed the pattern, so as to establish longer runs. It is, for such reasons, hard to compare, as to popular appeal, a Renaissance and a current drama.

GLOSSARY

The following items are given not as a full list of theatrical terms, but as a convenient explanatory compendium of terms employed in this volume.

Auto sacramentale (Spanish): A short religious play presented out of doors in Spain, at the Feast of Corpus Christi. The autos flourished in the sixteenth and seventeenth centuries; Lope de Vega* wrote some 400 of them. The form was brought to its fullest power by Calderon*. For a discussion of similar plays in English, see Everyman*.

Catharsis: The purification that Aristotle deemed the effect of tragedy, which "through pity and fear effects the purging of these emotions." The present writer feels that the chief, the validating, effect of the theatre is not this, but a sense of exaltation. Tragedy sets a man erect, defying the odds, the gods or other forces against which he stands firm; thus spiritually he conquers, even as his body is torn. Comedy sets men erect through laughter at these outer forces, irresistible but irrelevant to the inner spirit of man.

Comedy: See Catharsis; Komos.

Commedia dell' arte (Italian): The "comedy of masks", flourishing especially during the early Italian Renaissance. Conventional figures — Pantalone, Pierrot, Columbine, recognizable by their costumes — performed in dramas of which the actors were given the skeleton plot, but for which they improvised the words at each performance. Deceits wrought upon the old man, clowning, and amorous intrigue, in these plays, carried the tradition of the ancient Roman drama, as in Plautus*, on toward the beginnings of the modern theatre, as in Goldoni*.

Deus ex machina (Latin): The god from the machine. In some of the ancient plays, a god appears at the end, to straighten out the human complications. As coming from Mount Olympus, the god was lowered by a machine from the roof to the amphitheatre floor. Hence, any arbitrary adjustor of complications at the end of a play is spoken of as a god from the machine.

Dramatic Irony: The attitude that arises when a situation appears in one light to a character in a play, but in quite a different light to other characters or to the audience. The most obvious instance of this is in cases of mistaken identity, as when, in The Comedy of Errors*, twins are confused. Dramatic irony may add to tragic power, as when the understanding audience watches Oedipus drive unwittingly to his doom.

Three attitudes upon which the dramatist can play are Surprise, Suspense, and Dramatic Irony. Surprise, taking the audience unawares, is the least lastingly effective. Shakespeare uses it seldom; once, when Othello tells how he took the turban'd Turk by the throat and stabbed him—thus!—as he kills himself. Some modern mystery plays have borne program requests not to tell their ending, lest the pleasure of surprise be lost. Suspense, holding the audience in poised expectancy, is a constant, an essential, element in the theatre. It advances to a richer level of interest in dramatic irony, wherein the expectant audience is also — like the gods on Olympus — aware of the forces shaping events still hidden from persons of the drama. This sense of sharing in the movement of destiny is part of the drama's rouse of the human spirit.

Gamos (Greek): The union of the sexes. Greek comedy usually ends with a feast (see *Komos*) that culminates in sexual union. Eight of the extant comedies of Aristophanes* end with a gamos. The modern theatre continues this pattern, for, while most tragedies end in the churchyard, most comedies end in the church.

Hamartia: *See Hybris.*

Hybris (also *hubris*; Greek): Originally meaning violence, assault and battery, hybris was applied, in the Greek drama, to the more basic attribute, inordinate pride. Aristotle found tragedy rising when a noble person, through some inner flaw (hamartia), brings about his own destruction. Chief of the flaws to which the great are prone is hybris, pride.

Hamartia, although Aristotle said that the fall of a truly just man would be not tragic but revolting, is not essential to tragedy (see *Catharsis*). Tragedy may rise from the difference in two codes, or from opposed loyalties in a person truly noble. Much of the Spanish drama presents such persons, caught in a situation where honor conflicts with love. Tragedy may be seen as intrinsic in man, inevitably rooted in the world order, so that the hero by his very nature is doomed: to act as his conscience bids, as his being must, is to summon disaster. Sophocles' *Antigone**, for example, presents a situation where to act properly is to die. The martyr, indeed, the noble person that, like Shaw's Joan of Arc, goes willingly or at least wittingly to avoidable death for a principle or ideal, may mark the deepest tragedy.

The notion that crime (or hamartia) produces the tragedy is the root of the idea of poetic justice, or dramatic justice, which degenerated to the retribution applauded in every melodrama as the villain bites the dust. The tragedy is both subtler and deeper when the only "hybris" involved is that caught in *noblesse oblige*, the pride, better, the self-respect and fortitude that hold along the proper path even to the crack of doom.

Komos (Greek): Festival, revel. The song of the religious festival, the *komoedia*, developed into the comedy. *See Gamos.*

"Tragedy", in origin, means song of the goat: the sacrifice or scapegoat, through whom the sins of the community are expiate. *Oedipus** is a clear example. This is one source of the sense of universality in great drama: what happens to him is happening for all.

Off-Broadway: In the metropolitan New York district, but not part of the commercial theatre, which centers around Broadway, from Times Square (42d Street) to Central Park (59th Street).

Poetic Justice: *See Hybris.*

Scène à faire (French): An obligatory scene. A moment of theatrical crisis toward which the play's action has been moving, and which the audience must be shown.

Stichomythia: Dialogue in which two persons speak alternately in a line or half-line apiece, in quick exchange of argument, with pat epigram, catching up of the other's words, and sharp retort. A marked characteristic of the dramas of Seneca*, it was often employed in the Renaissance, as in Shakespeare's *King Richard III**.

Succès (French): Success; used in several phrases that have become theatrical parlance:

Succès d'estime: A financial failure, critically well received.

Succès fou: A smash hit.

Succès de larmes: A play that drowns the audience in tears.

Succès de scandale: A financial success, because of daring subject or treatment, or the star's recent sensational divorce, or other reasons apart from the merit of the play.

Succès de théâtre: A success because of imaginative direction, or superb acting, or further elements that the other theatre arts add to the playwright's. Often a play acts much better than it reads.

Surprise: *See Dramatic Irony.*

Suspense: *See Dramatic Irony.*

Ten-Twen'-Thirt': Term drawn from the price of admission (ten, twenty, and thirty cents) and applied to the violently active melodrama in the late nineteenth and early twentieth century theatre in the United States (similar "blood-and-thunder" plays were equally popular in France and England) in which, amid much physical action, virtue is brought to the brink of ruin before its ultimate triumph. *See The Streets of London**.

Tragedy: *See Catharsis; Komos.*

Unities, the Three: The Unities of time, place, and action, according to which a play should present but one story (with no subplot), confined within a single city and limited to a single day. Drawn from observations of Aristotle, never fully heeded by the ancients, these "unities" were hardened into rules during the Italian and the French Renaissance. Largely ignored in Spain and England (Shakespeare in but one play, *The Tempest**, comes near to observing them), the three unities were maintained in the French theatre—so firmly that, when *The Cid** failed to follow them, its author was rebuked by the French Academy — until they were broken, in a great theatrical upheaval, by Alexandre Dumas* and Victor Hugo*.

Universality: The sense, within a work, that the characters—whether individualized and recognizable as persons, or presented as types or symbols—reach beyond their circumstances to wider implications. What is happening to these persons happens, or might happen, to us all.

On both the physical and the psychological planes, every work of wide scope reaches through three distances. Physically, there is, first, the immediate setting, let us say of the New York money market. Beyond this stretches the wider background of similar fields in other times or places, Threadneedle Street, the Bourse, the Rialto. Still farther though pressing closely around, and often in sharp contrast, is the rest of the world, art or science as opposed to business, the slums that abut upon the havens of wealth. Thus the great work encompasses the world. Psychologically, there is, first, the individual with his particular quirks, his personal responses. Within him, there are also the attitudes and reactions characteristic of his race, class, or group: the lawyer; the Scot; the millionaire, or the bourgeois struggling to make ends meet. Deeper still, though perhaps basically determinant, stir the impulses, appetites, affections common to every human being. Thus the great work embraces all mankind.

The means by which a work establishes this sense of universality are a self-locked hold. *Hamlet** attains it, partly because of the poetry in which the thoughts are clothed, partly because of the human limitations of the characters and the seemingly accidental (life-like) nature of the events. *Everyman** expresses it directly, ignoring the individual and establishing its wider meaning through characters that are universal symbols: the main figure *is* every man. *Strange Interlude** less fully conveys this sense of universality, partly because it lacks poetry, partly because of the very thoroughness with which Nina Leeds is shown in every possible relation with the other sex, a mathematical completeness that, within the realistic mood, makes a unique rather than a representative structure. However attained, it is in the measure of such universality, gleaming beyond the particular events of the drama, that the work achieves lasting significance.

Verisimilitude: The appearance of truth or reality. This is desirable in realistic plays and in the naturalistic drama, which seeks to present "a slice of life". Otherwise, the audience comes to the play ready to grant what Coleridge called "the willing suspension of disbelief". Credibility is not essential to good drama. The events in the ten-twen'-thirt' melodramas of our fathers' youth were no more improbable than the events in the blood-and-thunder melodramas of Shakespeare's time. Ghosts and witches, who thronged before believing audiences in the Elizabethan theatre, came in cohorts again upon the New York stage in the enlightened years of 1950-1951: *Bell, Book, and Candle; Great to be Alive; The Lady's Not For Burning**; *Gramercy Ghost.* On the 1955 stage, the devil defeated a baseball team in *Damn Yankees,* gave a simpleton his pin-up dream girl in *Will Success Spoil Rock Hunter?* There is no greater actuality in *A Midsummer Night's Dream** than in *Peter Pan** or *Alice in Wonderland* or the *Odyssey.* However one may judge for education or for propaganda, for art the likelihood of the happenings in a play is immaterial; what matters is their consistency — their consistency with the pattern the play sets for itself. Within the structure and mood of its own world, whether realistic or in any vein of fantasy, the events must accord with the established expectancy. This consistency with the norms of the world within the work is what is meant by truth in art. One impossibility may seem out of time and place; on two impossibilities one can erect a new world. The work is first judged in reference, not to all human knowledge, but to its own coherent growth of mood and structure. The test of truth in art is to have made it. Beyond and after this rises the question of universality, of relation to the life outside the work.

TO ROBERT AND CAROLYN

All plays are arranged under the names of their authors, who
are listed alphabetically. If an author is represented by more
than one play, his plays are dealt with chronologically. An
asterisk (*) after a title mentioned in the text indicates that
there is an article under that title in the volume. An index of
titles appears at the end of the book.

CATO OF UTICA   *Joseph Addison*

Joseph Addison (1672-1719) appeared on the British scene at a
time when writers were first exploiting the printed word as political
propaganda. With the establishment of the *Tatler* and its successor, the
Spectator, the first newspapers to be widely imitated all over Europe,
Addison, who contributed to the latter, found an expectant throng at
the opening in 1713 of this blank verse tragedy, in which he depicts the
resolve of Cato to resist the tyranny of Caesar and restore freedom to his
country or to die.

The striking and majestic lines of this play were originally interpreted
as applying to the current political situation in England. The Whigs saw
their Marlborough in the heroic martyr Cato. The Tories saw him in the
tyrant Caesar. Since each party vied with the other in its plaudits, the
play was a great success. Pope and other poets wrote verses in its praise
and it was translated into French, Italian and German. In book form the
play ran through seven printings during the first year of its publication.

Samuel Johnson called *Cato* "rather a poem in dialogue than a drama,
rather a succession of just sentiments in language than a representation of
natural affections, or of any state probable or possible in human life."

Many critics today consider *Cato* the supreme example of the English
neo-classical tragedy. Allardyce Nicoll, for example, says that, "The
whole drama is as logical as a treatise on philosophy. Addison's style
is the triumph of familiarity; he rises to no grand heights of eloquence and
he seldom descends to poverty of expression."

Despite the absence of the political fervor that gave *Cato* its initial
prominence, it remains a majestic and moving drama.

THE COUNTY CHAIRMAN   *George Ade*

According to the *New York Herald Tribune* (July 23, 1939), this play
ushered in "a new era of authorship for the American stage, our theatre
up to that time having leaned heavily upon playwrights of other lands."
Significantly, the comedy was first produced by Henry W. Savage, whose
Garden Theatre in New York was "dedicated to American plays by
American playwrights."

George Ade (1866-1944) certainly supplied Savage with delightfully
typical American figures in typical American situations. Shortly after
the play's premiere in South Bend, Indiana (Ade's native state) on
August 29, 1903, the *Chicago Record Herald* observed that the author
had created "human, reasonable, sharply defined people, some of them
pompous, loquacious, and vain, some of them sly and mendacious, some
of them silly and vulgar, some of them sturdy, dominant, and adroit.
But all of them are real."

The County Chairman came to New York on November 24, 1903, for a
run of 222 performances. Later, it became popular throughout the

1

country, achieving 110 performances in Chicago. A film version made in 1935 starred Will Rogers. The Players' Club staged the play in 1936 as its annual revival. With James Kirkwood, Alexander Kirkland, Rose Hobart, Mary Ryan, Dorothy Stickney, and Linda Watkins in the cast, the Players' production revealed that this delightful comedy still had the power of making its people seem real. Thomas R. Dash called the play " a positive delight . . . a lampoon on pettifogging politics that is salty in both its humor and its satire . . . Ade's quips and sallies on politics and politicians are barbed wires smeared with honey." The play scored again on the occasion of another revival in 1939.

The story of an election fight motivates *The County Chairman*. Young Tilford Wheeler, opposing the unscrupulous Judge Elias Rigby for the office of County Prosecuting Attorney, is steered to victory by county chairman Jim Hackler. Wheeler also wins the judge's daughter.

This play claims merit mainly for Ade's portrayals of the town loafer, the town flirt, a Negro factotum and a barefoot youngster with a home-made fishing pole, and the other local figures.

Ade took the names of his characters from a list of delinquent tax-payers posted in a Vicksburg, Mississippi, courthouse. In essence, his play presents, with simple charm and lusty vitality, a gently satiric but authentic portrait of American small town life.

THE SUPPLIANTS   *Aeschylus*

This is the earliest extant Greek drama, the first of the seven plays by Aeschylus (525-455 B.C.) that have survived (almost ninety were apparently written). The worthy scion of a distinguished Athenian family, Aeschylus used the tales of the Greek gods and heroes as the spearheads of his searching inquiries into basic human problems.

Drama during Aeschylus' early days was a matter of ritual. Aeschylus was in large measure responsible for its theatrical growth. Although *The Suppliants*, produced about 492 B.C., has the originally religious chorus of fifty members to serve as its protagonist, there is also a distinct player, second to the leader of the chorus. If, moreover, as Aristotle says, it was Sophocles that introduced the third actor into the drama, Aeschylus in his trilogy the *Oresteia* was prompt to make use of the added player.

At annual contests, the Greek dramatists presented three serious plays and one satyr-play, all four usually based on a single theme. Thus, *The Suppliants* is one play, the first of a trilogy. The other two, *The Egyptians* and *The Daughters of Danaus*, have been lost, so that it is impossible to say how Aeschylus fully developed his theme.

A number of mystical, religious interpretations of the drama have been put forth, but basically *The Suppliants* is a story of love and freedom. The fifty daughters of Danaus, having fled their native Egypt for Argos, the home of their ancestress, Io, beg protection against the fifty sons of Aegyptus. Pelasgus, King of Argos, is thus confronted with the problem: shall he grant the privilege of sanctuary, so highly esteemed by the Athenians, to the daughters of Danaus, at the possible cost of war? Or shall he refuse that privilege, perhaps to find the altars of the gods polluted with blood? After some hesitation, he offers them sanctuary and refuses to turn them over to the herald of Aegyptus. The play opens with the prayer of the chorus of Danaids to the benevolent Zeus and ends with the hope that he will continue to favor them, "for the hands of thy saving are sure."

The Egyptians probably carried the story on through the eventual success of the sons of Aegyptus, to the enforced marriage of the maidens, whom their father Danaus commanded to kill their husbands on their wedding night. Only one daughter, Hypermnestra, in love with Lynceus, spared her husband on that fatal night. In the third play, *The Daughters of Danaus,* Hypermnestra was probably brought to trial, and defended by Aphrodite, thus manifesting Aeschylus' belief in the universal power and the claims of love.

Some of the most violent dramatic conflicts in *The Suppliants* arise when the herald of Aegyptus and his cohort seek to capture the fifty maidens. Their Egyptian costumes are themselves striking, the dark masks contrasting with white robes traced with formal patterns in gold. The lines of the herald are sung alternately with those of the daughters of Danaus, during "a frenzied symbolic dance". The Chorus, as Gilbert Murray has described it, is "pursued by a hideous rabble of negroid slaves from Egypt, led by a brutal Herald. The effect is somewhat dream-like: the virgin pursued by the ravisher, the white girl pursued by something black and dreadful, the Greek woman—or, as we should say, the English woman — pursued by a creature of foreign speech." The impact of such choral scenes on the Athenian audience can hardly be recaptured today.

Even in the corrupt text of *The Suppliants* that has come down to us, the language is rich yet simple. It has been compared in magnificence to certain passages of Isaiah. In simplicity of movement and beauty of form, this earliest European drama sets a standard that every subsequent period has found it hard to equal.

THE PERSIANS   *Aeschylus*

Written in 472 B.C., this is the only surviving Greek tragedy that deals with an actual historical situation, as opposed to the legendary or myth-ological themes of the other dramas. Dealing with a battle in which Aeschylus himself had fought and in which the very existence of his city was at stake, the play depicts the enemy of Athens without rancor. The Persians are vigorous human beings who maintain their dignity even in defeat. As Gilbert Murray has remarked, "There is no hatred of them, no remotest suggestion of what we now call 'war propaganda'."

The great conflict between the Greeks and the Persians is presented by Aeschylus to the Athenians from the Persian point of view. The glory of Athens is made manifest only in the Persian picture of the significance and the enormity of their defeat.

The action of *The Persians* takes place in Susa, the capital of the Persian Empire, in 480 B.C., the year of the battle of Salamis. Atossa, the widow of Darius and mother of Xerxes, awaits word of her son's victory. A messenger brings news of disastrous losses on land and sea. The ghost of Darius joins in Atossa's lamentation; then Xerxes himself appears, crushed by the blow that has stricken his host and his farthest hopes.

The ordinarily trite consideration that pride goeth before a fall is turned in *The Persians* to a pondering of basic ethical concepts in the Greek drama: great or prolonged prosperity breeds satiety (koros), leads to pride, boastfulness, insolence (hybris) and thence to ruin (ate). Aeschylus' ethical fervor is combined with an intense patriotism. A panegyric could be no more inspiring than the description the Persian messenger gives of the great battle of Salamis; it is perhaps the most famous passage in all Greek poetry. Thus, *The Persians* accomplishes the unique feat of awakening sorrow for the defeated foe together with respect for the righteous victor.

The choregus (patron who paid the expenses) of *The Persians* was the great Athenian lover of democracy, Pericles. In 472 B.C. the play won first prize.

The Persians was performed at the Sorbonne, Paris, in 1936. During the same year, Eva Sikelianos worked on a production for the American Federal Theatre project, and in 1939 she helped dancer Ted Shawn with a "visible song" arrangement of the opening chorus of the play at Lee, Massachusetts. A version by Gilbert Murray was broadcast in England in 1939. In beauty, dignity, and moral power, *The Persians* is one of the great dramas of the world.

SEVEN AGAINST THEBES   *Aeschylus*

Certain stories of the earlier Greek heroes attracted the fifth century dramatists again and again. One of the most popular was the legend of the curse on the house of Laius. The story of Oedipus is told by Aeschylus in *Seven Against Thebes* and by Euripides in *Phoenissae.** Where these two plays leave off, the story is again taken up by Sophocles in his *Antigone** and *Oedipus at Colonus**.

Seven Against Thebes is the last play of a trilogy. The lost plays are *Laius, Oedipus,* and the satyr-play *The Sphinx.* The group received first prize at the annual tragedy contest of 467 B.C.

Seven Against Thebes is the story of Oedipus' sons, Eteocles and Polyneices, whose blind father, when they mistreat him, lays upon them the curse of their mutual doom. The two sons are pledged to rule alternately over Thebes; but, when Eteocles' year is up, he refuses to relinquish power to his brother. Polyneices therefore brings a force from Argos to besiege the city. While the Argive host is driven back, the brothers meet in battle and kill one another. As the Thebans prepare to bury Eteocles, at the end of the play, Antigone, his sister, defies the order that Polyneices' body be left for the dogs and swears she will give him fit burial.

Aeschylus in *Seven Against Thebes* is concerned not with divine but with human justice. In Eteocles he has created the first truly tragic hero in ancient drama: a man noble and worthy, but with the "tragic flaw" that works his own undoing. Eteocles loves his city. That is his crime: his love of it (or of power in it) led him to break his pledge to share its rule with his brother Polyneices. Polyneices too was wrong in summoning alien aid against his native city. The issues are argued in stark, sharp phrases—an early example of the short, alternately spoken lines called stichomythia.

The Theban women are terrified by the attack on the city as they hear the shrieks of the wounded, the clash of shields, the thunder of charging horses and the whinnies of agony as the steeds are cut down, the rumble of chariots, the thud of heavy stones against the gates; they are reassured and comforted by the King. When the King rages toward combat with his brother, the women try to calm him and dissuade him from the crime of fratricide. Though he senses his doom, the King resolves that "Honor is the prize, not life prolonged!" Of the four cardinal virtues, only fortitude remains in his breast. The chorus await, shuddering, until the bodies of the brothers are brought in. Their sympathy goes to both, as they recognize the fickle shiftings of human nature. And they wonder how peace and good can result from evil that calls forth further evil.

Aeschylus may be tracing a parallel between the story of Polyneices and the political situation of his own day. Themistocles, hero of the battle of Salamis, 480 B. C., condemned of plotting with the Persians against the Greeks, had just been ostracized and exiled, and had joined Artaxerxes in Persia. Aeschylus does not mention the name Thebes; throughout the play, he uses the archaic term, City of Cadmus: in the invasion that culminated in the decisive battle of Salamis, Thebes had been on the side of the Persians.

The practice of enumeration of heroes, familiar to the Greeks in the public recitations of Homer, is indulged in *Seven Against Thebes*. Eteocles names the Argive leader in charge at each of the seven gates of the city, briefly characterizes him, and describes the device on his shield. He then names the Theban leader that is to defend the gate. Polyneices, incidentally, does not appear in the play.

Seven Against Thebes was quite popular in ancient times. Aristophanes deemed it familiar enough for the satire of *The Frogs**, which he directed against its martial theme and its lofty language, which sometimes approaches bombast. But Aeschylus was a dramatist of power and a poet of dignity and measure. In *Seven Against Thebes*, the high standard of his ethics and the beauty of his expression shine through a tragic story.

PROMETHEUS BOUND   *Aeschylus*

In the trilogy of which *Prometheus Bound* is the one surviving play, Aeschylus ponders one of the most perplexing problems of all time—the existence of evil in the world. If the divine power of the universe is accepted as both omnipotent and benevolent, the problem is indeed a complex one. Seeking a solution, Jews and Christians look upon the serpent, which led Adam and Eve to eat of the fruit of the tree of knowledge, as an instrument of the powers of darkness, and upon Lucifer, the light-bearer, as a fallen angel.

Prometheus, "the fore-thinker", (as was probably shown in the lost first play of the trilogy, *Prometheus the Fire-Bearer*), taught man the use of fire. But Aeschylus, veering from his usual concept, in *Prometheus Bound* depicts Zeus as a jealous tyrant, who punishes Prometheus for having brought that knowledge to man. The Biblical story offers a parallel to that of Aeschylus: "And the Lord God said, Behold, the man is become as one of us, to know good and evil; and now, lest he put forth his hand, and take also of the tree of life, and eat, and live forever: Therefore the Lord God sent him forth from the Garden of Eden" (*Genesis* 3, 22-23). Prometheus, however, by possession of a secret regarding the future of Zeus, is able to secure his freedom, as was probably depicted in the last play of the trilogy, *Prometheus Unbound*.

The portrayal of Prometheus as the "suffering servant" and stricken benefactor of mankind brought Aeschylus before the city magistrates on charges of impious disrespect to the gods. Alexander Harvey in *The Freeman* (Jan. 31, 1923) surmised that in summoning Aeschylus the magistrates discerned political satire in *Prometheus Bound*: "Io, transformed into a heifer, stands in the Aeschylus scene for the young lady with whom the politician newly in power in Athens is hopelessly infatuated. This politician is referred to in the play only as Zeus, precisely as the wife of that politician becomes Hera or Juno for stage purposes, Prometheus being the candidate for office, whose defeat led inevitably to his ostracism. The situation is so familiar to a student of ancient Athenian politics that the names of all the parties in the case — with the exception of the heifer—might be gleaned from a somewhat casual perusal of any history of Greece." The trilogy was written about 465 B.C.

Aeschylus' full estimate of Prometheus, of course, is lost with the other plays of the trilogy. Shelley sought to reconstruct *Prometheus Unbound* in 1819, writing a version in which Demogorgon, the all-pervading spirit and primal power of the universe, takes form as the child of Zeus and Thetis. He hurls Zeus over the battlements of heaven, and Prometheus is unbound by Heracles to introduce on the earth a reign of love, freedom, and peace based on individual self-control.

The Aeschylean conclusion of *Prometheus Unbound*, however, if we reconstruct the lost play aright, would show Zeus, on learning from Prometheus that "the son of Thetis will be greater than his father," abandoning his intention of marrying Thetis. And Prometheus, for revealing his secret, would be set free. What is important, here, is that Zeus is the first god to be pictured as learning from experience. Aeschylus offers the concept of the perfectibilty of god. And if man is made in god's image . . .

Prometheus Bound has little external action, for, after Prometheus is borne onto the stage at the opening of the play, he remains chained to a rock throughout the rest of the drama. Inwardly, however, the play is anything but calm. "It seethes," as John Mason Brown phrased it, "with a defiance that reaches beyond the limits of earthly challenge and involves the very elements themselves." The fact that all the characters save Io are super-human adds to the weight of its mighty issues. In lofty language of great poetic beauty, Prometheus bears his torture with quiet resolution. His endurance, as well as his thought, challenges the evil of the world, however highly placed the evil-doer.

"I have been reading *Prometheus Bound*," Gerald Manley Hopkins once wrote to E. H. Coleridge. "It is immensely superior to anything else of Aeschylus I have read . . . It is really full of splendid poetry; when you read it, read with it Shelley's *Prometheus Unbound*, which is as fine or finer, perhaps a little fantastic though." Despite his supernatural characters, Aeschylus is never fantastic; his spirit is noble yet wholly down on earth.

Among the English translations of *Prometheus Bound* are the dignified 1899 version by Paul Elmer More and the more vibrant one by Edith Hamilton, which was staged in New York in 1930. William Vaughn Moody wrote a play on the theme entitled *The Fire Bringer*, 1904. Recent performances of Aeschylus' play in Greek have been given at Syracuse, Sicily, 1921; Delphi, 1927; Bath, England, 1932; and in the United States at Randolph-Macon College, 1934, and at Wellesley College, 1936. American performances in English include one at New York University, 1930, and another at Yale, 1939.

The beauty, power, and pertinence of Aeschylus' protest against tyranny, even when divine, remain bright and challenging to our time. Foe of the traditional, Aeschylus was, nevertheless, steadfast in his quest of the ideal.

ORESTEIA   *Aeschylus*

Oresteia is the only trilogy of which all three plays have come down to us from ancient Greece. Aeschylus' last work, and by contemporary repute his best, *Oresteia* won first prize in the contest of 458 B.C. Its three plays are certainly the most dramatic and most majestic of his extant dramas. In them we see most fully the pattern of Aeschylus' thought, turned upon the topical problem of public justice as opposed to the private blood-feud.

Oresteia tells of the curse on the house of Atreus, as it works its tragic doom even unto the third generation, when there is promise of final release. The curse was laid upon the house long before Aeschylus takes up the story, when bitter blood was spilled between Atreus and his brother Thyestes. The sons of Atreus, Menelaus and Agamemnon King of Argos, however, lived in peace until Menelaus' wife, Helen, was snatched by Paris of Troy and the Greeks rallied to avenge the deed. Warned that the Trojans could be defeated only if Iphigenia, daughter of Agamemnon and Clytemnestra, were offered to the gods, Agamemnon reluctantly consents to her sacrifice. During the ten year siege of Troy, Clytemnestra broods over the killing of her daughter and grows to hate her husband. She takes as her lover Aegisthus, son of Thyestes and therefore bitter enemy of Agamemnon. Together, they plot the murder of the king, should he return from the Trojan War. He comes, and they kill him. His return and murder are the story of *Agamemnon*.

The second play of the trilogy, *The Choephori* (*The Libation Bearers*), named after the chorus that goes with Electra to Agamemnon's tomb, is the story of the return of Agamemnon's son, Orestes, who with his sister Electra avenges the murder of his father by slaying Aegisthus and Clytemnestra. The Furies (Eumenides) gather about Orestes, symbols of his tortured conscience.

The third play, *The Eumenides,* tells of Orestes' pursuit by the Furies. Enanguished by their unrelenting chase, Orestes appeals to Apollo, is tried by the goddess Athena and a jury of twelve Athenians, and is declared free from guilt of blood. The curse of the house of Atreus is spent.

The tragic story of the house of Atreus has attracted many playwrights. Euripides left us two *Iphigenia** plays, an *Orestes**, and an *Electra*. Better known in present-day translations and revivals is Sophocles' *Electra**. The Roman Naevius wrote an *Iphigenia* in the third century B. C. Seneca's *Agamemnon* (about 60 A. D.) is one of his weakest tragedies. Erasmus translated a version of the story in 1524; Racine's *Iphigenie* was first produced at the French court in 1674; and the Englishman John Dennis wrote a version in 1700. Shortly after this, the Italian Apostolo Zeno, court poet to the Holy Roman Emperor Charles VI, presented a musical version, the most successful of his sixty operas; Gluck's opera on the theme was first heard in 1774. Goethe's first prose draft was written in 1779; he finished the work in 1787, three years before Schiller's version. Jean Moréas wrote a French version in 1903, and in 1941 the German Gerhardt Hauptmann's play vividly contrasted the calm of Iphigenia with the passion of Electra.

Among the many versions or adaptations of *Agamemnon* after that of Seneca are one by James Thomson, poet of *The Seasons,* and another by Count Vittorio Alfieri*. The latter also wrote an *Orestes,* following the Italian Rucelli of the fifteenth century. Voltaire's *Oreste* appeared in 1750.

Most popular of the episodes in the tragedy, in ancient as in recent times, has been the story of Electra. It was in the French version by Jolyot de Crébillion (1709) that Adrienne Lecouvreur made her debut at the Comédie-Française in 1727. Modern treatments of the theme have been made in various lands: a violent version by Hofmannsthal* in German, 1874, on which the opera by Richard Strauss is based; one by the Spanish Benito Pérez Galdós, 1901, from an anti-clerical point of view; one by the French Alfred Poizat, 1907; one — with modern and trivial images — by Jean Giraudoux* in 1937; and still another, an existential drama called *The Flies*,* by Jean-Paul Sartre. In addition, there is Eugene O'Neill's trilogy *Mourning Becomes Electra*,* with its gloomy American setting during the War between the States. The entire trilogy was condensed into three scenes in the dramatic version of the poem *The Tower Beyond Tragedy* (1925) by Robinson Jeffers.

In his trilogy, Aeschylus sought with profound thought to combine concepts of divine and human justice. Early in *Agamemnon* he sets the theme in the chorus: Zeus, the one god, "that name of many names", has so ordered the world that "Men shall learn wisdom, through affliction schooled". Throughout *Agamemnon* and *The Choephori,* the hideous course of that affliction unfolds as crime breeds vengeful crime. And in *The Eumenides,* Athena charges the jury at Orestes' trial: "Thou shalt do no unjust thing . . . Let no man live uncurbed by law, nor curbed by tyranny." Aeschylus gives scope to Athenian pride; for Athena tells the court it is to continue dealing justice thereafter, thus assigning ancient origin and divine sanction to the Areopagus, the court which the Athenians properly regarded as the cornerstone of their state.

The jury trying Orestes is evenly divided, as indeed justice in this case must be, for Orestes is traditionally right in avenging the murder of his father, but cruelly wrong in slaying his mother. Athena then tempers justice with mercy and sets Orestes free. Here is Aeschylus' richest thought on the problem of good and evil. It approaches the Christian view: Man, by forces within and circumstances without, is driven against his will to evil, to be redeemed by something less akin to justice than to love. Even the Furies (Erinyes) are changed by Athena into goddesses of grace, while the Athenians rejoice in the glory of the justice of their great city. (The word *Eumenides,* which was used by the Greeks as a euphemism for the Furies, literally means daughters of grace.) Thus out of the tragic pattern of life, as it rises to its peak, suffers, and sinks to death, Aeschylus derives a basic moral order.

The trilogy is marked by its simplicity; to our Shakespeare-trained minds, it seems almost barren of imagery. It is free from figures such as Shakespeare loved to weave, elaborated for sheer delight in the beauty of their image and sound. Rarely indeed — the *London Times* (September 25, 1948) found Clytemnestra's picture of a wife's anxiety over her husband at war a rare exception — does "the sheer intensity and completeness of the poet's insight almost outrun his immediate dramatic purpose." The drive of the emotions is unbroken, and direct.

The plays of the trilogy have had recent performance. The first American production of *Agamemnon* was at Harvard University in 1906. It had a powerful effect. Other performances have been at Chapel Hill, North Carolina in 1929; at the University of California, Los Angeles in 1932; and, along with *The Choephori*, at Ogunquit, Maine in 1937. *Agamemnon* was staged in London in 1934 and 1936. The *Choephori* was given in New York in 1908 and in Los Angeles in 1933. Los Angeles saw *The Eumenides* in 1934; New York, in 1942.

After 2400 years, the power, beauty, and nobility of the work of Aeschylus are still deeply felt. In his own time, too, his plays were highly valued. Aristophanes, in *The Frogs**, has Dionysus go down to Hades to bring back Euripides and, for the good of Greece — after some gentle satire and weighing of their virtues — return with Aeschylus instead.

Aeschylus was particularly skillful in his portraits of women. Clytemnestra is pictured masterfully. The *London Times* (June 18,1934) reminded us that she "is not merely a bad woman who has had an adulterous intrigue during her husband's absence, and resorts to murder in order to cover her tracks. She is above all an outraged mother, whose whole being is concentrated on avenging her murdered daughter. And although throughout the play the sympathy of the audience is meant to be against her, Aeschylus was careful not to depict her as a vulgar murderess or an inhuman monster. And at the end of the play, though her hatred against her murdered husband is by no means exhausted, she is more and more overcome by the fear that in her vengeance she is after all merely the instrument of the Doom that broods over the House of Atreus."

Even more pitifully drawn is Cassandra, daughter of the King of Troy. Brought to Greece a prisoner by Agamemnon, she is cursed with the power of foreseeing the future but not being believed. She cries out upon Agamemnon's blind approach to his doom, then goes to her own death beside him.

In *The Choephori* there is an equally revealing portrait of Electra, an instrument of vengeance yet a heart-wrung woman. With sensitive reticence, Aeschylus lets us see no more of Electra, once her brother has advanced to the killings. And Orestes himself, having slain Aegisthus, hestitates before his mother. He has to be reminded of his vow before he can lift his sword against her.

The dramaturgic skill of Aeschylus is shown in the opposition of his characters. Agamemnon's pride, for example, prevents his understanding the veiled warning of the chorus on his return. He accepts Clytemnestra's excessive show of welcome and walks the crimson carpet she has spread as if he were a god. Thus the Queen's hypocrisy easily outmatches his astuteness, as her double-edged words press with sharp irony upon the audience. But in the next scene, Clytemnestra loses her grasp on power before the calm and silent Cassandra, who knows the fate in store for all. Not until Clytemnestra has rushed away in futile fury does Cassandra speak. Then in sorrow and dignity she goes to her doom. Through such opposition pathos and irony are deepened to plumb the soul.

A new use of the chorus can be traced to *Oresteia*. The chorus of *The Eumenides* is as active as in earlier dramas. Resting, at first, while Orestes seeks refuge at the innermost altar of Apollo, the Furies murmur at the summons of Clytemnestra's ghost. They gather force and fierceness until they move like baying hounds upon the trail of Orestes. Horribly masked, in weird and ghoulish round, they weave a terror with their dancing, and the glee of their closing in on their victim is beyond the capture of words. When these Furies first appeared in the Athenian theatre, we are told, women fainted and babes were prematurely born. In the two other dramas of the trilogy, however, the chorus takes a different role. Its figures are less participants than spectators. They guide and share the emotions of the audience, responding to events as beholders would respond. Thus they draw the audience into the drama with a profound effectiveness.

In this greatest work of the earliest known dramatist lies the secret of great theatrical art: the spectator become participant. Each of us, looking at any other mortal in our daily span, might say "There, but for the grace of God, go I." The theatre extends no such withholding grace; it absorbs us into its spell so that, in its problems and its passions, "There go I!"

FEAR   *Alexander Afinogenov*

The conversion of a Russian scientist to the Soviet point of view is the subject of this unusual play. Professor Ivan Ilich Borodin, director of the Institute of Physiological Stimuli, comes to the conclusion that the vast majority of persons in the Soviet Union live in a constant state of fear. Eighty percent of human actions, he concludes, are stimulated by fear — the other twenty percent by opportunism. Charged with treason for his views, and imprisoned, he discovers that he had taken into account only the noisily dissatisfied. The great mass of the Soviet people, he decides, far from being victims of their fears, are swayed by a great enthusiasm. Borodin becomes a true "friend of the people."

One of the most vivid of the Soviet dramatists, Alexander Afinogenov (1904-1941) had his career cut short by a Nazi bomb during an air raid on Moscow. His first three plays were based on themes from abroad. *Robert Tim* (1923) told the story of a revolt among the weavers of nineteenth century England; *South of the Slot* (1926) was taken from Jack London's story of a San Francisco strike; and *At the Breaking Point* (1926) was a study of German unrest at the end of World War I. *Fear*, Afinogenov's greatest drama, was written after he had based three other works on Soviet themes.

Banned in 1931 as counter-revolutionary, *Fear* later opened at the State Dramatical Theatre in Leningrad and at the Moscow Art Theatre. For more than two years, it was the most popular play in the U.S.S.R. It was presented frequently until 1938, when another shift in "the party line" took all Afinogenov's plays off the Soviet stages.

American productions of *Fear* include one given at Vassar College, 1934, from a translation by Dorothy B. Coleman, Adelaide G. Brown, and Nikander Skelsky; another during the same year under the direction of Erwin Piscator at the Dramatic Workshop, New York, from a translation by Leon Dennen; and one at Syracuse in 1935.

It is a matter of speculation whether or not the ending of *Fear* was rewritten so as to serve Soviet purpose before the play was acceptable to the Soviet stage. In commenting on the Vassar production, the *New York Herald Tribune* (January 14, 1934) reported: "Save for the last scene, which does not ring true to the rest of this poignant piece, no capitalistic critic could be more critical of the shortcomings of Marxism as applied by Stalin and his followers. In the denouement one suspects the coarse hand of the censor."

The conversion of Borodin in the play prophesied the 1948 shift of all U.S.S.R. scientists to "the party line," particularly the shift of the biologists to the "support of the charlatan Lysenko" and the abandonment of the universally accepted principles of genetics.

Afinogenov's picture of the efforts of individuals to adjust themselves to the Soviet order is unsparing. A professor is dismissed because he has no Marxist background. Former aristocrats beg on the streets, among them an admiral's daughter, whose son denies his parentage in the hope of being accepted by the Communists but is nevertheless thrown out of the party to rejoin his mother in beggary.

The citizens accepted in the play as loyal Soviet subjects do not escape the dramatist's satire. Of the fearful eighty percent, Afinogenov said: "The dairymaid fears confiscation of her cows; the peasant, forcible collectivization; the Soviet worker, perpetual purging of the party; the political worker, the accusation of lukewarmness; the scientific worker, the accusation of idealism; the technical worker, the accusation of sabotage. Of the opportunistic twenty percent, he wrote: "They are the owners of the country. They enter institutions of science with arrogant faces, stamping their boots, laughing and chattering loudly. But for them there is brain fear; the brain of the worker fears the overtaxing of his ability that develops into persecution mania."

Allowing for the shift in the play's ending, propaganda perfunctory and perforce, *Fear* is a vivid and dramatic picture of the state of mind of the citizenry of Soviet Russia.

UNCLE TOM'S CABIN   *George L. Aiken*

In 1851 Gamaliel Bailey, editor of the *National Era,* a weekly published in Washington, D. C., wrote Harriet Beecher Stowe (1811-1896): "My dear Mrs. Stowe — I enclose a $100 bill. Please send me a story — anything you choose." The result of that letter was *Uncle Tom; or, Life Among the Lowly.* Like its own character Topsy, the story "just growed"; it appeared in book form as *Uncle Tom's Cabin* in 1852.

In response to a request from Asa Hutchinson, a friend, for permission to dramatize the story, Mrs. Stowe replied: "If the barrier which now keeps young people of Christian families from theatrical entertainments is once broken down by the introduction of respectable and moral plays, they will then be open to all the temptations of those who are not such, as there will be, as the world now is, five bad plays to one good. However specious may be the idea of reforming dramatic entertainments, I fear that it is wholly impracticable, and, as a friend to you, should hope that you would not run the risk of so dangerous an experiment. The world is not good enough yet for it to succeed."

However, since Mrs. Stowe had not reserved the dramatic rights to *Uncle Tom's Cabin,* unauthorized productions sprang up on all sides. The version written by George L. Aiken (1830-1876) for actor-producer George C. Howard was the first to reach the stage. Opening in Troy, New York, on September 27, 1852, this version, (it ended with the death of little Eva) ran for over a hundred nights. Aiken, then aged twenty-two, was a member of the company; his payment for the dramatization was a gold watch. He played the role of George Harris. Mrs. Howard played Topsy and her daughter Cordelia played little Eva. No one one wanted to play the oily fellow who introduces himself with the remark: "I am a lawyer, and my name is Marks"; this role, finally thrust upon young Frank Aiken, brother of the playwright, became one of the most famous comedy parts on the American stage.

During the run in Troy, a sequel was added to the play, showing Uncle Tom's life as a slave on Legree's plantation. With this version, the company repeated its success in Albany and in Boston. In the latter city a rival version, already on stage when the Aikens and the Howards arrived, ran for 103 performances.

The editor of the *Atlantic Monthly* took Mrs. Stowe to see the play— the first theatrical "entertainment" she had ever attended. "We entered privately," he reported, "she being well muffled . . . I never saw such delight upon a human face as she displayed when she first comprehended the full power of Mrs. Howard's Topsy. She scarcely spoke during the evening, but her expression was eloquent, smiles and tears succeeding each other through the whole . . . Drawn along by the threads of her own romance, and inexperienced in the deceptions of the theatre, she could not have been keenly sensible of the faults of the piece or the shortcomings of the actors . . . The Eliza of the evening was a reasonably good actress and skipped over the floating ice of the Ohio River with frantic agility. The Uncle Tom was rather stolid—such a man as I have seen preaching among the Negroes when I lived in Kentucky."

On August 23, 1852, another version, by Charles W. Taylor, strangely omitting Eva and Topsy, opened at Purdy's National Theatre in New York and ran for but eleven nights. The Aiken version, however, played at the same theatre, at a higher admission price, and with three performances daily, for over a year. The poet William Cullen Bryan and the actor Edwin Forrest were among those that wept at Cordelia Howard's characterization of Eva. Mrs. Howard played Topsy continuously for thirty-five years, and G. C. German, the Uncle Tom of the original cast, acted no other part during the rest of his life.

Since popular sentiment in New York in 1853 was generally anti-abolitionist, the local press was cold toward the play. An editorial in the *New York Herald* ended with the following admonition: "We would advise all concerned to drop the play of *Uncle Tom's Cabin* at once and forever. The thing is in bad taste—is not according to good faith to the Constitution and is calculated, if persisted in, to become a firebrand of the most dangerous character to the peace of the country." The play remained popular, and within a decade the country was torn by civil war. The stage version of *Uncle Tom's Cabin*, even more than Mrs. Stowe's book, helped to solidify Northern sentiment against slavery. It pressed home the moral issue and prepared the people for the War between the States.

There have been some twenty different stage versions of *Uncle Tom's Cabin*, all fairly closely following the plot of the novel. When financial straits force the kindly Shelbys to sell their slaves, the mulatto Eliza, rather than be separated from her baby, runs away with it into the snow storm. Bloodhounds follow close upon their trail, but she carries the babe out onto the ice of the Ohio River, leaping from floe to floe until safe on the Nothern shore. Uncle Tom is sold to a trader, but George Shelby promises to redeem him. While sailing down the Mississippi, Tom saves little Eva, whose father, St. Clare, buys him. Tom lives happily with them and Eva's playmate, the lively Negro girl Topsy, until the frail Eva dies, and St. Clare is stabbed to death. Tom is then bought at auction by the brutal planter Simon Legree, who hates him for his independent spirit. Legree demands: "Ain't you mine, body and soul?" Tom replies that his soul is God's, and Legree has him savagely flogged. The lawyer Marks now confronts Legree with evidence of his having killed St. Clare; Legree fights, and Marks shoots him. Tom's old master, Shelby, arrives as Tom is dying, and vows to work for the freedom of the slaves.

This story was invariably supplemented with Negro plantation scenes, songs and dances, and with many spectacular effects—the famous crossing of the river on the ice was followed by a fight on the edge of a cliff between Eliza's husband, George Harris, and the slave-dealer pursuing her, until the Quaker Phineas Fletcher heaves the slave-dealer into the torrent below; and always there came the final vision of little Eva in heaven, her outstretched arms blessing her father and her beloved Uncle Tom.

As early as 1853 there were three dramatizations of *Uncle Tom's Cabin* playing at one time in London, and two in Paris. In February 1862, four companies opened in New York within a single week; the Old Bowery version had horses as well as hounds chasing Eliza. Jubilee singers added to the show became a popular feature. For fifty-seven consecutive years, ten to twenty *Uncle Tom* companies were on continuous tour of the United States, and three to five in Great Britain. Some of the companies were beneath even small town tolerance; one western paper reviewed an *Uncle Tom* show with the remark: "The cast gave the bloodhounds poor support."

In the 1880's, the first attempts were made to show the play in the South. In Georgia, the actors fled as the scenery was smashed. In Kentucky, a law was enacted forbidding performances of the play. By now, however, *Uncle Tom's Cabin* has been shown in Texas, Arkansas, Louisiana, Missouri, and Mississippi. A Soviet Russian production of 1949 pictured the United States as the land of lynchings; Uncle Tom, accordingly, was not flogged to death, but hanged.

The Aiken version of *Uncle Tom's Cabin*, by far the most frequently played, was revised in 1933 by A. E. Thomas for the Players' Club annual revival. Otis Skinner, who made his stage debut in Philadelphia in 1877 as Uncle Tom, played the same role in this revival. Lois Shore played Eva; Fay Bainter, Topsy; Ernest Glendenning, St. Clare. Also in the cast were Cecilia Loftus, Minnie Dupree, Gene Lockhart, Thomas Chalmers, and Pedro de Cordoba. The production glowed with surprising lustre. Richard Lockridge warned: "Several of the big scenes will get you if you don't watch out . . . The slave-market scene, for example, is stirring drama in which the violent taking of sides is unavoidable . . . It is not only authentic Americana; it is in its own rights a pretty grand evening." The *New York Herald-Tribune* reported that the blasé audience came to scoff but "remained to sniffle as the bright spirit of little Eva was exhaled, and Uncle Tom suffered his sable martyrdom . . . The Players make the old prejudiced and hateful show an exciting entertainment."

Uncle Tom's Cabin, which John Mason Brown has called "the greatest grease-paint curiosity of all time," helped make American history. Its record of performances is unparalleled in the annals of the theatre.

DECLASSEE

Zoe Akins

Few plays have aroused more critical controversy than *Déclassée*, the story of a high-born Englishwoman who falls down New York's social scale. Probably written as a counter-attack to Somerset Maugham's *Our Betters*, which presented the rise of American bounders in the scale of London, *Déclassée* brought Ethel Barrymore to New York's Empire Theatre in 1919.

As portrayed by Zoe Akins (b. 1886), Lady Helen Haden, one of "the mad Varricks" of England, is a glamorous and noble woman, despite her downward journey. Having written compromising letters to a young adventurer, Ed Thayer, she refuses nevertheless to keep quiet when she discovers that Thayer is a card-cheat. Thayer thereupon gives the letters to her husband, the coarse and bibulous Sir Bruce, and Lady Helen is impelled to leave both her husband and her native England. Taking up residence in New York, she is reduced to pawning her last pearl, though wooed by Randolph Solomon, "the American rival of the British Museum." When Thayer turns up, Solomon offers to withdraw his attentions. Misunderstanding Solomon's offer, Lady Helen goes despairingly out, and is run over and killed. Her final moments are made happy by Solomon's tender affection.

Alexander Woollcott (October 7, 1919) led the chorus of praise that the play brought to Zoe Akins. "At the zenith of her powers and in the fulness of her queenly beauty," he said, "Ethel Barrymore came back to town last night in the richest and most interesting play that has fallen to her in all her years upon the stage." The play, he continued, held "the audience spellbound, held it enthralled even through such a lingering and luxurious death scene as has not been vouchsafed to this hurried city in our day and generation." Heywood Broun seconded Woollcott's praises: "Some of *Déclassée* is gilt, but it would be pretty thankless and risky business to try to scrub it off. . . . Enough of the new play is pure metal, and rich and rare, for us to shout for it all."

Kenneth MacGowan sent up a warning flare: "Let a play like *Déclassée* beware! America so seldom produces a drama with body and brain and character to it that when such a piece comes along its road is set with a small forest of critical thorns. We mentally collect its few shortcomings instead of recollecting its many singular and unusual virtues. We fuss around with a little slackness of exposition here and forget a great rightness of feeling there, and an eternally true and constant sense of human character throughout. We run it down by comparing it favorably to Pinero . . . *Déclassée* has wit, breeding, self-respect."

The opposition was led by Alan Dale: "Really, the play was such an amusing mixture of cheap family heraldry and cheezy stories, that it could scarcely pass muster even with the uninitiated. It was mostly 'told' in conversation at tables . . . the company had nothing to do but pretend to drink cups-o'-tea and chat around the theme." *Theatre* magazine came to Dale's support: "Were it not marred by an impossible third act, it would be almost a good play . . . no human being could linger for fifteen minutes and be able to talk as splendidly as does Miss Barrymore after being crushed by a taxi. It is the death of Camille over again."

Supported by Claude King and Clare Eames, Ethel Barrymore played *Déclassée* for several seasons. The play was adapted for the silent screen in 1925, with Corinne Griffith as Lady Helen, and a talking version was filmed in 1935. The play itself has been revived several times; once by Ethel Barrymore in 1935.

Though the plot is melodramatic, the dialogue is lively. The characters are honestly and carefully drawn; their motives natural and widely true. *Déclassée* is a vivid example of the transformation of the "society" play into the psychological drama. The social conventions within the play, like the social strata themselves, may seem a bit remote from our less polished and more leveled time; but, granting the conditions, which were real enough in their day, *Déclassée* probes a basic motivation of life. A tense drama, it presses the basic problem of integrity, certainly no less urgent in our time.

THE TEXAS NIGHTINGALE   *Zoe Akins*

Considered by many authorities to be Zoe Akins' best play, *The Texas Nightingale* (originally entitled *Greatness*) had the shortest run of any of them. After getting under way in Dayton, Toledo, and Chicago, it opened in New York at the Empire Theatre on November 20, 1922. It closed on December 16, a notable *succès d'estime*.

Heywood Broun hailed the play as "the most important and interesting work Zoe Akins has ever done." Described by Broun as "authentically romantic without being sentimental" and the *New York Times* (November 22, 1922) as "gentle of heart and cheerful in every aspect," this comedy presents one episode in the spangled career of Pearl Jones "the greatest Brunhilde of the age." First known as Hollyhock Jones of Waco, Texas, then as "the Texas nightingale," and finally as Brasa Canava, Pearl sings and marries her way up to the Everest peak of the musical world. When she is about to take her fifth husband, one Sascha Block, a violin virtuoso fifteen years her junior, Raymond Tillerton, Pearl's grown son by her second husband, objects. Raymond himself plans to marry a flapper from the chorus of a musical show; and mother objects. In order to win Raymond over, Pearl calls in the boy's father, Steven Tillerton. But the boy is forgotten and the violin virtuoso plays his tunes in vain, for Pearl's eyes grow starry once more as she gets a fresh look at her second husband.

While several plays have presented the life of the prima donna, none has been so successful in making the prima donna both strange and human, lovable and changeable, swiftly fulminous and as suddenly rainbowed with honey smiles and baby talk. Pearl Jones is opulent in voice, purse, and profanity. Even *Variety* commented on Zoe Akin's frequent use of the word "tart." Pearl Jones was everyone's darling, and everyone's demon.

Her first husband caught her right out of Waco High. A drunken undertaker, he used to send her second-hand funeral lilies; he liked to hear her sing. With a voice that could drown the brass bands of the Lone Star State, Hollyhock Jones sang her way into the arms of Steven Tillerton, who borrowed $8,000 to send her abroad for vocal training. There the Texas Nightingale found a third husband in the composer with whom she studied. He was followed by a sculptor who rounded her into marble before she left him flat. Now—as Brasa Canava, serene, supreme —she is looking with eyes aquest for novelty and youth upon Sascha.

Husband number two, Steven Tillerton, is probably the only mate who truly loved her, and surely the only one who understood her. There is gentleness in the scenes between Steven and Pearl—although Zoe Akins knows when to cut a tender scene with a comic line. There is a good measure of compassion, too, despite the conflict, in the scenes between the mother and the impractical poet son. Most touching of all, however, are the scenes between the father and son, who beneath carefully chosen words try to feel their way into one another, with the tender and tense hesitancy of the parent and child that know one another but slightly.

A Texas Nightingale thus adds to its sparkling dialogue, to its "outrageously funny second act" (New York Journal, November 22, 1922), "quite as much heart as humor" (New York Globe, November 22, 1922). Alexander Woollcott declared Zoe Akins' A Texas Nightingale "not only the best play she has written, but one of the three or four most artful and civilized comedies the American stage has yet produced." George Jean Nathan, surprisingly, concurred with Woollcott, calling the play "beyond question as graceful, as witty, as original, and as amiably penetrating a comedy as the American Theatre has given birth to."

Chicago did not take kindly to the play, according to Charles Collins, of the Chicago Post (October 24, 1922). He called Zoe Akins' "extravagance unabated but her sense of the theatre almost exhausted"; and he felt the singer's son to be a "wretched little pest, a shrill repellent insect of modernity . . . written with a peacock's plume and violet ink." But the New York critics were unanimous in their praises. Heywood Broun (December 17, 1922) exclaimed that the brilliant and authentic comedy ran for such a short time because it had been "mauled and dog-eared by a ruinously inferior performance."

The Texas Nightingale was presented in Pasadena in 1940; but as far as New York is concerned, the play remains an example of good drama destroyed by bad production. It awaits a production that will transfer its rich qualities to the stage.

THE OLD MAID   Zoe Akins

A dramatization of one of the four novels of Edith Wharton's series In Old New York, this distinguished play opened at New York's Empire Theatre on January 7, 1935, with Judith Anderson and Helen Menken. It brought Zoe Akins the critical disagreement she usually evokes—and the Pulitzer Prize. The story of a tense but secret struggle between two sisters for the emotional possession of a child, the play is more quietly and simply written than most of the works of the author.

Delia, refusing to wait until the poor artist she loved made good, married and was soon widowed and left well off. Meanwhile the artist, having consoled himself with Delia's sister Charlotte to the extent of fathering her child, went abroad, never to return. For respectability's sake, Delia raised the child, who is given to believe that her mother, Charlotte, is merely her "old maid" aunt. When the play opens, the girl is grown, and the two sisters wage desperate war for her love.

As the New York Times put it, "Under the serene surface of a well-bred life in the New York of a hundred years ago, the velvet-pawed struggle goes on for two decades . . . With so much human emotion whipped up into passion, The Old Maid ought to be a masterpiece. This reviewer cannot pretend to know exactly why it it a good deal less than that."

On the other hand, Arthur Pollock described The Old Maid as "delicately carved in age-colored ivory, a beautiful picture of a day that is past, its romance and prim passion and tender sentiment . . . straightforward, astringent drama, moving in a direct, slender line, outlining its story without adornment." And the *New York World Telegram* reported that the play "never relaxes its emotional strength. Seldom does the theatre yield such plastic substance into the hands of actors who know how to mold a performance."

In their *History of the Theatre* (1941), George Freedley and John A. Reeves attribute to this "sentimental" play the establishment of the New York Drama Critics' Circle award: "The fact that so poor a play as this received the Pulitzer Award stimulated so much criticism that the New York Critics' Circle instituted its own award for the best play of the season, feeling that the Pulitzer judges either had lost their critical standards or were too likely to be overruled in their judgments by the Advisory Board." Freedley and Reeves neglect to mention that the critics had themselves been harassed by criticism from playwrights, producers and theatre goers. The Circle and its annual award grew, in part, out of a sense that the critics might find some safety in united action.

The Old Maid was presented in Vienna in 1937 as *The Two Mothers.* No doubt because it calls for two extremely sensitive actresses, the play has not been widely taken up by summer or college theatres. Without well contrasted stars, it would be as wooden as an antique show. With effective acting, however, the very quiet of its surface makes its depth profoundly moving. *The Old Maid* is a powerful psychological study, a grim picture of a hatred engendered by rivalry in "mother love."

SAUL   *Count Vittorio Alfieri*

This is the best play by Count Vittorio Alfieri (1749-1803), one of Italy's finest dramatists. In a severe style, suited to the patriarchal age it depicts, it moves with dramatic grandeur through the last days of the mad King Saul.

Taken from the *First Book of Samuel,* in the *Bible,* the story begins with the submission of David to King Saul. A fugitive, David plans to surrender while Saul's son, Jonathan, and his daughter, Michal, David's wife, try to dispel from the King's heart the suspicion and hatred of David that his uncle, Abner, has planted there. When David, by showing a piece of cloth cut from the robe Saul had worn in the Cave of En-gedi, proves that he had once had Saul in his power and spared him, the King once more receives David into his favor. Together, they plan a campaign against the Philistines.

Roused again by Abner, Saul appears in a spell of madness. David sings and soothes the King, but when his song grows warlike, the King rages against him. David flees; the battle plans are changed; and the Philistines, victorious, kill Jonathan. As Abner spirits Michal away to safety, Saul, in quiet majesty, rather than surrender kills himself.

Alfieri's tragedy *Saul,* published in 1777, has been universally acclaimed. The playwright himself, in dedicating *Saul* to Abbot Tommaso Valperga, said that "perhaps wrongly, I am singularly pleased" with the play. His judgment was not wrong. Matthew Arnold, however, spoke of the play's "narrow elevation" and called Alfieri a "noble-minded, deeply interesting man, but a monotonous poet." Mme. de Staël found "a superb use of lyric poetry" in *Saul.* Schlegel felt that among Alfieri's works the play was "favorably distinguished from the rest by a certain Oriental splendor, and the lyrical sublimity with which the troubled mind of Saul finds utterance." Emiliani Giudici believed that "in Alfieri art once more achieved the faultless purity of its proper character: Greek tragedy reached the same height in the Italian's *Saul* that it touched in the Greek's *Prometheus*, the two dramas that are perhaps the most gigantic creations of any literature."

A dignity animates the characters of *Saul* and their actions. Although their station in life may be as high as it is unique, their motives and their emotions are understood and shared by the beholders. Even Saul, whom Alfred Bates called "perhaps the only heroic madman in classical drama," stays within the bounds of human sympathy. At the end of the play, his sanity returned, Alfieri's Saul is a pitiable figure. Shorn of power, surrounded by enemies, he nevertheless defies defeat and challenges the fear of death in a reaffirmation of the will, the dignity, and the stature of man. From such a stand rises the exaltation born of tragedy.

The basic theme of *Saul* is one to which Alfieri turned again and again: the staunch defying tyranny. While *Saul* was less immediately pertinent to Alfieri's compatriots than others of his plays, they felt in it the fervor of Alfieri's drive against oppression.

A version of the play by André Gide was produced at the Vieux Colombier, Paris, in 1922, with Jacques Copeau. The role of Saul was a favorite with the great actor Salvini.

The *Christian Science Monitor* said of a comparatively poor production of the play: "One feels in some particularly audacious and vigorous scenes a truly Shakespearean breath. All the work is filled with the sober force of the classics. The style is lucid and harmonious. And if— apart from certain scenes which reach an intensely pathetic grandeur— one does not feel much emotion, at least one is constantly and acutely interested, owing to the incomparable literary qualities of *Saul*."

After writing *Saul*, Alfieri himself said, "Here I lay down the buskin forever."

MYRRHA   *Count Vittorio Alfieri*

Outstanding among the later tragedies of Vittorio Alfieri, *Myrrha* (*Mirra*, published 1783) retells from Ovid a story of incestuous love.

Myrrha, the only child of Cinyras, King of Cyprus, and of Cecris, is betrothed to Pereus, heir to the throne of Epirus. At one moment, she seems eager for the wedding, at another, she seems alarmed. Disturbed by her behavior, Cecris asks Myrrha's old nurse, Eurycleia, to discover what disturbs the girl; then Myrrha decides to marry Pereus on the morrow, saying, however, that she expects to die.

Cecris recalls having once boasted that more people came to Cyprus to worship her beauty than to worship Venus. It was on that day that Myrrha's behavior had changed; we may assume that her fate is visited upon her by the goddess, to punish her presumptuous mother. As the hymns of the wedding chorus swell, Myrrha suddenly becomes hysterical, as if she were attacked by a swarm of Furies, and Pereus kills himself. Myrrha's father, Cinyras, demands to know with whom Myrrha is in love. "With you!" she exclaims and seizes her father's dagger to plunge it into her breast.

Alfieri has told us what suggested this theme to him: "I happened to come across, in Ovid's *Metamorphoses,* that very warm and truly divine conversation of Myrrha with her nurse. It made me burst into tears, and the idea of making a tragedy of it flashed into my mind." *Myrrha* proved so moving that Byron reportedly fainted when he saw the play.

In his published works, Alfieri says that he placed *Myrrha* between the two plays called *Brutus,* "to serve as a whet to the appetite of those that would otherwise be sick of hearing of nothing but liberty and Rome." The theme of the play is indeed different from Alfieri's usual stories, which hang upon tyranny and freedom, as in the two plays in which he traces the course of the fight of the Roman patriot Brutus against the tyrant Tarquins. Once attracted, in *Myrrha,* by the character of the unfortunate maiden, Alfieri became interested in the problem of revealing her incestuous love, so that the play, as Schlegel saw it, is "a perilous attempt to treat with propriety a subject equally revolting to the sense and the feelings." Alfieri himself thought that he had been successful in his treatment of it. "In my opinion," he said, "the strictest mother in the strictest country in Europe might take her daughters to see this play without any dangerous emotions being aroused in their breasts. And this is not always the case when chaste virgins are taken to see many other tragedies founded on the most lawful love."

Alfieri saw *Myrrha* presented, with great success, with Madame Pollandi. The play was a favorite with Madame de Staël, at whose suggestion it was presented in Paris with La Marchionni. The role of Myrrha was Adelaide Ristori's finest part; she appeared in it in New York in 1867.

Myrrha tenderly probes a woman's heart. It is fired with the passion and eloquence that make Alfieri a noble representative of Italian literature.

ONE, FEW, TOO MANY and THE ANTIDOTE   *Count Vittorio Alfieri*

In his few comedies, no less than in his great poems and tragedies, Count Alfieri reawakened a national consciousness among his people. "He discovered Italy," said Massimo Taparolli d'Azeglio, "as Columbus discovered America, and initiated the idea of Italy as a nation. I place this merit far beyond that of his verses and his tragedies."

Alfieri's best comic work—and the most pointed of his political plays —is the group of four satires: *One, Few, Too Many,* and *The Antidote,* written about 1800. The four comprise an examination, in dramatic terms, of different forms of government. Written, like his tragedies, in iambic verse, they press home Alfieri's attitude toward freedom and toward government of the people for the people.

The comedy *One* examines the monarchy of Darius, King of Persia. In terms set by the oracle, a new king is to be chosen by the neighing of the first horse after sunrise. His horse brings the monarchy to Darius. Alfieri's play describes how the groom, apprized of the terms of the oracle, pricks his horse into neighing first. The grateful monarch sacrifices the steed to the sun and raises a statue in its honor.

The comedy *Few* deals with the oligarchy of the family of the Gracchi in Rome. Alfieri pictures their struggle to remain in power and their defeat and humiliation, in the campaign for the consulate, by Fabius.

The comedy *Too Many* portrays the democracy of Athens as viewed through the ironic eyes of Alexander the Great of Macedon. Of the two parties in Athens, that of Demosthenes constantly warns against the aims of Alexander, while that of Aeschines continuously calls for appeasement. Alternately, the two parties are courted and mocked, wooed and scorned by Alexander and his courtiers. Alfieri exposes the jealousy, venality, and general baseness of most of the representatives of the people, of the leaders sprung from the people.

The first play of the group describes the complete disregard of the tyrant for his subjects; the second, how the few manipulate the people to their own selfish and self-centered ends; and the third, how the people themselves, divided and incompetent, are stupid when well-meaning and selfish when shrewd.

The solution? Alfieri suggests it in the full title of the fourth comedy: *Mix Three Poisons and You Will Have Their Antidote.* Taking an island of the Orcades as his locale, Alfieri used contemporary situations to support his idea that monarch, aristocrat, and the common man must unite in the national interest and, with patriotic zeal, effect a proper government.

In the four comedies, as in his tragic dramas, Alfieri treats the great heroes of history like ordinary mortals. More than in his tragedies, however, he strips them of the grandeur in which history has draped them, thus bringing them to the level of the politicians, the citizens, the leaders of his time and thus making his political concerns concrete and near to home.

"When the fiery love of freedom shall have purged Italy," said Emiliani Giudici, "the Alfierian drama will be the only representation worthy of a great and free people."

A SUNNY MORNING   *Alvarez Quintero Brothers*

The brothers Alvarez Quintero—Serafin (1871-1938) and Joaquin (1873-1944)—are the most prolific of twentieth century Spanish playwrights. Their collaborative efforts have produced as many as six plays in a single year, while their total output amounts to almost 200 burlettas, farces, and comedies. Most of their plays abound in local color. The chief value of their work lies in the kindly portrayal of the varied types of their native Andalusia, whose motives, but more especially, whose sentiments are deftly and tenderly described.

Most popular of the Quintero plays outside of Spain is the one-act *Mañana de sol (A Sunny Morning)*, 1905, which was performed in New York at the Neighborhood Playhouse in 1917; by Eva Le Gallienne in 1928 and 1935; and which has been played frequently in the "little theatre," as well as by college groups.

Based on a poem from the *Doloras*, 1846, of Ramón de Campoamor, *A Sunny Morning* presents two crotchety old folk, Don Gonzalo and Doña Laura. Meeting on a bench in a public park, over a pinch of snuff they fall into conversation, only to discover that, years before, they had been deeply and romantically in love with one another. A sentimental "lace valentine," this comedy is as radiant as the sunshine after a spring shower. With tender humor and neat characterization the irony of the situation is subdued, as the passions of youth become a remembered flame that, for a moment, stirs beneath the settling ashes of age. Recollected in tranquillity, their old love quickens the tenderly ironic smile of a charming play.

THE LADY FROM ALFÁQUEQUE   *Alvarez Quintero Brothers*

Liveliest of the Quintero brothers' longer plays is the two-act comedy *La Consulesa (The Lady from Alfáqueque)*, written in 1914. Produced in London in 1928 and again in 1933, in New York by the Civic Repertory Theatre with Alma Kruger in 1929, and widely performed in Europe, this play, more than any other of their some 200 plays, has made the Quintero brothers internationally known.

It is a delightful comedy of a woman in a big city who cannot forget the small town that was her childhood home. Doña Fernandita, wife of a wealthy Madrid manufacturer, idolizes everything and everybody, the almond cakes, the saints, the poor relations, from her home town Alfáqueque. As a result, a constant stream of guests makes her home a minor bedlam, a pleasant but constantly chaotic, crowded household, over which her adoring and tolerant husband watches with amused and greatly abused patience. One day a poet, Felipe Rivas, arrives from Alfáqueque. Fainting from the worries of a secret danger, he stays on, heartily welcomed by Doña Fernandita. Exercising the prerogative of the poet, he makes love to three of the girls. When Doña Fernandita discovers that he is not really from Alfáqueque, and that the danger threatening him is the danger of having to work, she finally admits that she has been imposed upon. As she gathers strength to tell Felipe to leave, he launches into a new poem on the glories of Alfáqueque. Her anger smooths to rapture, as her husband looks on with reasonable doubt, and the curtain falls.

While the play neatly captures the local atmosphere, with the idiosyncrasies of an overpolite Spanish gentleman and a ubiquitous but befuddled priest, it has wider implications even in these figures, as well as in its portrayal of poor relatives. It suggests, without malice but with quiet understanding, that differences in conduct and outlook between dependents and those who are financially and socially secure are to be expected and accepted. Equally universal is the play's basic theme. As pointed out by the *New York Herald Tribune* (January 20, 1929), Doña Fernandita could be any American small town woman whose husband's work holds her in Manhattan.

Shrewd, but unfailingly amusing, this delightful play does not always use new materials, but it lends the old a warmth of humor and a zest for life. Its externals are but slightly heightened for drama, its essence is widely true. Reported the *Boston Transcript* (May 16, 1929): "The Quinteros' humor, again, eschews current modes, being as far from wisecracking as it is from buffoonery . . . unpretentious, honest, good-natured, made from foibles and idiosyncrasies as the pleasing part they are in the common lot . . . They neither gird at Doña Fernandita nor guy her. They are content to smile, wonder, sigh, and look the other way. Don Pascual, who makes the best of his wife and her infirmity after this fashion, is their spokesman. For them, a hint is better than italics. How grown-up they are, how wide-minded and honest-minded, too, how good tempered as well! Americans need them and their works, not only for two hours' pleasure in the theatre but also for mental and moral good." *The Lady From Alfáqueque*, their most mellow work, is a heart-warming and heart-lifting comedy. In plays to which Joaquin contributed lightness and gay wit and Serafin the more philosophic view, they combined realistic externals with an inner content that makes their work a pattern of delight.

THE ARCADIANS   *Mark Ambient*

Here is a fresh and lively combination of what theatre-folk call the
"girlie show" and the gay fantasy of an amusing story. Mark Ambient
(1860-1937) co-authored it with fellow-Englishman A. M. Thompson
(1861-1948).

The play opens in an Arcadian dell, where maids and youths enjoy
primal innocence and a care-free happiness. Their curiosity is aroused by
reports of a country, England by name, where the truth is not always
told, where the inhabitants have found an ingenious substitute called the
lie. Their wonder is satisfied when James Smith, a middle-aged Lon-
doner, descends upon Arcady from a balloon. Finding that they have
little liking for Smith's lies, the Arcadians dip him in a well, from which
he comes forth a truth-telling young man. The Arcadians then christen
him Simplicitas.

Successful with Smith, the Arcadians resolve to cure his countrymen
of the lying habit. They journey to England, where they visit the Askwood Race Track and set up the Arcadian Restaurant. Eventually, they
decide to return to Arcadia before they too become liars. They leave the
English to their fate.

In the second act, at the race track, there are two contrasting choruses:
the diaphanously clad but innocent maids of Arcady; and the sophisticated
ladies in Directoire gowns who come to Ascot ("Askwood") to watch
the races and the men. This contrast, not of the sexes, but rather of
the awareness of sex, is delightfully effective.

Mrs. James Smith is at the races too, enjoying the country and a brisk
flirtation, little knowing that her husband is the handsome young "stranger" nearby. Eileen Cavanagh is also there; her sweetheart Jack Meadows
has all his money on an entry. The Arcadians, understanding animal talk,
know which horse the horses have decided will win. Simplicitas rides
him. Thus girlies and gags join in amusing situations.

The music by Lionel Monckton and Howard Talbot is tuneful and
pleasant; the lyrics, fresh and clever. Among the more popular songs
from the play are "The Pipes of Pan," "Since the Days Before the Flood,"
"The Dear Little Girl With a Bit of a Brogue," "Charming Weather."

The Arcadians opened in London on April 28, 1909, with Frank Moulan
(of Gilbert and Sullivan fame) as Simplicitas-Smith and Julia Sanderson
as Eileen. It ran for 809 performances. "It is long since anything on the
light opera stage of London has been seen that can be compared for prettiness, cleverness, and melody to *The Arcadians*," reported *The Times*.
During the following season, the play repeated its London success in New
York.

With a swirl of Arcadian nymphs and the sweep of English ladies, this
delightful play gives a fanciful approach to the eternal problem of truth-
telling and to the eternal mystery and mastery of sex.

WHAT PRICE GLORY?   *Maxwell Anderson*

The son of a Baptist minister, fervent and serious in all his work, Maxwell Anderson (b. 1887) is among the foremost American playwrights.
After teaching for a while, he turned to journalism, which he abandoned
upon the success of *What Price Glory?*, written with Laurence Stallings
(b. 1894) in 1924.

What Price Glory? is the soldiers' play of World War I, the first realistic drama to come out of that conflict. The plot of the play is far less important than the picture it gives of the thoughts, feelings, and actions of the common man at war. Three corporals, like the "three weird sisters" in *Macbeth,* create the mood of the play; the life of the ordinary serviceman during his off hours, the hours of "sweating it out" and of swearing, supplies the story. There is plenty of fighting, but not with the enemy.

A semblance of plot is woven around the bitter rivalry between two members of a Marine unit—Captain Flagg and Sergeant Quirt. In a French town near the front, the latter steals the Captain's girl, Charmaine. The two men are pummeling one another when the command is given for their return to the front. Kissing Charmaine a blithe farewell, they dash off together—friends.

What Price Glory? opened on September 4, 1924, and ran for 299 performances. Because it depicted members of the armed services as subject to spells of profanity in their unguarded moments, Rear Admiral Charles Plunkett complained to Secretary of the Navy Wilbur, that the production violated a federal law prohibiting the wearing of the United States uniform by nonservice men *except on the stage, providing nothing is done to bring discredit on the services.* Following upon a visit from New York police, three profane expressions were removed and the honor of the Marines was seemingly restored.

Stallings, who had served in the Marine Corps, first thought of developing his ideas into a musical show. Anderson wrote it as a play; Stallings then went over it, as he said, "to give it local color, the living, realistic touch." The genesis of the play was vividly described by Heywood Broun in the *New York World-Telegram* of August 2, 1933, "I think that *What Price Glory?* deserves to rank very close to the top of the list of enduring American plays," he concluded, "but it contains its own particular solace for those who still believe in war."

When *What Price Glory?* was first produced, Percy Hammond (September 5, 1924) called it a ruddy gem. But, he added, "like several other pleasures, it is too good to be true." Alexander Woollcott, on the other hand, was highly enthusiastic: "No war play written in the English language since the German guns boomed under the walls of Liege, ten years ago, has been so true, so alive, so salty and so richly satisfying."

Considering the possibilities of *What Price Glory?* as a motion picture, a Hollywood executive described it as having "some of the most unreal situations I have ever seen. It is acclaimed a great play by all the critics, but I cannot see it with a spyglass either as a play entertainment or picture." Despite this sharp report, it was filmed in 1926 with Victor McLaglen, Edmund Lowe, and Dolores Del Rio; and again in 1936 and 1952. The play toured through the years 1926 and 1927, and was performed at Amherst College in 1938.

Despite the rough-house, the rough language and the "anti-romantic" attitude of *What Price Glory?,* the play assumes a basic faith in man, a recognition that—swear as he may, sneer or scorch with cynicism as he will—beneath the callous epidermis is a tender core. For some things a man will die. Although it is not preached, but rather is felt behind the actions of the soldiers, this basic perception makes *What Price Glory?* something more than a mere play about soldiers with their guns down. It is a driving drama of unspoken ideals.

SATURDAY'S CHILDREN

Maxwell Anderson

In 1927, while seeking the mode best suited to him in the theatre, Maxwell Anderson found neat expression in this pleasant comedy of domestic life. He had previously attempted a tragedy, *White Desert* (1923) and had written three plays in collaboration with Laurence Stallings; *What Price Glory?* (1924), *First Flight* (1925), and *The Buccaneer* (1925)—of which only the first achieved significance. But on his journey to what George Freedley and John A. Reeves call "a high standard of near perfection," he wrote this "restrained and sympathetic comedy of young love and middle-class domesticity."

Saturday's child, according to the nursery jingle, works for a living. In the play, Bobby discovers this truth, after having put aside her stenographer's notebook to marry the attractive lad in the outer office, Rims O'Neil, whom she has won through a trick devised by her sister. During the first year of their married life, the couple is beset, not only with the problem of earning a livelihood, but with the strain of making a happy life together. Bills inundate their dreams of domestic harmony, but as Bobby sits forlornly desolate at the close of the play, Rims, who has slammed the door, climbs back to her up the fire escape. Love has conquered all.

With Ruth Gordon and Roger Pryor, *Saturday's Children* proved both amusing and moving. Opening in New York on January 26, 1927, it received a wholehearted welcome. Alexander Woollcott observed: "This is so vociferous a season in the theatre that one wonders how the shy, gentle, steadfast comedy will ever make itself heard above the uproar, will ever get word to the nameless, countless millions who would find an evening of warming satisfactions in its truth, its wisdom, and its deep, tender charm . . . subtle interplay of loneliness and fear and deceit and blundering ignorance and hope and hungers of the heart." Gilbert W. Gabriel went even further in his praise, finding that the season offered "no play of better quality of fun and charm and cozy truth . . . this tussle between a gawk in peg pants and a girl in mutiny has become something as important and arresting as a tide of armies and emperors at Austerlitz."

Brooks Atkinson wondered over the play's literary qualities: "One suspects Mr. Anderson of being more a man of letters than a man of the theatre. As the reviewers invariably say upon such occasions, *Saturday's Children* profits quite as much as it loses by that weakness."

The English production of 1934, with Colin Keith-Johnson, changed the young couple's names to Joy and Robin.

Anderson is a provocative though uneven writer. His attempts at drama in verse are often somewhat pretentious. Of these, *Night Over Taos,* 1932, which describes the last stand of Pablo Montoyas, feudal lord of Taos, New Mexico, against the surge of American "progress," and *The Masque Of Kings,* 1937, based on the shooting of Crown Prince Rudolph of Austria and Baroness Mary Vetsera in a hunting lodge at Mayerling, which pictures the Crown Prince as opposing his father's tyranny, will be less lengthily remembered than the simple, warm, and human study of young folk fighting for happiness in *Saturday's Children.* Revived frequently, especially by college groups and summer theatres, it presents in a humorous and provoking way the problems of struggling for a livelihood and finding a common ground of living.

GODS OF THE LIGHTNING   *Maxwell Anderson*

The indignation that frequently burns in Maxwell Anderson was
never more intense than in this drama written in collaboration with
Harold Hickerson, based upon the trial and execution of Sacco and Vanzetti in Massachusetts in 1927.

As told in the play, a paymaster is killed during a mill strike. Macready, a firebrand of the I.W.W., who had instigated the strike, and
Capraro, a pacifist, are arrested for the killing. Given a trial in which
every legal trick is turned against them, they are found guilty and
executed. That they are both innocent is not so much as questioned in the
play; in fact, a premise of the play, which with thin disguise follows the
fortunes of Sacco and Vanzetti from their arrest to their death, is that
they are martyrs. The district attorney plays upon the prejudices of a
picked jury; and the judge, with self-righteous patriotism, is bent upon
destroying the two "foreign radicals."

Advance reports of the play keyed the public to expect a violent
attack upon an "arrant injustice." At its opening in New York, October
24, 1928, officials of the Department of Justice and of the State of Massachusetts were in the audience to take notes.

The public, too, took notice of this "strong, harrowing drama," excellently performed by Leo Bulgakov, Charles Bickford, Horace Braham,
and Sylvia Sidney. But the intensity of public feeling over the Sacco-
Vanzetti case, and the sharp one-sidedness of *Gods of the Lightning*,
prejudiced the reception of the play. Thus Percy Hammond, with cold
reservation, observed: "It might have been a better, if a less moving,
play, if it had dramatized the tragic doubt concerning the guilt of Sacco
and Vanzetti instead of deliberately ignoring it . . . The authors do not
give Law and Order a better break than Law and Order gave Sacco and
Vanzetti. They shut their ears to evidence and summon the tumbril for
their victim without listening to the defense." At the other extreme,
Robert Littell exclaimed: "My growing dislike for courtroom scenes was
washed violently overboard by the blast of defiant flaming courage so
admirably delivered by Mr. Bickford, by Horace Braham's quieter but no
less moving appeal, by Mr. Bulgakov's sinister, withering confession, and
by the awful feeling that this was all true and could never be righted or
undone."

The authors combined their intense feeling with sufficient dramaturgic
skill to make *Gods of the Lightning* a rousing piece of propaganda. Like
most propaganda, however, the play appeals only to those already convinced of the soundness of the cause it champions. Equally melodramatic, but with a deeper psychological probing and a less violent
eloquence, Maxwell Anderson pictured the possible consequences of the
Sacco-Vanzetti case in his *Winterset**. There is, nevertheless, enough
sound theatre in *Gods of the Lightning* to make it a forceful dramatic
study of the powers-that-be destroying opposition through legal murder.

ELIZABETH THE QUEEN   *Maxwell Anderson*

Originally entitled *Elizabeth and Essex*, this drama in verse made its
bow in a brilliant production by the Theatre Guild in New York on November 3, 1930, with Lynn Fontanne as Elizabeth and Alfred Lunt as Lord
Essex. In 1932 it was again produced in New York, with Mildred Natwick

and Vincent Price, and it has been revived somewhere in the country almost every year. In 1941, it was recorded on disc for the blind by Mady Christians and Wesley Addy.

The play is written in a crisp prose that alternates with a loose blank verse. At times, as in the banter between the court ladies and the fool in Act II, Scene 3, the patter and the puns of its prose are a rather obvious and consequently dull imitation of such effects in Elizabethan plays. The essential theme of the play, however, is presented in strong, dramatic terms and, in usually vigorous prose or swift if uninspired verse, it moves with speed and power.

Elizabeth is torn between her indomitable will, her need to hold her power, and her love for Essex. Aging, she desperately loves the gallant young Essex, and he loves Elizabeth. But Essex, too, suffers the need for power. He wishes to share the throne as Elizabeth's equal. Loved by the people, but snared by his enemies, Raleigh and Cecil, into a command in Ireland where all English expeditions fail, Essex returns to capture London and the palace. By promising to share the throne, Elizabeth tricks him into dismissing his guard, whereupon she has him arrested and taken to the Tower. The stubborness of both Elizabeth and Essex leads thence to his execution.

Maxwell Anderson slipped a number of interesting literary references into the play. Much, for example, is made of a performance of Shakespeare's *Richard II**, given supposedly in support of Essex' rebellion, since it portrays the deposition of Richard; later, when the Queen hopes that Essex will sue for pardon, the players attempt to distract her with scenes of her favorite character, Falstaff.

Despite such allusions to the period of the play, and despite the date of its events (1601), the psychological responses and complexities of the characters are essentially of our own time.

The power of the characterization of Elizabeth and Essex is felt despite the language of the play rather than because of it. The fateful spur to power pricks within the individual; and the intensity, as reading reveals, is in the play itself. The critics, however, inclined to attribute it wholly to the performers. Thus the *New York World* (Nov. 4, 1930) concluded: "By far the most remarkable feature . . . is the playing of the Queen by Lynn Fontanne." John Mason Brown went further: "The Lunts outdistanced not only the material with which they were working but all of those who stand near them on the stage . . . they converted what threatened to be a very much beruffed and cross-gartered adventure into a high-voltage and exciting evening in the theatre."

Elizabeth the Queen certainly provides a challenge to great actors.

BOTH YOUR HOUSES   *Maxwell Anderson*

Here is another of Anderson's plays in prose. Written as an attack upon corrupt politics, it has been praised for its "forthright courage, savage vigor, and enlightenment."

Both Your Houses opened in New York on March 6, 1933, played through the season, and won the Pulitzer Prize. Changing conditions have not weakened the message of the play.

"A plague o' both your houses," says Mercutio in *Romeo and Juliet**, as he becomes mortally entangled in a quarrel of others. Anderson borrows the phrase *both your houses* to refer to the two political parties which in his play embroil and destroy a young and naive Congressman. Appointed to the Appropriations Committee, this youthful legislator watches aghast as a bill is fattened into a political pork barrel. Unable to check the dishonesty of his colleagues, the young Congressman proceeds to pile additional items into the bill until it seems to him so extravagant a measure that it will die of its own wastefulness. Both chambers thereupon pass the bill by a great majority. "Our system is—every man for himself, and the nation be damned," the Congressman protests.

"And it works!" cries the politician, as the final curtain falls.

With a brilliant cast—Shepperd Strudwick played the young congressman, supported by Mary Phillips, Morris Carnovsky, Jane Seymour, J. Edward Bromberg, and Walter C. Kelly—and with racy vernacular dialogue, so vehement a play inevitably evoked partisanship. It may indeed be questioned whether the political leanings of the critics did not tilt their judgment of the play.

Brooks Atkinson found *Both Your Houses* the most stirring and direct of the theatrical attacks upon the depravity of representative government. "It is not only an angry crying of names and causes but an excellent play that will interest those whom it is convincing . . . a remarkably actable play." John Anderson, on the other hand, while feeling the fervor of the play, denied it any other merit: "The drama turned around . . . and bit the hand that taxes it . . . Maxwell Anderson doesn't, unfortunately, make it very dramatic, thereby defeating its own purpose." Robert Garland called it "an unhappy hangover from the Hoover administration . . . a bellyache inherited from a former and less fortunate era . . . and unexpectedly dull, as entertainment goes." John Mason Brown, however, found virtue in Anderson's characterization: "By giving his graftees a break, by drawing them as human beings rather than as Boucicault bankers or Desperate Desmonds from the comic strips, Mr. Anderson proves his wisdom as a dramatist."

After *Both Your Houses* had received the Pulitzer award, the *New York Herald-Tribune* observed that it lacked "those qualities of imagination and poetry that have touched Mr. Anderson's other plays. It is a straightforward, workmanlike job of theatrical muckraking . . . As a so-called propaganda piece, it comes a bit late and is blanketed by much that fills the actual air. As drama, it is photographic and literal, and slogs a bit too persistently along the one rather raucous, combative line."

Both Your Houses is an effective, somewhat savagely satiric, yet basically realistic picture of corruption at work on the roots of democracy.

MARY OF SCOTLAND   *Maxwell Anderson*

Beginning with a sweep of Puritan prose and surging into vigorous verse, *Mary of Scotland* is another play in which Maxwell Anderson vividly dramatizes history, depicting the six sad years that begin with the return of Mary from France in 1561, and end with her imprisonment by Queen Elizabeth of England in 1567.

Although Puritan John Knox abominates his Catholic Queen and her Scottish lords fear her frailty, Queen Elizabeth hates her as a young and beautiful rival to the throne. At the end of the play, Mary becomes aware that the critical events of her career—her marriage to Darnley, the murder of her secretary Rizzio, the murder of Darnley, her marriage to Bothwell, the rebellion, the truce—were all the results of traps deliberately set by Elizabeth for her own particular ends.

In having Elizabeth visit the imprisoned Mary at the close of the play, Anderson forges history to his dramatic purpose, creating a great scene wherein the crafty, plausible, but indomitable Elizabeth of England meets the meek, yet proud and undaunted Mary, Queen of Scots. Mary has the one shaft in her quiver to sink into Elizabeth's heart, for Elizabeth, politically victorious over Mary, has been a hater, a schemer, a liar, and a barren woman—while her victim has known a rich life, with love and its fruition, a child.

The simple power of the verse of *Mary of Scotland* places it among Anderson's best writings. It was originally presented in New York on November 27, 1933 (it ran for 248 performances) with a superb cast including Helen Hayes as Mary, Philip Merivale as Bothwell, and Helen Menken as Elizabeth. Katharine Hepburn later played Mary in the motion picture version.

If the scales of history are tipped to attract the sympathy of the audience, the playwright's enthusiasm rather than his honesty is at fault. As emphasized by Brooks Atkinson in his review of this play, Anderson "has not always succeeded on the stage, but he has never failed in integrity". Atkinson, indeed, gave *Mary of Scotland* his fullest praise: "This is the drama of heroes . . . a drama that is streaked with greatness. It has restored the English language to its high estate as an instrument of lustrous beauty;" and in his Sunday "second thoughts" he called the play "one of the finest pieces of writing in the collected works of the American Drama".

In *Mary of Scotland*, Anderson deals more with individuals than with ideas. The characters of the play are not there to set in contrast ideals or theories of government so much as to portray the struggle of two women, two rulers, for power.

VALLEY FORGE
Maxwell Anderson

This play is especially interesting as a twentieth-century view of the eighteenth century. If, as has often been said, history offers a lesson to our day, it is no less true that we see the past through our own eyes.

Valley Forge portrays the American Revolutionary forces during the dreary winter of 1778, when their fortune was at its lowest ebb, when Washington had to fight not only the British, but the double-dealing war-weary among the colonists; the Congress, with its petty disputes, indecisions, and delays; the impatient among the merchant class, whose business had been damaged by the war; the homesick and the deserters among his worn-out, rag-wrapped men; and the fierce winter's cold. Earlier histories, borne on the surge of rugged individualism in the United States, showed Washington as the dominant leader, who by the power of his personality and iron will held together the shriveling remnants of his half-starved and half-frozen forces. But Anderson's *Valley Forge*, with the mass-impetus and emphasis of our time, shows a discouraged, defeated General, who meets with the British Lord Howe in a shack on a Delaware River island in order to seek terms of surrender; a General who is reproached by the rank and file (the proletariat!) of his men and who, through their determination (mass-pressure!), is brought to a new resolve. We behold not the leader rallying his men, but the men inspiriting their commander. Thus does the twentieth century interpret the eighteenth.

Valley Forge opened at the Guild Theatre on December 10, 1934, with Philip Merivale as Washington and Margalo Gillmore as Mary Philipse, the charming lady who accompanied Howe and brought to Washington word of the French alliance. It played 58 performances.

Arthur Pollock called *Valley Forge* "as articulate as lightning and made eloquent by liquid language that is often liquid fire". The play, however, rather haphazardly shifts from prose to an irregular, often prosaic verse.

Estimates of this work differ greatly. Brooks Atkinson, for example, said: "Formal English seems better suited to English and Scottish courts than it does to the ragamuffins of a cruel Valley Forge winter . . . It is hard to worship a great character in the theatre without slopping over. To tell the truth, *Valley Forge* gives a splash or two." Freedley and Reeves in their *History of the Theatre* (1941) said, likewise, that "high regard is a poor substitute for drama and the life of Washington . . . is a poor subject for playwrights."

A more definite dissatisfaction was registered by Percy Hammond: "Its routine romance enters and exits punctually, its humor is the expected and bitter jocularity of the Colonial doughboy, and its story that of a Cause which, lost for a while, turns up in the nick of time, triumphant. Although fastidious drama-lovers may object to its orderly procedure, poets and patriots will find in it much that will agitate their sympathetic souls."

John Anderson (no relative of Maxwell) was very much impressed. He called the play "a noble work, its author's full-seasoned best, a play stirring with passionate eloquence and majestic drama, at the deep roots of American history . . . something that he can be proud of, and something that we, the inheritors of this rediscovered Valley Forge, can be grateful for as history, entertainment, and, if it please you, warning."

WINTERSET   *Maxwell Anderson*

This is Maxwell Anderson's finest drama and one of the few great American tragedies. It offers an imagined aftermath of the Sacco-Vanzetti case, which had furnished Anderson the theme of his *Gods of the Lightning*.

Mio, the son of one of the two executed men, hopes to clear his father of the judgment against him. Judge Gaunt, who had handed down the verdict, cracks beneath the pressure of conscience. He and Mio are drawn to the home of one Garth, a witness to the murder for which the two men were condemned but who had never been called to testify. The real killer, Trock, watches Garth and, in order to keep himself clear, kills Mio; and Mio's sweetheart, Mirianne, dies with him.

No one who saw *Winterset* during its New York run will forget the grim setting designed by Jo Mielziner: A slum district beside a river, where tenement wall and natural rock rise to the great loom of a bridge. The cheerless basement of a tenement with pipes running outside its walls, a large steampipe crossing low on the stage—a rat-hole where cowards and killers might hide, but where the poorest could look to-

wards the bridge, and dream. The vividness of the setting was matched
by the acting of Eduardo Ciannelli as Trock, Margo as Mirianne, Richard
Bennett as Judge Gaunt, and Burgess Meredith as Mio.

The play opened in New York, September 25, 1935, and toured the
country for five years. It had the distinction of winning the first award
of the New York Drama Critics' Circle. Margo and Burgess Meredith
starred in the motion picture version of the play in 1936, and it was
presented in New York, 1945, by Equity Library.

Looking back upon a wrong committed by a previous generation,
Winterset saw beyond the immediate facts of that wrong into the larger
issues of faith, justice, and integrity. When the sin of their father is
visited upon the sons and daughters of *Winterset*, Anderson achieves,
not the flare of indignation that was his *Gods of the Lightning*, but the
even flame of steadfastness and truth. Even his verse is ennobled by
the depth and fullness of his perception. His language is at his simplest,
most effective, and most beautiful.

Brooks Atkinson, in his first review of the play, said, "There are moments when the verse seems superfluous or ostentatious," but he retracted after reading the play: "I called the final lines 'formal and prolix.' They are not. They are as hard and cutting as emerald dust and
a fair token of the philosophy and style of a fine American drama . . .
By comparison with *Winterset*, journeyman drama has a pettiness that
is almost contemptible . . . *Winterset* ought to be, not an incident, but
an event, in the theatre."

The critics, as is usual in the case of Anderson, met *Winterset* with
divided opinions. Percy Hammond called it "a murky drama." John
Anderson commented: "Maxwell Anderson has stirred the embers of
a poet's wrath . . . [the play] achieves one superlative scene in the second act and leaves the rest of the evening lost in articulate emptiness."
The scene he singled out is that in which the gangster, the judge, and
the executed man's son together come face to face with the truth. Robert
Garland was disappointed: "*Winterset* isn't the fine play it set out to
be. Instead, it is a murder melodrama in masquerade, a gun-and-
gangster thriller with poetic aspirations."

The action of the play draws its title from the time symbolically
chosen for its happenings. There is the chill of remembered cold in
Winterset; but after it comes the warmth of love, even of exaltation.

HIGH TOR   *Maxwell Anderson*

A combination of melodrama and farce, of Hudson River legend and
contemporary satire, of smiling surface and serious depth, *High Tor* is
the most delightful of Maxwell Anderson's plays. It is, as Brooks Atkinson declared, " the gustiest fantasy in the American drama".

High Tor is a crag looming 832 feet above the Hudson River, along
the Palisades below the town of Haverstraw. The owner, Van Van Dorn,
a young American who loves the mountain for its beauty, refuses to sell
it to a crushed-stone firm. Mixed in the tangle of the play are two
local politicians trying to swindle the lad out of the property, three fellows who have robbed a bank in nearby Nanuet, a company of Dutch
sailors waiting for Henry Hudson to come back for them, a philosophical
old Indian, a maiden of today, and a young seventeenth century lass,

Lise. The Dutch sailors stuff the two rascal politicians into a steam
shovel and hoist them up for a night. Van falls in love with the wraith
Lise but at the end of the play, in a return to reality, he sells the crag
and with the modern maid, Judith, goes west toward fresher mountains.
The end of the play may seem a surrender. Indeed the *New York
Daily News* spoke of the "unbelievably shallow conclusion" that Anderson had embodied in the last words of the Indian, "Nothing is made by
men but makes, in the end, good ruins." The *News* overlooked an earlier
reflection by the Indian on the olden days: "Then, as now, the young
braves were for keeping what was ours, whatever it cost in blood. And
they did try, but when they'd paid their blood, and still must sell, the
price was always less than what it was before their blood was paid."

The dialogue is for the most part spirited, amusing, and imaginative.
Atkinson, after the opening night, thought some of the verse "too lyric
to be dramatic", but upon reading *High Tor*, he declared: "My admiration, especially for the verse, has on the whole increased."

Following their wont, the critics disagreed sharply over the play.
After its world premiere in Cleveland on December 29, 1936, *Variety*
with its usual elegance said that the play delivered "another kick in the
pants for the machine age—without arriving at any definite attitude,
and without gripping the listener . . . Very little danger is there, of
his new one copping any sort of prize, except a medal for being the
season's most confusing play." But after *High Tor* opened in New York,
on January 9, 1937, with Burgess Meredith, Peggy Ashcroft, and John
Drew Colt, it won the New York Drama Critics' Circle award.

Nonetheless, New York opinion was divided. Richard Watts considered *High Tor* one of Anderson's "strongest and most arresting plays".
But John Anderson found the play's fantasy disappointing: "In dramatic poetry especially, there must be a complete unity, maintained
against all intrusion, and held surely against dramatic irrelevance. *High
Tor* repeatedly breaks its own spell by a clash of moods, and since the
mood here is the chief thing, I found the illusion in fragments . . . It
would be a fine bubble if it didn't have a pinhole in it." In direct disagreement, John Mason Brown declared: "One false step, one lapse
into the mundane, the heavy-handed, or the conventional, and its enchantment would vanish. But vanish it does not. Because, even while
it is dealing with a spell cast upon those who are brought together one
stormy night on a haunted mountain up the Hudson, *High Tor* succeeds
in casting a spell of its own. It is a magic spell which finds Mr. Anderson doing the best, most creative and original work of his distinguished
career."

Maxwell Anderson has his home on South Mountain Road in the
shadow of High Tor. The nearby Nanuet bank really had been robbed.
Anderson's neighbor, William A. Caldwell, commenting on the play in
the New Jersey *Bergen County Evening Record*, said, "I will swear I
can call the two politicians by name. Can it be that Maxwell Anderson
is busting a first-rate scandal story on the New York stage instead of in
the local gazettes?" The owner of most of High Tor, Elmer Van Orden,
who holds the deed by grant of George III, after seeing the play, swore
that he'd never sell the mountain. Thus the Hudson's High Tor may
remain a lift of beauty in the Palisades, as Maxwell Anderson's *High Tor*
remains a lift of beauty in the American drama.

High Tor has frequently been produced by community and college theatres. While recognizing the inevitable advance of the industrial age, it plays upon nostalgia with light humor and tearful fantasy; and it discloses the spirit of man unbound by the chains of the material world.

KNICKERBOCKER HOLIDAY   *Maxwell Anderson*

Maxwell Anderson went on a holiday romp when he wrote *Knickerbocker Holiday*. He goes back in music and song to old New Amsterdam, with Washington Irving contemplating the days of Pieter Stuyvesant and occasionally cautioning the citizens of that time as, standing at one side of the stage, he prepares "Father Knickerbocker's History of New York".

In truth, however, Anderson's is only a busman's holiday. For the story of his play opens with young Brom Broeck in the stocks. Something in the air he breathes and the food he eats makes Brom love freedom and that love brings him into conflict with Governor Stuyvesant in whom we see a prototype of the Fascist of recent years. Thus, Anderson's charming scene of the New York Battery in the seventeenth century is but a foreshadowing of the problems of the twentieth century. With appropriate music and due melodrama, the girl whom the authoritarian Stuyvesant wants to marry chooses freedom in wedlock with Brom.

The music is by Kurt Weill; the lyrics are by Anderson. Among the more memorable songs of the play are: "There's Nowhere to Go But Up", "How Can You Tell an American?", and that lovely melody, "September Song", which Walter Huston (as old Stuyvesant) projected touchingly as he lifted Pieter Stuyvesant's silver leg rhythmically.

Opening in New York on October 19, 1938, *Knickerbocker Holiday* was the second production of the Playwrights' company. It ran for 168 performances and was made into a motion picture in 1944.

Several critics frowned at this attempt at the light fantastic. Brooks Atkinson said the play was "beautifully staged . . . and there is much to recommend it in the way of intelligent showmanship and excellent music. But Maxwell Anderson's style of writing leans toward the pedantic in a brisk musical setting. He cannot trip it quite gaily enough for the company he is keeping". John Mason Brown concurred: "A good idea gone wrong . . . its humor, except in the lyrics, is of an obvious, old-fashioned kind." Walter Winchell, using his columnist technique in his review, cracked down, "The theme extends over a period of 300 years, but the show seems much longer."

The play was heartily welcomed, on the other hand, by Arthur Pollock. To him it was "light, amusing, and gracefully done"; he observed that Anderson shows "that democracy is better than Fascism because Democracy is governed by amateurs and since government by amateurs is less efficient it is more fun for those governed . . . The most literate musical comedy we have ever had in this country unquestionably, musical comedy the purpose of which is to have meaning and amiability at the same time. Musical comedy, that is, that we should shout with joy to find in the theatre at last".

Despite an occasional heavy-handed touch, *Knickerbocker Holiday* achieves a delightful blend of charm and satire. It is at once nostalgic and immediate, olden in flavor, contemporary in theme.

KEY LARGO   *Maxwell Anderson*

The noble concern of Maxwell Anderson with the larger issues of life
led him in *Key Largo* to disclose the evasions by which the honest man
may seek to justify his continuing existence in the midst of wrong-doing.
King McCloud, in the play, is given two chances to weigh the value
of life. The play's prologue shows him on a hilltop in Spain, whither he
has led a group of American volunteers to fight Franco. Faced with hopeless odds, King leaves and his comrades die. In the main body of the
play, King comes to Key Largo, situated on the far edge of Florida, to
tell the D'Alcalas of their son Victor's fate in Spain. He finds the home
of the blind father and his daughter Alegre commandeered as a hideout
of gangsters. Through the vision of the blind man and the faith of his
daughter, King recovers his integrity, kills the gang's leader, and dies in
victory over himself.

Key Largo brought Paul Muni back to the New York stage on September 27, 1939, after seven years of motion picture work. Jose Ferrer
played Victor; Frederic Tozere, the gangster; Harold Johnsrud, the blind
D'Alcala, and Uta Hagen, Alegre. In 1948, a movie version was made.

As usual with the work of Maxwell Anderson, *Key Largo* met with
differences of opinion among the critics. According to John Mason Brown:
"If it has intermittent moments of interest, it never rises to excitement.
It has all ripples and no waves, and frequently its ripples are far apart."
Sidney B. Whipple, however, called it "the finest and most passionately
sincere work he has accomplished in recent years." Brooks Atkinson
said: "'Mr. Anderson has drowned the best part of his work by pouring
golden words over it uncritically. Sometimes the poet is the enemy of
the dramatist, and this is one of those occasions." George Jean Nathan
remarked that Anderson "substituted so much bantam blank verse and
so many one-finger intermezzi for simple and forthright drama that the
final impression was of a toy music box ambitiously debating a machine
gun." Richard Lockridge felt differently: "The very simple and certainly
essential fact about *Key Largo* is that no other play we have seen this
season approaches it in stature . . . It is not the duty of poets to be comforting. It is their duty to lift thought and emotion beyond the everyday,
to hold human aspiration in the hollow of their words. As Mr. Anderson
does."

The *New York Daily Worker* apparently considered Maxwell Anderson too idealistic in deeming honor and integrity more important than
life. It called *Key Largo* another version of the East Indian rope-trick:
"Yogi Anderson throws his rope in the air to hang suspended in a vacuum
of rationalization . . . Death before dishonor is an easy conclusion which is
fast becoming a formula with Mr. Anderson, who will continue to be an
imperfect great artist until his own driving honesty, which is so endear-
ingly evinced in every beautifully written line, brings him to a more
demanding and thrilling declaration — life with awareness and conviction."

Key Largo contains much scorching commentary on evil in the world.
In it Anderson recognizes that without courage there is no integrity, and
he expresses that recognition in terms of swiftly moving drama.

JOAN OF LORRAINE   *Maxwell Anderson*

Within a year of his major fiasco, *Truckline Café*, Maxwell Anderson achieved a success with *Joan of Lorraine*. However, when the play opened in New York on November 18, 1946, the crowds that overflowed the lobby were not there to see what sort of dramatic challenge Anderson was bringing to his critics; they were attracted by the glamour of movie star Ingrid Bergman as St. Joan.

Miss Bergman was cast in the play as the actress Mary Grey assigned the title role in a production of Joan of Arc. On an almost bare stage, the action of the play takes place at rehearsal scenes. In the play depicted, a compromise between Joan and the politicians of her day seems unnatural to the modern actress who is to play Joan. In fact, rehearsals are stopped as she and the director discuss the matter of the compromise. At one point, the actress is about to quit the play. Finally, however, in the middle of a scene, she awakens to the realization that life demands a compromise on non-essentials if the living are to hold steadfast to basic ideals.

To many, Anderson seemed to base his play on a truism; George Jean Nathan went so far as to say that Anderson "enjoys all the attributes of a profound thinker save profundity." The fact remains, however, that in many fields of thought and action today, precisely this issue of compromise is being fought; and many highly-placed persons could use the lesson learned by the actress Mary Grey while playing Joan.

The sneer many today bestow upon the word compromise suggests —if it does not demonstrate—that the theme of *Joan of Lorraine* is both vital and timely. Beyond the issue of compromise the play also presses home the idea that all men live by faith, despite the fact that the articles of their faith cannot be verified. Faith nourishes itself to strengthen humankind.

An excellent cast helped assure the play's success. Ingrid Bergman was supported by Sam Wanamaker in the dual role of the director of the rehearsed play and the Inquisitor within that play. Other performers included Romney Brent as the Dauphin, and Joanna Roos.

Once again the critics were divided. "Like all Mr. Anderson's dramas, this one is sincere," said Brooks Atkinson. "Unlike some of them, it is written in excellent prose; and it is informal, like an intelligent discussion among people of high principle who are seriously wondering about sublime problems. Toward the end it seems, perhaps, to be overwritten and to be groping among abstractions, words taking precedence over ideas. But that does not alter the general impression that Mr. Anderson has written an engrossing play that is variously poignant, rhapsodic, and genial, and much above the common level of the theatre."

Somewhat less cordial, Richard Watts admired Ingrid Bergman's acting but found the play "by no means completely satisfactory or successful . . . Where *St. Joan** soared, *Joan of Lorraine* remains pedestrian . . . The plot device does not greatly help dramatically . . ." Significantly, the modern framework was omitted from the motion picture version of 1948, in which Ingrid Bergman again played Joan; only the story of Joan of Arc was presented.

George Jean Nathan, as urbane as ever, drew a number of devastating comparisons in his review of the play: "The impression one gains from it is of a Readers' Theatre performance of Percy MacKaye's *Joan of Arc* directed by a second cousin of Pirandello and interrupted from time to time by some old patent medicine doctor faith and hope messages from Mr. Anderson and with a popular screen actress as ballyhoo. In essaying

the Maid of Orleans theme, Mr. Anderson plainly accepted a pretty difficult challenge. It is not surprising that, from any viewpoint a bit loftier
than that identified with Broadway, he has not succeeded, except at the
box-office, which is seldom disturbingly critical. The list of his silent
challengers is too formidable. Shakespeare has outpoetized him; Schiller
has outfelt him; Barbier has outdramatized him: Twain has outwitted him;
Shaw has outthought him; even MacKaye has outwritten him."

Against such adverse opinions, Robert Garland was all praise: "The
theatre is itself again . . . a heady mixture of drama and melodrama,
bitterness and beauty, romance and reality, belief and disbelief"; and
Arthur Pollock called *Joan of Lorraine* one of Anderson's best: it "has
sunshine in it . . . the clearest and the warmest treatment that the Joan
of Arc story has enjoyed in the theatre."

What makes *Joan of Lorraine* an outstanding play is the way it presses
an old theme to a modern problem, the way in which it presents the
argument over the compromises made by Joan on minor things, and her
firm resolve, unto death, on a major issue. By her faith, Joan answers the
practical, material demands of our time. Yet the play makes clear that
compromise has its place in the practical but not in the spiritual world.
Through its dramatized answer to an eternal problem, *Joan of Lorraine*
gives good measure of the three hoped-for rewards of the theatre: entertainment, enlightenment, exaltation.

BAREFOOT IN ATHENS   *Maxwell Anderson*

The title of this play indicates Anderson's approach to the story of
Socrates, the philosopher who, when his fellow-citizens condemned him,
preferred taking the hemlock in his Athenian democracy to living under
tyranny abroad.

Anderson presents Socrates as a simple man, amid the concerns of
his family and his daily dealings with his shrewish but devoted wife,
Xantippe. Since this simple man is utterly devoted to the truth, he must
always search.

Balanced against Socrates in the play are zealots at home and the
conquering King Pausanias of Sparta. The latter is a genial tyrant who
likes to be called Stupid; but — in the words of John Chapman — "Stupid
is not so stupid as he appears; he is the practical politician, the fascist, the
communist, the dictator. He is baffled by the bungling inefficiency of
Democracy and prefers a practical business management of man's affairs
—but somehow he is drawn to it. Socrates' starry vision of a free society
fascinates him in spite of himself." Pausanias offers Socrates shelter in
Sparta, but Socrates will suffer his freedom to be stifled only by death.
Socrates' enemies at home — leaders of the conquered city when Pausanias withdraws — are less tolerant than the foreign tyrant. In the
trial scene that marks the major movement of the play, they charge that
he is a corrupter of the minds of youth, emphasizing that all three leaders
who brought on the downfall of Athens— the tyrant Charmides, the
shifter Alcibiades, and the quisling Critias — had been pupils of Socrates.

Maxwell Anderson allows Socrates' arguments for democracy no
straw-man victory. No one sees more clearly than Socrates himself the
dangers of democracy: "Perhaps freedom offers temptations that some
minds are not able to resist. When a man is free he is free to choose
wrong or right. In a free city no man chooses for another." The fact that

some men — Socrates' own pupils — make the wrong choice, preferring wealth and power to tolerance and justice, is human weakness, not democracy's fault. The jury may not always reach a righteous verdict — two "agorasses," (Anaxagoras and Protagoras), who boldly pursued their thoughts were exiled by their fellow citizens — but at least a man is held not guilty until convicted by his peers. Finally, some men seem by nature slaves — like the executioner; but Socrates' simple and essential democracy of human fellowship sparks even in him the wonder of the dream. For democracy proffers man the only path to his proper goal: freedom in the quest for truth. Written in simple but at times glowing prose, *Barefoot in Athens* is one of Anderson's most poetic plays.

A further virtue of the drama is the unobtrusive way in which it suggests the parallel with life today. There is no lesson pressed, no sermon preached. We watch Socrates in Athens of the fifth century B.C., but we think also of the twentieth century, now. And we recognize that democracy has deeper roots in the world today, since it no longer rests on a majority enslaved; but it faces the same great problems welling out of the nature of man: indifference and corruption within, jealousy and tyranny abroad. Such a choice as Socrates' keeps the ideal alive. Such a play as Anderson's keeps the theatre worth while.

Over a dozen playwrights before Anderson wove dramas about the Greek thinker. The Scot Amyas Bushe wrote his *Socrates* in 1762; the French François Pastoret, in 1789; the Italian Giovanni B. Lorenzi, in 1826. August Strindberg* included him in a trilogy, *Moses, Socrates,* (pub. 1922), and *Christ*. Georg Kaiser* wrote *Alcibiades Saved* in 1920; Clifford Bax, *Socrates* in 1930. One-act plays include *The Death of Socrates* by Laurence Housman*, 1925; *The Husband of Xantippe,* by Conrad Seiler, 1929; and *The Trial of Socrates,* by Alfred Kreymborg, 1947.

Anderson's *Barefoot in Athens* had its premiere in Princeton, New Jersey, on October 12, 1951, and went to New York on October 31 for but 30 performances. A few cuts in the printed version — for example, the omission of the discussion of the law requiring unmarried women to wear high-slit skirts to help replenish the Athenian population —speeded the action. In spite of this, Brooks Atkinson insisted that the play "has all the virtues except brilliance and vitality," and Walter F. Kerr, guest reviewer for the N. Y. *Herald-Tribune,* commented that it was "curiously without zest." John Chapman felt that it did not "strive for emotional heights or depths . . . The burden of the comedy is not so much that Socrates is worth fighting for or weeping over, but that he is worth thinking about" — an attitude which would probably have pleased the old Greek himself.

But *Barefoot in Athens* roused many with the keen excitement of a drama of embattled ideas. Richard Watts, Jr., called it "the most impressive work for the theatre (Anderson) has provided since the distinguished days of *Winterset** . . . a powerful and admirably evocative play." Robert Coleman considered it "a stirring, stimulating, and affectionate study of the philosopher with the ugly face and the glowing soul. It catches the wit, the essential dignity, the mind and the heart of the genius who spurned riches to teach men how to think and to question . . . It is Anderson at his best, and that, in our opinion, is the best that America has to offer."

In its simple picture of the family life of the questioning philosopher, as in the surge of his trial and the quiet nobility of his dying, *Barefoot In Athens* searchingly presses the weakness yet the high value of democracy in an unready world.

ANATHEMA   *Leonid N. Andreyev*

The gloom and despair that marked the life of Andreyev (1871-1919) — he attempted suicide three times — pervades this play, the greatest of the dramas of this Russian playwright.

In the prologue, Anathema sits at heaven's gate, demanding knowledge. What kind of god, he asks, has created this kind of world? Denied an answer, he goes to live with the saintly David Leizer, a Jew who gives everything — his love, his toil, and the 4,000,000 rubles left him by a brother in America — to the poor. David wishes to do good quietly, unobserved, but the people seek him out and worship him. When his wealth is used up, however, the mob turns on him and stones him. In the epilogue, Anathema, again at the Gate, is told that "David has his immortality," to which he replies that in David's name men will be murderers.

Originally produced in Andreyev's native land, *Anathema* was suppressed after 37 performances for giving too favorable a picture of the Jews. As has been pointed out by translator Herman Bernstein, Andreyev attributed to David "the qualities of Christ and subordinated them to the Russian Jew . . . For this, he was accused of blasphemy. He was excommunicated, and his play was suppressed by the Holy Synod. At a special ceremony, presided over by Archbishop Germogen of Kiev, black candles were lighted, and the play was anathematized."

In New York, *Anathema* was presented in Yiddish, opening on November 25, 1910. The *New York Tribune* — the only English-language paper to review it — said that it was "universal in interest, rich in poetic symbolism,and profound in philosophical conception."

Enacted again in Yiddish, February 7, 1923, with Maurice Schwartz as Anathema and Muni Weisenfreund (later known as Paul Muni) as David, the play was most favorably received. *The New York Times* spoke of "Andreyev's tremendous tragedy" as "a spectacle notable for poignance, vehemence, and color."

As a result of the hearty reception given the Jewish production, *Anathema* was brought to Broadway on April 10, 1923, in a translation by Herman Bernstein. A mixed welcome followed. "What to a Russian audience," said John Corbin, "is profound philosophy set forth in luminous symbols, seemed to an American audience pompous vaporings— a meaningless story enveloped in turgid verbosity." The *New York Sun* called David Leizer "a doddering old fool who ought to have gone to heaven years before the play started." J. Ranken Towse, however, observed that "there can be no question of its descriptive or imaginative power."

Although *anathema* has come to mean an accursed person or thing, the word literally meant consecrated, devoted. The play pictures Anathema as relentlessly dedicated to the quest of knowledge — whereas most men, as Andreyev sees them, will deny or destroy truth for wealth and power. Andreyev felt that *Anathema* was his masterpiece. It combines realism with allegory, and drives home the idea that, despite the sense of doom, man ever batters at the barriers of ignorance, hate, and greed.

HE WHO GETS SLAPPED   *Leonid N. Andreyev*

This is the greatest of Andreyev's studies of the tortured soul. It is
the story of a gentleman called "He" who comes to live among circus
folk. Given the part of a clown, he endures an inordinate amount of
slapping. The wiser and more beautiful his words, the more the public
laughs when he is slapped.

All is not well inside the circus world. The bare-back rider, Consuelo,
whom everybody loves, is to be sold by her father to the wealthy Baron
Regnard. As the time for the wedding approaches, Consuelo becomes
frightened; "He," who has also come to love her, shares a fatal dose of
poison with Consuelo, and at her death the Baron commits suicide. Thus,
Andreyev tells us that even in the world of make-believe there is no
escape from the doom of human weakness.

Written in 1914, the play was produced by the Theatre Guild in New
York in 1922, and ran for 182 performances. In the cast were Helen
Westley, Margalo Gillmore, Richard Bennett, and Louis Calvert. The
play was well received. Alexander Woollcott called it "alive in its every
moment, and abrim with color and beauty." The play was revived in New
York in 1944 by Equity Library and again in 1946 by the Theatre Guild
with Stella Adler and Dennis King in the cast. Of the latter production,
Louis Kronenberger observed that the first half had "a tingling, hopped-
up excitement, a highwire exhibition of the emotions . . . After that,
everything started to crumble. The falsity remained, without the lure."
Many critics found in the play "much that is exciting, and much that
will arouse the softer sentiments."

Tyrone Guthrie directed a London production which *Theatre World*
(August 1947) considered "an outstanding piece of theatre." Harold
Hobson, in the *London Sunday Times* (June 17, 1947), gave special credit
to the production: "The stage is never still: clowns and conjurers, in
yellow tinselled garments, lion-tamers and jockeys, dart continually
across it." Mr. Hobson felt, however, that the play, at the end, "dissolves
into the shadow of a shade" because Andreyev "does not seem to make
up his mind whether this is an abdication or a release, whether the Prince
("He") is a coward or a philosopher. The play wanders directionless,
and the Prince, who started by being a real, if mysterious, figure, ends
only as a vague abstraction of the world's resignation from responsibility."

The original New York production provided a noteworthy instance of
"slapping" in the experience of the Negro author, Claude McKay, who
attended the play with artist William Gropper. McKay recorded the
experience in the *Liberator* (May, 1922): "The stubs were handed to
Gropper and we started towards the orchestra. But the usher, with a
look of quizzical amazement on his face, stopped us. Snatching the stubs
from Gropper and muttering something about seeing the manager, he
left us wondering and bewildered. In a moment he returned, with the
manager. 'The — wrong date,' the manager stammered, and taking the
stubs marked 'Orchestra,' he hurried off to the box-office, returning with
others marked 'Balcony' . . . I had come to see a tragic farce, and I
found myself unwillingly the hero of one. He who got slapped was I.
As always in the world-embracing Anglo-Saxon circus, the intelligence,
the sensibilities, of the black clown were slapped without mercy." It is
pleasant to note that the "Anglo-Saxon" reaction to this incident did much
to end racial discrimination in the New York theatre.

But Claude McKay also struck a sharp blow at the despair portrayed by Andreyev. "Dear Leonid Andreyev," he wrote, "if you had only risen out of your introspective Nihilistic despair to create the clown in the circus of hell, the clown slapped on every side by the devil's red-hot tongs, yet growing wiser, stronger, and firmer in purposeful determination, seeking no refuge in suicide, but bearing it out to the bitter end, you might have touched me." In taking the path to death, however, "He" and the girl, like Antigone and Oedipus of Greek drama, maintain against life's overpowering evil the upright stand of human dignity. *He Who Gets Slapped* remains a continuing challenge, both to performers and to intelligent audiences.

THE WALTZ OF THE DOGS   *Leonid N. Andreyev*

In a letter to his English translator, Herman Bernstein, Andreyev pointed out that his entire life is expressed in *The Waltz of the Dogs*, written in 1914. "It will be crowned not with laurels, but with thorns," he predicted.

The play opens as Henry Tile, in the apartment he has taken for Elizabeth, his bride-to-be, receives word from her that she is already married. Henry's woe is increased when his brother, Carl, who intends to steal his money, becomes Elizabeth's lover. Henry decides to rob the bank where he works and set sail for America. In his cups, he tells a friend, Feklusha, and a stranger, Happy Jenny, of his plans and he boasts of the power over men and women the money will bring him.

Carl and Elizabeth meet with Feklusha in Henry's apartment. Feklusha tells Carl that he has persuaded Henry to take out considerable insurance, and, in anticipation of murdering Henry, he exhibits a forged suicide note. Carl and Elizabeth leave the apartment before Henry returns. Henry smells her perfume; then with unusual calm, he sends Feklusha away, plays the piano, leaves the stage — and a shot is heard in the wings.

The title of the play is the name of the song, a sort of "Chopsticks" on the high keys, which Henry plays. It is a descriptive piece, representing pet dogs dancing on their hind legs as a lump of sugar is dangled over their heads. Henry plays it when he receives the news of Elizabeth's marriage; Feklusha and Happy Jenny, like begging dogs, tipsily dance to it; and with high-pitched symbolism, Henry plays it before he takes his life at the end of the play. It marks, said Alexander Woollcott, "the pathetically docile measure which we humans will tread for the sweet cake of the occasional lump of sugar." A silly little tune, Andreyev makes it a sinister chiming.

The Waltz of the Dogs had its New York premiere at the Cherry Lane Theatre in Greenwich Village on April 25, 1928; it was so well received that in a fortnight it moved up to Broadway. Robert Littell called it "one of the strangest, emptiest, and bitterest plays on record . . . a dreadful skeleton of negation that should be kept locked in the closet." The *New York Telegram* declared it to be Andreyev's "final thumbing of the nose at an existence as frozen and forbidding as his own steppes."

THE DYBBUK   *S. Ansky*

Stimulated by the Dreyfus case while living in Paris, S. Ansky (Solo-

mon Z. Rappaport, 1863-1920) began to explore Jewish folklore. He was
struck by the legend of the *dybbuk,* the spirit of a dead person which enters another's body when its work is incomplete. He wrote a first version
of *The Dybbuk,* called *Between Two Worlds,* in 1914, in which he contrasted the other-world of love with this world of reality.

As developed ten years later in *The Dybbuk,* the spirit of Chanan,
who dies when his love for Leah is thwarted, enters into Leah's body, so
that when her family prepares a rich match for her, the spirit of Chanan
cries out against another bridegroom. When the rabbi exorcises the
dybbuk, Leah falls dead and, completing the work of the *dybbuk,* rejoins her beloved Chanan.

In the play, the fight for personal happiness on the part of Leah and
Chanan is balanced against the patriarchal authority of the rabbi, "the
eternal tree of the House of David." As Ansky himself put it, "The play
is, of course, a realistic one about mystical people . . . Both Chanan and
Leah — and also the rabbi — are right, and furthermore are justified in
their struggle."

The Dybbuk was written in Russian in 1917, at the suggestion of Stanislavski of the Moscow Art Theatre. Banned by the censor, it was translated into Yiddish and rehearsed by the Vilna Troupe, but it was again
suppressed. Chaim Nachman Bialik, the greatest Hebrew poet of our age,
made a Hebrew adaptation, which was also banned. Ansky, however,
liked the Hebrew version so much that he retranslated it into Yiddish,
in which form the play had its world premiere in Warsaw in 1920. It has
become the main piece in the repertory of the famous Habima Players,
formerly of Moscow, now of Tel-Aviv.

In 1921 *The Dybbuk* was produced at New York's Yiddish Art Theatre.
An English version, by Henry G. Alsberg and Winifred Katzin, directed
by David Vardi of the Habima Players, was given at the Neighborhood
Playhouse in 1925. With Mary Ellis as Leah, supported by Albert Carroll
and Dorothy Sands, the latter production moved uptown to Broadway in
1926. During 1926, the play was also revived in Yiddish and presented in
New York by the visiting Habima Players. In 1927, New York's Second
Avenue saw a Yiddish version with marionettes. A motion picture production was made in 1938. Among the more recent New York revivals
of the play are an Equity Library production in English in 1947, and the
Hebrew version again by the visiting Habima Players in 1948. An
operatic version by Lodovico Rocco made its bow at La Scala in Milan on
March 24, 1934, and in New York in 1936; another, by David Tamkin,
composed in 1931, had its world premiere at the New York City Center
on October 4, 1951.

Most comments on all the versions stress the play less than the production. Thus Richard Watts said of the 1926 English version: "It prob-
aly would seem to the alien spectator little better than superstitious drivel
but for the perfect staging." Alexander Woollcott declared that no other
production of the season could "compare in moving and memorable
beauty with *The Dybbuk;*" but Brooks Atkinson found that the muted
tones and mysterious movements of the cast in the third act "seem somewhat tedious, and the audience begins to emerge from the spell."

Of the Habima production in Hebrew, opinions have differed. In 1926
Alan Dale insisted that its players had an utter disregard for all the
essentials of the theatre; "They were crudely true and blatantly droll . . .
I was not gripped or held absorbed. Nor was my imagination touched

for an instant." Gilbert W. Gabriel said: "One is terribly aware of its power, of the huge energy of this conception; but one cannot love it, hold it close." The eerie dance of the beggars at the wedding feast was termed by Brooks Atkinson "one of the theatre's immortal creations."

The significance of the play was aptly expressed by its English adapter, Henry G. Alsberg: *"The Dybbuk attempts to give the quintessence of the Jewish ghetto, to fix forever the intense reality of the religious life and beliefs of the Jewish masses, just at the moment when the inroads of modern civilization were driving this life and these beliefs out of existence."* The inroads of modern war, and the horrors of genocide, have now more completely made *The Dybbuk* an evocative picture of a vanished past.

THE GREEN GODDESS   *William Archer*

As a London critic, William Archer (1856-1924) helped clear the stage for the drama of realism. His translation (1880) of *The Pillars of Society** introduced Ibsen to the English theatre. As a playwright, however, Archer is remembered for his romantic melodrama of smooth-fingered Oriental intrigue, *The Green Goddess*.

With a keen sense of dramatic situation, the critic-turned-playwright wove his plot. Dr. Basil Traherne, Major Anthony Crespin, and the latter's wife, Lucilla, whose plane has made a forced landing in the almost inaccessible territory of the Rajah of Rukh, are a troubled triangle. The Major is a suspicious dipsomaniac; his wife and the doctor are in love. The suave Rajah, a Cambridge graduate sporting a monocle and a long cigarette-holder, courteously informs them that, when the English execute some of his tribesmen on the morrow, they must also die. "The priests," he says, "demand the sacrifice of the white goats" to their Green Goddess. He can perhaps persuade them to spare the lady, if she will enter his harem.

Deftly and swiftly the story moves on: The Rajah, who has a wireless set, tests his "guests" by having his man Watkins send a message: "The Lady has come to terms, will enter His Highness' household." Crespin, who is an operator, gives not a blink. Later, the party gags Watkins, heaves him out of the tower, starts to broadcast for help, when the Rajah enters and shoots Crespin. Did his calls get through? Next morning, as the sacrifice is to begin, a British plane arrives, and Lucilla and Dr. Traherne are free to return "to civili— to India."

It is Crespin who, when they first meet the Rajah, thus expresses their hope of escape. The Rajah responds: "To civilization, you were going to say? Why hesitate, my dear sir? We know very well that we are barbarians. We are quite reconciled to the fact. We have had some five thousand years to accustom ourselves to it. This sword is a barbarous weapon compared with your revolver; but it was worn by my ancestors when yours were daubing themselves blue and picking up a precarious livelihood in the woods. — But Madam is standing up all this time. Watkins, what are you thinking of? Some cushions!" Such a mixture of civilized urbanity and pagan ruthlessness led the *London Times*, after the London opening (September 6, 1923, for 416 performances), to call *The Green Goddess* "a thrilling melodrama with all the old situations and all the newest embellishments; a play which is not only thrilling but also 'amusing' in the best sense of the term, with its literary allusions, its

picture of Oriental savagery veneered with Occidental culture, its cocktails and its Perrier Jouet 1906." Mischievously, several of the London
papers exclaimed "It isn't Ibsen!"

The Green Goddess had its premiere in Philadelphia, December 16,
1920; the Philadelphia Inquirer called it "a superb and horrible cameo of
a human devil with exquisite manners." The play opened in New York
January 18, 1921, and had a run of 440 performances. The New York Mail
labelled it "one of the most fascinating melodramas — intelligent and, if
you like, refined, but also a bully show"; and the New York Star (January 26) recognized it as "a well constructed piece of dramatic writing . . .
The interest is cumulative, the suspense thoroughly justified by the stage
proceedings, and there is not a wasted line or situation . . . written deftly,
economically, and to excellent purpose."

In addition to the fascinating portrait of the Rajah of Rukh, as suave
a villain as ever bowed before a fair heroine, there is a neat sketch of
his valet Watkins, a cockney with a criminal record and a grudge against
all English gentlemen, such as those now fallen into the Rajah's hands.
The servant's mean cruelty, and his master's gentle ruthlessness, make
stirring contrast to the English composure of the captured three.

George Arliss, in America and England, gave one of his most rounded
portrayals as the Rajah of Rukh. The play has been very popular. Cyril
Maude broadcast in it, in 1936; and Orson Welles, in 1939, toured in a
twenty-minute condensation of it, which the Hartford Courant (February
15, 1939) characterized as "indubitably melodrama at its peak of perfection." The Green Goddess is indeed, with polished villain and brave heroine, an outstanding example of the melodrama of the bestial claw in the
velvet glove.

THE SUPPOSES   Lodovico Ariosto

An attentive student of the Latin classics, Ariosto (1474-1531) wrote
several plays in imitation of the comedies of Plautus. They were widely
hailed, being the first comedies that, in lively verse, presented to Italy
the swift intrigues and amusing incidents that were the substance of
Roman drama.

Most effective of Ariosto's comedies, and the most influential in passing
along the Roman comic tradition, is The Supposes, written in 1503. It is
in plot a typical Roman intrigue of mistaken identity, and in spirit a
genially satiric character-gallery drawn from the Ferrara of Ariosto's
day. The story is a complicated one. Erostrato, come to Ferrara to study,
falls in love with Polinesta, daughter of the wealthy merchant Damon. To
enter her household, Erostrato changes name and place with his servant
Dulipo. Helped by the usual bawdy Nurse, he gains access to the maiden
and, revealing his identity, wins her heart. Meanwhile, Polinesta's father
wants her to wed a wealthy old Doctor of Laws, Cleander. The false
Erostrato (the servant), appearing as Cleander's rival, brings a false
father with him. Erostrato's real father, Philogano, meanwhile arrives.
Suspecting false play, he hires a lawyer — none other than Cleander! —
to ferret out the truth for him. The merchant sees his "servant" with
his daughter and imprisons him; Erostrato's danger leads Dulipo to
confess the impostures. Further complications end with the marriage of
the loving couple. This story became the subplot of Shakespeare's The
Taming of the Shrew.

With considerable incidental comedy, the play is really a satire, directed against doctors, and against customs-house officials, who, in those days of active trade among the Italian city-states, had many opportunities for profitable irregularity.

A prose version of *The Supposes* enacted during the 1509 carnival at Ferrara proved instantly popular. The version in verse was staged for Pope Leo X in 1519; and with many minor changes, it was printed in 1542. Within a quarter of a century, it had been adapted in French by Jean de la Taille and in English by George Gascoigne (1525-1577). Gascoigne's *The Supposes* was produced at Gray's Inn Court in 1566. It is in vigorous prose; although it lacks some of the polish and the gaiety of Ariosto's play, it affects the alliteration and other verbal devices of the Euphuistic style.

Though the plot is largely an amalgam of Terence's *The Eunuch** and Plautus' *The Captives**, the Italian of Ariosto's *Gli Suppositi* has a distinctive quality of its own. "Everywhere in these lively scenes," said R. Warrick Bond in *Early Plays From the Italian* (1911) "we feel the working of the same gay fancy; we find the same constructive imagination, as enabled Shakespeare to transmute and vivify the materials he found. The initial information is given without artificiality . . . The admirably natural action evolves with rapidity and smoothness . . . The absence of love scenes is partly a heritage from Latin comedy, which excluded respectable girls from the stage, partly a consequence of Italian custom, which discouraged their appearance in the street."

The Supposes is in essence a lively interfusion of the earliest elements of the drama.

THE ACHARNIANS   *Aristophanes*

Written about 425 B.C., *The Acharnians* satirizes the war policy of the Athenians and especially the leader of the war party, Cleon.

After the death (429 B.C.) of Pericles, who had started the Peloponnesian War "over three hussies," political power was shrewdly wielded by Cleon, whose war policy was cowardly, mean, and cruel. At his orders, the population of Megara was systematically starved; and in 427, at his insistence, the death of all males in the rebelling city of Mytilene was ordered, along with the enslavement of the women and children. The order was revoked, but similar ones, later in the War, were not. As a result of his attack on Cleon in *The Babylonians*, Aristophanes was brought before the City Council. The charges against him were dismissed, and the next year his comedy *The Acharnians* was produced.

The chorus of Acharnian charcoal-burners in Athens was a timely choice for the play. During the Spartan invasion of Attica, Acharnae was overrun and her citizens forced into Athens for shelter. The play portrays the Athenian Dicaeopolis ('honest citizen') who, when he finds that even the god Amphitheus ('the god on both sides') is manhandled by the police for advocating peace, decides to negotiate a private peace of his own. Arrested for treason by the Acharnians, he successfully defends himself; and while the general, Lamachus, dolefully dresses for battle, Dicaeopolis prepares for festive and feminine joy.

The plot of the play, as of a modern musical comedy, gives but scant measure of its worth. The Old Comedies were gaily costumed and played with music and merriment. *The Acharnians* is representative of the pattern they followed; in fact, if all the other comedies had been lost, we should still, from this one, know the general nature of the Old Comedy. It opens with a "bright idea" (in *The Acharnians,* Dicaeopolis' decision to sue for a private peace); a debate follows, interrupted by occasional lyrics and frequent comic questions or remarks. Always, however, the "bright idea" triumphs. Then comes a long speech by the leader of the chorus (with choral comment), the *parabasis,* in which the theme of the play is discussed seriously, and counsel offered to the Athenians. The end of the *parabasis,* the *pnigos* (choker), was spoken as rapidly as possible, much like the "patter-song" of a Gilbert-and-Sullivan musical, a modern art form close to the Aristophanic comedy. From this point on, the structure of the play is looser. There is usually a series of episodes — bawdy, slapstick, uproarious — showing how the "bright idea" works out in practice and ending with the *comos,* or gay revel with wine, women, song, and the *gamos,* the union of the sexes. Thus in one play are mingled beautiful lyric poetry, serious political satire and advice on the issues of the day, and broadest farce.

At a time when Athens was in the midst of a life-and-death war, with Cleon dictating Athenian policy, Aristophanes included the following words in the *parabasis* of *The Acharnians:* "I scoff at Cleon's tricks and plotting; honesty and justice shall fight my cause; never will you find me a political poltroon, a prostitute to the highest bidder."

Incidental political satire is evident throughout the play. Dicaeopolis is given samples of three kinds of peace-treaty, which he tastes like wine. He rejects the five-year truce; it would merely provide time to recoup losses and rush along in an armament race. Likewise, he rejects the ten-year truce; it would be used for cementing alliances and finding new allies. He welcomes and ratifies the truce of thirty years, both on sea and on land, with its aroma of nectar and its glad message of "Go whither you will" — unbarred by hostile hand or iron curtain. Beneath the swift and bawdy comedy the ruin of war is shown when a starved Megarian puts up his daughters for sale, pretending that they are sows.

Aristophanes shoots straight shafts of satire at many Athenian figures, especially at the tragic dramatist Euripides*. Throughout the very years when Aristophanes was urging the people toward peace, Euripides wrote play after play exalting the glory of the martial spirit of Athens.

The Acharnians won first prize at the Lenaean Festival in 425 B.C.; two older and already famous playwrights, Cratinus and Eupolis, took second and third place.

The first American production of *The Acharnians,* in Greek, was given at the University of Pennsylvania on May 15, 1886. The *New York Times,* the day before, declared: "The humanity of today has no interest in the personages of the comedies of Aristophanes or in the events they deal with . . ." On May 17, however, the *Times* retracted: "It is an excellent example of the poet's liveliest style, and the text is pure and comparatively easy to master. The performance, contrary to the expectations of many, was remarkably bright and entertaining . . ." The production was brought to New York in November, when the *Times* (November 14, 1886) reported: "The action of the comedy is brisk and amusing, and much of its wit is easily understood ages after the great comic poet's death."

Still using the ancient Greek tongue, but in modern dress, with comic policemen and a messenger on bicycle, a performance was given at

Bradfield College, England, in March 1930. Finally presented in English
by the Balliol Players, *The Acharnians* proved, according to the *London
Times* (July 8, 1938), "almost as topical in A.D. 1938 as it was in 425 B.C.
. . . At the close one felt that a sense of humor can do as much to end
a war as to win it." *The Acharnians* is a rapid flow of tumbling comedy
and keen satire, still pertinent and still alive.

THE KNIGHTS   *Aristophanes*

Written in 424 B.C., this drama is perhaps the most sharply political,
and therefore least comical, of Aristophanes' plays. It was directed
against Cleon, the leader of the war party, at the height of his glory. To
it, for the first time, Aristophanes put his own name; and he himself (no
other daring) wore the mask of the role of Cleon. It may have been for
his courage, as much as for his wit, that the play was awarded first prize.

In the year 424 B.C., which was marked by the biggest Spartan set-
back in the Peloponnesian War, the Athenians defeated the Spartan fleet
at Pylos, leaving a detachment of Spartan heavy infantry isolated on
the nearby island of Sphacteria. Cleon reached Pylos just as General
Demosthenes, having burned down the island forest, prepared to attack
the exposed Spartans. Cleon took over Demosthenes' command and assumed credit for the victory. The Athenians granted him a golden
garland, the great privilege of dining at the Prytaneum with the descendants of the national heroes, and a seat of honor at the theatre. From that
seat of honor, the first play Cleon saw was *The Knights*.

The Knights has five characters; one, Demos, represents the people;
three others are actual leaders of the day. Nicias and Demosthenes (the
general; the orator lived a century later) ponder how to get rid of the
demagogue Cleon. They hit upon the bright idea of getting an even
greater rogue than he. Thus Cleon, represented as a Paphlagonian tanner
(leather was his family's trade), is opposed by a sausage-seller. The
play is a succession of contests between the two (in terms of their trades,
often with obscene dialogue) for the favor of Demos. Between them,
they mention all possible ways — equally applicable to our time — of
buying or seducing popular favor. The play ends with the rescue of
"Thirty-year Truce," a young girl whom Cleon was holding prisoner, and
the reduction of Cleon to the status of a sausage-seller at the city gates;
Demos is restored to his olden beauty.

Throughout the play Cleon is attacked. His corruption and bribery are
symbolized in the dishes he prepares for Demos: "You chew the pieces,"
Cleon is reproached, "and you place small quantities in his mouth, while
you swallow three parts yourself." Again: "You want this War, to
conceal your rogueries as in a mist, so that Demos may see nothing of
them, and, harassed by cares, must depend only on yourself for his bread."
Bluntly, the chorus sing: "Oh! happy day for us and our children if
Cleon die!"

The political force of *The Knights* is so intense that its comedy is incidental. The play, nevertheless, is a good illustration of the fact that
ridicule is a more potent weapon than anger. It has been said that reformers see good only in the past, shame in the present, ruin in the future.
Aristophanes, however, hopefully pictured an aroused and reformed citizenry, moving toward the community's best interests. And Cleon — after
he received one more Aristophanic thrust in *The Wasps** — was sent

by vote of the Athenian citizens into active military service, where his
inefficiency and cowardice led to his ignominious death in 422 B.C. He
was succeeded, unfortunately, not by a more honest man, but by an even
more corrupt demagogue, Hyperbolus, to whose scoundrelly ways and
warlike policies Aristophanes had given anticipatory attention (lines
1300-1316) in The Knights.

The play was presented in Oxford, England, in 1897.

In his attacks upon the corrupt, war-wishing leaders of Athens, Aristophanes did not spare the citizens themselves. He rebuked them for their
gullibility, for the ease with which they were swayed by high-sounding
words and empty promises, for such universal characteristics, in fine,
that The Knights is still politically pertinent and probing.

THE CLOUDS   Aristophanes

In The Clouds Aristophanes turned from politics to education, to
attack the Sophists who were then spreading their ideas throughout
Greece, especially to attack the newly developed art of pleading, that
made "the worse cause seem the better." With characteristic courage,
Aristophanes singled out Socrates, the most prominent of the new teachers. But he also foisted upon Socrates all the extreme practices of the
school, of which the Socrates of history was in no wise guilty.

So potent was the influence of The Clouds that Plato in The Apology
pointed out that, when on trial for his life in 399 B.C., Socrates found it
harder to dispel the picture of him that the Athenians knew from The
Clouds than to answer the specific charges leveled against him. Robert
Browning, in his Aristophanes' Apology, took pains to picture the playwright as attacking not the individual but the school.

The extant version of The Clouds is a revised one, often read but never
performed in ancient times. Made about 421 B.C., it contains a reference
to Cleon's death, which occurred in 422. In The Knights, Aristophanes
had dismissed the playwright Cratinus as outmoded, bidding him go sit
among the spectators. To Aristophanes' chagrin, the very next year
Cratinus took first prize with his Wine Flagon. Ameipsias took second
place with his Konnos, which also attacked Socrates. The Clouds, over
the audience's heads, had to be content with last place. In the parabasis
of the revised version, Aristophanes rebukes the "unrefined" public for
not preferring his play, which, he points out, turned from lewd and low
comedy to deal with higher things.

To treat of the "higher things," Aristophanes introduces a chorus of
clouds; "their unsubstantial mistiness," as Henry Ten Eyck Perry indicated in Masters of Dramatic Comedy (1939), is "a good symbol for the
practical weakness of abstract reasoning." Socrates himself is suspended
in a basket, because the earth's moisture sucks the intellect dry: "I could
not have searched out celestial matters," says Socrates, "without sus-
pending judgment, and infusing my subtle spirit with the kindred air."
Thus hanging aloft, he does all his thinking in the clouds.

The play opens with Strepsiades ('son of a twister') in debt. He hits
upon the bright idea of having his son study with Socrates, to learn to
out-argue the creditors. Just Discourse and Unjust Discourse present
their advantages; Strepsiades chooses the latter, as the way to confute
the laws. But when his son emerges from the school and uses the lessons,
he does so not to save Strepsiades, but to justify thrashing him. There-

upon Strepsiades sees what a fool he has been to trust the new education, and sets fire to Socrates' Think-Shop.

Aristophanes' attack on Socrates is shrewdly advanced and captures the philosopher's physical peculiarities — his refusal to wear sandals, his need of a haircut, his dislike of hot baths — in order to carry along the more serious charges. The fire in the finale doubtless struck a note of actuality in the contemporary audience, for there had been physical attacks upon the Sophists in various parts of Greece, as well as in southern Italy, where a mob had burned the Pythagorean school at Croton.

"It had required courage to attack Cleon," observed Henry Ten Eyck Perry, "but it took skill to oppose Socrates, and perhaps partially as a result of the difference in the caliber of their subjects, The Clouds is a much richer and more intricate piece of work than either The Acharnians* or The Knights*." In structure, the play is more like a tragedy (therefore, more like the New Comedy) than a typical Old Comedy play, i.e., instead of being divided into two sections by a long parabasis, it moves more directly in a single drive to the climax. In other respects, too, The Clouds shows Aristophanes' power. The songs of the chorus are among the most beautiful lyrics in Greek literature. The metrical forms are effectively varied with the thought; Just Discourse, for example, speaks in dignified, rolling anapests, while Unjust Discourse flaunts his pretensions in pert iambics.

The scenic arrangement of The Clouds, while simple, was undoubtedly effective. Thornton Wilder in the New York Times (February 13, 1938) referred to it in defending the devices of his play Our Town*: "In its healthiest ages the theatre has always exhibited the least scenery."

The Clouds was a favorite among Aristophanes' plays in earlier times; 127 manuscripts of the comedy survive from Byzantium and medieval Italy. (This number is exceeded only by the 148 of Plutus.)

The Clouds was performed in Greek at Oxford, England, in 1905 and 1938. It was also presented in Greek at Swathmore College, Pennsylvania, in 1939. Of a performance at Williams College, Massachusetts, in June 1933, Clayton Hamilton wrote: "It is always interesting to be reminded at first hand that the human sense of humor has altered very little in the last 2500 years . . . Its satirical exposition of the topsy-turvy mental means by which an upstart younger generation may be taught to confute its conservative elders by ingenious argumentative devices, is not at all inapplicable to conditious on many of our college campuses at the present time . . . It still excels in comic force a majority of the timely products of these more journalistic days."

THE WASPS   *Aristophanes*

Aristophanes renews his attack on Cleon, the leader of the war party of his time, in this stinging travesty of the jury system as it was developed—or debased—by Cleon. Supposedly to prevent bribery, juries were constituted not of twelve, but of hundreds of citizens. Cleon increased the fee for jury service; during the hard years of the Peloponnesian War, when the farms outside Athens were ravaged by the Spartans, many a family eked out a wretched existence with the pay of its older men for jury service. With the young men at war, the large body of jurors was an important element of Cleon's power.

The Wasps, written in 422 B.C., presents the effort of Bdelycleon to make his father Philocleon (the names mean "Hate-Cleon" and "Love-Cleon") give up jury duty. Philocleon is a convicting juror; he (and his friends, the chorus of jurors clad as wasps) pride themselves on a record with nary an acquittal. Philocleon, confined to the house by his son, tries all sorts of schemes to get out and go to court. Bdelycleon, while persuading his father that the jurors are mere tools, has the bright idea of arranging a trial at home. The old man is tickled at the thought. They try their dog, Labes, for the theft of a Sicilian cheese. (The general Laches had been accused by Cleon of misappropriating funds for army supplies.) When Philocleon is fooled into voting for acquittal, he is so shocked that he turns away from jury service and gives himself over to the delights of feasting and frolicking, as a free citizen should.

The Wasps was carefully constructed, and once more put Aristophanes into the winning place at the Lenaean contest. There is deft characterization in Philocleon. The choral ode pays fine tribute to the deeds of the older men of Athens. There are both irony and sympathy in the picture of the old men going to jury service, guided by little boys; there is irony, mingled with tenderness, in the picture of the welcome Philocleon receives from his wife and daughter, when he comes home with his three obols at the end of a jury day; and there are satire and humor in the lessons in behavior that Philocleon takes before starting on his new life of gaiety, as well as in the contrasting misconduct of his carousal.

Aristophanes delighted in inconsistencies and in what his audience must have recognized as outrageous and facetious misstatements. In The Clouds he mocked his rival, Eupolis, for having copied the stock practice of having a drunken old woman perform an indecent dance; but in The Wasps he does the same thing himself with a drunken old man.

The theme of The Wasps is sufficiently general to have wide application. The only comedy of the French dramatist Racine, Les Plaideurs (1668), is a version of The Wasps written in terms of Racine's day, although Racine condemns the court procedure as a whole, whereas Aristophanes attacked only the abuses of the jury system.

Aristophanes' work is the more powerful. Matthew Arnold mentions one reason for that power: "The boldest creations of a riotous imagination are in Aristophanes based always upon the foundation of a serious thought." He had, furthermore, the faculty of piercing the surface of a social sore to the core of the disease. He always distinguished the integrity and the good will of the individual citizen from the personal ambition of the leaders on the one hand and the malleability of the mob on the other. Thus Gilbert Murray could properly say, in terms of our time: "If Aristophanes disliked the ascendancy of the mob as heartily as the Morning Post, he hated militarism and cruelty as much as the Manchester Guardian, and he exposed the absurdity of the world's solemn façades as vividly as a 'Low' cartoon."

PEACE   Aristophanes

One of the happiest, warmest, and most exuberant of the comedies of Aristophanes is his Peace, which was written after reverses on both sides of the war and the death of two leaders, Cleon of Athens and Brasidas of Sparta, had renewed negotiations. The Spartan ambassadors probably attended the Great Dionysia of 421 B.C., in which Peace won second prize (The Tradies of Eupolis was first; The Clansmen of Leucon, third). Prospects of a rapid end of the war were bright, and within the year, the treaty of peace was signed.

The hopeful mood of Athens is captured in the play's story. Trygaeus (the 'vine man') carefully rears a dung-beetle, until it is strong enough to bear him to Olympus to beg Peace of Zeus. He learns from Hermes that the angry Zeus has pitched Peace into a well, leaving the Hellenic world in charge of the god of war. Persuading Hermes to help him and his chorus of husbandmen, Trygaeus brings Peace back to earth. He also brings Opora, goddess of harvests, for himself, and Theoria, mistress of festivals, for the Athenian Senate. The play ends as the wedding feast is being prepared.

The delightfully playful quality of Peace bubbles out in all sorts of romping. Astride the beetle, Trygaeus plans to use his phallus as a rudder, in case of need. He tells the audience that from heaven they looked like rascals; from earth, the same, only bigger. Striving to extricate Peace from the well, the men work, as Eugene O'Neill, Jr. has phrased it, "with great enthusiasm and greater inefficiency. The difficulties are delightfully Hellenic; the Boeotians are only pretending; Lamachus is in the way; the Argives laugh at the others while they try to profit from their troubles; the Megarians are trying hard, but are too undernourished to be of much use; some of the Greeks are pulling one way and some another."

When Trygaeus gets back to earth with the three beautiful women, humor turns to love-making and festive sports. The chorus sings: "What I love is to drink with good comrades in the corner by the fire when good dry wood, cut at the height of the summer, is crackling; it is to cook pease on the coals and beechnuts among the embers; it is to kiss our pretty Thracian while my wife is at the bath." With good-humored anticipation, the amorous delights quicken the home-bound warriors.

With the same warm good humor, Aristophanes touches upon more serious concerns. In the parabasis, he reminds the audience (by quoting four lines from The Wasps) that he has never attacked women or obscure persons, but only the very greatest. He then changes immediately to a jesting tone, asking not only the peace-loving to give him victory in the dramatic contest, but also the bald, for he is one of them: "Do not grudge the prize to the poet whose talent shines as bright as his own bare skull!" (Aristophanes was then twenty-four years old). When Peace comes to earth, Aristophanes pictures the great dismay of those whose interests are promoted by war. First, the diviners and oracle-mongers, who profit from bad times, seek a share in the festivities, while at the same time they proclaim that the bonds of peace must be broken. (History soon showed their words were sadly true.) Then come the war profiteers, the manufacturers of weapons, breastplates, trumpets, shields. They bewail the coming of peace, and try to sell their surplus supplies, which (as is the case with government equipment today) go for odd sums for odd uses: the helmet crests for table dusters; the spears to split into vine-props; the breastplates and helmets for less public purposes. Combining scatological and erotic humor, good-natured satire and fantastic fable, Peace is the merriest of the comedies of Aristophanes.

A French version, 1932, of Peace by François Porché was performed in England in 1936, without enthusiastic reception. In the United States the students of Swathmore and Haverford Colleges combined to present the Greek play in May, 1941. The necessities of bowdlerization for public performances would remove much of the play's sparkle; but *Peace* shows Aristophanes in his lightest and liveliest mood.

THE BIRDS

Aristophanes

In the stress of a disastrous war, Athens in 414 B.C. tightened her belt and her temper. Rebellion and sacrilege were followed by widespread persecution. Direct criticism of persons and events was dangerous; it was a time to dream. During that year, Aristophanes wrote *The Birds*, a brilliant flight of the imagination. Rich, mellow and mischievous, the play was awarded second prize at the contests of that year; it is today generally considered Aristophanes' best work.

In *The Birds*, Peisthetaerus, ("Plausible") seeking a happier land, gets the bright idea of persuading the birds to establish their rule. Strategically placed between heaven and earth, they could dictate both to the gods and to mortals. The delighted birds at once erect the great wall of their new city of Cloud-Cuckooland. The Athenians, hearing of the new state, quick to seek fresh fields for exploitation and eager to acquire the advantages of wings, come ten thousand strong to colonize the land. Peisthetaerus drives them away as pests. Meanwhile the gods, barred from contact with the earth and starving for want of sacrifices, send Poseidon, Heracles and Triballus to treat with the birds. Peisthetaerus cajoles and bribes Heracles into awarding him the hand of Basileia ('Sovereignty'). The play ends with the celebration of their union.

On this fanciful framework Aristophanes wove some of his finest poetry, and some of his freshest fooling. The lyric song of the nightingale (lines 209-259) is among the greatest in Greek poetry, and the *parabasis* of the chorus of birds, with its recurring call, *tiotiotiotiotinx*, is delicate and charming. When the chorus addresses the judges, it promises them all sorts of benefits if they award the play the prize, but warns them that if they do not, they had better protect their heads with metal discs, such as are placed over statues, for the birds will befoul them when they go abroad.

Aristophanes makes the impossible quite plausible. When word comes that the great wall of Cloud-Cuckooland is built, no one wonders at the speed. Instead, the birds boast that they have raised it all by themselves, without human aid; and in the preposterous details of the construction— thirty thousand cranes from Libya brought the stones; plovers bore up the water; the geese used their web-feet as spades—the absurdity of the whole is at once heightened and slipped beyond the barriers of incredulity. Guards are posted and beacons burned, to intercept the messengers of the gods.

Among those that come to enjoy the benefits of the new city—those whom Peisthetaerus drives away—are a poet who seeks inspiration in the clouds; a geometer who plans to lay out the city scientifically; a dealer who hopes to sell the new laws for the city; an informer who thinks wings will help him in his trade; and a tax-supervisor from Athens.

While Aristophanes lays about him with a vigorous hand, it should be noted that he does not repudiate democracy; he denounces those that seek personal profit from its institutions.

In Goethe's youthful drama *The Birds, After Aristophanes*, 1778, Hopeful and Truefriend look for a Utopia in the clouds; but, once winged, they are borne on a burlesque extravagance far from Aristophanes.

Recent adaptations of *The Birds* include a notable óne in French by Fernand Nozieres in 1911. In English, *The Birds* was produced at Berkeley, California, and Mt. Vernon, Iowa, in 1934; at Bar Harbor, Maine, in 1935; at East Hampton, Long Island, in 1936. Donald Oenslager made a series of designs (some of them were reproduced in *Theatre Arts*, June 1929) for a version of *The Birds* set in the airplane age, with Peisthetaerus as a go-getter flying off with the birds, in the finale, to conquer the universe. A deft English adaptation by Walter Kerr was presented at Yale University in May 1952.

The Birds is the last play of Aristophanes in which there is a fully developed *parabasis*, i.e., the long ode of the chorus that divides the drama. Translating this, Swinburne called Aristophanes "the half divine humorist in whose incomparable genius the highest qualities of Rabelais were fused and harmonized with the supremest gifts of Shelley." We seldom, today, think of a dramatist as a lyric poet; but, in the blending of free ranging humor and high soaring verse, there is no one that comes within a thousand starry twinkles of Aristophanes.

LYSISTRATA   *Aristophanes*

This is the most modern of Aristophanes' comedies. Produced in 411 B.C., when Athens was on the verge of ruin in the Peloponnesian War, the play urges a pan-Hellenic peace and offers a unique means to achieve it.

Lysistrata, leader of Athenian women, persuades the fair sex of Greece to adopt her proposal to refuse themselves to their husbands until the men make peace. With the help of Lampito, a husky damsel from Sparta, she holds the frailer women to the line. Sex-starvation proves too much for the men, and the play ends with peace and marital joy.

No other of Aristophanes' comedies is so unified and so logically presented. The women are neatly portrayed: a few are stern and immovable, untouched by the men's sore desire; but the majority, especially the sweet Kalonike, find excuses to leave the Acropolis for their husband's embraces. Only the arrival of Cinesias, his phallus upreared to symbolize the men's impatient need, saves the situation. Lysistrata sends Cinesias' wife, Myrrhine, to gather strength from her husband's need of her. Myrrhine teases and tempts him, until he will have peace at any price. When the Spartan Herald and the Athenian Magistrate, in fact all the men, gather together, with swords down, but with their lances of flesh tipped high, to humble their war-time hates so that they may tumble their peace-won mates, they make one of the funniest scenes the theatre has ever beheld. For its "mad indecencies," said August Wilhelm Schlegel a century ago, *Lysistrata* "is in such bad repute that we must mention it lightly and rapidly, just as we would tread over hot embers."

In all of *Lysistrata*—and, for that matter, in all of Aristophanes—the fun with sex is frank, but never suggestive. Moreover, it is put to good use. The sexagenarians of the chorus, no less than the sex-agonized soldiers, point the phallus of nature at the follies of war. And for all the hearty laughter, "no Greek poet," as Henry Ten Eyck Perry emphasized, "not even Sophocles, has more tenderly dealt with maidenhood's soft season" than Aristophanes in this play.

Lysistrata expresses a most unusual fairmindedness considering the desperate straits of Athens in 411 B.C. Its author sees no special breed of evil in the enemies of Athens. Among the Athenians, however,

Peisander, who had fomented a briefly successful rebellion, is accused of favoring the war because it covers his thieveries. The Spartan woman, Lampito, states, "No doubt we shall persuade our husbands to conclude a fair and honest peace; but there is the Athenian populace: how are we to cure these folk of their warlike frenzy?", to which Lysistrata replies, "Have no fear; we undertake to make our own people listen to reason."

It is recorded that a pupil of Melanchthon, at Basel in 1532, read Aristophanes in order to contrast his obscenities with the purity of the Christian Church, in which connection it may be suggested that whereas to the pagan Greek woman was beauty to behold and love to enjoy, the fig-leaf after the Garden of Eden made Christian woman a secret and a sin. The delights of the Greek, as mirrored in Aristophanes, may be pagan, but they are not perverse.

The first effective revival of *Lysistrata* in recent times was produced by Maurice Donnay in Paris in 1892. The best was probably the production of the Moscow Art Theatre, in a version by Dmitry Smolin, 1923, which was brought to New York in 1925. Of the latter, Brooks Atkinson (December 14, 1925) said that it wrought "the organization of all the theatrical arts, vocal, scenic, and plastic, into a perfect projection."

The Moscow Art version was adapted in English by Gilbert Seldes. Opening in Philadelphia, it reached New York on June 5, 1930, for a run of 252 performances, followed by a long tour. The cast included Violet Kemble Cooper, Ernest Truex, Miriam Hopkins, Eric Dressler, Hope Emerson, and Sydney Greenstreet. In 1935, the Maurice Donnay version was presented in New York as an *Ode to a Grecian Urge*; the production was as heavy-handed as its title. Fay Bainter appeared in the Seldes version in 1931; Nance O'Neil, in 1933; the Coburns, in 1935. Westport, Connecticut, saw the play in 1936 and 1937, and again in 1948 in a "modernized" version with June Havoc. The Federal Theatre presented an "African version" in Seattle in 1938; an all-Negro cast brought the play to New York again in 1946. George Jean Nathan remarked that the Seldes adaptation "apparently has been dirtied up." Robert Garland declared, "Fall flat it does, right on its double-entendre. Sex is made actually uninteresting." Aristophanes, however, survives all such perversion of his work.

The Seldes translation of *Lysistrata,* published with superb drawings by Picasso, is lively, and makes a good theatre production. More literal translation does perhaps fuller justice to the Greek, which has qualities of universal portent that o'erleap the comedy, demonstrating that laughter can open wide the door to truth.

THESMOPHORIAZUSAE   *Aristophanes*

Written in 411 B.C., *Thesmophoriazusae* (The Women at the Festival of Demeter) is one of the freshest and most frolicsome of Aristophanes' comedies. A farcical attack upon the work of Euripides*, it is constructed much like a modern play, with a plot that moves gaily and speedily to a climax.

If it were not for the limited appeal of its subject, the play would undoubtedly be Aristophanes' most popular drama today.

The play pictures a gathering of the Athenian women to celebrate the Eleusinian mysteries at the festival of Demeter, goddess of fruitfulness, from which all men are barred. Warned that the women plan to punish

him for showing only the evil-doers of their sex in his plays, Euripides
has the bright idea of persuading his father-in-law, Mnesilochus, to go to
the festival disguised as a woman in order to see whether he can defend
Euripides against their charges. The manner in which Mnesilochus is
detected by the women and the various attempts made by Euripides to
rescue him are highly comic. At the end, Euripides makes peace with the
women, promising not to reveal their pranks to their husbands when the
men come back from the war.

Throughout the play shafts of satire are constantly directed against
Euripides, or against his young disciple, the playwright Agathon. Euripides' frequent use of stage machinery, the prettiness of his dialogue, the
emphasis he places upon devices rather than fundamentals, his supposed
concern for dramatic effectiveness instead of spiritual depth or poetic
beauty, all are given attention. When Euripides swears to come to the
rescue of his father-in-law if necessary, the old man tells him to keep in
mind that it's the heart and not the tongue that swore—thus recalling the
line in *Hippolytus** by which Euripides had shocked the Athenians: when
Hippolytus threatens to repudiate an oath, he says, "It was the tongue
that swore, and not the heart."

The heaviest of the charges against Euripedes concerns his many portraits of women in the excesses of love: of women whirled into adultery
or deception; of women attempting to rid themselves of illegitimate children, or kidnapping to conceal their sterility. Such matters may have
entered superficially into the great themes of Aeschylus and Sophocles;
but, Aristophanes charges, with Euripides they are the groundwork of
his dramatic structure and the chief subject of his studies.

At the festival in the *Thesmophoriazusae*, Aristophanes draws double
humor from his charges. In the first place, the women do not deny the
evil attributed to them; they merely call for punishment of Euripides
for revealing it. Nor does Mnesilochus, in defense, deny Euripides' attack; instead, he lists many more evil actions of women, declaring that
they should be grateful to Euripides for not having mentioned these.
Thus Aristophanes flays both the Athenian women and the playwright.

Once Mnesilochus is caught, he casts about for ways to escape the
women's clutches. He tries half a dozen different ways, each taken from
a drama by Euripides.

The deftness of the allusions and quotations, the neatness with which
episodes from Euripides are fitted to the situation of his father-in-law in
the *Thesmophoriazusae*, must have kept the Athenans engulfed in waves
of laughter. Beneath what seems a purely aesthetic concern, Aristophanes
was aware of the implications that Euripides' work held for the welfare of
the state; he makes this abundantly clear in his next play, *The Frogs**.

THE FROGS   *Aristophanes*

During the six years between Aristophanes' previous two plays and
The Frogs, Athens had recalled from exile the great leader Alcibiades.
He did not enter the city, however, until after four years of naval successes. Then, with the loss of an engagement with the Spartan Lysander,
the fickle Athenian government sent him into exile once more. Lysan-
ships, and another wave of executions and exiles swept the land.

Written during these crucial years of the Peloponnesian War, and shortly after the death in 406 B.C. of both Sophocles and Euripides, *The Frogs* combines patriotic fervor with its satire. It opens with Dionysus, the god of tragedy as well as of wine, waiting before the battle of Arginusae, reading Euripides' play *Andromeda*. Impelled to bring Euripides back from the underworld, Dionysus, disguised as Heracles (the only one that ever drew a mortal back from Hades), with his servant Xanthias enters the underworld. Ferried across the lake of the dead by Charon, Dionysus finds the newly arrived Euripides disputing with Aeschylus the throne of tragedy. A trial is held, in which each tragic dramatist points to the flaws of the other's work and recites the virtues of his own. None can decide between them save that, when scales are brought, Aeschylus' verses outweigh Euripides'. Dionysus determines to select the one "whose advice may guide the city true." He returns from Hades with Aeschylus. Thus, against the realism, the reason, and the sophistry of his day, Aristophanes urges a return to the dignity, the valour, and the integrity that had brought glory to his city.

Incidental political references are made throughout the play. Several, for instance, stress the fact that, in the recent battles, slaves that had volunteered for military service were given their freedom, while many true Athenians were still ostracized or exiled. This point is further pressed in the *parabasis,* the main choral ode, in which Aristophanes vigorously pleads that, in view of the crisis, Athens should forgive and recall her exiles. His exhortation so stirred the Athenians that, by public demand, the play received the unprecedented tribute of an immediate second performance, at which Aristophanes was presented with an olive wreath from Athena's sacred tree on the Acropolis.

The literary references in the play, however, are much more fully developed. Aristophanes repeats earlier charges he had made against Euripides, especially those of *The Thesmophoriazusae**; but he develops and adds to them. In addition to attacking Euripides' realistic, even colloquial and undignified, style, he accuses him of immorality and sophistry. In a final blow, when Euripides reminds Dionysus that the god has sworn to take him back to earth, Dionysus replies with the fateful words from Euripides' own *Hippolytus**, "Only my tongue has sworn."

Although Aristophanes makes no effort to be fair when balancing Aeschylus against Euripides, by no means does he leave the earlier dramatist unscathed. After giving some examples of Aeschylus' high-flown phrases, his pompous and straining compounds, which make Euripides cry out, "Let us at least use the language of men!", the great length of Aeschylus' choral odes and his frequent undramatic silences are attacked. Aristophanes presents Aeschylus, however, with dignity and poise; Euripides, with a quick ease that verges upon impudence.

It is Euripides, nevertheless, that gives the answer that the ages have echoed. When Aeschylus challenges him to tell on what grounds a poet should be admired, Euripides responds: "If his art is true, and his counsel sound, and if he brings help to the nation, by making men better in some respect." Aristophanes—as indeed all his works show— was not unaware of the poet's duty to entertain, but his immediate purpose in *The Frogs* joined him with Euripides, whose plays rang with patriotic fervor. Aristophanes knew that, beyond the rouse of a crisis, Athens had need of the dignity, the sense of honor, for which Aeschylus stood firm.

In recent years, *The Frogs* has been produced in many parts of the world: in 1936 at Missoula, Montana; in 1936 and 1937 in England; in 1938 in Minnesota (Winona State Teachers' College), with names changed to those of modern politicians and dictators; in 1940, in New South Wales. Of the 1936 English performance, the *London Times* (March 4) commented: "After twenty-three centuries this comedy does still win the laughter of all spectators, and that not only in its more boisterous moments. The audience naturally and properly revelled in the broad humour of the earlier scenes . . . The schools of Aeschylus and Euripides will always have their disciples, and it might be a profitable exercise for a satirist of today to set contemporary dramatists on the stage in an imitation of *The Frogs*."

In an interesting anticipation of modern economics, Aristophanes in the *parabasis* of *The Frogs* compares the *Kaloikagathoi* (the noble young aristocrats) to the good coins of old, driven out of circulation by the bad new ones.

In America, *The Frogs* has developed a tradition at Yale University. In the early 1890's the Greek students (perhaps after Dionysiac festivals) would sing, under the professors' windows, the refrain of the chorus of frogs that is sung while Dionysus crosses the underworld lake: the cry has been incorporated into the Yale cheer—"Bre-ke-ke-kex, co-ax, co-ax!" Monty Woolley staged a production of the play at Yale in 1921, with Stephen Vincent Benét handling the choruses. Some bright classicist, more recently, noticed that in the swimming pool of the new Yale gymnasium the seats rise round as in the Greek Theatre, while at one end the wall has three doors and benches beyond a platform. Consequently, in November 1941, an aquatic production of *The Frogs* was given there, with floats and underwater lights, with a surprisingly effective movement. John O'Reilly reported, in the *New York Herald-Tribune:* "Aristophanes was the Rodgers and Hart of his day. His slang was more than pungent and his choruses were snappy . . . The undergraduate translation of the work of this ancient satirist is hot . . . When Bacchus and his faithful slave, Xanthias, are being paddled across the River Styx by Charon, with the Yale swimming team in froggy headdress swimming figures about the boat and croaking 'Bre-ke-ke-kex, co-ax, co-ax,' it presents a spectacle that would make Billy Rose turn an envious shade of batrachian green."

Those that read or see *The Frogs* with some knowledge of the desperate military and pig-headed political situation of Athens when the play was produced, recognize the courage and wisdom of Aristophanes. Even without such knowledge, his playfulness and his power—his unique combination of slapstick, serious satire, bawdry and beauty—shine through.

ECCLESIAZUSAE   *Aristophanes*

In 404 B.C., the year after Aristophanes' *The Frogs**, Athens surrendered to Sparta and the walls of the city were thrown down. The government of Athens changed hands several times until Thrasybulus, exiled in 404 by the Thirty Tyrants, overcame them in 403, re-established the Athenian democracy and offered amnesty to all Athenians in exile. During these tumultous years, all sorts of political expedients were considered, if not tried. "Love of novelty," says Chremes (the ordinary citizen) in *Ecclesiazusae*, "and disdain for tradition are our ruling principles."

It was in this atmosphere that Aristophanes presented his *Ecclesiazusae (Women In Parliament)*, a travesty of the communistic ideas of the period, with women in control. Men having made such a mess of the world, Praxagora communes with her lamp as the play opens, why shouldn't she do better? She gets the bright idea of having the women of Athens, disguised as men, slip into the Assembly early and vote power into their own hands. "Let us save the ship of state," she cries, "which nobody now seems able to sail or to row." When Chremes hears that the women are to be given the reins of government, he exclaims "That's the only thing we haven't tried!"

Thus the women gain political power. Although their speeches praise their conservatism, in action, they at once set up a communist system. All property is to be turned over to the state, and the women and children are to be held in common. If children do not know who their parents are, Praxagora argues, they will respect all their elders.

The rest of the play shows the "bright idea" in practice. As might be expected, the citizens are less eager to give their wealth to the state than to enjoy the free banquets which the women have substituted for the law courts. Free love brings other complications. To be fair, it is ruled that no man may enjoy a young woman until her elders have first been satisfied. There is a most amusing scene in which a girl has her lover snatched away by three successively older and uglier hags. Despite such minor troubles, however, life seems to move joyously, as the final chorus moves to the great feast. Yet deftly the bubble is pricked, when the sumptuous spread of the public banquet is announced, by the suggestion that each citizen bring his own portion of soup.

The *Ecclesiazusae* was the first play presented in the contest of 392 B.C.; there is no record of the judges' decision. Its continuing timeliness is shown by the fact that, in a New York 1954 performance, 130 lines were cut, lest, it was protested, the play seem pro-Communist.

We do not know what Aristophanes wrote during the thirteen years after *The Frogs*, but in several ways the *Ecclesiazusae* marks a transition to a newer style of comedy. It retains the bawdry of the early plays, with occasional thrusts of political satire, and its general spirit recalls the revolt of the women in *Lysistrata** and the travesty on utopian ideas in *The Birds**. But its form has changed. Most of the play is in a new meter (iambic trimeter); and there is no central choral ode *(parabasis)*, only a dance. The chorus, indeed, has dwindled in importance; it has no entrance song, and it is long offstage. The play more closely approximates the latter-day five-act structure. Its setting is typical of the New Comedy: a city street, backed by a row of houses. Even the names of the characters begin to show a change: *'Praxagora'* is, as in the earlier plays, an invented name, meaning 'active in the market place'; but Chremes was a common name among the citizens of Athens—the first such name to be used by Aristophanes. The fourth century, indeed, brought new masters and new devices; the great days of Greek tragedy and of the Old Comedy had passed.

The *Ecclesiazusae* should not be left without mention of the glorious dish to which the citizens address themselves in the final banquet—the longest word in any Indo-European tongue: *lepadotemachoselachogaleo-kranioleipsanodrimypotrimmatosilphiotyromelitokatakechymenokichlepi-*

kossyphophattoperisteralektryonoptokephalio kinklopeleiolagoiosiraioba-
phetragalopterygon. This more-than-a-mouthful includes, as Oates and
O'Neill note in *The Complete Greek Drama* (1938) "limpets, slices of salt
fish, thornbacks, whistle-fishes, cornel-berries, a remoulade of leftover
brains seasoned with silphium and cheese, thrushes basted with honey,
blackbirds, ringdoves, squabs, chickens, fried mullets, wagtails, rock-
pigeons, hare, and wings ground up in new wine that has been boiled
down."

No successor has succeeded in boiling down the essence of Aristophanes. In many little touches of humor, in deft darts of satire, as well
as in over-all conception and execution, Aristophanes is in full and
unique command of the comic vein in the *Ecclesiazusae.*

PLUTUS   *Aristophanes*

This is the last extant work of Aristophanes. We know, however, that
he later wrote two more comedies, which were produced by his son,
Araros. One of these, *Cocalus,* seems to have set the pattern followed by
Menander* and other writers of the New Comedy.

Athens in 388 B.C. was in the midst of distressing times. Material and
moral poverty was widespread. No one dared to attack the leaders as
Aristophanes had done in his earlier works. The comedies in the contest
of that year disguised contemporary issues in mythological terms. Aristophanes took as his subject Plutus, the god of wealth. The play marks
a shift from political to economic concern.

Chremylus, a citizen of Athens, upon asking the oracle how his son
might grow successful without becoming a scoundrel, is told to follow
the first man he sees when he leaves the temple. That man, raggedy,
old, and blind, turns out to be none other than the god Plutus. Chremylus
conceives the bright idea of curing Plutus of his blindness, so that he can
look about and reward honest men with his wealth. Poverty appears, to
argue that she too is of value to mankind; but Chremylus will have none
of her. His slave, Cario, leads Plutus to the temple of Asclepius to have
his sight restored. An amusing account is given by Cario of his night in
the temple. The rest of the play follows the usual Old Comedy pattern,
showing the consequences of the bright idea. A threadbare, just man is
rewarded. An informer is bereft of his trade. An old woman loses a
gigolo, for he no longer needs her cash. Hermes, god of thieves, likewise
starves for lack of sacrifices; he takes a job, in his capacity as god of
games, at the great games Plutus inaugurates. The play ends with a procession moving to install Plutus on the Acropolis. Indeed, Athens had
sore need of his resources.

There is much fun in *Plutus,* but only mild satire. When the blind
Plutus remarks that it is a long time since he has seen a good man, the
slave, Cario, looking over the audience, says: "That's not surprising. I,
who have clear eyes, can't see a single one." Chremylus declares that
"whatever is dazzling, beautiful, or charming in the eyes of mankind"
depends on wealth; and when Poverty recites her benefits to mankind,
it is not Plutus, but the citizen Chremylus that answers her. Poverty argues that, "Modesty dwells with me, and insolence with Riches," and that
the desire for wealth distorts the thinking of the citizens. When Poverty
leaves, she prophesies, "One day you will recall me," but she does not
reappear in the play.

Plutus, like the *Ecclesiazusae**, is a mingling of the old style and the new. The chorus is reduced virtually to a group that dances between the episodes of the action; and although the gods are involved in the story, the humans are neither heroes nor kings, but ordinary citizens concerned with domestic affairs. The impudent, confidential slave, a stock figure of later Greek and Roman comedy (first suggested by Xanthias in *The Frogs**) is fully developed in the figure of Cario.

The general nature of the mild satire in *Plutus,* and the universal appeal of the story, made it through Byzantine and medieval times the most popular of all Aristophanes' plays. No fewer than 148 manuscripts of *Plutus* survive, over twenty more than of the next in popularity, *The Clouds**. Altogether, Aristophanes illuminated Athenian society; when Dionysius, tyrant of Syracuse, wanted to learn more about Athens, Plato sent him the plays of Aristophanes.

Plutus was performed in Paris, in 1938, in a version by Simone Jollivet. Pierre Audiat in *Paris-Soir* (February, 1938) declared: "Plutus was not alone; Taste accompanied him . . . The first act is, in itself, a perfect masterpiece . . . What! Already, in the fourth century before our era, Aristophanes made that subtle criticism of wealth in society! With very broad comic effects, he put across the nicest nuances. He saw the role of poverty—not to be confused with misery—in the social body; he saw that leveling by wealth would destroy all ties of solidarity between the members; he set the ideal to attain: that wealth enter the dwellings only of honest folk. And he said this neatly, strongly, without pedantry, without preachy-preachy, in the midst of sharp laughter and salty wit." This French version picked up and realized Poverty's prophecy of her return: at the end, it effected a union of Plutus and Poverty in a city where only workers thrive.

The old Greek plays reveal that the social panaceas of our time are no novelties fresh-sprung from the brow of Karl Marx; their virtues and their weaknesses alike were shrewdly foreseen two dozen centuries ago. It is not merely the proffered panaceas, but human nature, in which their virtues and their weaknesses are rooted, that Aristophanes gently but shrewdly holds for our smiles in *Plutus.*

THE GOD OF VENGEANCE   *Sholem Asch*

Novelist on biblical themes and dramatist of Jewish life, Sholem Asch (b. 1880) is best known in the theatre for this study of a ghetto brothel keeper.

Presented first in Yiddish in 1907, *The God of Vengeance* swept rapidly all over Europe. Reinhardt produced it in Berlin, 1910, with Rudolph Schildkraut. A production in English, also starring Schildkraut, opened at the Provincetown Playhouse, New York, December 20, 1922, with Morris Carnovsky and Sam Jaffe, and was moved to Broadway on January 21, 1923. After 133 performances, it was interrupted by the police and declared by the judge to be a desecration of "the sacred scrolls of the Torah." An English production in London in 1923 and a Yiddish production there by the Vilna troupe in 1926 were also closed. The play was presented without interference in Germany, Austria, Poland, Russia, France, Holland, Norway, Sweden, and for a whole season, in 1916, in Italy.

The play pictures the sins of the father being visited. Yekel (Yankel)

Shapshowitch, married to a former prostitute, maintains a brothel in the basement of his home. He is, nevertheless, a pious, God-fearing man. He commissions a scribe to copy the Torah and he hopes to marry his daughter, Rifkele, to a rabbinical student. But Rifkele is debauched by Manka, one of the women downstairs, whose lover plans to use the girl in a rival house. Tortured by her father to reveal what has happened, Rifkele cries "I am my mother's daughter!" Yekel, in disappointment and fury, defies and denies his God. He drives his wife and his daughter back to the brothel, and is left a lonely, desolate man. The God of the Jews has exacted his pound of flesh.

"The love between the two girls," Asch has explained, "is not only an erotic one. It is the unconscious mother-love of which they are deprived . . . I also wanted to bring out the innocent, longing for sin, and the sinful, dreaming of purity. Manka, overweighed with sin, loves the clean soul of Rifkele; and Rifkele, the innocent young girl, longs to stay near the door of such a woman as Manka, and listen within." The picture of brothel life, and of Rifkele's curiosity and temptation, is so real as to grip the emotions with both pity and horror.

The play provoked a sharp division of opinion in the press. "We know there are sewers and cess pools", reported the *New York Telegraph* (December 31, 1922). "Indeed, they are very necessary components of everyday life; but the theatre is scarcely the place for their representation." Most of the reviewers defended the play. The *New York Sun* (December 20) claimed that "in spite of two episodes such as we have never before seen on the stage, (the play) is, in our opinion, a highly moral drama."

Some of the papers managed to turn from defense to analysis. The *London Jewish Chronicle* (May 28, 1926) said that Asch "plumbs 'lower depths' than Gorki*, is as harrowing as Andreyev* — by simpler means." And although it described the play as "ugly, sordid, and repellent beyond any other play that has yet been presented on the contemporary English-speaking stage," the *New York Call* (December 21, 1922) said that "*The God of Vengeance* is nonetheless a powerful, realistic study of humanity in its most degraded form, expressed with that fierce vitality which is one of the characteristics of Yiddish drama . . . It has an unmistakable Oriental quality in its religious and ethical mood, in its sexual standards, and in the lyric beauty that gleams now and again out of the muck and filth of debased human life."

Asch meant only the surface of his play to be individualized. "Call Yekel John and instead of the Holy Scroll place in his hand the crucifix," he said, "and the play will then be as much Christian as it is now Jewish." Bernard Shaw presents a Christian brothel-owner in *Mrs. Warren's Profession**; but he is concerned chiefly with the economic aspects of the problem, whereas Asch lays bare the tortured soul of a male counterpart of Mrs. Warren. *The God of Vengeance* strikes deep to the core of environmental influence and ethical concern, and its brothel setting gives a sensational spur to its intrinsic dramatic power.

CHU CHIN CHOW   *Oscar Asche*

By turning the successful pantomime *The Forty Thieves* into an extravaganza with music by Frederick Norton, Oscar Asche (English, 1871-1936) achieved in *Chu Chin Chow* a delightful spectacle and gorgeous musical drama. Opening in London August 31, 1916, in the midst of World War I, *Chu Chin Chow* attained the longest run of any musical on the London stage, 2,238 performances, a record surpassed, by a mere ten performances, only by the recent New York run of *Oklahoma**. *Chu Chin Chow* has several times been revived in London: 1929, 1935-6, 1940, and 1941. The New York production, which opened on October 22, 1917, with Tyrone Power, Florence Reed, Henry F. Dixey, ran for 208 performances. Marjorie Wood and Lionel Braham went on the road with it in 1919; and a film was made in 1934 with Fritz Kortner and Anna May Wong.

Chu Chin Chow, a giant of malign and inhuman visage, his robe ablaze with embroidered dragons, and his fingers tipped with silvered talons like those of a bird of prey, is really Abu Hassan, the leader of the forty thieves. Ali Baba and the other characters of the tale all appear as the play moves through the familiar story from the *Arabian Nights*. Ali's son, called Nur-al-Huda, is in love with the slave girl, Marjanah.

Among the picturesque scenes that adorn the extravaganza are the feast of a thousand candles in a moonlit orchard and the dance of the jewels, which come to life as Ali Baba uncovers them in the robbers' cave.

Observed the *St. Louis Post-Dispatch* (December 2, 1919): "Raptures of color and sound, ecstasies of youth and beauty, and since man is so constituted as to find esthetic joy in evil, transports of grossness and monstrosity — these are the pagan beatitudes of the senses that burn with a devouring flame throughout that stupendous embodiment of romance, *Chu Chin Chow*."

The plot upon which *Chu Chin Chow* is built, with the drowning of the forty thieves in their jars of oil, is of course, as the *Toronto Star* (April 29, 1919) reminds us, "a rather grim and gory story, but nevertheless human." The play naturally stresses the love between Ali's son and the slave girl, who discovers the thieves hiding in the jars. Among the songs are the vigorous "We Are the Robbers of the Woods," the traditional song of the cobbler; the sentimental and very popular "Any Time Is Kissing Time," and a rousing love chant of the wild women of the desert.

The artistic director of the Metropolitan Opera House, Giulio Gatti-Casazza, called *Chu Chin Chow* "truly a beautiful spectacle, spirited and full of action, charming in its fantasy, a delight to eye and ear." And Enrico Caruso called it "one of the most artistic and most absorbing entertainments I have ever attended." With a lavishness that both London and New York have since surrendered to Hollywood, *Chu Chin Chow* remains the most successful of the spectacular musical comedies, a surpassing capture of Oriental color, fiery passion, and tender romance.

MR. POIRIER'S SON-IN-LAW   *Emile Augier*

The early plays of this French playwright (1820-1899) were written in verse. Later, Augier turned to prose dramas exalting the virtues of middle class life. In his day the old nobility of France was being absorbed into the ranks of the prosperous bourgeoisie. Without being blind to the faults of the newly-rich, Augier in a number of "thesis plays" examined the interrelationship of the aristocrat and the bourgeois. His best play, one that Francisque Sarcey said will always remain a classic, is *Mr. Poirier's Son-in-Law* (*Le Gendre de M. Poirier*) 1854, a dramatization, with Jules Sandeau (1811-1883) of Sandeau's novel *Sacs et Parchemins*.

Old Poirier, in the hope that his money will bring him a peerage, has married his daughter to a ruined marquis, Gaston de Presles. The Marquis ignores his wife, however, to pay attention to the frivolous Mme. de Montjoy, only to get himself financially entangled. When his wife saves his honor for a second time, the Marquis awakens to the fact that he loves her; the better qualities of both aristocrat and bourgeois are brought to the fore. At the end of the play, Poirier's ambitions are sheared, but the union of his daughter and the Marquis promises sound growth for France.

The role of Poirier was a favorite of Coquelin's, and until 1914 the play was highly popular in France. Frequently performed in the United States by French groups and classes, it was presented there professionally in 1904 by Cazelle's French company, and in 1918 by the Vieux Colombier. The *New York Dramatic Mirror* (November 12, 1904) commented on "the play's red blood of human passions and backbone of truth to life." In 1927, the dramatist Jacques Deval* expressed the general French opinion, that *Le Gendre de M. Poirier* "has not lost anything of its freshness, nor of its humor and emotion."

Mr. Poirier's Son-in-Law is a "well-made play," a type that later degenerated into expertly but mechanically contrived potboilers. In Augier and Sandeau's drama, the situation is real, the characters are natural, the feelings humanly warm. Born of a contemporary social problem in France, the play strikes to the heart of human nature everywhere.

BERKELEY SQUARE   John Lloyd Balderston

Suggested by Henry James' story *The Sense of the Past* and written with some assistance from J. C. Squire, *Berkeley Square* is the story of Peter Standish, an American visiting England in 1926, who becomes his English ancestor of the same name in the year 1784. Peter tries to enter into the life of the eighteenth century to which he has reverted, but, with the knowledge of a twentieth-century man, he succeeds only in creating uneasiness. The Duchess of Devonshire, for example, rather naturally resents his referring to her as an outstanding figure of an interesting historical period. Only in Helen — through their mutual love — does Peter wake no fear; but Helen had died some hundred years before the twentieth-century-Peter was born. Love helping, he lets her glimpse the future by peering long into his eyes. In keeping with eighteenth-century historical fact, Peter proposes to Kate Pettigrew; but when the twentieth century comes sadly back to him, it is the time-o'erleaping love of Helen Pettigrew that gives him memoried solace.

The play's tangle of time calls for explanation. Our ordinary sense of time is similar to that of a person in a river boat, whose view of the river's course is obstructed by overhanging banks and wooded bends ahead; time in the supernal view of Peter is as that of a person in a plane, to whom the whole course of the river is at once in sight.

Presented in London October 6, 1926, *Berkeley Square* ran for 181 performances, the first play by an American author (Mr. Balderston was born in Philadelphia in 1889) to achieve a long run in England before its production in the United States. London saw it again in 1929 and 1940. It opened in New York on November 4, 1929, with Leslie Howard and Margalo Gillmore, and ran for 229 performances. Somewhere in the United

States, it has played every year since. The theme of Berkeley Square recurs in the sentimentalized musical, *Brigadoon**.

The love of Peter and Helen, with his knowledge and her sense of its time-torn fate, keeps the delicate and tender story "on a plane of preternatural tragedy," according to the *New York Times* (November 5, 1929). The play evokes a soft pathos, rather than a tragic power. The *New York Telegraph* (November 6, 1929) observed that it quietly conveys the effects "of heartbreak and sorcery, of rich and breath-taking beauty, of bewilderment and tender fancy." Balderston's play "soars to high wit and original beauty" in its suggestion of the power of love, not only to level ranks, but to hold its spell steadfast in strange two-way journeying along the corridors of time.

MERCADET THE PROMOTER   *Honoré de Balzac*

Of the five plays which he wrote, novelist Honoré de Balzac (1799-1850) saw four produced—all failures. The fifth, *Mercadet le faiseur,* sometimes called just *Le Faiseur* (*The Promoter*), presented with Geoffroy at the Gymnase August 24, 1851, was a great success. It is still in the repertoire of the Comédie Française. Some critics believe that this play, built on the schemes and speculations of a man desperately in debt, is drawn from Balzac's own experiences.

Mercadet is in the intellectual tradition of the French satire of the money-manipulator. Its main figure is much the same sort as Le Sage's Turcaret*, save that Balzac is gentler with the man and, by an offstage *deus ex machina,* provides a happy ending. Mercadet blames his troubles on a partner Godeau, who has absconded. He manages his creditors so shrewdly that they begin by angrily demanding their money and end by lending him more. He persuades one to invest in his new invention, a barricade-proof pavement— "on which and with which no barricade is possible" — at once a satire on the absurd speculative projects of the day and an invention that, after the political upheavals of 1848, the business-men and governments would eagerly desire. He borrows money from another creditor by announcing his daughter Julie's betrothal to the wealthy Count de la Brive — only to discover that the Count is himself overwhelmed with debts. Mercadet then urges the count to masquerade as the absconder Godeau, returned penitent and rich. Madame Mercadet dissuades the Count; but lo and behold! the real Godeau returns (offstage) rich and penitent, frees Mercadet from his debts, and enables Julie to marry the poor clerk Minard whom she loves.

Mercadet le faiseur has been widely played. Within a year of its Paris premiere (which showed a version shortened from the original five acts to three) a German adaptation was presented in Berlin, and an English adaptation — *The Game of Speculation,* by George Henry Lewes (which calls Mercadet Mr. Affable Hawk), at the Royal Lyceum Theatre, October 2, 1851—in London. It was revived several times in London. Edmund Got enacted Mercadet at the Comédie Française in 1868; the play was presented at Balzac's centennial in 1899, and with music by Darius Milhaud in 1935. New York saw it first in English at the Broadway Theatre, September 21, 1857, with revivals into the 1900's. It was produced in Edinburgh, 1877; in Milan, 1882. New York saw it in French (Le Théâtre des quatre saisons) opening December 26, 1938. Chile saw a production in 1950.

Despite the convenient twist of its ending, the play has won almost unanimous praise, especially for the character of Mercadet. He is, observed
the London *Athenaeum* in 1879, "perhaps the most remarkable figure of
modern comedy . . . No half-hearted schemer is he, but a man sanguine
in his belief in himself, and justly sanguine, since some at least of his
schemes have in them the elements of assured success." The *New York
World-Telegram* of December 27, 1938, noted that the figures of the play
"make a vivid gallery, with their conflicts and calculations, and from the
butler Dustin up to Mercadet they are a cross-section of humanity
anywhere."

Balzac's prose is a far cry from the emotional depths of Shakespeare,
but a twinkling eye has turned its shrewdly realistic gaze upon the
middle-class businessman who "plays the market." As Marcel Barrière
remarked in 1899, "never have the greed and lack of principles that
characterize a certain class of speculator been exposed more scathingly."
Among the neat touches in the play is the opening picture of the servants
who, sizing up the situation, become impertinent in the hope that they
will be discharged and thus collect their wages; they complain that
Monsieur and Madame Mercadet do not even pay heed to their insolence.
Indeed, Mercadet so plausibly pictures a rosy future that the cook pays
the tradesman out of her own savings. In such details, and in the superb
portrait of a master manipulator, the kindly satire and keenly observant
realism of Balzac the novelist give life to his one great drama, *Mercadet*.

GRINGOIRE   *Theodore de Banville*

This one-act prose comedy glorifying the poet possesses not only
delicacy and taste, but effective characterization and touching drama.
It is perhaps the best of the writings by Theodore de Banville (1823-1891),
a moderately popular French poet-playwright of the nineteenth century.

The play shows King Louis XI of France taking a fancy to a wandering ballad-maker, Gringoire. The King tests Gringoire's manliness, to
see, as Homer Lind (who made an English version of the play in 1901)
put it, "whether that poet's soul can so shine through his ragged raiment
that he can win a young and beautiful woman in spite of his appearance."
Gringoire is placed in danger by the King's jealous and treacherous
barber. He proves worthy, and the King decides that "a plain-spoken
poet is a better friend than an evil-tongued barber." Louis punishes the
barber, makes Gringoire Court Poet, and arranges his marriage with the
enamoured young maiden.

The great Coquelin played Gringoire in 1889. The *London Times*
(August 14, 1935) called Gringoire "a well-judged mixture of simplicity,
impulsiveness, and heroism." The play is indeed a quietly touching evocation of the frank, simple directness of the olden maker of ballads, whether
standing erect before the monarch of his kingdom or bowing devotedly
before the lady of his love.

THE BLACK CROOK   *Charles M. Barras*

Theatrical history turned a distinctly new page when *The Black Crook*
opened at Niblo's Garden in New York on September 12, 1866. Originally planned as "an original magical and spectacular drama," the play
was elaborately transformed into a song and dance musical, with beau-

teous ladies in tights or ballet costumes doing the first high kicking the
New York Times' critic had ever seen. It started the trail that led past
Lydia Thompson, Pauline Markham, Billy Watson's *Beef Trust*, to the in-
creasing nudity of the burlesque show, the fan, bubble, or dove dances of
Sally Rand, to Gypsy Rose Lee, Margie Hart, and the other ecdysiasts,
artists of the strip-tease of our day.

Though the trail would probably have been blazed in any event, its
start with *The Black Crook* was burned into history. Jarret and Palmer
had imported a ballet troupe for the opera *La Biche au Bois* at the N. Y.
Academy of Music. From London, Paris, Berlin, Milan, the loveliest of
feminine beauties were summoned, including Rita Sangelli, Betty Regal,
Da Rosa, Paglieri, and fourteen-year-old premiere danseuse Mlle. Marie
Bonfanti. But the Academy of Music burned down.

William Wheatley, preparing Barras' play for Niblo's Garden, sniffed
a bargain, and bought the dancing girls. For all practical purposes he used
Barras' script as "a clothesline on which to hang pretty dresses" — thus
leaving the young ladies the more displayed. Barras was given an extra
$1500 as consolation for clear miss-handling of his plot. At a total cost
(then deemed tremendous) of $50,000, the play was opened and ran
sixteen months, into January 1868. It grossed $1,100,000. (A musical based
on this fire-story, *The Girl in Pink Tights*, ran in New York in 1954.)

New York City, aburst with profiteers from the Civil War, was ready
for such lavish display. Barras' plot, in truth, gave opportunities for many
contrasting colors. Hertzog, "the black crook," makes a pact with the
devil: he can live through every year in which he tempts a soul to Satan.
The humble painter Rodophe looks like an easy victim, for Count Wolfen-
stein has fallen in love with Rodophe's sweetheart Amina, and locked
Rodophe in a dungeon cell. Freed by Hertzog, Rodophe swears bloody
vengeance. But he kills a serpent as it is about to snare a dove, and
the dove is the Fairy Queen Stalacta. The Queen, of course, warns
Rodophe, and with her aid, the Count is killed. Thus Hertzog, with no
soul to offer the devil, is borne off to hell, and the lovers are reunited.

The play offered countless opportunities both for the mechanical
effects and "transformations" in which the age delighted, and for dances
of grotesque demons and delicate fairy maidens. Act I ended with a
demon incantation in a wild glen, a phantasmagoria of horrors rising to
tempestuous power. The finale of Act III showed the demons invading
Queen Stalacta's lake-lovely grotto. And at the close, as the *New York
Tribune* (September 17, 1866) raved: "All that gold, silver, and gems and
lights and women's beauty can contribute to fascinate the eye and charm
the senses is gathered up in this gorgeous spectacle." No lovers ever had
more elaborate glory to grace their union. The presentation lasted from
7:45 p.m. to 1:15 a.m.

The play swept the city into a storm. The *New York World* (September
17, 1866) declared; "As a drama *The Black Crook* is a pretentious boast;
that is, what little is left of it, for it is known that nothing but the name
and a few dreary 'carpenter's scenes' have survived the stage manager's
process of stuffing it with pageant and gorgeously spectacular transformations . . . It would have been wiser to have presented the *Colored Crook*
as a pantomime, not that the players are professional pantomimists, but
they could certainly express their sentiments of heroic virtue and hopeful
revenge quite as satisfactorily by dumb show as they do now by Bowery
word of mouth . . . During the two hundred and odd years of its existence

New York has never enjoyed the presence of so beautiful, varied, efficient, facile, graceful, and thoroughly captivating a corps de ballet." Joseph Whitton, treasurer of Niblo's Garden in 1866, looking back thirty years later, remarked: "I have said nothing of the literary merits of the *Crook* for the best of reasons: it had none. This, however, is no serious fault."

Shortly after the play's opening the city's clergymen rose up in arms; their Sunday sermons merely increased the week-day attendance at the play. James Gordon Bennett railed against it in editorial after editorial of his *New York Herald*. There is a suspicion, however, that his was a roundabout friendly gesture. The continuing abuse the *Herald* poured upon *The Black Crook* certainly kept the play in the public mind. A sample: "Nothing in any other Christian country, or in modern times, has approached the indecent and demoralizing exhibition at Wheatley's theatre in this city . . . Let all husbands and parents and guardians who value the morals of their wives, their daughters, and their wards, bear a watchful eye on their charges, and keep them from the walks of Niblo's Garden during the reign of *The Black Crook*." Ladies who went to the play wore long veils, as their respectable sisters of Queen Elizabeth's days wore masks.

Popular discussion kept the play going for 475 performances, with occasional "embellishments," duly reviewed. In May 1867 a grand-ball-room scene was added. Although Marie Bonfanti continued to be the star of the ballet, other dancers were added to the cast—among them Mme. Billon, an agile man ("Mexico alone can equal M. Van Hamme in the number and variety of his revolutions"), and a baby ballet ("a march of intricate military evolutions performed by over a hundred youngsters, varying in height from 35 to 45 inches") led by la petite Ravel, aged four.

In 1869, not long after its first run, *The Black Crook* was revived. Still the play remained hidden by the grottos and lakes and demon dens of the gorgeous scenery, and by "the bewildering forest of female legs." Kate Santley and Jennie Lee rose to fame in it in 1871. There were other New York productions about every second year till the century's end. Through the country, *The Black Crook* played almost continuously until 1909, the longest road run of any musical. Christopher Morley and his boonfellows produced it in 1929, with ballets arranged by Agnes de Mille, as part of their Hoboken laugh-at-the-old-plays exhibit; the superior, sophisticated laughter was muted by the production's beauty. It was done more simply, by the Federal Theatre in Los Angeles, in 1936.

As a literate drama, *The Black Crook* makes no claim; it remains a clothesline (now somewhat frayed) on which to hang such beauties as an enterprising director may assemble. Its original production will be remembered primarily because it brought the first surge of burlesque, with toss of skirts and spin of tights and lift of lissome legs, onto the American stage.

THE LITTLE MINISTER   *James M. Barrie*

When James Matthew Barrie (1860-1937), beloved Scotch writer, visited New York, Charles Frohman was seeking a play for Maude Adams. With considerable change, *The Little Minister*, one of Barrie's early novels of Scotch life, was dramatized, and Lady Babbie, the wild gypsy with red rowans in her hair, came to the stage of the Empire Theatre, September 27, 1897, to give Maude Adams her first starring role.

The play tells of the capture of Gavin Dishart, young Presbyterian minister in the narrow and suspicious village of Thrums, by the vivacious and wayward Babbie. Dressed as a gypsy, Babbie is in the woods to warn the striking handloom weavers that the soldiers are coming for them; Gavin is there to see that the weavers do not resist the law. Before the soldiers, Babbie declares she is Gavin's wife. To protect her, he remains silent, and by Scotch law they are wed. They meet again at Lord Rintoul's, where the Lord's daughter, Lady Babbie, claims Gavin, while her suitors swear Gavin is wed to a gypsy girl. The offended congregation is reconciled, and the suitors are foiled, as they learn that the gypsy girl and the Lady are one.

The *New York Dramatic Mirror* (October 2, 1897) found *The Little Minister* "at times prosy and inactive, and it frequently verges upon incoherence. Miss Adams . . . gave life, color, and rare delicacy to the highly improbable Lady Babbie." The play was better received in London, where it opened on November 6, with Cyril Maude and Winifred Emery. The *London Graphic* (November 13, 1897) praised Barrie's "removing what was merely episodical, giving to his story a compactness which it did not have before, and concentrating the interest upon its real dramatic feature, which is the development and final triumph of the love of the Little Minister for his wild and wayward temptress." Bernard Shaw, who had seen the Shakespeare play the night before, reported: "*The Little Minister* is a much happier play than *The Tempest**. Mr. Barrie has no impulse to throw his adaptation of a popular novel at the public head with a sarcastic title (*As You Like It**), because he has written the novel himself, and thoroughly enjoys it . . . The popular stage, which was a prison to Shakespeare's genius, is a playground to Mr. Barrie's . . . He has apparently no eye for human character; but he has a keen sense of human qualities, and he produces highly popular assortments of them." Barrie's combination of nine-tenths fun and one-tenth sentiment struck Shaw as most toothsome; he felt that *The Little Minister* "has every prospect of running into the next century."

It ran, in London, for over 200 performances. In the United States, Maude Adams played Lady Babbie frequently until 1916. In 1925, Ruth Chatterton revived the role, with Ralph Forbes (her husband in the play as in life) and J. M. Kerrigan. Heywood Broun commented (March 23, 1925): "There is something of genius in writing a tale of Prince Charming and making that same prince assume the habiliments of a young Presbyterian parson." Stark Young made some reservations, finding "the mood thin though arch and the situation forced and squeezed a trifle dry for every sweet or whimsical effect possible to it. On the other hand, there are spots full of the old (sic) Barrie savour, and motivations, like that of the elders and kirk members and their devotion to the young minister, that are lovable and delightful."

The generation that remembers Maude Adams continues to love the gypsy lady; but to every generation *The Little Minister* brings the tender stir, the universal quickening of hopefulness and ardor, the wild rouse of woodland freedom from urban restraints, the joy of love and make-believe, of misunderstanding and making up, that curl in the heart of romance.

THE ADMIRABLE CRICHTON   *James M. Barrie*

In this play the humor and charm of Barrie take on the savour of satire as the claims of equality and rank are examined. Barrie called the play "a fantasy", but its roots are spread through loam of truth.

Believing in "the equality of man", Lord Loam has his three daughters join with the servants in monthly teas, to the equal discomfort of both and the disgust of Crichton, the butler, who insists that "social inequalities are right because they are natural." On a cruise around the world, Lord Loam and his daughters, with one maid, Tweeny, and Crichton, are wrecked on an uninhabited island. As they dwell there for some time, natural inequalities make the competent Chrichton their leader. Lady Mary, the most self-reliant of the ladies, is about to enjoy the privilege of being his bride when a ship is sighted; Lady Mary wants to stay on the island, but Crichton sounds the signal and reverts to his butler's role.

Elaborately produced in London by Charles Frohman, directed by Dion Boucicault, *The Admirable Crichton* won great success, with H. B. Irving as Crichton, supported by Henry Kemble, Gerald du Maurier, Irene Vanbrugh (Lady Mary), Sybil Carlisle, Muriel Beaumont, and Pattie Browne. The English press reacted pleasantly to the picture of a butler better than his lord. Said the *London Times* (November 18, 1902), "It is a bewildering and amusing piece of topsy-turvydom, but it all comes out all right when they return to Lord Loam's house in London in the last act."

The play came to New York a year later, November 17, 1903, with most of the English cast, but with William Gillette as Crichton. Democratic America received it with delight. The *New York Dramatic Mirror* suggested that the plot resembled that of Sydney Rosenfeld's *A Modern Crusoe*, 1900, itself like Ludwig Fulda's *Robinson's Island,* both of which are serious sociological problem plays, remote from Barrie's light touch and mellow mood. The theme of Barrie's play was earlier touched in Gilbert's *The Gondoliers**.

There have been many revivals of *The Admirable Crichton.* It was put on film in 1921 as *Male and Female,* with Gloria Swanson; a talking version, *We're Not Dressing,* was produced in 1934. Among recent revivals on the stage was one in 1931 with Walter Hampden, Fay Bainter, Herbert Druce, Ernest Glendinning, Estelle Winwood, and Effie Shannon.

At the time of the latter revival, Brooks Atkinson (March 10, 1931) observed: "If there is anything priceless in Barrie it is the dainty allusiveness of his writing . . . He can catch all the emotion in the world in a buoyant phrase." Robert Garland dissented: "The occasion was gala and, if I may say so, dull . . . the whimsey scarcely worth retelling in these hard-boiled post-war days." To which William Allen White's words are fitly counter-poised: "Barrie is one of the few living dramatists who can dramatize the thesis that man on this planet is, on the whole, with his many foibles, a noble creature, following out through many zigzags the unchartable purpose of God; and who with that thesis can be gay and lovely and charitable and never dull."

With light humor, amusing story, and deft character portrayal, the play tilts a warning finger to those that accept without question the proffered social panacea that would level all folk in assumed equaliy.

PETER PAN   *James M. Barrie*

This play, Barrie's most successful, is the story of the boy who wouldn't grow up. It will never grow old.

Peter Pan drops in on the Darling children. In spite of the efforts of their nurse, the dog Nana, he teaches Wendy and her brothers to fly. They soar with him to Never-Never Land, where Wendy becomes the mother of the lost children who live underground and in the hollow trunks of trees. Adventures with Indians and pirates follow. The pirate chief, Captain Hook, is followed by a crocodile that, having devoured the Captain's hand, seeks the remainder of his meal; but the ticking of a clock the crocodile has swallowed always warns the Captain. There is desperate war between the children and the pirates. Peter's friend, the fairy Tinker Bell—visible only as a dancing light—swallows the poison Hook has prepared for Peter. To save her life, Peter appeals to the audience: Do you believe in fairies?, and as the audience applauds Tinker Bell's light grows bright again. Peter leads his forces onto the pirate ship, and the desperados walk the plank. Wendy goes home, promising always to return, for the spring cleaning, to Peter's house in the tree-top in Never-Never Land.

When Barrie wrote *Peter Pan* in 1904, he took it to Beerbohm Tree, whom he visualized as Captain Hook. Tree at once warned Frohman: "Barrie has gone out of his mind. I am sorry to say it; but you ought to know it. He's just read me a play. He's going to read it to you, so I am warning you. I know I have not gone woozy in my mind, because I have tested myself since hearing the play. But Barrie must be mad. He has written four acts all about fairies, children, and Indians running through the most incoherent story you ever listened to; and what do you suppose? The last act is to be set on top of trees!" Later, Tree said he'd probably be known to posterity as the man that had refused *Peter Pan*.

Both in London, and in New York, the play was an instant success. Maude Adams will always be associated with the title role, which she played again and again, although many others have essayed it: Cecilia Loftus in 1906, Ann Harding in 1923, Marilyn Miller in 1924, Eva Le Gallienne in 1928, and Betty Bronson in a movie version in 1924. J. Edward Bromberg is one of many that have endeared to audiences the part of Nana, the dog-nurse; he played the part in 1928-1929.

Young and old alike respond to the appeal of *Peter Pan*. Those who maintain—as many do—that it is a children's play, the *Boston Transcript* chided (May 8, 1929): "Fools and slow of heart! It is middle age's own tragicomedy—the faint, far memories of boyhood and girlhood blown back in the bright breeze of Barrie's imagination." Percy Hammond made the same point on November 7, 1927: "*Peter Pan* is as young as it was eighteen years ago—but I am not." The *New York Times* (January 2, 1916) made the point more precisely: "*Peter Pan* is not children at play, but an old man smiling—and smiling a little sadly—as he watches children at play."

"And if there be anybody," said the reviewer of London's *King* (January 14, 1905) "who can sit through the performance without an occasional tear, I can only wish for him that he may some day have children of his own, and will then understand why in the first and last scenes so many eyes around him were moist and so many throats felt in them the lump that a tender emotion brings."

Tenderness is in the play, but deeper things are there as well. Charles Frohman, Maude Adams' producer and close friend, spoke as his last words as the Lusitania went down, Peter Pan's words in the mermaid scene when he too expected to drown: "To die must be an awfully big adventure."

Peter Pan came back to New York April 24, 1950, with music and songs by Leonard Bernstein. Jean Arthur played Peter; and Boris Karloff, both Wendy's father and Captain Hook (Ernest Lawford played both roles in New York in 1905). Jean Arthur played Peter ingratiatingly, with pert mischief; but Karloff burlesqued the Pirate as though he were playing Gilbert and Sullivan instead of Barrie. Bernstein's music, on the other hand, improperly approached the sentimentality the rest of the production strained to avoid. For those that could not remember Maude Adams, the quality of Jean Arthur's work gave validity to this interpretation of Peter. The production attained 321 peformances, a record for the play. Mary Martin appeared in a musical version in 1954.

Playful and alive, tenderly gay with undertones of pathos, reaching through fantasy to the truths that time must cull, *Peter Pan* (approached only by Maeterlinck's *The Blue Bird**) captures the essential child each of us hopes to hold throughout our days. Small wonder that it is produced in London every Christmastide.

WHAT EVERY WOMAN KNOWS   *James M. Barrie*

In life's intertangling of the sexes, Bernard Shaw saw woman as the huntress, love being but a disguise for the "life-force" that must find continuance; Barrie, on the other hand, emphasized the tender and tolerant, protective mother-feeling of a loving wife. Barrie's attitude was most fully developed in *What Every Woman Knows*.

When John Shand breaks into the Wylie house in this play, he does so in search of learning, not money. The Wylies have the best library in their little Scotch town. They also have the unmarried Maggie. Catching John in unlawful entry, the Wylies bargain with him: they will put him through law school if he will marry Maggie. The bargain kept, Shand goes on to Parliament, becoming a popular leader. When he is attracted to Lady Sybil Lazenby while Maggie is away from him, Shand discovers how much his success has hinged upon Maggie, whose sense of humor gives sparkle to the ideas of her intelligent and hard-working but humorless husband. Shand manages to see the irony and humor of the situation, and the way is cleared for the happiness of John and Maggie.

What Every Woman Knows opened in London in September 1908, with Hilda Trevelyan (Maggie), Gerald du Maurier (John), Lillah McCarthy, Edmund Gwenn, and Mrs. Beerbohm Tree. It was an immediate success. The play came as a Christmas present to Broadway on December 23, 1908, with Maude Adams and Richard Bennett. It has since been continuously popular. Maggie has been played by Helen Hayes (1926, 1938); Frances Starr (1931); Pauline Lord (1931); and Muriel Kirkland (1942). In 1946 the American Repertory Theatre revived the play, with June Duprez (Maggie), Richard Waring (John), Ernest Truex, Philip Bourneuf, Walter Hampden, and Eva Le Gallienne. It was filmed in 1921 with Lois Wilson and Conrad Nagel, and again in 1934.

Of the Broadway premiere, *The New York Dramatic Mirror* (January 2, 1909) commented: "What every woman knows is that Eve was made not from Adam's rib but from his funny-bone . . . Perhaps it is not his best play, but it is as good as any of the others, no matter how paradoxical that may sound. And the role of Maggie was made for Maude Adams."

Critics have expressed curious ideas as to Barrie's intent in writing *What Every Woman Knows*. Freedley and Reeves said in *A History of the Theatre* (1941): "The thesis that every prominent man is a fool and that an intelligent wife must struggle to prevent his learning it, is distinctly depressing." (Freedley apologized in part by calling the play, after the 1946 revival, "the most delightful Scottish comedy of them all.") And Alexander Woollcott (April 14, 1926) said that the play was written "in support of Barrie's favorite conviction that all women have the wisdom of the serpent and that all men are but lummoxes." As a matter of fact, John Shand is both hard working and intelligent; he has both ambition and drive, together with a recognition of his potentialities. What he lacks is a sense of humor, the ability to stand off and look and laugh at himself—which Maggie manages to supply. That a woman can twist a man around her little finger is another matter, and, as Shaw and Barrie agree, a common masculine susceptibility.

There abide in *What Every Woman Knows* the quintessential qualities of Barrie. It has satire, "tenderized" by humor; it has charm, and the author's love of life; it has understanding without malice, understanding that humbles a man without lessening his dignity; it has a rippling and ripening of character; and it has a swift and easy flow of plot. The Wylies in the play are alarmed at what a Scot may do with £300 of education; Barrie shows what a mind of understanding and a heart of love can do—which is indeed what every woman knows.

A KISS FOR CINDERELLA   *James M. Barrie*

Those that are warmed by the sentimental will find a cozy hearth in this tender dream-story of a London drudge whose happiness comes in the form of a policeman.

Miss Thing, a char-girl in the everyday world, is in truth Cinderella, to herself and to the little war orphans she cares for at her home, which she calls "Celeste et Cie". The year is 1916. Miss Thing has four little ones: English, French, Belgian, and Gretchen ("who is not Swiss"). The friendly policeman on the beat watches over her one chilly evening when, having repeated the story of Cinderella to her wards, she sits outside awaiting the Fairy Godmother.

Cinderella goes to the ball. Her Prince is, of course, the handsome policeman. After her delirious dream she awakens, once more Miss Thing, in a convalescent home. But her prince, the policeman, comes to make her happy ever after. She makes him promise to propose twice, so that she can enjoy the fine flush and pride of refusing a man; then— "Quick, David!"—she accepts his proposal with all the high phrases she has been saving for such a glorious eventuality.

The Cinderella story is one of the basic themes of folklore. Barrie's variation is gracious, tender, playful, touching. Though sentimental, it is neither maudlin nor mawkish. Opening in London on March 16, 1916, with Gerald du Maurier (156 performances), and in New York on Christmas Day of the same year with Maude Adams (155 performances), the

play has had numerous London and New York revivals, and has been
produced many times throughout the English-speaking world. Luise
Rainer made her New York debut in a 1942 revival of the play.
A Kiss For Cinderella has worn well. The *Boston Transcript* reported
on December 27, 1926: "Whoever saw the play in 1917 awaited it eagerly
again; in 1926 departed not unblessed . . . Curtain, boy, a quick curtain!
Such eye-wetting humor is out of the fashion." The *London Times* (December 26, 1937) declared: "After a somewhat tedious first act, this curious mixture of a play charms with the fanciful absurdity of its second,
and in the third the author is shown at the top of his playwrighting form."
In a more searching estimate Allardyce Nicoll has said: "He comes as
near as any modern dramatist to that atmosphere out of which was created the Elizabethan romantic comedy . . . Part of this atmosphere Sir
James Barrie secures by making concrete the fancies of the mind, by
mingling together the dream and the reality. In *A Kiss For Cinderella*
. . . the fairy-tale has entered into the common London world . . . His
humour is perfect, and his skill in weaving the two worlds thus together
has enabled him to establish in modern English dramatic literature an
almost unique type of expression."
   One might expect the timely references in the play to grow out of
date. Indeed the *London Times* (December 28, 1937) remarked that "The
references to the War and to wounded soldiers are a warning to fanciful
dramatists to keep their families pure." Yet it was in the midst of a
second World War that Mark Barron, of the *Boston Post* (March 15, 1942)
declared it "too sugary for such hardbitten times as these."
   If you have a sweet tooth, *A Kiss For Cinderella* is a delicious morsel.

DEAR BRUTUS   *James M. Barrie*

   One of the most enchanting, as well as enchanted, of Barrie's plays,
Dear Brutus took London by storm. It opened on October 17, 1917, with
Gerald Du Maurier, and ran for 365 performances. Among its many re-
vivals, one in 1941 (124 performances) starred John Gielgud. The New
York opening, December 23, 1918, not only was a similar triumph for
William Gillette, but it awakened American theatregoers to the charm
of a young actress, playing Margaret, by the name of Helen Hayes.
   The title of the play, and its theme, are drawn from two lines of
Shakespeare's *Julius Caesar**: "The fault, dear Brutus, is not in our
stars, But in ourselves, that we are underlings." This idea is emphasized
by a character in the play, who says: "Fate is something outside us.
What really plays the dickens with us is something in ourselves. Something that makes us go on doing the same sort of fool things, however
many chances we get."
   The characters of the play are week-end guests of Mr. Lob—another
name for the elfin Puck, whose many pranks include the transmogrifications in Shakespeare's *A Midsummer Night's Dream**. In *Dear Brutus*,
the dream is on Midsummer Eve.
   The garden behind Lob's house becomes a wood. As his guests wander
there, we see that it is the "Wood of What Might Have Been," where
each guest is given the chance to relive a basic situation in his life, the
circumstances of which are shifted or changed in scale. The philanderer
Purdie, for example, relives the time that his wife Mabel had caught

him kissing Joanna, but, in the woods, he is married to Joanna and trying to tempt Mabel to a kiss.

But there is one change for the better. Dearth, the unhappily married artist, in the woodland meets his dream-daughter, Margaret. We see her as a girl about seventeen, in short green skirt and soft green cap, tossing beechnuts about, while her father works at his easel. All of Barrie's magic lifts that tender scene. It is bright with the love of father and child, a love that reaches out to the unhappy woman they meet in the wood, who in the life outside is Mrs. Dearth, to give her of its bounty. And outside the wood, the dream of love continues to hold its power, sending the artist and his wife off together, richer, happier, reconciled.

Although New York reviewers are inclined to shy from the sentimental, *Dear Brutus* swept down their guards. The *New York Times* declared: "'Sentimental Tommy' has found the way to dramatize character and fate in terms that illuminate our minds as inevitably as they delight our risibilities and our nether regions of the heart." But highest praise went to the Margaret scene; the *Times* said it "has all the spiritual comprehension and the wistful beauty in affection of Barrie at his best."

Dear Brutus is deservedly a favorite play with college and community groups. It was played in England during the Blitz. On January 28, 1941, just as Joanna pushed Purdie away, with a warning "Listen!" and he responded "I think I hear some one!" the air-raid sirens shrilled overhead. A wave of laughter swept the audience and the cast.

At every performance of *Dear Brutus*, there are softer overtones, as each in the audience relives his cherished or regretted hour and, caught in the drama's spell, resolves to bring his later days nearer to the brighter aspects of What Might Have Been.

The peculiar genius of Barrie as playwright, says James Agate in his review of this play in *At Half-Past Eight* (1923), "consists in his bringing from the back of his mind the simple things which lie behind the mind of the spectator. They are the things which, but for the twist of kindly laughter, would be unbearable." The secret of *Dear Brutus* is that it induces surrender. If you yield to its woodland magic and to its tender mood, criticism withdraws as you shape your own fancies, with the genial if somewhat cynical help of Mr. Lob. Less captured, more captious, critics still recognize that *Dear Brutus* works with the same power as brings to tender spirits the spell of *Peter Pan**. Barrie, like Peter—for those that have walked with fairies—is youth, eternal youth.

LA VIE DE BOHEME   *Théodore Barrière*

The most famous stories of bohemian life in Paris are those of Henri Murger, contained in his *Scènes de la vie de Bohème* (1847). Working with Murger, Théodore Barrière (French, 1823-1877) based *La Vie de Bohème (The Bohemian Life)*, 1849, on Murger's tales. The play was an instant success.

It was adapted in English by Dion Boucicault* under the title *Mimi* (the title also of a 1935 film version with Douglas Fairbanks and Gertrude Lawrence). In 1896, Clyde Fitch* in the United States wrote his drama *Bohemia,* with Henry Miller, Viola Allen, and William Faversham in the cast; in this version the happy Mimi is restored to health at the end. Two operatic versions entitled *La Bohème* have also been written. The one by Ruggiero Leoncavallo was first played in Venice in 1897; the other, with book by Giacosa and Illica, and music by Giacomo Puccini, first played in Turin in February, 1896, is one of the most popular of Italian operas.

Mimi is the sweetheart of Rudolph, the poet, one of the four boon companions leading a happy-go-lucky life in a garret in the Parisian Latin Quarter, about 1830. Rather than marry a woman he does not love, Rudolph has turned from his family and a fortune; he is happier in gay poverty with his friends. Marcel, the painter, is in love with Musette, a lively lass who leads on the wealthy Alcindoro, then leaves him with the dinner bills. Schaunard, a musician whose frequently erring wife constantly returns to him, and Colline, half philosopher, half dreamer, complete the quartet. But Mimi, who is sickly, watches Rudolph lured by one of the girls of the Quarter; she thinks he has abandoned her, and pines away. Rudolph returns to his one true love, and the despairing and ecstatic Mimi dies in his arms.

La Vie de Bohème, in its many versions, was invariably a success. The *New York Sun* said that the Clyde Fitch adaptation roused "a great deal of laughter on account of its scintillant wit and characteristic good humor, and there was still more of undemonstrative appreciation of its lifelike aspects." However, the sweet savouring of sadness in the story, the love and the anguish, together with the irresponsible ways of the artists, deepen in mood with music. Among the best-liked moments of song are the first act solo "They Call Me Mimi" and the succeeding duet "O Lovely Maiden" (O soave fanciulla!). It is chiefly as Puccini's *La Bohème* that Barrière's play and Murger's story are constantly heard around the world today.

WHITE WINGS   *Philip Barry*

A backward view — hind end first — of the American days when the horseless carriage was replacing the horse, a view touched with nostalgia and tinged with satire, is provided by Philip Barry (1896-1949) in *White Wings*. Too fragile and sentimental in its story and too oblique in its devices for the public taste, the play opened in New York on October 15, 1926 and, though deftly performed by Winifred Lenihan, Tom Powers, and J. M. Kerrigan, and praised by the critics, it quickly failed. Even when it was presented with music by Douglas Moore (written in 1935) at Hartford, Connecticut, February 9, 1949, the production was not considered suitable for Broadway.

"White Wings," the present generation may not know, were the street-cleaners who, in initially white uniform, with brush and barrel on wheels swept up and away the city's drift and the horses' droppings. In the fantasy of the play, theirs is a proud profession, with a membership as elect as any exclusive fraternity. The Inches pride themselves on having been White Wings since the Flood. The last of the family, Archie Inch, is in love with Mary Todd, whose family in Detroit are building the first automobiles. The staunch Archie, true to his family tradition, has sworn to stick to his profession until the last horse is gone; the equally determined Mary shoots the last horse in town.

When *White Wings* was first produced, Brooks Atkinson called it "a completely mad play . . . Mr. Barry has thrown into this satiric fantasy all the 'spare parts' of his dramatic workshop — charming conceits, fables and fairy tales, puns, low and high comedy, occasional Rabelaisian jibes, cynical head thumpings and gestures of despair. All these things he has strung on a tenuous thread of events, never clear, frequently dull." Alexander Woollcott said that "Much of White Wings is delightful; some of it deeply, nourishingly so, with such a freshness of invention and so airy a mockery that the heart is rejoiced . . . an often hilarious, sometimes tender, rueful little play."

The city blare of horns and the red lights of city crossings — regiment the theatregoers as they may — cannot dim the sparkle or diminish the antic mischief of White Wings, which grins at the opposing drives of tradition and progress with equal gusto, making sport of each.

HOLIDAY   Philip Barry

The problem pricked by Barry in Paris Bound (1927) is more deeply probed in Holiday, a distinctly witty play which opened on November 26, 1928, in New York, with Hope Williams and Donald Ogden Stewart, and ran for 229 performances. It has been played frequently around the country. It was produced in New York by Equity Library in 1945.

Two attitudes toward life are contrasted in Holiday. The young lawyer Johnny Case, engaged to Julia Seton of the wealthy Setons, as the play opens, meets and startles her family by announcing that he intends to retire (on some oil deal profits) to enjoy life while young. In ten years or so, after he has tasted life, he says, he may settle down to work. Julia sides with her conservative father, who thinks Johnny is crazy, but Linda Seton and her ebrious brother Ned understand Johnny's point of view. It becomes apparent that Julia has no deep love for Johnny Case; and when, the engagement broken, Johnny boards an ocean liner, it is Linda that ships aboard with him.

"A mad, mad gambol!" said reviewer Robert Coleman; "It tells a serious story in as light-hearted a fashion as e'er a serious story has been told . . . intimate, gay, irresponsible, effective." Barry succeeded in combining a swiftly moving and absorbing story of emotional conflict with a sharp opposition of two points of view regarding the social and ethical problem involved. "In the sparkling new piece at the Plymouth," Robert Garland held, "there is a great moral lesson . . . the old fight between spirit and matter. Old whines in new bottles, as it were." Barry has, said Gilbert Gabriel, "the gift of blowing big, gay bubbles which break right under your nose into cool, stinging little truths."

The dialogue of Holiday has the merit of speed, with a colloquial freshness that does not depend upon curent slang; hence it has lasting virtue. It appealed only partially, however, to St. John Ervine, visiting from England, who wrote for the New York World (November 27, 1928) that "the dialogue, mostly composed of abrupt, brief sentences, varies oddly in its quality, and is full of unexpected sparkles followed by stretches of lustreless stuff." To Americans, it seemed more valid. Representative praise and a good analysis were combined in the Boston Transcript (April 5, 1929): "Even when the playwright is most fertile in his own devices, it seems in character with the speaking personage, the moment in the play, the social, even the scenic, background. Throughout, with allowance for the two or three outsiders (as it were) who must be foils, it is a quick-flowing banter, here nonsensical, there comic, now serio-comic, again darting in and then darting out for self-revelation; palaver when it is frailest; wisdom or feeling when for an instant it shows its muscle. A speech of this day and no other; of a social class and environment; devised and conducted to convey trait, thought, faith, and emotion through a brightly glittering yet semi-transparent envelope. A speech of speeches for the theatre, since it incessantly beguiles audiences; as often as not he also entraps them into something near belief." *Holiday* makes its persons seem natural human beings; they are not mere mouthpieces of a point of view. The question it poses, of the opposition of material ambition to artistic appreciation and enjoyment of life, grows important because the lives of its persons are entangled in the answers. Cleanly, humanly, wittily, the alternatives of long drudging and early joying are set in *Holiday*.

HOTEL UNIVERSE   *Philip Barry*

The problem of the "lost generation," drained of faith and of zest for life by World War I and its disillusioning aftermath, is viewed through the various needs and bafflements of an assorted group of persons in Philip Barry's *Hotel Universe*. Gathered on the terrace of a house in the south of France, and living, or so they feel, "on borrowed time," these half-dozen intelligent folk, self-critical and aware of Freud, fight through to the promise of a readjustment of their lives. Some of Barry's writing in *Hotel Universe* is too tangential to grasp easily, but much of it is at his brilliant best.

The gathering at the home of Stephen Field and his daughter, Ann, is a varied one, though all in it feel that life has been drained of any purpose. Norman Rose is there, in love with music and with Alice Kendall, but entangled in the responsibilities of his wealth. There, too, are Tom and Hope Ames; he, tortured with a sense of sin since he turned away from a planned priesthood; she, so much a mother that she forgets she is Tom's wife. Lily Malone, the dancer daughter of a ham actor that she idolized, is there, plagued with the fear of her own insufficiency. "You can have my public," she says to Ann, "if you'll give me your heart." Ann Fields alone needs no defense of dreams or bitter words. She has always given rather than sought. She is troubled, nevertheless, over Pat Farley, who had once loved Ann, but later wooed another girl, who committed suicide.

With slanting satire and gibe, with playful banter that may flare into angry quarrel, these young folks thrust at themselves through one another. Lily shows a scar where she had pressed a razor-blade across her wrist. "That's right, Actress," says Pat, "do your stuff. God's out front tonight." Lily responds: "Will you tell the Kind Gentleman I enjoyed his little piece, but found no part in it for me?" Into their despair comes old Stephen Field, a physicist who has made his peace with the three worlds: the temporal world of daily motion, the inner world of constant adjustment, and the ultimate timeless world where all things find their place. With a mystic psychanalytic drive, Stephen becomes to these tortured folk a piece of their past they can relive, through which they break free of their fears to find strength to face the future. When Stephen slumps, unseen, but stricken unto death, in his great chair, Pat and Ann beside him look forward to a life they will share.

Hotel Universe opened in New York April 14, 1930, with Ruth Gordon, Glenn Anders, Franchot Tone, Earl Larimore and Morris Carnov-

sky. London saw it in 1932. It has had many productions in the United
States. It was given in New York by Equity Library in 1947 and at
Boston College in August, 1949.

The critics were not single-minded as to Barry's success in carrying
over its theme. Richard Lockridge (April 21, 1930) said: "*Hotel Universe* is a play of philosophy, and its philosophy is not very clear. But
it is a great deal more than that. It is an adventure among strange
dreams; an equilibrium established between stranger forces . . . It is
a brave adventure in the country beyond the moon. There are flickering
moments when from this adventure there comes back the music of
unearthly trumpets." The *Boston Transcript* (May 27, 1930) declared
that Barry equipped his characters with "minds that work quickly, if
not too deeply; with lips that open readily to darts of humor, jets of
capricious fancy, thrusts of wit, intimate and therefore piercing gibes."
London felt that the adjustments at the end of the play weakened its
power. "It is extremely easy," remarked the *London Times* (November
16, 1932) "with the assistance of ghosts or marvels to present an exciting situation, but it is extremely difficult to round it off without disappointment . . ." (Played without break in New York, the continuous
action of *Hotel Universe* was given one intermission in London.) The
end, though it lessens the tension—as endings should—is the inevitable
result of the play's movements.

The persons of *Hotel Universe* are natural, alive; they have problems,
and out of their problems rises the basic thought of the play. "Mr.
Barry never forgets," said Arthur Hobson Quinn in the *New York
Herald-Tribune* (May 25, 1930), "that drama proceeds primarily not
through ideas but rather through emotions. Indeed, my one criticism
of the play lies in the fact that our sympathies are so strongly enlisted
in the joys and sorrows of the characters that there is a certain strain
after two hours from the very intensity of our interest." That interest,
however, is not merely held by the play, it is quickened with a rouse of
the emotions and kindled by thought. There is reward in the sense of
fulfillment when the death of Stephen is counterpoised in the rebirth of
Pat. There is a measure of awe, too, in the recognition that we ourselves
are passing patrons of the *Hotel Universe*. Perhaps not fully enlightened,
we are nonetheless lighted up, by Barry's play.

TOMORROW AND TOMORROW   *Philip Barry*

The sensitivity of Barry's portraits of intelligent persons straining in
the grip of ethical problems is richly illustrated in *Tomorrow and Tomorrow*. Opening in New York on January 13, 1931, with Zita Johann,
Osgood Perkins and Herbert Marshal, the play ran for 206 performances.
It has been staged fairly often around the country; a 1941 production
starred Ruth Chatterton. The title, taken from *Macbeth**, suggests that
at the play's close time "creeps in his petty pace from day to day." Yet
the printed play bears a motto from the *Bible* (*II Kings*, 4) where
Elisha makes fertile the Shunammite, then saves her son, much as
Nicholas Hay does for Eve Redman in the play.

Eve is happily married to a successful and breezy businessman and
loyal college alumnus, Gail Redman of Redmanton, Indiana. However,
their union has not been blessed with the child Eve yearns for. Nicholas
Hay, psychiatrist, comes to town to lecture. He is their guest. He and

Eve fall deeply in love, and then part. Eve has a child. Several years later, as a young child, Christian Redman falls so seriously ill mentally that Eve sends for Nicholas, who finds the mental block and cures the child. He and Eve also find that love still binds them. Although she tells him that the child is theirs, not Gail's, the ties with Gail and the need within Gail hold Eve to her husband, as Nicholas once more takes leave of his happiness.

Tomorrow and Tomorrow, said Brooks Atkinson, shows Barry "at the top of his form . . . He evokes fresh beauty from characters unfamiliar to our tired stage . . . the ability to flavor tenderness with humor and the greatness of heart to meet anguish with compassion . . . Until the heart-breaking last two scenes his convictions are a little inarticulate, but they have lustre, gentleness, and beauty." The *Boston Transcript* (November 3, 1931) stated: "This newfound sensibility, flowering from *Hotel Universe**, enables Mr. Barry to invest the whole play, except when the factotum and the elderly doctor are crackling for laughs, with understanding and compassion. They mist it, more than once, with beauty; clothe the scenes about the imperilled child with a pathos free from every theatre-hokum; wind through speech that feigns lightness and triviality because feeling underneath runs deep and full."

The preparation for the important scenes of *Tomorrow and Tomorrow* is a bit lengthy. Gilbert Gabriel, indeed, complained that "two acts are employed upon this nobly sweet impregnation" — although such "nobility" as emerges is in the after-decisions rather than in the amorous act. The characters, however, are built solidly and they have stature; the problem of the play takes its value from their human ways; the ethics is embedded in the action. The dialogue, too, has the Barry touch of freshness and simple spontaneity. All in all, *Tomorrow and Tomorrow* provided stimulus to the emotions, satisfaction to thought, and exaltation to the spirit.

THE ANIMAL KINGDOM   *Philip Barry*

Several of Barry's plays seem to defend the conventional moral values of married life. In *The Animal Kingdom*, however, he reverses the accepted roles of the wife and the mistress, showing that his ethical concern goes beneath legal codes to attain more fundamental standards of conduct.

Set among the wealthy sophisticates of suburban Connecticut, *The Animal Kingdom* tells the story of Tom Collier, playboy, aesthete, publisher, who, after living for three years with the tasteful Daisy Sage, marries, as the play opens, beautiful Cecilia Henry. Cecilia tries to keep Tom to a practical path. It takes Tom somewhat over a year to recognize that his wife is using her physical appeal to make him betray his aesthetic ideals for mundane advantages. Once his eyes can break from Cecilia's beauty to look at her soul, Tom goes back to his true mate, Daisy.

In this play Barry again interests us in a personal problem, with warm, engaging humans, beyond whom the basic issues of the play are shadowed. Even Cecilia is a natural woman, not at all unlike many we see about us. Especially lifelike is the portrait of Richard Regan, Tom's ex-prizefighter butler and friend. Cecilia urges Tom to fire Regan, who does not fit into the formal home she plans; while Regan, unable to stand the stuffy atmosphere of Cecilia's home, tries to summon courage to tell Tom he's quitting. At the end, the two leave Cecilia together.

The Animal Kingdom opened in New York on January 12, 1932, with Ilka Chase and Leslie Howard, and ran for 183 performances. Ann Harding and Myrna Loy appeared with Howard in the film. In 1937, John Barrymore played a radio version. There have been numerous productions of the play, about the country. The critics received The Animal Kingdom warmly. "Discussing the integrity of a group of cultivated moderns," said Brooks Atkinson (January 13, 1932), "Mr. Barry has preserved his own integrity as an artist and a believer, and illuminated his thesis with splendor . . . The Animal Kingdom brings great loveliness into the theatre." John Mason Brown commented: "The conflict between 'Business' and 'Art' — or, if you will, Money and Self-Expression, or Society and Personal Freedom— has long been a skirmish that has interested Mr. Barry. But never has Mr. Barry stated it more skillfully or more poignantly than in The Animal Kingdom . . . Mr. Barry is the most genteel, the most 'knowing' and sophisticated of our dramatists."

Barry's dialogue flows with a sparkle, yet seems always to belong to the speakers. The wiles of Cecilia to woo Tom from his past are natural and defensible, until, almost imperceptibly, they become her wiles to dictate his future. The one aspect of the play not clearly motivated is the marriage itself. Why, one asks, after three years with Daisy Sage, should Tom have turned to Cecilia Henry? His turning shows the sheer force of physical beauty, for the world of material pleasures—"the animal kingdom" — wherein Cecilia loved to graze, held no lure for Tom. The Animal Kingdom bears the shape of an irresponsible, light-hearted and light-headed triangle play, save that its points are sharp and, this time, in the triangle, the wife is base.

HERE COME THE CLOWNS   Philip Barry

The plays of Philip Barry seem, in retrospect, to move toward more and more fundamental aspects of man's living. In Here Come The Clowns, Barry reaches a final question, the problem of good and evil, of God. Since God is hard to face directly, Barry approaches the problem roundabout. He does it through a group of vaudeville folk in a café next to their theatre. They are ordinary folk, minor vaudevillians and stagehands, just plain Christians. Stirred by a German Illusionist, Max Pabst, they begin to question themselves and their value to life.

They are an odd assortment, these entertainers, the "clowns." Among them is the ventriloquist, who through the slant words of his grinning dummy eases his anguish over his wife's cruelty and deceit, and her fondness for the girls that tag after her; and there is the midget, poignant and savage as he tells the story of his life, of how the dancing boy — who for a moment fears the midget may be his father — hates him! And there is Dan Clancy, the down-and-out stagehand, who seeks God. Dan's wife had married him because she was expecting a baby, then left him for its father. Reflecting on such things, Dan wonders: Perhaps the Devil won in that ancient battle with the Lord, and the world is ruled by evil. Dan has been tried, tested, somewhat as Job. When he hears the vaudeville house owner declare that "evil exists so we may know good; hunger, that we may appreciate food," Dan senses that he is hearing Satan. But the sinister power of the Illusionist backfires: Dan decides that man himself has created good and evil. Therefore there is hope, for with man lies the decision; man can destroy evil.

Based on the novel *War In Heaven* (1938), *Here Come The Clowns* opened in New York on December 7, 1938, with Eddie Dowling, and played 88 performances. It has been produced about the country fairly frequently since. Richard Watts called the play "a tortured, sardonic, confused and confusing play; an embittered mystic allegory of Good and Evil. It is a play that is beautifully written and only partially thought out; it is garrulous and obscure and as bewildered as its people; and it is almost continuously absorbing." Even in the *Daily Worker*, Michael Gold recognized *Here Come The Clowns* as an "honest cry out of a man's heart."

It may not be possible to set against every person and every speech in the play its symbolic significance; but it is certainly impossible not to feel the earnestness of the author. While this earnestness may militate against clarity, it contributes to the emotional power and dramatic drive of a deeply provocative and thought-evoking play.

THE WIZARD OF OZ   *L. Frank Baum*

When Lyman Frank Baum (American, 1856-1919) wrote the story *The Wonderful Wizard of Oz*, he and his illustrator, William W. Denslow, had to raise the money for its publication in 1900. Since then some 9,000,000 copies of that fanciful book and its fourteen sequels have been sold. The movies took over the story in 1938, producing it in technicolor with Judy Garland, Bert Lahr, Ray Bolger, Jack Haley and Frank Morgan. Dramatizations have been played in community and school theatres all over the country. With music by Paul Tietjens, *The Wizard of Oz*, "a musical extravaganza," opened in Chicago, June 16, 1902. In New York this production made its debut on January 20, 1903; there it ran for 306 performances and was revived on November 8, 1904.

The familiar story begins with a cyclone that carries Dorothy Gale's house from Kansas to the Kingdom of Oz. Among the Munchkins who inhabit Oz, the Good Fairy grants Dorothy two wishes; one she wastes, but with the other she brings the straw man Scarecrow to life. With the Scarecrow and the Cowardly Lion, she sets forth for the Emerald City, hoping that the Tin Woodsman, who has oiled his joints and joined the party, will have his heart restored by the Wizard and that the Scarecrow will be given brains. The lion, taking them on his back, leaps the unbridgeable chasm into the city. There they discover that the wizard, Sir Wyley Gyle, is a fraud. They journey on to Dreamland, whence Dorothy is returned to her Kansas home, while the others settle down to live happily ever after.

The staging of Julian Mitchell made the original production of *The Wizard of Oz* superbly memorable. It opened with a wild storm of swirling lights and shadows. When the travelers fall asleep in a poppy field and the good witch sends a frost to make the poppies droop and the sleepers wake, each poppy flower becomes a radiant girl. The dances in the production were numerous and varied. "There are evolutions," said the *New York Mail and Express* (January 21, 1903), "by marching women to remind us of *The Black Crook**, and the same women are displayed in pantomimic choruses in the modern Mitchell manner."

The dialogue of the play is lively, and often funny. The *Mail and Express* asserted: "Not since the burlesque of Lydia Thompson's time have we had so many puns in a play — and most of them so apt as to be worth making." Moreover, there are hilarious bits of comic action, such as the burlesque of football by the Scarecrow and the Tin Woodsman—played originally by the excellent team of David C. Montgomery and Fred A. Stone. To say that the new piece is a hit, commented the *New York Dramatic Mirror* (January 31, 1903), "is putting it mildly. There is enough material in it to make three or four ordinary musical comedies, and it is staged with a lavishness that is simply stunning. As a production, *The Wizard of Oz* has never been excelled in its class in this city."

With music and merriment, fantasy and spectacle, gay antics and lively dancing, colorful scenes and odd costumes, *The Wizard of Oz*, like the best Walt Disney films of a later day, gives a good measure of frolicsome and wholesome fun to the warm in spirit of every age.

THE DAUGHTER OF THE REGIMENT   *Jean François Alfred Bayard*

Opera buffa in two acts, *The Daughter of the Regiment* is one of the liveliest of light operas. The book is by Jean François Alfred Bayard (French, 1796-1853) and Jules H. Vernoy; the music is by Gaetano Donizetti (Italian, 1797-1848).

Set in the Swiss Tyrol in 1815, the play centers around a foundling, Marie, who has grown up as the adopted child of the 21st Regiment of Napoleon's Grand Army. Sulpice, the Sergeant that found her, objects to her love for Tonio, a Tyrolean peasant; but finally Tonio is accepted into the company. Then, however, the Marchioness of Birkenfeld comes to claim Marie as her niece. In the castle, where the Marchioness admits that Marie is her own child, "the daughter of the regiment" feels hemmed in, chafing at the lessons a young lady must take. To her great joy, the soldiers come, with Tonio now a captain. At Marie's plea the Marchioness relents and the young lovers are reunited.

The Daughter of the Regiment is one of the few musicals of its kind that is still played. It was first performed in Paris, February 11, 1840; in New Orleans for its American premiere, March 7, 1843; in New York, in September of that year. London first saw the play, in English, December 21, 1847 and there was a Command Performance for Queen Victoria November 8, 1893. Among those that have sung the role of Marie are Jenny Lind, Adelina Patti, Frieda Hempel, Luisa Tetrazzini, and Lily Pons.

The play tells its story in warmly human terms, pleasantly expanded through the music. It is "a delightful work," commented Pitts Sanborn in the *New York World-Telegram* (December 30, 1940), "melodious, sprightly, admirable in its relishing verve. The Metropolitan presented it with such dash and drollery, and Lily Pons as the vivandiere was so utterly delightful, that no doubt is possible about its being one of the season's hits." The play retains, said the *New York Times* (February 2, 1941) "the secret of the earthy antic that is broad, without losing the warm human undertone that makes comedy endearing." *The Daughter of the Regiment*, in its appealing story, lively music, and friendly warmth, remains deservedly a favorite among light operas.

THE BARBER OF SEVILLE   *Pierre Beaumarchais*

Set in Spain, but thoroughly French in spirit, *The Barber of Seville* was a potent dramatic instrument in rousing the middle-class against the aristocracy, for the imminent French Revolution. The play survives as an amusing comedy and as a light opera.

Pierre Augustin Caron (1732-1799) — he called himself Beaumarchais — was a bourgeois French liberal. He began work as a clockmaker, then turned to commercial affairs (he financed the purchase of supplies for the American colonies, for which he was never repaid). As musical instructor to the daughters of Louis XV, he had opportunity to observe the extravagance and heedlessness of the nobles. In 1767 he wrote a lively domestic comedy, *Eugénie*, tale of Eugénie's love of, seduction by, and eventual marriage to Lord Clarendon. His next play was a failure. Then, the five-act *Barber of Seville*, after a year's ban by the King, opened at the Théâtre Français on February 23, 1775. The play fell flat; but Beaumarchais condensed and rearranged it, and it became a lasting hit. Marie Antoinette acted Rosine in 1785, inviting the author to watch her performance with the royal guests.

The play was made into a motion picture in 1914 and 1947. Although there are occasional revivals of Beaumarchais' comedy, it is best known in this country as Rossini's comic opera (Gioacchino Antonio Rossini, Italian, 1792-1868). This opera was first performed in Rome in 1816; London in 1818; New York, in English, in 1819. It opened in 1853 at both the Broadway Theatre and Niblo's Garden in New York. Marcella Sembrich sang it, first at the Metropolitan Opera House, December 15, 1883. It is the only one of Rossini's operas that has held a continuous place in repertory. The play itself is frequently performed by college and little theatre groups; it was produced in New York in 1939, in French, by Le Théâtre des Quatre Saisons.

The Barber of Seville pictures the devices by which Rosine (Rosina in the opera) evades the advances of her amorous old guardian Bartholo, and succeeds in marrying her beloved young Lindoro, who turns out to be the Count Almaviva. The lively episodes of the story are swept into constant interest by the barber, Figaro, who fusses about, imagines himself indispensable, gives vitality to the play, and serves as an amusing but forceful vehicle of Beaumarchais' satire against aristocrats. As Austin Dobson has said, Figaro is "perpetually witty, inexhaustibly ingenious, perennially gay . . .the irrepressible mouthpiece of the popular voice, the cynical and incorrigible laugher . . . who opposes to rank, prescription, and prerogative, nothing but his indomitable audacity or his sublime indifference." Figaro is not merely the best incarnation of the stock theatrical character, the intriguing servant, in the tradition of Menander*, Plautus*, and Molière*; he is a typical French bourgeois, with the Revolution already in his heart, but laughter always bubbling as his first line of attack. His gay, irrepressible spirits, refusing to take the aristocrats at their own evaluation as a superior breed, helped rouse the citizens that on July 14, 1789, stormed the Bastille.

"Simple in plot," Brander Matthews has said, "ingenious in incident, brisk in dialogue, broadly effective in character-drawing, *The Barber of Seville* is the most famous French comedy of the eighteenth century — with the single exception of its successor from the same pen." Even in the twentieth century, with its revolutionary appeal tamed by the march of history, *The Barber of Seville* is a lively presentation of character and a gay theatrical romp.

THE MARRIAGE OF FIGARO   *Pierre Beaumarchais*

Written about 1776, *The Marriage of Figaro* was at once banned by Louis XVI. "The King does not want *The Marriage of Figaro* played," Beaumarchais declared, "therefore it shall be played." It achieved quite a vogue through readings at the homes of nobles. A private performance, arranged for June 13, 1783, was stopped by the King after the audience had assembled. It was finally released, and performed to great acclaim at the Comédie-Française, April 27, 1784. Three persons were killed in the crush to see the play. After an original run of 75 nights, *The Marriage of Figaro* continued to be a great favorite. It was played by Coquelin (first in 1861), and revived in Russia by Stanislavsky. But, like Beaumarchais' other great comedy, *The Marriage of Figaro* is best known as a comic opera. With music by Wolfgang Amadeus Mozart (Austrian, 1756-1791), it had its premiere in Vienna on May 1, 1786; in New York at the Metropolitan Opera House, 1895.

The factotum Figaro of *The Barber of Seville** has become the center of intrigue in *The Marriage of Figaro*, as Count Almaviva, though now married to Rosine, covets Figaro's fiancée Susanne, and tries to thrust Figaro into the arms of his aging housekeeper, Marceline. A rendezvous with the Count is made for Susanne, which Rosine intends to keep; complicated misunderstandings and surprises ensue; Marceline turns out to be Figaro's mother; and all ends happily.

As the central figure, Figaro even more shrewdly than in the earlier play sends flaming darts of satire against the abuses of the times, in the spirit of the impending revolution. Brander Matthews called the play "as adroit as its predecessor, and the hits at the times are sharper and swifter and more frequent."

Figaro is both a wit and a buffoon. Buffeted by the Count on every pretext, he bounces up again, buoyant, irrepressible, indestructibly alive. The servant is superior to the master in everything except social status. Figaro is an individualized figure in a long tradition, stemming from the shrewd slave of ancient Greek comedy, here, as occasionally in earlier times, fraught with social implications. Comic sense and courage peered together from the searching eyes of Beaumarchais, creating in Figaro one of the world's great comic characters, fit fellow to Falstaff or Pantagruel.

THE KNIGHT OF THE BURNING PESTLE   *Francis Beaumont*

The best plays of Francis Beaumont (English, 1584-1616) were written in collaboration with John Fletcher (1579-1625). Most amusing among them is the riotous farce *The Knight of the Burning Pestle*. Written some two years after *Don Quixote* (published in 1605), it followed the Spanish novel in its burlesque of the romance of chivalry, popular and excessive in that day.

With swiftly humorous prose, lively song, and a blank verse that is at times vigorous, at times deliberately prinked and panoplied with figures, *The Knight of the Burning Pestle* moves tumultuously on three levels of action. The Induction, like the Induction of *The Taming of the Shrew**, serves to introduce two actors onto the stage among the gay bloods of the audience seated there. The actors represent a London grocer and his wife. The grocer protests against the play about to be performed, *The London Merchant*, crying that there have been enough attacks on citizens from the stage. If they can't put on a better play, at least let them put a grocer into this one. They can't spare any actors? All right, his apprentice, Ralph, will play the part. Ralph comes on stage, spouts a few lines from Shakespeare's *Henry IV*, is given a costume, and carries on. Throughout the play, the grocer and his wife comment upon the course of the action, and upon Ralph's performance.

The romantic comedy *The London Merchant*, save for the interruptions, runs the familiar course from thwarted love to happy ending. In addition to its action, there is the mock-heroic extravaganza, encouraged by the grocer's wife, in which Ralph, as the Knight of the Burning Pestle, rejects the Princess of Moldavia for a cobbler's maid in Milk Street. This story constantly interrupts the original plot, though actually linked with it only at occasional and minor points. Through Knight Ralph (with Squire and Dwarf) there is considerable satire of the military fervor then aflame in London and kindled by such dramas as Heywood's *Four Prentices of London* and Kyd's *Spanish Tragedy**, which is parodied in the final blank verse of the Beaumont-Fletcher play. Finally, there is the direct, realistic satire of the merchant-grocer and his assertive wife.

The overstrained romanticism and heroics then popular made the first audiences unsympathetic to *The Knight of the Burning Pestle*. When the play was printed in 1613, the dedication admitted that "the world, for want of judgment, or not understanding the privy mask of irony about it (which showed it was no offspring of any vulgar brain) utterly rejected it." Gradually, however, the play grew in popularity. It was presented in 1635; during the Restoration, Nell Gwynne performed in it. Up to the nineteenth century, indeed, it shared in the general popularity of the Beaumont and Fletcher plays, which were performed more frequently than Shakespeare's; as Dryden said in 1668, "two of theirs being acted through the year for one of Shakespeare's or Jonson's."

Recent revivals of *The Knight of the Burning Pestle* include two in London: 1920, with Noel Coward; 1932, at the Old Vic, with Sybil Thorndike and Ralph Richardson. In the United States, there have been many productions; among them, at Pasadena, 1929; Missoula (University of Montana), 1936; off-Broadway, New York, 1938 and 1954. Poland saw the play in 1949.

In reviewing the 1920 London production, the *Christian Science Monitor's* correspondent objected to the style in which Ralph was acted: "Beaumont and Fletcher intended him to take himself as seriously as the Knight of La Mancha, of whom he is almost certainly a reflection. But Noel Coward plays the part with his tongue patently in his cheek. The scene with the Princess of Moldavia, in particular, is rendered as sheer farce." The Old Vic production was wiser, as noted in the *London Times* (January 5, 1932): "Much of *The Knight of the Burning Pestle* is remarkably similar, both in spirit and in shape, or lack of it, to a present-day review . . . The Old Vic Company have brought all their graces and ability to the task of making the inner play in *The Knight of the Burning Pestle* appear as bad as possible. With the gallant help of Miss Thorndike

as the Citizen's Wife, the result is an evening of most spirited slapstick."
The 1635 edition of the play indicates the authors' purpose, "to move
inward delight, not outward lightness; and to breed (if it might be) soft
smiling, not loud laughing; knowing it, to the wise, to be a great pleasure
to hear counsel mixed with wit, as to the foolish, to have sport mingled
with rudeness." In the last words of the play, the grocer's wife (anticipating Gilbert's *The Pirates of Penzance**) begs sympathy for Ralph
because he is an orphan. But the doubly fathered comedy *The Knight of
the Burning Pestle,* still lustily amusing, has held well over the years;
in it, Beaumont and Fletcher looked keenly and kindly into the extravagances of both romantic pretension and middle-class assurance.

THE MAID'S TRAGEDY   *Francis Beaumont*

The fierce passions and cruel lusts that sear *The Maid's Tragedy* make
it the most powerful tragedy of the two playwrights, Francis Beaumont
and John Fletcher, whose works are almost unanimously accorded second
place to Shakespeare's in Elizabethan drama and in popularity outranked
Shakespeare's for over two centuries. Adapted as *The Bridal* (London,
June 6, 1837) by James Sheridan Knowles, the story maintained its
popular hold; Macready revived it constantly for twenty years. In New
York City, when Macready opened in the play with Charlotte Cushman
on December 6, 1843, *The Spirit of the Times* (December 9) reported that
"the whole performance gave entire satisfaction."
The play begins with an arranged marriage. The King of Rhodes has
his mistress Evadne wed the young courtier Amintor, who at the King's
bidding relinquishes his own beloved Aspatia. After a lively nuptial
Masque, Evadne scornfully tells her husband that he is but a cloak for
the King. But Melantius, Evadne's brother and Amintor's friend, discovers the situation and so awakens Evadne to the debasement of her lot
that she takes upon herself the task of revenge. With equal scorn, she
now reproaches the King with his lust and slays him. Before the tangled
passions can be cleared, Evadne dies by her own hand and Aspatia in
disguise is slain by Amintor, who with remorseful love joins her in death.
The scene in which Evadne reveals the true conditions of their marriage to the unsuspecting Amintor is full of pathos and horror. The
happy lover comes to the nuptial bed, where Evadne halts him. "The
dreadful intensity of the dialogue," said J. St. Loe Strachey in his introduction to the *Mermaid Series,* "the hollow grace and gentleness of Amintor's earlier phrases, the frenzied weakness of his utterance as the scene
proceeds; the brutal scorn and still more brutal pity of Evadne, as she
tortures her husband before she lets him hear the shameful story she
had never meant to hide, blister the heart, and leave the fancy seared
and deadened."
There is irony, next morning, in the gay mockery of the couple's
friends, and double irony in the anxiety of the King, who now begins to
doubt whether Evadne has been true to him. The cup of degradation
runs over. Aspatia alone is not bespattered, despite the scorn of Amintor.
As Charles Lamb has said: "While we pity her, we respect her, and she
descends without degradation. So much true poetry and passion can do
to confer dignity upon subjects that do not seem capable of it."
Samuel Pepys thought *The Maid's Tragedy* too sad and melancholy.

Charles II had other thoughts; the play was banned in his reign, until Waller wrote a new fifth act, in rhyme, keeping the king alive.

In various adaptations, *The Maid's Tragedy* was revived up to the mid-nineteenth century; and, in cut versions of the original, in 1904 and 1908, in London. The full version, including the mythological masque, was given in London in 1921, with Sybil Thorndike as Evadne. *The Stage* (November 17, 1921) remarked: "One can easily understand why, apart from its lofty and beautiful language, it has engaged the attention of so many prominent actors and actresses ever since its inception. It is full of splendid acting parts, and one is always finding emotion treading on the heels of real or potential tragedy, as in the finely written Quarrel Scene between Melantius and Amintor . . . In spite of much gore and many coarse expressions characteristic of the period, its main effect is eminently moral and uplifting . . . The performance of Miss Sybil Thorndike as Evadne must have been very near the poet's ideal. In the earlier scenes, before remorse or fear comes, this king's concubine was that most tragic of all things, a human being with a dead soul; and Miss Thorndike, with her flinty, smirking demeanor and joyless laughter, made one feel its deadness." Speaking of the same production, the *Christian Science Monitor* (December 27, 1921) said "It is an extremely well-constructed stage play, teeming with intensely dramatic situations, affording excellent acting opportunities, and decorated with poetry that gives scope to the elocutionist as well as to the player."

With the advent of the Stuarts, the flowering of drama under Elizabeth, though still in gorgeous blossom, began to show the overbrightness and profusion of incipient decay. The audience, habituated to horror, as it were defied the dramatist to shock its jaded senses; situations and characters were framed rather to startle than to ring true. "Both the beauty and the latent decadence of this new style," said Allardyce Nicoll, "are to be traced in *The Maid's Tragedy* . . . the temper of the blank verse, which seems, in its vague rhythm and frenzy, premonitory of the dramatic decay to come." It is also, of course, and legitimately, premonitory of the degeneration and death of the figures within the play.

The emotions in *The Maid's Tragedy,* though pressed for sensation, stem naturally from the situations, to make a fiercely surging drama, with dialogue attuned to passion's drive and the grim and fateful, tortured ends of lust.

LA PARISIENNE   *Henri Becque*

The position of Henri Becque (French, 1837-1899) in French drama, is a matter of dispute. Freedley and Reeves in *A History of the Theatre,* 1941, include him among "the names associated with naturalism." However, S. A. Rhodes, in *A History of Modern Drama,* 1947, separates him from the naturalists. Becque himself said: "I have never had a great liking for assassins, hysterical and alcoholic characters, and for those martyrs of heredity and victims of evolution." He is quiet in his effects, slipping in a trenchant phrase quite unobtrusively, reaching his climaxes without hubbub and to-do. At the same time, his plays are constructed without orthodox pattern; and, while they do not slice life through the viscera, they do present, in naturalistic phrasing, "a slice of life". As a pioneer of the new movement in the drama, Becque unquestionably stands clear. His *Les Corbeaux (The Ravens;* translated as *The Vultures)* inaugurated the modern social drama, and his *La Parisienne* is the first of the modern triangle comedies.

The Vultures, 1877, was rejected by seven producers, and its first run, at the Comédie Française in 1882, consisted of three performances before tumultuous audiences. Equally unattractive to producers, but much more favored of the public, was *La Parisienne*, presented at the Renaissance Theatre in 1885. It is famed in France as the outstanding example of *comédie rosse* (gay light comedy masking a bitter irony and cynical realism). *La Parisienne* was again presented at the Comédie Française in 1890 and later by Antoine at the Théâtre Libre, with Réjane. New York saw *La Parisienne* in French in 1904 with Réjane and in 1924 with Mme. Simone. London saw the play, January 29, 1934, and again in 1943, in an English version called *A Woman of This World*, by Ashley Dukes. *La Parisienne* was a great success all over Europe, especially in Italy. The Ashley Dukes version, now called *Parisienne*, was revived in New York for two weeks opening July 24, 1950, with Faye Emerson, Francis Lederer, and Romney Brent, in a sadly dated production.

La Parisienne is not a triangle play in the usual sense. Clotilde Du Mesnil manages her adulterous life with a strict regard for propriety and for the well-being of her quite happy husband. She discards her lover Lafont when the dismissal helps her husband to a better social and financial position and also keeps Clotilde herself from being too readily taken for granted by her lover. Later, when young Simpson is beginning to weary of Clotilde's somewhat demanding ways and carefully preserved charms, she is ready to yield to Lafont's feelings and accept him as lover once more. But all the time, the interests and reputation and happiness of M. Du Mesnil are thoroughly safeguarded.

The brilliant dialogue of Becque calls for a simple naturalness in the performance. There is never any build-up to an effect, yet the impact when it comes seems most natural, springing neatly from the character and the action.

Despite Clotilde's delicious and malicious pleasure in her own adroitness, she is completely at ease only with her husband. With him, the guards are lowered; the battle of the sexes has its truce. They are good friends. To M. Du Mesnil, her friend, if not to M. Du Mesnil, her husband, Clotilde is always loyal. She deceives him as a woman, but remains a clever and competent helpmeet.

La Parisienne has been most favorably reviewed. Desmond McCarthy, after the 1943 London production, with Michael Redgrave as Lafont, declared that the play "can be enjoyed as much by those who do not reflect as by those who do, which is equivalent to saying that it is first-rate comedy." The *New York Globe* (November 19, 1904) stated: "It moves briskly and surely. It is adroitly dovetailed, yet not a joint is visible. The dialogue has a dry crispness that points its wit with bright suggestion. The insight into character is of the keenest, yet the traits that it discovers are set with the lightest of hands in the clear, dry light of sane, witty, sometimes sardonic, truth." One of the earliest, *La Parisienne* is also one of the best, of the modern French comedies of sex.

JACOB'S DREAM   *Richard Beer-Hoffmann*

Out of the "Young Vienna" group, Richard Beer-Hoffmann (Austrian, 1866-1945) was moved by an intense concern for his Jewish people. His best play, *Jacob's Dream*, 1918, reconstructs a story from *Genesis* of the constant trials and holy mission of the Jews. A second play of a projected trilogy, *Young David*, 1933, shows the testing of the future king of Israel, and continues the mood of exhaltation and high destiny.

Jacob's Dream pictures Esau, the elder son, selling his birthright, and Jacob by trickery winning his father Isaac's blessing. It continues through Jacob's dream, his wrestling with the angel of the Lord (in the play he wrestles Semal, Satan), his change of name from Jacob to Israel ("prince prevailing with God"), with the prophesy of eternal woe but eternal life.

A highly stylized production of *Jacob's Dream* was given in New York, January 3, 1927, in a Hebrew version by the Habimah Players. The scenery rose at weird angles; the actors wore grotesque make-up and used extravagant gestures; lurid flashes of lightning broke through inhuman noises echoing from the wings.

The people in the play, especially Esau and his Hittite wives, are rude and primitive; Jacob alone is gentle and pensive, as though the burden of the future were his own. The play, said the *Boston Transcript* (April 3, 1928) "is the expression of a nation, a scattered, sometimes driven and fugitive nation, but nonetheless a nation very powerful in its leavening influence upon all the nations of the world . . . The satisfaction in wealth of Ahalibama, the lust of power of Basmath [Esau's wives] are overspread with spiritual exaltation and exultation: the race goes on."

There is a power of poetry in *Jacob's Dream*, as well as the almost naive directness of the medieval Latin church plays. It is, said the *New York Evening World* (January 4, 1927) "as touching as the sincerest of lyric operas and as picturesque as the dream of an imaginitive child . . . beautiful lines of the dialogue, with their vigorous simplicity, shading sidelights on traits that are never-changing fundamentals of human nature . . . the text of the play has the sweep of true genius." Present events have not belied the olden prophecy, of which *Jacob's Dream* is a moving and beautiful reiteration in the drama.

BIOGRAPHY   *S. N. Behrman*

In this deftly written social comedy, S. N. Behrman (American, b. 1893) looks with keen objectivity upon our human ways and finds them faulty but amusing. *Biography* is a comedy of compromise in a world concerned for appearance.

The central figure in the play is Marion Froude, a third-rate painter with a flaming love of life. Richard Kurt, a young editor with intense convictions, has persuaded the colorful Marion to write her autobiography for his magazine, much to the alarm of assorted lovers. Especially alarmed is her first lover, Leander "Bunny" Nolan, a candidate to the U. S. Senate from Tennessee, who has a prospective father-in-law of immense respectability. Pressure shuts Marion's story from Kurt's magazine, whereupon Kurt leaves his job, insisting that his personal integrity and the safety of civilization depend upon his freedom to publish her story. Marion wishes she might change Kurt, but recognizes that in doing so she would destroy what she loves in him. She destroys her manuscript instead, and Kurt goes on his reforming way alone.

With Ina Claire, *Biography* ran in New York, opening December 12, 1932, for 267 performances. London saw the play, April 25, 1934, with Ina Claire and Laurence Olivier. Ilka Chase enacted it on the road in 1934. There was general agreement among the critics that, in *Biography*, Behrman had enriched his art, had "become the master of his art"; said the *New York Times* (January 22, 1933), "the one master of high comedy we have in America", added Gilbert Gabriel.

The play is presented from the point of view of Marion. Her outlook on life is deemed tolerant; and her easy loving, morally advanced. Nolan, by contrast, is an old-fogey; Kurt, contemptuous, bitter and over-intense. Life should be taken leisurely, savouring its beauty. Kurt tells Marion that she treats life "as though it were a bedroom farce". But within such bias, the characters are revealed intimately, amusingly, with economy and pricking point.

London enjoyed the play. Charles Morgan (writing from London to the *New York Times*, May 20, 1934) observed that *Biography* "has a freshness, an honesty and an intelligence which English audiences, tired of empty theatrical tricks, can scarcely fail to recognize." The play has, said *Theatre World* (June, 1934) "an underlying wisdom, despite the frothy wit of the dialogue, and a true gift for character drawing." *Biography* is the best of the social comedies of Behrman, all of which are penetrating, polished analyses of sophisticated persons seeking to live life as an art.

RAIN FROM HEAVEN   *S. N. Behrman*

As the sores of the pre-World War II period grew toward a head, the urbane mind of Behrman sought to weave within the matter of his comedy the opposing attitudes toward the world. In *Rain From Heaven*, with a measure of complacent cocksureness tipping the scales, he pictured smart society learning to make basic social discriminations.

The various attitudes in the play are expressed in the home of the wealthy and tolerant widow, Lady Violet Wyngate. (In the printed play, she is Lady Lael Wyngate.) Her guests make an odd assemblage. They include: Hugo Willens, a refugee German music critic, whose great-grandmother was a Jew; Phoebe Eldridge, who had an affair with Hugo in Munich and still feels possessive; Phoebe's husband Hobart, an American financier who is planning a Fascist Youth organization for England; their daughter Joan, in love with a Russian refugee musician who's trying to forget his past; and Hobart's younger brother, Rand, deeply in love with Violet. The reactionary Hobart, trying to break the liberal Lady Vi's hold on Rand, announces that Phoebe has told him that Vi is her successor with Hugo. Rand turns on Hugo, calls him a Jew; Violet, taking the insult, declares: "He is both my lover and my guest." Hugo is only the latter, but he appreciates Violet's gesture, which marks her recognition of the danger that the shrewd Hobart and the emotional Rand bring upon the world. Lady Violet would marry Hugo, but he too has come to recognize that one cannot run from prejudice; Hugo goes back to Germany to fight.

Rain From Heaven is deftly constructed. Balanced against Hugo, who learns that flight is futile, is the opportunistic Russian musician who tries to hide from his past. The play is also neat in dialogue. When the Hobarts have turned upon him, Hugo exclaims: "To be accused simultaneously of killing Christ and giving birth to Lenin—quite a feat!"

Its emphasis on contemporary values helped make *Rain From Heaven* a success. The play, in fact, originated from an article, *The Sentimental Journey of an Exile* by Alfred Kerr, which Behrman read in the *New York Times* (August 27, 1933). It had its world premiere in Boston, December 10, 1934, and came to New York, a Theatre Guild production, December 24, with Jane Cowl, for 99 performances. Peggy Wood played in it in 1936. Although clever and polished, with basic points as permanent as prejudice, *Rain From Heaven* presents particular circumstances that belong to a world now wiped away. It seems likely, therefore, that it will be seldom revived.

Looking back a week after the opening, Richard Watts (December 30, 1934) gave high encomium to the play: "It is one of the curious qualities of M. Behrman's dramas that they seem to receive most of their praise in retrospect . . . *Rain From Heaven* is in every way the finest of Mr. Behrman's works, the most mature and thoughtful, the richest and the ripest and the one most artful in its workmanship. It reveals the characteristic Behrman dramatic method at its highest point as it employs the genuine spirit and quality of high comedy for purposes that are earnest and important and contemporary." The play presents, Watts continued, "Behrman's testament of affection for the gracious, urbane spirit of the genuine English liberal, his scornful smile of disapproval for the clumsy, boorish Nazi philosophy, and his tolerant and quizzical contemplation of such problems as intolerance, political exile, economic fear posing as idealistic crusading, and dullness of spirit masquerading as the lust for adventure." An obviously basic, though subtle, fault in *Rain From Heaven* is its tolerance of the things taken for granted as worthwhile in Lady Violet's set and its—though (heaven forbid!) never vehement — disapproval of the things "the right people" would not do. That is, the drama poses its problems with a bias, however urbane, however smilingly assumed. The fact that most in the audience share the play's presuppositions and values may have made it acceptable to contemporaries, but lessens its holding power over the years. *Rain From Heaven* is so gently urbane we almost overlook that it is smug. Hobart, the villain, is too deeply dyed. Lady Violet, on the other hand, marks in a measure an unconscious satire on her sort. Thus *Rain From Heaven* presents a polished picture of the self-righteous liberal in a wry world no one can easily judge.

NO TIME FOR COMEDY   *S. N. Behrman*

In the World, as it moved toward the year 1939, the slick society comedy that was Behrman's forte seemed to him a vacuous impertinence amid portentous world affairs. Hence he said, "Why not dramatize my own dilemna, write a comedy on the impossibility of writing comedy?" The result is a triangle play with sociological trimmings.

No Time For Comedy is both a comedy and an examination of the comic dramatist in serious times. The author in the play, Gaylord Easterbrook, has written many star comic parts for his wife Linda. Now, having fallen under the spell of Amanda Smith, a romantic woman who deems herself most understanding, he is urged to fight for immortality and Loyalist Spain. Linda, failing to wean her husband away—his natural sympathy for the underdog combines with Amanda's appeal—as a last resort throws him into Amanda's arms. Philo Smith, Amanda's banker husband, tries to console Linda; but Philo has no feeling for the underdog. Linda, watching her husband pack, is inspired: Why not dramatize their problem? Easterbrook, caught in the spell, thinks it a good idea for a play, but how can they end it? Amanda calls; it is time for her and Easterbrook to leave. He hangs up on her; and that is the ending.

The ending is an effective turn. As Harold Hobson, writing from London, said in the *Christian Science Monitor* (April 19, 1941): "Every artist must sympathize with Gaylor Easterbrook's quandary. The play, therefore, is both topical and serious in theme, though in characters and story it is reminiscent of most of the brittle drawing-room comedies that have been written since Noel Coward* first showed how profitable it is to present worthless people doing worthless things . . . It is evident that the only satisfactory ending to the play can be Easterbrook's recognition of the fact that his essay in the portentous is nothing more than a sham, running clean contrary to the bent of his abilities."

Philo Smith calls his wife "a Lorelei with an intellectual patter"; but it is clear that the two wives embody, if they do not symbolize, two attitudes toward the urgent world. Amanda presses for embattled partisanship: Recognize the right, then fight for it. Linda eases towards the continuance of things that are good: You have a proper job in the world, why let enemies interrupt it? Since Linda holds Easterbrook at the end, reviewer Richard Watts could say (April 23, 1939): "There is no more persuasive advocate of the gospel of urbane liberalism than Mr. S. N. Behrman. His prose style is so graceful, his wit so sprightly, his mind so tolerant and his viewpoint so modest that he becomes the most winning of the drama's counselors . . . The play of his ideas is so mellow and bantering and he is so clearly bent upon saving the gracious amenities of life in a world determined to destroy them—." But Harold Hobson pointed out that Behrman's play but skates the surface of the problem: "The idea that tragedy is a more seriously significant form of art than comedy is a delusion . . . It is folly to abandon culture when culture is one of the things that make civilization worth while. And I can assure Mr. Behrman that an audience whose individual members have been bombed quite as much as is comfortable did not in the least find his comedy out of place or inappropriate." Easterbrook should continue to write comedy not merely because that's his forte, but because such plays have a worthy place in the world.

No Time for Comedy opened in New York April 17, 1939, with Laurence Olivier, Margalo Gillmore, and Katharine Cornell in her first modern comedy role. It ran for 185 performances, with 261 more on tour. London saw the play March 27, 1941, with Diana Wynyard and Rex Harrison, for 348 performances. The play's announced background, of the author "profoundly affected" by the tendencies of the times, affected the reviewers. Thus *Time* (May 1, 1939) declared that Behrman "too often makes sex a mere come-on for ideas, none of which he accepts. He is a kind of ideological window-shopper." *No Time for Comedy*, despite the author's preliminary protest, skates over the thin ice of political and social ideas, but plunges with delight into the perfumed pool of sex.

THE HEART OF MARYLAND   *David Belasco*

The shrewd showman David Belasco (American, 1854-1931) capped a sentimental melodrama of the War between the States with a rousing climax characteristic of the sensational thriller, to create the most popular of the dramas of "the blue and the gray", *The Heart of Maryland*. Opening in Washington October 9, 1895 and in New York October 22, with Maurice Barrymore and Mrs. Leslie Carter, the play was showered with superlatives. *The Heart of Maryland*, said the *New York Dispatch* (October 27) "is beyond doubt the most perfect and carefully constructed dramatic work that Mr. Belasco has yet brought forward". The *Sun* called it "the best war play of them all"; and the *Dramatic News* (October 29) considered it "the greatest American play up to this time". The play was revived annually through 1902, and was frequently played throughout the United States until the World War took the theatre from the War between the States.

The romance runs through a typical Civil War tale of divided families. General Hugh Kendrick is in command of the Confederate forces with headquarters at "the Lilacs", the Maryland home of the Calverts; his son Alan is a Cavalry Colonel of the Union Army. Alan, in love with Maryland Calvert, a loyal Southerner, comes disguised as a Confederate officer in hope of meeting her. Maryland's brother, a true-blue Union man, trying to carry Confederate plans to Alan, is mortally wounded, and sends his sister in his stead. Unwittingly Maryland betrays Alan to southern Col. Fulton Thorpe, and General Kendrick condemns his captured son to death. The General is killed in battle and Thorpe, now in command, promises to spare Alan if Maryland will sign a statement that she has betrayed the Southern cause; but when Thorpe seeks to embrace her, Maryland stabs him and frees Alan. The dying Thorpe orders the alarm bell sounded, for pursuit of Alan. Maryland dashes up the stairs to the belfry and reaches the bell just in time to catch desperate hold of the moving tongue; she hangs onto it as it swings back and forth, high in the misty night; her hands are bruised and bloodied, but the bell is silenced and her beloved saved.

With dialogue more terse, direct, and simple than was usual with Belasco, *The Heart of Maryland* conveyed a vivid sense of war-torn spirits, on both sides greatly daring for what they deemed the right. "Here was a drama without horses or boisterous guns," Vance Thompson pointed out in the *New York Commercial Advertiser*. "And yet so convincing was it that the characters moved as in the blown smoke of a battlefield . . . An admirable play, absolute in its unity of impression, a synthesis of war . . . a well-made play, at bottom a melodrama, but lit with romance and informed with the subtle realism not of fact but of mood. Nothing of its kind could be better done." The strength and beauty of the play, observed the *New York World* (October 27, 1895), "are not limited to the clearly drawn characters. The minor touches are sure and faithful indications of a keen study of human na-

ture. They give balance and finish to stage pictures of splendid breadth."
James Huneker epitomized the praises in the *Morning Advertiser*: "The
thrills relieved each other in squads last night. Every war play I have
ever seen was here in some form or other . . . but the synthesis was the
work of the master hand."

The tremendously rousing climax of *The Heart of Maryland*, as the
audience well knew, was suggested by the poem of Rosa Hartwick
Thorpe, *Curfew Must Not Ring Tonight*, written in 1882 and long a
favorite for recitation.

The one adverse criticism the play received appeared in the *Illustrated American* of November 11, 1895: "The introduction of the device
is so obviously artificial, its employment is so forced, so patent is it that
the play was built around the incident instead of the incident's growing
out of the action that, despite its admitted theatric qualities, it loses
most of its dramatic effect." Although Charles Frederic Nirdlinger in
this review challenged the "ignorant or careless or venal or intimidated
criticism that proclaims such a piece . . . to be a master-work", his protest remained a lonely one (though to us his point bears considerable
merit); and *The Heart of Maryland*, along with William Gillette's *Secret
Service** and Bronson Howard's *Shenandoah**, is one of the best three
mixtures of sentiment and melodrama that strove to bring the intertwining conflicts of the Civil War to life upon the stage.

MADAME BUTTERFLY   *David Belasco*

In January 1898 *Century* magazine published a short story by John
Luther Long (1861-1927) entitled "Madame Butterfly". David Belasco
received a letter from a stranger, suggesting that he dramatize the story.
Belasco read *Madame Butterfly*, discharged his reader for having cast it
aside, and in two weeks completed the play.

Madame Butterfly, with Blanche Bates, opened in New York March
5, 1900; in London, April 28. It was excellently received in both cities.
The staging was especially praised; in particular, the lighting of one
scene held the audience enthralled through fourteen minutes of silence
onstage, as the heroine awaits her love until dark fades to dawn. Giacomo Puccini (Italian, 1858-1924) saw the Belasco play in London and,
with Italian book by Illica and Giacosa, fashioned the story into an
opera. In two acts, opening February 17, 1904, at La Scala in Milan, the
opera was hooted off the stage. The whole of Belasco's play was in
Puccini's second act. Puccini added prior details; then made a third
act by dropping the curtain for the night watch. In three acts, *Madame
Butterfly* was tried again at Brescia, May 28, 1904, and was a success.
Opening in Washington, D. C., in October, 1906, the opera came to New
York November 12, 1906, and played forty-nine times in seven weeks.
Puccini was in New York for the Metropolitan performance of Febru-
ary 11, 1907, with Farrar, Caruso, Scotti, and Homer.

Madame Butterfly tells the story of Cho-Cho-San (Madame Butterfly) and the American naval lieutenant, Pinkerton. Finding himself
stationed for some time at Nagasaki, Pinkerton contracts a "Japanese
marriage" with Cho-Cho-San, which leaves him free, the broker assures
him, whenever he wishes. Cho-Cho-San, however, loves him and, defying the curses of her uncle, an old bonze (native priest), she renounces

her religion to be forever his. (This much is the first act of Puccini's opera; the second act begins three years later—when Belasco's play starts.)

Pinkerton, with his American bride, returns to Japan. He asks the American consul, Sharpless, to break the news to Cho-Cho-San. She has had a baby boy, named Trouble (when her husband returns to her, the child's name is to be changed to Joy) and has refused Japanese offers of marriage, confident that she will be happy when Pinkerton returns. Sharpless is too touched by Cho-Cho-San's joy at word of Pinkerton's return to give her the bitter news. Night comes; the child, then the maid, fall asleep; Cho-Cho-San keeps watch. Next morning, she consents to rest a little, to look her best when Pinkerton comes. He arrives but, on learning of her devotion, leaves while Cho-Cho-San is still asleep. She comes out in time to hear Pinkerton's American wife offer to take care of the child. Grasping the situation, Cho-Cho-San drapes her son in the American flag, and commits hara-kiri.

Belasco's play made a deep impression. "It is rarely," said the *New York Dramatic Mirror* (March 17, 1900) "that theatregoers are privileged to witness so exquisitely artistic a performance . . . the pathetic story is told with unusual artistic skill. There is no pretense of theatricalism, or of unnecessary comedy . . . a gem of the purest water." In London, *The Mail* (April 30, 1900) called *Madame Butterfly* "very weird and strange and beautiful . . . treated in such deliberate and fantastic fashion that the glamour and power of it have an effect of aloofness and strangeness, that mask the real horror of the tragedy; while its pathos and its pitifulness are not lost, it has nothing of brutality . . . one of the most pathetic little plays imaginable."

Belasco, in addition to the imaginative staging, added a few pathetic touches to Long's account, such as Cho-Cho-San's blindfolding of the baby before committing suicide, and having her errant lover return, for her to fall dying into his arms. She kills herself with her father's ceremonial sword, which bears the words: "To die with honor when one cannot live with honor."

Belasco's play was revived, again with Blanche Bates, in 1914, in a benefit performance. It was successful, although by that time it had been largely supplanted by Puccini's opera, which the *New York Sun* (October 20, 1913) called "the most popular opera in America today." *Madame Butterfly* has indeed been widely sung; by Geraldine Farrar; by Grace Moore (also over radio, 1937); by Gladys Swarthout, who also sang in a film version in 1937. The play was first filmed in 1915; and Sylvia Sidney was in a 1932 film. The Japanese Tamaki Misera was famous as Madame Butterfly in the United States, 1915-1930; the opera was played in Japanese, in Tokyo, in 1937. It was withdrawn from the repertoire of the New York Metropolitan Opera House after December 7, 1941, until January 1946. Licia Albanese, who made a spectacular debut at the Metropolitan in 1940, as Cho-Cho-San, sang the role for her tenth anniversary with the Metropolitan in 1950.

The music of *Madame Butterfly* flows almost uninterruptedly with Japanese melody. In the first act "Evening is falling", a calm duet of Cho-Cho-San and Pinkerton, grows to the passion of "O Night of rapture!" In the second act the "letter scene" is followed by a delightful "Flower duet" as Cho-Cho-San and Suzuki decorate the house for the returning Pinkerton. The last act opens with a "vigil theme", as Cho-Cho-San waits for the dawn in a scene that marks a high point of the Belasco drama.

Both the opera and the drama have been very well presented, with "the seven veils of cloud-capped Fujiyama and a wealth of picturesque Oriental devices" in what the London Times (July 14, 1905) called "a rare and perfect use of local colour." The sentimental plot of Madame Butterfly seems to current taste, however, less suited to straight drama than to opera. The music, with its charming sense of the faraway, helps distance not only the story but the emotions involved in it, so that it becomes a touching dream-play, with sadness and beauty intermingled in a story of a love in which the simple faith and dignity of Cho-Cho-San prefer, to the lingering futility of wretched days, the sharp clean stroke of death.

THE DARLING OF THE GODS   David Belasco

Belasco's theatrical powers reached their high point in The Darling of the Gods, which he and J. Luther Long wrote for Blanche Bates after her success in Madame Butterfly*. The play, with Miss Bates and George Arliss, opened in Washington, D. C., November 20, 1902, and came to New York, December 3. Although it took from 8 p.m. until 12:30, The Darling of the Gods ran for 186 performances. London saw a Beerbohm Tree production of the play, December 28, 1903, which ran for 168 performances, and a revival in 1914.

The play opens with a dark scene in the mountains, where the Princess Yo-San, "the darling of the gods," groping her way home from the temple by lantern light, is rescued from brigands by Prince Kara. Himself an outlaw, Kara is the leader of the ten Samurai who have rebelled against the Emperor's edict abolishing their class. Prince Kara and Yo-San fall in love. They meet again in the palace of the neutral father of Yo-San, the Prince of Tozan, who gives Kara a "feast of a thousand welcomes". But the Emperor's Minister of War, Zakkuri, has a thousand assassins posted. They wound Kara; Yo-San shelters him in her apartments. Zakkuri captures Kara; and in the Minister's great hall, dominated by a hideous idol, he forces Yo-San to listen to the sounds from the fiery torture-room below, until she reveals the hiding place of Kara's band. Kara is set free; Yo-San hastens to warn him and arrives in time for them to die together. In the epilogue, Yo-San gropes her way upward through the mists, after a thousand years in hell for her betrayal, to sunlit clouds where she is reunited with her love.

The Darling of the Gods was raised above melodrama, the reviewers felt, by its pictorial sumptuousness. At the feast, geishas dance, maidens sing, acrobats display their feats, personages of high rank move with splendid ceremony. With flashing poignard a geisha, favored, then spurned, by Zakkuri as he is drawn to Yo-San, leaps at the Minister. Her shrieks are later heard from the torture chamber. There is music throughout the play, whether of soft voices or faint strings, or crescendo to loud trumpets and brazen gongs. "The embellishment of the simple plot", said the New York Mail and Express (December 4, 1902) "is delicately fanciful and powerfully literal . . . gentle as the caress of a lady's palm at times; at others, violent as a ruffian's fist. These very different elements in the play are illustrated in ways fitting to each, always rapidly, and generally with commotion though never with confusion." In London, too, *The Darling of the Gods* was deemed an "illuminated melodrama", but, according to *Country Life* (January 9, 1904), "the melodrama is disguised by the most beautiful illumination ever seen upon the stage of His Majesty's Theatre . . . exciting all the way through."

Since the theatre is a cooperative art, with author, director, designer, composer, and performers joining skills and fusing their functions into a single accordant work, *The Darling of the Gods* gave an unusual opportunity to lift a rousing melodrama into a spectacle of power and beauty.

SATURDAY NIGHT   *Jacinto Benavente*

While most of the plays of Jacinto Benavente y Martinez (b. 1866) present, with a skeptical yet tolerant optimism, the society of his native Madrid, the dramas that have won him international recognition are those that turn from the comedy of manners to a more universal, emotional range of the drama. Outstanding is his *Saturday Night*, 1903, which opposes royal affection and duty to motherly love.

The play centers around Imperia, once the starving model of the sculptor Leonardo, who is now luxuriously installed on the Riviera as mistress of Prince Michael of Suavia. The young Prince Florencio, enamored of Imperia's daughter, is killed in the swirling gaiety of a sailors' dive. His murder is covered from the police by simulated intoxicate dancing as the gypsy orchestra wildly plays. Michael becomes king; but Imperia refuses to join him until her dying daughter sends her away.

There is a measure of symbolism in the story of the play. The sculptor's greatest work, for which Imperia posed, is a statue depicting the triumph of the will. As the *New York Post* said (October 26, 1926): "The story of a lady who has known the love of princes and who strives rather clumsily to save her daughter from the decadent maze of ugliness to which she has descended, becomes a philosophical thesis on the relation of love, life, reality, and will." The will, Benavente seems to feel, in contrast to our impulses or our desire, may direct our lives to valid goals.

The play was presented in New York October 25, 1926, the first production of Eva Le Gallienne's Civic Repertory Theatre, with Miss Le Gallienne, Egon Brecher, and Beatrice Terry. It is excellently constructed; each of its five scenes rises to a climax, yet furthers the single drive of the whole drama. Particularly effective is the murky tavern scene, where revelry and philosophy are brought together, until the murder of the Prince creates a frenzy of pretended gaiety to hide the tense emotions resulting from the deed. In varying moods, from laughter to thoughtful observation to fierce dramatic drive, *Saturday Night* is a study of the opposition, long prominent in the Spanish drama, of devotion and duty, of the conflicting pull of two aspects of love.

THE BONDS OF INTEREST   *Jacinto Benavente*

Although most of Benavente's plays, of which there are more than a hundred, are satiric studies of upperclass life in Madrid (his lifelong home), his masterpiece, *The Bonds of Interest*, 1907, is an unlocalized fantasy. As Crispin points out in the Prologue, it is "a little play of puppets, impossible in theme, without any reality at all."

Crispin is the traditional shrewd and trickful servant who devises schemes that seem always to grow more tangled but that carry his master Leander through to triumph at the end. After Crispin's lies establish the credit of himself and the penniless Leander, the two men live in luxury and manoeuvre so that Leander may win the purse of Silvia, daughter of the wealthy but suspicious and niggardly Polichinelle. With the help of the imposing, though impoverished, Dona Sirena and her maid Columbine, the match is well advanced.

Two obstacles, however, arise: Leander falls in love with Silvia, and his creditors storm him. Unwilling to deceive the maiden he loves, Leander tells her of his true state. Meanwhile Crispin points out to the creditors that the only way they can be paid is for Leander to marry Silvia. They turn upon Polichinelle and—they will be paid. Crispin leaves the happy pair, with a warning to Leander that "the bonds of love are as nothing to the bonds of interest."

What lifts *The Bonds of Interest* beyond the banality of a retold puppet-story is its combination of kindliness and keen, satiric observation. The play, said Brooks Atkinson (October 15, 1929) "is commedia dell' arte in spirit, but it is also the work of the sardonic, pointed Jacinto Benavente." The figures, named as puppets, have human traits; Benavente implacably notes and exposes their frailties. He shows both the good and the bad side of his characters; let him who lacks the latter stand as judge.

The Bonds of Interest was presented in New York in 1919 as the first play of the newly organized Theatre Guild, with Helen Westley, Dudley Digges, and Augustin Duncan. In 1929 it was revived by Walter Hampden; it has intermittently found favor among amateurs.

Rivaling *The Bonds of Interest*, in the minds of some critics, is Benavente's *The Evil Doers of Good*, 1905, which, by satirizing the complacent, superficial, smugly parading good folk, defends the ideal of moral tolerance. These two plays, with *The Passion Flower**, were instrumental in establishing Benavente's reputation outside of Spain. He was awarded the Nobel Prize in 1922.

The translator of *The Bonds of Interest*, John Garrett Underhill, observed that "the comedy is so deft and so facile that it is easy to pass its significance by. What the playwright sets out to say is that every man has within him two irreconcilable selves, the good and the bad, the generous and the base, the Dr. Jekyll and Mr. Hyde." This thought is coated, in *The Bonds of Interest*, with smiling comedy and playful romance; through a puppet foreground, it gives a view of the underlying traits of human nature.

THE PASSION FLOWER   *Jacinto Benavente*

Apart from the general tone and type of Benavente's plays, *La Malquerida* (translated as *The Passion Flower*) brought him international repute and with *The Bonds of Interest** helped win him the Nobel Prize in 1922.

The Passion Flower, in a superb Castillian atmosphere, is a gripping tragedy of peasant life, of the proud Spanish folk whose passions are a religion, quite as their religion is a passion with them. In the play, the widow Raimunda has remarried, but her daughter Acacia never calls Esteban "Father". Acacia breaks off her engagement with Norbert, and on the eve of her marriage to Faustino, Faustino is killed. A smouldering sense of guilt flashes into flame when Acacia, bidden to embrace Esteban as a father, finds herself held in his arms as a lover. Acacia's servant Rugio, who killed Faustino, frees Norbert from suspicion of the crime, by talking in his cups. Raimunda then accuses her husband of helping Acacia in the murder; arrested, he shoots his wife, bringing death to the only one in the family guiltless in thought and deed.

Written in 1913, *The Passion Flower* became a success all over Europe. It opened in New York, with Nance O'Neil, on January 13, 1920, and ran for 144 performances. Miss O'Neil and Leslie Banks acted in it in London in 1926. The play is a deeply moving picture of suppressed desires; at first unrecognized, love masquerades as hate, then boils fiercely as will battles emotion, until the passions explode to wreck the family. Two well-meaning persons and an innocent one are drowned in passion's flood.

The melodramatic aspects of this story are subdued by the simplicity of its setting and the restraint of its presentation. As the *Boston Transcript* stated (October 10, 1921), the story "unfolds gradually but inevitably, as solid tragedy must do . . . Since Benavente has brought to it so many ripened qualities of mind it must hold for many a day a high place in modern drama." Engrossing, carrying the audience somberly in its sway, *The Passion Flower* has a blood-red beauty in its grim revelation of tortured souls.

INVITATION TO THE VOYAGE   *Jean-Jacques Bernard*

Jean-Jacques Bernard (b. 1888) is the son of Tristan Bernard, French author of many light comedies. Early in his career he turned from the usual modes of drama to create what has been called "the theatre of silence". He seeks, said Thomas H. Dickinson in *Continental Plays* (1935) "to give voice to the unspoken, to dramatize the intangible overtones of experience". Perhaps it would be more accurate to call his "the theatre of reticence". For, as *Le Théâtre* (March 2, 1924) pointed out, "in actual life one keeps intimate concerns within oneself, talks of daily banalities, reveals moods and feelings by imponderables—an intonation, a gesture, a pause. Thus his characters reveal their preoccupations while speaking of other things. A subtle art, in which the smallest detail takes on a suggestive value."

In the *London Observer* (January 12, 1930) Harold Hobson described Bernard's approach: "Into the full-throated theatre of France, with its resonant past and its grand tradition of virtuosity in declamation, comes M. Bernard, as quiet as a mouse. It is a pensive mouse that strays into that historic cage of lions, a mouse with an ear for all the whisperings of the troubled spirit and with a mind to ponder them before the hand recreates them in his own terms of muted scene and dim suggestion . . . There is uncanny cleverness in his ability to reveal the seething tumult of suppressed eruption by showing only the tremors on the surface-soil."

Some critics feel that Bernard's best play is *Martine*, 1922, a sensi-

tive study of a country girl enticed by a city charmer. However, his
most widely popular play, and the one that most fully exhibits his rare
and sensitive touch, is *Invitation to the Voyage*.

Invitation to the Voyage—the title is that of a poem by Baudelaire
—opened in Paris February 15, 1924, in five scenes, and was revived
there in four scenes October 17, 1926. It was translated as *Glamour* in
1927, and played in London in 1930 as *Illusion*. In New York, it was
played, as *L'Invitation au Voyage*, by Eva Le Gallienne, October 4, 1928.
London saw it again, under its French title, in 1937 and 1948. Though
its delicacy and subtlety make it difficult to present, *Invitation to the
Voyage* is a delightful and touching, and widely played picture of a
woman waking from a wistful dream.

The action, if it can be called such, involves the family of Olivier
Mailly, well-to-do manufacturer of hobnails, in the Vosges. Into the
Mailly home comes Philippe Valbeille, to spend a few days at the factory
before setting off for the Argentine. We do not see Philippe at all,
throughout the play. Offstage, he plays tennis with Olivier's daughter
Jacqueline, he gives Olivier's wife Marie-Louise a volume of Baudelaire's poems, and he departs. For two years, Marie-Louise is in love
with the idea of distant places, and the man that has gone there. When
he returns, she has dinner with him. His conversation is more banal,
more filled with financial figures and industrial concerns, than her husband's, and Marie-Louise hurries thankfully back to her husband and
home.

The deftness of the drama was well described by the *London Times*
(February 4, 1947): "This piece not only dispenses with a hero, but
for story dares to give us no more than the tracing of a day-dream inspired in the mind of an ineffectual woman by a perfectly commonplace
young man whom we are never permitted to see. Marie-Louise has all
the domestic blessings—a pleasant house in delightful country, an affectionate husband, a charming child; but real people and real things have
never been a part of her inner life. It is the departure of Philippe for
Argentina which suddenly invests his figure with the strangeness and
beauty of lands unvisited, and during the two years of his stay abroad
he is the most wonderful thing that has ever happened to Marie-Louise.
But he returns, she goes to meet him, and instantly recognizes the commonplace creature who utterly failed to solicit her imagination when he
lived in her house. With dialogue exquisitely apt for the purpose, brilliantly glancing and never explicit, the author chronicles the progress
of this romantic illusion. He shows how its ending influences the woman's attitude to those about her. We may suspect that the change is
but temporary and that the same kind of romance will soon come to her
again, but she has served to make exciting drama of a day dream and
to give the life of an introvert palpitating theatrical reality."

The portrayal of the husband matches in sensitivity that of the wife.
He is the more intelligent. Indeed, according to *Stage* (April 22, 1948),
"if her husband had beaten her, betrayed her, or been anything but
understanding and kind, the whole thing would never have happened."
Or, once it had begun, only his patience could have helped it to this
end. For three of the play's five scenes, there is no mention of Marie-
Louise's love for Philippe. Yet the birth of love and the longing it inspires, the almost fevered eagerness and the agony that grow with it,

are subtly conveyed. Olivier divines his wife's love, and he, too, follows its course, with gathering jealousy and anxiety—all without an explicit word between them. Nor is any confession needed for Marie-Louise's repentance and Olivier's pardon. Understanding and faith of husband and wife have been enriched. And it is unlikely that Marie-Louise will slip from Olivier again, for she has had her voyage.

The characters in *Invitation to the Voyage* are natural, well-rounded, finely drawn human beings. Although the play is, as the *New York American* (October 5, 1928) said, "utterly devoid of action, as the regular playgoer comes to know it, *L'Invitation au Voyage* carries and sustains, once it swings into rhythm, a suspense that relaxes only with the final curtain. . . . It is drama that is poignant and real and that dominates its audience until the final denouement." It is a rich, rare, sensitive dramatic capture of a wish-fantasy; by its unveiling of the inexpressive, it has widened the resources of the theatre.

JOHANNES KREISLER   *Rudolf Bernauer*

On the lightning-tipped peak of expressionism there waves a banner bearing the legend *The Wonderful Tales of Conductor Kreisler*. In this drama, by Carl Meinhard and Rudolf Bernauer (German, b. 1880), all the devices of modernist theatrical presentation, expressionist style, burst and flare upon the anguished stage.

Produced in New York, December 23, 1922, as *Johannes Kreisler*, the play spun the critics in their seats. The *New York World* called it "one of the most amazing experiments our theatre has seen"; the *Mail* set it down as "a notable evening, perhaps even an historic one." Most of the play's forty-one scenes take place in Kreisler's mind.

The play begins with the aged Kreisler in his friend Theodor's room, about to tell the story of his life. Several times we return to the room, to pick up the realistic thread of the story. The many other scenes show the story Kreisler tells, touched with the hallucinations of a weary old man looking back at ardent youth, and at successful but ever unsatisfied maturity.

Kreisler, the youth, dreams of his uncreated masterpiece, an opera about Undine; in all his loves, the man sees the figure of this maiden. First he sees his ideal in sweet young Julia Mark, but Julia's priest wants her to enter a convent and her parents want her to marry a wealthy man. Johannes, caught kissing her, is sent away. He sees his ideal next in Princess Euphemia, in Potsdam, where his opera is to be produced. But the Lord Chamberlain guards the princess, and the jealous directors of the theatre, when Kreisler refuses to insert an irrelevant ballet, reject his opera. Nonetheless, as a successful composer, Kreisler frequents the opera-house; his third Undine-ideal is the singer there. She dies in his arms. And as he ends his story, in Theodor's room, Kreisler dies.

The swift changes and eerie effects that carry along this story were made possible by dividing the stage into six smaller stages, on various levels; a transparent curtain covered the whole, and sharp spotlights set their intense glow on the action, leaving all else dark. (The actors were led from scene to scene by guides in black, unnoticed by the audience.) Thus, against a hideous background speared with a toppling cross, Kreisler in fancy watches his Julia tortured by the priest and the millionaire. In blinding darkness these two, and the Lord Chamberlain, come to mock Kreisler as he sleeps. With pendulous heads and convulsive limbs, they cavort in a niggling dance. Against their spell Kreisler strives with music from his opera *Undine*, which he conducts in ever more frenzied beat; then in desperation he swings the baton at one of the men, then at another. Their heads fall off—we see them cleanly decapitate: bodies rigidly erect, heads rolling on the floor. He strikes at the third; the baton fails, and Kreisler falls unconscious. It is a veritably drunken scene. Less eerie, but equally surprising, is the scene in which the opera-singer, putting all her love in her expiring voice, by its supreme power lifts Kreisler from his box and floats him down to the stage, so that she can enjoy a last kiss, and die in his arms. These are but the more imposing of the many devices and details that add to the power of the presentation and combine to create an overwhelming impression. While the audience is engrossed, there is no sense of stage-trickery, of artificial capture of the emotions. The emotions are held, beyond thought. The *New York Mail* (December 24, 1922) reported that "the novelty of this fantastic melodrama is unimpeachable"; and Stark Young (January 10, 1923), stated that the action grows "tauter as the play progresses, and takes on toward the last a definite convincingness."

Johannes Kreisler is built up of fact and legend, around the life of Ernst Theodore Amadeus Hoffmann (1776-1822), composer and teller of grotesque tales, about whom Offenbach wove his *Tales of Hoffmann* (1881). Some of the music from Hoffmann's opera *Undine* is used in *Johannes Kreisler*, and much of the eerie fantasy of his fantastic tales is recaptured in the drama, as lovely moments—such as the "breathlessly beautiful ballet" by Fokine—are nudged aside by pageantry of terror.

In the New York production, staged by Frank Reicher, Jacob Ben-Ami played Kreisler; all three women—for in Kreisler's fancy all three are but manifestations of the one Undine—were played by Lotus Robb. All that is enacted in Kreisler's story comes to us colored by his mind, by his persecution complex, his hallucinative imaginings, his disordered mingling of the fancied and the real.

Out of the phantasmagoria that attack and supplant Kreisler's dream, the play is builded. Too difficult a staging task for frequent revival, it remains a challenge to imaginative direction. Created in the heyday of expressionist production, it reveals, in all their emotional surge and eerie swirl, the full powers of expressionism in the theatre.

THE THIEF   *Henry Bernstein*

The "brutal drama" has no more powerful playwright than Henry Bernstein (French, b. 1876). Accomplished architect of dramatic situations, he tightens the passions in the angry snarl that summons a scène à faire, then raises the emotions to such a storm that the spectators are tied to their seats by an inner intensity. Usually, there is the strewn wreckage of the storm in the calm of the final scene. In *The Thief*, as Jean Toulet is quoted by S. A. Rhodes, in *A History of Modern Drama* (1947), Bernstein "dissects the human heart with a kitchen knife."

The plot of *The Thief*, 1906, is novel, neat, and gripping. A young couple, Richard and Marie-Louise Voysin, are guests at the Lagardes' chateau. Twenty thousand francs are stolen. The detective names the nineteen-year-old Fernand Lagardes, who, admitting his guilt, is ordered by his father to Brazil. But Richard finds 6,000 francs in his wife's letter-case. Also aware that her undergarments are of choicest quality, he accuses her of the theft. Relentlessly he beats upon her, until she confesses that she has been stealing to buy pretty things with which to hold his love. Richard's mind now whips to a jealous fury: Why did Fernand confess? The boy, in love with Marie-Louise, was shielding her. Marie convinces Richard that this was but the boy's infatuation. She confesses her theft to the Lagardes, and the young couple, instead of Fernand, leaves France for Brazil.

The intensity of these situations is hard to convey off the stage. The second act takes place in the Voysins' room, with but the two there. Subtly the husband's suspicions are gathered, swiftly they are roused, ruthlessly he questions, and superbly the wife rallies in her own defense. *The Thief* holds a warning, said Dorothy Dix, when the *New York Journal* published the play (February, 1908), "a warning for every foolish husband who admires good clothes on other women, but doesn't put them on his own wife." Bernstein, according to the *New York Sun* (October 20, 1907), "is more than masterful and direct. He is vehement with a well-nigh irresistible vehemence." He can write, the *Boston Transcript* concurred (October 13, 1908), "an eminently dramatic narrative and then fling it across the footlights with such vigor and speed that the spectator who would hold judicially aloof is caught willy-nilly into it . . . Pace, power and mechanism are no less the qualities of his plays than they are of a Mercedes or a Fiat . . . He could hold his audience impaled on an interrogation point, like an excited butterfly on a pin, whenever he would." So highly wrought were the players themselves that during the 1907 New York run of *The Thief*, during its tremendous second act, Daniel Frohman used to signal from his studio over the Lyceum Theatre stage, when his wife Margaret Illington grew overemotional, playing Marie-Louise to Kyrle Bellew's Richard.

While Bernstein is ever ready to display power, he can also command subtlety. After his wife's confession, Richard calls Fernand over, intending to scold the boy. The shamefaced but plucky Fernand comes, and Richard bids him: "Say goodbye to her." Marie-Louise ends her talk with Fernand: "Goodbye, my friend, my brother."

The Thief was a great success in Paris. It opened in New York October 19, 1907, for a run of 281 performances. It was, the *London Mirror* (January 8, 1908) said, "the most discussed play in London", where it opened November 21, 1907, with Irene Vanbrugh and ran for 186 performances. The English version calls the couple Mr. and Mrs. Richard Chelford; the boy, Harry. Alice Brady and Lionel Atwill played *The Thief* in New York for 83 performances, opening April 22, 1927.

The action of the play takes place within twenty-four hours. The theft has already occurred when the curtain goes up; we watch only the crisis, which bludgeons our sensibilities, as with a swift surge of passion *The Thief* makes drama out of situations that drive uncomfortably home. The characters are not deeply probed, but they are truly seen; the story is plausible, straightforward, and pile-driver strong.

SAMSON   *Henry Bernstein*

Of Bernstein's "brutal" melodramas, the most powerful and most popular is *Samson*, 1907, the story of a man who tumbles his world upon himself and his enemies, to find happiness amid the rubble.

Anne-Marie, daughter of the Marquis d'Ardeline, in love with Jerome Le Govain, finds herself forced to marry Maurice Brachard, a former wharf rat and dock laborer, who has bullied his way to great financial power. Returning unexpectedly from London, Brachard finds Anne disheveled and upset. She does not tell him that she turned away in disgust from the orgy Govain had prepared; nor does she deny that she's had a lover. Brachard suspects Govain, and holds him in a room, at first by taunts, and then by force, until a fall of copper rates on the Bourse, manipulated by Brachard, wipes out Govain, and ruins Brachard as well. Brachard explains to Anne that he acted from love. She is deeply touched, and when she is urged by her family to seek a divorce, replies: "No, I was not rented to Brachard; I was sold to him."

There are two long speeches in *Samson*: one, at the end of the play, when Brachard tells his wife that he has always loved her, and compares himself to Samson; the other, his famous speech to Govain, on honor. While Brachard holds Govain prisoner, Govain challenges him to a duel, and on his refusal taunts him as a cur and a coward, without honor. Brachard retorts:

"Ah! You talk of honor. I wasn't brought up on honor, so I'm not supposed to have any . . . In all this affair of honor, there's nothing but stinking dishonor from end to end." The speech, rousing in itself, is accentuated by the shouts of the newsboys in the street as the copper market falls and falls.

Written for Sacha Guitry, who played it in Paris, *Samson* reached London, February 3, 1909, for 120 performances. New York saw it, opening October 19, 1908, with William Gillette, and Constance Collier in her American debut, for 140 performances. James K. Hackett took it on tour through 1909. Everywhere the play was greeted with enthusiasm. Arthur Brisbane devoted an entire number of his *New York Evening Journal* to the play and its author. "You wonder what Bernstein will do next," said the *Boston Transcript*. "Doubtless he will write a play that it will be dangerous to undergo without an anaesthetic . . . The deadliest of all hatreds pours itself forth in a torrent of such revilings, such taunts, such plain names for hidden things, as surely can seldom, if ever, have been heard on the stage before."

The Indianapolis News (April 2, 1909) pointed out that the English version of *Samson* overstressed the excitement: "It is rapid, violent, thrilling, but it is mere melodrama. The plot is still there, but the subtle and masterful analysis of characters, which is the very basis of Bernstein's art, has almost disappeared, and has been replaced by a rapid dialogue—which, however, leaves the spectator breathless." The characters are psychologically true in the French version; but, even there, they are shown for the tumult of their passion rather than, as in some of Bernstein's later plays, for the complexity of their motives. As Bernstein has said of his work: "I am an impressionist . . . To me, this means two things. First, it consists of seizing the culminating moment of a human life, a moment created by conflicts perhaps somewhat ex-

treme, but always essentially human. Secondly, I do not try to reproduce what my eyes perceive according to certain classical and artificial
rules, but to give a visual impression, vivid and definite . . . The artist
in me revolts at the mere suggestion of a play to demonstrate a superfluous truth. I am quite unequal to put upon the scene anything other
than a bit of humanity troubled, trembling, bleeding."

A strong study of a strong man—a rich man who finds the needle's
eye and enters heaven—a man who by tumbling himself and his enemy
together wins redemption, *Samson* is a sound melodrama with a fierce
theatrical drive.

JUDITH   *Henry Bernstein*

The *Book of Judith* has provided the story of many plays. It remains
the finest and most astonishingly vivid and convincing in all that wonderful story-budget known as the *Apocrypha.*

"The mountains shall be drunk with blood, and I will fill their fields
with the dead," saith Nabuchodnosor. And the Assyrians come down
like a wolf on the fold; their huge army of more than 170,000 footmen
sweep across helpless lands until they are stopped by the hardy little
hill tribe of Israelites at the town of Bethulia. Seizing the springs at
the bottom of the hills, the invaders sit, carefree, confident, to starve out
the defenders. With the threat of drought and starvation, however, the
beautiful widow Judith doffs her mourning, bedecks herself, and descends with her handmaid to the enemy camp. There she rouses the
lust of the Assyrian leader, Holofernes. Getting him drunk, with his
own falchion she hacks off his head, and carries it back in triumph, to
the glory of her people and her God.

Among the plays based on this story are versions by Lorenzo Giu-
detti (Italian, 1621); Johann Gottfried Gregori (in German, for the
Russian Czar Alexis, 1674); Christian Friedrich Hebbel (German, 1839);
Gedaliah Belloi (Yiddish, 1870); Thomas Bailey Aldrich (American,
Judith of Bethuliah, 1907); T. Sturge Moore (English, 1911); Anton H.
Tommsarre (Estonian, 1921); Henry Bernstein (French, 1922); Emil
Nikolaus Reznicek (Czech, *Holfornes,* 1923); René Morax (French Swiss,
1925; as an opera with music by Honegger, 1926); and Jean Giraudoux
(French, 1936).

The earliest versions merely dramatized the Biblical story. Hebbel,
however, whose drama is largely a succession of lively pictures, offered
a complicated psychological study of Judith. Having heard of the sexual
prowess of Holofernes, Judith, teased and tempted, persuades herself
that she can save her people by testing it. In Holofernes' tent, she recognizes that her motives are personal, not heroic; and she kills Holofernes because her integrity is besmirched. A counterpart to this explanation of Judith's motives was planned for a drama, never written,
by the Russian Chekhov*, who saw Judith as going forth to kill Holofernes, then falling in love with him.

The opera of Morax, presented at Monte Carlo February 13, 1926,
with Mary Garden in Chicago, January 27, 1927, by action and music,
according to the *Boston Transcript* (February 5, 1927) stressed "the
brutish savagery of the animal who, straining the woman to his breast,
assures her at the same moment of his inflexible determination to deliver

her city to the flames and put her people to the sword." Yet it showed
Judith unhappy at the end: "I yield my life to God, so that I may forget." Still another interpretation of Judith's conduct came from Giraudoux; in his play, Judith finds Holofernes a charming and accomplished
man; she freely becomes his mistress, finally killing him because she
refuses to be no more than a passing fancy in his life. Closest to the
Bible, of recent versions, Moore's *Judith*, acted by Lillah McCarthy in
London, 1916, showed the widow's reluctance to kill, her horror at the
task she somehow was inspired to undertake, and her final desperate
deed rising as much from frenzy at her ritual defilement as from a driving patriotism.

Most powerfully dramatic of all versions is the *Judith* of Henry
Bernstein. Staged by Antoine, with sets by Soudekine and costumes by
Leon Bakst and with the role of Judith acted by Mme. Simone, *Judith*
at its Paris premiere October 11, 1922, offered tense drama and a superb
spectacle of Oriental lavishness and lust. Bernstein's version depicts
Judith as a naturally frigid woman. Surprising her lustful maid Ada
in the arms of a man, Judith questions her with excited curiosity, recognizing that she herself has never known passion. In roused curiosity
and a mingling of hope and patriotism, she approaches Holofernes. He
divines her purpose; but they both fall in love. Holofernes offers Judith
his sword; she offers him her self. In revulsion, next morning, she slays
the man. Back in Bethulia, Judith realizes that she has been truly
smitten with love. She goes forth to the mountain where Holofernes'
head is spiked, and—while at her feet an enamoured captain of her people kills himself for vain desire—Judith mourns the lover and foe whom
she has slain.

Bernstein's treatment of the Judith story is, as the *New York Clipper*
(November 8, 1922) remarked, "more symbolical and philosophical than
usual with him, but he still has the splendidly gripping themes that have
helped to make his fame." Robert de Flers, reporting from Paris in the
Boston Transcript (December 2, 1922) observed that Bernstein's Judith
"appears so vivid that for a time we take her as one of our contemporaries." Of the vivid scene in which Holofernes senses Judith's intent
and she fears torture, Flers said: "This tremendous scene, profound
in its sudden shifts, its voluptuous premonitions, its violent theatrics,
making a life-like bit of psychological research applied to two souls
reacting upon each other, is a masterpiece."

Bernstein's *Judith* is not only a vivid historical drama but also a living portrait of a complex, intense, magnificent woman.

THE BARRETTS OF WIMPOLE STREET   *Rudolf Besier*

One of the most famous of romances, the wooing of Elizabeth Barrett by the young Robert Browning, is the subject of *The Barretts
of Wimpole Street*, by Rudolf Besier (English, 1878-1942). The play
discloses the cloistered, almost imprisoned life of the Barretts, while
Browning shakes the bars to free Elizabeth from the influence of a
sadistic father. Before Browning's coming, her one friend had been
her dog, Flush. There is little plot to the play, but it includes the first
visit of the famous poet with his invalid admirer, the expression of
their love, and the gathering strength and resolution of Elizabeth to

marry Browning and flee her dusk-held domicile. Around the lovers, the other Barretts chafe and brood.

The play is written with a rich sense of human integrity that well befits its subject. It has, as John Mason Brown said (February 10, 1931), "a dignity that in no way detracts from the quality of one of the great romances in English literature, even if it does not succeed in capturing its full fine, frenzied nature. It gains immeasurably, too, in both its character and style, from the skillful and frequent use that Mr. Besier has made of actual lines from those almost daily letters that passed between Browning and Elizabeth Barrett when she was still an invalid—and a prisoner—under her warped father's domination at 50 Wimpole Street."

The father, indeed, is the most considerable figure in the drama. Thus, the *New York World* (February 10, 1931) called the play "a curious mixture of charming recapture of the love of two famous poets and of the kind of deep-dyed, all-wool hiss-the-villain melodrama that one expects in plays about cruel sex-starved, half-incestuous old farmers in the backwoods of New England. It is a father and daughter play, a study of fantastic parental tyranny and jealousy, with Robert Browning almost incidental, an impetuous, spirited, human, and normal figure who rushes in to make mad love to a lady he has barely seen." The *New York Herald-Tribune* attempted to belittle the plot: "It is a story based on the eternal verities of the triangle composed of the wicked Dragon, the gallant Knight, and the beautiful Lady in distress." But the story is really more complex, as the *Outlook* (February 25, 1931) observed: "Along with considerable brains and a dominating personality, the father, Edward Moulton-Barrett, is distinguished by hypocrisy and marked incestuous tendencies. He bullies or makes thinly veiled love to the members of his family."

Perhaps the grisly nature of Mr. Barrett discouraged American producers. *The Barretts of Wimpole Street* had its premiere at the Malvern Festival, August 18, 1930, and opened in London, September 23 for a run of 529 performances. Yet in the United States, twenty-seven managers or stars rejected it before Katharine Cornell made it her first venture as actress-manager. It opened in New York, February 9, 1931, for 370 performances. On tour, a storm and flood blocked the company's way to Seattle, Washington, on Christmas Eve, 1933; the audience waited, and at 4 a.m. stood and cheered the troupe for a great performance. During World War II, *The Barretts of Wimpole Street* was shown to many appreciative G.I.'s in the European theatre of military operations. In 1945 Margalo Gillmore and Patricia Collinge wrote a book—the title was the same as that of the play—telling the story of the G.I. tour. The play has also been produced in Copenhagen, Stockholm, Oslo, Vienna, Budapest, and Australia.

The Barretts of Wimpole Street has been Katharine Cornell's greatest success. She revived it in New York with Brian Ahearn, March 26, 1945.

LOVERS' BREAKFAST   *André Birabeau*

André Birabeau (French, b. 1890), as *La Petite Illustration* aptly said in its issue of July 31, 1937, has written many "excellent and Parisian plays, some vaudevillesque, some inclining toward ironic and sentimental comedy, but all rising from precise and picturesque observation of characters and customs". The best of his dramas are those that, with deft and delicate psychological understanding, probe the spirit and examine the problems of children.

Birabeau's first use of children in the drama was in the one-act *Lovers' Breakfast*, a tender and delicate piece of sustained sensitivity. Presented, 1929, as one of a group at the Comédie Française, *Lovers' Breakfast* won enduring success. It was acted in French, in New York, in November, 1936 and April, 1941.

The story is a simple one. A divorced father, by an accident at once amusing and poignant, gains the love of his small son and loses the love of a long-desired woman. Completely forgetting that it is the boy's day to visit him, the father has arranged a lavish repast for his first rendezvous with the woman. The boy arrives; the woman, up to then unaware of the child's existence, grows annoyed, and soon leaves. The boy, not grasping the situation, sees all the delicacies, and his heart opens. All these good things for him? Then his father really loves him? And the father, controlling his exasperation, watches, and grows to appreciate and love the boy.

Within its single act, *Lovers' Breakfast* captures two hearts in a mellow moment and with tender certainty traces the growth of sympathy between father and son.

DAME NATURE   *André Birabeau*

At once searching and tender, smiling and serious, Birabeau's drama of adolescent love, *Dame Nature*, is, as *L'Illustration* (February 22, 1936) suggested, when the play was produced at the Theatre de l'Oeuvre (February 13), "as if Daphnis and Chloë, as if Paul and Virginia had had a child."

The story is simple, but novel. Leonie Perrot, left to her own resources at fifteen, runs a little stationery shop near the school where Paul, about the same age, is a pupil. Paul's parents make home a hell for him. Despising one another, they live together "for the child's sake". Unwittingly they neglect and mistreat him, for he is the symbol of their bondage. Paul and Leonie console one another. When they learn that they are to have a child, they are bewildered, but Paul accepts his responsibilities with adult and loving earnestness. The parents, at first, are aghast. But, as Arthur Pollock remarked (October 4, 1938), the urgency "teaches the children a great deal, and they are happy. It teaches the parents even more, and they are happy too."

The play moves constantly through touching, ironic, or amusing situations. The doctor who tells Leonie she is to have a child insists on seeing the prospective father; from the anteroom comes an anxious, bewildered boy of fourteen! The wondering reaction of the children to the phenomenon of childbirth moves to a gathering of resolve and resources for the emergency. There is a poignant scene in which, absorbed in a miniature shooting gallery, Paul suddenly remembers his beloved Leonie's state.

Paul's mother is a vain woman. Wishing to be thought still young, she keeps Paul in short pants; he's just too big for them. There is a ridiculous, at once absurd and poignant, children's Christmas party, at which Paul is manipulating a Punch and Judy show for his play-mates when a friend brings word that he's a father.

Things happen to Paul's parents, too. When the mother, on a first indignant impulse, goes to see Leonie, she thinks the girl is having an affair with her husband. Aghast at the truth, she turns to her husband. The discovery of the spiritual innocence of Leonie and Paul reawakens the decency of the older couple. Watching Paul help Leonie in the store, they surreptitiously slip money into the cash register—and love slips back into their hearts.

With Gallic wit and Gallic delicacy, Birabeau keeps the tender sentiments from growing sentimental. Granted the situation, he unfolds its consequences with psychological insight and truth. "He handles most ingeniously," said *L'Illustration* (February 22, 1936) "the shiftings of this comedy that might easily have become a problem play and that remains from beginning to end freshly innocent, when it might easily have become scabrous".

Dame Nature, in an adaptation by Patricia Collinge, was produced at Westport, Connecticut, in the summer of 1938, with great success. It was then brought to New York, September 26, 1938, by the Theatre Guild, with Lois Hall and Montgomery Clift as the children, Jessie Royce Landis and Onslow Stevens as the parents. Arthur Pollock called the play "all tenderness". The *New York World-Telegram* headed its review (September 27): "Poignant moments and humor mingle." The general New York reception was, however, but half-hearted; the adaptation dragged in the second act, and the brightness, lightness, good taste, and delicacy of the original were, as John Mason Brown moderately phrased it, "rendered into wooden English". In the original, *Dame Nature* is superbly entertaining; and in the picture it gives of spiritual awakening in a crisis, it is exalting, too.

PAMPELMOUSSE — *André Birabeau*

The rash of ardent American plays on racial prejudice, especially on discrimination against the Negro, gives piquancy to Birabeau's deft handling of the subject, in *Pampelmousse*. He presents the problem as it arises among children; and there is delight in watching the honesty and the directness with which the children face the issues, as contrasted with the roundabout, shame-faced evasions or downright prejudices of their elders. A pampelmousse (small grapefruit), explains the author, resembles "a slightly bitter orange or a somewhat sweet lemon, and my play has at once that bitterness and that sweet."

The setting for the theme is ingenious. In a small French town, where slander is quick-tongued, the engineer Guillaume Monfavet is taken seriously ill. His wife discovers that Monfavet has been supporting an illegitimate son. She feels it her duty to send for the boy, so that he can say his last farewells to his father. Her brother brings the boy. Monfavet recovers, but the eight year old child is there. A Negro, the child was born to Monfavet during his three years' work, away from his family, in the Congo.

Noel, or Pampelmousse, as they call the Negro child, becomes a problem. The legitimate children are at once shocked and delighted. The two mothers-in-law of the Monfavets are horrified. The neighbors buzz, intrigued. The boy himself is a superb study in hurt pride, grim resolution, hatred breaking down before good treatment, and growing normal understanding and love. Jean Pierre (age 16), Catherine, and younger Patrick Monfavet decide to vote whether to accept Pampelmousse as a brother. As they hesitate, he asks whether he may vote, too; when they say yes, he votes No! Whereupon, at once and unanimously, they overrule him and take him in.

The children grow fond of Noel. When the question of sending him back to school arises, they work on their paternal grandmother until she consents to keep the child. Then a neighbor comes in, and it becomes clear to the Monfavets that the town gossips, having seen Mme. Monfavet's bachelor brother bring the child, have decided that Noel is the result of a bachelor indiscretion. The elders jump at this way out of the scandal, and the children are just as happy, for Noel will be a neighbor, even though living with their maternal grandmother.

When Pampelmousse was first produced in Paris, 1937, a few papers cried scandal. The French Colonial Minister went to see the play, and praised it. So did most of the press, to judge by excerpts appearing in La Petite Illustration, July 31, 1937. La Republique held that Birabeau "marvelously understands the language of youth." Correspondence Havas reported that the play "brings to the surface troubled aspects of the human soul." L'Ami du peuple summed up the play's double power: "It is not only a gay comedy, one of the most irresistibly amusing, rich in laugh-compelling comments and insinuations that we have seen in a long time; it is also a comedy in which, suddenly and effortlessly, the tone elevates, and deep feeling springs, as easily as the humor, from the comic situation".

The American adaptation of Pampelmousse did scant justice to the subtlety and poignancy of the play. As Little Dark Horse, with Cecilia (Cissy) Loftus, Lily Cahill, and Walter Slezak, after a summer tryout it came to New York, November 16, 1941, to be buffeted by the reviewers. Brooks Atkinson insisted it was presented as "a comedy for guffawing . . . the huge joke of passing an unwelcome child from one person to another and trying to get him out of sight." George Freedley protested that "miscegenation may be funny to the French, but it is not a laughing matter in this country." Little Dark Horse unfortunately gave us no ground for judging how laughter might purge our emotions on the subject. The American version ends with Pampelmousse sent back to school and obscurity, instead of being admitted to the family— however obliquely, in smiling French acceptance of reality—as one of the Monfavets.

Through its laughter, Birabeau's Pampelmousse faces clearly and realistically what may at best be called an awkward situation; and, clear-eyed, it shows that, left to themselves, children can teach their elders how to deal with discrimination, how to accept all humans for their own human values. To exhibit this, with a tender portrait of young Noel; to snare all the humor in the embarrassed elders, and all the poignancy and nobility in the entangled youngsters, and thus to

create a play at once comic and cosmic in appeal, is the achievement of
Birabeau in *Pampelmousse*.

BEYOND HUMAN POWER   *Björnstjerne Björnson*

Friend and precursor of Ibsen*, Björnstjerne Björnson (Norwegian,
1832-1910) began his theatre writing with romantic historical dramas
based upon old Norse sagas. Most memorable is the trilogy (the first
act in verse, the other eight in prose) *Sigurd the Bastard*, 1862, which
with vivid historical perspective shows how the death of the pretender
Sigurd leaves the way clear for an equitable choice of ruler.

In *The Newly-Weds*, 1865, and *A Bankruptcy* and *The Editor*, 1874,
Björnson antedates Ibsen in the development of the social problem play.
However, the only play of Björnson that makes bid to stand beside Ibsen's is *Beyond Human Power*. Largely because of this play Björnson
was awarded the Nobel Prize in 1903.

Beyond Human Power is really two separate plays, written twelve
years apart, on the single but broad theme that man's grasp of the universe is both short and feeble. The first play, called *Pastor Sang*, in
1883, centers upon Pastor Sang's belief that his prayer can cure his wife,
who is critically ill. At his prayer she sleeps, unmindful of the crash
and roar of an avalanche that sweeps close by but spares the church and
house; and to his prayer she awakens, strong with love. And as they
rejoicing kiss, she falls back and dies. The assembled ministers argue
as to whether they have witnessed a miracle, while, with puzzled mind
and broken heart, Pastor Sang murmurs "This was not the meaning"
as he too falls dead, upon her corpse.

Beyond Human Power was a success in London in 1901 with Mrs.
Pat Campbell, who brought the play to New York, January 18, 1902.
(On January 9, the Sargent School pupils there had staged the play.)
Its American reception was mixed. The *New York Commercial Advertiser* (January 10) reported the play "entirely original in subject and
wholly sincere in treatment, and dramatic, though with little action,
through the very sincerity of its conception . . . It is a living drama, a
moving picture of human souls." Later (January 20) the paper called
it "a spiritual drama, which deals with no question, but cuts open a
few human beings, turns the light of imagination upon them, and shows
them struggling with undertakings and concepts beyond the reach of
man, or at least beyond his grasp." The *New York Tribune* (January
19), on the other hand, said that Mrs. Pat Campbell had "neither glamour in her proceedings nor magic in herself to divert attention from the
excessively lugubrious, morbid, dull and sometimes pernicious character
of the drama." The *New York Sun* (January 19) took middle ground,
praising the miracle as "a scene of exceptional power" and damning the
pastors' arguments over the miracle—an episode of rich irony, in the
original—as "a theological discussion that might send even a bishop
to sleep."

The second part of *Beyond Human Power*, 1895, (done in German in
New York October 7, 1902, and for its premiere in English, on Broadway March 31, 1905) presents the gulf not between reason and faith,
but between capital and labor. In a grim setting of poverty during a
protracted strike, Priest Falk proclaims the blessings of poverty, humil-

ity, and peace. Elias, on the other hand, although he comes directly from the corpse of Maren, who in wretchedness and despair has killed herself and her two children, urges the strikers to hold out. He and his sister Rahel argue over the strike. She says that death sets limits, to which he replies: "All that's worth while wins by going through death. If the workers will die for the cause, the cause will live." His are not idle words. In the citadel of the capitalists, atop the hill, when Elias announces that the place is locked, surrounded, and undermined, the leader of the capitalists, Holger, shoots Elias just as he gives the signal that dynamites the hall. Through the eyes of the workers' children, Rahel looks toward a day of social justice, but falls back upon the reflection that "heaven is in our hearts."

This play found New York even more unreceptive than had Part I, although the *New York Dramatic Mirror* (April 1, 1905) conceded that, "while the drama differs widely from the ordinary play in situation, plot and character, there is a dramatic intensity that carries interest."

Both plays have a greater proportion of sheer talk than we are accustomed to, with earnest argument on basic issues that holds intellectual attention, but without the wit that retains less devoted interest. The *Pastor Sang* story of *Beyond Human Power*, nevertheless, through the believable character of Pastor Sang and the fervor of his faith, as well as in the inevitable challenge life flings to such firm credence, has a strong hold upon its audience.

THE ROSE AND THE CROSS   *Alexander Blok*

The greatest Russian poet of his era, Alexander Alexandrovich Blok (1880-1921) is also the author of several plays. Disillusioned after the abortive Russian uprising of 1905, he drew his poetic pictures of life in symbolic drama touched with irony.

In 1906, Blok's play *The Puppet Show* was produced by Meyerhold. Part prose and part rhyming verse, this play looked within the usual Columbine, Pierrot, and Harlequin. In 1921, Blok wrote for Gorki* the play *Rameses*, which in the guise of a story of ancient Egypt set forth labor problems of Blok's day. Between these two plays, in 1912, Blok wrote the greatest Russian poetic drama, *The Rose and the Cross*.

Although rehearsed by Stanislavsky, *The Rose and the Cross* has never been publicly performed in Russia. Just as the Soviets look askance upon the end of Blok's poem *The Twelve*, the greatest poem of the 1917 revolution, so they are uneasy about the implications of *The Rose and the Cross*. Set in thirteenth century France, it portrays a fair lady who, enamoured of a troubadour beheld in her dreams, scorns the full-hearted devotion of a worthy knight. Her jealous and brutal husband imprisons her in a lonely turret; but in vain. When her illusions as to the troubadour are shattered, the lady surrenders, not to the knight, but to a comely page. The knight's last act, before he dies of grief (and of the wounds inflicted by his master's foes) is to help the conceited young page to climb into the lady's chamber. Since Blok, in his poems, intertwined symbols of the Lady Beautiful and of Russia, it is possible to read into the play the thought that national decisions do not go the worthiest way.

The play may, as the *London Times* (August 3, 1939) pointed out,

"appeal as a picturesque legend to those who accept it quite literally."
Viewed in such light or from the knight's point of view, according to
Nikander Strelsky in *The Columbia Dictionary of Modern European
Literature* (1947), *The Rose and the Cross* is "a transcendent utterance
of the poet's sense of the inseparable joy and suffering in life." More
poetic than intensely dramatic, with a quality that reminds many of the
plays of Maeterlinck*, *The Rose and the Cross* wins praise for the rich
investiture, for what the *London Times* calls "the mannered speech, the
complex symbolism, and the sharp, disillusioned thought wrapped in a
web of sensual sound and whimsical imagery", that make it the most
colorful Russian contribution to the poetic drama.

THE STREETS OF LONDON   *Dion Boucicault*

The long theatrical career of Dion Boucicault (originally Bourcicault;
Irish, 1822-1890) began when he left home to go on the stage. He was
eighteen when, under the pseudonym Lee Moreton, he wrote his first play.
The nineteenth century spate of melodrama with rousing theatrical
effects reached its full spring flood with Boucicault's *The Sidewalks of
New York*. Based on the French melodrama *Les Pauvres de Paris* (*The
Poor of Paris*) 1856, by Edouard Brisebarre and Eugène Nus, Boucicault's
play replaced the maudlin and moralizing sentimentality of the French
with a vigorous sweep of action.
The play opened in New York, December 9, 1857, with E. A. Sothern.
It was also enacted under the title *The Poor of New York*. In both versions the setting and characters were made wholly American; the panic
of 1857 was introduced, along with the vivid spectacle of a blazing building, with a real fire engine and horses clanging onto the stage.
Since the copyright of plays did not hold across the English Channel or
across the Atlantic, with its title changed to *The Poor of London* and with
appropriate changes of characters and locale, Boucicault's play was
rushed over to England, where two translations of *Les Pauvres de Paris*
(*Fraud and Its Victims* and *Pride and Poverty*) were already playing,
in 1858. Boucicault's drama was revived in London under the title *The
Streets of London*, August 1, 1864. It then ran for 209 performances, and
by all indications—if one counts other transmogrifications and motion
picture versions—it has been played somewhere ever since. In London,
with changes by W. A. Darlington, it was revived again on December
20, 1932 for 158 performances, and again in 1943. In New York, as *The
Streets of New York, or Poverty is No Crime*, it was played in 1931 with
Rollo Peters, A. P. Kaye, Romney Brent, and Dorothy Gish; in May
1951 it was revived by the Henry Street Playhouse on Grand Street.
In its various manifestations, *The Streets of London* tells of the plight
of the widow Fairweather and her two children Lucy and Paul, after
the dying Captain Fairweather has been swindled of £20,000 by the
scoundrelly banker Bloodgood. The Hon. Mark Livingstone, also rendered penniless, can refurbish himself by marrying Bloodgood's heartless, mercenary, and title-hungry daughter, Alida. But seeing Lucy,
barefoot in the snow, selling flowers in front of the Opera House, Mark
falls in love with her, and love, as the audience hopes, works to its
triumph. The widow Fairweather in desperation tries to dismiss the
family troubles with charcoal fumes; the fire brigade clangs to the res-

cue; and Bloodgood and his clerk Badger wrestle in the flames until the clerk jumps through the window with the receipt for the Captain's £20,000. Then Mark's wedding with Alida is interrupted; the foiled fury Alida is replaced by the gentle Lucy; the wretched Bloodgood, forgiven because of his love for his daughter, leaves to lead "a better life"; and young Paul Fairweather beseeches the audience, if their hearts have been touched, not to forget the poor of London.

Not to be outdone in theatrical thrills, Augustin Daly offered in New York, August 12, 1867, a melodrama entitled *Under the Gaslight; or Life and Love in These Times*, in which Laura Courtland was thrown from a pier (in later productions, a high tower) into a river, and the one-armed veteran Snorkey, tied by the villain to a railroad track, was rescued by Laura from beneath the cowcatcher of the approaching train. Daly patented this train effect, but before he could open the show in England, April 20, 1868, to protect his patent there, a new version of Charles Selby's old melodrama *London by Night; or The Dark Side of the Great City* opened, with its hero tied to the track before an onrushing train. In September, 1868, the same device was used in Miss Hazlewood's *London by Gaslight*; and in Boucicault's *After Dark, a Tale of London Life* of the same year, the rescuer breaks through a cellar wall as the victim lies in the London underground.

Well into the twentieth century, such melodramas were the rage throughout England and the United States. From their price of admission, they came to be known as the "ten-twent'-thirt' melodramas", and they gave more than their money's worth of thrills.

It became fashionable during the second quarter of the twentieth century to present burlesque revivals of the ten-twent'-thirt' melodrama, often in beer-gardens, with old-time songs and vaudeville skits between the acts and the audience loudly hissing the double-dyed, handle-bar-moustached villain. Some of the plays lent themselves to this treatment, but the better ones turned the tables upon their producers, and evoked anew the olden spell of vivid melodrama. This was especially the case with Boucicault's *The Streets of London*. When the play was revived in Australia, the *Sydney Herald* (September 4, 1937) reported, "The audience took it seriously." If this seems provincial, hearken to the reaction of theatre-wise London to a revival of January 1943. *The Daily Express* declared: "By the end it was the actual melodrama, rather than the parody of it, that moved the audience." *The Sunday Referee* added: "It lives still, as any authentic work of art must . . . *The Streets of London* is grand entertainment." Finally, the *Spectator* said: "From the technical point of view, the play is an amazingly strong piece of work . . . brilliant entertainment."

Deftly constructed, with theatrical effects of breath-taking power, *The Streets of London* is one of the first, and one of the greatest, of the many-sided, heart-wringing, spine-tingling spectacular ten-twenty-thirty melodramas, which for a century made popular theatrical fare.

THE OCTOROON   *Dion Boucicault*

In the tense days preceding the Civil War, it was inevitable that melodrama should take up the subject of miscegenation. The best of the early plays on this theme is Boucicault's *The Octoroon; or, Life in Louisiana,* which opened in New York December 6, 1859, with Joseph Jefferson playing the Indian, Wah-No-Tee. London saw the play open on November 18, 1861, and again on February 10, 1868. It was revived in this country frequently until 1910, and sporadically since, with productions in 1929, 1930, 1932, and one by the Federal Theatre in 1936. What seemed a bold subject for the theatre in 1859 was still deemed daring ninety years later, when it was presented in the movie *Pinky.*

Boucicault's play, indeed, brought editorial fire from the press. The abolitionist *New York Tribune* (December 7, 1859) took the drama as occasion for a fulmination against slave civilization: "The love—the impossible love of a high-souled generous young man, for one damned among women, though lovely, feminine, and with all the eternities of love glowing in the gentlest of bosoms——because out of eight parts of her nature one was derived from African blood—gives rise to a tragic drama, with some tremendous scenes in it—some of which would grind to the last trituration of shame and horror the barbarism that claims supremacy of the Government of this country, from the head of the White House down to the tide-water—down to below low water mark." The *New York Herald,* on the other hand, suggested that the inflammatory subject of slavery were best avoided on the stage; to which Boucicault (December 5, 1859) made answer: "I believe the drama to be a proper and very effective instrument to use in the dissection of all social matters . . . It is by such means that the drama can be elevated into the social importance it deserves to enjoy. Therefore I have involved in *The Octoroon* sketches of slave life, truthful I know, and I hope gentle and kind." Boucicault withdrew as stage manager of the play shortly after the New York run began, saying that his life was in danger if he continued.

The octoroon is Zoe, a handsome girl on the Peyton Plantation of Terrebonne in Louisiana. Salem Scudder, from New England, manages the plantation, but even his shrewdness cannot save it from the Peytons' apparent lack of concern; all is to be sold. Actually, Jacob McCloskey has killed the Negro boy Paul and stolen, from the mail pouch Paul carried, the letter from the London bank with Peyton money to save the plantation. McCloskey lusts after Zoe, who is loved by George Peyton, but to whom she denies herself because her one drop of colored blood in every eight "creates a chasm between us as wide as your love and as deep as my despair." George could save the plantation by marrying rich Dora Sunnyside; instead, he tells her of his love for Zoe Sunnyside buys in the plantation, but McCloskey keeps bidding for Zoe, and finally gets her for $25,000.

Melodramatic action and theatrical effects now crowd into the play. Zoe, to escape McCloskey's loathed embrace, takes poison. But her death is avenged. The plate in Scudder's camera is developed—McCloskey had knocked it over while struggling to overcome Paul—and the picture shows the crime. To avoid arrest, McCloskey sets the cotton-boat Magnolia on fire, then leaps into the water. But the Indian Wah-No-Tee, who "with an air of primitive ritual" had gathered up the dead Paul and his belongings, tracks down the murderer McCloskey to a duel of death in the swamps.

The Octoroon was the first play to make use of the camera trick—the accidentally exposed plate that exposes the villain. Its melodramatic devices and action drive steadily along; and it presents a problem that has lost none of its timeliness. In England, the ending was altered: Zoe hears of McCloskey's guilt soon enough to keep her from taking the poison; and she marries George.

The power of the play has held throughout the years. In 1893 the *Boston Transcript* (May 23) declared: "Its action is swift, its color vivid, its dialogue catchy: the galleries are enraptured, the parquet good-humoredly entertained; the revival, a popular success." In 1929, the *Transcript* (January 23) said: "The audience was as sympathetic and as serious as though sitting before the trial of Mary Dugan, A.D. 1928." The *New York Times* called *The Octoroon* "a piece packed with dynamite when it was first produced, just before the Civil War, and still tingling with perfectly sound theatrical thrills."

The characters, even in minor parts, are vividly etched. *The Octoroon* is melodrama that trembles on the somber brink of tragedy.

THE COLLEEN BAWN   *Dion Boucicault*

One of the most popular melodramas of the nineteenth century, *The Colleen Bawn; or, The Brides of Garryowen*, was the first play to dwarf the art of the actor through the use of mechanical devices and the resources of the stage. It must have been immensely thrilling that night in New York, March 29, 1860, when the blarney boy Myles-na-Cappaleen first dived to the underwater entrance of the cave where he hid his illicit distillery and swam up again with the supposedly murdered heroine Eily in his arms.

The play was popular all over the United States until World War I. The Irish Repertory Players revived it in New York in 1933. It was made into a film called *The Lily of Killarney* in 1929, and another called *The Bride of the Lake* in 1934.

The Colleen Bawn opened in London, September 10, 1860 for a run of 165 performances. Bell's *Life in London* recorded that on February 2, 1861, "Her Majesty and the Court went to the Adelphi Theatre to see that wonderful piece of dramatic and sensational vitality, *The Colleen Bawn*." Bernard Shaw, who saw a revival of the play January 25, 1896, complained that the use of real water in the rescue scene destroyed the illusion, and chuckled over the two players' taking their bows sopping wet; yet he found *The Colleen Bawn* "far superior to the average modern melodrama." The play was adapted in French, October 17, 1861, as *Le Lac de Glenaston*, by Adolphe d'Ennery, whose *The Two Orphans** the English borrowed with equal alacrity. There was an English burlesque of the play, *The Cooleen Drawn*, by H. J. Byron in 1862; another called *Eily O'Connor* opened at Wallach's Theatre in New York the same year.

Laura Keene had asked Boucicault for a play. He wrote her that he had it; sent her some Irish melodies to be scored and some Killarney scenes for the sets; and the first act went into rehearsal while he was writing the second. The play was scarce a week in the writing. What fired Boucicault were the dramatic possibilities of a novel *The Collegians* (1829) by Gerald Griffin. Based on a true story that had earlier been dramatized in *Eily O'Connor; or, The Foster Brother* by J. Egerton Wilks and presented in London July 23, 1831, with Ellen Tree, *The Colleen Bawn* (which is Irish for the "white maiden") depicts the distress and

final happiness of Hardress Cregan of the Irish gentry and the peasant
girl Eily to whom he is secretly married. For family reasons, Cregan
is pressed to marry the heiress Anne Chute. His foster brother, Danny
Mann, learning of the secret match and misunderstanding Cregan's desire, gets Eily into a boat and leaves her unconscious in the cave that
the high tide fills. Told that Eily has killed herself, Cregan consents
to the marriage with Anne. In the meantime Danny, dying, confesses
his deed. He is overheard by Cregan's enemy Carrigan, and at the wedding Cregan is arrested for Eily's murder. Then, as the *New York Tribune* put it, (March 30, 1860) Eily herself arrives, "in a state of serious
objection to the marriage of her husband to another woman." Eily and
Cregan are joyfully rejoined, and there is an old lover for Anne to fall
back on. "These are the main features of the story," said the *Tribune*,
"about which are grouped many minor incidents of interest, which all
add to the beauty of the play, and make it one of the most intensely
interesting of melodramas."

In the actual case of 1820 on which the play is based, a man named
Scanlan, who had secretly married Eily O'Connor, of Garryowen, a sub-
urb of Limerick, tired of her, killed her, and threw her body into the
Shannon River. The horses drawing Scanlan to the gallows balked,
refusing to cross Shannon Bridge, a "manifestation of the abhorrence of
heaven at the crime." Boucicault shifted the crime so as to leave Scanlan (Cregan in the novel and the play) innocent and still in love with
Eily; and he turned the river scene into vivid theatrical action by introducing Myles' dive (Boucicault played Myles) and rescue of the unconscious Eily. Laura Keene originally played Anne Chute, wearing a
green riding habit; Frances Starr, 1905 and later, in a huge feathered
hat, with riding whip. Thus the finery of high life was contrasted with
the picturesqueness and humor of the peasant folk. "Unlike the conventional Irish play," said the *Boston Herald* (March 14, 1905), "Boucicault's appeals to every class of theatregoer, to each succeeding generation, and will do so as long as wit, humor, pathos, and dramatic interest
attract people to the theatre." The play is livened with songs, too.

On the eve of its seventieth birthday, the *Boston Herald* (June 10,
1929) called *The Colleen Bawn* "a play of perennial popularity"; the
Transcript said: "Plentiful and diversified are the incidents of the play
—comic, pathetic, sentimental, homely, what you will—as changeful as
an Irish day of sun and shower." With its spectacular water scene and
the steady drive of its varied action, *The Colleen Bawn* is deservedly one
of the most popular of all romantic melodramas.

RIP VAN WINKLE   *Dion Boucicault*

Performances of *Rip Van Winkle* are literally innumerable; even the
various versions of the play are beyond accurate count. The story first
appeared in *The Sketch Book* of Washington Irving in 1819. It is the
story everyone knows, of happy-go-lucky, luckless Rip, who, henpecked
by his wife, Gretchen, seeks refuge with his dog in the Kaatskill Mountains, and there comes upon the old crew of Hendrick Hudson playing at ninepins, sips some of their liquor, and falls asleep for twenty
years.

The first production of Rip's tale seems to have been in Cincinnati in

1826. There was another there in 1829, and one in Philadelphia. In 1830, James H. Hackett played Rip in New York, in a version "altered from a piece written and produced in London." Hackett kept on playing the part and altering the play. In 1849 his company took on a new man in the role of the innkeeper, one Jefferson (Joseph Jefferson 4th, 1829-1905). Ten years later, Joe Jefferson appeared in his own version of *Rip Van Winkle*. It failed, but Jefferson struggled along with the play for five years, when Dion Boucicault wrote a new version for him. This opened in London, September 4, 1865, and ran for 172 nights. It opened in New York September 3, 1866, and for the rest of his life Jefferson acted Rip. In Chicago, just before he retired, Jefferson, comfortably tucked into the forest floor, actually fell asleep one night onstage. The curtain rose; and all was silent, until from the gallery someone cried: "Do we have to wait for the whole twenty years?" The prompter pinched "Rip", and his waking groan this time was real. When Joe Jefferson withdrew from the stage, his son continued for some years the role of Rip.

Although Joe Jefferson and Rip Van Winkle today seem almost one figure, the actor in his time had many rivals. In the 1870's, indeed, both McKee Rankin and Robert McWade were thought by many to be superior in the role. Each performer sought new turns of phrase or bits of business. Thus, while Jefferson merely mentioned his dog Schneider, McWade had an actual dog onstage. Coming into the woods, he tied the dog to a sapling; twenty years later, the skeleton of a dog was shown high on a tree that had grown in the middle of the meantime. The waking Rip looked around, spied the skeleton, and said ruefully, "Ah, Schneider, you barked up the wrong tree that time!"

In the Boucicault version, Rip, on his return, finds his wife remarried. In the version used by Beerbohm Tree (1900) Gretchen was a more pleasant figure. It was not her shrewishness that drove Rip to drink, but his drinking that set her to complaining; she refused to marry the eager Diedrich (who wanted the land even more than the lady), and on Rip's return he found a wife with open arms.

When Cyril Maude played Rip in 1911, after his sleep Rip was so covered with leaves—his beard and the moss grown one—that he seemed truly a part of the forest floor. He is, truly, in the groundwork of the American theatre.

Rip Van Winkle has also attracted composers. In 1855, an opera on the story by the American George F. Bristow ran for a month in New York. In 1881, *Rip Van Winkle*, to music by Robert Planquette, played in Paris; in 1882 in London for 323 performances; then in New York. This version was given a modern dress in 1933, with Rip as a radio announcer, put to sleep by bootleg gin; the election returns after the Revolution are broadcast to the village. Franco Leoni's version was heard in London in 1897, with book by Edgar B. Smith; the *Illustrated London News* (September 25, 1897) protested: "Imagine a skirt-dance in the Catskill Mountains!" Although there was a children's version by Edward Manning in 1932, the musical form of *Rip Van Winkle* that has best endured is the one by Reginald De Koven (1920), which still finds almost annual revival among operatic troupes.

The Dion Boucicault version remains the most popular, partly because it was endeared to a theatre generation by the acting of Joseph

Jefferson. Boucicault managed to make Rip appealingly human. What in Irving is a mere, though interesting, legend, is made a calamity befalling a weak but not wholly unworthy man. As William Winter, in his book *Joseph Jefferson*, declared: "There is no trickery in the charm . . . Rip Van Winkle's goodness exists as an oak exists . . . Howsoever he may drift, he cannot drift away from human affection. Weakness was never punished with more sorrowful misfortune than his. Dear to us for what he is, he becomes dearer still for what he suffers and (in the acting of Jefferson) for the manner in which he suffers it." Eleanor Farjeon, in her Foreword to *Rip Van Winkle: The Autobiography of Joseph Jefferson* (1950), quoted a friend visiting America: "In this land of short memories I find two names which are remembered by everybody—George Washington and Joseph Jefferson."

When Jefferson, as Rip returning from his long slumber, was told that Rip was no more, he used to say, sadly, "So poor Rip is gone", and point to heaven; a villager pulled at his hand until it pointed down. The audience knew better; a tender affection has kept *Rip Van Winkle* among the elect.

THE SHAUGRAUN   *Dion Boucicault*

A "shaugraun" is a "merry rogue", such as Boucicault himself has been pictured; and Conn O'Kelly, the shaugraun of his favorite play, was Boucicault's favorite role. Conn is a lovable rascal, a blarney boy, "the soul of every fair, the life of every funeral, the first fiddle at all the weddings and patterns in the parish." He is also a revolutionist in the Irish uprising, who wins his love despite his politics.

The Shaugraun depicts the wild romp of Conn's, as he goes about in the ragged red coat, kit on his back, that became known all over the English and the American stage. Conn bounds in and out of cabin windows, scales prison walls, leaps over church ruins, with nimble wit and laughing careless courage. He helps the Irish gentleman, Robert, against the English officer, Molyneux, a fine fellow himself, though he must do his duty. After Conn attends the wake for his own (feigned) death, he revives to do battle with a pair of ruffians, and tricks the English soldiers into firing the two shots at night that mark the signal for their own doom.

Opening in New York, November 14, 1874, *The Shaugraun* ran for 143 performances. F. B. Chatterton tried to put it on at the Adelphi, London—British law did not then protect a play if it were first produced abroad—but the actors Mr. and Mrs. J. C. Williamson refused to perform it when they learned that Boucicault wanted to appear in it himself. He opened in London, September 4, 1875, and had a run of 119 performances.

The play provided one of Boucicault's best roles, and was frequently revived after the turn of the century. In one New York revival, the then sheriff Al Smith and state senator Jimmy Walker played the villain and the hero of the play.

The chief virtue of *The Shaugraun* lies in the character of Conn. His genial ways and irrepressible good humor make him a mixture of Rip Van Winkle and Robin Hood, a sort of Irish Tyl Eulenspiegel, a picaresque rascal with love of his country in his heart.

THE CAPTIVE   *Edouard Bourdet*

Hailed throughout Europe as a daring psychological study rather than a social satire, *La Prisonnière (The Captive)*, by Edouard Bourdet (French, 1888-1945) was the first dramatic presentation of antagonistic sexual impulsions, forming a triangle in which a man and a woman are rivals for a woman's love. It reveals the stronger force as that of the woman, although she herself does not appear in the play.

Irene de Montcel, wishing to stay in Paris to be near Monsieur and Madame d'Aiguines, asks her friend Jacques Vivien to pretend to be engaged to her, so that she will have an excuse to stay. Loving her, Jacques consents. When in jealousy he speaks to his old friend d'Aiguines, Jacques discovers that it is not the man but his wife for whom Irene is staying. Despite his friend's warning, Jacques marries Irene when she pleads with him to save her; but when they return to Paris, the spell returns. Pinning on a corsage of violets, sent by Madame d'Aiguines, Irene goes vibrantly forth to meet the woman she loves.

The sharp, clear-cut picture Bourdet gives of the magnetic power between the two women and of the havoc it makes of two marriages swept *The Captive* to success all over Europe. Within a month of its Paris premiere in May, 1926, Max Reinhardt presented it in Vienna, with Helen Thimig. The foreign correspondent of the *New York Review* (May 12, 1926) reported: "There is not a line in *La Prisonnière* that is 'smutty' and there is not a scene that is in the least salacious . . . the play grips and holds the interest from the opening scene." The talk between the two men, the *Review* continued, "is admirable in its tact, its honesty. It is one of the most powerful and moving scenes in the drama of recent years."

In London *The Captive*, banned by the censor, was produced privately in 1927 and 1934; and in French in 1929. It received both high praise and vehement abuse.

The New York production opened September 29, 1926, with Basil Rathbone and Helen Menken, and ran for 168 performances despite various efforts to stop the play. When it was haled to court as "salacious and objectionable to civic morals", producer Frohman withdrew and publisher Horace Liveright became its sponsor. After the New York raid, February 9, 1927, the cast issued the statement: "Far from feeling that we have engaged in the commission of a crime for the past six months, we feel that we have been privileged in using our talents in a play of the highest literary merit and social value." *The Captive* ran for five weeks in Cleveland. Among the cities in which it was raided and closed were Detroit and Los Angeles.

Most reviewers praised the play. Gilbert W. Gabriel reported: "Here is a thoroughly absorbing, admirable and, incidentally, respectable play . . . a compelling, always engrossing and dramatic thing. As a piece of play building, it is remarkably skillful . . . fine glamour across its griefs, wit ingrained in its sincerity." Brooks Atkinson called it "a hard, brittle chronicle, horrible in its implications, terrible to contemplate at times, but sincere and cleanly finished."

For a time after *The Captive* was played, there were many burlesque skits that travestied its story; and there was a drop in the market for violets, which in the play signify Irene's illicit love. In a more measured view, *The Captive* remains not only the first modern dramatic treatment of Lesbian love, but a probing and poignant study of a woman struggling with a passion stronger than her will.

THE HIDDEN SPRING   *Roberto Bracco*

The Neapolitan Roberto Bracco (1862-1943), who started out as the author of farces of contemporary life, made his mark with serious realistic dramas in which the psychological interest is predominant.

The spell of subconscious desire is the undercurrent of *The Hidden Spring* (1905), the most imaginative and poetic of Bracco's dramas. It pictures the influence of a neurotic, self-centered mind. Stephan Baldi, a faded poet always of more promise than fulfilment, seeks fresh inspiration in the already tarnishing glamour of the titled adventuress, the Princess Meralda Heller. Stephan blames his wife, Teresa, because of her middle-class clumsiness, with having stifled his talent. Although he lacks the courage to run off with the Princess, his wife, a submissive creature, leaps to her death.

Various realistic details, such as an ex-soap manufacturer's dunning Stephan for payment on some antiques, give natural substance to the story, the psychology of which is deeply true. There is an interesting indication of how, in life, suggestions from various sources join like links in a causal chain: a strolling beggar and his woman dance and sing; the "friend" in their song is death; and Teresa before her fatal leap remembers and repeats the lines.

Popular in Italy, *The Hidden Spring* opened in London, September 24, 1922. Its perceptive quality and emotional power set Bracco among the great playwrights of the world.

THE PRIVATE LIFE OF THE MASTER RACE   *Bertolt Brecht*

The best known plays of Bertolt Brecht (German, b. 1898) are avowedly *Lehrstücke*, propaganda plays. In most of his works, Brecht has drawn upon earlier writers, shaping their ideas to contemporary use. With Erwin Piscator, Brecht was a founder of the "epic theatre", which used the stage as an instrument of education for the masses. Piscator was the director of plays; Brecht, the poet-adapter. Their most original contribution was perhaps the mingling of realistic and expressionistic modes to picture portions of contemporary civilization. Their sort of dramatized harangue gave birth, during the American Federal Theatre years, to *The Living Newspaper* (see *Hoppla!**). Brecht developed it in *The Private Life of the Master Race*.

Written in the United States, *The Private Life of the Master Race* had its world premiere in Berkeley, California, June 7, 1945. New York saw it on June 12, with Albert and Else Basserman, and Clarence Derwent. The play, in seventeen scenes, is a documentary of events from 1933 to 1938, showing how the Nazis took over Germany. In New York performance, the scenes were cut to nine. They vary in length and in satiric power. Some are scarcely more than swift "black-outs", for example, the scene in the prison yard, with the prisoners walking silently in two opposite circles: Two bakers exchange words each time they pass: "What did they get you for? Look out!" Next round, the answer: "For not putting bran in the bread. And you?" Next round: "For putting bran in the bread"! Curtain. Three scenes are outstanding. In one, a radio announcer tries to praise his sponsor's product, working against three uncooperative guests on the air; in another, a venal judge is shown seeking an acceptable pretext to justify his decision; and in the third, an informer is ironically portrayed, with psychological overtones.

The *New York Times* (December 17, 1944) said of the published play, that "except for a few aridities suggesting the schoolroom rather than the barricades, the play is intensely dramatic." The call to the barricades, however, is the core of the work, which does not pose a problem or present a conflict. It is a call to arms. "To prevent any sentimental identification with his characters, Brecht changes them with every scene; the only constant prop is a panzer which rumbles offstage and occasionally appears, holding twelve chalk-faced soldiers. This is not for unity but for 'interruptions' calculated to jolt the average audience out of its habits." The audience must not sit back and watch; it must join the crusade. Such was the aim of epic theatre, which was most moving to those already at one with the playwright's motives. Hence *The New Masses* praised Brecht for "social analysis done with the keenest psychological perceptions, a broad historical grasp, a deep poetic vision, a subtle dramatic sense."

Among the other plays of Brecht, four call for brief mention. His *Mother*, based on Gorki's novel (1907), a picture of Russia during the rebellion of 1905, was vividly produced by Piscator in Berlin; but the English version, which opened in New York November 19, 1935, was an overstrained, hyper-emotional kindergarten for Communists.

Most successful of Brecht's plays, all through Europe, was his version of Gay's *The Beggar's Opera**, produced as *Dreigroschenoper (Three Penny Opera)*, 1928. Although Eric and Maya Bentley felt that this play "summed up a whole epoch in European culture," American opinion was highly critical.

In 1947, the Experimental Theatre in New York put aside its contemplated production of a study of Galileo, *Lamp at Midnight*, by Barrie Stavis, for another play by Brecht, *Galileo*, which Charles Laughton had translated and, opening July 30, 1947, had acted in Los Angeles. In New York (December 7, 1947) *Galileo* was revealed as an episodic piece, with a coarse, calculating scientist, fond of the fleshpots, an unscrupulous sensualist. The translation destroyed Brecht's poetry; but the picture of Galileo as a victim of economic determinism and gluttonous desires is in the original.

In *Galileo*, propaganda was incidental. It was even less important to *The Good Woman of Setzuan*, which Brecht set in China. John Gassner in his *Masters of the Drama* (1945) said that in *The Good Woman of Setzuan* Brecht, "the ablest German poet, reaches the peak of his dramatic powers." With an Oriental leisureliness and a supernatural story, the play seeks universal significance.

Peter Lorre once declared that "Brecht is the poet of our generation and to my mind its greatest writer." Despite the enthusiasm of admirers, he has done little that today seems to qualify him for such high praise. His ideas are obvious; his pace pedestrian. The one swift-moving and really dramatic of his works is *The Private Life of the Master Race*.

THE THREE DAUGHTERS OF M. DUPONT   *Eugène Brieux*

The works of Eugène Brieux (French, 1858-1932), first presented by Antoine's Théâtre Libre, were "melodramas of ideas". Driving didactically, with theatrical effectiveness but little imaginative power, poetry, or vision, they were punching propaganda for a social cause, but tended to fade with the changes they helped to bring about in the social scene.

The first important play by Brieux was *Blanchette*, 1892, an attack upon society's attitude toward young women that wish to teach. Somewhat similar in theme, but far more significant, is *The Three Daughters of M. Dupont*, in which Brieux analyzes the opportunities open to the average young woman in quest of fulfilment. Angèle, the oldest daughter, seduced in her youth, lives precariously beyond the pale, in Paris. Of her sisters, Caroline is a parching old maid, and Julie finds her husband to be a niggardly tyrant who will not even allow the expenses incident to childbirth. Julie plans a divorce; but the sordid lives of her sisters persuade her that a loveless marriage is the least intolerable of a woman's alternatives. The wanton and the unwanted bow to the wed woman.

The Three Daughters of M. Dupont, translated by St. John Hankin, was given a "private" performance by the Stage Society in London, 1905, and a public production in 1917. The *London Telegraph* (March 14, 1905) said that "rarely has there been a more utterly pessimistic play . . . It would be desolating if it were not also stupid, pathetic if it were not so wholly extravagant . . . The play was received with a good deal of applause by those earnest devotees who condone theatrical and hysterical nightmare if it comes under the guise of dramatic liberty." Twelve years later, the *Pall Mall Gazette* (June 8, 1917) called it "a magnificent acting play . . . a bright and racy genre comedy . . . There was a rattling jollity of satire right up to the verge of horror . . . With all its trenchant sincerity of motive, the play has a certain falsity of exaggerated cynicism."

In New York, translated, produced, and acted by Laurence Irving, the play was similarly criticized. The *New York Times* (April 13, 1910) echoed the London press: "There is, unfortunately, almost always an audience in this city for anything that is violent, abnormal or extreme." Charles Darnton dismissed the drama as "entirely foreign to the American public." The *New York Dramatic Mirror* was stirred, however, from its usually conservative position to remark (April 23, 1910) that "M. Brieux refrains from preaching, and is broad enough in his method to exercise a universal appeal. He handles the subject of M. Dupont and his three graces with a skill that hardly affords a parallel since Balzac."

Although the self-sustaining, self-respecting spinster is today quite common in our midst, the basic alternatives of *The Three Daughters of M. Dupont*—marriage, wage-earning industry, wage-earning profligacy— still sprout as the horns of enough dilemmas to keep it the freshest of Brieux' social problem plays.

THE RED ROBE   *Eugène Brieux*

This play has an astounding theatrical force as it moves relentlessly to picture the perversion of justice by ambition. "Had I been an English citizen," said its author, Eugène Brieux, "instead of writing a play against the abuse of justice by a judge, I might have had to illustrate the same abuse by a lawyer." In the United States, the protagonist might well be a district attorney.

The story of the play centers on a simple French peasant, Etchepars, who is accused of murder. Ambitious for the red robe of a judge, Mouzon and Vagret do their best to convict him. Vagret, regaining his integrity, withdraws; but Mouzon presses on. To discredit the testimony of Etchepars' wife, Yanetta, he discloses a scandalous episode of her early life, which her husband did not know. As a result, when Etchepars repulses her, Yanetta kills Mouzon.

When the play was presented in Paris, 1900, the star Réjane ironically suggested the title La Robe Rouge, saying that people would come to the theatre expecting excitement over a new dress. The play, however, carried its own excitement. In New York, it was performed in German at the Irving Place Theatre in 1902; and by Réjane and a French company in 1904. The latter production provoked the New York Dramatic Mirror (November 14, 1904) to say: "Justice is free, but it costs a lot to get it." The first American production in English opened in Yonkers on January 14, 1920 and was called The Letter of the Law. It came to New York on February 23, with Lionel Barrymore, Clarence Derwent, and Louis Wolheim. The report from Yonkers called the play "tiresome and full of sermons," but when it reached New York, the critics were impressed. Heywood Broun said that the fundamental complaint "holds true of American law, and probably of Patagonian law as well." Burns Mantle said that the play exposed "relentlessly the prosecution that becomes the persecution of the poor." The New York World called it "a potent example of the good use to which the dramatic stage can be put when it raises its voice against social wrong." The Telegram declared: "The play delivers its message in the terms of extraordinarily effective acting drama . . . It employs real persons, in whose fate you share, and sets them in situations of dramatic power and pathos. The dramatist who can do this is entitled to all the sociology he likes."

The Red Robe discloses the manner in which unscrupulous men in legal posts can bring ruin upon a family. It is considered by many to be Brieux' finest drama, although less notorious than his Les Avariés, 1901 (Damaged Goods), a study of the physical consequences of syphilis and of the dread and secrecy smudged across the disease, which was a succès de scandale in many countries.

Though changing times have lessened the interest of his plays, Brieux himself did not lose interest in the "social and moralizing" drama. In 1925, he offered a prize of 30,000 francs for such a play. Of the several hundred manuscripts submitted, none was found acceptable. The later social dramatists were more concerned with picturing the general collapse of standards, the loss of ideals, the disintegration of society. The dramas of Brieux remain vivid, melodramatic studies of social abuses and social evils, of which each age must find and cure its own. Brieux was chiefly concerned, however, not with the specific social evil, but with the basic human attitude that permits such an evil to grow. Of the continuing dangers to justice in the ambitious designs of its supposed guardians, The Red Robe is a stirring dramatic picture.

A BLOT IN THE 'SCUTCHEON   *Robert Browning*

The plays of a poet are frequently considered "closet drama", rather for reading than for acting; but *A Blot in the 'Scutcheon*, written by Robert Browning (English, 1812-1889) at the request of William Macready, was performed effectively. It opened in London on February 11, 1843, with Helen Faucit. A quarrel between Browning and Macready led to the withdrawal of the play, but it made a vivid impression and was revived in 1848 and several times since. Lawrence Barrett kept it in his repertoire from 1879 to 1888; Marie Wainwright and Viola Allen were in his cast. It was presented in New York in 1893, and again, by Mrs. Sarah Cowell Le Moyne in 1905.

Written in swift blank verse, Browning's drama tells the story of an eighteenth-century English family proud that their name is free from stain. Lord Tresham, however, learns that his sister, Mildred, is granting assignations to her lover. He intercepts and stabs the unresisting man, discovering too late that he has killed Lord Henry Mertoun, Mildred's betrothed. Mildred, on hearing the news, dies of a broken heart, and her brother takes poison.

What in summary may sound perfervid is in the play emotionally attuned to its period and its characters. Productions of the play have, in general, won more than respectful interest. True, the *New York Times* on June 23, 1893 declared: "Browning's tragedy has already been tried on the stage, and has been found wanting"; but the same paper made amends on May 2, 1905, when it declared that *A Blot in the 'Scutcheon* "should not be missed by anyone having at heart the real interest of the stage."

To the 1905 production with Mrs. Le Moyne, only the *New York American* took exception, calling the play "a rather commonplace story of clandestine love." The *Tribune* thought that the average playgoer might not be entertained, but that "Browning's prodigality of ideas, his depth and virility of feeling, his sincerity of passion, and his warm, rich, vivid diction may well be brought to public attention in a playhouse the doors of which open where the Philistine passes." *Theatre* magazine (May, 1905) called the drama "an intellectual treat, and an emotional experience, too, notwithstanding the poet-dramatist's undramatic manner of clogging the action with studied soliloquies and elongated dialogue."

The dramatic monologues of Browning established a new genre in poetry, the words of one person often revealing more than one life. Such poems as *My Last Duchess, Rabbi Ben Ezra, Fra Lippo Lippi, Andrea del Sarto, The Bishop Orders His Tomb at Saint Praxed's Church*, show, in various moods, in monologue form, an essentially dramatic spirit. While no work of Browning's shapes itself wholly in terms of theatrical production, the same dramatic spirit as in the monologues gives *A Blot in the 'Scutcheon* a drive and a power that with sharp clarity evoke a vanished past.

SICKNESS OF YOUTH   *Ferdinand Bruckner*

The "lost generation", which survived World War I without zest for life and without direction, is grimly caught in *Sickness of Youth*, by

Ferdinand Bruckner (Theodor Tagger, Austrian, b. 1891). Produced by Reinhardt in Berlin, 1928, the play was also a hit in Vienna; and in Paris, 1931, it ran for over 300 performances. In it Bruckner gave dramatic expression to a state of mind widely characteristic of the youth of Europe.

Two medical students, Marie and Desirée, are close friends. When Marie's lover, a poet who is bored by her materialism, leaves her, Desirée comforts her more intimately. But Desirée declares that youth is the only part of one's life that is either necessary or desirable. She urges Marie to suicide, and sets the example by taking an overdose of veronal. The weaker Marie turns wildly to the unscrupulous lecher Freder. Freder has been intimate with Desirée; he has sent a maiden into a career as a street-walker; and now the frantic Marie teases him on to murder her.

Sickness of Youth is a powerful picture of the heart-hunger of desolate souls quivering between a fever for life and a revulsion against living. In Europe between the two World Wars, the play rang widely true. As Freder remarks, "Youth is a sickness from which few recover." The Romantics knew the ailment; in many of the 'tween-war generation, it turned chronic.

Bruckner's business was conducted by his wife; his identity as Theodore Tagger was oddly revealed. After the success of *Sickness of Youth*, a producer, in rejecting a script written under his legal name, asked him, "Why don't you try to write like Bruckner?" In a suit of Reinhardt's, Bruckner was subpoenaed and Tagger appeared.

Sickness of Youth was presented in New York in 1933 and again in 1937, both times in a greatly toned down version. In the original, the play is a searing study of the neurotic, desperate youth of Europe between the two wars, clutching at the straws of life.

THE CRIMINALS   *Ferdinand Bruckner*

Although Bruckner's *Races*, 1933, has been hailed as the first anti-Nazi play, there are grim foreshadowings of the Nazi terror in his earlier play *The Criminals*, 1928. Presented by Reinhardt in Berlin, in the last year of the Weimar Republic, *The Criminals* spreads over a broad canvas a picture of the decay and corruption that were rotting toward Hitler. In panoramic view, the play presents a half-dozen life stories. At one moment, the stage represents six rooms in an apartment house, which light up successively or at once; at another, it is a hall of justice, with three cases being tried simultaneously in three courts.

The Criminals is the most vivid and most successful dramatic picture of this troubled time. It has been produced in twenty-two languages. New York, however, saw it only in the summer theatre, at Green Mansions, in 1938, and at Erwin Piscator's Dramatic Workshop in 1941, with Herbert Berghof, and Lili Darvas, who was in the Berlin production. Bruckner shows, said the *New York Sun* (December 23, 1941), "the confusion of the people, the uncertainty of the nation's thoughtful men, the slow breaking down of the ideal of abstract justice. He tells of a boy sucked into Nazism and made a murderer, of a young woman who kills a baby she cannot feed, and of a cook who strangles her lover's paramour and lays the blame on the lover himself. And he shows us these people brought to trial before bewildered judges, while the real criminals escape."

Ernestine, the cook, is an embittered woman; the amorous waiter Tunichtgut (Ne'erdowell) is hanged for her crime. Too late the young Nazi discovers he is in the wrong movement; too late the liberal, the intellectual, learns that life calls for action. "The true criminals of present-day society," said *Cue* (December 27, 1941), "are the intellectuals who sit idly by while social forces are being directed by stronger hands into channels that lead to revolution, international murder, and national suicide."

The more specifically anti-Nazi play, *Races*, was produced in Zurich, November 1933, and in Vienna, Paris, and London. The Prague production of 1934 was cancelled because the actors refused what they feared would be their last roles. The Theatre Guild presented *Races* in Philadelphia, March 17, 1934, with Mady Christians and Clarence Derwent; it was not brought to New York. A New York production at the Heckscher Theatre, 1935, revealed that the adaptation was verbose, too frequently sermonizing—though the *New York Herald-Tribune* called it a vivid "picture of a nation drawn to the breaking point, the pattern of mob hysteria sweeping away men's reason, a rant against the world's most ghastly horror." The play shows the young medical student Karlanner at first breaking with his Jewish fiancee and aiding the Nazi persecutions; then, gradually disillusioned, helping the girl to escape, and surrendering himself to the Nazi tyrants.

There is less sermon and more power, as well as wider scope, in *The Criminals*. Bruckner, said the *New York Post* (December 20, 1941), "crowds the agony and disillusionment, the economic and moral degradation, the decency, the bewilderment, and the underground intrigue of a whole nation into a single Berlin apartment house . . . Interest mounts steadily as the evening goes on." The adaptation in English omits the homosexual intimations in the play, and tones down other aspects of the empty and bitter lives; but Bruckner's *The Criminals* scorchingly flares upon the sordid intensities, the morbid apathies and the shrewd, cruel, and desperate villainies that mushroom in the fetid atmosphere of a world between two World Wars.

DANTON'S DEATH   *Georg Büchner*

The twenty-two year old Georg Büchner (German, 1813-1837), fired by the French Revolution, wrote the play *Danton's Death*, which more than any other captures the hopes and fury and disappointment of that tremendous time. "I felt myself crushed down", Büchner declared, "under the ghastly fatalism of history. I find a horrible sameness in all human nature, and in men's relationships to one inevitable power. Individuals are so much foam on a wave, greatness the sheerest accident, the strength of genius a puppet play—a child's struggle against an iron law—the greatest of us all can only recognize it; to control it is impossible. *Must* is the cursed word to which human beings are born." In such a mood, in order to finance his escape from arrest for political plotting, Büchner wrote *Danton's Death* in 1835—stealthily, on his father's surgical table, in spite of paternal prohibitions and fulminations.

The play was finished in a fortnight; but the police came before the money, and Büchner fled.

In twelve swift scenes—anticipating the technique of the expressionists—the play evokes the spirit of Revolutionary days, as Robespierre and St. Just set the crowds aflame and the more moderate Danton and the poet Desmoulins go to their death. (Danton was arrested Mar. 31, 1794, and executed April 5.) The fiery Robespierre is the essence of revolutionary zeal; Danton is the calmer advocate of bourgeois reform. One of the two must fall; and in passionate times, invariably the calmer individuals succumb to the hungry mob. *Danton's Death* fills the theatre with the fickle, lurid, terrifying cyclone of the Revolution, the surging blood-drunk mob, and sets in contrast to this scenes of individual action: Danton with his young wife; Desmoulins and Danton reflecting upon the cruelty of the times; the husband beating his wife—(onlookers side with the wife until diverted to attack a young man who uses a handkerchief and therefore must be an aristocrat); the lamenting Lucile Desmoulins who, when the tumbrils carry her beloved to the guillotine, cries "Vive le roi!" and thus invites her doom. The most striking scenes of all are those of Robespierre's inciting of the Convention, and of the defense of Desmoulins and Danton.

The play forms a prodigious spectacle, with torrential mob scenes, drunken brawling on the street, bellowing and gathering frenzy at the Convention, surging passions at the trial. "I doubt if any stage in this country has ever before witnessed anything so impressive", said R. Dana Skinner in the *Commonweal* (January 4, 1928) "so moving, or so filled with magnificent vitality, as the scene in the Convention during the trial of Danton."

The single-eyed fanatic, Robespierre, embodies the basic heartlessness of the humanitarian doctrinaire. But love and beauty persist, evoked by the two women beloved of Danton and of Desmoulins who, though not prominent in the play, give a splendid, almost romantic quality to the hard historical realism. Tempestuous passion, pathos, human integrity, and poetic beauty surge to tragic exaltation in Büchner's masterpiece.

Danton's Death was not acted for some sixty years. The People's Free Theatre presented it in Berlin in the 1890's; Munich saw it in 1913; Reinhardt directed it in Berlin in 1919. Reinhardt's production came to New York, December 20, 1927, with Vladimir Sokoloff (Robespierre), Paul Hartmann (Danton), Arnold Korff, Lili Darvas, Tilly Losch, Harald Kreutzberg, and Herman Thimig. There were forty-seven named roles on the program, and hordes of soldiers, revolutionaries, citizens screaming for blood. In the Convention and trial scenes, voices called out from all parts of the theatre to carry the audience deep into the drama's mood. "It is a landmark in European drama," said Gilbert W. Gabriel, "a play apart from the spectacle it affords. Its many swift, short scenes may hurl themselves up to a pitch of clamor, the free-handed illusion of a world gone mad . . . but the writing of each of these scenes has a weight, a terror or a beauty, of its own."

A Mercury Theatre production in 1938, staged by Orson Welles, who played St. Just, added one effective device, a backdrop of a thousand masks. These little faces, said the *New Yorker* (November 12, 1938) were "illuminated with such hellish ingenuity that, as death draws nearer for Danton and his friends, they come to look like skulls, have a macabre effect, suggesting the millions grimly watching and waiting all over France." However, the crowding masks and the constricted stage of the Welles production gave it a static quality alien to the surge and swell of Büchner's drama. "Wells reduced it," said Freedley and Reeves in their *History of the Theatre* (1941) "to a series of soliloquies delivered in the manner of arias."

A version of *Danton's Death* by Stephen Spender and Goronwy Rees, presented in England in 1939, captured, according to the *London Times*, (March 24) "much of the poetry, the tempestuous passion, and the pathos of Büchner's masterpiece." An opera was made of *Danton's Death* by Nikolai Lopatnikoff in 1933; another, by Gottfried von Einem, was played at the Salzburg Festival in 1947.

More episodic, less spun in one connected story than Romain Rolland's *Danton**, which was also presented by Reinhardt, Büchner's *Danton's Death* is not merely a forerunner of the episodic expressionist drama, but a vivid and turbulent masterpiece, picturing men who carry into the teeth of Revolution, and hold against the gnashing of mob violence, the calm and lofty assertion of human dignity and measured values.

WOZZECK   *Georg Büchner*

At his death in 1837 Georg Büchner left unfinished a succession of scenes he called *Wozzeck (Woyzeck)*. In an expressionistic pattern later followed by Georg Kaiser*, *Wozzeck* presents the story of a poor ex-soldier, a serf whom emancipation has torn from the soil, and who lives from hand to mouth. A certain rough tenderness holds him to his mistress and their child, to support whom he sells himself as a guinea pig to a medical crank. Marie seeks relief from drudgery with a drum-major, whose boasts, along with jibes of the doctor and a captain, make Wozzeck aware of her infidelity. He slits her throat and throws the knife in a pond; then, for fear that it will be recovered, goes in after it and is drowned. The play ends with the little boy riding his hobby-horse, with no grasp at all of what is happening around, even though the other children shout·to him that his mother is dead.

Wozzeck was presented in Berlin in 1928, and elsewhere in Germany; the significance of the play lies in what one sees beyond the characters. Kurt List, in the *New Leader* (May 14, 1941), declared that *Wozzeck* "more and more has come to be the keynote of modern times." This uprooted serf symbolizes our social dislocation in a senseless world. In the captain is manifest the power of the petty bureaucrat; in the drum-major, the complacent vanity of the stupid male; and in the doctor, the wanton cruelty of the so-called scientific mind, in the name of humanity and the quest of immortality growing inhumane and deadly. In the disorderly existence in which he can divine no purpose, Wozzeck stumbles around.

Wozzeck had its London premiere December 22, 1951. The *New Chronicle* called it "an astonishing work, a solitary masterpiece . . . One leaves the theatre incredibly moved."

The mood in which Wozzeck's ideas are conveyed is one of melodramatic violence: "a sketchy expressionism, the brute force, the free rein of passion . . . atmosphere of sheer terror." This mood is at once organ-

ized, conveyed, and rendered bearable by the music of Alban Berg
(Austrian, 1885-1935), who in the years before 1921 converted *Wozzeck*
into an opera. It is the first full-length opera to make extensive use
of atonality and other devices of modern music; it introduces symphonic
elements and employs ballet technique. The opera was first heard in
Berlin on December 14, 1925; in Prague, 1926; Leningrad, 1927; New
York, 1931—in New York, and at the Salzburg Festival, in 1951. Harold
Taubman, in the *New York Times* of August 26, 1951, said that "the terrible and purging impact . . . of *Wozzeck* would haunt the audience
for days to come." Expressionistic in form, slantwise in allusiveness,
Wozzeck reaches across a century as a bitter commentary on the cruelty
and confused helplessness of modern times.

RICHELIEU   *Edward Bulwer-Lytton*

Edward George Earle Lytton Bulwer-Lytton, first Baron Lytton of
Knebworth (English, 1803-1873), wrote his best novels and his only plays
(*The Lady of Lyons*, 1838; *Richelieu*, 1839; *Money*, 1840) while serving
in Parliament.

A five-act play written in blank verse, *Richelieu* is a resounding
political melodrama. It was a prime favorite of the nineteenth century
theatre, when the stage with its huge projecting "apron" favored the
rhetorical star. In *Richelieu*, William Macready found one of his most
successful roles; Edwin Booth was at his best as the wily Cardinal; and,
according to *The Season* (January 14, 1871, looking back ten years),
"he who saw Edwin Forrest play Bulwer's *Richelieu* saw the very perfection of the actor's art."

The play deals with the plot of the Count of Baradas and the Duke
of Orleans to destroy Cardinal Richelieu (1585-1642) and make Louis
XIII of France their puppet. Baradas and the King both covet Richelieu's ward, Julie, but the Cardinal gives her to the Chevalier de Mau-
prat, who thereupon shifts his allegiance to the Cardinal. After difficulties and dangers, Richelieu reveals to the King the intrigues of Baradas and Orleans, who are then banished.

The 1839 preface to *Richelieu* acknowledged that a scene in the fifth
act was drawn from *The Fifth of March* by Alfred de Vigny, but *The
Season* (date above) charged that most of the story was drawn from
A Tale of Romance, by G. P. R. James. Bulwer-Lytton has, however,
merely followed history. Macready, who had already produced Bulwer-
Lytton's *The Lady of Lyons*, objected to the interpretation of Richelieu:
"Bulwer has made the character particularly difficult by its inconsist-
ency: he has made him resort to low jest, which outrages one's notions
of the ideal of Cardinal Richelieu, with all his vanity and suppleness
and craft." Bulwer-Lytton, however, had made the Cardinal human; he
persuaded Macready to read the play to the company, which was
enthusiastic.

London saw the play with Macready and Helen Faucit, March 7,
1839, and thereafter almost yearly, down the century. Edwin Booth
played Richelieu from 1861 to 1882. On his Cincinnati opening, Booth
was too drunk to play; his manager's plea saved him from critical castigation; and the next night he scored a blazing triumph. Henry Irving
carried Richelieu along, from a run of 114 performances opening Septem-

ber 20, 1873, with revivals as late as 1904. His 1873 success prompted the burlesque *Richelieu Re-Dressed,* by Robert Reece, which opened October 27, 1873, for 110 performances.

The American premiere of *Richelieu* was in Philadelphia, the farewell performance of actor Harrington, May 13, 1839; in the same year, September 24, Edwin Forrest gave a munificent production, with costumes and sets of Paris in 1641, costing the then considerable sum of $600. Among others who have included *Richelieu* in their repertory are Lawrence Barrett, Robert Mantell, from 1904, and Walter Hampden, who acted in a three-act adaptation by Arthur Goodrich, December 25, 1929, and on to 1940. Henry Irving alternated *Richelieu, Hamlet*,* and *Macbeth** so much that many began to think all three plays were by Shakespeare.

Out of performances of *Richelieu* grew the most disastrous rivalry in theatre history. William Macready, after creating the role in London, played it in 1843 at the Park Theatre in New York. The American actor Edwin Forrest followed him in the same theatre in the same play. Most of the critics favored Macready; the rivalry was born. Two years later Forrest, visiting England, was booed and hissed by the London audience. He had his revenge in Edinburgh when, watching a performance of *Hamlet,* he himself hissed at the way Macready as Hamlet fluttered about Ophelia and did a "fancy dance" with his handkerchief in the play scene. Again in America in 1848-1849, Macready was scheduled to play Macbeth at the Astor Place Theatre. On May 7, in the surge of anti-British feeling, he was so bombarded with hisses, howls, and more solid objects that the performance could not continue. Ned Buntline, creator of Buffalo Bill, was one of the anti-British instigators of the riot. Urged by Washington Irving and others to try again, Macready raised the curtain on May 10, 1849. There was another riot; the militia interfered; and when the theatre and the street outside were cleared, there were left lying thirty-six wounded and twenty-two dead.

Richelieu, though the dialogue is in a rhetorical blank verse now out of fashion, retains its forcefulness. The *New York Telegram* (December 26, 1929) found "a lively gusto throughout the play". Two of its lines are widely known: "The pen is mightier than the sword" and "In the lexicon of youth . . . there is no such word as fail." The play affords a still striking and emotionally sustained portrait of Cardinal Richelieu and of the tempestuous times he helped to mould.

COX AND BOX   *Francis Cowley Burnand*

This light, slight, amusing musical farce continues to hold a place on the stage, often presented as a fore-piece to one of the shorter Gilbert and Sullivan operettas. It is the liveliest work that Sullivan composed before his association with Gilbert.*

Francis Cowley Burnand (English, 1836-1917) reshaped for Sullivan's music the old farce *Box and Cox,* 1847, by John Maddison Morton (1811-1891). This farce had been a hit on both sides of the Atlantic. *The Spirit of the Times* (January 8, 1848) declared: "This week a very amusing farce just arrived from London, entitled *Box and Cox,* has enlivened the patrons of the Olympic Theatre into very ecstasies. It is one of the most amusing pieces we have ever seen; and from its commencement to its termination, is a series of the most ludicrous and mirth-provoking events we have ever had the pleasure to observe."

Burnand's play, 1867, is a burlesque on the earlier farce. After a production in New York, Richard Watts (January 18, 1939) said it was "to be enjoyed strictly as a museum piece"; Robert Coleman used the same words: "something of a museum piece". But in recent days of rooming shortage, when "hot beds"—sleeping quarters used continuously, in three eight-hour shifts—came into our slums again, the situation in *Cox and Box* did not seem too remote. Cox, a hatter, works by day; Box, a printer, works by night. Bouncer, the landlord, has rented the two of them the same room. All goes well, until the time comes—the time of the play— when Cox has a day off, and stays home. When Box arrives, misunderstandings begin; these combine with the desperate efforts of the landlord to keep the two from the truth, to carry along the farce.

The farce is ingenious, though the satire is dated. It is mainly as what the London *Era* in 1875 called "Sullivan's very melodious operetta," that the lively and amusing *Cox and Box* survives.

CAIN   *Lord Byron*

It seems natural that among the most striking dramas of the great rebel poet, George Gordon Byron, Sixth Baron Byron (1788-1824), should be a picture of Cain, earliest of rebels. *Cain*, 1820, which Byron called a mystery, shows the son of Adam wondering why he must work because of another's fault, questioning himself and then Lucifer as to God's purposes and God's arrangement of the world. In a spirit of revulsion against the unthinking piety of his brother Abel, Cain strikes him down. Then, regretting his rash deed, Cain with his sister Adah and their little son Enos goes forth into exile.

The boldness of the conception of the drama—one scene depicts the gateway to the Garden of Eden, another the great flight through space toward Hell as Lucifer disputes with the Angel of the Lord—and the daring of its religious challenge, awoke strong protest against the play, which has never been performed in England. Mrs. Piozzi (Hester Thrale Piozzi, 1741-1821, friend of Samuel Johnson) declared: "The yellow fever is not half so mischievous." Defenders were as vehement. Shelley cried: *"Cain* is apocalyptic—a revelation not before communicated to man."

The production of *Cain* in New York, April 8, 1925, was its world premiere in English; it had been produced earlier at the Moscow Art Theatre in Russian. The play has much power, although the *Evening World* said that its main virtue resides "in its declamatory strength—in the florid turning of the lines." The *New York Times* found that it "achieves real dramatic grip in its last act."

Cain draws significance from the tumbling force of Byron's verse, and from his conception of the chief character. Lucifer describes several restrictions placed upon the world before the creation of man, with pre-Adamite beings more intelligent than man wiped out by fiat of the Lord. Yet while Lucifer is the conventional rebel, defiant of power that is not his, Cain is pictured as the first thinking man, the questioner—"the Thinker" much as Rodin shaped him—brooding over the basic, elemental evils of the world. Until Cain's questions are answered, the play will have a relevance and retain its searing power.

OUR BOYS   *Henry James Byron*

Our Boys, by Henry James Byron (1834-1884), was the first English
play to achieve a run of over 1,000 performances. Opening on January
16, 1875, *Our Boys* ran until April 19, 1879, when, though still popular,
it closed to make way for a sequel, *Our Girls,* having surpassed all earlier
successes with an unbroken run of 1,362 performances. Among its several
revivals, that of February 6, 1884, had 263 performances; that of September 14, 1892, 137. New York saw *Our Boys* September 18, 1875, and frequently thereafter until the early years of this century. In 1907, when a
production was given in Italian, the *New York Dramatic Mirror* (April
13), noted that *Our Boys* had been played by nearly every amateur organization in this country and in England.

The story of the play has the appeal of love triumphing over parental
opposition. It contrasts wealth in the country with city deprivation. Act I
is laid at the home of Perkyn Middlewick, a retired and wealthy cheese-
monger and butterman. Balanced against this rough but good-hearted
self-made man is Sir Geoffrey Champneys, aristocratic heir of a long line
of baronets, whose home in the charming countryside is the scene of the
second act. Talbot, the baronet's son, is in love with Mary Melrose, who
is poor. His friend Charles, son of the butterman, is in love with Violet
Melrose, who is rich, and who scorns the uncultured Perkyn. Both boys
are forbidden to marry their choices. The third act finds them in Mrs.
Patcham's London garret, earning a precarious living at literary work.
Here they are visited by the girls, and by their fathers. Their independence and their constancy win them forgiveness and love.

Our Boys has considerable, if to us somewhat obvious, humor. The
two fathers are neatly contrasted: the aristocrat, haughty and formal;
the businessman, bluff and jovial, uneducated but as wholesome as the
products of his dairies. He is, like many characters from Shakespeare on,
a bit of a Malaprop, who hurls his "ultapomatum" at his son. Both
fathers are strict, yet basically decent and desirous of serving the best
interests of their sons. *Our Boys* is a play without villains.

The play was critically well received in both London and New York.
In London, the *Illustrated Sporting and Dramatic News* (January 23,
1875) said: "The excessive humour of the dialogue overpowers all
critical consideration of the improbability of the characters and principal
incidents . . . Those who go to the theatre for real enjoyment, to have a
good laugh and to revel in witticisms poured forth without stint at every
instant, cannot possibly do better than occupy places at this theatre during the performance of *Our Boys.*" The *New York Tribune* (September
20, 1875) called the play "fresh and charming . . . for at least two-thirds
of the way genuine comedy, and it is, all the way, a delightful piece of
literary and dramatic work."

The wit seems too purely verbal today; the characters not probed as
dramatists since have learned to probe them. *Our Boys* might now do
well in a musical version; its wholesome and elemental humor made it
the first play of a thousand and one nights on the British stage.

THE WONDER-WORKING MAGICIAN   *Pedro Calderón*

After an apparently wild youth, Pedro Calderón de la Barca (Spanish,
1600-1681) became attached to the court and was commissioned to write

spectacular plays—in which the mechanic and the scenic designer out-vied the dramatist—for the theatre of Philip IV of Spain at Buen Retiro. He was knighted for his *The Three Oldest Wonders* in 1636. Although ordained a priest in 1651, at the King's wish he continued writing plays. More and more of his 120 plays, however, were *autos sacramentales*, allegories of the mystery of the Eucharist. Calderón wrote his last secular play at the age of eighty-one, and was at work upon an *auto* when he died.

Calderón wrote plays of many types—palace comedies, historical plays, symbolic dramas (such as *The Wonder-Working Magician*, 1637, of which Shelley made a free translation), plays on the theme of jealousy, *pundonor* (point of honor) plays, cloak-and-sword dramas, and the *autos*, in which he was unrivalled. In every type, he proved himself an exquisite poet, sometimes extravagantly baroque, sometimes refreshingly direct and simple, admirably skilled in dramatic technique and full of the spirit of the devout, patriotic, chivalrous, artificial society of his time.

Calderón's most powerful play, rich in character development through tense dramatic conflict, is *The Wonder-Working Magician*, in which he presents the temptations and martyrdoms of Saint Cyprian and Saint Justina, who were put to death by the Governor of Antioch in A.D. 290. The scholar Cyprian falls in love with the poor Justina, a Christian maid whom Lelius, son of the Governor, also loves. When Cyprian is rejected by Justina, the devil disguised as a magician promises him the maid in return for his soul. The piety of the maid, however, protects her against the devil's wiles, although Lelius is led to believe her wanton. A simulacrum of the maid, conjured up by the devil, turns into a skeleton beneath Cyprian's gaze. The Governor, disliking the influence he thinks Justina has upon his son, orders the Christians arrested, and the maiden slain. Cyprian confesses, and goes to martyrdom by her side.

The main mood of the play is one of human goodness struggling against the temptations to which the flesh is heir. With cascades of rhetoric, elaborate diction and stage device, with strict observance of the rules of decorum, are combined a devout spirit and an inner simplicity of faith that sustain the power of *The Wonder-Working Magician* and through it sum up its age.

THE MAYOR OF ZALAMEA   *Pedro Calderón*

El Alcalde de Zalamea (*The Mayor of Zalamea*), c. 1650, is written with a simplicity that contrasts sharply with the flowery rhetoric of Calderón's cloak-and-sword dramas and with the elaborate and majestic structure of his religious works. Like many others of his time, he freely adapted and revised plays of earlier dramatists, including some by his rival Lope de Vega*; and from a rapid improvisation of Lope's came the finished masterpiece that is *The Mayor of Zalamea*. Freest of all Calderón's plays from far-fetched symbols and high-heaped figures, *The Mayor of Zalamea* is a sober and realistic problem play. A tale of seduction lightly undertaken but dearly paid, it is pertinent today because the center of its action lies in conflict between civil and military authorities such as may recently have occurred in many parts of the world.

A proud and prosperous man of humble birth, the farmer Pedro Crespo has civil authority in a town through which the army is passing. When his daughter Isabel is ravished by an hidalgo captain, Don Alvaro,

Crespo maintains that however loyal to his country a man may be, his honor is his own. He therefore arrests, then executes, the captain. King Philip II, passing through, checks further trouble by commending the mayor's action. Thus in Spain, the heart of conservative morality and monarchic devotion, a liberal thought took root: the notion that the *pundonor* (point of honor) applies not only to nobles but to all honest men.

The vigor of *The Mayor of Zalamea*, its straightforward and courageous drive, can still be felt. It was presented in Milwaukee in 1903; in New York in German in 1907; in Chicago in 1917, with Leo Dietrichstein as the Mayor; and again in New York, for one English performance by the Readers' Theatre, January 27, 1946. Arthur Pollock then called it "a fluent, vivid, wise drama." James Fitzmaurice-Kelly, in the *Encyclopedia Britannica*, referred to the play as "one of the greatest tragedies in Spanish literature"; and the playwright Benavente* has declared that "had Calderón written no more than *The Mayor of Zalamea* and *Life Is a Dream*, he would still be accounted one of the master dramatists of the world."

The first two acts of *The Mayor of Zalamea* present a pleasing picture of life in a Spanish country town, upon which the irruption of the troops breaks harshly. In the play, with simple dignity and forcefulness, Calderón probed deeply into a moral problem entangled in a political situation of continuing concern.

R. U. R.   ·   *Karel Capek*

After his first play, a lyrical comedy entitled *The Robber*, 1920, Karel Capek (Czechoslovakian, 1890-1938) wrote the full-bodied melodrama, *R. U. R.*, which has driven sharply home the thought that man may become slave to the machine.

The play introduces Russum's Universal Robots, mechanical men manufactured wholesale for every purpose—male robots for factory, farm, and battlefield; female robots as shop clerks, typists, and maids. The robots are designed to do nothing but relieve humans of all toil, until Helena Glory, President of the Humanitarian League, persuades their creator, Dr. Gall, to "better" the condition of the robots by giving them nerves and feelings. Almost their first feeling is one of hatred for their maker, man. Rising in rebellion, they wipe out the entire human race, save the mason Alquist. With the formula for their manufacture destroyed by the disappointed Helena, Alquist tells them he can do nothing to continue their species without dissecting one of them. A robotess is chosen; but when a robot volunteers in her place, Alquist sees the love agleam in their eyes and knows he is not needed.

Opening in Prague in 1921, Ŗ. U. R. came to New York on October 9, 1922, for 184 performances, with Basil Sydney, Helen Westley, and Louis Calvert. It opened in London, March 24, 1923, for 126 performances, with Basil Rathbone and Frances Carson, and was revived in New York in 1930 and 1942. During the latter year, it was also played by marionettes. The play has been very popular in college and community theatres; there were three off-Broadway productions in 1935.

The critics were highly enthusiastic in their reception of *R. U. R.* The *Illustrated Sporting and Dramatic News* (May 26, 1923) said of the London production, "In the last act, when the audience and one feeble old man on the stage are the only humans left alive, and the stage is filled with swaggering, Prussianized robots, we feel almost nervous as to our own safety." Heywood Broun was even more moved after the New York premiere: "Against a bloody sky the audience sees the head of the Robot leader as he climbs up the balcony, and then more and more sweep into the room and exterminate the feeble garrison. Not more than ten or twelve actors clad in the uniform blue of the Robots actually enter the room, but the director has managed to create the effect that millions are on the move. The movement is quite the most terrifying one we have ever known in the theatre." Years later, when Capek was dead and Europe overrun by mechanized men, Broun said (December 27, 1938) "I remember it still as one of the most frightening experiences I have ever seen in a theatre." Alexander Woollcott called the play a "murderous social satire." The *New York Sun* (October 10, 1922) called *R. U. R.* "a supermelodrama, of action plus ideas."

When he observes the havoc wrought by the robots, the sole human survivor, Alquist, recalls that there are prayers against drought, against most natural disasters and human diseases, and wonders why there has never been a prayer against progress. (The present writer supplied one in the *Folio*, 1923.) But Capek, wiser than his mason, did not attack progress; he levelled his satire against mechanization, against the soulless growth of instruments of power; and out of a cataclysm that obliterates civilization (such as our split-atom age fears from another war) Capek saw the regeneration of the human spirit. The double prophecy of doom and resurrection gives *R. U.`R.* power and persisting appeal.

THE INSECT COMEDY   *Karel Capek*

"A bug-eye view of the human race" was presented by the Capek brothers in *The Insect Comedy*, 1921 (also translated as *The Insect Play*, *And So Ad Infinitum* and *The World We Live In*), an ingenious satire à la Gulliver, through the behavior of insects exposing the foibles of man. Karel Capek, novelist and playwright, wrote the drama with his brother, the novelist and painter, Joseph (1887-1945).

The action of the play begins with a human wanderer, a broken-down student left stranded by World War I, who falls asleep, watching an insect. As he dreams, the world of insects takes on human size and human speech. Butterflies, in trifling dalliance, fight for the favors of a poet. Beetles, rolling a monster ball of dung, hoard their pile and steal it. A cricket, fatuously proud, cricks over his hungry brood until it is devoured. Brown and yellow ants, totalitarian both, whip up their industry for war, and when the leader of the victorious yellow ants cries, "I am Ruler of the world," the indignant human tramples him down.

Throughout all this insect activity, there is a chrysalis on stage, to which something tremendous is to happen. From it is born a Mayfly, which, after some late moths promise it eternal life, flutters and falls dead. Exhausted, the human being joins the troop of death.

After a brilliant success in Europe, the play opened in New York as *The World We Live In*, with a cast of two hundred, on October 31, 1922. Adapted by Owen Davis, with verses by Louis Untermeyer, it was, according to Alan Dale, received "with crescendo interest by a fascinated audience." The *New York Times* somewhat caustically commented that "somewhere these butterflies, beetles, and ants must have been contaminated by the example of rather degenerate humans . . . a travesty conceived in the spirit of the wartime pacifist and the peacetime hater of progress." Alexander Woollcott called it "as bitter and despondent and resentful a play as this city has seen in our time . . . far and away the handsomest and most ambitious project of all Brady's adventuring in the theatre . . . a thrilling and magnificent spectacle."

The size of the cast and the complexity of the production have kept the number of revivals to a minimum, but the play was seen again in New York in 1948.

London accorded *The Insect Play* an even heartier reception than New York. An adaptation by Nigel Playfair and Clifford Bax from a translation by Paul Selver opened, May 5, 1923, with Claude Rains, John Gielgud, Marie O'Neill, and Elsa Lancaster. There were revivals in 1936 and 1938; the latter included Joyce Redman as Mrs. Cricket. James Agate in the *London Times* (June 28, 1936) quoted his own earlier praise of the play, adding that "with the possible exception of *Everyman*, the allegory in this play fits better than in any other that I know . . . But the play has a good deal more than satire. It attains in the character of Chrysalis to both beauty and pathos . . . Let not the normal playgoer be afraid of this piece, which is just as highbrow as he likes to make it, and is intensely amusing and arresting throughout."

The insect world, as seen in the play, is one of incessant struggle, savage and heartless competition. It depicts life as less a progress of living than a postponement of dying. Only here and there, among the most ephemeral of creatures, are there moments of hope and wonder, or of quickly dispelled impulses of happiness. The Capeks, nevertheless, have made the play continuously absorbing. In it we watch the pompous, cunning, and ruthless actions of the insects until we are carried along with them. Their application to human life is an intellectual exercise that comes after the emotional flow of the drama itself.

THE MAKROPOULOS SECRET   *Karel Capek*

Those who are familiar with Bernard Shaw's *Back to Methusaleh** will find quite a different consideration of longevity in Karel Capek's *The Makropoulos Secret*, 1922. Capek's aged ones do not achieve the indefinite prolongation of life that results in the "intellectual ecstasy" of Shaw's ancients. In their three-hundred-year spells of renewal, they do not even attain the wisdom and earnestness of purpose that animate Shaw's tricentenarians. *The Makropoulos Secret*, indeed, dramatizes the thought that we should be content with one life span as it is.

In Capek's play, complications in the law courts reveal that Emilia Marti, a Viennese opera singer, is really Ellena Makrops, born in the sixteenth century. Her father, a Greek alchemist at the court of Emperor Rudolph, had found a formula for longevity, which requires renewal every three centuries. His daughter has stayed young, as Ellena MacGregor, as Eugenie Montez, and now as Emilia Marti, achieving new careers with her successive regenerations. Life, to her, is a round of love affairs, with an ever-widening edge of boredom that grows to disgust and then to horror when her own son Gregor and then her great-great-grandson Janek unwittingly fall in love with her. When they dis-

cover the truth, Janek kills himself, and his sweetheart Kristina destroys
the formula. Emilia is quite content to have her centuries end.

The Makropoulos Secret, the New Yorker observed (February 6, 1926)
presents "as weird and engrossing a theme as six nightmares and twenty-seven love affairs can conjure." The London Observer (July 13,
1930) said that it "makes strangeness palpable."

The London Times, (September 13, 1931) however, regretted the
gradual lapse of years into weary boredom: "After immensities of leading up, the thing led up to turns out to be almost nothing at all . . . at
the end, the play has only allayed curiosity without satisfying the mind."
Contrasting Capek with Shaw, the Times did not allow the Czech playwright the privilege of his own purpose. In Back to Methusaleh, Shaw
shows a longer life leading to wisdom. Capek, on the other hand, inquires into what longevity can mean to us. Be content with your allotted span, he concludes: With agelessness such values as good and bad,
such feelings as faith and hope, lose their meaning; endurance becomes
a fully foreseen, drab, changeless span of boredom: Happiness requires
change and hinges upon uncertainty. The boredom in The Makropoulos
Secret, however, does not tinge the audience, whether it prefers Shaw's
ascetic optimism or Capek's view of banal years.

SHADOW AND SUBSTANCE   Paul Vincent Carroll

The problems of faith—of rigid adherence and tolerant acceptance—
are pressed to dramatic intensity in the plays of Paul Vincent Carroll
(b. 1900), Irish-born schoolmaster of Glasgow, Scotland. His Things
That Are Caesar's, 1932, written with Teresa Deevey, centered the two
attitudes in the Hardy family; with a bigoted mother and a free-thinking father, the daughter tries to work out her own happiness. The play
won the Abbey Theatre Prize.

Shadow and Substance, 1934, sets a similar opposition in the household of the Very Reverend Thomas Canon Skerritt, whose brilliant mind
and acid wit have to be attuned to the small minds of the townsfolk of
whom he is the spiritual mentor. A young and crusading schoolmaster
has written a book against intolerant rigidity, which, issued anonymously,
enrages the town. The Canon, upon learning that schoolmaster Dermot
Francis O'Flingsley is the author of the work, discharges him. A naive
serving maid, Brigid, has the sympathy of Dermot in her beliefs that
she has talked with St. Brigid, while the Canon, whom she loves equally
well, sternly bids her to dismiss the thought. When the townsfolk learn
that Dermot is the author of the book that has scandalized them, Brigid,
running to save him from their wrath, is hit by a rock and killed. Dermot and the Canon are left to ponder the excesses of virtue, as the
sacrifice of the maid breaks through the Canon's intellectual shield.

Carroll's portraits of the schoolmaster and the Canon are superb.
Especially the latter is drawn with sympathy, with understanding of his
devotion, and of the submission of his fine intellect to the simple station
where the Lord has posted him. The Canon's faith is intellectual rather
than emotional, his view of life is almost aesthetic rather than ethical.
He says: "Catholicism rests on a classical, almost abstract love of God
rather than the frothy swirl of emotionalism." Brigid, who loves him,

says: "His pride would need the tears of a hundred just men and the soul of a child to soften it." Her soul sufficed.

The beauty and power of *Shadow and Substance* were at once recognized. The play was a hit in Dublin, where it opened on January 25, 1937. In New York it opened on January 26, 1938, with Sir Cedric Hardwicke, Sara Allgood, and Julie Haydon, and ran for 274 performances, winning the Drama Critics' Circle Award as the best foreign play of the year. London saw it on May 25, 1943. It has been shown widely in the United States. On its New York opening, John Andersen declared: "No play that has come this way in many a long lost night has filled a theatre with such passionate eloquence, such probing power, and such spiritual beauty." *Stage* (February 1938) stated: "The tragedy—which leaves the Canon at last facing his icy abstractions alone, sees her happily dead with her faith unscarred—builds grandly, in the hands of a true playwright and prophet."

Shadow and Substance, reminding us that a great drama may soar without consent of sex, is built upon natural persons, earnest and honest in their different sorts. It is a drama that probes deeply into the ways by which goodness itself may engender evil and examines the opposition of dogmatic austerity to the emotional necessities of the heart.

THE WHITE STEED   *Paul Vincent Carroll*

The White Steed, 1938, more specifically presses the problem of the letter and the spirit, the strict and the tolerant, than Paul Vincent Carroll's earlier plays. Its title is taken from the old Irish legend of Ossian, son of Finn, who was borne by the lovely goddess Niam to the land of eternal youth, where he dwelled with her for three hundred years. When he returned to earth, he found no heroes—only little black-haired men. Trying to show them how the olden warriors met their tasks, Ossian slipped from his white steed, touched the earth, and crumbled into dust.

In the play, a dreaming, liberal woman returns from England, to find the Irish oppressed and ignorant, dominated by selfish, rapacious masters. She hoists a schoolmaster on the "white steed" of her zeal to bring reform. His rebellious impulses are clouded by drink, and opposed both by young Father Shaughnessy, who pins the hope for the world on laws and their strict observance and by old Canon Matt Lavelle, who is paralyzed below the waist, but tolerant and forgiving. When the priest organizes a vigilante committee the Canon asserts himself, to establish the simpler ways of kindly faith.

Presented in New York January 10, 1939, with Barry Fitzgerald and Jessica Tandy, *The White Steed* ran for 136 performances, and became the second Carroll play to win the Drama Critics' Circle award. London saw the play with Wendy Hiller.

While it is more limited in its appeal than *Shadow and Substance**, *The White Steed* again reveals Carroll's ability to penetrate his characters and portray their soul-struggles. His problems rise out of contrasted natures, both good, opposed neither in starting-point nor in goal, yet by temperament driven to methods that clash. *The White Steed* "is a play of bone and sinew" said *Variety* (January 18, 1939), "of passion and tenderness, tears and laughter. It is timely yet timeless, earthy yet exalted. It electrifies the mind and enkindles the heart."

Combining realism with beauty, the play has at times a homely humor that keeps it close to the Irish soil and a lilting poetry and spiritual surge that lift it to the Irish heavens. Carroll, said Brooks Atkinson (January 11, 1939) "straps winged words to his white steed and trails flaming phrases through the empyrean." That the world has shriveled to a waste land, from the golden days of yore, is no new notion; *The White Steed*, quite the contrary, rings with affirmation of the worth of the present-day world, of the value of simple faith and a gentle heart. It brings such assurance with beauty and dramatic power.

. A BOLD STROKE FOR A WIFE   *Mrs. Centiivre*

Mrs. (Susannah Freeman) Centlivre (English, 1167?-1723), wife of the cook to Queen Anne, wrote eighteen plays, one of which, *The Wonder! A Woman Keeps a Secret*, 1714, provided Garrick with one of his most successful roles; and two—*The Busybody*, 1709, and *A Bold Stroke for a Wife*, 1718—have characters whose names have added words to the language.

A Bold Stroke for a Wife involves a pair of lovers, Colonel Fainall and Anne Lovely. Anne's guardian is the Quaker Obadiah Prim. To win his consent, the Colonel pretends to be "the quaking preacher", Simon Pure. After all is settled, "the real Simon Pure" arrives.

This play was presented in London, February 3, 1718; and it was the first professional production in New York, at the Nassau Theatre, November 9, 1750. Although its plot is in the usual vein of Restoration comedy, the play was at first not very favorably received for, in spirit, it was already approaching the sentimental comedy of the later eighteenth century. Instead of suggestive situations and cynical lines, with wit so singly sexed that it can hardly be said to have a double-meaning, *A Bold Stroke for a Wife* relies upon more innocent complications and a dialogue in which the sparkle of erotic wit is replaced by a milder but warmer gleam of humor. Consequently, after but few revivals over a period of sixty years, *A Bold Stroke for a Wife* became quite popular in the 1780's and 1790's, when sentimental drama held the English stage.

One sign of the play's popularity was the production (February 25, 1783) of *A Bold Stroke for a Husband*, by Mrs. Hannah (Parkhouse) Cowley (1743-1809). This showed Donna Olivia acting as a termagant to drive away her persistent suitors. Her maid, Minette, impersonates Olivia to interview Don Julio, and he becomes the successful wooer of Olivia. The sentimental mood is at its height in this artificial comedy. It was played in New York, at the John Street Theatre, May 19, 1794; and by Fanny Davenport in 1872.

A Bold Stroke For a Wife looks ahead to the sentimental comedy of the later 18th century. It is not mawkish, but mellows its artificial story with the glow of natural feeling, and a rich element of Simon Pure charm.

ALL FOOLS   *George Chapman*

Next to Ben Jonson*, George Chapman (English, 1559-1634), is the most learned and most erratic of the Elizabethan dramatists. Within one play, he rises to great heights and sinks to extravagant bathos. His first play, *The Blind Beggar of Alexandria*, 1596, is faulty to excess. "Of all the English play-writers," said Charles Lamb, "Chapman perhaps approaches nearest to Shakespeare in the descriptive and didactic, in passages which are less purely dramatic . . . In himself he had an eye to see and a soul to embrace all forms . . . I have often thought that the vulgar misconception of Shakespeare, as of a wild irregular genius 'in whom great faults are compensated by great beauties', would be really true, applied to Chapman."

Chapman's present-day fame rests largely on Keats' sonnet in praise of his translation of Homer (*The Iliad*, in 14-syllable rhyming lines, 1611; *The Odyssey*, in heroic couplets, 1615). Of his plays, two comedies, and four tragedies on French themes, are powerful enough to be still rewarding.

All Fools, 1599, is Chapman's best comedy. More than any other of his plays, it follows an ingenious plot (drawn from the *Heautontimorou-menos** of Terence) to a fit climax. The play is a realistic satire; it shows the influence of Ben Jonson, both in its pervasive cynicism and in its portrayal of the characters, who are less individuals than personifications of humours.

The main movement of *All Fools* is in the intrigue centered on the vain and dictatorial knight Gostanzo, who believes that his spendthrift son, Valerio, secretly married to Gratiana, is a paragon of bachelor virtue. Gostanzo's friend, Marc Antonio, has two sons: the elder, Fortunio, is in love with Gostanzo's daughter, Bellonora; his brother, Rinaldo, is a gay young blade, who seeks "to win renown by gulling". Rinaldo tells Gostanzo that Fortunio has married Gratiana. As a result Gostanzo is led unwittingly to give sanction to the wedding of both his son and his daughter.

The comedy was played in 1599 under the title *The World Runs on Wheels*; it was presented before King James as *All Fools But the Fool*. Much of the bustle of the turbulent and colorful Elizabethan age is caught in this lively comedy.

EASTWARD HOE   *George Chapman*

As Swinburne has said of *Eastward Hoe*, "In no other play of the time do we get such a true taste of the old city life, so often turned to ridicule by playwrights of less good humour, or feel about us such a familiar air of ancient London as blows through every scene." The play was written by George Chapman in collaboration with Ben Jonson and John Marston. The title is drawn from the cries of the boatmen on the Thames.

Eastward Hoe, 1605, tells of the efforts of Sir Petronel Flash to dodge his debts and—beguiling the vain and ambitious Gertrude with tales of a nonexistent estate eastward in England—to escape with her wealth to Virginia. Caught in a storm on the Thames, he is brought back and his ruse discovered. Nevertheless, he and Gertrude seek to make a match of it.

The value of the work lies in its ripe display of characters. A. H. Bullen has said: "Of the merits of *Eastward Hoe* it would be difficult to speak too highly.   To any who are in need of a pill to purge melancholy this racy old comedy may be safely commended."

The play was popular for a century.   In 1685 Nahum Tate combined it with Jonson's *The Devil is an Ass* to make his own farce, *The Cuckold's Haven*.   In 1751 Garrick revived it as *The Prentices*.   From it Hogarth drew the idea for his prints the *Industrious* and the *Idle Prentice*.   Then the play lapsed from the stage.   There was a production at Cambridge, Massachusetts, in 1903; another at Columbia University, New York, in 1947, which showed that *Eastward Hoe* is still richly entertaining.

For a time, the play sent its authors to prison.   Accounts vary as to just what in *Eastward Hoe* displeased the new king (James I, crowned 1603) and his Scottish followers.   There are references to the now proverbial canniness and thrift of the Scot; it is said that one of the actors imitated the King's brogue.   The influx of Scots friends and followers of James was undoubtedly resented by the Londoners; in one passage (Act III, iii, lines 40-47), speaking of the advantages of Virginia, Seagull wishes the Scots would all go there: "For my part I would a hundred thousand of 'hem were there, for we are all one countrymen now, ye know; and we should find ten times more comfort of them there than we do here."   This passage is not in the later quartos, nor in the version James himself laughed at when he saw the play in 1614.   But in 1605, on complaint of the newly created knight Sir James Graham, the authors were sent to prison and were sentenced to have their ears and noses cropped.   Again, accounts vary.   Some say all three spent some time in jail.   Others say Marston, who really wrote the lines in question, escaped punishment.   Jonson, in his later conversations with Drummond of Hawthornden, declared that Chapman and Marston were arrested, and that he voluntarily associated himself with them in the jail.   At any rate, the plea of powerful patrons soon brought them forth unscathed.   At a dinner Jonson gave to celebrate their release, his mother showed the poison she had secured for her son and herself if he were disgraced by ear lopping . . . The triple collaboration made *Eastward Hoe* a genial yet searching picture of London ways and characters.

BUSSY D'AMBOIS   *George Chapman*

After *All Fools**, Chapman tried another comedy, *Monsieur d'Olive*, 1606, which opens with a fine Elizabethan ring but soon thuds into inconsequential rhetoric.   At the same time, he worked on *Bussy d'Ambois*, the first of his best four plays, tragedies drawn from French history, which use the theatre to present almost contemporary situations, as a playwright today might choose a plot from yesterday's newspaper.

Bussy d'Ambois, 1607, tells the story of Bussy, a noble but penniless Frenchman, whom the Duke of Guise and Monsieur (the brother of the king) raise in the favor of Henry III of France.   They hope to use Bussy as their tool; when they discover him to be both independent and honorable, they seek to destroy him.   Bussy and Tamyra, Countess of Montsurry, are in love.   Monsieur reveals this fact to the Count.   Tamyra, forced by torture, writes Bussy to come to her; he is intercepted, and killed.

Bussy d'Ambois is the most popular of Chapman's plays. In printed form it ran through some ten editions in the seventeenth century. Bussy was a favorite role of Nathaniel Field (1587-1663). By 1641, three stars had vied as Bussy; the play was acted fairly frequently for the next 150 years. Dryden, having enjoyed a performance, was so disappointed on reading the play that he flared against it in his dedication to *The Spanish Friar*, 1681: "I have sometimes wondered, in the reading, what has become of those glaring colours which amazed me in *Bussy d'Ambois* upon the theatre; but when I had taken up what I supposed a fallen star, I found I had been cozened with a jelly; nothing but a cold, dull mass, which glittered no longer than it was shooting; a dwarfish thought, dressed up in gigantic words, repetition in abundance, looseness of expression, and gross hyperboles . . . a hideous mingle of false poetry, and true nonsense." Dryden's indignation was in part justified, for the play contains the worst, as well as the best, of Chapman. Bussy himself is a towering figure, invincible in both love and war, succumbing only to treachery. But the drama is at times swift and violent, at times impeded by turgid and extravagant rhetoric. Yet, as William Lyon Phelps has said, "When the mighty spirit of Chapman—for he had a mighty spirit—does get the better of its environment and finds its true voice, we are swept along resistless on the rushing torrent."

Chapman drew the historical facts of the life of Bussy d'Ambois from the contemporary Latin history of J-A. de Thou. The play is unique among English dramas in that it makes a finer figure of Henry III than even the French make of him; and the Duke of Guise, hated in England as the villain of the St. Bartholomew's Day massacre, is shown in sympathetic guise. Chapman (and later Dumas, who tells the story in his *La Dame de Montsoreau*) veers from history in having the King's brother, instead of the King, betray Bussy and the Countess to Montsurry.

Bussy d'Ambois has a sequel, *The Revenge of Bussy d'Ambois*, 1610. In this tragedy Bussy's brother, Clermont d'Ambois, urged by Bussy's ghost to avenge his death, reasons and delays somewhat like Hamlet; he will take only honorable means. Forcing Montsurry to a duel, he kills him. Then, hearing that his close friend and patron, the Duke of Guise, has been assassinated, Clermont throws off the evils of the time by killing himself.

HARVEY   *Mary Chase*

Those that have had no personal experience with a pooka will meet one most amusingly in *Harvey*, and will come almost to believe that they see the invisible six foot, one and a half inch rabbit that has become the boon companion of Elwood P. Dowd. A fellow who notes that the sober persons of the world are also inclined to be dyspeptic, grouchy, mean, and generally intolerant and unendurable, Elwood prefers to be pie-eyed, good-natured, and happy. In his ebrious hours, he becomes attached to the big pooka, Harvey, who accompanies him everywhere. His deeply concerned but somewhat silly sister, Veta Louise Simmons (whose daughter intensifies her mother's quality) thinks Elwood might be better off in a sanitarium; but signals are switched and it is Veta who is confined. By the time she is released, she too is making eyes at Harvey. *Harvey*, written by Mary Chase (American, b. 1907), was at first called *The White Rabbit*; then it was decided to call the white rabbit Harvey. Boston liked the play when it opened there, October 17, 1944. The *Post* called it "a mad, sweet, and soundly sane comedy of a mild, sweet screwball who was kind, gentle, polite and comical." *Harvey* came to New York November 1, 1944, took the Pulitzer Prize in its six foot, one and a half inch stride, and went on for 1,775 performances. Elwood was played by Frank Fay (then by James Stewart, Joe E. Brown, James Dunn, Jack Buchanan, the play's producer Brock Pemberton, and Bert Wheeler). Elwood's sister Veta was, for the most part, played by the superbly competent Josephine Hull. Harvey remained blandly invisible, but, as Robert Coleman said (June 7, 1948), "continues to give a marvelous performance. That is probably because the world's most famous Pooka becomes a creation of every member of the audience."

The press bubbled over with praise of *Harvey*. Robert Garland, for instance, called it "stage sorcery at its whimsical best, with gaiety, gusto, and guts." Even George Jean Nathan announced that "The Nathan Fife and Drum Corps parades today in honor of Mary Chase's *Harvey* . . . an evening of intelligent laughter."

There is good fun in the play from the efforts of Elwood's associates, at first to convince him that Harvey does not exist, then, gradually, to get a glimpse of the creature. There are amusing caricatures of psychiatrists and more usual citizens. There is, basically, the pleasure many folks derive from the spectacle of someone who, though possessed of the failings to which mankind is prone, is fundamentally good and ultimately triumphant. *Harvey* is a modern transmogrification of *Rip Van Winkle**. But one should not take the play as a prescription.

THE SEA-GULL *Anton P. Chekhov*

Anton P. Chekhov's grandfather was a Russian serf who saved enough to buy his family's freedom. Anton's father struggled unsuccessfully to make a living; Anton (1860-1904), while studying medicine, helped support the family by writing short stories for humorous periodicals. Later, he turned to the writing of brief dramatic sketches.

In all his work, Chekhov manifests deep sympathy for the peasant and the poor, combined with keen observation of the various levels of society into which his work as a physician gave him intimate entry. "As a doctor," he said, "I have tried to diagnose the illnesses of the soul." As for his writings, he observed, "I have no doubt that the study of the medical sciences has had an important influence on my literary work: they have considerably widened the range of my observation, and enriched me with knowledge, the true value of which to me, as a writer, can be understood only by one that is himself a doctor . . . I do not belong to those fiction writers that take a negative attitude toward science; nor would I belong to the order of those that arrive at everything by their own wits."

When *The Sea Gull* opened on October 17, 1896, at the Alexandrinski Imperial Theatre in St. Petersburg, the audience, familiar with the comic skits Chekhov had written previously, laughed at the wrong moments. On December 17, 1898, the two-months-old Moscow Art Theatre presented *The Sea Gull*, and the Moscow Art and Chekhov soared to fame together. In the cast were Stanislavski (Trigorin), Meyerhold (Treplev, the young poet), Olga Knipper, whom Chekhov later married (Irina), and Roxanova (Nina). So important was the production in the history of the new group, that the emblem of the Moscow Art Theatre has, ever since, been a sea gull.

In the play, the sea-gull is a symbol of the restless young Nina, who turns from the devoted love of the young dreamer and poet, Konstantin Treplev, to run off with the older writer Trigorin. After two years, the bored Trigorin returns to his earlier mistress, the fading actress Irina, Treplev's mother. Treplev, as an artist, has meanwhile abandoned the quest of new forms, in order to set down, direct, the outpourings of his soul. These outpourings, he would again dedicate to Nina; but she joins a traveling theatrical company, and Treplev kills himself.

Over this story hangs a fog of frustration, a sense of lives frittered away. The actress Irina lives on the glamorized memory of a second-rate past. Trigorin is drawn to Nina because she worships in him the things he'd have liked to be, but is not, the true success he has been too smug a drifter to achieve. Each of the persons in the play is a study in wasted potentiality. Such a tone-quality is best shadowed forth in moments of silence, and as Kenneth Tynan remarked in *He That Plays the King* (1950), Chekhov applied in the drama his observation that the normal condition of man is not "one of endlessly reshuffled conversation, but dead quiet . . . By exploiting this mood of stage silence, Chekhov immeasurably magnified the importance of speech. For him action is the interval between pauses; for other playwrights pauses are the intervals between actions. All the big battles in Chekhov are fought in the silences between the lines." It is in silence that intimacies ripen, that confidences—and decisions—prepare.

The Sea Gull has been given superb productions in English as well as in Russian. The best in London—James Agate called it "endlessly beautiful"—opened May 20, 1936, with Edith Evans as Irina, Peggy Ashcroft as Nina, John Gielgud as Trigorin, Stephen Haggard as Treplev, and Leon Quartermaine. The *London Times* (May 21, 1936) declared: "*The Sea Gull* is among the supreme masterpieces in the theatre, having, particularly in the first and second acts, a fluidity and ease that by their perfection make the heart turn over. To these qualities are added, as the play advances, a terrible insight into human weakness that has created the scene of Nina's clinging to her unwilling lover, and the superb pity that enabled Chekhov to reach, without strain, the tragic climax of the last act." It opened again in London November 16, 1949.

New York has seen four outstanding presentations of the play: the Washington Square Players (May 22, 1916), with Helen Westley (Irina), Mary Morris (Nina), and Roland Young (Trigorin); a Bulgakov production (April 8, 1929) with Dorothy Sands, Barbara Bulgakova, and Walter Abel; the Civic Repertory (September 16, 1929) with Merle Maddern, Josephine Hutchinson, Jacob Ben-Ami, and Eva Le Gallienne; and the Theatre Guild, opening March 28, 1938, with Lynn Fontanne, Uta Hagen, Alfred Lunt, Richard Whorf, and Margaret Webster. Equity Library revived the play, April 3, 1945.

Brooks Atkinson said of *The Sea Gull* (April 9, 1929): "It is written in words of sheer light; it illuminates everything it touches." On September 17, 1929, he called the Constance Garnett translation "a strange, sombre, infinitely sympathetic sweep of truth." The Lunts used a version by Stark Young which brought the play nearer to the directness and simplicity of diction of the original. On March 29, 1938, Atkinson spoke of "lines which echo mortality . . . pure expression, limpid and translucent . . . the tragedy of indifference."

Chekhov's deep sympathy wells in *The Sea Gull*, but it does not cloud his comprehension of heartbreak and futility. He can mix farce with tragedy, and, out of laughter at our follies, distill tears for our fate. Somehow, from the very mire of despair, his clear vision and his compassion rise to a gathering hope. The melancholy of *The Sea Gull*, though not heroic, does not fling but somehow wafts a challenge. Out of the picture of depression, an exaltation wells.

UNCLE VANYA   *Anton P. Chekhov*

Chekhov's play *Ivanov*, 1887, spoiled by the censor and the actors, was not given proper performance until the Moscow Art Theatre produced it in October 1904, after Chekhov had died. His play, *The Wood Demon*, 1888, closed after six performances; it pictures a poet dreaming over the growth of the forest and the future flourishing of the land. In the mood of the first of these plays, and with ideas of the second, Chekhov in 1897 wrote his second great drama, *Uncle Vanya*.

The play depicts the lives of a group on the estate of a retired professor, Alexander Serebryakov, a pompous fellow who has returned, with his young second wife, Yelena, to write his masterpiece. His daughter by his first wife (Sonya), his first wife's mother, and her brother (Uncle Vanya) grow increasingly unable to endure the professor's assumption of superiority. Finally Uncle Vanya takes two shots at the professor, misses, and life resumes its weary way around the seasons.

Played in the smaller cities during 1898, *Uncle Vanya* was offered to the Imperial Maly Theatre in Moscow. When the management demanded revision, Chekhov gave the play to the Moscow Art Theatre, where it opened October 26, 1899, with Stanislavski as the cynical looker-on Dr. Astrov. In 1924 the Moscow Art Theatre played *Uncle Vanya* during its New York season. It was produced in New York in English in 1927; also in 1929 with Morris Carnovsky; in 1930 with Lillian Gish, Walter Connolly, Osgood Perkins, Joanna Roos, Eugene Powers, Kate Mayhew, and Eduardo Ciannelli; and in May, 1946, by the old Vic Company, with Ralph Richardson, Lawrence Olivier, Mary Leighton and Joyce Redman.

Speaking of *Uncle Vanya*, Chekhov said: "The whole meaning and drama of man lies in internal and not external phenomena." To capture such meaning demands performance. As Granville Barker has observed, the printed play is like an opera libretto; the acting supplies the music, creates the mood. Prince Mirsky pictured the play as a symphony, in "the orchestration of parts . . . the resultant mood is achieved by the complex interaction of human voices."

Uncle Vanya has been called "a gloomy essay in stagnation"; it is rather a picture of well-meaning muddlers imposed upon by mediocre men with a sense of self-importance. "An extremely unhappy affair," said the *London Times*, (December 19, 1935), after a broadcast of the play, "and Vanya himself writes its epitaph in his superb answer to the comment that the day is fine and not too warm. 'A fine day,' says Uncle Vanya, 'to hang oneself.' Had Uncle Vanya attempted to hang himself he would almost certainly have failed, for everybody in this play is doomed to fail in the simplest tasks they undertake. Doomed is the word, for what could so easily bear an uncomfortable resemblance to burlesque is turned by Chekhov's genius into a truly tragic story of people thwarted and broken by their sensitiveness and their perception of their own thwarted potentialities." Even the decent persons are dull, yet Chekhov spreads over their dullness the quiet glow of genius. James Agate saw the play as "an embroidery upon the theme of apprenticeship to sorrow."

Some knowledge of the Russian temperament is requisite to a full understanding of the play. As the London Times (February 6, 1937) said, "The English tendency is to treat the attempt [to shoot the Professor] and the wild quarrel that precedes it as extravagant farce, for the plain reason that only in farces do Englishmen so wildly express their feelings as these Russians do in this scene." It was probably a failure to take this difference of temperament into account that led the New Yorker (May 25, 1946) to say that Uncle Vanya seems at times "a deliberate and wicked parody of all Russian drama."

No other of Chekhov's four great plays has won such divided opinions as Uncle Vanya. The New York Times (April 16, 1930) called it "the least interesting of Chekhov's major dramas"; on the same day the New York World declared it "the finest of Chekhov's plays; Chekhov's plays, at least four of them, are the finest plays of this century; and Jed Harris' production of Uncle Vanya is the best Chekhov that America has seen in a language it can understand." This judgment was affirmed by James Agate in At Half Past Eight (1923), where he called the play "quite perfect. I shall never know exactly 'what it means,' but then I do not know that I hunger for that knowledge. It is, and that suffices."

Tuberculosis kept Chekhov from seeing Uncle Vanya in Moscow; and in May, 1900, the Moscow Art Theatre went to Chekhov's home in Yalta to enact the play for him. On that visit, Gorki * saw the play, and was drawn to write for the theatre.

The dramas of Chekhov and Gorki best suit the "Stanislavski system," the quest of which is a "psychological realism" that bids the actor seek "self-justification" for his every action and prescribes "improvisation" in which the actor pretends to be the character in many situations not in the play, so as to grow more fully into the personality. For a play such as Uncle Vanya shows the everyday situations of ordinary folks; the initial genius of the author demands the rounded cooperation of the actor and of the theatre for full realization of the emotional impact and the mood. In Uncle Vanya the characters look forward to a time when, lengthily, they may rest; yet Chekhov suggests what the English poet Milton stated: They also serve who only stand and wait. Uncle Vanya is the drama of man's lifelong waiting.

THE THREE SISTERS   *Anton P. Chekhov*

Perhaps the pressures created by Chekhov's own confinement in the country gave impetus to his depiction of the boredom and frustration of small town life. In The Three Sisters, 1900, the reiterant desire to go to Moscow, to Moscow, is coupled with a greater faith in the future than in the earlier plays; at least it gives the feeling that this life, not alone the life hereafter, bears some hope.

The three sisters of the play want to break away from their petty provincial lives to join in the gaiety and activity of the great city. The eldest, Olga Prozorov, is an old maid school-teacher who hates her work and whose life outside the school is barren. Masha is married to a commonplace man; she has a brief affair with Battery Commander Vershinin. Irina, the youngest, works in a telegraph office; she is engaged, but her fiancé is killed in a duel, leaving her to lapse into drudgery. Their brother Andrey, of whose help they have high hopes, secretly mortgages their property and marries a country girl, Natasha. "Coming coyly into the Prozorov family," said Lewis Nichols (December 22, 1942) "she eventually is a vixen and a harridan, driving them off and at the end in violent control of their lives." With their hopes of escape gone, the three sisters find purpose only in work, until—some time—life's deeper purpose will be revealed.

The Three Sisters opened January 31, 1901 at the Moscow Art Theatre with Olga Knipper, (who in May, 1901, married Chekhov) as Masha. It was an instant success, and has since been the most frequently performed of Chekhov's plays. The Moscow Art Theatre production was given in New York, 1923, with five members of the original cast. The Civic Repertory Theatre, with Eva Le Gallienne, Beatrice Terry, and Rose Hobart, presented the play in 1926 and for six years thereafter. The American Laboratory Theatre produced it in 1929 and 1930. London saw it at the Old Vic in 1935; in 1938 with John Gielgud, Peggy Ashcroft, Michael Redgrave, and Leon Quatermaine, and in 1951, with Ralph Richardson, Diana Churchill, Celia Johnson, Margaret Leighton, and Renée Asherson. It has been seen all over the United States, and is constantly revived. Of the first performance in English, Gilbert W. Gabriel said (October 27, 1926): "Out of the nineteenth century no wiser nor more sensitive drama was anywhere born."

The best American production of The Three Sisters opened December 21, 1942, with Katharine Cornell (Masha), Judith Anderson (Olga), Gertrude Musgrove (Irina), Ruth Gordon (Natasha), Dennis King (Vershinin), and Edmund Gwenn (the philosophical doctor). Lewis Kronenberger stated: "One of the finest plays in the modern theatre was received last night with one of the most notable casts in living memory." Its director, Guthrie McClintic, was wise in not letting his wife (Katharine Cornell) see the script until she had heard it read aloud. Judith Anderson, upon reading the play, said that it didn't amount to much, and the sisters were obviously crazy, but she'd go along with the others; but, listening to a scene in rehearsal, she was moved to tears. The greatness of the play is fully illuminated by a great production. Robert Coleman said (December 22, 1942): "Like a big, sluggish river, it is not very exciting of itself to watch. But impelled by exciting acting, it can become a fearsome, potent force to see."

After the Russian Revolution, The Three Sisters was acclaimed as a herald of that storm. In the play Irina's fiancé, the Baron, who has never worked, exclaims: "The time is at hand, an avalanche is moving down upon us, a mighty clearing storm which is coming, is already near and will soon blow the laziness, the indifference, the distaste for work, the rotten boredom, out of our society. I shall work, and in another twenty-five or thirty years every one will have to work. Every one!" Imagine how Soviet audiences cheer those words till the rafters ring!

Moving quietly, with rich comic moments none the less steeped in pathos, where tragedy lapses into a sense of futile drift, and hope digs its spurs into cloud-flanks of despair, *The Three Sisters* at once films our eyes with tears and brightens them with vision. Through the Prozorov family we share the frustrations and the enduring courage of the world.

THE CHERRY ORCHARD   *Anton P. Chekhov*

Developed more quietly than his other plays, as Chekhov smilingly pointed out, his masterpiece, *The Cherry Orchard*, 1903, has "not a shot in it" as it depicts futile, wasteful aristocracy incapable of managing affairs, allowing control to pass into more competent hands. "All Russia is our orchard," cries the student in the play, giving symbolic meaning to its title. When the aristocratic Madame Ranevsky, together with her fussy brother whose plans evaporate into words and her amiable but ineffectual daughters, must leave their estate, a practical middle-class merchant, whose grandfather (like Chekhov's own) had been a serf, buys the cherry orchard. He plans to have the trees cut down in order to make way for surburban homes. With the house locked and the old servant, unnoticed, left behind to die, "Life," as the servant says, "has slipped by, as though I hadn't lived." The final curtain falls as strokes of the axe are heard in the orchard. A new life, a new world, is to begin on the morrow.

Chekhov felt the throbbing of an enwombed new day. While writing *The Cherry Orchard,* he said that the new play would be "something entirely different, something cheerful and strong. We have outlived the gray dawdle." Scarcely a year passed before the abortive revolution of 1905, and twelve years later came the complete overturning of Russian life.

The Cherry Orchard opened at the Moscow Art Theatre on Chekhov's birthday, January 17, 1904. It was forbidden by the censor in 1906. After 1917, however, it became, along with Gorki's *The Lower Depths* *, the most popular play in Soviet Russia. A gala performance was given by the Moscow Art Theatre on January 17, 1944, at which time Eva Le Gallienne and Joseph Schildkraut were performing the play in New York. Miss Le Gallienne had first played it in 1928, with Alla Nazimova; it was also played in New York in Yiddish during that year. The Moscow Art Company performed it in the United States in 1923-24, to a total of 244 performances, the Chekhov record in the United States.

Ward Morehouse was apparently not impressed by the Le Gallienne production. He called *The Cherry Orchard* (January 26, 1944) "a play of inaction . . . crowded with pauses, sighs, chuckles, and irrelevancies. There is incessant prattling by minor characters." Robert Garland felt the deeper impact of the play: "It is, fundamentally, one of the most skilfully contrived and most heart-breaking comedies in the modern theatre."

Gorki has said that Chekhov portrays "the tragedy of life's trivialities." Beyond such tragedy, however, there is in the play the ruthless inevitability of the coarse, but competent new order, which wipes away the refinements of the order that has fallen into decay. Lopahin, the practical neighbor of *The Cherry Orchard,* is indeed the boor the aristocrats find him to be, but he is no treacherous villain. At first, he tries to help the aristocrats to save themselves. It is not until their heedless impracticality and fluttering incompetence make disaster imminent, that he steps in to direct events and to steer their benefits in his own complacent direction. Perhaps Chekhov intended to show in that complacence the first signs of the new order's own decay. The Soviet audience may not like such an interpretation, but there are touches in *The Cherry Orchard* of continuing prophecy. "The old order changeth, yielding place to new"; and the sadness, the inevitability, the hopefuness, and the consequent disappointments of the flux of time have no more poignant dramatic expression than in *The Cherry Orchard*.

The play was produced in Los Angeles, June 6, 1950, with Eugenie Leontovich and Charles Laughton. On March 29, 1950, an adaptation by Joshua Logan, which transposed the Russia of *The Cherry Orchard* to the United States of *The Wisteria Trees* on a Southern plantation about 1890, opened in New York with Helen Hayes. In spite of Logan's serious efforts as both adapter and director, most of the changes he made either melodramatize or romanticize the starker work of Chekhov so that they lessen the irony and weaken the calm, implacable movement that give power to *The Cherry Orchard*.

MAGIC   *G. K. Chesterton*

Although Gilbert Keith Chesterton (English, 1874-1936) did not become a Catholic until 1922, his interest in religious forces and problems was earlier made manifest in such essays as *The Defendant*, 1901, and *Heretics*, 1905. His one play, *Magic*, which opened in London November 7, 1913, is hinged upon supernatural forces.

Magic is an oddly delightful play. Patricia, niece of a duke, encounters and is attracted to a stranger in the Duke's garden. She is disappointed to learn that he is the conjurer hired for their entertainment. But after the conjurer, who believes in the supernatural and cannot explain his "tricks", demonstrates his talents and his faith before her agnostic young brother, an unsure clergyman, and the Duke, she is ready to go away with him. The conjurer, however, tries to dissuade her. He tells her of his mother's hardships, after she had married a wandering fiddler. "She might have worn pearls," he points out, "by consenting to be a rational person." Patricia retorts "She might have grown pearls by consenting to be an oyster." And she holds her man.

The play ran for 168 performances in London, 1913-14; it was revived there in 1923, 1925, and 1942. New York saw the play in February, 1917, in 1929, and in 1942 with Julie Haydon and Eddie Dowling.

In London, William Archer, writing in the *Star*, November 8, 1913, said that the play "must be seen by everybody." The *Graphic* found it "a magical masterpiece in thought and feeling. It is elusive and wonderfully suggestive. It is touched at times with the eloquence of high poetry, and so, of course, it is tremendously emotional." The *Illustrated London News* (November 15, 1913) thought the play showed Chesterton at his best: "His buoyant personality makes itself felt, his wit gives delight, his freakishness and his mysticism alike obtain expression . . . Quaint, bewildering, argumentative, grotesque as is his story of the way in which a belief in fairy lore permeated a fussy duke's household, it is told in something of a dramatic fashion; it is developed through action and clash of character; it does really present a conflict of wills and standpoints, and this culminates in a climax immensely exciting and bordering on the horrible."

New York received the play favorably, but more calmly. Heywood Broun, himself not yet a Catholic, called it (February 13, 1917) "the eloquent expression of a revolt against the materialistic conception of the universe," adding that Chesterton "writes with such charm as to make even asceticism seem attractive." Twenty-five years later, John Mason Brown (September 30, 1942) called *Magic* "a remarkable tour-de-force."

Quietly, but with a gentle growth to deep power, *Magic* is a dramatic suggestion that science is less than the sum of human understanding, that the course of love, of life itself, remains a divine mystery.

THE MASK AND THE FACE   *Luigi Chiarelli*

Among the many plays of Luigi Chiarelli (Italian, b. 1885) *The Mask and the Face* has justly achieved international fame. It inaugurated the "grotesque" school of drama in which the spiritual upheaval of the first World War found bitter or wry expression.

The Mask and the Face is an attack upon those social fetishes which are intended to simplify and sweeten life but actually complicate and distort its movement. The strict and rigidly formal Count Paolo Grazia, finding his wife Savina unfaithful, has not the heart to do "the proper thing" and slay her. Instead, he sends her secretly abroad and "confesses" to having drowned her. At the trial, his lawyer produces a man who testifies to Savina's profligacy; and the jury absolves Paolo. The women of the city then pester him with such admiring and amorous attention that he resolves to call Savina back in order to rid himself of them. Meanwhile a body found in a lake is erroneously identified as Savina's. Paolo must attend the funeral, during which Savina arrives. Honored as a murderer, Paolo is now in danger of being arrested as a fraud. As the *London Times* (April 13, 1934) observed: "Life is a burden to him until she returns. After that it is a nightmare—but, fortunately, exposure reduces him to laughter, a relief he has never known before; and he who has once laughed, the dramatist seems to say, is safe for eternity." Loving and laughing, Paolo and Savina slip away during the funeral, suggesting, as did Barrie at the end of *What Every Woman Knows**, that while there is laughter there is hope.

The "grotesque" element in *The Mask and The Face* is not obtrusive. It takes shape in the novel action of the avenging husband and in some of the sharply satiric situations. At the funeral, for example, Chiarelli builds drama on the irony of Paolo's real feelings and the mask of sorrow he must assume; and in a scene where Savina faces the man who has denounced her at the trial, further irony rises through our learning that she really had never been unfaithful to her husband. Through such moments the play grows, as Domenico Vittorini declared in *A History of Modern Drama* (1947), into "an intriguing, strong, and impressive drama." The last act, especially, is a gem of comic invention.

Chiarelli wrote some half-dozen routine plays before *The Mask and the Face* and several afterwards in which the "grotesque" technique is more apparent. The best of the latter is *The Ladder of Silk*, 1917, a satire of political ambition, in which the aims of the earnest, honest Roberto are contrasted with the ambitions of the vain, shallow, but shining dancer Désiré, who rises to the rank of minister. Désiré makes a fluent address, grandiloquent of liberty and justice; the crowd applauds, and out of ingrained habit Désiré goes into his dance.

The Mask and the Face opened in Rome, May 31, 1916. London saw it in a version by Chester B. Fernald on February 5, 1924; again May 27, 1924, with Leslie Banks as the lawyer, for 232 performances. Fernald changed most of the men's names: Count Paolo became Count Mario. He also quickened the action at the end of the play: Savina hears her own funeral services; Mario is not allowed to confess, his friends saying to do so would ruin his career; Savina appears and dumbfounds the women who have been making eyes at Mario; the funeral procession still waits as the curtain falls. This ending scants the transformation of the husband, but it snaps along the action. The London Sunday Pictorial called Fernald's version "one of the most nearly perfect comedies of our times." A closer adaptation, by Somerset Maugham, was also presented in London, in 1934 and 1946. New York saw the play September 10, 1924, with William Faversham; again, in the Maugham version, May 8, 1933, with Judith Anderson and Humphrey Bogart.

The play was most favorably reviewed. The Boston Transcript (November 11, 1925) spoke of its "nimble and witty handling of a brilliantly original plot" whose characters are "sparingly but unmistakably individualized in the give and take of drawing-room conversation." The Stage (June, 1933) said that Chiarelli seems able to "grab a word and give it the precise emphasis that will carry it through the house like a shot of electricity."

Despite the favorable reviews, The Mask and the Face was not a success with the American public. "It springs", according to the New York Herald Tribune (May 7, 1933) "from an intellectual milieu already rather overripe." Which is one way of saying that Europe takes the problems of marital fidelity more seriously than the United States: To the sophisticate American playgoer, Paolo seems to be making a mountain out of a Venus-mound. The Mask and the Face, nevertheless, is a striking and dramatic satire on convention and reality. With considerable incidental comedy, it moves warm characters through intense concerns.

MIRACLE AT VERDUN   Hans Chlumberg

In Verdun cemetery, after World War I, the French and the Germans lay huddledy-muddledy in one mass grave. Before the astonished eyes of the caretaker, a veteran French sergeant, and a German tourist who had fought at Verdun, the dead begin to rise. Taking their crosses upon their shoulders, the French and the German dead exchange salutes and stagger off on their homeward march. Word of their resurrection sweeps ahead of them: to the French Minister, abed with his mistress; to the German, with his Frau; and to the English, with his pipe. But however lyrically the dead had been mourned, they are not now wanted. The Ministers call a conference to consider the problems brought by the reawakened dead: widows have remarried; other men have replaced the dead in factory and on farm. Ordered back, the dead, with scorn for the postwar world they have glimpsed, return—futile sacrifice—to their common grave. Only the two survivors, the French caretaker and the German visitor, remain.

This is the story of *Miracle at Verdun,* written by Hans Chlumberg (Austrian, 1897-1930). Told on a stage dark save for a great luminous cross, with seventy in the cast, and with motion pictures of the war to carry the mood, *Miracle at Verdun* made a great impact upon its audiences. Leipsig saw it in October, 1930; New York, with Claude Rains, March 16, 1931; London in 1932 and 1934. The *London Times* (September 21, 1932) said the play was "armed with dignity and sometimes even with splendour." It praised particularly (October 26, 1932) "the scene in which the risen dead, lying amid the waving corn, remember their lives, their meditations ranging as lightly and as stirringly as the wind across the corn."

By the intrusion of specific problems, such as the unemployment that would be created by these millions come back to life, the playwright asks us to accept the miracle literally—which of course we cannot do—and thus weakens its power as a symbol. Nevertheless, the play was profoundly touching. It is the best symbolic drama of war's human cost and wan futility to come out of World War I.

KIND LADY   *Edward Chodorov*

One of the most thrilling psychological melodramas is that of the "kind lady," kidnapped in her own home, which Edward Chodorov (American, b. 1911) wrought from the story *The Silver Mask* by Hugh Walpole. Tried out in 1934 at Southampton, Long Island, and in the summer theatre with Effie Shannon, *Kind Lady* came to the Booth Theatre in New York on April 23, 1935, with Grace George and Henry Daniell, for 102 performances. The play continued on the road until it returned to New York, again with Grace George, in 1940. It still finds frequent revival about the land.

In a prologue, the door of Mary Herries' house is opened to a banker. The play is the story he hears, and the epilogue shows what he does about it. In the play Mary, a kindly lady, who lives, in lonely old-maidenhood, befriends a street beggar on Christmas Eve. The beggar's wife appears and falls ill, and the doctor forbids her to leave the house. The intruders impose upon the lady; when she makes a desperate effort to expel them, they circle and close around her in silence. She then recognizes—as does the audience—that she is prisoner in her own house. This heart-catching discovery brings down the curtain of Act One. The invading family begin to sell the valuable paintings in the house, and seek to break the lady's will power, in order to gain control of her wealth. They announce to her few friends that she has gone on a long trip; they permit her to have contacts only with one or two outsiders, whom they warn to expect a crazy story. The outsiders consider her insane; indeed, her kidnappers impress upon her that she is insane. When a representative comes from the bank, the lady finds herself alone with him. Will he too think she is insane? The audience—and the kidnappers—wait to learn. They learn that he gives credence to her story and effects her release.

The situation is ingenious and excellently developed. "We thought we'd better bring Aggie with us," says the beggar's wife, introducing an inquisitive and kleptomaniac child, who is one of three characters that speak scarcely a word, but who, by their sinister and silent actions, add to the foreboding terror of the play. Few figures in melodrama have been subjected to such mental torture as the "kind lady." Moving gracefully into her riper years, half-trusting, half-fearful of life, generous, yet ashamed of her impulses—manifestly naive, seemingly weak—when the criminals reveal their purpose, she staunchly holds the fortress of her soul.

After the New York premiere, Arthur Pollock (April 24, 1935) reported that "the things that happen thrill to the last degree." John Anderson was afraid that the play would "drive sweet old ladies to going around the town on Christmas Eve kicking handsome young beggars in the face, and jerking the whiskers off the sidewalk Santa Clauses."

Brooks Atkinson (September 4) found the play, in the 1940 revival, "just as tingling now as it was in 1935, when it first began to tighten nerves in this vicinity, and Miss George is playing it with greater sensitivity and skill." Combining a natural sympathy for virtue in distress with a plausible situation, *Kind Lady* is a quietly terrifying play, one of the stage's best psychological melodramas.

THE TIDINGS BROUGHT TO MARY *Paul Claudel*

This tender and touching drama—its original title was *L'Annonce faite à Marie*—by Paul Claudel (French, b. 1868), is a breath of quiet beauty in a straining world. A modern mystery, a nativity play, it has its climax on the Christmas Day when Joan of Arc crowns the French king at Rheims Cathedral, when concerns of the world—the pressures and pains, the passions and bitter distractions of life—fade into the great symbol of mankinds's eternal rebirth.

In the play, the saintly Violaine in compassion kisses Pierre de Craon, the great builder of churches, who has become a leper. She contracts the disease, and her jealous sister, Mara, marries Jacques, the former fiancé of the now blind and ostracized Violaine. On Christmas Day the compassionate and saintly Violaine restores to life her weeping sister's child. As simple as the soil are the characters of the drama: the peasant mother, who is left alone at the end of the play; and the father with a Crusader's fervor.

The Tidings Brought to Mary was presented in Paris in 1912 and has been frequently revived. The Theatre Guild presented it in New York on Christmas Day, 1922; Montreal saw it in English in 1939; New York viewed it in French in 1942. In Montreal, *Le Devoir* (April 1, 1939) commented that "even translated, Claudel continues great" in spite of the loss of "that savour of the word, that rhythm of the style, that breath which overturns syntax and sings like nature herself, who does not always follow our rules." *Les Nouvelles Littéraires*, Paris, (June 20, 1946) expressed the view that the play "is in every respect one of the rare French works of this half-century, which can be listed among the masterpieces of the world theatre. It stands at the peak of Claudel's dramatic art."

Deftly suggested, beyond the immediate story of the play, are the stir of a military cavalcade, the rapt dedication of Joan of Arc, and the infinite implications of man's redemption. "It is only the unseen," said Heywood Broun, "that can ever be utterly convincing. It is curious that the theatre, which began in the church, has for the most part forgotten this vital fact, upon which all religion is founded." *The Tidings Brought to Mary* recaptured that early, devoted fusion of theatre and church, inducing an exaltation akin to worship.

Something of the deep effect of this quiet play is conveyed by the words of Stark Young (January 10, 1923): "Miss Jeanne de Casalis and Miss Mary Fowler, in the scene where the child is brought to life, really succeed in creating an ecstatic moment. And Miss Helen Westley, as the woman who has borne the burden of the lives around her and, when she is grown dry and empty, is abandoned by her husband and children for their separate pilgrimages, has something about her that is like the picture of his mother Dürer drew, something like an old and worn and exhausted bitter soil, like blood and ashes mingled . . . And as Claudel's play draws to an end we know what the tidings are: that a child is born to men, a perpetual renewal of life among men through beauty and passion and the mystical power of thought. And we see in the play the objects and the actions and the life around them become one; and the bread these people break is not only bread but all life; and all life is included and renewed in the bread." Beauty takes dramatic form in the love of man that wells through *The Tidings Brought To Mary.*

SEVEN KEYS TO BALDPATE   *George Michael Cohan*

A staunch American and a great man of the theatre, was George M. Cohan (1878-1942). He came on the stage early, in *Peck's Bad Boy* (1890); then he toured in vaudeville in "The Four Cohans," with his father and mother and sister Josephine. He wrote, produced, and performed in many plays and musicals. A deft and shrewd craftsman, with a light finger on the theatregoer's pulse, Cohan wrote, in *Seven Keys to Baldpate,* the most popular and the best murder mystery farce.

Based on a novel by Earl Derr Biggers, *Seven Keys To Baldpate* pictures the tough time had by William Hallowell Magee in winning a bet. On a stormy night, caretaker Elijah Quimby lets Magee into a lonely house on top of Baldpate Mountain where, Magee has wagered, he will write a play in twenty-four hours. Quimby assures Magee that his is the only key to the house. Nevertheless, Magee is interrupted by a gang of thieves, a murderer, a pretty reporter (Mary Nolan), and a policeman who wants to slip off to Canada with the thieves' loot. Many thrilling and amusing complications sweep through the storm upon the much-tried Magee. Finally the owner of the house appears and informs Magee that all these persons were sent by his friend Bentley to create a disturbance in order to prevent Magee from winning the bet. Mary, however is real, Magee responds; he's found her, the rest doesn't matter. And the curtain falls. Then Magee comes out with a manuscript. He phones Bentley: He's won the bet. All these events and creatures are the invented story of Magee's play, *Seven Keys To Baldpate.* Over the phone he says: "The critics? I don't care a darn about the critics. This is the stuff the public wants." And the curtain falls.

Driving to Hartford for the premiere (September 15, 1913) of *Seven Keys To Baldpate,* Cohan and the star, Wallace Eddinger, were injured in an automobile accident; Cohan, with a broken collar-bone, took over the star's part. The play came to New York, September 22, to run 320 performances. Clayton Hamilton stated in *Vogue,* (November 1, 1913): "The material is trivial, and the cleverest of craftsmanship was required to develop it into the very successful entertainment that is now crowding the Astor Theatre."

London saw *Seven Keys to Baldpate,* September 12, 1914. In the United States, the play is a constantly revived favorite. It was chosen, in 1935, for the Players' annual revival, with Cohan as Magee, Zita Johann as Mary, Josephine Hull, Walter Hampden, James T. Powers, and Ernest Glendinning. "A song and dance man and Yankeedoodler," said H. I. Brock in the *New York Times* (May 19, 1935)) "had written a mystery piece that was so good a satire on all the other mystery pieces that it was about the best mystery piece of them all." Charles Darnton called the proceedings "the wildest fun that has run riot on the stage in ages." More recently, Magee was enacted (June 9, 1948) by William Gaxton.

The lively and absurd events of *Seven Keys to Baldpate,* having little connection with reality, have not grown dim with time. The characters are not rounded; they are there only for the story. Yet this gather-all of mystery tricks turned farcical, remains a highly amusing sample of what "the public wants."

RAIN   *John Colton*

Somerset Maugham's short story, *Miss Thompson,* was rejected by *Cosmopolitan Magazine,* then using most of Maugham's work, and accepted by the *Smart Set.* Upon reading proof, John Colton (American, b. 1889) suggested that the story be turned into a play. "Why don't you write it?" asked Maugham. With Clemence Randolph, Colton did, calling it *Rain.*

Opening in Philadelphia, October 9, 1922, *Rain* came to New York, November 7, with Jeanne Eagels. It ran for 648 performances, then closed because Miss Eagels, quarreling with Actors' Equity, went to Europe. When she returned, she joined Equity and *Rain* reopened, September 1, 1924 to play 104 more performances. It then went on tour for a total of 1420 performances. Two other companies toured with the play at the same time. London saw *Rain,* opening May 12, 1925, for 150 performances; again in 1924. *Rain* has been played quite frequently all over the United States. Tallulah Bankhead acted in it in New York, opening February 12, 1935, wearing Jeanne Eagels' necklace and hand bag, "to the cheers and salvos," said the *New York Times,* "of one of the most enraptured audiences ever gathered in a New York theatre." The *New York Sun* in 1935 listed 60 actresses that had played the role of Sadie Thompson—among them Alice Brady, Helen Menken, Shirley Booth, Marjorie Rambeau, Winifred Lenihan, June Havoc (in a poor musical version in 1944), and fan dancer Sally Rand. Lenore Ulric acted the part in 1941; in 1949, the strip-teaser Margie Hart. A silent motion picture of *Rain* was made with Gloria Swanson and Lionel Barrymore; a talking film starred Joan Crawford and Walter Huston. The play is of the strongest appeal to an emotional actress, for it is, as the *New York Times* said (November 8, 1922) "a drama of altogether extraordinary grip and significance."

Maugham's story springs from notes he made on a trip to Pago Pago, a port on a volcanic jut in the South Pacific. In these notes, Maugham described a woman who was sailing from Honolulu to escape arrest:

"Plump, pretty in a coarse fashion, perhaps not more than 27. She wore a white dress and a large white hat, long white boots from which the calves bulged in cotton stockings." There was a missionary on board, "a tall thin man, with long limbs loosely jointed. He had hollow cheeks and high cheek bones. His fine, large dark eyes were deep in their sockets. He had full, sensual lips, and wore his hair rather long. He had a cadaverous air, and a look of suppressed fire." The woman became Sadie Thompson; the man, the Reverend Alfred Davidson.

In the play, the two are held, during five days of continuous rain, in the hotel-store of Trader Horn of Pago Pago. Sadie plays her phonograph; she is ready to go to Sydney with an ardent marine, marry him, and lead an exemplary life. But she reckons without the Reverend Davidson and his frigid wife, who abominates the pleasure-loving Sadie. Davidson persuades the governor to deport Sadie to San Francisco. In a scorching scene, Sadie turns upon her persecutor and rends him. She blasphemes, then succumbs to his religious spell. But the long-repressed Reverend succumbs to her sexual spell. In the morning, Sadie plays her phonograph loudly: the Reverend Alfred Davidson has cut his throat. The governor permits Sadie to start for Sydney with her marine.

Rain is built upon the familiar "hour-glass pattern" (best represented in the novel by Anatole France's *Thais*), of two persons whose paths cross as one moves toward regeneration and the other toward destruction. The play is drenched with atmosphere and tense with mounting melodramatic power. The role of Sadie Thompson is vivid, with opportunity for superb histrionics. Of the emotional drama built upon the repressions and the explosions of sex, *Rain* is a scorching example.

THE DOUBLE DEALER   *William Congreve*

Turning from law to literature, William Congreve (English, 1670-1729) found himself in one year the author of two successful comedies and launched on the brief career that set him supreme among playwrights that depict the narrow world of gallantry and society intrigue.

More highly polished and with even sharper darts of wit and satire than *The Old Bachelor*, its predecessor, *The Double Dealer* opened in London with Mrs. Bracegirdle in November, 1693. Although it was considered by many to be too sharp in its satire of fashionable society, Queen Mary's request for a Command Performance set the seal of royal approval on the play. Dryden, with Commendatory Verses, put his weight on the play's side.

Maskwell is the double-dealer in the play. He covets Cynthia, daughter of Sir Paul Plyant, who is engaged to Mellefont, nephew and heir of Lord Touchwood, whose wife covets Mellefont. While pretending to be Mellefont's friend, Maskwell tells Plyant that Mellefont is intriguing with Lady Plyant and also manages to have the suspicious Touchwood find Mellefont in Lady Touchwood's chamber. With Mellefont thus disgraced, Lord Touchwood informs his wife that Maskwell is to wed Cynthia. When Lady Touchwood reproaches Maskwell for this treachery, however, Lord Touchwood overhears. All is straightened out, and Mellefont and Cynthia are united.

Maskwell has been played by Thomas Sheridan and Basil Sydney. Lady Froth, "a great coquette . . . pretender to poetry, wit, and learning" was played by Kitty Clive. Peg Woffington played Lady Plyant, "insolvent to her husband, and easy to any pretender." There is some incongruity in the violence of Lady Touchwood's amorous desire for Mellefont amidst the more artificial intrigues of Brisk and Careless and the Froths and the Plyants. But the wit, the crackling dialogue of dalliance, and the satiric thrust are evident throughout. After the 1916 London revival, the *Pall Mall Gazette* noted that "the richness of its satire and the music of its dialogue are still pungent and pleasing." The *Daily Chronicle* remarked: "Here the English comedy reaches its highest perfection, a perfection from which even the genius of Sheridan and Goldsmith is a decline . . . According to modern standards, all the ladies are lax and all the gentlemen loose. But actually Congreve suffers neither virtue nor vice upon the stage . . . Congreve's wit is all headwork. There is never a heartbeat in all his comic theatre."

The Double Dealer is a heady draught of sparkling drama, a relentless set of portraits of pleasure-bound gallants and especially of luxurious ladies, in the dreg-depths of a dissolute society.

LOVE FOR LOVE   *William Congreve*
Resentful of the treatment they were receiving at the Drury Lane

Theatre, several of its stars built the Lincoln's Inn Fields Theatre. They opened it on April 29, 1695, with Congreve's *Love For Love*. The play was so successful that the actors gave the dramatist a share in the theatre; he was to write a play a year for them. Actually, however, he wrote but two more dramas.

Love For Love is another complicated intrigue of amours. Sir Samson Legend, exasperated by the expensive ways of his son Valentine, will pay Valentine's debts only if he signs over his inheritance to Ben, his younger brother. Valentine signs the preliminary bond, then feigns madness to avoid signing the final conveyance. Wealthy Angelica, who has been keeping Valentine at arm's length, woos Sir Sampson into a marriage proposal and gets Valentine's bond. Despite his frivolous ways, life means nothing to Valentine without Angelica. When he hears of her engagement to his father, he reaches for the conveyance to sign, whereupon Angelica destroys the bond and confesses her love for Valentine.

The incidental action of the other characters in the play adds much to its lively movement. Ben, a plainspoken man of the sea, is intended by his father to marry Miss Prue, "a silly awkward country girl" eager to learn what love is all about. Tattle, "a half-witted beau, vain of his amours, yet valuing himself for secrecy"—the descriptions are Congreve's —is always on the brink of teaching Prue, and always interrupted; he hurries off to marry the rich Angelica, but (on a plan arranged by Valentine's servant, Jeremy) finds himself wed to Mrs. Frail, whose virtue is no stronger than her name. Prue's father, Foresight, "an illiterate old fellow, peevish and positive," prides himself on being a proper astrologer. The figure of Foresight "was then common," said Johnson; "Dryden calculated nativities; both Cromwell and King William had their lucky days." The elegance and the brilliant wit of *Love For Love* are thus balanced by elements of farce rising from these varied figures.

Every period has liked *Love For Love*. The *Tatler* and the *Spectator* gave it frequent praise, the latter (No. 189) calling it "one of the finest comedies that ever appeared upon the English stage." The play's wit shines in "a gorgeous blaze which dazzles us almost to blindness," said

Macaulay, who also praised "the constant movement, the effervescence of animal spirits" in the play. William Hazlitt said that the play presents the highest model of comic dialogue: "Every sentence is replete with sense and satire, conveyed in the most polished and pointed terms. Every page represents a shower of brilliant conceits, is a tissue of epigrams in prose, is a new triumph of wit."

Love For Love has also been continuously popular on stage. A recent London production, opening April 8, 1943, with John Gielgud, Leslie Banks, and Leon Quartermaine, attained 471 performances. A New York production of 1925 was directed by Robert Edmond Jones, who also supervised the Players' annual revival production of *Love For Love,* which opened June 3, 1940, with Dorothy Gish, Peggy Wood, Violet Heming, Cornelia Otis Skinner, Dudley Digges, Bobby Clark, and Romney Brent, and Walter Hampden speaking the Prologue. A production with John Gielgud opened May 26, 1947. In the summer of 1936 Eva Le Gallienne was in a Westport, Connecticut, production with Dennis King, Rex O'Malley, and Van Heflin, using a version in which lines from Congreve's *The Way of the World* * were inserted.

In London, when *Love For Love* was given as a benefit for Betterton, the *Tatler* (April 12, 1709) said that its reception "gives an undeniable instance, that the true relish for manly entertainments and rational pleasures is not wholly lost." Two centuries later, in New York, *Time* (June 9, 1947) commented: ". . . where most Restoration writers were gross, Congreve was graceful. His people air their low thoughts in high language; his scandalmongers are witty; his sluts have style." John Mason Brown (June 14, 1947) said the play is written "by as superlative a stylist as ever employed prose in the form of dialogue."

The pretended madness of Valentine is usually burlesqued. It roused Gielgud, as Harold Hobson noted in the *Christian Science Monitor* (July 3, 1943) "to a magnificent frenzy of mockery of all the similar scenes in Shakespeare", including Gielgud's own work as Hamlet. But Gielgud found deeper moments too; particularly, the one where Valentine, forsaking his pretended madness, asks Angelica to own her love for him and she repels him. The power of this passage was well caught by John Hobart in the *San Francisco Chronicle* (November 11, 1945): The scene lasted " for only a minute or two, but during it Gielgud held us under a spell. For here, in the midst of Vanity Fair, with its cynicism and insincerity, its protocol of wit, its preoccupation with appetite, was an honest man, speaking his most private thoughts, and who, ironically, was to be repulsed. By the sheer magic of his acting, Gielgud suddenly made us understand that this unobtrusive scene was the great climax to which the whole play had been leading—the exposure of an honest heart. And *Love For Love* then brushed, as all great comedies must, against tragedy—just for the one poignant, passing moment, before it returned to its high, heartless Restoration ways."

Along with such constant praise, *Love For Love* has been continually attacked on the score of immorality. Congreve himself came off second best in his reply to Jeremy Collier's *Short View of the Profaneness and Immorality of the English Stage* (1698). Lamb defended Congreve's works from the charge of immorality, but, says Harold Hobson, "hardly secured an acquittal." The play's fine ladies, Hobson avers, "are brilliant, for they are decked with jewels, but they are unwashed." It might, of course, be stated that it is usually wrong to accredit (or besmirch) an author with his characters' failings. Congreve in *Humour in Comedy* declared: "If anything does appear comical or ridiculous in a woman, I think it is little more than an acquired folly or an affectation. We may call them the weaker sex, but I think the true reason is because our follies are stronger and our faults are more prevailing." He does not spare the weaker sex in his plays; his purpose is to display, not to defend them. *Love For Love*, as the *New York Times* (June 30, 1936) remarked, is "full of what Dr. Johnson called 'gay remarks and unexpected answers' . . . the flashing stuff of his great artifice, carrying its modish sin with delicate balance and wicked wit."

Valentine calls after the lawyer whom his pretended madness sends scurrying: "Ha! You need not run so fast, honesty will not overtake you." Those that enjoy brilliance of wit, sharp satire deftly poised and bull's-eye-darted, will be overtaken with delight at *Love For Love*.

THE MOURNING BRIDE   *William Congreve*

At the age of twenty-seven, William Congreve wrote his one serious drama, his greatest contemporary success, *The Mourning Bride,* 1697, which was presented by the best performers of the period. Mrs. Anne Bracegirdle, the most versatile actress of the day, created the role of Almeria; Elizabeth Barry, the greatest tragic actress of the century, the role of Zara. The play was produced constantly throughout the eighteenth century, and had a Command Performance on February 24, 1785, with Sarah (Kemble) Siddons and Elizabeth Kemble.

The play is a surge of action, of counter-surprise and foiled intrigue, centered on Almeria, daughter of King Manuel of Granada, and Alphonso, son of King Anselmo of Valencia. The fathers are enemies; the children, secretly wed.

King Manuel orders his daughter to wed the son of his favorite, Gonsalez. A fiery African princess, Zara, who rescues and falls in love with Alphonso, is captured with him by Manuel, who desires her. Fearing that Zara will help Prince Alphonso, Manuel substitutes himself for the imprisoned prince, and is mistakenly slain by Gonsalez. Zara, thinking Alphonso dead, takes poison. Almeria is about to do the same, when the released Alphonso arrives in triumph.

Macaulay stated that *The Mourning Bride* "stands very high among the tragedies of the age"; Johnson thought certain passages of the play superior to any others in English drama.

There wells through the rhetoric of *The Mourning Bride* the power of a vigorous and earnest spirit, the forceful rouse of a champion of decency and fair-dealing. There is more drive of plot to this serious play than to Congreve's comedies. The drama maintains the tradition that extends from the Elzabethan blood-and-thunder plays to the violent melodramas of the nineteenth century. In a period of predominantly comic drama, it strikes a strong and somber note.

THE WAY OF THE WORLD   *William Congreve*

Paradoxically, *The Way of the World,* 1700, the greatest of William Congreve's plays, was so poorly received that the author resolved, and kept his resolve, to write no more for the theatre. Despite the best efforts of the stars Thomas Betterton and Ann Bracegirdle, the scintillating wit of the play—"There is as much bullion in it," said Pope, "as would serve to lace fifty modern comedies"—was too much for its early audiences. Congreve wrote it at the age of thirty, and lived for thirty years more without writing another line for the theatre.

The Way of the World was later recognized as a great play. It opened at the new Covent Garden Theatre on December 7, 1732, and has been played more than any other English comedy since. Swinburne has called it "the unequalled and unapproached masterpiece of English comedy," and Edmund Gosse considered it "the best written, the most dazzling, the most intellectually accomplished of all English comedies."

The increasing emphasis on morals produced a decline in the stage popularity of Congreve's plays, although all five he wrote were produced, in bowdlerized versions, in 1776. Productions were few through the Victorian regime.

London saw The Way of the World in 1942 with Godfrey Tearle, Edith Evans, and Peggy Ashcroft; New York saw it in 1924, 1925, 1927, 1931, and 1954. The 1931 production, by the Players Club, engaged Walter Hampden, Fay Bainter, Dorothy Stickney, Cora Witherspoon, Ernest Cossart, and Moffat Johnson. A sparkling production was given at the Johns Hopkins Playhouse, Baltimore, in November, 1949.

The Way of the World shows how Mirabell and Lady Millamant manage to achieve matrimony despite the jealous obstruction of Millamant's aunt and guardian, Lady Wishfort. Intrigue and cozenage form the substructure upon which Congreve's wit and worldly wisdom coruscate and cascade. As William Hazlitt has said: "The style of Congreve is inimitable, nay, perfect. It is the highest model of comic dialogue . . . The fire of artful raillery is nowhere else so well kept up." Note that the comedy intended by Congreve is not the humorous variety, warm with emotion, light with animal spirits, as in Shakespeare; it is the crackling of the intellect, the sparkling of wit, as in Molière. In this vein, as Voltaire estimated, "Congreve raised the glory of comedy to a greater height than any English writer before or since."

The Way of the World is no romantic comedy like the spring-tide sunny dramas of Shakespeare, but a play of wit like the glint of sun on a lake of ice, where expert skaters cut fancy figures, and slide more lightly where the ice is thin. Objection has been made to the morals of Congreve's characters—though they are more exemplary than those of most contemporary dramatists—but such objections were routed by Charles Lamb: "I feel the better always for the perusal of one of Congreve's comedies. I am the gayer at least for it; and I could never connect those sports of a witty fancy in any shape with any result to be drawn from them to imitation in real life . . . The Fainalls and the Mirabells, the Dorimants and the Lady Touchwoods, in their own sphere, do not affend my moral sense; in fact, they do not appeal to it at all . . . They have got out of Christendom into the land—what shall I call it?—of cuckoldry, the Utopia of gallantry, where pleasure is duty, and manners perfect freedom. No good person can be justly offended as a spectator, because no good person suffers on the stage . . . No peace of families is violated, because no family ties exist among them . . . No deep affections are disquieted, no holy wedlock bands are snapped asunder, for affection's depth and wedded faith are not of the growth of that soil." There is profound observation in Lamb's words, for, while tragedy shows the dire consequence of violating ethical and social laws, comedy, like love itself, laughs at such locks.

Millamant is a truly rich creation. While she is self-designed in elegance, refinement, wit, and high assurance, the tapping toe of a woman genuinely in love peeps beneath the petticoat of her artifice. Millamant, observed Leigh Hunt, "pushes the confident playfulness of a coquette to the verge of what is pleasing; but her animal spirits and good nature secure her. You feel that her airs will give way by and by to a genuine tenderness; and meanwhile some of them are exquisite in their affected superiority to circumstances."

The *Manchester Guardian* called the 1924 London production "the choicest and most piquant thing the English theatre has done this year." Percy Hammond disagreed sharply; looking around on opening night (June 1, 1931) of the Players Club revival, he announced: "During intermission I counted twelve persons in the stalls who can write better comedies than *The Way of the World* . . . Mr. Congreve's corpse." Allardyce Nicoll walked middle ground: "Congreve is the perfect stylist, but he is by no means perfect in his plot construction or his truth to character. For a *bon mot* he will sacrifice both the one and the other . . . The precision and balance of the prose are exquisite."

Most critics today would still deem quite moderate the judgment of the *London Chronicle,* after a Drury Lane performance of November 14, 1758: *The Way of the World* is "a comedy which for poignancy of wit, delicacy of humor, regularity of conduct, propriety of manners, and continuity of character, may (if ever work might) be reckoned a finished piece." Behind the froth of recherché clothes, the tapping of snuffboxes, the powdering of curly wigs, the high fantastic fashioning of amours, *The Way of the World* has vitality enough to quicken audiences, as Lady Wishfort says, "to all futurity."

THE GREEN PASTURES   *Marc Connelly*

Out of the simple picture of man's earliest days that a Southern pickaninny might conceive, Marc Connelly (American, b. 1890) fashioned *The Green Pastures,* which surged into the hearts of all beholders. Alexander Woollcott in the *Ladies' Home Journal* (September, 1935), called it "the finest achievement of the American theatre in the hundred years during which there has been one worth considering."

Starting in the Louisiana Sunday School of the Reverend Deshee, *The Green Pastures* moves through seventeen scenes of Biblical times, after a fish-fry in heaven, with Gabriel smoking "ten cent seegars." In that scene, the jubilant singing of spirituals is suddenly hushed by the most awesome entrance cue in the history of the theatre: "Gangway!" the Angel Gabriel cries, "Gangway for de Lawd God Jehovah!"

De Lawd leaves the angels' fish-fry to create Adam and Eve. He then follows humanity on its uneven course—driving off Cain; rescuing Noah when crap-shooting revelers and revilers are left to drown; leading Moses, after a Minstrel Show magic competition with the Egyptian high priests, along the road to the promised land; putting into the trumpets of Joshua the compelling rhythm that seems the Negro's heritage today; sweeping wrath upon the Harlem cabarets of ancient Babylon; and finally moving on to another angelic fish-fry at which, after looking along the course of creation, the Lord of Wrath envisages the Crucifixion and knows that he must also be the Lord of Mercy. When He thunders upon erring and sinful humanity, however, it is man's Job-like faith in God that restores God's faith in man.

Attempting to explain the deep appeal of *The Green Pastures*, John Mason Brown spoke of its moving simplicity; Alexander Woollcott, of its innocence. "Perhaps those whom it most readily moves to tears" said Woollcott, "are people who are crying in the dark and cold, weeping for something their world has lost." The author himself remarked that what touched him, while writing the play, was the way "these untutored black Christians have adapted the contents of the Bible to the consistency of their everyday lives . . . with terrific spiritual hunger and the greatest humility." Their picture, at times garish, at times is fraught with the simple wonder of the dawn.

An equal humility, and a great daring, must have animated Marc Connelly. He succeeded in being both colloquial and reverent in bringing the actions of the Lord—even when He "passes a miracle"—to the level of comprehension of the simplest human.

For all its warm reception, *The Green Pastures* had no easy road. No Broadway producer would touch the play; the subject seemed anathema. It was finally backed by a Wall Street man new to Broadway. Then came the problem of finding someone to play de Lawd. Broadway and Harlem casting agencies were at a loss. Connelly remarked that he must come "from heaven"—when in walked sixty-five-year-old Richard Berry Harrison. Born in Canada of runaway slaves, Harrison had never been on the stage, but had long wandered, as bell-hop, porter, itinerant elocutionist. Assured by his Bishop that it was all right to enact the part, Harrison accepted. He made a simple, magnificent figure of de Lawd, a cross between a benign pastor and a paternal plantation owner, with flashes of majesty. As he was making up for the 1657th performance, Harrison fell ill: "Hold me up, Charlie," he pleaded; "the world needs this play at this time." He was buried beneath a blanket of 1675 roses.

The Green Pastures opened in New York February 26, 1930, and had a run of 557 performances. It returned to New York, after a country-wide tour, in 1935. In some places, however, the play was forbidden. In Philadelphia and Washington, the law against child actors was invoked. One Willmoore Kendall, a blind preacher of Miami, Oklahoma, reminded his congregation that de Lawd was not God, but "the Afro-American's anthropomorphic personification of God." From the *London Daily Mail* came the indignant protest of J. H. Barton: "How any creature can dare to personate and caricature our ineffable Holy God passes understanding. That the actor is not struck dead is only another of the multitudinous proofs that God is long-suffering and plenteous in goodness and mercy." London, where representation of deity onstage is forbidden, banned *The Green Pastures* as sacrilegious; Russia banned it as too religious, "too servile in its démodé piety."

In Europe, the play was produced only in Sweden. In the Stockholm production, after the cleaning women had mopped and dusted Jehovah's office—where Gabriel's trumpet of Doomsday hangs enticingly on a hat-peg—one of the women picked up her bucket and nonchalantly flew out of the window. These charwomen wore dust-jackets over their wings in the New York revival that opened March 15, 1951, with William Marshall as de Lawd. The play was warmly welcomed by the reviewers; but an earnestness in our lives, with many plays and motion pictures attacking discrimination, made the childlike conception of Biblical days, with its sinner-or-saint morality, seem too blandly condescending. In another few decades, it may again seem like a timeless legend.

Marc Connelly drew *The Green Pastures* from sketches by Roark Bradford, which had been collected as *Old Man Adam an' His Chillun* (1928). The Sunday School prologue is Connelly's addition. Robert Garland, with parallel passages, showed that much of the play's language was taken directly from the book; Brooks Atkinson analyzed the nature of Connelly's changes and came to the conclusion that "all that is so inexplicably transfiguring about *The Green Pastures* is Mr. Connelly's personal contribution."

Those that have seen *The Green Pastures* are likely to agree with Alexander Woollcott that it is "an experience which will thereafter be a part of their lives as long as they live." In its simplicity and reverence, even through the pictures of innocent fish-fry jollity and of guilty Babylonian revels, *The Green Pastures* captures the primal wonder of man about the upward march of living.

AARON SLICK FROM PUNKIN CRICK   *Beale Cormack*

There is another world of make-believe beyond the Hudson, said *Harper's* magazine (March, 1938), "unnoticed by the metropolitan critics and unknown to first nighters, but of astonishing proportions, health, and vigor . . . The most popular plays of the past fifty years have been *Among the Breakers, Mr. Bob,* and *Aaron Slick from Punkin Crick.* Any one of these classics of the crossroads has established a record which makes even that of *Abie's Irish Rose** seem very small-time stuff indeed." Any consideration of the theatre must glance at the favorite fare of the 300,000 or so amateur groups in the United States, each of which produces a play or two every year.

"By long odds the most popular drama this country has ever known," Merrill Denison declared in *Harper's,* is *Among the Breakers,* written in 1872 by George Melville Baker. He estimated that "some 140,000 audiences have gasped over its revelations and felt uplifted by its sermon." *Among the Breakers* is a simple melodramatic heart-tugger about a lighthouse keeper and the fifteen-years' wait of his wife at the foot of his light.

Apparently the second biggest selling play ever published for amateurs is *Mr. Bob,* c. 1893, a comedy of mistaken identity by Rachel E. Baker, the daughter of the author of *Among the Breakers.*

Aaron Slick From Punkin Crick, "the greatest of all rural comedies," according to *Life* (March 14, 1938) had a later start than these two record holders, but it already challenges their records. Written in 1919 by Lieutenant Beale Cormack, it has undoubtedly been performed some three or four times daily ever since. Once it played in forty-three different towns on the same evening. It has been seen by more persons than saw all the plays on Broadway in the past seven years. A string of other folk dramas, from *Silas Smidge of Turnip Ridge* through *Abba San of Old Japan* to *Mrs. Plaster of Paris,* have taken cue from its rhyming title.

Aaron Slick From Punkin Crick brings villain Wilbur Merridew and his sly sister, Gladys May, from the city to fleece the simple Oklahoma farmer folk. Finding oil in the spring of widow Rosy Berry, Wilbur buys her farm for $20,000. With the cash the widow, followed by her bashful suitor, Aaron Slick, goes to the big city. At a Chicago cabaret, Aaron is tempted by the Girl in Red, "daring symbol of the lures of a big city", but he outwits her. Then the outraged Wilbur, finding that oil had been poured into the spring by Aaron Slick, demands the return of his money. Aaron is charged with fraud. All looks black until Clarence, the tenor waiter, shows his detective badge and arrests Wilbur "for that little job in Ioway two years ago."

From beginning to end, there is horseplay galore in *Aaron Slick from Punkin Crick*. The productions themselves are usually on the same scrambled, good-natured level.

Such plays are gladly given and gladly seen all over the land. They are evidence and reminder, in these days of two-dimensional spectacles and plays, of the tremendous appeal of the full-bodied art of the theatre, even when it is only folk-entertainment or folk-enlightenment on the lower brink of art. "The whole business is hoke", said *Variety* (July 12, 1939) when *Aaron Slick From Punkin Crick* ventured within commuting distance of Broadway (1933, Provincetown Playhouse in New York; 1939, Tarrytown in the suburbs). But one man's hokum is another man's hope. *Aaron Slick from Punkin Crick* may represent the first grade of theatrical fare, but at that level it is first grade.

THE CID   *Pierre Corneille*

The greatest play of the first great French tragic dramatist, Pierre Corneille (1606-1684), *Le Cid* was written in 1636 after the Spanish play, *The Youthful Exploits of the Cid*, by Guillen de Castro y Bello (1569-1631). It deals with the problem of love and honor (the Spanish *pundonor*) in the career of "the Cid" (from the Arabic *Sayyid,* Lord), the Spanish hero Don Rodrigue Diaz de Bivat, who died in 1099 and whose beloved, Ximena (Chimène), entered a convent in 1102. The play is centered on the climactic moment of their lives when, despite his love for Chimène, the Cid challenges and kills her father to avenge an insult to his own father. Thereupon, despite her love of the Cid and despite his great victory over the Moors, Chimène is obliged by honor to bring about his death. A compromise, however, develops in the form of a duel: Chimène says she will wed whoever slays Rodrigue; the king says she shall wed whoever wins. Don Sancho, who loves her, is killed by Don Rodrigue, whom she loves. The King grants her a year to mourn her father, before they marry.

Corneille did not merely repeat the time-worn formula of the struggle between love and honor in *The Cid*. His hero is bent upon the pursuit of glory, which love, joined with honor, impels him to seek. "The originality of the analysis of passion in *The Cid*," said Octave Nadal in *Love in the Works of Corneille* (1948), "springs from this discovery: love and honor do not enter into conflict; they conspire together." The conflict lies between the quest of glory and the drive of love.

The Cid marked the peak of Corneille's rebellion against the literary domination of Cardinal Richelieu, who imposed the "law" of the dramatic unities upon the playwrights of the time. Corneille had first been attracted to the theatre when Mondory's troupe visited Rouen, where Corneille was practicing law. He wrote the comedy *Mélite*, which Mondory produced in Paris in 1629. Richelieu, under whose sponsorship the French

Academy was coming into being, insisted upon observance of the three unities—of time, of place, and of action—and Corneille, to show his distaste for these, wrote another comedy, *Clitandre*, 1632, "obeying all the rules of the drama, but having nothing in it." Richelieu than hit upon the notion of assigning five authors, each to write one act of a play; Corneille accepted one such assignment. Refusing a second, he wrote *Le Cid*.

Playing through the opening days of the year 1637, *The Cid* raised a storm of controversy. France was then at war with Spain. Since the Queen was Spanish, Richelieu, leader of the war party, did not dare openly oppose the play. He had, however, made stringent regulations against duelling, and in the play Rodrigue fights two duels within twenty-four hours. But *The Cid* was praised by the King, and presented three times at court. Three hundred years later (when *The Cid* was presented via radio in 1938) Burns Mantle called it "the first smash hit in the history of French drama."

In 1637, however, friends of the Cardinal protested vigorously. Over a score of poems and pamphlets carried on the controversy. Most influential was the *Observations on "The Cid,"* by the brother of Mlle. de Scudéry, Georges, which charged the play with being undignified in subject, with showing poor judgment, with breaking the rules, and with having many faulty verses. Georges appealed to the newly formed Academy, and Richelieu ordered Corneille to submit to the Academy's judgment. In 1638, *The Opinions of the French Academy on the Tragicomedy "The Cid"* condemned both its subject and its denouement. Corneille was vanquished. He dedicated his next play, *Horace*, 1639, to Cardinal Richelieu and was elected to the Academy.

Polyeucte, produced in 1642, also stands against time. A picture of the Christian Polyeucte whose martyrdom effects the conversion of his wife Pauline, it was long played at the Comédie-Française, annually, before and after Lent. *Les Nouvelles Littéraires* said of it (March 4, 1937): "Here the great man finds his place again, first. The Father. To him we owe all, including Racine, Molière, Victor Hugo, Claudel. He has been subject to eclipses; but the periods indifferent to him condemned themselves . . . For Sarcey, Polyeucte is a man who sacrifices his woman. One might say that he sacrifices woman."

In *Polyeucte,* as in *The Cid,* there is a transmutation of the usual concept of love; love becomes part of a deeper drive. As the *London Times* (December 4, 1948) observed: "In *Polyeucte* there is an apparent conflict between the claims of Divine and human love; but for Polyeucte human love is the first step toward sanctity and sacrifice. It is only by choosing Divine love that a proper value is placed on human love, and the reconciliation of opposing claims produces the moral transformation that is common to the characters of all Corneille's greatest plays."

Increasingly, however, it became clear that Corneille's work did not accord with the spirit of his time. Unfortunately, he seems to have been convinced by his critics; he tried to write what was wanted. He failed. And he watched himself being superseded by dramatists more attuned to the age, especially by Racine*.

Corneille's works have been divided into four periods: that of spontaneous creation, of *The Cid*; that in which he repented and was taken into the Academy; that of gallant historical romances—*Pompée*, 1643, and other plays exhibiting the "tender reasonableness" and the artificial style of the day; and that of his doomed rivalry with Racine. These periods mark a steady descent in his talent; his gifts never found fuller expression than in *The Cid*.

As late as 1660 Corneille was still apologizing for the "irregularities" in *The Cid*. He altered the opening and the ending, to make it seem that Chimène did not intend to marry Rodrigue. Productions since have wisely returned to the original version.

The drama of Corneille, as in *The Cid*, does not stir the audience to pity or horror, but rather quickens its awareness of the heroic, the assertion of individual integrity in the face of disaster. Thus, in his first tragedy, *Medea*, 1635, when, after losing her husband and killing her sons, Medea is asked what she has left, she replies "Moi, dis-je, et c'est assez!"—"Myself, I say, and that is enough!" The audience grows exalted in contemplation of such greatness as transcends doom. But the appeal of the tragedies is thus directed to the intelligence more than to the emotions. The heart may be touched, but the mind is uplifted.

In his concept of human dignity, Corneille is "sublime without ever losing elegance." He may lack the pellucid regularity of Racine, but he has complete command over all the appropriate resources of the language. As Edith Hamilton said in *Theatre Arts* (August 1937): "The power of definite and complete expression is the very heart of Corneille's drama. He is not only able to put into words all that he has in mind; he depends almost wholly upon words for his interest. There is practically no action in his plays. What the actors do is to talk to, or, rather, to argue with each other. It is excellent argument if Corneille's premises are granted, admirably logical, sharp-cut, maintaining an astonishing degree of intensity." The eloquence of the speeches, the dignity and grandeur of the rhetoric, the sweetness and power of the versification, and the validity of the characters, give *The Cid* commanding stature.

Corneille's characters and their motives approach the complexity of life more than those of any other dramatist save Shakespeare. For dramatic effectiveness, emotional power, and psychological insight, the two interviews of Chimène and Rodrigue are twin peaks of the drama; but throughout, their relationship is marked by the most subtle interplay. This is traced in some detail in Lacy Lockert's introduction to his translations from Corneille, and he notes: "Jules Lemaitre has cleverly observed that they often express not the sentiments which they have, but those which they think they ought to have; that they are conscious of the noble figure they cut, each in the other's eyes, and that they want to compel each other's admiration and prove themselves worthy of being loved; that constantly in all their anguish they thus are, after a fashion, making love to each other: it is a very delicate and beautiful touch."

The Cid was produced in English as early as January 26, 1637, in a translation by Joseph Rutter. Samuel Pepys saw a production of this version some time later, when its style was outmoded in English verse, and he wrote in his *Diary*, December 1, 1662: "I saw *The Valiant Cid* acted, a play which I have read with great delight, but it is a most dull thing acted, which I never understood before: there being no pleasure in it though done by Betterton and by Yanthe and another fine wench."

Colley Cibber's version of *The Cid*, called *The Heroick Daughter*, opened November 28, 1712, with Mrs. Oldfield, and was revived several times. Its printed preface (1718), which praised the influence of Richard Steele in the theatre but slighted Joseph Addison, precipitated a controversy; Mist's *Journal* (October 31, 1719) sneered at it, saying that Cibber "very modestly confesses he has infinitely outdone the French original."

The French have always been receptive to *The Cid;* it has remained a favorite in French repertoire. As the *London Times* remarked (November 9, 1924): "There are Frenchmen who have gone every year of their lives to hear *The Cid.*" In 1907, director André Antoine, at the Odéon in Paris, gave a "facsimile" of the original performance.

The great French tragedian Mounet-Sully brought *The Cid* to the United States in March, 1894; it was presented at Hunter College, New York City, in October 1936. A new translation of the play (with five others of Corneille's) by Lacy Lockert was published in 1952.

On the occasion of a Comédie-Française production in London, the *Times* (May 31, 1934) said: "In his preface to *The Cid* Voltaire observes that Corneille was the first writer, after the deplorable attempts of the Spanish and English theatres, whose tragedies were sufficiently regular to move the audience to tears. And, of course, he was more or less right. Nothing but perfect regularity could save those sustained and purely artificial conflicts of love and honor, of public and private duty, which seem to have been constructed for the express purpose of matching the formal antitheses of rhetorical verse." What gives *The Cid* power is the pressure of its romantic subject upon its mainly classical form.

TONIGHT AT 8:30   *Noel Coward*

Nine sketches by Noel Coward (English, b. 1899), usually presented in three groups on successive evenings, are joined in the theatre under the title of this play. Directed and acted by the author, with Gertrude Lawrence, they were successful in London in the spring of 1936, acclaimed in Boston in the fall, and achieved a triumph on their opening in New York on November 24, 1936, with a run of 118 performances.

In 1937, the sketches were presented in San Francisco with a cast including Helen Chandler, Estelle Winwood, Bramwell Fletcher, Mary Astor, Claud Allister, and Carol Stone. Individual sketches from the group have been frequently performed in little theatres. Six of them were presented again in New York in two groups, opening February 20, 1948, with Gertrude Lawrence, and with Noel Coward directing but not playing a part. Independent though the pieces are, they are all character sketches, mainly of persons reflected from various facets of English life.

1. *Hands Across the Sea,* a masterpiece of organized irrelevance, pictures visitors to the witless Lady Maureen, just back from a trip around the world. She mistakes the couple that had entertained her at Malaya for a couple she had met at Penang. With a scramble of persons and 'phone calls and flying tangents of conversation, including a stranger whose errand is never ascertained, the piece tells no story but is a superbly satiric picture of flighty folk and their social irresponsibility.

2. *Fumed Oak* is a caustic picture of lower middle-class Cockney life. Henry Gow, long dominated by his bossy mother-in-law, his nagging wife, and his adenoidal daughter, reveals that he has been secretly saving; in a swirl of petty triumph, he leaves his family. In this brief sketch, Coward achieves a searing picture of a lower-middle-class family —marred only by a sense that the author despises what he depicts.

3. *Shadow Play*, a danced and crooned episode, shows Simon telling Victoria that their rapture cannot last. An overdose of sleeping powder brings memories through delirium, and they decide to try all over again. This is a semi-satiric, sentimental trifle, deftly done.

4. *Family Album* presents a Victorian family, gathered in 1860 for the reading of their father's will. A few drinks break down their reticences and pretenses—"To hell with father!"—and we discover that the youngest daughter, who has given years of care to the old man, has destroyed a will in which he left everything to a mistress. The faithful butler, who had witnessed the destroyed will, stands by the family. Ironic and comical, the sketch is a picture which sympathy and satire, blending, make both poignant and absurd.

5. *The Astonished Heart*. After twelve years of happy married life, a successful psychiatrist is lured by his wife's former schoolmate, who is piqued by his indifference. When she wins him, she stops the affair. Though he loves his wife, his body—or his vanity—requires the other woman; rebuffed, the psychiatrist jumps out of a window. Lightly moving, these characters suggest troubled depths.

6. *Red Peppers* is a rowdy, gusty picture of a cheap variety team, a married pair of ham vaudevillians, who act together onstage, but quarrel offstage, while hoping for a better billing in the theatres out of town. This is the most uproarious and richly comic sketch of the group.

7. *Ways and Means* shows an extravagant, impecunious, and incurably silly couple, talking in bed, wondering how to avoid eviction from their rooms in the Villa Zephyre on the Côte d'Azure, when a theft happily provides the wherewithal for continuing their inane existence. The complete emptiness of the couple's life is revealed beneath the swift movement and easy laughter.

8. *Still Life,* one of the more serious sketches, shows the final rendezvous of a man and woman—each married—who have been meeting in a railway refreshment room. Recognizing that continuance would be too sordid, they decide to part; ironically the gushing of a garrulous friend interrupts their last farewell. This sketch contains the best character drawing, the most sympathetic figures, and the mellowest writing of the group.

9. *We Were Dancing* is another frail piece set to music. A man and a woman meet at the Country Club at Samolo, Maylasia; they dance; they fall in love. The woman asks her husband to release her. The three talk through the night, and in the light of morning all is as it was before. With the dawn comes the yawn. The sentiment and the satire battle in the audience' mind and heart.

On the first presentation of these playlets, the critics found them of uneven merit. James Agate in the *London Times* said of *Hands Across the Sea*: "Every second of this admirable skit is not only perfect theatre but first-class satire." He objected, however, to the determined respectability of Coward's middle-class characters, as opposed to the determined irrespectability of the "Mayfairies," W. A. Darlington of the *London Telegraph* declared that in *Fumed Oak* Coward "reveals a new power of seeing simple ordinary humanity for what it is. . ." While Agate called *Shadow Play* "a revue number interminably spun out," Darlington felt that "the theme is handled with great delicacy".

The New York critics were more receptive, as the papers of November 25, 1936 attest. Brooks Atkinson called *Fumed Oak* "a little masterpiece of sour-puss dramaturgy." John Anderson deemed *Hands Across the Sea* "hilariously malevolent." Robert Coleman said that *The Astonished Heart* showed "an iceberg heaving over a volcano." The works as a whole, John Mason Brown characterized as "vaudeville sketches of a kind that you used to dream of seeing, but never saw, when vaudeville was in its heyday." And Richard Watts called Noel Coward "one of the great figures of the modern theatre."

The revival in 1948 did not fare so well. It ran for but 26 performances, and found the critics unenthusiastic. George Freedley, it is true, called the sketches "still as delightful as ever." But Atkinson—exempting *Red Peppers* and *Fumed Oak*—exclaimed: "Don't look now, but 12 years have disappeared. Although Gertrude Lawrence is a superwoman, she cannot restore a world that has been lost." And John Chapman found the occasion "like trying to get a bang from the leftovers of an Elsa Maxwell party which I'd never been to."

Louis Kronenberger gives a fuller analysis: "Mr. Coward himself is so very important a symbol of our time, so very successful and clever a writer for our age, that it somehow seems one's duty to try to account for one's distaste. Just why should so much of him, in the midst of exciting our laughter, set our teeth on edge; and just why should so little of him ever excite us to laughter more than once? . . . We can be sure only of his satiric perceptions, never of his sense of values. We cannot be sure, for instance, whether he regards the hard-up couple in *Ways and Means* as unspeakable, or merely unfortunate . . . Yet he is enough in the line of the Congreves to make us wonder why he merely emerges as the most gifted jack-of-all-trash of our age. His very versatility—his sorties into the sentimental and fantastic and melodramatic— explain it a little; your true master of social comedy keeps his gifts in a cool dry place, and his eye consistently on the object. Coward, too, I suppose, always keeps his eye on the object; but the object is always his audience: he's first and last and always a showman. That is his real vulgarity—a vulgarity of intentions. Hence we are happiest with him when he is writing pure fantasy or farce, a *Blithe Spirit** or a crazy ditty; when there is no possible meaning, when there is only an effect."

To the supercilious, all things are superficial. Noel Coward may, as some of his critics aver, enjoy the society he is satirizing. Precisely! For the best satire—not savage, but sunny and supple and searching—is based on the excesses of those we love. With the deftness of a chef with an onion, Noel Coward peels off the outer layers of the persons he presents and usually finds material enough to flavor a goodly dish; and sometimes, at the end, there is what remains when one has peeled an onion—tears. The sketches comprising *Tonight at 8:30* are a permanent picture of a fading society.

BLITHE SPIRIT   *Noel Coward*

A light-hearted mixture of fantasy and mirth, *Blithe Spirit*, the first play to present an astral bigamist, was literally a howling success. Opening in London during World War II (July 2, 1941), it ran for 1,997 performances, while three other companies toured England. It came to New York on November 5, 1941, with Clifton Webb, Peggy Wood, Mildred Natwick (as the medium), and Leonora Corbett (her American debut), and in spite of Pearl Harbor the play ran for 657 performances. It has been played frequently around the country; in 1949 at Syracuse, it was present-ed as a bawdy Restoration farce.

The play pictures the plight of Charles Condomine, novelist, widower, and husband. He permits the bicycle-riding medium, Mme. Arcati, to hold a seance at his house; and behold, his seven-years-dead wife Elvira materializes and refuses to leave. As she is visible only to Charles and the audience (and later to the mediumistic maid), the living wife, Ruth, is naturally hard to convince that Elvira has returned. Both wives are jealous to such a degree that Charles is relieved when an accident makes him twice a widower. Happily he prepares to sail abroad. As he jestingly bids the two wraiths a gay goodbye, toppling vases and falling pictures show that now both women are haunting him.

"So deft is Noel Coward's writing," said *Life* (December 8, 1941) "and so skillfully does he skim the thin, slick ice of his inventions, that *Blithe Spirit* emerges as the most amusing bauble on the United States stage." John Anderson declared that the theatre where *Blithe Spirit* was showing was "just the place to die laughing," but he would be a hardy ghost that would care to face those cunning and mischief-making females. Never-theless the antics of the wraiths are amusing to watch; their early rivalry, Charles trying to play them one against the other, and their final joining to plague their single man, make delightful theatre.

The play, said John Mason Brown, "is as audacious in its subject matter as it is expert in its treatment. In it Mr. Coward turns death into the merriest of merry topics and the dear departed into the gayest of gay companions. . . . Just when you would swear that his theme is bound to become as tedious as a coloratura's solo concert, Mr. Coward changes the register, and by doing so gives his performance a new lease on life. He does this effortlessly, with infinite suavity,with a perfect control of his materials, with an eagle's eye for what is unsuspected or unexplored in a situation, and with all those side-splitting irrelevancies which are so much to the point and add so to the delights of Mr. Coward's writing when it is at its best. If his play lacks body, remember that it deals with shades. But its spirit is of the blithest." Just as *Arsenic and Old Lace** makes a farce of murder, *Blithe Spirit* turns the return of the dead into gay comedy.

THE MAGNIFICENT CUCKOLD   *Fernand Crommelynck*

Born of a theatrical family, Fernand Crommelynck (Belgian, b. 1888) took to writing plays when he was eighteen (1906). He was on the stage until 1921, when he was set free for writing by the swift success of what he called "a lyrical farce"—his masterpiece *Le Cocu magnifique* (*The Magnificent Cuckold*).

A grand rouse of irony and biting satire, with Roman candles of color-ful dialogue and flaming pinwheels of figurative speech, *The Magnificent Cuckold* depicts the pride, then the suspicion and jealousy, of a possessive husband who drives his wife to the very infidelities he fears. The husband, Bruno, struggles between the vanity of having his wife Stella coveted, and himself envied by all men, and the vanity of having her as his exclusive prize. He compels Stella to exhibit her charms to his cousin Petrus. Detecting a glint of desire in the man's eyes, Bruno needs assur-ance of his wife's fidelity; he deliberately exposes her to temptation. A

sort of second self of Bruno, Estrugo, constantly baits Bruno's jealousy
and renews the prick of suspicion, until in his mind a phantasmagoria of
his wife's indiscretions develops to a point where tragedy mingles with
farce: A line of impatient lovers awaits outside her door, kept in order by
a policeman and entertained by circus acts. Then, in a touching balcony
scene, Bruno himself approaches his wife, disguised; she recognizes him
and accepts his advances, whereupon he, misunderstanding, reveals himself and casts her off. Wishing to be faithful, she is driven to unfaithfulness, fleeing from her plagued and plaguing husband with a herdsman.

The Magnificent Cuckold is at once madly swirling and realistic. It
externalizes the inner movements of the spirit in a way that suggests
the odd turns and intense drives of expressionism. The play was given
an interesting "constructional" (also called "constructivist") setting by
L. F. Popova, which has become the model for other productions. Two
platforms on the stage, with stairs leading up to them, are connected by
a plank; the skeleton of a house stands behind the right hand platform,
and off to the left are the great wings of a windmill. American designer
Albert Johnson made sets for the play, but it has not yet had professional
performance in the United States. In 1932, a London performance was
directed by Theodore Komisarjevsky, with George Hayes and Peggy
Ashcroft.

In Rabelaisian rouse and swift, tumultuous satire, The Magnificent
Cuckold exposes individual weakness and suggests universal ills: Is it
not the same fear that in the field of international affairs, for instance,
brings on armament races and suspicions and consequent conflicts, the
very disasters nations are seeking to avert? The world is a cuckold that
works toward its own betrayal.

The cuckold became a frequent figure in the drama during the
twenties, a symbol of the betrayal of the hopes of man. In 1922, Paris
saw Dardamelle, or The Cuckold, a play by Emile Mazaud. More grim
is Hinkemann (Crippleman), written by Ernst Toller*; this tragedy,
with symbolic significance, combined the themes of the cuckold and the
castrate.

Two of Crommelynck's later plays continue the mood and, to some
degree, the wider implications of The Magnificent Cuckold. Corinne,
(1929), a mixture of symbolism and romance, pictures a girl who would
rather die than see her dream of life polluted by reality. A more important work, A Woman With Too Small a Heart (1934) is a searing
satire on cold efficiency. With effective byplay and radiating fancy,
Crommelynck develops an intensity in his plays and wraps an envelop-
ing atmosphere of meaning around their stories, to lift what might seem
surface comedies of sex to the level of dramas of man's deepest problems.

him   E. E. Cummings

In 1922 Edward Estlin Cummings (American, b. 1894) came to wide
attention through an autobiographical story, The Enormous Room, which
pictures, with fantasy and grim realism, the lives of prisoners in a
French concentration camp during World War I. Thereafter he became
notorious for several volumes of poetry, in which sentimentality and
cynicism were cloaked by typographical distortion. Refusing capitals
and punctuation marks, running words together and breaking syllables
at the ends of short lines, Cummings was alternately hailed as the devel-

oper of new poetic resources and damned as an obscurantist and poseur. In 1927, he capped the climax of his career with the publication of the farcico-tragic surrealist fantasy drama, *him*.

In the spring of 1928, *him* was produced at the Provincetown Playhouse, in New York's Greenwich Village. In 1948, at the same theatre, The Interplayers gave it an "anniversary" production.

The program of the original production bore a "warning" which stated: *"him* isn't a comedy or a tragedy or a farce or a melodrama or a revue or an operetta or a moving picture or any other convenient excuse for 'going to the theatre'—in fact, it's a play, so let it play: and because you are here, let it play with you. Let it dart off and beckon you from the distance, let it tiptoe back and snap its fingers under your nose, let it creep cautiously behind you and tap you on the back of the neck, let it sweep up at you from below or pounce down on you from above, let it go all around and over and under you and inside you and through you. Relax, and give this play a chance to strut its stuff—relax, don't worry because it's not like something else—relax, stop wondering what it's all 'about'—like many strange and familiar things, Life included, this PLAY isn't 'about', it simply is. Don't try to despise it, let it try to despise you. Don't try to enjoy it, let it try to enjoy you. Don't try to understand it, let it try to understand you."

him's public, according to Robert Littell in the *New York Post,* "laughed, when it did laugh, only at mention of bodily functions and some of those words that small boys chalk up on blank walls." The play is, indeed, a deliberate mixture of the banal and the bawdy, the obvious and the obscure, the realistic, the fantastic, the fanatic.

The play's opening displays a backdrop on which is painted a doctor anaesthetizing a woman. Through two holes where the heads of the doctor and the patient should be painted, protrude the living heads of a man and a woman. Onstage are three withered female figures, knitting: the three weirds, Miss Stop, Miss Look, and Miss Listen. The doctor introduces to them Mr. Anybody, whose name, he says, is the "nom D. ploom" of Everyman, Marquis de la Poussière, who is "him."

The hero of Cummings' first play is earnestly writing a play. Gradually we discern—as through a glass, darkly—through "him's" conversations with his girl-friend "me" and through slanting slaps at life and the theatre, that we are watching the struggle of a man to find reality, to discover the basic value in the world. "him" faces himself in a mirror, and the image he sees kills his real self. Moreover, "him" is not sure of "me": She loves him, but is it she, or the picture she makes of herself, or the picture he makes of her, that attracts him? In other scenes, the moods of which vary from derision to anguish, "him" similarly examines life to test its values.

"him" looks at life in terms of the theatre; he shows "me" scenes from the play he has not written. The scenes are a succession of skits. First, three drunks reel about a wistful maiden lady. Then a silk-hatted Englishman carries his "unconscious" around in a trunk; a policeman, when he looks into this, falls dead. Next Rome burns while Mussolini, the cardboard Caesar, fiddles with some fairies. The 1948 production made Mussolini look and act like Groucho Marx. Finally, in America, gruesome figures reach out of the hell-hole of poverty to die for a crumb of bread; Negroes enact a lively version of "Frankie and Johnny"; a circus barker extols his display of freaks, climaxed by the Princess Anankay, Huemun

Form Divine: A woman appears, completely draped in white, with a newborn baby in her arms; the crowd recoils, and the three Weirds cry "It's all done with mirrors!" The woman in white looks up; she is "me."

Immediately "me" and "him," alone on the stage, look around, and "me" points out that their room has only three walls. "Out there," "me" declares, are people, real people; but "him" cannot believe her. As he looks incredulously at the audience, the curtain falls.

Thus the play ends with the grim reflection that truth is the one thing everyman cannot believe. The impossibilty of ever being certain about anything, about values, about the world, even about oneself, twists Cummings along such wry indirections that we are often uncertain of his specific intention, though his general drive is clear. Mockery of the world, scorn of its folly, hatred of its evil, run through the play; but these are subordinate to the hero's (everyman's) tortured quest of himself. It was therefore misplaced emphasis when the 1948 cast acknowledged the curtain-call by singing "Yes, We Have No Bananas." At least in our mental mirror, we are fully equipped.

him received high praise from the advanced-guard literary reviewers. "For God's sake," exclaimed William Rose Benét, "be a little glad for such a Fourth of July!" Conrad Aiken declared the play "brilliant, and full of brilliance." Stark Young found a strange verbal excitement in the play: "There were fantastic combinations, a mad music of ideas, a real poet's intensification of the word, image, and tone, a heightening of the beat, that seemed to me fresh and blessed in the theatre."

The Broadway reporters, on the other hand, almost unanimously rejected the play. Alexander Woollcott insisted: "Its satire is accomplished by all the clichés of the day, and its black despair is that of the pimply-faced schoolboy announcing (within earshot) that he means to end it all." Percy Hammond saw "dozens of actors throwing fits and babbling the daffy outcries of idiots afflicted with rabies in its dullest form." Robert Littell felt that Cummings was trying "to chew up *Processional* and Frank Sullivan and Ring Lardner and Mike Gold and Jean Cocteau into one great loony quid and squirt the juice at us . . . And every now and than it is exactly like stepping on something extremely nasty in the dark."

Only John Anderson sensed a richer value: "Behind the eloquent delirium of such writing there is fierce sanity flaring out across parts of *him* and making them memorable. . . . Against the struggle of an artist to find himself, Mr. Cummings sets a scalding mockery of the whole theatre."

him still has little general appeal; but, as Anderson said, "though it can have little popular interest, *him* is a provocative event in the theatre." *him* should, indeed, be part of the required course for would-be playwrights. Its excesses are such as they will naturally avoid; its attack on the banal, on the easiest way, and its probing for the basic issues, may chasten them. It will stimulate, irritate, challenge, and hold the alert mind.

THE DAUGHTER OF JORIO   *Gabriele D'Annunzio*

Best known as a novelist and poet, Gabriele D'Annunzio (Italian,

1863-1938) turned to the drama by way of New Testament parables. His first important play, *The Dead City*, 1898, was enacted by the famed Eleonora Duse for twenty-five years.

The Daughter of Jorio, set among the simple, superstitious peasants of D'Annunzio's native Abruzzi, rises to peaks of intense beauty, with torrential feeling, flashing energy, passionate imagination, religious fervor, and superstitious frenzy, as it pictures the interwoven lives of the lovers Aligi, a shepherd, and Mila, the daughter of a sorcerer. The father of Aligi comes to the lovers' cave to take Aligi back to his betrothed in the village; passions rise until Aligi strikes and kills his father. To save Aligi, Mila declares that she is guilty, that by sorcery she had turned the deed upon Aligi. Even her lover believes her story, as she is borne off to be burned. (This climactic turn, of the woman's confessing to witchcraft to take blame from the man she loves, was earlier used in the successful drama *The Sorceress* by Victorien Sardou*.)

The Daughter of Jorio has been widely performed in Italian, as far as Sydney, Australia, where it was presented in 1937. Mimi Aguglia flamed in it around the world; more moderately, Marinella Bragaglia revived the play's intense emotions. Of the latter's performance with the Sicilian players, the *London Times* (February 28, 1910) declared: "These violent delights are tempered by much curious folklore from the Abruzzi and diluted—almost drowned—in floods of D'Annunzian eloquence . . . Signora Bragaglia plays that hunted creature Mila di Codra with less frenzy and more beauty than did Signora Aguglia, who was a wild-cat and nothing else." A fuller picture of the impression made by the play and Signora Aguglia can be gathered from the review of the *Boston Transcript* (January 20, 1909), during the actress' American tour: "La cosa trista, la cosa malvaggia—the woeful thing, the fateful thing of evil, stalked ominously through the first act, and, indeed, through all the play when once the softer picture of the three sisters singing shrilly and with reiterated refrain over the bridal gowns had dissolved . . . a strange, wild world, remote, as it seemed, from all normal things, yet for the time and for long afterward of poignant and haunting reality . . . There is no doubting the play's beauty as poetry, its power as drama, its vividness as a picture of passionate and pagan life, its insistent horror— and its insistent fascination."

The contagious power of D'Annunzio's superabundant energy and lust for life is nowhere more manifest—eloquent, hauntingly beautiful and pitiful, humanly exalting, deeply dramatic—than in *The Daughter of Jorio*. Some critics have seen an intricate symbolism in the play, of the wild yet essentially good powers of nature, doomed to be forever misunderstood by the narrow greeds and creeds of man. It may, however, be accepted for its vivid surface story, melodramatic but alive and moving, of the woman who sacrifices all, not merely her life but her good name, for love. *The Daughter of Jorio* is one of the most colorful presentations of such sacrifice.

COSI FAN TUTTE   *Lorenzo Da Ponte*

This comic opera (known in English as *Everybody's Doing It* or *The School For Lovers*) is a gay and lively play of amorous intrigue. The book is by Lorenzo Da Ponte (Italian, 1749-1838, born a Jew as Emanuele

Conegliano, baptized a Catholic by the bishop whose name he took, migrated to the United States in 1805). The music which sparkles through the whole play was written by Mozart.

Cosi Fan Tutte was presented in a command performance before Emperor Josef II of Austria on January 26, 1790. It has been very popular in opera repertory and with light opera groups. The story, set mainly in Naples, centers upon cynical Don Alfonso's wager with Fernando and Gratiano, that their sweethearts, the sisters Dorabella and Isidora, are accessible to other suitors. Pretending to be called away to war, the two men disguise themselves as foreigners and woo the fair but fickle ladies; then they discard their disguise and rebuke the faithless ones. Don Alfonso, his wager won, assures the men that a little harmless flirtation is not only harmless, but quite the vogue—"everybody's doing it"—and the lovers are reconciled.

A lively factor of the fun is the sisters' maid, Despina. Made part of the plot, she introduces the "foreign gentlemen". Disguised as a doctor, she revives the men when the girls' early obduracy drives them to "suicide"; disguised as a notary, she prepares the marriage contracts when the girls decide to yield. There is an unusually swift swirl of comic action in the play, a crescendo that rises to its peak when Fernando and Gratiano, returning from the "war," dash out in chase of the "foreigners," and come in again using the manners and accents they had assumed when in disguise.

A variant form of *Cosi Fan Tutte,* used especially in English, pictures Dorabella and Isidora as seeing through the disguises of their lovers and leading them on to punish them for their presumption. This at once makes them less fickle and more sympathetic to the conventional conscience, and adds a suggestion of such irony as is more deeply sprung in *The Guardsman,* by Ferenc Molnar*, which leaves wholly unanswered the question as to whether the succumbing lady saw through a similar disguise. The best English version is by Ruth and Thomas Martin.

The press has constantly praised *Cosi Fan Tutte.* In the *New York Times* (March 7, 1924) Deems Taylor took especial note of the decor by Joseph Urban. In London, the *Times* (April 25, 1930) declared: "We are transported at once into a world of fantasy, where anything may happen." It is a gay, gracious, ingratiating world of make-believe. With music that charms as it carries the playful mood of the story, *Cosi Fan Tutte* is a delightful dalliance of drama.

THE DETOUR   *Owen Davis*

Out of the ten-twenty-thirty cent theatre of lurid melodramas, with a hundred plays such as *The Gambler's Daughter* and *Nellie The Beautiful Cloak Model* to live down, Owen Davis (American, b. 1874) made a long detour to the realistic theatre, with authentic and understanding pictures of American country life. The best of these are *Icebound** and *The Detour.*

The Detour presents the wan hopes of Helen Hardy, who, after her marriage to the Long Island farmer Steve, transfers her dream of an artistic career to their daughter Kate. When Steve wants to enlarge the farm with the money Helen has saved to send Kate to art school, Helen decides to go to New York with Kate. But Kate, overhearing an art critic declare that she has no talent at all, has sense enough to settle down with a neighbor, Tom Lane. When Tom's garage is attached for debt, Helen's savings all go to clear it; but indomitably she begins to save again for the grandchild. Of such bourgeois solidity, and of such hopes, is our civilization made.

However devious their ways, these characters are basically good. They are, moreover, clearly seen, well drawn, authentic. They are everyday folk in commonplace situations; but, as *Current Opinion* observed, "the amount of nutriment that Mr. Davis has managed to extract from these unpromising materials would surprise even the believer in sensation." There may be a bitter pill in the final thought that the dreary round must be renewed for another generation; but that pill purges us to a more hopeful mood: "One of the finest moments in any play," said Benjamin de Casseres in the *New York Globe,* (September 1, 1921) "is the last moment in *The Detour,* when Helen Hardy drops ninety cents in the vase to begin saving for the unborn grandchild."

The Detour opened in New York on August 23, 1921, with Effie Shannon and Augustin Duncan. It has been frequently revived in community theatres. The play has light moments, as in a scene of the sale of some antique furniture, but its chief value lies in the simple, direct portrayal of the ordinary lives of ordinary people, who by their very simplicity rise to dignity and importance. *The Detour,* said Alexander Woollcott, is "a thoughtful human play, one that has more than its share of wisdom and kindly humor and knowledge of folks." The *New York Telegram* generously declared: "The tradition that Mr. Davis is not a dramatist but a play factory has been demolished." The *Tribune* called *The Detour* "so faithful in its picture, so pungent in its observation, and so real and eloquent in its characters, that one regrets one's sneers at Mr. Davis's previous tawdry ineptitudes." Certainly these earlier plays were not dramaturgically inept, for Owen Davis had at least one play on Broadway every season for thirty-seven years. The craft of the melodrama manufacturer is invisible, though at work, within the dramatic directness of *The Detour,* in its sound study of simple folk on an American farm.

ICEBOUND   *Owen Davis*

Encouraged by the reception of *The Detour,** Owen Davis tried another play of the same sort—this time set in New England. Opening in New York, February 10, 1923, *Icebound* ran for 171 performances and won the Pulitzer Prize.

According to the author, "Few serious attempts have been made in the direction of a genre comedy of this locality. Here I have tried, at least, to draw a true picture of these people, and I am of their blood, born of generations of Northern Maine small town folk, and brought up among them." The characters in *Icebound* seem hewn of that stern and rockbound coast.

The Jordan family are waiting for Mother Jordan to die so they can share the inheritance. They include the crusty old shopkeeper, Henry; his oppressive wife, Emma, and Nettie, her daughter by an earlier marriage; the forlorn old maid, Ella; and a poor relative, Jane Crosby, who is Mother Jordan's companion, and whom they plan to send packing as soon as the old lady dies. The youngest son, ne'er-do-well Ben Jordan,

returns, sent for by Jane at his dying mother's wish. Ben had fled years
before to escape an arson charge; he seems as dissolute and opinionated
as ever; he is quarreling with Henry when their mother dies.

Mother Jordan leaves everything to Jane Crosby, who takes a shine
to Ben. She buys a new dress to impress him, and hopes to reform him.
Nettie, however, puts on the new dress and swirls it into Ben's embrace;
but the thought that he may go to jail scares her off. Jane, having persuaded those concerned to drop the arson charge, announces that she is
leaving and turning over the farm and all the inheritance to Ben, as his
mother would have wished when he proved worthy. Ben proves that
he is worthy by asking Jane to marry him.

The whole Jordan family is, the *New York Tribune* said (February
12, 1923), " a bickering, unlovely lot, from Henry, the hypocritical small-
town storekeeper, to young Nettie, who is cattish and shows omens of
sex." In the play, Ben remarks that the Jordans were "half froze before
we was born."

Icebound has been played quite frequently about the country; in 1936,
Owen Davis, Jr. played Ben. The play manifests the skill in construction
that kept pace swift and interest tense through a hundred lurid melodramas, together with a capture of character—vivid, biting, clear as pond
ice—grown out of close acquaintance and dramatic power.

THE SHOEMAKER'S HOLIDAY   *Thomas Dekker*

The Shoemaker's Holiday, by Thomas Dekker (English, 1570?-1632?),
was the first dramatic presentation of the rising spirit of personal independence, the forerunner of democracy, in England. In it, apprentices
hold to their rights against arrogant nobles; a shoemaker becomes Lord
Mayor of London, and talks on familiar terms with the King. That such
an attitude was in high vogue may be seen in the fact that the premiere
of the play was a Command Performance before Queen Elizabeth, on
Christmas, 1599.

There is less concern with the plot than with the activity of Simon
Eyre, master of "the gentle craft" of shoemaking and of his lively journey-
men, and more interest in the picture of faithful Jane than in the main
love story. Jane, the wife of the lame journeyman Ralph, refuses Ham-
mon's advances and his gold. Dekker himself, in a dedicatory note to
"all good fellows, professors of the gentle craft," stated the argument of
the play: "Sir Hugh Lacy, Earl of Lincoln, had a young gentleman of
his own name, his near kinsman, that loved the Lord Mayor's daughter of
London; to prevent and cross which love, the Earl caused his kinsman to
be sent Colonel of a company into France: who resigned his place to
another gentleman his friend, and came disguised like a Dutch shoemaker to the house of Simon Eyre in Tower Street, who served the Mayor
and his household with shoes: the merriments that passed in Eyre's house,
his coming to be Mayor of London, Lacy's getting his love, and other
accidents, with two merry Three-men's songs. Take all in good worth
that is well intended, for nothing is purposed but mirth; mirth leng-
theneth long life, which, with all other blessings, I heartily wish you.
Farewell!"

The Shoemaker's Holiday is Dekker's earliest extant play. Acted in
1599 as *The Gentle Craft,* it was published under its present title in 1600.
Its technique is as good as Dekker ever achieved; its philosophy is simple

and homely: "A pound of care pays not a dram of debt." Dekker's genuine enthusiasm for the simple aspects of London life is contagious, as his experience of London ways was intimate. The comedy, said Ernest Rhys, "is indeed the most perfect presentation of the brightness and social interest of the everyday Elizabethan life which is to be found in the English drama . . . The craftsman's life, merging in the citizen's, is the end and all of the play; the King himself is but a shadow of social eminence compared with the Lord Mayor. Simon Eyre, the shoemaker, jolliest, most exuberant of all comedy types, is the very incarnation of the hearty English character on its prosperous workaday side."

Simon Eyre is a figure out of history; as is mentioned in the fifth act, he built Leadenhall in London in 1419 and became Lord Mayor in 1445. The real Simon Eyre was a draper, but, since Leadenhall, in Dekker's day, was used as a leather market, it was natural to picture him as a shoemaker.

The Shoemaker's Holiday was sure to appeal to its audience, said Charles Dudley Warner, "especially the pit, where the tradesmen and artisans with their wives applauded, and, noisiest of all, the apprentices showed their satisfaction: here they saw themselves and their masters brought on the stage, somewhat idealized, but still full of frolic and good nature." That the play still appeals to its audience has been made manifest by numerous revivals, especially in college theatres, and by a lively professional production of the Mercury Theatre, with Orson Welles, in New York, which opened on New Year's night, 1938. Sidney B. Whipple's comment emphasized the idea of democracy: "It is the puissant Earl of Lincoln who, attempting to meddle with the right of a 'young, fair, and virtuous maid' to marry his kinsman, is confounded in the final scene." John Mason Brown stressed the sheer fun of the production: "For all its baffling complexities of plot and subplot, the play in which they caper continues to be what its author would have saluted, and we gladly welcome, as 'fine, tickling sport' . . . Theirs is a philosophy of joy. Hum, let's be merry whiles we are young; old age, sack, and sugar will steal upon us, ere we be aware . . . It is the gayest and most unblushing excursion into Elizabethan low comedy which contemporary playgoers have been privileged to enjoy." The natural humor of *The Shoemaker's Holiday* has kept its flavor fresh along the years.

OLD FORTUNATUS   *Thomas Dekker*

Based on a German folk tale set down in 1509 and turned into a play by Hans Sachs in 1553, the story of the beggar Fortunatus who, offered one of Fortune's gifts—wisdom, strength, health, long life, beauty, or wealth—chooses the last, was played at Henslowe's Theatre about 1595. Four years later, Henslowe commissioned Thomas Dekker to write a sequel to this; instead, he worked into one drama the story of Fortunatus and his two sons, the virtuous Ampedo and the covetous Andelocia. With Prologue and Epilogue written for the occasion, *Old Fortunatus* was presented before Queen Elizabeth in the Christmas celebration of 1599.

In the play, Vice and Virtue (added by Dekker) contest the world. Fortunatus, given a purse that never empties, spills cataracts of gold and is greeted gladly everywhere, as Vice sets greed agape in the souls of men. The eagerness of the Sultan of Babylon to learn the secret of

Fortunatus' wealth leads the Sultan to tell of his wishing hat that transports the bearer wherever he desires to go. Fortunatus promptly steals the hat. From the peak of his preening triumph, however, Fortune tumbles Fortunatus to the grave.

Andelocia, despite the distress of his virtuous brother Ampedo, carries to greater heights his father Fortunatus' excess, seeking especially to win Agripyne, daughter of Athelstane, King of England. Agripyne is also wooed by the Prince of Cyprus and by the devoted Orleans of France. The purse and the hat give Andelocia a temporary hold over Agripyne; but the faithfulness of Orleans wins her love. Time and his own recklessness strip Andelocia of his talismans; and both brothers are borne down to ruin, while, under the eye of the pure sovereign (the virtuous Queen Elizabeth), righteousness and the true devotion of Orleans triumph.

Old Fortunatus was long popular. It appealed, as Charles Dudley Warner said, "to the spirit of the time, when men still sailed in search of the Hesperides, compounded the elixir of youth, and sought for the philosopher's stone . . . Here Dekker the idealist, the poet of luxurious fancy and rich yet delicate imagination, is seen at his best." Despite the range of the play, to Cyprus and Babylon, the good Englishman Dekker feels happiest amid scenes of his native land.

Old Fortunatus has, as Gamaliel Bradford pointed out, "passages of the richest imaginative poetry"; yet it plays the gentle game in true Euphuistic fashion, or, as in Molière, it parries questions in the bantering duel of sex, as when Agripyne asks "whether it is more torment to love a lady and never enjoy her, or always to enjoy a lady whom you cannot choose but hate?" Charles Lamb declared: "The humor of a 'frantic lover' is here drawn to the life. Orleans is as passionate an inamorato as any Shakespeare ever drew."

Also like Shakespeare, Dekker was aware of the limitations of the theatre, though he justified cramming vasty fields into the cockpit and the wooden O, declaring that the theatre is to the earth as the earth is to the universe. A vivid mixture of magic and melodrama and morality, of satire and sentiment, of far-fetched folk and honest English feeling, *Old Fortunatus* gathers into its mingling of poetry and prose many of the best characteristics of the Elizabethan drama.

SATIROMASTIX   *Thomas Dekker*

In the Elizabethan War of the Theatres, Ben Jonson hurried his satire *The Poetaster** to put it on stage before the attack he had heard Dekker was preparing. Although Dekker and Jonson, in 1599 and 1600, had collaborated in the writing of two plays, Jonson's love of the classics and his precise, methodical workmanship were in such sharp contrast to Dekker's romantic tendencies and slipshod habits that Dekker could be persuaded to enter the lists, in behalf of Marston and his friends, against the satiric, "humorous" poet. Taking a romantic play which was then in the writing, Dekker added an extensive satirical element, and called the mixture *Satiromastix (Satire's Scourge); or, The Untrussing of the Humorous Poet.* Allardyce Nicoll called this, of all the War of the Theatres plays, "easily the wittiest and most entertaining." It was presented privately by the Children of Paules and publicly by the Lord Chamberlain's company in 1601, and first printed the year following.

Into *Satiromastix*, Dekker brought many of the characters from

Jonson's *The Poetaster*: Horace (Jonson); Crispinus (Marston); Demetrius (Dekker himself); Captain Tucca; Asinius Lupus. Most of the abuse of Jonson comes from the coarse mouth of the swaggering Captain Tucca, whom Dekker made an amusingly exaggerated burlesque of Jonson's own Tucca, the liveliest figure in *The Poetaster*. In *Satiromastix*, the Captain alludes to Jonson's work in his stepfather's brickyard —"poor lyme and hayre rascall"; "foul-fisted Morter-treader"—and even makes reference to Jonson's narrow escape from hanging after a duel. He mocks Jonson for his shabby clothes; Jonson set the pattern for this in *The Poetaster*, taunting both Crispinus and Demetrius with their defective doublet and ravelled satin sleeves—though more nobly Horace in *The Poetaster* chides Augustus Caesar for a glancing mention of his lack of wealth.

Who the chief victim of Dekker's satire is, Captain Tucca leaves the audience no need of guessing. In addition to frequently quoting or parodying *The Poetaster*, he addresses Horace as Asper and as Criticus, both names Jonson had used for himself in his own plays, and he complains: "A Gentleman or an honest citizen shall not sit in your penniebench Theatres, with his Squirrel by his side cracking nuts; nor sneak into a Tavern with his Mermaid, but he shall be satyrd and epigramd upon, and his humor must run upo' the stage: you'll have Every Gentleman in's humour and Every Gentleman out on's humour." Identification could hardly be pinned more clearly upon Jonson.

At the end of the play's satire, King William Rufus of England, at whose court the action takes place, delivers Horace over to Crispinus for punishment. Horace is given an oath to take, analogous to the palinode in *Cynthia's Revels** and the oath of Crispinus and Demetrius in *The Poetaster;* then punishment such as Crispinus' emetic is pondered. Horace is finally tossed in a blanket and crowned with a crown of thorns.

Perhaps, in 1609, when writing, in *The Gull's Horn-Book*, the satiric chapter on *How a Gallant should behave himself in a Playhouse*, Dekker looked back laughingly upon these matters, remembering how Jonson had laughed at Crispinus' (Marston's) kinky hair and "little legs"; for in this chapter Dekker wrote: "Now Sir, if the writer be a fellow that hath either epigrammed you, or hath had a flirt with your mistress, or hath brought either your feather, or your red beard, or your little legs etc. on the stage, you shall disgrace him worse than by tosing him in a blanket, or giving him the bastinado in a Tavern, if in the middle of his play you rise with a screwd and discontented face from your stool to be gone." Doubtless friends of the playwrights took such steps in the War of the Theatres.

The attack upon Jonson quite overbalances the original story of Dekker's play, which deals with the marriage of Sir Walter Terill to Caelestina at William Rufus' court, and with Caelestina's taking what she thinks is poison but turns out to be a sleeping potion, to escape the unwanted advances of the king.

Dekker's attack upon Jonson, however, is gentle, almost amiable; it does not emulate the sharpness and arrogance of Jonson's words. Demetrius, in *Satiromastix*, admires the good qualities of Horace. No lasting enmity resulted from the dramatic exchange of fire. Dekker was in reality scarcely more than an amused bystander, who joined the fight for the fun. When it was over, all were friends again. In 1604, Jonson collaborated with Marston and Chapman in the writing of *Eastward*

Hoe*, for which all three spent some time in the King's gaol; and later that year, Marston dedicated his drama *The Malcontent* to Jonson. It should be noted, however, that, in 1619, Jonson told Drummond of Hawthornden that Dekker was a knave.

In dismissing the disputants in the play, King William Rufus says: "True poets are with art and nature crowned." The genial Dekker gives ample evidence in *Satiromastix* that he is graced with such a double crown.

THE HONEST WHORE   *Thomas Dekker*

High folk and low mingle in the two plays by Thomas Dekker titled *The Honest Whore* (Part One, 1604; Part Two, 1630). Although their locale is labeled Milan, their characters are English—Dekker, London-born, seldom strayed from his native city—and are such as might in his day have been seen on the London streets. Dekker's voluntary visits to taverns and enforced visits to prisons made him thoroughly familiar with the frequenters of both. *The Honest Whore,* though its theme has kept it from frequent production, most characteristically represents Dekker's genius.

In the first part, the Duke of Milan seeks to separate his daughter Infelice and Count Hippolito. He spirits the girl away, and holds a funeral for her, while he seeks to have Hippolito poisoned. The harlot Bellafront, by falling in love with Hippolito, though he scorns her, is redeemed from her wanton ways. Doctor Benedict, instead of poisoning Hippolito, informs him of the treachery and deceit. Infelice meets her lover in Bethlem Monastery where, after a display of madmen to amuse the audience, the two are married.

Interwoven with this plot are the efforts of Viola, wife of Candido, the linen-draper, to break down her husband's patience. Neither the rudeness of the rakes who are his customers, nor the devices of his wife which finally lead him also to Bethlem, annoy Candido. The Duke frees him, blesses Hippolito and Infelice, and orders Matheo, who had first misled Bellafront, to marry her.

In the second part, Matheo becomes more spendthrift and dissolute. Hippolito, married, now desires Bellafront, and Matheo for profit would have her turn whore again. Bellafront's father, Orlando Friscobaldo, disguised as a servant, watches over her. After a parade of harlots at Bridewell prison, to amuse the audience, Hippolito and Matheo, their villainies exposed, presumably reform.

The characters are well drawn throughout the play, which, with its mingling of serious and comic parts, is a forerunner of the problem play of our own time. In his picture of the whore turned honest, as Ernest Rhys observed, "Dekker has used his realistic method with terrible sincerity, and yet with so cunning a grasp of the nettle of shame that with its sting it yields a fragrance as of the perfect flower of love." Bryan, the Irish footman, is a good caricature of a type then frequent in London. Candido, the linen-draper, is perhaps too saintly in his forbearance, but he drives home the political intention that Dekker makes clear in his last line: "A patient man's a pattern for a king." Failure to heed such warnings led, within a dozen years, to Cromwell's revolution.

The father of Bellafront is the finest creation in the play. William Hazlitt exclaimed: "Old honest Dekker's Signior Orlando Friscobaldo I shall never forget! . . . Simplicity and extravagance of style, homeliness and quaintness, tragedy and comedy, interchangeably set their hands and seals to this admirable production. This 'tough senior,' this impracticable old gentleman, softens into a little child; this choke-pear melts in the mouth like marmalade . . . The story has all the romance of private life, all the bearing up against silent grief, all the tenderness of concealed affection: there is much sorrow patiently borne, and then comes peace."

Swinburne, in *Nineteenth Century,* (January, 1887), especially praised Dekker's handling of "the reclaimed harlot, now the faithful and patient wife of her first seducer; the broken-down, ruffianly, light-hearted and light-headed libertine who has married her; and the devoted old father who watches in the disguise of a servant over the changes of her fortune, the sufferings, risks, and temptations which try the purity of her penitence and confirm the fortitude of her constancy. Of these three characters I cannot but think that any dramatist who ever lived might have felt that he had reason to be proud . . . —the crowning evidence to the greatness of Dekker's gifts, his power of moral imagination, and his delicacy of dramatic execution."

Though its situations may seem remote, *The Honest Whore* is rich with characters and motives that stir about us every day, and ripe with sound reflections on human woes and ways.

THE TWO ORPHANS   *Adolphe D'Ennery*

Hailed as "a story that never grows old," *Les deux orphelines* (*The Two Orphans*) was one of the most popular plays of the late nineteenth century and, in several ways, has become a part of American theatrical history. The story was taken by Eugene Corman to the already successful playwright Adolphe D'Ennery (French, 1811-1899) whose dramatization of it opened on January 29, 1874, and took Paris by storm. In those days before international copyright protection, French hits were rushed into English; a London adaptation of *The Two Orphans* by John Oxenford opened in September, 1874, and ran for nine months in competition with another version called *The Blind Girl's Fortune.*

In New York, Hart Jackson—one of the first adapters to deal with foreign playwrights, rather than steal their plays—prepared a version of *The Two Orphans* which Albert M. Palmer, with considerable reluctance, presented on December 21, 1874, at his Union Square Theatre. A blizzard kept the theatre empty on opening night, but the play recovered and ran until the following June 15; it was, in fact, the chief instrument in breaking Lester Wallack's czarlike hold on the New York theatre.

Kate Claxton was in the original New York cast, as Louise; in 1889, she took over the rights and in 1902, and again in 1909, published warnings to all theatre managers that she was the sole copyright owner. In 1904 Grace George starred as Louise. The play was revived again in 1911. In 1926, New York saw an all-star production with Robert Loraine, Wilton Lackaye, Jose Ruben, Fay Bainter, and Mary and Florence Nash.

In Chicago, two versions—Oxenford's and Jackson's—were presented during the summer of 1875. In Brooklyn, on December 5, 1876, the theatre in which *The Two Orphans* was playing to a packed house took fire; over 300 spectators and several of the cast were killed. Kate Claxton emerged as the heroine of the occasion and survived to carry the play to stages all over the country.

The Two Orphans is today more familiar as *The Orphans of the Storm,* D. W. Griffith's silent film with Lillian and Dorothy Gish.

In the play, two Normandy foster-sisters, Henriette and the blind Louise, seeking relatives, reach Paris in a swirling snow storm. Henriette is abducted by a scoundrelly noble; Louise is ensnared by a hag of the Paris slums who makes her go begging in the streets. Rescued by a gallant chevalier, Henriette finds Louise in the hag's hovel. When the hag's pickpocket son, Jacques, bars the girls' way, his crippled brother, Pierre, "leaps into manhood" and dies fighting Jacques while the girls escape. At the end, Louise finds her countess mother, whose noble husband opens his heart to them both, and a doctor promises to restore her sight. Henriette is happy with her chevalier. The audience is happy, too.

"For thirty years," commented the *Boston Transcript* (September 13, 1904), "the American theatregoing public has thrilled and wept over the sad adventures of the orphaned Louise and Henriette in the great city of Paris, has had its gorge rise at the pitiless cruelty of the besotted hag La Frochard, and her brutal son, Jacques, has given unstintedly of its sympathy to his crippled brother, Pierre, has mingled its tears with the sorrowful Countess de Linières, and has entered heart and soul into the bitter-sweet love idyll of the Chevalier de Vaudrey and Henriette; and there is no reason to suppose that it will not go on thrilling and weeping for countless years to come. *The Two Orphans* is, beyond question, one of the strongest, sanest, and best constructed of melodramas, so true in its portraiture, so probable in plot and so continuously appealing that it can never grow stale."

The Parisian audiences probably wept even more, for the American version omits some of the heart-pulsing episodes of the original. Louise's sufferings at the hands of La Frochard are softened; the actual death of the crippled Pierre is averted by the timely arrival of the chevalier; and there is also omitted the Countess's confession that Louise is the love-child of a matrimonial indiscretion, as well as the forbearance of her elderly and august husband.

Never having been "fresh," never quick with aught but theatrical fire, *The Two Orphans* cannot grow "stale." Its lapse from constant performance serves as a reminder that the motion pictures have largely taken from the theatre the wide, unsophisticated public that, without great regard for character growth or literary polish, enjoys a stirring story well told. Such an audience, for almost half a century, found complete melodramatic suspense and arousal in *The Two Orphans.*

HER CARDBOARD LOVER   *Jacques Deval*

Dans sa candeur naive, 1926, by Jacques Deval (French, b. 1893), adapted by Valerie Wingate and P. G. Wodehouse as *Her Cardboard Lover,* was the deftest of the frou-frou comedies that effervesced in Paris after the first World War. (Better known, though less lively than *Her Cardboard Lover,* is Deval's *Tovarich,* 1933, which Robert E. Sherwood adapted in 1936. In *Tovarich,* the topsy-turvy world that followed the Russian Revolution is ironically shown.)

The story of the play is simple. Simone, being pursued by her still loving ex-husband, is fearful of yielding. She hires a penniless young man, who has declared his devotion, to be her "cardboard lover" and to guard her from such weakness. By his unfailing good-humor, but equally by his shrewd tactics, the young man turns Simone's heart toward himself. His kiss, at the final curtain, wins from her the admiring exclamation (the play's closing words): "That's not so cardboard!"

During the preliminary tour of *Her Cardboard Lover* Simone was played by Laurette Taylor, but Jeanne Eagels had the part when it opened in New York, March 21, 1928, with Leslie Howard. The play has been widely and succesfully played. Tallulah Bankhead acted in it in Liverpool in 1929, and it is a very popular summer-theatre piece. With deftly drawn figures moving in a cardboard world, *Her Cardboard Lover* smiles at life's complications as it ironically captures an amusement tinged with melancholy, that's not so cardboard!

A TAILOR-MADE MAN   *Gábor Drégely*

The tailor's apprentice who, in the Budapest farce, *The Son of Fortune,* 1908, by Gábor Drégely (Hungarian, b. 1883) is an unscrupulous though not unpleasant schemer, became, in Harry James Smith's adaption, *A Tailor-Made Man,* an honest if adventurous American go-getter. In both tongues, and throughout Europe, the play was a great success.

In the Hungarian play, Kormos, the tailor's assistant, knows himself destined for greater things. He reads Szontagh's unpublished manuscript *Gentlemen and Workers;* he listens at doors, when he delivers suits, to absorb society ways; at length, he puts on a dress suit left at the shop for pressing, goes to a reception at the Reiners', and impresses the Prime Minister. He publishes Szontagh's book as his own, is elected to Parliament, offered a substantial dowry to marry Emma Reiner, and promised a Cabinet post. In the meantime, Szontagh, having discovered Kormos in a rendezvous with his wife, plans—along with Emma's rejected suitor— to expose him. Each of the accusers, however, is persuaded that he'll be better off letting Kormos become Minister; and the tailor's apprentice moves triumphantly on.

In the American version, John Paul Bart dons the dress suit, but he uses Sonntag's book only to get ideas that help him solve the labor troubles of the financier Nathan, head of a shipbuilding trust (whom, instead of a prime minister, John captivates,). There is no love-making with Sonntag's wife—a high comic spot in the original, as the woman is more amorous than the ambitious man—and although the society Stanlaws try to interest Bart in their daughter, Corinne, he does not succumb. Instead, he tells the whole tale to the press before the envious Sonntag can expose him, goes back to the tailor shop, and marries the humble tailor's daughter, only to be lifted again by Nathan to supervise his new labor relations program.

The American version, with its true man risen from the ranks in the land of opportunity and nerve, lacks, as E. J. Gergely pointed out in *Hungarian Drama in New York* (1947), "the cynical acceptance of human frailty" with which the original ends; and its final note "of integrity and hope" is more sentimental than the original. Smith, indeed, achieved such a transformation as to make his version seem a genuine American work, "saturated with Americanism," said *Current Opinion* (November, 1917). *The Forum* (March, 1918) said that the play is "reminiscent of the Englishman's remark, 'Americans and Englishmen are both great bluffers, with the difference that the American makes his bluff good';" and the

New York Telegraph (December 22, 1918) called the adaptation "the funniest American comedy ever written."

A Tailor-Made Man opened in New York August 27, 1917, with A. P. Kaye and Grant Mitchell, for a run of 398 performances, the longest run of any play adapted from the Hungarian. (Second is Molnar's* *The Play's The Thing,* with 326 performances.) The *New York Tribune* stated: "*A Tailor-Made Man* is comedy of a kind that is rare and delightful . . . here and there it rises to points at which it is a real comment on life and destiny. And it is comment that is well flavored and full of relish." The chief figure of the drama caught the interest of the *Times:* "The character was solidly based in psychology, the thought ever underlying the action and peeping out at odd corners of the countenance before a word was spoken. Therein lay its power of convincing, and its sterling humor." There is, in *A Tailor-Made Man,* an amusing basic situation, with developments through which a natural character moves in ways that make the play both a lively comedy and a kindly and searching light on human nature.

ABRAHAM LINCOLN *John Drinkwater*

Great men of history are a constant lure to playwrights; yet it is exceedingly difficult to compress the surge of a lengthy and eventful career into the compact form of an evening's drama. In most cases, the famous figure becomes little more than a wax-museum exhibit, an effigy in an historical tableau, a mouthpiece of the author's ideals, or a fellow whom the author labels, say, Lincoln, but who for significance and vitality might just as well be called John Doe. Of the many plays that have been written about the United States' most beloved President, two rise to lasting worth: *Abe Lincoln in Illinois*,* by the American Robert E. Sherwood; and the English John Drinkwater's *Abraham Lincoln.*

John Drinkwater (1882-1937) was director of the Birmingham Repertory Theatre, and for it pondered an historical play. As he tells the story in the *Pictorial Review,* (December, 1920), "The choice was made as objectively as though Lincoln had been a Pharaoh or an Alexander of old. . . My aim had been toward the essential and universal qualities of Lincoln; and upon the dramatic presentation of these the play must stand or fall."

Abraham Lincoln proved of considerable interest to many audiences. After its Birmingham premiere, October 12, 1918, the play went to London, where it opened on February 19, 1919, for a run of 466 performances and reopened, August 6, 1921, for 173 more. The first New York production came December 15, 1919, and ran for 311 performances. The play is still quite popualr everywhere. Walter Hampden played in it in 1939; the King and Queen of England watched a performance in 1940; it was a hit in Japan in 1946. Alexander Woollcott called it "a moving, exciting, and forever memorable experience." President Hoover declared: "I never enjoyed a play more in my life."

Inevitably episodic, *Abraham Lincoln* shows its hero in six significant situations: First, amid homely surroundings, notified of his nomination and accepting it in dedication to the cause of justice: Second, in the grim and painful decision to hold Fort Sumter and to deny secession: Third, in an interview with two women, a war profiteer's wife who cries for bloody vengeance and a widow whose son has been killed in the War, when in shining tolerance he stands (almost alone in history) with Christ, as one who loved his enemies: Fourth, in a challenge to his Cabinet and the issuance of the Emancipation Proclamation: Fifth, at the moment of Lee's capitulation and the chivalrous terms of "Unconditional Surrender" Grant: and finally, in the box in Ford's Theatre, April 14, 1865, when he was assassinated.

Throughout this pageant, Drinkwater keeps Lincoln within the human mold by countless homely touches: the English ambassador finds the President busy blacking his boots; Grant's orderly comes upon him asleep, stretched across two chairs in the General's headquarters. Drinkwater's Lincoln is a sad and weary man, called by destiny, and unwillingly come, to play a decisive role in the movement of his country toward the realization of its ideals.

On both sides of the ocean, reviewers agreed as to the merit of the play. Kenneth Macgowan (December 16, 1919) exclaimed: "The thrill of the theatre—the surge of history—the lift of the creative imagination: these three things made a rare and exciting evening . . . The appeal of John Drinkwater's creation goes beyond the appeal of Lincoln himself, great as that is . . . the language of *Abraham Lincoln* is the language of the Bible—strong, simple, true." James Agate in the *London Times* (March 18, 1943) looked back to the first performance he had seen, in 1921, and declared that then "Quite suddenly I 'got' Lincoln in the way people 'get' religion."

The lofty nobility of Lincoln, coupled with his simple humanity, is drawn with power and passion through the well chosen and finely wrought episodes of Drinkwater's play.

ALL FOR LOVE   *John Dryden*

John Dryden (English, 1631-1700) began writing plays quite in the Restoration mood of licentious wit and bawdry. From about 1670, he wrote a play a year for some fifteen years.

Dryden's first play in blank verse, and his best play, is a version of the story of Antony and Cleopatra, *All For Love, or The World Well Lost.* Observing the unities of time, place, and action, more exactly "than perhaps the English theatre requires," Dryden concentrated on the final days of the fated lovers, when Antony is besieged in Alexandria by Octavius Caesar. Starting at the point Shakespeare reached in Act IV, Dryden reduced the speaking parts from thirty-four to ten and the scenes from forty-two to one for each of the five acts. Dryden concentrated also on the all-encompassing love of the doomed couple, in contrast to Shakespeare, who in *Antony and Cleopatra** set in conflict the urge of private love and the drive of public power, with Antony's disaster hung upon his failure to choose between his personal feelings and his political career. In Dryden's drama, the disaster springs from the tortured jealousy of Antony's all-consuming love. Antony's general Ventidius, his friend Dolabella, and his wife Octavia have persuaded him to leave Cleopatra and join in friendship with Octavius, when a gust of suspicion that Dolabella will succeed him with Cleopatra flings him back into the Egyptian's open arms.

Cleopatra is likewise wholly enamoured of her Roman. She is bemused in love beyond resourcefuness, incapable of the wiles and lures wherewith Shakespeare shows "the gypsy of the Nile" seeking to win and hold her Antony. In Dryden, it is love complete, love the conqueror; and all for love. A false report of Cleopatra's death fells Antony on his sword. Cleopatra comes to him as he dies, and sets the asp upon her soft arm, that had often held her Antony.

Without the majestic sweep of Shakespeare's, Dryden's play has a soft, sweet power of its own. Shakespeare's tragedy has largely supplanted Dryden's on the stage. When Dryden's was presented, however, opening May 27, 1946, by Equity Library (the first New York production since 1797), George Freedley said that it "plays astonishingly well . . . makes an extremely interesting performance on the stage." Another revival opened at Fordham University on December 6, 1951, "to complete the cycle," it was smilingly announced, represented on Broadway by the Oliviers' alternating productions of *Antony and Cleopatra** and *Caesar and Cleopatra**.

There rises from *Antony and Cleopatra* a sympathetic flow of emotion, and an impulse of respect, for two great persons torn between their passion and their thrones; out of *All For Love* wells a deeper spring of sadness and of pity for two great lovers whom the wide concerns of empire condemn to die for love.

THE MAN WITH A LOAD OF MISCHIEF   *Ashley Dukes*

Ashley Dukes (English, b. 1885) has had a varied career in the theatre. He is well known as a critic. He has, since 1933, been manager of the little, experimental Mercury Theatre where T. S. Eliot's *Murder In the Cathedral** was produced. He has adapted a number of plays from the German and the French, including *The Machine Wreckers** and *The Man Who Married a Dumb Wife*.* Of his several original dramas, only the first, the romantic comedy *The Man With a Load of Mischief*, has lasting merit.

The Man With a Load of Mischief pictures a swift idyll of a stormy night on the Bath-to-London road, these many years ago. A beautiful lady, once a famous Covent Garden singer, now the mistress of a prince, is running from that prince and from a nobleman who also desires her. The noble libertine, rejected, and lecherous in his cups, sets on his valet, Charles, to woo the lady. Charles, who had heard her sing years before and had always adored her, turns out to be a manly, self-respecting, understanding fellow, and as the prince arrives the lady goes off with the man. The noble finds consolation with the maid.

This simple story takes its title from the sign of the roadside inn where the lady takes refuge from the storm, a sign that shows a portly old amorous baron bearing a ribald young blonde upon his back. There is little substance to the drama; it is fetching but conventional, entertaining but sentimental. Its value lies in its delicacy and its neat style.

The Man With a Load of Mischief opened in London, December 7, 1924, and was revived there June 16, 1925 for a run of 261 performances and was played again in 1933 and 1942. New York saw the play, October 26, 1925, with Ruth Chatterton; Westport, Connecticut, in 1932 with Jane Cowl. The *New York World* (October 27, 1925) called it a "sedately indecorous and beautifully written romance," and Arthur Pollock said it is "a comedy wise as well as delicate." The *London Times* (September 24, 1933) also praised the play, discerning that "this lovely little romance of the Regency has a sense of style and a distinction that are missing from most modern plays."

So delicate is the drawing, so fine-spun the sentiment, that the subtle satire may be missed. The picture of the nobleman, addicted to fleshly pursuits, wholly unobservant of his valet Charles' true worth, gives a fuller flavor of independence to Charles' quiet poise and self-respecting love. The movement toward the assertion of human worth regardless of title and station, however, establishes a sound core of dignity within the polished gallantry and dukely dastardry and romantic rouse of the delicate and charming comedy, *The Man With a Load of Mischief.*

THE TOWER OF NESLE   *Alexandre Dumas, père*

Henri III and his Court, 1829, by Alexandre Dumas père (1802-1870) was the first French romantic drama.

Dumas' second, and most successful, romantic melodrama was *The Tower of Nesle,* in which Mlle. Georges (Marguerite Josephine Weimer) appeared in 1832. It is based upon actual scandalous incidents in French history, involving the wives of three French kings, brothers all: Louis X (King, 1314-1316), Philip V (1316-1322), and Charles IV (1322-1328). The wife of the first, the licentious Marguerite of Burgundy, chose her lover each day, enjoyed her amours by night in the Tower of Nesle, and let the waters of the Seine cover the favored one before sunrise. She was strangled by order of her husband. Associated with her in these amorous and lethal enterprises were her two sisters-in-law.

Dumas' play, *The Tower of Nesle,* is built mainly upon a duel of wits between Marguerite and a captain who, with incriminating papers scrawled with her secrets, forces his way to the prime ministershp, until his overweening ambition tumbles them all.

The Tower of Nesle remains a melodramatic favorite of the French theatre. It is, indeed, a vivid and still stageable piece, the forerunner of a host of less literate plays, which degenerated into the "ten-twenty-thirty" melodrama of our grandfathers. When Dumas' drama was presented in Chicago in 1927, directed by Whitford Kane at the Goodman Theatre, the *Chicago Journal* (October 10) said "It is gratifying to report that the Dumas piece, for all its demands, is better than anything the Goodmanites have previously done."

In Paris, Robert Kemp reported of a revival, in *Bravo* (October, 1930): "The newest play? Undoubtedly *The Tower of Nesle,* of which, in twenty months, we'll observe the centenary. What a delight to find in it so much innocence, life, ridiculous and charming passion! It's the history of our grandparents of 1832, ardent, candid, childlike, thunderous." When it was made into a motion picture, in 1937, *La Critique cinématographique* called the play "a strong, powerful work, masterfully constructed, and spun of steel, for it has preserved its attractive qualities through the generations." In 1938, Richard Le Gallienne, writing from Paris for the *New York Sun* (August 27), said that *"The Tower of Nesle,* produced at the Porte Saint Martin Theatre May 29, 1832, has never stopped running in some Paris theatre since, a record that no other playwright has ever matched."

Dumas turned from plays to novels; he is best known for his two romances published in 1844: *The Three Musketeers,* and *The Count of Monte Cristo.* We are told that his many sprawling romances were written with a staff of "ghosts," but his earlier plays were singly and carefully constructed. The complicated intrigue of the plot is skilfully carried to a strong climax. The characters are seen on the surface only, but—especially in *The Tower of Nesle*—they are dynamic, and they drive toward their goals with an energy of mind and will that still gives power to the play, one of the vivid melodramas of the romantic stage.

CAMILLE   *Alexandre Dumas, fils*

The greatest 'tear-jerker' of all time is this drama of the lady of the camellias, the Parisian courtesan Marguerite Gautier, who gives up the young man she loves, Armand Duval, at his father's plea. Only as she is dying from tuberculosis does Armand learn that Marguerite really still loves him; he rejoins her, and she breathes her last in his arms.

Alexandre Dumas, fils (French, 1824-1895) based his novel *La Dame aux camélias* (Camille) on the actual story of Alphonsine du Plessis. While waiting penniless, in a Marseilles tavern, for a remittance from the generous but often pinched Dumas père, Alexandre within three weeks turned the novel into a dramatic pot-boiler. Surprised when its performance was forbidden by the censor, Dumas left France. When Emperor Napoleon III removed the ban, Dumas was even more surprised at the play's immediate and sensational success. Opening on February 2, 1852, it played for the then unprecedented run of over 100 performances. *Camille* has been played by many stars: by Sarah Bernhardt in France and on several American tours; by Eleanora Duse, who opened her American tour with it in 1893; by Jessie Bonstelle, Margaret Anglin (with Henry Miller), Nance O'Neil, Olga Nethersole, Helena Modjeska (with Maurice Barrymore), and by Forbes Robertson (in England in a version by James Mortimer called *Heartsease*), Margaret Anglin, Eva Le Gallienne in 1931 and 1935, Lillian Gish in 1932, and Jane Cowl (with Rollo Peters) in 1933. In addition, there have been several motion picture versions of the play, one with Norma Talmadge. In 1917 Ethel Barrymore acted in a version that vainly strove to "modernize" the drama, introducing a prologue in which Duval goes to an auction of Marguerite Gautier's effects after her death; he spends the night in her room, and the play is his vision as he relives those days in retrospect.

Of the social attitude behind the play, Brooks Atkinson said in *The Civic Repertory Magazine* (March, 1931): "If life was ever like that, life must have been terrible. Of all the cant, hypocrisy, and purple-plush punctilio the *Camille* school of ethics is the most despicable. What a genius these folks had for muddling human relationships and inventing bogus crises out of whole cloth!" This, however, he added, "has no bearing upon such theatrical fustian as *Camille*. *Camille* is festive. . . . With such people, dressed in costumes that delight the eye, gaiety is no more than common civility; and it dispels a good deal of the tedium that plucks at the fringe of such verbose plays as *Camille*." As for Eva Le Gallienne's performance as Camille, Atkinson was quite ecstatic.

Percy Hammond (1922) liked Lillian Gish even more: "I have seen two dozen Camilles, ranging from Barrymore to Bernhardt—some of them chill, some of them passionate—but they all left me with eyes undimmed, excepting Miss Gish and Duse." Miss Gish herself said of her revival: "We went up into the attic of the theatre and took out of its treasure chest—tenderly, I hope—one of its loveliest pieces."

Henry James, in the year of Dumas' death, looked back to earlier impressions: "Written at twenty-five, *La Dame aux camélias* remains in its combination of freshness and form, of the feeling of the springtime of life and the sense of the conditions of the theatre, a singular, an astonishing production. The author has had no time to part with his illusions, but has had full opportunity to master the most difficult of the arts. Consecrated as he was to this mastery, he never afterwards showed greater adroitness in keeping his knowledge and his naiveté from spoiling each other. The play has been blown about the world at a fearful rate, but it has never lost its happy juvenility, a charm that nothing can vulgarize. It is all champagne and tears—fresh perversity, fresh credulity, fresh passion, fresh pain."

William Winter, who made *Camille* the chief weapon in his attack on realism in the theatre, preferring its theatrical effects to the bare bones and dirty crusts of current thesis plays, wistfully recalled the Camille of Madame Modjeska as "faultless in delicacy and superb in completeness."

Those familiar with the opera will recognize that the story of *Camille* is told in *La Traviata (The Castaway)*, by Francesco M. Piavé, with music by Giuseppi Verdi, which opened in Venice in 1853 and in New York in 1856 (later, at the Metropolitan Opera House with Marcella Sembrich and at the Academy of Music with Adelina Patti, both in 1883). The operatic version calls the heroine Violetta Valery; the hero, Alfredo Germont; it moves the story from nineteenth-century Paris to the days of Louis XIV. Otherwise, it follows the play very closely. A failure on its first production, *La Traviata* scored a distinct success in revised form a year later; it holds today a high place in any repertoire of Italian opera.

Camille holds a similarly high place in the theatre. Sentimental rather than sublime, it is one of the first, as well as one of the greatest, of the plays that have drawn women "to enjoy a good cry" in the theatre. Yet for all its sadness, as Willa Cather aptly sums it up, "it is always April" when *Camille* is played.

THE DEMI-MONDE   *Alexandre Dumas, fils*

Dumas invented the term *demi-monde,* as the title of the play that proved to be his best and, in France, his most popular. He is said to have written it to counteract the bad moral impression made by *La Dame aux camélias**, which had been severely censured at first; but *Le Demi-Monde* in its turn startled and shocked society—many of whose members doubtless had uncomfortable shivers of recognition. The play, indeed, was not presented at the Théâtre Français, but opened at the more liberal Gymnase on March 20, 1855.

Mlle. Rose-Chéri, as Suzanne, la baronne d'Ange, electrified the house. Suzanne, as the *New York Herald-Tribune* of December 11, 1926, described her, is "a lady with a past who, having arrived at a certain age, is trying valiantly to escape that past and exchange her bogus title and imaginary husband for a genuine title and a real man. . . a woman of the world with brains, with courage and the nerve to fight it out as long as there is a ghost of a chance and a loophole of escape." Suzanne's former lover, Olivier, however, without revealing their amours, is too masculinely high-minded to permit her to ensnare the honest soldier, Raymond de Nanjac, who loves her. Olivier's trap exposes Suzanne, and she is left at the end with only another old lover's wealth for consolation. Hence the play may be called a "high moral drama," as— observed the *New York Tribune* of November 12, 1859—"comedies more than usually full of demi-reps are now popularly termed."

The Demi-Monde was at once and lengthily popular on stage and in print. The book version went through six editions in its first year. From the Gymnase, the play was soon taken into the repertoire of the Comédie-Française, which also presented it frequently in London and, with Cecile Sorel, in New York in 1922 and 1926—the most popular play of her series.

Watching *The Demi-Monde,* one is held by the character of Suzanne. The play, said the *New York Mail* (November 15, 1922), "proves that when a woman sets out to love she has at her command an arsenal of weapons that range from pity and tenderness to passion and hate, and that she can wield them with the mastery of a finished strategist in battle. And it proves, too, that the spectacle of a woman marshaling her forces in such a fray is a spectacle for the gods and man to revel in."

While in performance the figure of Suzanne dominates the stage, *The Demi-Monde* gathers varied figures into a many-sided picture of the fringe of high society, "where husbands are never found." These persons are neatly caught in the crisp prose dialogue; among them, Valentine de Santis who, having left her husband and squandered the settlement he made on her, seeks now to reassume his name and his fortune, and La Vicomtesse de Vernières, who has kept her niece Marcelle nearby, to help give liveliness to her frittered and frivolous hours. A second major motif of the play is the contrast between the innocent Marcelle and the demi-dissolute society around her; she manages to maintain her maidenly attractions and is rewarded with the hand of Suzanne's high-minded former lover, Olivier. Olivier de Jalin, in truth, eats his cake and has it too; he participates in the demi-mondaine doings while he harangues against them; he draws all he can from the society he disdains, then withdraws from it to the world of respectable matrimony. The *New York Post* of November 15, 1922, called Olivier "a moralist so preposterous that even the contemporary critics of the play were inclined to regard him as a spot on the sun of the dramatist's genius"; but Dumas had merely condensed the essentially truthful picture of a man that sows his wild oats while carefully building a fence around his own farm. This double standard was almost universal at the time. Dumas saw in the opposition of Olivier and Suzanne the struggle of *l'honnête homme* against *la femme fatale;* but, as M. W. Disher pointed out in *Blood and Thunder* (1949), "the character of Olivier has undergone, if only because moralizing is no longer tolerated on the stage, a thorough metamorphosis from hero to prig."

Dumas' writing in *The Demi-Monde* is at its best. The play's construction moved toward the pattern of the "well-made" play of Sardou* and Scribe*. The exposition is especially effective: the past of the various characters is gradually revealed; a bit of information slips out, as it were, neatly at a critical moment—a method Ibsen* is often said to have brought to the modern theatre. The persons and the situations in *The Demi-Monde* are true to Dumas' time, and the drama was a vivid document of social criticism. *The Demi-Monde* took the stage as a colorful capture of an aspect of life, and it holds the stage as a well-wrought drama rooted in lasting elements of human nature, as self-indulgence seeks to wear the garments of propriety.

ANDRE   *William Dunlap*

The success of Tyler's *The Contrast** turned the portrait painter William Dunlap (American, 1766-1839) to writing for the theatre; his first produced play was *The Father; or American Shandyism,* at the New York John Street Theatre, September 7, 1789.

The success of *The Father* kept Dunlap long in the theatre; he became a shareholder of the Old American Company in New York; he adapted some thirty-five plays from the French and the German, the most popular being *The Stranger,* 1798, by August Kotzebue*; and he wrote thirty original plays, the best being *André,* 1798, and *The Italian Father,* 1799. In 1832, Dunlap wrote the first *History of the American Theatre.*

Major John André (1751-1780) seems to have been an engaging fellow; even the Americans felt for him a sympathy such as none entertained for Benedict Arnold, with whom André negotiated in an attempt to take West Point. Dunlap's *André* (revised in 1803 as *The Glory of Columbia*) is tightly knit. It presents the efforts to save the already condemned André. Pressure is brought by young Captain Bland, an American whose life André had saved and whose father, Colonel Bland, is held by General Clinton as hostage for André. André's English sweetheart, Honora, also pleads for him, but General Washington, touched though he is by André's own generous nature, holds firmly to his sense of duty and has the execution proceed.

André had its premiere on March 30, 1798, at New York's new Park Theatre. Recent productions include one in New York in 1917, one in 1940, and another in 1941 at Tappan, New York, where André was tried and executed. At the premiere, the scene in which Bland, disappointed at the failure of the pleas for André, rips down the American flag and flings it to the ground, created a riot. The management apologized, and the scene was removed. There are, nevertheless, several vivid scenes in *André,* the best play of the American Revolution by a man that lived through it.

BROADWAY   *Philip Dunning*

This play remains significant for its full dramatic capture of the false glamour of the prohibition era in New York. As Alexander Woollcott said: "Of all the scores of plays that shuffled in endless procession along Broadway in the year of grace 1926, the one which most perfectly caught the accent of the city's voice was this play named after the great Midway itself, this taut and telling and tingling cartoon. . . . The theatre is at its best when it is journalistic, when it makes its fable and its parable out of the life streaming down its own street, when the pageant on its stage is just a cartoon and a criticism of the land and the day lying across the sill of the stage door. So journalistic is *Broadway* that . . . its manuscript could scarcely have been delivered through the ordinary snail-paced channels. It must have come in over the ticker."

Philip Dunning (American, b. 1890), who wrote the play with George Abbott (American, b. 1887), and who peddled it for three years before Jed Harris produced it, said that he was "casting a challenge to the so-called silver screen . . . I set out then to write a play of continuous action occurring in a background that adhered to its prototype in real life with utter fidelity. As an indication of the pace at which the action moves, there is the fact that in the three acts of *Broadway* there are more than three hundred entrances and exits."

In its summer tryout at Atlantic City, the play was called *The Roaring Forties* (the New York night-club and theatre district stretches from Fortieth to Fifty-Second Street). It opened in New York at the Broadhurst Theatre on September 16, 1926, as *Broadway,* and caught on like wildfire. Never before did a drama gross a million dollars in thirty-seven weeks. (It cost but $9,000 to produce.) *Broadway* ran in New York for three years, while it was being played elsewhere by ten other companies, four of them abroad.

St. John Ervine called the English production "very crude, very direct, and very real." The *London Mail* said, "Much of it seems exceedingly vulgar; and no revue producer has dared undress his chorus to the extent of the girls supposed to represent the cabaret troupe." The English Lord Chamberlain, in truth, ordered some changes. He deleted about 30% of the profanity, changed "God!" to "Gee!", and subdued "Make your hands behave!" to "Stop!"

Two movements are intertwined in *Broadway*. There is the melodramatic rivalry of the gangsters, with Steve Crandall as big boss of the bootlegging racket; and there is the sentimental story of sweet Billie Moore, of the chorus at the Paradise Night Club, and her sweetheart, the hoofer Roy Lane. Steve, however, also has designs on Billie, and when the gangster shoots an uptown rival, somehow the police find Roy holding the murder gun. Things look bad for Billie and Roy; but when the uptown gangster's girl friend shoots Steve, the lovers are free to hope for happier days on Broadway.

Some critics were not sure of the play's appeal. Brooks Atkinson observed that it often has "the illusion of motion even when it is not progressing at all," but he felt that it was on the whole a "firmly packed melodrama." Alan Dale insisted that "this ingenious chatter of Broadway has nothing at all to interest anybody but the residents of near-Forty-Second street." The *New York Telegram* concurred with Dale. However, the play's stage history, including wide production among college groups, and "little" and summer theatres, shows that the rest of the country thrilled to the picture of life on the Gay White Way.

The play was twice converted into a motion picture: in 1929, with Lee Tracy and Sylvia Field; in 1942, with Pat O'Brien, Janet Blair, and George Raft (who played the part of "George Raft, the hoofer"). A new stage version, *Broadway 1941*, was attempted by Philip Dunning, with a shift from bootlegging to labor racketeering. *Variety* called the new version "antiquated by the host of gangster shows and (especially) pictures that followed and improved on it." The original remains, however, the best melodramatic picture of the "roaring twenties" along New York's "roaring Forties."

THE GLITTERING GATE   *Lord Dunsany*

Edward John Moreton Drax Plunkett, Lord Dunsany (Irish, b. 1878), who turned his Irish whimsy to the writing of short plays of Oriental mystery and horror, first came to the stage with his best play, *The Glitter-*

ing Gate, a one-act drama, which W. B. Yeats produced with the Abbey Players in Dublin, 1909.

Through the minds of two burglars that have died on the job, the play presents an ironic and whimsical satire on hope. In "the lonely place" before the "Gate of Heaven," Jim—who was hanged—tilts empty whiskey bottles, only to be mocked by far-away laugher, while the more recently dead Bill takes out his jimmy and works. The glittering gate swings open, to reveal only the blooming great stars. Bill is aghast, as the mocking laughter rises, and Jim exclaims: "That's like them. That's very like them. Yes, they'd do that!"

The Glittering Gate opened at New York's Neighborhood Playhouse on March 6, 1915, and became popular all over the United States. The *Milwaukee Leader,* after a 1917 production, called Dunsany "the most imaginative dramatist now using the English language." *The Glittering Gate,* as well as Dunsany's later plays, allows for imaginative staging and lighting. The language is simple, yet fraught with tense anticipation and muted suggestion along the brink of terror.

The emptiness of the hereafter envisioned in *The Glittering Gate* has caused critics to seek to reassure their readers. It has been suggested that Dunsany meant to show merely that there is no heaven for such as Jim and Bill, but the *London Referee* (March 25, 1920) was more consoling: "The stars are not, after all, a negation. Their only fault is that they are as far away as before. And we have to remember the possibility of more 'gates' than one to the Heavenly estate." The play remains quietly ironic.

The later dramas of Lord Dunsany were less universal in their evocation.

Current trends have lessened the vogue of Dunsany's dramatic moods, his fantasies of the macabre, but within that genre, and with a more delicate sensibility than Poe, Dunsany remains a dramatic master.

NJU   *Ossip Dymov*

Ossip Dymov (O. Perlmann, b. 1878), who wrote in Russian then translated his plays into Yiddish, composed one stark drama, produced as a striking contrast in lights and shadows, the ten moving scenes of *Nju.* (Nju, pronounced Nee-oo, is a Russian diminutive for Annie.) Acted in Austria, Poland, Germany, and France, as well as in 400 Russian cities, *Nju* had its English premiere in Los Angeles, October 31, 1916, and came to New York on March 22, 1917. Everywhere it found critical welcome as a powerful drama of the everyday. "Nju is a restless young creature," said the *Los Angeles Graphic* (November 4, 1916) "who really has too much in this life—that is, of the material things—and therefore imagines there are heights of ecstasy due everyone in this mortal existence. . . . the neighbors gossip over her bier, and life goes on again undisturbed in her little world." The play is an exercise in life's irony.

The story of *Nju* is a sordid one. Nju leaves her husband for a young poet, but, respecting the poet's demand that he be kept "unfettered," she rents an apartment for herself and her seven-year-old son. The poet finds a new source of inspiration in a gypsy cabaret singer; Nju finds release in poison.

Throughout the drama, vivid realism is mocked by attendant irony.

"The scenes between the husband and wife," said the *Los Angeles Tribune* (November 1, 1916), "between the two men, and the big episode in which the three take part, are remarkable bits of life. One cannot call them stage craft, for they are simply life as it is, neither of the stage nor stagey." Vivid, too, is the ballroom scene, with the dancers silhouetted against a curtain, while on the fringe of their gaiety disaster gathers. Ironic and poignant are the utterances of the seven year-old boy, while the adults are weeping for his dead mother. At the funeral scene, the irony is less subtle: the lover haggles with the florist, who in his turn confuses the wreaths of the husband and the lover; and before the burial is complete, the poet is reciting, to a young woman in black, verses that he had already whispered to Nju.

Dymov's play, according to the *New York Globe* (March 23, 1917) "reveals to us human characters as they are seldom revealed on the stage. . . One should not go to see *Nju* expecting the ordinary rule-made play, nicely dovetailed, with climaxes at the right moments, the characters filled with mechanical motives as a watch is filled with cogs and springs. The people in it do not behave like watches, registering sixty minutes every hour. . . They are different, because they say right out the things we think and keep to ourselves, not only things of the utmost moment, but the trivial, irrelevant things that come into our heads at odd times, nobody knows why or how." This sense of the naturalness of the persons, the implacability of events, and the indifferent onward flow of life, gives distinction to the simple lines and subtle implications of *Nju*.

BRONX EXPRESS   *Ossip Dymov*

Ossip Dymov combined symbolism and fantasy with realism in his greatest play, *Bronx Express,* in which he managed to extract poetry from the New York subway. First produced by the Jewish Art Theatre in New York in 1920, with Jacob Ben Ami, *Bronx Express* was revived in Yiddish in 1925. Meanwhile, in an English adaptation by Owen Davis, it was enacted in 1922 by Mr. and Mrs. Coburn. The play blends satiric portraits of Bronx life with ironic symbols of American business methods in a way that combines sweet charm and sharp sting.

In the Bronx express, Chatzkel (in the English version, David) Hungerstolz is a nightly straphanger on his way home from ill-paying work as a buttonmaker. His daughter Leah is foolish enough to love the impractical writer Joseph Hayman and to despise Jacob Katzenstein, a wealthy manufacturer who, if she weds him, will set David up with his own button factory. When David puts on the pressure, Leah runs away. That night, by chance just short of miracle, David gets a seat in the subway. He falls asleep, and dreams.

In the dream, David is in Florida. Wealth surrounds him. Miss Murad smiles and the Gold Dust twins gleam upon him; Aunt Jemima grins in the flesh. The figures in the subway advertisements have come to life— the Smith Brothers are especially imposing—but they all talk in terms of high finance, symbolizing "the push, the drive for success, the heartlessness, of American business." Uneasily through the dream the subway rumbles. In the millionaire's Florida mansion, dancers cling to straps hung from the ceiling; the doors are subway exits; a turnstile gives access to the ballroom; the hand towel is the *Subway Sun*. Awakened, David is less positive that money is all-important. A fellow-straphanger suggests that bluff may pave a highway to success; David tries it on the manufacturer, and gets the financing, leaving Leah free to marry her writer man. The first and third acts of *Bronx Express* are set in the well-kept but impecunious flat of the Hungerstolzes in the Bronx. The steampipes are too near and too noisy for Leah's dream of art, though her Joseph is as yet an author only by ambition. "Can you make a pair of pants?" David asks him. "Can you make buttons? Then what good are you?" Leah's little brother Sammy is well drawn, his current American slang and city ways contrasting with the speech and manners of his parents, still colored with the old world from which they have come to "the land of opportunity." Opportunity did not knock; but neither do the Hungerstolzes. They have a certain pride of place. David, in a trying moment, shouts at the janitor: "Loafer! Irisher! Spoil the Bronx!" And his wife, returning from the callous and grotesque grandeur of Florida—where she has been entangled in David's dream—gives vent to a heartfelt and homey cry: "Gott sei Dank, this is the Bronx!"

The fantasy of *Bronx Express* anticipates that of *Beggar on Horseback**; the realistic episodes have the quality of grim struggle in the city that has often gloomed the Yiddish and American stage. In *Bronx Express,* the two moods complement one another, out of the fantasy breeding hopefulness, a less dreary, less mercenary drive, to lighten the later living. The *New York Globe* (April 27, 1922) called the play "an original and imaginative piece of work, with the saving grace of a significant idea." Alexander Woollcott described the Florida figures as "a nightmare company, through whose mazes wander from time to time the pathetic figure of the old man's wife and the frightening figure of his lost Leah. Here is fantasy conjured up out of the humblest stuff; here is a blend of never and every day."

Some that have dwelled too lengthily along its teeming ways have been tempted to applaud the statement that Art is the quickest way out of the Bronx. The play *Bronx Express,* however, shows the obverse of such coinage: out of the Bronx, Ossip Dymov has made art.

THE GREAT GALEOTO   *José Echegaray y Eizaguirre*

Until he was forty-two, José Echegaray y Eizaguirre (Spanish, 1832-1916) grew through a career as a scientist and a statesman. In 1874 he wrote two plays; their success encouraged him to devote himself to the theatre. Altogether, he wrote some sixty-five plays. He is best known for *el gran Galeoto* (translated as *The Great Galeoto,* 1895).

The play is dedicated to "everybody," and *everybody* is its theme. It presents the effects of surmise and suspicion, of the whispered word of gossip in the world. Around Ernest, secretary and adopted son of Julian, and Julian's wife Teodora, false rumor rises, until a duel is fought, Julian dies, and the false suspicion of the world thrusts the innocent two into each other's arms. That which started as a lie grew in power until perforce it became the truth.

Galeoto is the book in which Paolo and Francesca were reading on the fateful day whereof Dante tells; Galeoto (Galahad) it was that brought together Launcelot and Guinevere. Throughout Italy and Spain, Galeoto is the name used for a go-between; in the play, Galeoto is the world's gossip that unites the lovers.

Echegaray, said Benito Pérez Galdós, "broke up worn-out forms and imbued the actor's art with a new strength and new resources." His novelty, however, was in large part a return to the past; and, in 1904, when he shared the Nobel Prize with the Provençal poet Frédéric Mistral, the new generation of Spanish writers protested against the award. Echegaray, with modern themes and sharp juxtapositions and stark conflicts, returned to the forms of the romantic drama and managed even to set into his modern considerations the old ideals of chivalry and conjugal honor.

Such ideals are manifested in several of Echegary's dramas, of which the best known, after *The Great Galeoto,* are *The Son of Don Juan,* 1892, and *Mariana,* 1892.

The Great Galeoto was produced in Chicago on October 22, 1906. The *Chicago Sun* praised its depiction of the power of gossip: "The lifting of an eyebrow, the unfathered innuendo, an intimation that all the world would disclaim having made: these accomplish everything—inspire doubt, fan doubt to flaming hate, pillage a man's peace of mind, blast the fair name of his house, his wife, his friend." In a lecture at the time, William N. Guthrie exclaimed, of the Galeoto, the gossip that is go-between: "Prodigious hero! Enormous central personage! Titanic conception! For here a whole city is your hero, every man and woman in the community your central personage and—most amazing stroke—your hero never appears upon the scene."

The version of *The Great Galeoto* presented in New York as *The World and His Wife* on November 2, 1908, was adapted by Charles Nird-linger and starred William Faversham as Ernest, with Julie Opp as Teodora. The *New York Dramatic Mirror* (November 14, 1908) called it "a marvel of play building . . . remarkable construction that makes the succession of comparatively commonplace incidents lead inevitably to the conclusion." *The World and His Wife* has been frequently revived by college and little theatre groups: 1911, 1914, 1927, 1934, 1939.

The *Boston Herald* (January 11, 1927) said that it "plays stirringly, with scarcely a moment that is dull."

Echegaray is content to make his characters clearly drawn and baldly opposed types; his passions spring from principles and may remain as abstract; his dialogue is less natural than rhetorical, less welling from the heart than lilted by the mind. From such characteristics, however, grows an intense dramatic effect. *The Great Galeoto* electrified Madrid; its author revitalized the theatre of Spain and broadened the local stage once more to the status of world theatre.

MURDER IN THE CATHEDRAL   *T. S. Eliot*

In this verse play about Archbishop Becket of Canterbury, poet Thomas Stearns Eliot (English; born in U.S., 1888) presents a very different aspect of the story from that pictured in the drama *Becket,* by Tennyson. Eliot's play deals with the motives behind the Archbishop's martyrdom and brings the issues involved in that twelfth century strug-gle into focus in the twentieth century.

The play is in two parts, with an interlude of the Archbishop's Christ-mas sermon of 1170. It has a chorus of Canterbury women who speak some of Eliot's finest poetry and link the high ritual of the high people with the common life of the day. The chorus opens Part One, which

presents Becket returning from his seven years' exile. (For his story, see
*Becket**.) In Part Two, the Archbishop defies four knights and is slain.
The four knights then step forward; in prose now and, said Eliot, "quite
aware that they are addressing an audience of people living 800 years
after they themselves are dead," each tries to justify his deed, so that
through this defense we discern that the forces that create martyrs and
saints are still at work in the world. The priests have the last word —
a prayer for mercy.

Murder in the Cathedral is a chronicle of Becket's torture of mind and
agony of spirit. All the other characters are merely labeled, "Priest,"
"Knight," "Tempter." Save in the knights' words at the close, Becket's
soul is the one concern. He is tempted in various ways: by worldly
pleasure and temporal delights; by power and prestige, as he ponders
turning over the king to the ambitious barons. The greatest temptation
of all is martyrdom, the urge to do the right thing for the wrong reason,
to sacrifice himself, not because he has "lost his will to the will of God,"
but out of pride. By resisting the temptation of sainthood, Becket proves
himself saintly.

Murder in the Cathedral runs swiftly, in easy verse, with many words
of Anglo-Saxon origin; the verse itself recalls the Anglo-Saxon in its
use of stresses, alliteration, and assonance. Eliot in writing the play
wished to avoid Shakespearean echoes, and kept the vesification of
*Everyman** in mind. John Anderson (March 21, 1936) called the result
"the finest dramatic poetry written in our time." Particularly in the passage where Becket makes his decision, where his nature finds true expression in complete surrender to God's will, does the poetry rise in simple yet solemn nobility and power.

The play was first shown at the Canterbury Festival in June, 1935. It
came to London, November 1, 1935, for a run of 180 performances, and
reopened October 30, 1936, for 154 more, and was played there again in
1937 and 1947. In the United States, *Murder in the Cathedral* was shown
at Yale University, December 20, 1935; in New York, March 30, 1936, and
again in 1937. It has also been widely shown around the country.

Reviewers have found the play not only literate but dramatic. "A
tragedy of the first distinction," said the *London Times* (November 2,
1935). "Its mode is the original dramatic mode of ritual; its theme is the
theme out of which drama itself, and some would say even religion, first
grew—the story of the priest-king who is slain for his people . . . The one
great play by a contemporary dramatist now to be seen in England."

In America, Brooks Atkinson (March 21, 1936) declared: "For exaltation, for earthly terror and spiritual submission, *Murder in the Cathedral*
is drama restored to its high estate"; and Howard Barnes found that
"it testifies eloquently to the compelling power of poetry wrought to
significant stage terms . . . a fervent and moving drama with moments
of majestic beauty."

Eliot is a practicing advocate of the use of verse in drama. In the
narrative portions of a play, however, he said in 1949: "The verse should
be unnoticeable . . . Here the purpose of the verse should be to operate
upon the auditor unconsciously so that he shall think and feel in the
rhythms imposed by the poet without being aware of what these rhythms
are doing. All the time these rhythms should be preparing the audience
for the moments of intensity when the emotion of the character in the
play may be supposed to lift him from his ordinary discourse—until the

audience feels, not that the actors are speaking verse, but that the characters of the play have been lifted up into poetry." The application of this
procedure in plays of contemporary significance, however, reveals its
drawbacks. The demands of neither poetry nor drama are satisfied in
Eliot's *The Family Reunion*, 1939, which shadows forth Orestes and the
Furies of Aeschylus* with a group in a north-of-England mansion, or in
his *The Cocktail Party* (originally *One-Eyed Reilly*) 1949, which has remote resemblances, Eliot has told us, to Euripides' *Alcestis*.* Especially
is this true of *The Cocktail Party*; obvious though earnest in its ethical
implications and muddled in its symbolism, this play is one, as John
Mason Brown observed, that "everyone seems to understand until asked
to explain it."

In spite of the current spate of plays in prose and the frequent flatness
of plays in verse, the greatest dramas have had their beauty and power
enhanced by the poetry of their expression. In *Murder in the Cathedral*,
Eliot's fervor and his theme meet in harmonious fusion, showing that
great poetic drama is not limited to treasures of the past, but can be a
constant and a contemporary vitalizing force.

THE POLISH JEW (THE BELLS)   *Erckmann-Chatrian*

Erckmann-Chatrian (French: Emile Erckmann, 1822-1899; Alexandre
Chatrian, 1826-1890) collaborated on numerous novels, most of which are
historical. Their one memorable drama, *The Polish Jew*, 1869, is a gripping story. It has a superb acting part in the role of a prosperous inn-
keeper, the mayor of an Alsatian town, who is haunted by an old crime.
Long popular on the French stage, where it was first played by Benoît
Constant Coquelin (Aîné), *The Polish Jew* was turned into an opera in
1900, with book by Henri Cain and Pierre Gheusi and music by Camille
Erlanger. Almost immediately after the play's French premiere, two
English versions were produced. The first, opening in London, November
13, 1871, was F. C. Burnand's *Paul Zeyers*, or *The Dream of Retribution*.
The second, opening there November 25, 1871, put on in desperation when
the Lyceum Theatre was in sore straits, gave Henry Irving his first great
triumph and a role to which he repeatedly returned for thirty years; it
was the Leopold Lewis (1828-1890) melodrama *The Bells*. In New York,
James W. Wallack played Mathias in *The Bells* in 1872-73, according to
the *Oxford Companion to the Theatre* (1951), "most terrifyingly."

The story opens on Christmas Eve, 1833, in a little town of Alsace. The
innkeeper and Mayor, Mathias, respected by all, the wealthiest man of the
town, is about to marry his only child, Annette, to Christian, a sergeant
of police. As the talk goes round, Christian is told of a mystery unsolved
for fifteen years: A polish Jew came to the inn to buy grain and thumped
his money-bag on the table; the next day, his horse and his coat were
found in the snow beneath the bridge. As this story is being told, a Jew
enters and tosses his money-bag on the table. Mathias shrieks and falls
in a fit. Fearful for his health, he hastens the wedding. When he counts
out Annette's dowry, the clinking of the coins seems to him the jingling of
sleigh bells. Terrified, he dreams that he is on trial for having murdered
the Jew and disposed of the body in a lime-kiln, and that he is forced to
re-enact the crime. In the dream, the executioner approaches. . . The
wedding guests find Mathias dead, and give sad testimony of their high
regard for an honest Mayor.

Coquelin played Mathias as a murderer without remorse or fear; Henry Irving, once the arrival of the second Jew betrays Mathias to the audience, played the part as though pursued by fear of detection and by remorse. When Irving celebrated the twenty-fifth anniversary of the role, the *London Observer* (November 26, 1896) hailed it as "a great day in the history of stage triumphs." As late as 1901, the *New York Tribune* could still say, "His performance is unique, and it remains unapproached and unapproachable." H. B. Irving, in 1909, enacted his father's role. The play is popular in the current repertoire of Butler Davenport's Free Theatre in New York.

The Bells is a great, perhaps the greatest, "one-part" melodrama; but it is morbid, shrewdly built to break upon the spectator's nervous excitability. The *New York World* (April 14, 1926) exclaimed: "He must have been an actor that could make *The Bells* ring true!" But the play sought no ring of truth, it sought to shock. In plays of this sort, the question of truth does not trouble the audience; they come not to be taught but to be moved. The *New York Tribune* (April 14, 1926) called *The Bells* a "drama of continuous thrills." The *London Times* (October 5, 1933), of a revival with Martin Harvey, declared: "The scenes of the eve-of-the-wedding party and of the ghostly trial are those that engross us most. But all through the evening we are sufficiently intent upon Mathias not to be worried by the stitled, old-fashioned dialogue, and to ask only those questions which the story intentionally suggests as we listen to the sound of the ghostly bells." Theatre-wise folk may find *The Bells* crude; but the ringing reaches below reason to grislier depths in us all, as the justly famous melodrama shows conscience bringing its own retribution, as the unrecognized murderer shrinks in horror to his doom.

JANE CLEGG   *St. John Ervine*

Although he was born (1883) in North Ireland and was director of the Abbey Theatre of Dublin in 1915, St. John Ervine spent most of his years in London, where he was drama critic of the *Post* and, later, of the *Observer*. (In 1928-29, he was in the United States as visiting critic of the *New York World*.) His plays are not so much Irish in local color, as English. The early ones ring with a round attack upon religious zealotry and intolerance; the later ones seem, on the whole, society-drama potboilers. Between these, however, Ervine wrote two earnest and rewarding psychological studies of humans caught in wretched circumstance, *John Ferguson** and *Jane Clegg*.

Jane Clegg is a sordid story of lower middle class life. Jane, who has been living for twelve years with her stupid, lying and unfaithful husband, Henry, their three children, and her fussing but weak-willed mother-in-law (who always gives in to Henry, but wonders why Jane doesn't stand up to him) at length has a chance to make a stand. With a little money her uncle has left her, she resolves to educate her children. She tries to summon the courage to leave Henry; but Henry, in debt to a bookie, cashes a check belonging to his firm, and it looks as though Jane's money will have to go to keep her children's father out of prison. In talks with the firm's cashier and the bookie, Jane learns that Henry has been lying again; he has used the money to buy tickets to Canada for himself and a lady friend. Calmly Jane bids him farewell and prepares herself for the new burdens of life with her mother-in-law, who is ready to spoil her grandchildren as she had spoiled Henry.

This sordid story is simply told in effective dramatic terms. The play opened in Manchester, April 21, 1913, and moved to London, with Sybil Thorndike, on May 19, 1913. It was revived in London in 1922 and again in 1944. The Theatre Guild presented it in New York opening February 23, 1920, for a run of 158 performances, with Helen Westley, Dudley Digges, and Margaret Wycherly.

In 1920, the *New York Post* (February 24) called *Jane Clegg* a notable example of modern realistic drama: "There are hundreds of women like Jane Clegg—patient, honest, simple, dutiful, affectionate creatures originally—wholly disillusioned and brought near to heartbreak, and driven finally to desperation by the constant neglect, petulance, and egotism of such ne'er-do-wells as her husband—though their portraits are seldom sketched so sympathetically." The *New York World* remarked that the play "rings as true as steel . . . distinguished by its unpretentiousness . . . You must always look below the surface to find the uncommonly fine quality of it." After the 1922 London revival, James Agate in *At Half-Past Eight* (1923) declared the play "a masterpiece small in scope but of perfect craftsmanship and truth, a slice torn out of the heart of things . . ." In 1944, the *London Observer* (October 1) said: "This little classic of the domestic school is too well built to show signs of reportorial wear and tear."

Although sympathy tends to flow entirely to Jane, the playwright does not that heavily tip the scales. In such wretchedness as the Cleggs', relieved only by Jane's endurance and her steadfast determination to do her best for the children, there is no character deliberately evil. Henry's mother dotes on him; it is lack of intelligence, not lack of love, that, indulging Henry, spoils him. Although a weakling, Henry has a certain ingratiating quality about him. He knows his own failings; he feels how futile it would be to strive to rise out of himself. He knows, moreover, that Jane is a fine woman; that's what makes it hard to live with her. Her life is an example he cannot follow. It is much more comfortable to relax with his Kitty, to slump with her on a level where no moral questions rise. We need not approve, we may not condone, but we surely can understand Henry.

Such insight brightens the surface sordidness of *Jane Clegg*. Richest is the portrait of Jane herself, a memorable study of an honest woman overborne by life, in a searching, realistic drama.

JOHN FERGUSON   *St. John Ervine*

A powerful character study, *John Ferguson* is the story of a crippled farmer who keeps firm hold on faith, although life makes of him a second Job. The play is St. John Ervine's most popular and his best. Dublin first saw it in 1915; London in 1920; New York in 1920, 1921, 1926, and again in 1928 and 1933 with Augustin Duncan, Richard Whorf, and Miriam Hopkins, (who also played it on the road). Joyce Redman played it for television in 1947.

The February 23, 1920 opening of *John Ferguson* with Helen Westley, Augustin Duncan, and Dudley Digges, was a crucial one for the New York Theatre Guild. It was their second production; although it cost them only $3,000, they had but $19.50 in their treasury on opening night. The play ran for 177 performances, and made it possible for the Guild to go on to its gratifying future.

Set on a farm, instead of on the squalid city street of *Jane Clegg*,* the play tells a grim story of misshapen lives. John Ferguson, crippled, sits in his chair, watching the evil around but knowing that God intends all for the best. His daughter, Hannah, despises the timid grocer, Jimmy Caesar, but consents to marry him to save the farm from Henry Witherow, who intends to foreclose his mortgage. Witherow overpowers and seduces Hannah. He is killed, and Jimmy is arrested. But the weakling Jimmy, despite his wild threats, had cringed away from vengeance. It is Hannah's brother, Andrew, that has shot Witherow, and he will not let Jimmy die for his deed. Hand in hand, Andrew and Hannah start for the police, while John, left alone behind them, seeks comfort in the Bible, crying "Absalom, my son!"

This story of mortgage, rape, and murder is saved from the rawness of melodrama by the simplicity of its telling and by its closeness to the soil. Its characters are natural, they strive to overcome their own weakness; their earnestness is real, their heart-throbs are living. Jimmy Caesar (as created by Dudley Digges and acted later by J. M. Kerrigan) is a memorable portrait of a wistful weakling, a good-natured, well-meaning fellow who cannot screw his courage to the sticking-place. Small wonder that the strong-willed Hannah should despise him, and shrink from marrying him even to save her crippled father's farm!

George Freedley, in *A History of Modern Drama* (1947), called the "rape of Hannah not entirely convincing." To others it seems an inevitable act. At one point Hannah slaps Witherow's face, an indication that sparks have flown between them; and, as she comes upon him right after her "engagement walk" with the weakling Jimmy, what could be more natural than for her indomitable spirit to surge for a moment toward the high-willed Witherow? In the very breath of her resistance, her yielding pulsed! Ervine has subtly probed the depths of that proud spirit.

Lesser figures are clearly drawn, too. Among these is Clutie John, "away in his mind," who wanders in and out with his whistle and words of daft wisdom. Work? says Clutie; "There's plenty can work, but few can whistle." But he cannot whistle death away. Ervine presses home the final irony: After the death of Witherow, a letter comes from John's brother in America, with money to pay the mortgage installment, overdue. Bitterly, Hannah declares "One man's dead, and another's in jail in danger of his life, because my Uncle Andrew forgot the mail day."

John Ferguson, said the *New York Evening World* (May 13, 1919) "grips us with its reality . . . a play of the soil, with Irish blood running wild and leading to a tragedy so terrible that in the end it makes old age —the most tragic thing in life—a hopeless, empty contemplation of existence." And the *New York Sun* (October 19, 1926) added: "It is a play burning deeply, mercilessly, unforgettably; a drama tense with the suffering and defeat of men."

The defeat of men, but the triumph of human values. Beneath the eyes of their God-trusting father, Hannah takes Andrew's hand and they walk forth, head high, to suffer the consequences of his deed. Such nobility within the sordid circumstance, the ring of truth blending with the ring of justice, gives beauty and distinction to *John Ferguson*.

THE MAN OF MODE   *George Etherege*

Sir George Etherege (1635-1691) set a new fashion in English comedy. His first play, *The Comical Revenge; or, Love in a Tub*, 1664, was the first Restoration prose comedy, though the serious portions are in heroic couplets. In its lively, realistic, roustabout comic scenes, the play established a pattern followed by William Congreve*, Richard Sheridan*, and especially Oliver Goldsmith in *She Stoops to Conquer**.

The best of Etherege's plays is *The Man of Mode; or Sir Fopling Flutter,* which held the stage for over a century. A production of February 24, 1728, included in the cast Mr. and Mrs. Colley Cibber, Wilks, Oldfield, and Mrs. Barton Booth. Horace Walpole in his *Thoughts on Comedy* (1775) observed: "*The Man of Mode* shines as our first genteel comedy; the touches are natural and delicate, and never overcharged . . . almost the best comedy we have."

The Man of Mode presents society at the height of jeweled coquetry, with the code that conceals emotion under epigram and polish or insolent carelessness. The chief character, Dorimant, is a portrait of Lord Rochester. Around him statelily move, in coiled intrigue, Sir Fopling Flutter, full of the latest Parisian plums of fashion and wit; the poet Bellair; together with Harriet—quite a match for Dorimant—and the other ladies whose amorous fencing with the gallants, on mutual quest of gaiety, must suffice for plot. As with Congreve, wit and dalliance take the place of story.

The Man of Mode opened with Mr. and Mrs. Betterton, March 11, 1676; Dryden had written an epilogue for it, and the King was in the audience. Although surpassed by later comedies in the field, it has sparkling dialogue, and its character drawing is as keen as it is shrewdly aimed.

ALCESTIS   *Euripides*

The lives of the three great Greek tragic dramatists span the period of Athen's glory. Aeschylus* fought in the battle of Salamis, which drove back the Persians and inaugurated Athens' proudest and most triumphant period; young Sophocles* led the chorus in the paean of praise at the games celebrating that victory; and Euripides was born on the island of Salamis on the day the battle was fought. Euripides' first extant play, *Alcestis*, was produced in the year (438 B. C.) that marked the completion of the most perfect building of Greek architecture, the temple of the virgin Athene, the Parthenon, "glory of the Acropolis." Although Euripides left Athens in 408 for the court of the King of Macedon, he and Sophocles died within a year, just before the utter defeat of Athens in the Peloponnesian War. Sophocles dressed his actors and chorus in mourning on the news that Euripides had died.

Throughout Greece, not in Athens alone, Euripides was held as the foremost dramatist. He was somewhat unpopular, personally, during his lifetime, but his fame grew rapidly after his death. Of his 88 plays, only five won first prizes (one posthumously), but through the fourth century before Christ he was far more popular than either Aeschylus or Sophocles. As a result, more of his plays—a total of 19—have been preserved.

Euripides (480-406 B. C.) was the most "modern" of the three great playwrights. Sophocles, who was in friendly rivalry with Euripides for many years, declared that he himself pictured men as they should be; Euripides, as they are. The legendary demigods and heroes of Greek literature became in Euripides' plays great figures on the human level, where their emotions and motives were examined. In many situations, Euripides restudied basic ethical problems, treating them more realistically than did the other dramatists. His realism was carried over to costumes as well; over a half dozen plays of Euripides in which the chief characters wore rags are mentioned by the comic dramatist Aristophanes in *The Acharnians**.

Euripides also played more upon the emotions of the audience, seeking not so much the exaltation of tragedy as the arousal of pity, even to the point of sentimentality. Quintilian praised him for his power of pleading and debate. Longinus remarked, in the third century after Christ: "Euripides is most assiduous in giving the utmost tragic effect to these two emotions—fits of love, and madness. Herein he succeeds more, perhaps, than in any other respects, although he is daring enough to invade all the other regions of the imagination."

In the actual construction of his plays, also, Euripides strove to approximate the pattern of life. He often pushed the chorus casually aside, treating it as no more than a lyric interlude. His dialogue is natural, conversational. While he was capable of great poetry, he seldom launched into lofty flights during the action of the drama. His entrances are deftly and naturally managed; in *The Suppliants**, for example, two characters come in talking; in *Iphigenia in Aulis**, a Messenger rushes in interrupting a conversation. Thus, in all aspects of the drama, Euripides came closer than Aeschylus and Sophocles to the modern realistic spirit.

Finally, in his emphasis on contemplation, his sharing of the aristocratic disdain of public life that developed in Athens, Euripides exhibited that indifference to earthly affairs which led Athens to lose its dominant place among the city states of Greece. "Blessed is he that has attained scientific knowledge," Euripides declared, *"that seeks not the troubles of citizenship,* nor rushes into unjust deeds, but contemplates the ageless order of immortal nature, how it is constituted and when and why."

Euripides' first play, *Daughters of Pelias,* an episode of the Medea* story, won him third prize, the last place among plays chosen for presentation. *Alcestis* won him second place in the contest of 438 B. C., in which Sophocles took first place.

Euripides used the olden myth of Admetus and Alcestis to illuminate human character. The intent of the *Alcestis* is to study the effect of his weaknesses on an otherwise good man. It has been prophesied that Admetus, King of Thessaly, must soon die—unless, Apollo adds, someone will volunteer to die in his place. His aged father refuses to volunteer. Admetus' wife, Alcestis, offers herself as the sacrifice: "How could a woman show her husband greater honor, than to wish to die in his place?" Alcestis dies; but Heracles, grateful for Admetus' hospitality, fights with Death and restores Alcestis to her remorseful husband. It is the gentleness, the softness of Admetus that wins Apollo to grant the boon of life, and wins Heracles to bring back Alcestis. The came softness, however, leads the King to accept his wife's sacrifice, and to agree to marry the masked woman Heracles brings in, even before he knows it is his tru wife come home. The whole picture of the man, of his weaknesses and their recognition, is natural and appealing.

Juvenal, in the second century after Christ, mentioned a performance of *Alcestis*. In modern times, the play has had many adaptations. French versions include those by P. Quinault, 1674, and Lagrange-Chancel, 1694. Handel composed music for it in 1727; Gluck made it an opera, 1762-1764. Wieland wrote a German version in 1773-1774, followed by a series of articles in which he stated that he preferred his own work to Euripides', which drew a fierce attack from Goethe, *Gods, Heroes, and Wieland*. Ducis wrote a French version in 1778; Alfieri, an Italian in 1798; Herder, another in German in 1802. Browning told the story in *Balaustion's Adventure*, 1871, suggesting that King Admetus accepted Alcestis' sacrifice not because he was a cowardly egotist but for the sake of his people; this conception was followed by the German Hugo von Hofmannsthal, who in *Alkestis*, 1911, pictured a brooding, introspective king, his "reason whirled by passion into dreamland." William Morris includes the story in his *Earthly Paradise* (1868-1870).

English versions of the *Alcestis*, too, have been fairly frequent. One by Blanche Shoemaker Wagstaff was presented in New York in 1910. Edith Wynne Matthison and Charles Rann Kennedy opened the Melbrook Theatre with *Alcestis* in 1922. The Gilbert Murray version was enacted at the Carnegie Institute of Technology in 1935; Horace Gregory called it "a veritable text of what to avoid in adaptation of Greek verse into English." Of a 1936 version by Dudley Fitts and Robert Fitzgerald, Gregory remarked: "The entire play is given a masculine quality that all other versions lack . . . I believe a performance would be extraordinarily successful." His words were proved true by a production at Cambridge, Massachusetts, in 1938. Richard Aldington also made a translation, in prose, in 1930.

Ruskin said that the *Alcestis* sums up "the central idea of all Greek drama." It exemplifies Aristotle's conception of the tragic hero, who through the flaws in his character brings misfortunes upon himself. It is a searching study of natural human emotions and deeds, with both Admetus and Alcestis effectively and sympathetically drawn. Despite the many versions since his day, Euripides' *Alcestis* remains the most successful dramatization of the story.

RHESUS   *Euripides*

Rhesus may be the only tragic drama that has come down to us from ancient Greece that is not from the pen of one of the three great tragic dramatists. Gilbert Murray believed it to be Euripides' work, probably presented at the founding of Amphipolis in Thrace in 437 B.C. Others believe that it was written a century later, in a deliberately simple and archaic style. The chorus, for example, opens the action, as is not the case in any other play after Aeschylus. The play, also, contains twenty-nine words found nowhere else in all Greek literature.

On the other hand, the chorus, of Trojan guards, is treated in lively fashion, far from the archaic; the various men on guard, for example, call out individually from their places of watch, and later, they chase Odysseus through the camp. The scene is the Trojan War; the Greeks have been losing, and the Trojans, under their general Hector, have moved out from the city onto the plain toward the Greek ships. In the play, Dolon sets forth to spy for the Trojans; he is killed by Odysseus and Diomedes, who in disguise have penetrated the Trojan Camp. Meanwhile help has come to Troy with Rhesus, King of Thrace, who is scolded by Hector for having waited until the Trojans are ahead. Rhesus boasts that he will wipe out the Greeks. Sent by the goddess Athena, Odysseus and Diomedes kill Rhesus and drive off his horses. Hector orders an assault upon the Greeks.

Opinions of the *Rhesus* are sharply divided. Philip W. Harsh called it "probably the poorest of all extant Greek tragedies," while Eugene O'Neill, Jr. affirmed that it "contains within it the essence of tragedy." The tragic mood rises mainly from the portrait of Hector, in early confidence and continuing assurance, despite the underlying feeling—"Come forth and fight for Ilion ere the end"—that defeat is the ultimate doom of the Trojans. Hector reproaches Rhesus for having waited until the war is almost won to bring his aid, but mourns him sincerely when he is slain.

Rhesus is the only Greek drama in which the action occurs at night, and, though of course the performances were given in broad daylight in the open air Greek theatres, the sense of darkness is well suggested and well sustained.

The *Rhesus* is the only surviving play of the few based on stories from the *Iliad;* its events are related in the tenth book. In the Homeric story, the spy Dolon, abjectly seeking to save his own life, tells Odysseus and Diomedes that Rhesus is coming. The play makes more use of the gods: Athena tells the two Greeks of Rhesus' arrival; the Muse of the Mountains carries off her dead son Rhesus, cursing Odysseus and Diomedes, along with Helen, who has emptied a thousand cities of good men. The dramatist added a few other effective theatrical devices: Odysseus uses the Trojan watchword (gotten from Dolon) to delude the guard; the Greeks return the wolf-skin disguise of Dolon, whose death is thus revealed to Hector; and the Thracian charioteer accuses Hector of having killed his king, Rhesus, when it is Hector's own cause that Rhesus' death has endangered.

Aside from the lyric of the shepherd piping and the nightingale calling —"changeful and old and undying"— there is little adornment in the swift movement and simple style of the *Rhesus.* The usual choral odes are in the main replaced by the staccato words of the sentinels, whose night watch is broken by the comings and goings of warriors and spies. The dialogue is direct, carrying the action swiftly along. The play is as rich in excitement, in physical stir and struggle, as any of the ancient dramas.

MEDEA   *Euripides*

The tetralogy of Euripides that included *Medea* fell into last place in the contest of 431 B.C., in which the victor was Euphorion, son of Aeschylus, with Sophocles second. *Medea*, the first play of the tetralogy, was followed by *Philoctetes, Dictys,* and the satyr-play *The Reapers.* Since then *Medea* has become one of the most popular plays of all ancient drama.

Medea is the most powerful example of the truth of the adage, Hell hath no fury like a woman scorned. More interested in women than other contemporary dramatists, Euripides in this play had the problem of making Medea's awful revenge seem probable. Jason, for whom Medea had betrayed her family and abandoned her native land, in order to improve his state puts Medea aside and marries the daughter of Creon, King of Corinth. Medea alternately rages and broods over her lot. Then she poisons Creon and his daughter. She allows Jason to live, but in order to drive him to the last brink of helpless grief she kills the two young boys, his sons—and hers.

Despite all this desperate slaughter, Euripides by many subtle touches keeps Medea natural. In her, fully developed in the drama for the first time, we watch the conflict of a divided soul, as love and jealousy contend. She holds her children close, in fierce maternal love, as though to protect them from the thoughts that are gathering within her. She is balanced against a base and calculating Jason, who takes all Medea's help as his due, and then grows contemptuously abrupt with her. From the cold, scheming, and specious arguments of Jason, Medea's passion grows more torrid, and when she slays her children we can understand her action even as we shudder in horror of the deed. Hence we feel no basic injustice when the dragon-drawn chariot, in the upper air, bears Medea and the boys' bodies safely away, leaving Jason in anguish on the ground.

Medea is also the first independent woman roundly drawn in the drama. She utters the first dramatic protest against woman's lot:

> Men say we women lead a sheltered life
> At home, while they face death amid the spears.
> The fools! I'd rather stand in the battle line
> Thrice, than once bear a child.

This cry is heard faintly in the dramas of Nicholas Rowe, *The Fair Penitent**, 1703, and *Jane Shore**, 1714, but it does not sound clear again until Ibsen's *A Doll's House**, 1879—2300 years after *Medea*.

Euripides' *Medea* appeared in the first year of the Peloponnesian War, when Athens hated Corinth and therefore rejoiced that the Corinthian royal family met death in the play. The theme became very popular; a dozen later Greek and Roman playwrights used the story. Seneca's version removed all sympathy from Medea; it excused Jason's marriage as part of his desire to get the best he could for Medea and his children in a strange country; it made Medea a cold-blooded murderess, and started the tradition that turned her into the most notorious cruel witch of the ancient world. But she became a famous figure; there are representations of Medea on the walls of Herculaneum and Pompeii, and Julius Caesar paid a great price for a painting of her. King Alexander the Great of Macedon often quoted *Medea*; his own mother, put aside for a Cleopatra (not Caesar's and Antony's), killed his father, Philip (336 B.C.). The Roman Brutus, dying at Philippi (42 B.C.), uttered his cry for vengeance in words from *Medea*: "God, be not blind to him that caused these things!" The Roman Emperor Caracalla, just before his assassination (217 A.D.), quoted the lines that close the play:

> In many a way is the gods' will wrought;
> For things deemed sure, they bring to nought,
> And things none dreamed of, they dispose.
> Even such, this story's close.

With the same words, Euripides ended four other dramas: *Alcestis**, *Helen**, *The Bacchantes**, *Andromache**.

With his mastery of theatrical effects and his psychological insight, Euripides was the most discussed of ancient dramatists. His original and striking remarks were often quoted; but his rationalism and his rhetoric were frequently attacked. Among the comic playwrights (as in Aristophanes' *The Frogs**), it was as usual to deride Euripides "as to throw nuts to the spectators or to rob Heracles of his meal." Written about 60 A.D., *Medea* is one of Seneca's most effective trage- dies. Politics no longer interfering, he shifts the sympathy somewhat to- ward Jason; the fact that Jason plans to have the children stay in Corinth gives color to his claim that he is really abandoning Medea for the chil- dren's sake. Seneca's version, on the other hand, heightens the spectacle of horror. Medea kills one of the children onstage, before the audience; she kills the other on the roof as not only the audience but also Jason watch; then she flings their bodies down to their distraught father. Though too gruesome for modern presentation, Seneca's tragedy has a stateliness within its horror.

The power of the story of Medea carries over into modern versions and productions. French playwrights on the subject include de la Peruse, 1553, Corneille, 1634, Longepierre, 1694, Pellegrin, 1713, and Legouvé, 1849. An English version by Glover (at Drury Lane, London, 1767) makes Medea temporarily insane when she kills the children; Creon is slain by the Corinthians; Jason, abandoning his bride, turns back to Medea and provides a happy ending. Samuel Johnson wrote a burlesque translation of a chorus of *Medea*, in the Gray's *Elegy* stanza. He also, as F. L. Lucas pointed out, "produced a serious version of the same passage which, although the modern reader will not find it easy to distinguish from the comic one, had the distinction of being copied out, together with the original Greek—over 220 words in all—in a circle an inch and a half in diameter, by Porson the great Euripidean critic." In Lessing's tragedy *Miss Sarah Sampson*, 1775, the deserted mistress cries "See in me a new Medea!" as she poisons her rival. Grillparzer holds close to the original *Medea* in his play of 1822; William Morris tells the story in his poem *The Life and Death of Jason* (1867).

A modern handling of the theme is Maxwell Anderson's *The Wingless Victory*, a tragedy of the African Oparre who, having saved the life of a Yankee sea-captain (as Medea saved Jason's) goes back with him to New England, where, finding herself estranged and abandoned, she kills their children.

The story of *Medea* finds a vehement modern objector in James Agate. In *At Half Past Eight*, 1923, Agate grants "the exquisiteness of Professor Murray's translation", but he fails to find nobility in hate. "The only pity in the *Medea* is expressed by the Chorus, a boring lot of young women feebly enlarging upon what has gone before like a poor parson marring a good text . . . I cannot find tragic interest in monstrosity. Strip the *Medea* of its poetic clothing, and only the monstrous remains . . . Medea, we feel, deserved more than she got. That cruelty turned her into a vile thing is not the fault of cruelty, but of the degenerative metal upon which it was exercised. Medea was essentially not noble, but base. That she should go gadding about Pallas' plain in a golden chariot is, to an English mind, scarcely a fitting reward. What propriety was here to the Greek mind I can but guess; watching the play in the English theatre of today, I care nothing for such fiddle-faddle. We have outgrown these too big emotions. Opera is their sphere, with Strauss to make divine hash of them." Fortunately, stripped of its poetry, *Medea* does not exist. Shelley anticipated and in part answered Agate, in his Note to *The*

Cenci*, where he states that the pleasure in the poetry mitigates the
pain of the moral deformity. Beyond this, what comes upon most spectators of an outstanding production of *Medea* is not a calculation of the
deserts of the crazed, rejected wife, but an awesome contemplation of
the tremendous power of human passion, of the two sides of the coin of
love-and-hate that—more than any golden mintage—rules the world.

Of recent American performances of Euripides' *Medea*, Margaret Anglin's was outstanding. *The Brooklyn Eagle* (February 21, 1918) declared:
"Margaret Anglin is probably the greatest actress on our stage today . . .
playing the part with a tigerish ferocity that is simply appalling." Margaret Anglin alternated the *Medea* with Sophocles' *Electra**; Clayton
Hamilton in *Vogue* (April 1, 1918) contrasted the two: "It would be easy
enough to argue that Sophocles, in his *Electra*, has surpassed, in sheer
dramatic power, the appeal that was subsequently made by Euripides,
in the *Medea*. But this traditional and scholarly adjudication would be
divorced from the verdict of the contemporary public. There can
scarcely be a doubt that the New York theatregoing public prefers the
Medea." The preference may have come because revenge involving
matricide is less easily understood, and less frequent, than jealousy that
sacrifices the children to hurt the hated spouse. The public was deeply
stirred by Margaret Anglin.

Other productions of the *Medea*, vivid but less notable, came in 1919
and in 1920 with Ellen van Volkenberg in the Gilbert Murray translation.
In the same translation, another production was given in 1944, when
George Freedley (February 21) held out a staff to a project then going
the rounds: "Gilbert Murray's somewhat stilted acting version did little
to make the evening a happy one . . . a knowing producer would certainly try to enlist Judith Anderson." In 1946, Robinson Jeffers' version
of *Medea* was dedicated to Judith Anderson; on October 20, 1947, she
opened in the role, and in the second outstanding *Medea* production of
our time took New York by storm.

"Perhaps *Medea* was never fully created until Miss Anderson breathed
immortal fire into it last evening", raved Brooks Atkinson. "For theatric
force, human passion, female ferocity," said Louis Kronenberger, "*Medea*
stands virtually alone." Judith Anderson won the Drama League award
for the best performance of the year. She enacted the part, opening September 12, at the 1951 Berlin Festival, where Maria Fein opened September 26 in the Grillparzer German version of the story. "A superlative
performance by Judith Anderson is the chief distinction of *Medea*," said
Howard Barnes, preserving enough detachment to recognize that, save
for the flame and flow of her work, the New York 1947 production was
"more declamatory than melodramatic". In truth, the Robinson Jeffers
version of the play alters parts, does not capture the Greek spirit, and
exaggerates Medea's horror to the point of hysteria.

In 1946, also, Jean Anouilh wrote a French modernization of *Medea*,
making the tortured queen a foul-mouthed Russian gypsy who, at the
end, burns in her own caravan, like the victim in a sordid and cheap sex
crime story.

The *Medea* of Euripides, in spite of the faults of translations and the
folly of adapters, burns with an intensity of truth and tortured souls that
time has not weakened.

HIPPOLYTUS   *Euripides*

In *Hippolytus*, 428 B.C., Euripides shows the consequences of violating the golden mean of the Greeks: nothing too much. Since Hippolytus has too much disdain for love, Aphrodite puni..hes him by putting into the breast of his young step-mother, Phaedra, an overpowering passion for the young man. The play makes a searching and dramatic study of the interactions of three persons—Theseus, his young bride Phaedra, and Hippolytus, his son by the Amazon queen—caught in the first full-scale dramatization of the "eternal triangle".

The subject attracted Euripides. *Hippolytus* is his second attempt at the subject; it may be, indeed, a revision of his earlier, lost, *Hippolytus Veiled*. Never in ancient times were the vagaries of the "tender passion" more carefully analyzed, more subtly shown. When Phaedra becomes aware of her love for Hippolytus, she fights against it, even fasting for three days to destroy her desire. It is not Phaedra, but her Nurse, that first mentions Hippolytus' name; it is the Nurse, urging Phaedra to action and swearing Hippolytus to silence, that tells him of Phaedra's love. When Hippolytus rejects her, Phaedra hangs herself, leaving a note accusing her step-son. Hippolytus, saying "With my tongue I swore it, never with my heart", goes to break his oath of silence and tell Theseus the truth; at the crucial moment, however, he remains silent, and preserves Phaedra's secret and good name. When Hippolytus is dying, under his father's curse, the goddess Artemis tells Thesus the truth. Hippolytus, less disdainful now, recognizes that the greatest sufferer of the three is the doubly bereft Theseus, who remains alive. The first triangle in the theatre is a tragic one.

The power of love is vividly pictured by the Nurse: "Cypris goes to and fro in the heavens; she is upon the wave of the deep; and from her all things arise. She it is who sows and scatters love, whose children all we on earth confess ourselves to be." This first dramatic flowering of romantic love is a distinct contribution of Euripides. "The buoyant romance of the lost *Andromeda*," said F. L. Lucas, "with its rescue of the heroine from the sea-monster at dawn by the young hero, to whom she cries with a strange anticipation of the very words of Miranda to Ferdinand in *The Tempest*, 'Take me, O stranger, as thou wilt, for maid or bride or slave of thine', the jealousy of Medea, the dark, unhappy loves of Phaedra and Stheneboea, the perverse passions of Canace and Pasiphae —all these were treatments of a theme which, hackneyed today, was then a fiercely criticized innovation on the stage. 'None knows of a woman in love in any play of mine', is the boast of Aeschylus in the *Frogs** of Aristophanes, as he denounces Euripides on this very ground; but since Euripides there has lived not one great dramatist who could make the same disclaimer."

The effect of these first dramatic pictures of love must have been great indeed. Thus Lucian, in the second century after Christ, tells that, late one spring, after a troupe of strolling players had performed Euripides' *Andromeda* at Abdera in Thrace, the citizens neglected their work, roving through the meadows and groves, singing a song from the play, "O Love, high Lord both over gods and men!" until the winds of autumn cooled them back to sanity. Even allowing for the exaggeration of Lucian's satire, we must recognize the strong appeal of the new theme of "romantic" love.

The deep respect of the Athenian audience for an oath made one line in *Hippolytus* notorious. When Hippolytus threatens to tell his father the truth, averring "With my tongue I swore it, never with my heart", the audience booed. Euripides was perhaps raising the question whether to break an oath secured under false pretenses was a violation of Greek morality; notice that the young man, when the time comes, keeps his word though it means his death. Yet Aristophanes in no less than three plays (*The Acharnians**, *The Frogs**, *The Thesmophoriazusae**) attacked Euripides for the line, and Cicero made comment upon the equivocation.

In most later versions of the story, emphasis is shifted from Hippolytus to Phaedra. Seneca's play *Phaedra*, about A.D. 60, one of the Roman's best, makes several changes. The gods Euripides introduces (Aphrodite at the beginning, her chaste rival Artemis at the end) are omitted, as is also the strong scene between Hippolytus and his father. But Seneca made three important additions that humanize the motivation in the drama. He presented a scene between Phaedra and Hippolytus, in which she herself tells him her love; effectively her embarrassment and shame are shown as Hippolytus at first fails to understand her; the scene is rich in pathos. Then Phaedra, in person, denounces Hippolytus to Theseus. Only when Hippolytus' mangled remains are brought in does she break down, confess the truth, and kill herself.

Racine's French *Phèdre*, 1677, combines elements of the Greek and the Roman drama; retaining the three episodes of Senesa just mentioned, it adds a new motive. Hippolyte rejects Phèdre not from chastity, but because he is himself in love; this adds jealousy to Phèdre's gathered wrath. She is the utter victim of her passion: "C'est Vénus toute entière à sa proie attachée." The French play *Phèdre and Hippolyte*, 1677, by Nicolas Pradon, written in competition with Racine, was proclaimed by Racine's enemies as a better play than *Phèdre;* the consequent controversy in verse is known as the War of the Sonnets. Pradon's play—as also the highly praised English *Phaedra and Hippolytus*, 1708, by Edmund Smith—is now neglected; but Racine's *Phèdre* is by many considered his masterpiece. The part of Phèdre, first played by Marie Champmeslé, was played also by Adrienne Lecouvreur, Marie Dumesnil, and Rachel. Sarah Bernhardt deemed Phèdre one of her richest roles. The play is Racine's most moving and most enduring drama of passion and undying love. It was presented in an English version by Bernard Grebanier, at the Dramatic Workshop, New York, in February and March 1953, revealing beauty and moving power.

D'Annunzio's Italian *Fedra*, 1909, is, in fervid style, exaggeratedly romantic.

There have been a number of recent productions of *Hippolytus*. About 1858, Julia Ward Howe wrote a version for Charlotte Cushman and Edwin Booth, but the manager's wife coveted the role of Phaedra and the version was not produced until Margaret Anglin took it over in 1911. In 1935 the play was presented at the Old Vic, in London; in 1936, in the Gilbert Murray translation, at the Carnegie Institute of Technology; and in 1937 at Albright College, Pennsylvania. In 1950, Rex Warner made another English translation of the play.

What was called a "free adaptation" of Euripides' *Hippolytus* by Leighton Rollins was presented by the Experimental Theatre of the American National Theatre and Academy in New York in 1948. In reviewing that production, Brooks Atkinson declared that *"Hippolytus reveals the gods and their earthly victims in a series of sadistic relationships requiring the services of a licensed psychiatrist. Living in a fantasy world of primitive taboos, the characters of ancient Greek tragedies can certainly get into some harrowing dilemmas . . . Hippolytus is framed by gods whose code of ethics conforms to the most enlightened practices of modern gangsters, although the gods, of course, speak finer verse."* It is obvious that Rollins' "free adaptation" conveyed no sense at all of Euripides' use of the gods as symbols of natural forces.

A heart empty of love will have other torments. Excess of love, excess of continence, alike bring train of evil. Its psychological study makes the *Hippolytus*—in spite of the interference of the gods, who are no less symbolic than the three witches in *Macbeth*—one of the most modern in spirit of the ancient Greek dramas.

THE CHILDREN OF HERACLES   *Euripides*

The *Heracleidae (Children of Heracles)*, 427? B.C., was written at the beginning of the Peloponnesian War, and its patriotic purpose was undoubtedly more important to Euripides than its dramatic style. Athens at that time was by many in other lands considered a tyrant state, with imperialistic, selfish designs; the play pictures Athens, as she seemed to her loyal sons, the home of justice and the refuge of the oppressed.

After the death of the Dorian hero Heracles, his children, accompanied by Heracles' mother, Alcmena, and his old friend, Iolaus, are driven across Greece by their father's ancient enemy, Eurystheus, King of Argos. No city will shelter them, until they come to Athenian Marathon. The King of Athens protects them, and the defeated Eurystheus is led to death.

The play is thus a reproach, which Eurystheus in his dying words makes clear, to the Dorian descendants of Heracles for joining the foes of Athens in the Peloponnesian War. The martial courage of the Athenians is glorified in the play, also the spirit of self-sacrifice, although it is the daughter of Heracles, Macaria, who unflinchingly offers herself when the oracle says that a maiden's death is prerequisite to victory. There is pathos in Macaria's words, and steadfast courage, but there is also an implicit reproach to the Dorians of Euripides' day.

There is considerable action on the stage in *The Heracleidae* for a Greek drama, when, for example, the Argive herald seizes the children of Heracles and knocks down old Iolaus. A dramatic device used in the *Bible* story of Samson is found in this play: Iolaus prays that his strength may be restored to him for just one day, and it is he that captures King Eurystheus. Perhaps Euripides meant also to taunt the enemies of Athens, then gathering in conceit of superior power, for the messenger tells of the fall of King Eurystheus of Argos, "whose fortune now doth preach a lesson clear as day, to all the sons of men, that none should envy him who seems to thrive, until his death; for fortune's moods last but a day."

The abundance of such contemporary references has kept *The Children of Heracles* from frequent modern production, but in the spiral of history, we have come around to times not unlike Euripides' own.

ANDROMACHE   *Euripides*

Euripides' *Andromache*, 426 B.C., was first presented, not at Athens, but probably at the court of the King of the Molossians, whose favor Athens was seeking at the beginning of the Peloponnesian War; the king traced his ancestry back to Achilles through Andromache's son, Molossus.

Though she gives the play its name, Andromache drops from sight midway; the contemporary situation seemed more important to Euripides than any unity of plot. In the first part of the play, the lives of Andromache and her son, Molossus, are threatened. Andromache, Hector's widow, has been borne off as a slave to the son of Achilles, Neoptolemus (also called Pyrrhus); Molossus is their child. But Pyrrhus is married to Hermione, daughter of Menelaus, who in jealousy would slay Andromache and Molossus. Menelaus seizes them, but they are saved by the intervention of old Peleus, Achilles' father. At this point, Euripides' hatred of Sparta, rival of Athens in the Peloponnesian War, shifts the play's movement. Orestes, nephew of Menelaus of Sparta, comes in. He kills Pyrrhus and goes off with Hermione. The play ends when the goddess Thetis descends "from the machine" and declares (as the witch shows of Banquo, in *Macbeth**) that Molossus shall be father of a long line of kings.

Hatred of Sparta is doubly emphasized in *Andromache*. It is pressed in the irony of the fact that the house of Achilles, who was sacrificed to win the Trojan War, is destroyed by the house of the Spartan Menelaus, which had caused the war and gained most by it. More directly, hate pours with the words of Andromache to Menelaus: "O citizens of Sparta, abhorred by all men, ye tricky schemers, masters of falsehood, contrivers of evil plots, with crooked minds and devious devices and never an honest thought, it is unjust that ye should thrive in Hellas."

Euripides' venom against the Spartans led him to vilify even the god Apollo, whose Delphic oracle had promised aid and victory to Sparta in the war. He also attacked the comparative freedom of Spartan women (although in *Medea** he had, conversely, condemned the conservatism of Athens), robing Spartan Hermione in garments to reveal charms that decorum would allow but to be surmised. Euripides' characterizations were also influenced by the political intentions of the play. Andromache is a lofty-minded figure, who retains her queenly dignity even when she is snatched away to be slain; Hermione, on the other hand, is both vain and cowardly; and her father, Menelaus, as not in Homer, is treacherous, craven, and cruel.

Andromache has not been among Euripides' most popular plays. Racine wrote a French version, *Andromaque*, which was produced November 17, 1667. By bringing in Pyrrhus, who does not appear in Euripides' play, Racine gave his drama greater coherence. Racine, in fact, made numerous inner changes, altering the psychology so that his characters move with the restraint and dignity of seventeenth-century French courtiers. Of the chain of thwarted lovers—Orestes loves Hermione who loves Pyrrhus who loves Andromache—Racine made the women more subtle and altered the ending: Andromache, though still devoted to her late husband Hector, is not untouched by the love of so powerful and renowned a warrior as Pyrrhus; yet she marries him only to save the life of her son and plans to kill herself thereafter. The jealous Hermione makes the suicide unnecessary; she sends Orestes to kill Pyrrhus, then, railing at him for having obeyed, she kills herself over Pyrrhus' body. Orestes goes mad.

The beauties of Racine's play are, in the main, untranslatable; they are matters of balance not merely in the plot but in the verse structure, within the speech, within the sentence, within the phrase. The pellucid quality of the diction, the serenity of the rhythm, almost belie the emotional intensity, so that persons reading the play in translation may feel that Racine is cold. He is controlled, but intensely emotional.

An English adaptation of Racine's *Andromaque* was made by Ambrose Phillips in *The Distressed Mother*, 1712; Mrs. Siddons played in it. Junius Brutus Booth played Orestes in the French version in New Orleans in 1828. The Gilbert Murray translation of Euripides' *Andromache* was presented in London in 1901; a French translation of Euripides was performed in Paris in 1912 and in 1917.

In her performances of Racine's *Andromaque*, Rachel always played Hermione; Sarah Bernhardt always chose Andromaque. When "the divine Sarah" visited England, the *London Graphic* (July 5, 1879) indicated why she preferred that role: "Its attributes are rather tenderness and pathos than strong passion; but it is probably for this very reason chosen by Mlle. Bernhardt, whose outbursts of fury have always a strained and exaggerated air; whereas her tender, pathetic utterances are exquisitely soft and moving . . ."

Racine's *Andromaque* is a great and unified drama of characters under emotional stress; Euripides' *Andromache*, a vivid dramatic portrayal of the tensions and involvements that persisted, beyond the legendary battles, in Euripides' own battle-scarred Greece.

HECUBA   *Euripides*

One of the three most popular of Euripides' dramas in ancient times (along with *Orestes* and *The Phoenician Women*), *Hecuba*, 424? B.C., was much read during the Middle Ages and later continued popular in France. The hapless Queen of Troy was well enough known to Elizabethan England for Shakespeare to have Hamlet bid the Players "Say on: come to Hecuba" and to marvel at the actor's real tears over the Queen's fate: "What's Hecuba to him, or he to Hecuba, That he should weep for her?"

Hecuba has drawn tears from uncounted audiences as Euripides shows her meeting misfortune proudly as a queen. Two blows fall upon her in the play. The first strikes grievously at Hecuba's heart, but was to be expected among the horrors of the fall of Troy; her daughter Polyxena is sacrificed in memory of the Greek hero Achilles. The second blow comes from the unexpected treachery of a friend. When the Trojan War was but a threat, Hecuba sent her youngest son, Polydorus, to the friendly King Polymestor of Thrace, with ample gold. With the defeat of the Trojans, Polymestor slew the young prince and appropriated his wealth. Learning of this treacherous deed, Hecuba's wild grief changes to a cold fury; she plans and carries through the killing of King Polymestor's two children and the blinding of the King.

The character of Hecuba is presented with sympathy and understanding as Euripides pictures the overpowering emotions of the mother, seventeen of whose nineteen children are dead, and the hardening of her feeling into a bitterness and resolve that coldly wreak her vengeance. At the end of the play, the Greek Agamemnon, judging between Queen Hecuba and King Polymestor, declares that the Thracian king has been properly punished for his treachery. The blinded King thereupon prophesies the death of Hecuba's last child, Cassandra, a slave in Agamemnon's train, and the same fate for the conquering Agamemnon.

The ghost of Polydorus, Hecuba's son, opens the play, announcing the fate of the characters. Passed along in the dramas of Seneca, this ghost was the forerunner of the many apparitions that thronged the theatre—the ghost of Hamlet's father, the visions of Macbeth, and in the minor plays of horror the wraiths that rushed forth in very battalions—until they were (for a season!) laughed away by the ancestors stepping from their picture frames in Gilbert's *Ruddigore**.

Some critics have felt that the hearing of Hecuba and Polymestor before Agamemnon takes disproportionate space in the play. The development of this scene is doubtless a reflection of the interest Athenians at the time took in oratory and argument.

The writing of *Hecuba* is brilliant throughout, with many epigrams and passages of moving beauty. Commenting on a performance of the play in Greek at Holy Cross College in June, 1926, the *Boston Transcript* praised Euripides' "craft and masterdom as playwright, fervor and splendor as poet . . . Winged often are the free-rhythmed speeches, many-voiced, of the chorus . . . World without end, sound and sight remain potent in the theatre. Out of *Hecuba* and Euripides, they span these three and twenty centuries—alien tongue but eye and ear still holden."

Hecuba was presented in 1916, as part of Sarah Bernhardt's New York repertoire. A new translation, by H. B. Lister, was published in 1940. In beauty of expression, pungency of thought, and capture of character, *Hecuba* still holds a high place among the world's great dramas.

CYCLOPS   *Euripides*

The *Cyclops*, 423? B.C., is the one extant satyr play. In the dramatic contests of the fifth century before Christ, the tragic poets were expected to present a tetralogy, three tragedies followed by a satyr play. The latter, if we may take the *Cyclops* as representative, was a travesty of the theme handled seriously in the tragedies. It was much shorter than the serious dramas; the *Cyclops* has but 709 lines. (For length of other plays, see *The Phoenician Women**.) Basically, the satyr play was perhaps closest to the early religious dance drama. The dramatic contests were held at the Great Dionysia festival, in March, and the chorus of the satyr play consisted of satyrs; Silenus (son of Pan and foster-father of Dionysus, god of wine and revelry) was always a character, and Silenus and the chorus wore phalluses, as in the old Dionysiac fertility rites.

Euripides, in the *Cyclops*, burlesques the story of Odysseus and the Cyclops Polyphemus, as told in Book Nine of Homer's *Odyssey*. Arriving before the Cyclops' cave in Mount Aetna, Odysseus in exchange for wine buys cheese and sheep from Silenus, who is Polyphemus' slave. The Cyclops surprises Odysseus and his men, and pens them in his cave. There, Polyphemus eats two of Odysseus' companions, gets drunk on Odysseus' wine, and is blinded by Odysseus. The cowardly satyrs, who had refused to help Odysseus, now mislead the blind Cyclops, who bumps his head against the rocks while Odysseus and his men escape.

Save for its brevity, the satyr play has the form of the tragedies: five sections separated by choral songs. The structure and the plot development are very simple; the language is lively with colloquial and slang expressions that were not used in tragedy. Odysseus, however, maintains his dignity, both in action and in speech; indeed, his sobriety and earnestness seem deliberately poised against the ribaldry of the others, to make their tipsy revelry more amusing. Drunken Polyphemus, for example, wants to make love to the drunken Silenus.

The *Cyclops*, however, is not all ribaldry and slapstick; Euripides' satire plays upon more than the old legend. It has Polyphemus laugh with scorn at mortals that wage war over one indecent woman. And the leader of the chorus inquires about Helen, upon the fall of Troy: "After capturing your blooming prize, were you all in turn her lovers? For she likes variety in husbands." Through Polyphemus, Euripides looks with no friendly eye upon those persons that worship "the belly, the greatest of deities". And he has Odysseus point out the misfortunes, the widespread sorrow, that the Trojan War brought, not to the defeated Trojans, but to the conquering Greeks.

[In the name that Odysseus gives the Cyclops, James Joyce found a searching symbol. "My name is No-man," says Odysseus, so that the Cyclops will not recognize his real name; but, in the Greek, this is not a far-fetched change: the name that *Odysseus* gives is *Odys*. This, said James Joyce (in a conversation), prefigures the situation of the artist. The artist must always give all of himself. If he tries to withhold any part of himself, it is inevitably the god (the *Zeus*) in him that is sloughed, and no man (*Odys*) indeed that remains!]

Euripides' *Cyclops* is an amusing travesty, scarcely more than a skit, but quite actable. The French comedian Coquelin enjoyed playing Silenus. The ancient Greeks, after the deep emotional drive of the tragedies, must have had high hilarity with the satyr play.

HERACLES   *Euripides*

The *Heracles*, 422? B.C., is one of Euripides' most effective dramatic studies of the growth of character through suffering. The hero, Heracles, King of Thebes, returns from his labors to find his wife, Megara, and their sons about to be slain by the usurper Lycas. Heracles kills Lycus, but the gods set a madness upon him, so that he also kills his wife and their children. When the madness is lifted, Heracles at first would kill himself, but recognizing that suicide is the coward's evasion, he decides to endure whatever fate may send. On this note of high resolve, the tragedy ends.

Seneca's Latin version of the drama, *Mad Hercules*, about A.D. 60, emphasizes the Stoic qualities of the hero, making a number of minor changes from the Greek. Most effective is Seneca's leaving Hercules, after he awakens from his madness, uninformed about the murders: he sees the blood on his own arrows and thus becomes aware of his guilt. On the whole, however, Seneca's formal construction lacks the emotional appeal of Euripides' drama.

Opinions of Euripides' *Heracles* vary considerably. Some critics place the play much later in Euripides' life because it pictures the evils of old age, but no poet would advance such an argument. The play emphasizes the friendship of the Athenians and the Dorians, as did other plays written near the beginning of the Peloponnesian War.

On the ground that the two movements in the play—Heracles' triumph and Heracles' downfall—are not well-knit, other critics consider the play inferior, but the theme of the play is the very change of circumstance that overtakes Heracles, and his reaction to it. The French nineteenth century critic Henri Patin declared that *Heracles* "comes near to being the most pathetic and the most lofty" of all Euripides' dramas. At the end of the nineteenth century, the English critic A. W. Verrall said: "For power, for truth, for poignancy, for depth of penetration into the nature and history of man, this picture of the Hellenic hero may be matched against anything in art."

The English poet, Robert Browning, paid the play high tribute. In his poem *Aristophanes' Apology* (1875), in which he discusses the Greek dramatists, he says, "Accordingly I read the perfect piece", and follows this line with his own translation of Euripides' *Heracles*. The last line of the *Apology* is "Glory to God!—who saves Euripides!"

Browning's words might serve as our last on *Heracles*, save that Heracles' own words in the play serve as a guide both for individuals and for nations, not only of his time but of our own: "Whoever prefers wealth or power to the possession of good friends, thinketh amiss."

ION   *Euripides*

Toward the beginning of the Peloponnesian War, Euripides wrote several plays to rouse enthusiasm for and devotion to Athens. *Ion*, 421? B.C., presents the story of the founding of the Ionian (Athenian) race and reminds the citizens that they have a divine ancestor, Apollo, the god of light and culture.

The play begins with a long prologue wherein the god Hermes tells of the events before the play's action starts. Creusa, daughter of Erechtheus, King of Athens, has had a son by the god Apollo. She had the infant exposed, but it was saved and given to the priestess of Apollo at Delphi to rear. Creusa in the meantime has married Xuthus; childless, she and Xuthus have come to the temple at Delphi to be blessed with offspring. At this point of the story, *Ion* begins.

The oracle informs Xuthus that, when he leaves the temple, the first person he encounters will be his son. He meets and embraces Ion. Creusa, jealous at this, prepares a poisoned drink for Ion, but a dove drinks from the cup and reveals the poison. For the attempt on Ion's life, Creusa is being led to her death, when the priestess brings out the casket of relics that were found with the abandoned infant, and Creusa identifies herself as Ion's mother. Athena appears at the end, prophesying the long "inheritance of a noble house" that will glorify Athens through the descendant of Apollo.

Ion is one of Euripides' plays (like *Iphigenia In Tauris**) in which there is a swift drive of story, a definite interest roused by the events themselves, apart from any religious or patriotic intent. Ingeniously, Euripides makes Ion and Xuthus interpret the oracle so as to believe that Ion is Xuthus' actual son, born of an early escapade; neatly he plays upon the jealousy of Creusa, who thinks herself excluded and seeks to kill the one who (as with shrewd dramatic irony Euripides has let the audience know) is actually flesh of her flesh.

For the development of these points, and for the final revelation, Euripides makes extensive use of question and answer, as in sharp dialogue one character speaks a line and the other responds. This device played upon the current interest in pleading and argument; it is the form that developed into the "Socratic method" of reasoning. Euripides shows that it can lead both to true and to false conclusions. Perhaps a sad echo of the time, too, is the desire Euripides puts in Ion's heart, rather to remain in the beauty and peace of the temple than to go forth to dwell among the envies and greeds of Athens.

Some critics have felt that Euripides was attacking the anthropomorphic religious beliefs of his day; he seems to show Apollo as a carefree ravisher and he argues against the current practice of sanctuary, by which a criminal might seek refuge in the temple: "The righteous and the wicked should not have the same consideration from the gods." That such was the dramatist's purpose is contradicted by many points in the play: Ion's solemn charge to the gods to give examples of justice to mankind; Ion's sad thought, when he believes himself Xuthus' bastard, that the Athenians, "proud of their high race", are thus brought low— and this reflection is obvious contrasting preparation for the final disclosure, which Athena affirms and emphasizes, that Ion (hence the Athenians as well) is offspring of the god. At the close of the play, the chorus says—with sound psychology—that the pious man may be justly confident, "for the good at length obtains the reward of virtue; but the wicked, such is his own nature, never can be happy."

Ion was a popular play. Its influence on later Greek drama was considerable. "With its recognition of a lost infant by its trinkets," F. L. Lucas has said, *Ion* "is the obvious parent of all those fourth century and Roman comedy plots with their quiverfuls of missing offspring identified at the crucial moment, and a more distant ancestor of the long-lost heirs with strawberry-marks of modern melodrama."

Performances of *Ion* were rather frequent during the nineteenth century. When August W. Schlegel produced his version of the play at Weimar in 1803, Goethe had to intervene to stop the hissing, but the objection was to the translation, not the play. In England in 1837, William Macready played Ion in a version by Thomas N. Talfourd; other productions followed in 1838, 1839, 1840, 1844, 1853, 1855, and 1857; Mary Anderson played Creusa in 1878 and 1881. In addition to the dramatic concision of its style, *Ion* sustains interest as a vivid and moving story.

THE SUPPLIANTS   *Euripides*

Appearing when the Peloponnesian War had lasted as long as the Trojan War (it was to continue until 404 B.C. and end in the downfall of Athens), *The Suppliants*, 421? B.C., is another of Euripides' political dramas. A decade of war had made the Athenians more solemn, and the play emphasizes the importance of man's heeding the will of heaven. A particularly important duty, in wartime, is the performance of the proper funeral rites for the dead. Thebes had refused to permit the burial of the Athenian dead after the battle of Delium in 424 B.C. What more fit occasion for the story of *The Suppliants!*

The suppliants are the mothers and children of the champions of Argos who were slain in the siege of Thebes. (That siege is pictured in Aeschylus' play *The Seven Against Thebes**.) The triumphant Thebans refused permission for the burial of the dead, and the Argive mourners have come to King Theseus of Athens to beseech his aid. Theseus defeats the Theban army and recovers the bodies of the dead heroes of Argos, so that they are accorded fit burial.

The political significance of the play is such that one suspects it played a part in history. At the time it was written, Athens and Argos were not friendly. The play not merely reminded the Argives of the former generosity of the Athenians, it set down the oath of friendship that had passed between them in older days. The goddess Athena, in a "descent from the machine" that closes the play, sets the oath for the men of Argos: "We Argives swear we will never lead our troops to war against this land, and, if others come, we will repel them." In the year after *The Suppliants* was acted, Argos and Athens cemented a new alliance.

The purpose of the play, and his love of his country, naturally led Euripides to exalt Athenian virtue. Athens is shown as the guardian of law, both human and divine. Scorning political expediency, shrinking from no peril, the city forwards the just cause of the weak against the strong. A number of the play's thoughts, however, rise beyond the immediate occasion to command a universal appeal.

The so-called law of the "classic unities"—really invented by the Renaissance—by which all a play's action is confined to a single city and a single day, is not observed in *The Suppliants;* for in it Theseus and his army (offstage) go to Thebes, defeat the Thebans, and bring back the bodies of the Argive champions. The funeral pyre is then reared onstage, and the audience watches while from a high rock the widowed Evadne leaps upon her husband's burning corpse. This vivid incident is not, as some critics have declared, irrelevant to the major drive of the play; rather, it reenforces with a deep emotional appeal the reasoned projection of Argos' woe and need, and Athens' generous aid. *The Suppliants,* indeed, rich in rousing challenge, stirring thoughts, and high ideals boldly maintained in action, is one of the most vivid and presently pertinent of all Greek dramas. Its ritual has modern analogy, in our return of the soldier dead for appropriate burial. Its thoughts, and its ethical impulsion, are still to be heeded in our day.

THE TROJAN WOMEN   *Euripides*

In all literature there is no picture of the devastation and the sorrow wrought by war more moving than Euripides' *Troades* (*The Trojan Women*), written in 415 B.C. It is the "mightiest of all mighty denunciations of war," said John Mason Brown, when the Edith Hamilton translation was produced in New York in 1938, "which Euripides wrote 2,350 years ago and which even now (perhaps we should say, especially now) is as timely as if it had been written yesterday."

Although the play probably cost Euripides his Athenian citizenship, as

Brown pointed out, it won him the gratitude of the world: "None of the many dramatists who have excoriated the savagery and waste of war in the theatre's long history has faced its miseries so fearlessly, or stated them in such simple, moving, and eternal terms as did this ever-prodding Greek . . . This is why his tragedy speaks so poignantly to us who are thinking neither of Troy nor a plundered island, but of Shanghai, Madrid, and the future's cloudy skyline. His drama is ageless in its beauty, its brutality, its majesty . . . It is realism of the finest, most enduring sort because it is a picture, at once accurate and dateless, of the human spirit in agony."

In 416 B.C. the Athenians swarmed upon the island of Melos, which was trying to preserve its neutrality in the Peloponnesian War (427-404 B.C.) . In a surge of totalitarian hate, the Athenians killed all the men on the island, and ravished all the women and children into slavery. No one made public protest. But within the year, while the same leaders were planning a similar drive upon Sicily, Euripidies produced *The Trojan Women*.

A pageant of sorrow, *The Trojan Women* pictures the rapine and destruction and enslavement that followed upon the fall of Troy. Young Astyanax, son of Hector and Andromache, is snatched from his mother's arms and hurled from the Trojan walls. The women of Troy, watching their sons and husbands die, hearing the topless towers of Ilium crash and crumble in the smoke and dust, are borne away to slavery. Distraught, Trojan Cassandra foretells the doom of the Grecian house of Atreus. Greek Menelaus, recapturing his wife Helen, finds his victory hollow in his heart. Emptiness, and the presage of doom, thus perch upon the victor as upon the vanquished.

In *The Trojan Women*, Euripides has none of the shining belief in Athenian ideals that marks his earlier political plays. The justice of democratic Athens has been belied by the events of the Peloponnesian War. A hopeless grief rises out of the murky doom. All man can do—as the Trojan women show, when, led by Queen Hecuba, they move to the Greek ships—is to meet his fate with dignity and courage. It is the pulse of such steadfast courage in heavy misfortune that adds to the pathos and poignancy of *The Trojan Women* the exaltation that springs from tragedy.

The choice of such a subject, which thrust upon the Athenians a reminder of their own crimes, helps explain why Euripides was not popular in his own day, in his own city. When it was first presented, the tetralogy of which *The Trojan Women*, the sole survivor, was the third play (with *Alexander; Palamedes;* and the satyr-play *Sisyphus*) won only second place. Yet the power of the play could not be withstood. When he beheld *The Trojan Women*, Alexander of Pheras (who died in 359 B.C.) left the theatre in the middle of the play; but he sent word to the actor that he left not because of the performance, but because he did not wish men to see him weeping for Hecuba when he had, dry-eyed, watched many of his own victims. (The power of the drama persisted through the ages; remember Hamlet's comment on the Player: "What's Hecuba to him, or he to Hecuba, that he should weep for her!") The scene of the killing of the young Astyanax, Gilbert Murray has said, "is probably the most harrowing in Greek literature."

In other ways, too, Euripides seems to have pressed the story home to his own people. Twice he emphasized that the Trojan War was started over a woman; first the allusive Cassandra says that "one woman's beauty made their myriads fall"; then, more bluntly, the leader of the chorus of women cries: "O ill-starred Troy! For one alien woman, one abhorrèd kiss, how are thy hosts undone!" Gossip in Euripides' day had it that the Athenian Pericles precipitated the Peloponnesian War over two sluts belonging to his mistress Aspasia . . . Shortly after the presentaton of *The Trojan Women*, Euripides left Athens. He was sheltered at the court of King Archelaus of Macedon, and his later plays, (the *Bacchantes; Iphigenia at Aulis,* etc.) were produced in Athens by his son.

Seneca's Latin version of *The Trojan Women*, about A.D. 60, is his finest tragedy. In its picture of the horror and futility of war, the insolence of the victors—with the irony of their own imminent disasters—the play reaches depths of emotion, and the formal Latin rhetoric achieves the exaltation of poetry. The occasional lyric songs have a rich beauty and pathos, especially the one in which the old Trojan mother, pointing out to her child a distant cloud of smoke, tells him that this is the only sign by which to know their home.

A German version of Euripides' *The Trojan Women*, by Franz Werfel*, 1913, was hailed by critic Wolfgang Paulson as "a milestone in the history of the expressionist theatre." New York, however, has been content to view the play in less contorted guise. In the Gilbert Murray translation, Euripides' play was produced by Granville Barker in 1915; it was enacted again in 1923, with, according to the *New York Times* (November 9, 1923), "a painfully timely significance since the late armistice . . . a directness and fulness of effect." The same translation was used in 1941, when Margaret Webster staged the play and played Andromache; Walter Slezak, Dame May Whitty (Hecuba), Johanna Roos, and Tamara Geva (Helen) were in the cast, and the conquering soldiers wore Nazi uniforms. In the meantime, Edith Hamilton's translation, 1937, was used in a January 1938 New York production: Atkinson found it "much sharper and crisper" than "Gilbert Murray's otiose and Victorian rhymed translation." In April, 1938, the Federal Theatre presented a version by Philip H. Davis of Vassar College.

As Euripides wrote the play, however, and in an adequate translation, *The Trojan Women* contains exquisitely poignant lyrics—the words of Hecuba beginning "Lo, I have seen the open hand of God" approach the sublime— and in its presentation of the horrid aftermath of war has had few equals in the drama, and has still to be surpassed.

IPHIGENIA IN TAURIS   *Euripides*

The suggestion has been made that *Iphigenia in Tauris*, 414? B.C., is an early example of "escape" literature, that Euripides, discouraged by the turn of events in the Peloponnesian War and by the decline of Athens' idealism under the strain of her many losses, deliberately sought to forget the present in exciting adventure of far-off times. After a production of *Iphigenia In Tauris* by Mr. and Mrs. Coburn, the *New York Dramatic Mirror* (August 6, 1913) said: "Had it been written today—and, indeed, it might have been— it would come under the head of thriller. Stripped of its classical mysticisms, it could well be an intrigue of the Italian Renaissance, and as to its emotions—well, it is the same old human nature."

In this play Euripides uses a variant episode of the Trojan legend. Both Aeschylus and Sophocles picture Iphigenia as sacrificed at Aulis so that the Greeks could win the Trojan War. According to Euripides' version, Iphigenia was spirited away from the sacrificial altar by the goddess Artemis. When the play opens, she is serving as priestess of Artemis' temple in Tauris, held there by Thoas, King of the Taurians. An inhospitable people, the Taurians sacrifice to the goddess all strangers that come to their land.

And now, on his wanderings, still at times driven mad by the Furies that have tormented him since he killed his mother, Iphigenia's brother Orestes comes to Tauris, accompanied by his faithful friend Pylades. Captured and held to be sacrificed, Orestes and Pylades are questioned by Iphigenia; Orestes begs that he be killed and his friend spared; and in what Aristotle called the best "recognition scene" in all the Greek drama, Iphigenia and her brother learn each other's identity. King Thoas comes to watch the sacrifice. Iphigenia tells him the strangers are polluted with matricidal blood; the goddess must be cleansed. While the King watches, Iphigenia leads the goddess' statue forth from the temple, followed by Orestes and Pylades. When word comes to King Thoas that they have all taken ship and fled from Tauris, the goddess Athena comes "from the machine" to tell Thoas who the strangers are and forbid his pursuit.

The play did not require the final descent of the goddess; apparently Euripides introduced it purely for its spectacular effect. For *Iphigenia in Tauris* is built for the story interest, with a straight and swift dramatic drive, and less psychologoical concern than is usual in Euripides.

On the stage the play is unquestionably vivid. Voltaire, who saw a performance when he was eighteen, declared thaat it gave him his first impetus toward writing tragedy. Goethe took part in a production of his prose *Iphigenie auf Tauris* at the court of Ettersburg in 1779. In 1780, Goethe rewrote the play in iambics, and during his trip to Italy in 1787, he gave the play its final shape. Still in iambics, it took on some of the calmer beauty of Greek tragedy. It presents less action but more character study than Euripides' play, is indeed Goethe's psychological masterpiece in the drama. Goethe changed the ending, having Iphigenie escape not by tricking the Taurian King, but by telling him the true story and trusting to his better nature, which her own candor and trust help to bring into play. Goethe's drama was translated into Finnish by Elino Leino; and in modern Greek it was acted in New York by Marika Cotopoulis in 1930. F. L. Lucas has said of Goethe's version: "Reading the two plays together, one is struck by the greater nobility of the German, the greater grace and truth of the Greek . . ."

The Gilbert Murray translation, the most effective to date, was presented by Harley Granville-Barker in 1915 in the Yale Bowl and in the College of the City of New York stadium with a cast including Lillah McCarthy (Iphigenia), Ian Maclaren (Orestes), Lionel Braham (Thoas), Claude Raines, Philip Merivale, and Alma Kruger. In 1932 and 1935, there were productions at the University of North Carolina.

In Aristotle's discussion of dramaturgy he mentions *Iphigenia In Tauris* favorably no less than five times. For sheer story interest, it is perhaps the most vivid of the Greek dramas.

HELEN   *Euripides*

This play, written in 412 B.C., presents the sort of character popular among the Greeks—an ingenious, resourceful man who works his own problems to a successful solution. In many ways similar to the dramatist's

Iphigenia In Tauris*, it is thoroughly interesting for the story itself, which is told with rapidity of action and rouse of plot.

There is, for modern minds, a further interest in *Helen* in that it presents a little-known variation of the legend of the Trojan War. As the orthodox and familiar story goes, the goddess of discord, Eris, not having been invited to the wedding of Peleus and Thetis, tossed into the midst of the gathered guests an apple with the inscription "for the fairest." Hera, Athena, and Aphrodite claimed the prize. None of the gods dared state which was the fairest of these three goddesses, and the decision was left to Paris, son of King Priam of Troy. Each of the goddesses sought to bribe the young man; Aphrodite promised him the fairest woman on earth (who chanced to be Helen, wife of King Menelaus of Sparta). Paris gave the decision to Aphrodite and his winning of Helen precipitated the Trojan War.

Naturally, the two other goddesses were jealous, and from their jealousy springs the variant story. In this version, Hera sent a wraith in the semblance of Helen with Paris to Troy, spiriting the real Helen off to Egypt, to be sheltered by King Proteus until the conflict was over. This is the situation as revealed by Helen in the prologue of Euripides' play.

Helen opens before the tomb of Proteus and the palace of his son Theoclymenus, seven years after the fall of Troy. The new king hopes to force Helen to marry him. Menelaus, Helen's husband, shipwrecked and tempest-tossed, arrives; when he learns how Helen has been preserved from Paris, they are reconciled. With friendly aid of Theonoe, sister of Theoclymenus, Helen pretends to have had word of the drowning of Menelaus; the King grants her a ship to perform the funeral rites at sea, and Helen and Menelaus sail away in safety.

The handling of the character of Menelaus, King of Sparta, is noteworthy. Whether hopes of peace in the Peloponnesian War moved Euripides, or just a desire to forget all the hardships and hard feelings of the conflict, we cannot now say; but he depicts Menelaus not as a hated Spartan, but simply as a tried and resourceful human, striving for happiness.

The story *Helen* tells, of a wraith at Troy while the genuine Queen Helen is lodged in Egypt, gave Euripides opportunity for caustic comments on the power of the seers, who supposedly knew hidden truths yet guided the Greeks while for a decade they waged an unnecessary and ravaging war. Again we may suspect a personal tone and contemporary reference in the play's comments on ten years of conflict to no purpose.

The swift movement and discerning reflections of *Helen* make it not only a lively story but a drama that probes the soul.

THE PHOENICIAN WOMEN   *Euripides*

One of the most frequently played dramas in ancient times, Euripides' *Phoenissae* (*The Phoenician Women*), 410? B.C., echoes through ancient history. From *The Phoenician Women*, Julius Casear took his motto: "If one must do wrong, best to do it for a kingdom, and in all else do right," a thought that became, in Shakespeare's words, "Caesar did never wrong but with just cause." A bit later in Roman history, Mamercus Scaurus inserted in one of his plays a line from *The Phoenician Women*, "We must endure the folly of the powers that be"; the Emperor Tiberius took this as a personal affront and had Mamercus put to death.

Euripides wrote seven plays on various phases of the Theban story, of which *The Phoenician Women* and *The Suppliants** survive. Euripides' version differs in several respects from the tale as told by Aeschylus in *The Seven Against Thebes** and by Sophocles in *Oedipus the King**. Antigone, on the roof of the palace of her brother Eteocles, King of Thebes, watches the hosts of her brother Polyneices, come to attack the city, for Eteocles has denied Polyneices his turn to rule. Jocasta (the mother and wife of Oedipus; in this version she has remained alive after Oedipus blinded himself) seeks to persuade her two sons to peace, but proud Eteocles brooks no conciliation. The two brothers kill each other. Creon, taking command in Thebes, orders the attacking Polyneices to be left unburied, orders Oedipus to leave the city, and strongly urges Antigone to marry Haemon (Creon's son; thus cementing his power). Antigone refuses the marriage, preferring to accompany her blind father in his exile, but she swears first that she will perform the funeral rites over her brother Polyneices. The play ends as she leads Oedipus away.

The Phoenician Women has a much more complicated plot than Aeschylus' *The Seven Against Thebes*. With an unusually large number of characters, it is one of the longest Greek plays (1766 lines), exceeded only by Sophocles' *Oedipus at Colonus** (1779 lines).

As Antigone looks from the palace wall at the opening of the play, a guard tells her who the besieging champions are. Euripides undoubtedly meant to attack Aeschylus' method of handling this situation, which was to have Eteocles say, "To tell you the name of each [champion at the seven gates] would be a grievous waste of time, when the foe is camped beneath our very walls." Euripides, also—as he frequently does, to increase the pathos—introduces more children, such as the little son of Creon, Menoeceus, who kills himself when it is prophesied that the city will be safe if he should die. The chorus, which gives the play its name, strikes a new note: the Phoenician women are maidens on their way to serve in the temple of Apollo at Delphi; they have just stopped at Thebes and are more objective observers than the usual chorus composed of citizens concerned in the action.

Seneca's version of *The Phoenician Women,* in Latin about A.D. 60, is more formal in structure, more rhetorical in style, than the Greek. Seneca's choral odes divide the play into five acts, a division that became the standard. Seneca's *The Phoenician Women* was the model for *Gorboduc** by Sackville and Norton, which, as F. L. Lucas has pointed out, is "the first English play in the Senecan form, the first regular English tragedy, the first English drama in blank verse." The jealousy, the fratricide, the sententious speeches, the formal structure, are all from Seneca.

Euripides is the subtler playwright. His having the two brothers meet as their mother pleads with them to be reconciled, affords opportunity for contrasted characterization, and Euripides effectively sets the reasonable but wronged Polyneices against the arrogant and wilful Eteocles. The harsh conflict of wills gives an inner force to the drama, so that the play drives with sustained power to the closing doom. Then Oedipus walks to exile in the quiet dignity that gives man stature, that lifts *The Phoenician Women* with tragic exaltation in its close.

ORESTES   *Euripides*

Full of dramatic incident, surging with swift emotion to tragic heights,

Orestes, 408 B.C., was deservedly one of the most popular of Euripides' dramas. Along with his *Hecuba** and *The Phoenician Women**, it was the most frequently read during the Middle Ages, and since then, though not frequently performed, it has retained its high repute. A. W. Verrall has called it "one of the triumphs of the stage, which may still be described as supreme of its kind . . . For excitement, for play of emotion, for progression and climax of horror, achieved by natural means and without strain upon the realities of life, it has few rivals in the repertory of the world."

The story of *Orestes* is one of the few of Euripides in which the descent of the god from the top of the theatre is used not merely for the spectacular effect, but as the essential device to resolve the conflict in the drama and to produce a happy ending. There is enough else in the play that is spectacular. It opens in Argos, a week after Orestes has killed his mother and her lover. Orestes, ravaged with spells of madness, is watched over by his sister Electra. Menelaus refuses to shelter him from the citizens, who pass upon Orestes and Electra sentence of death by their own hands. With the help of his friend Pylades, Orestes seeks to seize Helen, back from Troy; when she slips away, they take her daughter by Menelaus, Hermione. While Menelaus watches impotently from below, Pylades and Orestes hold Hermione on the roof of the palace, up which soar flames enkindled by Electra. Amidst the flames Apollo appears, and orders them to cease their struggles. He bids Orestes wed Hermione, Pylades wed Electra, Menelaus return to rule Sparta; Helen, he transports to dwell among the gods. The play ends, like *Iphigenia In Tauris** and *The Phoenician Women**, with the chorus, as it files out, uttering a prayer for victory in the dramatic contest.

The critic Aristophanes of Byzantium, in the third century B.C., commented on the remarkable power of *Orestes* when performed, despite the fact that every character in the play is evil. Pylades, though partially redeemed because he is acting not in self-interest but for friendship's sake, suggests the killing of Helen. Menelaus, the Spartan king, is ungenerous, forgetful of former benefits, and cowardly; Aristotle, indeed, mentions him, as pictured in *Orestes,* as an instance of "unnecessary baseness."

Swift and stimulating in its picture of the frenzied Orestes, the play gives us the most vivid study of an abnormal psychological state in the ancient drama. Of the opening scene, in which Electra watches while Orestes wakes, the French critic Henri Patin remarked: "This scene, in its sentiment, language, arrangement of the dialogue, and grouping of the different ideas, is an epitome of the Greek tragic genius, for the study of which it is almost, in itself, sufficient."

In the legendary material of this drama Euripides has built one of his most moving plays.

IPHIGENIA IN AULIS   *Euripides*

In Euripides' *Iphigenia in Aulis,* 407? B.C., which the French critic Henri Patin has called "the most perfect of his plays," the old legendary material is translated into a romantic story with human, natural characters. The well-motivated actions carry swiftly along in a plot that could be used today.

Aeschylus and Sophocles, as well as Euripides, have told the story of Iphigenia, the daughter of Agamemnon and Clytemnestra, who, on the island of Aulis, was given in sacrifice by her father so that the Greeks might have safe journey to Troy. All three playwrights have Agamemnon lure Iphigenia to the island by sending word that she is to be married to Achilles. From that point, Euripides adds dramatic device after device, all flowing naturally from the initial situation. He has Agamemnon, the father, repent and write a letter home, telling Clytemnestra not to bring the girl. But the suspicious Menelaus, burning for revenge for his wife Helen's going to Troy, waylays the messenger. Not only Iphigenia, but her mother Clytemnestra comes to Aulis. When Clytemnestra greets Achilles as her son-in-law, he is dumb-founded, and the deceit of Agamemnon is disclosed. Then Clytemnestra bursts out in fury against her husband Agamemnon, reminding him of his murder of her former husband and child (a fact not found in Homer) and confessing that her marriage to him was a forced and hateful one. Achilles, too, is wroth. In his anger at being made a pawn of Agamemnon's deceit, he comes to defend Iphigenia against those ready to sacrifice her. At this turn of events, Iphigenia proves her loyalty and courage; since the safety of the Greeks depends upon the sacrifice, she is ready to die for her country. As the priest strikes, the spectators see on the altar, instead of Iphigenia, a wild doe of the hills. The gods have taken the noble Iphigenia to abide with them.

The natural movement of the characters in the play is supported by sound portraiture. Iphigenia is one of the loveliest maids in the Greek drama. Devoted to her father, she runs to embrace him, happy with thought of her marriage to the great hero. In sharp contrast is her despair when she learns that Achilles was but a decoy to lure her to the island. She is noble in her final resolve and dignified in her dying. Achilles is natural, too. Ready to fight the whole army to save Iphigenia, he does not, however, stand in the way of her duty—perhaps he even is relieved—when she determines to give herself to the sacrifice. Clytemnestra, the doting mother, then the domineering wife, is just the sort of person that could murder her mate. Agamemnon, on the other hand, is just the sort of man one might wish to murder: good-natured, well-meaning, but desirous of praise and power and too weak-willed to oppose the wishes of the mob. Menelaus, the Spartan—here pictured when Sparta was winning the war against Athens—is the only consistently scoundrelly figure, but even he is given natural motives, so that his actions are understandable. The gallery of human figures, sharply etched, in *Iphigenia in Aulis*, is unmatched elsewhere in the Greek drama.

Euripides also makes effective use of dramatic irony, as in Agamemnon's mortification and secret shame when Clytemnestra and Iphigenia, newly come to Aulis, rejoice in the approaching marriage, and he knows that his daughter is doomed.

Numerous writers have pointed out the similarity of Iphigenia's death to Abraham's sacrifice-offering of his son Isaac, and also to Jephtha's sacrifice of his daughter, in the *Bible*.

Unfinished at Euripides' death, *Iphigenia in Aulis* was presented by his son at the contest in Athens in 405 B.C. In the trilogy with *The Bacchantes**, it won first prize. In the modern period, it was translated by Erasmus in 1524; made into a French play, *Iphigénie*, by Racine in 1674, one of his best; and into an opera by Gluck just a hundred years later.

Schiller translated *Iphigenia in Aulis* in 1788; while working on it, he declared: "Often the execution is such that no poet could better it; but at times his tediousness spoils my enjoyment and my labor." Of the creator of *Iphigenia in Aulis,* Goethe exclaimed: "Have all the nations of the world possessed a dramatist worthy to hand him his slippers? . . . Over the scenes of Hellas and its primitive body of legends, he sails and swims like a cannon-ball in a sea of quicksilver and cannot sink even if he tried."

Euripides, however, can soar, as those who saw Margaret Anglin as Iphigenia in New York in 1921 will remember. The play revealed its persisting power in a revival at Columbia University in November, 1950. In dramatic movement, in character portrayal, in thoughtful phrase and liquid style, Euripides' *Iphigenia in Aulis* soars in surpassing beauty.

THE BACCHANTES   *Euripides*

About 407 B.C. Euripides accepted the invitation of King Archelaus of Macedonia, at whose court he lived for the year until his death (at the fangs of Archelaus's hunting dogs, legend says). In Macedon, Euripides probably saw some of the orgiastic rites of the worship of Dionysus. His spirit, already heavy with disillusion at Athens' conduct in the Peloponnesian War, found in those religious excesses further cause for sombre brooding over human nature. His play *Bacchae* (*The Bacchantes*) pictures the consequences of the frenzied, often hysterical, celebration of the feast of the god of wine.

The Bacchantes (Dionysus is the Greek name of the Roman Bacchus) pictures the coming of Dionysus to impress his worship on Thebes. The old men welcome him, but young King Pentheus considers his worship harmful to the state and binds the god. Laughing Dionysus sets the women into ritual ecstasy on the hilltops; he slips his bonds, hypnotizes Pentheus into dressing as a woman so that he may behold the "mysteries"; and off in the hills the maddened celebrants, the bacchantes in their reveling frenzy, leap upon and destroy Pentheus their king. Pentheus' own mother Agave, thinking she has killed a lion, bears back Pentheus' head with rejoicing song—then gradually she recovers from her Bacchic fury to recognize her son's severed head in her hands. The god has paid the city for its neglect of him.

The attitude of Euripides toward religion cannot be grasped from *The Bacchantes,* especially as portions of it (including part of a climactic speech by Dionysus) are lost; but the dramatist seems to be emphasizing the danger of excess, the need of faith. There are no other extant plays based on this theme—but one line of a play, *Pentheus,* by Aeschylus. There are, however, many other signs of Athenian interest in the wilder and more emotional aspects of the worship of the wine-god in Dionysiac frenzy. Countless vases and jars of the period show maenads with drums; young Dionysus is laughing among them, and Silenus constantly leers. About 420 B.C. a temple to Dionysus was erected in Athens near the theatre where the dramatic contests were held as part of the festival of the Great Dionysia; on the temple wall is a painting of Pentheus' punishment for opposing the god.

Many critics have considered *The Bacchantes* one of the most tragic of dramas. The scene in which the frenzied Agave, coming to her senses, finds herself holding the head of her own son whom she has killed is so

terrible that modern audiences would protect themselves from its impact
by denying its credibility. Yet even that horror comes home to us. R. P.
Winnington-Ingram observed in 1948 that "the play has an immediate
relevance to the worship of Dionysus in Greece, being a priceless document for the history of Greek religion. At the next remove it is relevant
to all emotional forms of religion in all ages, and particularly to those
that manifest the power of the group. But similar manifestations occur
in connexion with objects not specifically religious, and so the scope of the
play is widened to include the phenomena of group emotion in all social
and political life." Robert Graves found the relevance of the actions in
The Bacchantes more deeply imbedded in our souls: "This tearing apart
of the young man by the Bacchantes may seem far removed from modern
life, but the archives of morbid pathology are filled with such stories . . .
An English or American woman in a nervous breakdown of sexual origin
will often instinctively reproduce in faithful and disgusting detail much
of the ancient Dionysian ritual. I have witnessed it myself in helpless
terror." Euripides anticipated Freud by 2,500 years.

The Bacchantes was presented after Euripides' death by his son. When
the dramatist died, Aristophanes in *The Frogs** declared: "His works have
perished with him." Two months later, in the Great Dionysia of 405 B.C.,
Euripides' trilogy won first prize with *Iphigenia in Aulis** and *The Bacchantes.*

In the ancient world, *The Bacchantes* was very popular. When invited
to Syracuse as tutor to Dionysius the Younger, the philosopher Plato refused a purple robe Dionysius offered him, quoting from *The Bacchantes*
a line (836) objecting to effeminacy; whereupon Aristippus took the
robe, quoting from the same play (lines 316-317) a remark that true
worth is not easily corrupted. Plato was dismissed.

In 53 B.C., *The Bacchantes* was being performed by strolling Greek
players before King Artavasdes of Armenia and King Orodes of Parthia,
when Parthian horsemen rode in with the head of Crassus (with Caesar
and Pompey, member of the first Roman triumvirate). The actor playing
Agave, Jason of Tralles, took the actual head of Crassus and used it for
the head of Pentheus in the play.

For elements other than its horrid press of emotion, *The Bacchantes* is
outstanding. The two old men, Cadmus, grandsire of Pentheus, and the
prophet Tiresias, are excellently drawn; and there is a vivid portrait of
Pentheus himself, who opposes the Dionysiac cult for the good of his
people, but gradually is drawn under the hypnotic spell of the god. The
actual poetry of *The Bacchantes,* furthermore, is of surpassing beauty—
especially, the lyric odes of the chorus, which are among the most lofty
and the richest in love of nature in all the ancient drama. Eugene O'Neill,
Jr. expressed the critical consensus in calling *The Bacchantes* "one of
Euripides' greatest artistic creations." Macaulay declared it "a most
glorious play . . . as a piece of language, it is hardly equalled in the
world." The choral odes, original in their power and beauty, are em-
bellished versions of the traditional chants of the Bacchic mysteries; the
magnificent chorus, lines 64 to 169, follows not only the tenor but the
terms of the ritual paean. *The Bacchantes* is indeed, as Cedric H. Whitman called it in *Sophocles* (1951), "a shattering paean of unreason, a
hymn to the god of the beautiful but meaningless world."

The description of the wild sweep of the reveling Bacchantes through
the wild woods mingles poetry and strangeness in ecstatic surge before

the wakening horror. Nowhere else in the Greek, if indeed in any drama, is there such a mingling of beauty and terror, of wild exultation and bitter woe, as in *The Bacchantes*.

THE CHIEF THING   *Nikolai Nikolayevitch Evreinov*

From the time when, at five, he was first taken to a play, the theatre was in the soul of Nikolai Nikolayevitch Evreinov (Yevreinoff; Russian, b. 1879). He wrote a play at the age of seven. Later, he became a circus performer, actor, director, and critic, as well as playwright. Evreinov felt that the will to dramatize was as basic as the urges of self-preservation and sex. After a spell of symbolism, he developed the monodrama, a type of play in which all the persons and acts are seen through the eyes of a single character. He made use of this form in *The Presentation of Love*, 1909, and especially in *The Theatre of The Soul*, 1912.

Evreinov's fullest dramatic expression of his ideas is in *The Chief Thing*, 1919, first performed at Petrograd in 1921. It was produced as *Quintessence* by the Harvard Dramatic Club in 1925, and New York saw it in March 1926. It has also been translated as *The Theatre of Happiness*. In Paris it was played in 1936 as *The Comedy of Happiness*. The author calls it "a comedy for some, a tragedy for others."

The Chief Thing is a dramatic parable of man's search for happiness. The Paraclete (Comforter) comes, not quite as promised in the *Bible* (*John*, 14, 15): "When the Paraclete is come, whom I shall send unto you from the Father, even the spirit of truth," for in Evreinov's play, the comforter feeds only the illusions, which seem to him essential to human happiness. "It is more comfortable to be lied to a little than to be unhappy much." The Comforter comes in the guise of a fortune-teller, who listens to the complaints of the occupants of a drab boarding house and then engages three actors to bring spiritual relief to the unhappy household. As Brooks Atkinson (March 23, 1926) summed it up, the fortune-teller has heard "a bizarre procession of customers—the woman whose husband has left her for other women; the boarding-house drudge whose daughter wants love at any price; the actor who fattens his salary as a detective . . . Suddenly the scene shifts to the stage of a provincial theatre where a rehearsal of *Quo Vadis* is in progress. Now, passing for an eccentric American theatrical producer, the Paraklete [hires three of the actors] to bring joy to the lugubrious household, to play the lovers to aching hearts." The comic actor philanders with the dry and distasteful school teacher; as an insurance agent, the second actor makes love to the landlady's eager daughter; as a servant, the soubrette consoles the student contemplating suicide. However, the actors dislike their assigned roles and quarrel among themselves. The director scolds them back to their jobs, while the audience watches the two levels of action. Their contract ended, the actors unmask before the boarders and press home the moral of the play; all join in a riotous harlequinade at the success of the hoax. As the curtain falls, Columbine pokes out her head and asks about the audience—who plays for them the roles they need? The thoughtful, she concludes, may draw their own moral.

This "gayly colored prankful romp of a play," as Alexander Woollcott called it, makes free use of theatrical devices and other resources of the theatre. It combines a realistic picture of the boarding house folk with a symbolic use of the players—theatre folk hired to act a part "in real life" on the stage—to press home, in terms of drama, a searching thought. The chief thing in life is happiness, *The Chief Thing* suggests, and only a combinaton of fact and fable, the feet of reality asprout with the wings of illusion, can help us to attain it. A more profound view would perhaps behold happiness as a byproduct rather than a goal, but for those that deem it most to be desired, *The Chief Thing* presents a gay story that presses a sober point home.

THE BEAUX' STRATAGEM   *George Farquhar*

George Farquhar (1678-1707) has been called the last of the Restoration dramatists, but the wit of the plays of this Irish playwright rises above the ethical indifference of his predecessors. To them, a gentleman was a natural rake; Farquhar's beaux may start out as gay deceivers, but love works to the good in them.

Farquhar's first connection with the theatre was as an actor. After badly wounding his opponent in a duel scene in Dryden's *The Indian Emperor,* he abandoned the stage and began to write. His first comedy, *Love and a Bottle,* 1699, was a success. He followed it with *The Constant Couple,* 1700, in which Robert Wilks made a hit; its sequel, *Sir Harry Wildair,* 1701, was not so popular. Succeeding plays increased neither Farquhar's reputation nor his fortune; indeed they left him in dire straits.

In 1707, during his last six weeks, while he was living on funds provided by Robert Wilks, Farquhar wrote his mastepriece, *The Beaux' Stratagem,* a lively social comedy which shows no trace of the fatal illness he was undergoing. He lived scarcely beyond the third night of its performance (the night the receipts went to the author), but he knew that the play was a success and that his two daughters would be provided for.

The play pictures two gentlemen, Archer and Aimwell, without resources but quite resourceful, who decide to work together toward a wealthy marriage. Archer passes as the servant of Aimwell. While the latter woos Dorinda, daughter of the wealthy Lady Bountiful, Archer and Mrs. Sullen, the mismated daughter-in-law of Lady Bountiful, fall in love. Aimwell comes to love Dorinda and confesses that he is penniless. Then honesty is rewarded; Aimwell's elder brother dies, leaving him title and estate. Mrs. Sullen wins a divorce, enabling the two couples to be both virtuous and happy.

The Beaux' Stratagem was for some time one of the most frequently played English comedies, enjoying constant revivals for a century. Opinions as to the morals of the play, however, have differed. In her preface to an 1808 edition, the pious playwright Elizabeth Inchbald observed: "It is an honor to the morality of the present age, that this most entertaining comedy is but seldom performed . . . Plays of this kind are far more mischievous than those which preserve less appearance of delicacy." But the 1829 preface says that the play "is absolutely a *sermon* compared with the productions of Wycherly and Vanbrugh; and, though this 1829 edition is assigning it but moderate praise on the score of decency, it may serve to show that Farquhar, at least, improved on the morals, if not on the wit, of his predecessors."

In *The Beaux' Stratagem,* Farquhar achieved a great success that broke with more than the ethics of Restoration drama. The scene of the comedy is a provincial town, Lichfield, and although two of the characters sigh to be in London, they no longer believe that city the sole habitat of endurable gentlefolk, nor that there are tolerable talk and admirable action only within earshot of Westminster chimes.

Several of the minor characters in the play have won lasting attention. Scrub, the servant of Squire Sullen, is a gem of his kind, one of the liveliest English descendants of the slave in the classical drama who holds the secrets and forwards the designs of the lovers. Boniface, the beaming innkeeper, was so popular that his name became proverbial for a genial host, and similarly "Lady Bountiful" became the general term (even to the heroine of an early "comic strip") for a wealthy and generous though somewhat gullible woman.

In the United States, *The Beaux' Stratagem* has also fared well. In New York, it was played in the first season of the New Theatre, 1732; at the Nassau Street Theatre, in 1750; and it was the opening piece for Hallam's American Company at the John Street Theatre, December 7, 1767. In Massachusetts, the House of Representatives in 1790 denied the petition of Hallam and Henry to open a theatre, but in 1792 an English company played *The Beaux' Stratagem* in Salem and Boston. It was presented again in Boston in 1807, a hundred years after its premiere.

More recent revivals include the Players Club presentation in New York and on tour, 1928; one at the Mohawk Drama Festival, 1937; one with Aline MacMahon in Charleson, 1939; and another, with Brian Aherne, at Woodstock, New York, summer of 1948. The Players Club cast included Lyn Harding, Raymond Hitchcock, James T. Powers, Helen Menken, and Fay Bainter. A London production opened May 5, 1949, for 532 performances.

Brooks Atkinson (June 5, 1928) called the play "delightfully entertaining—a bundle of humors and rhymeless merriment." Alison Smith, in the *New York World,* declared that Farquhar's "intimations of a forthright and genuine consideration of life beneath the cynical persiflage of his stage bring a fresh breath into the studies of coffee house and boudoir." *The Beaux' Stratagem* matches the wit and the lively movement of the best of the Restoration comedies, while replacing their irresponsible licentiousness with a deeper understanding and a kindlier portraiture of the basic good qualities in human nature.

THE TRAGEDY OF TRAGEDIES   *Henry Fielding*

Author of what many consider the greatest English novel, *Tom Jones,* Henry Fielding (1707-1754) wrote a few farces and two satirical burlesques—*Pasquin* and *The Tragedy of Tragedies; or, The Life and Death of Tom Thumb the Great*—for the theatre. The latter was first produced as *Tom Thumb, a Tragedy* at the Haymarket Theatre, April 25, 1730, and achieved the then remarkable record of 36 performances by the season's end. Revived at the Haymarket with alterations and the full title, March 24, 1731, the play was again warmly welcomed. Its satirical thrusts were sharp, showing that spiritual balance and true majesty have no essential connection with size or power; its little hero with a great soul embodies an attack on those who write in the grand style without great ability, or those who deem themselves good rulers because they occupy the ruler's seat. The play thus evoked the ire of the authorities and was a major cause of the Licensing Act of 1737, which virtually set the Lord Chamberlain's censorship over the English stage.

Popular throughout the eighteenth century, *The Tragedy of Tragedies* was performed in the new Nassau Street Theatre in New York, October 22, 1753. It was presented in London as a burletta with music by Kane O'Hara, October 3, 1780; previously two musical versions were produced in 1733. Recent productions include one at the Malvern Festival in 1937 and one at the University of California in 1938.

This play is set at the Court of King Arthur, father of the fair Huncamunca, husband of domineering Queen Dollallolla. The King is in love with the captive queen of the Giants, Glumdalca. Both the Queen and the giantess love tiny Tom Thumb, "a little hero with a great soul"; Tom loves Huncamunca. Also in the play are the conjuror Merlin, "in some sort father to Tom Thumb"; the Ghost of Gaffer Thumb—every tragedy must have its ghost; Lord Grizzle, Tom's rival for Huncamunca's hand; three courtiers, Noodle, Doodle, and Foodle; and two maids of honour, Cleora and Mustacha. Huncamunca, according to the list of characters, is "equally in love with Lord Grizzle and Tom Thumb, and desirous to be married to them both." Tom Thumb kills Grizzle; on his triumphant return Tom is swallowed by a cow. Noodle reports this to the court, and the bearer of ill tidings is killed by the Queen. Cleora, who loves Noodle, stabs the Queen; Huncamunca kills Cleora; Doodle kills Huncamunca; Mustacha kills Doodle; the King kills Mustacha then himself. On this universal doom the curtain falls.

Fielding's burlesque stands worthily in the line of English dramatic burlesques, between *The Rehearsal* and *The Critic**. In addition to the satire implicit in the absurd story, contemporary audiences laughed at the many lines that parody passages of then popular plays. In the printed edition of *The Tragedy of Tragedies* annotations by "H. Scriblerus Secundus" point dagger-thrusts home.

This play, said Allardyce Nicoll, is "decidedly Fielding's happiest work." It is decidedly his most popular play, and the court scenes, with song and pantomime, were made into gorgeous and grotesque spectacles. The songs grew into favor and are still pleasant. But *The Tragedy of Tragedies* suffered the tragedy of its own good fortune: it laughed the excesses of poetic tragedy out of the theatre and thus destroyed its main excuse for being. While the particulars of its satire are thus outmoded, its nonsense is still amusing; and pretension still requires such drubbing as is delivered in mock-serious earnestness with a midget piledriver in Fielding's most forceful and most amusing play.

BARBARA FRIETCHIE   *Clyde Fitch*

The rousing patriotic episode that took place in Frederick, Maryland, on October 10, 1862, celebrated in Whittier's poem of Barbara Frietchie, forms the basis of this play by Clyde Fitch (1865-1909). It opened in New York October 23, 1899, with Julia Marlowe as Barbara and Arnold Daly as her rejected Southern suitor.

For dramatic purposes, the 96-year-old Barbara Frietchie becomes a young Southern girl in love with a northerner, Captain Trumbull. Their marriage is interrupted by the call to arms. When two sharp-shooters in her house await the passing of the Captain, Barbara succeeds in getting one drunk, then shoots the other in the arm. Later, the Captain, wounded by Barbara's Confederate suitor, is brought to Barbara's house; she pleads with her suitor and her father to give the Captain the quiet he needs.

Captain Trumbull dies. Barbara takes the bloody Stars and Stripes from his bosom, and waves it from the balcony as the Confederate troops roll through her home town. Their leader looks up:

> "Who touches a hair of that girl's head
> Dies like a dog! March on!" he said.

The patriotism and martial spirit of *Barbara Frietchie* caught the public. A deftly constructed play, it has several mounting climaxes in the last act, capped by the historic incident for which everyone waits.

So popular was *Barbara Frietchie* that, in the fashion of the time, it was soon travestied in the burlesque *Barbara Fidgety* by Edgar Smith, in which Mabel Fenton duplicated Julia Marlowe's costumes, David Warfield played the crazed Southern suitor, and Weber and Fields assumed the roles of political "heelers."

The operetta *My Maryland,* which opened in Philadelphia, January 25, 1927, for a 41 weeks' run, and in New York, September 12, 1927, for 312 performances, appeared to be so similar to *Barbara Frietchie* that the Fitch estate sued for plagiarism. This operetta with music by Sigmund Romberg has continued to enjoy popularity. Among its lingering songs are "Dixie", "The Same Silver Moon", and "Your Land and My Land."

My Maryland holds popularity not only through its music, but also through its compact presentation of Fitch's story with all its freshness, felicity, and power.

CAPTAIN JINKS OF THE HORSE MARINES   *Clyde Fitch*

Though shallow in its characterization and now familiar in its design, the lively and gay *Captain Jinks of the Horse Marines* was in its time one of the most talked of plays in New York. When it opened on February 4, 1901, it gave Ethel Barrymore her first stellar role and Broadway 168 performances of romantic dash and gay delight.

Clyde Fitch, said Alan Dale, "is certainly a wonder . . . The hero and heroine are so unconventional that you never know what they are going to do next . . . *Captain Jinks* is brimming over with fizzing novelties. No men and women who appreciate real genuine human humor—every line funnier than a whole book of 'jokes'—could fail to laugh." The *New York Evening World* called the play "one of the most delightful comedies New York has ever known." With five plays on Broadway at the same time— *Sapho, Lovers' Lane, The Climbers, Barbara Frietchie**, and *Captain Jinks*—Clyde Fitch became the king-pin playwright.

There was more laughter when Edgar Smith's revue *Fiddle-Dee-Dee,* a burlesque of *Captain Jinks,* bounced along with David Warfield a hilarious Jinks, with Fay Templeton making ludicrous the graceful "Grecian bend" of Ethel Barrymore, with De Wolfe Hopper as the ballet master, and with a bevy of ballet girls played by males.

Ethel Barrymore proved a success in *Captain Jinks* again in 1907, and on the radio in 1936. A musical comedy made from the play, *Captain High Jinks,* opened September 8, 1925, with book by Frank Mandel and Laurence Schwab, lyrics by B. G. De Sylva, and music by Lewis E. Gensler and Stephen Jones. It ran for 167 performances, but moved slowly, lacking both the pace and the punch of the play. Ethel's niece, Diana Barrymore, was in a revival of the play, in 1941, at White Plains, New York, along with Gregory Peck, Jose Ruben, Philip Bourneuf, and Winston O'Keefe. *Captain Jinks* was seen again in New York in 1946 (off

Broadway) and 1948 (Fordham University). It is a bit dated, but amusingly quaint, and romantically charming.

The title came from a song (words by William H. Lingard, music by T. Maclagan) which Lingard brought from London to the Theatre Comique in New York, in 1868: "I'm Captain Jinks of the Horse Marines, I feed my horse on pork and beans, And often live beyond my means: I'm a Captain in the Army." The nonsense song made a sensational success, was used as the title of Fitch's play, and was sung in the 1931-1941 revivals of *The Streets of New York**. Lingard, incidentally, was the first of the long line of popular female impersonators.

The play begins on a New York dock, where newspapermen and others wait to greet the great singer Madame Trentoni, an American girl named after her native city, Trenton, who has won fame abroad. Among those waiting are the Purity Ladies, who have come to beg her not to sing in the "immodest" opera *La Traviata,* and Captain Jinks. The latter has wagered with his comrades that he can win the actress; if he succeeds, they all will live on what she earns for him. The inevitable happens: the officer and the lady fall in love; she learns of the wager and is brokenhearted. Not even her manager and ballet master, "Papa" Belliari, can persuade her to sing—until out of her wretchedness she cries "I'll sing to every woman's heart in that house." Then the genuineness of Captain Jinks' love reawakens her to joy.

Variations of this theme have scuffed its novelty, but there is undeniable deftness and lightness in Fitch's handling. The plea of the Purity Ladies is a slantwise attack upon the reception of his own play *Sapho* (from the story and play by Alphonse Daudet), the star of which, Olga Nethersole, went to jail. Belliari is a richly comic creation. The intertwining of the fuss and fret of theatrical preparations, the confused rehearsal of the ballet, with the officers' interest in their wager and Jinks' predicament in regard to Madame Trentoni, help make *Captain Jinks of the Horse Marines* a capitally amusing play.

THE STUBBORNNESS OF GERALDINE   *Clyde Fitch*

Staged and produced by its author, *The Stubbornness of Geraldine*, 1902, presents, in the satiric atmosphere of an international society comedy, a pleasantly sentimental picture of the "stubbornness" of faith and true love. Geraldine Lang, a young American woman on her way home from a prolonged stay abroad, meets the Hungarian Count Carlos Kinsey. They fall in love. Upon their arrival in the United States, Geraldine's friends try to convince her that Carlos is a villain and a fortune-hunter. The final report on Kinsey shows him to be honest though poor.

The sentimentality of the story is relieved by the deftness of Fitch's dialogue and by the liveliness of the action. In the original production, the first act was vividly staged on a highly realistic ocean liner. Two levels of deck, funnels, and rigging comprised the set. As Geraldine leaned over the rail while Count Carlos serenaded her, the vessel rose and fell. "When the swells came," said the *New York Herald* (November 3, 1902) "and one poor woman had to be led away by the stewardess, there were several susceptible persons in the audience who confessed afterwards that they were afraid for a minute they, too, would have to withdraw." In the second act, the setting was no less vivid; the dialogue was spoken by persons climbing up and down a hallful of trunks.

Fitch, said the *Commercial Advertiser* (November 4, 1902) "has dealt with his material so deftly, so gracefully, has worked out little incidents here and there with such clevernes, that one loses sight of the slenderness of the story." Of the plays of Fitch, said the *New York Herald,* "certainly none has been more delightful than *The Stubbornness of Geraldine.*"

The play opened in New York on November 2, 1902, and was revived almost seasonally until 1908. Its success and the sentimentality of its heroine made it a fair target for travesty. On December 18, 1902, Weber and Fields produced *The Stickiness of Gelatine* by Edgar Smith. In this burlesque, Fay Templeton played Gelatine Pang, William Collier was Vi Bumpson of Tombstone, Arizona, Lew Fields played Count Carless Kidney, and Joe Weber was Fraulein Krank.

Both plays were successful. *The Stubbornness of Geraldine* is an outstanding representative of American social sentimental comedy.

THE TRUTH   *Clyde Fitch*

The most popular of Fitch's plays is *The Truth,* written for Clara Bloodgood, who had starred in Fitch's *The Climbers* and *The Girl With the Green Eyes.* After opening in Cleveland on October 16, 1906, *The Truth* came to New York the same night as Fitch's *Straight Road.* It had a run of only two weeks, but it toured successfully throughout the United States. It was also popular all over Europe and in Australia. London saw the play open on April 6, 1907, for a run of 170 performances, with Marie Tempest, to whom the published version was dedicated. Shortly after the play appeared in book form, Sarah Bloodgood killed herself in Baltimore (December 1907), thus ending the American tour.

The Truth shows how the habit of lying can add to the complications of life. Eve Lindon, separated from her husband, but desiring a reconciliation, suspects Becky Warder of encouraging the flirtatious Lindon's attentions. Eve voices her suspicions to Becky's husband, who catches Becky in a lie and sends her packing. Becky, "artless and artistic in her fibbing," seeks the help of her father, who initiates a further deceit by informing Warder that Becky is ill. Warder, learning of the deceit, comes prepared to trap Becky, but she surprises him by telling the truth. The story moves along with speed, with neatly constructed situations and effective climaxes.

The play is notable for well-turned details, and for "fat" minor parts, such as those of Becky's father and Mrs. Genevieve Crespigny, his boardinghouse landlady. It has more fidelity to life and less satire than Fitch's *The Climbers,* 1901, which was a great success in New York, though London rejected its characters as cold-blooded boors.

Of *The Truth,* the *Boston Transcript* (December 11, 1906) observed: "Since his rediscovery of the moral element in human affairs, Mr. Fitch has written plays that are natural and convincing in a degree that could never have been predicted from his earlier work, with no loss of the lightness and smartness that were once its chief merits ... lightness that is not altogether frivolity, but rather the filmy and rose-tinted veil that most sophisticated people throw nowadays over their most serious actions."

Clyde Fitch once said of *The Truth:* "The first two acts are capital—and the last two are labor." This jocular confession of the creative effort does not indicate the lightness and speed of the entire play. While it glances amusingly across the surface of the deep problem of truth, it both stimulates and entertains.

THE CITY   *Clyde Fitch*

Clyde Fitch died in France three months before *The City* was produced. Since it was his last play, Fitch deemed it his best; but his comedies have shown greater lasting power. *The City* is a stark, and, for its time, a breath-taking melodrama. Its central point is that, contrary to the notion pressed in many contemporary plays, the city does not corrupt but tests a man.

The play pictures the collapse of the Rand family. The younger folk long for the city, but old George Rand "would rather be *It* in Middleburg than *Nit* in New York." His secretary, George Hannock, a drug fiend who has a hold on Rand, demands money and, refused, threatens to shoot himself. Old Rand dies of shock. The family moves to New York where, urged on by Hannock, George Rand Jr. becomes a candidate for governor. Teresa Rand, in the city, wants a divorce. Hannock has secretly married Cicely Rand. George, learning this, tells Hannock he has married his half-sister: Hannock shoots Cicely, but is stopped before he can shoot himself. He reveals that the Rand fortune was questionably amassed, at the expense of the Vorhees family, and George relinquishes it to Eleanor Vorhees, whom he loves.

The characters of *The City* are vividly drawn. The two sisters are well contrasted, "the one capricious and a little perverse, yet true at heart and unconscious of evil," as the *Baltimore News* put it (December 27, 1910); the other "frivolous and obstinate, yet with her principles likewise firmly anchored." The men are even more sharply limned—particularly Hannock going down hill and George struggling against circumstances not of his making.

Vivid as these figures are, it is the situation in which they find themselves that transfigured the public. When Hannock, for the first time on the English-speaking stage, used the expression "You're a goddam liar!", and when the audience recognized that Hannock had married his half-sister, Charles Darnton reported that it "caused women to shriek and men to shout over the nerve-wracking scene." "It is loaded to the muzzle with thrills," the *New York Press* observed. Louis V. DeVoe declared, in the *New York World,* that the play was "the greatest example of purely melodramatic writing that has yet been accomplished by one of our native contributors to the stage." William Lyon Phelps observed in the *Hartford Courant* (December 14, 1909): "*The City* is one of the most powerful dramas ever composed by an American . . . Furthermore, it is a drama that has as its driving force a great idea; it is a play full of excitement and full of cerebration."

The City opened in New York on December 21, 1909, with Walter Hampden as George Rand, Jr., with Tully Marshall as Hannock, and with Mary Nash and Lucile Watson. It ran for 194 performances.

Not everyone found the play completely praiseworthy. The *New York Dramatic Mirror* (January 1, 1910) dissented in regard to the climactic moment of the play: "Tremendous in its effect on the audience as this scene is, it owes its success to a purely morbid, ultra-sensational coup bodied forth in language exceeding the limit of all hitherto attempted freedom of speech on the American or any other stage, and superheated with a hysterical frenzy that could not fail to communicate itself to the onlookers."

Today the language of the big scene in *The City* falls upon too accustomed ears; even the impact of incest comes with the lessened force of a known situation. Without the power of poetry to sustain its fire, a mere situation, however blazing when first flung upon the stage, dims like a dying torch. The characters in *The City* are natural, but their relationships seem contrived for the sake of achieving a melodramatic story. Hence, the story may shock us into roused attention, but it does not bind us with a lasting spell.

THE TWO NOBLE KINSMEN   *John Fletcher*

Best known for his dozen or more collaborations with Francis Beaumont*, John Fletcher (English, 1579-1625) also wrote some sixteen plays alone. He may have worked with Shakespeare on *Henry VIII* and Shakespeare may have had a finger in the making of *The Two Noble Kinsmen* (printed in 1634), Fletcher's best play.

The story of *The Two Noble Kinsmen* was told by Boccaccio in his *Teseide* and is *The Knight's Tale* of Chaucer's *Canterbury Tales*. The noble kinsmen are Palamon and Arcite, prisoners of Theseus, king of Athens. Theseus is married to Hippolyta, queen of the Amazons—their nuptials are celebrated in the opening scene of *The Two Noble Kinsmen,* and also in Shakespeare's *A Midsummer Night's Dream**—and Palamon and Arcite love Hippolyta's sister Emilia. They compete for her in a tournament; Arcite wins, but shortly after is thrown from his horse and, dying, bids Palamon and Emilia wed.

To this tale, Fletcher added some episodes that enrich it with pathos. The imprisoned Palamon is freed by the gaoler's daughter, who loves him and, when he spurns her, goes mad. The lover she has disregarded follows her faithfully, and his description of her is as touching as that of the mad Ophelia in *Hamlet**. Indeed, said Kenneth Tynan in *He That Plays the King* (1950), "her mad scenes are exquisite, and better written, I think, than Ophelia's."

The authorship of *The Two Noble Kinsmen* has stirred more controversy than that of any other Elizabethan play. A drama about Palamon and Arcite mentioned in accounts of Queen Elizabeth's entertainment at Oxford in 1566 is ascribed to "Master Edwards of the Queen's Chapel." In the diary of theatre manager Philip Henslowe mention is made of a new play on the subject as of 1594. Critics are now generally agreed that the play was written by two writers of quite different style and temperament. The weaker portions, assigned to Fletcher, are marked by a large proportion of double (feminine) endings and a small proportion of run-on lines. The parts not by Fletcher are probably Act I, Scene 1 (except lines 1-40); most of Scenes 2, 3, and 4; Act II, Scene 1; III, 1 and 2; most of IV, 3; V, 1 (except lines 1-19), part of 3, and 4 (except lines 99-113). These portions are very close in style to *The Winter's Tale**, *The Tempest**, and *Henry VIII**, and give basis to the suggestion that Shakespeare lent a hand. However, the characterization—especially of the rather coarse heroine, Emilia—is less Shakespearean than the style.

Whosoever the hand that penned them, the non-Fletcher parts of *The Two Noble Kinsmen*, as C. F. Tucker Brooke pointed out in *The Shakespearean Apocrypha* (1908), contain "some of the most brilliant of

Jacobean poetry." The play is easily the best of the few in the shaping
of which Shakespeare may have had a minor share.

THE MINOR   *Denis I. Fonvizin*

The first Russian play of lasting worth, the one Russian play of the
eighteenth century still performed, is *The Minor,* 1782, by Denis Ivan-
ovitch Fonvizin (also von Visine or von Viezin; 1744-1792). The play is
often listed with *The Inspector General*, Woe From Wit*,* and *Enough
Stupidity in Every Wise Man*,* as among the greatest Russian comedies.

The Minor, sometimes translated as *The Young Hopeful,* is still laughed at on the Soviet stage, not so much for its neat satiric shafts as, in the
words of H. W. Dana (*A History of Modern Drama,* 1947) for its "horrible
example of the product of privilege." The play centers upon sixteen year
old Mitrofan, a completely spoiled, vulgar, boorish son of an aristocratic
family, who maintains that a noble needs no education. A former German
coachman supposedly instructs Mitrofan in science. A priest remarkable
for his pious bearing and ignorance corrects Mitrofan's grammar. An old
soldier, whose inspiration comes from a liquid not bottled at the fount of
learning, tries to teach Mitrofan arithmetic by applying the ruler to his
anatomy. His loving mother, Mrs. Simpleton (Prostakova) coddles her
darling boy, much as Mrs. Hardcastle in *She Stoops To Conquer*;* and,
much as Tony Lumpkin, the boy turns without gratitude or affection and
rends his mother. Why should he study geography? Cannot his coachman drive? All he needs is an heiress to marry, which is duly arranged.

Although the satire in *The Minor* is obvious, and the characters are not
deeply etched, there is much that is amusing in the comedy even today.
It has been continuously popular in Russia; Gogol*, in a school production, played the mother's role. The play sets laugher as a broadside
against presumptuous ignorance.

'TIS PITY SHE'S A WHORE   *John Ford*

The greatest tragedy of the prolific John Ford (English, 1586-1640?),
'Tis Pity She's a Whore, is a sombre story of incest, of the deep love be-
tween Giovanni and his sister Annabella. The latter, with child, marries
Soranzo, but her husband learns their secret. Anticipating punishment,
Giovanni kills Annabella, then slays Soranzo, and is slain.

On the picture of this doomed love, Ford lavished all his skills. As
Havelock Ellis has said, "he concentrates the revelation of a soul's agony
into a sob or a sigh."

The women of Ford's plays, especially Annabella, are probed more
tenderly yet more deeply than those of his contemporaries. He writes of
women, observes Havelock Ellis, "not as a dramatist nor as a lover, but
as one who had searched intimately and felt with instinctive sympathy
the fibres of their hearts." Ford was not content with the gay or the
majestic surface; he sought the soul.

'Tis Pity She's a Whore still finds occasional presentation. Maeterlinck's French translation, *Annabella,* was acted in Paris in 1894. New
York saw the play in 1925-1926 and 1935; London had a revival in 1934;
Hartford, Connecticut, viewed it in 1943. The 1926 production was advertised as *'Tis Pity.* The full title, the *New York Times* (Jan. 24, 1926) explained, was "too stout by far for our delicate ears." The *Times* added:

"Yielding all the connotations of this abnormality to the sweep of inevitable tragedy instinct in the theme, Ford composed a great work, shrouded in black like the paid murderers who cross the stage three times." W. A. Darlington, in the *London Daily Telegraph* (December 31, 1934) called *'Tis Pity She's a Whore* "work of a supremely dramatic imagination and a mind typically of the Renaissance. John Ford's ability to pile horror on horror's head was something better than the luridness of the author of a 'penny blood'." The passion and the penetration, the temerity of the theme, and the tenderness of the treatment, make *'Tis Pity She's a Whore* a truly majestic achievement, a sombre searching of entangled and blasted souls.

PERKIN WARBECK   *John Ford*

This "chronicle history" (1634), quite different from Ford's other plays, is one of the best English historical dramas. With vivid characterization, vigorous blank verse, and an objectivity that makes no man a villain, Ford sweeps through a stirring story of the aftermath of the War of the Roses.

Lancastrian Henry VII was on the throne of England, when Perkin Warbeck (1474-1499) claimed to be Richard, Duke of York, second son of Edward IV of England, and sought help from James IV of Scotland to take the English throne. The play deals with the last years of Warbeck's life, when James married Warbeck to Lady Katherine Gordon against her father's wish; but James later deserts Warbeck's cause. Upon landing in Cornwall, Warbeck is defeated and led to execution.

In the prologue to *Perkin Warbeck,* Ford attacks "the antic follies of the time"; his play, he declares, must rest on "truth and state." King Henry is shown as a monarch truly devoted to his people. Yet Warbeck is sympathetically drawn; his wife's devotion wins even his enemies' hearts. The resolution and fortitude of Warbeck sustain the drama to the end. It closes with a sense of justice done.

Perkin Warbeck was at times used as a political weapon. It was reprinted in 1714, when a revolt was brewing in Scotland, and it was revived in 1745, when "Bonnie Prince Charlie" (Charles Edward Stuart, 1720-1788) readied his claim to the throne. The story has attracted other playwrights (Schiller left a sketch of a play called *Warbeck*), but Ford's drama remains perhaps the best chronicle play in English outside of Shakespeare's.

THE MAN WHO MARRIED A DUMB WIFE   *Anatole France*

Among the many novels and satirical works of Anatole France (Jacques Anatole François Thibault; French, 1844-1924), little heed is paid his early verse play, *The Corinthian Wedding,* 1876; but popularity pours upon the constantly revived dramatic anecdote, *The Man Who Married a Dumb Wife,* 1912. In this playlet flash the keen wit, the deft satire, the "irony and pity"—his favorite formula for one's attitude toward life—that in 1921 brought Anatole France the Nobel Prize.

In the third book of *Gargantua and His Son Pantagruel* (1535) by "Alcofribas Nasier," we are told that there was enacted at the University of Montpellier "the highly moral comedy of the man who had espoused and married a dumb wife." If this play be not an invention of François Rabelais, it is lost; but two paragraphs of *Gargantua* tell the simple story. A man marries a dumb wife. He has her cured. Thereupon, she talks so incessantly that, not being able to render her dumb again, he makes himself deaf.

The plot was utilized by Molière in his *Doctor In Spite of Himself** and it is the basis of the intrigue in Jonson's *Epicoene**. Anatole France presents it without complications, neat and self-sufficient. Master Botal, a judge, is the rashly amorous husband; Catherine is the wife whose flood-gates of speech are suddenly loosed.

In New York, March 1915, a Granville Barker production, with O.P. Heggie, Lillah McCarthy, and Ernest Cossart, revealed the riches of the play. The quaint medieval costumes and the sets, of restful proportions and simplicity in contrasting colors, first brought designer Robert Edmond Jones to wide attention. Scarely longer than a vaudeville sketch, *The Man Who Married a Dumb Wife* achieves distinction by the clarity of its style, the neatness of its satire, and the kernel of truth within the chaff of its amusing story.

TWELVE THOUSAND   *Bruno Frank*

The most successful of the many dramas by Bruno Frank (German, 1887-1945) is this story of the blocking of an army of German mercenaries intended for British use against the American colonies. (Historically, some 29,000 Germans were sold into service in the American Revolution by Prussian nobility.)

A deal designed to provide funds for the private pleasures of a petty duke is negotiated in *Twelve Thousand*, 1926. Faucitt of England represents the British crown. Piderit, secretary of the Duke, is upbraided by his two farmer brothers, who do not know that, with the help of the liberal Baroness of Spangenberg, Piderit has notified the King of Prussia of the pending transfer of troops. A Prussian Colonel arrives, forbidding the twelve thousand mercenaries to cross Prussian territory, thus cutting off their access to the sea. When the action of Piderit is discovered, the Colonel saves him by giving him safe-conduct to America, "where a man stands on his own, by inherent right, an equal among equals, free."

A strong satire against little despots and a vigorous plea for the democratic way of life, *Twelve Thousand* is primarily a drama; its ideas slip across behind the action. Thus the *New York Sun*, (February 18, 1928) stated: "The presentation is so direct and clear, so devoid of dramaturgic tricks, and so tranquil that one is scarcely conscious of the inherent propaganda until after the dramatic suspense has been resolved." Gilbert Gabriel (March 13, 1928) called it "a play of severely classic cut . . . a finely wrought affair, an admirable sword-knot of humanitarian historical romance . . . To Germans of today this formal garden of a Germany of Frederick's day must flower with special meanings and messages. Unmistakable are the references, no matter how done up in satins and white wigs, to the perversions of monarchy, the rights of common men."

Twelve Thousand has been shown in almost 400 theatres in Europe, where indeed it marks a parallel and provides a lesson for our times. For Americans, too, there are ringing sounds in this obverse of the coin of the

Hessian mercenaries our fathers met across the Delaware. After the New York opening, March 12, 1928, with Basil Sydney and Mary Ellis, Alexander Woollcott remarked: "For the American playgoer, the play gains fourth dimension by the sounds of the Liberty Bell and the musketry at Lexington, which, borne faintly on the winds from across the sea, furnish a curiously heightening incidental music for the unfolding of the fable." John Anderson observed: "Frank has contrived to strike a parallel between the rights of men in his unnamed state and the rights of the colonials against whom they were supposed to fight, and he does so in terms of unfailing interest. It is history in the baby grand manner, a huge panorama caught to its final detail in exciting miniature."

The British saw the play from still another angle. After the London opening, September 15, 1931, of *Twelve Thousand*, the drama critic of the *London Times* (September 20) declared: "It has dignity, form, and real thought; and it voices some sound old arguments—too often neglected in these days of dictators and Soviets—for the liberty of the individual." It is, however, not by virtue of its arguments, but through neat characterizations, the sharp oppositions of men and ideas, and the simple but searching dialogue that shapes these, that *Twelve Thousand* grows to distinction and dramatic power.

SUMURUN   *Friedrich Freksa*

Out of the *Arabian Nights* by way of theatre magic and Friedrich Freksa (German, b. 1882) comes the wordless play *Sumurun*, 1910. In nine major scenes, linked by episodes of street life and swift passage, its pantomimed action, with music by Victor Hollander, carries us through the hazardous journey to happiness of the cloth merchant Nur-al-din and the radiant Sumurun, beautiful wife of the old Sheik.

The play opens with a chalk-faced hunchback quarreling with an old woman snake charmer over the sale of a dancing girl to the old Sheik. The dancing girl teases, almost tortures, the hunchback, who loves her; she has set eyes of favor upon the Sheik's son. At the bazaar, the Sheik's wife Sumurun sees and desires the merchant Nur-al-din. Intrigues follow with black-winged feet. The hunchback is poisoned and thrust in a sack, but the old woman shakes the bhang from his throat and he recovers. The dancing girl plays upon the Sheik's son until, to possess her, he agrees to kill his father. The plot fails and, chasing his son to the women's quarters, in spite of Sumurun's desperate dancing to distract his attention, the Sheik finds Nur-al-din hiding there. As the two fight, the hunchback creeps behind and kills the old Sheik, freeing Nur-al-din and Sumurun to enjoy their love. The hunchback—who is also the showman—pulls the curtain down.

Produced by Max Reinhardt, *Sumurun* ran for three seasons in Berlin. London saw it January 30, 1911; New York, January 16, 1912. In a condensed version, Gertrude Hoffman played Sumurun at the New York Palace Theatre, with the harem girls swimming in an Oriental pool. The play was seen in Los Angleles at the Federal Theatre, July 1939, with Gene Lockhart starring in a cast of 200.

Spectacular, colorful, swift-moving, *Sumurun* has the power and passion of the spoken drama, with the grace and beauty of the mimed. "The action is so swift and convincing," said *Theatre Magazine* (February, 1912) "that there are many moments when you forget the actors are silent." The play, it continued, "is sensuous, barbaric, primitive, yet at the same time it is vitally human . . . The scenes, like the music, have a repellent charm, alluring and antagonizing at the same moment. You feel, in looking at them, that the inner veils have been rent, and you have been shown not its stage portrayal but the veritable Orient."

The production of *Sumurun*, with the Sumurun waltz, the languorous lures of "the beautiful slave of fatal enchantment," the bustle of an Oriental bazaar, the shifty pedlars and beggars, the street sounds and odors, and the softer sounds of song and dance and illicit amours within the guarded chambers, the wafted scents of the harem, the slave girls Sheik-picked in many lands—all these brought a fusion of the arts of the theatre that was in essence a new technique. Looking back, *Theatre Arts* (January, 1944) observed: "Winthrop Ames not only introduced Max Reinhardt to the American public, but gave the new stagecraft a marked impetus when he brought *Sumurun* to New York in 1912." *Sumurun* shows, through the sumptuous presentation of an oft-told tale, the power of the theatre, even without words, to soar to heights of beauty and to pulse with emotional power.

THE JOURNALISTS   *Gustav Freytag*

The most popular of all German comedies is *The Journalists,* by Gustav Freytag (1816-1895). It opened December 8, 1852, in Breslau and has been played in Germany probably more frequently than any other play. Much of the material for the play came directly from the life of the author, who from 1848 to 1870 was co-editor of a Leipsiz liberal journal.

Freytag is perhaps best known outside of Germany for his pattern of a five act play known as "Freytag's pyramid," developed in his book *The Technique of The Drama* (1863). In this pattern exposition is allotted to Act I; Rising Action, to Act II; Climax, to Act III; Falling Action, to Act IV; Denouement— in tragedy, Catastrophe—to Act V. This pattern is roughtly applicable to Shakespeare's plays; more impatient times short-ened the pattern to four acts, then three, lopping off the end, so that now the climax and the denouement virtually coincide.

In *The Journalists,* Colonel Berg is sharply opposed to Oldendorf, suitor for his daughter Ida's hand, because Oldendorf is an editor of the Liberal paper, *The Union,* which has attacked an article by Berg in a Conservative journal. Oldendorf runs for Parliament; Berg, flattered by the Conservative leader Sender, becomes the opposing candidate. The Conservatives plan to buy *The Union,* but Adelheid, a young heiress friend of Ida, buys it to keep it Liberal. Its editor, Bolz, wins over a most influential Conservative, the wine merchant Piepenbrink, with whose help the election goes to Oldendorf. The Colonel discovers that the Conservative leader, Sender, is an insincere opportunist. Oldendorf, elected, resigns from the paper, thus reconciling the Colonel to the match with Ida; and Adelheid and Bolz make a second happy pair.

There are several especially vivid scenes in *The Journalists,* evocative of various milieux incidental to the action. The picture of the editorial sanctum, first of the kind in the drama, is colorful and real. There is also a lively party at which various types of well-to-do citizen are neatly dis-played. "The work is not only skilfully wrought out," said Thomas B. Bronson in his introduction to the play (1910), "but it is a life picture pure and simple. While dealing chiefly with one class, it takes in many. It is ... charming with its sunshine and joyousness, and convincing with its verisimilitude ... true to German life, temperament, and character." Fresh and refreshing in its kindliness and understanding of the characters, colorful in its pictures of the time, lively and natural in its story, *The Journalists* well deserves its continued popularity.

THE LADY'S NOT FOR BURNING   *Christopher Fry*

The best writer of English dramatic verse today, Christopher Fry (b. 1907), blossomed suddenly, with five of his plays produced in London in two seasons. His chief plays to date are *Venus Observed* and *The Lady's Not For Burning*. The latter is a story of witchery and love in the year 1400. Jennet Jourdemayne, hunted as a witch, seeks refuge in the home of Hebble Tyson, Mayor of the English market town of Cool Clary. A discharged soldier, a sardonic misanthrope, Thomas Mendip, tries to divert the charge from her by claiming to have murdered the man she is accused of having turned into a dog. All refuse to believe him, while taking her guilt for granted—until the tipsy return of the supposed victim clears the girl. Then she and Thomas go off together. Moral: love at least helps us to tolerate the unendurable.

Upon this slight story, Fry has woven a pattern of observation and reflection, spangled with bright imagery. His figures form an exciting blend of familiar objects and new attitudes; he reawakens the eye to the fresh strangeness of the world.

Fry wrote *The Lady's Not For Burning* as resident playwright of the London Art Theatre, which produced it on March 11, 1948. On May 11, 1949, it opened at the London Globe, with John Gielgud and Pamela Brown, for 294 performances. The same players brought it to New York, opening November 8, 1950, for 151 performances.

Praise for the play was almost unanimous. Harold Hobson, writing in the *Christian Science Monitor* of June 4, 1949, found it too continuously brilliant: "It dazzles too consistently. It is like the long, hot sun of the tropics, which makes one throb for a little shade ... With his belts of Orion, his astrolabes and his metaphors from Archimedes, his familiarity with the obscurest saints, his knowledge of all learning, and his restless penetrating wit he astounds and a little wearies. If only now and again he were somewhat dull, how much more entertaining he would be! ... Yet entertaining he certainly is."

As in all of Fry's plays, there is a sense that the riches of language are being renewed. New figures are minted from nature's ore: "When the landscape goes to seed, the wind is obsessed by tomorrow." Beyond the felicity of phrasing and penetrant wit and incisive wisdom of *The Lady's Not For Burning*, there is the high lilt of romance, of the joyous spirit that accepts life as a challenge worth the taking. In this play, man walks with smiling, slightly self-mocking hopefulness towards the dawn.

MISS LULU BETT   *Zona Gale*

Of her various short-stories and novels of the lives of simple folk in America, Zona Gale (American, 1874-1928) dramatized two. *Mr. Pitt*, 1924, gave an excellent role to Walter Huston; *Miss Lulu Bett*, dramatized in a week, opened in New York, December 27, 1920, for a run of 176 performances, and won the 1921 Pulitzer Prize.

Though it moves with dramatic intensity through exciting situations, *Miss Lulu Bett* is essentially a study of small town life and characters. Lulu is a spinster of thirty-four years and many tribulations, living with her sister Ina and Ina's husband, Dwight Deacon, a dentist and local justice of the peace. As *The Outlook* pointed out, Ina "is vain, shallow, and selfish"; Dwight is "pompous, dictatorial, and self-righteous." Both are amazingly well pleased with themselves for their kindness in giving Lulu the shelter of their roof-tree. "They are possessed of two children, the younger of whom in particular impels the spectator to reach out for nonexistent hairbrushes at her every appearance. She is certainly one of the most spankable stage children we have seen in many years. The sixth member of the family group is the mother of Lulu and her sister, an aged woman bordering on senility, whose mind combines attributes of keenness and understanding with that tragic forgetfulness which marks the approach of oblivion."

In this household Lulu is the untiring drudge, bound to dull and continuous toil by the tyranny of little things, until Dwight's brother, the jovial wanderer Ninian, arrives, sizes up the situation and quickens the glow of life in Lulu. Invited to go with the others to a show, Lulu leaves behind the dull droop of the shabby drudge, and blossoms with at least the incipience of charm.

They jest gaily along until Ninian and Lulu go through a mock marriage. Dwight, a magistrate, reminds them that the ceremony is binding. Ninian confesses that he doesn't know whether his first wife is dead. Dwight and Ina browbeat Lulu into silence to save their own reputation. Lulu, finally rebellious and regardful of her self-respect, prepares to leave when Ninian, having learned that his first wife is safely dead, tells her he wants the wedding to hold.

The Cinderella theme, of which *Miss Lulu Bett* is a variation, is a perennial favorite because self-pity and wishful thinking are among the most popular of recreations. Women readily identify themselves with Lulu Bett, weep over her burdens, and smile victorious in her rebellion and her transformation. With kindliness and understanding, even in its presentation of the self-satisfied married pair, the play creates a mellow mood, a sense of friendly hopefulness for life in America.

STRIFE   *John Galsworthy*

Better known as a novelist, John Galsworthy (English, 1867-1933) also wrote some dozen plays, the best of which are concerned with problems of social justice.

A sharply ironic picture of the conflict between capital and labor, *Strife* was produced both in London and New York in 1909. The play begins on what proves to be the final day of a winter-long strike at a large industrial plant. John Anthony, chairman of the Trenatha Tin Plate Works, refuses to yield an inch; David Roberts, leader of the Workmen's Committee, is equally uncompromising. While Roberts is seeking to maintain morale among the workers, word comes that his wife has died. In his absence, the men vote to return to work. At the same time, the company's directors force Anthony to resign. The terms of the final agreement, however, are precisely those that were proposed by the union official and the company secretary before the strike had begun.

The play made heavy impact upon its early audiences. The *Manchester Guardian* declared that "in tragic power, in insight and philosophy, and in style, the play is one of the masterpieces of our time." Charles Darnton stated of the American production: "*Strife* is uncompromisingly true, scornfully honest, and bitterly outspoken."

The American production, which opened November 17, 1909, with Louis Calvert, A. E. Anson, Ferdinand Gottschalk, William McVay, Albert Bruning, Pedro de Cordoba, and Beatrice Forbes-Robertson, changed the locale to the Ohio River Valley, but most critics felt that the mood of the play remained essentially English. The *New York Times* considered the play "beyond question among the most notable, the most interesting, and the most adroit of contemporaneous dramas." But the *Times* critic added: "It might have been a still more potent and satisfactory drama than it now is if it had dealt more definitely with a specific instance and not ended with an implied moral, of by no means universal application."

Strife has had several revivals—at Ithaca in 1924; London, Manchester, and Glasgow saw it in 1933.

The vaunted objectivity and even-mindness of Galsworthy's dramas is perhaps most nearly exemplified in *Strife*. In its quest of objectivity, however, it loses some of the vigor that comes from the fervent espousal of a deeply-felt cause. Yet it remains one of the most powerful theatrical presentations of the struggle between capital and labor.

JUSTICE   *John Galsworthy*

Galsworthy's greatest play, *Justice*, came upon the British in 1910 with such a severe indictment of the penal system, and effected such an arousal of public indignation, that the nation's prison administration was reformed. *Justice* is indeed a powerful play. Its scene of solitary confinement, without a spoken word, is one of the most harrowing in the modern drama. After beholding this scene, Winston Churchill, then Home Secretary, reduced the allowable period of solitary confinement in English prisons from nine months to four weeks.

The play tells the story of William Falder, a law clerk who, to help the woman he loves break from her cruel husband, commits forgery, is found guilty, and is sentenced to three years in jail. Upon parole, his past haunts him, driving him from job to job. His former employers offer him a place, but the parole officer comes to arrest him for failing to report; the harassed Falder leaps from a stairway to his death.

First performed in the United States by the Hull House Players in Chicago, 1911, *Justice* came to New York, April 3, 1916, during a period of prison reform. With a cast including Cathleen Nesbitt, O. P. Heggie, Henry Stephenson, and John Barrymore (Falder), it took the city by storm. Thomas Mott Osborne, late warden of Sing Sing, said after opening night: "*Justice* does not come under the head of an amusement, for it is too pitifully somber, but there never has been a time when a play of such character would have so much chance of success as at present, when the local world is so stirred over prison reform." The *New York Review*, next day, added: "Mr. Galsworthy's play throws the big light on 'causes.' It helps you to understand how and why people go wrong. It paves the way to divine love and forgiveness . . . We can thank Mr. Galsworthy for giving us a drama of real uplift and one which has punch enough in the last act to satisfy the most determined low-brow." Channing Pollock saw the production as a crusade: "At the club there was but one topic, and in the street. Overnight the theatre has ceased to be a toy, a plaything—and had become a vital part of every day . . . *Justice* is not a play; it is an emotional experience, a tragedy in which you participate . . . the tremendous force of the treatment is in its simplicity and reticence." Other critics were less willing to enlist in the crusade; in the May, 1916, issue of *Theatre*, for instance, the success of the play was attributed mainly to the performance of John Barrymore: "He was one of the accidents, so to speak, that make for this unexpected success of a play not adapted to entertainment or even edification."

The power of *Justice* is indisputable; less can be said for its objectivity. The forgery is committed, not out of the mere prosaic desire to make money, but in order to free a sweet and harmless young mother from the brutality of a cruel husband. Also, though Falder is arrested while about to depart for South America with Ruth Honeywell, and returns to her as soon as he is released, Galsworthy takes pains to assure us there has been no sexual intimacy between them. So honest, so innocent, are these two victims of society that we almost expect a smile of heavenly approval for Falder's breach of man-made law. Indeed, the play closes with the words: "He's safe with gentle Jesus!"

Justice was revived in various parts of the United States in 1922, 1927, 1937 (Federal Theatre), and in London in 1922, 1928, 1932, and at a Galsworthy Festival in 1935.

It is interesting to note how critical opinion has shifted over the years. Leon M. Lion observed in the *London Era* of July 11, 1928: "The play stands now, as it did all those years ago, more as an indictment of the physical and mental horrors comprised in prison routine. Mr. Galsworthy, as always, has stated his case with the utmost fairness and clarity . . . Never, surely, was a play so subtly wrought, so carefully built up, as this one; how, with the firmest of blows, the hammer is wielded so that each point is driven in immovably!" In the *London Times*, after the April 1935 production, the same Mr. Lion observed: "It always was and still remains a mighty fine piece for sentimentalists priding themselves on their austerity, and for loose thinkers taking delight in their clearsightedness . . . What can it have been which in 1910 bluffed us into mistaking this piece of special pleading for a master-stroke of high unescapable tragedy?"

The fervor of a cause leads its adherents to give enthusiastic welcome to works that advance it—the more so when that cause seems at humanity's core. *Justice* today seems as obvious and as partisan as the novels of Dickens, though stodgier and less exuberant. It remains, however, a milestone in the drama of social fairdealing, which in every generation will wring new indignation and new pathos from abiding problems.

THE PIGEON   *John Galsworthy*

A pigeon whom any wastrel can pluck is Christopher Wellwyn, artist, lover of mankind, and the title figure of this play. Into his home, despite his daughter's protests, he brings various fag-ends of humanity's coursing. To his daughter's charge that his almsgiving habits are a disgusting luxury, he concedes that he is a "sloppy sentimentalist"; but Christopher Wellwyn is an individual with a distinct and individual soul determined to oppose the pressure of organized charity to have its recipients conform.

Among those whom Christopher shelters are Gwinny Megan, a forlorn flower girl; old Timson, a rum-soaked cabby; and Ferrand, a philosophical French vagabond. Christopher gives them a chance to live in concord with their own natures, saving them from the demands of machine conformity, from the call of the vicar to moral redemption, from the summons of the magistrate to discipline and punishment, and from the examination of the professor for scientific treatment and reshaping.

Christopher's efforts are in vain. Timson drinks himself deeper into Christopher's wine. The happy-go-haywire Ferrand seduces Gwinny; and the girl, fished out of the Thames by the police, is fined for attempting suicide. Undismayed, Christopher simply moves to cheaper quarters so that he may still have money to go on "helping" the needy.

The Pigeon opened in London January 30, 1912; in New York, Galsworthy saw the premiere on March 11, 1912, with Frank Reicher as Ferrand. The gentle, perceptive quality of this tenderest of Galsworthy's dramas was at once recognized. The Boston Transcript (March 12, 1912) called it "not fantastic at all, but a profound comedy, with all its outer humors, of the maladjustment of the great machine, civilization, to the individual who is different." The play, it continued, "chastises manners with a smile, but a smile that is rueful, perturbed, sometimes almost misty with the pity of things . . . Behind the observation is the sympathy that discovers, the feeling that understands, while the two wing and order the artistry to just expression."

Whitford Kane played Christopher in England, when The Pigeon was revived in 1928; he also played in a New York revival of 1922. New York saw the play again in 1930. It has not had many little theatre productions because The Pigeon challenges non-professional groups where they are weakest—in the subtleties of acting.

"The Pigeon has probably more true thoughts and important thoughts on its particular subject than any other English play touching a sociological subject", commented Kenneth Macgowan (February 3, 1922). "This is because Galsworthy approaches his problem from the human end. He builds character and lets character reflect. The double result is that the play itself becomes sound drama and the players find something to work with." Sociologists will of course dispute Galsworthy's thesis; but The Pigeon gives us an eloquent and dramatic exaltation of the integrity and essential right of privacy and freedom of each individual soul.

LOYALTIES   John Galsworthy

In this play John Galsworthy searchingly examines the ideal of loyalty while telling a vivid and dramatic story.

The story deals with the insistence of De Levis, a wealthy Jewish businessman week-ending in a Christian home, on an investigation of the theft of £1,000 from his room. Accusing a retired Army captain, Dancy, of the theft, De Levis is called a "damned Jew." Dancy's friends rally to him. As a result, De Levis is blackballed by an exclusive club and the matter is pressed in court. Then circumstances darken for Dancy.

His lawyer withdraws from the case, advising Dancy to leave the country; and, as his loyal wife delays the police, a shot is heard from the next room: Dancy at the end is loyal to his standards. The pistol keeps faith. "Keeps faith!" echoes a friend in the final words of the play: "We've all done that. It's not enough."

The trouble with loyalties is that each person feels noble in clinging to his own. Delineated in the play are the conflicting loyalties of the soldier, the gentleman, the Jew, the lawyer, and the wife. Galsworthy presents these loyalties in a tense drama.

Loyalties opened in London, March 8, 1922, and was seen there again in 1928 and 1932. New York saw it in 1922 (September 27) and in 1932 with Eva LeGallienne; and college and other groups have presented it with some frequency.

Its quality still holds. The *New York Tribune* (April 2, 1922) reported that "*Loyalties* is the most subtle, and at the same time the least 'preachy', of all Galsworthy plays." The *Christian Science Monitor* (March 28, 1922) said unequivocally: "*Loyalties* is Galsworthy's best play . . . Galsworthy presents his problem with extraordinary fairness and impartiality, and shows himself as good a judge as he is an artist."

On the other hand, the *London Times* (August 23, 1932) praised the play on the very ground that "it is free of the elaborate air of impartiality that causes some of Mr. Galsworthy's work to resemble a scolding by too just a parent." There is some truth in the charge that Galsworthy presents De Levis as not only a Jew but also a cad. He is willing to drop the charges if admitted to the club. There is reason for his being considered, as Percy Hammond (September 28, 1922) put it, "a little repellent to his acquaintances in London Christian society . . . He did things in the wrong way, even when they were right things." In truth, this aspect of De Levis was singled out for praise by James Agate in *At Half-Past Eight* (1923). One may, however, feel that balance was achieved by Galsworthy in making Dancy at least as obnoxious as De Levis. Unquestionably Galsworthy presents De Levis in the right; and De Levis' insistence on his rights is no more vehement than is natural in a society that has—in its own loyalties—turned upon him.

Out of the inevitable clash of hopelessly irreconcilable loyalties the emotional poignancy and the intellectual terror of the play lift it to lasting power.

BLOOD WEDDING   *Federico García Lorca*

Although the fame of Federico García Lorca (Spanish, 1899-1936) had temporary glow from the fact that he was shot in Granada by Franco adherents, it rests solidly upon his work as the leading poet and poetic dramatist of his generation in Spain. Although university trained, Lorca chose his themes from the simple people of his native Andalusia, and for three years (1931-1934) he guided a traveling theatre, La Barraca, which brought classics of the Spanish stage to the people. In addition to a considerable body of distinguished poetry, and several light farces, Lorca wrote a group of three serious plays that set him high among Spain's playwrights. All three—*Blood Wedding,* 1933, *Yerma,* 1934, and *The House of Bernarda Alba,* 1936—present the same theme: the tragedy rising from frustrate women yearning to be fulfilled.

Blood Wedding deliberately moves within a non-realistic realm. Unlike those of the two other serious plays by Lorca, its characters, save for Leonardo, have not names but labels— the Mother, the Bride, Leonardo's Wife. Among the figures in the drama are Death and the Moon. With prose that breaks into poetry at intense and climactic moments, the play presses home the concept of human fatality. Without any conscious will, the characters are drawn to their destiny. The one person named, Leonardo, seeks his own destiny, but no more than the others does he shape its end. He and the Bride run off on her wedding day; the Bridegroom hunts him, and in fierce knife-combat both are killed. The three women—Leonardo's wife, the ravished bride, and the bridegroom's mother—mourn together.

It is the Mother who holds the play together. A knife thrust has already taken her husband away, and her other son—killed by Leonardo's kin. A brooding sense of doom hangs over her thoughts, hardly to be dispelled by the haunting beauty of the procession and dance before the wedding, for it is from that dancing that Leonardo disappears with the Bride.

Played in Madrid and Buenos Aires in 1933, Blood Wedding was enthusiastically received. It played successfully in Brazil, Italy, France, Portugal, Sweden, Norway, Denmark, Finland, Russia, Czechoslovakia, England, Canada, South Africa, Israel, and Ireland. In the United States, it has been well received in university theatres, but twice failed in New York. A Neighborhood Playhouse production on Broadway, February 11, 1935, under the title Bitter Oleander, with Nance O'Neil, Effie Shannon, and Eugenie Leontovich, ran for 24 performances. This version conveyed neither the taut violence nor the folk-quality of the original. Richard Lockridge (February 12, 1935) liked it more than most reviewers; he called it "a classic tragedy of love" and said that "at its best the play has poignant beauty . . . For all the stylization, the emotions are simple, unforced and untortured, real." As Blood Wedding, the play was presented by New Stages, off Broadway, February 6, 1949, in a formalized production that, for all its sombre speech, had more of the quality of a brooding dance. The pathos, and much of the beauty, were felt, but the drive of drama was not carried across.

Although Blood Wedding sprang from a newspaper account of an incident in Almeria, Lorca deliberately generalized his treatment of the story. His brother, in the Introduction to Three Tragedies of Lorca (1947) relates that the play matured in Lorca's mind for years, then took but a week in the writing. In poetic beauty and intensity of feeling, with heavy sense of the implacable hand of fate, Blood Wedding and its two companion plays are the most poignant presentation of the love-starved and barren woman in the modern poetic drama.

THE BEGGAR'S OPERA   John Gay

John Gay (English, 1685-1732), apprenticed to a mercer, became known through several poems and plays before he wrote, following a suggestion by Swift, the one work that has given him enduring fame, The Beggar's Opera. This musical play was a satire on Italian opera (which for a time it drove out of style) and on the conniving with the London underworld of unscrupulous politicians.

In the midst of the play's underworld figures, the audience recognized the portrait of a judge who had recently been fined the enormous sum of £30,000 for taking bribes; they saw in the character of Peachum the living presentation of an actual informer (later hanged); and they had the delight of watching the Prime Minister and Chancellor of the Exchequer, Sir Robert Walpole, cry "Encore!" to the satire on himself. (Walpole had his revenge; *Polly*, the sequel to *The Beggar's Opera*, was forbidden the stage.)

The Beggar's Opera, produced in 1728 by John Rich at Lincoln's Inn Fields, was an instantaneous success, setting a record for its day of 62 performances. It "made Gay rich and Rich gay." Until 1773, it was regularly presented every season at both Drury Lane and Covent Garden. In 1773, the play was suppressed as "encouraging theft and other enormities." After its license was renewed, the play continued on the boards almost every season for 170 years. In 1728, its first year, it was played in Dublin by a cast of children under ten years of age.

Buxom Lavinia Fenton, the first Polly Peachum, within the year was married to the Duke of Bolton. *The Beggar's Opera*, in fact, lifted more actresses to the peerage than any other play. It was involved in other matters, too. When Covent Garden instituted its higher scale of prices with a revival of *The Beggar's Opera*, September 15, 1809, there were nightly riots for over a fortnight before arbiters decided that the increase was justified. In America (where the first performance was given in New York in 1750) the play was a favorite of George Washington's; the charms of the current Polly Peachum are said to have precipitated the duel between Alexander Hamilton and Aaron Burr.

With clever songs neatly interwoven with the dialogue, *The Beggar's Opera* gives an amusingly satiric picture of the disreputable London world of the eighteenth century, with a story that might well have happened, and still rings true. Captain Macheath, highwayman, is secretly married to Polly Peachum; when her father, who is both a fence and an informer, learns of this, he betrays Macheath to the authorities. Macheath, always gay and gallant, wins the heart of Lucy Locket, daughter of the Newgate Prison warder, who helps him escape. "By treating this material," Allardyce Nicoll observed, "almost in a spirit of romance, by artificializing, by jesting, by exaggerating, Gay has been able to create a new world of his own."

The Beggar's Opera has been one of the most frequently revived plays in the English theatre. In New York, however, it was not seen from 1870 until the Arthur Hopkins revival of 1920. A London revival, which opened June 5, 1920, ran for 1,463 performances. The British company that came to New York in 1920 had but a short run at the Greenwich Village Theatre, but toured successfully for eight years and then returned to New York. The *New York Times* then (March 28, 1928) called it "that incomparable blend of racy satire and song." The play has since been frequently performed. In 1940 it was shown at the University of California, at Yale University and in London (directed by John Gielgud).

In 1928, Bertholt Brecht wrote a German version, *Die Dreigroschenoper*, with music by Kurt Weill, which, retranslated into English as *The Three-Penny Opera*, has had some success; it was made into a motion picture in 1933. London was cool to Brecht's version, an experiment in "epic theatre" which, though set in 1837, seemed of the twentieth century. The scenic artist Mordecai Gorelik explained that Brecht sought to create "the social web of circumstances which can alone precipitate and qualify the story. The primary task of the *Opera* was not to parade the peculiar behavior of eighteenth century or twentieth century criminals, but to depict the connivance of criminals with supposed guardians of law and order." The more manifest social concern of Brecht did not improve his version.

More recently, December 26, 1946, there was presented in New York still another adaptation of *The Beggar's Opera*, with book and lyrics by John LaTouche and music by Duke Ellington. Called *Beggar's Holiday*, it was set in twentieth century Harlem, the Negro section of New York. John Chapman called the play "the most interesting musical since *Porgy and Bess*"; and Brooks Atkinson, who hailed it as "a gutter gavotte danced to the beat of an original, fresh, and animated score," seemed to prefer it to the original; Gay's version, he claimed, "always had more prestige than entertainment." (History proves, however, that the entertainment is what won the prestige.) The LaTouche version, Richard Watts declared, "doesn't come off"—and the public agreed. For La-Touche, in his effort to make his characters sympathetic, smiled also upon the vices in which they indulge—an error of which Gay is happily free. The liveliness of *The Beggar's Opera* came freshly through a production off Broadway in 1950, with thirty-five of the songs that at various times have brightened the play, and at Columbia University in 1954.

Long without rival, *The Beggar's Opera*, the first of the great satirical musical comedies, is a play that is both excellent fun and a sharply pointed travesty of the abuses of its time. Both the abuses and the fun abide.

TRIAL BY JURY   *William Schwenck Gilbert*

The wit, satire, and sprightly humor of William S. Gilbert (English, 1836-1911), accompanied by lively songs set to the superbly accordant music of Arthur S. Sullivan (1842-1900), continue to delight theatregoers everywhere. The D'Oyly Carte Company, a permanent London troupe exclusively devoted to his operettas, is eagerly welcomed on its periodic trips to the United States, where the plays are even more frequently performed than in England. At one time, forty Gilbert and Sullivan companies were simultaneously touring the States. Almost 5,000 performances of the plays are given by amateur and professional companies every year—a record not approached by any other playwright, even Shakespeare.

Trial by Jury, the first Gilbert-and-Sullivan success, was presented in London on March 3, 1875, as an afterpiece to Offenbach's *La Pericholo*. It opened in Boston on December 2, 1876, and in Chicago on January 7, 1877. Described as a "dramatic cantata," it is the only one of the operettas without any spoken dialogue. For the first time in comedy since Aristophanes, it uses the chorus as an integral part of the story—a satire on breach of promise suits. When the fair plaintiff declares that her betrothed is fickle, he responds that he is doing what comes naturally. After considerable frolicsome foolery and mocking of court procedure, the play ends with the judge's decision to wed the plaintiff himself.

It has been suggested that, in writing the play, Gilbert had in mind the trial of Bardell vs. Pickwick as depicted in Dickens' *Pickwick Papers*.

He evidently also had in mind, and made the scene resemble, the Clerkenwell Sessions House, where he himself had practised law.

It would be impossible to list all the times and places *Trial by Jury* has been played. In New York, it was presented in a full length marionette version in 1940; in modern dress in 1942; in its regular costume presentation, many times before and after.

The London premiere was at the Royalty Theatre, of which the manager was Richard D'Oyly Carte (1844-1901). Recognizing their possibilities, he commissioned Gilbert and Sullivan to write a two-act opera for the company he organized. He leased the Opera-Comique, then built the Savoy Theatre, and all the later Gilbert and Sullivan operettas are associated with the D'Oyly Carte company, "the Savoyards."

THE SORCERER   *William Schwenck Gilbert*

"Oh! My name is John Wellington Wells, I'm a dealer in magic and spells," sings the head of the old established firm of sorcerers with office at Seventy Simmery Axe (St. Mary Acts), in *The Sorcerer,* the first of the Gilbert and Sullivan operettas to be presented, November 17, 1877, under the management of D'Oyly Carte at the Opera-Comique.

Founded on a story in a Christmas issue of an 1876 magazine, with borrowings from *The Elixir of Love* and the *Bab Ballads* (*The Cunning Woman*), this operetta builds its fun on a slight plot and the love philtres of John Wellington Wells. It pictures two lovers so happy that they hire the sorcerer to spread love around; such incongruous pairing develops that the happy ending is achieved by his removing the spell.

In *The Sorcerer* first appeared the patter song, a riotous racing rhyme that challenges the speed of the singer, and the one type of song in which Gilbert grew increasingly expert.

The patter song had an ancient forerunner in the strangler song (so-called because the singer might choke on it) of the comedies of Aristophanes. Indeed, across the ages Aristophanes and Gilbert and Sullivan are fellow spirits unmatched.

John Wellington Wells was first played by George Grossmith, who until he took the role was a police-court reporter by day, an entertainer by night. His son, and more recently Martyn Green, have succeeded him in the magician's role, which carries the bulk of the humor of the play.

The Sorcerer first takes full stride in comic operetta. It contains not only typical Gilbertian bubbling fun, and fund of wit and satire, but some of Sullivan's most catchy tunes. It began the series that, as William Archer says, "restored the literary and musical self-respect of the English stage."

H. M. S. PINAFORE   *William Schwenck Gilbert*

Gilbert and Sullivan first won their wide public with *H. M. S. Pinafore; or, The Lass That Loved a Sailor,* which D'Oyly Carte produced on May 25, 1878, for a run of 700 performances. The initial criticisms, however, were not all favorable. One now unknown prophet declared: "In the story itself there is not much of humor to balance its studied absurdity . . . a frothy production, destined soon to subside into nothingness." It has become the most popular of all the Gilbert and Sullivan operettas.

Pinafore (with *The Mikado**) has most successfully undergone translation into German, and there is a Spanish version, *Pinafor,* 1885.

International copyright not yet existing, *Pinafore* was at once pirated
in the United States. It opened in Boston in 1878 and in New York early
in 1879. *The Spirit of the Times* (February 15, 1879) disparagingly commented: "we fear very much that those managers who have pinned
their faith to *H. M. S. Pinafore* will find that they have trusted too
strongly to public favor . . . it has scarcely those elements that will command the long lease of popularity which entrepreneurs would seem to
anticipate." The more astute William Winter, in the *New York Tribune,*
called the play "one of the neatest, brightest, funniest operatic burlesques
in any language . . . The bright, fresh, sparkling music will take the
popular fancy at once . . . There are lines that are destined to be famous."

Winter was right; the vogue of *H. M. S. Pinafore* grew into a craze.
By the Spring of 1879, eight rival companies were playing the operetta
in New York. At Haverly's Theatre, in May, a children's company opened
in morning and afternoon performances, with an adult company in the
evening. (A London production by children opened January 17, 1880,
and was highly praised; *The Illustrated London News* declared that the
adult companies could take hints from the youngsters.)

In London, the popularity of the play grew slowly, in large measure
as a result of the American furore.

As early as February 21, 1879, the San Francisco Minstrels presented
in New York a burlesque of Gilbert's play, *His Mud Scow Pinafore,* using
Sullivan's music and featuring Admiral Porter, "bottled for use," Captain
Corkonian, and a motley crew. At the peak of the play's popularity, over
ninety professional companies were playing *H. M. S. Pinafore* in the
United States.

In July 1879, at Providence, Rhode Island, 63 performances of *H. M. S.
Pinafore* were given on a full-rigged ship anchored in a lake; Buttercup,
the Admiral and the cousins and the aunts were rowed from shore to
ship. In the following month the play was again presented on a real ship
in real water at New York's Madison Square Garden (then on 25th
Street). In 1935 a ship production was played off Jones Beach, New
York. A Negro company, headed by Bill Robinson and Avon Long, produced in 1945 a musical comedy called *Memphis Bound,* in which a
stranded show-boat company puts on a performance of *H. M. S. Pinafore.*
The D'Oyly Carte Company, of course, includes the play in its repertoire
every season.

Plot ideas for *H. M. S. Pinafore* were drawn from six of the *Bab
Ballads.* The play is a travesty of the once popular "shiver-my-timbers"
nautical melodrama, with incidental satiric thrusts at politics and jingoistic patriotism. Just before the play opened in 1878, Disraeli had appointed W. H. Smith, a publisher, as First Lord of the Admiralty; hence
the punch in the song ending:

> Stick close to your desk, and never go to sea,
> And you all may be rulers of the Queen's Navee!

On this satire Queen Victoria delivered her characteristic dictum: "We
are not amused" (for details, see *The Pirates of Penzance**).

The plot of *H.M.S. Pinafore* revolves about the ambitious Captain Cor-
coran, who wishes his daughter Josephine to marry the Rt. Hon. Sir
Joseph Porter, First Lord of the Admiralty, although she loves the plain

tar Ralph Rackstraw. Villainous Dick Deadeye tries to help the Captain foil the lovers until the bumboat woman, Little Buttercup, reveals that Ralph and the Captain had been exchanged in the cradle—whereupon Ralph becomes Captain and marries Josephine, while the Captain becomes a common sailor and marries Little Buttercup. (The plot trick of a revealed substitution to solve the play's dilemma is a satire on theatrical fare of the 1870's; Gilbert used it again in *The Gondoliers*.*) The songs hold their place among Gilbert and Sullivan's best.

Amusing plot, swift wit, and lively varied songs combined to make this work the first sweeping success of Gilbert and Sullivan. It has remained a lasting favorite; only *The Mikado* comes near, in frequency of professional and amateur performance, to *H. M. S. Pinafore.*

THE PIRATES OF PENZANCE   *William Schwenck Gilbert*

Queen Victoria was quite displeased at the political satire in *H. M. S. Pinafore**. In *The Pirates of Penzance; or, The Slave of Duty*, Gilbert proffered a mock apology, but the play continued his satire.

The Pirate King declares that many a crowned monarch has to do more dirty work than he. The "very model of a modern major general" knows no more of military tactics and gunnery than a novice in a nunnery. The timidity of the police force is laughably brought home. Then, at the close of the play, comes a sudden change. The pirates, having overpowered the police, stand with drawn swords over their prostrate prisoners, until the captured police sergeant cries, "We charge you yield, in Queen Victoria's name!" At once the conquering pirates throw down their swords and kneel, crying:

"We yield at once, with humbled mien,
"Because, with all our faults, we love our Queen."

Queen Victoria, who had little sense of humor, never forgave Gilbert. She early knighted Arthur Sullivan, composer of oratorios, cantatas, of "Onward, Christian Soldier," and of the Queen's favorite song, "The Lost Chord." When, in March 1891, a special performance of *The Gondoliers* was given before Queen Victoria "the piece was described," Gilbert has recorded, "as 'by Sir Arthur Sullivan', the librettist being too insignificant an insect to be worth mentioning on a programme which contained the name of the wig-maker in bold type!" Gilbert was knighted by King Edward VII in 1907; he accepted the belated honor because, he explained, "I am the only dramatic author upon whom, *qua* dramatic author, it has ever been conferred." The *London Times* inquired: "Is the knighthood compensation for the temporary ban that was placed on *The Mikado,* or a reward for the sublime mockery of the Peers in *Iolanthe?*"

The Pirates of Penzance is built on word play. Frederic, an orphan apprenticed to the pirates (his nurse misunderstood the word "pilot"), is in love with Mabel, one of the daughters of "the very model of a modern Major-Gineral." Freed from his apprenticeship at the age of 21, Frederic helps the unhappy and timid police, who have been sent against the pirates. Then comes "the most ingenious paradox": Frederic has been apprenticed until his twenty-first *birthday;* since he was born on February 29, leap year, he still has some sixty-two years to serve the pirates! A "slave of duty," Frederic warns his pirate masters of the police trap, and the police themselves are caught in it. Honesty and love triumph only through the power of "Queen Victoria's name."

Other "pirates" led Gilbert and Sullivan to journey to the United States to oppose the unauthorized productions of their works with an "official" production of *H. M. S. Pinafore.* The authors stayed to direct *The Pirates of Penzance,* which opened at the Fifth Avenue Theatre, with an English cast, on December 31, 1879; thus they secured United States copyright. The British rights were meanwhile obtained by an unannounced performance in a private theatre in the remote sea-side village of Paignton, South Devon. In the cast was a Mr. R. Mansfield, who later toured in the Gilbert and Sullivan operettas and grew to be the famous star, Richard Mansfield.

The Pirates of Penzance opened in London on April 3, 1880, for a run of 363 performances. The play was very popular in the United States. The Bostonians produced it in September 1880, with the first all-American cast; soon after, three companies were on the road. Tony Pastor (February 7, 1881) presented at his Broadway theatre *The Pie-rats of Penn-Yan,* with Sullivan's music; this travesty gave Lillian Russell her first playing role. Alice Brady appeared in *The Pirates of Penzance* (1912); and among the men who have made names in its roles are George Grossmith, Frank Moulan, and De Wolf Hopper.

Among the countless productions of *The Pirates of Penzance,* that of Winthrop Ames is outstanding. Brooks Atkinson (December 7, 1926) averred: "On the word of Gilbert-and-Sullivan maniacs, whose mad eyes lit up the audience everywhere last evening and whose gestures endangered the safety of the common spectators, this is the best revival of *The Pirates* yet seen in the Milky Way." Alexander Woollcott nominated Winthrop Ames for the presidency of the United States.

"Gilbert's pirate king," William Archer stated, "seems to us an almost inconceivable caricature, but he does not exaggerate the poses and gestures that had been accepted as serious art until well on in the nineteenth century." The sense of travesty has gone, but the rippling wit, the amusing songs, the arrant nonsense of it all remain.

PATIENCE
William Schwenck Gilbert

Patience; or, Bunthorne's Bride is many folks' favorite among the Gilbert and Sullivan operettas. It is a light and light-hearted spoofing of the "aesthetic craze" of the period in which it was written.

Based on the *Bab Ballad* "The Rival Curates," this operetta is a delightful satire on the poets that used "to walk down Piccadilly, With a poppy or a lily In their medieval hand" to fascinate the ladies. Bunthorne, the fleshly poet, loves the milkmaid, Patience; his rival Grosvenor, the idyllic poet, wins all the other maidens. But a revolt from the affectedly poetic ways duly arrives. When Grosvenor swears to be always a commonplace young man, Patience accepts him; the dragoons pair off with the other ladies; and the discomfited Bunthorne is left with his buncombe.

Gilbert was afraid that in *Patience* he had written merely a topical satire, which would soon lapse into oblivion. The *Illustrated London News* (June 18, 1881) saw that it was more: "This is at once the most subtle and most incisive of all the contributions to the exhaustive satire of aestheticism . . . To say ridiculous things with a grave face is but half Mr. Gilbert's method . . . He respects no one; and he shows ourselves not 'as others see us', but as we see ourselves. *Patience* . . . is terribly true.

It is a satire of a human weakness, more than of a society craze. It will live in literature when the other plays and poems are long ago forgotten."

Allardyce Nicoll found in *Patience* "an enduring literary charm and a wit which is itself symptomatic of the change coming over English theatrical literature . . . This opera is one long good-natured but severely critical attack upon that atmosphere which Oscar Wilde, the author of the *Poems,* strove to establish in London. It is the answer of wit to that outworn romanticism which called itself the aesthetic movement."

After opening at the Opera-Comique on April 23, 1881, *Patience* was transferred on October 10 to the new Savoy Theatre, built by D'Oyly Carte especially for the Gilbert and Sullivan operas—the first public building in England lighted by electricity. *Patience* ran in the two houses for 578 performances. Gilbert directed it, as he did all the operas, with an iron hand, sure and firm. (He had a model stage at home, with little figures representing the players, on which he worked out all the situations and movements in advance.) With specific reference to *Patience* he recorded that "the actors and actresses were good enough to believe in me and to lend themselves heartily to all I required of them," but George Grossmith, a star of the play, thought differently: "Mr. Gilbert is a perfect autocrat, insisting that his words shall be delivered, even to an inflection of the voice, as he dictates. He will stand on the stage beside the actor or actress, and repeat the words, with appropriate action, over and over again until they are delivered as he desires."

The rippling wit of Gilbert in *Patience* has been graced with an exceedingly bright score. John Mason Brown, who has called *Patience* his favorite of the operettas, says, "I know of no other score that tingles so incessantly with melodies which refuse to be forgotten, or that boasts lyrics which are more ingenious in their rhyming or amusing in their subject matter."

In sustained tomfoolery and in mockery of pretense, with merriment and tender music, none of the operettas is superior to *Patience*.

IOLANTHE   *William Schwenck Gilbert*

Having approached the pinnacle of popular approval with three plays whose titles begin with a P, Gilbert and Sullivan were hesitant about making a change. To play safe, they chose a subtitle that doubled the P and on November 25, 1882, presented the fantastic opera *Iolanthe; or, The Peer and the Peri,* which ran for 398 performances.

Iolanthe, based on "George and the Fairies" in the *Bab Ballads,* is a fusion of topsyturvydom and fairyland. After a period of exile at the bottom of a well for having married a mortal, the fairy Iolanthe is pardoned. She visits her son, Strephon, who is " a fairy down to the waist, but his legs are mortal." Strephon, who has grown up as an Arcadian shepherd, loves Phyllis, a ward of the Lord Chancellor. Various Lords in love with Phyllis lead her to surprise Strephon kissing the ever-young Iolanthe. Subsequently, the Lord Chancellor decides to give Phyllis to the most eligible suitor—namely, himself. But the Queen of the Fairies intervenes: Strephon will go into Parliament and throw the House of Lords open to competitive examination. Iolanthe then reveals that Strephon's father is the Lord Chancellor; the Peers marry the Fairies;

the Queen of the Fairies marries Private Willis, the Parliament sentry; and Strephon and Phyllis are reunited.

This moonshine story is accompanied by some of Gilbert's choicest satire on the law and the House of Lords. The "highly susceptible Chancellor" has two songs in this satiric mood: "The Law is the true embodiment of everything that's excellent," and "When I went to the bar as a very young man." Best known and best of all is the Sentry's Song, outside of Parliament: "When in that House M. P.'s divide, If they've a brain and cerebellum too, They've got to leave that brain outside, and vote just as their leaders tell 'em to."

In addition to its satirical songs, *Iolanthe* is bright with lilting lyrics of love: "I'm to be married today, today"; "None shall part us from each other"; "Faint heart never won fair lady," and more. The finale of Act I is one of the most lively in the operettas, with the Peers and the peris challenging one another in various rhythms and languages. And the nightmare patter song of the Lord Chancellor is far and away the most surprising, ingenious, and brilliant such piece in all literature.

As the Gilbert and Sullivan operettas appeared, the British press grew so fond of each one in turn that the next seemed inferior. Thus *Punch* insisted that "as a musical or a dramatic work *Iolanthe* is not within a mile of *Pinafore* or a patch on *Patience*." However, its gay tunes, sharp shafts of satire, and good-humored romping fun have endeared *Iolanthe* to generations of playgoers. It is comparatively difficult for amateur groups to produce because of the well from which Iolanthe rises, the wings that the Sentry sprouts, and other fairyland embellishments. But it is a joy to hear and see well done. The Winthrop Ames 1926 production in New York was one of the best.

PRINCESS IDA   *William Schwenck Gilbert*

The "whimsical allegory," *The Princess,* a one-act piece written in 1870, became *Princess Ida; or, Castle Adamant,* "a respectful operatic perversion of Tennyson's *Princess*", in 1884. It is in three acts; all the other operettas are in two. *Princess Ida* opened on January 5, 1884, for a run of 246 performances.

The play presents a bevy of scholarly maids who have shut themselves away from all male company, declaring themselves the superior sex. Some young men—including Prince Hilarion—enter the feminine retreat, Castle Adamant, in women's clothes. They are exposed, but while the women man the battlements, Hilarion and his friends overcome Princess Ida's brothers. The women are at the men's tender mercy. Lady Blanche, Professor of Abstract Science, wondering what to do, consults "the five Subjunctive Possibilities—The May, the Might, the Would, the Could, the Should"—and the women decide that they "should" succumb to love's enduring call. *Princess Ida* invites comparison with Shakespeare's *Love's Labor's Lost**, which treats the same theme with the sexes reversed.

In *The Princess* some of the male parts were performed by actresses. In *Princess Ida*, as in all his operettas, Gilbert did not allow women to dress as men. His choruses, furthermore, were always clothed in garments that could have been worn in a drawing-room. The *New York Times* (April 14, 1925) remarked: "The theme is nothing more or less than Rabelaisian . . . But *Princess Ida* emerges . . . as a deft comedy always in the best of taste and, as one of the songs puts it, 'most politely, oh, most politely'."

Princess Ida is not performed so frequently as the other operettas—partly because the dialogue, all in blank verse, lacks the sparkle and spontaneity of Gilbert's prose dialogue, and partly because the subjects of the satire have lost their freshness. "Women's rights" no longer lead to fights. Nevertheless *Princess Ida* has a considerable fund of humor.

When it is played, *Princess Ida* proves its worth. The *New York Post* (April 14, 1925) reported: "All responded to the quaint quips of Gilbert and to the wonderful songs of Sullivan as if they were hearing them for the first time and enjoying them to the full." And the *New York Telegram* (October 13, 1936) called *Princess Ida* "gay as ever," hailing two of its episodes as "the coyest moments in the whole repertory."

Despite the passing of the issues on which Gilbert centred this satire, there is much still valid humor and good-natured frolicking in *Princess Ida*.

THE MIKADO   *William Schwenck Gilbert*

The most popular of all the Gilbert and Sullivan operettas, *The Mikado; or, The Town of Titipu*, opened in London on March 14, 1885, for a run of 672 performances. It has been more frequently played by professionals and amateur groups throughout the world than any of the other operettas. Its wide appeal is attested by the fact that there have been three versions of it in German alone.

Although the atmosphere is that of an absurd Japan—the Japan we see "on many a vase and jar, on many a screen and fan"; Gilbert had Japanese teach the original cast the drape of their costumes and the play of their fans—the satire in *The Mikado* is directed against the English. Gilbert was both surprised and indignant when, during the delicate international situation of 1906-1907, performance of *The Mikado* was forbidden for fear of offending Japan. G. K. Chesteron was moved to remark: "Gilbert pursued and persecuted the evils of modern England till they had literally not a leg to stand on; exactly as Swift did under the allegory of *Gulliver's Travels* . . . I doubt if there is a single joke in the whole play that fits the Japanese. But all the jokes in the play fit the English . . ."

In *The Mikado,* Ko-ko is Lord High Executioner; Pooh-Bah, Lord High Everything Else. Ko-ko, in love with Yum-Yum, yields her to the wandering minstrel Nanki-Poo on the latter's promise to die at the end of the month so that Ko-ko may have an execution to report to the Mikado. Meanwhile, the Mikado arrives, seeking his son, who has run away from marriage with the Midako's daughter-in-law elect, the more-than-middle-aged Katisha. The kindly Ko-Ko and the timorous Pooh-Bah falsely report the execution—only to learn that the "wandering minstrel" is the Mikado's son. Ko-Ko placates Katisha by suing for her hand, and Nanki-Poo is enabled to stay alive, married to Yum-Yum.

All the songs are delightful. Some are delicate and charming: "A wand'ring minstrel I", "Three little maids from school", "Brightly dawns our wedding day." Some—like "The flowers that bloom in the spring", the tit-willow song, and "There is beauty in the bellow of the blast"—combine lightness and laughter. Some are lively tumbling of good spirits and gay fun, with more than a hint of wisdom. The "little list" of folk that won't be missed is usually brought up to date for fresh perform-ances of *The Mikado*. Gilbert himself set the precedent for this in a children's version of *The Mikado*—his last literary work.

Performances of *The Mikado* have been too numerous to detail. The first American amateur production was in Yonkers, New York, in 1891. There was a performance at the New York Metropolitan Opera House, December 5, 1900. Among those that have delighted audiences in the play are George Grossmith, William Danforth, De Wolf Hopper, Frank Moulan, Martyn Green. Fritzi Scheff played Yum-Yum in 1910, with Alice Brady making her debut as the third little maid, Peep-Bo.

In New York, 1885-1886, three companies played *The Mikado* while law-suits tangled. One company, during the curtain speeches cele-brating its 500th performance, was dumbfounded to see the Ko-Ko from the company across the street dash in costume onto the rival stage, and cry—pointing to the other Ko-Ko: "He's not upon my list, he sadly would be missed," and dash off again. He had effectively stolen his rival's thunder.

In 1939 two Negro companies appeared in versions of the play: the Chicago Federal Theatre produced *The Swing Mikado,* which visited New York, opening March 1; and in New York, March 23, *The Hot Mikado* introduced the famous "Bojangles" Bill Robinson as the Mikado. Both were well received. To Brooks Atkinson (March 2, 1939) it seemed "an original notion to slide *The Mikado* into the groove of black and hot rhythm"; Robinson's company, he observed, substituted "Harlem frenzy for an amateur swing serenade." However, the two companies were not first to hit upon the idea of "Sepia Savoyards." In 1886, Thatcher, Prim-rose, and West's Minstrels celebrated the 200th performance of "the most successful afterpiece ever produced on the minstrel stage"—Ed Marble's *The Black Mikado.* The program announced 'Mick-ah-Do the Great, J. P. O'Keefe; Ko-Ko, Billy Rice; Pooh-Bah, his Cabinet, Ed Marble; Yanki-Poh and the three little maidens all unwary, plus Ah-There, Stay-There, The Yeddo Coconut Dancers and other curios too numerous to mention."

The popularity of *The Mikado* gives no signs of abating. The work is fresh and lively throughout, with the best-knit plot of the operettas, songs that spring naturally from the situations, and a constant spurting of humor and amusing topsyturvy. "In my humble opinion," George Ade once declared, "*The Mikado* is the best light opera ever written in Eng-lish." Hosts of enthusiasts will concur.

RUDDIGORE   *William Schwenck Gilbert*

Though tempted to a new preference by every fresh production, the author of these lines, who has seen every professional Gilbert and Sullivan company in New York since 1908, concurs in fine with Gilbert himself, whose favorite of the operettas was *The Yeoman of the Guard,** and whose second in favor was *Ruddigore.* (The original title, *Ruddygore,* so shocked Victorian London that Gilbert, ever considerate of the ladies, changed the spelling to *Ruddigore*).

Ruddigore; or, The Witch's Curse was not one of the most popular of the operettas, although, opening in London January 22, 1887, it ran for eight months (288 performances) and netted Gilbert some £7,000. Based upon an early sketch of Gilbert's, *Ages Ago,* with ideas from the *Bab Ballads* ("The Modest Couple"), *Ruddigore* satirizes the "naughtycal" melodrama of the day, which brought the hero sailor home from the bounding main to foil the bold bad baronet who covets the innocent maid.

The "bold bad baronet" in *Ruddigore,* Sir Ruthven Murgatroyd, is a really good fellow at heart. He has inherited the family curse and (like a perverted Boy Scout) must commit a crime a day or die. To avoid this fate, Ruthven disguises himself as a farmer, Robin Oakapple; but his foster-brother Richard (home from the sea), his rival for the hand of sweet Rose Maybud, reveals Robin's true identity. The ancient Murgatroyds step down from their family portraits and force the present Murgatroyd to continue the family career of crime. Finally he finds a way out: since he will die if he does not commit a crime, to refuse to commit a crime is tantamount to suicide—and suicide *is* a crime; hence by refusing to commit a crime, he commits one. This paradox—in Gilbert's land of topsyturvy—frees Robin to marry Rose, and the fishing village of Rederring rejoices with Castle Ruddigore.

This "supernatural" opera contains Sullivan's liveliest and most varied score, Gilbert's most varied and deftest lyrics, and many shafts of humor in the dialogue. Two aspects of the play perhaps weight it against popular favor. The theme—with the ancestral curse, and Mad Margaret, who with her reformed Murgatroyd becomes a district religious visitor—lacks the airy grace and light-hearted charm of *The Mikado** or *The Gondoliers*.* Moreover, the end comes rather abruptly. Although sudden turns end others of the operettas, the final turn in *Ruddigore* is a play on words, on the technical fact that suicide is a crime. This lessens the satisfaction at the play's close.

A more deft thrust, at a more universal impulse, is the device hit upon to keep the reformed Mad Margaret from lapsing into a passion. She and her husband agree upon a word, and whenever she seems ready to fly off the handle, he calls out, to warn and calm her:—"Basingstoke!" "Basingstoke it is!" and she is calm.

There are numerous humorous songs in varied mood in the play. The lightsome love song and the tender plaint are also sung in rich variety.

When *Ruddigore* was first produced, the press objected even to this title; but Sullivan had the good sense not to allow Gilbert to change it, as he suggested doing, to *Kensington Gore.* Gradually, however, the bad baronets grew into favor.

In the United States, *Ruddigore* has won a chorus of praise. Gilbert W. Gabriel (August 11, 1931) declared: "Sullivan never wrote handsomer music than the famous ghost scene, nor wittier music than the duet of Sir Despard's and Mad Margaret's conversion. Nor was his collaborator ever more intrinsically droll." The *New York Herald-Tribune* (October 18, 1936) agreed that *Ruddigore* is "one of the most tuneful and humorous of their entire series." In this and in their next work, *The Yeoman of the Guard,* the talents of the pair are at their peak.

THE YEOMEN OF THE GUARD   *William Schwenck Gilbert*

Gilbert felt that *The Yeoman of the Guard* was the best of the Gilbert and Sullivan operettas; "and he was right," agreed his biographers, Sidney Dark and Rowland Grey, "the best thing they had done or were ever to do—a perfect work of art." *The Yeoman of the Guard; or, The*

Merryman and His Maid opened October 31, 1888, for 423 performances.

In this operetta, Gilbert came nearest to making his quips and cranks and wanton wiles convey genuine portraits. His Phoebe Meryll, biographers Dark and Grey maintain, is "the most fascinating and human character he ever created"; and the melancholy Jaques, whom Shakespeare presents in *As You Like It**, has an active brother in Jack Point, the strolling jester of *The Yeomen*. Many see in this sad merryman Gilbert himself, who, at the public comand—"Come, fool, follify!"—was brave enough to declare, "I ply my craft and know no fear, I aim my shaft at prince or peer," yet shrewd enough to know that "he who'd make his fellow-creatures wise should always gild the philosophic pill."

Rising to the challenge of Gilbert's more serious character study and more rousing and natural plot, Sullivan composed some of his most developed and effective music for *The Yeoman of the Guard*. The duet of the Merryman and his Maid, "I have a song to sing, O," is the finest music in the operettas, a masterpiece of cumulative sound and sense. Music critics have compared the opening song, "When maiden loves, She sits and sighs", sung by Phoebe as she spins, with the spinning chorus in Wagner's *The Flying Dutchman*.

The *Pall Mall Budget* (October 11, 1888) hailed the new operetta as undoubtedly in for a long run: "The delightful melodies, the plaintive ballads, the catching choruses, the lovely trios and quartets which are scattered so profusely through this new work, will give pleasure to millions . . . Sir Arthur surpassed his former efforts." The *London Times* (July 17, 1939) said: "There is more substance to *The Yeomen* than to the purely comic operas. Sullivan responded to its humanity and romance with music such as he could hardly write for Gilbert's merely cynical constructions." And in 1941, *The Yeomen of the Guard* was presented in London as "a dramatic play with music," emphasizing the romantic and pathetic interplay of characters.

The plot of *The Yeomen of the Guard* is serious, and intricately knit. Jack Point, a strolling jester, loves his singer, Elsie. He consents, however, for a hundred pounds, to have Elsie marry Colonel Fairfax, a prisoner within London Tower. Fairfax is to die within the hour; he wishes, by leaving a widow, to divert the inheritance from the relative responsible for his imprisonment and death-sentence. But Phoebe, daughter of the Sergeant of the yeomen of the guard, loves Fairfax. While singing a wooing song to the head jailor, "Were I thy bride", she steals his keys and releases Fairfax. The jailor discovers the secret; to silence him, Phoebe must grant him her hand. Reprieve comes for Fairfax, who stays married to Elsie, and Point falls fainting as the curtain falls.

Brooks Atkinson (January 24, 1939) remarked: "Criticism of the D'Oyly Carte productions should, and generally does, consist of rhapsodic encomium." His words most aptly apply to *The Yeomen of the Guard*.

George Grossmith, who had starred in most of the operettas, acted Jack Point in *The Yeomen of the Guard*, then left the company. The great collaboration was nearing its end. It had one more great satiric frolic to come, *The Gondoliers**, but it had reached its richest combination of earnestness and topsyturvy in *The Yeomen of the Guard*.

THE GONDOLIERS   *William Schwenck Gilbert*

Annoyed at the temperaments and inflated egos of their stars—George Grossmith left the Savoyards, August 17, 1889; Jessie Bond refused to renew her contract for less than £30 a week—Gilbert swore: "We'll have an opera in which there'll be no principal parts." And in *The Gondoliers* three men are equally entangled with three women. The men's identities are mixed; the two gondoliers (one of whom—but no one knows which—is supposed to be the king of Barataria) sing duets in which they divide the words, sharing even the silly syllabification. Gilbert was a thorough man.

The Gondoliers; or, The King of Barataria opened at the Savoy Theatre on December 7, 1889, for a run of 554 performances. It earned the most money of all the operettas. Over 70,000 copies of the songs were sold in a few days. In March 1891, Queen Victoria saw a command performance at Windsor Castle; the Queen had been sharply displeased by Gilbert's satire, and *The Gondoliers* was listed on the program as "by Sir Arthur Sullivan" (for details, see *The Pirates of Penzance**). The *Pall Mall Budget* (December 12, 1889) called the new play "an admirable specimen of melodious topsy-turvydom, in which neither author nor composer can be said to have fallen short of the Savoy standard. The humor of the libretto is unflagging, and the music is written in Sir Arthur Sullivan's brightest and most fascinating vein, and the whole surroundings of the piece are as picturesque and full of colour as possible."

Barataria, readers may recollect, is the island of which Don Quixote made his man Sancho Panza the governor, with queer results. In *The Gondoliers*, it is the island which the two gondoliers (ruling as twins until they learn which is king) set out to democratize. Whichever is king was betrothed in infancy to the daughter of the haughty Duke of Plaza-Toro. This fact embarrasses the gondoliers, because they have just been married to two charming Venetian girls. The Grand Inquisitor is distressed at their marriages, and also at the workings of democracy in Barataria, until it is revealed that the real king is Luiz, the drummer boy of the Duke of Plaza-Toro, whom the Duke's daughter loves.

Sullivan had more trouble with the music for *The Gondoliers* than for any other of the operas. His accomplishment was worth the trouble. The songs are his most varied; they are delightful in rippling merriment; they swing mock-martially, with rolling drum, for the "celebrated, cultivated, underrated Nobleman, The Duke of Plaza-Toro", who leads his regiment from behind; and they prick home their barbs of satire. But they demand the most skillful of choruses; they call for tricky ensemble singing by the principals. Winthrop Ames, whose Gilbert and Sullivan productions have been among our best, said he wouldn't risk *The Gondoliers* with his troupe. "What *The Gondoliers* may lack", said the *Boston Transcript* (April 14, 1937) "in the matter of the usual gimlet-like wit, it makes up for in richness of color, grace, and lovely musical compositions." Its love songs are especially sparkling.

It is rich, too, in gay satire of snobbery, whether of aristocrat or of democrat. The gondoliers intend to improve Barataria by leveling *up*, not leveling *down*, hence:

> The Lord High Bishop orthodox—
> The Lord High Coachman on the box—

The Lord High Vagabond in the stocks—
They all shall equal be!

But the Grand Inquisitor, in a clever and lilting song, reminds the new-born democrats, "When everyone is somebodee, Then no one's anybody!" Originally, in this song, at the line "Up goes the price of shoddy", Sullivan introduced a few bars from *Yankee Doodle Dandy*. An American, present at a rehearsal, objected, and Sullivan removed the musical satire.

In *The Gondoliers*, we watch the twin kings, in a joint patter song, "embark without delay On the duties of the day." We see excitement boil and subside, and boil again in song, while between their passionate moments the excited ones peacefully sing "Quiet, calm deliberation Disentangles every knot." We hear the Grand Inquisitor's reassurance: "Of that there is no manner of doubt", when the mystery is greatest as to which is the king. We see and hear the gavotte of the Venetians who are being taught court manners, and the gayer romp, "We will dance a cachucha, fandango, bolero." We observe the pomp of the Duke of Plaza-Toro and the majesty of his wife, who, giving her daughter counsel, sings of how "I tamed your insignificant progenitor—at last!" And we note how the nobles (like moving picture stars today) lend themselves to causes for a fee.

It is folly to ask which of the Gilbert and Sullivan operettas is "best." Yet the *London Times* (January 26, 1938) said that *The Gondoliers* "has good claims to that distinction, especially today. For one thing, nothing in the libretto has dated."

When *The Gondoliers* first came to New York, it was savagely attacked in the *New York Herald*, and *The World* (January 8, 1889) said that "The general verdict is that it is not up to the standard of the former works . . . The general effect is cheerful and inspiriting, but that the individual numbers are to be compared with those of *Patience**, *Iolanthe**, *Ruddigore**, or *The Mikado**, is absurd." Opinions changed, especially after the American debut of the new D'Oyly Carte company, September 3, 1934, and by March 4, 1942, Richard Watts, Jr. expressed the "general verdict" when he said that *The Gondoliers* is "a musical pleasure." The last line of *The Gondoliers*, indeed, is "We leave you with feelings of pleasure." There could be no more fit farewell to Gilbert and Sullivan.

The rest of the story of the two collaborators takes a darker tone. During the run of *The Gondoliers*, D'Oyly Carte spent £140 for a carpet for the theatre. Gilbert protested that this was an excessive sum. Sullivan sided with D'Oyly Carte. Buried resentments over prestige, over light versus serious music, swelled up, and the long and genial association came to an end. Later, Gilbert and Sullivan were reconciled, and produced two more works together. Both failed. (On May 29, 1911, while swimming to save a young woman, Gilbert died by drowning.)

Isaac Goldberg, in a tribute to Gilbert, stated that "there is no figure of the past or present to whom Gilbert can be likened." He most resembles Greek Aristophanes*, that other staunch shaver of sham, who two thousand years earlier brought poetry and music together with mirth and social criticism, in a merry melange of satire and beauty. Between them, and since, they have no parallel.

SECRET SERVICE   *William Gillette*

For a stirring melodrama of war, in the days when war still carried
the cloak of courtesy and gentlemanly dealing with a gallant foe, there
is fire in the episode of the War Between the States presented in *Secret
Service*, 1895, by William Gillette (American, 1855-1937). *Secret Service*
remains, as William Archer has called it, "the best play of its type."

William Gillette, author and actor, tried out *Secret Service* in Philadelphia, May 13, 1895. He withdrew the work for improvement, however,
and played all the next season in his farce *Too Much Johnson*. With himself as Captain Thorne, Gillette reopened *Secret Service* in New York,
October 5, 1896. It ran for over 300 performances, followed by 150 in
Boston, by a two year run in England, and another successful season in
New York. Gillette (turning from his adaptation of *Sherlock Holmes*, in
which he played intermittently from 1899 to 1932) starred again in
Secret Service in 1915. The play has had frequent community theatre
production, and was seen in 1948 at the Putnam County Playhouse, New
York.

The play is set in Richmond at the close of the War. Lewis Dumont,
disguised as a Captain Thorne, a secret agent of the Northern forces, and
Edith Varney, daughter of a Southern general, are in love. Arrelsford, a
Southern agent, also in love with Edith, watches Thorne closely—while
Thorne's brother, a prisoner surrounded while escaping, shoots himself
to avoid betraying Thorne. But Arrelsford sets a trap and, while Thorne
is telegraphing a misleading message, shoots him in the hand. Thorne is
led away to be shot.

Edith has had her faithful Negro slave unload the guns; she tells
Thorne to fall when they fire. He will not, unless she admits that she
loves him. Modesty and Southern loyalty combine to keep her still.
"Sergeant, look to your guns," says Thorne. "Thank you." "You're welcome." And the men reload. But the Southern surrender is announced;
this saves Captain Thorne, and permits Edith to admit that she loves him.
Arthur Hobson Quinn, in *A History of the American Drama* (1936) regretted that the saving of Thorne turned "a tragedy of uncommon power"
into no more than a vivid melodrama.

Secret Service seemed, to its day, not merely a rousing spy melodrama
of the late war, but "a remarkable contribution to the stage of any land."
Such was the judgment of no less a critic than James Huneker, writing in
the *New York Sunday Advertiser*, (October 11, 1896), who said . . . "I
can instance no other play by an American writer where the main current takes on such delightful, swirling eddies, and remember, the rush of
the action never halts. The unities of time and place are rigorously adhered to. Even the diversion and sweet foolery of the young lovers melts
into the story, and from being at first blush subsidiary, determines in
reality the denouement. This is supreme art. The strands of this stirring
tale are woven closely, yet is the fabric ever elastic, human, and not
merely a triumph of the dramatic weaver's art."

There is a deftness of structure in *Secret Service* that utilizes all the
resources of the stage, including silence. A most effective bit of wordless
action comes as the curtain rises, with, as the *New York Journal*, (September 27, 1898) described it, "the Richmond girl sewing for the hospitals,
who enters the quiet room, crosses to a table to gather up some forgotten

bit of work, her hesitating glance toward a window, where we see the flash of the siege guns, her weary glance through the parted curtains, and her silent exit. There is no reason why a thing so simple should be so tremendously impressive save that it is absolutely genuine. In the play's humor, its pathos, its heart-stirring climaxes, the same directness of treatment is maintained." "Above all else," said Arthur Hobson Quinn, "it is the absolute reality of the characters that is effective. Without a bit of heroics, they all move under the shadow of danger, playing the game."

The power of the play's hold, and the change in the public estimate of chivalrous conduct, are alike shown in an episode during the play's revival in 1915, a revival that the *New York Dramatic Mirror* (November 13) called "as effective as its first presentation nineteen years ago." When, on Edith's refusal to declare her love, Thorne tells the sergeant to look to his guns, a voice from the gallery cried "You damned fool!" A ripple of laughter bespoke the relaxing nervous tension, and in a moment the house was caught again in the drama's flow. Of the scores of melodramas drawn from the conflict of the Blue and the Gray, with love that crosses the lines, although closely followed by Bronson Howard's *Shenandoah** and David Belasco's *The Heart of Maryland**, the most gallant, gripping, and vital is *Secret Service*.

SIEGFRIED   *Jean Giraudoux*

Jean Giraudoux (French, 1882-1944) was well known as a novelist, original in thought and in the structure of his works, before he turned to the theatre. He first won wide attention with the novel *Simon le Pathetique*, (1918). His novel *Siegfried et le Limousin*, 1921, was awarded the Goncourt Prize; his first play was a dramatization of this novel, as *Siegfried*.

Giraudoux' years in German universities gave him background for the story, which sets a forgotten and forgetting Frenchman in Germany, after the first World War. A German nurse, Eva, finds a man wounded on a battlefield, without memory or identification. She nurses him, then becomes his secretary, as under the name Siegfried he becomes counselor of state and the liberal leader of the German people. The reactionary von Zelten, Siegfried's political rival, suspects that Siegfried is a minor French writer, Jacques Forrestier, reported "lost in action"; he imports Forrestier's fiancée, Genevieve Prat, to identify him. Genevieve comes, supposedly to teach French to Siegfried, who feels drawn to her. His identification is made. The two women urge their opposite claims: Eva tells him 60,000,000 people want him as leader; Genevieve says there's a little French poodle mourning its master. Siegfried returns to France. The close of the play bears the mellow hope that the good on both sides will prevail.

Such a fusion of Frenchman and German gives opportunity for showing the best of both countries. There are several emotional scenes in the play, and the conflict between the two women for Siegfried is a touching one, with audience sympathy finely balanced. Personal relationships, however, are on the whole subordinated to a searching and disillusioned picture of the ironies of political fame and fate, and the distortions of professional or jingoistic patriotism.

Produced in 1928, *Siegfried* ran for a year in Paris. Courtney Bruerton reported in the *Christian Science Monitor* (May 26, 1928) that the author showed "rich imagination and a great talent for poetic fantasy in realistic settings. . . . Most original figure in French letters for many a day." *L'Illustration* (May 19, 1928) said: "To hear Giraudoux is one of the rare pleasures of the spirit . . . The lack of likelihood in the story matters not; it is but a pretext for a development often profound and always sparkling on the German and French soul."

Siegfried was performed in New York in French, opening February 20, 1929; and in May of the next year in an English translation by Philip Carr at the Civic Repertory Theatre. Jacob Ben Ami was Siegfried; Eva Le Gallienne, Genevieve; Margaret Mower, Eva; Egon Brecher, von Zelten; also in the cast were Donald Cameron, J. Edward Bromberg, and Burgess Meredith (doubling in two minor roles).

The play, despite the flourishes of Giraudoux' imagination, holds its characters and situations in sharp relief. It was very well received in New York. Marc Connelly in the *Nation* (November 5, 1930) said *Siegfried* was "the first play I have seen in which the device of the amnesia victim has been used with artistic dignity." Howard Barnes (October 21, 1930) said Giraudoux "clothed this skeleton of a plot with rare artistry, and the climaxes of his dramatic movement are poignantly moving." Brooks Atkinson felt that the author "engenders beauties of thought and feeling quite unfamiliar to the stage. . . . occasionally drops into interludes of brisk Gallic irony, and turns one incidental scene in a frontier railway station into a vastly amusing caricature of French petty officialdom."

The scene at the railway station marks Siegfried's return to France, and brings home the irony of the change from a leading political figure before whom all bow to an ordinary citizen who must bow to border regulations and be tangled in red tape. With rich imagination, deft pressure of irony, and a subtle but sophisticate spirit, *Siegfried* manages to be both a neatly developed document for peace between nations, and a stirring play.

ONDINE   *Jean Giraudoux*

Since Baron Friedrich Heinrich Karl La Motte-Fouqué wrote *Undine* (1811), his story of the water spirit that loved and caused the death of a mortal has had wide popularity and many retellings. The opera *Undine* (1816, libretto by La Motte-Fouqué) with music by the composer and novelist Ernst Theodor Amadeus Hoffmann, became in turn the inspiration for Jacques Offenbach's *Tales of Hoffmann* (1880). The opera *Undine* was performed in England in 1843; in Berlin in 1932; in Vienna in 1936 and 1938. A play *Undine* by J. Benedict was presented in London in 1839; and *Undine* was a Christmas pantomine in London, 1858; a play by R. Reece was performed in London in 1870. (The legend was first set down by the sixteenth century Paracelsus in his *Treatise on Elemental Spirits*).

A version of *Undine* was first played in America at the Chestnut Street Theatre in Philadelphia on New Year's Day, 1822. Joseph Jefferson (grandfather of the Joseph that created the role of Rip Van Winkle) played the fisherman; Henry Wallach played Sir Huldbrand, the knight doomed by the love of Undine. The production was most spectacular, with underwater grottos, falling trees, and tumbling cascades.

In New York, in 1839, the noted Taglionis presented a ballet, *Undine*, which the *Spirit of the Times* (August 3, 1839) reviewed favorably. In New York also there was a play *Undine* by Grant Stewart in 1901. In

Germany, the play *Undine,* by Albert Lortzing, based on the original story, was presented in 1931.

The most recent, and the best, of the dramatic versions of the tale is *Ondine* by Jean Giraudoux. Directed by Louis Jouvet, *Ondine* opened in Paris with Jouvet as Hans and Madeleine Ozeray as Ondine on April 27, 1939. It was given once in English in New York, May 19, 1949; then, opening there February 18, 1954, with Audrey Hepburn, won the Critics' Circle award as the best foreign play of the year.

In the La Motte-Fouqué version, the nymph Undine is reared by fisherfolk whose daughter has been kidnapped. The knight, Sir Huldbrand, encounters Undine; they fall in love. Undine is snatched back by the water-folk, and the Knight marries Bertalda, who is really the fisherfolk's daughter. The bride calls for a drink from the old well, and Undine is forced by the water-spirits to rise with the waters and bring about the death of the knight. Out of this tale, Jean Giraudoux created a supernatural fantasy that is also a human allegory, a poetic play with satiric overtones and shadings of wisdom and sadness.

In the Giraudoux play, Ondine, transparent as water, loves Hans von Wittenstein zu Wittenstein, opaque as earth. She is told by her uncle that Hans will die if he prove untrue. At court, Ondine mocks the courtesies and hypocrisies of the nobles. Her uncle, posing as a court magician, speeds the years along; Ondine disappears, and Hans is to marry Berthe. Now Ondine comes to save Hans; she tries to pretend that she was unfaithful first; but her love is too wholehearted for deception; it fools no one. Hans does not understand Ondine's attempt at self-sacrifice, but his love for her reawakens, and he dies. In the space of three sounds from the waters, Ondine has forgotten her mortal interlude, and is again one with the water-nymphs.

After the Paris production of *Ondine,* American opinions varied. The *New Yorker* correspondent (July 8, 1939) stated "It's a poor play, and nowhere does it touch on the fears and hopes now moving Frenchmen's minds, but Frenchmen flock to see the piece, which, for a relief, deals with the unreal." The reviewer for the *Christian Science Monitor* (June 3, 1939) was more sympathetic: *Ondine,* he said, "has indeed the fluidity of water, its freshness, its carefree babbling, and also here and there its pools hidden in the green shade, its still serenity, its depth, most of all its transparency."

The French newspapers were unanimous in enthusiastic praise of *Ondine.* All found the production superbly spectacular, yet delicate: "One of the most exquisite creations of Louis Jouvet," said Robert de Beauplan in *La Petite Illustration* (August 26, 1939). Several critics emphasized that Giraudoux had in *Ondine* most successfully combined reality and fantasy. "Never," said Pierre Audiat in *Paris-Soir,* "has Giraudoux been more accessible in his flashes of irony and philosophy; never has he gone farther in the exploration of the emotions." Most penetratingly, James de Coquet in *Annales* observed: "He seizes with uncommon clearness of vision the nature of things, the essence of forms, the course of events. Once in possession of these truths, so that they could be set down in figures and formulas, he gives them back to us in the colors of a dream . . . First he reduces things to their simplest expression, then he raises them to their highest power . . . He does not rest content with telling a story or demonstrating a truth; he must also lead the beholder into an imaginary world, far from our own in all appearances, yet very close in the character of its inhabitants." London saw *Ondine* in 1953.

The fairy-tale world of *Ondine* indeed comes close to our own, as the nymph Ondine loves Hans so much, and suffers so much for him, that she almost becomes human. As there is pathos—and all loving womanhood—in her attempt to sacrifice herself for Hans, so is there irony, and all natural indifference, in the forgetfulness of Hans that comes upon her as she, a force of nature, remains immortal while human generations die.

In addition to its poetry and its wisdom, *Ondine* is not without satire. The simple, superstitious fisherfolk are not spared, yet there is a kindliness in their exposure that becomes less gentle in the presentation of the absurdities and the hypocrisies of the court; and there is a searching comment in the manner in which Hans' doom is to be announced: when the peasant speaks poetry, the noble will die.

Ondine is a truly colorful and fanciful fairy-tale, delightful to behold, charming to the ear and the eye; it is also a moving and thoughtful picture of man's brief hold upon life and love in the endless indifferent flow of nature. In short, it is a play rewarding to the heart and to the mind.

THE MADWOMAN OF CHAILLOT   *Jean Giraudoux*

Most rewarding of Giraudoux' slantwise satires of the life of our time is *The Madwoman of Chaillot* (*La Folle de Chaillot*), 1943, which was produced in Paris, directed by Louis Jouvet, on December 19, 1945.

Vogue (March 1, 1946) considered the first production especially "notable for the inspired acting of Marguerite Moreno as the Madwoman, and Louis Jouvet as the Ragpicker; for the imaginative fantasy of Christian Berad's settings." After this production ran for over a year, Jouvet tired of a single role and returned to repertory. He has not revived the play since Mme. Moreno (aged 82) died.

A translation by Maurice Valency opened on Broadway December 27, 1948, with Martita Hunt (the Madwoman), John Carradine (the Ragpicker), Estelle Winwood, Clarence Derwent, and Vladimir Sokoloff. The costumes and the settings—a café terrace, and the vast cellar of the Countess—were brought over from France. In spite of unimaginative direction, the brilliance of the play shone through. It ran for 368 performances and, after a tour, returned to New York June 13, 1950, for two weeks at the City Center. Martita Hunt was also in the cast of the London production which opened February 15, 1951, for 68 performances.

The Madwoman of Chaillot pictures a half-demented but quite competent and confident old crone who discovers that there is evil in the world and proceeds to dispose of it. A syndicate of astute exploiters plans to extract oil from the ground beneath Paris; the mad Countess, to save Paris from being destroyed by their greed, invites them, followed by journalists and sundry greedy groups, to her cellar, whence an endless staircase leads forever down. Thinking to find oil, they step down. "The pimps who little by little have taken over the world" thus removed, the clean world is left to the common people, the men of good will, the pure in heart.

The lucky Frenchman is born not with a silver spoon in his mouth, but with a golden pen in his hand. The French theatre-public believes, says Giraudoux, that "the soul can be made to open naturally, like a safe, with a word, and dislikes the German oxyhydrogen blow-torch method."

Hence the flashes of improvisation in *The Madwoman of Chaillot*: sometimes they gambol for the sheer delight of verbal and mental play; sometimes they flicker with an eerie light over dark places within the human soul; sometimes they turn like a great revolving searchlight across contemporary life. "The logic of the scene", as Brooks Atkinson said (January 9, 1949), "seems to be impeccable, but the effect is crack-brained, original, and delightful . . . This vagrant style naturally suited Giraudoux, who was too sophisticated to believe in easy solutions but never lost faith in people and never renounced a young man's dreams of a happy world." When seen through Giraudoux' eyes, said John Mason Brown (January 15, 1949), "the mundane regains its wonder, the expected becomes unpredictable." Several critics compared the mood of the play with that of Lewis Carroll's *Alice* books. In Brown's opinion the Madwoman's was "the most hilarious and maddest tea-party given since the Dormouse, the March Hare, and a certain Hatter entertained Alice."

Those that complain that Giraudoux' cure for the evils of the world is too simple, overlook the fact that the cure is devised by the mad woman. Giraudoux not only looks with glint of irony at the evils of society; he also satirizes those that would adopt panaceas for social ills. In the seemingly mad cascading of the playwright's fancy, there is a subtle method as *The Madwoman of Chaillot* lights Roman candles over the gauds and the greeds, the shoddies and the needs, of human kind. Where realism must reckon with despair, Giraudoux focuses fantasy to light the intelligence with good theatre and brighten the vision with hope.

ALISON'S HOUSE   *Susan Glaspell*

With her husband, George Cram Cook, Susan Glaspell (American, b. 1882) organized The Provincetown Players, a group that first produced the plays of Eugene O'Neill and staged the Cook-Glaspell satire on amateur Freudians, *Suppressed Desires*. More seriously, more poetically, more trenchantly, *Alison's House*, which opened in New York December 1, 1930, probes a basic problem of human behavior.

The play's action takes place a score of years after the death of Alison Stanhope, when the family comes upon a manuscript of poems written by Alison. The poems reveal genius, but they also reveal that Alison had quietly suppressed a deep love for a married man. The question therefore arises as to whether the poems should be made public. Interest in the play centers on the various characters' attitudes toward the question and the influence upon them of the still living spirit of Alison. Aunt Agatha wants to burn the "confessions of a great but misguided soul," but the generation after Alison's is more matter-of-fact; the callous nephew, and the flippant niece, Elsa, who has attempted to meet a similar problem by running away with a married man, vote to release the poems.

Alison's House moves rather slowly for two acts, with a poetic rather than a dramatic power; only in the last act does it rise to intense drama. "The final scene containing the battle of wills", said the *London Times* (October 12, 1932), "has merit not only as a contest between the living but for its power to evoke, in Alison's bedroom, the influence of the dead . . . The problem seems a genuine one, and is ably used to exhibit the characters of those that discuss it." Because of the thin dramatic texture of the play, some of the critics (Lockridge, Atkinson) demurred when it was awarded the 1931 Pulitzer Prize.

There is, however, compensating merit in the play's quiet evocation of spiritual values, of an integrity that overlasts brief mortality. Thus R. Dana Skinner, in the *New York Times* (May 17, 1931), observed: "The play says nothing more clearly than the simple fact that Alison Stanhope became great through denying herself a love which she thought wrong. This, of course, is a challenge to nine tenths of modern thinking. It is an old idea, and a mystic one, that 'as we die to ourselves we live to a greater life.' It is because Alison could do what Elsa could not that Alison lived after death, made her presence felt in every corner of the great house and in the moments of crisis in the lives of each member of the family. I grant you this is not a popular idea today, but it has on its side the greatest poets since history began. It rips to pieces the smug egotism of today; but is it any the less profound and stirring for striking a radical blow?"

Although the scene of *Alison's House* is transplanted from New England to Iowa, Alison's story is patterned upon that of Amherst-bound Emily Dickinson (1830-1866), whose life is also the basis of our most moving modern dance ballet, Martha Graham's *Letter To the World*. Out of the sheltered life and heart-held love of a great poet, Susan Glaspell in *Alison's House* fashioned a tender, touching, and understanding play.

GÖTZ VON BERLICHINGEN   *Johann Wolfgang Von Goethe*

With the publication of *Götz von Berlichingen* in the summer of 1773, Johann Wolfgang von Goethe (German, 1749-1832) took the younger generation of Germany by storm. He became the hero of the day, the "German Shakespeare", the founder and leader of the *Sturm und Drang* (Storm and Stress) movement. *Götz von Berlichingen*, together with the novel *The Sorrows of Young Werther* (1774), brought Goethe his widest surge of popularity in the flush of the Romantic Rebellion.

The *Sturm und Drang* was rooted in three emotions: worship of Shakespeare, desire to "return to nature", hatred of all things French. All these are found in Goethe's *Götz von Berlichingen*, especially in the first version, written in the last months of 1771, and not published until after Goethe's death. The 1773 version was revised in 1787, and again, with Schiller, in 1803, for presentation on the Weimar stage.

The first version of *Götz von Berlichingen* shows the romantic enthusiasm of the youthful Goethe. In a 1771 lecture on Shakespeare, he said: "The first page of his that I read made me his for life . . . The unity of place seemed to me irksome as a prison; the unities of action and time, burdensome fetters to the imagination." And *Götz von Berlichingen* is rather a series of vivid episodes than a tightly knit play; its five acts have 103 scenes. On reading the first version, Herder remarked: "Shakespeare has quite spoiled you." The 1773 version was pruned of many of the excesses, especially in diction. But the play retains something of Shakespeare's power of characterization, of a sense of the tumult and rouse of life, and of a vivid immediacy of action and truth. For these qualities, as the *Encyclopedia Britannica* observes, the play remains "irresistible in its appeal, even to a modern audience." Something of Goethe's indebtedness to the English Shakespeare was repaid; Sir Walter Scott translated *Götz von Berlichingen* in 1798, and it is supposed to have suggested his *Waverly Novels*.

The first version of the play was called *Götz von Berlichen of the Iron Hand,* after a sixteenth century robber baron who had lost his hand in battle with the authorities of his day. Goethe worked hard with history to convert Götz into an honest malcontent, a true lover of freedom, disrespectful of laws yet loyal to the Emperor. The play shows Götz active in the Peasants' War (1516); besieged and promised freedom, then treacherously held; tried, and at the trial rescued by his friend Sickingen on his promise to keep the peace; and again leading the peasants, against Würzburg in 1525, when he is captured and killed.

The ending of Götz is not historical; he lived on until 1562. Some episodes grew out of a love story Goethe added to history—no doubt suggested in part by his own sense of guilt; he had just turned away from loving Friederike Brion, daughter of the pastor of Sesenheim near Strasbourg (the story is told in Goethe's autobiographical *Dichtung und Wahrheit, Poetry and Truth,* 1811). The play opens with Götz' capturing his former friend Weislingen, who had gone over to the side of the Bishop of Bamberg. Weislingen renews his friendship, and his pledge to marry Gotz' sister Maria; then, returning to Bamberg to arrange his affairs, Weislinger is lured by and marries the beautiful and unscrupulous Adelheid von Waldorf. Later, Weislingen holds Götz prisoner; at Maria's plea, he spares Götz—and is himself poisoned at his wife's command. Adelheid is then sentenced to death by the Secret Tribunal. Adelheid is an inhuman creature, compounded of villainy and beauty. In the 1773 version, Goethe cut her role ruthlessly, so much that some scenes had to be restored to make the role acceptable to the actress. Save for Adelheid, however, Goethe had his own life in mind, for he wrote to a friend, "Poor Friederike will be somewhat consoled to find the faithless lover poisoned."

Excessive as *Götz von Berlichingen* may be, in its youthful exuberance —Goethe later repudiated it as "a Gothic crime against the majesty of art"—the play has many virtues. It is picturesque, rich in the color of the period. Its presentation in Berlin, opening April 12, 1774, inaugurated a new tradition; instead of dressing, as thitherto, in the clothing of the contemporary French court, the actors wore authentic costumes of the time in which the play's action is set. The episodes are vivid and vigorous, especially the drives against the Swabian Bund and the Heilbronn Councillors. The humanism of the sixteenth century, and its early romantic aspects, are interspun with the romanticism and sentimentality of Goethe's own time.

Götz von Berlichingen remains a tremendous melodrama rather than a tragedy. The *Teutsche Mercur* (September 1773) hailed it as "the most beautiful, the most captivating monstrosity." A devotee of French literature, Emperor Frederick the Great, in his *On German Literature* (1780) called *Götz von Berlichingen* "a detestable imitation of the bad English plays." Won by its hero-picture, Napoleon, in his talk with Goethe in 1808, complimented Goethe as a dramatist. But the German scholar Hermann Hettner made the essential observation—"the end is sad, not tragic" —when he pointed out that Götz' death, the hero's fall, as developed in the play, depends too much upon the wickedness of the world, not on his own error, and arouses the personal concern and the pathos of melodrama, not the exaltation and the grandeur of tragedy.

Götz von Berlichingen has, nevertheless, not only a tumultuous power but a surging beauty. "There are indeed few poetical productions," said the literary historian Wustmann, "in which the quality of the language is so remarkable as in Goethe's *Götz von Berlichingen*. This peculiar charm, moreover, does not rest on any one feature specially prominent, but on a happy combination and blending of the most diverse elements."

When *Götz von Berlichingen* was presented in New York, January 15, 1908, the *New York Dramatic Mirror* (January 25) called it "a red-letter event in the history of the German drama in this country." In 1902 the play was fashioned as an opera with music by Carl Goldman. Historically, it was one of the most influential of all dramas. Intrinsically, it remains a tumultuous dramatic presentation of the conflict between individual liberty and the necessary progress of society toward order sustained by law.

FAUST   *Johann Wolfgang von Goethe*

The legend of Faust, a popular German folk tale supposedly based on the life of a real man who died about 1545, was first printed in the German *Volksbuch* of 1587. There was an English ballad on the subject in 1588; the great play by Christopher Marlowe* was written during the next year. During the Reformation, the legend was utilized for anti-Catholic propaganda, Faust being represented as a student of the Jesuits. Early versions of the story picture Faust as seeking material prizes: wealth, power, beautiful women; later, he is shown seeking more spiritual goals, until in Goethe his desire is equated with the highest, selfless quest of man.

Christopher Marlowe, in the opinion of the *London Times* (September 23, 1949), gave Faust "his true greatness when he divined the secret vitality of the story and made Faustus symbolize the human spirit's hunger for experience and power in the phase of the English Renaissance when that hunger was at its keenest. The symbol was too powerful to be confined even within the limits of a masterpiece. He found his way to the showman's booth and was immensely popular as a puppet. Swift saw him come off second-best to Punch. A gentleman walking in Smithfield in 1701 reports a performance at Bartholomew Fair of *The Devil and Dr. Faustus* [which is also the title of a motion picture shown in 1950]. It was as a wooden doll on wires that Goethe first saw the masterpiece upon which he was to labor intermittently throughout his creative life. Germany in the days of *Sturm und Drang* was as fascinated by the figure of Faust as Renaissance writers and showmen, and many *Fausts* were written while Goethe was at work. The creative spirit of the second coming of humanism found expression in the infinitely significant figure of the man who sought the same end."

The Faust legend captured the yearnings of the late Middle Ages, during which it arose. The goals of humanism, Faust achieves by the Devil's power: he hears blind Homer sing; he brings Alexander back to life; he weds immortal Helen. "That for which Faustus sold his soul", observed John Addington Symonds in *The Italian Renaissance,* "was yielded to the world without price at the time of the Renaissance."

In 1775 Goethe wrote his first, simple draft of the story, now known as the *Urfaust* (*Original Faust*).

In a play without firm dramatic structure—in quick, shifting scenes such as Goethe found in Elizabethan drama—but with some of the world's greatest poetry, Goethe gives his version of the Faust story. The First Part, completed in 1808, opens (like *The Book of Job**) with Mephistopheles in Heaven winning permission to tempt man. On earth, Faust agrees that the Devil may have his soul if the Devil gives him one hour so perfect that he would not have it pass. Chief of the seductions which Mephistopheles presents is the charming and innocent Margaret (Gretchen), whom Faust seduces; then, killing her brother who interferes, he leaves her to drown their child and to die.

The Second Part of *Faust* (completed in 1831, and so formless and complex that it is rarely acted) pictures Faust turning from the pleasures of the senses to the joys of the spirit, to a quest of aesthetic beauty and human worth. Helen of Troy is given to Faust. Their son, Euphorion, symbolizes at first the union of the classical and the romantic; then, more generally, the urge of mankind toward beauty. Both Euphorion and Helen, however, soar off into flaming air: beauty cannot be kept; ambition must hold its roots in earth. Faust then devotes himself to helping his fellow-men; he wears through years of service until finally, old and blind, he declares himself content. He has lost his wager, but he has found his way: and his soul is transported to Heaven.

Though the First Part is still frequently performed in Germany, *Faust* has undergone many transformations. The Hungarian Nicholas Lenau (N. N. von Strehlenau) rewrote *Faust* as an epic drama in 1835. Michel Carré made a French version, *Faust and Marguerite*, in 1850, which follows Goethe's Part One rather closely, but stresses the lighter moments of the play. The opera of Charles François Gounod (his first success), 1859, is based on Carré's version. London had earlier seen two forms of Part One. A version by George Soame, 1825 and 1827, was written in the style of the early nineteeneth century romantic drama, a mixture of song and dialogue, of Marlowe and Goethe and *Don Giovanni*, with Faust stung by a serpent in the final scene. Then came "the comic *Faust*", a version by Lema Rede, 1849, set in contemporary London, with the Devil played as a buffoon. In 1863, and for some years after, London saw an English adaptation of Carré's French version of the German play. Of this adaptation, The *Spirit of the Times* (January 3, 1863), reviewing a Niblo's Garden production in New York, said: "The text bears no resemblance to that of Goethe's *Faust*. And it is well that it does not, for any attempt to put the original on the stage would be almost as absurd as an attempt to play *Paradise Lost* . . . Mephistopheles is . . . a limping, vulgar, noisy fellow, grinning like a monkey at every word or movement, and outraging all the proprieties of time and place with his loud ejaculations and perpetual boisterousness."

In Gounod's version, Faust is transported to hell; but in the opera of the Italian Arrigo Boito, *Mefistofele*, 1868, he is saved. Faust goes to hell again in *The Damnation of Faust* by the Frenchman Louis Hector Berlioz, which was presented as a dramatic cantata in 1846 and first played as an opera in 1880.

Notable among later *Faust* productions was, first, that of Henry Irving in a version by W. G. Wills played continually in London and New York from 1886 to 1896. Irving's performance as Mephistopheles was generally condemned, but Ellen Terry as Margaret won high praise. The production was highly praised by the *New York Dramatic Mirror* (November 12,

1887) and Clement Scott in the *Illustrated London News* (May 5, 1894).

Perhaps the best English acting version of Part One is that of Stephen Phillips, based on Bayard Taylor's translation of *Faust,* which Beerbohm Tree presented in 1908. Clayton Hamilton felt that "it compresses into comparatively few scenes the unrestraind sweep of Goethe's epical inventiveness . . . and reduces his main ideas to the simplicity demanded by a theatre-going public that yawns while it asks to be amused." Walter Pritchard Eaton, however, thought it a rather tawdry device to have the witch (drawing from Goethe's Part Two and Phillip's imagination) show Faust visions of Helen, of Cleopatra, and of Messalina. But Eaton conceded that there is a masterly touch in the witch's showing Faust the image of Margaret in prison, her dead baby at her feet. The sight wakes all the decency in Faust and Mephistopheles is foiled. "This is an idea", said Eaton, "quite in accord with Goethe's poem, and perhaps the best contribution of the new drama."

Of the original German work, James Huneker stated that "Goethe is not bound by the Faust legend; it is merely a springboard for his fantasy and wisdom." In weighing a performance of the play at Frankfurt, the *London Times* (August 15, 1939) declared: "Of the main themes, the lesser is the problem of the co-existence of good and evil; the greater, that of the insufficiency of man, who can aspire, god-like, to all understanding and all riches of existence and yet remain, when all is had, empty and unsatisfied."

Goethe's main idea was to picture human helpfulness as redeeming the soul; whereas Marlowe's was to picture a man who has gained the whole world at the cost of his soul. The frequent performance of Goethe's Part One without Part Two, however, has led many to consider the Gretchen episode as the main story. Thus Charles Lamb, in a letter to Harrison Ainsworth in 1823, before Part Two was written, declared: " 'Tis a disagreeable, canting tale of seduction, which has nothing to do with the spirit of Faust." In Part One, Goethe probes depths of human pathos; in Part Two, he soars to heights of human majesty.

When the Henry Irving version of *Faust* was revived (January 3, 1927) with Gene Lockhart as Mephisto, the *New York Times* reported that it "turns a poem into a melodramatic costume tragedy, but there is something living in the play that histrionics cannot thwart." The next year (October 8, 1928), the Theatre Guild in New York presented a version by Graham and Tristan Rawson, with Dudley Digges (Mephisto), George Gaul (Faust), Helen Chandler (Margaret), Gale Sondergaard (the Witch), and Helen Westley (Martha). Later productions include one at Chapel Hill in 1932; one at Los Angeles, 1938, directed by Max Reinhardt, who in the same year produced a motion picture version with Walter Huston as Mephistopheles, Conrad Nagle as Faust, Margo as Margaret, and Lenore Ulric as Martha; and one by Equity Library in New York in 1946. Altogether, there have been over forty English versions of Goethe's play.

London saw *Faust* in German in 1852, 1853, 1901, and 1930; a performance by the Münchener marionettes in 1931, and the *Urfaust* in the centennial year of 1932. New York has also seen quite a number of German productions of Part One; recently, at the Barbizon Plaza, one opening November 28, 1947, with the eighty-year-old Albert Bassermann as Mephistopheles and Uta Hagen as Margaret. The year 1949, bicentennial of Goethe's birth, saw further revivals of *Faust.*

The symbolism of Helen, in Part Two of *Faust,* has been deeply explored. In *The Classical Tradition* (1949), Gilbert Highet discusses various ways in which her impact on Faust may be interpreted.

In his recent book *The Fortunes of Faust* (1952), E. M. Butler refers to more than fifty translations of Goethe's play into English and almost as many retellings of the legend after him. Among the latter are fragments by Shelley, a serious play (*Gretchen*) by W. S. Gilbert*, Valery's *Mon Faust,* Thomas Mann's novel, *Doktor Faust* (1947), and Dorothy Sayers' *The Devil to Pay* (1945).

Faust, Eugene O'Neill has said, is "the one classic drama which is closest to the American mind of today." Though its turbulence and its tumultuous organization keep it from frequent full revival, *Faust* is certainly one of the world's greatest poetic dramas. Its story, being a legend, is timeless in that it can be interpreted anew to fit the fashions and the urges of every time; its theme is timeless and universal, being not merely man's questioning and heartbreak over good and evil in the world, but the quenchless thirst of humanity for meaning, for value, for direction on this dark journey we call life.

THE INSPECTOR-GENERAL   *Nikolai Gogol*

Revizor (*The Inspector-General*), by Nikolai Vassilievitch Gogol (1809-1852) is the greatest Russian comedy. Its idea was suggested to Gogol by the poet Pushkin, perhaps from an actual happening. Gogol had already abandoned an unfinished play about an intriguing government official because he knew it could not pass the censor. But *The Inspector-General* was taken by the playwright Vassili Zhukovski to the Czar, who was so amused by it that he ordered it performed. Its devastating satire of corrupt petty officialdom has been played ever since throughout Russia, throughout the world.

The Inspector-General displays a small town whose officials hear that the Inspector General is on a tour of inspection. The town hospital is filthy; the judge raises geese in the court room; the school superintendent draws his staff from the asylum; local accounts are in an incredible state. Dressed in the latest fashion, a nobody with haughty airs arrives from St. Petersburg. He is wined and dined, offered the Superintendent's best suits, the mayor's daughter, everybody's purse. When he leaves, by intercepting a letter they guess to be the secret report of the inspector, the town officials learn that they have been imposed upon. As they are gathering fury, hurling blame upon one another, a soldier announces that the Inspector General has arrived.

The Inspector-General was played in Moscow and in St. Petersburg in 1836. New York saw it in Yiddish, with Maurice Schwartz, for sixteen weeks in 1923; then Schwartz played it in English, opening April 30, 1923. It was revived December 23, 1930, with Romney Brent, Dorothy Gish, Eugene Powers, and J. Edward Bromberg. The Moscow Art Theatre presented the play in New York, in Russian, February 17, 1935. It was played there again in Russian in 1949. In English there was a New York production by Equity Library in 1947. A film based on the comedy, with Danny Kaye in a setting moved to Middle Europe, was released in 1949.

In some Russian provincial theatres, the producers were afraid to stage *The Inspector-General* in the 1830's and 1840's. In Rostov-on-Don, when at the end of the play the "real" Inspector General Skvosnik-Dmykhanovsky shouts "I'll send you all to Siberia!", Governor Zaguro-Zolorovsky jumped onto the stage and shouted, "You are insulting the authorities! I'll send you all to Siberia!!" He ordered the cast arrested; when shown the *exprimatur* of the St. Petersburg censor, he stomped out of the theatre.

When *The Inspector-General* was first shown in New York, only a few reviewers recognized its value. The *Call* (October 10, 1922) called it "a vivid human document, one of the famous comedies of all literature . . . Historically and socially, *The Inspector-General* has a value quite apart from its dramatic significance." Later performances were more widely hailed. In 1935, the *American* (February 18) said: "It is a living, universal farce, a great farce forever funny." Robert Garland called it "a political prank, a hilariously funny slapstick satire." More solemnly, of the centenary Leningrad production, B. M. Shushkevich, the director, declared in the *Moscow Daily News* (June 24, 1936): "I wanted to transmit the social force of laughter."

In 1929 a highly stylized production was given by Vsevolod Emilievich Meyerhold in Paris—the production for which the great Russian director Meyerhold is best known. This production romped about so freely that at length Balieff (the famous director of the Chauvre-Souris) rose in the audience and cried "Give us Gogol!"

In hilarious satire, with a clean integrity of malice, Gogol has pilloried for all time the petty, ignorant, grafting, rascally official, caught in one of the world's greatest comedies.

THE SERVANT OF TWO MASTERS   *Carlo Goldoni*

Although without the dramatic vitality of his later work *The Mistress of the Inn**, *The Servant of Two Masters* by Carlo Goldoni (Italian, 1707-1793) retains a considerable measure of liveliness and power. Written in 1740, it is still played in Italy. It was revived in German by Reinhardt in Vienna (1923), in Berlin (1924), and in New York, with Lili Darvas, Hermann and Hans Thimig, and Vladimir Sokoloff, January 9, 1928. Cambridge saw the play in English on June 8, 1935—the first time that a Cambridge Dramatic Club production used women—and it was revived there again in 1936, when Yale University also produced the play. The Barter Theatre played it in 1941; the New York Dramatic Workshop in 1954.

The Servant of Two Masters is built upon an intrigue involving two pairs of frustrated lovers. It is a comedy, somewhat after the Roman style, of confusions and mistakes, further complicated by the fact that Florindo, who loves Beatrice, meets Beatrice disguised as a man and deems her a rival. Most of the play's fun revolves upon the always hungry Truffaldino, who acts as servant both to Florindo and to the disguised Beatrice. He persuades both masters to order him a dinner, but his double-stuffing ends (with the play) when Beatrice's identity is revealed, and she weds Florindo.

The high point of the play is Truffaldino's final enjoyment of his meal, "an orgy among the edibles," said the *New York Post* (January 10, 1928), "giving the stage the general appearance of a delicatessen store wrecked by a tornado."

In *The Servant of Two Masters*, Goldoni had not yet broken away from the established patterns of comedy; especially, the use of stock figures. The triteness of such figures was especially noted by the *London Times*, June 10, 1935, but a later review (October 23, 1936) conceded "they are nevertheless a lively lot . . . the intricate pattern they weave with their borrowed intrigues makes a charming effect." Considerable slapstick enlivens current productions, but *The Servant of Two Masters* is sustained by Goldoni's good nature, gay spirits, and amused capture of the foibles of folk familiar to us all.

THE MISTRESS OF THE INN   *Carlo Goldoni*

In French and in Italian, Goldoni wrote well over 200 plays; by far the most famous of these is *La Locandiera* (*The Mistress of the Inn*, also known as *Mine Hostess* and *Mirandolina*).

La Locandiera was first presented in Venice, December 26, 1751. It is still very popular in Italy. Duse played in it in Paris, London, and, in 1893, New York. Stanislavski presented it in Moscow, December 2, 1898, and in New York, 1923. In English, *The Mistress of the Inn* was shown in Los Angeles in 1935, in New York by Eva Le Gallienne, 1926 on. As *Mine Hostess,* in adaptation by Clifford Bax, London saw it August 17, 1944. Equity Library, New York, produced it in 1947; the Hedgerow Theatre in 1948. In 1936, presented by the "First Collective Farm Arts Theatre" in a Moscow competition, it won first prize.

Robert Browning has said that "Goldoni, good, gay, sunniest of souls", reflects in his plays "the shade and shine of common life." These qualities, together with the pleasures and profits of innkeeping, are delightfully presented in *The Mistress of the Inn*, the story of the merry and independent Mirandolina, who is wooed, mainly for her wealth, by the niggardly old Marquis of Forlipopoli, and the eccentric Count of Albaforita. Mirandola, however, sets her cap for the woman-hating Cavalier, the Black Knight of Ripafratta. By flattery and good food she wins the Cavalier, then tumbles him aside for her head-waiter, Fabrizio. For she knows that the best way to secure her freedom is within the walls of matrimony.

A good deal of the play's fun is supplied by two actresses, Ortensia and Djaneira (omitted in the Duse version), who come to the inn; they pretend to be ladies of quality but on the slightest provocation behave like ladies of the evening. Mirandolina sees through their pretensions, and provides scope for their whole-hearted, lusty vulgarity. While all this fun, combined with kindly satire, keeps the action lively, the provident Mirandolina takes care to stuff not only her guests but the money-box of the inn.

"Papa Goldoni", as the Italians call him—father of the friendly comedy of manners, original in its mood though in its manner based on Moliere*—continues to be popular.

Of Eva Le Gallienne's production of the play, *Variety* (December 1, 1926) observed that it was "an amusing satire, in style quaint now and fan-like; but the essence of its characterizations is still of a piece with the quirks of human nature." In London, Harold Hobson said in the *Observer* (August 20, 1944): "This is a classic alternative to some modern methods of making antic hay."

Goldoni's conception of character was dynamic; he saw men as the instruments with which their own will could fashion a personality. The conception gives vigor to his figures and vitality to their movements. As Francesco de Sanctis points out in his *History of Italian Literature* (1931), "Goldoni has a marvelous gift for finding situations in which the character can be developed to the full . . . The author proceeds on his way swiftly and directly, without stopping to meditate or look into his soul, or to plumb the depths; but stays on the surface, content and joyous." This surface joy, rising from characters tinged with gentle satire and seen with sharp but amused eye, radiates from *The Mistress of the Inn.*

SHE STOOPS TO CONQUER   *Oliver Goldsmith*

Oliver Goldsmith (Irish, 1730-1774) seems to have been a blunderer as a man. After rejection for ordination and failure to earn a living as a physician, he took to literature. *She Stoops to Conquer* is based on an awkward situation from his own life.

At first the play had trouble in reaching the stage. Samuel Johnson, Goldsmith's friend, pressed it through to production at Covent Garden, where it opened, May 15, 1773. Although a claque almost spoiled the play's effect by over-applause, it was a hit. King George III enjoyed it; and it ran for 13 performances to the end of the season. Revivals were produced almost every year until the end of the nineteenth century. Four editions of the play were printed in its first year. The title was suggested by Dryden; Goldsmith's original name for the play, *The Mistakes of a Night*, was kept as subtitle. At first, since the play did not employ the high-flown, over-colored speech then in vogue, actresses disdained the parts; but soon they were quarreling for roles, and Goldsmith wrote several Epilogues to satisfy the temperamental ladies. Garrick, sorry he had not taken the play for Drury Lane, wrote a Prologue.

Controversy over the play reached beyond the theatre. Johnson declared that no comedy in years had "answered so much the great end of comedy—making an audience merry;" but Horace Walpole demurred: "It is not the subject I condemn, though very vulgar; but the execution. The drift tends to no moral, to no edification of any kind . . . It is set up in opposition to sentimental comedy, and is as bad as the worst of them." In the *London Packet,* "Tom Tickle" attacked the play; considering the attack a personal one, Goldsmith thrashed the publisher and was fined £50 for his pleasure.

The story of *She Stoops to Conquer* springs from a misunderstanding. Young Marlow, "one of the most bashful and reserved young fellows in all the world," with his friend Hastings goes to visit the Hardcastles, a match having been proposed between him and Kate Hardcastle. At night, Tony Lumpkin, Hardcastle's step-son, directs the two young men to an "inn," which is really the Hardcastle home; and Marlow treats Hardcastle bluffly, as the landlord, while he makes bold advances to Kate Hardcastle. Recognizing his misunderstanding, Kate "stoops" to the role of servant, so that Marlow may not be shy. The comedy rises mainly from the misunderstanding, but several of the characters are in themselves truly comic creations.

She Stoops to Conquer has been almost as popular in America as in England, being revived in Boston, for example, in 1870, 1871, 1874, 1875, 1876, and 1877. In New York a musical version by Stanislaus Stange,

The Two Roses, was presented, opening November 21, 1904, with Roland Cunningham and Fritzi Scheff.

Many stars have performed in *She Stoops to Conquer*. Among them are Charles Kemble, Mrs. Langtry, Fanny Davenport, Rose Coghlan, Annie Russell, Julia Marlowe, Mary Shaw, Sidney Drew, Robert Mantell, and Cyril Maude. In New York, there was an all-star revival in 1905; another, the Players' Annual, in 1924, with Basil Sydney (Marlow), Dudley Digges (Squire Hardcastle), Ernest Glendenning (Tony Lumpkin), Elsie Ferguson (Kate Hardcastle), Helen Hayes, Pauline Lord, and Selena Royle; and still another in 1928, with Wilfrid Seagram (Marlow), Lyn Harding (Squire Hardcastle), Glenn Hunter (Tony), Fay Bainter (Kate), and Patricia Collinge, with Pauline Lord delivering the Prologue. The first performance of the play in the United States was at the New York John Street Theatre on August 2, 1773. More recent ones have come in 1933, 1934, 1936, 1937, 1938, 1940, and 1942. In 1949 it was played at the Old Vic in London with Michael Redgrave.

Of the 1924 revival, the *New York World* (June 10) declared: "This piece, which has made snobs of high school sophomores the land over and supplied safe fuel for languishing stocks, seemed in its glory." In 1928, Alexander Woollcott called the play "a singularly durable comedy"; Brooks Atkinson said it is "shot through with the homely simplicities of a pastoral jollification"; Allardyce Nicoll has pointed out that the play does not, like its predecessors, deal in pointed wit, but warms with an all-pervading humor. There is a basic love of mankind throughout; even the satiric strokes are friendly.

Revived as the first of the City Center series in New York, December 28, 1949, with Maurice Evans presenting a new prologue, and Celeste Holm, Ezra Stone, Carmen Matthews, and Burl Ives in the cast, *She Stoops to Conquer* again found the critics delighted. Atkinson singled out Tony Lumpkin as "one of the most objectionable brats in dramatic literature;" but noted that the play as a whole is stamped by "the good-hearted simplicity of Goldsmith's lovable genius."

Horace Walpole complained that *She Stoops to Conquer* "tends to no moral"; and, indeed, it presses no ethical point. But the play is so abounding in good humor, in gay and gentle and good spirits, that not only its fun but its fresh wholesomeness is infectious: it does not preach morals, it makes one better for the beholding. *She Stoops to Conquer* is the roast-beef-and-pudding, the ale-and-fare-well spirit of England, at its laughing heartiest.

CAPONSACCHI   *Arthur Goodrich*

This vivid play was drawn roundabout from the story of Count Guido Franceschini, beheaded in Rome for murder, February 22, 1698. Pope Innocent XII interested himself in the case. The story is told in an old volume that the poet Robert Browning picked up in Florence; from it he wove his poem *The Ring and the Book,* which presents the story from various points of view. The actor Walter Hampden received a letter from a stranger, Rose A. Palmer, suggesting that Giuseppe Caponsacchi in Browning's poem would be an excellent role. Hampden passed the thought along to his brother-in-law, Arthur Frederick Goodrich (American, 1878-1941), who with Miss Palmer wrote the play. Browning's poem gives most attention to the count Guido; writing for Hampden, Goodrich centers attention on the canon Caponsacchi.

In the play, Caponsacchi is a romantic young monk, who tries to rescue Pompilia from her husband Count Guido Franceschini, who is slowly torturing her in order to extort her family's wealth. Sensing the monk's love of Pompilia, Franceschini tries to catch the two together. Caponsacchi escorts Pompilia to Rome, then leaves her; when ruffians murder Pompilia and her parents, both the Count and Caponsacchi are put on trial.

The play opens in the court of justice in the Vatican, before the trial. The Pope conceals himself behind a curtain as the trial begins and by flash-backs presents the story. At the end, the Pope, recognizing that the judges will bow to the popular fury, steps out and delivers judgment, exonerating Caponsacchi and leaving Franceschini to the executioner.

The play was first presented in Indianapolis in 1923 as *The Ring of Truth*. Revised and entitled *Caponsacchi*, it came to New York October 26, 1926, for 269 performances. Walter Hampden kept it in his repertory for many years. In 1931 Goodrich used the story as the book of an opera, at first called *Tragedy in Arezzo*, then *Caponsacchi*, with music by Richard Hageman. The opera had its premiere February 18, 1932, at Freiburg, Germany; and was performed in Vienna, 1935; at the New York Metropolitan Opera House, February 4, 1937, with Lawrence Tibbett (Guido) and Helen Jepson. The opera was not favorably received.

The play *Caponsacchi*, however, moves with sensitive handling of the strong emotions involved, and swift, terse dialogue. Some hundred lines from Browning's poem are so neatly fitted into the text that it is hard to single them out. Indeed, said Clayton Hamilton in the *New York Times* (February 13, 1927), Goodrich "so steeped himself in the spirit and the atmosphere of Browning that he has enabled himself to make the play of *Caponsacchi* with the full connivance and approval of the poet." "It is a robust play," said the *New York Sun* (October 27, 1926), "with a story that is a story, and no tendency to suggest what can just as well be told . . . It is curiously alive. It is illusion builded out of granite. It proves once more that vitality is not a modern discovery, and that brave hearts and flashing swords have not lost their power strangely to move."

Suggested beyond the events of the play are the gay licentiousness of those Italian times, the corrupt politics and the intrigue of noble and churchman, which give color to Guido's false charges against his wife and the monk.

Caponsacchi is an unusual figure, a churchman whose romanticism is well cloaked by his priestly garb and who guides his beloved with all innocence, in simple love and dignity and quiet heroism. His character gives to the drama the true glamour of the romantic play. *Caponsacchi* is an intense and sensitive costume melodrama of innocent beauty wronged and villainy punished.

GOD, MAN, AND DEVIL   *Jacob Gordin*

The Yiddish drama as an art form was substantially advanced in the United States by Jacob Gordin (1853-1909), who migrated from the Ukraine in 1897 and in the same year created a sensation with his play *Siberia*. His best play, a variation on the theme of Goethe's *Faust**, is *God, Man and Devil* (1900).

Like Goethe's play, *God, Man, and Devil* has a Prologue in Heaven, where the disputatious, mocking Devil argues with audacious sarcasm; yet the Lord (heard as a Voice from the wings) deigns to wager that Satan cannot win a pious soul. The Devil brings riches to the poor Jewish scribe Herschele, of the town of Dubrovna, and leads him along the paths of temptation. Herschele deserts his wife, Pesse, for a younger woman. He opens a prayer-shawl factory, in which he exploits his neighbors, until Mottel, son of his best friend, is killed at the loom. Awakening to a sense of his sinfulness, Herschele then knows only one way to free himself from the evil influence, and he commits suicide.

The New York premiere of the play was December 10, 1903, with Bertha Kalich. It has remained popular in Yiddish repertory. New York saw it most effectively performed by Maurice Schwartz, Celia Adler, and Miriam Elias in December 1928. Schwartz presented it in London, August 19, 1935. Schwartz played the role of Uriel Masik, the Devil, the peddler of lottery tickets who sells to Herschele on credit.

The *London Times* (August 20, 1935) felt that *God, Man, and Devil* was pretentious, "unduly strained, in an attempt to impose a spiritual significance upon material that is, in essence, no more than melodramatic and spectacular." Its judgment, however, overlooked the long tradition of such plays, not only through Goethe's more majestic treatment, but in Yiddish and other folk theatre; the essential element in the play is as old as the fall of man. The play was more receptively welcomed in New York, where John Anderson (December 22, 1928) called it a "sumptuous allegory", and the *Telegram*, "a serious-minded and meaningful play . . . decidedly worth while."

There is good drama in the contrast of Herschele's two homes: the first is squalid but clean, and cold, with everyone trying desperately (and amusingly) to keep warm; the second is rich but gaudy, with bad taste and vulgar display. And there is excellent drama in the spiritual change within Herschele: at first the simple, poor, but pious and pity-full man; then the rich niggard, scheming to grind his former friends into roubles. When Herschele rediscovers his values, it is with the prayer-shawl stained with Mottel's blood that he hangs himself. The language of the play is simple and realistic throughout.

The prologue of *God, Man, and Devil* ends with a chorus of Angels, chanting the Jewish trinity: "Truth is eternal, eternal and one; The good and the beautiful are the truth." In its Yiddish setting and tongue, *God, Man, and Devil* dramatically reasserts the eternal and ultimate power of the man who nestles this credence in his soul.

THE LOWER DEPTHS   *Maxim Gorki*

Alexei Maximovich Pyeshkov (Russian, 1866-1936), left to fend for himself at the age of nine, drifted through Russia, grubbing at many jobs, was imprisoned as a revolutionary, and wrote some short stories under the name of Maxim Gorki (Maxim the Bitter). In 1900, several years after he organized a peasants' theatre in the Ukraine, he was in-vited to Chekhov's villa at Yalta, where the Moscow Art Theatre under Stanislavski was rehearsing. Shortly thereafter he wrote two plays, with Stanislavski's encouragement.

The first of the two, *The Petty Bourgeois* (also called *The Middle*

Class and *The Smug Citizen*) was weakened by censorship, but still aroused a storm when it opened the new Moscow Art Theatre on October 25, 1902. On December 31 of the same year, *The Lower Depths* was presented. It had been censored in advance (over 50 passages were deleted), but the play achieved the greatest triumph in the history of the Moscow Art Theatre. It was revived, on Gorki's return to Moscow in 1928, after the Revolution, with the full text and almost the whole original cast. On its thirtieth anniversary, the author's birthplace, Nizhni-Novgorod, was renamed Gorki, and the theatre was rechristened "The Moscow Art Theatre in the name of Gorki". In the meantime, the play was produced in London in 1903 and 1911; in Berlin (as *Nachtasyl*) for 500 performances in 1908. In New York it was presented by Arthur Hopkins as *Night Lodging* in 1919; the Moscow Art offered it in Russian in 1923; it was revived as *At the Bottom* in 1930, as *The Lower Depths* in 1943 and at the City College in 1947; an all-Negro version, *A Long Way From Home*, was produced by the Experimental Theatre of ANTA, opening February 9, 1948. Other American performances include one in Cleveland, 1933; Dallas, 1934; Hollywood, 1935.

Following the Stanislavski method, of living oneself into the character, the Moscow Art players prepared for the premiere of *The Lower Depths* by visiting the slums and meeting such detritus of the human race as slumps through Gorki's drama. Derelict thief, convict, run-down gentleman, one-time actor ruined by alcohol, receiver of stolen goods, philosophic ragged greybeard, whiner, aging prostitute, and profiteer seek anodynes or wait for death in this dreary drama. Into the midst of the wastrels comes the optimist Luka, who tells them that "no one is so low as to deserve the degradation of another human's pity." He converts them to hope, but during a murderous brawl, Luka simply goes off, and the derelicts drift back into hopelessness. The drunken ex-actor Satin, after telling them that weaklings need Luka's lies but the strong man can face the truth—breaking into a hopeful paean: "Man is higher than a full belly! Man is born to conceive a better man."—proceeds to hang himself. In the brawl, the proprietor of the cheap lodging-house, Kostylov, is killed; his sister-in-law in jealousy cries murder against his wife and the thief her lover, and they are taken to jail.

The events in *The Lower Depths* are of less importance than the portraits. These are devastatingly drawn, and have been superbly acted. In Russia, Ivan Moskvin played the wanderer, Luka; Mrs. Chekhov played Nastya, the prostitute. A superb cast—Gilda Varesi, Alan Dinehart, Pauline Lord, Edward G. Robinson, and E. J. Ballantine—starred in the New York production of 1919, but the critics had mixed reactions. The *New York World* (December 23) was impressed: "No pen has ever traced on paper a more stark, shocking, loathsome, and yet strangely fascinating story of the flotsam and jetsam, the scum and dregs of miserable, abandoned, and hopeless humanity. It is, perhaps, not a play at all, but a slow-moving graphic panorama of unrelieved woe. Nevertheless, truth is stamped indelibly upon it; it is the work of a master of dramatic realism." But the *New York Times* remarked thaat "the average playgoer would be bored to extinction." The *Herald* deemed it "remarkable in being one of the most idly and feebly constructed plays ever written by an important author . . . a triumph of the dismal and the dirty may be of literary value, but for drama he has neither impressiveness nor coquetry. . . . As the play goes on you begin to look eagerly, even impatiently, for the doing in of a lot of the characters, but in spite of many spats—the word being employed in its most literal salivatory sense—there were comparatively few fatal atrocities . . . This is the mire out of which Bolshevism grew, and Gorki was one of the workers who spattered the mud into parlors."

When the Moscow Art brought its Russian production to New York, January 15, 1923, the critics, judging by the acting only, thought the play a sardonic comedy. Arthur Pollock said the production resembled the earlier ones "as a clown an undertaker." Only the *Times* (January 16, 1923) was bold enough to admit that, despite having read and seen the play several times, "two acts had passed before we could tell which was Mr. Katchaloff as the degenerated Baron, and which Mr. Alexandroff as the drunken actor." In this play of character revelation, the language barrier proved insurmountable.

In 1930, however, Leo Bulgakov (who had made his debut in *The Lower Depths,* in Moscow, 1911, and stayed in the United States after the Moscow Art visit in 1923) directed the play in English, with a cast that incuded John Wexley, E. J. Ballantine, Walter Abel, and Edgar Stehli. The translation into modern slang was ludicrously inept, but the production was vibrant and deep-toned.

The Negro version, *A Long Way From Home,* with Mildred Smith, Josh White, Fredi Washington, and Edna Mae Harris, was an almost line by line transportation of *The Lower Depths* into a slum flop-house in Durham, North Carolina. Celine, losing her lover Joebuck to her younger sister Marcy, goads her landlord husband into torturing the girl— with the same murderous consequences as in the Russian original. The setting, with the consumptive dying in the filthy room below, the cluttered yard outside, the mounting steps to the poolroom above, effectively evoked the drab atmosphere of the drama.

Gorki called the Russian Revolution "the sunniest and greatest of all Revolutions." Certainly there is no sun in the wretched world he pictures in *The Lower Depths,* the forerunner of that Revolution, which embodies what Gorki himself called "the terrific force of the theatre."

THE LOVE FOR THREE ORANGES   *Carlo Gozzi*

In mid-eighteenth century Italy, two playwrights were rivals for popular favor. Pietro Chiari (1711-1785) won tremendous success with now forgotten dramas combining monstrous events and impossible characters. Almost equally successful was Carlo Goldoni*, whose plays proved more enduring as they were based upon the new belief in the human will as the director of human destiny. While these two dramatists were vying for popular favor, Carlo Gozzi (1720-1806) turned from reality back to the marvelous with the use of old stock favorites from the comedy of masks, the commedia dell' arte that the people loved. Gozzi drove Goldoni into France, and Chiari into oblivion. From France, the more realistic comedy of manners returned to wreak revenge upon Gozzi. But in the meantime Gozzi's type of play— the *fiaba*: romantic fable— had its golden hour.

The Love For Three Oranges, 1761, one of the most delightful of Gozzi's *fiabe,* survives outside of Italy in the opera of Prokofieff, which had its world premiere in Chicago, December 30, 1921. A prologue presents the Glooms, who call for a tragedy; the Joys, who ask for a comedy; the Empty Heads, who clamor for a farce; and the Cynics, who hush the hubbub so that there may be anything at all. Then the story begins, combining several fairy tales. The three Oranges are three princesses, in the spell of the wicked enchantress Fata Morgana. The Prince Tartaglia, who would free them, is ill; the only cure is for him to laugh; but nothing can make him, until a foolish antic of Fata Morgana herself sets the Prince guffawing. Fata Morgana then lays upon him the task of finding the "oranges," and joining with one in mutual love. The friendly devil Farfarello works his bellows to speed the Prince along. The fat cook who guards the oranges is beguiled by some magic ribbons, while the Prince rescues the fair maidens thus imprisoned. Two of the Princesses die of thirst in the desert; but after Fata Morgana and the other forces of evil are outwitted, the third Princess and the Prince are united in love, and live happily ever after.

The opera, performed in New York at the City Center in 1950, bears traces of Gozzi's commedia dell' arte liveliness, especially in the masks and the antics of the cook and the jolly devil.

The play is a combination of fairy tale and caricature. With Prokofieff's music, said Virgil Thomson in the *New York Herald-Tribune* (November 2, 1949), it is "a kind of masterpiece, richly imagined, fresh, animated, and ever so skillfully composed. It is full of atmosphere and wonder and kidding." The spell of the music may be modernistic, yet the merry mood of Gozzi's play sparkles with the artificial but ever charming appeal of the timeless fairy tale.

TURANDOT   *Carlo Gozzi*

The most charming and the most popular of Gozzi's *fiabe* (romantic tales) is *Turandot, Princess of China*, 1762. In this great success of its day, Gozzi made his happiest combination of the two elements that characterize his dramas: old legended folk story and the rollicking improvisations of the commedia dell' arte.

The story of Princess Turandot came to Gozzi from China by way of Persia. The proud Princess, of beauty and intelligence unparalleled, will give her hand only to the man that solves three riddles; those that try and fail must die. As the play opens, the Prince of Persia, twelfth to fail, is being led to his death. The Prince of Astrahkan, in humble disguise as Calaf, enters the contest, and gives the right answers (Hope, Blood, Turandot). Seeing the Princess still loath to marry, Calaf says that if, on the morrow, she can answer his question, he will end his life. The question is: "Who is that King's son, and of what stock is he, who was a beggar, porter, menial, yet in good fortune more unfortunate?" Princess Turandot surmises that Calaf means himself, and she spends the night trying to discover his real name. Unwittingly Calaf reveals his identity. Princess Turandot announces it the next day—then stops his dagger: "You shall live for me."

Mixed with the romantic charm of the olden story is a great deal of horseplay. Tartaglia, the High Chancellor; Pantalone, the Prime Minister; Brighella, the Captain of the Court Pages; Truffaldino, the physician— all these, in name and nature, are added to the story from the commedia dell' arte. Their general line of action is indicated; but Gozzi supplied no dialogue for them; their words and their antics were improvised at each performance. Presented at first with grotesque masks, but always with gorgeous costumes, *Turandot* is a lively spectacle as well as an entertaining drama.

The late eighteenth century Germans found in *Turandot* a welcome relief from the formal French classical theatre. Schiller translated the play for production at Weimar; Goethe fell under its influence. More recently, *Turandot* was given an elaborate production, in a new adaptation by Karl Vollmoeller, by Reinhardt, in 1911; in an English version by Jethro Bithell in London in 1913. In Russian, *Turandot* was the last and greatest production, 1922, of Eugene Vakhtangov; an English adaptation of this version came to New York in 1926. In all of these productions, the element of spectacle was emphasized, adding the pleasures of the eye to the other gifts of the drama.

Turandot, and indeed all of Gozzi's dramas, John Addington Symonds has pointed out, are superb material for operatic libretti. With *The Love For Three Oranges* and *Turandot*, Symond's words proved prophecy. *Turandot* became an opera in 1924, the book by Giuseppe Abrami and Renato Simoni and the music by Giacomo Puccini (Italian, 1858-1924), the last duet and the finale completed by F. Alfano after Puccini died. The opera makes several changes in Gozzi's story. Calaf's father, the dethroned Tartar King Timur, is in the opera instead of his old tutor, Barak, as in the play; Timur is seized and is to be tortured to tell the Prince's name, when Liu, Timur's slave girl who loves Calaf, cries that she is the only one that knows his name and stabs herself. Conquered by Turandot's beauty, Calaf embraces her; she warms to his ardor and at dawn he whispers her his name. The next day, before the Emperor and all his court, Turandot announces: "His name is—Love!" and falls into the Prince's eager arms. In the opera, the Emperor's counsellors are named Ping, Pang, and Pong; but there is more humor in the pranks of Gozzi's figures. To Gozzi's story Ferruccio Busoni also wrote music, employing Chinese scales and other exotic devices, that was first played in Rome, April, 1940. The mingling of spectacle, fantasy, and fun in *Turandot* makes it a gay and lovely entertainment for the romantic youthfulness in us all.

THE MADRAS HOUSE   *Harley Granville-Barker*

Harley Granville-Barker (English, 1877-1946) was a force in the theatre that extended far beyond the influence of his plays. As an actor, he played Jack Tanner in the first production of Shaw's *Man and Superman**. As a director and producer, he managed the London Court Theatre, where he introduced simpler productions, with considerable attention to effects of lighting.

The Madras House develops its story in what has been called the symphony style—its four acts being four movements around the lives of the Huxtable and Madras families, and the great women's emporium that they own. First we see the six frustrated, unmarried Huxtable girls, who vainly strive, through local charity or watercolor painting, to give some meaning to their empty lives. Then we behold the several hundred spinster employees of the Madras House, who, corralled by the "living-in system," are doomed to dried-up years—from which one of them has burst to unmarried motherhood. We see the mannequins, parading in seductive finery copied from Parisian cocottes. Finally, in Philip's wife,

Jessica, we see the attractive modern woman, whose beautiful flowering springs from the dead leaves of the workers in the store.

The author's fullest examination of the position of women is in the third act, when the partners meet to discuss an American millionaire's offer to buy the store. Among them is the head of the house, Charles Madras, called back from the Mohammedan land where he has been seeking refuge from woman's interference in politics, business and other parts of "man's domain."

Produced in London in 1910, *The Madras House* met but moderate welcome. It was played in 1921 at the New York Neighborhood Playhouse with Whitford Kane, Montague Rutherford, Albert Carroll, Eugene Powers, and Aline MacMahon. A program note by the author admitted that the external story of the play was somewhat dated, by the disappearance of the "living-in system"—which had never gained foothold in the United States—"by which the several hundred employees of a large department store are herded, men and women, in a mixture of barracks and boarding-school." Alexander Woollcott (October 31, 1921) found the play "alive and entertaining, a dramatization not of a human being but of a human problem. Its characters drift on and off its scene most casually, but the protagonist that marches through its four abundant acts is not a person. It is a question. How are the brains of the world to be cleared and the work of the world to be done, when that world is necessarily peopled with mutually exciting creatures and its energy so largely devoted to fomenting that excitability? . . . Variants of the woman question in a man-made world are provoked by every scene of *The Madras House*." The *London Times* (May 9, 1938), after a performance of Act I of *The Madras House*, called it "a pretty and malicious period piece . . . a recognizable but vanished past."

While the particular circumstances of women workers have changed, the basic attitudes and expectations remain. *The Madras House* continues to be a brilliant satire of the man that is a Turk at heart and the woman that is a siren at bottom.

IN ABRAHAM'S BOSOM   *Paul Green*

One of the starkest dramatic pictures of the Negro's lot in the southern United States and of his efforts to improve his station is *In Abraham's Bosom*, 1925, by Paul Green (American, b. 1884). Set in the turpentine country of North Carolina, the story shows, in seven stages of doomed struggle, the attempt of Abraham McCranie to rouse his people to a sense of dignity and a worthiness of freedom.

Son of the white Colonel McCranie, Abraham persuades his father to grant him a school. But when the Colonel dies, Abraham's white half-brother, Lonnie, is antagonistic. The Negroes—partly in submission to Lonnie's attitude, partly out of resentment of Abraham's imperious insistence (he whips an unruly student, for example, just as any of them might be whipped by a white man), and partly out of shiftlessness and lack of hope—drift away. The Whites check Abe's efforts to start another school. They disperse a meeting he has called. In a quarrel, Abe kills his half-brother; then stands at the door of his cabin as the white men come to shoot him down.

Douglas, Abe's shiftless son, thinks he knows the Negroes' place: "at de bottom, doin' de dirty work foh de white man, dat's it. An' he ain't

gwine stand foh us to be educated out'n it, nuther. He's gwine keep us
dere. It pays him to." But Douglas' father, standing in his doorway
awaiting death, repeats: "We got to be free . . . "

An earnest group with faith in Paul Green's drama presented it on
December 30, 1926, at the Provincetown Playhouse, New York City. The
production cost them about $1500; for a while the company received no
salaries. Good reviews kept *In Abraham's Bosom* running for 116 performances, and it reopened to packed houses when in the spring of 1927
it was awarded the Pulitzer Prize. It has since been quite frequently
played around the country.

There was at first some feeling that the play dragged a little, was too
slow or long. By November 29, 1927, however, the *Boston Transcript*
reported that much pruning had made its seven episodes "abrupt, instant, concentrated." The range of the drama, said the *New York Times*
(December 31, 1926) "runs all the way from the boisterous and infectious
gaiety of the race to the religious ecstasy and the madness of the hunted
and baffled creature of mixed blood who is the central tragic figure. But
they are all combined into a whole in which the bitterness that lies at
the core of things is kept free of any accusing animus as between black
and white." The *New York Herald-Tribune* (January 1, 1927) called
the play "a tragedy so charged with primitive emotion and the terrible
longing of the human spirit that the Provincetown's narrow walls could
scarce contain its fury."

The episodic development of *In Abraham's Bosom* has not been firmly
knit into a single drive. The dialogue has the ring of authentic folk
speech and the undertone of a sermon. Felix Sper in *From Native Roots*
(1948) maintained that "too many addresses and prayers maintained at
high pitch create a condition midway between Biblical exhortation and
political oratory." That very mood, however, helps make the play a
challenging dramatic picture of the downtrodden striving to rise to
dignity and freedom.

Paul Green has written some half-hundred one-act and longer plays
on themes rising out of the folk, their background, their loves, and
their aspirations. His most poetic and most powerful picture is *In
Abraham's Bosom*.

SPREADING THE NEWS   *Lady Augusta Gregory*

Lady Augusta Gregory (Irish, 1859-1932) was one of the three chief
figures and the most effective organizer among those that established the
Irish Literary Theatre in Dublin in 1899 and thus gave impetus to the
Irish drama. Of her various one-act plays, her satire. *Spreading The
News*, 1904, is the most popular. In the play, Bartley Fallon shuffles down
the road to Jack Smith's, carrying a pitchfork. Rumor runs ahead that
he intends assault. On the wings of gossip, battery breeds murder, and
on his return Bartley is arrested. Love of Jack's wife is suggested as his
motive, and Bartley's wife swears dire vengeance. Then the unsuspecting Jack Smith saunters in. It's clear he is a ghost; then—who can
believe Bartley was merely returning a borrowed tool?—Jack also is
arrested.

"There is nothing", said the *New York World-Telegram* (November 1,
1932) "more surely real . . . [it is] incisive and amusing satire." *Spread-*

ing the News remains a gem of humor, of sly satire, and of warm understanding of human nature in Ireland.

THE RISING OF THE MOON   *Lady Augusta Gregory*

This deft and charming one-act play, written in 1907, opens with a Police Sergeant on guard near a quay. Alarm is out for an escaped Fenian patriot. A ballad singer engages the Sergeant in conversation, which drifts toward the past. The Sergeant ponders the fate that made him a policeman instead of a patriot rebel; he joins the ballad singer in old patriotic songs. As the ballad singer chants, a boat approaches; and the Sergeant realizes that his companion is the escaped prisoner. Restraining himself, he lets the patriot go away; then, thinking of the £100 reward, he says, "I wonder if I'm as big a fool as I think I am!"

The Rising of the Moon was presented in New York, opening February 24, 1908, with W. G. Fay as the ballad singer and F. J. Fay as the Sergeant. The *New York Dramatic Mirror* (March 7, 1908) felt that "it might belong in any nation in which patriotism is divided." The Irish Players from Dublin's Abbey Theatre presented the play in New York, opening November 20, 1911, with Arthur Sinclair the singer and J. M. Kerrigan the Sergeant.

The Rising of the Moon has been enacted numberless times by amateur groups and little theatres. It was played in New York in 1928 at the Provincetown Playhouse; in 1932 and 1933 by the Abbey Theatre; in 1937 at the Y.M.H.A.; in 1938 by the Irish Repertory Players in a benefit performance.

One needs no Irish blood to enjoy the charm and nostalgia of this patriotic idyll. Nor has the success of the cause it proclaims, and from which its songs well, dimmed the murmurous effulgence of *The Rising of the Moon*.

WOE FROM WIT   *Alexander S. Griboyedov*

At the age of twenty-seven, Alexander Sergeievich Griboyedov (Russian, 1795-1829) wrote the play *Gore ot Uma*, 1822, which, according to H. W. Dana in *A History of Modern Drama*, "many have considered the greatest of all in the history of Russian drama." Among the titles under which the play has been translated are *Woe From Wit, Too Clever By Half, The Disadvantages of Reason, The Misfortune of Being Clever, Intelligence Comes To Grief, Too Thoughtful to be Happy, Wit Works Woe*, and *The Bane of Wisdom*.

The play is a social satire, picturing the "million torments" of a sensitive, honest, and intelligent fellow in a world largely inhabited by less wise and more time-serving individuals. The young intellectual, Chatski, returns to Moscow after three years abroad; he finds "new houses, but the same old prejudices." At the home of the retired Czarist official, Famusov, Chatski sees Famusov's beautiful daughter Sophia, wooed by the conservative Colonel Skalozub, who expects to be a general, but giving herself to her father's secretary, Molchalkin. The secretary is a servile sycophant; the colonel, a substantial fool. Chatski expresses his opinion of Moscow society so vehemently that Sophia exclaims, "He's not in his right mind!" Her opinion of Chatski spreads.

Then, while Chatski and Sophia are separately hidden, Molchalkin tells
the pretty maid, Liza, that he loves her and is playing up to Sophia only
because her father is influential. Furious, Sophia breaks in and dismisses
Molchalkin. Chatski comes out, enraged that Sophia should have preferred that sycophantic cad, and now Famusov comes in and scolds the
two for having a rendezvous. Full of despair and disgust, Chatski quits
Moscow.

There is one vivid scene in *Woe From Wit* of Chatski and his liberal
friends reading revolutionary verse by Pushkin and voicing the need of
reform, but most of the thirteen episodes of the play are keen and clever
satiric pictures of the empty-headed society of the day and of those
that, by flattery and fawning, batten upon it. Dotards, redoubtable but
purposeless dames, serf-owners, bribe-takers—the upper froth and scum
of Moscow society—are all captured in the drama's lively flow. Circulated
in thousands of manuscript copies, *Woe From Wit* was forbidden publication or production, and was not played in full until 1869. Since then, it
has been a prime favorite.

In many ways breaking with tradition, the 1928 Meyerhold production
roused heated argument. On a wide stage, Meyerhold had stairs at both
sides to elevations beneath which were curtained nooks; a balcony in the
center gave further level and scope for the action. In the scene where
Famusov entertains Moscow society, across a long table some thirty self-
satisfied aristocrats and their hangers-on faced the audience. Satire and
humor romped around the stage.

Written in short lines of trickily rhymed verse that give the effect of
conversation, *Woe From Wit* is an intellectual delight. Situations, as well
as characters and their dialogue, augment the irony.

At the age of thirty-four, Griboyedov, while on diplomatic service,
was murdered by a mob at Teheran. In his *Woe From Wit*, he left a
masterpiece of the comic stage, a scintillant satire of society, and a
powerful play.

THE GOLDEN FLEECE   *Franz Grillparzer*

The plays of Franz Grillparzer (1791-1872), the leading classical
dramatist of Austria, are written in melodious verse. Viewing the ideals
of his day with keen insight, he cut through their hopefulness to a weary
pessimism. He foresaw the path of European civilization "from humanism through nationalism to bestiality."

The best of Grillparzer's plays is his trilogy *The Golden Fleece*, 1820,
which includes the one-act play *The Guest-Friend*, the four-act *The
Argonauts*, and the five-act *Medea*.

The Golden Fleece presents the story of Jason, who leads the
Argonauts in quest of the golden fleece, and of Medea the sorceress of
Colchis, who helps him to secure the fleece and who then is cast aside
and wreaks gruesome vengeance. (For other dramatizations of Medea's
story, see Euripides*.) Medea towers above the other figures in the plays,
yet Grillparzer keeps her within the range of human motivation. His
emotions are ardent, yet his mind is clear, and his style achieves classical
purity. Actresses—Fanny Janauscheck brought a German production to
New York in 1867; Blanche Bates starred in a Thomas W. Broadhurst
version of the story in San Francisco, 1923; and Judith Anderson gave
fervor to a Robinson Jeffers reshaping of Euripides' play in New York,

1947—may drain Medea's passion to the dregs, but the poetry of Grillparger gives the story at once the flush of living blood and the coolness of classic marble.

Arthur Burkhardt made an English translation of *The Golden Fleece* in 1942 in which the power, if not the poetry, of the plays is manifest. Grillparzer subdues violence with beauty, and the spirit of renunciation in his plays is counterbalanced by the serenity and vitality of their expression.

THE FAITHFUL SHEPHERD   *Giambottista Guarini*

The pastoral motif running through all literary forms reached a dramatic peak in the play of the Italian Giovanni Battista Guarini (1538-1612), *Il Pastor Fido* (*The Faithful Shepherd*) at the close of the sixteenth century.

Ferrara was the center of activity for the pastoral drama. There the pastoral dramatic poem of Torquato Tasso, *Aminta* (*Amyntas*) was produced in 1573. When Tasso was imprisoned, Guarini succeeded him as court poet at Ferrara, and *The Faithful Shepherd* was produced there in 1590.

The Faithful Shepherd is distinctly effective as a dramatic work. The pattern of its plot became the traditional one for pastoral drama, with its entanglement of lovers. Mirtillo loves Amarilli the shepherdess; she returns Mirtillo's love, but is betrothed to Silvio, who loves only to hunt. Dorinda loves Silvio. Mirtillo and Amarilli are condemned to death through the double-dealing of Corisca, a woman corrupted by the city and the evil machinations of the satyr, who represents the grosser aspects of nature. In the forest, Silvio mistakes Dorinda for a wolf and wounds her; then his heart is softened toward her. And it is discovered that Mirtillo is actually the Silvio (son of Montano) to whom Amarilli should be betrothed. Thus, love conquers all. The play, incidentally, contains a long ecstatic description of the virtues of a kiss.

Most of the events in *The Faithful Shepherd,* as in classical drama, occur offstage and are reported, but there is sound theatrical tension in the scenes of Corisca and the satyr, and the meeting of Silvio and Dorinda after he has wounded her is skilfully as well as tenderly wrought. The play, said Francesco De Sanctis, "has two actions that interpenetrate each other in a completely natural way and are wonderfully grafted into each other; the characters are well conceived and well drawn, and their peculiarities are perfectly fused. The surface is smoothed to the last degree of elegance, and the verse is easy and clear and musical. In construction and technical skill this little poem is a jewel." Charming little madrigals adorn the play, as in the comedies of Shakespeare.

The Faithful Shepherdess, about 1610, by John Fletcher* is a direct imitation of Guarini's play. In Fletcher's drama, Clorin has sworn to be faithful to her dead lover; Thenot so admires this fidelity as to love Clorin for it. Perigot loves Amoret and is loved by Amarillis. The wanton Cloe turns from Daphnis to Alexis. With the help of a magic well, complications intertwine, but are cleared in the final unions in a drama of quiet charm and poetic beauty.

The dramatic mode and mood of *The Faithful Shepherd*—"How magnificent it all is! What a marvel of construction!," said De Sanctis— have fertilized a charming and fruitful field in many lands.

DEBURAU   *Sacha Guitry*

Among the various biographical plays of Sacha Guitry (French, b. 1885)—in some of which his father, Lucien, acted; in some, Sacha himself—none is more deft and more tenderly touching than the story of the prince of pantomimists, *Deburau*, 1918.

Jean Baptiste Gaspard Deburau (1796-1847) was trained as an acrobat, and failed. The fool and the butt of his family, he turned to pantomime and became, as David Belasco has said, "probably the greatest performer of Pierrot that ever lived." He played at a rather obscure theatre devoted to acrobats, jugglers and the like, until in 1839 Jules Janin proclaimed in the *Journal des débats*: "Gaspard Deburau, the greatest actor of our time, has revolutionized the actor's art . . . If you have nothing else to do, go to the Theatre des Funambules; whatever else you have to do, go to the Funambules—*and see Deburau!*" It was at a performance of Deburau's that Dumas met Marie Duplessis, whom Dumas set down in his drama *La Dame aux camélias**. She figures in Deburau's life, as well.

As presented in the play, Deburau, peerless among the moon-face harlequins, is a lonely man. Admired and sought by many women, he shows them a portrait of his wife to ward them off. And his wife elopes. In single devotion Deburau follows his art; then he meets Marie Duplessis, and has two loves: his art, and his mistress, Marie. Subtly the drama traces the change in him. Deburau's serenity disappears; he is, in the words of W. L. Courtney in the *London Telegraph* (January 6, 1921), "no longer master of his emotions; he deserts his home; he is constantly in the house of Marie Duplessis. And the tragedy of it is that she has already become tired of him; while on the threshold of her flat appears the young man, Armand Duval, whose association with her is the theme of *La Dame aux camélias*. In a touching scene Deburau comes to her rooms, bringing with him his son, Charles, 10 years of age, and a bird in a cage, believing in his naiveté that such domesticity as he required would be found in the home of his beloved. He finds Armand Duval there and humbly takes his leave. He is not one to tear a passion to tatters; he accepts defeat with gentle stoicism more affecting than torrents of rhetorical passion."

His heart slowly breaking, Deburau gives up acting. But, jealously, he will not let his son, save under another name, carry on his career. Finally, yielding to persuasion, Deburau appears again at the Funambules. He is an utter failure. Then he turns and helps his son prepare for his debut, while outside the barker cries "A new Deburau! A young Deburau! A handsome Deburau! A better Deburau!"

Opening on February 9, 1918, for matinees only (Paris was under German fire), Sacha Guitry as author and actor made a sensation in *Deburau*. In an adaptation by Granville-Barker* the play had its English premiere in Baltimore, July 12, 1920, with Lionel Atwill and Elsie Mackay. Coming to New York, December 23, 1920, it ran for 189 performances. It opened in London, with Robert Loraine and Madge Titheradge, January 5, 1921, and was revived in 1935 with Morgan Farley. *Theatre* magazine (February 1921) called *Deburau* "a really fine play, a play of genuine human feeling, one that quickens the pulse, and stirs the emotions."

There is strong appeal in the worthy man who bears with fortitude the misfortunes of life. On a tragic scale, we see such a figure in *Oedipus**. Nearer our own human level, lonely but not forlorn, buffeted but not beaten, betrayed but not bitter, sad but not despairing, and out of the lees of life straining the wine of courage, wanly smiles Deburau.

FLORADORA *Owen Hall*

This refreshing play by Owen Hall (pseudonym of James Davis, English, 1853-1907) has given lovers of light music a legended song—the unforgettable double sextet "Tell me, pretty maiden, are there any more at home like you?" Other tunes and a sufficient story make it one of the liveliest of comic operas.

The play opens in the Philippines. Dolores, daughter of the concocter of the perfume "Floradora", is in love with Frank, Lord Abercoed, manager of the firm that owns the perfume. The head of the firm, Gilfain, who has acquired the business illegitimately, hires Tweedlepunch, a detective disguised as a traveling phrenologist, to clear Dolores out of the way. Lady Holyrood, wanting Frank for herself, joins the conspirators. Frank, suspecting, is discharged; Dolores sets off after him to Britain. In Wales, Gilfain holds Abercoed Castle, but Frank breaks in. Tweedlepunch tells so fearful a ghost story that Gilfain confesses and restores the castle to Frank and the perfume to Dolores. The two join hearts and hands; Gilfain takes over Lady Holyrood; and his daughter Angela pairs off with Captain Donegal of the Life Guards.

This typical musical comedy plot, written in 1899, is furbished with gay music by Leslie Stuart (T. A. Barrett, 1864-1928).

Opening in London on November 11, 1899, *Floradora* ran for 455 performances; it had bright revivals in 1915 and 1931. In the United States, after a New Haven premiere, the show ran in New York (from November 10, 1900) for 552 performances, then toured for eight years. It played in New York again in 1905, and—with Gilfain changed to an American millionaire, and a sextet of six pretty stenographers and six English dudes—gave another 126 performances there beginning April 5, 1920.

The Floradora girls set the fashion in America for chorus girls' marrying wealth. Nightly they were besieged by stage-door Johnnies; orchids bore hidden gifts of jewels; champagne was drunk from slippers. Five of the six girls, snatched by tycoons, soon had to be replaced. Marjorie Relyea early married a nephew of Andrew Carnegie who dropped dead the night of the New Haven opening. Vaughn Texsmith (of Texas) married a New Jersey silk manufacturer. Marie Wilson got a Wall Street man, Frank Gebhard. Anges (Mrs.) Wayburn divorced Ned to marry a Johannesberg diamond king. Daisy Green had to be content with a stock broker from Denver. Margaret Walker, apparently, just had to be content.

So famous is *Floradora's* sextet song that "Tell me pretty maiden" has been heard all over the world. At a Navy benefit show in 1942 it was sung by Leonora Corbett, Eve Arden, Sophie Tucker, Tallulah Bankhead, Peggy Wood, Gertrude Lawrence, and, kneeling before them, Ed Wynn, Vincent Price, Clifton Webb, Danny Kaye, Boris Karloff, Eddie Cantor.

When *Floradora* returned to New York in 1905, the *American* (March 28) hailed it as "the most generally popular musical comedy ever sung hereabouts." The play itself is not badly tarnished by time. Only a song

or two from *Show Boat** and possibly from *Oklahoma** seem likely to
rival the popularity of the *Floradora* sextet.

GASLIGHT   *Patrick Hamilton*

Among recent "shockers", few have had more success than *Gaslight,*
1938, by Patrick Hamilton (English, b. 1904), presented in New York as
Angel Street, and on the screen twice(once under each title). A hit in
London, the play opened in New York on December 5, 1941, and ran for
three years. It was revived in 1945, 1946, and 1948. In the first New
York production Vincent Price and Judith Evelyn enacted the married
pair and Leo G. Carroll the detective. The City Center revival of
January 22, 1948, starred Jose Ferrer and Uta Hagen.

The play is set in a private house on Angel Street in London during
the 1880's. Pretending to be considerate, Mr. Manningham tortures his
wife, seeking to drive her into insanity (in which state her mother died).
Old Police Inspector Rough, when Manningham is out, convinces Mrs.
Manningham that her husband committed murder in the same house
fifteen years before, that he has now returned, and is seeking to get rid
of his wife so that he may continue his hunt for jewels he did not find
at the time of the murder. The horrified Mrs. Manningham is left to wait
for her husband to return and betray himself. He almost does away with
her—then, realizing he is caught, seems almost to persuade her to his
aid—before in gloating triumph she delivers him to justice.

The devices of melodrama are deftly used, with constant breathhold-
ing suspense. The author, said Brooks Atkinson (December 6, 1941)
"never raises his voice much higher than a shudder . . . never strays outside the bailiwick of dark, soft-footed nervousness."

Some of the play's devices are, if seriously intended, not well coordinated. The Inspector, for example, hides in the clothes-press, yet Manningham, who goes in and changes his suit, unaccountably does not find
him. Such flaws led Louis Kronenberger (December 6, 1941) to declare:
"The second act is thin and has to be padded out with a great many
little tricks and pieces of hokum. But the last act regains some of the
power of the first, and this ending, a kind of psychological denouement
which comes after the plot has run its course, is a smash." Robert Coleman (January 23, 1948), on the revival of *Angel Street,* offered another
explanation; he saw the play as at once a thriller and a satire on vintage
thrillers: "There are those who put *Angel Street* on a pedestal, who conceive it as a deep psychological study. Let them. We've always thought
it was a hokey chiller-diller that burlesques its breed with tongue in
cheek. So apparently does the City Center Company's director."

Angel Street may be contrasted with *Kind Lady**, as a model of suspense built and maintained by successive turns of action and tricks of
dramaturgy. At the end of the first act, when Rough has convinced Mrs.
Manningham that her husband is a murderer, the basic suspense of the
play appears to be over. Yet the author holds the audience in poised
expectancy through two more acts, and at the very end, while we do not
know whether or not Mrs. Manningham is yielding to her husband's
hypnotic blandishments and desperate persuasion, a high peak of intensity is attained. In its quiet crescendo of psychological pressure,
Angel Street stands out among melodramas of suspense.

SHOW BOAT   *Oscar Hammerstein II*

Like Ol' Man River, *Show Boat* just keeps rolling along. Come of age for a fortnight at the New York City Center in 1948, it proved just as winsome and winning as when, twenty-one years before, it started its career on December 27, 1927, and had a run of 572 performances. It has been successfully revived a number of times since, notably in 1932 and in 1948, when it ran for 417 performances. Stars in it have included Norma Terris, Charles Winninger, Paul Robeson, Dennis King, and Helen Morgan.

The music of this perennially popular musical comedy is by Jerome Kern (1885-1945); he and the author, Oscar Hammerstein II (American, b. 1895), together created what John Mason Brown has called "by all odds the most engaging musical romance known to our stage." Brooks Atkinson called it "the most beautifully blended musical show we have had in this country." The thrill that comes once in a lifetime swept over critics as well as less hardened playgoers when they heard, in immediate succession, the three songs, "Only Make Believe", "Ol' Man River", and "Can't Help Lovin' Dat Man"—which later in the evening were followed by the almost equally engaging "Why Do I Love You?" and "Just My Bill" (the words of the latter were contributed by the English humorist P. G. Wodehouse). *Show Boat* was also most favorably received in England in 1928, and was remembered there a score of years later, when Harold Hobson called the music of *Oklahoma** "the freshest and most melodious we have heard in a musical comedy since *Show Boat.*"

The story of *Show Boat* at once exhibits and burlesques the life of the Mississippi River traveling troupe. Captain Andy of the "Cotton Blossom" takes his company upstream and down; we see them in the 1880's, at small town landings, with a barker urging in the curious; we watch part of an old-time melodrama interrupted by two hill-billies who take the villain in earnest. Andy's daughter Magnolia falls in love with gambler Gaylord Ravenal; married, he takes her to Chicago, where we watch the sideshows and stir of the 1893 World's Fair. Loving her still, but penniless, Gaylord deserts Magnolia and her daughter. Magnolia becomes a music hall singer, then a radio star. Twenty years later the two are reunited on the old "Cotton Blossom."

Interwoven with the plot are other episodes involving the comedy team and the star of the company, Julie, whom Magnolia loves. Julie turns out to be a Negress passing as white; her white husband, when the southern sheriff comes to arrest him for miscegenation, quickly pricks her with a knife and sucks the blood so he can swear he has Negro blood in him. Years later, Julie (after singing "Just my Bill"), at the Trocadero Music Hall, gets herself put out of the night club show to give the deserted Magnolia her chance to get started as a singer. The range of emotions played upon is wide, as the play's movement bears us from the picturesque to the pathetic, from the humorous to the sentimental, from burlesque melodrama to romantic love. Incidentally it affords a survey of the growth of the American dance, with the early two-step, the swishing skirt dance, the clog, eccentric dances, tap, waltz, a touch of the can-can, and variegated group work.

The play follows Edna Ferber's 1926 fiction best seller closely—"positively slavish," said the *New York Times* in 1927, adding that it has "about every ingredient that the perfect song-and-dance concoction should have." The *New York World* declared that "the amazing result has been the preservation of most of the old-time pathos and sympathy that made the story what it was."

Playgoers today would call the plot of *Show Boat* "corny"; but the corn is sweet, and there are flowers amid the stalks. The dialogue, as well as the story, has the lift of humor. In its color and story, its ability to laugh at itself, its muted sadness and irrepressible gaiety, its superb songs, its deft and agile dances, *Show Boat* is the most American of American musicals.

FINIAN'S RAINBOW   *E. Y. Harburg*

Opening January 10, 1947 for a run of 723 performances, *Finian's Rainbow*, by E. Y. Harburg (American, b. 1896) and Fred Saidy, with music by Burton Lane, is a musical show of the highest quality, with a social conscience. Pleasantly imaginative in conception, with deft lyrics, delightfully melodic tunes, and concordant dances, the play laughs gaily at the prime stupidity of racial prejudice.

The story springs out of a leprechaun, Og, who follows his stolen pot of gold. Finian McLonergan brings it and his grand-daughter Sharon from Glocca Morra to Missitucky, to plant the gold and grow wealthy. (Have not the Americans buried their gold, and created great industries based upon it?) Much merriment and mischief develop before the folks learn that the greatest treasure buried in a land is what human labor develops from nature's resources. A southern Senator, a prejudiced fellow with designs on the land, is, through the magic of the pot of gold, turned black. He must therefore consort with Negroes; he joins a traveling quartet and becomes pure white inside. Even when his external whiteness is restored, the Senator remains a wiser and a more tolerant man.

Truly ingratiating were the three who came from Ireland: Albert Sharpe as Finian; Ella Logan as Sharon; David Wayne as Og, the leprechaun. The most beguiling song of the play is Sharon's wondering "How are things in Glocca Morra?"

On some of the play's details the critics disagreed. Louis Kronenberger enjoyed the fact that there is "message in its madness," but Brooks Atkinson found that "its stubborn shotgun marriage of fairy story and social significance is not altogether happy." Similarly, in London, Harold Hobson in the *Sunday Times* (October 21, 1947) insisted that "one seeks in vain for unity"; the American aspect of the play, he felt, "could hardly be bettered," but he too spoke of its "unhappy marriage" with the fanciful Irish legend.

In a lavishly colored first-act finale, "Come-and-Get-It-Day", all the poor folk in Rainbow Valley, Missitucky, prance about, bedecked in the gorgeous costumes that poor folks conceive in their dreams of sudden wealth. John Chapman delighted in this: "Seeing is believing . . . the costume designer rates a prize for this alone"; Atkinson rejoiced in the leprechaun; of Og's song "Something Sort of Grandish", he declared: "It and he should be inscribed in the Hall of Fame." John Mason Brown considered the same song "coy to the point of inducing emesis." All agreed with George Jean Nathan, however, that "the show is so superior to the common run of light entertainment that finding fault with it is much like finding fault with a charming supper simply because there is a little hole in the napkin."

Many Broadway dramas have attacked prejudice with indignation and in the fire of their own zeal have been consumed. *Finian's Rainbow* lets its social conscience peep through its fantasy and join in the laughter. We absorb the lesson; we remember the fun. At the end of *Finian's Rainbow,* there was the pot of gold.

THE DYNASTS   *Thomas Hardy*

An epic-drama of Napoleonic times, this play of three Parts, nineteen Acts, and 130 Scenes (Part I, 1904; Part II, 1906; Part III, 1908), is one of the grandest works of modern times. Written by Thomas Hardy (English, 1840-1928), mainly in blank verse, partly in other meters, with descriptive passages in prose, it presents a great panorama of English and European life and warfare from 1805 to 1815.

Part I opens with the House of Commons called at threat of Napoleon's invasion of England; it includes Napoleon's coronation at Milan, the battles of Ulm, Austerlitz, and Trafalgar, the death of Nelson and of Pitt. Part II sweeps on past the Prussian defeat at Jena, through the war in Spain, to Napoleon's divorce from Josephine and marriage with Marie Louise. Part III carries us to the 1812 invasion of Russia, the battle of Leipzig, Napoleon's abdication and return from Elba, and Waterloo.

Significant in the drama, beyond the military exploits and great figures of the time, are two other levels of the action: constantly the scenes shift from statesman and general to farmer and camp-follower, as episodes of humble life show how the higher events seep down and change existence for all; and, above the conflict, great Spirits soar—the Spirit of the Years, the Sinister Spirit, the Ironic Spirit, the Spirit of the Pities (each with its chorus), the Shade of Earth, and the Recording Angels— giving the earthly events their place in the cosmic scheme.

Although such a work, turbulent and magnificently moving in the reading, might seem destined to remain a "closet drama", *The Dynasts* has had several performances. It was seen first in London in an arrangement by Granville-Barker, November 25, 1914. In 1916, the Dorchester Dramatic Society at Weymouth presented scenes from Trafalgar to Waterloo, arranged and linked for continuity by Hardy himself. And Hardy saw the work played again, by the Oxford University Dramatic Society; he was the first living playwright to be presented at Oxford since the Restoration.

Helped by a Reader, and with choruses rendering Strophe and Antistrophe, the productions proved the dramatic power of the play. *The Dynasts,* said the *Christian Science Monitor* (March 7, 1920) "relies for its effect on the simple and almost unstudied interest of each incident, and on the gradual unfolding of a definitely religious attitude to human affairs; impersonal, but at the same time strangely tender." Its author, said the *London Times* (February 10, 1920) "sees with an eye almost microscopic as well as with the mighty vision of a seer or spirit . . . While he offers a dramatic presentation of ideas on the greatest problems of human existence, and sees armies like caterpillers, he moves you to laughter or tears or excitement with the rich details of human character and plants your feet firmly on the village green or in the harbor inn." One of the greatest poem-dramas of our century, *The Dynasts* has a majesty and a dignity in its wide sweep, and searches the human spirit from the humblest to the sublime.

THE WEAVERS   *Gerhart Hauptmann*

The work of Gerhart Hauptmann (German, 1862-1946) coincided with the growth of the "new theatre movement" and the rise of social consciousness at the end of the nineteenth century. His most powerful social drama grew out of his father's stories of the 1844 revolt of the weavers in the Silesian Mountains. (Heine has a poem on the theme.) *The Weavers,* 1892, was stopped by the Prussian authorities after the first performance because of its socialist tendencies, but it was continued in the subscription performances of the Free Theatre. The play was also forbidden in provincial Germany and in many sections of Austria-Hungary.

New York saw the play in German at the Irving Place Theatre, opening October 14, 1894. The *New York World* said that "Its power comes simply from a curious, an almost repellent, accent of truth . . . The talk is positively ghastly, in its brutal, its ferocious, commonplace character." The *New York Sun* contrasted Hauptmann with Dumas, noting that the Frenchman, intending a sermon, gives us a play; the German never gets beyond the sermon: "*Die Weber* is sincere, it states terrible facts with terrible energy . . . but it does all this directly not incidentally; and therefore it is not a great or a good play, and there may be some doubt if it is a play at all."

By the time of the 1915 New York revival (December 14) in English, opinion had changed. *Theatre Magazine* (January 1916) called the play "one of the most stirring of realistic dramas dealing with modern social conditions. . . . the undercurrent of ferocity which breaks through at the climax is gripping and intense." Emanuel Reicher, who had been one of the first in Germany to hail Hauptmann, supervised this production. The *New York Dramatic Mirror* (December 25, 1915) contended that the play was probably the most graphic picture of human misery ever written: "The conventionalities of theatrical construction are disregarded . . . If it were a mere sop to sensationalism, or a case of special pleading, it would have its little day, and pass with the falling leaves; but it is not. It is the work of a poet with a deep insight into the philosophy of life and society, but it is supplemented in this instance by the work of an artist who has instilled life and verity into its scenes."

The Weavers was the first play with a composite hero. Despite the gallery of sharply etched individuals, the protagonist is the group of desperate weavers who rebel against wretchedness and starvation. Their bullying manager and their vain, vulgar capitalist employer are little more than caricatures, but there is a fierce power as the weavers go from the cheery tavern to destroy the house of their employer, a grim loom of future revolt in the suppression of the tumult by the soldiers, and a sharp stab of irony when a stray shot kills, at his work, the old weaver who has held aloof from the conflict.

Productions include a revival in 1937 at Yale University, another in 1937 by the Federal Theatre in Los Angeles. The play is generally recognized as not merely one of the earliest, but one of the best dramas of social conflict.

HANNELE   *Gerhart Hauptmann*

The first play in the world theatre to have a child as its heroine was

Hauptmann's sensitive study of the last days of an abused and wretched girl, *Hanneles Himmelfahrt* (*Hannele's Journey to Heaven*), 1893, known in English as *Hannele* (*The Assumption of Hannele*). Hannele is an illegitimate child who, brought up in a pauper's home, was taken by Mattern the mason, a drunken ruffian whose cruelty killed Hannele's mother. To escape this brute, Hannele tries to drown herself. She lingers in a spell of delirium as life obtrudes upon her vision of heaven; then she dies.

There is touching pathos as well as tender truth in Hannele's picture of the world to come. For heaven offers the things Hannele missed on earth—meat every day instead of hardened crusts, a white robe and Cinderella slippers replacing her rags, and a mother's undying love. A picture compounded of fairy-tales and a child's naive notions of religion, spun in a fevered spirit, the play is, as the *Boston Transcript* said (December 26, 1909), "a strange, moving medley, grotesque and pitiful; yet, as all who have studied childhood know, well-nigh inevitable."

The visions of Hannele, though faithfully reported, mark a step of the author away from the naturalism of his earlier plays. The emphasis, however, is still upon things humanly caused, the correction of which is in the power of humans—the brutality and drunkenness of the mason are the results of poverty and ignorance. Not until *The Sunken Bell**, 1896, did Hauptmann move to the thought that tragedy is inherent in man's nature, that our very being, not merely our social circumstances, may lead us to our doom.

The pathos and implicit protest in the picture of Hannele perhaps contributed to the difficulties the play encountered. Hailed on the Continent, *Hannele* was banned in England (save for a private performance February 29, 1904) until 1908, and it was not played again until 1924. In New York, after one performance, May 1, 1894, the play was banned as blasphemous. It was played again in 1908, in both English and German, without hindrance. Minnie Maddern Fiske and Holbrook Blinn starred in it in 1910. In 1946 it was presented in the Berkshires (summer theatre) and at Piscator's Dramatic Workshop in New York.

Set in Silesia, the play is written partly in Silesian dialect, in prose, and partly in simple, moving verse. Hauptmann, said the *New York Times* (May 2, 1894), "has avoided purely literary forms, his language is appropriately simple, and he rarely misses just the right word." Nevertheless, the *Times* moved to protest that "in the presence of such an assemblage of 'first nighters' and 'rounders', the performance seemed horribly sacrilegious." By 1908, the *London Leader* (December 9) questioned how anyone could object to such a "singularly restrained and beautiful treatment of the teachings of Christianity." And in America the *Boston Transcript* (date above) said that "Femininity and piety were surely seldom so wholly and so truly mingled . . . We find it all delightful, partly because in its very crudity it is precisely natural; partly because of the very human tenderness with which the author has treated it, and partly because it is, all in all, an exquisitely poetical piece of work." In essence, *Hannele* gives us the first picture, tender, searching, poignant, of a child protagonist building wretchedness into beauty.

FLORIAN GEYER   *Gerhart Hauptmann*

Encouraged by the success of *The Weavers**, Hauptmann in 1895 tried the same group technique in a panoramic drama of the Peasants' Rebellion of 1525, *Florian Geyer*, which reproduces not only the events and the social-political background but the very language of the time. Instead, however, of showing only the group struggle of the serfs for greater freedom, as the play progresses Hauptmann centers attention more fully upon their leader, the liberal knight Florian Geyer, whose fight ends with his betrayal and assassination.

Well received on its first production, the play was even more popular after two score years had made its sixteenth century events timely once again, when Max Reinhardt gave it a tumultuous production in 1920. The *London Times* (July 9, 1938) declared that "Because of its didactic earnestness, a quality rated highly in German drama, and still more because it can be taken as a parable showing the awful consequences of failure to observe the rules of 'Follow-my-leader', this tragedy of the Peasants' War is today accorded a favor hitherto denied it . . . The play has much incidental power and poetry, for beside the passages of stirring patriotic appeal there are scenes of more intimate and more genuine sentiment . . . the splendour and horror of the period were suggested with uncommon skill. In particular, we do not remember a production in which the use of sound effects was more telling—the distant singing, the noise of war, the clatter of armour on the cobbles."

This excellent example of naturalistic drama effectively intersperses scenes of quieter personal emotion among the surging emphases of the peasant crowds. The turbulence is well managed, so that there is a definite dramatic progression. The later stress on Geyer remains a flaw. "The trouble is," said the *Times*, "that Geyer's fate is not effectively shown as the summing up of the tragic conflict." Geyer's ruin falls on him from his own weakness as a man, his indecisiveness, his failure to assume leadership at the crucial moment. Thus "The War becomes a setting for a subjectively treated drama of Geyer's downfall." This shift in emphasis sends the drama driving in two directions, but it remains a stirring and vivid picture of a rebellion defeated not by its lack of virtue or even of might, but because bickering, division from within, distrust and hesitant leadership clog its own mains. Thus the play dramatically points a lesson that might fitly be more heeded today.

THE SUNKEN BELL   *Gerhart Hauptmann*

In this play, Hauptmann turned from naturalism in a poetic, romantic flight that combined realism and fantasy with a use of symbolism somewhat similar to that in Ibsen's *Peer Gynt**. Produced in Berlin in December 1896, it created an unprecedented furore, and for several years it continued to be the most popular and most discussed drama in Europe, winning almost immediate translations into French, Russian, Danish, Italian, Hungarian and English.

Something of the feelings that the play aroused is conveyed in a Berlin despatch of March 13, 1897, to the *New York Times*: "It met with unsparing criticism on the part of the public, and not a little ridicule . . . moderate success in Vienna, while the Paris version has been received with the liveliest reprobation. The setting of *Die Versunkene Glocke*, its outside of Nixie-man and fairy nymphs, witch, and 'little people' of the woods, gnomes of the metal-bearing rocks, and satyrs of the hills, is as delightful to children as *Rip Van Winkle**. To children of a larger growth its morality seems a trifle queer, because Hauptmann has taken pains to show that the bell founder had no cause whatever to leave his devoted wife and hie him to the wilds in company with his fairy love, Rautendelein . . . And so the general verdict is that *Die Versunkene Glocke*, if not a silly play, is a highly immoral one, since the fleshy side of his sinning is naturally more evident than the spiritual . . . [Still] the fact remains that *Die Versunkene Glocke* holds the stage, and exercises on all a distinct charm quite its own."

Considerable admiration greeted the play when it appeared in English. Reported the *London Sketch* (April 13, 1898): "An unpremeditated flight into the ether of pure idealism has placed Gerhart Hauptmann, the uncompromisingly realistic . . . on the highest pinnacle of literary fame." In New York, the *Herald* (March 27, 1900) said of the production with E. H. Sothern: "Last night's experience proved anew that poetry is of absorbing interest in whatever tongue it finds utterance . . . The final scene of the fourth act, with the apparitions of Heinrich's children, the darkness lowering over the rock plateau, and the deep clang of the sunken bell rising from the lake below, is one of the weirdest and most impressive episodes seen on the New York stage in many years." The *Sun*, however, refused to take seriously the deeper meaning of the play.

By 1907, the tide of critical appreciation was sweeping back from symbolism. When E. H. Sothern and Julia Marlowe revived the play, the *Tribune* (February 6, 1907) called it "a dreary, foggy, puerile exposition of the discontent that is naturally sequent on an ill-assorted marriage . . . but the epidemic of 'symbolism' has struck the stage, and, like other epidemics, it must run its course . . . complex, obscure, inscrutable medley of trite domestic detail, fairy pranks, and transcendental flummery."

Through its human figures *The Sunken Bell* shows the eternal struggle of the artist who must have his feet on earth though his spirit be in heaven. As Heinrich's forsaken wife flings herself into the lake, it is her dead hand that rings the artist's bell. Heinrich, returning with his sad children to the world of men, drives Rautendelein from her humanity. There is left to him only the goblet of death, which Rautendelein proffers. In more poetic terms, Hauptmann is presenting the same quest of freedom that marked his *Lonely Lives*. Individual freedom and social justice are his alternate, often his intertwined, themes.

None of Hauptmann's earlier plays reaches the level of *The Sunken Bell* in poetic beauty and symbolic grasp. This play is the richest expression in the German drama of the late nineteenth century quest (as in Ibsen's *Peer Gynt**, as in Maeterlinck*), through fantasy and beauty, through a reality that borders on the dream, of the basic values and meaning of human existence.

THE YELLOW JACKET   *George C. Hazleton*

Although J. Harry Benrimo admitted that he and George C. Hazleton (American, 1868-1921) barely "knew enough Chinese to swear at a laundryman", their drama *The Yellow Jacket*, 1912, is the most charming and enduring of the plays in the Chinese manner. The novelty of its presentation, the delicacy and poignant tenderness of its movement, softly conquer the seat of judgment, and win response from the heart. Clayton Hamilton declared it the most successful play of American authorship produced within his memory; the *Christian Science Monitor*

(November 11, 1916) averred that "by many, *The Yellow Jacket* is considered the finest play written in America;" and Heywood Broun (November 10, 1916) declared: "You like the play, not because it is curious, but because it is beautiful."

When *The Yellow Jacket* opened, however, its fragile, exotic beauty won but a *succès d'estime*. Although the critics praised it, "Auditors couldn't agree whether it was comedy, tragedy, farce, or burlesque," reported the *New York Sun* (November 5, 1912), "but they did agree it was both a novelty and a success." Connoisseurs saw the play again and again. Enrico Caruso during the first run attended thirty-five performances; Sir Herbert Beerbohm Tree crossed the Atlantic to have a look at it; and Charles Frohman prophesied, "This play will be seen all over the world."

The Yellow Jacket opened in London in 1913; by 1916 it had been seen also in Berlin (Reinhardt), Moscow, Shanghai, Hungary, Poland, Czechoslovakia, Norway, Spain, Japan, Sweden, Denmark and Holland. The Coburns took the play all over the English-speaking world and gave it successful revivals in New York in 1916, 1921 and 1928. A summer production in 1941 at Marblehead, Massachusetts, used Harpo Marx as the Property Man (the inimitable original was Arthur Shaw); *Life* (September 1, 1941) called it "the most interesting of the 150 shows produced so far this summer." The play still finds frequent performances.

Hazleton and Benrimo insisted that neither the plot nor the method of production was Chinese save in the most general fashion. The stage arrangements were, however, drawn from the old Jackson Street Chinese Theatre in San Francisco. The story itself has all the intricacy, all the naivete, of a Chinese legend. When Che Moo, first wife of the provincial governor Wu Sin Yin, bears a sickly son, the governor wants to get rid of her so that a second wife can give him a healthy heir. The farmer hired to destroy Chee Moo kills instead her treacherous maid and takes the wife and child to hiding. Years later, the second son, Wu Fah Din, the Daffodil, has succeeded his father and has his mind set on marrying the beautiful maiden Plum Blossom. The sickly babe Wu Hoo Git has grown into an accomplished youth. With the help of a philosopher and his own talents, Wu deposes the unrighteous ruler, and takes the throne and the beauteous Plum Blossom.

The presentation of this story invests the tale with an exotic charm that adds novelty and frequent amusing moments to its beauty and emotional appeal. Most important is the supposedly invisible Property Man, a blasé individual who sits at the side of the stage drinking tea when he is not arranging or sustaining scenery in full sight of the supposedly unseeing audience. He holds a bamboo pole beside the two lovers: it's a willow tree; he drapes a scarf along two teakwood stands: it's a boat wherein the lovers share their dreams.

"For our part," said Heywood Broun (November 10, 1916), "neither Griffith nor Ince ever made us see a drifting boat and a moonlit river as do Chow Wan and Wu Hoo Git as they sit on a few chairs and point across a bare stage . . . Only the hard of heart and the dull of eye can see anything except the picture which the mind conjures up. And if you laugh when Chee Moo ascends to the spirit land on a ladder, you are among the utterly damned who shall never know the true felicity of the theatre."

With gorgeous costumes, kindly face or villainous mask, each character on its first entrance explains its role in the play. The baby in Act One is, without disguise, a block of wood. When the treacherous maid is beheaded the Property Man hides her face with a red cloth and throws a red pillow (her head!) on the ground, while she walks off. And yet by the magic of make-believe, while we smile at these devices their artificiality quickly becomes a convention; we note them, we are amused for a moment, and we are caught again into the emotions of the play. We are touched by its tenderness, moved by its beauty.

During its early stages, the authors called the play *The Peacock Feather*, then *The Child of Chee Moo*; finally, they took the yellow jacket, symbol of royal power, as the title. The play starts with a pleasant address by the "Chorus," who asks the audience not to encourage the actors by too great signs of favor. The original "Chorus," the noted tenor Perugini, was stone deaf; he took his cues from the actions of the other characters. There is plenty of action in the play; indeed, the Property Man keeps it moving at a smart pace. If a warrior brandishes his sword too long, the Property Man calmly takes it from him and puts it in the closet. Or if the Property Man grows bored with the dialogue, he may begin to dust the dragon's head. Such interruptions, of course, are timed for a relaxing smile before the unbroken sweep to a climax, when the emotional flow rises undisturbed. There is at once a savoring of remote beauty and a nearly touching tenderness in the legend plucked out of the reign of time and set for continuing delight in *The Yellow Jacket*.

MARY MAGDALEN   *Christian Friedrich Hebbel*

Out of the poverty and wretchedness of his early days, Christian Friedrich Hebbel (German, 1813-1863) wrote *Maria Magdalena*, 1844, a prose tragedy of ordinary life, a problem play of contemporary concern written when Henrik Ibsen*, usually deemed the pioneer in this field, was a youth of sixteen. The magdalen is Klara, daughter of the joiner Anton, who has been seduced by an ambitious fellow, Leonhard, who wants to marry her for her dowry. Although Klara loves a secretary, family pressure leads her to accept Leonhard. But he learns that there is no money for her dowry and seizes the arrest of her brother as a pretext for breaking their engagement. The brother is cleared, but Leonhard will not return, and Klara drowns herself. The secretary challenges Leonhard to a duel, kills him, but himself is fatally wounded. Klara's father sadly recognizes that the old concepts do not fit the new generation.

The play presents a vivid contrast of the generations and studies with penetrating psychological insight the relations of Klara and her world. The author owed to his own troubled environment "his sharp directness of speech, and to his peasanthood a raw facing of unvarnished facts", according to translator L. H. Allen. With a glowing passion and a true sense of dramatic drive, Hebbel won fame throughout Europe as a powerful playwright.

Mary Magdalen was played at the German Theatre in New York in 1907. Despite its long monologues and asides, despite its unpleasant situations and violent incidents, the *New York Dramatic Mirror* declared that the play had "withstood the ravages of time excellently". The story moves with no comic relief to its tortured ending, but it sets in sharp

contrast individual impulses and social codes, and it is one of the earliest vivid examples of the modern problem play which flooded the
western stage after Ibsen.

HEROD AND MARIAMNE   *Christian Friedrich Hebbel*

The best of Hebbel's dramas picture a person in conflict with environment. Out of the different impulsions of personal integrity and social
convention, tragedy rises. The immediate driving force within the
drama may be a specific emotion, as jealousy in *Herodes und Mariamne*,
1850, but beneath is the more basic contrast of the individual and his
world.

The story of Herod the Great (73?-4 B.C.) and his second wife
Mariamne has been told by many playwrights: in French, in *Mariamne*
by Alexandre Hardy, 1610; by François Tristan l'Ermite, 1636, whose version made Richelieu weep; and by Voltaire*, 1724. Voltaire's play failed
at its premiere because a remark in the pit started the audience laughing just as Adrienne Lecouvreur, as Mariamne, took her poison; shortly
after, revised, it was a success. In English, Stephen Phillips* wrote
Herod in 1900; and in Hebrew there is one by Falek Halpern, produced
in Palestine in 1937.

An English version of Hebbel's play, written by Clemence Dane,
opened in Pittsburgh October 26, 1938, with Katharine Cornell and
Florence Reed, and Fritz Kortner in his American debut. Besides cutting Hebbel's soliloquies and asides, Dane's adaptation neglected the
play's psychological perceptions to emphasize the fierce jealousy of
Herod; the production died on the road.

All the Herod plays present the same basic story. In continuing suspicion of his beautiful wife, Herod when departing on his campaigns
leaves secret orders that if he falls Mariamne is to be slain; on returning,
he kills her guards. She learns of and protests against these orders;
this quickens his jealousy, for he assumes that she has employed her
feminine charms to seduce the guard. Mariamne disdains to deny this
and is condemned to die, leaving Herod sunken in a morbid spell. In
Hebbel's psychological approach to this story, however, the jealousy of
Herod is subordinated to the self-respect of Mariamne. A woman of
dignity and moral force, she cannot consent to continue living in a world
where a woman is no more than a man's possession. By such clear
and dramatic presentation of the problem of individual integrity, and the
tragic consequence of upholding ideals for which the time is not yet
ripe, Hebbel made his mark as a dramatist.

THE GOOD HOPE   *Hermann Heijermans*

The dramatic power and reforming zeal of Hermann Heijermans
(1864-1924) have made him the most popular playwright of the Netherlands. His work is mainly of the naturalistic sort, influenced by Ibsen*
and by Hauptmann*. His *Op Hoop van Zegen* (*The Good Hope*), 1900,
played over a thousand times in the Netherlands, has won lasting fame
abroad.

"The Good Hope" is the name of a ship in the play, which bears its
crew to their death. The scene is a Dutch fishing village, every cottage
of which has given victims to the sea. Kniertje, a sturdy fisherman's

wife, though she has thus lost her husband and her elder sons, with fatalistic calm watches her last two sons going to sea. The rough and high-spirited Geert goes willingly but the sensitive Barend clings to the door-post, and Kniertje herself sends him off. The women at home gather and talk of earlier losses; the younger women find it hard to bear. Geert's sweetheart, Jo, is pregnant; she breaks down and shrieks out the horror of waiting. The foreboding is heavy—and prophetic; for ship-owner Clemens Bos, with "The Good Hope" well covered by insurance (like Bernick in *The Pillars of Society**) has let it sail unseaworthy; all that returns is the body of Barend clinging to a spar. There is fierce resentment among some of the fisher folk, but death is all men's destiny: Kniertje, still looking ahead with courage, gets a bowl of soup from Bos's wife, and the townsfolk cheer Bos for his contribution to the widows and orphans fund.

The play touched so closely to conditions in the Dutch fishing industry that it produced vehement agitation leading to the revision of the Ships Act in 1909. In London, *The Good Hope* opened, with Granville Barker playing Barend, April 24, 1903; it was played again in 1904 with Ellen Terry. New York saw the play February 11, 1907; and again, with Alma Kruger as the mother and Eva Le Gallienne as Jo, October 18, 1927. It has been played frequently around the country, being of considerable artistic as well as theatrical power.

The Good Hope is in a sense a group play like *The Weavers**; especially in the third act, when its power comes from the townsfolk together, from the fishing community, humor-full, enduring, even in the loom of death. At the same time, in the individual portraits, there is a precision of detail that recalls the seventeenth century Dutch masters. "It was the truth of human nature and human circumstance," said the *Boston Transcript* (April 23, 1907), "of the pain and the hardness of life; and, shorn as it was of ordinary dramatic trappings, dramatically it still prevailed." And as the *New York Dramatic Mirror* said (February 23, 1907): "What is best of all is the poetry swinging through the lines, the poetry of the sea, the poetry that more than all else symbolizes the inevitableness of fate."

The pressure of sorrow in the play seemed to some too weighty to bear. Thus the *London Telegraph* (April 25, 1903) found *The Good Hope* "replete with horrors and agonised scenes crowded into the four acts pell-mell, one melodramatic situation succeeding another, until through sheer iteration of woe the very faculty of sympathy is blunted." And of the young Barend's spell of frightened refusal to board the ship, the *Telegraph* questioned "whether so frank and terrible an exhibition of poltroonery should ever be put in all its naked ugliness on the boards." But the boy recovers; the play too lifts its head, bringing calm after the storm and the courage to bear the human lot. *The Good Hope* is both an ironic and symbolic title of man's endurance and faith on the ultimate journey.

MISTER ROBERTS   *Thomas Heggen*

One of the most amusing and popular plays to come out of World War II is unquestionably *Mister Roberts*, fashioned by Thomas Heggen (American, 1919-1949) and the stage-wise Joshua Logan (b. 1909) from the former's book of the same title about life on the *U.S.S. Reluctant*, a supply vessel far from the centers of actual conflict. The conflict within the play rises from Mister Roberts' efforts to be transferred to more active service and the efforts of the martinet captain to keep him. The play, however, is important only for its amusement value; its intellectual and spiritual values are on the level of the comic strip. It opened in New York, on February 18, 1948, for a run of 1157 performances. Some 214 performances were given in London in 1950. A Paris production failed quickly.

Take the word of a sailor, John Mason Brown, ex-Navy lieutenant, who, when at the helm of the New York Drama Critics' Circle, said: "As a play, *Mister Roberts* may lack importance. At times it may come perilously close to slapstick. In its ultimate range, it may be limited by its fidelity to the juvenile mind and emotions . . . But . . . it is gloriously accurate in realizing its intentions. It finds supreme showmanship informed by very human values. It is superlative theatre; a miracle of production." A mere landlubber, Louis Kronenberger (February 20, 1948) also enjoyed the play, but with reservations: "Personally, I thought *Mister Roberts* too long . . . What plot there is, is that of a boy's book with some bad words thrown in." John Chapman declared that "If it were boiled down, there wouldn't be much to this comedy. But who would want it boiled down? It should be left as it is."

Mister Roberts is one of the rare cases in which the spirit and mood of a work run away with its theme and its form, and in a madcap sweep command the public's plaudits. Its humor tumbles you along, topsy-turvy, so that only away from the theatre are you likely to see how puerile is the point of view of the play's story and how that story is beaten about for the sake of humor.

The basic idea, if there is any, is to make Mr. Roberts a hero for wishing to get into active service. His country is fighting a grim war for its very existence, and he is doing an excellent job sustaining morale at a dull but essential task; but he is bored and his country's need be damned! So the Captain is pictured as straining "for a record" merely in order to win a citation and a potted palm. Hence all the pranks played on the captain are supposed to have our sympathy and we should root for the man that wants to shirk his duty and go forth to be a hero. There isn't any sense of human dignity rising from the play. It may best be considered as a sort of *Hellzapoppin* variety show set to a plot.

Too often, unfortunately, the play's humor is maintained at the expense of the story. At the climax of the conflict between the captain and Roberts, when the captain's precious potted palm is heaved overboard, the humor obscures the symbolic significance of that action. Most spectators, it is true, gladly accept the rowdy succession of episodes— escapades and pranks such as navy men enjoy reviving and revising for their cronies. The humor is so predominant that the reported death of Roberts in action rings inappropriately at the end. The authors are deft; they make the best job they can of this ending; but the rowdy mood, the continuing fight of the *Reluctant's* crew against their captain, call for a different clincher. Nevertheless, despite its shortcomings, *Mister Roberts* remains important as the first dramatic hit to mirror the war in the comic-strip mind.

THE LITTLE FOXES   *Lillian Hellman*

The plays of Lillian Hellman (American, b. 1904) present humans pressed in the throes of perverse passions—jealousy, hatred, greed. That the public favors such figures may be judged from the fact that out of six plays by Miss Hellman five have been hits. Two of the Hellman plays, colored by bitterness, deal with one family. These are *The Little Foxes*, which opened February 15, 1939, with Tallulah Bankhead and Patricia Collinge, for 410 performances, and *Another Part of the Forest*, which opened November 20, 1946, for 191 performances. The latter was a hit in Moscow in 1949 under the title *Ladies and Gentlemen* . The two plays present an unrelieved picture of greed and hate.

The Little Foxes (its title is taken from the *Song of Solomon*: "the little foxes, that spoil the vines") is a picture of rapaciousness working its own ruin. In Snowden, Alabama, about 1900, we see the end of the ruthless drive for power and wealth of the profiteers and carpet-baggers who have all but swallowed the milder-willed folk of the South. Petty, mean, grasping Oscar Hubbard has married timid and shrinking Birdie Bagtry, who dips her fear and aversion in wine. The older Ben Hubbard is shrewder and more controlled, but no less grasping. Their sister Regina, married to gentle Horace Giddens, is the most eager-clawed of them all. When Horace, sick of the Hubbards' vulpine dealings, refuses to join their latest project, Regina by not reaching over for his heart medicine lets him die. Although her daughter Alexandra breaks free, Regina in proud isolation holds the family power.

The characters of the play, etched in vitriol, are obnoxious, but not too unreal. "Between the crude short-changer Oscar," said *Time* (February 27, 1939) "and his greatly aspiring sister is the difference between a rat and an eagle: Not instinctive, but icily calculating, is their family sense: the same greed that divides them among themselves unites them against others . . . With such implacable people Playwright Hellman has dealt implacably, exerting against them a moral pressure to match their own immoral strength. Both the Hubbards and their playwright-inquisitor are a pitch too relentless for real life. But it is the special nature of the theatre to raise emotions to higher power, somewhat simplifying, somewhat exaggerating, but tremendously intensifying. Playwright Hellman makes her plot crouch, coil, dart like a snake; lets her big scenes turn boldly on melodrama. Melodrama has become a word to frighten nice-belly playwrights with; but, beyond its own power to excite, it can stir up genuine drama of character and will. Like the dramatists of a hardier day, Lillian Hellman knows this, capitalizes on it, brilliantly succeeds at it." Howard Barnes (November 1, 1949) called the play "a grim and numbing tragedy . . . One of the memorable events of the modern theatre"; and Atkinson hailed it as "one of the theatre's keenest dramas".

The author declared in the *New York Herald-Tribune* (March 12, 1939): "I wanted especially to write about people's beginnings, to deal with the material that in most play construction is antecedent to the action, to show how characters more frequenly shown in the maturity of their careers get that way . . . It seemed to me, in *The Little Foxes*, an essay in dramatic technique as well as an interesting business to depict a family just as it was on the way to the achievements that were to bring it wealth or failure, fame or obloquy. At the final curtain, the Hubbards are just starting to get on in the world in a big way, but their various futures I like to think I leave to the imagination of the audience. I meant to be neither misanthropic nor cynical, merely truthful and realistic." Miss Hellman remains too external to the characters—presenting them as seen from the outside, by an onlooker who condemns, instead of with their own inner self-justifications—to achieve a sense of full truth; but she is certainly scorching.

Almost as much intensity surges through *Regina*, which opened in New York October 31, 1949, a musical version of *The Little Foxes*, written and composed by Marc Blitzstein, a powerful melodrama with many moments in which the music heightens the emotional quality of the play. Among such moments are the opening, which admirably illustrates Regina's character as she hushes the innocent merriment beneath her window; Birdie's tipsy singing of her cowed and frustrate life; and the closing contrast, after Regina lets Horace die, of the mourning Negroes outside the house and the quarreling family within.

The few persons in the play not wholly driven by powerful passions are weaklings. Alexandra, the exception, is the least rounded character in the play. Her father, Horace, is not well developed; he makes one feeble stand but his will cannot match his wife Regina's ruthlessness. Birdie, the *New York World-Telegram* (March 4, 1939) noted, "is beaten, crushed, and whipped into a state of fearful timidity and docility." However, she picks a swift moment's courage out of her own despair to help Alexandra escape the Hubbard will.

The play's blackguards, greedy, unscrupulous, hot-tempered folk, are shown with an incisive intelligence, a blunt, straightforward speech, and a sense of strong situation, that make *The Little Foxes* memorable.

SHORE ACRES   *James A. Herne*

After his rural melodrama, *Hearts of Oak*, 1879, and the sincere character study *Margaret Fleming*, 1890, actor-playwright James A. Herne (originally James Ahern, American, 1839-1901) combined the two modes and wrote *The Hawthornes*. It opened in Chicago, May 17, 1892, as *Shore Acres Subdivision*, which title was soon changed to *Uncle Nat*. Revised as *Shore Acres*, the play opened in Boston February 20, 1893, with the author as Uncle Nat, ran there for 100 performances, and found wide and continuing success. It was a hit in New York, opening October 30, 1893.

A review in the *London Telegraph* (May 22, 1906) captured the mood of the play and much of the story: "It has pleasant and bright elements, a great deal of engaging domesticity; it also has brief and vivid episodes where something like dramatic intensity is reached. But it has the thinnest story which was ever extended through four acts . . . It is as though amid scenes out of *Peter Pan* were wedged some old Adelphi piece portraying the fortunes of an ambitious farmer, a scheming and designing villain, a revolting daughter, and the return of the daughter and her recently wedded husband in the midst of the falling snows of Christmas Eve. The last is perhaps the most archaic touch of all. Possibly it is this mixture of incongruous elements which makes the play a little difficult to describe. It is at once homely and melodramatic. It contains the oldest of stage incidents, tricked out with the newest of stage elaboration."

The farmer, Martin Berry, is owner of Shore Acres, and keeper of the lighthouse on Frenchman's Bay. The villain, Blake, wants to marry Martin's daughter, Helen; he also persuades Martin to cut up Shore Acres into building plots. Uncle Nat returns from the War between the States in time to stop this, and to save Shore Acres when the land boom collapses. As Helen and the doctor are eloping through a storm on the bay, the furious Martin wants to put out the lighthouse beam; in the play's one moment of fierce excitement Nat struggles with him there, and manages to keep it burning. In the last act, with mutual forgiveness, the Christmas stockings are hung, the turkey is dressed, basted, and cooked to the olfactory delectation of the audience, and in closing silence Uncle Nat looks around on a peaceful and contented world.

Save for the one episode of struggle, the play's characters in the main move with the cool ease typical of New England. The *Boston Commonwealth* (February 25, 1893) called it "truthful, vivid, and moving." An editorial in the *Boston Transcript* (May 19, 1893) observed it had "much that is vital and genuine." New York reviewers were equally enthusiastic. Alan Dale (November 1, 1893) found it "so absolutely satisfying to truth, that one marvels at the directness of the touches that are apparently aimed carelessly." The *World* (November 26) noted that it had "exquisite touches of both idyllicism and realism." The *Journal* (October 31) called *Shore Acres*, simply, "the best American play that we have had."

As theatre, *Shore Acres* deserved its popularity. The dialogue abounds in quaint and gentle humor. If the story seems obvious, it is because melodramas since have explored and exhausted its variations. If the characters seem familiar, it is because they have been endlessly copied. *Shore Acres* remains the venerable father of a considerable brood.

PORGY   *Du Bose Heyward*

Porgy, the crippled Negro of Catfish Row, Charleston, South Carolina, whose diminutive body housed an indomitable spirit, has had his story told in several forms. From his novel *Porgy*, 1925, Du Bose Heyward (American, 1885-1940) and his wife Dorothy fashioned a play, 1927. In 1935, with book by Du Bose Heyward and lyrics by Ira Gershwin, George Gershwin fashioned what he called the "grand opera" *Porgy and Bess*. In 1942, by reducing the recitatives to dialogue, and other simplification, Alexander Smallens gave the musical the more appropriate status of a "folk opera".

The story itself is one of violence. The play opens with a crap game at which bully Crown kills Robbins; when Crown flees, his girl Bess takes shelter with Porgy, who has always worshipped her from afar. His tenderness wins her affection, but when, at a picnic, Crown appears and summons her, Bess cannot resist. She comes back to Porgy, however; and when Crown seeks her in Catfish Row, Porgy kills Crown. While Porgy is being questioned by the police, the inconstant Bess goes off to New York with the carefree and pleasure-promising Sporting Life. On Porgy's release, he sets out in his rickety goat-cart to find New York and Bess.

Around these violent deeds pulses the warm life of crowded Catfish Row. The opening scene, of morning in the square, is rich in color and sound. The very noises grow in a rhythm of dawning: we hear snoring, then the taps of an early hammer, the swish of the morning broom, the sharpening of knives in the fish shop; then closer together or in concert the opening of windows, the banging of shutters, the flapping of towels, the beating of eggs, until the diapason is rounded with the human voice breaking into the cheery song "Good morning, brother!"

Two mass scenes in the play rise to great power: that in which all Catfish Row is gathered in Serena Robbins' room before her husband's burial, as the singing of spirituals rouses the Negroes, and that other dark scene in which the folk are huddled against the raging hurricane and a flash of lightning shows Crown at the threshold, Crown the bully and murderer, but now the only one that dares to brave the storm, dashing forth to rescue the frenzied woman whose husband is out on the waters. Alexander Woollcott (October 11, 1927) called the first scene "one of the most exciting climaxes I have ever seen in the theatre."

Many homely touches highlight the play. Vendors of food call their wares through Catfish Row. The gossip of the women, the gambling of the men, the stir of the fishermen preparing their nets, add considerable color. As a consequence of this fulness, Porgy becomes only the most prominent figure in a crowded panorama. "His simplicity, his frank rascality," said Commonweal (November 2, 1927), "his moments of grandeur, his confused vision of his limited universe—these all become the summing-up of forces eddying about him, a reflection, too, of the whole passion of a race . . . flashing with the ardor and the sultry magnificence of folk melodrama."

Porgy opened in New York on October 10, 1927, and ran for 217 performances, with 137 more on its revival the next year. It was seen in London in 1929. The play continues to be popular around the country, though in the larger centers it has, in the main, been replaced by Porgy and Bess. The opera, first produced October 10, 1935, ran for 120 performances, and did not cover its cost; the 1942 New York revival (January 22) ran for 286 performances with a return, after its tour, to the New York City Center in 1944. It was played in Zurich in 1945. It was revived again in 1952, with a brilliant cast, for export to Western Europe as a sample of American musical-theatrical culture.

The operatic score is fortified by frequent and delightful songs, including "Summer Time", "I Got Plenty O' Nuttin' ", and "It Ain't Necessarily So!". There is a constant surge of emotion in the opera. It rests, said Brooks Atkinson (February 1, 1942) "on a barbaric foundation of whirling terror, superstition and excitement . . . Even the gaiety is passionate." However, there is a loss of the cheery, everyday atmosphere that the play Porgy somehow maintains against the violent action; the opera lacks "the limpid give and take of community life." The songs and music of the opera are amusing or feelingful, but the pathos of the human story, of a staunch soul denying defeat, blends more successfully with the essential cheeriness within the tumult and trouble of a poor Negro community in the play.

THE FOUR P'S   John Heywood

Court entertainer for King Henry VIII, John Heywood (English, 1497?-1580?) looked clearly at the abuses of his time, spoke boldly against them, and left one monument, the interlude of The Four P's, written about 1530.

An interlude is a dramatized anecdote or argument short enough to be presented between courses at a feast. Often it is little more than a versified conversation in dialogue. Such is The Four P's, "a newe and a very mery enterlude of a Palmer, a Pardoner, a Potycary and a Pedlar," each of whom, in his speeches, reveals his character, well set off by contrast; and each of whom, in his way, is an arrant knave. Through these persons, Heywood struck home at the society they helped fashion.

A Palmer is one whose branch of palm is a sign of great merit, betokening a pilgrimage to the Holy Land. A Pardoner is one who carries blessings from the Pope, holy relics, or other means of shortening one's stay in Purgatory; often, he promised forgiveness of all sins past and yet to be committed. A "Potycary", or apothecary, was understandably an ignoramus, and frequently a quack. The Pedlar was usually a "snapper-up of inconsidered trifles", as ready to steal as to sell. These four P's come together in Heywood's interlude, and out of their chatting rises a contest as to which can tell the biggest lie.

The dialogue is very neatly interwoven and moves to an amusing climax. When the men meet, each parades the merits of his profession. When the Palmer boasts of his wide travels, the Pardoner tells him he could have stayed comfortably at home and bought salvation. Too many of your promises, retorts the Palmer, are lies—and the contest is on. The Pedlar refuses to take part. Modestly he declares that he cannot match the others; they make him judge. Later, when the Potycary is displaying his wares, he tries to bribe the Pedlar; unsuccessful, he declares in surprise, "Forsooth, ye be an honest man!"

Among the holy relics the Pardoner displays are "Of All Hallows' the blessed jawbone . . . the great toe of Trinity . . . the bees that stung Eve under the forbidden tree . . . a buttock-bone of Pentecost." The English folk, in the very midst of King Henry's dispute with Rome, must have relished the satiric sting in such items.

The Pardoner's story pictures a woman redeemed from hell because Lucifer is glad to be rid of her lashing tongue. Thereupon the Palmer expresses surprise; in all his travels, he protests, he has never seen a woman who lost her temper. At once he is given the prize for the biggest lie.

The Four P's is a delightfully indigenous draught of merry England. The four characters are well pictured by their own speeches. The rhymed couplets have vigor; a native dramatic faculty carries the movement along. The dialogue of The Four P's, said John Addington Symonds, "exhibits far more life, variety, and spirit than many later and more elaborate creations of the English stage."

One may wonder whether, when he wrote the drunken porter's fantasy of Hell-gate in Macbeth*, Shakespeare remembered The Four P's. The play presses no moral; it rises entirely out of love for fun, and is significant as recognizing that entertainment is its own justification. Unquestionably the best of the English comic interludes, still richly humorous in its racy anecdotes and neat denouement, The Four P's points the way towards the Renaissance growth of the drama.

A WOMAN KILLED WITH KINDNESS   Thomas Heywood

Thomas Heywood (English, d. 1650?) seems to have devoted his active years wholly to the theatre. Beginning as an actor with the Lord Admiral's Company in 1598, later with the Queen's Players, he became a prolific playwright. He admitted authorship of some 220 plays.

The simplest and most effective of Elizabethan domestic dramas, according to Allardyce Nicoll, is A Woman Killed With Kindness, 1603. Here, with unaffected, sincere sympathy, with language direct and of the English soil, in a play that moves without artifice, Heywood tells a story that touches the heart and manifests a Christian spirit unusual in his, or any, time.

The story is simple. Frankford, discovering his wife in the arms of his friend Wendoll, banishes her—to live in comfort, but without ever seeing him or their children again. In remorse, she pines away and dies. At her death-bed, Frankford grants her the forgiveness that is her last request.

What gives the drama its distinction is the noble spirit of the author. "In all those qualities that gained for Shakespeare the attribute of gentle," Charles Lamb declared, Heywood "was not inferior to him—generosity, courtesy, temperance in the depths of passion; sweetness, in a word, and gentleness." Lamb saw Heywood as "a sort of prose Shakespeare. His scenes are to the full as natural and affecting. But we miss the poet." It is Nicoll's opinion that the play displays "a universality of atmosphere; and contains, both in language and in portraiture, a strength which comes close to that of Shakespeare himself."

The two opening scenes show contrasted levels of charm and merriment as we watch the gentlefolk and the servants at the Frankford wedding celebration. The third scene presents another of the vigorous brawls Heywood knew how to handle—this one over a wager between Sir Charles Mountford and Sir Francis Acton as to the skill of their hawks. Later there is an excellent scene, with play of words while Frankford, Mrs. Frankford, and Wendoll play at cards. Touching in its simplicity, yet dramatically most effective, is Frankford's hesitation before he enters his wife's chamber, where he expects to find—and does find—her lying with her paramour. Frankford withholds his sword—quite the opposite of Hamlet at Claudius' prayers—so as *not* to send them to death "with all their scarlet sins upon their backs."

The subsequent talk between the husband and wife is deeply scored with pathos. Mrs. Frankford, broken and contrite, speaks, as John Addington Symonds noted, in "monosyllables more eloquent than protestation".

Most of Heywood's plays have an almost independent sub-plot; this one, brought into homely English terms from an Italian novella by Illicini, pictures the plight of Sir Charles Mountford after the hunting brawl.

Mistress Frankford's gown in a 1662 performance cost six pounds and thirteen shillings—exactly thirteen shillings more than Heywood was originally paid for the play.

The play has not been recently presented in New York, though two scenes of it were enacted at the MacDowell Club in 1922. It was produced at the Malvern Festival in England in 1931, with Ralph Richardson as the faithful servant Nicholas. The *London Times* (August 5, 1931) found in it "many a happy touch . . . the unfolding drama challenges the judgment at every turn." *A Woman Killed With Kindness* is a simple and dramatic picture of domestic tragedy, with natural yet tender play of passions in a gentle soul.

THE RAPE OF LUCRECE   *Thomas Heywood*

Of the various plays Thomas Heywood wrote on classical themes or legends, the best known is *The Rape of Lucrece*. The story of the play was originally told in Livy's history of Rome and in Shakespeare's poem of the same name as the play. It is a stark tale of the beginning of the Roman Republic in 509 B.C. While Collatine, a Roman general, is at camp, Sextus, son of Tarquin the Proud, slips off to Rome and rapes Collatine's wife—the proud and chaste Roman matron Lucrece. She summons her husband, tells him what has occurred, and stabs herself. The patriot Brutus, drawing the sword from her breast, swears to sheath it in the tyrants' hearts, and leads the revolution that replaces Rome's kings by chosen consuls.

In Shakespeare's poem, only the last fifty of its 1855 lines mention Brutus' hopes, and only the very last couplet tells that public consent led to "Tarquin's everlasting banishment." Heywood, on the contrary, gives almost the whole fifth act to the bloody consequences of Tarquin's rape and Lucrece's suicide. Porsena, King of the Tuscans, seizes the opportunity to march against Rome, and Heywood sweeps through episodes of this conflict. We see the heroic stand of single-handed Horatio at the bridge; we watch Scevola, caught trying to kill Porsena and threatened with torture, calmly hold his own hand in the torch-flame; we see Brutus the first Consul fight Sextus Tarquinius till they both fall dead—and promise of peace and freedom shines over Rome. Heywood's phrases and allusions in his play show his familiarity not merely with Shakespeare's poem, but also with his dramas, especially *Hamlet** and *Macbeth**.

The play is one of striking and poignant contrasts. First we see the simple and refreshing homelike quality of Heywood's domestic dramas in the early scenes of Lucrece and her maids. Later, in Act IV, after watching the ravished and despairing Lucrece wake in the hateful arms of Sextus, we hear Valerius at camp sing a charming song to the dawn. In another moment, however, Valerius is singing a bawdy song about the general's wife, Lucrece; and when the clown comes from Rome with the message from Lucrece, the clown and Valerius sing a still more suggestive catch.

The songs, incidentally, contributed a great deal to the play's popularity and made outstanding the minor part of Valerius. The play, according to Alan Holaday's study (1950), was written in 1594, the year of Shakespeare's poem, and revised in 1607. Its first printed version, 1608, contains thirteen songs, inserted in the drama, says Holaday—all save "Pack, clouds, away"—"with blithe disregard of artistic propriety"; the fifth edition, 1638, contains twenty-two songs, many of which were quite popular.

Several other playwrights have told Lucrece's story. The Italian Alfieri covers it in his *Brutus*, published in 1783 (see *Myrrha**); in England Nathaniel Lee wrote *Lucius Junius Brutus*, about 1680; John H. Payne, *Brutus, or The Fall of Tarquin*, 1820. In France, François Ponsard wrote *Lucrèce* in 1843.

Five years later, at the Théâtre de la Republique (its name just changed from Théâtre Français) the entire Provisional Government and an excited populace watched Rachel in *Lucrèce*, cheering wildly at every reference to the earlier, Roman revolution, especially at Brutus' remark, "It is easier to destroy than to restore." The brother and the nephew of Napoleon were in the audience. At the end of the evening, Rachel, kneeling with the tricolor pressed to her heart, sang the *Marseillaise*.

In the twentieth century, André Obey wrote a French version of the story, which Thornton Wilder translated, and Katharine Cornell brought to the American stage: *The Rape of Lucrece*, in Cleveland, November 29, in New York, December 20, 1932.

The music drama *The Rape of Lucretia*, which opened in New York December 29, 1948, with book by Ronald Duncan and music by Benjamin Britten, is an operatic form of the Obey version.

The varied moods of Heywood's play, without the almost ascetic quality of the twentieth century version, but with a lusty vigor of life and a love of mankind and of justice, remain the best dramatic capture of the old Roman story.

THE IDLE INN   *Peretz Hirschbein*

After writing realistic dramas and plays influenced by Maeterlinck* in which the mood was the major element, Peretz Hirschbein (Russian; came to U.S. in 1911; 1880-1949) moved to his best work in plays, often dramatized folk tales, of simple village Jews in their poor but picturesque environment. The best of these plays, with an almost idyllic charm, is *The Idle Inn*, 1911, in which there is a complicated intrigue, natural and supernatural.

Bendet, father of fair Maite, and Mendel, father of Leibush, decide to have their children marry. For a wedding gift, Bendet plans to move the old Idle Inn, which is a white elephant on his hands, and make it his wedding present to the couple. The spirits haunting the inn resent the move; they come to the wedding disguised as merchants and interrupt the ceremony. This happily does no harm, for Maite is already secretly married to Eisik (Itzik). With Eisik, she runs off to the Idle Inn woods, and the spirits frighten away the pursuers. To break the spell Bendet sets fire to the inn; but Eisik comes back to Bendet's home—which also burns—and carries off Maite forever.

Played in Yiddish by Jacob Ben-Ami in 1919 (the first production of Emanuel Reicher for the Jewish Art Theatre), *The Idle Inn* (also called *The Haunted Inn*) was presented in English in New York on December 20, 1921 with Ben-Ami, Sam Jaffe, Louis Wolheim, and Edward G. Robinson. It was revived in 1936 by the Federal Theatre. The reviewers praised the play highly. The *New York Globe* (December 21, 1921) mentioned its "curious and seductive flavor" and singled out the wedding scene for its ruddy and vigorous beauty: "It is a scene overflowing with vitality. Nothing at all like its charm and its comedy has been seen on Broadway."

The combination of unusual atmosphere and of folk legend, however, weakens the impact of the drama. The alarms and the interference of the ghosts are at odds with the realistic elements of the story; the quaintness does not compensate for the consequent lack of emotional drive. Yet it has a haunting quality and a color and vigor that make this folk play a still rewarding drama.

DEATH AND THE FOOL   *Hugo von Hofmannsthal*

Hugo von Hofmannsthal (Austrian, 1874-1929) summed up, in effect, Austria as the meeting-ground of many cultures. In his work, as Richard Alewyn has described it, "there is the magic of the *Arabian Nights* and the severity of the medieval morality, the passionate roar of Dionysian

Greece and the morbid charm of dying Venice, the rustic purity of Corinthian peasants and the mellow abundance of the Renaissance, the naive grace of Mozartian rococo and the apocalyptic gloom of the baroque." Although he adapted works of many periods of the drama, from Aeschylus to Otway, Hofmannsthal's plays have a richly poetic and colorful quality of their own; moreover, they lend themselves to elaborate production and scenic effects. Max Reinhardt staged many of Hofmannsthal's dramas, and several of his works were set to music by Richard Strauss: *Electra*, 1909; *Ariadne at Naxos*, 1910; *Der Rosenkavalier (Knight of the Rose)*, 1911; *Egyptian Helen*, 1928.

Hailed as a poet at the age of sixteen, Hofmannsthal was also a precocious playwright. At seventeen he wrote his first play and before he was twenty was convinced of the futility of trying to hold the world of beauty apart from the world of ugly reality: art and life are one. The inevitable failure and waste of such effort, of the attempt to keep aloof from the taints of life, are most poetically and effectively presented in *Death and the Fool*, 1893.

The play is more concerned with idea and mood than with events and characters. Claudio, pondering his days, reflects that he has had all his wishes, but merely as a spectator, without any sense of real participation, without feeling life's many joys and sorrows. In the guise of a musician, Death comes; and Claudio pleads that he has not yet really lived. Death recalls various episodes—of his mother's love; of the woman whom he has discarded; of his faithful friend—to show Claudio that life has been lavished and wasted upon him. Finally Claudio welcomes the passage from "life's dreaming into death's awakening."

The wide range of Hofmannsthal's plays constitutes the fullest poetic exploration of the soul in modern drama, with the persistent presentation of the folly of withholding oneself, the need and the fruitfulness of full participation in life. In many of his works, this thought is clothed in lavish color, in flaming emotional hues, with opportunities for rich or symbolic costumes, elaborate staging, and strikingly baroque or stylized acting. It is maintained at its simplest, with charm, pathos, and power, in his early poetic drama *Death and the Fool*.

RASMUS MONTANUS   *Ludwig Holberg*

Born in Bergen, Norway, Ludwig Holberg (Danish, 1684-1754) turned from the Latin of his day to found the Danish national literature. Professor, author in every literary form, he raised Scandinavian literature to a level of international worth. Between 1722 and 1727 he wrote twenty-eight plays.

In *Rasmus Montanus*, 1731, the leading character is the butt of a satire on the snobbery of learning that apes foreign ways and sneers at what is local and homey and of the native soil. The student son of the well-to-do peasant Jeppe Berg, Rasmus comes back from Copenhagen crammed full of Latin and disputatiousness. He shocks his parents by his air of superiority and the neighbors by his outlandish ideas. He actually tries to convince the bailiff that the world turns round. When the wealthy freeholder Jeronimus finds that Rasmus is not jesting, he wants to break the engagement between his daughter Lisbed and Rasmus. Toward his brother Jacob, the son whom Jeppe had kept at home to give a hand with the work, Rasmus is condescending; he expects Jacob to wait upon him. Gradually, however, the situation changes. The Deacon, who wept when Rasmus by chop-logic proved he was a rooster, out-shouts Rasmus in almost-remembered Latin until the neighbors think he has out-argued the student. But Jacob's common sense refutes Rasmus' long-winded disputation. At length an army lieutenant comes, tricks Rasmus into accepting "press money", and orders him off to military service. Rasmus then sees the folly of his superior ways; he is let off and happily rejoined with Lisbed.

The satire is merrily and clearly pressed home. The play may lack the fire of passion, but it has the twinkle of intelligence. "There is no complexity of plot-making," said Brander Matthews in his *Chief European Dramatists* (1916), "the characters are drawn in the primary colors, and the story moves forward with the swift simplicity of a fable." Technically, *Rasmus Montanus* makes one useful innovation often credited to Lessing: the locale of the scenes changes only at the ends of the acts; there is but one set called for throughout an act. *Rasmus Montanus* is still performed in Scandinavia; it has survived two centuries as a lively and amusing satire on presumptuous pretension.

DOUGLAS   *John Home*

The most celebrated of Scottish tragic melodramas, *Douglas; or, The Noble Shepherd*, by the Reverend John Home (1722-1808), stirred keen controversy on both sides of the Cheviot Hills. Refused by the English producer David Garrick, it was produced in Edinburgh in 1756. Amid the tumult of patriotic enthusiasm one triumphant voice cried, "Whur's yer Wully Shacksper noo?" The Scot David Hume called the tragedy "one of the most interesting and pathetic pieces that was ever exhibited in any theatre . . . with the theatric genius of Shakespeare and Otway, refined from the unhappy barbarism of the one and the licentiousness of the other." Samuel Johnson, however, defied the Scot Boswell to show him ten consecutive good lines in the play.

In spite of partisanship, *Douglas* was a hit the next year, 1757, at Covent Garden in London, with Peg Woffington, and Spranger Barry as young Norval. Mrs. (Ann Street) Barry's most successful role was as Lady Randolph in the play, which she enacted constantly until her retirement in 1798. Sarah Kemble Siddons played Lady Randolph first in 1784. The *Gentleman's* magazine of February, 1757, recorded that the Scotch Presbytery raised strenuous objection to a minister's writing a play and to other ministers' attending performances. Nevertheless, *Douglas* was frequently revived for over a hundred years. In 1819 the play was converted by Thomas Dibdin into a spectacular melodrama; a burlesque version was presented in 1837.

The story springs from a feud between the clans of Malcolm and Douglas. In secret the son of Douglas, saved by the son of Malcolm, becomes his friend and marries his sister, Matilda. Both young men are killed in battle, leaving Matilda to bear the Douglas' child. She sends it away with a trusted nurse, who is drowned in a flood. Matilda, now the Malcolm heiress, is wooed for her wealth by the scheming Glenalvon, from whom she saves herself by marriage with Lord Randolph.

We are told all this during the first act, which begins when assassins secretly set upon Lord Randolph by Glenalvon are driven away by a young stranger, Norval. His jewels identify Norval to Matilda as her

son, and she reveals the secret to him. Their friendliness leads Glenalvon to provoke Lord Randolph's jealousy. Norval, refusing to fight
Randolph, is stabbed in the back by Glenalvon; he kills the villain but
himself also dies; and Lady Randolph leaps off a cliff.

Despite the Scottish praise lavished on the tragedy, *Douglas* is in the
main a pedestrian drama. However, it was a famous play and still acts
well because, as even the *London Times* (November 29, 1935) admitted,
it has a "compact and exciting plot, strong verse, and occasionally magnificent rhetoric". At the Edinburgh Festival of 1950, the performance of
Dame Sybil Thorndike showed that Lady Randolph can still be deeply
moving. There is considerable action, colorful swishing of kilts in the
play, which with dignity if not depth gives vivid presentation to a moving story.

FAIR AND WARMER   *Avery Hopwood*

In the second decade of the present century, there developed on
Broadway a species of simperingly salacious, rollickingly risqué drama
that came to be known as the bedroom farce. Chief concocter of such
liqueured bonbons was (James) Avery Hopwood (American, 1882-1928),
with *Fair and Warmer*, 1915; *The Gold-Diggers*, 1919; *Ladies' Night* (in
a Turkish Bath), 1920; *The Demi-Virgin*, 1921.

First of the genre and best of the bedroom farces is *Fair and Warmer*,
which opened in New York November 7, 1915, for 377 performances, and
played in London, opening May 14, 1918, for 497. It combines the amusing opportunities of tipsiness and sex with surface innocence, picturing
two ingenuous, unsophisticated young folk trying to be naughty. Billy
Bartlett believes a man's place is the home, beslippered beside his wife;
Mrs. Bartlett likes to go out on parties. Mrs. Jack Wheeler, on the
other hand, is a home girl whose husband believes that a man should
go out, on principle, at least once a week. Left alone, Mrs. Wheeler and
Billy Bartlett decide to concoct a compromising situation to make their
spouses jealous. Never having prepared a drink, they mix malignant
cocktails. Through moments and movements hilarious to watch they
seek to be mutually seductive, but succeed only in growing tired and
bored; then they drink to keep awake. Naturally, they fall asleep. The
other two, returning, find them in the bedroom in what indeed seems a
compromising situation—mirthfully readjusted.

The reviews of the play sound like blurbs. Alexander Woollcott
reported: "You are quite likely to spend two hours in immoderate
laughter"; Heywood Broun hailed it as "among the most amusing plays
New York has seen"; the *Telegraph* called it "the best farce of this season, and one of the best of any season." Declared the *Globe*: "Not only
the cleverest and most amusing thing Mr. Hopwood has done, but one
of the cleverest written by an American pen." When the play reached
Boston, even the *Transcript* (June 21, 1927) unbent to declare it "broad,
obvious—and never failing."

There is in plays of this sort no more than a mental fornication, a
tinsel dallying and sparkler trifling with "insinuendos" of amours. There
is a gentle pricking of the risibilities with the risqué, a deft and never
too daring display of ripening charms, a proferring that withholds, a
refusal that half tenders. Such plays do not, as some rigid moralists have
fulminated, convert the theatre into a bawd; they may, indeed, serve as

the Aristotelian catharsis, purging the audience "of such emotions." Certainly they entertain; and none of them more deftly and more gaily than *Fair and Warmer.*

PRUNELLA   *Lawrence Housman*

Prunella; or, Love in a Garden by Lawrence Housman (English, b. 1865) is a charming blend of play, pantomime, and opera. It opens in a garden "where it is always afternoon." Although lessoned by Aunt Prim, Aunt Prude, and Aunt Privacy, Prunella listens to the mummer's lure of Pierrot, chief of the strolling players, who serenades her as she climbs down a ladder. While Prunella hesitates the statue of Love in the garden wakes and plays its viol. As Pierrette, Prunella goes away with her Pierrot. Two years later the sole surviving aunt, Privacy, sells the garden to a rich stranger. He is Pierrot, now despairingly seeking Prunella. He explains to Privacy: "She left me . . . I had been gone a whole year; but I came back again. You see now—it is not I who left her; she didn't wait for me long enough."

Pierrot wants to hear of the old troupe, to help him forget Pierrette; and Scaramel gives him word: "Coquette. Hmm. Her modesty's down at ankle now, like a slipt garter. Romp's a little heavier on the bounce than she used to be. Tawdry's much as usual, but dressed worse than ever, and costing more. The old faces, master, as you desired?" Then one disconsolate face slips in, of one to whom Pierrot had earlier sung "Little bird in your nest, are you there, are you there?" At first she does not recognize the rich stranger, but Pierrot is brought home to her by love: the statue floods with light and plays its viol, and the garden grows loud with song.

Prunella opened in London December 23, 1904, with Harley Granville-Barker, who collaborated in its writing, as Pierrot. The music by Joseph Moorat was in constant flow beneath the dialogue, surging for the songs. The movements, almost as in pantomime, gave a fragile, delicate artificiality to the fantasy. The play was revived in London in 1906, 1907, 1910, 1930, 1933 (in the Priory Garden at Orpington, a perfect setting), and in 1937. In New York it opened October 27, 1913, with Ernest Glendinning as Pierrot and it ran for 105 performances. Sylvia Sidney played Prunella in 1926, when the *New York Telegram* (June 16) called it "an exquisite little fantasy . . . in just the proper key of visionary romance."

"There is a curious mounting something in Mr. Housman's rhythms," said the *New York Tribune* (October 28, 1913), "in the music which serves as an undercurrent to most of the lines, in the exquisite beauty and harmony of the colors and movement, which captures the doubtful spectator and is altogether perfect of its kind"; and the *Mail* called *Prunella* "as tender in sentiment as the love of a child, and worldly wise as the philosophy of a graybeard."

Prunella is a favorite, and a challenge to perform, in little theatres. The stock figure Pierrot is here a poetic symbol of the casual fancy that turns away, then recognizes the true worth of what it has left behind. In a delicate, dream-like blend of poetry, pantomime, music and drama, *Prunella* shows us such a fancy ripening into love.

SHENANDOAH   *Bronson Howard*

Bronson Howard (1842-1908), whose most popular play was *Shenan-*

doah, a vivid melodrama of the War Between the States, was significant in several ways in the growth of the American theatre. Upon the success of his light comedy *Saratoga*, 1870 (produced in England as *Brighton*, 1874), he became the first American to make a living solely from his plays. With *Young Mrs. Winthrop*, 1882, he presented the first serious study of American life on the stage. After *Shenandoah* (rewritten from his *Drum Taps*, produced in Louisville, Kentucky, about 1868) made a poor start (as a five act play) in Boston in 1888, a four act production by Charles Frohman opened in New York September 9, 1889, with Wilton Lackaye, Henry Miller, and Effie Shannon, running for 250 performances. In Chicago the next year *Shenandoah* reached over 100 performances; for more than a decade it was exceeded in popularity in the North only by *Uncle Tom's Cabin**, on which the stars forever shone.

Shenandoah opens in Charleston, South Carolina, with Colonel Kerchival West, officer of the United States Army, declaring his love to Gertrude Ellingham. An explosion takes her to the window; it was a shell over Fort Sumter. She says to her beloved: "We are enemies now!" Gertrude must also part with her school friend Madeline West, beloved of her brother, Colonel Robert Ellingham of the Confederate States Army. The plot intertwines the usual Civil War episodes of parted lovers and spies, but reaches its climax when the defeated and withdrawing Yankee forces hear the approaching hoof-beats of Sheridan's great ride, and the General calls out his famous command, "Turn the other way!", to shift the fortunes of the battle and the war. The last act of the play, with the war ended, presents a rousing review of the Union troops and unites the happy lovers.

Excellently intertwined in the war plot is the jealousy of old General Haverill as his young wife's letter, taken from their gallant son's body by the spy Thornton, is found by the General on the wounded Colonel West. Superb, too, is the manner in which Gertrude is torn between her southern patriotism and her northern love, until in a sudden heart-wrung cry she urges on her own horse that is bearing Sheridan to save the day for the North.

Superlatives crowded the reviews of *Shenandoah*, especially for "the greatest battle scene ever shown upon the stage". A New York Academy of Music production included 250 men, many "late members of the U.S. Artillery, most of them from Manila where they have seen active service", and ended with a charge of over fifty horses across the resounding stage. Jack, the horse assigned to Sheridan throughout the run of the play, grew so attuned to the part that a dozen trainers could not hold him when his cue came; once when Sheridan was not in the saddle on time he galloped across the stage without him. "The government should open a recruiting station at the Academy," declared the *New York Dramatic Mirror* (May 17, 1898), "there would be a rush of volunteers after the performance of *Shenandoah*." It is impossible, the *New York World* stated (October 7, 1894) "to conceive that stagecraft can go any further than this scene takes it."

More than the fervor of Sheridan's ride gave *Shenandoah* its popularity. "Its clever character drawing and dialogue," said the *Boston Post* (October 7, 1890) "are in Howard's best and most polished vein . . . Love, war, and the varied emotions of the most stormy period in all our latter history are blended in one effective and consistent impression." "Its pathos is always deep and true," commented the *New York Tribune* (August 31, 1894); "Its humor is natural and appropriate, and its interest is that of human lives and human hearts."

Little more need be said. A 1917 production of *Shenandoah*, with Tyrone Power, was presented in Los Angeles. Along with David Belasco's *The Heart of Maryland** and William Gillette's *Secret Service* Shenandoah* remains, as the *New York Herald* called it in 1894 (August 31): "the most interesting, the most exciting, the most dignified of modern military dramas."

THEY KNEW WHAT THEY WANTED   *Sidney Howard*

After several adaptations from the French and an original melodrama of the Italian Renaissance, Sidney Howard (American, 1891-1939) came into his own with *They Knew What They Wanted*. With superb plot construction and a colorful capture of the fervor and vitality of life in the United States, the drama displays that gift of character portrayal which remains Howard's major achievement.

The story is set in a grape vineyard in California. Old Tony, whom Prohibition has made rich, writes to Amy, a waitress he had seen in San Francisco, proposing marriage. The proposition catches the lonely girl, and she comes to Tony, eager and hopeful. When she arrives, Tony's young helper, Joe, doesn't know what to make of her cordial though nervous greeting, until Tony—whose reckless driving to meet Amy's train ended in a ditch—is brought in on a stretcher. Then Amy discovers that Tony, timid because of his age, had sent her Joe's picture instead of his own.

What with Tony's broken legs and Amy's broken heart, the inevitable happens between Amy and Joe. But as she nurses her husband, Amy comes to recognize his sterling qualities. His ever cheery optimism, his understanding, his generous affection, awaken her love. But she is pregnant. It tears her heart to tell Tony this and to tell him she is leaving him; but Tony's need and Tony's love reach out to her. The casual Joe, an I.W.W., and a wanderer at heart, goes off; Amy and Tony in regathered love prepare a home for their child.

Howard has stated that the plot was "shamelessly, consciously, and even proudly derived from the legend of Tristan and Iseult".

They Knew What They Wanted, with Pauline Lord, Richard Bennett and Glenn Anders, opened November 24, 1924. Charges of immorality were made, and on April 26, 1925, the play was examined by a Broadway play-jury and cleared. The same day it was announced as the winner— the Theatre Guild's first—of the Pulitzer Prize, for "raising the standard of good morals, good taste, and good manners." The play has remained continuously popular. Tallulah Bankhead appeared in the London production in 1926; various companies in the U.S. have included June Havoc and Sally Rand as Amy. There was a New York revival, October 2, 1939, with June Walker; another, February 14, 1949, with Paul Muni. The film (1940) directed by Garson Kanin, starred Carole Lombard, Charles Laughton, William Gargan, and Frank Fay.

There was some objection, when the play was first produced, to its picture of unfaithfulness on the very night of a wedding and also to the husband's forgiveness of his wife's action. *Theatre* magazine (February 1925) called the drama "an unusually well-constructed play, smudged up with repellent situations." There is, however, a searching truth, almost an inevitability, in Amy's first reaction to the deception; her chagrin and her touched pride, and the picture of Joe she has come with, all drive her to Joe's arms. There is equal, but more winning, truth in Tony's forgiveness. Indeed, with his amusing Italian accent and curious ways, Tony is one of the most engaging figures of the modern American theatre.

The play as a whole, in Gilbert Gabriel's words (November 25, 1924), is "a winning little idyl of the California vineyards, nonetheless fond and sunny for the thumbprint of reality that is on it . . . a happy, lovable play. Yet it is a shrewd one, too, and sharp". Time has not altered this judgment of *They Knew What They Wanted*, which remains a colorful and a dramatic story, revealing finely responsive traits of human character.

NED McCOBB'S DAUGHTER   *Sidney Howard*

Many of the elements of the old-fashioned folk melodrama—including city villainy, country shrewdness, and even the overhanging mortgage and the impending child—are present in this play. What lifts it above that level is the salty savor of Carrie Callahan, the New England daughter of Captain Ned McCobb, and the richly human solidity and warmth with which she takes life and its complications. Rekindling the oldtime rural sure-fireworks with the fresh breeze of his own temperament, Sidney Howard has given us a play that bears the pine-smoke and the maple sugar of New England.

Carrie, in the play, has troubles enough; she has never told her father of the unsavory past her husband George has left behind in New York. They must raise $2,000 or George will go to jail for holding back fares on the Maine ferry where he works. Old McCobb dies of a stroke, but lawyer Grove tells Carrie the farm has already been mortgaged by her father to get George out of an earlier scrape. George's brother, Babe Callahan, arrives from New York with a plan to use the farm as a rum-running depot for his bootlegging. He offers to put up the money to save George; desperately Carrie agrees. Then Babe insists that she keep her children on the farm. As "blinds", they can ride the loads of hay under which the liquor is concealed. Through Babe, Carrie learns that George's earlier "scrape" involved money to get her helper Jennie a doctor when she was going to have a child. At this last straw, Carrie humps her back and, with the imminence of Federal agents, outwits the bootlegger, sends the Callahans flying, and saves the day and the future for the McCobbs.

Presented by the Theatre Guild on November 29, 1926, with Clare Eames, Alfred Lunt, Margalo Gillmore, and Dudley Digges, the play ran for 129 performances. It is still popular. It was acted at Sing Sing in 1938 with Mildred Natwick; at San Antonio in 1948, with Peggy Wood.

The play is a racy one. Not only is Carrie herself effectively drawn, but each figure stands distinct, clearly limned with deft revealing strokes. Every character is a "character". As the *Boston Transcript* (October 4, 1927) declared: "Not once does Mr. Howard's hand slip or his invention falter . . . His mind does not relax nor his pen halt until speech has

added trait to trait and each several quality translated itself into immediate deed . . . Soon this gusto and abundance become an irresistible
exuberance of the theatre." *Ned McCobb's Daughter* is, in essence, a
rural melodrama converted by dramaturgic skill and power of human
portrayal into a lively picture of a sturdy character in a crisis.

YELLOW JACK   *Sidney Howard*

The year that Paul De Kruif's *Microbe Hunters* was published (1926),
Sidney Howard suggested to the author a dramatization of the eleventh
chapter, which tells the story of the confirmation of the mosquito as the
carrier of yellow fever ("yellow jack"), a finding that made possible
the completion of the Panama Canal. With the help of De Kruif, Sidney
Howard somewhat later found the time to write such a play, and on
March 6, 1934, Broadway was pleasantly surprised with *Yellow Jack*.
The play was hailed by Brooks Atkinson as "of tremendous importance
to the stage . . . enlarges the scope of the modern theatre," and by the
New York Herald-Tribune as "a kind of minor miracle . . . it is almost
as if, through the adroit use of lights, visible characters, spoken words,
pause and spacing, and nothing else, life were given to an article in
the encyclopedia."

The isolation by Army doctors in the Canal Zone of the mosquito as
the carrier of yellow fever involved some opposition from conservatives
and old fogies at Washington and elsewhere. Mainly it was a question of
securing and observing two sets of four volunteers. One group was to
live in a tent, filthy and foul with blankets and clothing of men who had
died of the fever, but free of mosquitoes; the other group in a tent as
clean as scientific prophylaxis could maintain it, but to which the mosquito was given full access. Out of the persistence of the "theorizing
old fool" who entertained the mosquito theory, out of the enthusiasm
and self-experiments of the doctors—one of whom died in the quest—
and out of the seemingly dull waiting of the volunteers, Howard built a
play of quiet but gathering intensity. "Without question", said producer
Gilbert Miller, speaking of producer Guthrie McClintic's offering,
"*Yellow Jack* is one of the greatest productions I have ever witnessed in
the American theatre." Stephen Vincent Benét called the play "the
finest thing ever done in the theatre by an American."

The story is advanced with complete realism of detail. The characters are natural, and the volunteers are effectively differentiated: the
eloquent, almost grandiloquent Irishman; the radical Jew; the lazy
Southern lad; the man who wants to be a sergeant. The language and
the attitudes of the speakers, moreover, are not only natural; they are
historical. Only the staging departed from the realistic treatment. The
various scenes were presented on a single setting, a simple stage archi-
tecturally disposed in various levels, with steps and curving bars marking off the doctors' office or the encampment site. Sufficiently suggestive
and admirably apt, the staging permitted a rapid flow of the story.

Howard was perhaps justifiably afraid of the seeming barrenness of
his theme, with an impersonal nurse as the only female in the cast and
the villain literally an insect. For emotion he at times turned to theatrical standbys. As John Mason Brown (March 10, 1934) pointed out, he
is "not above running up the American flag when he thinks he needs it,
playing taps to guarantee a flood of tears, and closing many of his scenes

with good old tag lines." Howard need not have resorted to such devices. The play holds its audience and is indeed a constant favorite with community groups. It was seen again on Broadway in 1947.

The theatre has often made reference to or incidental use of scientific discoveries. Rarely has it, as in *Yellow Jack*, made discovery itself the dramatic theme. The play was hailed by *Stage* magazine (April, 1934) for depicting the heroism of science, which enlists not to kill men, but to save them: "The antagonist is so small as to be nearly invisible, even to the fine eye of the microscope, but deadly enough to call forth a strange and glorious kind of dramatic conflict . . . If there is one thing that differentiates our age from the age of antiquity, it is the faith in experimental science. If modern drama is to have a similar grandeur, it must not exclude such science from its theme. *Yellow Jack* has accepted that theme, and projected it with splendor . . . a notable contribution to the American theatre."

Unfortunately, the theatrical promise foreseen in the first quoted comment, and the last, has not been fulfilled. Stories of great scientific achievement have been frequent in motion pictures, which more smoothly than the drama can course through a laborious and hopeful life. *Yellow Jack*, therefore, remains distinctive as the dramatic presentation of a gallant fight of men against a long defiant foe of man.

A TRIP TO CHINATOWN   *Charles Hale Hoyt*

In the last decade of the nineteenth century, the increasing popularity of the ten-twen'-thirt' melodrama was matched by that of the lively farce with interpolated songs and dances that was one of the forerunners of the present-day musical comedy. Chief among the writers of such farces in the United States was Charles Hale Hoyt (1859-1900). Anna Held made her American debut and Maude Adams her first New York appearance in plays by Hoyt. His most popular play was *A Trip to Chinatown; or, An Idyl of San Francisco*. With its premiere in Philadelphia, January 26, 1891 and opening in New York on November 9, 1891, it ran for 657 performances, a record not broken until *Lightnin'* crackled in 1918. The dancer Loie Fuller made her serpentine "skirt dance" famous in *A Trip to Chinatown*. The play opened in London on September 29, 1894 for a run of 125 performances.

The characters in the play never get to Chinatown but the audience gets considerable fun by the way. Indeed, the destination is only a trick by which Ben Gay, a wealthy and strict widower, is persuaded to let his daughter Tony and his nephew Rashleigh Gay go out with Norman Blood, Isabelle Dame, and some other friends, (im)properly chaperoned by the widow Mrs. Daisy Guyer. Their intention is to go to the masquerade ball at the Cliff House. Mrs. Guyer's letter to Rashleigh making the arrangements is delivered to old Ben by mistake; he interprets it as a billet doux making rendezvous, and he goes to meet the widow, first at the Riche Restaurant, then at the masquerade ball. After countless misadventures and tipsy venturing the younger folk surprise Ben in the midst of his pleasures and out of his discomfiture win greater freedom.

One manuscript of the play sets the last act not at the ball but in Ben Gay's home gymnasium (which permits the ladies to appear in shorts); here, Ben is exposed by his "I. O. U." on the Riche Restaurant menu.

Much of the fun of the play rises from Ben's old friend Welland Strong, who constantly checks his temperature and announces how much each gay spurt is taking off his life, but insists on joining the youngsters in all their reveling. There is a deal of dancing at the ball, and all the men, young and old, chase a high-kicking masquerader who turns out to be Mrs. Guyer's maid. The *Boston Transcript* (February 10, 1891) could well say that the play presents "a world in which conversation consists of diffusive slang and warmed-over waggishness, a world where high kicking is a high virtue, where a lady is reckoned as well and becomingly dressed in inverse ratio to the extent of her raiment, and where any and every member of society is prone, as well as expected, to break out at any moment, and with or without provocation, into song, dance, or other irrelevancy."

The songs in the play were epoch-making. Three by Percy Gaunt are "The Bowery," "Push Dem Clouds Away," and "Reuben and Cynthia." A song interpolated at a Milwaukee performance stopped the show; this was "After the Ball" (1892) by Charles K. Harris, which has sold well over five million copies. "Reuben, Reuben, I've been thinking" and "the Bowery, the Bowery, I'll never go there any more" are classics of popular song.

A Trip to Chinatown was constantly played for a decade. The *Philadelphia Record* in 1893 summed up its appeal: "The curtain goes up on silly merriment and almost three hours later the curtain comes down on silly merriment." Several years later (January 28, 1896) the *Boston Transcript* reported that the play captured "all that is most original and best in Mr. Hoyt's peculiar talent; in its way, it is a gem." Outside of sophisticate circles, *A Trip to Chinatown* still has much to please, and a little refurbishing would make it still shine on Broadway.

HERNANI   *Victor Hugo*

The French Romantic drama, surging free from two centuries of classical rule, reached flood tide with the work of Victor Hugo (1802-1885). Already hailed as a leader by the young Romantics, Hugo in his preface to the play *Cromwell*, 1827, issued the direct challenge: "Let us take the hammer to poetic systems. Let us tear down the old plastering that conceals the façade of art. There are neither rules nor models; rather, there are no other rules than the general laws of nature."

In accordance with his own precept, Hugo wrote *Hernani* (1830), and at the prospect of its presentation at the Théâtre Français, blood began to boil. Seven members of the Academy petitioned Charles X to keep the theatre closed "against all productions of the new school, and reserved exclusively for writers who really apprehend the beautiful and the true." With kingly modesty Charles replied, "In literary matters my place, gentlemen, is only, like yours, amongst the audience."

As January 1830 moved along, classicists eavesdropped at rehearsals, caught snatches of the play and parodied them before the production. A burlesque of *Hernani, Hounded by the Horn*, even beat it to the stage. The Théâtre Français company itself was cold to the drama. Hugo received threatening letters. The painter Charlet offered him a bodyguard of four janissaries; boldly Hugo declared that on opening night he would dispense with the usual claque. Instead, the young artists of Paris rallied to him, led by Gautier in a new rose-colored waistcoat. Their passes to the theatre were red slips marked Hierro! (Spanish for "iron"—their mood for the evening). And on February 25, 1830, *Hernani* opened. The hisses of the classicists and the cheers of the romantics so drowned the play that hardly a word was heard from the stage all evening. For almost a hundred nights the tumult continued. Duels were fought over the drama's merits. Finally, *Hernani*, Romanticism and freedom won. The play stands as a milestone in the history of the French drama. On its centenary, February 25, 1930, Edmond Rostand, at a great celebration, read a poem "A Night at *Hernani*."

The story has all the turbulence and violence of the Spanish "cape and sword" drama, in which the *pundonor* (point of honor) drives young love to rapturous death. In the year 1519 the outlaw Hernani is in love with Doña Sol, who is betrothed to her old guardian Don Ruy Gomez. Don Carlos (King Charles V of Spain) covets her. Knightly obligations and the laws of hospitality out-balance jealousy. Don Carlos saves Hernani from Ruy Gomez; then Hernani spares the King, and Ruy Gomez hides Hernani from the King's pursuit. In thanks, Hernani gives Ruy Gomez a horn and his word that he will end his life when Ruy Gomez sounds it. Together they now pursue the King, who has carried off Doña Sol, and Don Carlos is saved only by the bells that announce his election as Holy Roman Emperor. Don Carlos grants amnesty to all below the rank of Count. Doña Sol exclaims that this spares Hernani, but the outlaw proudly proclaims his noble birth. The Emperor pardons him and sanctions his marriage with Doña Sol. But on the bridal day, Ruy Gomez sounds the fateful horn. Doña Sol snatches and shares Hernani's poison and Ruy Gomez also kills himself.

This surge of romantic heroism, of pride that dooms its owner, of love where "all is true, and all is good, and all is beautiful, and naught is wanting," Hugo has couched in majestic lyrical verse, with striking images, stark contrasts, and bold dramatic conceptions. Even without the excitement of the classical ire and romantic verve that led to "the battle of *Hernani*," the play is striking enough to have been a great success. Its tumult, however, was part of the aesthetic and political turmoil of the day; those that cheered the play also helped put Louis Philippe on the throne in the revolution of July 1830.

The English felt the disorder as well as the power of the play. The *Foreign Quarterly Review* (October 1830) declared: "We cannot better compare M. Hugo's drama than to one of those Gothic castles, amidst which he has placed its scenes; it is vast and striking from the magnitude of its outline, varied from the accumulation of materials it contains, powerful from the wild strength which has been employed, or, rather, wasted in its construction; but, like it, incoherent in its plan, and mixed in its architecture; with pillars where it is impossible to trace any connection between the capital and the base, shapeless chambers, where meanness sits side by side with magnificence, and dark and winding passages, which terminate after all in a prospect of a dead wall, or an empty courtyard."

In 1844 Verdi based his opera *Ernani* on the Hugo play. Sarah Bernhardt acted in *Hernani* in London in 1879 and in the United States in 1887. Mounet-Sully brought it to America again in 1894, when the *New York Times* (March 27) said that in it, "passion never became effusive, nor heroism absurd" and the *Boston Transcript* (May 12, 1894) found it crowded with "people who have much of the stuff of humanity in them, whom we can imagine real, and whose emotions and actions we can reckon with . . . their humanity pierces the artificial, whimsical fantasticism of their surroundings, and to a great extent condones it. Surely there are few more emotionally powerful scenes on the stage than that terrible struggle between Hernani, Doña Sol, and Ruy Gomez in the fifth act."

The *Boston Transcript*, however, observed (April 12, 1930): "It is very evident that *Hernani* has become hopelessly old-fashioned for the modern stage." It is seldom acted; but it is often read. For, as the *Transcript* added, "it is sustained by the glory of the poet, by the brilliancy of the verse, and by a celebrity rare in the history of literature." Historic as *Hernani* stands, the drama of Hugo found few followers; only Rostand* has richly explored the Romantic vein. The characters are hollow as trumpets—but they make a trumpet sound. Dynamic in movement, superb in the vivid rhetoric of its verse, *Hernani* opened the French theatre to the romantic drama; it remains an outstanding example of the type.

RUY BLAS   *Victor Hugo*

After several unsuccessful prose plays, Hugo returned to poetic drama in a surge of resounding rhetoric. In 1838 he produced his most popular play (in France, second to *Hernani*), the heroic romantic *Ruy Blas*, which tells the story of a lackey who pretends to be a prince—and earns the grade.

Don Salluste, humiliated by Queen Maria of Spain, tries to persuade his cousin, Don César de Bazan, to help him gain revenge. Although a sort of ne'er-do-well, Don César refuses to take such action against a woman, whereupon Don Salluste introduces his valet Ruy Blas at court as Don César, with orders to make love to the Queen. Ruy Blas really loves her, and she warms to the man, making him her prime minister. Ruy Blas, in truth, is a firm, wise, and just counsellor. Complications ensue with the arrival of the real Don César, but Don Salluste orders Ruy Blas to arrange a rendezvous with the Queen. Breaking in upon them, Don Salluste tells the Queen to abdicate or he will expose her. The Queen is ready to go with the man she loves. Thereupon Ruy Blas reveals his true station. As the Queen shrinks back, Ruy Blas says to Don Salluste "I was your lackey; I am your executioner." He kills Don Salluste, takes poison, and dies knowing that the Queen loves him as a worthy man.

Many great actors have played Ruy Blas, a number of them doubling in the same performance as Don César. The original (November 8, 1838) was Frédérick Lemaître. Most effective of the early performers was Charles Albert Fechter, who played Ruy Blas in London in 1860 and in the United States in 1870. "Nothing could be finer of its kind," said the *London Times* (October 29, 1860) "than Ruy's declaration of love to the Queen, so exquisitely was the fire of passion tempered by the feeling of respectful devotion, and with such eloquence of speech and action were the words poured out." Sarah Bernhardt first played Queen Maria in 1867; she took the role to London in 1879, with Mounet-Sully as Ruy Blas, Febvre as Don Salluste, and Coquelin as Don César. The play was most favorably received; the *Sketch* (July 12) "doubted whether in the whole range of the French drama there is another play its equal in intense power and dramatic feeling . . . from first to last full not only of dramatic but of human interest . . . many passages not only excellent in their places as forming part of a drama, but master-pieces of literature and deep thought." Oscar Wilde gave the actress her enduring sobriquet, "the divine Sarah."

Edwin Booth had *Ruy Blas* in his repertoire for a dozen years, from 1877. The play was so popular in the 1870's as to be the subject of several English burlesques. When Salvini opened in the United States as Ruy Blas, the *New York Herald* (December 20, 1893) noted that he "left little to be desired." The actor Edward Vroom went to court to enjoin Salvini from doubling as Don César; Vroom in another theatre was playing both roles, under-emphasizing the earnestness of Ruy Blas for the sake of Don César's humor. A version by the poet John Davidson was presented in London in 1904 as *The Queen's Romance*, with Mrs. Pat Campbell.

Recent productions have won praise for the play itself. Of a 1933 production, in English adaptation by Brian Hooker, with Walter Hampden, the *New York Times* (July 24) stressed "Hugo's literary characteristic of placing social and class inequalities in dramatic juxtaposition. These inequalities are made glowingly vivid . . . through violent conflicts of personal ambition, hatred, villainy, love, and hide-bound tradition . . . The whole play moves in brisk tempo, with fine regard for the inherent romanticism and the final tragic climax." When the Comédie Française brought the play to London in 1934 there were some reservations. The *Telegraph* (May 24) said that it evoked "a grand, sonorous, rhetorical world with big manners and sweeping gestures . . . perhaps, a trifle too stilted for modern consumption;" and the *Times* (May 21) declared that "*Ruy Blas,* once a stormy banner flouting the winds of classicism, is worn and tattered now." These reservations may have been due to the fact that the title role in 1934 was played by the seventy-year-old Albert-Lambert, who had been appearing in it for fifty years.

In 1938, at Central City, Colorado, Robert Edmond Jones staged the play with Bramwell Fletcher and Helen Chandler, in what *Variety* (July 20) noted as "the biggest success of the seven annual play festivals." And again in London, the *Times* (June 8, 1945) spoke of the play's "purple passages like banners hung on some donjon's walls." *Ruy Blas* was a success in Paris once more in 1948. In the same year, Jean Cocteau turned it into a film with Danielle Darrieux and Jean Marais.

This widely successful play, though summary in its psychological development, is stark and strong in its emotional appeal, and one of the most striking of romantic melodramas in the amplitude and verve of its lyric outpouring, the power and beauty of its poetic form.

THE COMEDY OF LOVE   *Henrik Ibsen*

Born in the small Norwegian harbor town of Skien, Henrik Ibsen (1828-1906) was a shy youth, rendered more sensitive by his father's going through bankruptcy. In Skien and in the neighboring village of Grimstad, where he served six years as an apothecary's apprentice, he became a permanent rebel against the narrow middle-class atmosphere he breathed. In 1850 he went to Christiania, where he starved as a journalist; the next year, he accepted a post at the new Norwegian

National Theatre in Bergen. For this theatre, he wrote four plays.

In 1857, Ibsen returned to Christiania, where conditions discouraged him, but where he began to work in a newer vein. *The Comedy of Love,* 1862, a poetic reworking of the prose *Svanhild,* 1860, of which only one act was written, is his first play with a contemporary setting. It is constructed somewhat like an opera, with a duologue between hero and heroine toward the end of each of its three acts, and male choruses at the beginnings of Acts I and II and at the end of Act III. With ingenious, irregular rhyming, swift and sparkling versification, and brilliant dialogue, it is Ibsen's liveliest satire, especially of the conventions and complacencies of the upper middle class, and the social pretenses that often underlie courtship and marriage. It is his closest approach to the "triangle play" of opposed suitors. It was violently attacked as immoral and unpoetic, with especially sharp words against Straamand, the first satirical portrait of a minister on the Norwegian stage.

The basic theme of *The Comedy of Love* rests upon the hierarchy set by the Danish existentialist philosopher Sören Aabye Kierkegaard (1813-1855) of the aesthetic, the ethical, and the religious attitude in human development. The plot, however, springs from the novel *The Sheriff's Daughters* (1854-5) by Camilla Collett. Falk ("Falcon", the high-flying poet) offers Svanhild the privilege of serving as his Muse; she rejects him. He then determines to turn his poetry into action; his manifestation of independence and will-power wins Svanhild's love. She discovers, however, that in the ecstasy of their mutual love they have already achieved their highest moment; life thereafter can offer only a tapering off and fading of their love; and she turns from the temporary lover to a permanent husband, Guldstad ("Goldtown", the solid bourgeois).

The battle of the moral Guldstad and the aesthetic Falk for the hand, if not the heart, of Svanhild strikingly resembles the struggle in Shaw's *Candida**; neatly in both plays the dismissed suitor is given comfort that would appeal only to an aesthete. More definite in *The Comedy of Love* is the capitulation of the ideal before the practical, which recurs in *An Enemy of the People** and is, indeed, a basic movement in Ibsen's plays.

Although Ibsen has in *The Comedy of Love* abandoned the elves and fairies of his earlier plays, he retains, amid the caustic contemporary satire, romantic elements such as the garden setting, the music and the twilight, and the "romantic renunciation," with the casting of their rings into the fjord, as at the peak of their passion the lovers part.

The Comedy of Love was presented in Christiania in 1873, in Helsinki in 1889, in Copenhagen in 1898. Paris saw the play at the Théâtre de l'Oeuvre in 1897. Its premiere in English was in New York, March 23, 1908. It was presented in London, November 22, 1924. The play had a number of notable productions in Europe during Ibsen's centenary year, 1928.

The greater power and pertinence of Ibsen's later plays have unfortunately thrown into comparative obscurity this lively and searching play.

BRAND   *Henrik Ibsen*

The question of recognition of one's mission in life and of devoting oneself to it at any cost, was very much on Ibsen's mind when he wrote this play in Rome in 1866. Brand is a stern pastor, whose motto is "All or Nothing." Through him, Ibsen shows the dangerous power of will without love. While the play pictures the destruction an iron will can bring upon its possessor and upon those around, who must be left free to make their own choice, it surges to an exaltation of faith in the spirit of man, "the one eternal thing."

Returning to the fjord valley of his youth, Pastor Brand challenges his country-folk to renew their faith. Young Agnes, about to run off with an artist, weds Brand and follows him. Brand fights the petty avarice of his mother, the self-seeking of the Mayor, the feeble humanitarianism of the doctor, the shrewd cynicism of the schoolmaster. As he denounces a church built on hypocrisy and compromise, his wife and child die of the cold of the countryside and the cold absolutism of his spirit. There is a conflict, implicit in his family's fate, between God as a force for order and God as a force for love. When Brand exhorts his congregation to follow him to the true church, he starts up the mountainside; and though the cold drives his congregation back, Brand continues the climb. An invisible choir warns him: "Earth-born creature, live for Earth!" The phantom of his wife appears, and pleads with him; he spurns, through her, the "spirit of compromise," the "falcon" that lures forever. And the rifle shot of Brand's last follower, the gypsy girl Gerd, fired to drop the falcon, loosens an avalanche that sweeps down and overwhelms Brand. Over the covering snow a great voice calls: "He is the God of Love."

Although *Brand* presents an eternal challenge in the idea that faith is essential though suffering is inevitable, the play's exhortation to Ibsen's countrymen had a more immediate application. When in 1864, as part of Bismarck's plan for the unification of Germany, Prussia and Austria invaded Denmark, Norway stood by, neutral. The result was that the defeated Danes abandoned all claim to the duchies of Schleswig, Holstein and Lauenberg. Ibsen—whose love for his country was deepened by his prolonged stay abroad—felt that Norway's action was a betrayal. The fierceness of his patriotic fervor gave particular point to the exhortations of Brand. Ibsen later declared, "Brand is myself in my best moments."

Brand was warmly received by a public that largely shared Ibsen's indignation. Its printed form ran through four editions within its first year. Although the play was not intended primarily for production, Act IV was enacted at the Christiania Theatre in 1866; the whole play was presented there in 1876, in 1885 in Stockholm, in 1895 in Paris, and in 1898 in Copenhagen and Berlin. The full production requires six and a half hours. Act Four, separately, has been much more frequently and more widely performed; it was given in London in 1893 and in New York in 1910. In its entirety, Brand was produced at Yale University in 1928 (Ibsen's centenary), at Litchfield, Connecticut, in the summer of 1938, and at Cambridge, England, in 1946.

Brand is written in four-foot rhyming verse; iambic for the more familiar and colloquial scenes, trochaic for the peaks of vision and passion and sober thought. The poetry is vivid, at times direct, at times mystic, always bearing an undertone of earnest emotion and a cloak of beauty. In 1906, C. H. Herford observed in the introduction to his translation of the play, that only those English readers "who can imagine the prophetic fire of Carlyle fused with the genial verve and the intellectual athleticism of Browning, and expressed by aid of a dramatic faculty to parallel which we must go two centuries backward" can understand the fascination of the play. Writing in *Black and White* on December 19, 1891, William Archer called *Brand* "one of the simplest, noblest, and most absorbing dramas in literature . . . among the two or three supreme poetic achievements of this century . . . the poet's farewell to popular theology—his passionate declaration that ideal Christianity is impossible, while possible and actual Christianity is a base compromise . . ."

This noble drama of a God of love whose "caress is chastisement," and of a faithful one who will not compromise but who summons mankind to the stern and stark alternatives of all or nothing, takes an imperious hold upon every reader. It poses the paradox of the human spirit: the absolute is destruction, yet compromise is a living death. *Peer Gynt**, the companion drama, is the wan comedy of eternal compromise; *Brand* is the bright tragedy of steadfast holding to one's high ideals.

PEER GYNT   *Henrik Ibsen*

In his dramatic poem *Peer Gynt,* 1867, Ibsen wrote a counter-movement to *Brand**. In Peer, all is compromise; instead of holding firmly to faith, though it lead to death, he abandons everything that may interfere with living. His life becomes inevitably a life of the senses. In *Brand* love means chastisement and death; contrariwise, in *Peer Gynt* love means forgiveness and life.

A happy-go-lucky lad, who drains each moment of its opportunity, Peer Gynt, boastful at a wedding, makes off with the bride, Ingrid, and after a night, abandons her; he dallies with the girls of the hillside farms; he accepts the virgin Solveig, who gives her life to him. He then returns to his dying mother, Aase, and in a tender make-believe drives her through St. Peter's gate to her eternal home. Away again, he comes upon the mountain trolls, and instead of man's motto, Be thyself, he accepts that of the trolls, Exist for thyself. Obeying this motto, Peer wanders lengthily. In a wild fourth act (not in the original plan of the play) he goes to Morocco with millions made in America. When the millions are stolen, he wanders in the desert and comes upon the Emperor's horse and jewels which were abandoned by frightened thieves. He meets Anitra, daughter of a Bedouin chief, who dances for him; he bears her off with the jewels. From behind the Sphinx at Gizeh comes a German, who takes Peer to the madhouse at Cairo, where a language reformer and other lunatics—among them a minister who thinks he's a pen, while everyone insists on using him as a blotter—hail Peer as their king, the Kaiser of Self-hood. Come home, he finds himself a legend. Peer then meets the button-moulder (Death); men, like buttons, are designed to have a definite shape in order to hold things together in the world, but Peer has "set at defiance his life's design." By never being firm, he has never been himself. He is destined for the melting-pot, unless in truth he can find himself—which he does, in Solveig's heart. It is Peer's recognition of his error that wins the grace of his salvation through Solveig.

The phantasmagoria of *Peer Gynt* confused many of the critics when it first appeared, even as others hailed it. Clemens Petersen, the most influential critic in Copenhagen, maintained it was "full of riddles that are insoluble because there is nothing in them at all." He called some of the playwright's devices "thought-swindling . . . not poetry, because in the transmutation of reality into art it falls halfway short of the demands both of art and of reality." As Ibsen had said earlier he'd be interested to hear what Petersen thought of the play, he now protested vigorously: "My book *is* poetry; and if it is not, then it will be. The conception of poetry in our country, in Norway, shall be made to conform to the book." This prophecy has been more than fulfilled: *Peer Gynt* was hailed by Alrik Gustafson, in *A History of Modern Drama* (1947), as "the great national poem of Norway."

Even Georg Brandes, though he later changed his mind, found the poetry and thought of the drama all wasted. The fourth act, he said, "is witless in its satire, crude in its irony, and in its latter part scarcely comprehensible . . . Contempt for humanity and self-hatred make a bad foundation on which to build a poetic work. What an unlovely and distorting view of life this is! What acrid pleasure can a poet find in thus sullying human nature?" Today the play is recognized as not merely a satire, but also a song to love.

In its entirety, *Peer Gynt* has seldom been performed. Ibsen recognized that the play required cutting and suggested that in place of Act IV there could be a great musical tone picture, suggesting Peer Gynt's wanderings all over the world, in which "American, English, and French arias occur as alternating and disappearing motives". At Ibsen's request, Edvard Grieg wrote the *Peer Gynt* suite, which is probably more widely familiar than the play. With Grieg's music, *Peer Gynt* was produced in Christiania in 1876, in Copenhagen in 1886 and 1892. In 1895 it was played in Stockholm, then it went on tour through Scandinavia. Paris saw it in 1896, at the Théâtre de l'Oeuvre; Vienna saw it in 1902. Richard Mansfield acted the role of Peer in the first performance in English, omitting Act IV, at the Chicago Grand Opera House, October 29, 1906, and later in New York. In 1923 the Theatre Guild produced the play with Joseph Schildkraut (Peer), Dudley Digges (the Troll King), Edward G. Robinson (the Button-Moulder), and Lillebil Ibsen (Anitra). The production was directed by Komisarjevsky. In 1924 Basil Sydney took on the role of Peer. Since 1930, *Peer Gynt* has been performed virtually every year by college theatres. New York saw it again, off Broadway, in 1949, and with John Garfield in 1951. The first American presentation of the complete play was at Amherst, Massachusetts, in 1940.

Peer Gynt was produced in Edinburgh in 1908. In London, the Old Vic Company presented it in 1922 and 1935 and, with Ralph Richardson as Peer, in September, 1944.

Despite the frequency of its performance and the variety of its acting versions, theatre critics in England and the United States have not given wholehearted praise to *Peer Gynt*. The first American production, for example, was dismissed by Albert Pulvermacher in the *New York Staats-Zeitung*: "What we saw on the stage was a hodge-podge of mere madness."

The Theatre Guild production of 1923 made clear enough the surge and sweep of the drama, but it left the critics divided. Heywood Broun (February 7, 1923) stated: "To the eye it is the most beautiful thing the Guild has ever done . . . Instead of being clearer when put upon the stage, more fog drifted into *Peer Gynt* than when we read it . . . The last two scenes are eternal drama. It has always seemed to us that the death of Aase is one of the most moving scenes ever written for the theatre." Alexander Woollcott declared: "To one who found the Jessner production in Berlin a singularly narcotic influence, the Guild revival seems an unexpectedly tonic and spiritual thing. *Peer Gynt* is an undisciplined, unedited play, a tremendous unfiltered stream fed from the springs of Norwegian folk lore and carrying with it no end of rubbish that fell in by chance as it was being written. The very process of cutting it down to the limits of a tolerable three hour and a half performance betters it some, and we could bear it if the entire gimcrack fourth act were dropped entirely. This . . . would leave intact all of the beauty which has kept the play alive for fifty years."

The English were even less hospitable to the Norwegian gallimaufry. On September 3, 1944, James Agate observed in the *London Times* (of a production that used Dame Sybil Thorndike as Aase, Ralph Richardson as Peer, Nicholas Hannen as the Troll King, Laurence Olivier as the Button-Moulder, and Joyce Redman as Solveig): "Last week, in an unguarded moment, I let slip my private opinion that Ibsen's *Peer Gynt*, like some other world-masterpieces, is all very jolly and boring! I withdraw and apologize abjectly. I now declare that there is neither iota nor scintilla of jollity in this cavernous and gloomy masterpiece. . . ."

Despite the reservations of some critics, *Peer Gynt* holds firm place, not only as a national, but as a world masterpiece. The Norwegians naturally found in it many allusions to themselves. Björnson*, whose idyllic stories of peasant life Ibsen may have been satirizing, generously declared: "*Peer Gynt* is a satire on Norwegian egoism, narrowness, and self-sufficiency, so executed as to have made me not only laugh and laugh again till I was sore, but again and again give thanks to the author in my heart—as I here do publicly."

Although Peer Gynt comes partly out of Norwegian folk-tale, as do the trolls, the main story is Ibsen's invention; and as the adventures carry Peer around the world, so are the implications universal. *Brand* said that each man must hold to his faith and his ideals; *Peer Gynt* shows that each man must find, and be, his self. Bacchanalian and pagan in its imagery and rout, Christian and concerned in its thought and deeper feeling, Ibsen produced a unique and ebullient masterpiece in *Peer Gynt*.

EMPEROR AND GALILEAN   *Henrik Ibsen*

For several years, Ibsen worked upon a theme that had caught his interest when he went to Italy in 1863. In 1873 were published the two parts, *Caesar's Apostasy* and *The Emperor Julian* (five acts each—originally planned as a trilogy), of *Emperor and Galilean*. The play captures some of the surging beauty Ibsen felt on first crossing the Alps; there is a descriptive grandeur in its scenes, a majesty in its scope. It is based on Italian history in its most critical moment: at the peak of the battle between paganism and Christianity—a struggle which Ibsen believed will always repeat itself. Hence he called the play "a world-historic drama." Though he set its action in the past, he felt its pertinence to the present, and he wrote it in prose to create the illusion of reality.

The philosophy of *Emperor and Galilean*, which Ibsen deemed his greatest work, is clear. We watch the downfall of Julian; we observe how readily the people turn from one ruler to the next; but we note also that Ibsen, whose previous two non-realistic plays, *Brand** and

Peer Gynt*, had pictured extremes, reaches here toward an eclectic compromise. As Julian is dying, he exclaims: "Beautiful earth—beautiful life . . . Hold fast to wisdom." Ibsen's "wisdom" led him to a hope that there might ensue a "third empire," a combination of pagan vigor and Christian love, a fusion of erring flesh and groping spirit in the maturity of the human race. Ibsen saw in the political confederations of 1871 the beginning of such a unification of mankind, the political union that must precede, but must be complemented by, the spiritual union. The spiritual lack leads to the failure of Julian in the tragedy *Emperor and Galilean.*

Though hardly intended for stage performance, *Emperor and Galilean* was produced in Germany in 1896 and again, as part of the celebration of Ibsen's seventieth birthday, in 1898. It found production in Norway in 1903. In the reading, the sincere quest of Julian for higher meaning in the world gives fervor to the wide sweep of the drama, and reveals the dignity and exaltation of the human spirit, even in his failure. Looking at the dead pagan Emperor Julian, the Christian Basil says: "It dawns on me like a great and radiant light, that here dies a noble, shattered instrument of God." Whoever strives sincerely, though he reach not the goal, serves the good cause. *Emperor and Galilean* is stout testimony to the worth of such service.

PILLARS OF SOCIETY   *Henrik Ibsen*

Since events in Europe did not justify Ibsen's hopes of a gathering spiritual force, he turned to a succession of plays about everyday life with the second of his all-prose contemporary dramas, *Pillars of Society.* In the deliberate turn to commonplace themes, his English friend and translator, William Archer, thinks that Ibsen went too far, that this is "of all Ibsen's works the least characteristic, because, acting on a transitory phase of theory, he has been almost successful in divesting it of poetic charm."

This play is chiefly an exposure of sanctimonious hypocrisy, of the shaky pedestals that support the "pillars of society." The career of Consul Bernick, the leading citizen of a small but thriving Norwegian seaport, is founded on a lie: fifteen years earlier, he managed to shift onto his brother-in-law, Johan, gone to America, his own amorous indiscretion and a rumor of embezzlement. Bernick has, however, for the fifteen years, been a stalwart citizen, making the town a better place to live in and a richer field for his own double-dealing.

Faced with a threat of exposure, as the play opens, he plans to have the returned Johan sail on an unseaworthy ship—only to hear that his son has run away on the same vessel. Shocked to his senses, Bernick makes a decision and—though he learns in time that the ship has not sailed—before an assemblage of citizens confesses his earlier and present sins.

Two years in the writing, *Pillars of Society* opened at Copenhagen on November 18, 1877, with immediate and striking success. It was enthusiastically received throughout Scandinavia and German-speaking Europe. In 1878, there were productions at five Berlin theatres within a fortnight; by the turn of the century, it had been played over 1200 times in German. In France and England, the play was more tardily welcomed. Lugné-Poe produced it in Paris in 1896. A single London performance on December 15, 1880, was Ibsen's first appearance in the English theatre; there was another performance in 1889 and two more were given in 1901.

Pillars of Society came more lengthily to New York; it was played in German, opening December 26, 1888, and frequently thereafter; in English, it opened on March 6, 1891, to the usual Anglo-Saxon reception of Ibsen. The production, said the *New York Dramatic Mirror*, "served to show the dreariness of the one play of Ibsen's that seemed to give some promise . . . The work is verbose and tiresome . . . His 'realism' is evidently the commonplace unavoidable in a writer who has not the dramatic instinct nor the technical knowledge that permits a playwright of ordinary capacity to make a drama interesting and theatrically effective. In our humble opinion Ibsen is the veriest tyro in the art of playwriting. His pieces are sermons written in dramatic form . . . Even the wildest of Ibsen faddists cannot fail to vote him an intolerable bore when he is acted."

In spite of this reception, the play has had numerous revivals in New York; notably in 1904 with Wilton Lackaye and William O. Hazeltine; in 1910 with Holbrook Blinn, Henry Stephenson, Fuller Mellish, and Minnie Maddern Fiske; in 1913 with young Edward G. Robinson; in 1931 with Moffat Johnston, Rollo Peters, Romney Brent, Frank Conlon, Edgar Stehli, Fania Marinoff, and Dorothy Gish.

By 1904 the *New York Dramatic Mirror* had changed its mind about the play: ". . . as fresh and as real today as when it was penned . . . To an average audience perhaps more appealing than are the majority of Ibsen's plays . . . Whether the drama is presented in Christiania or Cincinnati, its shafts of truth are pretty sure to strike as near home as one's next door neighbor."

Interwoven with the main theme of social pharisaism, Ibsen also stressed the drive of women toward moral and economic independence, which motivates his next play, *A Doll's House**. In *Pillars of Society*, this emphasis is clearly shown in the contrast of three women. Martha, Bernick's sister, is all of the old generation: she fits into the pattern sketched in the first draft of *The Pretenders*: "to love all, to sacrifice all, and be forgotten: that is woman's saga." Dina, who marries Johan, is all of the new generation; she makes her own decisions; she does not yield to conventional claims. Standing between the two is the Bernicks' old friend, Lona Hessel; firm in her strength to turn Bernick toward the truth, when catastrophe comes she is equally firm in her devotion: "Old friendship does not rust." This may be, as Archer says, the only play of Ibsen's "in which plot can be said to preponderate over character": the plot is ingenious, naturally developed, skilfully drawn together, with several powerfully theatrical scenes; yet the character of Bernick is probed with shrewd insight, and the women are neatly balanced in searching and sympathetic portraits.

In this play, Ibsen emerges as a searching analyst of the social scene, pondering universal human impulses in contemporary terms.

A DOLL'S HOUSE   *Henrik Ibsen*

With *A Doll's House* Ibsen broke the chains of the nineteenth century well-made play with its happy ending. He also emerged as a world dramatist, for, although *A Doll's House* was not his first great play, it was the first to be widely performed and vehemently discussed in many tongues.

Before the play opens Nora Helmer, brought up in sheltered happiness, forges a check in order to help her sick husband. Krogstad, a clerk in Helmer's bank, after holding the forgery over her, returns the check; but in the meantime the attitude of her husband, Torvald, opens Nora's eyes. She has boasted that Torvald "wouldn't hesitate a moment to give his very life for my sake"; instead, he turns upon her and scolds her roundly for forging the check, though she has done it to save him. And Nora recognizes that she has been, not a true companion, but a toy; she leaves her husband to find herself. The last sound in the play is the slamming of the downstairs door.

The closing of that door was heard around the world, in the surging battle for women's rights. Published and produced in Copenhagen (where it was Fru Hennings' greatest success), *A Doll's House*, 1879, within the year was played all over Scandinavia and Germany. Argument over the play—over the right or wrong of Nora's declaration of independence—so monopolized conversation and engendered such heated controversy that discussion of the play was by prior agreement barred at social gatherings.

Copyright laws did not then protect the text of plays, and Ibsen, confronted with perversions of the play's end, himself wrote a happy ending, in which the thought of her children works in Nora until she stays at home. Ibsen preferred, he said, "to commit the outrage myself, rather than leave my work to the tender mercies of adaptors." It is quite possible, indeed, that Ibsen originally planned a happy ending—which comes when Krogstad returns the forged check—but that the characters grew too real for such an outcome. Assuming a happy ending as Ibsen's original intention, however, explains certain inconsistencies in Nora, who seems at first too shallow for the great change that comes.

A rather remote adaptation of the play, called *Breaking a Butterfly*, by Henry Arthur Jones* and Henry Herman, was presented in London in 1884, but *A Doll's House* was not shown there until Janet Achurch enacted Nora with great success in June 1889. In America, Helena Modjeska had performed *A Doll's House* in Louisville, Kentucky, as early as 1883, but it was not until 1889 that it came to, and stirred, New York, in a version called *A Doll's Home*. "The Ibsen cult is not likely to achieve popularity in this metropolis," said the *New York Dramatic Mirror* (December 28, 1889) "if we may judge by the impression created by *A Doll's Home*. However profitable the study of the piece is to the sociologist, it is by no manner of means pleasurable from the playgoer's standpoint. Nora, the heroine, is a mixture of Frou-Frou and Featherbrain. She is of little dramatic value, because she is a freak rather than a type, and freaks are not welcome in the dramatic world . . . [Ibsen] develops both character and plot in a tedious, halting fashion, using no lights and no genuine dramatic contrasts . . . The dialogue is wearisome—an arid desert without oases . . . It is a dose that will make even the Ibsen cranks quail."

Ibsenites, however, rallied to the play, and it has been frequently revived. Actresses are attracted by the variety and increasing depth of the chief role, as the heedless and happy Nora, who dances the tarantella and skips to the masquerade ball, wakens to a responsible life.

In his introduction to *A Doll's House* (1906), William Archer remarked, "When Nora and Helmer faced each other, and set to work to ravel out the skein of their illusions, then one felt oneself face to face with a new thing in drama—an order of experience, at once intellectual and emotional, not hitherto attained in the theatre." Among the actresses who have partaken of, and transmitted, that experience, are the Germans Lucy Mannheim, Hedwig Niemann-Raabe, and Agnes Sorma; the French Réjane; the Italian Duse; the Russian Vera Komisarjevsky; and in English, Alla Nazimova, Minnie Maddern Fiske, Ethel Barrymore, Eva Le Gallienne, and Ruth Gordon.

A Doll's House has been popular in college theatres since 1920. The best recent Broadway production opened December 26, 1937, with Jed Harris directing a version by Thornton Wilder in which Ruth Gordon played Nora; Dennis King, Helmer; Sam Jaffe, Krogstad; and the screen star Paul Lukas made his Broadway debut as Dr. Rank. Atkinson called this production "one of the finest Ibsen revivals in years . . . Nora trying to hold the world back with a desperate tarantella; Nora driven nearly out of her mind with apprehension; Nora quietly coming into her own inheritance of personal pride and taking command of the situation—these are the portions of the play that Miss Gordon has completely mastered . . . the moral and spiritual triumphs of Nora are still full of the fire of life." And while John Mason Brown felt that "both specialists and general playgoers are forced to admit that their interest in A Doll's House nowadays is more academic than human," Robert Coleman declared that "the Norse giant's play still retains the ability to enlist and to hold the interest of modern audiences." The revival achieved a record run of 144 performances.

In A Doll's House there lingers a romantic juxtaposition of contrasted effects, not found in the later Ibsen social dramas. The tarantella, the Christmas tree, the toy-shop mood of the early scenes, are almost blinding in their brightness, held before Nora's dark self-questioning, and the cynical bitterness of her friend Dr. Rank. Despite these intrusions of an earlier dramaturgic method and mood, A Doll's House is a pioneer play in structure as well as in theme. It abandons most if not all of the tricks of the "well-made play" (though the confidant remains), and builds what has been called "the drama of retrospective analysis." The play starts, like the classical epic, in medias res, in the midst of things, when the events that will produce the crisis have already occurred, and the gradual revelation of the past as part of the present gives a double forcefulness to the happenings. This technique has been widely used by playwrights after Ibsen.

In idea, A Doll's House is a pioneer in the dramatic presentation of women struggling for independence, for equality of consideration and of treatment with men. Beyond the conflict of the sexes, however, the play continues Ibsen's dramatic portrayal of the basic conflict, of the individual against the mass, of personal integrity against the crust of convention and the rust of social mores and concerns. It is a world growing up, not merely a Nora, that is called upon to slam the door of its "doll's house."

GHOSTS   *Henrik Ibsen*

Opposition to Ibsen rose to a furious howl with his Ghosts, 1881. Intended as a sort of sequel to The Doll's House*, in which Nora had refused to submit to social conventions, *Ghosts* pictures the life of Mrs. Alving, who does submit. Many critics of the time, however, mistook the son, Oswald, as the central figure of the play. Nor has this error lapsed; Freedley and Reeves in their *History of the Theatre* (1941), thinking they are praising *Ghosts*, declare "This play holds its own . . . the problems of inherited disease, insanity, and euthanasia are still as great as they were sixty years ago." The same emphasis marks the summary of the play in Sobel's *Theatre Handbook* (1940; 1948).

Her love for the pastor Manders checked by his concern for convention, Mrs. Alving has devoted her life to a conventional hiding from the world of the dissolute, diseased nature of her husband, a retired ship captain. She has sent her son abroad, to shield him from the knowledge. As the play opens, Mrs. Alving, who is erecting an orphanage in her late husband's name, welcomes home her son Oswald, only to learn that he has come home to die—of inherited syphilis. He makes his mother promise to give him a deadly drug when insanity comes. The captain's illegitimate daughter, Regina, goes off to a life of pleasure, as the orphanage burns down and Mrs. Alving kneels beside Oswald, who is insanely calling, "The sun! Mother, give me the sun." His mother's concern for keeping up appearances has brought disaster down upon them all.

Oswald is often taken as the "ghost" of his father, but Ibsen's concern was larger, as Mrs. Alving reveals in the play: "I am half inclined to think we are all ghosts, Mr. Manders. It is not only what we have inherited from our fathers and mothers that exists in us, but all sorts of old dead ideas, and all kinds of old dead beliefs and the like."

Nazimova—who played Regina in St. Petersburg and Mrs. Alving throughout the United States—emphasized the same point: "It is only a very imperceptive person that sees in *Ghosts* the presentation of a single social problem. The true ghosts of the play are a whole legion of outmoded beliefs and ideals. They are dead ideas of conduct with which we have been brought up, notions of duty and obligation, conceptions of law and order which, in the lines of the play, I characterize as 'the cause of all the unhappiness in the world.'"

Ghosts is the first play fully utilizing the new technique of Ibsen. It is as "modern" as his ideas, which leap from his own time's conventional reticences to a forthrightness scarce seen since ancient Greece. Spare, stripped of all romantic trimmings and unnecessary adornment, it is austere in its direct and undeviating drive. While Pastor Manders may be somewhat of a type, the other characters are deeply revealed; we see them clear to the soul.

Ibsen's chief technical advance comes in the exposition of earlier essential facts as a part of the present drama. Each item—the late Captain Alving's dissolute nature, his being Regina's father, Pastor Manders' early rejection of Mrs. Alving's love—is revealed to the audience just when its impact is most forceful. This method, which had not been used in the drama since Sophocles' *Oedipus**, became both a model and a challenge.

Another stark quality of *Ghosts* is its objectivity. Some have said that it is a sermon; but if so, it is one only in the sense that there are sermons in stones, books in the running brooks. There is validity in Ibsen's protest: "They try to make me responsible for the opinions certain of the characters express. And yet there is not in the whole work a single opinion, a single utterance, which can be laid to the account of the author. I took good care to avoid this. The very method, the order of technique that imposes its form on the play, forbids the author to appear in the speeches of his characters. My object was to make the reader feel that he was going through a piece of real experience; and nothing could more effectually prevent such an impression than the intrusion of the author's private opinions into the dialogue. Do they imagine at home that I am so inexpert in the theory of drama as not to know this?"

The charge of sermonizing, however, was the least of the accusations hurled against the author of *Ghosts*. Amid what Ibsen called a "terrible uproar in the Scandinavian press," only two staunch voices rang in his praise—that of Björnson*, whose early realistic plays had already appeared, and that of the greatest of Scandinavian critics, Georg Brandes.

The play was not produced until August 1883, with August Lindberg playing Oswald, first at Helsingborg, Sweden; then on tour through Scandinavia. Later that year *Ghosts* was played in the Royal Theatre at Stockholm. In 1899, when the National Theatre opened in Christiania, *Ghosts* was accepted in the repertory. Its first production in Germany was a private performance at the Stadttheater in Augsburg, April 1886. On September 29, 1889, it opened at the Freie Bühne (Free Theatre) of Berlin, which presented *Ghosts* as its initial offering. Berlin's Free Theatre, like that of Paris (Théâtre Libre) avoided censorship by a subscription scheme that made performances legally "private." The first production of Ibsen in France was given at the Paris Free Theatre on May 29, 1890. By the same subscription device, the Independent Theatre in London presented *Ghosts* on March 13, 1891. In the meantime, *Ghosts* had been forbidden in St. Petersburg, on religious grounds.

Ibsen expected that *Ghosts* would be attacked. "It may well be," he wrote in January, 1882, "that the play is in several respects rather daring. But it seemed to me that the time had come for moving some boundary-posts. And this was an undertaking for which a man of the older generation, like myself, was better fitted than the many younger authors who might desire to do something of the kind. I was prepared for a storm; but such storms one must not shrink from encountering."

The play encountered considerable opposition in England; a storm of abuse followed the Independent Theatre production. The *Hawk* called the play "merely dull dirt long drawn out." *Truth* agreed that it was "not only consistently dirty, but deplorably dull." W. St. Leger, in *Black and White*, declared: "No one . . . could have been converted by the representation of that lugubrious diagnosis of sordid impropriety . . . The Ibsen craze is merely a cave of Adullam, to which resort all who would fain do some displeasure to Mrs. Grundy . . . There is not one theory, not one phrase, which bears the stamp of new thought, or of the vivid representation of the old. Some of his apologists see in *Ghosts* a great moral lesson—a moral lesson so great that, apparently, it is to excuse the writer for presenting to us a play which is dramatically as dull as it is generally unsavoury. And this new lesson is that the sins of the fathers are visited on the children! . . . His characters are prigs, and pedants, and profligates. Their lives are, no doubt, of interest to themselves, as the lives of the least estimable of creeping and crawling creatures are esteemed in creeping and crawling circles; but how any critical, let alone any wholesome mind can find pleasure in contemplating these morbid creatures it is hard indeed to comprehend." Clement Scott, in the *London Times*, called the play "an open drain; a loathsome sore, unbandaged; a dirty act done publicly; a lazar-house with all its doors and windows open."

Among Ibsen's defenders were his English translator William Archer, George Bernard Shaw, and Justin McCarthy. The latter declared: "I think . . . that *Ghosts* is, for the days that pass, a great play; that it is in no sane sense unclean; that whether we like it or do not like it, it is obviously the work of a man of genius, and that above all things it is intensely interesting and intensely vital . . . I do not think that a more moral play than *Ghosts* was ever written . . . Sin was never more sternly unmasked, its shamelessness, its degradation never more mercilessly arraigned than in this tragic work of art, which is worth a wilderness of sermons."

Ghosts gradually worked its way to other theatrical centers. It was played in Italy in 1892. Its American premiere, on January 5, 1894, at the Berkeley Lyceum, New York, was hailed by William Dean Howells as "a great theatrical event—the very greatest I have ever known." In the same year, the play encountered censorship in Boston. Though long forbidden by the English censor, it was again seen in "private" productions in London in 1893 and 1894, and by 1900 was an accepted repertory play throughout the world. After an early New York production, opening May 29, 1899, directed by Emmanuel Reicher, the *New York Dramatic Mirror* (June 10) observed: "Some there were whose hearts and minds could not endure the hammer blows of the Norwegian dramatist's pessimism, and they moved noiselessly from the playhouse before the curtain fell . . . No less than as a philosopher and thinker is the Norwegian great as a dramatic craftsman. *Ghosts* is constructed with the scientific accuracy that a master engineer employs in building a suspension bridge. Every strand in the network of dialogue has its duty to perform in supporting the main theme. Every character, too, is as truly a part of the whole, and as necessary a part, as is each pier in the engineer's structure . . . to the analytical mind it presents itself as a monument of absolute truth."

In 1929 Alexander Moissi acted in New York in the Reinhardt German production of *Ghosts*. Nazimova played it in English at the New York Empire Theatre, with Romney Brent, in the season of 1935-1936. There have been productions of *Ghosts* every year since. A recent New York production was that of Eva Le Gallienne in 1948.

The timelessness of *Ghosts* is, of course, relative. In 1926, after a production with Lucile Watson, Jose Ruben, Hortense Alden, and J. M. Kerrigan, Gilbert W. Gabriel reported that he found it "the most completely dated and withered of Ibsen's plays." In 1935, Brooks Atkinson, praising Nazimova's performance, called *Ghosts* "now . . . only a temperate statement of an ugly thought with a milk-and-gruel attack upon authority and pious idealism." Atkinson partially retracted in 1948 (February 18): "Since *Ghosts* is planned and written by a master craftsman of the old school, it can still be made exciting by great acting or by a novel point of view . . ."

Unfortunately, the 1948 Broadway production was not effective. As Robert Garland said: "The fresh 'translation' credited to Eva Le Gallienne and the stale direction discredited to Margaret Webster help not at all." It was better received in England, with Beatrix Lehman, at the Festival of Britain in 1951.

There is the crux: every generation must continue the struggle against the chains of "convention," the clinging and clanking of outmoded ideas. Because of its stark presentation of this fact, the power of *Ghosts* remains in the reading, and in proper presentation. The play has admirably served its author's purpose, for *Ghosts* has set more "minds in motion" than any other drama of the last hundred years. It was, in many lands, the clarion call to realism and sharpness of technique, to freedom of thought and expression, in the modern drama.

AN ENEMY OF THE PEOPLE   *Henrik Ibsen*

The reactions of the public to Ibsen's previous plays strengthened his feeling that the majority, the conformers, had to be jolted from their smug sense of righteousness. His next play, *An Enemy of the People*, which his indignation hurried, was published in Copenhagen in November, 1882.

This play takes a literal pollution as symbolic of the "swamp" in which the people's conscience had sunk. The noted health baths of a south Norway town, Doctor Stockmann discovers, are polluted; when he wishes to proclaim this fact, the "responsible" folk of the town denounce Stockmann as an enemy of the people for desiring to destroy their profits. Against the politicians and the press, Stockmann is powerless; he can console himself only with thoughts of the future, and with the closing reflection—an individual consolation out of a social defeat—that "the strongest man in the world is he that stands most alone."

Ibsen himself found consolation in the lonely rebel. Speaking of Dr. Stockmann in a letter to Georg Brandes, he declared: "The majority, the mass, the multitude, can never overtake him; he can never have the majority with him . . . At the point where I stood when I wrote each of my books, there now stands a fairly compact multitude; but I myself am there no longer; I am elsewhere and, I hope, farther ahead."

Going down to defeat, Stockmann nevertheless refuses to be "beaten off the field by public opinion, by the compact majority, and all that sort of devilry . . . I want to drive it into the heads of these curs that the Liberals are the craftiest foes free men have to face; that party-programs wring the necks of all young and living truths; that considerations of expediency turn justice and morality upside down, until life becomes simply unlivable." The battle of the baths has been lost, but the battle against hypocrisy goes on.

In spite of the personal indignation that spurred the drama, Ibsen is by no means onesided in his presentation. He stirs in Dr. Stockmann a surge of energy and a genial humor; the aristocratic idealism of the man is beyond the grasp of the townsfolk. At the same time, he rouses in the good doctor a zealot's insistence, an uncompromising failure to grasp the other issues involved. Where a more moderate person might have won the town to take effective steps against the pollution of the baths, Dr. Stockmann by his insistence on instant public action, which would wipe out the town's income from the baths, succeeds only in turning every leading citizen against him.

An Enemy of the People, though William Archer called it Ibsen's "least poetical, least imaginative" work, is nevertheless a satirical comedy of technical excellence, buoyant good spirits, and surging vitality. In March, 1882, Ibsen wrote his publisher: "It will be a peaceable production, which can be read by Ministers of State and wholesale merchants and their ladies, and from which theatres will not feel obliged to recoil." It was, indeed, quite popular. Within three months of its publication, it was played in Christiania, Bergen, Stockholm, and Copenhagen. Holland saw the play in 1884; Berlin, not until March 5, 1887, but frequently thereafter. In Paris, it was presented in 1895; on March 29, 1898, and in 1899; in 1895 and 1899 anarchist demonstrations accompanied the productions. In England, Beerbohm Tree, playing Dr. Stockmann first on June 14, 1893, appeared frequently in the part up to 1905. Its New York premiere was in 1895. Walter Hampden acted Dr. Stockmann first in 1927, then revived the play frequently until 1937. In that year (February 16) Richard Watts remarked that the play "continues to strike out with sardonic power, while its implications remain inescapably modern." Calling it a "mighty provocative play," Brooks Atkinson satirically observed: "Now that we have arrived at the golden age when governments and society welcome the truth in all things and never put convenience ahead of scientific enlightenment, *An Enemy of the People* is less pertinent." An adaptation by Arthur Miller* was produced in New York in 1950 with Frederic March, Morris Carnovsky, and Florence Eldridge. Miller "pepped up" the dialogue with many a "Damn!" and with current slang, but turned Dr. Stockmann, as Howard Barnes saw him, into a figure "part Galileo, part a man who refuses to testify whether he is or is not a Communist. The form and context of the original drama were far better than they are in the present reworking of the plot."

In any democracy, Ibsen's points call for pondering, lest the most well-meaning man find himself "an enemy of the people."

THE WILD DUCK   *Henrik Ibsen*

In two respects, *The Wild Duck*, 1884, marks a shift in Ibsen's thought. His earlier social dramas were concerned with themes; *The Wild Duck* is concerned with individuals. His earlier poetic plays raised the question of compromise—whether or not to hold absolutely to ideals. In *The Wild Duck* Ibsen begins to question ideals. Ibsen was going through a period of self-questioning; *The Wild Duck* is in a sense a spiritual autobiography. Little Hedvig in the play is modeled upon his own sister Hedvig, dearest to him of all his relatives. Gregers Werle, who insists upon telling the truth, to "ennoble" those whose lives have been lived in the shadow of a lie, is an ironic self-portrait of the Ibsen that wrote *Brand**; Dr. Relling, the cynically despondent philosopher who sees through the shams and pretenses of people, is the Ibsen that now questions. One actor, in the role of the doctor, made himself up to look like Ibsen.

Freedley and Reeves in *A History of the Theatre* (1941) esteem *The Wild Duck* as Ibsen's "most appealing play"; many deem it his best one. After a 1936 production, W. A. Darlington, in the *London Daily Telegraph* (November 4) observed: "It may be a matter for argument whether *The Wild Duck* is the best of Ibsen's plays, but there is hardly room for doubt that it is the most durable."

In technique, *The Wild Duck* marks Ibsen's richest use of the "retro-

spective method." Only in *Ghosts* does as much of the essential action
take place before the play begins, and in *Ghosts* the events are simple,
almost bare. In *The Wild Duck* the whole play grows through our learning the tangled course of life that has already been run. And, as
William Archer said in his introduction to the play (1908), "as every
event is also a trait of character, it follows that never before has his
dialogue been so saturated, as it were, with character-revelation." In
no other Ibsen play do we feel that the characters and events are so real.

Through its story, *The Wild Duck* suggests that there are cases in
which falsehood is essential to happiness, that there are persons who
cannot carry on without a "life lie." Gina Ekdal is a practical soul; her
shrewd commonsense keeps on a steady keel the household and the
photography business of her dreamer husband Hjalmar. Their daughter Hedvig is a happy little creature; she loves the wild duck that old
Ekdal, Hjalmar's father, has tamed and keeps in the attic. Like the
Ekdals, the wild duck grows accustomed to its tame existence. But
Gregers Werle, "suffering," as Dr. Relling puts it, "from an acute attack
of integrity," insists upon telling Hjalmar that old Werle is contributing
to the support of the Ekdal household, and may indeed be Hedvig's
father. Hjalmar, contrary to Greger's expectation, is not ennobled by
the revelation; he thrusts little Hedvig from him, and the girl goes into
the attic and shoots herself.

Gregers speaks of maintaining one's ideals; Dr. Relling tells him he
should speak, rather, the native word—lies. "Rob the average man of
his life lie," says the doctor, "and you rob him of his happiness at the
same stroke." "If you are right and I am wrong," says Gregers at the
end of the play, "then life is not worth living." Dr. Relling responds:
"Oh, life would be quite tolerable, after all, if only we could be rid of
the confounded duns that keep on pestering us, in our poverty, with
the claims of the ideal."

Presenting this idea in terms of character-development, Ibsen has
created several of his most interesting figures. Little Hedvig is his most
heart-warming, tender child. Her nature is interwoven with that of
the wild duck in the attic, which grows tame and fat, but which is
really at home only in the forest. Hjalmar once says that he would
like to kill the wild duck; it is to show her love for Hjalmar that Hedvig
goes to the attic and kills the little human bird Hjalmar has thrust
aside—herself. Here, more moderately than in the later plays, Ibsen
seeks to strengthen his psychological presentation by the use of symbols.

The figure of Gina is another triumph of character creation. Blanche
Yurka enacted her role vividly in the New York Actors Equity production, which opened February 24, 1925.

Perhaps Ibsen's major creation in the play is Hjalmar Ekdal, at once
a deeply pathetic and a broadly comic man; egoist, sentimentalist, poseur,
dreamer, and failure, he lives on Gina's practical management and his
life-lie. The fact that Ibsen has set this richly comic Hjalmar in circumstances that lead to tragedy—has even made him the fulcrum on
which the crisis lifts—has misled the more solemn commentators. Thus
Thomas Mann, looking for an image in which to cast his own dislike of
the contemporary public, pontificates, in "Mankind Take Care," in the
Atlantic Monthly (August 1938): "Put before an audience of today . . .
a play like Ibsen's *The Wild Duck*, and you will see that in the course
of thirty years it has become quite incomprehensible. People think it

is a farce and laugh in the wrong places. In the nineteenth century there was a society capable of grasping the European irony and innuendo, the idealistic bitterness and moral subtlety of such a work. All that is gone . . ." Contrast with this the observation in the *London Times* (November 6, 1936), made of a revival of *The Wild Duck* in modern dress: "Of all Ibsen's plays it is most likely to disturb the moral and intellectual complacency of a modern audience"; or the remark of the *London Observer* (November 8, 1936) that "Dr. Relling diagnosing 'rectitudinal fever' is a national necessity in any country"; or Bernard Shaw's "Where can I find an epithet magnificent enough for *The Wild Duck!*"

Published November 11, 1884, *The Wild Duck* was, within four months, played throughout Scandinavia. Berlin saw it in March 1888; Paris, at the Théâtre Libre, in 1891 (when the dramatic dictator-critic Francisque Sarcey called it "obscure, incoherent, unbearable.") It came to London through the Independent Theatre Society, on May 4, 1894, when Clement Scott said: "To make a fuss about so feeble a production is to insult dramatic literature and to outrage common sense." London gave it a public performance in 1897; in 1905, Granville Barker played Hjalmar there. It was performed in Chicago in 1907, but New York did not see it in English until Nazimova played Hedvig in 1918. The thoughts of several critics were expressed by one who wrote that Nazimova's "bobbed sparkling black hair, that breathed a strangely missisvernoncastle spirit of rollick" broke the spell of the play; but Louis Sherwin in the *New York Globe* (March 12) said: "Last night I saw an Ibsen play acted as it should be acted . . . It was the most hilarious performance of an Ibsen play I ever saw, and the most commonsensible."

There being no single starring role in *The Wild Duck*, it has been less often performed than poorer plays that provide good acting vehicles. It is, however, frequently revived by repertory groups. There was a notable New York production in 1925 with Blanche Yurka as Gina, Helen Chandler as Hedvig, and Tom Powers as Gregers; Blanche Yurka played Gina in revivals up to 1937. There were other New York productions in 1938 and (Equity Library Theatre) in April 1944 and May 1945 with Albert and Else Bassermann.

The Wild Duck suggests that truth, like other valuable commodities, should be used sparingly. But it presents this thought in an observation of life at once so genial and so searching that *The Wild Duck* may well claim highest place in the field of domestic drama. In *The Wild Duck*, realism and symbolism, comedy and tragedy, integrate and fuse.

ROSMERSHOLM   *Henrik Ibsen*

Written in 1886, this play is the last of Ibsen's dramas based on social themes, and the first of his profound psychological studies. It is Ibsen's starkest tragedy.

When the play opens, the cultured and distinguished Johannes Rosmer, roused by the imperious Rebecca West, is ready to turn from his conservative post and take active part in the liberal and progressive movements of his day. Gradually, however, Rosmer becomes aware that the driving will of Rebecca, perhaps innocently and unconsciously at work, had pushed his wife Beata to suicide; his faith in his mission is broken. Rebecca sees but one way to restore it, namely, to kill herself; but

Rosmer joins her and together they leap from the foot-bridge into the millrace that had earlier borne away his wife.

There is a parallel in the careers of Ibsen himself and Rosmer. Both were at first conservative; both turned liberal and were scorned therefor; and both found the change hollow. Ibsen visited Norway in 1885, just after the Liberal party triumph over the King and his Ministers destroyed the King's right to veto the decisions of Storthing (Congress). Ibsen found his countrymen turned into "cats and dogs," with snarling personal antagonisms that precluded urbane discussion of principles. "This impression," Henrik Jaeger has pointed out, "has recorded itself in the picture of party divisions in *Rosmersholm*. The bitterness of the vanquished is admirably embodied in Rector Kroll; while the victors' craven reluctance to speak out their whole hearts is excellently characterized in the freethinker and opportunist, Mortengard."

Ibsen himself, in an address to Norwegian workingmen (June 14, 1885), declared: "There remains much to be done before we can be said to have attained real liberty. I fear that our present democracy will not be equal to the task. An element of nobility must be introduced into our national life . . . Nobility of character, of will, of soul."

Although the actual incidents of *Rosmersholm* were suggested by a similar tragedy in the life of a Swedish Count, the theme of the play is the attempt of persons of nobility to square their life with their ideals or, as Ibsen himself said, "the struggle with himself that every serious-minded man must face in order to bring his life into harmony with his convictions." Rosmer is caught in the fateful dilemma of a constructive and progressive social purpose and a personal progress that has been reared on destruction. Rebecca West is pressed by an iron will that equally redeems and dooms.

Rosmersholm is knit with intricate skill. It employs the retrospective method as superbly as *The Wild Duck**, but the characters are more deeply sounded. The drama of the richly eventful past unfolds within the drama of the present in a complex yet clear and stately harmony.

Rosmersholm was published on November 23, 1886, and within four months played throughout Scandinavia. Ibsen saw the first German production at Augsburg in 1887. The play was produced in Vienna and in Paris by Lugné-Poe (who took his French Company on tour into Scandinavia), in 1893. In Italy, Duse enacted Rebecca West.

In Germany *Rosmersholm* is one of Ibsen's most popular plays, but in English it has never had a whole-hearted reception, though it was performed in London in 1891 and 1893 and in New York in 1904 and frequently thereafter. Minnie Maddern Fiske played Rebecca in 1907, and at intervals for eleven years. The Stagers' production opened on May 5, 1925, with Margaret Wycherly, Warren William, J. M. Kerrigan, Josephine Hull, and Arthur Hughes. Eva Le Gallienne played Rebecca in 1935; Equity Library Theatre put on the play in 1946 and 1947. London saw it again in August 1950.

Of the comments on the first English production, that of the *London Illustrated Sporting and Dramatic News* (March 7, 1891) is representative: "The filling-up of the play was the merest commonplace of domestic platitude. But the composition of the piece was no stronger than the comedy. I do not speak only of the straggling nature of the incidents and the want of action, but of the dramatic thinness of the work . . . With regard to the story of *Rosmersholm*, those who profess to know tell us it is a politico-social revelation . . . All that I gathered from the very dismal performance is that when a weak man loves a bad woman, the only thing open to both of them is to commit suicide . . . But where is the justice of awarding the same fate to a woman who deserved hanging and the man who should simply have been locked up for a fool? . . . The only emotion from beginning to end was the uncontrollable laughter produced by the naive comicality of some of the serious lines." In America, although the *New York Dramatic Mirror* (April 9, 1904) allowed that "*Rosmersholm* is at once one of the deepest and—in the printed pages—one of the clearest of Ibsen's plays," it found that "the joy of anticipation was the only joy experienced by the auditors. The presentation was in almost every respect a disappointment."

Looking at the Stagers' production, the *New York World* (May 6, 1925) said that *Rosmersholm* was "like a fine granite chapel . . . all the cunning in design of its creator was preserved in the material provided by the builders. Yet somehow it was a chapel from which the worshippers had fled. There was a classic chill about it unrelieved by the warm humanity of hymns and whispers of life among the columns." By 1935, Brooks Atkinson (December 6) called the play "the mirror of a dead society," and John Mason Brown agreed that it was "tedious and talky and dated." Yet in 1947 George Freedley (November 25), speaking of the Equity Library production, said "*Rosmersholm* has got the season off to an auspicious start."

The unrelieved seriousness and unremitting introspection of *Rosmersholm* make it a heavy burden for the Anglo-Saxon spirit, accustomed to the comic interlude within the tragic drive; yet the play remains a masterpiece of psychological drama. Beneath the intellectual conflict of tradition and liberalism surge the ingrown forces and subconscious drives to which many persons awaken too late to dam before they themselves are damned.

THE LADY FROM THE SEA   *Henrik Ibsen*

In 1888, Ibsen published *The Lady From the Sea*, another psychological study of a woman caught in the quest of integrity. Nora, in *A Doll's House**, breaks free at the play's close, going forth to find herself. Ellida, in *The Lady From the Sea*, discovers that with freedom comes power to accept responsibility, comes decision. When her husband leaves to her the choice, whether or not to go off with her sailor wooer, Ellida chooses to remain at home.

The play is touched with a pleasant dry humor and tinged with tenderness, especially in the invalid Lyngstrand and in Ellida's younger step-daughter, Hilda.

The Lady From the Sea was played in Scandinavia and in Germany early in 1889, and has always been popular there. At a Weimar production, on March 14, 1889, Ibsen, then sixty, was given a laurel wreath. London saw the play in 1891 and 1902; Paris, in 1892. New York saw it first on November 6, 1911, with Hedwig Reicher. Duse included it in her American tour, in New York in 1923, across the country in 1924. Revivals came in New York, with Blanche Yurka in 1929; in 1934; in 1948, an Equity Library production; and with Luise Rainer opening August 7, 1950, in a production that emphasized the personal story and slurred the general problem of integrity and freedom of choice, which remains most significant in our time.

HEDDA GABLER   *Henrik Ibsen*

Without wholly putting aside social satire, Ibsen places greater emphasis on individual psychology in this play than in any of his previous works.

Freedley and Reeves in their *History of the Theatre* (1941) call *Hedda Gabler*, 1890, "a character study pure and simple." Its namesake is neither simple nor pure—though quite attractive. Alrik Gustafson in *A History of Modern Drama* (1947) suggests that Hedda is "so repulsive in her cold, clammy spiritual sterility that we are attracted to the phenomenon as we are to a poisonous snake." Grant Allen, on the other hand, says Hedda is "the girl we take down to dinner in London nineteen times out of twenty." Hedda's is indeed a hypersensitive soul; she shrinks from all that is gross and prosaic. She desires power, but seeks it only along decorous avenues. Fastidious to excess, she avoids not evil but ugliness; rather than become tangled in a sordid, underhand liaison, she shoots herself.

Married to a dull pedant, George Tesman, Hedda finds his devotion to his aunts and his drudgery ways unbearable. In envy of an old schoolmate who has helped another writer, Eilert Lövborg, with his manuscript and has won him from drinking, Hedda lures Eilert back to his liquor and burns his supposedly lost manuscript. She then sends her pistols to Eilert, who shoots himself. When Hedda's cynical but observant friend, Judge Brack, indicates that he knows about the pistols, and expects Hedda's favors in return for his silence, Hedda finds one more use for the pistols, pointed at her beautiful but oh-so-bored self.

Freedley and Reeves call *Hedda Gabler* "perhaps Ibsen's best play." Written in colloquial prose, it has but seven characters, covers but two days, and its well-knit plot observes strict unity of place and action.

Published December 16, 1890, the play was performed in Munich, with Ibsen in the audience, January 31, 1891, with Frau Conrad-Ramlo as Hedda. In Copenhagen, Fru Hennings opened as Hedda, on February 25; Constance Brunn starred in Christiania the following night. The production with Elizabeth Robins, in London, April 20, 1891, made quite a stir, as did the Paris production, December 17, 1891. Mrs. Fiske brought the play to New York in 1903. Others who have played the proud Hedda include Eleanora Duse, Katina Paxinou, Mrs. Pat Campbell, Nance O'Neil, Alla Nazimova, Clare Eames, Emily Stevens, Blanche Bates, Blanche Yurka, and Eva Le Gallienne. Productions have come almost yearly in the United States; from Nazimova, whose first English role was Hedda in 1906 and who revived the part constantly, with excellent productions in 1918 and in 1936-1937, to Eva Le Gallienne, who enacted Hedda 'with the Civic Repertory Theatre in 1928, 1929, and 1930, and played the part again in 1939, 1941, and 1948. Such actresses are drawn to the part by qualities that led Justin Huntly McCarthy to say in the London *Black and White* (April 25, 1891): "*Hedda Gabler* is the name, to my mind, of Ibsen's greatest play, and of the most interesting woman that he has created . . . She is compact with all the vices, she is instinct with all the virtues, of womanhood." But the great Danish critic George Brandes said: "What deep impression can it make upon us, that such a creature throws her life away?   It is with but cold regret that we see her lying dead on the sofa in the inner room."

Hedda Gabler presents no social theme; its action, with a few changes in details of setting, could occur almost any place in our time.   Ibsen stated, in a letter of December 4, 1890, to his French translator, Count Prozor: "It was not my desire to deal in this play with so-called problems.   What I principally wanted to do was to depict human beings, human emotions, and human destinies, upon a groundwork of certain of the social conditions and principles of the present day."   This detachment of the playwright led to mixed judgments.   Brandes declared: "In no earlier work of Ibsen has it been so difficult to discover what the poet wishes us to learn, or rather what is his underlying sentiment . . . it seems as though Ibsen this time has not had anything at heart which he particularly wishes to say—although surely his artistic conscientiousness has never been greater than in this play, and his technical mastership has never been more brilliant . . . In *Hedda Gabler*, it seems to me that Ibsen is at his best only as a calculating artist, not as the sympathetic poet."   Yet William Archer called the play "surely one of the most poignant character-tragedies in literature."

When Blanche Bates (with Minnie Dupree, J. H. Benrimo, and Albert Bruning) opened in *Hedda Gabler* in Philadelphia, the *Ledger* (February 13, 1904) exclaimed: "What a hopeless specimen of degeneracy is Hedda Gabler!   A vicious, heartless, cowardly, unmoral, mischief-making vixen."   The *New York Sun* of April 18, 1918 cried out: "What a marvel of stupidity and nonsense the author did produce in this play! It is incredible to think that only a score of years ago the audience sat seriously before its precious dulness and tried to read something into its lines."   Thirty years later (February 25, 1948) the *New York World-Telegram* had other words: *Hedda Gabler* "completely escapes the perennial blight of an Ibsen play—datedness—in its timeless theme of a woman revenging herself on the lover she rejected to her regret.   In the title role, Eva Le Gallienne turns in an all-stops-out performance that ranks with Judith Anderson's *Medea**."

The sentimentalist may be repelled by the photographic indifference of Ibsen's portrait; Ibsen presents, he neither condones nor condemns, the ways of the hapless Hedda.   But few women have been more clearly and more completely revealed in moving drama.

THE MASTER BUILDER   *Henrik Ibsen*

Master Builder Solness (to translate the original title literally) was written after Ibsen had returned to his native land "to arrange his affairs."   It is the first of the four plays he wrote in Christiania, and bears a symbolism that, while it has universal application, is also autobiographical.

Much of the drama is spun through conversation between Halvard Solness, architect, and the young Hilda Wangel, for whom he had once hung a wreath on a church steeple.   He is no longer building churches, he tells her, only "homes for human beings."   With the eager zest of youth, Hilda encourages Solness to build houses with high towers, perhaps even castles in the air.   Spurred on by her, despite his fear of dizzying peaks, Solness climbs with a wreath to the pinnacle of his new house—and falls to his death.

In the play's vague, mysterious atmosphere, says William Archer, "though the dialogue is sternly restrained within the limits of prose, the art of drama seems forever on the point of floating away to blend with the art of music." Others have been less sympathetic, finding the mixture of symbolic and realistic elements confusing and Solness comprehensible only as a pathological study. Thus the *London Times* (February 24, 1893) declared: "The most ardent votaries of Ibsenism must be in some doubt as to whether a further prosecution of the cult is advisable. They must have left the theatre with an uneasy feeling that the master was laughing at them up his sleeve. It is only on some such hypothesis that the strange composition of the latest of Mr. Ibsen's plays can be accepted as the work of a wholly sane writer." With pretended sympathy, the *Theatre* (All Fools' Day, 1893) inquired as to the possible meanings of the play: "There is room for a score of interpretations . . . Presumably there is more in the play than meets the eye. Otherwise it is a very uneven, exasperating, and inconclusive jumble of brilliance and dulness, lucidity and obscurity . . . the characters of Solness and Hilda are vague, elusive, utterly lacking in sustained reality. At every turn, moreover, they bring one into a blind alley, and turn one back with the sense of having been rudely made a fool of."

Fifty-four years later, Harold Hobson declared in the *Sunday Times*, with reference to a production of *The Master Builder* that opened January 1, 1947: "I find this play, like the universe and the way of an eagle in the air, incomprehensible. But, incomprehensible or not, there blows through this play a loud and gusty wind of genius, which . . . sets everybody tingling with an invigorated and refreshed excitement . . . This is an evening to remember."

Published in December 1892, *The Master Builder* was first presented in Berlin with Emanuel Reicher on January 19, 1893; then in London the following February 20 with Elizabeth Robins. Christiania and Copenhagen saw the play on March 8, 1893. Lugné-Poe enacted Solness in Paris, opening April 3, 1894. The New York premiere was January 16, 1900. Other New York productions came in 1905; in 1907 with Alla Nazimova and Walter Hampden, in 1926 with Eva Le Gallienne and Egon Brecher, who revived it for a number of years. The work was brushed aside by the *New York Dramatic Mirror* (November 18, 1905) with the exclamation: "Enough for this week's recrudescence of Ibsenity." In London, the *Times* (March 15, 1936) called a revival of the play "enchanting." It was performed again in 1948 with Donald Wolfit and Rosalind Iden.

The later reactions show that the critics discerned order beneath the first semblance of confusion. Some saw it as the drama of a sickly conscience prodded by a conscience more robust, as the conservatism of age is pressed by the insistent seeming radicalism of youth. Solness' inability to climb as high as he builds thus symbolizes man's inability to act as freely as he thinks. Others, finding the symbolism and the psychology both true, examined the play on its realistic level. Thus the *London Observer* (March 15, 1936), calling it "an enthralling play," observed: "Here is no plain tale from the Norwegian hills, but a complex parable whose narrative surprises flower . . . with astonishing richness and fecundity from outset to denouement. Here, if anywhere, Ibsen begins where lesser dramatists leave off."

There is an autobiographical symbolism throughout the drama. The churches Solness builds represent Ibsen's historical and romantic plays. The homes for human beings are his plays of domestic realism, his social dramas. The towered buildings, "castles in the air," point toward the spiritual dramas, with psychological problems and symbolical overtones. Like Solness, Ibsen was insistently pressed by the younger generation.

The intertwining and overlapping of subject and symbol—surface story and suggested thought—make *The Master Builder* unique among the plays of Ibsen, the least derivative and most original of all his works.

LITTLE EYOLF   *Henrik Ibsen*

This is Ibsen's grimmest and most pessimistic study of a conflict of egos in the basic battle of self-deception versus integrity.

Alfred Allmers, dreaming and theorizing for his projected book on "Human Responsibility," has himself evaded responsibility all his life. Supported by his wife's wealth, Allmers remains a "restive and reluctant windbag," blind to things around him because he lives on a dream. Alfred's wife, Rita, requires full possession of her husband: "I don't care a bit," she tells him, "for your calm, deep tenderness; I want you utterly and entirely—and alone!" She even wishes out of the way their nine-year-old son, the crippled Eyolf, on whom Alfred lavishes his tenderness; and the sensitive child, following the old hag they call "the Rat-Wife" to the fjord, is drowned. The horrified parents see the floating crutch; they are haunted by "the wide open eyes" that seem to stare at them from the depths. Their recriminations turn to self-examination; they recognize that Eyolf, amid their egocentric concerns, has been "a stranger child," and they resolve to devote their lives to aiding poor, crippled stranger children, as the problem of "human responsibility" takes on living meaning.

Published December 11, 1894, *Little Eyolf* was presented in Berlin on January 12, 1895; in Christiania, several days later; in Copenhagen, March 13; in Paris in May. Chicago (with an amateur company, in Norwegian) and Boston saw it in 1895; London, on November 23, 1896, with Janet Achurch (Rita), Elizabeth Robins (Asta), and Mrs. Pat Campbell (the Rat-Wife). New York saw productions on May 13, 1907; in 1910, with Nazimova and Brandon Tynan; in 1926 by the Theatre Guild, with Margalo Gillmore, John Cromwell, Reginald Owen, Clare Eames, and Helen Menken; and by Equity Library in 1942. Pasadena staged the drama in 1941. London saw the play again in 1945.

As in most of his plays, Ibsen's suggestion of the supernatural can be realistically explained. Thus the Rat-Wife, who recalls the Pied Piper of Hamelin and may be a symbol of death, is also an actual Norwegian figure, such as used to come to drive the rats from Ibsen's own boyhood school. The basic idea in *Little Eyolf* is dramatic, personal not ethical; as the individuals grow, the meanings also develop.

Declared the *Boston Evening Gazette*, on May 27, 1895: "It is difficult to believe that Mr. Ibsen really knows what he wishes to say . . . His utterances are about as clear as are the landscapes when they are obscured by the mists that rise from his native fjords." But even the *New York Dramatic Mirror* (Ibsen's early enemy in America) on May 25, 1907 was discerning enough to say of the drama: "While on the surface it appears as little more than a study of opposing temperaments, it has a greater depth of poetry and a far more subtle motive than the better known of his modern plays . . ." The *London Observer* (June 17, 1945) found that the play retains its power: "Here is the very north wind of love; Ibsen has no more chilling picture of conjugal misery. Even so, given the right cast, the play—as the current Embassy revival proves—can hold its audience."

There have been dissenting voices. Alan Dale, after a Theatre Guild matinee performance (February 2, 1926), exclaimed: "Happy, happy little Eyolf! He was drowned in the fjord at 2:45, leaving the play in misery—and us . . . It was dull, drab, dark green, and terrible." Yet William Archer considers the death of Eyolf "surely one of the most inspired situations in all drama" and the play as a whole "a terrible and beautiful work of art."

Little Eyolf has a driving power of self-probing that sustains the interest long after the external action of the drama has ended. The play is one of awakening. The pity, and the pessimism, rise from the fact that no one in the audience, as probably not Ibsen, believes in their final recovery and resolve. The *New York World* (February 3, 1926) pictured Alfred and Rita "self-deceiving as they settled back into the inertia of their ignoble marriage, she really wanting nothing in the world but his physical presence, he happy in finding a new face to put on the essential coziness of being supported by her gold and her green forests. Of a rebirth, of a new courage to face the accusing eyes from the depths of the fjord, there was nothing. And I begin to doubt if Ibsen believed there ever was."

It is precisely as a study of the self-deceiving ego, of the blinders one sets upon one's own eyes—even again after catastrophe has for a moment torn them off—that *Little Eyolf* continues to have validity and appeal.

JOHN GABRIEL BORKMAN   *Henrik Ibsen*

This play, written in 1896, was Ibsen's last intense drama of individual psychology. It is of interest especially as it shows Ibsen looking back upon, and weighing, his career.

John Gabriel Borkman opens with an intensity of feeling as Ella confronts her twin sister, Mrs. Gunhild Borkman, after a silence of eight years. Above them paces John Gabriel Borkman, self-imprisoned by hatred, after having been released from jail. Avid for power, Borkman had renounced Ella, whom he loved, to marry Gunhild, who could further his career. He feels no compunction for the embezzlement for which he'd been sentenced; if he'd been let alone, he bitterly reflects, he'd have doubled the money for everyone. And as Borkman paces his room, waiting for society to call upon his talents, the two sisters below struggle for power over Borkman's son, Erhart, who in the heedless passion of youth scorns both his mother and his aunt and goes away with the knowing widow next door. The unwanted Borkman walks out into the storm to die; over his body the sisters at last join hands.

This bitter study of individuals gathers meaning from its portraits. In it we find what Dumas sought in a drama: a painting, a judgment, and an ideal. For through the vivid portraits of the two sisters and the man they loved we discern the bitter end of ruthless self-seeking, the lees of the wine of self-concern and quest of power; and we behold how the killing of love slays what is best in man. Yet in Borkman's final vision, where the poet complements the dramatist as the doomed man tells his dream—weaving "a network of fellowship all round the world" —though his unscrupulous means dragged him to failure, Borkman in his dying moments holds high the ideal.

Published December 15, 1896, *John Gabriel Borkman* opened at Helsingfors in two theatres (one in Swedish, one in Finnish) on January 10, 1897; within the month, it was played all over Scandinavia. Germany took it up quickly, as did London, May 3, 1897, with Elizabeth Robins, and New York, in November of the same year. On March 19, 1897, the *New York Times* reported from Berlin that "the drama exhales an atmosphere of respectability mildewed and eaten away by vice." The play was revived in New York in 1915; by the Civic Repertory with Eva Le Gallienne in 1926, 1927, and 1928; by Eva Le Gallienne again, November 12, 1946, with Margaret Webster, Victor Jory, and Ernest Truex.

Every New York production has won mixed reviews. The *New York Dramatic Mirror* of April 21, 1915, noted the differences of opinion. Chapman, Garland, and Barnes were negative. Chapman: "Theatrical claptrap of an astonishingly cheap quality." Garland: "These woe-is-me-ers woe-is-me-ing on the frosty outskirts of Norway's Christiania are out of this world. And they certainly should be!" Barnes: "The rescue of the Ibsen drama from comparative neglect has been effected with more pains than flourish." Other critics were deeply impressed. Morehouse: "a play of gnawing and sustained bitterness . . . steadily engrossing theatre." Watts: "this low-pitched but oddly arresting drama of anticlimax took on an absorbing sense of power and truth." Atkinson: "Put *John Gabriel Borkman* down as a tone-poem written out of Ibsen's angry passion, and dub the current performance a masterpiece . . . with the rhythm of a dance of death and the tone of a song of doom."

The swift movement of *John Gabriel Borkman* strictly observes the "unity of time." The time of the events is no more than the time of the performance. Yet at the end the intensity slackens somewhat as the dramatic drive gives way to a lyric exaltation before doom. Comparison with *Pillars of Society** shows the greater poetic power of the later play. In both dramas a business man of great ability has committed a crime; in both the man is torn between two sisters; in both he has turned from a woman he loves to a woman who can help his career. But *Pillars of Society* seems cluttered, and its end, if not tawdry, tame, beside the stark and inevitable movement of *John Gabriel Borkman*. Imagination and beauty combine with truth, to give the play grim yet magnificent power.

ARMORED TRAIN 14-69   *Vsevolod Vyacheslavich Ivanov*

The first successful Soviet play, produced in Moscow and in Leningrad in 1927, the tenth anniversary of the Russian Revolution, was *Armored Train 14-69* (also called *The Armored Train*), by Vsevolod Vyacheslavich Ivanov (b. 1895). Based on an actual event, the capture of a White Army train by a band of peasants, the play combines vivid history with rousing propaganda. Its underlying idea is that those that control the machine control human destiny; therefore the workers must take over the machines.

As the play opens, the peasants are watching the tracks from the roof of a ruined church. They plan to capture the armored train, which will soon pass by. Since they must not damage the tracks, the only way to stop it is for some one to throw himself in front of the engine. "Who will volunteer?" calls the leader, Vershinen. In the expectant silence, a voice cries, "Why not you?" Vershinen agrees. Then his adjutant says the leader is needed; he will go instead. At the tracks, when the engine roars near, a Japanese comrade thrusts the adjutant aside and leaps to his devoted death. A shriek, grinding of brakes, pouring down of the peasants, then the train appears wreathed with the smiling peasant conquerors.

Armored Train 14-69 has been frequently revived throughout Russia; in Moscow, elaborately at the Theatre Festival of 1933. It was presented in New York in Yiddish in 1931 and in English, at the Dramatic Workshop, in 1934. The *New York Times* (November 26, 1931) felt that the play came alive, "by reason of that religious quality which runs through most of the plays of contemporary Russia." John Mason Brown (March 28, 1934) said that it called for "extended program notes and explanatory lectures between the scenes." A presentation less of a conflict than of a gathering surge of devotion that brings victory in its armored train, the play is a vivid example of the use of the theatre for the ends of propaganda.

MICHAEL AND HIS LOST ANGEL   *Henry Arthur Jones*

Coming from a strict Welsh background at a time when the English stage was flooded with adaptations of French melodramas and farces, Henry Arthur Jones (English, 1861-1929) worked seriously for the improvement of the theatre, with both plays and criticism. Among his critical works are *The Renascence of the English Drama*, 1895, and *The Theatre of Ideas*, 1915.

After the success of his play, *The Silver King*, 1882, Jones sought to examine, sincerely and fully, in dramatic terms, social problems of his day. He wrote over sixty comedies and domestic dramas, of which he considered *Michael and His Lost Angel*, 1896, his masterpiece. To protect the copyright, the play was opened the same day, January 15, 1896, in London and New York; eager to have a proper presentation in America, Jones sent over, on forty phonographic cylinders, his own reading of the lines.

The story is a simple one. After insisting that Rose Andrews confess her sin before all the congregation, the Reverend Michael Faversham finds himself likewise a transgressor. In love with his charming and wealthy parishioner Audrey Lesden, he goes to his lonely island to pray for strength, and finds himself and the lady alone on the island over night. After making public confession of their transgression, Michael retires to Italy, where Mrs. Lesden, who has followed him, dies in his arms.

Michael and His Lost Angel won greater critical than popular acclaim. Forbes-Robertson and Marian Terry (though Audrey was written for Mrs. Pat Campbell) played it in London; Henry Miller and Viola Allen, in New York. There was some doubt as to just what Jones was trying to demonstrate, and a considerable body of playgoers objected to the Church as the locale of the love scene between Michael and Audrey. Clement Scott, in the *Illustrated London News* (August 8, 1896) said: "I read the play before I saw it acted, was delighted with it," and he quoted critic Joseph Knight, who had declared: "In some respects the loves of Michael Faversham and Audrey Lesden seem to take rank with the masterpieces of human passion; if not with Romeo and Juliet, with Cupid and Psyche, with Paul and Virginia." Then Mr. Scott added: "The church scene offended me, not because it was a church scene, but because as seen on the stage it was vulgar, ineffective, not to say ridiculous. The scene read well, and it acted badly. Voilà tout!"

The play received kind words from Bernard Shaw, who remarked that Jones's works grow, they are not just stuck together: "When I respond to the appeal of Mr. Jones's art by throwing myself sympathetically into his characteristic attitude of mind, I am conscious of no shortcoming in *Michael and His Lost Angel* . . . I unhesitatingly class Mr. Jones as first, and eminently first, among the surviving fittest of his own generation of playwrights." Shaw went on to tell how he would have given both Michael and Audrey a tragic self-realization. He also suggested that what drives Rose Andrews to confess should be not a lugubrious preaching of mortification and wrath, but a contagion of Michael's bounding and rapturous faith in the gladness of an open and contrite heart—a joy of life that is at once the minister's power and his doom.

The theme of *Michael and His Lost Angel* has been interpreted as an insistence on the single standard—what is loss for the goose is loss for the gander—and as the idea that justice without mercy, meted out to others, will some day strike home. The play, however, is better considered as a study of human relationships. The happy love of Audrey Lesden, which admits no obstacle to its expression, founders upon the ascetic ideals of Michael, whose passions plunge him into the depths.

Even the "lost angel" of the title brought different interpretations. Most critics assumed that the lost angel is Audrey, for she tells the minister that he might inspire her to saintly ways—but at too great sacrifice. The *New York Herald* (January 16, 1896) however, said: "The lost angel is Michael's dead mother, whose portrait is lugged in for a little tawdry sentimentality that had better been spared."

The *Home Journal* summed up the reception of the play: "*Michael and His Lost Angel* is a powerful, interesting, and instructive play, well-built, clearly told, and with an objective purpose . . . The matters in this piece by which it has failed to win popular approval are easily perceived. *Michael and His Lost Angel* is consistently serious; it lacks that odious thing, 'comic relief'; it is wholly without action; it consists in a series of duologues between two persons; it seems to have, although it does not possess, sacrilegious elements; its hero is a pitiful fellow, and its heroine has no qualities that earn applause. We may grant all these things without losing our esteem for the artistic treatment of the play, its excellent construction, its clear portrayal of character, and its powerful situations. As a work of dramatic art, *Michael* is almost flawless; as a popular diversion it is abundant in faults . . . We regret that there are not enough people in town to support a performance which is one of the most intelligent achievements of the modern theatre."

The church scene was removed in New York after the first performance, but that was too late. The pious were already repelled; the curious could no longer be satisfied. The *Times* (January 16, 1896) said, "The failure was deserved, complete, irreparable." There was a reading of "the uncensored version" of the play in New York, October 30, 1913; but *Michael and His Lost Angel*, though imitated, has not been revived. It remains one of the best English problem plays of the late nineteenth century before the surge of Ibsen and of Shaw.

THE LIARS   *Henry Arthur Jones*

With shafts of comedy, Henry Arthur Jones in *The Liars* aims at the heart of society, its conventions and its petty evasions. Skilfully constructed, deftly told, *The Liars*, 1897, was Jones' most popular play. Written for Charles Wyndham and the Criterion Company (with Mary Moore), *The Liars* came to New York in 1898, with John Drew. It was a hit on both sides of the Atlantic, and was revived often in the United States, notably in 1915 with Grace Moore and Conway Tearle.

The play is set in English society. Lady Jessica, feeling herself neglected by her husband, Gilbert Nepean, meets the diplomat Edward Falkner at the "Star and Garter", where they are seen by her brother-in-law George. To clear Jessica, her sister Rosamond and her cousin Dolly join in an invented story, to which they make their men folk testify—until the unwitting Edward tells a conflicting story. The counsel of Jessica's old friend Sir Christopher keeps her from going off with Edward, who departs alone; while Gilbert, become aware of his error, begs Jessica to give him another chance.

When the play opened in London, its quality was quickly recognized. Observed A. B. Walkley in the *Speaker* (October 9, 1897): "The reality of the tragedy is not disguised by the somewhat cheap and facile conclusion . . . the comedy of the surface must be worked for all it is worth, and the tragedy of the undercurrent must be discreetly veiled." Walkley, however, put his finger on the high spot of the play; "There is one moment when we can all laugh without stint. It is in the capital scene of the play wherein Lady Jessica's friends engage in the concoction of a story which shall blind the husband . . . The facile fluent lying of the women, the helpless floundering of the men, the irritation of the one sex at the other's want of skill at the game and the blank amazement of the unskilled sex at the rich and ready resource of the skilled—all this, as I have said, is excellent comedy." Even Bernard Shaw, who usually pricks at his forerunners on the English stage, declared that Jones had extracted from this situation "all the drama that can be got from it without sacrificing verisimilitude, or spoiling the reassuring common sense of the conclusion."

Allardyce Nicoll has called *The Liars* a landmark in the history of modern drama: "The true comedy of manners is realistic in aim, but from the very fact that its main objective is the displaying of the manners of society it is artificial; it aims at the realistic depiction of artificial life, and frequently the success of the picture depends upon the subtle contrast instituted by the dramatist between the external veneer of society manners and the evidences of natural man (and woman) peeping through the veil. This quality often appears in the present play, and contributes much to its permanent interest." In its realistic capture of this artificiality, *The Liars* marks, said Nicoll, the beginning of a new period in the drama.

In New York, *The Liars* was favorably received. The *Dramatic Mirror* (October 1, 1898), however, regretted that "the three wives, Lady

Jessica, Lady Rosamund, and Dolly, are silly, frivolous, and heartless. Their respective spouses are dolts of incredible density." The *Mirror* refused to have its "ideals of the stability of the English character . . . shattered by even so careful an observer of manners and morals as Mr. Jones." *Harpers Weekly* (October 8), preferred the play to the production; it called *The Liars* "a far better play than one is permitted to appreciate. . . ."

Revivals found *The Liars* still effective. The *London Outlook* (April 20, 1907) declared it "one of the few plays that never stale." Of the New York 1915 production, Charles Darnton (November 19) said there is "still a great deal of interest and entertainment"; and the *Dramatic Mirror* (November 20) stated: "In the neatness of his characterization, in the effect of his spontaneity of wit, Henry Arthur Jones proves as magnificent a calculator, as expert a dovetailor, as the playwrighting world has produced." Neatly woven, with broad but savory strokes of characterization, beneath its amusing surface *The Liars* carries sobering thoughts of a widespread weakness of mankind.

EVERY MAN IN HIS HUMOUR   *Ben Jonson*

Although Ben Jonson (English, 1573-1637) collaborated in the writing of a few earlier dramas, *Every Man in his Humour*, 1598, is the first play from his pen alone. At once it marked a new type in the English theatre. Jonson was aware of the novelty he had provided; in the prologue he scorns the drama that ranges widely through lands and years, like many plays of Shakespeare.

For the history play and the romantic comedy of Shakespeare, Jonson substituted the satiric comedy of humours. The word "humours" refers to the four moistures that, in medieval physiology, were held to determine a man's temperament, making him sanguine, choleric, melancholy, or phlegmatic. By the time of Jonson, the term had come to be applied to a man's dominant foible or passion; *Every Man in his Humour* turns its shafts upon the eccentricities and affectations of London types. There are Edward Kno'well, the town gull, whose father is over-solicitous of his son's behavior; Well-Bred, from the country; the lively Cob, the water-bearer; and especially Captain Bobadill, a boastful and cowardly soldier, condescending, affecting a niceness in his habits and associations, without humor in our sense of the term, but thoroughly phlegmatic in Jonson's. Gentlemen, merchants, and a genial magistrate, Justice Clement, are variously displayed in the drama.

The plot of the play, amusingly carried along with varied disguisings of Kno'well's man Brain-worm, revolves about the jealous merchant Kitely, whose wife proves credulous and jealous too, once her suspicions are aroused. The two meet at Cob's house, each thinking the other to adultery inclined. Kno'well, on the watch for his son, is mistakenly assumed by Kitely to be his wife's paramour, but young Kno'well has meanwhile been tied in lawful matrimony to Kitely's sister Bridget, and at Justice Clement's chambers the misunderstandings are cleared away. In the course of the story Bobadill, the haughty soldier, submits to a thrashing.

While the persons pictured in the play are as authentic English types —London types—as any in the theatre, they had their prototypes in the Greek drama, and indeed are embodiments of universal failings. When the play was first presented in 1598, it had Italian localities and names; these were changed to English in the version of 1606, when the play was revived at the time of the visit of the King of Denmark to his daughter Queen Anne. The characters are drawn from every level of life, as might well come within the compass of Jonson, a gentleman by birth, a citizen by training, a craftsman and a soldier by necessity, a scholar and a poet by nature, an actor by choice. The Prologue, announcing Jonson's satiric intention, was first printed in the 1616 folio edition of the play. Since Jonson holds up to ridicule all excess, and with the sharpness of his intellect almost mocks all enthusiasm, it is understandable that in this edition he omitted young Kno'well's praise of poetry, in which a genuine fervor richly rings. It might be noted that a great bulk of the play is written in vigorous—indeed, at times too full of oaths for the censor!—plain English prose.

In the first production of *Every Man in his Humour* by the Lord Chamberlain's servants at the Globe Theatre, the actor Shakespeare was listed as having a part. The play was revived after the Restoration, in 1675; in 1751 Garrick first played Kitely, who became one of his favorite roles. In the preface to his acting version, Garrick said of Jonson: "The basis of his dramas is one master-passion; to illustrate which, he brings forward a variety of strongly contrasted characters, drawn with the profoundest skill: the incidents maintain a perfect consistency; he never throws his personages into ridiculous situations to make the unskilful laugh . . . His too lofty contempt for the million forbade him the use of pantomimic aid; nor would he sacrifice his own severe judgment to escape or insure the catcalls of their censure or applause . . . When the passion he set out with is illustrated, his play is done . . . The scene is laid in domestic life; the characters are striking and original; and the incidents are kept within the pale of probability. In depicting jealousy working in the bosom of a plain citizen, Jonson may stand in comparison with Shakespeare: indeed, Kitely is altogether a more masterly-drawn portrait than Ford (in *The Merry Wives of Windsor**)."

Through the eighteenth and first half of the nineteenth century, the play continued popular. Cooke and Kemble alternated in the part of Kitely; Macready also acted the part. Charles Dickens played Bobadill, making *Every Man in His Humour* the first production of his noted amateur company in 1845. In New York, the *Spirit of the Times* (April 4, 1846) commented of a revival that the comedy "has a peculiar adaptability to the stage where, when in proper hands, it cannot fail to convey a good moral, as well as to amuse."

The first American production was at New York's John Street Theatre in 1769. Of a 1905 performance at Stanford University, California, with even the audience in Elizabethan guise, *Stage* magazine observed that "its principal interest to a modern audience lies in the historical view it gives of the development in our social and economic conditions and in the realization that while our manners, our costumes, our pet hobbies and our chosen extravagances may change in three centuries, the fundamental 'humours' which make every man, remain unaffected by the swing of time." It seemed even more contemporary when revived in England in 1937 with Donald Wolfit and Rosalind Iden, marking the 300th anniversary of Jonson's death. Ivor Brown stated that "Iden Payne's production fully justifies the choice of play . . . a light and nimble masquerade of cozeners, gulls, and pretenders." And the *London*

Times declared: "At no other time can one imagine such a conjunction of scholarship with quick and close observation of everyday affairs . . . not only in the slang and catchwords of their time but in language of wonderful richness and variety . . . It is surprising how real many of these types of a vanished age become."

Though the age has vanished the persons persist, and Jonson's picture of the "humours" of men has lost none of its validity and force.

EVERY MAN OUT OF HIS HUMOUR   *Ben Jonson*

In his second play, *Every Man Out of His Humour*, 1599, also enacted by the Lord Chamberlain's company, Jonson followed the pattern of his previous hit, but the experiences between brought certain modifications. There is a greater measure of self-confidence, even of self-applause. There is a sharpness of satire, increasing to sarcasm, in the attack upon the follies of the time. Writers that have attacked Jonson are represented in the play: Carlo Buffone the jester may be Marston; Fastidious Brisk has been identified as Daniel; more directly, in two figures irrelevantly introduced, Orange and Clove—the character Cordatus calls them "mere strangers to the whole scope of our play"—the dramatists Dekker and Marston are satirized. On the other hand, the attack on human weaknesses, while more fully elaborated, is also more generalized; it is not so much individuals as representatives of common failings the audience watches on the stage. It opens, like Shakespeare's *The Taming of the Shrew**, with an Induction, in which Asper and two friends, Cordatus and Mitis, argue about the purpose of comedy. Turned 'out of his humour', Asper becomes a character in the play, called Macilente. Between episodes, the two friends continue the argument.

Various persons move about, exposing their natures, finally reveal them to themselves, and thus achieve improvement. In the printed copy of the play, Jonson gives a sketch of each character, from which we may cull examples: Puntarvolo, "A vainglorious knight, over-Englishing his travels, and wholly consecrated to singularity"; Carlo Buffone, "A public, scurrilous, and profane jester . . . His religion is railing and his discourse ribaldry"; Deliro, "A good doting citizen . . . a fellow sincerely besotted on his own wife."

Jonson's theories are presented mainly by Cordatus, described as "the author's friend; a man inly acquainted with the scope and drift of his plot: of a discreet and understanding judgment; and has the place of a Moderator." In the Induction, Asper, who represents the author, rejects the dramatic unities, demanding for himself the freedom the ancients took, to alter and add to the drama's form and range. He recognizes the necessity of pleasing the audience, but insists that the audience seek more than pleasure, "and come to feed their understanding parts". At one point in the play, Mitis (who presents the views of Jonson's opponents) declares it would be more fun if in the story there were "a duke to be in love with a countess, and that countess to be in love with the duke's son, and the son to love the lady's waiting-maid"; whereupon Cordatus rests upon Cicero's definition of comedy: "the imitation of life, the mirror of manners, the image of truth."—Not a bad, nor a petty, goal; and in this play attained by Jonson.

The fustian and highfalutin phrases of Marston are neatly burlesqued in the speeches of Clove, but Jonson's own prose and occasional blank verse are vigorous and apt, with many effective figures and blunt but trenchant phrases.

For the performance of the play before Queen Elizabeth, Jonson wrote a special epilogue, altering the end so that Macilente loses his envy through beholding the Queen and feeling the force of her virtue; the London public objected to this panegyric, being then resentful of Elizabeth's treatment of their favorite the Earl of Essex, on his return from Ireland. (Essex was executed for treason in 1601.)

In *Every Man Out of His Humour*, Shakespeare comes in, if not for attack, at least for a few mocking allusions. When Clove and Orange are displaying their learning, they casually toss off the remark "Reason long since is fled to animals, you know"—a thrust at Antony's "O judgment! thou art fled to brutish beasts And men have lost their reason." Later, when Puntarvolo seals Carlo Buffone's lips with wax, Buffone's last words are "Et tu Brute!" It has been suggested that this, besides its comic intent, sends a wink to the audience at Shakespeare's ignorance, as Caesar's dying words were different, and in Greek: *Kai ou, teknon* (You too, my son?)

Its episodic nature makes *Every Many Out of His Humour* less interesting to ages not so vividly caught in its figures; there is no record of its professional performance after 1682. There is too much learning in it, also—quotations from Erasmus and from the classics, frequently in Latin—to make for effective presentation before a modern audience, but reading reveals much that remains pungent and pertinent. *Every Man Out of His Humour* remains a brilliant example of satiric drama.

CYNTHIA'S REVELS   *Ben Jonson*

Although *Cynthia's Revels*, 1600, was intended for the Court—under Elizabeth's successor, James I, Ben Jonson became the chief writer of Court Masques—it is an intense and earnest satire on the weaknesses and the vices of the day. "The genial laughter of the painter of humours," said C. H. Herford, "contracts to the scornful smile of the satirist. Through the various plays, the motley crowd of Humours falls back and the figure of the poet gradually emerges into distinctness, assailing them now with sarcasm and invective as Asper [in the preceding play], now with serene disdain as Horace [in the play following], now with sorrowful indignation as Crites. It is difficult not to feel that this last, above all, brings us to the very heart of Jonson's moral virtue, and none of his verses ring truer than those of the great and mournful speech of Crites which closes the first act of the *Revels*." In the play's dedication "To the special Fountain of Manners, the Court", the same earnestness is apparent: "It is not powdering, perfuming, and every day smelling of the tailor, that converteth to a beautiful object: but a mind shining through any suit, which needs no false light, either of riches or honors, to help it."

In no play of Jonson's is there greater scorn of any standards save those set by the intelligence. Crites—Jonson himself—and "the Lady Arete, or Virtue" are the two upright humans in the play; Cynthia (Queen Elizabeth) appears only at the end to watch the Masque and to call for correction of the follies she beholds.

In the Induction, three actors come quarreling onto the stage; each wants to speak the Prologue. They draw lots; one of the losers says that in spite he'll tell the argument of the play. Cupid and Mercury, on their way to serve as pages at Cynthia's court, come upon Echo, singing ("Slow, slow, fresh fount, keep time with my salt tears") over the Fountain of Self-Love where her Narcissus drowned. Of the court are Hedon, the Voluptuous, and Anaides, the Impudent; coming to the court are the traveller Amorphus, the Deformed, who has drunk of the water and tells of its wonders, and a citizen's heir, Asotus, the Prodigal. The ladies include Philautia, the Self-Loving; Phantaste, the Giddy Wit; Argurion, the Money-mad; their guardian Mother Moria, Folly, and her daughter Gelaia, heedless Laughter. All imbibe the waters of the Fountain of Self-Love, and drink in the fatal folly.

The follies exemplified in these figures then strut upon the stage. They plan a school of Courtship, conduct a contest in Court-Compliment, and join in the games of the day. To adorn the courtiers for a Masque come the tailor, the barber, the perfumer, the milliner, the jeweler, and the feather maker. Cynthia enters to watch the Masque and counter-Masque. Each "vice" wears the mask of the converse virtue. Thus Gelaia becomes Aglaia, "delectable and pleasant conversation, whose property is to move a kindly delight, and sometime not without laughter"; Phantaste enacts Euphantaste, "a well-conceited Wittiness." When they unmask, Cynthia sees them as they are and leaves their correction to Crites, who orders them to sing a palinode appeal to be cured of their follies—and to make pilgrimage to drink of the Well of Knowledge.

At one point in the play, Jonson has Mercury say to Crites: "Sir, you have played the painter yourself, and limned them to the life." Nor did he overlook the theatre. "Limn" was a favorite word of Marston's, and Marston—with his vanity, his craving for distinction, his pretentious, affected syle—is portrayed as "the light voluptuous reveller", Hedon, in whom Marston's traits are travestied. Mother Moria, Folly, is similarly compared with "one of your ignorant poetasters of the time, who, when they have got acquainted with a strange word, never rest till they have wrung it in, though it loosen the whole fabric of their sense." More general examination of the theatre is made in the opening attack on the conventional Prologue and in the burlesque of the various types of gallant that sit upon the stage. Of the songs in the play, that of Hesperus before the Masque—"Queen and huntress, chaste and fair"—is among Jonson's most beautiful.

The language of *Cynthia's Revels* is vigorous, though occasionally long-winded; twentieth century taste would find the play static and deem it a dramatized character sketch rather than a drama. It was, however, quite frequently played at the Blackfriars (Jonson's relations with the Lord Chamberlain's company had ended), and was long popular at Drury Lane. *Cynthia's Revels* combines the powerful portraiture of the satirical drama with the pageantry and spectacle of the Court Masque. As long as audiences enjoyed bright spectacle as much as quick action, *Cynthia's Revels* held a high place on the stage.

THE POETASTER   *Ben Jonson*

In this play, written in 1601, Jonson put aside most of his concern with current vices and devoted himself to the dramatists that had been having a fling at him. Though it is set at the court of Augustus Caesar,

there is no doubt that Horace is Jonson; Crispinus is the playwright
John Marston* and Demetrius the playwright Thomas Dekker.*

Jonson rushed the writing of *The Poetaster* to reach the stage before
his rivals. It was completed in fifteen weeks, instead of the full year
usual with Jonson. Better than most of his other plays, it holds closer
to a single dramatic drive.

Captain Tucca, a foul-mouthed braggart and bully, overflowing with
boisterous spirits and rich vocabulary (perhaps a portrait of an actual
person of Jonson's time, one Captain Hannam), incites Crispinus and
Demetrius to defame Horace, who pleads before Caesar for justice and
accepts the great Vergil as judge. Lines from Marston's plays *Antonio
and Mellida** and *Antonio's Revenge** are read; Crispinus and Demetrius are convicted of envy and put under oath to refrain from further
attacks on the poet: "Neither shall you, at any time, ambitiously affecting the title of the Untrussers or Whippers of the age, suffer the itch
of writing to over-run your performance in libel, upon pain of being
taken up for lepers in wit and be irrevocably forfeited to the hospital
for fools." (Here is obvious allusion to Dekker's *Satiromastix; or, The
Untrussing of the Humorous Poet.*) In addition, Horace is permitted to
administer an emetic to Crispinus, who vomits up some thirty bombastic
or unusual words—*gibbery, lubrical, magnificate; spurious snotteries,
oblatrant, furibund*—twenty of which are drawn from Marston's plays,
down to the last *obstupefact.*

In his concentration upon the literary quarrel, Jonson did not neglect
the more general satire. In the background of Horace's successful
defence are the loving citizen Albius and his ambitious wife, who dotes
upon the Court; and Ovid, who's in love with Caesar's daughter and
who lashes out at lawyers and boastful soldiers. For these attacks,
Jonson was brought before the Lord Chief Justice, but protesting that,
as claimed in his *Apologetical Dialogue,* "my book has still been taught
To spare the persons and to speak the vices," he was exonerated.

Even though Jonson hurried the writing of the play, the persons he
chose for characters made allusions to classical literature inevitable.
His handling of the great personages is superb. Of his portrait of Augustus, Lamb has said: "Nothing can be imagined more elegant, refined, or
court-like than the scenes between this Louis the Fourteenth of antiquity (Augustus) and his literati. The whole essence and secret of
that kind of intercourse is contained therein: the economical liberality
by which greatness, seeming to waive some part of its prerogative,
takes care to lose none of the essentials; the prudential liberties of an
inferior which flatter by commanded boldness and soothe with com-
plimental sincerity." In his use of the ancient works, however, Jonson
was spendthrift beyond dramaturgical prudence. As Herford has stated:
"Few richer minds than his ever created drama; few so critical in
temper so easily mistook their intellectual abundance for artistic wealth,
or pursued the track of the ancient poets with so complete a disregard
of the reserve, the austerity of classic art." Jonson gives us in this
play an emendation of Marlowe's translation of one of Ovid's love poems
(15th Elegy, Book I); a song from Martial; in the last act, twenty-eight
lines from the *Aeneid* (Book IV, 160-188); and—added in the 1616 edition; Act III, Scene 2, on Horace's first appearance— an almost bodily

borrowing of one of Horace's satires (I, Book II). Original to Jonson, however, and noble in spirit, are the several tributes to Vergil. Some critics like to think that Jonson here compared Vergil with his contemporary Shakespeare, but his other comments—as that Shakespeare had never blotted out a line; would he had changed a thousand!—seem to void such likelihood. Vergil more probably represented, if any contemporary, Jonson's close and admired friend, Chapman.

The Poetaster is the best example in the English drama of a particular quarrel turned to the ends of general satire. Through it the caustic vehemence and the noble integrity of Jonson shine.

VOLPONE   *Ben Jonson*

Into a gorgeous flowering of Renaissance tapestry, Ben Jonson wove his most savage attack upon the evil of his time. Instead of a motley crew of "humours," he shows in *Volpone; or, The Fox*, 1605, various faces of the same vice—cupidity. His vehemence as a moralist, moreover, is here coupled with his indignation at those that looked upon the theatre as antechamber to the brothel, "my special aim being to put a snaffle in their mouths that cry out 'We never punish vice in our interludes'!"

"No such revolting figures as Volpone and his instrument Mosca," said C. H. Herford, "had yet been drawn with such sustained and merciless vigor, for the English stage. The hideous occupations of the parasite and the 'captator,' stock subjects of every Roman satirist, are reproduced with incomparable vividness before the relatively innocent English public . . . Of all professedly comic scenes, surely the most ghastly is that where Volpone's human playthings, the dwarf, the eunuch, and the hermaphrodite, entertain their master with 'songs' in which the intentional 'false pace of the verse' parodies their own imperfect humanity."

The same greed that leads Volpone (fox) to sham mortal sickness bends the various gulls, itched on by Mosca (gadfly), to give Volpone their wealth, hoping to be his heir: Voltore (vulture) the advocate, who would make out the will in his own favor; Corbaccio (raven), who would betray his own son; Corvino (crow), who would yield his own wife to Volpone's lust; Lady Would-Be, who would be all things to him, though Volpone cannot bear her constant chatter, her fussing over appearances, and her long-worded and long-winded pretense to learning. When Corbaccio's son, present by chance, rescues Corvino's wife from the attempted ravishing, Volpone is taken to court. Supremely impudent, he summons his gulls to lie for him, and in the flush of victory pretends to be dead, leaving as his heir—Mosca. And now the gadfly, who has been urging Volpone on, turns upon his master and tries to hold everything; as a consequence, their deceptions are exposed, and both lose all.

Played at the Globe Theatre in 1605, *Volpone* was an instant success; it was revived at once when the theatres were reopened with the Restoration (1660); and it was played frequently during the next century. In 1921 and in 1923, the Phoenix Society gave a few performances of *Volpone,* and it was played at the Malvern Festival in 1935 and at Bir-

mingham in 1937. Donald Wolfit, producing it in London on January 1,
1938, called his the first production there for a century and a half. The
London *Times* in 1935 (erroneously) declared: "In his own day, Jonson
was an author for the few, and the English public continues to be estranged by the formalism of *Volpone* . . . At Malvern we learn among
other things how to endure our own satirical masterpieces, and there
was no abatement of satire in tonight's production. Briskly as the
crow, the raven, and the vulture were drawn by the clever fly into Volpone's traps, Mr. Wilfrid Lawson saw to it that the farce was dominated
by the sulphurous horror of an intelligence immensely alert in the pursuit of evil, and there was terror as well as laughter in the play. There
was nothing of the cackling dotard about this Volpone. A fox in his
flaming make-up, he was in essence a man whose cruelty and cunning
and intellect had grown with age and were ripe for mischief on the
grand scale."

Stefan Zweig adapted the play in German for a Berlin production of
1927. A hit, this version was also played throughout Germany. It was
translated into French by Jules Romains (filmed with Harry Baur) and
into English by Ruth Langner for an elaborate 1928 (1929, 1930, 1933,
1934) production by the Theatre Guild in New York and a 1929 production in London. The New York production in 1928, virtually an all-star
one, included Alfred Lunt (Mosca) and Dudley Digges (Volpone).

Never having seen any version of *Volpone,* the New York critics
gave glad greeting to Zweig's adaptation. They were fortified by the
statement of R. G. Noyes of Harvard University that Zweig's version
possessed a "compression, unity, heightened irony, conformation to the
demands of the modern stage" that the original lacked. Alexander
Woollcott acclaimed it "a gay and gaunty and slightly rakish feather in
the Theatre Guild's cap." Brooks Atkinson called it "heavy in the central scenes, played straight without the poisonous edge of satire. But
it begins with a flourish of buffoonery, and it concludes with a spectacular hailstorm of flashing gold coins. In between, the ingenuity of
a complex plot and the rowdiness of Jonson's greedy characters make
Volpone a welcome diversion." When the English saw the American
translation of the German version, they were less enthusiastic. Sir Nigel
Playfair quoted a friend: "If you want to make money, produce the
version of *Volpone* they are doing here." To which Sir Nigel added:
"I do want to make money, and so, most meritoriously, do most of my
brothers in the craft. But I hope there exists in London an undertaker
with a sufficiently macabre imagination to invent a suitable form of
memorial service for anyone of us who follows her advice."

When the critics saw Jonson's own *Volpone* done by Donald Wolfit
at the Century Theatre (February 24, 1947) for the first time in New
York, they recognized the superiority of the original. Robert Garland
declared: "It took the comedy almost three and one half centuries
to get from London to New York. It was worth waiting for." Of the
Guild version he added: "Even with Digges, Lunt, Westley, Gillmore
and the Guilded likes of them, it was neither Jonsonian nor joyful. At
the Century, it is both of these." Richard Watts, Jr., concurred: "Quite
a triumph in a play that has freshness for New York audiences . . .
For all its sneering hatred, it is such an inventive, bawdy, hilarious, and

perversely gay comedy that, instead of being distressing, it is vastly entertaining, though certainly in a cynical fashion . . . not virtue that triumphs, but evil that outsmarts itself."

Wolfit's London production of Jonson's *Volpone* opened April 9, 1947. Harold Hobson of the *Sunday Times* called it "a piece which, if it resembles a catalogue of diseases, a doctor's dictionary, is nevertheless a considerable work. *Volpone* has the teeming life of worms in a rotting corpse, and Mr. Wolfit plays it with all the fifty-seven kinds of relish."

In January 1948, Jose Ferrer and Richard Whorf, with John Carradine as a stalking, stooped, and black skeleton of a Voltore, brought *Volpone* to another success at the City Center. Kronenberger objected to their reducing the satire to clowning farce, but the production was undeniably amusing. The play was revived again at the Stratford Festival of 1952.

It is clear that after a century and a half of neglect, *Volpone* has come back into its own. Swinburne earlier recognized its worth from the reading; he felt a coursing in the play of that "life-blood which can only be infused by the sympathetic faith of the creator in his creature— the breath which animates every word . . . with the vital impulse of infallible imagination." Desmond McCarthy has astutely pointed out that the chief quality of Volpone is not his evil, but his delight in the artistry of his devices.

Jonson's figures may seem abstract in the reading, but the virtue of the stage is that it gives living body to an author's figments. In the acting, Jonson's people are caught in the acid ink of a master pen. They continue to live in the continuing fire of human passion.

EPICOENE   *Ben Jonson*

The most popular of all Ben Jonson's plays for 250 years, *Epicoene; or, The Silent Woman,* 1609, still is an effective stage piece, but its emphasis has shifted from satiric comedy to farce. To many critics today, cruelty rather than humor glints in the tricking of a man who hates noise into a mock marriage with a "dumb" woman who turns out to be a noisy scold.

In the play, young Dauphine offers to free his uncle Morose of this nagging wife, if Morose will deed Dauphine his estate. When the transfer is signed and sealed, Dauphine reveals that the "wife" is a boy, disguised and imposed on Morose to win the property. This trick may have seemed a good joke three hundred years ago, but the sympathy of the modern audience veers toward the duped old man. Thus W. A. Darlington, after a 1936 performance, went so far as to say that "Dryden's verdict seems little better than nonsense nowadays."

In his *Essay on Dramatic Poesy* (1688), Dryden praised *Epicoene* for the manner in which it observes the dramatic unities, then added: "The intrigue of it is the greatest and most noble of any pure unmixed comedy in any language: the conversation of gentlemen, in the persons of Truewit and his friends, is described with more gaiety, air, and freedom, than in the rest of Jonson's comedies: and the contrivance of the whole is still more to be admired because it is comedy where the persons are only of common rank, and their business private, not elevated by passions or high concernments, as in serious plays." The characters in the play, however, do not advance beyond the stage of "humours"; nor is there growth, through the course of the play, in the persons' natures. Only at the end of the play, when bang! the head hits the hard wall of experience, is there awakening and consequent hint of change.

The *London Times*, (August 3, 1938), after an Oxford production for which John Masefield wrote an Epilogue, made a measured judgment: "That the plot is brilliantly contrived is undeniable, but much of it serves the end of a rather cruel and insensitive humor . . . It is difficult to understand how this astonishing eloquence of dialogue, this miraculous fertility of illustration and metaphor, should accompany the unkind cozening of a poor old gentleman with a very natural distaste for noise . . . the characters, though they are wonderful caricatures, are much rougher in their outline than in their speech, and they must submit, in spite of their powers of discourse, to many rude indignities of farce."

The early success of the play is marked not only by frequent performances, but by printed editions in 1609, 1612, 1616, 1620, etc. It has been translated into the major European tongues, plus the Portuguese. Samuel Pepys mentioned *Epicoene* in his *Diary* five times. On April 15, 1667, he took his wife to the play and on the next day noted that "Knipp tells me the King was so angry at the liberty taken by Lacy's part to abuse him to his face, that he commanded they should act no more, till Moone (Mohun) went and got leave for them to act again, but not this play. The King mighty angry; and it was bitter indeed, but very fine and witty. I never was more taken with a play than I am with this *Silent Woman,* as old as it is, and as often as I have seen it. There is more wit in it than goes to ten new plays."

A 1735 production of *The Silent Woman* had as the afterpiece Moliere's* *The Mock Doctor; or, The Dumb Lady Cured;* Anatole France's *The Man Who Married a Dumb Wife* is another version of the same theme. An adaptation of Jonson's play in 1776 by Colman made the mistake of having a woman (Mrs. Siddons) play Epicoene, and when the character was revealed as a "boy" at the end, the audience felt, not surprised, but cheated.

Inevitably, Jonson reaches out to ranges of satire beyond the play's main drive and shows us types of the day, sharply satirized. Yet the satire remains general; no particular person is travestied although common follies are ludicrously displayed. "The utmost effect," said C. H. Herford, "is got out of the few but felicitously chosen characters."

The two hundredth anniversary of Jonson's death led to revivals of *Epicoene*—as in London in 1936 and 1938, and at Fordham University, New York, in 1939. Though the novelty of its plot, with the final curtain surprise, has lost its freshness, the play still has a humor and a sting that reward imaginative revival.

THE ALCHEMIST   *Ben Jonson*

Many critics deem *The Alchemist,* 1610, the best of Ben Jonson's comedies. Coleridge went so far as to declare the swift-moving plot one of the best three in literature. It owes much to Giordano Bruno's *The Candle-Maker* (1580), a surprisingly vivid mixture of effective realism, lively indecency, and keen observation. In *The Alchemist,* as C. H. Herford points out, "Jonson, for the first and also for the last time, found a subject in which all his varied faculty could run riot without injury to the art quality of his work. The profession of alchemy, at once notorious and obscure, with its mountebank reputations and its mystic pretensions, its impenetrable Kabbala of subtleties, and its Rembrandtesque profusion of sordid and squalid detail—the most impudent, venerable, and picturesque of social plagues—was the fittest subject then to be found in Europe for such comedy as his."

From its first presentation to the end of the eighteenth century, *The Alchemist* was frequently played. Comparatively neglected during the nineteenth century, it has recently been restored to popular favor. A presentation in London in 1899, appropriately enough at Apothecaries' Hall, brought playgoers the robust humors of its satire, the imposing range and richness of its language—its blank verse is superbly adapted to natural dialogue and ranges from luxurious poetry to brisk and bawdy repartee—and the plain, downright fun of its coursing plot. There was a revival in 1904 at Cambridge, Massachusetts. More important were the productions at Malvern Festival in 1932 and in London in 1935, with Ralph Richardson as Face and Sir Cedric Hardwicke as Drugger. In New York, the depression of 1931 was lightened by a production, and London saw the play again in 1947. New York enjoyed a revival in 1948 with José Ferrer as Face.

The story opens in the London plague of 1610. Lovewit leaves the city to avoid the plague. His servant, Face, lets into the house an alchemist, Subtle, and his punk, Doll Common. The three join forces to cheat the folk around. Among their victims is Sir Epicure Mammon, who hopes that Subtle will find him the philosopher's stone, which turns what you will to gold. Tangled in their devices are also Dapper, a lawyer's clerk; Drugger, a tobacco-man; a pastor of Amsterdam, Tribulation Wholesome, with his deacon Ananias—satiric portraits of Puritans, extended in *Bartholomew Fair**—the willing widow Dame Pliant and her brawling brother, Kastril. (The names, as you notice, catch at the characters. Kestrel, a hawk, was a term then applied in contempt to a boisterous ruffian.) A gambler, Pertinax Surly, suspects the impostures; he comes disguised as a Spanish grandee to expose the rascals, but the unexpected return of the owner of the house, Lovewit, makes Subtle and Doll Common flee. Face faces it out, and wins his master's pardon by marrying him to the quite content Dame Pliant.

Recent productions have won *The Alchemist* almost unanimous praise from the critics. The *New York Post* called the 1931 revival "a brawling, full-blooded, wholesomely bawdy thing, volleying its broad humors of a fresher time across three hundred years, to burst in laughter on a twentieth century target. Soothsayers and charm-vendors still flourish, taking pretty pennies from the wallets of the children of this scientific age. But aside from that, *The Alchemist* is a joy because of its perfection as a piece of dramatic craftsmanship." The *London Times,* (April 2, 1935) remarked on the present timeliness of the characters: "The petty tradesman and the ambitious clerk, the young gentleman who is determined to be a dog, and the old one who creates a fool's paradise of infinite self-indulgence, in fact the whole company of the dupes and the self-deceived can still be seen flocking to the doors of any occultist charlatan or vendor of tickets in the Irish Sweep." Ivor Brown said in the *London Observer*, (January 19, 1947): "Ben trovato, indeed! . . . Jonson went crashing into the theatre with a matchless torrent of polysyllables, Latinities, and lickerish rhetoric as gross as grand . . . Richardson's look of moon-calf innocence as he gulls and pills lackwit and greedyguts alike, and the superb incantations of alchemical bosh, are a simple, eternal, irresistible type of fun."

The New York 1948 revival, which opened May 6 at the City Center, was likewise hailed. The *Sun* enjoyed its "ample sheaf of fat roles." The *World-Telegram* called it "a first-rate dramatic hit." Only the *Times* dissented, with the statement: "Coleridge seems to have been well off the beam on this one. Its story is tedious in the telling today, and there have been some better plots in recent memory which have been blown off the stage."

The wealth of Jonson's language in *The Alchemist* makes a lavish display, apart from its contribution to the plot's movement. The delighted imaginings of Sir Epicure as he translates his fancied wealth into dreams of bedding and banqueting, lift just over the sunset brink of genuine splendor to the ludicrous, and woo us, as we laugh, to share his fancies.

Allardyce Nicoll discerned Jonson's deepening horror at the corruption of his time: "This note is continued in *The Alchemist* and in *Bartholomew's Fair*, two of his finest comedies. In the former all the men are either rascally or rapacious, the women vain and libertine; in the latter Jonson's lash falls with no sparing hand upon the Puritans and on current hypocrisy. These are among the best comedies in the English language, but the coarseness and even the brutality of Jonson's later style detract considerably from their beauty." Of these words, James Agate declared: "Read 'add' in place of 'detract,' and I agree." The vigor, the blunt and even brutal presentation, are part of the beauty.

In writing *The Alchemist*, Jonson was, as usual, conscious of his orderly method and insistent upon his pride of place as a dramatist. Throughout the sixteenth century playwriting was deemed either a schoolmaster's exercise or the shift of a poet for his purse's sake. The profession owes much of its later prestige to Jonson's integrity and sense of the theatre's high office. In his Preface to this play, Jonson wrote with vehemence of the art of the theatre, against those that "think to get off wittily with their ignorance . . . For it is only the disease of the unskilful to think rude things greater than polished: or scattered more numerous than composed." And in his Prologue to the "judging" audience, Jonson scorned the usual bending to plead for plaudits, and spoke with the same honesty as in the play itself he attacked not evildoers but the evils of the time.

Dryden sought to deny the originality of the story. Before Jonson's own edition of the play (1616), there had been presented before King James, at Cambridge in 1614, Thomas Tomkis' comedy *Albumazar*, twisting the ninth centry astronomer Albumazar into a tricky astrologer and wizard, who transforms the boorish Trincalo into the shape of his absent master, with humor sought in the consequent absurdities. When this play was revived in 1668, Dryden wrote a Prologue in which he claimed that Jonson based his play on Tomkis'. As the two plays have very little in common—the *Albumazar,* though revived again by Garrick, is not only different in story, but lacking the gifts of language and satire—and as, furthermore, Jonson's play was enacted in 1610 and first printed in 1612, the relationship Dryden claims is nonexistent.

The reaction of Garrick to *The Alchemist* shows that it indeed has "fat" parts, and that genius needs not the star's place in order to shine. Garrick always took the little role of Abel Drugger, the tobacconist who is planning to open his own shop, and who comes to Subtle to be told how the planets fall, for favorable disposition of his wares in his store. What an actor long dead has made of a part, it is hard for later generations to recover, but we may glimpse something of Garrick's capture in his widow's memory. When Kean first appeared as Richard III, Garrick's widow drove to his lodging and presented him with the sword her husband had used in the part; some months later, she paid him a second call, and said: "Sir, you can play Richard; you cannot play Abel Drugger." Abel is but one of a dozen comic parts, rich in their opportunities, true and fresh in their satire today as when first set down, that bustle through the gay rioting of *The Alchemist.*

BARTHOLOMEW FAIR *Ben Jonson*

Despite his classical learning, Jonson was one of the most typical Englishmen of all time; he could not avoid writing about his home and his true love—London. After the failure of his second tragedy, *Cataline,* in 1611, he returned to comedy with *Bartholomew Fair,* 1614. In this play there is less savagery than is Jonson's wont; a more genial tone pervades it; so that the Londoners could recognize themselves and still be amused at the vivid and colorful pictures of their gross enjoyments.

From about 1150 until 1855, the churchyard of the priory of St. Bartholomew, Smithfield, London, was the scene of a fair on Bartholomew's day, August 24. In Jonson's time, the occasion was one of gay frolicking; and, of course, every type of gull was matched by a scheming knave. The whole of Jonson's play, after the opening scene, is at the Fair. On the broad canvas he set many characters: the ginger-bread woman and the roast-pig woman; the puppeteer; the ballad-singer who is a receiver for the pickpocket; the Captain who is a pimp for the blowsy bawds. Chief of those gulled is the young simpleton Bartholomew Cokes, come from the country to be married; overjoyed at the fair, he buys all that he sees, until he is robbed of his purse, his cloak and sword, and his bride-to-be. Amid all the crowding folk walk Littlewit, his submissive and pregnant wife whom he has persuaded that she has an insistent longing for roast pig, and the gluttony Rabbi Zeal-of-the-land Busy. The manners of these outwardly pious Puritans, and the tricks played upon them, were not the least reason why the Elizabethans made a favorite of the play.

Bartholomew Fair was revived immediately upon the Restoration; several command performances were given before King Charles II, who especially enjoyed the character of Cokes. The Puritan leader Collins, taken to the play, thought for a while (so deft is Jonson's satire) that he was watching a sympathetic portrait of Puritan life; he shouted in fury when he saw Rabbi Busy thrust into the stocks. Although he partakes gluttonously of the feast, the Rabbi protests that he is going to the Fair against his will and only to guard the pregnant Win-the-Fight Littlewit and her mother, the wealthy widow Dame Purecraft.

There is another group of Puritans at the Fair. The zealous Justice Adam Overdo has served on the Fair's pie-powder court (*Pie-powder,* from French *pied poudreux,* dusty foot: a special medieval court called to deal summary justice to the vagabond beggars, cutpurses, and brawlers that sought the opportunity afforded by the crowding, happy, heedless throngs at the fairs). And Justice Overdo, wishing to see things at first hand, mixes with the crowd disguised as a fool: "They may have seen many a fool in the habit of a justice; but never till now, a justice in the habit of a fool." Yet the naive Overdo is himself beguiled by the sharpers; he mistakes the cutpurse Ezekiel Edgworth for an innocent boy, deems the madman wise, is put in the stocks for a pickpocket, and at the end discovers that the person he is about to sentence as a drunken bawd is his own wife.

Meanwhile, two gentlemen about town, Winwife and his friend Tom Quarlous, have been pursuing Dame Purecraft, on whom Rabbi Busy also has matrimonial designs. Justice Overdo has arranged a match between his well-to-do ward Grace Welborn and his country-bred brother-in-law, young Cokes. At the fair, Winwife and Quarlous meet and covet Grace; she dislikes Cokes so much that anyone else looks lovable: Winwife wins her in a game of words, but Quarlous steals the license.

The Elizabethans are so well caught in the comedy that they might indeed have continued the action at home after the play. The characters are rude and crude, using broad language, painted with broad strokes; but those were broad, bustling, brawly times. They are superbly sketched, with neat markings subtly held to the brink of caricature. Littlewit prides himself on his cleverness; never a quirk or a quiblin but he apprehends it and brings it before the constable of conceit. Justice Overdo is, like many of us, an honest but simple fellow. Only Zeal-of-the-Land Busy steps over the brink of caricature. The Elizabethans were well acquainted with such long-winded sanctimonious argument as that by which he justifies the Puritans' going to the fair.

Some little known features of the Elizabethan theatre survive in the Induction to the play. The booke-holder (whom we call prompter) ridicules the stage-keeper for presuming to deem himself a critic. There were two stage-keepers, usually in hideous false-face masks, on the Elizabethan stage. They furnished pipes and tobacco to the gallants seated there; they drew the curtain of the inner stage; and, if necessary, they helped curb the unruly in the audience. In an 1881 production of *Hamlet**, William Poel used a pair of such curtain-drawers.

Recent performances of *Bartholomew Fair* have been mainly by community or college groups. These include one in Boston in 1908; another in London (at the Merchants Taylors' School: the fair was originally held for drapers) in 1936; one at Bryn Mawr in 1939. In 1950 the play was presented at the Edinburgh Festival and at the Old Vic in London. It is still a lively and homely play.

EXILES   *James Joyce*

The one drama of novelist James Joyce (Irish, 1882-1941) *Exiles,* 1916, manifests the interest in intellectual analysis that pervaded his writings. Joyce's material is sex, even "the eternal triangle"; but of it he has worked a picture of tortured lives, too intellectualized for wide popularity, yet drawn from the inner core of tragedy. The most exalting type of tragic disaster is that which comes, not from villains without, nor from the pressures of society, but from good qualities within—a doom foreseen, and that may be avoided, but instead is freely chosen, elected as the noble, or, better, as the natural way of life. Such a choice, on one level, is that of Dick Dudgeon in *The Devil's Disciple**; on another level, it is that of the martyrs of all time. In *Exiles,* Joyce pictures a modern liberal doomed to torture by the inconsistencies of his ideals.

Richard Rowan, a writer, and Bertha have lived together, in love, but unwed, for a decade. Their best friend, the journalist Robert Hand, visits them. Sensing an attraction between Robert and Bertha, Richard tells Bertha she is free and leaves the two alone. Bertha needs a commanding spirit; she lacks the self-sufficiency of Richard. Loving him, she begs Richard to forbid her going to Robert. But Richard, having achieved his own freedom, insists on freedom for her as well. She goes. When she returns, Richard refuses to allow her to tell what happened. The audience is permitted to feel that Bertha has been faithful to him, but Richard, himself tangled in the contrary tugs of freedom and love, is condemned to continuing doubts and torture.

On an intellectual level, the tension in *Exiles* is that of high-powered electric wires. "The whole is lifted," said the *London Times,* (February 16, 1926) "and throbs, like *King Lear,* with a capacity for suffering more startling even than the situation in which it is manifested."

Exiles was published in 1918 and first produced in German. New York saw it at the Neighborhood Playhouse on February 19, 1925; London, a year later. In the New York *Playbill,* Ernest Boyd wrote: "Technically, *Exiles* is an Ibsenite play, but for Ibsen's symbols and solutions Joyce substitutes doubts and irresolutions that are typically modern . . . All its action is psychological and cerebral, and its strength lies in the superb delineation of character, notably that of Bertha, an instinctive woman, in the hands of a man who feels through emotional analysis rather than through emotion itself . . . The people of this play are exiled from happiness, from the tranquility of doubts that can be stilled, into suffering."

It is possible to interpret Richard's nobility in quite another way. The free man, the anarch, by imposing his own freedom on others becomes a tyrant. Of the moment when Richard tells Bertha that she is free, the *London Times* commented: "At this point you begin to wish that someone would kick Richard, who is possibly a psycho-realist but certainly a cad . . . We see in Richard a self-tormentor, a man with a perpetual grievance against life as it is lived, and yet with an absorbing interest in that life and a curiosity to see it actually lived under his eyes—a curiosity which leads him to actions that can only be qualified as odious." This judgment of the *Times* is based on Richard's application of the Golden Rule: Do unto others as you would have them do unto you. If made specific, the rule fails because natures differ; it might better read: Do unto others what they would want you to do unto them. There may be flaws in this, too, as a general principle of action, but Richard's conduct serves soberly to remind us that different natures demand different attitudes. Bertha is not, shall we say, "ready" for the freedom Richard insists is man's only good. Perhaps, indeed, freedom is not everyone's path to righteousness: in our Father's house are many mansions. By presenting—with sharp analysis, gripping dialogue, and ruthless penetration—the opposition of these two natures, and the tortures set upon both by their very nobility, James Joyce has given us in *Exiles* a drama of intellectual power and high distinction.

FROM MORN TO MIDNIGHT   *Georg Kaiser*

In the great decade of dramatic expressionism which began in 1914, Georg Kaiser (German, 1878-1945) was the outstanding playwright. Germany hailed him, presenting in those ten years 26 of his dramas, which were promptly produced throughout Europe. The most popular of his works, and the most enduring, is the tragedy in seven scenes, *From Morn to Midnight,* written in 1916.

The play is expressionistic in its devices—that is, it seeks to externalize states of mind. It is a monodrama; all the characters and events are seen through the eyes of a single person. In its development, the drama is what Kaiser called a "think-play." Sweeping along with intense emotional power, it is the illustration of an idea.

The person through whose eyes we watch the multiplex happenings of the day and trace the author's thought is a bank cashier. Rebellion long pent in him flares with a whiff of perfume, as a lady awaits identification for a letter of credit. Off he goes to her with 60,000 marks—to discover that this glowing, seductive stranger is a perfectly respectable mother. He leaves her, then, for a carousing day of freedom, of frenzied spending at the races, at an all-night cabaret, with a sobering pause at the Salvation Army. But everywhere he remains imprisoned by his stodgy past and by his sense of guilt and of the imminence of retribution. As the police draw near, the bank clerk anticipates his capture and shoots himself.

The theme of this "think-play" is the persistence of illusion. In each scene, the cashier sloughs one illusion, only to have another cloud his mind. First is the simple sex illusion; the swirl of a silken skirt foreshadows a conquest. Then, on his flight, there is the illusion that he can laugh at death, at disillusion. Fear looms over him and shrouds him, to prove such laughter hollow. The next illusion is that he has proper place in some more glamorous sphere than his conventional home. Like most persons that dream exotic, golden dreams, he is a habit-ridden home-body; the rouse makes him restless, not full of zest. At the race track, he breaks the illusion that free spending frees the spirit, and at the night-club, that money can buy more than mechanical favors. The last illusion of the man in the play is that men have learned the futility of living for money. He learns that lesson—learns, indeed, the futility of living at all. Freed of illusions, he takes his life, leaving the illusion that life might be worth living to those watching the play.

From Morn To Midnight was produced in Berlin by Max Reinhardt. In New York, The Theatre Guild offered it for two special performances, in May, 1922, in translation by Ashley Dukes. Encouraged by the play's reception, The Guild opened it in June for a regular run. The critics were respectful, but deemed the treatment a bit difficult for American audiences. Maida Castellun, in the New York *Call*, called it "an amazing emotional drama . . . crashing to its doom while terror and sardonic humor seize the spectator, as well as the clerk, who tastes life only while he is gambling with death . . . There can be no question about the arresting quality of its spiritual telegraphy, its swift staccato dialogue, its explosive soliloquies, its soul-shattering revaluation of the pleasures and duties of life." Audiences have since become more fully acquainted with the expressionist technique, but *From Morn to Midnight* remains a challenge to the imaginative producer. It has been widely revived in community theatres, for beyond its technical challenge is a searing picture of the wish-dreams of an ordinary man come horribly true.

SHAKUNTALA   *Kalidasa*

The "bridegroom of poetry", Kalidasa, is believed by the Hindus to be a contemporary of the Shunga king Agnimitra, who lived about 100 B.C. Western scholarship tends to place him about the fifth century after Christ. This greatest of the classical Sanskrit poets composed two epics, a long lyric, and three dramas. The first two of his plays, *Vikramorvashiya* and the *Malavikagnimitra*, are based on romantic Hindu legends of their kings.

The third is Kalidasa's world-famous masterpiece, the greatest example of the heroic type of Sanskrit drama. *Shakuntala (Abhijñana Shakuntala); or, The Fatal Ring*, presents a love story in which grace, tenderness, and humor unite with grandeur and sublimity. Reverenced in India almost as a sacred drama, it has found translation and wide production in modern tongues.

The story is an early legend about the parentage of the great Hindu hero Bharata. King Dushyanta of India, come to the forest to hunt deer, stays to wed Shakuntala, fair foster-child of the hermit Kanwa. The demigod, Durvasa, knocking at the hermitage gates and unheeded by the love-rapt Shakuntala, puts the curse of forgetfulness on the King, who has returned to his palace. Shakuntala's friends—she knows nothing of the curse—plead with Durvasa, who relents enough to grant that the king will remember, if ever he sees the ring he has given Shakuntala. Shakuntala, now a mother, goes to the King's court; she has lost the ring, and the King thinks her claim is part of a plot against him. Shakuntala is carried, by the nymph her mother, to the home of the gods.

Six years later, a fisherman brings to the King a valuable ring found in the stomach of a carp; the King remembers and mourns. Then he is summoned by Matali, charioteer of the god Indra, to do battle with the Demons. Returning victorious, King Dushyanta admires a noble boy at play with a lion cub. He sees the royal birthmark on the boy's hand; it is his son. King Dushyanta and Shakuntala are reunited.

The play is, as the *New York Times* commented (April 9, 1919), "one of the few great love dramas of the world. It is as fresh to us today, and as moving, as a play of the Shakespearean era. Its dramaturgy is

absolutely Elizabethan, even in surprisingly minute details; and its spirit
of ingenuous passion, of maidenly charm, and of lyric loveliness, finds
its nearest counterpart in the predecessors of Shakespeare, especially
Robert Greene. Not infrequently it rises to the level of the great master
himself."

Most modern productions of *Shakuntala* in India are given, not in
Sanskrit, but in the various vernacular tongues, but the play is still
enjoyed in the original. It represents, said V. Raghavan in the *Encyclopedia of Literature* (1946), the best style of Sanskrit composition, "the
Vaidarbhi style; graceful, simple, free from bombast, exaggeration, or
over-ornamentation, precise, suggestive not verbose. Poetic imagination is often and justifiably estimated by the variety and striking beauty
of a poet's similes; here too Kalidasa excels. The poet's wise observations strewn all through his writings show his abounding knowledge."

First translated by William Jones in 1789, *Shakuntala* has been rendered in Western languages more than fifty times. Goethe was especially
attracted to the play, seeing it as a progression from the blaze of physical love, by purification through separation, to the sublimation in the
union of true souls. Rabindranath Tagore developed this thought: "The
motif of the play is the progress from the earlier union of the first act,
with its earthly unstable beauty and romance, to the higher union in the
heavenly hermitage of eternal bliss described in the last act. The drama
. . . was meant to elevate love from the sphere of physical beauty to the
eternal heaven of moral beauty . . . *Shakuntala* stands alone and unrivalled in all literature, because it depicts how restraint can be harmonized with freedom. All its joys and sorrows, unions and partings,
proceed from the conflict of these two forces."

The child is a symbol Kalidasa uses for the union, the blending, that
happily ends this conflict. At the beginning of the play, the hermit bids
King Dushyanta not to kill the deer: the maiden Shakuntala has a pet
fawn. The fawn disappears through the sad days of her journey; it is
replaced by the child of Shakuntala and the King, through whom the
final union is effected.

Shakuntala was played in London in 1899, and in 1911 in a version by
Lawrence Binyon, with Sybil Thorndike. Helena Thimig played in
Shakuntala in Germany. It was Alexander Tairov's first production in his
Kamerny Theatre, Moscow, 1914. New York saw the play in 1919 and
1926; Pittsburgh, at the Carnegie Institute, in 1936. *Shakuntala* was the
first feature film to be made in India, 1947. The story has been woven
into a dance and its moods have been caught in program music.

The climactic episodes of the drama reach emotional depths and
surging tender beauty. "The wilding vigor of the heroic child", said the
New York Times (April 13, 1919) "and his father's joy in recognizing
him, give color to an episode of the utmost humor and beauty, and strike
a mood of joy which is consummated in the King's reunion with Shakuntala." But pervasive qualities of the play are equally outstanding; as the
Times continued: "Nothing is more striking in the art of Kalidasa than
the manner in which he achieves salient character without ugliness,
reality without prosaic realism."

The supernatural elements of the story blend so harmoniously into
the tale that they become an accepted symbol of the eternal forces striving through the characters. These elements help to widen but do not

weaken the emotions aroused; they add universality to the particular story and gather up into a great and single fabric the many strands of beauty. *Shakuntala* has the perennial youth of a vibrant masterpiece of the dramatic art.

LUTE SONG   *Kao-Tong-Kia*

It is possible to classify the plays of the Ming Dynasty in China, roughly, as northern or southern. The North China drama was in the main concerned with historical and legendary (supernatural) events, while the South China drama was in the main concerned with romance. Both expected the audience to stay lengthily in the theatre; the dramas were as much danced as acted, with stately movements and elaborate costumes; and the dramatic episodes were interspersed with lyric poetry, often of considerable power and beauty. Outstanding among the plays of South China was *P'i P'a Chi (The Story of the Lute)*, written by an obscure provincial schoolmaster, Kao-Tong-Kia, in the mid-fourteenth century, and adapted for court presentation (in twenty-four acts) by Mao-Taou in 1404. Played before the Ming Emperor Yuan Lo, and by strolling companies throughout China, the drama became a classic. It has been played often ever since, and was recently produced in the New York Chinese Theatre. In fact, it was Will Irwin's hearing *P'i P'a Chi* in San Francisco's Chinatown theatre about 1910 that led to its production in English. (The Chinese audience cried like children, Irwin tells us.) Developed from an 1841 French version of *P'i P'a Chi, The Lute Song* was adapted by Sidney Howard and Will Irwin, with lyrics by Bernard Hanighen and music by Raymond Scott. It was presented in 1930 at the Berkshire Playhouse; in 1944, by the adventurous Catholic University of Washington, D. C. On February 6, 1946 a superb company—including Mary Martin and Clarence Derwent—opened at the Plymouth Theatre, in New York, "with $185,000 worth of scenery, lights, and costumes" by Robert Edmond Jones.

Lute Song is a sad story of family fortunes, in the true Chinese manner. A young student, successful in the examinations, leaves his wife and doting parents. Become a magistrate, he is forced by the prince's edict to marry a princess; nor can he send word to his family. His parents starve. His first wife, as a mendicant nun, begs her way across China, seeking her husband. When they meet, the Princess wife, being of noble heart, helps to bring about the reunion.

This tale, despite the attempt to retain the Oriental coloring—which led Robert Coleman and others to declare that "Jones, in our opinion, is the real star of the evening"—was sadly transmogrified into an overdressed musical. It had a few good lyrics but on the whole it was wrecked by Broadway pretentiousness, sumptuousness, and expensive shoddy. John Chapman called it "arty as all hell"; Burton Rascoe headed his review: "Authentic, No Doubt, and a Bore". George Freedley was as strangely altered as the play; in his *History of the Theatre* (with John A. Reeves, 1941) he says of *P'i P'a Chi* that "its lugubrious story of filial piety is rather sickening to the western mind"; in his review of *Lute Song* (Feb. 6, 1946), he called it "one of the most touching plays, in incredibly beautiful production." George Jean Nathan was probably thinking of the Chinese original when he wrote: "What is slight about it is the characteristic Chinese butterfly-wing approach to it, and what is simple about it is the customary and relishable Chinese practice of avoiding complexity where simplicity will better serve . . . charming, delicate, and leisurely story . . ."

For the original Chinese has merits that the adapters have caught as those that seek to snare the secret of genius, and copy only its cough. All entrances, the Chinese convention dictates, are made from the right; all exits are made to the left. The bridal veil is red, the color of blood; mourning color is white, the pallid hue. These external conventions are carried over into *Lute Song*. But *P'i P'a Chi* is rich in Chinese culture, and in satire of Chinese ways. It satirizes the Imperial examinations, wherein tests in classical literature and verse writing are given prospective canal builders and road-menders. It satirizes the ubiquitous grafter (long a disastrous element in Chinese life), and the arbitrary user of power (still dangerous in any land).

P'i P'a Chi is the only play that presents, sympathetically, the three great Chinese religions: Confucianism, Buddhism, Taoism. The genii, the supernatural elements that the simpler Chinese accept, the talking animals, are aspects of the ancient Taoism. The student Tsai-Yong and his family are Buddhists.

The Prince in the play exemplifies the reaction from the liberal Buddhist attitude, to the deep-rooted, noble but conservative family piety of Confucius. Indeed, many of Prince Nicou's remarks in the play are direct quotations from Confucius. Thus *The Story of the Lute* deservedly became a Chinese classic, combining as it does a tender and realistic story with poetry of beauty and ideas of grace and truth, together with a satire of general abuses and a wide picture of the richly colored Chinese life.

SQUARING THE CIRCLE   *Valentine Petrovich Katayev*

The Russian novelist and playwright Valentine Petrovich Katayev (b. 1897) combines an earnest sense of Soviet values with a keen recognition of the incongruities that resulted from the rapid and cataclysmic social upheaval in his land. Watching or reading his plays in English, one must remember that many adaptations increase the satiric attack on social abuses; otherwise, it would seem strange that the author is still at large in the Soviet Union. He has not, indeed, always escaped censure. *Pravda*, on January 16 and 17, 1950, launched a 10,000 word blast (contradicting its earlier praise) against Katayev's novel *For Soviet Power!* Katayev responded: "I promise my readers to radically rework the novel."

Katayev's amusing farce *Squaring the Circle*, 1928, ran for some 800 performances at the Moscow Art Theatre, and by now has had over 20,000 performances in the U.S.S.R. There have been several versions of the play in English; the one by Charles Malamuth and Eugene Lyons opened in Philadelphia September 17, 1935, and came to New York October 3 for a run of 108 performances.

Since it is by far the most successful Soviet comedy, the play has been called "the Soviet *Abie's Irish Rose*"*. It pictures two Communists, Vasya and Abram, sharing one room, to which they bring their brides, Ludmilla and Tonya. At first they draw a chalk line to separate the families, but Tonya wants to prettify the place. "If curtains are bour-

geois," she says, "you had no reason to take me to the marriage bureau"
—and a curtain is stretched across the room.   Within each couple, however, there develops a deeper division: Vasya is an earnest Communist,
Ludmilla wants to wait on him like a middle-class wife; Abram is earthy
and self-concerned, Tonya would rather buy Soviet books than eat.   The
ill-assorted couples develop tempers that go from bad to worse, until a
Communist Party officer, like a benevolent god from the machine, gives
his approval as the two couples interchange.

Katayev is careful to indicate that the errors and follies he shows are
neither committed nor countenanced by the right people.   Yet he does
pin for laughter many of the Party clichés, and, especially through the
sentimental Ludmilla, stabs at excesses in Soviet life.   Extremes outside
the U.S.S.R. could thus agree about the play.   *The Park Avenue Social
Review* (November 1935) reported it has "plenty of laughs for both pro-
letarians and tycoons"; and *The New Masses* (November 12, 1935) announced it "should delight friends of the U.S.S.R. and warm the hearts
of 'neutrals'—despite a few of its remaining innuendos."

At the close of the play, the future looks on, through the little child,
Sasha.   "Tell us, Sasha, will you go on marching and building, or will
you destroy it all?"   The child turns a silent, uncomprehending face as
the curtain falls.   This dual quality of the play, satire and searching, is
caught in the comment of Joseph Wood Krutch, in the *Nation* (October
23, 1935): "In the first place, it is a lively, knock-about farce making
simple-hearted fun of the more obvious paradoxes of Soviet life.   In the
second place, it is a piece which manages very adroitly to reconcile this
boisterous satire with a subtly effective profession of fervent faith in the
Communist enterprise.   In the third place, it is also a play provided with
an elusively ironic conclusion which is bound to leave the audience wondering just how deeply it is intended to cut, and which in all probability
left some Soviet officials wondering whether or not the author had succeeded in putting something over on them after all.   Katayev's art is not
merely a weapon, it is a two-edged weapon . . . *Squaring the Circle* is,
to change the metaphor, a dance on eggs which seems to be conducted
with boisterous abandon until one realizes that by some miracle none
of the eggs have been broken."

Squaring the Circle is not only the most amusing drama of self-
criticism the Soviets have produced, but their liveliest farce.

BEGGAR ON HORSEBACK   *George S. Kaufman*

The finest fruit of the collaboration of two experienced journalists
and men of the theatre, George S. Kaufman (American, b. 1899) and
Marc Connelly*, is the fantastic comedy *Beggar on Horseback*.   The
story and much of the technique of the play are taken from the German
satire *Hans Sonnenstresser Goes Through Hell*, 1912, by Paul Apel. Trans-
planting the characters to an American scene, with many comic inventions of their own, the American authors concocted a hilarious satire of
the money-centred life.   The title of the play was taken from the proverb
"Set a beggar on horseback and he will ride a gallop", which means that
sudden riches are soon spent, that the proper use of any value demands
preparation and understanding.

The play opened in New York with Roland Young and Osgood Perkins
to music by Deems Taylor and a delightful pantomime danced by Grethe

Ruzt-Nissen on February 12, 1924. The story is a simple one. The young and struggling composer, Neil McRae, in love with Cynthia Mason, the girl across the hall, contemplates—urged on by Cynthia—marriage with the wealthy Gladys Cady, so as to gain freedom for his creative work. In a dream, he marries Gladys, and envisions his enslaved life; he kills his in-laws, and is sentenced to work in an "art production factory". When he awakes from this nightmare, Cynthia gives him her hand. The basic situation is sentimental; the dream device with the awakening turn is a familiar one. What gives *Beggar on Horseback* its distinctiveness is its rich satire, its good-humored but unsparing wit, and the freshness of its individual comic devices by which machine-age efficiency and money values are lampooned. The banal mother-in-law with an appalling nasal voice, who knits and nods and gossips, is bound to her rockingchair; the father-in-law, Cady, has a telephone strapped to his vast, self-satisfied middle and on his golf bag is a stock-market ticker.

The dream shows the overpowering effect of great wealth by a multiplication of butlers: almost a score of them stand, formidable, forbidding, in the composer's way, helping to bind him to convention. When the dream-murder has been committed, newsboys rush down the theatre aisles with copies of *The Morning Evening*, which has big headlines, full details of the crime, a picture of the accused, and a special article headed "No Crime Wave, Says Commissioner". A ragtime burlesque of courtroom and trial follows; the verdict is announced through a loud-speaker. In the "Cady Consolidated Art Factory", to which the composer is condemned, novelist, song-writer, poet, painter, sit in cages at work on art as anodyne. When the composer determines to make a break for freedom, he discovers that the cage is unlocked; all he needs is the will to walk away. Then he awakens and chooses poverty, love, and freedom.

The critics gave the play a most hearty reception. "All the good qualities of the heart and of the head," said Alexander Woollcott (February 13, 1924), "went into the making of this wise, witty, and leaping comedy"; and John Corbin declared: "It bristles with sly and caustic satire, brims with novel and richly colored theatric inventions, and overflows with inconsequent humor and the motley spirit of youth . . . It is all quite mad, utterly delightful, and inerrant in touching off our mundane fads and follies."

Beggar on Horseback opened in London on May 7, 1925. It has been popular everywhere and is a favorite with community theatres. Swift in its flow, and topsy-turvily satiric in its ridicule, *Beggar on Horseback* is a tilting of laughter against the idea that money makes the man.

ONCE IN A LIFETIME   *George S. Kaufman*

The feeling that the motion picture industry was a threat to the theatre was decupled when, in 1929, the first talking pictures were heard. The theatre, "the fabulous invalid", has, of course, never been the same since cinemanufacture, but it is far from moribund. More than once, it has smiled indulgently at the grandiloquent and resplendent Hollywood. The most genial yet devastating of these theatrical glances at the movies is *Once In A Lifetime* by George Kaufman and Moss Hart. It still deserves Gilbert Gabriel's comment (September 25, 1930) that it is, "in its own loose, loping, sly-eyed way, the funniest satire the movies have yet had."

When "sound" reverberated in Hollywood, it startled the actors of the silent films. What had they to do with English! *Once In A Lifetime* pictures a rescue team, around whom many aspects of the Hollywood spectacle are pricked in the full of their foibles. A refugee from vaudeville, Jerry, seeing a talking picture in New York, decides to entrain for Hollywood. His friend May suggests opening a voice-culture school and, with the simple-minded and semi-literate George Lewis, they launch forth. The impression they make on film magnate Herman Glogauer approximates that of a snowflake on the mid-Pacific—until George angrily gives Glogauer a piece of his mind. Since no one else has ever dared let Glogauer even glimpse a mind, the magnate at once makes George boss of the studio.

Meanwhile, there is shown the making of a film on a Hollywood set, a wedding scene of super-supreme splendor, though the "Bishop" sends for a racing-sheet just before the camera clicks. The famous playwright, with a sumptuous workroom at the studio, has been six months without an assignment. The Boss has dodged a script-writer scene after scene, then comes out crying "Masterpiece!" after the writer shrewdly left his manuscript in the Boss's bathroom. The presently-successful scorn the not-yet-arrived, while quick oblivion envelops the has-beens. There is broad and deft capture of the sham and the shame, the flimflam and the flame, of Hollywood. George Lewis, the dumb-bell, reading *Variety* and cracking nuts with his teeth, finds Hollywood an easy nut to crack.

Once In A Lifetime opened in New York on September 24, 1930, with Jean Dixon and Spring Byington; it had an enthusiastic press and a run of 401 performances. "I laughed so steadily," George Jean Nathan reported, "that everyone thought it must be a couple of other fellows from Fort Wayne." Brooks Atkinson called it "a hard, swift satire, fantastic and deadly, and full of highly charged comedy lines . . . The skinning of Hollywood is neat and complete."

Kaufman staged the play in New York, making his stage debut as Lawrence Vail, the transplanted and lonely playwright. Hart staged it on the West Coast, playing the same part. *Once In A Lifetime* went to Birmingham, England, on January 28, 1933; to London, February 23. The *London Daily Mail* called it "the funniest play in recent years."

Once In A Lifetime has been popular with amateur groups; 1932 saw a production even in Hollywood High School. Now that the lush days of the movies are (at least temporarily) over, what with wars and recessions and radio and television, *Once In A Lifetime* remains a unique capture of the fabulous phantasmagoria that once was Hollywood.

OF THEE I SING   *George S. Kaufman*

A rousing musical comedy and an uproarious political satire, *Of Thee I Sing* by George S. Kaufman and Morrie Ryskind, with music by George Gershwin and lyrics by his brother Ira, is the only musical comedy to win a Pulitzer prize. Opening in New York on December 26, 1931, with William Gaxton, Victor Moore, and Lois Moran, *Of Thee I Sing* ran for 441 performances, then toured for 24 weeks. It has been revived often; in New York, at Jones Beach and at Randall's Island in 1937; and by Erwin Piscator in 1949.

The story is an amusing one. The political party that has nominated

John P. Wintergreen for President resolves to carry the country on a platform of love. A beauty contest is held; Wintergreen is to marry the winner. In the meantime, however, he falls in love with Mary Turner, a campaign worker who can cook wonderful corn muffins. In a whirlwind campaign, John publicly proposes to Mary in forty-eight states. The campaign speeches at the climactic Madison Square Garden rally are accompanied by a comic wrestling match and emphasized by placards with such slogans as "Wintergreen—The Flavor Lasts", "Vote for Prosperity and See What You Get." John is elected; inaugural and marriage are one ceremony.

However, Diana Devereaux, pride of the Southland and winner of the beauty contest, brings suit. Since "She's the illegitimate daughter of an illegitimate son of an illegitimate nephew of Napoleon", the French Ambassador interests himself in the case. Public sympathy swings to the deserted Diana; all that saves the President is Mary's timely announcement that he is about to become a father. What will the child be? The Supreme Court's decision is twins, one of each sex. As a consolation prize, Diana Devereaux is delivered to the moon-faced, roving-eyed Alexander Throttlebottom, the lost and forgotten fellow who was made Vice-President. All ends with a hey-nonny-nonny and a ha-cha-cha.

Many other touches of satire enliven the play; some press particular issues and personalities, some prick general foibles of our time. In addition, there is much good humor with lively or genuinely comic songs (the lyrics were written first, reversing the Gershwins' usual procedure). The title song illustrates one secret of the musical's success. It is drawn from the familiar anthem: "My Country, 'tis of Thee", but with a comic twist. In the musical the song goes: "Of Thee I Sing, *Baby!*" That is to say, the seriousness and the satire, the earnest intent and the comic spirit, are fused. There is one integrated movement, one drive of laughter throughout.

Of Thee I Sing brought wide ripples of laughter to the land. Brooks Atkinson called its authors "as neat a pair of satirists as ever scuttled a national tradition . . . transposed the charlatanry of national politics into a hurly-burly of riotous campaign slogans, political knavery, comic national dilemmas and general burlesque." Several reviewers, indeed, felt that, in such moments as the entrance of the six blue-bearded secretaries of the French Ambassador or the deliberations of the nine old men of the Supreme Court, we approached an American equivalent of Gilbert and Sullivan. This peak of high humor, however, is not maintained in the writing, but the Broadway production helped sustain the mood. As Atkinson said: "Satire in the sharp, chill, biting vein of today needs the warmth of Victor Moore's fooling and the virtuosity of Mr. Gershwin's music. Without them, *Of Thee I Sing* would be the best topical travesty our musical stage has created. With them, it has the depth of artistry and the glow and pathos of comedy that are needed in the book."

The 1949 revival showed that *Of Thee I Sing* remains timely. The strokes of satire are broad enough to smack firm upon general follies, while sparing individuals that fall. There were scattered votes, in the Wintergreen election, for Mickey Mouse, for light wines and beer, and for Mae West. Democracy votes for what it likes best. The public gave a hearty, and a deserved, vote to that leveling of laughter at democracy's failings, that self-mockery spun out of love, *Of Thee I Sing.*

YOU CAN'T TAKE IT WITH YOU   *George S. Kaufman*

The most madcap of all the George S. Kaufman-Moss Hart products is the picture of the completely irresponsible, completely captivating Sycamore family, *You Can't Take It With You*. With Josephine Hull, Henry Travers, and Paula Trueman, the play opened in New York on December 14, 1936, for a run of 837 performances and the 1937 Pulitzer Prize. It has beeen widely played since. England saw it in 1937 (Manchester, December 13; London, December 22) and New York enjoyed it again in 1945.

Root of the Sycamores is Grandpa Vanderhof. A quarter of a century before the play begins, he went up in the office elevator, reflected while rising that drudgery is a silly game, and came right down again. Ever since, he's been luxuriating at home; for variety, he attends commencements, throws darts, hunts snakes, and manufactures fireworks. Having sheltered a milkman who died without mentioning his last name, Grandpa has the milkman buried as Vanderhof. Since then he has opened no mail; thus he hasn't paid twenty-two years of income taxes.

The Sycamore family is made in Grandpa's image. His daughter Penelope is an aimless but eager muddlehead. Since the day a typewriter was delivered by mistake, she has been writing a play. It's about monks; she inquires: "If a girl you loved entered a monastery, what would you do?" Penelope is also a sculptor; Mr. De Pinna—an iceman, who has been their guest for eight years — poses for her, as a discus thrower. Easie practices ballet dancing; her husband, the xylophone. The fireworks explosives cook in the cellar. A tipsy actress comes in to give her opinion of Penelope's play. It is the wrong night for the supercilious, society Kirbys—but they arrive.

Tony Kirby wants to marry his typist, Alice Sycamore; he brings his family to meet hers. The Kirby brows wrinkle higher; their noses tip more loftily back—when F.B.I. men, suspecting the cellar gunpowder, carry them all to jail. The Kirbys' experiences in jail—while Mrs. Kirby is being searched, a tipsy strip-teaser sings an undressing song—knock them thump off their pedestal. They consent to the marriage. The curtain falls with Kirbys and Sycamores around the festive table as Grandpa says grace before the meal: "Well, Sir, here we are again. About all we need is our health. The rest we leave up to You."

Each of the figures in *You Can't Take It With You* is an individual study in oddity. The Kirbys, who represent orderly society in contrast to the irresponsible brood of Sycamores, are mildly satiric types. The two lovers, most nearly normal, seem almost an intrusion upon the genially madcap scene. Kolenkhov, the xylophonic husband of the ballet dancer, declares: "A Russian feels life chasing around inside him like a squirrel." The doings of the Sycamores, undirected by mundane motives, denying the monetary standards of humdrum life, responsive to the moment's whim and the apt suggestion, whirl around like the colored chips of a kaleidoscope.

The reviewers whirled into superlatives. John Anderson (December 15, 1936) said that *You Can't Take It With You* "puts the 'tops' in topsyturvy." *Time* magazine (December 28, 1936) said that the play "mounts into the stratosphere of literary lunacy." The *Brooklyn Eagle* (August 27, 1938) called the Sycamores "the goofiest but at the same time the

most likable family the legitimate stage has ever presented." John
Mason Brown (September 14, 1938) thought the entire piece "one of the
most lovable and uproarious products of our contemporary stage."

No doubt some of the contemporary references—to Father Divine and
to Franklin D. Roosevelt's attempt to hog-swallow the Supreme Court—
will date revivals unless deleted. But the substance of the play survives as a charade against grubbing and grinding and hoarding in a
world that can, instead, be enjoyed.

THE SHOW-OFF   *George Kelly*

Two of the most reliable figures in the theatre are the braggart that
is humbled and the genial incompetent that makes good. George Kelly,
(American, b. 1890), fused the two figures in *The Show-Off*, and achieved
what has been called "one of the three or four best comedies the modern
American theatre has had."

The play is an expanded version of a vaudeville skit. It depicts
Aubrey Piper, a $32 a week clerk in a railroad freight yard in West
Philadelphia, who talks as though he were an executive involved in tremendous deals. Amy Fisher adores Aubrey and his grand ways; her
family are less pleasantly impressed. They suffer still more after Aubrey
and Amy are married, for Aubrey's inefficiency runs into debts the family
must pay and when Amy's baby is due, Ma Fisher reluctantly gives them
shelter in her house. Despite his sister-in-law Clara's plain speaking,
Aubrey persists in his magniloquent ways—until his high assumption of
authority and his important airs double the amount offered for an invention of Amy's brother, bringing $100,000 and peace to the Fisher house-
hold. The show-off's bluff, at the last, comes through.

Opening on February 5, 1924, *The Show-Off* attained 571 performances and has since been very popular. It "combines a keen commentary
on human nature with a steady flow of scintillating dialogue," said
Kelcey Allen. When the play reached its first anniversary, Stark Young
pointed out the qualities in Aubrey Piper that take hold upon the audience: "For all his garish bluff, he makes a woman happier than her
mother has ever been, and happier than the childless sister whose well-
off husband is more than indifferent to her. The mother with her household, her stewing and fretting, and her blunt goodness, becomes a wistful
rhythm through the play. Aubrey has wild wings and a thick skin. He
is always second-rate, commonplace, and soaring. He is a liar with an
overwhelming truth of his own, a parrot among hens, the irony of art
over utility. He is an intolerable, inconsiderate breeze blowing through,
but from this on the room will be stuffy without him." "Of course," said
Heywood Broun, "it may truthfully be said that Aubrey lives in a fantastic dream world of his own creation; but once he has built his world
he stands by it. God himself has done no more."

Aubrey is a combination of comic butt and hero. He is a figure in
the tradition of Rip Van Winkle* and 'Lightnin'*, with a touch of the
grandiose braggart warrior, laughed at down the ages. *The Show-Off*
sets the eternal pretender against a characteristic background of our
time and, with touches of tenderness and pathos, builds his bluff into a
successful deal and a perennially amusing comedy.

CRAIG'S WIFE   *George Kelly*

Craig's Wife, the first full-length play by George Kelly not expanded from a vaudeville skit, won the 1925 Pulitzer Prize. It opened on Broadway October 12, 1924. London was hospitable to only ten performances in 1929, but Broadway liked it again in 1941, with Pauline Lord, and again in 1947, when *Variety* said that it "remains Grade A theatre." Although it lacks the genial spirit of Kelly's best play, *The Show-Off**, and occasionally presses its point too heavily, *Craig's Wife* is one of the most keenly etched, most devastating portraits of a woman in the modern theatre. The apparently devoted wife and loving home-maker, whose living-room reflects her excellent taste and her insistence on order, is gradually revealed as a woman who will sacrifice everything, including her husband's happiness, for the sense of security that springs from her hold on her home.

Under the guise of love, Mrs. Craig weans her husband from his friends, even from his business associates. The time comes when relatives, servants, and her finally awakened husband turn from her, leaving her with her home and her security—alone. With head high, she accepts the roses a friend brings for the departed aunt, then—first sign of misgiving—as though in a daze, she plucks the rose petals, and on the floor where up to now a flicker of ash would have aroused her fury, she lets fall the petals one by one.

The entire action of the play grows out of and turns ever back to Harriet Craig, whose early fears have built her into an unscupulously selfish woman. Every word of the play, said the *New York World* (October 13, 1924) "is dedicated to the steady, cruel illumination of Harriet Craig . . . To this one purpose of hers, she is faithful within the limits of her purely feline intelligence. That purpose expresses itself in a thousand ways, from her entirely cold calculation with regard to her husband to the watchful prowl she maintains behind her servants, running her sceptic finger over every lintel they have dusted, crouched for a vengeful pounce if one match-end or a rose petal is found on the rug." The portrait achieved is not only absorbing, but disturbingly true; it is the portrait, as Alexander Woollcott said, of "a woman who would rather have her husband smoke in hell than in her living room. At every matinee of this play there will be some uncomfortable squirming in the audience."

The action of the play extends only from 5:30 one evening until 9 o'clock the next morning. It shows, declared *Theatre* magazine (April, 1926), "genius in conception and craftsmanship." Without doubt, *Craig's Wife* is a penetrating portrait, especially revealing because it sinks below appearances to basic motives and bone-bred drives. In milder form, many a Mrs. Craig is taken as a model wife. As her character is brought to life before us, the development is as horrid as it is true.

THE SERVANT IN THE HOUSE   *Charles Rann Kennedy*

By far the most popular, and the best, of the plays by Charles Rann Kennedy (American, b. 1871) is *The Servant in the House,* which had its New York premiere on March 23, 1908, with Tyrone Power, Edith Wynne Matthison (the author's wife), and Walter Hampden. It had eighty performances, but ran again in 1909 and 1910; Hampden periodically revived it up to 1934. In 1925, it was produced with Violet Kemble Cooper, Helen Chandler, and Pedro de Cordoba.

The play is a picture of the triumph of brotherly love. It contrasts four brothers. One, a simple vicar, seeks funds for repairing his church. One brother, the famous and pious Bishop of Benares, has promised to help him. Another, the worldly Bishop of London, comes to share the prestige the pious bishop will bring, together with any more material rewards he can annex. The fourth brother, Robert, disowned by the family and become a socialist, returns, to repair the church drains. The Bishop of Benares comes among them disguised as a butler, Manson, to see what this household of God is like. By his piety and trustful love, he awakens a truly loving spirit in the household—save for the servant of Mammon, the Bishop of London, who departs incontinent. As Manson represents the Christlike spirit of love, so the drains represent the deep and hidden corruption that may beset the church; and in the end the vicar and the socialist go down to clean them together.

The Servant in the House created a sensation in Baltimore and Washington before it came to New York, where it was also hailed. The *New York Times* (March 24, 1908) called it "a play that is at once important in its discussion of ethical idealism as contrasted with worldly expediency and is yet an entertainment . . . an excellent piece of dramaturgy, which, while no doubt of interest because of the daring employed in the development of its central character—intended to represent the reincarnated Son of Man—has more legitimate values in a beautifully developed story and an assemblage of picturesque and sympathetic characters."

In 1925, Stark Young said (April 7): "People who once delighted in *The Servant in the House* need have no fear about going to see the revival. They will still like it." In lone dissent, Alan Dale declared that "the years have not improved Charles Rann Kennedy's arrant curtain lecture." The *New York Telegram* presented the majority opinion: "The morality of *The Servant in the House* is substantial enough to last as long as human relations come under the head of religion and as long as hypocrites and worldly-wise men exist to muddle those relations up. The impulse behind it is still strong and heady, distilled in a sincerity too hot for careless handling. Of all the several plays which have since its advent chosen to use the suggestion of Biblical repersonifications, here is far and away the one of quality."

The Servant in the House has a continuous drive of tense action, fortified by its observance of the "classical" unities of time, place and action. It has, in addition, a deep fervor and ethical force, as Manson turns turbulence into peace and hatred into love. Robert's socialism, bred of bitterness and anger, is yet informed with brotherliness and love. There is, moreover, a lyric quality in the dialogue that at times rises to high imaginative levels, as in Manson's description of his church.

The work of Charles Rann Kennedy, preeminently in this play, vividly recalls the origins of the drama in religion and demonstrates that man's deepest impulses and direst needs may still make not only noble but exciting theatre.

ARSENIC AND OLD LACE   *Joseph Kesselring*

"The funniest play about murder ever written," as the *Baltimore Sun* (March 26, 1941) called it, *Arsenic and Old Lace* has audiences on both sides of the ocean half-seas over with applause at poisoning. Opening in New York January 10, 1941, the play ran for 1,437 performances. London saw it first December 23, 1942; it ran for 1,337 performances and reopened in April, 1946. It was played in Spanish in Buenos Aires in 1942, and has had corpses in window-seats and audiences in stitches on every continent. It was the first play ever presented in sign language (at Gallaudet College for the deaf, Washington, D. C.). The author, Joseph Kesselring (American, b. 1902), we are told, intended the play as a serious melodrama; during rehearsals, its mood was changed to farce.

The play revolves about the sweetly homicidal mania of the mild old maid Brewster girls of Brooklyn, Martha and Abbie. The local police drop in for cosy comfort on cold nights; the women are charitable; everybody loves them. They have three nephews. Teddy Roosevelt Brewster, who lives with them, is amusingly cracked; he digs the Panama Canal in the cellar and he constantly charges up the stairs blowing a bugle for the taking of San Juan Hill. Nephew Mortimer, who loves the minister's daughter next door, is a drama critic. Mortimer discovers a corpse and then finds out that his aunts, with humanitarian motives, welcome lonely, friendless, homeless old men, ply them with elderberry wine spiked with arsenic, and bury them in Teddy's Panama Canal. This corpse makes their twelfth victim.

While Mortimer ponders what to do about his tender aunts, nephew Jonathan arrives. Abbie learns of him when she discovers a strange corpse in the window seat; "Now what can that be?" she wonders. Jonathan, a more direct homicidal maniac, is disguised as Boris Karloff (Boris Karloff created the role); he travels accompanied by his personal facelifter and plastic surgeon. Jonathan, as Abbie observes, always was a mean boy; he couldn't bear to see anyone get ahead of him: he too has accumulated his twelfth corpse. The police account for Jonathan, but Mortimer manages to arrange to have his aunts taken to a private "home". When the custodian arrives, the gentle ladies suggest that he have a drink before they leave. They serve him the arsenic and elderberry as the curtain falls.

We will not render lip-service to the two benign old ladies, but they almost capture our hearts. We are less concerned than amused when a playwriting cop, finding Mortimer tied in a chair (one of Jonathan's pranks), seizes the opportunity to read the critic his play. (The falling curtain spares the audience.) It is not less than inevitable that Mortimer, being a drama critic, is a bastard—and thus, spared the Brewster heritage of insanity, is free to marry the minister's daughter. Richard Watts Jr. claims (or confesses) that the drama critic is partly patterned after him.

Insanity not only runs in the Brewster family; it gallops. The dramatic effects—in the New York production of Howard Lindsay and Russell Crouse, directed by Bretaigne Windust—were equally cavorting. The climax was top-hatted when, during bows after the final curtain, up from the cellar streamed the thirteen murdered old men. The total impression, said *Time* (January 20, 1941) is "as if Strindberg had written *Hellzapoppin*." Certainly no such genial pair of lethal spinsters has elsewhere made murder so hilarious as in this corpse-ridden play.

MEN IN WHITE   *Sidney Kingsley*

The doctor has been caricatured or satirized in the modern drama, from the ailing Molière* to the vegetarian Shaw*. Sidney Kingsley (American, b. 1906), in *Men in White*, favorably presents his physicians in the atmosphere of a modern hospital. The old chief of staff, Dr. Hochberg, is an ideal surgeon, a scientist with a whole-hearted devotion to his profession. Dr. Levine, a once most promising interne, shows the social and intellectual poverty that may be pressed upon a physician whom an early marriage drives into the humdrum and wearing routine of ill-paid general practice. Between them stands young Dr. Ferguson, who wants a good career, while his fiancée, Laura, wants only a good time.

The problems implicit in these contrasted figures, however, are given scant attention in the play's rather trite story. Dr. Ferguson, happy at the success of a risky operation, kisses nurse Barbara Dennin. He thinks nothing of it, but Barbara goes to his room and waits for him. "The inevitable" grows between them until Barbara needs an emergency operation—which interne Ferguson is called to perform. Barbara dies. Laura, discovering the situation, is quickened to a sense of deeper reality. Dr. Ferguson leaves, to study abroad; a more understanding Laura accompanies him.

The play has, according to John Mason Brown (October 7, 1933) "a piffling script, mildewed in its hokum, childishly sketchy in its characterization and so commonplace in its every written word that it in no way justifies its own unpleasantness." But, as the *New York Herald-Tribune* (February 4, 1934) declared, "all this is the surface of *Men in White*. Beneath its innocently phony exterior there are problems, solved and unsolved. What, it seems to ask, are the Hippocratic pledges, and how obediently can they be observed? Must a young student of medicine consecrate himself absolutely to the duties of science, or should he be humanly selfish now and then and compromise with the ideals and the ethics?" Even beyond this, the power of the play lies in the atmosphere, in the general stir of life within hospital walls, in the medical aspects of the play, more significant than its love story.

We see the big, modern, city hospital from the inside, with its many facets: the loudspeaker calling the internes; the anxious inquiries of relatives and the professional calm sympathy of the nurses; the almost military precision of operation procedure; and also (as Arthur Ruhl pointed out in the *New York Herald-Tribune,* October 22, 1933) "the politics of the hospital board room; sharply revealing incisions into the lives of various kinds of patients . . . grouped round the central story in a swift sequence of scenes, vividly set, told with moving sincerity, without a trace of flub-dub or waste of words."

The "expert" was pleased with the picture: An editorial in the *Journal of the American Medical Association* praised the atmosphere of the play; doctors thronged to see it. They did object, however, to the earlier scene of the over-insulinated child; to the doctors, this is comparable to a sergeant's snatching papers from a general and issuing orders.

The second operating-room scene is indeed a major one. It was rehearsed over a hundred times. Nine-tenths of it is in pantomime; there are no speaking cues; each one is busy and cannot watch the others.

Sand-glasses were used to time washing and other actions, as the regular routine of an operation speeds upon the stage, with the doctor driving on, quick step by step, and the nurses in instant time with the required instruments. It is rich, said Brooks Atkinson, with "impact in the theatre, and it is warm with life and high in aspiration"; and, said Arthur Pollock, "it is a really remarkable drama. It will make you feel once more that there is nothing quite like the theatre, and never will be."

Men in White was presented by the Group Theatre in New York, September 26, 1933, with Morris Carnovsky, Alexander Kirkland, Luther Adler, and J. Edward Bromberg. It ran for 367 performances and was awarded the 1934 Pulitzer Prize. (The play jury unanimously recommended Anderson's *Mary of Scotland**, but was overruled by the Board of Trustees.) In London, *Men in White*, adapted by Merton Hodge to English medical practices, opened June 28, 1934, for a run of 131 performances. It played at the same time in London, Baltimore, Cleveland, Los Angeles, and Budapest; also in 1934, Myrna Loy and Clark Gable acted in a screen version. While it presents the problems of the medical profession through the medium of an obvious and sentimental story, the play is a shining example of how the theatre can create a living atmosphere and a moving mood. The swift surge of hospital events largely replaces the story; the characters gather a sense of human worth; the play speeds a vital emotional drive upon the stage.

DEAD END   *Sidney Kingsley*

This play by Sidney Kingsley (American, b. 1906) vividly captures the opposed extremes of city life. A gripping melodrama, it is, in the opinion of Arthur Pollock, "very close to being the last word in realistic playwriting and presentation." The street scenes, said the *New York Herald-Tribune* (November 10, 1935) are "so literal, so apparently genuine, that you are fascinated in the belief that you are a spectator at real events." Opening in New York October 28, 1935, the play ran for 687 performances, and it has become a little theatre favorite.

"We see the whole drama of our social order," said the *New York Times* (November 3, 1935) "concentrated in a foul and ugly tenement street that lies at the rear of an aristocratic apartment house and debouches into the East River . . . The jeering, bullying, slippery restlessness of the hoodlums, the pool of quiet around the artist who is sitting on the stringpiece, the tired anxiety of the older sister for one of the boys, the condescension of an apartment-house adventuress, the pompousness and assurance of the uniformed doorman, the nervous distaste of the rich for the mean street they have to follow—all this pother of a thousand and one Manhattan days, Mr. Kingsley has reproduced so literally that at first it appears to lack significance . . . Presently, however, you perceive that this casual pier scene represents in Mr. Kingsley's mind something of current social importance."

Some of Kingsley's shrewdest writing is in the interplay of the youngsters, for in them is the heart of this drama. Its story concerns Babyface Martin, come back to his boyhood haunts hunted by the police. He has taught little Tommy some of the gangsters' tricks; with them Tommy trips up the supercilious Philip Griswold, 2d, scion of wealth, and swipes his wrist-watch. The lame architect, whose emotional life is thwarted but whose ethical direction holds straight, promises Tommy's sister that the reward money for Martin's capture will be used to help Tommy. And perhaps not all of these lives will move, like Martin's, through violence to a dead end.

Rich in vivid moments and swiftly coursing emotions, *Dead End* keeps melodrama within the range of reality. Especially gripping, in their psychological truth, are Babyface Martin's moments with his mother and with his early sweetheart. As the *New York World-Telegram* (January 15, 1937) declared: "Many will remember Mrs. Martin's fierce denunciation of her son as a wonderful scene, but there is an equally dramatic sequel of even more significance—the recoil of Babyface. For even to his killer, Mr. Kingsley gives a human touch. Dismayed by her anger, Martin offers her money as a last gesture. She spurns it and turns away, leaving him with her awful curse. 'Well, whatdaya tink o' that,' says Hunk, Martin's trigger man. 'Whyn't ya slap her down?' 'Shut up!' says Martin. Although smarting, a shade of sadness crosses his face, which is relieved only when he thinks of his coming meeting with Francey, his one-time sweetheart. And then along comes Francey—now a diseased prostitute. Again Mr. Kingsley caps the drama of this meeting. Unlike the mother, Francey accepts Babyface's money—and asks him for an extra $20. One of these scenes would be outstanding in any play, but to introduce two in such a way that the second is in no way an anticlimax, is playwriting of a high order."

The appeal of wealth, of luxury, is one of the strongest along the dead end streets of the city, the breeding ground of go-get-it girls and of gangster elements. But we hear Evolution's warning, lest civilization be approaching its dead end: "Now, men, I made you walk straight, I gave you feeling, I gave you reason, I gave you dignity, I gave you a sense of beauty, I planted a God in your heart. Now let's see what you're going to do with them. And if you can't do anything with them, then I'll take them all away. Yes, I'll take away your reason as sure as I took away the head of the oyster; and your sense of beauty as I took away the flight of the ostrich, and men will crawl on their bellies on the ground like snakes or die off altogether like the dinosaur."

With a vivid setting by Norman Bel Geddes and a blending of blue and white lights that simulated out-of-door daylight so well the players needed no make-up, *Dead End* proved a strikingly realistic presentation, beyond the strong melodrama of its story, of a problem basically dramatic and crucial in all city life. Children at both extremes are problems, spoiled Philip as much as neglected Tommy; and as they grow the city will grow, to fruitful future or to dead end.

TOBACCO ROAD   *John Kirkland*

From the novel *Tobacco Road* (1932) by Erskine Caldwell (b. 1902), John Kirkland (American, b. 1901) fashioned a play of the squalid, exhausted, degenerate fag-end of southern farmers, "poor whites" on the hangdog and hookworm edge of extinction. It opened in New York on December 4, 1933. After a generally unfavorable reception by the reviewers and several weeks on the brink of closing, this initial production gathered momentum and rolled on to a total of 3,182 performances, closing May 31, 1941. It established a new record, broken since only by the 3,224 performances of *Life With Father*.* "I never saw all three acts of it," Ward Morehouse reported; but one man saw the whole play 34 times.

In the original cast, the lazy, pants-hitchin', cursin' reprobate Jeeter Lester was played by Henry Hull; his wife, Ada, by Margaret Wycherly. During the run, Hull was succeeded by James Barton, James Bell, Eddie Garr, and Will Geer. John Barton, James' uncle, played Jeeter on the road for seven seasons. London banned the play until August 1949, when, with the language toned down, it opened to general disfavor and remained for 109 performances. "Overstatement on such a scale defeats its object," said the *London Times,* (August 10, 1949). The *Chronicle* declared it was as though one lifted "a large flat stone, permitting us to observe the unpalatable insect life beneath." This also seemed true in the Negro Drama Group production seen briefly on Broadway in March, 1950.

Chief of the "insects" is Jeeter Lester. Determined to keep the worthless farm he no longer owns, he does nothing about it but loaf and swear, and beg or steal food from the neighbors. Sharing Jeeter's collapsing hovel is his wife, Ada, who longs for snuff and has retained a tigress's love for her fourteen year old daughter, Pearl, whom Jeeter has just sold into marriage to Lov Bensey for seven dollars. Lov comes in, complaining that Pearl has refused to sleep with him and has run away; while Jeeter's hare-lipped eighteen-year-old daughter, Ellie May, lures Lov, Jeeter steals off with Lov's turnips. Sister Bessie Rice, an itinerant preacher, arrives; a stalwart woman of forty, she looks at the impudent sixteen-year-old son Dude and decides that the Lord wants her to marry him. Dude agrees to this if Bessie will get him a new car and make him a preacher. Bessie herself performs the ceremony, and everybody peeks when Bessie drags her new husband indoors.

Meanwhile, Jeeter's bullied and shrunken old mother has got lost in the swamps; Jeeter says "I'll go look around one of these days." The owner of the farm comes to tell Jeeter he must pay $100 a year or go. Pearl turns up; Jeeter grabs her and holds her for Lov, who has promised him two dollars a week as long as he has Pearl. Dude and Bessie start their new car (already damaged by two collisions) to get Lov; Ada tries to stop them and is run over. In her dying breath she bites Jeeter's hand; the pain and surprise make him release Pearl, who runs away. Jeeter sends the eager Ellie May to take Pearl's place with Lov, and slumps back, as at the play's start, dozing on the sagging porch, alone left in the hovel of the unlovely Lesters.

Some of the reviewers were downright in their condemnation of the play. Richard Lockridge insisted it "achieves the repulsive and seldom falls below the faintly sickening." Gilbert W. Gabriel: "Let's admit it unsuccessful. It was jolly to read, it is only snickery to watch . . . *Tobacco Road* was never meant for footlights. They boil it down into mere streaks of salt and soot."

The swearing, the direct or sly references to sex, and the impulsions to its expression, the physical filth portrayed in the play seemed, to some, insuperable objections; to others, obstacles at times overcome by stronger values. John Mason Brown felt that the play sank under the deadening weight of "the live stock it chooses to parade as men and women." John Anderson agreed. Percy Hammond called the play "relentlessly ruttish and unclean," but maintained it was "a vividly authentic minor and squalid tragedy, lighted in the right spots with glowing and honest humor." The *New Yorker* (December 16, 1933) declared: "It would be possible to write a burlesque of *Tobacco Road* . . . but somehow you don't want to. There is a certain quality in the play . . . It has the strange disheveled dignity of sounding true." After announcing that "The theatre has never sheltered a fouler or more degenerate parcel of folks than the hardscrabble family of Lester that lives along the tobacco road," Brooks Atkinson added that "it has spasmodic moments of merciless power . . . and it leaves a malevolent glow of poetry above the rudeness . . ."

The characters are not deeply sounded; they seem on the level of the frequent cartoon figures of the shiftless hill-billy or poor white of the south. The episodes, however, hold the attention and despite the laziness of the characters the play moves swiftly along.

The great success of the play has evoked many explanations. Primary is the suggestion of the appeal of its naughtiness, the swearing and the sex: the pleasure the conventionally and timidly religious man takes in the profane, the pleasure the conventionally and timidly moral man takes in the libidinous. Samuel Grafton, in his column "I'd Rather Be Right," in the *New York Post,* (August 18, 1939) thought that: "It is the toleration of human weakness that is both funny and fascinating in *Tobacco Road*. Once again, maybe the public isn't so dumb." Jeeter Lester, however, is decidedly too dumb for philosophic acceptance of others' faults. It is more true to say that moral standards have lapsed; these characters have no sense of sin. Indifference—as in Jeeter's reception of his mother's failure to return from the swamp—is their chief characteristic, beyond the range of their own physical comfort.

A reason for the play's success may be found in the audience's sense of security and superiority in contrast to these caricature figures of the back road of human detritus. The very remoteness of their way of life adds to its attraction: what it sinful or intolerable among us becomes funny, once it is safely "way over there." The authenticity (to which reviewers referred) in the realistic setting and treatment of the drama compels us to watch with fascinated scepticism: Can such things be true? And the play to some extent works the miracle of faith; we believe because it is incredible. Here lie the deeper values in this poison-pen portrait, the relentless picture of the putrefying end of a once potent race of pioneers, that sprawled for a record time across the stage in *Tobacco Road*.

THE BROKEN JUG   *Heinrich Kleist*

Within the vehemence of the German *Sturm und Drang*, Bernd Heinrich von Kleist (1777-1811) lived turbulent days, sensitive and brooding to the brink of madness, until in jealous passion he shot his sweetheart, Henriette Vogel, and himself. His tormented life found echo in his intense dramas, which swing from despair to jubilation, which delight in sharp contrast of emotion. Even in his comedies there is a turbulence, as is shown in the thirteen scenes of his comic masterpiece, *The Broken Jug*, 1808.

In this play Frau Marthe Rull comes before the village judge, Adam, to claim damages for her broken jug from Ruprecht, the sweetheart of her daughter Eve. The district judge, Walter, present on a tour of inspection, watches the case. The jug has been broken by a midnight visitor to Eve's bedroom. This turns out to be not Ruprecht but Judge Adam himself, who, inventing a summons to Ruprecht for military service in the East Indies, has come to promise Eve to let the lad off in exchange for her favors. The trial ends with the ignominious flight of the exposed judge.

The play—translated into English in *Poet Lore*, 1939—gives an excellent picture of the life of ordinary folk, much in the style, as several critics have observed, of the Flemish masters of painting. "What an atmosphere of everyday reality is spread over it!" exclaimed Kuno Francke in *A History of German Literature* (1901). "How squarely they stand before us, this slovenly and slothful justice of the peace with his club foot, his blackened eye, and his big bald head; this sleek, thin, officious clerk, constantly on the alert for an opportunity to thrust himself into the position of his chief; this quarrelsome and loquacious Frau Marthe, not hestitating to drag the good name of her daughter into the courtroom if there is a chance of recovering damages for her broken jar; and, in pleasant contrast with all these, this sturdy peasant lad and his sweetheart, whose love, though sorely tried, is proven to be genuine and true!"

Natural as the development of the story seems, there is deft art in its construction. *The Broken Jug* has been called the comic counterpart of *Oedipus**, which it resembles in the skill with which the gradual revelation is achieved through constant action, the present progressing as it unveils the past. Presented by the Federal Theatre in New York in 1936, *The Broken Jug* proved still rich in its satire of hypocrisy and in its capture of the comic drama within ordinary happenings to simple folk.

PRINCE FRIEDRICH VON HOMBURG *Heinrich Kleist*

The uncompromising spirit of Bernd Heinrich von Kleist (German, 1777-1811), his refusal to accept the limitations life imposes, is marked in his serious dramas, by which he hoped, with a blending of Greek and Shakespearean elements, to lift the laurels from Goethe's brow.

Kleist's greatest drama, *Prince Friedrich von Homburg*, 1810, opens with the Elector of Brandenburg making plans for the battle of Fehrbellin (June 28, 1675) against the Swedes; Homburg, in charge of the cavalry, is to await the order for the finishing blow. Word sweeps across the field that the Elector is dead; Homburg charges, and gains the victory. He then declares his love to Nathalie, Princess of Orange. The Elector, however, is alive; and Homburg is condemned to death for disobedience. In the presence of Nathalie, Homburg abjectly begs the Electress to plead for his life. Nathalie, though scorning Homburg for his cowardice, intercedes, and bears him a letter from the Elector: "If you believe I have been unjust, say so, and I shall return your sword." Homburg refuses to make that claim, and publicly asserts the code of honor and patriotic service: a commander must first of all learn to obey. Expecting to die, he is now restored to freedom, honor, and happiness.

The drama, with its costumed spread through palace and dungeon, begins and ends in a garden; but beneath the melodrama and the flowered romance one may discern—as in Homburg's revulsion from the thought of death—a more realistic understanding of human nature. Christian Hebbel,* praising the play, pointed out that not death but no more than "death's darkening shadow" was needed to produce the "moral purification and apotheosis of the hero."

The play had its American premiere at Brown University April 29, 1935, and manifested a freshness and power that have kept its issues vital. The story has color, surging emotion, and dramatic substance.

MILESTONES   *Edward Knoblock*

The best plays by Edward Knoblock (American 1874-1945; naturalized a British citizen in 1916) are his adaptations and collaborations. The former include Vicki Baum's *Grand Hotel,* 1931, and *Hatter's Castle,* 1932; the latter, *The Good Companions,* 1931, with J. B. Priestley. The most successful of his original plays was *Kismet,* 1911, a fantasy out of the *Arabian Nights.* In the same year, he wrote the more substantial *Milestones* with the novelist Arnold Bennett (English, 1867-1931).

Milestones is an attempt to capture dramatically a half century of progress, summing up the world's advance in terms of the shipbuilding industry. Act I, in 1860, shows the days of wooden ships; Act II, in 1885, ships of iron; Act III, in 1912, ships of steel. John Rhead, pioneer in the field, grows to become a lord, the magnate of the industry. Throughout the play the Rhead and the Sibley families are intertangled, as the new generations revolt against the old. John's sister Gertrude lives a long life as a spinster, regretting the angry moment when she broke her engagement with Samuel Sibley, who went off and married a Yorkshire country girl. John keeps his family well in hand. His daughter Emily, to promote the family's rise, is married off to elderly Lord Monkhurst; only as a widow can she turn to the man she loves. At the end, however, Lady Rhead summons courage to defy her dominating husband and bring about her granddaughter Muriel's marriage to Richard Sibley.

Produced in London March 5, 1912, with Haidee Wright and Mary Jerrold, *Milestones* ran for 607 performances. In the New York production of September 16, 1912, Auriol Lee played the spinster, Gertrude. Charles Darnton (September 18) exclaimed: "Seeing *Milestones* is like seeing yourself grow old. Herein lies the real fascination of this curiously simple play." It was revived on both sides of the Atlantic in 1930; in London, with Clare Eames as Gertrude; in New York in the annual Players' production with Beulah Bondi, Dorothy Stickney, and Tom Powers. Through an industry and a family, *Milestones* gives a sense of the movement of civilization and a vivid picture of the way in which our instruments improve as we mortals pass, but our concerns and our foibles, our patterns and our passions, persist.

THE HUNCHBACK   *Sheridan Knowles*

Cousin of Richard Brinsley Sheridan* and man of the theatre, in which he acted as well as wrote, (James) Sheridan Knowles (Irish, 1784-1862) deemed *The Hunchback,* 1832, his masterpiece. In this judgment the public concurred, with a revival almost every year until 1900.

The play was accepted by Drury Lane, but the management wanted it postponed a season for revision. Sheridan thereupon took it to Charles Kemble, manager of Covent Garden, which was on the verge of bankruptcy. With Knowles as the hunchback and Fanny Kemble as his daughter, Julia, the play opened April 5, 1832. The performance of Fanny Kemble electrified London; the play saved the theatre. The drama opened in New York at both the Park and Richmond Hill Theatres on June 18, 1832, and on September 15 at the Bowery Theatre. Boston saw the play November 20, 1832 at the Warren Theatre, and the next night with Charles Kean at the Tremont Theatre. Rivalries of this sort both reflected and enlivened public interest. From the first, the role of Julia stole the honors from the title part. Among actresses that have played Julia are Ellen Tree, Helen Faucit, Charlotte Cushman, Ada Rehan, Viola Allen and Julia Marlowe.

The play challenges the idea of the influence of environment, which was gaining force in the humanitarianism of the day. It illustrates the thought that "pure gold in a gentle woman's heart will but shine the brighter when rubbed by the wicked of the world." The hunchback, Master Walter, rears Julia in a love that she returns. He acts as an elderly counsellor, not revealing—lest his deformity depress her—that he is actually her father. Sir Thomas Clifford loves Julia and she likes him, but when the opportunity comes she frolics like a butterfly in the gay social world, entranced by the attentions of the London blades. Modeling her ways on the frivolous city-bred Helen, she quarrels with the disapproving Sir Thomas and lends an ear to the seductive lure of the Earl of Rochdale. When Julia's eyes are opened, however, to the shams and shames of the city, she returns to Sir Thomas, and Walter discloses that he is her father and the rightful Earl of Rochdale.

William Winter said of the play that it "shows fine dramatic ability, the talent to evolve dramatic effects from a rational, coherent treatment of characters and incidents that are true and simple, and to do that in a romantic period of poetry, not in the hard, commonplace method of photographic prose." Similar praise came, after a performance by Julia Marlowe, from the *Boston Transcript* (February 15, 1896): "The good old play seemed doubly welcome . . . The Hunchback is one of those plays of that dramatic era when actions were supposed to speak louder than words, the result being an obscurity of plot which can only be clarified and made interesting by the highest order of acting . . . [it] has lived because it deserves to, not because it is merely popular."

So preeminently is *The Hunchback* an actress's play that reviewers have tended to fuse the performance and the play. Of an Ada Rehan revival, the *New York Times* (November 30, 1892) declared: "Julia has been a test role for young actressss since Fanny Kemble's time . . . The development of the traits of Julia's character is clearly and beautifully indicated . . . Julia's moods . . . are depicted with bewitching grace, with humor . . . with the deftest possible art . . . there is no lack either of force or of passion in the portrayal . . . It has the ring of truth."

Presenting a situation that has since grown hackneyed, *The Hunchback* makes no profound explorations of the human soul; yet it vividly presents a strong character bending under temptation, then rising clear. As a challenge of the human spirit against evil, it was staunchly popular.

MISANTHROPY AND REPENTANCE   *A. F. F. von Kotzebue*

The plays of August Friedrich Ferdinand von Kotzebue (German, 1761-1819) dominated the German theatre for thirty years and held the stage throughout Europe and in the United States for a full century. Kotzebue brought to the theatre the lush sentimentality of the Romantics, ushering in "the school of the drowned-in-tears", with melodramatic effects and violent action onstage.

Kotzebue's *Misanthropy and Repentance*, 1789, played in English as *The Stranger*, took one then daring step beyond its fellows: it ended with the forgiveness and happiness, not of an innocent, but of a transgressing heroine. Mrs. Haller's husband, though his life seems broken by her faithlessness, ultimately takes her back, softening to the children's pleas —which tender appeals continued to soften hearts in later tear-drenched melodrama. The first English version of the play showed Mrs. Haller stopping just short of infidelity; rejecting this, John Philip Kemble, with Mrs. Siddons and John Palmer, presented *The Stranger* in London March 24, 1798, in all its bold forgiveness of a woman that has sinned. The play's daring drew the crowds. "Few dramas have produced such controversy and such wide difference of opinion", observed the *Theatre* almost a century later (September, 1891). The play was frequently revived; Mr. and Mrs. Charles Kean were among those that played in it. John Palmer contributed a further shock to its history when he fell dead during a performance after speaking the words, "There is another, and a better, world."

The Stranger, like the rest of Kotzebue's plays, makes little claim to literary merit. Its tone was satirized in *Rejected Addresses,* by James and Horace Smith in 1812.

Despite the scorn of the sophisticate, however, the tears of the audience continued to flow. The *Theatre* (date above) testified: "Even in a poor theatre portions of the play, the later scenes especially, were invariably affecting," and the offspring of *The Stranger* have in this century become familiar in motion pictures and "soap opera". The play was the first great "tear-jerker" of the modern stage.

THE SPANIARDS IN PERU   *A. F. F. von Kotzebue*

In *The Spaniards in Peru; or, The Death of Rolla,* 1796, August von Kotzebue combined the sentimental strain of the Romantics, their exaggerated emotions and violent actions, with their exaltation of "the noble savage". The play depicts the resistance of the Incas to the tyranny of their Spanish conqueror, Francisco Pizarro (1470?-1541).

The Spaniards in Peru is the sequel to *A Virgin of the Sun,* which tells how Cora, daughter of the Inca of Peru, renounces her vestal vows for love of the Spaniard Alonzo. In the sequel Alonzo, wed to Cora, rallies the natives against Pizarro and is taken prisoner. Cora accuses the Indian Rolla, who also loves her, of having plotted his capture. Cora's infant child, lost in a storm, is brought to Pizarro. Rolla snatches the child; he is shot, but he bears the child across a cataract to safety before he dies. Helped by Elvira, Pizarro's Spanish mistress who has turned against her tyrannical lord, Alonzo kills Pizarro.

Adapted by Sheridan* as *Pizarro; or, The Death of Rolla,* the play opened at Drury Lane, London, May 24, 1799, with Mr. and Mrs. John Philip Kemble, Mrs. Siddons, and Charles Kemble. Its American premiere took place December 11 of the same year. The adaptation was so successful that it was retranslated and played in Germany. So strong was the appeal of *Pizarro* that William Taylor, who translated plays of Lessing and Goethe, wrote in 1830: "According to my judgment, Kotzebue is the greatest dramatic genius that Europe has evolved since Shakespeare." Although the play was attacked as theatrical hash and trash, *Gleason's Pictorial* (March 6, 1852) could remark, after a Boston production: "This standard play is too familiar to our readers to require any recapitulation of its plot; every school-boy has read it . . ."

In addition to putting "the noble savage" onstage, *The Spaniards in Peru* drew emotional effects from devices that became standard equipment in early melodrama: the prisoners or fugitives in the (often subterranean or undersea) dungeon or cave; the storm in the forest; the infant exposed; the rescue over a roaring torrent. Such visual appeals combined with the violence and sweep of Kotzebue's story to make the play the progenitor of a heady brood of popular melodramas.

THE SPANISH TRAGEDY   *Thomas Kyd*

Written by Thomas Kyd (English, 1558-1595?) in the early Shakespearean years, *The Spanish Tragedy; or, Hieronimo Is Mad Again*, 1589?, was the greatest Elizabethan stage success and the most popular English drama for a century. Licensed October 6, 1592, the play had numerous printings between 1594 and 1633. Familiarly known as *Hieronimo*, it was frequently alluded to in other works. "Its thrilling theme," Allardyce Nicoll noted, "with murders galore, ghosts, madness, and love, easily captured the attention of contemporaries, and even when, in later years, it was ridiculed by literary men with pretensions to taste, it kept its hold on the popular imagination."

Although Kyd's blank verse is rough, his construction and use of dramatic irony is effective and many of his melodramatic devices reappear in unnumbered blood-and-thunder plays thereafter. Even *Hamlet** following *The Spanish Tragedy* uses an opening ghost, the dumb-show, the play within the play as an instrument of vengeance, the innocent woman whom the horrors drive to madness and self-slaughter. Any criticism, said John McGovern and Jesse Edson Hall in the June, 1908, issue of *National Magazine*, "that dwells on the horrors of Kyd's drama falls with nearly equal harshness on *Hamlet*, and we think the general construction is the better in *Hieronymo*."

The Spanish Tragedy is set against the background of Spain's victory over Portugal in 1580. Andrea, the beloved of the Spanish lady Bel-imperia, has been slain by the Portuguese Prince Balthazar, who has in turn been captured by Horatio, son of the Spanish marshal Hieronimo. The play opens with the ghost of Andrea and the spirit of Revenge, but for much of the time Revenge sleeps. Balthazar is delivered to Lorenzo, the brother of Bel-imperia, who sees his own political advantage in marriage between his sister and Balthazar. He and Balthazar spy upon Bel-imperia and Horatio whom she has come to love; murderers then stab and hang Horatio, and Bel-imperia is carried off. The murderers themselves are slain so that they cannot betray their masters, but Bel-imperia sends Hieronimo word writ in blood of their villainy. Hieronimo, who himself has cut down his son's body, has spells of madness, but he is shrewd enough to awaken Revenge. He arranges a play, in which he and Bel-imperia, and Lorenzo and Balthazar, are to act. As part of the play's action, Hieronimo and Bel-imperia stab Lorenzo and Balthazar; Bel-imperia then kills herself. The audience onstage think this but part of the performance—then discover it is fatally real. Hieronimo bites off his tongue, so that he cannot be forced to speak. Given a quill pen, he motions for a knife to sharpen it; with the knife he stabs Lorenzo's father and himself.

Many of the lines of the play have a surging power; some, even the lift of beauty. However, the style is unsustained — so much so that Charles Lamb was led to stretch a resemblance into a collaboration, suggesting that the passages added in the 1602 edition are not by Kyd but by Webster, displaying "that wild solemn preternatural cast of grief which bewilders us in *The Duchess of Malfi**." Certainly the mad speeches of Hieronimo point toward the aberrations, the method in the madness, of Shakespeare's Hamlet.

Turbulent, melodramatic, for our taste long-winded, Kyd's play borrowed many elements, of ghostly avenger, of harrowing horror, from the Roman Seneca*; but the deeds of violence reported by messenger in the Roman drama were in *The Spanish Tragedy* enacted before the eyes of the audience on the English stage. It was the first and long the most popular of the blood-and-thunder dramas.

THE ITALIAN STRAW HAT   *Eugene M. Labiche*

Among the plays of Eugene M. Labiche (French, 1815-1888) written with sheer intent to amuse, is *Le Chapeau de paille d'Italie* (*The Italian Straw Hat*), 1851, which has enjoyed a great success and many years of revivals. "F. L. Tomline" (W. S. Gilbert*) rendered it into English as *The Wedding March*, which opened in London on November 15, 1873 and ran for 119 performances. Gilbert later rewrote it as an operetta, *Haste to the Wedding*, with music by George Grossmith, first enacted July 27, 1892. As *Horse Eats Hat*, September 22, 1936, adapted by Edwin Denby and Orson Welles, it was one of the high spots of the Federal Theatre in the United States. The antics of the farce are well fitted to the films and were set delightfully on the screen by René Clair.

On his wedding morning, a young man goes horseback riding; when he stops, his horse eats a hat of Italian straw instead of grass. The hat belongs to a woman with a jealous husband; she is now with an irascible Army man, who demands that the bridegroom at once replace the hat. The wedding party turns into a mad chase for the hat. It stops at a milliner's. The owner of the shop happens to be an old sweetheart of the bridegroom and wants to renew their amours. However, he manages to learn that the hat's only twin has been bought by a Countess. Off they go to the Countess only to find she is having a party. The bridegroom is mistaken for an entertainer; the wedding party makes itself at home at the Countess' feast. The Countess has given her hat to her niece. At the niece's home a suspicious husband awaits and the groom finds he's been chasing the very hat his horse has eaten. Everywhere the bride's father, Nonancourt, carries a pot of myrtle for the bride;

each time he encounters the groom he announces "Tout est rompu!" — "It's all off!"—whereupon the bride is at once embraced by a drooling cousin who had hoped to marry her. The right two are finally married at the City Hall in the course of the hunt for the hat. Everywhere, too, the bride's deaf uncle carries a gift box he refuses to set down; it turns out to contain an exact copy of the eaten hat! But before the groom can get it to the lady, her jealous husband appears, the wedding party is arrested, and the audience has worn itself with laughter.

Although the motion pictures quickly borrowed the stir and excitement of the chase, it still carries interest on the stage. The doings at the Federal Theatre production were characterized in the *New York Times* (February 28, 1936): "It was as though Gertrude Stein had dreamed a dream after a late supper of pickles and ice cream, the ensuing revelations being crisply acted by giants and midgets, caricatures, lunatics, and a prop nag. They pulled down the scenery and jumped into the aisles, were mummers of a Hallowe'en parade and the victims of slapstick from the age of innocence."

The ludicrous names of the French original are recaptured in the Gilbert version. The bridegroom is Woodpecker Tapping; the Uncle, Bopaddy; the Cousin, Foodle. The irate military man is Captain Bapp; his lady of the eaten hat is married to Major-General Bunthunder. Much of the Gilbertian humor is in the songs, but the music is not Sullivan's, and the absurdities of the story all stem from Labiche.

THE VOYAGE OF MONSIEUR PERRICHON   *Eugene M. Labiche*

Hailed by many as the chief comic dramatist of nineteenth century France, Eugene M. Labiche moved from light vaudevilles and lively farces to plays that, while no less amusing, were centred on a core of character or a nugget of thought. The best of these is *The Voyage of Monsieur Perrichon (Perrichon's Trip)*, 1860, which entertainingly presses home the psychological point that we are grateful to and like not those that have helped us but, rather, those that we have helped.

The play starts with the confusion of a railway station, and the Perrichons—a bourgeois husband who is proud, petty, and vain; a hopeful but muddled wife; their charming daughter Henriette; and six pieces of luggage—on their way to the Alps. Henriette has two suitors, Armand and Daniel. In the Alps, at the edge of a glacier, Armand saves M. Perrichon's life. The women shower Armand with attentions, but the shrewd Daniel pretends to slip and offers M. Perrichon the opportunity to save him. Thereafter Daniel sings M. Perrichon's praises and Perrichon centers his affections—and his daughter—upon the man that he believes he has saved. It is only when the cocksure Daniel boasts and Perrichon learns how he has been tricked that Henriette and Armand are united.

The psychological factor that motivates *The Voyage of M. Perrichon* is subtly traced and neatly developed. It may seem obvious now, but as the *London Times* (March 8, 1933) declared, it is "a platitude only because this once brilliant discovery has now been known for a long time. And it is worked into an excellent and amusing plot." Its structure is direct and clear; the dialogue is straightforward and without subtleties, but amusing and keen. When the play was written, according to the *New York Times* (November 2, 1937), "it was the fashion of the drama to caricature the bourgeoisie. It was the vogue among dramatists to imitate the simple diction and idiom of Voltaire. —For this last reason *The Voyage of M. Perrichon* has been academically perpetuated, so that few French classes, few French dramatic societies, have escaped it." But surely mere imitation could not ensure the continuously friendly greeting the play receives. Its situations are amusing, its basic point is both ironic and true.

When *The Voyage of M. Perrichon* was produced in New York in 1937 (in French, November 1) *Theatre Arts* of January 1938 observed "Le Théâtre des Quatre Saisons dusted off the gay comedy of Labiche and redecorated it with some of the glitter and wit it had a half century ago." In Paris *Le Monde* (February 6, 1946) remarked that "the humor remains alive." The play remains an excellent light-hearted, laughing dramatic picture of man's natural tendency to find virtue where it makes him shine.

PROCESSIONAL   *John Howard Lawson*

Set against blatant backdrops by Mordecai Gorelik, with a center piece announcing Bargains in Isaac Cohen's general store, *Processional*, "a jazz symphony of American life," came to the New York stage on January 12, 1925, with June Walker and Philip Loeb. The author, John Howard Lawson (American, b. 1894), expressed his debt to the old burlesque, "our one vital indigenous contribution to the theatre". The play is an attempt to picture a strike in terms of vaudeville and the jazz-beat of youth in the turbulent 'twenties.

The burlesque Jewish comic is a storekeeper in a West Virginia mining town. The Sheriff is drawn as in the early movies; the soldiers as in musical comedy; and there is a black-face Minstrel. Yet against this background all the vicious elements of a labor dispute sweep along—race prejudice, the Ku Klux Klan, and Dynamite Jim, the dumb miner. Dynamite Jim's eyes are gouged out, but he comes to see the light. Having seduced the jazzical Sadie Cohen, he furnishes the end of the play with the thought that she is pregnant with the future, that a reckoning day will come.

Despite its radical implications, *Processional* won wide critical acclaim. The *New York Times* (October 14, 1937) called it "one of the truly significant plays of the American theatre . . . a combination of drama and vaudeville, dancing, music, sentiment, horror and outrage, played on the stage and in the audience", and added (ten days later) that the play succeeded in "translating some of the economic festers and jingoisms of the United States into a brassy, turbulent vaudeville show that swaggered through the theatre like a bombastic drum-major, poking wry fun at sacred cows, crying 'faker' at the charlatans and sheriffs and occasionally standing back to discharge deadly fire at the enemies of justice. Although the humor was bitter, it was lively, and . . . filled the theatre with action and sound signifying something." Heywood Broun called the play "wholly engrossing, extraordinarily poignant, and altogether one of the finest things which has yet come out of the native theatre . . . I cleave to *Processional* as a play flooded with creation in full cry."

Other reviewers placed the play on an even higher dramatic level. "One can be purposely ridiculous, but only accidentally sublime," Gilbert W. Gabriel stated. "Out of the rude march of events and meanings, wilful absurdity, gross tragedy, the rankling, blood-knuckled stuff of a sarcastic vaudeville which makes up *Processional* darts ever so often a line, a phrase, of such beauty and burning as lights up the whole parade with wonderment. There is the awe of genius in this new production by the Theatre Guild." Similarly, the *Atlantic Monthly* (March, 1925) said: "To some, *Processional* is a weird hodgepodge, crude, uncouth, and repulsive; to others it seems a blinding revelation of a new mood of art, revealing in flashes a glimpse of the secret of human life. Paradoxical as this may seem, I am inclined to believe that it is a mixture of both. Life is a two-faced god. Bathos and pathos are two different aspects of his immortal visage. There is not even one step from the sublime to the ridiculous. The sublime is the ridiculous. The ridiculous is the sublime."

Processional was not played widely. A radio version was heard from Station WEVD in 1935. A revised version by the Federal Theatre, October 13, 1937, seemed to show that the play had caught a period in its own rhythm, but—being completely of its period—had but a fading hold. Though the play inspired a number of dramatists, no other of the genre had the power and impact of the prototype, which, in its violence and its mode of presentation, has left its mark on the American theatre.

THE GOLEM   *H. Leivik*

The Golem takes on significance as a dramatized legend symbolizing the eternal struggle of a people against oppression. According to Jewish legend, Rabbi Judah Low fashioned in Prague, about 1575, a "golem", a giant man made of clay, to help the Jews. After killing the tyrant who persecuted them, the golem (like Frankenstein's monster of a later day and the robots in *R. U. R.**) turned upon its own people and had to be destroyed. This story is presented against a background of rich local color depicting the Jews of the East-European ghetto.

In its picture of the messianic hopes of the Jews, the play poses the problem of physical force as opposed to spiritual power. There is symbolic coincidence in the fact that a recent production by the Habimah Players of Tel-Aviv opened in New York on May 15, 1948, the day the Jewish state of Israel came into being.

The life of the author is also linked with the problem of the play. Studying for the rabbinate, he was expelled for reading modern Hebrew works. He then became part of the revolutionary movement of his native Russia. Sentenced in 1906 to four years in prison and to exile in Siberia for life in 1912, he escaped the next year and made his way to New York.

Written by H. Leivik (Leivik Halpern, b. 1888), the play was published in Yiddish in 1921. Its first professional production was performed in Hebrew in 1925 by the Habima Players, who brought it to New York in 1927. The play was translated into English in 1928 (published in *Poet Lore*) by J. P. Augenlicht, and performed the next year. Motion pictures of the legend were made in 1921 and 1936; an opera with music by Eugen d'Albert was heard in Danzig in 1927; an oratorio with music by Vladimir Heifetz played at New York's Carnegie Hall in 1931.

American reactions have not been especially favorable to *The Golem*. The Yiddish Ensemble Art Theatre production in 1931, according to *Variety,* transformed "a theme and a plot that should have been treated with subdued reverence into a hybrid music-tragedy-comedy-farce" with the "story sequence submerged in a mass of extraneous horseplay". The *New York Herald-Tribune* called it "a grim artistic triumph," but the *New York Times* declared it "slow-moving, undramatic."

To the 1948 Hebrew presentation the *Times* was more generous: "Things happen plainly enough to engage an onlooker's interest and emotions . . . The final conflict is vivid enough to render translation unnecessary." George Freedley was blunt: "Let's face it. A highly stylized performance of worn-out plays in Hebrew is largely a pretentious bore to American audiences . . . *The Golem* was a tiresome piece in English even when well acted; but in Hebrew, in a dull and mannered performance, it seems interminable."

The Golem is, nevertheless, a dramatic monument to a period that has gone and to a question that remains unanswered: Must force be used, or can one rely on spirit, against the oppression of tyrants?

TIME IS A DREAM   *Henri René Lenormand*

The most somber and penetrating analyst in recent French drama is Henri René Lenormand (1882-1938). As a writer of thrillers for the Grand Guignol stage, he was well trained in devising strongly-knit plots and in playing upon the emotions of an audience. With psychological and psychoanalytical probing, he examined the soul states of turbulence and restlessness (*le théâtre de l'inquiétude,* his field has been called) that precipitate disaster. While a number of Lenormand's plays achieve distinction, the most representative is the vivid *Time Is A Dream,* 1919.

Less psychoanalytical than Lenormand's later plays, but equally involved in the currents of modern physical and psychical speculation, this gripping tragedy was presented by Pitoëff in Geneva in 1919 and later in Paris. It was shown at the Neighborhood Playhouse in New York on April 23, 1924, where it was preceded by a motion picture explaining the theory of relativity—for one of the ideas suggested in the drama is that past, present, and future all exist now.

In the play, Nico Van Eyden returns to his Dutch home healthy and hearty after a stay in Java. Just before his arrival, his sweetheart, Romee Cremers, has a vision of him drowning in a lake in front of his home in Utrecht. In spite of his sister's and his sweetheart's efforts to keep Nico cheery, a Dutch despondency settles upon him more and more deeply. The dull skies and the ancient and mouldy house weigh upon his spirit until he takes a boat, cuts through the reeds, and jumps into the water.

In six short scenes and with a simple story, Lenormand worked *Time Is A Dream* into a tense and absorbing drama. His Grand Guignol training stood him in good stead. "As a matter of fact," said the *New York Times* (April 24, 1924) "Lenormand's play is a popular thriller, which the playwright, interested in the theatre primarily as a vehicle for ideas, has elected to develop along philosophical lines rather than dramatic." At the same time, he achieved, as Alexander Woollcott recognized, "a beautiful and exceedingly difficult tragedy." Woollcott said that Nico's actions could be interpreted in either of two ways: that Romee's thoughts influenced Nico, or that Romee actually was granted prescience of the act to be. Lenormand gives more weight to the second alternative. If all time is now, some persons may have eyes attuned to the three-way vision: Respice, Adspice, Prospice. Certainly many have perceived their destiny approaching and have striven in vain to hold it off. The mystery of time and the adventuring of the soul are here fused into a quiet but intense drama.

THE FAILURES   *Henri René Lenormand*

Henri Lenormand's psychological probing is most gruellingly evident in *Les Ratés* (*The Failures*), a study of the degeneration and ruin of a playwright and his actress wife who cannot withstand the successive shocks with which life batters their loving but insufficient souls. Unable to bear the thought of her husband's starving, the actress sells herself to buy food. Her sacrifice exalts him, but he soon feels a backwash need of equal defilement. He goes to a prostitute. Love and poverty mix with liquor and reproaches down the sluice-way of weakening will until in a drunken frenzy the playwright strangles his wife and kills himself.

The characters of this sordid story are "He" and "She", implying that, mutatis mutandis, they might be you and I. "For each man kills the thing he loves"; Wilde's words are quoted in the play with the addition, "or the thing he loves kills him." With several other human failures in the background—the manager of the cheap touring company, the musician who composes into his cups—the drama presents fourteen sharply-etched episodes in the fated lives of the playwright and his wife.

The play was a great success when produced by Firmin Gemier in Paris, 1920 and by Reinhardt in Vienna. The Theatre Guild presented it in New York on November 20, 1923 with Dudley Digges, Jacob Ben-Ami and Helen Westley. The scenes, said Alexander Woollcott, are "so sharp, so swift, so silent, so simple. Some of them have great beauty. The last of them is superb, a very Whistler of grays and charcoal blacks and wan lights and only one splotch of color. It is a picture chill with dawn, grimy with poverty. It smells to heaven of murder and the morning after . . . a filling performance of a brutally honest play that trudges doggedly through the squalor of life." The *Boston Transcript* (March 4, 1924) called the play "a tragicomedy of self-deceit and self-pity, devotion and decay," but the *New York Sun* (November 21, 1923), saw beyond the love of each for the other to their mutual love of art and therefore to "the tragedy—perhaps the most heart-breaking tragedy in the world —of those in whose breast burns the sacred fire to attain the highest, but with so tiny and impotent a flame that it cannot light them through the crushing struggle of life."

With power and pity the play traces two spirits, generous yet poor, bewildered yet striving, devoted yet weak—much, indeed, like the majority of mankind—borne on too strong a tide of hours to their doom.

THE MERRY WIDOW   *Victor Leon*

When *Die Lustige Witwe* (*The Merry Widow*) opened in Vienna on December 30, 1905, its gay and lively airs took the city by storm. It became a great success all over Europe. Based on *La Petite Ville*, 1801, by Louis Baptiste Picard (French, 1769-1828), the best playwright of the

Napoleonic era, *The Merry Widow*, with book by Victor Leon (Austrian, 1858-1940) and Leo Stein (1872-1947) and music by Franz Lehar (Austrian, 1870-1948) opened in London June 8, 1907 and ran for 778 performances. By the time of its New York premiere, October 21, 1907, with Donald Brian and Ethel Jackson, there were a hundred "merry widow" variations romping on a hundred stages. The operetta ran for 419 performances in New York and started a vogue of "Merry Widow" hats, dresses, drinks, and conversation. London saw revivals in May 1923, in May 1924, in 1932, in March 1943, in September 1944, and in April 1952. The operetta was burlesqued in New York, January 2, 1908, for 156 performances. *The Merry Widow* itself was revived in New York in 1921, 1929, 1931, and 1932. On August 4, 1943, it opened for 318 performances with Jan Kiepura, Martha Eggerth, and conductor Robert Stolz, who had conducted the Vienna premiere. It was seen again in New York in 1944—this time at the City Center. It has had some 250,000 performances in twenty-four languages and is still in live repertory. There were film versions in 1911, with Wallace Reid and Alma Rubens; in 1925 with Mae Murray; in 1934 with Jeanette MacDonald and Maurice Chevalier, and in 1952 with Lana Turner.

The story is a simple one. Sonia of Marsovia, widowed young, takes her good looks and some twenty million francs to have a good time in Paris. Many men naturally seek her hand, but the Marsovian Ambassador, Baron Popoff, has instructions to see that she marries a Marsovian. The Baron picks as husband-to-be Prince Danilo. He and Sonia had loved before she married money; piqued, he is having a good time with Fifi, Jou-Jou, Clo-Clo, Lo-Lo, and other French girls at Maxim's. Sonia, too, is piqued at the thought that she should marry to order, but after considerable gaiety and roundabout dalliance, the old love wins through.

The Merry Widow has continued to be popular because its comedy is gay, wholesome, and fresh, but mainly because its music is tuneful, lively, and easily remembered. At the New York premiere the waltz "I Love You So" spurred a spontaneous demonstration of cheering and wild applause such as is seldom heard. *The Merry Widow* remains one of the most engaging and delightful of operettas.

MASQUERADE   *Mikhail Y. Lermontov*

Like Pushkin*, Mikhail Yurievich Lermontov (Russian, 1814-1841) was a poet more than a playwright. His impassioned ode to the Czar after Pushkin's death in a duel in 1837 led to his being exiled. He himself, at the age of 27, fought a duel so arranged that the loser would plunge off a cliff. Lermontov lost. Much of the fire and aristocratic recklessness of his brief life throbs in his greatest drama, *Masquerade*, written in 1835, when he was but 21 years of age.

The play pictures the effete aristocrat Arbenin, who prides himself on his disdain. In a gambling house, he lectures the reckless and passionate Prince Zvezdich, helps him recoup his losses, then takes him to a masquerade ball. A coquette gives the Prince her bracelet; it is that of Nina, Arbenin's wife, whom Arbenin instantly kills. On her funeral day Arbenin learns that the bracelet had been found by the woman who gave it to the Prince; he goes mad.

This powerful play, popular in Russian repertory, opened in one of Meyerhold's best productions on February 26, 1917—the eve of the Rus-

sian Revolution. It was revived all over Russia in 1941, the centenary
of Lermontov's death. Its chief figure, Arbenin, has been called the
Russian Othello, but his only resemblance to Shakespeare's Moor is that
he too mistakenly feels honor-bound to kill the woman he loves. In
character Arbenin is more Byronic than Shakespearean; indeed, as the
New Statesman and Nation (August 28, 1943) remarked, "there is something in him not only of the Byronic hero but of Baudelaire's dandy . . .
He stalks pleasure while condemning it, carries doom to the gambling
table and the ballroom, rescues a friend from ruin and then suspects
him." Through Arbenin, too, Lermontov attacks the heartless, frivolous,
dissipated Russian upper class. In irregular rhythm and rhyme, *Masquerade* is a vivid drama of a man blinded by his pose of superiority,
caught in a world of giddy pleasure, high spirits, and sudden doom.

BRIGADOON   *Alan Jay Lerner*

Seldom in a single season does Broadway rejoice in two musical shows
that prove lengthily haunting; but, scarcely two months apart, *Finian's
Rainbow** was followed by *Brigadoon.* Opening on March 13, 1947, the
latter won the Critics' Circle award as the best musical of the year. After
a successful tour it returned, May 2, 1950, for three more weeks in New
York. Some 886 performances were given in London, opening in 1949.

What chiefly lifted *Brigadoon* above similar plays was the complete
integration of the theatrical arts it achieved. The music by Frederick
Loewe, the dances by Agnes de Mille, and the book and lyrics by Alan
Jay Lerner fused in a rich union.

Brigadoon takes us to Scotland and to whimsyland, where two American hunters come upon the village of Brigadoon on the one day in every
hundred years on which it rises from the mists of magic to become a
living, pulsing village once again. When the town comes to life the two
hunters are entranced with its ways, and with two Brigadoonian maids.
So deeply is one of the men smitten that, after his return to the United
States, he journeys back to the forest glen in Scotland, where love works
its magic and bears him again to Brigadoon.

The heart of Brigadoon is MacConnachy Square. The name is a cue
to its Scottish fantasy, for James M. Barrie called his "unruly half—the
writing half" by the name of M'Connachie. George Jean Nathan noted
that the plot is "a pleasant, if strangely unacknowledged, paraphrase of
Friedrich Wilhelm Gerstächer's little German classic, *Germelhausen*".
The German story, written in 1862, does not have the final episode of the
modern man returning to the old-time girl in the vanished village. In
truth the American play might well have omitted this, too; for here, as
Kronenberger said, the piece "flops down to a banal Broadway level."

Especially attractive is the manner in which the dances, beautiful in
themselves, lead on the action. "A kind of idyllic rhythm flows through
the whole pattern of the production," declared Brooks Atkinson. "The
funeral dance, to the dour tune of bagpipes, brings the forestep of doom
into the forest." John Mason Brown concurred: "The austerity of the
old ballads is caught . . ."

The village of Brigadoon has more charm and reality than most
existing communities, and displays it in a feat musical.

TURCARET   *Alain René Le Sage*

In *Turcaret* (*Financier*), French novelist Alain René Le Sage (1668-1747)—author of the picaresque masterpiece *The History of Gil Blas of Santillane*—wrote the best French comedy between Molière* and Beaumarchais*. The play is as sharp a thrust at the financiers as Molière's *Tartuffe* is at the hypocritically pious. It is reported that financiers did indeed attempt to bribe Le Sage to withhold the play, reputedly offering him the then enormous sum of 100,000 francs. When Le Sage refused, and the play was a great success, the financiers worked their will upon the company. Although *Turcaret*, opening at the Comédie Française on February 14, 1709, was revived in the repertoire seven times before the Lenten closing, it was not played again when the theatre reopened after Easter. Not until 1730, when Le Sage's son, Montménil, entered the Comédie Française, did it reappear. A general prohibition of Le Sage's dramas seems to have been arranged. Subsequently he wrote only short farces to be played at village fairs.

Based upon Le Sage's one-act play *Presents*, the play pictures the downfall of "the eternal profiteer" in the shape of a tax-farmer under Louis XIV. [The King "farmed out" the right to collect taxes to the highest bidders; the Farmers General collected all they could wrest from the people, giving the King a stipulated sum and keeping the rest. The financiers reveled in luxury while the people were bled dry; even the King became a debtor, almost a prey. In 1707 all the King's tax revenue up to 1715 was already mortgaged. Thus both the noble and the rising bourgeois hated the tax collectors. This explains both the enthusiasm with which Le Sage's satire was greeted and the zeal of the financiers to drive it from the stage.]

In the play, Farmer General Turcaret, foolishly in love with a Baroness, is bled by the Baroness, who in her turn is bled by a Knight with whom she is infatuated. The Knight has the Baroness dismiss her faithful maid Marine and engage Lisette, a friend of the Knight's valet, Frontin. The latter is ready to suck money from any source among these knaves; Lisette is eager to pluck them by proxy in plucking Frontin. While the Baroness enjoys the prospect of marrying her wealthy provider (without surrendering her lover, of course), Turcaret's sister discloses the fact that her brother has a wife whom he is hiding in the country. While Turcaret lavishes a fortune on his lady-love, he does not even support his wife. Mme. Turcaret therefore comes to town, flirts with the Marquess de la Tribauderie, and with him visits the Baroness while Turcaret is there. The ensuing excitement ends with the arrest of Turcaret by his own associates. The wily Frontin, who has amassed 40,000 francs, remarks: "M. Turcaret's reign is now over and mine begins." Lisette's sly smile shows that she holds the reins.

This comedy of intrigue brushed with satire foreshadowed the didactic comedy of the nineteenth century. The characters—even the minor figures—are clear-cut and sharply defined. The Marquess, who stands a little out of the fray, is, as Richard Aldington said, "one of the great creations of French comedy, perhaps the finest dramatic portrait of the *petit-maitre* (elegant fop)."

The satirical power of *Turcaret* has dimmed, but it has not died. "It is a classic," said *L'Illustration* (February 18, 1928) "yet in many respects it seems modern . . . At moments it has the verve of Molière comedy; at others, by the sharpness of its satire and the realism of its characters, it suggests the daring flights of the Théâtre Libre." As a dramatic work, the play's chief fault is a lack of sympathy: we are glad to see everyone deservedly punished, but we are not pleased to see the scoundrel Turcaret succeeded by the rascal Frontin. Yet, as the French put it, *c'est la vie!*

MINNA VON BARNHELM   *Gotthold Ephraim Lessing*

Educated for the priesthood, Gotthold Ephraim Lessing (German, 1729-1781) preferred social criticism and the theatre. In 1766 the newly organized Hamburg National Theatre invited him to be its official poet. Not wishing to grind out plays to meet popular need, he refused the post, but he accepted appointment as critic and began the penetrating body of criticism known as the *Hamburg Dramaturgy*, deemed by many to rank next to Aristotle's *Poetics* among the world's considerations of the drama.

In 1767, Lessing's *Minna von Barnhelm* was produced at the Hamburg National Theatre. This first German comedy to present contemporary life was an immediate success; it has proved a lasting favorite. It was produced in New York in 1904 and in 1920, in German, at the Irving Place Theatre. Germany saw productions recently—in 1928, 1931, 1934; on the radio from Munich in 1937; and in Berlin in 1940. Of a 1937 London production, W. A. Darlington observed in the *Telegraph* (July 14): "To me, the play was a very pleasant surprise . . . By modern standards it is stiff and conventional, but there is no mistaking the life in it."

Modern standards have indeed made the central theme of the play seem less a basic social problem than a stickler's scruple. In the drama, a Prussian army officer, Major von Tellheim, is discharged on an accusation of embezzlement. Despite her faith in him, he releases the wealthy Minna von Barnhelm from their engagement. When he clears his honor, Minna for a time gives Tellheim a dose of his own medicine, pretending to have lost her fortune and to refuse him because of their unequal status.

The story is thin, but the characters are delineated with keen observation, with natural and sympathetic colors, and with a deep sense of integrity. The lofty concept of womanhood in it, and of the nobility of the army officer, helped keep the play a favorite on the German stage. "Since Sara Sampson and her lover perished by violence on the Frankfort stage," said Magnus, "the weeping heroine of everyday life has dominated the social problem drama." And since Minna taught her lover a lesson on the Hamburg stage, Sara's smiling sisters have shown the theatre that, given love and faith and a firm spirit, many social problems can be solved. In both types of social drama, Lessing was a vigorous pioneer.

NATHAN THE WISE   *Gotthold Ephraim Lessing*

After Lessing became involved in religious controversy, the authorities forbade his further critical writing on the ground that he "antagonized the principal doctrines of the sacred writings of Christianity." He therefore determined to try the theatre again. In the meantime, he had lost his wife and child; out of his grief and loneliness grew a spirit of tolerance and peace. The fierce attack his opponents expected in his new work proved, instead, a compassionate picture of understanding and love—Lessing's best play, *Nathan the Wise*, 1779. The plot was to some extent suggested by *Edward and Eleonora*, a play by James Thomson, published in 1739. Lessing called his play "the son of my old age, whom polemics helped to bring into the world." It was the rich product of his maturity.

Set in Jerusalem, the play presents a tangled tale through which to reach its moral of tolerance. A Christian knight is given permission by the Jew Nathan to wed his daughter Recha. The Patriarch of Jerusalem, learning that Recha is really a Christian child brought up by the Jew, wants to have Nathan killed. The case is brought before the Sultan Saladin, whose clear-sighted justice and objective tolerance set an example for Christian and Jew alike.

The most famous part of the play is the story of the three rings (also told in Boccaccio's *Decameron*), which Nathan tells in his defense before Saladin. For generations, Nathan says, a royal line had left the favorite son a most precious ring, a talisman of love and peace. At length came a king who had three sons, equally beloved. He called in a jeweler and had two duplicates of the ring made, and when he died each son claimed to be the heir. The judge ruled that each should hold a third of the kingdom; after years had gone by, the prevalence of justice and peace would prove which was authentic. Similarly, by the spread of love and justice and peace, humanity may know which is the true religion.

"If God held all truth in his right hand," said Lessing, "and in his left nothing but the ever-restless impulse toward truth, though with the condition of ever erring, and said to me 'Choose!', I should humbly fall at his feet and say 'Father, give me the left; pure truth is for Thee alone'." This recognition that to err is human was at the core of Lessing's spirit; it brought calm in the midst of passion, love in the midst of hate.

Produced posthumously, 1783, the play passed almost unnoted, but after Goethe and Schiller revived it at Weimar in 1801 it became tremendously popular and has never gone out of favor in the German theatre. It was the first play Max Reinhardt presented in Berlin after World War I. Burned by the Nazis in 1933, it was acted in London by a German company during World War II. In New York, the play has had numerous productions in German. In English, Erwin Piscator's 1942 Dramatic Workshop production was so well received that it moved to the Belasco Theatre on Broadway; the play was revived again at the Dramatic Workshop in 1944.

The Dramatic Workshop used an English translation of Ferdinand Bruckner's adaptation of Lessing's play. Bruckner*, said John Mason Brown (March 12, 1942) "denies the plot its multiplicity and suspense, exiles the Sultan to the wings and eliminates entirely such helpful characters as Hofi and the Sultan's chess-playing sister," but helps by omitting the "lost-baby combinations" at the end. Brown found the play powerful: "The blaze of Lessing's intellect and heart is such that no Nazi could hope to survive it." Robert Coleman stressed the play's "eloquent, timely, and timeless words . . . a literary landmark." Richard Watts was a dissenter; he called the play "a garrulous and undramatic work, with the nobility of its spirit atoning for its essential tediousness." Brooks Atkinson considered it "an admirable and profoundly moving play".

It is the simplicity and the calm of its plea for the brotherhood of man that give the play its permanent power. Robert Garland well said (February 22, 1944): "It is this quality of quietude, of composure and control, that gives the work its undeniable effectiveness . . . Something to think about, something to take home with you and treasure."

One may cavil at the end of the play (omitted by Bruckner) in its revelation that the Jewish Recha is a Christian after all (a twist also seen in *Gentleman's Agreement*, a 1948 novel) for this removes rather than solves the problems of interrelationship; but this is a detail in an otherwise superbly integrated dramatic study of understanding and love.

SPRINGTIME FOR HENRY   *Benn Levy*

One of the most popular farces among stock companies and summer theatres is *Springtime For Henry*, written by Benn Wolf Levy (English, b. 1900) in 1931. It is a crackbrained farce that turns the moral code topsyturvy and elevates the reckless spirit of man against the curbs of commonplace convention.

The story is absurdly simple and simply absurd. Henry Dewlip, a wealthy London automobile manufacturer, is a gay old roué; under the influence of his new secretary, Angela Smith, who likes "the Decent Thing", he reforms; then he relapses. But this story has many other twists. It turns out that the secretary, Angela Smith, is a self-made widow: she shot her husband in the Touraine. He was a Frenchman who brought two mistresses home to tea, an act which Angela thought a bit excessive and a bad example for their little boy. The jury acquitted her. It turns out, too, that when Henry reforms he gives up his flirtation with the wife of his best friend Jelliwell; this throws her back on her husband's company—to the desperate boredom of both. Jelliwell complains to Dewlip; his happiness depends upon his wife's having an extramural interest. The reformed Henry has also been boring his friends at the Club. So, out of regard for his fellow-men, Henry goes back to his rakish ways. As he proceeds toward the consummation of his intrigue with his friend's not unwilling wife, Jelliwell and Miss Smith disclose that they have discovered love in the mirror of one another's eyes.

This story came to New York on December 9, 1931, for a run of 199 performances. Its hilarious situations and slily twinkling dialogue were an instant joy. Leslie Banks (later, Henry Hull), Nigel Bruce, Helen Chandler and Frieda Inescourt excellently conveyed its "intelligently slapstick mood", said Robert Garland; "it had the audience in hysterics." When the play opened in London on November 8, 1932, it won equally favorable comment; the *Evening News* called it "that rarest of productions, a farce that does not insult the intellect."

Springtime For Henry is indeed, as Brooks Atkinson has said, "a marvelously demented bit of impish fancy. . . . the most skillful farce written in English in many years." The dialogue is as unexpected as it is hilarious. There are few funnier narrations in any drama than the story of Perseus and Andromache that Jelliwell tells to Angela. Situations and details of stage business continuously freshen the fun.

Especially effective in the play were the devices of Edward Everett Horton, who began playing Henry in 1933, and, after eighteen years of touring the United States, brought the play to New York on March 14, 1951. The date of the story was wisely set back to 1911, giving it a delightful period flavor.

In 1931, the play provided a lift of laughter against the depression. A decade later, the Texan *Dallas News* (April 6, 1940) called it "as complete an escape from the war, taxes, politics, the census, and canker worms as can be had outside a flagon of spirits." But a basic value of art, even comedy, even farce, is that it provides not an *escape from* but a *springboard to* a world where irresistible social and natural forces are irrelevant in the face of the soaring independence of man. *Springtime For Henry* continues to be a delightfully irreverent thrust of shrewd absurdity against the solemn forces that would burden and bind the spirit of man.

THE LONDON MERCHANT   *George Lillo*

The Merchant, better known as *The London Merchant; or, The History of George Barnwell,* presented at Drury Lane, June 22, 1731, created a furore, for George Lillo (English, 1693-1739) had written the first serious prose drama of which the chief figures are not of the nobility, the first domestic, or sentimental, tragedy. It was promptly translated into French, German, and Dutch. As Allardyce Nicoll points out, the play "was taken by eighteenth century Continental dramatists as prime model, inspired a Lessing* and a Diderot, and with them that whole school of bourgeois playwrights who led the way toward Ibsen*."

The London Merchant had its New York premiere at the Nassau Street Theatre on May 7, 1750. Very popular in the eighteenth century, it was familiar enough to the nineteenth to be parodied in the *Rejected Addresses of* James and Horace Smith (1812), and to be caricatured in Thackeray's satiric retellings of great works. It had a London production on June 2, 1927.

Based on an old ballad, the play tells the story of the destruction of the apprentice Barnwell by the courtesan Millwood. Under her influence he robs his employer, Thorowgood, then murders his uncle. For these deeds, Millwood and Barnwell are executed. The play tells its story directly and with force, but the characters are not deeply probed, and the story is by now long familiar. It is of importance as the first domestic drama in modern prose, pointing the way toward the most frequent type of play in our own time.

LIFE WITH FATHER   *Howard Lindsay*

Begun as a series of sketches in the *New Yorker* by Clarence Day (American, 1874-1935), *Life With Father* was issued as a book in 1935, then transformed by Howard Lindsay (American, b. 1889) and Russell Crouse (American, b. 1893) into a play that achieved the world's longest unbroken run. Opening at the Empire Theatre on November 8, 1939, it closed on July 12, 1947, with a record of 3,224 performances, forty-two more than its closest rival, *Tobacco Road**. Actor, manager, play doctor, and author Lindsay and Broadway journalist Crouse drew out of virtually no story, merely a series of lively episodes from Clarence Day's memories, a delightfully real picture of family life in a fairly well-to-do New York home of the 1880's.

Such plot as there is revolves around Mother Day's determination to have Father Day—whose parents had neglected the ritual in his childhood—consent to be baptized. But it is the wholesome vitality of the bewildering Days and their four red-headed sons that maintains the constant comedy.

Foremost, of course, is Father Day, by turns irascible and complacent, king-pin, cock of the walk, roaring "My Gawd!" in frequent anger, constantly concerned over the family expenditures and Mother's inability to keep accounts; yet tender and even sentimental on occasion. Mother Day, who bows to her proper master, is humorless and naive, yet knows how to turn a situation to her advantage. Through sheer misunderstanding she wins her way in money matters, as her love and warmth and bending persistence guard her brood. These are buoyant, living people. "Merely as a play it may be unimportant", said John Mason Brown, "but as a biography of everyone's family, except Caspar Milquetoast's, it is as shrewdly drawn as it is ingratiating". Brooks Atkinson called it "a perfect comedy".

It is such an amusing piece of Americana, such an "authentic part of our American folklore", as Atkinson said, that we might expect the play to be attacked by those that profess to despise the American way of life. The one dissenting critical voice did come from the Communist *Daily Worker*: "There is not a moment of honest joy or passion in its daguerreotype tableaux. Father is a stuffed shirt who never condescends to a lovable moment of human uncertainty. . . . When it becomes a matter of chivalry, understanding, and simple human compassion, we'll take one of Saroyan's drunks—in a pinch . . . *Life With Father* may be good propaganda, but it's bad art."

It's hard to see what these dramatized character sketches are propaganda for—other than the basic goodness of human nature—but, as deftly presented in *Life With Father*, they rise to excellent theatrical art. Howard Lindsay himself played Father Day in the original cast; his wife Dorothy Stickney played Mother. In the eight years of the play's run, those that played Mother Day included Lily Cahill, Nydia Westman, Margalo Gillmore, Dorothy Gish, and Lillian Gish. Several "generations" of young actors outgrew the roles of the Day boys.

In England the play opened June 5, 1947, and was received with polite enthusiasm. Critic Harold Hobson called it "simple, rollicking fun".

This epic of the brownstone front with its lively and genial picture of old New York went so gently into the hearts of its beholders as to win the play a preeminent place among long-loved productions in the American theatre.

MANDRAGOLA   *Niccolo Machiavelli*

The brilliance and the cynicism of the Italy of the Medici shine in this lively and bawdy drama. When the Medici family re-entered Florence in 1512, Niccolo Machiavelli (1469-1527), suspected of having plotted against them, was given "four twists of the rack" and sent into exile. He subsequently wrote *Mandragola*. Printed in 1524, it was supposedly based on an actual occurrence in 1504. When Machiavelli was restored to favor, *Mandragola* was presented before Pope Leo X at Rome; the Pope ordered a theatre built so that the people could see the play. Catherine de Medici and Henri II of France saw it at Lyons in 1548. *Mandragola* is, said J. A. Symonds in *Renaissance in Italy* (1876) "the ripest and most powerful play in the Italian language." Macaulay esteemed the play below only the best of Molière. Voltaire said he would surrender all of Aristophanes to have *Mandragola*.

The story is simple, in the Renaissance taste. Old Nicia wants a cure for his wife Lucrezia's sterility. Her would-be lover, Callimaco, disguised as a doctor, administers the fecundating mandrake (mandragola) root. But there is a hitch. The first one thereafter to lie with her, so they assure Nicia, will absorb the poison of the mandrake and be in peril of death. Nicia and the doctor seek a victim to purify Lucrezia; they pick—Callimaco.

This is, as the *Los Angeles Times* (April 22, 1935) averred after a performance in its city, "a lusty tale, which the brilliant wit of Machiavelli wove into a complicated intrigue, sinister yet ripe with the hearty swing of a swift medieval pungency." Around the intrigue move typical figures of the Italian Renaissance, shrewdly pricked with darts of satire or illuminated with beams of wit. Prominent among these is the cynical confessor, Frate Timoteo, a prime representative of mocking monks.

Two recent adaptations of *Mandragola* have been produced. A German version by Paul Eger, acted in Berlin in 1912 to music by Ignatz Waghalter, was presented in New York with book by Alfred Kreymborg, March 4, 1925. It contained some charming songs, especially one in praise of love, sung by Bianca, niece of old Pandolfo (the names were changed), but in general the pungency and wit of Machiavelli were not recaptured. There was more vigor and bustle in the Ashley Dukes adaptation shown in London in 1939, which, according to the *New Statesman and Nation* (December 23), was "not Machiavelli, but excellent entertainment."

Harold Hobson, in the *Christian Science Monitor* (March 9, 1940), noted a present significance in *Mandragola* in that "it windows a mentality that has deeply deflected the course of human events, and is said to influence the policy today of some leading figures of Central Europe."

The incidents of *Mandragola* were used as though they had happened to Machiavelli himself in W. Somerset Maugham's story *Then and Now* (1946). The gullible old husband, horned on his dilemma, might be offered a different remedy today, but the characters of *Mandragola* are still as full of life as the bawdy play is full of the joy of living.

THE SCARECROW   *Percy Mackaye*

Of the plays by Percy Mackaye (American, b. 1875), who has looked upon the theatre as an avenue of community expression and a force for general culture, the most effective is *The Scarecrow; or, The Glass of Truth*, 1908. In 1923 it was made into a motion picture starring Glenn Hunter, Osgood Perkins and Mary Astor.

"A tragedy of the ludicrous", the play is developed from Hawthorne's story of "Feathertop" in *Mosses From an Old Manse*. It is set in Salem, Massachusetts, at the end of the seventeenth century. Goody Rickby, "Blacksmith Bess", is shown seeking vengeance on the rigidly puritanical Justice Gilead Merton, who years before had fathered her illegitimate son, now dead. With the aid of Dickon, a Yankee embodiment of the Prince of Darkness, Bess constructs a scarecrow out of farmyard scraps and endows it, by means of a magic pipe, with the illusion of life. As Lord Ravensbane, she sends its forth to woo the Justice's niece, Ruth. Ravensbane not only wins Ruth from her fiancé, but he also falls deeply in love with her. When the "mirror of truth" reveals to Ravensbane that he is only a scarecrow, he breaks his magic pipe and falls. As he dies in Ruth's arms, the mirror reflects him once more—a man. Love has given him a soul; in the act of dying, he is born.

This combination of fantasy and folktale was presented in Boston on January 2, 1911, and went to New York on January 17 with Frank Reicher as the scarecrow. The *Boston Transcript* called it "an unusual, a distinguished play. [Mackaye's] first prose drama among four plays in verse, it is in many ways the most poetic . . . poetic prose, idiomatic yet beautiful, at times passionate, at others light and graceful." There is a simplicity in the telling, a casual naturalness of the dialogue, that heightens the effect of the drama.

The *New York Telegram* of January 19, 1911, called *The Scarecrow* "a play of more than common merit, a play in which dignity and beauty of thought, insight into character, firmness of construction, and development of dramatic interest combine in an impressive whole."

The play was produced in Berlin by Reinhardt in 1914; in Moscow by Stanislavsky in 1924. Louis Jouvet was rehearsing it in Paris, 1951, when he died. It was presented in New York in 1953.

Jack Lanthorne, otherwise Lord Ravensbane, constantly smokes his corncob pipe to "equilibrate the valvular palpitations of the heart". When Justice Merton wonders, Dickon whispers that this is the Justice's son by Blacksmith Bess Rickby; in fear of exposure, Merton consents to the marriage with his niece. Dickon is a shrewd, frisky, and proud fiend; he flatters himself that he has "dictated some of the finest lines in literature". But all the devil's devices collapse beneath the impalpable power of love.

The Scarecrow builds the fantasy of its folktale into a smiling allegory —at once amusing and challenging and sad—of the saving grace of love in the soul of man.

MONNA VANNA   *Maurice Maeterlinck*

When Maurice Maeterlinck (Belgian, 1862-1949) went to Paris in 1886, he joined the symbolists who were then in the thick of their fight against naturalism. To their exploration and exploitation of the soul, he added a dream quality, a pessimism, a brooding over man's destiny and his end in death. To emphasize the unreality of his dramas, Maeterlinck hoped that they might be played by super-marionettes. The theatre was, to him, "a temple of dream".

Set in fifteenth century Pisa, *Monna Vanna* (1902) is a tale similar to that of the Biblical Judith and Holofernes. Prinzivalle, leader of the Florentine army, offers to abandon the siege of Pisa if the governor's wife, the beauteous Monna Vanna, will come to his tent clad only in her mantle. Monna Vanna finds him a devoted admirer, who takes her untouched back into Pisa. Monna Vanna's jealous husband refuses to believe her innocence; Prinzivalle is arrested. Repelled by her husband's lack of faith, Monna Vanna "confesses" the deed her husband credits, takes the key to Prinzivalle's cell, saying she'll seek vengeance, and goes to free Prinzivalle and join her life to his.

The goal of man in death is, thus, no longer the limit of Maeterlinck's vision, although he continues to brood over the world's wretchedness. The play ends with the hope of love in mutual understanding and respect.

Written for Georgette Leblanc, later Maeterlinck's wife, *Monna Vanna* was a great success. It was for a time forbidden by the censor in England because "of one line" ('naked under her mantle', according to J. T. Grein in the *Illustrated London News*, March 1, 1924), until in 1914 Maeterlinck overcame the Chamberlain's scruples. Actually, Monna Vanna never removes her mantle in Prinzivalle's tent, and her costume is an unimportant detail. The play was well received in New York, both in German, opening December 17, 1903, and in English with Bertha Kalich, October 23, 1905. It was revived in 1917 with sets by Joseph Urban; again in 1919; and has since been produced in many American cities. Of the play, in 1905, the *New York Dramatic Mirror* said: "Symbolic and poetic as it is, there is in it the element of human appeal, and a dramatic strength his former plays have lacked". The *New York Tribune* called it "more than a series of theatrically effective situations . . . On its literary side is the picture it creates of the blended blood and beauty of Italy during the rebirth of learning . . . The third act combines the psychological subtleties of what has gone before with theatrical surprises piled one on the other, with elemental passions aroused to their highest pitch".

It may be said that in this play the quest of the soul drew the dramatist from symbolism to psychology. Andreyev*, in *Letters on the Theatre* (1912), announcing his own departure from symbolism in search of the soul, said of the earlier Maeterlinck plays that the spectator there was like a "perfectly sober person at a party where everyone else is drunk". Poetic and dramatic, subtle in its searching, *Monna Vanna* is a noble picture of a woman's heart, a woman's response to injustice and to love.

THE BLUE BIRD   *Maurice Maeterlinck*

In *The Blue Bird*, 1908, the gloom and pessimism of Maurice Maeterlinck's earlier plays are wholly dissipated by the sun of happiness and love. Here symbolism and fantasy combine with complete clarity in a charming play that has remained popular with theatregoers of all ages. Soon after it was written, the play was produced in Russia and in England. New York saw it in 1910, 1911, 1913, 1915, and 1923; Pasadena in 1929 and 1937; Seattle in 1934; Chapel Hill, North Carolina, in 1938. After its world premiere in Russia (September 30, 1908), the play enjoyed popularity in that country right up to 1930, in Stanislavsky's and other companies. It was revived there in 1936. At one time it was being shown by 59 different companies in almost as many countries.

The story concerns a poor woodcutter's children, Tyltyl and his sister Mytyl, who set forth on Christmas Eve to seek the blue bird of happiness, accompanied by Milk, Fire, Water, Bread, and Light, as well as by the Cat and the Dog. They first hunt for happiness in the past. In the land of memory, they find their grandparents, kept alive by the children's thoughts. Next they visit the Kingdom of the Future. Many adventures entangle them, including an escape from the forest in which the Cat would destroy them. In the end, they come back to find the blue bird of happiness awaiting them at home. They give the bird to a sick neighbor child. After the neighbor has tasted joy and the children have found happiness in the giving, the bird flies away.

The theme of the play charmingly grows through the quest of the children. Even through their joyous journey, we constantly glimpse the dark forces of the universe, lurking and watching for a relaxed moment in man's vigilance, ready to thrust humanity back into the seething depths of evil.

Maeterlinck visualizes the story of man as a lonely adventure in a hostile world. In a discussion of the play, he declared: "We are alone, absolutely alone on this chance planet, and, amid all the forms of life that surround us not one, excepting the dog, has made an alliance with us . . . In the world of plants we have dumb and motionless slaves, but they serve us in spite of themselves, and, as soon as we lose sight of them, they hasten to betray us and return to their former wild and mischievous liberty."

Maeterlinck's idea was further developed in a review of the play in the *New York Dramatic Mirror* (October 5, 1910): "every object, animate or inanimate, has its own soul or essence of being . . . All this symbolism is lost, however, in the panoramic splendor of the production . . . *The Blue Bird* may nest as long as it wishes to at the New Theatre, secure in the support of a wide popular interest in ornithology."

This play has indeed been popular all over the world. The reasons for its success were well put by the French statesman Leon Blum: "The originality of Maurice Maeterlinck, as a thinker, lies in his having united in a single system the Alexandrian or German mysticism and the Anglo-Saxon ethics, the mysticism of knowledge and the morality of practical life . . . But . . . it must not be assumed that *The Blue Bird* is pedantic and boring. It is the most pleasant, the most charming, often the most delightful, of spectacles . . . One feels constantly present that sort of imagination, special and rare, which consists in seeing and seizing, in the slightest concrete detail, or in the merest word, the way of giving expression to the abstract thought . . . a work both very lofty and very beautiful."

The play wears well. Upon seeing it in 1923 John Corbin observed that it had "grown" considerably: "Or perhaps it is we who have grown. In either case, the play is, or seems to be, of far greater stature both as the holiday entertainment which it is on the surface and as the wisely thoughtful and amiably humorous fantasy which it is fundamentally . . . By some magic of his own Maeterlinck has woven into this seemingly naive fantasy far more of wisdom and of humor, of penerating observation and of deeply quiet thought, than are to be found in many a ponderous tome." In London's *Saturday Review* (December 18, 1909) Max Beerbohm traced the progress of Maeterlinck from his early plays, when the problem of existence moved to the enigma of death, to the deathless joy of *The Blue Bird*: "For proper appreciation of Maeterlinck, you must have, besides a sense of beauty, a taste for wisdom . . . In his youth, the mystery of life obsessed him. He beheld our planet reeling in infinity, having on its surface certain infinitesimal creatures, all astray, at the mercy of unknown laws. And he shuddered . . . Little by little, the shudders in him abated . . . If we are but the puppets of destiny, and if destiny is, on the whole, rather unkind, still there seems to be quite enough of joy and beauty for us to go on with. Such is the point to which Maeterlinck, in the course of years, has won; and such is the meaning he has put into *The Blue Bird*."

Maeterlinck was constantly preoccupied with the basic problems of the human soul, which he approached at times more realistically, at times more fantastically, but always delicately, with a luminous aura of suggestion and symbol around the dramatic figures. Nowhere, however, has he achieved a happier and richer combination of his best qualities than in *The Blue Bird*.

FALSE SECRETS   *Pierre Marivaux*

The plays of Pierre Carlet de Chamblain de Marivaux (French, 1688-1763) were greatly influenced by the Italian commedia dell' arte. His first success, *Harlequin Polished by Love,* was presented by the Italian Comedians in Paris in 1720; his most successful play, *False Secrets* (in which Harlequin is the heroine's servant) had its premiere with the same company on March 16, 1737. Of Marivaux's thirty-two plays this one and three others are still in the French repertory.

Although some of Marivaux's characters are drawn from Italian comedy, they are not stock figures, but endowed with a graceful life of their own, among the solid bourgeois and the lesser nobles. In the generation before the French Revolution, Marivaux dealt not with social problems but with social dalliance. Gallantry and intrigue occupied society and the stage, but Marivaux was concerned less with the erotics than with the metaphysics of love-making. His elegance and ease of thought and expression (which gave birth to the word *Marivaudage*) and his exquisite though trifling dialogue are in delightful harmony with his delicate sentiment and refined analysis. The actions and reactions are less in the deeds than in the emotions of his characters. They tell not merely what they feel but what they feel the others feel they should feel. His is indeed the theatre of the salon.

False Secrets (Les Fausses Confidences) shows the scheming servant Dubois working by indirections to arrange a marriage between his former master, Dorante, and the beauteous, wealthy Araminte. Dubois whispers to Araminte that Dorante is madly in love with her. Like the disguised Rosalind in *As You Like It**, Araminte laughingly suggests that seeing her often may cure Dorante of his love; she employs him as her steward. From this point, as Arthur Tilley declares in *Three French Dramatists* (1933), "the gradual awakening of a reciprocal love in her heart is portrayed with a marvelous skill and delicacy." Araminte's ambitious mother, an impecunious Count, and a maid, Marton, who thinks Dorante is in love with her, add complications to the story. More important are the sparkle and interplay of sentiment, the gathered grace of "the kingdom of the tender."

Later periods grew in appreciation of Marivaux. Araminte was a favorite role of the famed Mlle. Mars, in the 1830's; and when Mme. Arnould-Plessy played the part in 1855, Théophile Gautier called it "one of the pleasantest in the theatre." The United States premiere of *False Secrets,* by the Madeleine Renaud - Jean-Louis Barrault Company, November 12, 1952, was the play's thousandth professional performance. The Renaud-Barrault production was a great success in New York, as it has been in Paris. After the French premiere Gabriel Marcel, in *Les Nouvelles Littéraires* of July 11, 1946, said that "the exquisite spirit of Marivaux is at its best . . . His good will is a grace as much as a virtue . . . The tenderness does not exceed the span of a sigh, an exclamation withheld; but the emotion the actor suppresses the audience feels." Out of artificial comedy Marivaux has fashioned real delight.

TAMBURLAINE THE GREAT   *Christopher Marlowe*

The advent of the plays of Christopher Marlowe (1564-1593) brought the English drama to its full freshet power in one great springtide surge. In the naked freshness of exuberant youth Marlowe opened the door to the modern theatre.

It may be that Marlowe is more poet than playwright. Certainly in his first play, *Tamburlaine the Great*, 1587, he presents less a well-knit story than a succession of dramatic episodes. Yet these episodes move with such vigor that they took Marlowe's unaccustomed age by storm.

The story of Tamburlaine (Timur the Lame, 1336?-1405) is drawn from the Spanish *Timur* (1543) of Pedro Mexia, translated in 1571 as *Foreste* by Fortescue. The First Part of Marlowe's play shows the Scythian shepherd, Tamburlaine, rising in power until he marries the daughter of the Sultan of Egypt, Zenocrate, and crowns her Empress of Turkey and Persia. The Second Part carries Tamburlaine further upon his career of conquest—kings draw his chariot, champions tremble at his name—until he is confronted by death.

The pomp and majesty of this play must have been especially rousing to the many who knew the court of Henry VIII. "The lures of Tamburlaine," said Lamb, "are perfect midsummer madness. Nebuchadnezzar's are mere modest pretensions compared with the thundering vaunts of the Scythian shepherd."

Marlowe lacked the creative imagination of Shakespeare, who boldly refashioned whatever he took; but he, too, made old material new. The wonder of Tamburlaine, said Havelock Ellis in his Preface to the Mermaid edition of the work, "lies in the wild and passionate blood, in the intensely imaginative form, with which he has clothed the dry bones of his story." The successive scenes are held together by the surging personality of Tamburlaine (whose sweep toward power and beauty was akin to the Elizabethan) and by the impact of Marlowe's words. (He was the first to reveal the power of blank verse in the English drama.)

Despite lapses into bombast and rant, the play is rich and forceful. Swinburne has said of this play: "In the most glorious verses ever fashioned by a poet to express with subtle and final truth the supreme aim and the supreme limit of his art, Marlowe has summed up all that can be said or thought on the office and the object, the means and the end, of this highest form of spiritual ambition." The poet in Marlowe makes the playwright soar. In his *History of Elizabethan Literature* (1887), Saintsbury avers that "Shakespeare himself has not surpassed ... no other writer has equalled the famous and wonderful passages in *Tamberlaine* and *Faustus*."

For many years *Tamburlaine the Great* (especially the First Part with its magniloquent lines) held the stage. In 1702 Nicholas Rowe condensed the two parts into one play: *Tamerlane*. Instead of a conqueror blood-thirsty and afire for power, Rowe paid tribute to King William by converting his hero into a calm, philosophic ruler.

Tamburlaine the Great had its American premiere January 26, 1758. It was played again in 1762, 1784, and 1799. In the nineteenth century, its popularity waned because of its long speeches and episodic structure. In England, it was revived at Oxford in 1933, when the Second Part was played for the first time since the seventeenth century.

Although long stretches of *Tamburlaine the Great* would stall on the stage today, many passages still flash with the fire that was Tamburlaine's—and Marlowe's.

The lasting power of the drama was demonstrated recently when Donald Wolfit acted Tamburlaine in an Old Vic company production which opened in London, September 24, 1951. Harold Hobson reported in the *Christian Science Monitor* of September 29 that "the play is packed with horrors which were preserved from becoming ridiculous only by becoming revolting", but he recognized it as "the most tempestuous, wildest, most frantic play in the English language."

Tamburlaine the Great remains tremendously important as the first flag Marlowe raised in that new realm he helped create—the modern English drama.

DOCTOR FAUSTUS   *Christopher Marlowe*

Probably first produced in 1588, *The Tragical History of Doctor Faustus* by Christopher Marlowe was not officially registered until 1601. The first edition was not printed until 1604; other editions followed in 1609 and 1616, the latter with many comic additions. The story (for its sources, see Goethe's *Faust**) is based on an old German legend, but the spirit is all of Marlowe's England and Elizabeth's.

Magic and hell are to Marlowe no symbol, no subject for irony, as with Goethe; they are hot, passionate reality. Doctor Faustus is a vivid figure of the times, a master of the alchemical knowledge of the Middle Ages, yet afire with the lust for power that marked the Renaissance. Against the earlier conception of duty to one's superiors, against the divinity of kings, against God himself, Marlowe for the first time in modern drama set the assertion of individual responsibility and individual worth. Yet, because of his position in time, his Dr. Faustus is torn between the two conceptions; Faustus seeks power, raising himself against the world, yet he acknowledges his sinfulness. He knowingly rebels against the rule of God, and he admits the justice of the doom for which the devils hale him off to hell. Legend has it that at one performance the actors noticed one devil too many amongst them; they spent the evening not at the tavern but in prayer.

While Marlowe thus raises the legend to a symbol of that rebellion of the individual against authority which characterized the Renaissance, he also spiritualized his drama, freeing it from the physical signs of hell-fire and the other material horrors that delighted the medieval audience (some of which were reinstated by the author of the 1616 comic additions). Marlowe's conception of hell itself, as existing wherever the damned may go, is more modern than that of either Dante or Milton.

In the article "Faust on the Stage" in *All the Year Round* (June 28, 1879), edited by Charles Dickens, the differences between Marlowe's and Goethe's Faust are pointed up: "Marlowe's work is the outcome of an undoubting mind, not the statement of a great problem yet unsolved. After the old simple fashion, Marlowe points his moral before he begins to adorn his tale . . . Goethe's earth and air spirits are abstractions; Marlowe's are concrete actualities; and throughout the Englishman's wonderful play there is no hint, any more than there is in a medieval mystery, that the events in it are either impossible or even improbable . . . This Mephistophilis is not the mocking fiend of Goethe, but rather the awful Lucifer of Milton . . . Not only is Faustus duly handed over to the foul fiend at the conclusion of the tragedy, but a perpetual conflict is maintained between his good and bad angels. He is shown, within the compass of eight days, the face of heaven, of earth, and of hell. The seven deadly sins appear before him, and describe their attributes; he is given every chance of repentance—in vain. His power to decide is assumed by the frequency of the appeals made to him. He is vanquished by one weakness—sensuality."

The lust for power that led to the excesses of the Renaissance—the slaughter of Montezuma and countless American Indians, the launching of the Armada, the very creation of the English Church out of Henry's spleen—is epitomized in Dr. Faustus, whom it scorches to hell. The visit of Dr. Faustus to Rome, in the play, with the Pope and the Cardinals burlesqued, pays tribute to the passions of the times. In the very year of the play's production, the 132 Spanish ships of the Invincible Armada set sail to bring the rebellious English back to the fold of the Church. On every side Puritan and Catholic stood, sword, dagger, pistol, and poison in hand. In the religious and political intrigues of the time, the government agent Christopher Marlowe lost his own life. Vigorously, but through the force of will rather than through physical force, Dr. Faustus chose his own path toward power though it end in damnation.

Out of this earnest presentation in *Dr. Faustus* of a theme that shaped his own life, Marlowe rolled his "mighty line". Amid the prose passages of the play, his blank verse takes more powerful and more beautiful surge than in the earlier *Tamburlaine**, which marked its first effective use in the drama. As Swinburne said in the Prologue to an 1896 production: "Then first our speech was thunder."

The dramatic power of *Dr. Faustus* has been manifest in a number of recent productions. The *London Telegraph* (July 25, 1934) observed: "Faustus is the one figure in English drama whose mind is shown at war with itself, and whose inner struggle is expressed by direct means." *"Faustus* at its best," declared Arthur Symons, "seems to me much finer than *Faust*." There can be no question that Marlowe's is a more effective stage play than Goethe's. American productions included one almost every year of the decade 1931-1941, somewhere in the United States; Orson Welles played Faustus and directed the Federal Theatre production in New York in 1937. Brooks Atkinson called his "a brilliantly original production . . . grim and terrible on the stage." To John Mason Brown this production suggested the spirit of the Elizabethan stage "in exciting modern terms." Richard Watts, Jr. noted that the play "contains some of the most haunting poetry in the English language." Those that find the writing uneven should note that only Act I, Scenes 1 and 2 of Act II, and 87 lines more of the twelve scenes up to the last of Act V, have come to us in Marlowe's own words.

There was a Federal Theatre production of *Dr. Faustus* in New Orleans in 1937; another in Boston in 1938; Rex Ingram played Mephistophilis in 1940. The play ran in London in 1940 during a defense blackout; the *New Statesman and Nation* (March 9, 1940) observed: "It is astonishing how well it acts, and how overwhelming is the effect of the sustained tragedy of damnation." In 1941, the play was presented in Los Angeles by six masked readers while dancers enacted the parts.

Marlowe was later denounced as an atheist; his plays give ample evidence at least of his questioning nature. Three of his four chief figures are infidels. All are vibrant with hot desire for beauty, power, wisdom; and they reach out beyond the limits of human grasp. The illimitable desire in Marlowe's plays turns them to tragedy. Lamb has looked into this relationship: "The growing horrors of Faustus are awfully marked by the hours and half-hours as they expire and bring him nearer and nearer to the exactment of his dire compact. It is indeed an agony and bloody sweat."

The spirit of Tamburlaine and of Faustus is Marlowe's own spirit, on the fervent quest that led him toward beauty, toward power—therefore toward danger and toward evil: a quest that resulted in four masterpieces and ended on a dagger's point.

Christopher Marlowe, who died in his thirtieth year, is the author of some of the greatest English dramas. Of these, *Dr. Faustus* probes most deeply into the soul of man.

THE JEW OF MALTA   *Christopher Marlowe*

Shakespeare is supposed to have drawn his Shylock in *The Merchant of Venice** after Barabas in *The Jew of Malta,* 1588(?). But the compound of villain and buffoon the Elizabethans saw in Shylock bulked concentrate, horrendous in Barabas.

The first impression the play makes is majestic; only Milton has surpassed Barabas' opening soliloquy, Swinburne has said. But as the incidents gather and break, the first grandiose conception of Barabas shifts to the caricature of a crafty villiain. Resisting the tax demand, when Malta must pay tribute to the Turks, Barabas has his properties confiscated. His house is turned into a nunnery. He poisons his daughter Abigail and all the nuns. He betrays Malta to the besieging Turks, who make him governor. Then, seeking to ensnare the Turks, he is caught in his own trap and spilled into his own boiling cauldron.

Charles Lamb gave these reasons why *The Jew of Malta* was not often played: "Barabas is a mere monster brought in with a large painted nose to please the rabble. He kills in sport, poisons whole nunneries, invents infernal machines. He is just such an exhibition as a century or two earlier might have been played before the Londoners, *by the Royal Command*, when a general pillage and massacre of the Hebrews had been previously resolved on." It was, in short, popular in its own day with much the same appeal as bear baiting. It was usually performed at Shrovetide, when the rowdy audience demanded low comedy and violent action. Today, occasions for reviving this play seem less frequent. It was performed at Yale University in 1940. London saw it in 1922 for the first time since 1818.

The *London Times* of November 12, 1922 declared that some "may, with some justice, ridicule the element of buffoonery in his comedy, the preposterous intrigue of his tragedy; but no one can deny the wild poetry, the raging sublimity of his words, the force, the passion, of his rhetoric and verse . . . The soul of the sea is in almost every line of Marlowe. His music surges up against our ears with tidal beauty. His power of rhythm is oceanic alike in its serenity and its tumultuousness. While we cannot bring ourselves to think seriously of the incidents in such a play as *The Jew of Malta*, whilst the skeleton of its plot is grotesque and absurd, there is always a magniloquent grandeur in its verbiage, a turgid beauty in its thoughts . . . It is a stage creation of undeniable vitality . . . there is throughout directness of characterization, swiftness of action, and felicity of dialogue."

At first, in vivid lines, Barabas prizes the beauty of precious stones, as well as the power of riches.

"The vigorous design and rich free verse of *The Jew of Malta*," Havelock Ellis points out, "show a technical advance on *Dr. Faustus**". While the beauty of the verse gathers turbulent power, the beauty Barabas desires is lost in his uncontrolled lust after power over men. Like all Marlowe's protagonists, Barabas reaches too far and topples.

In the development of the Malta Jew we find all the traits woven by Shakespeare into the Jew of Venice. "There is not a single note in Shylock," the *London Times* of November 12, 1922 declared, "that primarily Barabas does not indicate or suggest."

Despite the grim course of Barabas' plotting, *The Jew of Malta* surges not only like the sea, but like the spring, and morning. "Now Phoebus ope the eyelids of the day!" cries Barabas; and morning wakes with Marlowe on the English stage.

EDWARD II   *Christopher Marlowe*

The last of Christopher Marlowe's great dramas, *Edward II*, 1590?, is by many deemed his masterpiece. While it lacks some of the fire of his earlier verse, it is more fully integrated as a work of art, not so much a mere succession of stirring scenes as a coordinated and swiftly progressing drama. The characters, too, are more individually drawn. There are sensitive portrayals, especially of Isabella, Edward's Queen, and of young Edward III, the best drawn child in the Elizabethan drama. In *Edward II*, as Havelock Ellis said, Marlowe's "passionate poetry is subdued with severe self-restraint in a supreme tragic creation."

Edward II is a "history play" of the turmoil in England from 1307, when Edward, newly crowned, recalled his Gascon favorite Gaveston, to 1327, when Edward was forced by his wife Isabella and her lover Mortimer to abdicate, and was brutally slain. There is broad sweep of passions across the stage as the nobles resent the king's infatuation for Gaveston, whom they force Edward to banish. The domestic and the international intrigues are interwoven with a skillful hand. Isabella, at once a political pawn and a passionate woman, turns from Edward to Mortimer and from love to murder. "The reluctant pangs of abdicating royalty in Edward," said Charles Lamb, "furnished hints which Shakespeare scarce improved in *Richard II;* and the death scene of Marlowe's king moves pity and terror beyond any other scene in ancient or modern drama with which I am acquainted." Havelock Ellis expressed the opinion that "the whole of Shakespeare's play, with its exuberant eloquence, its facile and diffuse poetry, is distinctly inferior to Marlowe's, both in organic structure and in dramatic characterization."

First acted in 1592, *Edward II* was printed in 1594, 1598, 1612, and 1622. Although seldom performed nowadays, it has been broadcast both in England and in the United States in the "great plays" series. It was presented at Oxford in 1933; the *London Times* of February 10 of that year stated: "Although Marlowe's drama pursues its way without the relief of any lighter interludes in the Shakespearean manner, yet the play as it was performed tonight never appeared heavy or tedious." Of a production at New York's City College in May, 1948, George Freedley wrote: "One of the noblest and best of English tragedies . . ."

The words of Edward (opening Act V) after he has been imprisoned, have the nobility and fire of true majesty. We can readily understand how the boatmen on the Thames used to sing Marlowe's *Hero and Leander;* how Marlowe's young contemporary Petowe could declare that "men would shun their sleep in still dark night to meditate upon his golden lines." Truly, as Drayton declared, Marlowe "had in him those brave translunary things that our first poets had." He was England's first great dramatic poet—cut down in his thirtieth year. Tradition has it that he was slain over a wench in a tavern brawl, but research has shown that Marlowe was in the government secret service, and his death may well have been the outcome of such intrigues as still sunder the world today, and as he pictures, with power and sympathy, in his great historical drama, *Edward II.*

ANTONIA AND MELLIDA and ANTONIO'S REVENGE

John Marston

In sharp contrast to most of his contemporaries, John Marston (English, 1575?-1634) dedicated his works "to everlasting oblivion." Yet some of them still send clear echoes along the corridors of time. For a while, Marston was engaged in the "War of the Theatres" against Ben Jonson, who in *The Poetaster** attacked *Antonio and Mellida,* 1599?, and *Antonio's Revenge,* 1600?. William Gifford, who in the early nineteenth century edited Jonson, declared that these two plays of Marston's "are distinguished by nothing so much as a perpetual bluster, an overstrained reaching after sublimity of expression, which ends in abrupt and unintelligible starts, and bombast anomalies of language." A century later, however, the more objective Allardyce Nicoll observed that "of the sixteenth century revenge plays with thrilling and bloody plots . . . none is more entertaining than *Antonio and Mellida.*"

The two parts of the story were published in 1602 as "sundry times acted by the Children of Paules." In the First Part, Andrugio, Duke of Genoa, defeated by Piero Sforza, Duke of Venice, has been hiding in the Venetian marshes, with a price on his head. The son, Antonio, likewise outlawed, goes disguised to the court of Piero, whose daughter Mellida he loves. They run away, but Mellida is brought back. Then, in stately funeral procession, Andrugio bears the body of Antonio to Piero's court and claims the offered reward. Piero, now assuming neighborly forbearance and grief, says he'd give half his fortune, or his daughter's hand, to have the young prince alive again. Thereupon Antonio rises from his bier, and the two lovers are united.

The Prologue to the Second Part, *Antonio's Revenge,* is fraught with the dark presage of overhanging doom as are few passages in our literature. "This Prologue," said Charles Lamb, "for its passionate earnestness, and for the tragic note of preparation which it sounds, might have preceded one of those old tales of Thebes or Pelops' line which Milton has so highly recommended . . . It is as solemn a preparative as 'the warning voice which he who saw th' Apocalypse heard cry'." Piero had once courted Andrugio's wife, Maria; he now poisons

Andrugio, and presses himself upon the widow. He also has a friend of Antonio's slain and the body placed in Mellida's room to make it seem that she has been unfaithful. Antonio is told the truth in Elizabethan fashion by his father's ghost, but meanwhile Mellida has died. Maria has feigned acceptance of Piero's suit; at a banquet on the eve of their wedding, Piero is offered his own son to eat, then is hacked to death. Instead of taking control of the two dukedoms, Antonio seeks such peace as he can find in the seclusion of a religious house.

Through the glooms and horrors of this bloody story, Marston moves like a majestic storm—now with great lightning flashes and reverberant thunder roll, now with heavy drench of rain in the irksome dark. His tones are clear and massive, but occasionally he strains, especially in diction, on the quest of sublimity or awesomeness of passion, laying himself open to Jonson's satiric shafts.

In 1607 Marston entered the church and closed the door upon his brief writing career. *Antonio and Mellida* and *Antonio's Revenge* are his best plays, and in underlying nobility and dignity of spirit the most rewarding of the blood-and-thunder dramas.

CRADLE SONG   *Gregorio Martinez Sierra*

The tender picture of convent life in *Cradle Song*, showing the love of God that blossoms also as love of man, has made this gentle drama, everywhere, a *succès de larmes*. Countless audiences, since the March 1911 premiere in Madrid, have wept and smiled at this melody in dialogue by Maria and Gregorio Martinez Sierra (Spanish, b. 1881). New York first saw it on February 28, 1921; again, with Eva Le Gallienne, for 125 performances beginning January 25, 1927. It was also given there in Spanish in 1927, and in English in 1932, 1944, and 1955. It ran in London in 1926, for 109 performances; in 1931, 1936, and, in a Gielgud production with Wendy Hiller, in 1944. Los Angeles saw it in 1948. So moving is the quiet flow of the play that the *New York Telegraph* reviewer reported on January 26, 1927 that "an esteemed contemporary was blubbering, and working vigorously away at some chewing gum to hide this critical faux pas." The story of *Cradle Song*, however, is not sad; it is touchingly tender.

The play is set in a convent of Dominican nuns. There is one happening in each of the two acts, which spreads ripples like a pebble dropped into a quiet pool. In the first act, the Sisters receive two gifts: a canary, which sings continually; and a baby. In the second act the foundling, now a girl of eighteen, goes forth to be married. That is all. "The marvel is," said the *Telegraph* of March 1, 1921, "how the author could make so much out of so little."

The play is made up of little, genuine touches of human character. It moves through unimportant incidents that grow to significance because of the warmth, and the kindly humor, and the pervasive love, that shine in them. The prioress is a wise and understanding soul, who delights even in the high spirits of the novices. The vicaress has more acid in her devotion; she discerns the horns of the devil beneath the gentlest ripple of good fun. The doctor, who has brought the infant Teresa to the convent, and comes to escort her forth, enjoys the little shocks his privileged position permits him to give to the nuns.

Cradle Song seems to lure its reviewers to poetic expression. The *London Observer* of Sepember 6, 1931, called the play "aptly named, for it does not so much tell a story as croon a gentle melody . . . Such is Martinez Sierra's art that character is as sharply defined and emotion as clearly expressed as though its pious alarums and excursions were dramatically secular. It charms, indeed, no less by its continuous plainsong than by the stage picture it presents." "The tragedy," said the New York *Tribune* of March 2, 1921, "lies in the bereaved heart of the immured community at the parting—and particularly in the heart of one of the nuns riven from the object in which her maternal instinct had richly plied." "Meltingly beautiful," said Brooks Atkinson; and Alexander Woollcott exclaimed that to seek to analyze its beauty "would be like explaining the simple and ancient magic of chimes on frosty air . . . The gentle, fond raillery of this tender, rueful play is the work of hands at once gracious and infinitely grateful . . . it recaptures and holds cupped in its hands a little of the lost peace of the world."

As the curtain falls, the chapel bell summons the nuns together, and the spell of the play woos the theatre back toward its starting-place in religion, warming the theatre with its twinkling understanding and embracing love.

THE TRAGEDY OF NAN   *John Masefield*

The greatest play of the poet John Masefield (English, b. 1875) is the grim story of a simple, dignified country girl who is driven to destruction. *The Tragedy of Nan* shows Nan, after her father's execution for stealing sheep, taken into the home of her uncle, Pargetter, as a charity girl. A neighbor lad, Dick Gervil, promises to rescue her from her drudgery, but switches his attentions to her cousin, Jennie, when the aunt tells him of Nan's father's disgrace. He switches back when, her father's innocence belatedly established, Nan is to receive compensation. In a fury of revolt, Nan scorns the blood money, stabs the greedy hypocrite, and goes out to drown herself.

Produced in London, May 24, 1908, with Lilla McCarthy, and in New York, January 13, 1913, with Constance Collier, the play won critical acclaim. It toured the United States in 1918 with Alexandra Carlisle and Philip Merivale, who brought it to New York in 1920. Equity Library presented it in New York in 1945.

Not only are the dialect of the play, and the local atmosphere, admirably caught, but the personal story reaches out to universal impulses. As Masefield says in the Preface: "The vision of agony, or spiritual contest, pushed beyond the limits of the dying personality, is exalting and cleansing."

The reviews of *The Tragedy of Nan* stressed its power. The *London Observer* (October 3, 1943) said, "The play is the pelting of a pitiless storm"; and the *New York Globe* (February 18, 1920): "Its prose is as pungent and as beautiful as any in modern English drama." According to the *London Times* (May 3, 1932), Masefield's "conception of character springs from something rooted so deep in human nature that, though fashions in rustic drama have changed, we are still content to companion Nan with Tess as the representatives of all wronged women. Nor have improvements in play-making made the close and skillful interweaving of unflinching realism and genuine poetry seem any the less close and skillful."

Masefield, in *The Tragedy of Nan,* builds a succession of deeply ironic contrasts, as the simple but honest spirit of Nan is chafed to full attrition, first by the complacent relatives who feel that her love and her unending toil are their due, for taking in a poor relative, daughter of a criminal; later, by the smug assurance of the parson and the insensibility of the official when her father is cleared; finally, by the money-serving turncoat eagerness of her suitor. The play is a powerful and honest study of integrity driven by greed and stupidity to desperation and despair.

A NEW WAY TO PAY OLD DEBTS   *Philip Massinger*

There is a proud spirit, a dignity, a sense of human values, in the dramas of Philip Massinger (English, 1583-1640) who came, said Arthur Symons, as "the twilight of the long and splendid day of which Marlowe* was the dawn." Massinger collaborated on a score of dramas with Fletcher,* with Dekker,* and with Beaumont.* He is sole author of some thirty plays, the seven earliest of which are lost, having been used leaf by leaf for baking pie-crust by William Warburton's cook.

Razor sharp in its satire of contemporary manners, and the most popular Elizabethan play after Shakespeare's and Jonson's, is *A New Way to Pay Old Debts,* written about 1625. In this play, according to Allardyce Nicoll, Massinger "has shown his power of depicting boldly limned characters, and his fine knowledge of stage effect. Sir Giles Overreach is a perfect masterpiece, drawn with lines which seem to come between those of the 'humorous' style of Jonson and the individual style of Shakespeare. He is a man, and yet he is a monstrous type . . . *A New Way To Pay Old Debts* is essentially a theatre play; it acts much better than it reads, although its dialogue has a certain straight and rhetorical beauty of its own."

The central situation of this play was drawn from Middleton's *A Trick to Catch the Old One,* but the plot was based upon an actual political scandal of the time (1620), when the Jacobean monopolist and extortioner Sir Giles Mompesson was degraded from knighthood and banished. In the play, the wealthy but avaricious Sir Giles Overreach seeks to marry his daughter, Margaret, to the rich Lord Lovell, and to ruin, and secure the property of, his nephew Wellborn. Lord Lovell and Lady Allworth connive to fool Overreach, who unwittingly consents to his daughter's marriage with young Tom Allworth. When he finds out how he has been deceived, Overreach goes mad and is sent to Bedlam. (In some acting versions, Overreach has a stroke, and dies.) Wellborn gets his property back, and Lord Lovell weds Lady Allworth.

Few roles have been more desired by stars than that of Sir Giles. It was the greatest role of Edmund Kean (1787-1833). A study *The Amazing Career of Sir Giles Overreach,* by Robert H. Ball (1939), is devoted to the history of the part. For a decade, beginning 1816, Edmund Kean, Charles Kemble, and Junius Brutus Booth all essayed Sir Giles, and the reviewers took vehement sides. Looking back at Kean's debut, to the moment of Sir Giles' going mad, the *Theatre* (August 1, 1895) recalled:

"Not a few women, like Lord Byron, went into hysterics; the pit rose as one man and cheered; even the other players, hardened as they must have been in their art, were beside themselves with emotion. Mrs. Glover fainted; Mrs. Horn sobbed over a chair; Munden was so far spellbound that he had to be taken off by the armpits." A decade later, when Kean revived *A New Way to Pay Old Debts* at Drury Lane, his admirers and his detractors created a riot.

A New Way To Pay Old Debts actually won favor slowly; even when revived by Garrick it found no great success. Throughout the nineteenth century, however, it was performed in England almost every year. Edwin Booth brought it to New York in 1849, and kept Sir Giles in his repertoire until 1886, when the *New York Times* (February 17, 1886) reported that he showed Overreach "a man confident of his own power, stopping to use the meanest craft to gain his ends, of course, but never losing the sense of his own dignity and vast importance . . . the death of the usurer was powerful and realistic; the effect of the stroke of paralysis falling suddenly in a moment of violent passion was vividly manifested."

E. L. Davenport essayed the role of Sir Giles in 1871 in Boston, where Booth was also playing it; he took it to New York, and by 1874 had played the part more than 500 times. In 1922, Walter Hampden played Sir Giles.

A New Way to Pay Old Debts was presented in New York, by Equity Library, in 1945, in an arena theatre; George Freedley found it "curiously effective." Of a 1932 production the *London Times* observed that "it tells vigorously an interesting story that appeals to any age."

The money-seeking devices of Sir Giles Overreach seem too obvious to our more circumspect age, but *A New Way to Pay Old Debts* remains dramatically vivid and historically important.

OUR BETTERS   *William Somerset Maugham*

Among the studies of international society by William Somerset Maugham (English, b. 1874), *Our Betters* ranks high. It is a deft and pungent social satire.

In this play, Maugham portrays both title-hunting wealthy Americans and wealth-hunting titled Englishmen. Pearl, now Lady George Grayson, wants to arrange a match with Lord Bleane for her younger sister, Elizabeth. In the quest of social success, Elizabeth observes that spiritual values have been lost. She sees the back-biting, the scandalmongering, the infidelity, and the condescension of these sophisticated wasters toward a simple and happy American couple. She watches the gathering storm in her sister's affair with the dissolute Gilbert Paxton, on whom the Duchesse de Surennes has prior hold. Refusing the hand of Lord Bleane, Elizabeth turns back to the United States and her American sweetheart, Fleming Harvey.

Our Betters opened in New York, March 12, 1917, for a run of 104 performances. The London production which opened September 12, 1923, ran for 548 performances.

New York saw the play again beginning February 20, 1928, with Ina Claire and Constance Collier, for 129 performances. It has been frequently played about the country; Elsa Maxwell acted in it in 1941.

Maugham's dialogue is deft, and apt; it does not so much scintillate with its own wit as light up the characters in finely-barbed satire. The ways of the Americans abroad and their English playfellows are drawn with a lively but firm hand.

The *New York Graphic* (February 21, 1928) called the play "a smart, saucy, and seductive show." At the earlier production, some reviewers used harsh words. Heywood Broun (March 3, 1917) pontificated: "Immorality on the stage becomes indecent when it becomes overt. It also becomes bad art . . . The second, or overt, act of *Our Betters* just about ruins what would otherwise be an amusing entertainment." Broun's indignation perhaps grew partly from a repressed resentment of the kind to which Charles Darnton gave strong voice: "There is nothing so outrageous on our stage as an English play that makes Americans ridiculous." The English in the play are, of course, equally asinine wastrels, and the "immorality" is obviously satirized.

Noting that *Our Betters* had been preceded at the same theatre by the play of the eternal joy-girl, *Pollyanna,* the *New York Sun* wrote that Pollyanna "would excuse the dirt of making smart and often amusing dialogue out of illicit relations on the ground that the lily of a moral is naturally grown in a muddy soil." The "dirt," however, is in the eye of the beholder. The play, as Gilbert W. Gabriel observed, (February 21, 1928) is "in intent and style and beautifully bitter literacy, a good example of that comedy of bad manners which Maugham more or less invented."

Lively and ironic, deftly balanced with an observant mind and an accomplished pen, *Our Betters* pins the social butterflies and ambitious amoralists for our amused but also our enlightened regard.

THE CONSTANT WIFE   *William Somerset Maugham*

This play is a challenge to the double standard of morality. It depicts the charming Constance Middleton, fifteen years wedded to an eminent London surgeon. Providing Constance with an excellent home, John Middleton freely goes his own emotional way. Constance blandly wards off all attemps of relatives and friends to tell her of John's affair with her best friend, Marie Louise Durham; and when Durham himself comes with what he thinks is proof of the liaison, Constance convinces him that he must be mistaken. After he leaves, Constance lets Marie Louise and John know that she has known of their affair all along, but is behaving as a proper, "constant" wife. She then proceeds to make herself self-supporting, and announces to John that she is going to take six weeks' holiday with her old friend Bernard. Chagrined though he is, John sees that he is being given a dose of his own medicine, and he reconciles himself to being a constant husband on Constance's return.

Opening in New York, November 29, 1926, with Ethel Barrymore, *The Constant Wife* was an instant success. The London opening, April 14, 1927, was marred by a ticket error that sent half the pit into the stalls, creating a confusion that blurred the play. Not until ten years later did the London reviewers have proper view of it. Then the *Times* (May 20, 1937) said Maugham "has a story to tell; he has something to say which is both entertaining and, so far as it goes, true." The *Telegraph* of the same date called Maugham "one of the greatest craftsmen of our theatre . . . with brilliant and incisive dialogue."

As a craftsman, Maugham recognized the value of effective curtain incidents. He had ended *The Circle* with ironic laughter; in *The Constant Wife,* the final moments turn upon the husband the full irony of the "enginer hoist with his own petar."

The *Boston Transcript* (November 10, 1928) pointed out that the play appeals to those "preferring the smile of intelligent amusement to the guffaw of knowing derision" and admired the play's "exercises in pure reason . . . neatly decorated with verbal wit usually sardonic, minor ironies, vignettes of manners, contrast of characters." Yet it noted that, when Constance' old sweetheart returns, opportunity fed by jealousy breeds inclination, till, "catching these pebbles of sentiment in her shoe, pure reason goes alimping." This fallibility makes more engaging the portrait of the understanding woman.

The Constant Wife was revived in New York on December 8, 1951, with Katharine Cornell as Constance, Grace George as her mother, and Brian Aherne. In spite of unimaginative direction, the irony and sparkle of the comedy retained their hold.

THE BED BUG   *Vladimir Mayakovski*

Chief of the futurists, Vladimir Vladimirovich Mayakovski (Russian, 1893-1930) kept his eyes ever forward. When the Russian Revolution succeeded, he wanted to wipe out all the theatre of the past. On the first anniversary of the Revolution his *Mystery Bouffe,* November 7, 1918, began by having a group of workers rip down the old-style theatre curtain: henceforth the stage and the auditorium, won by the workers, are one.

Mystery Bouffe, like a medieval mystery, pictures a deluge of Revolution, with the upper classes seeking escape on a second ark. Confining the workers in the hold, they proclaim a Republic, which the workers discover is but a "Czar with a hundred hands." The workers break free; they move to the next world. After what they have endured, hell holds no horrors, but, on the other hand, heaven holds no satisfactions. They return to this world, to a paradise of their own making, the new Commune.

The earthly paradise that in *Mystery Bouffe* is undated but imminent, Mayakovski set fifty years away in *The Bed Bug,* 1929. In his next play, *The Baths,* 1930, he made the interval a hundred years. Before the end of 1930, he committed suicide. During his life, however, Mayakovski was the dramatic prophet of the Communist state. In terms of the theatre, he attained his goal most fully in *The Bed Bug.*

The Bed Bug (translated as *The Bug* in England, with the same meaning), a fantastic comedy in nine scenes, contrasts the Soviet citizens of 1929 and 1979. The first three scenes show us the remnants of the decaying bourgeoisie and some racketeers, including one Prisypkin, an aspiring fellow about to be married and eager to acquire such wealth as one can dishonestly gain under the Soviet system. The guests at the feast get drunk, there is a fire, and all are burned. The firemen flood the house, and the water freezes; Prisypkin, in the cellar, is drowned.

In 1979, in a completely Communist world, the cellar is unearthed; out of the ice, alive, come two 1929 creatures: Prisypkin in his tuxedo and a bedbug. Putting on their gas masks, the U.S.S.R. world-citizens approach these two survivors of an extinct civilization, while in a lecture at once pseudo-scientific and pontifically political, the similarities of the bed-bug and the human parasite are pointed out.

At once a farce and a dramatic lecture on what the good citizen should avoid, *The Bed Bug* has been extremely popular in Russia. It is probably the most effectively dramatized of the Soviet propaganda plays. Meyerhold first directed it; then it swept the country. It has been less successful abroad. Staged in New York in 1931, it held the Sun reviewer (March 20) but briefly: "The first three scenes end in fights, after beginning in shouts. The fourth scene consists of a brief report of a fire in which, as I understood it, all those that had appeared in the first three scenes were burned to death. This seemed such a happy solution of the whole matter, so precisely what any one would have wished for the characters who had appeared in the first scenes, that I did not risk the almost certain anticlimax." Indeed, structurally, the play becomes a lecture, with pointer, specimens, pomposity, and all. Yet, both to Communists and to those for whom Mayakovski could not tear down the curtain, the play has effective satire.

IF I WERE KING   *Justin Huntly McCarthy*

In this glamorously romantic drama by Justin Huntly McCarthy (Irish, 1861-1936), much of the legended life of the French poet François Villon (born 1431) is brought upon the stage. The play begins with a colorful tavern scene in which Villon, after confessing his love for a high-born lady, wounds in a duel the traitor, Thibaut d'Aussigny, Grand Constable of France. King Louis XI, incognito, hears Villon boast how, were he in power instead of Louis Do-Nothing, Dare-Nothing, he would whip the Burgundians. Louis makes Villon Lord Constable for a week, after which, unless the high-born lady take him in love, the poet is to die. During that week, Villon defeats the Burgundians, foils Thibaut's plot to kill the king; Villon's own life is saved when his tavern light-o'-love, Huguette, flings herself in the path of Thibaut's knife; and he wins the love of the lovely Katherine de Vaucelles.

At the end, when his week is up and Villon is on the scaffold, first his mother pleads for him; then Katherine speaks: There may be a thousand reasons, she says, "but the best of reasons for a woman's loving a man is just because she loves him, without rhyme and without reason, because heaven wills it, because earth fulfils it, because his hand is of the right size to hold her heart in its hollow."

Opening in New York, October 14, 1901, for 56 performances, *If I Were King* gave E. H. Sothern his first real hit. Cecilia (Cissie) Loftus, who had eloped with Justin McCarthy in 1894 and divorced him in 1899, was the first Katherine. Margaret Illington opened in the role of Katherine in London, August 30, 1902, for 215 performances. Other Katherines include Florence Reed in 1907 and Julia Marlowe in 1913. Revivals were given in London in 1934 and 1936.

If I Were King was enthusiastically received by the reviewers. *Town Topics*, for instance, declared "*If I Were King* is so exalted in sentiment,

so noble in speech, so gentle and universal in its humanity, and the
diversion of its lighter phases is so invigorating, that one is almost glad
that the author has done nothing to threaten its unquestioned favor
with the general public."

The surge of drama in the Villon story was given its inevitable musical
accompaniment in 1925 when Brian Hooker and W. H. Post wrote *The
Vagabond King*, with music by Rudolph Friml. With Dennis King as
Villon, *The Vagabond King* opened in New York, September 21, 1925,
for 511 performances. The London production, April 19, 1927, reached
480 performances. The musical was played all over Europe; it has been
frequently revived in the United States and in England, and has been
generally well received. The *London Observer* of March 21, 1937, said:
"If you like musical comedy, this one may well seem a masterpiece."
J. Walker McSpadden in *Operas and Musical Comedies* (1946) called
The Vagabond King "one of the best works of this brilliant composer,
and of the contemporary stage."

For its story, the musical closely follows the play. To the tender and
stirring tale, the musical adds equally tender and stirring songs: the
vivid "Song of the Vagabonds," the martial "To Hell With Burgundee,"
the casual "Love For Sale" of Huguette, and the favorite "Only a Rose."

Although the musical version is distinctly enjoyable, there is
swifter surge of noble feeling, delight in derring-do and tender love, in
the poetic romantic drama *If I Were King*.

THE MIDNIGHT REVEL   *Henri Meilhac*

Henri Meilhac (French, 1831-1897) and Ludovic Halévy (French, 1834-
1908) were masters of structure.

They built neat comedy dramas and swift farces, with little concern for character probing, but with every regard for lively situations. As a consequence many of their plays, with or without credit,
have provided the basis, the plot and groundwork, of other works. In
their original form, as they kept breaking upon a delighted public, Meilhac's comedies made half a century laugh. His collaborations with
Ludovic Halévy were produced from 1861 to 1881.

Le Reveillon (The Midnight Revel), 1872, was a frisky farce, which
Haffner and Genée, with music by Johann Strauss (Austrian, 1825-1899),
converted into the operetta *Die Fledermaus (The Bat)*. Opening in
July 1874, *The Bat* achieved only 16 performances, but the next season
it became a hit. It has grown to be the most popular of all light operas
and, as *Life* observed (December 14, 1942), "It remains just about the
prettiest operetta ever written." The boulevardier spirit of Meilhac, his
brilliant and fertile fancy, and the agile turns of his wit, sparkle with
the Strauss music throughout the play.

The story of the play is trickily complicated, with many opportunities
for slily patterned, laughing amours. Baron von Eisenstein, out on his
own recognizance, instead of going to jail decides to go first to Prince
Orlofsky's ball. When Eisenstein doesn't reach the jail, the Warden goes
to Eisenstein's, where the Baron's wife, Rosalinda, is dining familiarly
with Alfredo Allevante, who has serenaded his way into her home. A
true gentleman, Alfredo goes to jail as though he were the husband. But
Rosalinda, masked, goes to the ball, where her own husband madly flirts

with her. Also at the ball is her maid, Adele; dressed in her mistress' finery, she is a pert and pretty lass, and the Prince does more than flirt with her. After the ball, Eisenstein goes to the jail to begin his sentence. When the Warden, who has also been at the ball, finds two men who both say they are Eisenstein, he thinks himself more tipsy than is his wont. The wife is sent for, and after confusion, discovery, recrimination and forgiveness, the curtain descends before a happy audience.

The title, *The Bat,* is drawn from the costume the Baron's friend, the Notary Falke, had worn a while before, when the Baron tricked him into having to go home in broad daylight in that disguise. It is the Notary that persuades the Baron to go to the ball before going to jail, and in the resultant confusion finds his revenge. In the Reinhardt production, the roof of the Warden's office in the jail had the shape of a hovering bat.

After its false start, *The Bat* flew to success. By 1880, it had been played in 171 German theatres. The French (Wilder and Delacourt) wrote their own libretto, as *La Tzigane (The Gypsy).* Its American premiere was in Brooklyn, 1879. Translations of it have taken many names. In London, beginning December 30, 1911, titled *Nightbirds,* it had 133 performances. In New York, it started on August 20, 1912, as *The Merry Countess,* with the Dolly Sisters, and had 129 performances. Opening on October 31, 1929, as *A Wonderful Night* (with one Archie Leach, later somewhat more familiar as Cary Grant), it had 125 performances. On October 14, 1933, it reappeared as *Champagne Sec,* with Peggy Wood, and ran for 113 performances. There have also been *The Masked Ball; Fly-By-Night;* and more. In the meantime, in 1929, with the production freshened and beautified by Reinhardt, *Die Fledermaus* ran for 300 performances in both Berlin and Paris. That production came to New York, October 28, 1942, as *Rosalinda,* with Oscar Karlweis as the Prince, for 521 performances; to London, March 8, 1945, as *Gay Rosalinda,* for 413 performances.

As *Die Fledermaus,* it remains in light opera repertory everywhere. The New York Metropolitan Opera Company gave it a lively production in 1951, with book by Garson Kanin but strained and hard-to-sing lyrics by Howard Dietz. The most successful English rendering of *Die Fledermaus* is that of Ruth and Thomas Martin, first heard in San Francisco in 1942, the biggest hit of the 1949 summer season at Central City, Colorado, and of the 1950, in Cincinnati, Ohio, and on tour throughout the United States, as also the Kanin version, in the fall of 1951.

The delightful music of Oscar Strauss permeates *The Bat,* and gives further touches of charm and beauty to its piquancy, its fun, its colorful frolicking. Among the songs it is hard to choose. "Dove that has escaped" is the romantic serenade that opens Rosalinda's window, if not quite her heart. Other gay tunes are "Come with me to the ball"; a lively drinking song; and the Prince's popular "Each to his own taste, sir! Chacun à son gout!" *The Bat,* fledged from *The Midnight Revel* of Meilhac and Halévy, is deservedly the favorite among light operas.

CARMEN   *Henri Meilhac*

Out of Prosper Merimée's novel *Carmen* (1847), Henri Meilhac and Ludovic Halévy fashioned a play with music by Georges Bizet (1838-

1875), that was called a light opera but has since established itself firmly in all opera repertoires. It was not especially well received on its world premiere in Paris, March 3, 1875; Bizet died thinking it a failure. It had 15 performances in Paris up to February, 1876; then was not heard there for six years. In the meantime, however, it won plaudits around the world. It was played in New York first at the Academy of Music, October 23, 1879. In its first performance at the Metropolitan Opera House, December 20, 1893, Emma Calvé made her tumultuously welcomed debut. She sang the thousandth performance at the Metropolitan on December 23, 1904. Others that have sung the role of Carmen are Olive Fremstad, Rise Stevens, Adelina Patti, Rosa Ponselle, Mary Garden, Geraldine Farrar, and Gladys Swarthout. Carmen is a superbly challenging part, in a fiery play.

The story of *Carmen* is set in Spain, about 1820. Don José, commanding a troop of dragoons in Seville, flirts with Carmen, a gypsy girl working in a cigarette factory. After a fight among the girls, Don José arrests Carmen, but, fallen under her spell, lets her escape. Also under her spell, he insults a superior officer and joins Carmen's mountain friends, a gang of smugglers. José spurns the faithful Michaela, who has led him to his dying mother's bedside. He then watches Carmen, now bored with his jealous attentions, flirting with the famous bull-fighter, Escamillo. As Escamillo is returning successful from the arena, José in jealous fury stabs Carmen to the heart.

Carmen moves with a speed and a passion unusual in opera. It has, at least it had in the original version, moments of dialogue instead of recitative, as well as many memorable airs: especially Carmen's songs "Love is a rebellious bird"; the coquettish "Near the walls of Seville"; "When the gay guitars ring out," a lively gypsy tune; and her more defiant "In vain I sort the cards." There is a vivid opening march of the soldiers; later, a stirring smugglers' march. José has a vigorous song when he cries to Carmen: "You must hear me! This flower you once gave me is dishonored!" Best known of all is the Toreador song of Escamillo, a bravado cock-crowing that shivers along female spines.

The success of *Carmen* has given rise to other tellings of the story. It was presented as straight drama in 1869 both in London (version by Henry Hamilton) and in Boston (version by Marie Doran and Mollie Revel) without success; but Olga Nethersole made a hit in a play version on tour in the United States. A burlesque of the play, *Carmen-Up-to-Date*, by Henry Pettit and George R. Sims, music by Meyer Lutz, ran in London, opening October 4, 1890, for 248 performances. In New York, a Negro version, *Carmen Jones,* which opened December 2, 1943, followed the Bizet score, with book adapted to American Negro life by Oscar Hammerstein 2d, and restored dialogue instead of recitative. This "sizzling sexy saga of a rapacious Dixie wench," as *The Journal of Commerce* aptly called the Billy Rose production, ran in New York for 500 performances with Muriel Smith as Carmen, then toured the country and returned, May 2, 1946, for four weeks at the New York City Center. The cigarette factory was converted into a war-time parachute plant in a Southern town; the tavern became a hot-spot night club, with fantastically swank décor. Don José became Corporal Joe; Michaela became Cindy Lou; the toreador Escamillo became the prizefighter Husky Miller.

But Carmen remained her carefree, flirtatious, fiery self, and all the passion of the story was sustained.

Another recent transformation of Carmen, even more fiery, was into pantomime and dance, choreography by Roland Petit, who also danced Don José, in Les Ballets de Paris company, to the torrid Carmen of Renée Jeanmaire. This dance drama, seen in New York in 1949, turn d Carmen into a savage French apache, with one dance of desire that scorched the accustomed stage.

In its various forms accompanied by music, *Carmen* proves irresistible. As *Le Temps* (March 3, 1925) remarked on its fiftieth anniversary, "It charms the philistine and the cultured alike. It exercises a strange attraction in its mixture of primitive passion, frivolity, and fear. The red flower which the cigarette-maker holds between her teeth has not yet faded. It blooms anew every season." Its appeal strikes basic chords of lust and stormy passions, as well as higher tones of beauty and final atoning calm.

THE ARBITRATION *Menander*

By the time Alexander the Great of Macedon had gained ascendency over all Greece (335 B.C.), the Old Comedy had given way to the New Comedy—that is to say, the gods and heroes, as characters, had been replaced by the upper middle-class citizens of Athens, with their entourage of slaves, parasites, procurers, courtesans, pompous physicians and boastful soldiers. The stories of the plays, however, were not localized, but remained general tales of intrigue, romance with all its difficulties and happy ending—often with a surprise recognition at the close. The setting, too, was generalized: the stage became a city street or public square, with two houses in the background; the action was all outdoors.

In the opinion of the ancients, the greatest writer of the New Comedy was Menander (Greek, c. 342-292 B.C.). Of his hundred-odd plays, sections of three survive: *Samia, The Shearing of Glycera,* and *The Arbitration.* These fragments, said Goethe, "gave me so high an idea of him that I look upon this great Greek as the only man that can be compared with Molière."

Menander's *The Abritration,* written about 300 B.C., is not a farce, but a social problem play, with individualized characters excellently drawn, and with an approach to the interrelationships of the sexes that even today seems enlightened and advanced. The play, moreover, is admirably constructed and rich in thought of the highest moral tone. It is swiftly paced and effectively mounts in interest to an absorbing close.

The story, while intricate in detail, moves clearly along the usual pathway of misunderstanding to surprise recognition. The surprise is not that of the audience; a prologue informs us of the situation in advance. We know that the man who assaulted Pamphila during a festive night, the father of the babe she exposed, is the very man she later marries. With this knowledge, we can watch with amusement the complications that develop, sure that the happy ending will come.

The marriage, as usual in those days, was an arranged one, but the charming Pamphila and the upright, if somewhat stern, Charisius come to love each other. Thus, when Charsius learns of his wife's lapse, he is heartbroken. He moves away and embarks on a life of reckless extravagance; but he leaves untouched the courtesan he hires; he cannot get drunk; he cannot forget; and he cannot shake off his love of his wife. Then he hears his wife's father urge her to divorce the dissolute husband who has abandoned her. This she refuses to do. Her simple trust and integrity work upon her husband's spirit; ashamed of his excesses and transgressions, he determines to seek his wife's pardon. In the meantime, we have seen, step by step interwoven with this action, how the exposed babe is saved, then freed, then (presented by the courtesan) accepted as Charisius' bastard son, and finally recognized as a legitimate son and citizen, cementing the family ties of respect and love.

The Arbitration presents a moving and dramatic story. In the period of Athens' decline, it nobly maintained her best ideals of faith and self-respect and human dignity.

OLD HEIDELBERG   Wilhelm Meyer-Förster

Wilhelm Meyer-Förster (German, 1862-1934), used his own story Karl Heinrich (1899) in writing this romantic play.

Old Heidelberg opened in Berlin on November 22, 1902, took the city by storm and within two months was playing all over Germany and Austria and in Russia. Soon after, it was translated and produced in Poland, Denmark, Sweden, Greece, and Italy. It opened in London, in English, March 19, 1903, for 189 performances, and had revivals there in 1909 and 1925. In New York it was for some years the most popular play at the German Irving Place Theatre. Richard Mansfield played it in English, opening October 2, 1903. It was revived in 1910.

The story is a charmingly nostalgic one. Karl Heinrich, grandson of the King and heir to the throne of Sachsen-Karlsburg, comes from the stiff formality of his early training to spend a year at Heidelberg. There, by the banks of the Neckar, he joins in the student life, and he and Käthie, the pretty maid at the inn, fall in love. After four months of idyllic happiness, Karl is summoned to assume the responsibilities of the throne. Two years later, Kellerman, a tippler from the Heidelberg tavern, arrives at court to claim a promised job. Memories awakened, Karl revisits the college town. The students hail him with formal and solemn respect. Käthie tells him: "I shall marry my cousin; you, your princess. But we shall remember how we loved each other."

Old Heidelberg touched a tender chord. "In its own style the play is a gem," said the Boston Herald of December 22, 1903, "a dim, sad-colored gem, finely cut, perfectly proportioned . . . The author's hand is firm, exact, and cultured in expression, and his constructive skill is considerable. He produces exactly the effects he desires."

The songs can be discussed more fitly in connection with The Student Prince, a musical comedy that Dorothy Donnelly (American, 1880-1928) fashioned from Old Heidelberg, with music by Sigmund Romberg (b. 1887). The musical follows the story closely, with emphasis on the male chorus of students; it has been even more successful in English than the play. Opening in New York, December 2, 1924, it ran for 608 performances and had revivals in 1931, 1936, and in 1943 for 149 performances. The year 1945 marked its twelfth return to Philadelphia, and the musical has had equal popularity in other cities. London saw it in 1926, 1929, and 1944. On its New York premiere, the *New York Times* stated: "It is many a year since so glorious an opera has graced the stage of this city. From beginning to end it was a triumph." The *Sun* reviewer said he had "never heard an opera that was more alive," and the *World* called it "the finest, the most robust, and most stirring of all American light operas."

Traditional student songs are in both *Old Heidelberg* and *The Student Prince*. Many a member of the audience, beneath his breath, joins in as the chorus swells with "Gaudeamus igitur"; with the drinking song "Ergo bibamus"; with the traditional "Old Heidelberg"; with the universal "Hoch soll er leben!" To these the musical added a student's march; a "rough house" song; and love ditties such as the Serenade and the tender "Deep in my Heart."

There are moments of comedy in the play, drawn in good part from the contrast between Karl's formal valet, Lutz, and the rollicking students. Karl's old tutor, Dr. Juttner, dies while at his alma mater, giving a prior touch of pathos to the final scene between Käthie and Karl. But essentially the power of both *The Student Prince* and *Old Heidelberg* rests in the effective evocation of the spirit of youthful hours, of student ways in college days, in the nostalgia of memories of a happy, wholesome, and love-warmed time.

A TRICK TO CATCH THE OLD ONE   *Thomas Middleton*

Thomas Middleton (English, 1570?-1627) was a prolific playwright, in tragedy, romantic comedy, and political satire. His social satire of greed and intrigue, *A Trick to Catch the Old One*, 1607, the popularity of which led Massinger* to borrow its plot, is Middleton's most enduring drama.

Lucre, an old usurer, maintaining that it is better to be fleeced by one's kin than by strangers, secures to himself the property of his spendthrift nephew, Witgood. The latter persuades a courtesan to impersonate a rich widow; Lucre and a rival usurer, Hoard, at once compete for the new prize. Playing one against the other, Witgood recovers his property from his uncle, marries the courtesan to Hoard, and mends his profligate ways.

The picture of London life in *A Trick to Catch the Old One* is colorful and drawn with a swift, unerring hand. The play moves rapidly through a well-knit story. Swinburne praised "the vivid variety of incident and intrigue, the freshness and ease and vigour of the style, the clear straightforward energy and vivacity of the action."

The play was quite popular in its time, and had numerous revivals through the seventeenth century. Unlike most of Middleton's plays, much of it is in prose which retains the vitality of its tumultuous period.

DEATH OF A SALESMAN   *Arthur Miller*

With *Death of a Salesman,* Arthur Miller (American, b. 1915) at one stroke won the Critics' Circle Award, the Pulitzer Prize, the Antoinette Perry Award, and the distinction of having written the only play ever selected for circulation by the Book-of-the-Month-Club. The demand for tickets before and long after the Broadway opening on February

10, 1949, exceeded capacity and helped precipitate an official investigation of the fees charged by ticket brokers. The commonly careful John Mason Brown went so far as to say that the play "provides one of the modern theatre's most overpowering evenings."

In *Death of a Salesman,* many reviewers saw a searing indictment of the American way of life. It opens with Willy Loman's return to his Brooklyn home after an abortive start on a selling trip. Willy is sixty-three, and just cannot summon the concentration and the will to go on selling, even to go on driving his car. Flash-backs give glimpses of happier days, when Willy's two boys were growing up: Biff, the high school football star, and Happy, the worshipful younger brother. Their mother, Linda, was also happy; the household was thriving. Then Biff, rushing to his father in a crisis, discovers him with another woman, calls him a "phony," turns into a petty thief, and leaves home. Biff might have found himself as a farmer, but some family bond always brings him back, to quarrel with his father and leave again. Happy has grown into a complacent, self-centered lecher. Linda, loving and understanding her husband, defends him against the contempt of his sons, but can bring nothing to sustain Willy, as he wonders vaguely and glumly about the downward turn of life. Finally, his salesmanship slumps so low that he cannot even persuade himself to go on living. His insurance, he comes to think, makes Willy "worth more dead than alive."

The story is presented through a succession of scenes that flow freely through time. Some are in "the present"; some are in the past as it was (as the author sees it); some, apparently, are in the past as Willy sees it; and some scenes are entirely in Willy's imagination. Just which are which, it is sometimes hard to tell; but this physical confusion is important as a symptom of deeper confusions in the play.

The very theme of *Death of a Salesman* is a matter of sharp difference of opinion. John Mason Brown declared the play "the most poignant statement of man as he must face himself to have come out of our theatre." Miller himself, in commenting on the play, said: "Willy is Everyman who finds he must create another personality in order to make his way in the world, and therefore has sold himself." On the other hand, Miller has told the present writer that he had discussed his play with Harold Clurman, and that subsequently Clurman, in *Tomorrow* (May, 1949), had expressed Miller's intention "better than I could myself." Clurman was emphatically with those that saw a wide social significance in *Death of a Salesman.* The play, he declared, "is a challenge to the American dream . . . of business success . . . Salesmanship implies a certain element of fraud: the ability to put over or sell a commodity regardless of its intrinsic usefulness . . . The death of Arthur Miller's salesman is symbolic of the breakdown of the whole concept of salesmanship inherent in our society."

The critics did not agree. Willy's story is one of an individual's incompetence, not of society's insufficiency. Willy does not fail because his standards are false; he just fails to meet his own standards. Other men, he declares, can sit and get orders by 'phone; but he has to have his mistress pass him through to her boss. This is no criticism of salesmanhip. In fact, Willy's family life with his growing sons is very happy. The seeds of corruption in it are by no means inherent in Willy's occupation or ideals; they are, simply, flaws in Willy.

More than confusion and the failure to establish its theme mars *Death of a Salesman*. Willy's killing himself, telling himself it's to help Linda financially, is a dumb, pathetic step, that gives none of the exaltation of tragedy. Most of the minor figures in the play are left uncomfortably undeveloped; Willy's boss, his mistress, his brother, who's made a fortune in Alaska and in the jungle, are cartoon characters.

Most of the reviewers, nevertheless, praised the play. Brooks Atkinson called it "one of the finest dramas in the whole range of the American theatre"; John Chapman, "One of those unforgettable times in which all is right and nothing is wrong"; Robert Garland, "One of the lasting rewards that I, as a professional theatre-goer, have received in a long full life of professional theatregoing." The supersalesman, W. Howard Fuller, president of The Fuller Brush Company, in *Fortune* (May, 1949), sought to explain why salesman Willy Loman's story had such wide appeal: "Nearly everyone who sees it can discover some quality displayed by Willy and his sons that exists in himself and his friends and relatives. It is this close identity between the audience and the characters that lends such poignancy to the tragedy."

A few reviewers seemed disturbed by the play's success. Atkinson later remarked (May 29, 1949) that seeking the basis for its favorable reception would be "a job in mass *psychiatry* terrible to contemplate." Yet Dr. Frederic Wertham inquired before interviewing Arthur Miller for the *New York Times Book Review* (May 15, 1949): "What is the basis of its universal success? The people have spoken. But have they listened?" They attended, at any rate, 742 performances in New York. Lee J. Cobb, Gene Lockhart, Albert Dekker, and Thomas Mitchell in succession played the role of Willy Loman.

Partisan Review (June, 1949) saw in the play "an intellectual muddle and lack of candor that regardless of Mr. Miller's conscious intent are the main earmark of contemporary fellow-traveling . . . This is a very dull business which departs in no way that is to its credit from the general mediocrity of our commercial theatre . . ." George Ross in *Commentary* (February, 1951), discussing the Yiddish production of *Death of a Salesman*, had this tó say: "What one feels most strikingly is that this Yiddish play is really the original, and the Broadway production was merely Arthur Miller's translation into English." He suggested that Miller "make another try at a more imaginative translation of his material into English; the attempt might result in a more authentic and, by that same token, a more moving play." *Death of a Salesman*, in truth, is even closer than the early works of Clifford Odets* to the sob-stuff of the Yiddish drama.

Harold Hobson struck at this mixture of James Barrie and *Esquire* when he said that the play's "fusion, or confusion, of them is its greatest artistic defect, yet it may prove again its financial salvation. For the world is full of people who like to eat their cake and have it."

British reviewers were cool toward a London production which opened July 28, 1949, for 204 performances. Ivor Brown reported in the *New York Times* (August 28, 1949): "There were cheers for Paul Muni, but no tears for Willy Loman . . . Its pathos is more easily recognized in Brooklyn than in Balham . . . The play has an immediate, and specious, appeal because it makes the little man the hero . . . It is Lowman, not Highman, who throws Broadway into compassionate lamentation."

Viewed from overseas, *Death of a Salesman* lacked universality as well as sharpness of outline. Arthur Miller has exemplified, rather than caught into conscious art, the muddled strivings, the distorted rather than false ideals, and the consequent confused sense of guilt, of our time.

MR. PIM PASSES BY   *Alan Alexander Milne*

This play, written in 1919, first drew wide attention to the gentle whimsy of A. A. Milne (English, b. 1882). His *Wurzel-Flummery*, 1917, and *Make-Believe*, 1918, introduced the Barriesque vein without the full blowth of Barrie's charm.

Mr. Pim causes quite a commotion among the Mardens as he "passes by." Come from Australia with a letter of introduction, he tells a story of a scoundrelly drunkard on the boat, one Jacob Telworthy. George Marden is aghast, for this is the name of his wife Olivia's first husband, reported dead. Olivia loves George, but she's not especially pleased with the way he takes the news. When Mr. Pim mentions that the man died at Marseilles, and George wants the Church and the Law to renew the stamp of sanction on their union, Olivia exacts, first, a honeymoon in Paris, and then George's consent to the marriage of his niece Dinah and the impecunious artist Brian Strange. Mr. Pim, after his departure, returns to tell Olivia that his memory had tricked him; the name of the man he had met was not Telworthy, but "Polwhittle, Ernest Polwhittle."

This trifle is lifted into significance by the smiling love of Olivia, who waits for George to tell her that he loves her and Telworthy be damned. The play manages, as the *New York Clipper* of March 9, 1921, said, "to strike the emotions under the camouflage of foolery."

The London production, January 5, 1920, was a hit, as was the revival, February 20, 1928, with Marie Tempest. The *Stage* of February 23, 1928, praised the witty lines and odd twists of situation, and the oaks of emotion that spring from the acorns of event: "For what could be more trivial —or more stupendous—than the irresponsible utterances of this same muzzy-minded Mr. Pim, whose rare wanderings in and out of the play are so big with consternation or joy? The whole thing is as light as thistledown, and the strange and rather sad old gentleman seems to be able to blow it about whenever he chooses."

The Theatre Guild gave *Mr. Pim Passes By* a superb production on February 28, 1921, which had a run of 140 performances, with Laura Hope Crews, Phyllis Povah, Dudley Digges, Helen Westley, and Erskine Sanford. The last three were in the April 18, 1927, revival with Helen Chandler and Gavin Muir. Erskine Sanford appeared in the play again in 1938, with Uta Hagen. *Mr. Pim Passes By* has had many productions throughout the English-speaking world. I have found only one voice of disapproval, when on the brink of a World War, the *Sydney Herald* in Australia (June 5, 1939), shook its head over the "verbal padding used to fill out a cockleshell plot . . . too whimsically superficial in these days of realism and disillusionment."

THE TRUTH ABOUT BLAYDS   *A. A. Milne*

With less whimsy than in *Mr. Pim Passes By**, A. A. Milne set a serious situation into a comic frame in *The Truth About Blayds*, 1921. The

London Times of December 21, 1921, called the play "comic, both in the vulgar and in the strict sense: [Mr. Milne] provokes hearty laughter, and also calls up the serious emotions that are not too serious to be within the province of comedy."   In two ways—these only, for their moods are wholly unlike—*The Truth About Blayds* resembles Ibsen's *The Wild Duck**: both plays picture the havoc wrought by a sudden revelation, in a household dwelling comfortably upon a lie: and both seem to point the moral that not all truths are always to be told.

The play concerns ninety-year old Oliver Blayds, who is venerated as the last of the great Victorian poets, their equal and their friend. His daughter Isobel, who has relinquished the man she loves, the critic Royce, to devote her life to her father, comes from the latter's death-bed to announce to the family his confession: all his poetry, save the one book the critics damned, has been stolen from manuscripts left him by a long-dead friend.

The reactions of the family give rich irony to the play. Son-in-law Blayds-Conway, who is planning a biography of the genius, brushes the confession aside, and there is a condescending reference to "another Shakespeare-Bacon controversy." Isobel, indignant at having wasted her life on a fraud, wants to give the truth to the world at once, and rehabilitate the dead genius, Jenkins. Blayd's works have brought them all a tidy sum; the news that Jenkins had made his best friend, Blayds, his heir eases their financial worry, but does not ease their consciences. With the thought that the poetry, not the name of the author, is what matters, they decide not to waken scandal. Isobel finally accepts her Royce, and Blayds-Conway settles down to his biography, in which he promises to make reference to the Jenkins shadow in Blayds' background: "it is our duty to tell the whole truth about that great man." The satire is particularly effective in the way each relative completely loses all human feeling, all sense of personal relationship, in regard to old Blayds. He is just an antique; the question is, whether or not he is genuine.

The Truth About Blayds was a hit on both sides of the ocean. London saw it, December 20, 1921, with Irene Vanbrugh, Dion Boucicault, and Norman McKinnel. The *Telegraph* said it had "less sparkle than usual because there is more depth." In New York, the play opened on March 14, 1922, with O. P. Heggie, Alexandra Carlisle, Leslie Howard, Frieda Inescort, Gilbert Emery and Ferdinand Gottschalk. Alexander Woollcott called it "an engrossing play . . . wise, finely wrought." Percy Hammond remarked: "Any plagiarist who could steal, as Blayds did, his friend Jenkins' *Ode To Truth* and other works, and live to be ninety in the spurious glamour of their fame, is himself a poet of distinction. It was a beautiful achievement in mendacity, and we were all glad when it was decided last night to let it stand."

The play was revived in New York, April 11, 1932, with O. P. Heggie, Effie Shannon, Pauline Lord, and Ernest Lawford.

Pauline Lord also acted, the next autumn, in a sort of obverse story to *The Truth About Blayds*, the very successful *Prenez garde à la peinture* (1932), by René Fauchois (b. 1882) which within the year Emlyn Williams* adapted for England, and Sidney Howard* for the United States. In New York, as *The Late Christopher Bean,* it opened October 31, 1932, with Pauline Lord, Walter Connolly, Beulah Bondi, Clarence

Derwent, and Ernest Lawford. The English version (with Sir Cedric Hardwicke) was set in Wales; the American, in New England. It pictures Abby, the faithful drudge in a country doctor's family, the only one who had befriended the poor and neglected painter, Christopher Bean, until he died. Then a critic hails him as a genius; art dealers rush upon the doctor's family, whose greed is awakened. They rescue Bean's paintings from plugging leaks in the roof, from serving as backs to the chromos the doctor's daughter made. Abby resists their pressure to give up Bean's portrait of her; it turns out that she has eighteen further authentic Beans. It turns out, further, that the paintings the doctor has been setting the dealers at odds to buy are also Abby's; for she is the widow of the late Christopher Bean.

Pauline Lord played Abby again in 1938. June Walker assumed the part in 1934, with Geoffrey Kerr and Montagu Love; again in 1939. Others who have appeared in this popular play are Helen Mencken, Charlotte Greenwood, and Catherine Alexander. It has been a favorite of colleges and community theatres.

The Truth About Blayds remains Milne's most serious drama, an ironic comedy that lays bare the personal interest behind pretense.

COMUS   *John Milton*

Written by John Milton (English, 1608-1674) in 1634 as a masque, *Comus* was played at Ludlow Castle on September 29, 1634, to celebrate the inauguration of the Earl of Bridgewater as Lord President of Wales. Musician Henry Lawes was the Attendant Spirit; the Lady and her brothers were played by three children of the Earl.

Comus was frequently performed during the eighteenth and nineteenth centuries, and has often been revived. Among those that have played in it are James Quin and Mrs. Cibber; Peg Woffington; Mrs. (Anne) Spranger Barry; Mrs. Siddons, with Charles Kemble; Kemble with Ellen Tree; Madame Vestris; William C. Macready and Helen Faucit; Nigel Playfair; Phyllis Neilson-Terry; and Fay Compton. Its first performance in America was at the John Street Theatre in New York on June 21, 1773. In England its three hundredth anniversary was celebrated by a performance at Ludlow Castle. In the 1930's, annual outdoor summer productions were given; the *London Times* (July 21, 1935) called *Comus* "the most beautiful presentation at the Open Air Theatre," and in 1937 (July 22) referred to it as "an established favorite."

Comus is a deity invented by Milton, the son of Bacchus and Circe. In Milton's pastoral drama, a Lady, separated from her brothers in a forest, comes upon Comus reveling with his kind. Like Circe, Comus has a drink that transforms humans into beasts. He is pressing this upon the unwilling Lady, when her brothers, warned by the Attendant Spirit (in the form of the Shepherd Thyrsis), dash in and disperse Comus and his crew. The Lady is still held in Comus' enchanted chair; to release her, the Spirit summons Sabrina, goddess of the river Severn nearby. After an ode of thanks to Sabrina, the Lady and her brothers return to Ludlow Castle.

The story of Comus was in part suggested by Spenser's *The Faerie*

Queene, of which Book II ends with a Platonic image based on Circe and her beasts and Book III has, in Amoret, a kindred picture of chastity triumphant over lust. The underlying philosophy of *Comus* is a Christianized Platonism; true love abides in Heaven; earthly virtue is a discipline prerequisite to its enjoyment.

James H. Hanford in *John Milton, Englishman* (1949) suggested that *Comus* was Milton's deliberate reply to the libertine philosophy of his fellow student, Thomas Randolph: "In *The Muse's Looking Glass,* which Milton may well have seen performed, it is reasoned that Nature's bounty is an invitation to enjoyment and that he who would be continent commits a sullen injury against her. Comus rehearses this very argument, thereby prompting the Lady to open her virgin lips in chastity's defence. If the poet had indeed been offended by Randolph in his Cambridge days, to exhibit him as the corrupt son of Circe and Bacchus, confuted in his own palace by the voice of innocence and truth, would have been a very proper and a very Miltonian revenge. But there were many other Randolphs, and Milton is indeed standing against the whole lewd tradition of libertine and erotic verse."

Comus was published by Henry Lawes in 1637, as "so lovely and so much desired that the often copying of it hath tired my pen." In 1937, when it appeared in a beautiful Nonesuch Edition, the *Observer* called it "a poem in which more, I think, than in any other of Milton's, his formative and defining manipulation of our mother tongue is to be felt," and added: "However deeply impelled he may have been to read luxurious nobility a moral lesson, a Maske must be a Maske, and, for their dramatic purpose, the speeches in *Comus,* in all their rhetorical perfection, are almost all labored and too long." This judgment from the book, however, runs counter to that from the stage.

Through the years, *Comus* has been as popular on the British stage as Shakespeare's *Merry Wives of Windsor** and *As You Like It**. Its mood, with its reflections on morality and life, is akin to that of *The Tempest**. In form, *Comus* is a pastoral drama, a masque; in thought, it is a presentation of the power of virtue; in beauty, it is a poetic gem harmoniously set onstage.

SAMSON AGONISTES   *John Milton*

The final great poem of blind John Milton, *Samson Agonistes* (Samson Wrestling), 1672, though in dramatic form, was not, like his *Comus**, intended to be played. It was, however, produced in London on April 7, 1900, and in 1908, 1935, and 1938. The story is the familiar one of the Bible (*Judges* XVI). In prison at Gaza, blind Samson is visited by his Jewish friends, who form the Chorus, then by his old father, Manoa, who still hopes for his release, and by Delilah his wife, who asks forgiveness, but reveals herself still his evil spirit. Taunted by Harapha, a strong man of Gath, Samson is taken to the temple of Dagon, for the sport of the Philistines celebrating there. A messenger bears word of Samson's destruction of the temple, which took the Philistines down with him in death.

Following the pattern of a Greek tragedy (with chorus, and with action not presented but reported) *Samson Agonistes* also follows the spiritual course of Milton's life. Like Samson, Milton felt that he was

guilty of that noblest of tragic faults—hybris, rebellious pride. Like
Samson, Milton had to walk in darkness, stumble in the Valley of Humiliation, learn that God doth not need either man's work or His own gifts:
through full submission he might come again to serve. In Samson's
travail we find "the inner agony of Greek tragedy in its darker moments"
until the Greek catharsis is achieved.

On the title page of the play's text Milton quotes Aristotle's definition: "Tragedy is the imitation of a serious action . . . through pity and
fear effecting a purgation [catharsis] of such emotions."

It is the need of submission to the Lord that makes Samson seem to
some a passive, undramatic figure. Writing in the *Saturday Review* of
Dec. 19, 1908, Max Beerbohm denied the play any dramatic quality:
"Even Dalila, the one dramatically imagined person in the play, has a
taste for copybook headings." However, James H. Hanford, in his
John Milton, Englishman (1949), had this to say: "The resolution of
conflict is on a different level from anything we have met elsewhere in
Milton's work. There is no God from a machine. Samson accomplishes
his restoration to favor by his own effort. He is dynamic even in be-
wailing his hard lot or confronting the image of his guilt. His final
act, though felt to be divinely instigated, is yet an act of passion . . . It
is not right reason which triumphs, but the will of man."

Milton, as Cromwell's Latin Secretary, was opposed both to the
Catholic Church and to monarchy. His feeling against the latter rings
through the drama.

Samson Agonistes is a great poem cast in dramatic form. Its chief
classical model is the *Prometheus Bound** of Aeschylus, which it follows
in majesty of conception and character, as well as in general form, even
in such matters as having one character lengthily alone onstage. Like
Aeschylus, Milton achieves poetry of the highest order in *Samson Agonistes*. The play's ending rises to theatrical power. "The climax was
made exciting," declared the *London Times* of April 11, 1938, "by a
breathless but brilliant recitative effort on the part of the Messenger."
The best appreciation of *Samson Agonistes* as a stage piece is probably
that of the *Times* a few years earlier (July 24, 1935): "There is the
grandeur of the poetry . . . a grandeur which Milton himself never
surpassed, and there is also the intrinsic interest of feeling everywhere
in the play the poet's final reflections on his own experience, his blindness, his unhappy marriage, and the defeat of his spiritual and secular
ideals . . . While Samson laments in exquisitely subtle monologues over
what has passed, slowly forms the resolve to do some great deed and
steadily establishes the theme that man is regenerated by the use of his
will to resist temptation, the stage is more or less static . . . except in
the closing scene, which is magnificent in its swift drama."

The redemption of man through the exercise of his will, however
static the stage, is a dynamic conception and a powerful motivating
force. In *Samson Agonistes,* expressed in majestic poetry, the integrity,
the thought, and the feeling of Milton reach their dramatic height.

BUSINESS IS BUSINESS   *Octave Mirbeau*

The drive of a captain of finance, who puts success and power above
all else, is vividly, caustically shown in *Les Affaires sont les affaires
(Business is Business)*, 1903, by Octave Henri Marie Mirbeau (French,

1850-1917). A success in Paris, the play came to New York, in translation by Robert Hichens, September 19, 1904; and to London, translated by Sydney Grundy, May 13, 1905, with Beerbohm Tree.

The action of the play takes place at the chateau de Vauperdu, the country estate of the financier Isidore Lechat (the London version called him Isidore Izard). Once in jail and twice bankrupt, Lechat has risen by shady means to be the money king of Paris. He is no petty money-grubber; he believes in the mission of the great man of finance. His dealings have given railways, factories, and many jobs to the people. The aristocrats, the Porcellets, for instance, were bandits when they first wrested power from the people; the great financier today is a philanthropist.

This belief enablet Lechat unscrupulously to grind down individuals for his own good. Is not his good that of the state? He holds the Marquis de Porcellet tied in mortgages which he will release when his daughter Germaine marries the Marquis' son. Lechat's own son, Xavier, has all his father's unscrupulousness, with a pettier selfishness and without his father's vitality and indomitable will. Lechat's wife, always worried that the servants are robbing her, would trade their vast and formal estate for a cosy house with a little garden, and one servant whom she could keep under her eye.

Germaine loves her father's engineer, Lucien Garraud, who, broken by Lechat's double dealing, commits suicide; between her despairing sobs, Germaine cries wildly "Les affaires sont les affaires." The Marquis humbly consents to his son's marriage into the Lechat family, but Germaine, pouring out her hatred of her father and of his way of life, scorns the proposal, exclaiming, "I have a lover." Lechat drives her out, and she goes gladly. Meanwhile Lechat's son, Xavier, is killed in an auto accident. Lechat has a stroke. Two financial speculators arrive, hoping to trap the troubled man; he suspends his sorrow to outmanoeuvre them. The body of his son arrives; he continues to dictate, has the financiers sign his terms, then goes to look on his dead son, unremorseful, undefeated: big business, ruthless, concentred, proud.

The character of Lechat gives *Business Is Business* its power and its distinction. Neatly, the author has made him no villain, but a man proud of his mission: amassing power, spreading employment and comforts across the world. Neatly Lechat is shown at the business of getting the better of his associates. In a single flow of shrewdness, to have a nobleman as his son-in-law, he browbeats his unwilling daughter, flares out at his unhelpful wife, and wheedles the hesitant marquis. Since his wife is not the sort to flash in diamonds, Lechat is pleased, too, at the extravagant expenditures of his son. Lechat is the typical self-made man, "the modern billionaire." The *New York Dramatic Mirror* described him as "a citizen of nowhere and the curse of everywhere."

There were objections to the quality of the English adaptation of *Business Is Business*. The *London Leader* (May 15, 1905) stated that what is in French "a serious study of the character of a type of modern financier, vain and vulgar, but with a touch of greatness, becomes an almost farcical exaggeration, a fantasia on the grotesque." Reporting on the Paris production, the *London Telegraph* (April 21, 1903) said: "Full of the caustic and scathing humour which has always been M. Mirbeau's forte, it is well built up from the purely technical point of view of the stage, and . . . has real dramatic interest of situation as well as effectiveness of character study and dialogue."

Business Is Business has all the theatric power of a gripping melodrama of love and business, as well as a vivid dramatic portrait of the sort of financial wizard that is capitalism's ornament and curse.

THE NEW YORK IDEA   *Langdon Mitchell*

Although the cast of *The New York Idea,* when it opened in New York on November 19, 1906, included Emily Stevens, George Arliss, and Dudley Digges, the play is usually associated with Minnie Maddern Fiske as the fetching divorcee, Cynthia Karslake. Even before the Broadway run, her work was hailed. The *Chicago Record Herald* of Oct. 16, 1906, declared: "Pathos springs from laughter, and reverts to it, in the twinkling of Mrs. Fiske's eyes . . . Mrs. Fiske played with her audience —tossed laughter to it as she might in mischievous frolic have tossed thistles to stick on the garments of self-satisfaction." The play is a mixture of merry comedy and satire on divorce.

Langdon Mitchell (American, 1862-1935), son of the physician and novelist, S. Weir Mitchell, was basically serious in his intent. "The humor is only incidental," he stated in the *Boston Transcript* of January 19, 1907. "It is only such humor as happened to come to me, spontaneously evolved from the situation . . . I do not consider it a funny play but, on the contrary, a very serious one . . . The essence of this comedy sermon of mine is contained in Karslake's line: 'Ours was a premature divorce, and you are in love with me still'." Despite Mitchell, and despite the appalling increase in the divorce rate since it was written, the play holds to this day because of the humor of its situations.

Cynthia, the divorced wife of Jack Karslake, comes to stay with the family of her fiancé, Judge Philip Phillimore, for a few days before the wedding. She is liked by none of the Judge's conservative Washington Square family. When Cynthia's ex-husband and the judge's ex-wife call on business—Jack wants to sell his horse, named Cynthia K—the relationships have to be explained to the English visitor, Sir Wilfred Cates-Darby. Wilfred, who has come to America to marry wealth, is ready to take either of the ladies, but when Vida, the judge's ex-wife, sets her flirtatious cap for Cynthia's ex-husband, Cynthia decides she has to save the susceptible Jack from Vida's lures. In the process, the Karslakes discover that they are still in love. The venerable judge and his reverend brother are left waiting at the altar, and the discovery that the Karslake divorce was not valid, after all, speeds the closing reunion.

When first shown, *The New York Idea* seemed a daring, breath-taking play. The *Chicago News* of October. 16, 1906 called it "decidedly astonishing in its courage and ribald satire . . . The *New York Post*, however, reacted unfavorably to the out-of-town praises: "Instead of the hoped-for comedy . . . there was a sort of farce, or extravaganza . . . pert, audacious, nonsensical, utterly insignificant, and occasionally, unmindful of good taste." The sole aim of this play, the *Post* added, is "to extract laughter out of the least respectable possibilities of a notoriously scandalous institution."

The *New York Dramatic Mirror* of December 1, 1906 deemed *The New York Idea* "a satire of social circumstances, whose ridicule bites as deep and hurts as long as the tragic realism of one of Ibsen's dramas, though it is clothed in the pleasing robe of comedy . . . a marvelously vivid, coherent, and effective work." Later performances—Grace George played it around the land, and it has had frequent amateur and little theatre production—have emphasized the comedy. The satire seems a bit obvious and the characters are not deeply probed, but it remains good fun. As George Freedley said in 1948, *The New York Idea* is still "an amusing and frequently hilarious comedy." Brooks Atkinson was of the same favorable opinion.

Much of the liveliness and lightness of the play springs from the deft and sparkling dialogue. Striking out, lightly but neatly, at hasty divorce when the adage "Marry in haste and divorce in Reno" was beginning to shape the American mores, *The New York Idea,* compared in 1906 to the dramas of Ibsen and Shaw, remains an entertaining study of the eccentricities of smart society.

THE AFFECTED YOUNG LADIES   *Molière (Jean B. Poquelin)*

Jean Baptiste Poquelin (1622-1673)—he took the name Molière when he became an actor—is the greatest French comic dramatist. Indeed, as Saintsbury says in his *History of French Literature,* "If we leave purely poetic merit out of the question, and restrict the definition of comedy to the dramatic presentment of the characters and incidents of actual life, in such a manner as at once to hold the mirror up to nature and to convey lessons of morality and conduct, we must allow Molière the rank of the greatest comic writer of all the world."

An active man of the theatre, Molière was actor, manager, and playwright for his company. For some twelve years, he toured France with the Béjart family in "The Illustrious Theatre Company." On November 14, 1659, the one-act farce *Les Précieuses Ridicules (The Affected Young Ladies)* had its première. When it was played, early in 1660, before Cardinal Mazarin, King Louis XIV leaned incognito on the Cardinal's chair; he gave the company 3,000 livres; and "Monsieur," the King's brother, took the company under his protection. Molière was launched

Les Précieuses Ridicules was the first modern social satire. It ridiculed the feminine coterie then in high repute throughout France. Women such as Madame de Sévigné, Madame de Lafayette, Mademoiselle de Scudéry, gathered all the great figures of the day in their salons, seeking to improve the taste of the time, to avoid extremes of pedantry and vulgarity, to lend elegance to language and to manners.

Deriding the excesses of such gentlewomen, *Les Précieuses Ridicules* portrays two affected ladies come to Paris, where they spurn their lovers, seeking more delicate gallants. The lovers have their valets masquerade as gentlemen. They are greeted by the ladies in this fashion: "I beg you, Monsieur, do not be inexorable to this easy chair, which has been opening its arms to you for a quarter of an hour; satisfy its desire to embrace you." The valets match the affected talk of the ladies with grandiose absurdities, until the lovers, returning, force the valets to unmask—and properly lesson the ladies.

Mascarille, the comic valet, was acted by Molière; by Jodelet; most effectively in recent years by Coquelin (Benoit Constant Coquelin, 1841-1909). When he is unmasked, Mascarille takes off waistcoat after waistcoat (as does the gravedigger in *Hamlet**) in perennial comedy.

The satire struck home. All fashionable Paris attended the open-ing, but the coterie was cold; the play was banned for a fortnight. Molière protested that he was attacking only excess. After the King showed his favor, the play reopened and played to crowded houses, twice daily, at double prices, for four months. Amused audiences have rejoiced in its fresh fun and pungent satire ever since. But the hostility of the nobles, against the "presumptuous player," Molière, pursued the play-wright to his grave.

Everywhere *Les Précieuses Ridicules* has proved a delight. Of an American production, the *New York Dramatic Mirror* of October 13, 1888, reported: "An admirable skit . . . a bit of grotesque exaggeration of amazing proportions."

When *Les Précieuses Ridicules* was played in 1938, the *Post* called it "hilarious mockery"; in the same year, a copy of the first edition brought £880 in London. "Les Compagnons," of Montreal, played the farce in Boston and in New York in 1946.

A somewhat different attitude toward the satire is urged by Ashley Dukes. Writing for *Theatre Arts* (August, 1937) he said "In the appar-ent realism of Molière the most important thing is its poetic fabric . . . I should say that the comedies of Molière never moralize, in the usual sense, and we must see in them quite simply the most perfect expression of the French spirit, a new form of what Rabelais called *pantagruelisme* —a certain gaiety preserved in defiance of fortuitous events—an attitude of mind, which is distinctly superior to a moral."

There may be exaggeration rather than photography in *Les Pré-cieuses Ridicules,* but there is essential truth in its capture of preten-tiousness and continuing delight in its good-natured mockery.

THE SCHOOL FOR HUSBANDS   *Molière*

Paris saw the premiere of this exuberant comedy in June 1661.

Taking stock types from the commedia dell' arte—the lover, the valet, the pair of pretty girls, the outspoken maid—and hints from Terence's *The Brothers,* from Boccaccio, and from Lope de Vega, this play is yet fresh and original. Molière works into its hackneyed story a true, though comic, study of contemporary characters and attitudes. The sturdy, com-mon-sense citizen, frequent in the later plays, first appears here, to hold the balance of reason against excesses and passions.. Molière, says Brander Matthews, "made a more or less farcical complication carry social criticism, vivid and veracious."

In *The School For Husbands,* we meet Sganarelle, originally played by Molière. He has a ward, Isabelle (played by young Armande Béjart, whom Moliére married in 1662); Sganarelle, wishing to marry his ward, holds her in a tight circle of domestic tyranny, from which she is eager to escape to a lover's arms. Sganarelle's brother Ariste is equally in love with his ward, Léonore, and by his liberal treatment wins her af-fectionate regard. But love proves stronger than duty, and shrewder than guardians.

Voltaire regarded the play's movement as "probable, natural, and what is more, extremely comic." It seemed still charming and amusing in the version Arthur Guiterman and Lawrence Langner made for the

Theatre Guild, produced in New York in 1933, with Osgood Perkins and
June Walker, and the dancers Doris Humphrey and Charles Weidman.
For a tercentenarian, *The School For Husbands* has much vitality.

THE SCHOOL FOR WIVES   *Molière*

Produced in Paris in December 1662, this highly amusing play has
a story artfully woven for expectancy, suspense, and surprise.

Three characters in the play are excellently developed. Arnolphe
(originally played by Molière) is a man of forty, who has raised the girl
Agnes in sweet and simple innocence to be his wife. In a dozen amusing
soliloquies, Arnolphe reveals himself to us; jealous but not a dupe, to
awaken our laughter and sympathy. Arnolphe is, as noted by Paul
Benichon in *Morals of the Grand Century* (1948), "the most thoroughly
revealed figure Molière has given us of the bourgeois in love."

Agnes' very innocence, however, defeats Arnolphe. For when young
Horace makes love to her, she knows no reason why she should not respond. She is completely frank when Arnolphe questions her. Horace,
too, tells the old man of all his meetings with the ward of "M. de la
Souche", unaware that he is talking to that very man. The situations are
superbly handled—so deftly, in fact, that Voltaire insisted the play seems
to be all action when it's really all narrative, and Sainte-Beuve mar-
velled how interest is maintained in a five-act love story when the
audience doesn't see the lovers meet until the middle of the last act!

Through sycophant writers and rival theatrical companies, nobles
hostile toward Molière denounced the play on three grounds. Listing
a few remarks of double meaning, they called it indecent; in that it
seemed to approve revolt against one's lawful guardian, they called it
immoral; and, as Arnolphe's list of commandments for a wife might be
construed as a parody of a sermon, they called it impious. In the eyes
of Louis XIV, however, such satire served to strengthen his power, now
firmly held against the nobles. On the list of annual pensions in 1663
were Corneille (2,000 livres as "the foremost dramatic poet of the
world"), young Racine (800 livres, as "French poet"), and—the only
actor included—Molière (1,000 livres, as "excellent comic poet"). When
the King asked which writer under his reign had most honored France,
the poet and law-giver of the drama, Boileau, answered: "Molière." Yet
Molière saw himself not merely as a dramatist, but fully as a man of the
theatre. When he was offered membership in the French Academy
if he would stop acting, he refused. The seat was given to Racine.

The School for Wives was first performed in America at New York's
John Street Theatre on May 8, 1788. London saw it in the same year
with English setting and names. More recently, it was presented in New
York, in French, in 1933, by the Abbey Theatre in Dublin in 1934, and
in Montreal, then in New York, with Louis Jouvet in 1951.

To the many contemporary objections to this play, Molière answered
with a one-act prose comedy, *Critique of The School For Wives*, which
opened in Paris on June 1, 1663. A series of conversations, with characters neatly contrasted, of marvelous variety and vivacity, this "dia-
logued essay in criticism", remarked Brander Matthews, "is one of the
most adroit and characteristic of Molière's comedies." The *Critique*
evoked a number of responses, published, or performed by a rival com-

pany at the Hotel de Bourgogne; and Louis XIV, in his first direct command, ordered Molière to retort. He had a week's notice before presenting what he called (October 14, 1663) the *Impromptu de Versailles*. This ingenious handling of the problem begins with Molière's telling members of the company they are to perform. They suggest postponement; he says they must defer to the King's command. Then we watch Molière, the stage manager, conducting a rehearsal, telling the company what and how to act; Molière, the author, presenting his writing creed; and Molière, the man, in dignity defending himself against personal abuse. One character remarks that the best answer to criticism is another good play. (And, indeed, thereafter Molière never again responded to attacks.) Amid these displays of virtuosity, Molière freshened his satire with some lively sallies between man and wife (his own wife rejoined the company for the *Critique*, after bearing a son, to whom the King condescended to act as god-father). As in the *Critique* and the *Impromptu* Molière showed understanding and dignity in defending his art; so in *The School For Wives* and other plays he sets his own passions and pains in their proper perspective. He was often a victim, but never a dupe. Through his genius, his lapses and sufferings in life become sources of laughter and of a finer perception of truth.

TARTUFFE   *Molière*

On the sixth day of the Versailles Spring Festival of 1664, three acts of *Tartuffe* were presented.

There was at once a howl of protest from the pious; the Queen-Mother exacted a promise that it would never be shown again. After she died, the King authorized its production; it was shown in August, 1667, but with the King off at the wars, the Mayor of Paris closed the play. Not until February, 1669, when the Jesuits and Jansenists had quieted their feud and their fervor in "the Peace of the Church", did *Tartuffe* achieve a run. It was an instant and lasting success. "The best title of Louis XIV to the recollection of posterity," Lord Morley has said, "is the protection he extended to Molière."

What was this play, which roused such pious wrath? Into the home of the substantial citizen Orgon (originally played by Molière) comes cunning, hypocritical Tartuffe, who, palming himself off on an honest and refined family, tries to drive the son away, marry the daughter, corrupt the wife, ruin and imprison the father, and almost succeeds, not by clever plots but, at Taine described it, "by the coarse audacity of his caddish disposition." When Orgon's wife pretends to yield to Tartuffe, in order to let her husband hear, and the hypocrite is exposed, he brazens out the situation. Presenting Orgon's deed of gift, Tartuffe claims the house as his, and only a message from King Louis saves Orgon and sends Tartuffe to prison.

When an Italian company performed *Scaramouche and the Hermit*, Louis XIV said to Condé: "I'd like to know why those that are so scandalized by Molière's play do not object to this *Scaramouche*." Condé replied: "That's because this *Scaramouche* shows up religion and Heaven, about which these gentlemen care nothing; but Molière's comedy shows them up—and this, they will not allow."

The excellent workmanship of *Tartuffe* has won highest praise. The play is simple without being bare, direct without being obvious; it is powerful in conception, unswerving in movement, and, given the characters, inevitable in its situations and turns. Of its opening, Goethe exclaimed: "Only think what an introduction is the first scene! . . . It is the greatest and best thing of the kind that exists." Of the climactic drive, when the exposed Tartuffe turns with renewed demands upon his baffled victims, Brander Matthews wrote: "It is one of the most effective scenes ever shown in a theatre, startling when it comes, and yet perfectly prepared for and immediately plausible." When Molière's company took the play to London in 1879, the French critic Sarcey noted that *Tartuffe* was the easiest, if not the only, play for those unfamiliar with the language to watch with unflagging interest.

Only one great critic has objected to a structural aspect of *Tartuffe*. Taine considered the ending careless, for bringing the King casually in as a *deus ex machina*. Even the dramatic hack, Taine remarked, could tell that "the catastrophe of half of Molière's plays is ridiculous." But Scribe*—the "hack" *par excellence* of Taine's own time, the master of the well-made play—found the ending " has one great merit: without it, we should not have had the play, for Molière would probably not have been allowed to produce it, had he not given the King a role in it . . . Here is an honest man who has bravely served his country, and who, when deceived by the most open and odious of machinations, does not find anywhere, in society or in law, a single weapon wherewith to defend himself. To save him, the sovereign himself must needs intervene. Where can a more terrible condemnation of the reign be found than in this immense eulogy of the King!"

After its first vicissitudes, *Tartuffe* continued to have a varied history. Voltaire commented in 1739: "Scarcely anyone now goes to the *Tartuffe* that once drew all Paris." Napoleon said he'd never have permitted even the first performance of the play, yet he saw it several times, preferring a production of elegance and almost affected nicety to the direct, robustious presentation.

The Romantic movement paid fullest tribute to Molière. In 1800, Madame de Stael remarked: "We feel a vague sentiment of sadness in the most comic scenes of *Tartuffe*, because they bring to mind the natural wickedness of man"; in 1801, Chateaubriand said: "It is remarkable how the comedy of *Tartuffe*, by its extreme profundity and, if I may say so, by its sadness, closely approaches the tragic gravity." A one-act play, written by Merle and Désessarts in 1809, *Down With Molière,* could not stem the tide. From 1815 on, *Tartuffe* was welcomed by packed houses. Stendhal, in 1825, said of Molière that he "has seen clearly into the depths of the human heart" and hailed him as the greatest genius in French literature. The *Paris Globe* of March 18, 1826, declared: "In general, if the English tragedies hold more truth than our own, their comedies hold less; and we prefer Molière to Shakespeare, just as we prefer Shakespeare to Racine." Many outside the English-speaking countries feel the same. The popularity of Molière was summed up by Gustave Lanson in his *History of French Literature* (1894): "Hardly was he dead when all attacks, all jealousies, all reservations ceased; he was ranked as a genius, inimitable and without equal, and never perhaps has a reputation been sustained as consistently as his."

The traditional single set for *Tartuffe* was not varied until 1907, when *L'Illustration* pictured the five sets Antoine introduced for the different acts. Lucien Guitry ventured a new interpretation of the title role, which, however, even the English rejected. *The London Stage* (March 29, 1923), remarked that Tartuffe "untidy in appearance, with the boorish manners of a peasant, and an accent that smells of garlic, would never have been intimately received in Orgon's household . . ." Another change came with the very successful 1950 production in Paris, with Louis Jouvet; for this, the costume of Tartuffe, and the sets by George Braque, were a somber black. The end was arranged as a surprise tableau. the rear wall parting to reveal the King.

American performances include one in English, March 13, 1913, at the American Academy of Dramatic Arts with Edward G. Robinson as a sheriff's officer, one by Albert Lambert and Cecile Sorel in New York in 1922, one at New York University in 1938, and one in Boston in 1924. Of the last production, in the traditional vein, the *Boston Transcript* (March 13, 1924) said: "Molière so acted is exceeding good for an American audience to see and hear . . ."

Closest to the hearts of French playgoers, quickening the spirit with laughter even as it sobers and stirs the mind, *Tartuffe* remains the most vivid presentation of a hypocrite, preying upon the weaknesses of ordinary folk, etched in enduring drama.

THE DOCTOR IN SPITE OF HIMSELF   *Molière*

One of Molière's most amusing comedies is *Le Médecin malgré lui* (*The Doctor In Spite of Himself*), first played August 6, 1666, in three acts in prose. Suggested by a medieval painting, *The Rascally Apothecary*, the play was developed from an earlier farce of Molière's, *The Shuttlecock Doctor*.

The Doctor In Spite of Himself begins with Sganarelle, originally played by Molière, as a cunning but improvident woodcutter, once the servant of a doctor, now married to a shrew. Their neighbor Géronte has a daughter Lucinde, who loves Léandre; to avoid her father's choice, she pretends to be dumb. Various doctors fail to effect a cure.

In the meantime, Sganarelle has thrashed his wife, and she, in revenge, has told the neighbors that Sganarelle is a great doctor, who will not admit it unless he is beaten. Soundly beaten, Sganarelle diagnoses Lucinde's ailment, with a rigmarole jargon of mixed French and pseudo Latin, Hebrew, and Greek. However, when he takes Léandre as his assistant, Lucinde is forthwith cured. Sganarelle thereupon decides to remain a doctor.

The frolicsome, farcical satire of the play has made it highly popular. Fielding based a farce on it, *The Mock Doctor*, which opened in London in 1733 and reached New York in 1750. Gounod made an opera from Molière's play (the Prologue shows the court assembling to watch the comedy); it was heard first in Paris in 1857; recently in New York, 1936, and New Haven, 1941.

The Molière comedy has been translated numerous times, often with a changed title, such as *The Frantic Physician* and *The Doctor by Compulsion*. It is frequently played in community and college theatres. It was acted in Wilmington, Delaware, in 1943, with modern slang and colloquial dialogue. In New York, it was presented in adaptation by Anne Gerlette and the Czech comedian George Voskovec in what claimed to be the first professional production of the play in English. George Freedley (May 30, 1946) called this "certainly one of the best of the Equity-Library productions."

The Doctor In Spite of Himself was produced in Moscow in 1936. In the original French, New York saw the play in 1937, produced by Le Théâtre des quatre-saisons, which had toured the French provinces playing it in the open air. Of the play, as they performed it in a *commedia dell' arte* spirit, *Les Beaux Arts* (May 28, 1937) declared: "The humor of the situations still produces full-throated laughter." A French Canadian group, Les Compagnons, acted the play in Boston and New York in 1946.

As a human being, Molière walked in the valley of tears; as an artist, he knew both that life is too serious to be taken solemnly and—more important—that by laughter man reasserts his values in the face of defeat. Out of the buffeting of comedy, as out of the battering of tragedy, the dignity of the individual indefeasibly rearises.

THE MISANTHROPE   *Molière*

Since the Queen-mother had just died, *The Misanthrope*, June, 1666, was not shown at court. The depth and earnestness of the play's portrayals took the public slowly, but with increasing favor. George Brandes observed that "by most French critics this play is held to be the loftiest achievement of French comedy, the unapproachable masterpiece of the foremost of comic dramatists"; and George Eliot called it "the foremost and most complete production of its kind in the world."

Lord Morley noted its wide social range: "Without plot, fable, or intrigue, we see a section of the polished life of the time, men and women . . . flitting backwards and forwards with a thousand petty worries—and among them one strange, rough, hoarse, half-sombre figure, moving solitarily with a chilling reality in the midst of a world of shadows."

In her salon, the gay and charming Célimène receives the polite world of courtiers and women of fashion, whose varnish of politeness cannot quite conceal vulgarity of taste, polished without being decent, well-bred without being sincere.

Amid this group looms Alceste, insistently sincere. He tells the blunt truth, whether it be a question of his salvation or of a poetaster's love sonnet. He cannot endure the pretense, the affectation, that abound; yet his extravagance is as ridiculous as the others' foibles are bad. His rigid righteousness carries him to extremes. In love with Célimène, he alternates between jealousy of the courtiers whose company feeds her social sense, and impatience with her for enduring them. When she finally consents to marry him, he sets the condition that she abandon the world of fashion and its dazzling insincerities. She refuses; Alceste rushes off to the desert alone; the play ends as his friend Philente goes off to persuade him to return.

Alceste has no pettiness of soul; there are in his make-up true manliness, fervor, and force, but the acid of Célimène's etchings of the folk around has eaten into his soul; in contrast, he grows perhaps overproud of his virtue. He is essentially humorless.

"Célimène," said George Meredith in his essay on *The Idea of Comedy* (1877), "is worldliness; Alceste is unworldliness." Nowhere are two lovers more deftly set in contrast.

The Misanthrope lacks the close-knit structure of *Tartuffe** and the variety of incident of *Don Juan,* but its superb character portrayal wins every audience. Of Richard Mansfield's performance, the *New York Daily Mirror* of April 22, 1905, said: "The character of Alceste has little sympathy, for he appeals more to the reason, but Mr. Mansfield played him so sincerely, with such nobleness...he quite won our warm regard."

The performance of Jacques Copeau, in French, 1919, was greatly admired; that of Lucien Guitry, 1922, was not. The work of Cecile Sorel as Célimène won praise (in New York, in French, with Albert Lambert, 1922; with Louis Ravet, in 1926). The play was performed, in a verse translation, in London in 1935. The best recent production in English was in 1937, with Lydia Lopokova as Célimène.

Some critics discern an autobiographic tone in *The Misanthrope.* Molière and his wife were, at the time, estranged; he had reason to believe she was unfaithful. Yet onstage Madame Molière was playing Célimène to her husband's Alceste: what wonder if his jealous tirades lashed with genuine green fire! This suggestion, however, is weakened by the fact that some of Alceste's despairing jealousy is cast in words borrowed from Molière's *Don Garcie,* written long before his marriage.

THE WOULD-BE GENTLEMAN   *Molière*

In 1670 Molière presented before Louis XIV the five act prose comedy that is today his most frequently performed work, *Le Bourgeois Gentilhomme* (*The Would-be Gentleman*).

This picture of the *nouveau riche,* the wealthy citizen who would like to be accepted as a gentleman of fashion, is superb and perennial in its capture. The central figure, Monsieur Jourdain, like most of Molière's best figures, displays in excess a quality within us all. As in *Tartuffe** and *L'Avare,* we watch the disintegrating effects, within a single family, of the folly of its head. The quick-witted and outspoken Nicole, who rebukes Jourdain for his pretensions, ranks, with Dorine of *Tartuffe,* among the best of the maids in comedy—a stock figure lifted to a genuine character presentation.

The play comprises three acts of Molière's best character comedy, followed by two of fantastic farce. The first two acts show Monsieur Jourdain with his various instructors, learning to be a gentleman. In the third act, love enters the scene; for of course widower Jourdain and his daughter Julie must marry as befits Jourdain's hoped-for station. Jourdain aims at Dorimène, Marquise de Montignac, who loves an adventurer and swindler, Dorante, Comte de Chateau-Gaillard (Count of Jolly-Castle). For Julie, these schemers provide the Son of the Grand Turk, who naturally, cannot marry the daughter of a commoner; Jourdain is raised to the rank of "Mamamouchi". But the Grand Turk's son, who marries Julie, is just plain Cléonte, her lover, in disguise. Jourdain is left with his hopes of distinction dashed, but really the better off, as Dorimène and Dorante also decide to marry. The Turks come in for caricature at the end of the play, probably because the new Turkish envoy to the French court had displeased Louis XIV.

Monsieur Jourdain is, as Brander Matthews said, "a constant source of unquenchable laughter, as we behold him delighted to discover that he has spoken prose all his life without knowing it, and as we see him, pricked by the foil in the hands of Nicole, protesting that she is not fencing according to the rules." But there is more than laughter within this portrait. As the critic of the *New York World* (October 3, 1928) noted after the Civic Repertory opening of *The Would-Be Gentleman:* "Jourdain is a fool, a buffoon, a monster of ignorance, crudity, and complacency. But his befuddled destiny is played against a background of snobbish, contemptuous exploitation on the part of the gentlemen he envies; and some of this he dimly feels—and swaggers the more, to combat it. Before the genuine pathos in this picture your own contempt crumbles."

There have been innumerable productions, in various lands, of *Le Bourgeois Gentilhomme*. It was a favorite role of Coquelin. Firmin Gemier brought his French company to New York in 1924, with romping onstage and amidst the audience. The *New York World* (November 20) reported that "anything funnier or more finished than the Odéon's presentation of the delicious old comedy has not been seen in New York. It was comedy run wild, but never out of hand; absurdity carried to the last degree, but always adroit."

In English, The Civic Repertory presented the play in New York in 1928, in an adaptation by F. Anstey (acted in London in 1928, with Nigel Playfair) with Egon Brecher (Jourdain), Walter Abel, Donald Cameron, Alma Kruger, and J. Edward Bromberg. Pierre de Rohan, in the *New York American*, (October 3, 1928) commented: "Molière's immortal comedy has been preserved to us without the loss of a single flash of wit and without the necessity of modernizing a single allusion." Productions at college, community, and summer theatres have been numerous; *The Would-Be Gentleman* was presented at Cornell University in adaptation by Lady Gregory in 1929; with Jimmy Savo at Westport, Connecticut, in 1936; at the Mohawk Drama Festival in 1937, with Charles Coburn; at Yale in 1937 also; in 1939 at the University of California and at Pennsylvania State College; in Philadelphia, in 1941; at the University of Texas, with Walter Slezak, in 1942; and by the New York Equity Library in 1945.

With elaborate changes by and with Bobby Clark, *The Would-Be Gentleman* was turned into a masterly display of Clark's comic mannerisms, in a production that opened in New York January 9, 1946. Clark (like Molière) took many liberties. Though it ran for only 77 performances, the production was generally well received. Robert Coleman called it "a glittering rough-house of fun"; Howard Barnes, "a wonderfully funny show." If there were lapses, some felt, with Louis Kronenberger, that "the fault is mostly Molière's." However, Arthur Pollock insisted that the character comedy of the play, with all its deeper implications, had been sacrificed to the farce: "Clark has taken out all the flavor and, surrounded by a cast of pretty bad actors, simply grinds out the comedy all evening like a cement-mixer."

The original play is, of course, a fast and funny frolic; but it is also a searching exposure of human weakness, and in consequence a reassertion of human dignity. These qualities combine to make Molière's *The Would-Be Gentleman* both a provocation and a delight, one of the world's richest comedies.

THE LEARNED LADIES   *Molière*

Molière's *Les Femmes Savantes* (*The Learned Ladies*) was first produced in March 1672.

This five-act play in verse, which Brander Matthews called "the
ultimate model of high comedy", follows the fair sex in its fashionable
progression from the frills of preciosity (pricked in *Les Précieuses
Ridicules**) to the blue stockings of philosophical and scholarly conversation. It was favorably received, but not by Molière's aristocratic foes.

Again, as in *Tartuffe,** *L'Avare,* and *Le Bourgeois Gentilhomme,**
Molière drives home his theme through a single family; beyond them,
too, the social milieu is neatly caught and deftly laid bare. Two generations are shown. Of the old: Chrysale (played originally by Molière), well-intentioned but weak-willed, led by his dominating wife Philaminte, who has been educated beyond her intelligence; and Chrysale's
resourceful and sensible brother Ariste, whose flighty old maid sister,
Bélise, thinks all the young men are courting her. Of the younger generation, we see Chrysale's two daughters: the pretentious and self-important Armande, her mother's girl, and the simpler and more readily
satisfied Henriette (played originally by Madame Molière, then reconciled with her husband).

The play opens with a superb scene in which Armande mocks Henriette for taking her discarded suitor Clitandre; in Molière's deftest dialogue the nature of the two girls is revealed: the prurient prude who
shrinks, beneath a mask of would-be learning, from the normal responsibilities of a woman's life; and the charming, straightforward girl of
solid affections and simple ways. Philaminte, however, wants Henriette to marry the man she thinks is a paragon of wit and learning, Trissotin. When Uncle Ariste announces that the family money is lost, Trissotin withdraws, and the steadfast Clitandre gets Henriette, as old
Ariste reveals that his story of the lost money was just a device to
expose Trissotin.

The play is rich in contrasting characters. Trissotin is a sharp portrait of an actual person, the Abbé Cotin, who had translated Lucretius,
but had attacked Molière and his friend Boileau; two of Trissotin's
epigrams are drawn from the writings of Cotin, who in the play is pilloried for literary pretentiousness. "The comedy as a whole has a unity
of intent and a harmony of tone which Molière was rarely able to attain,"
wrote Brander Matthews.

Les Femmes Savantes pokes fun at pretentious women with Molière's
neatly barbed shafts of wit. Tucked into the dialogue are many apt
phrases, some of which have become proverbial: "seasoned with Attic
salt"; "grammar, which controls even kings".

It was a pleasant bow to the old master when the young women of
Hunter College, New York, produced *Les Femmes Savantes,* opening November 5, 1938, the tercentenary of the birth of Louis XIV.

THE IMAGINARY INVALID   *Molière*

Though the title figure in the comedy *Le Malade Imaginaire* (*The
Imaginary Invalid*) is a hypochondriac, Molière, while playing the role,
himself was seriously ill. He had a convulsion while taking the bur-

lesque oath at the end of the play, during the fourth performance, February 17, 1673, and died before his wife could reach his side.

The Imaginary Invalid carries along Molière's frequent attack upon the quacks and pretending physicians of his day. A sentence of the play—"Most men die, not of their diseases, but of their remedies"—was too nearly true in Molière's time for any but rueful laughter.

Argan, the hypochondriac, wants his daughter to marry a physician, so that there'll always be a doctor in the house. He is attended by a doctor, Purgon; an apothecary, Fleurant; and two other medicos, Purgon's brother-in-law Diafoirius, and young Thomas Diafoirius, whom Argan wants to marry his daughter Angélique. The girl, however, prefers another man. With the help of Argan's solid, clear-headed brother, Béralde, and the shrewd maid Toinette, who at one point puts on the disguise of a doctor, Angélique gets her Cléante. When Béralde suggests that Argan has learned enough to be a doctor himself, Argan agrees, and the play ends with the lilting farce of his induction into doctorhood, with the "right to purge and bleed and kill throughout the world."

The Imaginary Invalid (sometimes translated as The Robust Invalid) has been frequently and widely played. It is in the repertory of the Moscow Art Theatre and of the Habimah (Hebrew) Players. When the Coburns played it in New York, Arthur Hornblow in Theatre magazine (April, 1917) considered it "the funniest play of the season." The Coburns played it again in 1922, the tercentenary of the birth of Molière. The Old Vic, in London, showed it in English in 1929 in F. Anstey's sprightly version, with Martita Hunt as Madame Argan and Margaret Webster as the maid Toinette. It was presented again at the Old Vic, in French, in 1933, when the London Times observed that it had "plenty of wit, and kept fully alive its knockabout fun." Radio versions were broadcast from Munich in 1933 and from London in 1937.

Recent American productions were given at the Mohawk Drama Festival in 1936; at Tuscaloosa, Alabama, in 1939; at Great Neck, Long Island, in 1945; at Piscator's Dramatic Workshop, New York, in 1947; and in Delaware, Ohio, in 1948. Elisabeth Bergner starred in a revival entitled The Gay Invalid which opened in London, January 24, 1951. The play shows that the great comic spirit of Molière was vigorous and rich and vital to the end.

LILIOM   *Ferenc Molnar*

The suave and subtle comedies of Molnar (Hungarian, 1878-1952) neatly constructed, deft in dialogue, are admirable examples of plays written to entertain. Rarely does their author offer more than lively, slightly ironic, superficial theatrical fare.

Liliom, 1908, gains especial interest because it reaches beyond sentimentality and cynicism to probe a simple, ineffectual heart. It tenderly unfolds a tragedy of the inarticulate. "Liliom" (the nickname "Lily" means Toughy), a swaggering barker in a cheap amusement park, is watched with jealousy by his boss, Mrs. Muskat, as he flirts and then goes away with naive little Julie. Despite Mrs. Muskat's attempts to lure Liliom back, something holds him and Julie together. His impatience at his joblessness, his inarticulate love, his wordless urges, come out in beatings for Julie. Equally incapable of giving words to her thoughts and feelings, Julie somehow understands. When she tells Liliom they are to have a child, he seeks money for it; he permits "The Sparrow" to guide him in a hold-up attempt—which fails; and Liliom stabs himself to escape arrest. Again, beside the dying man, Julie understands.

At the Police Magistrate's Court up yonder, the unregenerate Liliom is sentenced to sixteen years in the purgatorial fires, after which he is allowed a day to return to earth and try to atone. On that day, he brings to his daughter Louise (now sixteen) a star he has stolen from heaven. Julie has told Louise her father was a fine man; when this "stranger" says he knew Liliom, who had beaten her mother, Louise scolds him for lying, and he slaps the girl. Liliom turns away with a sense of defeat, but Louise turns in surprise to her mother: the blow has borne no sting. "It is possible, dear," says Julie, with memoried love, "that someone may beat you, and beat you, and beat you—and not hurt you at all."

When Eva Le Gallienne, Helen Westley, Joseph Schildkraut, and Dudley Digges opened in *Liliom*, on April 20, 1921, its tender pathos won instant favor. The *New York Times* called it "Barrie done in terms of realism instead of sentimentality." Heywood Broun allowed: "There is some sentimental tosh in the play, but it is almost the best tosh we have ever heard." Alexander Woollcott was comparative: "There are such scenes of human squalor in it as Gorki might have written, but now and again there are dancing lights that Barrie might envy, and at times a cathedral hush settles over the play for those out front who have a prayer in their heart." *Liliom* was revived in 1932, again with Eva Le Gallienne and Schildkraut; Burgess Meredith was also in the cast, as he was again (this time with Ingrid Bergman) in 1940.

With music by Richard Rodgers, lyrics by Oscar Hammerstein II, choreography by Agnes de Mille, and the setting transplanted to the New England shore, the play reappeared on April 19, 1945, as the musical *Carousel*. Save for the transposition to New England, with a chorus of factory girls and fisher men, the story of *Liliom* is followed closely in *Carousel*. Songs and dances delightfully carry along the gayer mood: "June is bustin' out all over", "If I loved you", and "This is a real nice clam bake". The musical was welcomed with cheers. Robert Coleman (April 20, 1945) called it "beautiful, bountiful, beguiling". Ward Morehouse spoke of its "charm and compassion in musical play form . . . something rare in the theatre." It attained 890 performances in New York and 650 on the road, then went back to New York for four more weeks at the City Center. It well achieved the author's aim, to be "not *Liliom* with some songs added, but truly a musical play based on *Liliom*." A London revival of 1950 enjoyed 567 performances.

THE RED MILL   *Ferenc Molnar*

The theme of the damnation of man recurs in Ferenc Molnar's plays. It is the main motif of two of them: *The Devil*, 1907 and *The Red Mill*, 1923. The first shows Satan triumphant on earth; the second shows him defeated in hell.

The Red Mill is, in Molnar's words, "a play of Hell in Hell, nevertheless a morality play." Satan's chief engineer, Magister, has invented a machine, the psycho-corruptor, that speeds up the process of seducing a soul. It takes twenty years, we are told, to make devil's meat of the average New Yorker; the machine is guaranteed to do it in an hour.

Magister tells Satan that he will demonstrate the machine. Satan and his assistants sit in the orchestra pit, watching, while trolls, ogres, fiends, and hobgoblins swirl among the audience, and onstage a black curtain opens as Magister searches on earth—discarding a self-righteous schoolmaster, a love-protesting poet, a smug politician, a conventional clerk—for a wholly good man. He finally chooses the simple forester János, whose devoted wife Ilonka is preparing the evening meal.

The next act takes place in various parts of the red mill, the psycho-corruptor, as the puppets it manufactures out of damned humans work on János. The synthetic she-devil Mima leads János through a crowded catalogue of crimes. Among the infernal noises a bell rings every time János sins; soon there is a continuous chiming. At the end, János is about to slay Mima, who has repeatedly seduced and betrayed him. She begs for mercy, telling him that once she sent his mother a withered violet, long pressed in her prayerbook. Pure fiction, probably, but János is touched and forgives her. Thereupon the machine rumbles in the depths of hell, shivers, and, with a roar, blows up. János awakes beside his quiet cottage, a little late for Ilonka's evening meal.

With subtle and occasionally cynical humor, Molnar fashioned in *The Red Mill* a mixture of fancy, satire, and stagecraft that took Europe by storm. The *Neues Pester Journal* (Budapest) said: "Molnar went in quest of the salvation motif. With him he took the poet and the humorist. In this wise there came into being a work of arresting variety, a mystery pierced with laughter." *Der Tag* (Vienna) said "Molnar's Hell made my flesh creep."

The intricacy of the stagecraft snares the beholder in the play's mood, and fancy wings lightly over the whole. It is strongly tinged with satire in the first part, while Magister is seeking among men for a good soul to corrupt. It shines more balefully, with cynical glintings, when the fires of hell feed the impatient machine. In David Belasco's English version, both satire and fancy almost succumbed to the stagecraft. Writing in *The Bookman* (February 1929), Belasco stated that he considered the play "the greatest of the brain children of Ferenc Molnar", and "the stupendous work of producing it . . . one of the happiest and most soul-filling tasks of my career." His version, called *Mima*, opened on December 12, 1928, with Lenore Ulric, Sidney Blackmer, and A. E. Anson, and ran for 180 performances. Percy Hammond called the production "a combination of satire, extravagance, spectacle, morality, and grand opera." Belasco's phycho-corruptor was certainly a triumph of theatrical ingenuity. (Its pattern and plan can be found illustrated and explained in *The Scientific American* for March, 1929.)

The temporal victory of evil pictured in *The Devil* fades before the eternal triumph of good in *The Red Mill*, an amazing and amusing, an arousing and edifying, large-scale dramatic capture of life's basic drive.

THE GREAT DIVIDE   *William Vaughan Moody*

When Margaret Anglin was playing in *Zira* in Chicago, William Vaughan Moody (American, 1869-1910), a teacher of English at the University of Chicago, brought her his play, *A Sabine Woman*. It was a melodrama of backwoods violence and domestic sentiment. Margaret Anglin liked the play and tried it out while still in Chicago, April, 1906. With suggestions from Henry Miller, the play was revised. As *The Great Divide* it opened in New York on October 3, 1906, and altered the course of American drama. As late as May 1920, *Theatre Magazine* noted that *The Great Divide* is "said to be the best play written by an American".

Melodramatic in incident, *The Great Divide* is important because of the two characters it sets in conflict, both strong individualists, whose deeds loom above the more normal actions of Philip Jordan and the "lovable chatter" of his wife Polly. Philip's sister, Ruth, is alone in his Western ranch house one day, when three men break in. Two are rough desperados; the third, Stephen Ghent, as rough as the others, is of more substantial stock. They want to gamble for the girl; Stephen buys her from the other two, then protects her from their treachery. Ruth and Stephen marry; Ruth comes indeed to admire and love Stephen, but she cannot rid her spirit of the shame of having been bought. The feeling that she must somehow "cleanse the sin" sends her back to her conventional home in the East. Stephen sees the validity of her choice: "You belong here," he tells her, "and I belong out yonder—beyond the Rockies —beyond the Great Divide." Ruth comes to appreciate the core of gold within the rugged ore: "You have taken the good of our life, and grown strong," she says, "I have taken the evil, and grown weak—weak unto death. Teach me to live as you do!"

The first New York run of *The Great Divide* was 234 performances; it reopened on August 31, 1907, for 103 more. It played in London, opening September 15, 1909, and was revived in New York in 1917. It has been played often in little theatres. The power of the drama was at once recognized. The *New York Sun* (December 23, 1906) spoke of it in almost religious terms: "It is its splendid virtue that it brings us to the ragged edge of the great mystery of sin, and it is its more splendid virtue that it does not attempt to go beyond it . . . Moody begins in passion and he ends in mystery." The *New York Dramatic Mirror* (October 13, 1906) characterized it as "a drama that, from its interaction and clash of characters and the poetry both of its conception and of its lines, rises far above the mere theatric effectiveness of melodrama . . . It is this concept of the basic principles of things, this brushing aside of the superficial, the merely clever, that causes the play to set a new standard for the American drama."

"No man", said *The Mail* (October 4, 1906) "has set the breadth of Arizona against the narrowness of Milford Corners, Massachusetts, with so much art and so much eloquence."

The deep core of American individuality in such a figure as Stephen Ghent attracted the reviewer of the *Boston Transcript* (December 1, 1908), who saw in the play "the great divide between the ineffectual old and the vital new of American drama . . . The man is big in every dimension, physical and moral. There is nothing little about him. Even his faults are huge. He is planned on a grand scale; he requires an enormous forgiveness and brings the ampler virtues to merit it."

The theme of the play is sustained, and the events of the plot are deftly linked, by a chain of gold nuggets. With this chain Ghent buys the Mexican's "rights" to Ruth. The latter weaves blankets for tourists until she earns enough to buy the chain, the token of her shame, from the Mexican. She flings it away and goes back to her eastern home. Ghent recovers it, and carries it until Ruth accepts it and willingly wears it, free of the stigma, as a sign of understanding and ripening love... The play may well be considered the beginning of psychological searching in the American theatre.

THE PRIVATE SECRETARY   *Gustav von Moser*

Out of the very successful German farce of Gustav von Moser (1825-1903), *Der Bibliothekar,* Charles Hawtrey (1858-1923), the English actor-manager, wove one of the most popular English farces, *The Private Secretary.* The play opened in Cambridge in 1883 and was brought to London, March 29, 1884, for the then phenomenal run of 785 performances. It has been frequently revived. By 1900, the *Hull* (England) *Mail* estimated that the play had already "shaken the sides of the great British public 468,000 times." New York saw it September 29, 1884, with William Gillette, opening a run of 200 performances; Gillette revived it in New York, December 12, 1910, for a fourteen weeks' run. He played the title role more than 2,000 times, and the part was considered his best comic characterization.

The play presents a galaxy of varied characters, including, as the *Boston Herald,* November 15, 1910, listed them, "the shrinking country clergyman who, as a new tutor for a couple of lively girls, is hurled into the company of two gay young London blades, a dunning tailor, a sporty rich uncle from India, a languishing chaperon seeking spiritualistic manifestations, and a doting wife with unnumbered small children, all stirred into a rattling mixture of cross purposes, misunderstandings, and mistaken identities." The private secretary, the Reverend Robert Spaulding, is a meek fellow who wears galoshes, plays the piano, and always carries an umbrella. Douglas Cattermole, a wild young man who has accumulated a host of debts, persuades the timid Spauling to change places and names with him. Meanwhile old Cattermole from India, Douglas's rich uncle, comes back to help his nephew sow a few wild oats; he won't leave his money to any prissy pallid boy. The "nephew" he meets, the timid Spaulding in the gay blade's stead, disgusts him. Finally he and the tailor with his bill descend upon the innocent impostor and the complications are cleared away. Uncle Cattermole is pleased to discover that his nephew is a lively, high-spirited fellow after all, and the two girls are no less pleased with their swains, as the Reverend Robert Spaulding rejoins his sedate better half.

Much of the fun rises from the misunderstandings. The dialogue abounds in malapropisms, mispronunciations—Cattermole is called Cattleshow, Shattlemow, Mattercole—and other verbal play. The buffeted private secretary was born to be the butt of practical jokes, a fellow you like while you laugh at him. "His sufferings", said the *Boston Herald,* "excited such genuine sympathy that one felt half ashamed to laugh at the poor fellow."

"Farcical comedy that is worthy", the *New York Telegraph* commented (December 13, 1910) "has a quality in common with good wine—age adds to its flavor. As the droll Reverend Robert Spaulding . . . Mr. Gillette was delightful." The play provides perennial entertainment. Certain of its outer devices are now dated, but the basic situations and comic characters of *The Private Secretary* continue to justify its wide repute as one of the funniest of modern farcical comedies.

FASHION   *Anna Cora Mowatt*

The first American social comedy, and still the best of the early pictures of budding American society, is *Fashion; or, Life in New York,* by Anna Cora Mowatt (1819-1870). Beginning her theatrical experience with an amateur group in Flatbush, New York, then turning to the professional stage, Mrs. Mowatt designed the play wholly as an acting comedy. "A dramatic, not a literary, success was what I wanted." She had her wish. *Fashion* opened, March 24, 1845, and attained the then phenomenal run of 28 nights. Mrs. Mowatt had the pleasure of starring in her own play in London.

Fashion has lasted well; a 1924 revival in New York ran over seven months, and London in 1929 saw the "famous old comedy". Various groups have constantly performed the play all over the country; it played in New York again in 1941 and (Equity Library) 1948.

As in *The Contrast*, Fashion* shows the conflict between homely American ways and the supposed high society manners of old Europe. The action takes place in the home of the Tiffanys. The *Albion,* (March 25, 1845) described the Tiffanys as follows: "(He) is a New York merchant doing an extensive business, has risen from a peddler to his present importance, and conducting his affairs upon the high steam pressure of the day, becomes involved in and resorts to false indorsements for the support of his declining credit. Mrs. Tiffany, also of obscure origin, uneducated, vulgar, and full of pretension, aspires to lead in so-called fashionable society by extravagant display and aping of foreign manners." She wants her daughter Seraphina to marry Count Jolimaitre, a valet posing as a noble, who, while wooing the wealthy Seraphina, also flirts with the beautiful governess, Gertrude. Also, more honestly, attracted to Gertrude is Colonel Howard, U.S.A. Adding varied color to the play are such figures as the sycophantic and villainous bookkeeper, Snobson, and the poet, T. Tennyson Twinkle, who makes no less than seven unsuccessful attempts to read his poems in Mrs. Tiffany's drawing-room. The complications of the plot are disentangled by Adam Trueman, well-to-do farmer from Catteraugus, upstate. In Adam, the first diamond-in-the-rough American, there is moving power, as well as rustic earnestness. He reveals that Gertrude is his daughter and bestows her on Colonel Howard. Graciously the play ends with a restoration of honest manners.

Fashion is not without standby characters and situations, and it is indeed, as the *Chicago Journal* (December 7, 1926) remarked, "one of the earliest American manufacturers of hokum." Edgar Allan Poe, writing in the *Broadway Journal* (March 24, 1845), blasted the original direction for its "total deficiency in verisimilitude . . . the coming forward to the footlights when anything of interest is to be told; the reading of private papers in a loud, rhetorical tone; the preposterous asides." Nonetheless Poe went to each of the first five performances of the play, and his final judgment of it was that "Compared with the generality of modern drama, it is a good play; compared with most American drama, it is a very good play; estimated by the natural principles of dramatic art, it is altogether unworthy of notice." As literature, *Fashion* is of little consequence; as theatre (which, after all, was the author's aim) the play achieved and has held a prominent place on the American stage.

WHITE HORSE INN   *Hans Müller*

White Horse Inn is one of the most successful of spectacular musical comedies. It is based upon a farce by Oskar Blumenthal (German, 1852-1917) and Gustav Kadelburg, the comic actor (Austrian, 1851-1894), which was itself successful both on the Continent and (in adaptation by Sydney Rosenfeld) in New York in 1899 with Amelia Bingham and Leo Dietrichstein. *Im Weissen Rössl (White Horse Inn)* has book by Hans Müller (Austrian, b. 1882), and music by Ralph Benatzky and Robert Stolz. The musical version played over 1,000 performances in Vienna; it ran for two years (from September 1932) in Paris; had 416 performances (from November 1930) in Berlin, and has been seen throughout Europe as well as in Palestine, Africa, and Australia. London saw it, opening April 8, 1931, for 651 performances, and for 268 more beginning March 20, 1940. In New York, it ran for 228 performances beginning October 1, 1936, with Kitty Carlisle and William Gaxton, with lyrics by Irving Caesar. It is said to be the longest-run show in European history. "Never before", said *Play Pictorial* (May 1931) "has the London stage seen such an elaborate production." In New York, the Center Theatre spread the Inn and its Tyrolean surroundings across its wide stage and out along the sides. Everywhere the spectacle has been colorfully and lavishly adorned. Robert Coleman fitly warned his readers: "Bring along your St. Bernard and your skis."

The White Horse Inn is situated in the village of St. Wolfgang, on an Alpine lake. The proprietress, Josepha Voglhuber, has been loved by each of her head waiters; she turns from the present one, Leopold, to Valentine Sutton, an English solicitor and a guest at the Inn. Also present is Mr. Ginkle (McGonigle in the English version), the bathing suit king, now presenting his latest "Lady Godiva" model, and his daughter, Ottoline, whom Sutton admires. Leopold deliberately confuses the suites of Ginkle and Sutton, who are on opposite sides of a law suit. The Emperor Franz Josef, on hand for the Tyrolean festival, gives the proprietress some good advice. She settles back with her Leopold, and Ottoline bridges the Ginkle-Sutton abyss.

All in all, the play is lively, gay, and amusing. There are also a few good songs: "Star Dust", "The White Horse Calling To Me", and the rousing march "Good-Bye." Most appealing are the spectacles, swirling with dancers in variegated costumes. "The real heroine of the evening", said John Mason Brown, "is the wardrobe mistress." In New York, there was a cow-milking scene and song, with real cows in a village cowshed; the visitors for the Tyrolean festival arrived in a real, full-size motor omnibus, greeted with ballets and folk dances; a great revolving stage took them around the fair grounds, and to the public baths; the Emperor arrived by steamer, and the Tyroleans passed before him in review. As the *London Era* (April 15, 1931) declared: "All the resources of modern stage-craft have been used. Colour, light, music, and movement are perfectly blended in an entertainment that is almost breathless in interest . . . I rarely remember a more thrilling scene than the procession that preceded the arrival of the Emperor." The lavish display, the gay movement of light-hearted comedy, the tuneful and cheery songs, combine to make *White Horse Inn* one of the greatest world favorites of musical comedy.

THE CAPRICES OF MARIANNE   *Alfred de Musset*

Alfred de Musset (1810-1857) is widely known as the "enfant terrible" of the French Romantics, the poet of passion and regret, one of the fated lovers of George Sand. Among his published works is *Comedies and Proverbs*, a volume of charming, cultivated dialogue and keen psychology. Years after the publication of this book it was discovered that it contained plays that made delightful theatre pieces.

"The theatre of Musset", said Jacques Porel in 1936, "is a marvelous accident, unique in our dramatic literature . . . Poetry, in all its forms, irony, melancholy, mystery—in one sweep invaded the stage. A grave lightness, a sort of sweet madness, animates all these ambiguous personages. Each of them, even the most ordinary, seems to bestride a little cloud all his own. Their voices have the sonority of an echo. Beholding them, we feel freed from our chain of reason; we come out of ourselves to journey in unknown regions of the spirit."

Best of Musset's comedies is *The Caprices of Marianne*, published in 1833 and first produced at the Théâtre Français (at that time called the Théâtre de la République), June 28, 1851, introducing the new star Madeleine Brohan. Théophile Gautier, in his comment, regretted the changes and cuts in a "text that everyone knows by heart . . . Nonetheless, *Les Caprices de Marianne* won the most brilliant success, and will further popularize the author's name." It was frequently performed by Louis Delauncey from 1851 to 1887; in 1906 it became a permanent part of the repertoire of the Comédie Française.

The play is in two acts and nine scenes. It portrays young Marianne, married to ugly old Claudio and adored by handsome young Coelio. The timid Coelio sends his friend Octave to plead his cause; he does so well that Marianne is drawn to him. She sets a rendezvous with Octave, who sends Coelio; but Claudio has been watching, and Coelio is killed. Marianne would be consoled by Octave, but he says, "I do not love you; it was Coelio who loved you." Marianne, said *Le Théâtre* (February 11, 1906) "has 'caprices' in vain; she is not a coquette, *la grand coquette,* as they say in the theatre; she is *l'amoureuse,* the loving woman." Following a revival on October 16, 1922, *Le Théâtre* (November) called *Les Caprices de Marianne* "a work that does not age."

Once Scribe and Musset were discussing their work. "My secret", said Scribe, "is to amuse the public."

"My secret", said Musset, "is to amuse myself." When *Les Caprices de Marianne* was published, Musset (aged twenty-two, not yet entangled with George Sand) was asked where he had met this Marianne: "Nowhere", he replied, "and everywhere. She is not a woman, she is woman." The rest of the secret is the capture of character in sparkling dialogue, and the discerning vision that beholds and sets forth that irony which robs us of our pretenses and leaves us reduced to the simpler dimensions of human dignity and beauty. Alfred de Musset is amused at love's little subterfuges and more damnable ways, but he—and his audiences —remain in love with humans, and with love.

LIFE IS A JOKE TO HIM   *Johann Nestroy*

Of the scores of farces and melodramas written by Johann Nestroy
(Austrian, 1802-1862), mainly in Viennese dialect, that delighted the
Austrian public in the mid-nineteenth century, only one achieved international success. This is an amusing comedy of an aging small-town merchant who goes to the big city to have a good time and get a second wife.
Nestroy took the idea from the farce *A Well Spent Day* by John Oxenford (English, 1812-1877) and called it *Einen Jux will er sich machen*
(*Life Is a Joke to Him*). Thornton Wilder adapted it as *The Merchant
of Yonkers,* 1938 and revised it as *The Matchmaker,* a smash hit in 1955.

The Wilder version opens in the 1880's in the gilded drawingroom of
the elderly Yonkers merchant Horace Vandergelder. After berating his
niece Ermengarde for fancying a "scalawag artist", Horace goes off with
the pert minx Mrs. Molloy, a milliner, to have a gay time in the wicked
city of New York. Two of his clerks, also on a spree, engage Mrs. Molloy
in their champagne festivity, and Horace's old friend, Mrs. Dolly Levi,
née Gallagher, takes over as his guide and adviser. Her advice is that
Horace marry her; accepting it, he can no longer object to the union
of his niece Ermengarde and her artist.

The play opened in Boston, December 12, 1938, with Jane Cowl and
June Walker, and in New York, where it ran for five weeks, December
28. An over-elaborate production by Max Reinhardt slowed the rippling
pace of the comedy, which makes merry use of the well-tried tricks of
farce. Indeed, as the *Boston Transcript* (December 13, 1938) remarked,
the author "has penned a tongue-in-cheek satire on the conventions of
farce, decorating his gentle fable with all or anyhow a good parcel of
the traditions thereof . . . The jokes, if mild, are neat, and even they are
less important than the philosophical pleasantries that adorn the play."
"Sheer funny business", said the *New York Sun;* "Laughter-compelling",
declared the *World-Telegram.* Nestroy was a master of the popular
theatre, and Wilder has converted his Viennese comedy into a lively
American frolic, spiced with a little wisdom.

ABIE'S IRISH ROSE   *Anne Nichols*

The success of *Abie's Irish Rose* is testimony to the faith of an author
in her work. Anne Nichols (American, b. 1895?), drawing her plot from
an actual episode, wrote a play she called *Marriage in Triplicate.* Oliver
Morosco produced it in Los Angeles, where it ran for thirty weeks as
Abie's Irish Rose. Declaring that Morosco's option had lapsed, Miss
Nichols opened the play herself in New York on May 23, 1922. For four
months the play ran at a loss, sustained by Anne Nichols' faith and a
loan of $30,000 from gambler Arnold Rothstein. Then the play gathered
impetus and remained to achieve a run of 2,237 performances, the longest
in the history of the theatre, surpassed since only by *Life With Father**
and *Tobacco Road*.* All over the country the play established records:
29 weeks in Philadelphia; 35 weeks in Boston; 81 weeks in Chicago; 22
weeks in Columbus, Ohio. It ran 39 weeks in Detroit, and this picture
of inter-racial love was a hit there again in 1943, at the time of the second most disastrous race riot in American history. Around the world, it
ran for 128 performances in London, for eight months in Berlin; Will
Rogers saw a Chinese production in Shanghai.

The play brings together the Levys, their friends the Cohens, and the Murphys. Jewish Abie Levy introduces his Irish sweetheart to his family as "Rose Murphisky". When the couple are being married by a rabbi, Dad Murphy arrives from California with a priest; only the fact that the rabbi and the priest had worked side by side in the World War averts a race riot. The Levys want a grandson; the Murphys, a granddaughter. Miss Nichols makes the stork kind: the newlyweds have mixed twins, and all is well.

Numerous imitations have sought to swing on the tail of Anne Nichols' kite, among them *Kosher Kitty Kelly*, a comedy with songs and dances by Leon de Costa, which opened June 15, 1925, "a misdemeanor", according to Percy Hammond, "a merciless and incompetent bore", which nevertheless attained 105 performances.

Robert Benchley, needing a fresh weekly comment on *Abie* for his one-sentence summary of plays in the old *Life*, at first protested: "Come on now, a joke's a joke!", but subsequently he gave broad hints: "They put an end to the six-day bicycle races by tearing down Madison Square Garden. How about a nice big office building on the present site of the Republic Theatre?" Broun called *Abie's Irish Rose* the worst play of the season: "I don't think it will last six months"; five years later, he added: "*Abie's Irish Rose* is still a bad play. I don't think it will last forever." For fifteen years, it never stopped playing somewhere, and there is no sign that it has ended its career. New York saw it again in 1952 and 1954.

After the New York opening, the *Times* (May 24, 1922) commented: "We hope to be present at little Rebecca Rachel and Patrick Joseph Levy's second birthday, if not their Hudson-Fulton centennial." As the play continued, appreciation grew. The novelist Mary Austin was quoted by Alexander Woollcott (May 19, 1924) as saying: "It is quite true that the humor of *Abie's Irish Rose* is the humor of the comic strip. But what is the matter with the comic strip as an expression of folk humor? . . . It is also true that the plot and situations of Miss Nichols' play are old. They are exactly as old as *Romeo and Juliet* when the well known William Shakespeare found it in a book of popular tales. But Miss Nichols' treatment of the theme is not old."

A decade later, *Abie's Irish Rose* was still gathering momentum. Arthur Pollock in the Christian Science Monitor (May 18, 1937) observed philosophically that it is "really no older than ever it was, for it was ancient at birth." And on August 18, 1939, Samuel Grafton wrote in his *New York Post* column: "The one memory of this drama that lingers is the wonderful, warm note of racial tolerance on which the play ended."

The plot of *Abie's Irish Rose* was traced by George Jean Nathan to the farce *Krausmeyer's Alley*. When Anne Nichols brought suit against Universal Pictures for their screen series *The Cohens and The Kellys*, the attorneys, like Mary Austin, carried the plot back to *Romeo and Juliet*. Anne Nichols swore that she had read neither Nathan nor Shakespeare, but she lost the suit.

Combining sweet Irish sentiment as in *Peg o' my Heart** with broad Jewish humor as in *Potash and Perlmutter, Abie's Irish Rose* comforted, cajoled, and convulsed large sections of two important minority groups in the United States, and left everywhere widening ripples of good-natured laughter.

WINGS OVER EUROPE   *Robert M. B. Nichols*

When *Wings Over Europe*, 1927, by Robert M. B. Nichols (English, b. 1893) and Maurice Browne (English, b. 1881), let loose the threat of an atom bomb upon the startled world, few persons outside the cloistered halls of science would have guessed how soon the play's story would seem realistic. Brooks Atkinson (December 11, 1928) said that "the idea of their odd and original play is so preposterous that it is probably true, and it does credit to their intelligence and vision." The London *Illustrated Sporting and Dramatic News* (May 7, 1932) summed up the play's issue: "The youthful physicist, who idealizes human nature, believes his theory has brought the millennium. The politicians demur, fearing that mankind, given possession of illimitable power, will merely use it to bring about their own destruction."

The physicist in the play is Francis Lightfoot, an idealistic young man who has the secret of the atom bomb. The entire action of the play takes place in the British Cabinet Council Room at 10 Downing Street, where Lightfoot has brought to the British his proposal for international peace. Moved by all sorts of motives, the Cabinet turns him down. It wonders whether it can secure and destroy the secret, or imprison Lightfoot. When he threatens to blow up Europe, the War Secretary shoots him. Overhead is heard the murmur of metal wings as the Union of World Scientists sends a message to the Cabinet, ordering it to a conference to hear the scientists' orders for readjusting the world.

The theme of *Wings Over Europe* seemed fantastically remote; the play won artistic praise but little popular attention. It opened in New York on December 10, 1928, in a Theatre Guild production with Alexander Kirkland as Lightfoot, Morris Carnovsky and Ernest Lawford. London saw the play April 27, 1932, with Melville Cooper. Brooks Atkinson observed that although the authors ". . . let their imagination soar boundlessly . . . they succeed only spasmodically in keeping *Wings Over Europe* in terms of the theatre . . . Writing in deadly earnest, [they] express themselves not only in unrelieved conversation, but in conversation that is almost completely abstract." Richard Lockridge found *Wings Over Europe* "a drama ringing with the clash of idea upon idea and singing with that music words make if they are hurled high enough. . . . Its considerations are humanity and right and wrong . . . Its drama is the conflict of the ideal with compromise—with all the compromises we make to keep on living. It has to do—in intention at any rate—with finalities. It is exciting—and it slips away. In the end you are awaking slowly to the fact that the larger discussions of humanity and its difficulties fail quite to reach that poignancy which may lie in the little pointless doings of men and women." John Anderson was more impressed: "A completely fascinating play . . . as engrossing as a detective mystery, as searching and provocative as a telescope and as interesting as no play in this town has been in many months."

The London reaction was also mixed, though mainly favorable. D. B. Wyndham Lewis in the *National Graphic* (May 5, 1932) confessed: "I suffer from an unfortunate disability in the matter of plays about scientists with secret formulae enabling them to blow everything to smithereens. These ancient warshaken nerves get so jumpy with constant expectation of the big bang that after the last curtain I am generally seen leaving the theatre on all fours, jittering. *Wings Over Europe* delayed the big bang so long that when it didn't come after all I looked rather silly crawling out of the Globe in the accustomed position. Nevertheless, this play is highly interesting and unusual." The *Sketch* (May 11) called it a "remarkable play . . . satire, symbol, and moral rolled into one."

Wings Over Europe is unquestionably not only a prophetic but a vivid play. Its concern with a timely subject has made it popular for college and little theatre revivals. With its compelling theme, it combines sharp satire of politicians and the motives that underlie their decisions, in the portraits of the Cabinet ministers. Its chief flaw is the wholly impractical, almost blind, idealism of Lightfoot, whom Wyndham Lewis calls "so *exalté*, mystical, and Shelleyish, that I should not have been surprised to see him at any moment release a flock of pure white doves." In the world outside the theatre, however, when the atom bomb arrived, scientists proved themselves much the same as other muddled folk. *Wings Over Europe* vividly anticipated world events, and built a tense drama out of our most urgent world concern.

GORBODUC   *Thomas Norton*

The first English tragedy, *Gorboduc; or, Ferrex and Porrex*, 1561, marks the first use of blank verse in the English drama. It was written by Thomas Norton (1532-1584), in collaboration with Thomas Sackville (first Earl of Dorset, Baron Buckhurst, 1536-1608). It is a formal tragedy in the classical style. All the action of its five acts occurs offstage. The happenings are presented in either of two ways: they are related by a messenger, as in the Latin plays of Seneca, or they are performed in a dumb-show before the acts. The latter device is a development of the synopsis in the Greek prologues of Euripides; it became a feature of Elizabethan drama, occurring in *Hamlet** as an introduction to the play to catch the King.

Although classical in form, *Gorboduc* is English in its story. Ferrex and Porrex, the two sons of Gorboduc, a mythical British king, are supposed to divide their father's kingdom; but Porrex drives his brother from the land. Ferrex, returning with an army, is killed by Porrex. Then their mother, who loved Ferrex more, kills Porrex.

It has been suggested that the play was intended as a warning to Queen Elizabeth of the dangers hanging over a country when the crown succession is unsure; therefore she should marry and have children.

The play was praised by Sir Philip Sidney in his *Defence of Poesy* (1595): "It is full of stately speeches and well-sounding phrases, climbing to the height of Seneca his style." By 1808, it seemed of only historical interest to Charles Lamb: "The style of this old play is stiff and cumbersome, like the dresses of its times. There may be flesh and blood underneath, but we cannot get at it. Sir Philip Sidney has praised it for its morality. One of its authors might easily furnish that: Norton was an associate to Hopkins, Sternhold, and Robert Wisdom, in the *Singing Psalms*. I am willing to believe that Lord Buckhurst supplied the more vital parts." Other authorities maintain that Buckhurst probably wrote the last two acts of the play.

Acted at the Inner Temple in 1561, *Gorboduc* was published in 1565 and again in 1570. It belongs now in the library rather than in the theatre; but it remains important as the first English historical play, the first English tragedy, and the first play to use blank verse.

JUNO AND THE PAYCOCK   *Sean O'Casey*

"Everyone was getting tired of the Abbey plays, so I decided to write one for them." These were the words of a 37-year-old Dublin brick-layer, Sean O'Casey (Irish, b. 1884). His first play was rejected, but his fourth attempt, *The Shadow of a Gunman*, was accepted and well re-ceived. The promise of the fourth play was richly fulfilled in *Juno and the Paycock*, 1924, which James Agate *(New York Times,* August 29, 1937) called "the greatest play written in English since the days of Queen Elizabeth." Juno—so named because she was born in June—is the suffer-ing and eternally hopeful wife and mother; her husband Jack Boyle is the self-satisfied strutter, the "peacock". Juno's son Johnny was hurt, as a boy, in the Easter Rebellion (1916) and lost an arm in a later up-rising. When a neighbor is killed, Johnny, whom his mother is called to identify, is accused of betraying the man and executed. To ingratiate himself with the family, the schoolteacher Charlie Bentham, who seeks the hand of Juno's daughter Mary, brings word that Boyle's uncle has left them a fortune; the family buys new furniture and holds a celebra-tion. But Charlie's news is a lie; he goes off, leaving Mary pregnant, whereupon Jerry Devine, another suitor, turns from her. Creditors carry off the new furniture while the Paycock and his tipsy crony Joxer Daly philosophize, and Juno gathers the debris to start to build anew.

Dublin greeted the play with cheers and resentment. London saw it, opening November 16, 1925, for 202 performances, and awarded it the Hawthornden Prize. The play was revived in 1927, in 1934, and with Sara Allgood and Arthur Sinclair in 1937. New York saw the play first on March 15, 1926; again in 1927, 1932, 1934, 1937, in 1940 with Barry Fitzgerald for 106 performances, and in 1947 at Piscator's Dramatic Workshop.

The play's tragic aspects have an impact that is increased by verbal understatement and a broad vein of comedy. "Mr. O'Casey does not drive his comedy home with a hammer, as he does his tragedy," said the *London Sphere* (November 28, 1925). "It seems to come almost before he is aware of it himself." But in all the tragic aspects, as James Agate said, "the play is keen and alive." The comedy, drawn mainly from the "Paycock" and Joxer Daly, is none the less amusing because these men are, at bottom, poignantly pathetic figures of a spent generation.

The Dublin city speech of O'Casey's characters matches the rural Irish dialogue of Synge.* "The beauty of words is a thing all but for-gotten by the London theatre, and our great indebtedness to Mr. O'Casey is for his rediscovery of words," said the *London Times* (June 27, 1934). "But beauty of language can disguise many forms of poverty, and there is no denying that Mr. O'Casey's rhetoric helps him over a number of serious lapses . . . We have the rich humor and the variously shaded pathos of his conversational passages, and the violent, unprepared-for assaults on the emotions of his 'drama'. The two main notes of the play are isolated; they alternate, but never harmonize. The only unity comes from Juno herself in her indomitable bravery, tenderness, and humour, who subdues the breaking waves within her heart. The contemporary theatre, nevertheless, has few things as rich to offer us." A later writer in the same paper (September 21, 1951) felt a greater unity in the play: "The language flows freely and at the same time acknowledges by instinct the restraint of dramatic economy. Through scenes of high humor and rich, racy fooling the tragic story moves on with that inevitability which is the mark of organic design." There are, nevertheless, in *Juno and the Paycock,* successive drives of feeling, rather than a sustained and gathering power. Though the disasters fall upon the members of a single family, we feel their severance rather than their union. The play thus presents a gallery of portraits—sardonic, bitter, hopeful, gentle—all touched with the shadow of doom, poetically and powerfully drawn and deeply moving.

THE PLOUGH AND THE STARS   *Sean O'Casey*

This play is a story of the Easter Week Rebellion of 1916, in which Sean O'Casey himself had participated. Young Jack Clitheroe, happy with his wife Nora, goes out to fight and is killed in the street; their baby is born dead and Nora goes out of her mind. Found in this biting picture of tenement life in Dublin are the gossipy but good-hearted Mrs. Gogan, the drunken old Peter, the quick-tongued but good-hearted neighborhood prostitute Rosie Redmond, boastful, drinking Fluther Good, and bitter Bessie Burgess, who curses the rebels for killing her son but who gets shot pushing Nora to safety from a window. It is indeed, as the *New York Post* called it (April 24, 1926), "A harsh and repellent bit of portraiture." But there is fire in it. "The word 'masterpiece' should be sparingly used," said the *London Times* (July 2, 1939). "This play is more. It is a blazing masterpiece."

Opening at the Abbey Theatre, Dublin, on February 8, 1926, *The Plough and the Stars* literally started a riot. The fighting is vividly described by O'Casey in his autobiography *Inishfallen, Fare Thee Well.* "Barry Fitzgerald became a genuine Fluther Good, and fought as Fluther himself would fight, sending an enemy, who had climbed on to the stage, flying into the stalls with a flutherian punch on the jaw. And in the midst of the fume, the fighting, the stench, the shouting, Yeats*, as mad as the maddest there, pranced on the stage, shouting out his scorn, his contempt; . . . his long hair waving, he stormed in utter disregard of all around him, confronting all those who cursed and cried out shame and vengenance on the theatre, as he conjured up a vision for them of O'Casey on a cloud, with Fluther on his right hand and Rosie Redmond on his left, rising upwards to Olympus to get from the waiting gods and goddesses a triumphant apotheosis for a work well done in the name of Ireland and of art. Then the constables flooded into the theatre, just in time. Rough and ready, lusty guardians of the peace. They filed into the theatre as Irish constables for the first time in their life; mystified, maybe, at anyone kicking up a row over a mere play. They pulled the disturbers out, they pushed them out, and, in one or two instances, carried them out, shedding them like peas from the pod of the theatre, leaving them in the cold street outside to tell their troubles to their neighbours or to the stars."

In a debate (March 26, 1926) with Mrs. Skeffington, who had led the opposition to his play, O'Casey declared: "I was not trying, and I never will try, to write about heroes. I can only write about the life I know and the people I know. The people in my plays form the bone and sinew, and ultimately, I believe, they are going to form the brain of the country as well. My critics evidently want to bring every one out of the public house. I want to bring every one into the public houses to make them proper places of amusement and refreshment."

London saw the play open on May 12, 1926, for 133 performances; and again in 1930 and 1939 with Sara Allgood and Maire O'Neill, who with Arthur Sinclair had also been in the New York premiere, November 28, 1927. New York saw the play again in 1934, and at the Provincetown Playhouse in 1947. "With startling realism," said Allardyce Nicoll, "O'Casey has done for the poor in Dublin what others have done for the peasantry, and his strength develops out of his intimate knowledge of the material with which he is dealing and out of his determination to keep true to the facts he observes . . ."

O'Casey's dialogue is rich, simple, and racy; it has overtones of beauty glowing through its truth. As Gilbert Gabriel put it (November 29, 1927), the play has the "power to riddle you with steel-lipped laughter, to crush you under the tread of its insurgent, pounding grief . . . 'There's always the makin' of a row in the mention of religion.' But O'Casey is no epigram shaker. The relish of his talk lies in its raciness and real-ness. Full flavored oaths abound . . . Then, when sorrow suddenly takes charge, the language is as lithe and beautiful."

The bitterness and the sharpness of irony that underlie *The Plough and the Stars* indicate the depth of emotion within the playwright, who, like Commandant Jack Clitheroe, had fought in the Irish Citizen Army of Easter Week. Clitheroe, like O'Casey, was a bricklayer. "Though it is a tale of Easter Week in Dublin," said the *London Times* (June 27, 1939), "*The Plough and the Stars* was not at any time a propagandist or even a topical play, and the qualities of critical insight into the follies and hero-isms of man which saved it from being so preserve it now from stale-ness. It is, indeed, an object lesson to imaginative writers who, wishing to see a contemporary scene and a controversial subject, find that what seems to be a work of art today is in peril of becoming stale journalism by tomorrow. Mr. O'Casey faces this difficulty and overcomes it, not in-deed by a romanticized avoidance of contemporary fact, but by pene-trating superficial fact and ephemeral controversy and building his play upon realities underlying them."

There is, however, sharp disagreement on this point. Thus the *London Times* of September 21, 1951, stated that, when reading the play, "we are moved by each separate scene, sharing in turn the confidence of each of its pitiful, shiftless characters, without ultimately being able to discover the motive of the play itself. The apparent formlessness is de-liberate." The *Oxford Companion to the Theatre* (1951), on the other hand, declared that "the satiric use of antithesis gives form to the play and, as a result, carries it beyond photography of life into interpretation." One cannot but feel, however passing the play's events, that its person-alities recur; and it is this capture of the essence of men's lives—the deg-radation, and the nobility, of their being—that through revealed charac-ter and pungent dialogue gives power and beauty to *The Plough and the Stars*.

THE SILVER TASSIE   *Sean O'Casey*

After vehemently defending *The Plough and the Stars** when it was attacked at the Abbey Theatre in Dublin, William Butler Yeats rejected Sean O'Casey's next play, *The Silver Tassie*, 1928, and bitter correspondence between the two men ensued. Said O'Casey: *"The Silver Tassie,* because of, or in spite of, the lack of a dominating character, is a greater work than *The Plough and the Stars.* And so, when I have created the very, very thing that you are looking for—something unique—you shout out: 'Take, oh take this wine away and for God's sake bring me a pot of small beer!'" Yeats replied: "It is all too abstract after the first act; the second act is an interesting technical experiment, but it is too long for the material; and after that there is nothing." O'Casey queried: "Really nothing? Nothing at all? Well"—and here O'Casey quoted Yeats—"Where there is nothing—there is God." The trouble with O'Casey, said A.E., is that "he tries to light every cigarette on the stars."

The "tassie" in the play is a loving-cup won by Harry Heegan, soccer champion, boxer, and all-around athlete. It has become an ironic memento to Harry, back from the war "dead from the belly down." In a Dublin tenement, surrounded by ne'er-do-wells and drifters who are heedless of life's deeper concerns, the jealous Harry pushes his wheelchair around after his old sweetheart and her new flame, who had won the Victoria Cross for rescuing the wounded Harry. In helpless fury, Harry dashes the silver tassie to the ground. In the second act, the horror of war is expressionistically bodied forth, as embattled soldiers face a great crucifix that shadows the stage.

The Silver Tassie opened in London on October 11, 1929, with Charles Laughton; in the same year the Irish Players presented it in New York October 24. Bernard Shaw called it "a Hell of a play . . . the hitting gets harder and harder to the end . . . What I see is a phantasmopoetic first act, intensifying into a climax of war imagery in the second act, and then two acts of almost unbearable realism bringing down all the voodoo war poetry with an ironic crash to the earth in ruins." Gilbert Gabriel (October 25, 1929) deemed it "a play with honest greatness riling and boiling in its thickened veins; a wrathy, rough-tongued, bitter-hearted brand of greatness which passes all understanding." Shown in Dublin by the relenting Abbey Theatre on August 12, 1935, with Barry Fitzgerald, *The Silver Tassie* found some defenders, but a pacifist play among the Irish was as a sheep among wolves. The *Dublin Irish Press* (August 13, 1935) declared that it showed "much genius much perverted." The *Irish Independent* asserted that "where there is any attempt for humor it's cheap farce, relying upon vulgarity for its effects. The intelligentsia and literati, who always have flocked to the Abbey on such occasions, roared at jokes the banality of which would have made an old-time music hall audience squirm." Across the Irish Sea the *London Times* (August 16, 1935) disliked the play, though for different reasons: "It is perhaps permissible to hope that Mr. O'Casey will return to his human beings as quickly as possible. In them, not in his philosophy, lies his strength."

When The Interplayers revived *The Silver Tassie* in New York, July 21, 1949, it was evident that the second act could not—what single act could?—convey the sense of the horrid waste, the enanguishing futility, and the global scope of present-day war. The play is not wholly satisfactory, said Brooks Atkinson (August 21, 1949), "because it arbitrarily introduces one act of expressionism in the midst of a realistic play, and not everything in the expressionistic act is as intelligible as the rest." The play is, nevertheless, Atkinson continued, "a trenchant drama by an indomitable writer who is incomparably gifted."

The vigor of the realistic portions of *The Silver Tassie* brings sharply ironic comedy and poignant tragedy wth keenly drawn portraits of Dublin folk, through which—rather than through the broader but vaguer, and not wholly successful, expressionistic reach toward universals—the play takes its power and significance.

WAITING FOR LEFTY   *Clifford Odets*

The first and thus far the best of the plays by Clifford Odets (American, b. 1906) is this one-act drama, suggested by the 1934 New York taxicab strike. Slanted from the point of view of the taxi drivers, the play is sharp in irony and unusually deft in propaganda.

The theatre becomes the meeting-hall of the drivers' union. The officers of the union are onstage and its members are seated amid the audience. As the rank and file voice their grievances, flashes of their lives are shown in the corners of the stage. Among the characters are Edna and Joe, whose children are put to bed without food and whose furniture has been taken away though the installments are three-quarters paid. Despite their circumstances, Edna urges Joe to insist on the union's demands or to strike. Other such scenes further expose the stunted, empty lives of the exploited drivers. As the union members await their leader, Lefty, he is brought in—dead, killed by company "goons". The members vote to strike.

Waiting For Lefty opened in New York on February 10, 1935, together with Odets' *Till the Day I Die*, which pictures the persecution of Communists under Hitler. The production of both plays cost less than $10; borrowed tables and chairs were the only scenery. After moving to a Broadway house on February 26, the plays ran for 168 performances.

In some cities, *Waiting For Lefty* has been banned as profane and un-American. It has been very popular, however, in Soviet Russia and among radical groups for, as Brooks Atkinson put it, it "argues the case for a strike against labor racketeering and the capitalist state" and is "clearly one of the most thorough, trenchant jobs in the school of revolutionary drama . . . soundly constructed and fiercely dramatic."

Perhaps Odets' most effective quality is the swift sense of reality in his dialogue. At the moment of their utterance, his words have the force not of stage colloquy "seeming" true but of living argument and action. This sharp and life-tongued dialogue gives a partisan reality and a surging power to the drama.

S.S. GLENCAIRN   *Eugene O'Neill*

When Eugene G. O'Neill (American, 1888-1954) registered in the fall of 1914 for George Pierce Baker's famous playwrighting course at Harvard, he showed Baker an already finished one-act play, *Bound East for Cardiff*. Baker pointedly said it was not a play at all, but it was the first of O'Neill's works to be produced.

"There was a fog on the night in 1916," said the *London Times* (April 10, 1948), "when Mr. O'Neill's first play to be publicly performed, a short sea-piece entitled *Bound East for Cardiff*, was produced in a fish-

shed on a wharf in Provincetown, on the coast of Massachusetts. The
fish-shed had been transfigured, and was now the Wharf Theatre, with a
'capacity' of ninety persons: a little smaller than the Bandbox in Bergen
in which Bjornson and Ibsen learnt their craft. The cast included the
author who, however, failed to convince his audience that his father
[who had played *The Count of Monte Cristo* some 6,000 times] lived
again on the stage. . . . The fog entered Mr. O'Neill's soul that night and
has remained there ever since." Three years later, O'Neill had completed
three other short plays of the forecastle. The four are usually presented
together under the collective title *S.S. Glencairn*.

Bound East for Cardiff is scarcely more than the portrait of a dying
man, Yank, in the sickly light of the fo'c'stle, and the helpless and almost
inarticulate grief of his comrades at sea. *The Moon of the Caribbees*
shows the ship at anchor, with harbor women bringing their wares and
smuggling liquor so that the men may have a party on board. *In the Zone*
is a war play: as the ship passes through a dangerous submarine zone,
spy talk leads the crew to suspect one of their members; they pry open
his box to find a letter from an English lady who loves him but says she
must give him up because he cannot give up drink. *The Long Voyage
Home* pictures a Swedish sailor, finally deciding to leave the sea and go
home; persuaded by his mates to have one last drink with them, he is
shanghaied to a brutal voyage.

"What tough-fibred sketches they are!" said the *Boston Transcript*
(January 31, 1929). "How powerfully the spirit of the sea comes through
the heavy, brooding maleness of the crews! . . . To encompass the loves,
hates, the comradeship and the superstitious ignorance of Driscoll, Yank,
Olsen, and the other shipmates, the glib competence of Broadway acting
would be scarcely muscular enough . . . These are the simplest of Mr.
O'Neill's plays . . . Nothing comes between them and the rugged form
of life; nothing yields until it is broken by the most unscrutable of forces."
They ran for 105 performances at the Provincetown Playhouse in New
York, opening November 3, 1924; and they have been played, as a group
or singly, in little theatres constantly since.

The Moon of the Caribbees was singled out by *Theatre* magazine
(July, 1921) as "an intense and poignant chunk of life." In *Bound East
For Cardiff*, the dying Yank describes the sailors' life: "Just one ship
after another; hard work, small pay and bum grub, and when we git into
port, just a drunk endin' up in a fight and all your money gone, and
then ship away again." "That is the complete cycle," said the *Boston
Transcript*, "as *S.S. Glencairn* and its able-bodied actors describe it . . .
It seems complete and final, and you know that you are also face to face
with life." But it is life in a fog, with no goal visible, no compass; one
cannot hear the bell-buoy near the bar. The *S.S. Glencairn* series are
superb photography, to be sure, but seeing them again at the New York
City Center, May 20, 1948, with Jose Ferrer, George Coulouris, and
George Mathews, one wondered whether they are anything more.

The latter-day experimentation of O'Neill's was but foreshadowed in
these one-act plays, which were perhaps only more tense, more stark in
their realism, than others of the many being written at the time. The
trend of O'Neill's work, however, is indicated by the fact that he himself
liked least the one with the most fully developed and climactic story:
"To me *In the Zone* seems the least significant of all the plays. It is too

facile in its conventional technique, too full of clever theatrical tricks . . . At any rate, the play in no way represents the true me or what I desire to express. It is a situation drama lacking in all spiritual import—there is no big feeling for life inspiring it." Just what a playwright, or a critic, means by "feeling for life", is hardly clear but, in any event, *S.S. Glencairn* is a tense and truthful portrait of the drab and drifting men who haunt—are they more than ghosts?—the dingy quarters of the tramp steamers of the world.

BEYOND THE HORIZON *Eugene O'Neill*

Eugene O'Neill's first full length play to be produced, and his first play to reach Broadway, *Beyond the Horizon,* opened in New York on February 2, 1920. It ran for 160 performances and won a Pulitzer Prize.

The play depicts Robert Mayo, a restless plowman whose dreams of the open road end in the squalor of neglected fields. About to ship for a voyage with his uncle, Robert tells Ruth Atkins, his brother Andrew's girl, that he loves her. She responds, and Andrew, who would have been a fine farmer, ships away instead. When he returns, a wealthy man with Ruth wholly out of his mind, he finds the farm in ruin and the marriage sodden. Robert and Ruth have slumped from mutual hate to dreary indifference. Robert, dying of tuberculosis, fevered, babbling, still looks beyond the horizon, dreaming the vain hope that when he dies Ruth and Andrew will find happiness together.

Through the 1930's, the play was produced by some ten college and community groups every year. In 1937, the year after O'Neill was awarded the Nobel Prize, it had its Scandinavian premiere in Oslo. In the same year Helen Hayes played Ruth on the radio, after a long dispute with the Federal Communications Commission over the use of what it labeled "profane and indecent lines", and Margalo Gillmore acted Ruth (without the lines Helen Hayes had retained) in a 1938 broadcast. In 1947 Equity Library staged the play in New York.

"O'Neill begins crudely but honestly and frankly with a scene in which two of his chief characters sit down and tell the audience the things they ought to know," said Heywood Broun (February 4, 1920), "but after this preliminary scene the play gathers pace and power, and until the final act it is a magnificent piece of work, a play in which the happenings are of compelling interest and, more than that, a play in which the point of view of everyone concerned is concisely and clearly set forth in terms of drama . . . The power of the play is tremendous . . . it is as honest and sincere as it is artistic." The *Boston Transcript* (February 5, 1920) observed that "since the days of *The Great Divide* no such significant piece has passed to our stage."

In England, the play was less favorably received. Charles Morgan, reporting in the *New York Times* (March 30, 1938) spoke of the "rigidity" with which O'Neill identified the two aspects of his thought with the two brothers, Robert and Andrew Mayo: "Andrew, keen, eager, practical, is a first-rate portrait . . . And the setting of the play—the father, the seafaring uncle, the life of the farm—all these are Andrew's natural background. His brother Robert is an invader of the play, not because he is a youth born out of his element, for that is natural and true enough, but because O'Neill has poeticized him and has written of him in a tone and idiom different from that employed in the writing of the rest of the play. For this reason, *Beyond the Horizon* gives an impression of being a studio piece. Its poetry is not fused with its observation."

Even sharper was the double-edged attack in the *London Times* (April 10, 1948): "Mr. O'Neill's technique has been extolled for its experimental character, but it is clumsy and sometimes surprisingly ingenuous. He was not a novice when he wrote *Beyond the Horizon*, yet that play, which has six scenes when three would suffice, is singularly incontinent and full of loose ends . . . This play is intellectually, as well as physically, tuberculous. Its lungs are full of holes. Mr. O'Neill does not let his audience off a single hacking cough . . . It is in this play that the theme of all Mr. O'Neill's plays is set out: frustration and disillusionment."

Beyond the Horizon is on the whole overdrawn, perfervid, not carefully wrought, as though the playwright's memories were too turbulent to be set in polished order. Partly for this reason, the play has a disturbing power. Its ultimate effect is not so much the exultation and the exaltation of purging tragedy as it is a sense of pity, almost of self-pity, at thought of what life can do to the ineffectual beings most of us mortals are.

THE EMPEROR JONES   *Eugene O'Neill*

Eugene O'Neill's power of presenting the breaking down of a human mind is nowhere more vividly displayed than in this short play of eight episodes.

The first scene sets the background for the story. From the sycophancy and cowardly hatred of Smithers, a trader and the only white man on a small West Indian island, and from the boastfulness of Brutus Jones, an ex-Pullman porter and ex-convict who has imposed himself as Emperor upon the superstitious natives of the island, we learn that Jones has amassed a fortune; also that he has cached a boat on the farther shore of the island against the day when the natives will revolt. We learn, then, that the day of revolt has come. Lightheartedly Jones sets forth for the forest and safety.

The rest of the play depicts the fantasied flight of Jones. Reaching the forest by dark, he grows less confident. Nameless fears take shape in his mind. His fancy gives body to his crime; he envisions the slave auction block, the slave ship, and the voodoo god of his ancestors. He dispels each vision with a revolver shot; to drive off the last, he uses the silver bullet he had been saving for himself. All this time he hears the throb of the tom-tom which had summoned the natives to revolt and which ebbs and floods with his emotions. Dawn finds Jones, half dead with fatigue and fright, not at the haven of the farther shore, but returned in a circle to the forest's edge, where a silver bullet moulded by the natives brings him down.

If racking the nerves be a function of the drama, *The Emperor Jones* fulfills it. In this it was highly successful, according to the *New York American* of October 13, 1926. The *London Times* (September 11, 1925) called the whole thing "one brutal attack on your nerves." "The tom-tom stunned us as it stunned the Emperor Jones," said St. John Ervine, "and if it had not stopped when it did, I should not have been surprised to see some of my less controlled colleagues climbing onto the stage and doing a war dance."

Brutus Jones, who after the first scene plays virtually a monologue, was acted in the New York premiere (November 1, 1920, for 204 performances) by Charles S. Gilpin. Paris saw the play in 1924; London, with Paul Robeson, beginning September 10, 1925. In German, the tom-tom apparently had less effect; the critics dismissed the production by Reinhardt in Vienna, 1926, as "melodramatic rot". The play has, however, continued to be widely popular. Dublin saw it in 1927 with a white actor playing Brutus Jones. 1932 saw it performed by puppets in Los Angeles. It was also made into an opera in 1932 with music by Louis Gruenberg; Lawrence Tibbett sang it at the Metropolitan in 1933. In 1933 it was also memorably filmed with Dudley Digges and Paul Robeson. Colleges and communities have frequently revived the play. Canada Lee acted in a radio version in 1945.

The Emperor Jones unquestionably is stirring. It brought a new thrill to the theatre with its impact of fear that sends a man back toward the brute, and its hypnotic and cumulatively bloodcurdling sound. It evoked, said Richard Dana Skinner, "a mood in the theatre never before felt."

Although he spells us into a state of emotional intensity, O'Neill does not find a way to lift us with its movement. The breaking down is completely effective, but the building up—as often in O'Neill—does not follow through. Though Heywood Broun (November 4, 1920) deemed *The Emperor Jones* "the most interesting play that has yet come from the most promising dramatist in America," he was constrained to add: "He has almost completely missed the opportunities of his last scene, which should blaze with a tinder spark of irony. Instead, he rounds it off with a snap of the fingers, a little O. Henry dido." The *London Times* (September 11, 1925) more bluntly observed: "Your Ah! of admiration ends in the Ugh! of repulsion." The sum total is negation, the conclusion is defeat. Since this powerful and compelling play is the drama of a man without faith, it can only rouse emotions, it cannot direct them. Bernard Shaw called O'Neill "a Fantee Shakespeare who peoples his isles with Calibans." *The Emperor Jones* remains on the level below thought.

DIFF'RENT   *Eugene O'Neill*

This play is a grim study of Puritan conscience, eating within a prim woman until her purity grows to cankerous lust. Emma Crosby rejects the hearty sea captain Caleb Williams because he admits having had relations with a native girl off in the South Seas. Thirty years later, Emma, still ludicrously clinging to the shreds of her youth, makes overtures to the cheap, wise-cracking Benny Rogers, veteran of World War I and no-good nephew of Caleb. Benny, despising Emma, is ready to marry her for the comforts she can provide him, but Caleb, still drawn to Emma, seeks release by hanging himself. The shock of his action, and of a brutal display of Benny's real nature, sends Emma after Caleb.

The play probes deeply into the emotionally unbalanced spirit of Emma and makes a vivid impression in performance. Its New York premiere, January 4, 1921, inaugurated a run of 100 performances. London saw the play October 4, 1921. *Diff'rent* has not often been revived because the depths of Emma's distress and self-humiliation are distressing to behold. The play is "hard to stomach", said the *New York Globe*

(February 1, 1921) "but only because it is so brutal, so bitterly nauseating. It is true enough, God pity us!" Joseph Wood Krutch (March 4, 1925) went so far as to say: "When I saw *Diff'rent* some years ago, I thought it the best American play to date, and I do not believe anything written since would make this an untenable opinion."

There was, however, some critical objection both to the structure and to the story of *Diff'rent*. As late as 1948 the *London Times* (April 10) challenged both. Referring to the principle of the unity of time—"to keep a play as far as possible within a single circuit of the sun"—the *Times* remarked: "To defy the alleged Aristotelian law, however, is one thing and to treat time as confetti is another. Thirty years separate the two acts of *Diff'rent*, a play which ends with incredible suicides."

O'Neill sought to explain the purpose of the play and answer some of the objections to it in the *New York Tribune* (February 13, 1921): "*Diff'rent*, as I see it, is merely a tale of the eternal, romantic idealist who is in all of us—the eternally defeated one. In our innermost hearts we all wish ourselves and others to be 'diff'rent' . . . Either we try in desperation to clutch our dream at the last by deluding ourselves with some tawdry substitute; or, having waited the best of our lives, we find the substitute time mocks us with too shabby to accept. In either case we are tragic figures, and also fit subjects for the highest comedy, were one sufficiently detached to write it. To me, the tragic alone has that significant beauty which is truth. It is the meaning of life—and the hope. Only through the unattainable does man achieve a hope worth living and dying for—and so attain himself. There are objections to my end, but, given Caleb and Emma, the end to me is clearly inevitable."

But Caleb and Emma do not "die for" their hope; they die because they have abandoned their hope. Thus they do not "attain themselves"; they simply shirk the consequences of their own mistakes. Their end comes not with a bang but a whimper. O'Neill thought he was writing a tragedy but the play seems essentially the detailing of a psychoneurotic case-history. The final exaltation, the sense of human worth, are sadly wanting.

THE GREAT GOD BROWN   *Eugene O'Neill*

What Eugene O'Neill sought in *The Great God Brown* is suggested in an article in the *New York P M* (November 2, 1946). A Black Irishman, the article explains, is a brooding, solitary man—and often a drinknig man too—with wild words on the tip of his tongue. He is one "who has lost his faith and who spends his life searching for the meaning of life, for a philosophy in which he can believe again as fervently as he once believed in the simple answers of the Catholic Catechism." Contrasting an artist and a business man, O'Neill in this play seeks the real person behind the masks one puts on for life, but reveals himself as a "Black Irishman".

In the play, William A. Brown and Dion Anthony inherit a building construction firm. They are both in love with Margaret. When she chooses Dion, he tries to become a painter. Failing at this, he goes back to work with Brown, hiding his sensitive spirit beneath a cynical mask. Twice he tries to take off the mask and reveal his true self to Margaret, but she shrinks away in fright. The solid businessman and financial success, "the great god Brown", often needs no mask, for he requires no defense against the world around him. Yet Brown envies the more sensitive and gifted Dion, who has sought peace from Margaret's maternal possessiveness in drinking and in Cybel, a prostitute whose earthy love is wide enough to understand Dion's yearning. When Dion dies alone with Brown, the latter assumes Dion's mask and Dion's place with Margaret. The confusion, however it strikes the audience, is too much for Brown: before Margaret and before a committee to inspect his designs for a new building he shifts from Dion mask to Brown mask and back, tears up the design, says that there's no harm done and in the mask of Dion announces that Brown is dead. The police find him in the arms of Cybel, who calls him "Dion Brown"; ecstatically he recites the Lord's Prayer, and dies. Cybel says that spring will always come again, "bearing the intolerable chalice of life." Margaret kisses Dion's mask, crying: "I will feel you stirring in your sleep, forever under my heart." And to the police captain, who says gruffly: "Well, what's his name?" Cybel replies, "Man." In the Epilogue, four years later, Margaret, wearing the mask of the proud, indulgent Mother, sends her three sons in to dance, while she sits on the Casino pier where, a score of years before (in the play's Prologue), Dion and she had become engaged. Her sons gone, Margaret removes her mask, takes "from her bosom, as if from her heart" the mask of Dion, and says again, "I feel you stirring in your sleep, forever under my heart."

Straining for essences, aching for a substance where faith is lacking, unable to establish a clear-cut synthesis of characters and theme, O'Neill is constantly driven to outer resources, building his plays to unusual length or striving, as in *The Great God Brown*, by external devices to reveal the inner truth. Although there was nothing new in the use of masks to indicate various aspects of one personality, O'Neill's use of the device seemed original in some quarters. Gilbert W. Gabriel (January 24, 1926) called *The Great God Brown* an "amazing new drama of bare souls and false faces." *Theatre* magazine (April, 1926) explained that "the mask is the protagonist of the play. It is the embodiment of an identity, a distinct personality." *Commonweal* had a reservation: "In his use of realistic masks—as distinct from the representative masks of old Greek tragedy—he has plunged into a new and fascinating mode of extending the scope of emotion and spiritual contrast on the stage. His courage and vision in this respect are not yet matched by ability to use the new medium." More bluntly, Robert Benchley (February 11, 1926) challenged the value of the device: "We seem to remember equally subtle changes and conflicts of characters having been expressed in the old-fashioned theatre simply by good acting."

The introduction of Cybel (named after Cybele, the great mother of the gods), as the compassionate, consoling, comprehending spirit, is also open to attack. Said Benchley: "If Samuel Shipman had written a scene in which a prostitute teaches the Lord's Prayer to a dying man, we wise boys would be tittering yet." And Heywood Broun commented that, for the words of that strumpet over the dead body of Brown, "the stage directions say they must be spoken 'with a profound pain'. It gives me one."

The scenes with Cybel (before whom Dion, the boy scared of life, sometimes removes his mask and relaxes and rests) are taut with O'Neill's rarely manifest humor—a bitter, sardonic, twisted laugh, a wry pun like the rubbing of salt on a wound.

The Great God Brown, opening in New York on January 23, 1926, ran for 271 performances. London saw it, opening June 19, 1927. New York saw it again in 1947 (Equity Library) and 1949 (C.C.N.Y.). Apart from its devices and details, the play is impressive. Gabriel called it "a deep-minded and compassionate fantasy, often thrilling in the brightness of its words, sometimes perplexing in the shadows of its meaning." "The new play," said *Commonweal*, "has high moments of rich spiritual insight, of abiding faith, and understanding of the mystic vale of tears." It is "a passionate cry of the artist in the modern world of commerce," said Freedley and Reeves in their *History of the Theatre* (1941). The spiritual torment of Brown, the business man, however, is as great as that of Dion the artist. For, O'Neill seems to inquire, who can find himself, then be himself, in this twisted world? Only tucked away in the dream of the mother-mistress does the vision of the man march on. To look at oneself unmasked is also blinding. Such are the ideas that seep through the tortured figures of *The Great God Brown*.

ANNA CHRISTIE   *Eugene O'Neill*

Out of Eugene O'Neill's drinking and seafaring days came one of the most vivid of his dramas. The saloon in which, according to George Jean Nathan, O'Neill used to sleep under the bunghole of a whiskey barrel is Jimmy-the-Priest's, where *Anna Christie* opens. Chris Christopherson, captain of a coal barge, hates "dat ole devil sea"; he has had his daughter Anna brought up, safe from its terrors, on a relative's Minnesota farm. Now, in the saloon, as he tells his mistress, Marthy, that she can sail with him no more, for Anna is coming to stay with him, and "She is goot girl, my Anna", Anna bristles in through the family entrance, orders a drink: "Gimme a whiskey—ginger ale on the side. And don't be stingy, baby!" And only Anna's father, onstage or off, is unaware that the girl is a member of her sex's oldest profession.

The sea that Chris hates cleanses Anna. Out of that sea through the fog comes Mat Burke, a shipwrecked sailor, to make honest love to her. In the peace and salve and release of her soul, Anna tells of her horrible days of ill-treatment on the farm, where her cousin had seduced her, and of her bitter life before joining her father. The fury of Mat flames against the fury and remorse of Chris; the men quarrel, then get drunk together, then return to be reconciled with Anna. The two men—still on the edge of mutual slaughter—have signed on the same ship; Anna will wait for Mat.

Originally entitled *Chris Christopherson*, the play was tried out with Lynn Fontanne as Anna; it was withdrawn in Philadelphia for revision. On November 2, 1921, it opened in New York as *Anna Christie*, with Pauline Lord, for 177 performances. The London production, opening April 10, 1923, ran for 103 performances. The play has been frequently revived: in 1941, Ingrid Bergman played Anna in Santa Barbara; in 1942 both play and film (the latter with Greta Garbo and Marie Dressler) were seen in Baltimore; June Havoc essayed the title role in 1948. In 1922 the play was awarded the Pulitzer Prize.

The authenticity of atmosphere, both saloon and sea, won considerable praise. A captain of the British merchant marine, author and twenty-two years a sailor, David W. Bone, commented in the *New York Times* (January 15, 1922) that the play "has brought our true environment to the boards." Praise went also to the characterization of Anna. In the *London Observer* (April 11, 1937) Ivor Brown likened her to "every broken blossom that ever drifted through a brothel and emerged to allure the lusty youth of the waterfront." After the New York premiere, Kenneth Macgowan stated: "Miss Lord's Anna Christie is the most perfect piece of naturalism I have ever seen on the American stage." One other naturalistic aspect of the play, its salty use of language, was noted by the *London Times* (April 8, 1937): "This is a comparatively early example of the many American experiments in inarticulacy . . . For here is not only the confused utterance and worn imagery of the illiterate, but Anna herself, in the crisis of her life, turns naturally to the 'language and gestures of the heroics in the novels and movies' with which she is familiar."

Despite the chorus of praise, the play aroused considerable controversy. The two main points of dissatisfaction were mentioned in the London *Punch* (December 6, 1944), which insisted that Captain Chris's "confusion between devil and deep sea is the play's most trying repetition", then bracketed the other objection with its praise: "For about five-sixths of its length—until, indeed, the author yields to the melting mood in the flat calm of a happy ending—the play is a tough, passionate drama, talking at the top of its voice and holding us with the gaze of the Ancient Mariner." "What is really the matter with this play," said the *London Times* (April 11, 1937), stressing the first point, "is that big red herring, the ocean. What is the strength of old Christopherson's 'Dat ole devil sea!' which he reiterates so often? Even in 1923 it didn't seem to have much point."

Although O'Neill provides little justification for Chris's deep distrust of the sea, *Anna Christie* is well motivated and constructed. However, the very critics who had previously lamented the unending dreariness and depression of O'Neill's plays, now objected to his happy ending, calling it unnatural and conventional. When O'Neill went so far as to boast, in the *New York Times* (May 11, 1924), that the last act "was the most courageous and original act of the play," the *London Times* (April 11, 1937) retorted: "Nonsense."

Anna Christie speaks vividly and powerfully of the sea and the sea's influence upon three quite different persons. Like the sea, from which it springs, it is turbulent; it is sunny, with sudden storms; and within the "very ordinary little drab", Anna, we can feel what is within most ordinary folk, the urge of a dream toward a finer self. This upward urging, mystic within the summons of the sea beyond the conventional drop of a happy curtain, gives the play considerable distinction.

THE HAIRY APE   *Eugene O'Neill*

This is another play by O'Neill that makes strong impact when first seen, but that on reflection seems to depend less upon any basic drive of thought than upon sheer emotional rouse. In this sense, it has been properly compared to the tales of Poe.

Subtitled "A Comedy of Ancient and Modern Life", *The Hairy Ape* is presented in eight scenes. When Yank Smith, a stoker who refers to himself as "the hairy ape", isn't seeking a society where he "belongs", he spends much time wondering why there are places where he does not belong. His wonder is on the level of a man first struggling with thought; twice the stage directions make him assume "the attitude of Rodin's *The Thinker*".

In the first scene, set in a ship's stokehole, Yank is comparatively articulate. Rejoicing in the power of steel and steam, he scorns his tipsy shipmate, who laments the passing of the old sailing ships. But Yank's assurance and security disappear when Mildred Douglas, a wealthy socialite with a pallid urge toward social service, enters his world. Slumming to see the stokehole, she gets a breath of his language, a gaze at his face, cries "Oh, the filthy beast!" and faints. His cocksureness destroyed by Miss Douglas' reaction, Yank goes awondering. His walk on Fifth Avenue—where manikins in mechanical accents utter banalities—lands him in jail. At I.W.W. headquarters he is taken for a fool or a spy and thrown out. Finally, at the zoo, he tries to shake hands with a gorilla, which crushes him to death and stalks off.

Opening in New York March 9, 1922, with Louis Wolheim and Carlotta Monterey (whom O'Neill married seven years later), the play ran for 127 performances. There was an unsuccessful attempt in May to suppress the play as indecent because of the language the stokers use. The play was later performed in Paris, 1922; in Moscow, 1923; in London, with Paul Robeson, 1931. Arthur Pollock (March 10, 1922) called it "not only absorbing, but astounding." Alexander Woollcott considered it "a bitter, brutal, wildly fantastic play of nightmare hue and nightmare distortion . . . now flamingly eloquent, now choked and thwarted and inarticulate . . . a turbulent and tremendous play, so full of blemishes that the merest fledgling among the critics would point out a dozen, yet so vital and interesting and teeming with life that those playgoers who let it escape them will be missing one of the real events of the year." Charles Darnton (April 19, 1922) was less enthusiastic: "It is only natural to feel deeply sorry for the poor furnace-feeding devils who are in a hell of a hole on an ocean steamship. You realize this, if no more, in Eugene O'Neill's pitiless play, *The Hairy Ape*, now cursing its luck at the Plymouth Theatre . . . It suggests nothing so much as despair run amuck. It is a strangely interesting play, though it pounds so persistently on one note that you may find it monotonous."

The *New York Herald-Tribune* in an editorial (April 20, 1922) drew an old moral from the play: "What does that horrifying final scene imply wherein the man-ape of the forest crushes the ape-man of the stokehole? . . . In this brutal death grapple, which equals in intensity any one Poe ever described, one can hear the old Poundtexts shouting: 'Except ye conquer the animal within you he will conquer you!' "

Heywood Broun, champion of the advance-guard, lashed out at *The Hairy Ape*. Its basic motivation, he maintained, is wrong. Yank prides himself upon his importance and his strength until Miss Douglas faints at sight of him. "This seemed to us a fear and horror distinctly flattering. Yank might well have swelled his chest a little further at the thought that the sight of his crude power had proved overwhelming. Other gods have never grown self-conscious and ashamed when mortals looked at them and could not endure it. Medusa might as well have wailed that she did not belong because some venturesome people looked and turned to stone." There is, indeed, no explanation, no proffered justification, of Yank's reaction. We must take O'Neill's word for it that this particular man was affected in this particular way. That, however, tears off the cloak of universal significance.

Certain details of *The Hairy Ape* call for examination. O'Neill says that the treatment of none of the scenes should be "naturalistic"; yet all give the impression of realism, except that of the marionette-like persons on Fifth Avenue. This one non-representational incident is, thus, obtrusive: "the slabs on either side," said Broun, "are overlarge for the fantasy." The engines in the stoke hole showed flaws for which O'Neill, though he sat in throughout rehearsals, should perhaps not be blamed. Bennett Cerf in the *Saturday Review* (September 25, 1948) recalled O'Neill's old crony who wrote: "I liked the show a lot, Gene; but for God's sake, tell that Number Four stoker to stop leaning his prat against that red-hot furnace."

A basic flaw in the play's construction is the playwright's neglect of Mildred Douglas. Carefully he builds up her background, her wealth, her artificiality, her boredom, her social interest (part pose out of boredom, part craving for sensation, part restless urge of the spirit). Then O'Neill fronts her with "the hairy ape". Thereupon she disappears from the play.

The Hairy Ape again confronts us with a fundamental fact about O'Neill; he can tear a passion to tatters, but he is always felling Humpty-Dumpty; he cannot put the pieces together again. But his analysis of the process of disintegration is unequalled in the American drama.

ALL GOD'S CHILLUN GOT WINGS   *Eugene O'Neill*

Critical opinion now places this play somewhat higher than when first it scorched the stage with its picture of an inferior and neurotic white girl who, in her frantic search for security, drags down a more sensitive and somewhat more intelligent Negro. In spite of O'Neill's statement (*New York Times*, May 11, 1924) that "Jim and Ella are special cases, and represent no one but themselves", the general problem of white and Negro is so closely touched in the play that it is bound to obtrude. No doubt it prevented immediate judgments from being objective.

The play is set "years ago" and opens on a lower New York street corner in a poor section, with one abutting street of white folk and one of Negroes. Children are playing together regardless of color, and little white Ella Downey has a crush on Negro Jim Harris. Years flow by. Ella has become the mother of an illegitimate child to prize-fighter Mickey, who sends his henchman Shorty to get rid of her. Shorty offers her a place in his "stable"; in a spin of revulsion against her life, Ella accepts the constant love of Jim. They marry, despite hostility on both sides of the color line. Two years in France, increasingly unhappy, make them feel they are dodging their fight, and they return to New York for Jim to continue his law study. But Ella, more and more torn and neurotic and in need of a sense of superiority, ever more distressfully plagues Jim. He fails in his examination, and Ella's mind cracks. Instead of crying "Nigger!", as she had been, she becomes again as she was in their earliest years and says "I love you, Jim." The Negro, exalted in his devotion, bends himself to the service of the mind-shattered White.

The early scenes of the play leap across time. Nine years elapse between the first scene and the second; five, between that and the third. It may be questioned whether a better, because a more tightly knit play, might not have omitted the scenes prior to the marriage of Ella and Jim, allowing those earlier days to glower through the consequent conflict. And surely the days in France—jumped over in the two years between Act I and Act II—the days in which the gulf between Ella and Jim first becomes conscious to them, make a scène à faire; the audience has a right to see that first flaring of Ella's suppressed hatred and the early efforts at adjustment.

The first scene, which endeavors to show that "the color line" does not cross childhood, is hardly convincing; it is difficult to believe that eight-year-olds in a crowded city have not already become aware of, and assumed, color attitudes. In any event, this scene was denied the first New York audiences. Just before the premiere, May 15, 1924, Mayor Hylan revoked the permit for children to appear in the play, and Paul Robeson and Mary Blair had to carry on after the first scene was read to the audience. The next morning the *New York Post* declared it "a pity that our colleague in criticism couldn't have withheld some of the other scenes as well. By collaborating judiciously with Mr. O'Neill he might have pared the piece down to the one-act play that it really is, dramatically, and made it a brief but poignantly moving tragedy." The *Post* concluded, however: "It is the same arbitrary O'Neill, who goes straight to the center of a situation and tears its heart out. Such procedure leaves the landscape a wreckage, but it is breath-taking." Seven years later, the *New York Herald-Tribune* (November 1, 1931) called *All God's Chillun Got Wings* "perhaps his greatest play."

Paul Robeson and Flora Robson acted in the play in London in 1933; it had earlier been performed there in 1926 and 1928. Attention was now turning to the two central figures, the portrayal of which is O'Neill's greatest strength in this drama. The *New York Times* had already (May 16, 1924) said that the picture of Jim "grips attention and tingles in the nerves." In measuring "America's greatest playwright" against England's greatest, the *London Times* (April 10, 1948) took the position that in *All God's Chillun Got Wings*, "Mr. O'Neill comes a terrible cropper, bringing no thought to his theme."

This play neither uplifts the spirit, nor points a path for the mind. As the *New York Evening World* (May 16, 1924) summed it up, "Mr. O'Neill's work proceeds from start to finish along a straight path of degeneration into a drab and dreary monotone of despair . . . In the end, the play has helped nothing and nobody by the measure of a single thought." But the anguish of it enters our bones. For O'Neill, however we may fail to take flame from him in spiritual exaltation or intellectual rouse, scrapes out the very marrow of our feelings.

DESIRE UNDER THE ELMS   *Eugene O'Neill*

This farmhouse tragedy is another O'Neill play that builds cumulatively to an effect of great power. It opened in New York, November 11, 1924, for 208 performances. With its frank language, its "distresses", as the *New York Herald-Tribune* called them, that range "from unholy lust to infanticide, and include drinking, cursing, vengeance and something approaching incest", the play was at once attacked. It was exonerated by a citizens' play jury in New York, February 25, 1925. In London it was banned by the censor until 1938; though it had a private production there, opening February 24, 1931, it was not publicly enacted until January 20, 1940. In Los Angeles the cast was arrested (February 18, 1926). Nevertheless, the play has been widely performed: Prague, 1925; Moscow, 1932; Stockholm, 1933; and it has been given by community groups in the United States, for its manner of production is a challenge to little theatre ingenuity. The play was revived off-Broadway by The Craftsmen, November 21, 1951, so effectively that they wished to transfer their production to Broadway, but were prevented by ANTA, which opened its own Broadway revival January 16, 1952.

To a New England farmhouse of 1850, old Ephraim Cabot has taken as his third wife young Abbie Putnam, who welcomes the security he offers. Two of his sons decide to go west, but Eben, who hopes to inherit the farm, remains behind, hating the new wife. Not having a son by Ephraim, Abbie seduces young Eben, and their child is born. Eben feels that he has avenged his mother upon his father. At the celebration of the baby's birth, Ephraim dances while the neighbors snicker behind the back of the seventy-six-year-old farmer. But the combined urge for security and lust in Abbie have melted into a love for Eben; to prove that she did not merely want an heir to claim the farm, she kills the child. Eben leaves to report the murder to the Sheriff, while Abbie tells the enraged Ephraim that it was not his child. When the Sheriff comes, Eben deepens in his love of Abbie enough to share the blame and go off to prison with her. In a surge of personality rare at the end of an O'Neill play, the main figures rise to face their bitter lot.

The power of the play is impressive. On its New York opening, the *New York Herald-Tribune* declared that "O'Neill again eats his heart out in the bitter torments of despair"—overlooking the fact that the play ends not in a slump of despondency but with a lift of resolution in the midst of disaster. The *Times* found it "essentially a story of solitude, physical solitude, the solitude of the land, of men's dreams, of love, of life." Gilbert W. Gabriel commented: "Some moments were vivid and great ones. Some sloughed off into maudlin dreariness. Some wrenched the clothes from gnarled, grimy farm folk. Others reclothed them in poetic masquerade and togas of deliberate oratory. It is a story so grim it will sour the spittle in most persons' mouths." Alexander Woollcott remarked: "A strong tide swept through it; it was hewn from the stuff of life itself; and it was marked from first to last with boldness and with imagination." Burns Mantle called it "stark, morbid, forbidding tragedy; a cheerless, fascinating, hopeless, thrilling human document."

As the title indicates, the drama develops variations on the theme of desire. Old Ephraim desires to maintain the farm and keep warm o' nights; sons Simeon and Peter desire freedom from the hard New England farm life; son Eben desires to hold on to what his mother had; and Abbie desires a home, security, then love. Rooted in insecurity and insufficiency, their desires are doomed to be frustrate.

The stage set of *Desire Under the Elms* is most effective. It shows the ground before the Cabot farmhouse, and the front of the building, with the windows of four rooms, two on each story. The walls of these rooms are removed at will, so that we watch the action outdoors, or in any of the rooms, or in several at once, with not only a continuity but an intimacy of action.

O'Neill's efforts to give symbolism and universal import to the play

are frustrated by the very complexity of the detailed incidents themselves; such a series of happenings and actions can bear no general application; it is possible only as a unique train of events involving particular
individuals.   Hence, again—as most often in O'Neill's plays—the accumulated power is lost as in a fizzling fuse.   Hence the reversal of Woollcott's first enthusiasm, and his conclusion that the play "falters feebly at
its climax and remained, when seen in retrospect after the final curtain,
essentially unimportant."

Despite O'Neill's usual failure to give an individual story universal
overtones, *Desire Under the Elms* has all his depth of human analysis,
his emotional power, and, in addition, a lift of courage and constancy at
the end that does not let the human spirit die.

LAZARUS LAUGHED   *Eugene O'Neill*

O'Neill's one play of high affirmation, of exalting faith in life, *Lazarus
Laughed*, tells the story of Lazarus of Bethany, whom Jesus (*The Bible:
John*, 11-12) has brought back from the dead.   His message that there is
no death, that all is life and love, brings him eager followers, many of
whom, including his parents and sisters, are slain.   With his wife, Miriam,
Lazarus goes to Rome, where his message troubles Tiberius Caesar and
his nephew Caligula.   Caesar's mistress, Pompeia, jealously poisons
Miriam, who lifts her dead frame for a moment to cry "There is only
life," then sinks back, still.   Tiberius orders Lazarus burned to death,
and Tiberius is killed by Caligula, who tries haltingly to achieve Lazarus'
exaltation.   He watches Lazarus laugh while burning.   Lazarus dies with
a final sigh of compassion as Caligula cries "Forgive me, Lazarus! Men
forget!"

The fullest tribute paid the play was by Lewis Mumford in a review
of the published version in the *New York Herald-Tribune* (November 20,
1927): "It was little less than an act of genius to seize upon the figure
of Lazarus to sum up in magnificent pageant and design the truth toward
which Mr. O'Neill has been striving.   What happens is something so
beautiful and stunning in Mr. O'Neill's hands that I am reluctant to take
it out of its context . . . Mr. O'Neill confronts Lazarus with the morbid
power and spiritual degradation of Rome, even as he must confront his
own affirmation of life with all the pathologies in the contemporary
Romes he has explored . . . Using every resource of dramatic art, from
the pageant to the mass, from the formal movement of figures masked as
in Greek tragedy to the intense realism of *The Weavers**, Mr. O'Neill has
expressed in a poetic form all that his previous plays have led to.   It is a
great, an exhilarating achievement."

Mumford's judgment of the printed play is unfortunately not sustained by performance.   The title-page calls *Lazarus Laughed* "a play
for an imaginative theatre", but the actual theatre cannot meet its demands.   What human organs of sound can, for example, convey the
ecstatic affirmation of Lazarus' laughter?   At one place in the play, the
laughter, according to the stage directions, continues for four minutes.
At the Fordham University production, April 8, 1948, the spirit of the
laughter was represented by music.   The *London Times* (April 10, 1948)
mercilessly pointed out that when the brother of Martha and Mary is
summoned from the tomb, Lazarus arrives in a "fit of giggles".   The

Times might have added that Lazarus talks endlessly, but says nothing comprehensible. The thought behind the play has no intellectual nor spiritual depth, nor does it develop in the course of the play. The idea of having the restored Lazarus laugh is not in the *Bible* nor in legend; it was O'Neill's invention. He seems to have liked it, for the entire play is a repetition of the strain: "There is only laughter." "O'Neill's own tragedy, and ours," said John Mason Brown in *Still Seeing Things*, "has been that though he possesses the tragic vision he cannot claim the tragic tongue."

There have been several public readings of the play; its complexity forbids frequent performance. The world premiere, at Pasadena, California, April 9, 1928, used 125 supernumeraries, besides a score of speaking parts. Every character save Lazarus is masked. In addition to the Semitic masks for Lazarus' family and early followers and the individual masks for the major figures, there are military masks, the masks for the various crowds, and the forty-nine different masks of each sex, for the seven choruses representing seven ages of life, each chorus containing seven different types of character.

The most vivid character in the play is Caligula, fearfully, desperately striving for faith. There is an anguish in him that comes across the footlights, as the exaltation and the endless faith of Lazarus do not. Thus even Brooks Atkinson, who declared (April 25, 1948) that beside O'Neill's vitality all else is superficial, also added: "The recent Fordham production of *Lazarus Laughed* painfully disclosed the poverty of his use of words when he is trying to express ecstasy or exaltation. Nor is O'Neill a thinker. Although he is always digging at the roots of life, his intellectual conclusions are hardly impressive. Under the impression that he is being profound, he habitually overwrites because he cannot prove a point except by repeating it over and over. As a conscious artist, O'Neill lacks grace."

There is a note of hysteria in *Lazarus Laughed*, not only in the frantic Caligula, but in the crowds that sway between a superstitious adoration of Lazarus and the bloody lust to kill. The theme of the play, as it emerges in the continuing action, is not so much the message of Lazarus himself, as the powerlessness of such a dream when fronted by fear. Fear, preventing faith, destroys the faithful. Caligula cries to be forgiven, because men forget. *Lazarus Laughed* shows that men will require forgiveness as long as they fear. It is a play that should soar in the heavens like a comet of fire. Even though O'Neill could manage no more than a sky-rocket, he stirs us with the impulse toward the light. Onstage, the play cannot realize its intentions, but even Thor could not drain the ocean through Utgard-Loki's horn. O'Neill has tried to gulp the mystery of life and death in a laugh.

STRANGE INTERLUDE   *Eugene O'Neill*

The nine acts of this Pulitzer Prize play required that performances begin at 5:30 p.m. when it opened in New York on January 30, 1928, running for 426 nights with Lynn Fontanne; Pauline Lord and Judith Anderson have also played its leading role. When Boston banned the play, it opened at nearby Quincy on September 30, 1929. London saw it February 3, 1931, with Mary Ellis and Basil Sydney. It was cut to three hours' playing time for Europe (Vienna, 1936). Lynn Fontanne acted in a radio version in 1946.

George Jean Nathan hailed O'Neill's play as "the finest, the profoundest drama of his entire career, a drama, I believe, that has not been surpassed by any that Europe has given us in recent years and certainly by none that has been produced in America." The *Boston Transcript*, (October 25, 1929) concurred: "It has affirmed his originality and power as a dramatist, his insight into the dark places of human living, his intrinsically tragic imagination, his ambition to widen and deepen the scope of the stage. His tendency to excess, his occasional obtuseness, his unconscious lapses, are less faults in themselves than the price his temperament pays for virtues."

Beyond its length, *Strange Interlude* marked the continuing of O'Neill's experimentation, in its use of "asides"—though "forethoughts" might be a better term. Time and again the characters utter their thoughts aloud before speaking to those around. The audience is thus carried along on two planes of reality: the outer, audible level on which the characters address and show themselves to one another; and the inner, self-conscious level of thoughts and recognized feelings.

The story revolves around Nina Leeds who, at her father's insistence, has waited to marry until her beloved Gordon comes back from the war; he does not return. In agony at not having given herself to him, Nina becomes a promiscuous war-bride, until, we are assured, she can clear away her neurosis by rearing her own children. Loving her hero still, she marries his male idolator, the ineffectual but wholesome Sam Evans, and by him becomes pregnant. Told by Sam's mother that there is insanity in the family, Nina aborts the burden; then, at old Mrs. Evans' suggestion, she picks a healthy man and has his child. Sam thinks the boy is his and although Nina and the real father, Dr. Edmund Darrell, fall in love, Nina refuses to leave or to disillusion Sam. Nina's friend, Charlie Marsden, watching all this, suspects and is jealous. The boy, named Gordon after Nina's ideal, resents Darrell's intrusion into the family life and thus comes to hate his actual father while he loves Sam. Finally Nina, piqued by her son Gordon's growing away from her, closer to his fiancée, Madeline Arnold, and closer to his "father" Sam, decides to tell Sam that Gordon is not his child. Sam's heart-failure prevents this. The love between Nina and Darrell has grown cold and empty, and Nina settles down "with drowsy gratitude" to warm the rest of her nights with "dear old Charlie" Marsden.

The examination of Nina Leeds is thorough and complete. She might seem, indeed, a more natural person were the analysis less thorough, for we note that (as in *Mourning Becomes Electra** with incest) O'Neill has taken pains to include every possible relationship of heterosexual love. We observe introspective Nina and her dream-ideal lover; her father; casual "lovers"; husband; father of her child, who becomes a true lover; understanding friend; and son. The study, granting all these relationships, and the quirks of the story (with its intruding insanity, and the son growing in the dream-lover's image) is psychologically profound, but the strain of granting all these fortuities, which in a novel might (through the 25 years the play covers) be clothed in explanatory and solidifying atmosphere, reduces the drama to a tour de force that is true in the details of its character observation, yet essentially false. O'Neill explores the caverns of love as one bearing light through a labyrinth; he reaches the Minotaur, but he holds no Ariadne's thread to lead him out to the sky once more.

The chief merit of the play, according to Gilbert W. Gabriel (*New York Sun*, February 6, 1928), is its use of spoken thought: "The whole worth—not only the novelty, the passing originality, but the whole big worth—of *Strange Interlude* is hung upon these soliloquies and asides. It is these that make dualism out of Sardoualism. It is these that plunge the play's violences back into deep vistas of each character's past, illuminate each of those memories and motives which play even greater parts than do the living bodies before your eyes." Brooks Atkinson, on the other hand (January 31, 1928) remarked: "One irreverently suspects that there may be an even deeper thought unexpressed than the nickel-weekly jargon that Mr. O'Neill offers as thinking." And St. John Ervine, in the *London Observer* (March 13, 1932) maintained that if *Strange Interlude* "were shorn of its last two acts and its valueless asides, it would make a moderately interesting play."

Analysis of the asides shows that they do not forward the action of the drama. In many cases, the character "thinks aloud" a thought or feeling, then speaks it. Dudley Nichols put his finger on the fault when he said in the *New York World* (January 31, 1928): "This is a psychological novel of tremendous power and depth put into the theatre instead of between the covers of a book." O'Neill—son of an actor whose work he despised—blunts the actor's part by his various devices: in *The Great God Brown** masks blank the mobility of expression; in *Strange Interlude* the double wording of thought or feeling dams the actor from creative expression. "The characters are automata," said Brooks Atkinson (May 13, 1928). Such intensity as develops springs from the emotional baring of the story, and the personal power of the performer, breaking through the artificiality and loquaciousness of the device.

"Whatever one may think personally of the story and the significance of Mr. O'Neill's long drama," said Atkinson (May 13, 1928, shortly after it was awarded the Pulitzer Prize) "it is a heavily-freighted piece of work, uncompromising, forceful, and sustained." The complex intertangled relationships of Nina Leeds and her men make the fullest study of a woman in the American theatre. It loses in intensity through the very logic of its completeness, but its analysis is as implacable as complete, making *Strange Interlude*, though unsuccessful in its experimental features, richly revealing. Elmer Rice in *Harper's Magazine* (Spring 1932) called it a "bitterly anti-feministic play", but O'Neill has merely laid bare a woman's soul.

DYNAMO   *Eugene O'Neill*

Critical opinion differs sharply as to the merits of *Dynamo*, O'Neill's most fully developed indictment of the rootless and faithless core of machine civilization. Planned as the first of a trilogy, O'Neill's own lapse of faith in the work kept him from writing the two succeeding plays. He had hoped, he says, for a unit of three plays "that will dig at the roots of the sickness of today as I feel it—the death of an old god and the failure of science and materialism to give any satisfying new one for the surviving primitive religious instinct to find a meaning for life in, and to comfort its fears of death with."

The stage of *Dynamo* shows the exterior and, at will, the interior of two houses, and the space between, in a small Connecticut town. In one house dwells the most serious Reverend Hutchins Light, with his narrow, not wholly resigned wife Amelia and their earnest son Reuben. Next door dwells the atheistic practical joker Ramsay Fife, superintendent of a hydroelectric plant, with his over-plump and sentimental wife May and their alert and slangy daughter Ada. As expected, Ada and Reuben fall in love, but the mocking disbelief of Fife and the black puritan severity of Reuben's father wring to anguish of doubt in Reuben's mind, and rip his will apart. He runs away, returning fifteen months later to find his beloved mother dead. "Electricity is God now," says Reuben to his father; he takes a job in Fife's plant. With a sense of guilt toward his mother, and a sense of sin with Ada, Reuben finds a Mother — the Great Mother, the creator and comforter—in the Dynamo. In the great dynamo room with its high galleries of switches and fretwork of wires, Ada protests that Reuben has been neglecting her, and that she loves him. They have, for the first time, made love. At first, Reuben tries to speak of it as natural—mere sex, neither mystery nor sin—then, falling under the spell of the dynamo, the overwrought Reuben feels defiled; he shoots Ada, and embraces the Dynamo. "Reuben's voice rises in a moan that is a mingling of pain and loving consummation, and this cry dies into a sound that is like the crooning of a baby, and merges and is lost in the dynamo's hum. Then his body crumples to the steel platform."

The play was produced in New York on February 11, 1929, with Claudette Colbert, Glenn Anders and Dudley Digges. St. John Ervine in the *New York World* admired O'Neill's "charming and tender love passage", but queried: "Is he obliged to go on with this Greenwich Village sentimental cynicism?" Back in England, Ervine was more blunt; he wrote in the *Observer* (March 13, 1932): "Some of his plays are of quite incredible stupidity: for example, *The First Man, Welded*, and a piece called *Dynamo*, which stupefied his admirers." Yet Brooks Atkinson, by no means a consistent admirer of O'Neill's, hailed the play (February 12, 1929): "At last he seems to have gotten the form of his drama in harmony with the universal theme he is fully developing . . . a drama of overwhelming stature . . . has epitomized the spiritual record of the scientific and machine era. . . . Writing on the most essential theme of modern life, Mr. O'Neill has strength and breadth, and a lashing, poetic fury."

Dynamo "contains some of O'Neill's finest writing" said Freedley and Reeves in *A History of the Theatre* (1941); and O'Neill defended himself against those that attacked the play's style, writing for the *New York Times* (March 3, 1929): "Jones once said that a very noticeable point about my plays was that I wrote primarily by ear for the ear, and that most of my plays, even down to the rhythm of the dialogue, had the definite structural quality of a musical composition. This, I think, hits the nail on the head. Willy-nilly, it seems, my stuff takes this form . . . I believe it to be a virtue, although it is the principal reason why I have been blamed for useless repetitions, which to me were significant recurrences of theme." Again, however, O'Neill, with true psychological turn but poor reason, defended the weakest aspect of his writing. He is neither poet nor musician. He wields not the baton but the scalpel. His words do not make harmony; they explore discord. They do not unite in a symphony; they dissect the human heart. O'Neill is equally astray on the question of the asides in Dynamo. He regards them, according to his notes (July 18, 1930), as a "hangover inclination to use *Interlude* technique regardless—that was what principally hurt *Dynamo*, being forced into thought-asides quite alien to the essential psychological form of its characters." Actually, their use here is better directed than in *Strange Interlude**. In the earlier play, the thought-aside announces speech that usually but echoes the thought; in *Dynamo*, the thought-aside motivates speech that begins where the thought leaves off. Insofar as there is any validity in this dual plane of revelation, it is more manifest in *Dynamo*.

Overwrought in the reading, the play, in sensitive performance, gains more measure, more power of imposing credence, more weight as a symbol. Being symbolic, its characters are drawn to represent contrasting attitudes—the superstitiously and rigidly pious; the mocker whose very atheism is a religion—rather than to embody warm humans. The intensity of its direct drive, nevertheless, and the clarity and simplicity of its theme—the failure of the machine age either to eliminate or to improve the idols at whose altars we fall—give *Dynamo* an intellectual force lacking in some of O'Neill's more humanly vibrant dramas.

MOURNING BECOMES ELECTRA   *Eugene O'Neill*

Following the plot pattern of the *Oresteia** trilogy of Aeschylus, *Mourning Becomes Electra* is O'Neill's most neatly constructed play. With names suggestive of the ancient Greeks (Ezra Mannon for Agamemnon, Orin for Orestes), O'Neill set his trilogy at the time of the American Civil War. "Homecoming" shows Christine Mannon, while her husband is at war, having an affair with an outcast cousin, Adam Brant. Christine's jealous daughter, Lavinia, discovering the affair, notifies her father whom she idolizes; on Ezra's return Christine poisons him. "The Hunted" shows Christine using her power over her son Orin to induce him to marry Hazel Niles. Her plan might have succeeded, but Lavinia and Orin overhear Brant and Christine planning to go away together. Orin shoots Brant and virtually forces Christine to kill herself. In "The Haunted", Orin and Lavinia, returned from a long voyage, have failed to rid themselves of "the curse of the house of Mannon". Lavinia seeks a way out in marriage with Peter Niles. Orin, after making more than brotherly overtures to Lavinia, in disgust of soul shoots himself. When Peter Niles is repelled by the morbid intensity of Lavinia's desire, she makes the Mannon home her living tomb.

The play takes five and a half hours to perform; in New York the curtain rose at 5 p.m. The play opened there October 26, 1931 for a run of 150 performances with Alla Nazimova, Alice Brady, and Earle Larimore. On tour, then in New York, were Judith Anderson, Florence Reed, and Walter Abel. London saw the play opening November 19, 1937 for 106 performances. Erwin Piscator produced it at his Dramatic Workshop, New York, in 1947.

There is a surging power in *Mourning Becomes Electra*. It is, thought the *London Times* (April 10, 1948) "O'Neill's masterpiece, and is superbly constructed." It moves, said John Mason Brown in *Seeing More Things* (1948), "with the white heat of tragedy", at least for the first two parts, "before the play became mired in Freud." The three parts, said Burns

Mantle (October 27, 1931) are "artistically important and physically wearying." More enthusiastically Gilbert W. Gabriel declared: "They capture a firmness of wording, a litheness of incident, a burning beauty, which insure them rightful place among dramatic masterpieces of the world today."

The length of the trilogy was scored vehemently by St. John Ervine in the *London Observer* (March 13, 1932): "Mr. O'Neill is a verbose author who declines to be economical in his writing. He will not use one word where he can use six, nor say in a sentence what he can say in a page . . . This spendthrift habit has grown upon him to such an extent that he cannot now write a play in less than thirteen acts . . . Only a born dramatist could have written the first nine acts of *Mourning Becomes Electra*; only a Greenwich Villager could have written the last four . . . Mr. O'Neill *knows* when to stop, but wilfully goes on." The *London Times* (March 10, 1932) pressed a further point: "O'Neill has asked of his chosen medium more than it has power to give. As though aware of this, he has tentatively introduced here and there groups of townsfolk— 'a chorus', he says, 'come to look and listen and spy on the rich and exclusive Mannons.' This was his way out; by using a chorus he might so have enriched his medium that his stage-directions and the play's spiritual intent were fully expressed in their comments. But having introduced his chorus, he makes surprisingly little use of them, preferring to hustle them off the stage and revert to the methods of direct naturalism. No play ever stood in greater need of a chorus than this trilogy. They might have been the tongue of its tragic spirit which, in their absence, cannot speak plain."

By the form and substance of his trilogy, O'Neill challenged comparison with Aeschylus. Their most obvious difference, said the *London Times* (April 10, 1948) is that Aeschylus loved mankind, while O'Neill "feels only contemptuous pity for it. The strongest passion animating his characters is hate." Clytemnestra had several substantial reasons for murdering Agamemnon — among them, his sacrifice of their daughter Iphigenia, an innocent child, to win back the wanton Helen. Clytemnestra herself, though a dutiful wife, had never loved Agamemnon; she was one of his spoils of war. The motives of Christine are vaguer and less substantial; she behaves, said the *Times*, like "a mawkish schoolgirl with a crude, novelettish mind." In Aeschylus' plays the crimes are open, even flaunted; in O'Neill's they are concealed, and sordid.

In two other ways, O'Neill loses power by deviating from the Greek spirit. In the classical trilogy, there are not only three plays but three stages of spirit: the curse, the doom, and the deliverance. These may also be envisioned as the Christian pattern of sin, penitence, and redemption; both approaches imply a religious understructure. Without such religious ground, O'Neill cannot show the reclamation; his trilogy but lengthens out the doom. Hence *Mourning Becomes Electra* does not achieve the catharsis that would purge audiences of fear and pity and send them asoar with exaltation; instead, it leaves them in a dismal slough of despond. Secondly, having added the element of incest, O'Neill is not content to leave it humanly individual, but, as in *Strange Interlude**, like a conscientious syntagmatist he must ring all the changes on his theme, compile a complete catalogue: Mrs. Mannon is drawn only toward her son, but Lavinia is stung with desire of her father and her brother; Orin, of his mother and his sister. Such a thorough surging of incestuous desire, while it may enlighten Freudian neophytes, and while it may pile horror upon horror in melodramatic pitch, will hardly seem to add to the play's credibility or to its art.

With all its shortcomings and long-windedness, *Mourning Becomes Electra* probes deeply into the tortured souls of Orin and Lavinia Mannon, and renders poignantly vivid the trail of their pitiful lives.

AH, WILDERNESS!   *Eugene O'Neill*

This is a strange, pleasant interlude among O'Neill's threnodies of disaster. Presented in New York on October 2, 1933, it ran for 289 performances and was revived there in 1941. London saw it in 1936, Oxford in 1946. It has been popular in community theatres.

Ah, Wilderness! is O'Neill's only play that follows the conventional pattern of contemporary comedy. Picturing the problems of a small-town family, it is an affirmation of the tolerance and goodness of the American way of life. Nat Miller, Connecticut newspaper publisher, has a problem, among his four children, in the shape of his rebellious son Richard. The boy's mother, Essie, is worried. Her own brother, Sid Davis, a good-natured fellow, has never amounted to anything because of his drinking; and Nat's sister Lily is an old maid from refusing to marry Sid. When rigid neighbor David McComber thinks Richard too wild for his daughter Muriel, the boy goes off on a binge and pretends to be as knowing as Belle, "the swift babe from New Haven", whose vulgarity and amorous readiness really scare him. On Richard's drunken homecoming, Sid takes charge. Then his father helps straighten Richard out and his sweetheart Muriel washes away the bitter taste of his wild oats with a pure kiss.

This sentimental vein, most unexpected in O'Neill, brought, as the *London Times,* (April 10, 1948) remarked, "mingled pleasure and surprise" and showed "how skillfully he can construct a play, how charmingly he can create presentable people."

Deftly and sympathetically produced, and with David's father understandingly played by George M. Cohan in New York and Will Rogers on the road, *Ah, Wilderness!* was received like an engagement present. The mood is, of course, more of a dream delight, a creation of wishful memory, than a living span of days, but, as Richard Dana Skinner said in *Eugene O'Neill: A Poet's Quest,* (1935): "This appealing and innocent and tender little comedy of adolescence is really much more important than it seems in the poet's unconscious scheme of things. It marked an end to that terrible fear which had made every symbol of youth appear like some hideous monster. It was unquestionably the beginning of a third and entirely new period in O'Neill's creative life, the period of full manhood of the soul."

Skinner's prophecy proved less accurate than his description; O'Neill returned to his restless seeking, moving downward to despair. Robert Garland (October 3, 1933) said of the play that it was "strong with the strength that is tenderness, warm with the ineffable sweetness of everyday life . . . It came with laughter, tears, and good old-fashioned sentiment. And with acting, settings, and direction that must have been made in heaven." George Jean Nathan maintained it is "a folk comedy of such truth in humor, such gentle and sympathetic raillery and such imaginatively photographic character that it must be given sound rank in the list of O'Neill's accomplishments."

In contrast with O'Neill's more experimental but more straining and perfervid plays, *Ah Wilderness!* provides a mellow evening and shows that sentiment and hopefulness, and the bounding bounty of youth, were at least once within the grasp of our grimmest dramatist.

DAYS WITHOUT END   *Eugene O'Neill*

In *Days Without End* O'Neill presents a tortured soul that in the end finds grace and salvation in the Catholic faith. John Loving—followed by a masked semblance, his worse self—is seeking a way of life. He is urged by his worse self to write a novel about the futility of life, to hate his virtuous wife, and to hate God for making him an orphan. After seeking for meaning among the religious faiths of the world, he tries atheism, socialism, Communism, anarchism—retaining, as Percy Hammond noted in the *New York Herald-Tribune* (January 14, 1934), "the bitterest features of them all." Although John finds love and peace in his wife, he can have no faith in love. It terrifies him to love so deeply; he therefore is deliberately unfaithful. His wife looks upon marriage as "a true sacrament", and when John confesses his infidelity she deliberately, though on the edge of pneumonia, goes out in a driving rain. While she lies at the brink of death John, who has studied all the religions of the East without finding faith, kneels praying at the foot of the Cross. As John prays his worse self writhes in agony, but his wife is uplifted and healed and brought close again to the cleansed John Loving, now fortified with faith.

Opening in New York January 8, 1934, the play turned the reviewers topsy-turvy. The Catholic *Commonweal* proclaimed that O'Neill had "at last written the play which, in its spiritual content, some of us dared to hope would emerge from the deep conflicts within his poet's soul." Gilbert W. Gabriel, one of O'Neill's most constant admirers, insisted the play was "a religious tract clumsily tied to unpicturesque claptrap and most threadbare working." John Mason Brown objected on similar grounds: "According to Mr. O'Neill, *Days Without End* is a 'modern miracle play,' but the description hardly seems accurate. For almost everything that was simple, straightforward, and disarmingly poignant in the miracle plays of old became tedious, ridiculously elaborate, turgid, and artificial in this fakey preachment of our own times." Perhaps some of this difference was implied when O'Neill called his a *modern* miracle play. Percy Hammond concluded his review: "I suppose that the best thing there can be said concerning *Days Without End* is that it is a lugubrious affectation lightened occasionally by Mr. O'Neill's inherited flair for obvious showmanship." Such a rightabout, indeed, was made by the reviewers that it might seem that some that had praised O'Neill because he was "radical" were now attacking him because he was returning to the Church. Several reviewers even issued the warning to Catholics not to expect O'Neill's conversion! "What most of the daily reviewers objected to", John Mason Brown felt it necessary to explain, "was not Mr. O'Neill's theme but the lamentable way in which (as they saw it) he had failed it." The Catholic Church, incidentally, did not place *Days Without End* on its White List of recommended plays.

London saw the play in 1935 and again in 1943. Its reception there was more favorable. "Not for a very long time," said W. A. Darlington in the *Telegraph,* (February 5, 1935) "has the Stage Society given us such an interesting play . . . In the theatre, with O'Neill's gift of seriousness and his superb dramatic sense, it becomes convincing and even enthralling." Charles Morgan, reporting from London in the *New York Times* (March 3, 1935) said that the play possesses "a justice and truth very rare on the stage. Here, for once, the battle was pitched in spiritual territory and not in the field of mere appetite. And the play had this other merit—that Mr. O'Neill has perceived and expressed the truth that we human beings are not good and bad by turns, but at the same time."

Whatever its shortcomings, the play moves with fervor and clarity along a path many in our age have trodden; it examines a problem fraught with deepest significance and shows a solution that those who cannot accept should at the least respect. In 1936, O'Neill was awarded the Nobel Prize.

The last line is a bridge to an earlier play. ("Life laughs with love.") This echo of *Lazarus Laughed** suggests that again O'Neill is presenting persons in whom faith is a resurrection, the opening of a door upon a new life. Not reason, but faith—passionate faith. For the key to O'Neill's power is passion. "It is as a distinguished emotion, rather than as a distinguished mind", said Richard Watts (January 21, 1934) "that O'Neill has become great." There is an exaltation at the close of *Days Without End* rare indeed in the plays of Eugene O'Neill.

THE ICEMAN COMETH   *Eugene O'Neill*

After a twelve-years' lapse in the production of his new plays, O'Neill's drama of illusion, *The Iceman Cometh,* written in 1939, had its premiere on Broadway, October 9, 1946. In this work, he went back to "the best friends I ever had", the derelicts in a New York saloon of 1912, and to his old depressive mood, his characteristic preoccupation with despair. "The Mr. O'Neill who wrote *Beyond The Horizon* in 1920" said the *London Times,* (April 10, 1948) "is the Mr. O'Neill who wrote *The Iceman Cometh* in 1946", and John Mason Brown (October 19, 1946), in discussing the latter play, quoted references to "Jimmy-the-Priest's, a waterfront dive", in an O'Neill interview of 1924. They could have gone farther and fared better; in the magazine *Seven Arts* of June 1917 is a short story, *Tomorrow,* by Eugene G. O'Neill, which is a detailed summary of *The Iceman Cometh.* O'Neill has, in the play, dramatized his earlier story.

The play opens in the saloon of Harry Hope, with a spread of back room tables on most of which lie the heads of sleeping bums. Among them we find Larry Slade, one-time anarchist; Pat McGloin, an ex-policeman; Willie Oban, a Harvard Law School alumnus; Piet Wetjoen, a General; and James Cameron (Jimmy Tomorrow), a correspondent. Harry Hope, once a ward heeler, hasn't gone out of doors in twenty years. The persons most alive are three streetwalkers—Margie, Pearl, and Cora—and the bartender pimp. A young frightened fellow, Don Parritt, comes from the West Coast; Slade, who at refuses to be the kid's confessor, gathers that the boy has betrayed his I.W.W. pals—including his mother; then Slade talks the boy into suicide.

None of these half-alive dreamers in Hope's haven considers himself down and out. They all "hit the pipe of the future". On that fateful tomorrow, each will venture forth and again do a man's job in the world. Their present interest centers upon the imminent coming of Theodore Hickman, "Hickey", a salesman who periodically leaves his wife "with the iceman" to enjoy a spree at Harry Hope's. His coming is a feast for all. But this time when Hickey comes, he brings a new faith which he insists upon imparting to Harry's soaks, has-beens, and tarts. Face yourself, he tells them; see yourself as you are, and you will change, you will act, you will be happy. Tomorrow is here. Against their will, as though hypnotized by his fervor, one by one they set forth; even househeld Harry Hope steps beyond his door. Then one by one they slink back, unable to face themselves or the life beyond the saloon. They discover that Hickey's faith itself is built on death; he has killed his wife, he tells them, to end her suffering over his infidelities and drunkenness. Hickey has himself summoned the police, and his departure is welcomed by the besotted cowards in Hope's saloon, who shrink back again behind their drinks and their illusions. "They will relapse with relief," said the *London Times;* "the swine return to their swill. They are, Slade asserts, converts to death." At the end of the play, in its printed form, Larry Slade slumps over a table; in the performance, he walks slowly toward the door through which the boy Don Parritt went to jump to death.

This shrunken universe of dregs and depression, of persons seeking consolation for life in drink and dreams, takes four hours to enact upon the stage. One speech of Hickey, telling why he killed his wife and urging the sodden souls to live their dreams, takes nineteen minutes. To all rehearsal suggestions that the play be cut, O'Neill was adamant: "Cut out a minute, and I'll add a half hour." Yet the one point on which all the critics agreed is that the play is much too long. John Mason Brown "kept wondering for an hour and a half when the play was going to begin." Ward Morehouse found it "too verbose, too slow in starting, too digressive once it was started." Kelcey Allen remarked that Act I began with most of the characters asleep and ended with most of the audience asleep.

Beyond this there was sharp division of opinion. Richard Watts (October 19, 1946) called the play "a drama of great emotional and creative power." Brooks Atkinson declared that it "ranks toward the top of his collected works . . . the drama that seems tediously wordy in the reading glows with promethean flame." Despite its verbosity, Morehouse felt that it is "one of the few plays of genuine stature brought to the theatre of the century's fourth decade." George Jean Nathan broke into cheers for his friend's return to the theatre: "Hallelujah, hosanna, hail, heil, hurrah, huzza, banzai and gesuntheit!" He called Hickey's peroration one of the most impressive pieces of writing in contemporary dramatic literature. On the other hand, Howard Barnes maintained that the play "has not increased O'Neill's artistic stature . . . more promise than substance." "One trembles to imagine", said John Mason Brown, "what people would think of *The Iceman Cometh* if it did not bear Mr. O'Neill's mesmerizing name." Sterling North headed his review of the printed play "Iceman Cometh Stinketh."

The play suggests a symbolic meaning which according to Atkinson becomes in the glow of the performance "no more than an unimportant afterthought." It has, however, troubled other reviewers. John Mason Brown suggested several possibilities: "What the drummer in Mr. O'Neill's drama symbolizes—whether he means death by robbing men of their life-sustaining dreams, or whether he (and the whole play) represent Mr. O'Neill's subconscious protest against those who have chaperoned and tidied up his own recent living—is a matter for individual conjecture. One thing is certain. Mr. O'Neill has turned on the meddlesome idealists as fiercely as ever Ibsen did."

The *London Times* (April 10, 1948) summed up the dramatist through his work by saying that "Mr. O'Neill . . . has no hope of anything better, here or hereafter. The world is futile and so are its inhabitants. There is no other world, and this one had better be ended . . . There is nothing here of courage and endurance, nothing of unflinching faith, nothing of self-sacrifice deliberately made. The O'Neill world is a dirty pub, frequented by drunks and disorderlies and shiftless loafers; and periodically raided by corrupt cops."

The lack of courage in the play, its "nothing of unflinching faith", suggests examination of Nathan's statement that the play yields "the profound essences of authentic tragedy." Each may frame for himself his own definition of tragedy; for many—for O'Neill himself (see *Diff'rent**)—tragedy rings with the affirmation of human worth or dignity. Out of the depths of physical disaster, one is borne to the heights of spiritual triumph. The simple reassumption of a staunch stand against overwhelming forces—human or superhuman—brings a companioning exaltation that makes tragedy a rich and a purging experience. O'Neill's world comes to its end in no such stalwart wise, not laconically bright-eyed against the terrors, but lengthily drooling evasions in its beer. It is as a picture of this piteous world of the coward, not as a tragic stand but as a pathetic fall—a picture the more heart-rending because the playwright is within the frame—that *The Iceman Cometh* makes its dark appeal.

ENOUGH STUPIDITY IN EVERY WISE MAN   *Alexander N. Ostrovsky*

The greatest single influence in the Russian drama has been that of Alexander Nicolaievich Ostrovsky (1823-1886). Half a hundred of his plays, some banned by the Czar, are still popular on the Soviet stage. Indeed, during the first decade of the Soviet regime, Education Commissar Lunacharski gave the theatre the slogan, "Back to Ostrovsky!" Born on the "wrong side" of the Moskva (Moscow) River among wealthy upstart philistine tradesmen, Ostrovsky in his greatest plays satirizes the social conditions of this rising class in Russian life.

The boldest in its ending, the most popular and perhaps the shrewdest of Ostrovsky's plays is *Enough Stupidity In Every Wise Man,* 1868. The wise man is Yego Dmitrich Glumov, who, recognizing that the world is built of knaves and fools, decides to climb over them to success. By flattery and cunning, by balancing prejudices and jealousies, utilizing the aid of a hired fortune-teller, Maniefa, Glumov wins universal favor. His fortune seems assured. He becomes the secretary to his millionaire Uncle, flirts with his Uncle's coquettish wife, and plans to marry his cousin Kurchaiev's fiancée, Mashenka. But Glumov's "stupidity" is that he has set down his real thoughts about everybody in a diary. Found by a busybody, the diary is read by the astounded and enraged millionaire to the assembled company. Then Glumov's cleverness truly asserts itself: he brazens it out before them, telling them that each would have loved to hear, privately, what the diary says about the others, and that their anger now labels them hypocrites, even as he—save that he has been more successful. Now, he adds, they need him for his silence. Thus Glumov succeeds in wheedling his way back into his Uncle's good graces and Mashenka's arms.

The drama has been played all over Russia in styles ranging from sheerest realism to farthest futurism. It was presented in New York in Russian by the Moscow Art group, December 5, 1923. A bit obvious in its characterizations, more nearly akin to caricature than to rich and rounded portrayal, *Enough Stupidity In Every Wise Man* presents a great gallery of Russian types who have their counterparts in every land, and it so exposes vanity, ambition, greed and clever hypocrisy that it shares with *The Inspector General** the greatest popularity of all Russian comedies.

VENICE PRESERVED   *Thomas Otway*

This play has long been hailed as the greatest English tragedy since Shakespeare. As late as December 18, 1910, the *New York Sun* drama critic maintained that "outside of Shakespeare there is no English tragedy that can compare in power, pathos, and passion with *Venice Preserved*." Today the play's plot and treatment seem rather melodramatic, but there is no mistaking, even now, the strong emotional impact in its tense opposition of the claims of loyalty and love. It is the masterpiece of Thomas Otway (1652-1685).

Based on *The Conspiracy of the Spaniards against Venice in 1618*, a work by César Vichard de Saint-Réal (Paris, 1674), *Venice Preserved; or, A Plot Discovered* presents the disastrous dilemma of Jaffier, a noble young Venetian who, against the will of her father, Senator Priuli, has married Belvidera. When Priuli seeks to oppress the impoverished pair, Jaffier joins the Spaniard Pierre in a conspiracy against the Senate. Belvidera begs Jaffier, for love of her, to save her father and the State. Yielding to his love, he reveals the plot to the Senate on its promise to spare the conspirators—a promise that it promptly breaks. On the scaffold, Jaffier stabs his friend Pierre, then himself; Belvidera, her mind and her heart broken, joins them in death.

With Thomas Betterton and Otway's beloved Elizabeth Barry, the play opened in London on February 7, 1682. It was a fiery success, and it was revived constantly for two hundred years: by Mrs. (Susannah Maria) Cibber, 1738; David Garrick, 1743; Spranger Barry, 1747 (for a decade Barry and Garrick alternated as Jaffier and Pierre, with Mrs. Cibber as Belvidera); Mrs. (Sarah Kemble) Siddons and J. P. Kemble, from 1774 to 1811; William Charles Macready and Eliza O'Neill, 1819; Charles Kean, 1820 and the next decade; Charles and Fanny Kemble, 1829; Macready with Helen Faucit up to 1837. New York first saw the play at the Nassau Street Theatre February 20, 1752. More recent performances include one in London, 1920; Oxford, 1932; and an elaborate production at Yale, 1933. Hugo von Hofmannsthal translated *Venice*

Preserved into German. The London production opening May 15, 1953, with John Gielgud and Pamela Brown, was called by Harold Hobson, in the *Christian Science Monitor* (June 6), "about the most contemporary play now to be seen in London . . . as much an example of *le théâtre engagé* as any work of Sartre or Camus". New York saw it in 1955.

The fiery speeches, the swift variations of passion, the conflict of motives, make *Venice Preserved* a superb acting play. Its prime value, as Allardyce Nicoll has said, "rests in its masterly construction and in its fine characterization, but its final impresson is added to by the nervous blank verse, essentially theatrical, which Otway, after many experiments in various styles, had taught himself to write." The character of Belvidera is warm and richly revealed, as she moves upon her own path too ardently to recognize where it may lead the man she loves.

There are some allusions to contemporary affairs in *Venice Preserved,* which added to its appeal. The Venetian Senator Antonio was recognized as a caricature of the Earl of Shaftesbury. England in 1682, with its "Popist plots," with one revolution not far behind it and a second just ahead, could find much pertinent in conspiracies and divided loyalties. Without such timely tugs of interest, *Venice Preserved* remains nonetheless a richly colored, invigorating drama. The tragedy results, not from villainy, but from the flaws in decent men, from Pierre's too inflexible resolve and firm-set faith, from Jaffier's love-swayed vacillation, which is redeemed by his manly action at the end. "Now, now," gasps the dying Pierre, "thou hast indeed been faithful. This was done nobly." Jaffier's is an old-fashioned nobility (if indeed, nobility itself seems not to many old-fashioned!) as *Venice Preserved* is an old fashioned play, that still trails clouds of glory.

TOPAZE   *Marcel Pagnol*

A hit in Paris, where it opened on October 9, 1928, *Topaze,* by Marcel Pagnol (French, b. 1895), with its warm humor and gentle irony, also scored in London and New York. Frank Morgan and Clarence Derwent headed the New York cast in 1930, which played 141 performances. A French company played it in New York in 1931, and the comedy has been revived frequently by little theatres and college playhouses. The play has been performed all over Europe, and remains an excellent ironic study of human nature.

Watching Topaze conduct a class of mischievous boys, we find him scrupulously honest and quite naive. He refuses to raise a student's marks to please an important patron of the Pension Muche, and is fired. To his great surprise he is offered a much better job. And gradually Topaze grows aware that he is being used as an honest front for dealings in community graft and that the lady who has befriended him and given him the work is the chief grafter's mistress. Thus wakened to the ways of the world, Topaze tosses aside his old adages, turns rogue, and deftly proceeds to supplant the grafter both in the spoils of the city and in the smiles of his mistress. As the curtain falls, his old pedagogue colleague is deciding to leave school to become Topaze's secretary, hoping also to reach the rainbow's end.

The play delights with the deftness of its portraits, the neatness and the fineness of its satire. Its theme—the decision of an upright person to match the manners of the world and play its "practical" game, with its implication that the honest man makes the best thief—while it may amuse a laissez-faire society, is hardly acceptable as a jest in these more bureaucratic days, when graft would be too large-scale for persiflagic trifling. The Broadway production of 1947 ran for one performance. But it is always a comfort to see the innocent tool turn on its cynical users, and in *Topaze* the characters are excellently drawn, the episodes humorously manoeuvred, and the dialogue crisply pertinent.

Benn W. Levy* made the English adaptation, which Gilbert W. Gabriel (1930) said lacked a little in raciness, vigor, edge: "It manages, though, to do Anglo-Saxon justice to the delicacies, whimsicality, little bendings of humanity that are most Gallic and most charming about M. Pagnol's play . . . a play that should tickle the humor of all students of what rogues these mortals be."

From its schoolroom scenes, which touch teachers with intimate humor and understanding satire, to those in which the emancipated manipulator of men masters the woman also, *Topaze* is a delightful capture of human nature devoted to truth, turning aside to acquire riches.

MARIUS   *Marcel Pagnol*

The three plays by Marcel Pagnol that deal with life in the port of Marseilles—*Marius*, 1929, *Fanny*, 1931, and *César*, 1936—are parts of a sentimental story of a wandering lad and the girl he left behind him. It is "a tale told by McFee and a score more seafaring novelists", said Gilbert W. Gabriel (November 18, 1930), "but never more deftly than Pagnol told it to the footlights, or more packed with the satisfaction of finely etched old salts, ferrymen, fishwives, and souses."

The story itself is simple. In *Marius,* the young shore boy Marius, the pride of his father César, hungers for the sea, but he is also drawn to Fanny, who truly loves him. Fanny gives herself to him; then, feeling how he yearns to be a sailor, she pretends, even though she is pregnant, that she never intends to marry him. Freed of this burden, Marius slips away and ships for a long sea voyage.

In *Fanny* the heart-broken girl marries the good-natured, stuffy old stay-at-home, M. Panisse. When Marius returns from his voyage, he again enkindles deep love in Fanny. Especially when he learns that the child is his, Marius is determined to take her from Panisse. Through César's determination, however, and through her own commonsense and concern for her child, Fanny stays with her substantial and steady husband, thus ensuring the child's respectability and sound future. The play *César* rounds out the story. The child, also named César, is grown; his real father, Marius, refusing to live nearby, works as a garage-man in a neighboring town. When Panisse dies, the son takes a motor boat to Marius to be repaired, so that he may size up his father. The two men like one another and Marius and Fanny are reunited.

Opening in Paris March 9, 1929 with Raimu as César and Pierre Fresnay as Marius, *Marius* took Paris by storm. The unpretentious flow of the simple story was colored by a superb characterization of the main figures and a deft capture of the many types that haunt the waterfront. *La Petite Illustration* (May 16, 1931) called the play "the poem of

Marseilles life . . . a masterpiece of spontaneity and good humor . . .
with skillful technique and sincere use of theatrical resources." *Le
Journal* declared: "We laughed all evening, with a richly tempered
laugh, and were moved as we should be by scenes that a slight shift in
emphasis would make tragic—so true is it that good comedy is drama
balanced by laughter." *Echo de Paris* saw in the play "neither ridicule
nor caricature . . . the love of the bartender Marius and the oyster-girl
Fanny is as touching, and their separation as poignant, as those of
Titus and Queen Berenice." *Comoedia* stressed the flavor of the play:
"The Old Port, the picturesque rough types, fishmongers, sailors ashore,
patrons of the saloon, the lazy life of the bar, sipping or guzzling drinks,
the violent but inoffensive disputes, the accent—that notorious Marseillaise accent as strong and as savorous as garlic in the pot—stories
whose charm lies wholly in their frame, and that happy southern indulgence in temperament, that good humor, that optimistic, cordial smile
of folk who do not fuss: all this forms a background painted with a
happy and easy verve, and a natural sense of comedy."

Played in New York November 17, 1930, as *Marseilles*, in an adaptation by Sidney Howard, with Dudley Digges, Allison Skipworth, and
Alexander Kirkland, *Marius* was not well received. Robert Littell protested that *"Marius*, when I saw it in Paris, seemed to me one of the
best shows I had ever seen," but in English "the smell of fish and harbor
has gone out of it." Brooks Atkinson found it a pleasant piece: "There
are romance and gallantry enough in it for a little sweet sadness at
the matinees. There is also low comedy enough for a burgher's evening
away from home . . . They cheat at cards, fly into petty tempers, wink,
leer, and scuffle as Daumier would enjoy imagining them . . . They relish
a bit of amorous deception as long as the conspirators are sufficiently
young."

As motion pictures, the works preserved their charm. Joined in a
single musical, *Fanny,* by S. N. Behrman* and Jushua Logan, they
largely lost their flavor. This play opened in New York November 4,
1954; the songs by Harold Rome, the singing of Ezio Pinza, the acting of
Walter Slezak, and a colorful though hodgepodge range of events from
waterfront dive to wistful dream, kept the musical running for over a
year.

French to the core, with simplicity, sincerity, humor, joy of living,
and a love that abides and endures, *Marius* and its companion pieces
glow with a serenity and a smiling sense of well-being beneath life's
vicissitudes, that look unafraid toward the future.

THE SOCIETY WHERE ONE IS BORED   *Edouard Pailleron*

Among the deft comedies of the French Academician Edouard Pail-
leron (1834–1899), *Le Monde où l'on s'ennuie (The Society Where One
is Bored)* 1881, has become a classic both of the French stage and of the
classroom. It is a shrewd but light-handed satire of the pretentious
and pompous society in which literary and political reputations are
sometimes made and often marred. The play was produced in London
in 1893, and has often been presented by student groups.

On the surface the play depicts a complicated set of amours. Roger
de Céran loves Suzanne de Villiers, the pretty adopted daughter and

heir of the Duchesse de Réville. Suzanne, however, has a "crush" on Professor Bellac who is also admired by the bluestocking English girl Lucy Watson. The main business of the drama, however, is not in matching these couples, but in making clear the character of the Professor and of the Raymonds. The Professor (drawn from life after Professor of Philosophy Caro of the Sorbonne) has made a name as "the ladies' philosopher", the savant à la mode; he is a neatly caught prototype of the latter-day popular lecturer and author of guides to "mature behavior". Paul Raymond, a young sub-prefect of a small town controlled by Roger's mother, the Comtesse de Céran, has taught his bride Jeanne how to bow and say the right word, with apt quotation, to win the Comtesse's favor and Paul's promotion. The play ends with Paul successful and Jeanne relieved of this duty.

Mildly pleasing in its romance, the play is superbly deft in its satiric delineation of literary and political pretenders of a sort that still seek prominence in our age.

DISRAELI   *Louis Napoleon Parker*

According to its author, Louis Napoleon Parker (English, 1852-1944), this "is not an historical play, but only an attempt to show a picture of the days—not so very long ago—in which Disraeli lived, and some of the racial, social, and political prejudices he fought against and conquered." Parker's portrait, richly and roundly drawn, is not only an effective dramatic seizure of Disraeli, but in performance the most famous of George Arliss's characterizations. *The New York Mail* (September 19, 1911), noted that "The play itself, with its story of international intrigue, is but the frame or background for the portrait, an artistic and harmonious setting with its lords and ladies in their picturesque Victorian costumes, its every detail blending to create the atmosphere of that golden age."

The play centers on the intrigues that preceded English control of the Suez Canal project, and ends with a reception to Queen Victoria, new Empress of India. Charles, Viscount Delford, who seems an idler but is an astute statesman, and the charming Clarissa Pevensey form a background to the intrigue. Disraeli's clerk, Foljambe, is a Russian spy, as is the vivacious Mrs. Travers. The shrewd Disraeli, aware of their interest, keeps them properly misinformed. But Russian manoeuvring manages to bankrupt Meyers, on whom Disraeli depends for funds for the Canal deal; whereupon Disraeli threatens to smash the Bank of England unless its head, Sir Michael Probert, grants him credit. This credit carries through the deal, which is celebrated in the reception to the Queen. At this point, personal concerns enter the story. Disraeli has been greatly worried over his wife's health. He receives a telegram, but does not dare open it; he is still holding it as his wife arrives at the reception.

The four-act play opened in Montreal January 23, 1911, and failed. It displeased audiences in Detroit, Toledo, Columbus and Chicago. The trouble seemed to come at the end of the third act, at which point, pressed by Disraeli, Sir Michael grants credit to cover the purchase of the Canal, and the curtain falls. In the new version, Sir Michael, forced to give Disraeli credit, goes. Then Disraeli, smiling, bows Mrs. Travers, who he knows is a spy, out of the room. Clarissa exclaims: "Oh, Mr. Disraeli, thank God you have such power!" Disraeli confides: "I haven't, dear child; but he doesn't know that."

After this change, business jumped from $3,000 to $15,000 a week. Opening in New York on September 18, 1911, the play ran for 282 performances; in 1913 it attained over 150 performances in Boston; in London, where it opened April 4, 1916, it reached 128. George Arliss played Disraeli also in a talking film, with Joan Bennett, in 1929.

It is more than the fact that Arliss played both roles that now brings thought of the Rajah of Rukh in *The Green Goddess**. There is in the man Disraeli a similar stroking with the velvet glove, the polished courtier concealing the shrewd and ruthless politician. Disraeli, fighting for the creation of the Empire, used weapons fitter to disrupt it. An excellent picture of the times, the means, and the man is built in the political melodrama *Disraeli*, still a powerful piece in the theatre.

THE TEAHOUSE OF THE AUGUST MOON   *John Patrick*

This play opened October 15, 1953, to win the Drama Critics' Circle Award, the Pulitzer Prize, and several other citations as the best of the year. It is presumably now past its thousandth New York performance; two companies have taken it on lengthy American tours, and some eighty foreign companies have presented it.

The play is a delightful combination of genial satire, deft staging, and warm sense of human fellowship. At once mellow and mocking, it was neatly fashioned by John Patrick (American, b. 1907) from the novel by Vern Sneider. Outwardly, it shows the natives of Tobiki Village, Okinawa, getting what they want by shrewd handling of the United States occupation authorities, but beneath the amusing patterns of the play we discern that democracy—decency in dealing with others— may, with the modicum of luck (or God's favor) all things human require, point the way to living together. East and West, that presumably impossible twain, do meet.

A genial interpreter, Sakini — played first by David Wayne in New York, Eli Wallach in London then New York, Burgess Meredith and Larry Parks on the road — sets the Oriental point of view before the audience, with touches of Oriental philosophy: "Pain makes man think; thought makes man wise; wisdom makes life endurable." Sakini is also interpreter, within the play, to Captain Fisby, whose task it is to democratize Tobiki according to Army Plan B. Fisby is not liked by his superiors, having one major fault: he does not know how to refuse what someone deeply wants. Thus somehow the jeep that is to take Fisby to the village carries also a heaped-up cargo of natives, with luggage and goat. On his arrival, among the natives' gifts to the Captain is a geisha girl, so that naturally instead of the Plan B schoolhouse it is a teahouse that gets built. Under Fisby's democracy the village thrives, especially as its sweet-potato brandy is a boon to the Army posts—until the literal-minded Colonel arrives and in horror orders the teahouse torn down. The United States, however, now heir to the process of muddling through, gives orders that restore the teahouse and one's faith in democracy, that make the natives happy, and the audience too.

Over and beyond the play's "rich and deliciously humorous and

touching qualities as sheer entertainment," said Richard Watts, Jr., "I
think the most enchanting quality of *The Teahouse of the August Moon*
is its smiling tribute to the human spirit and the capacity of mankind
for mutual understanding." The reviews were studded with such phrases
as "the delicacy of a porcelain bowl . . . the ease and airiness of a magic
carpet . . . the whimsy of spoken Gilbert and Sullivan." The moon of
August is the most mellow; more than any other play in a lustrum of
August moons, *The Teahouse* blends satire, comedy, charm, and warmth
of man toward fellow-man.

THE OLD WIVES' TALE   *George Peele*

As engaging a romp as has come to us from the Elizabethan theatre
is *The Old Wives' Tale,* written about 1590 by George Peele (English,
c. 1557-1596). Like Cervantes' novel *Don Quixote,* this play was intended as a satire on the romantic writings of the time. Its prose, and
occasional rhyme, and deliberately inflated blank verse, with here and
there a touch of mock Latin, present a merry mixture of reality and
make-believe, a potpourri that might well be called "The Follies of
Fairyland." Peele's first plays were written for the court; then, as in
The Old Wives' Tale, he carried qualities of the courtly style to the
public theatres.

The play begins with a combination of romance and reality as three
starving knights-errant, Antic, Frolic, and Fantastic, break in and find
hospitality with the plain smithy Crunch and his old goodwife Madge.
Madge begins her tale, and the fairies come romping—and out of the
fireplace bursts one of the characters of the story. Madge the narrator
joins the delighted spectators as the story she was about to tell unfolds
before our eyes.

The story is an amusing tangle of tales. Two brothers, Calypha and
Thelea, in quest of their sister Delia, who is held by the magician Sac-
rapant, are also made his prisoners. In the magician's power are Erestus
and his lady love; indeed, the sorcerer has changed bodies with Erestus,
who hobbles about as a bent old man, while the magician takes youthful,
vigorous strides.

A number of other legendary figures enter the story, such as
Lampriscus, a villager unblessed with two unmarried daughters who
find their fortunes at a magic well. The sorcerer is finally bested by
the knight Eumenides, with the help of the ghost of Jack the Giant
Killer, who helps because the knight has paid for Jack's burial. Sacra-
pant's victims are rescued, and Delia, beloved of Eumenides, turns out to
be the Sleeping Beauty. Madge prepares a cup of ale and some breakfast, as the drama ends.

Pleasantly contrasted, amidst this merry travesty of romantic and
fairy plays—the first dramatic travesty in English—are the village
dances and songs of the harvest men and maids and the tripping rounds
and lilting roundelays of the fairies. In the one recent American production of *The Old Wives' Tale* (at Middlebury College, June 20, 1911,
supervised by Frank W. Cady) the music arranged by Mrs. Maude S.
Howard found old English tunes for Peele's delightful songs: "All ye that
lovers be;" and the impatiently charming "Whenas the rye—".

The Old Wives' Tale is crowded with literary allusions, most of them intended to spice the satire. The mood of the play and certain of the relationships made Thomas Warton remark, in *Milton's Poems* (1791), that *The Old Wives' Tale*, "which might have been a favorite of his early youth," suggested to Milton the general movement of his *Comus*.

There is considerable amusement still to be drawn from Peele's extravaganza, which presents, as Allardyce Nicoll has said, "a peculiarly original handling of the romantic material. Stories of chivalrous adventure, of sorcerers, of spirits who rise amid thunder and lightning, had been popular on the stage for well over a decade, but such themes had been treated in a serious manner . . . By the use of a typical romantic colouring, this serious treatment of adventurous themes has been blended with burlesque, and real persons meet on the same plane with fictional characters who step out of the story and enact their own parts. It is not too much to say that we have here a kind of strange anticipation of Pirandellesque methods." Fresh after 365 years, *The Old Wives' Tale*, first of dramatic travesties, can hold its own against many more recent burlesques. With little change, it might make a merry Yuletide frolic in the theatre.

PAOLO AND FRANCESCA   *Stephen Phillips*

Dante Alighieri, a fellow-soldier of Francesca's brother Bernardino, first told Francesca's story in the fifth Canto of his *Inferno*. Her father, the Guelph lord of Ravenna, losing in battle to the Ghibelline Traversari, sought aid from his former rival, Malatesta di Verucchio, the notorious "mastiff" of Rimini. As seal to the pact of friendship, Francesca was sent in 1275 to marry Malatesta's son Giovanni. How she and Giovanni's younger brother Paolo fell flamingly in love, how they loyally sought to beat down the fire, how they were consumed—and by Giovanni killed— has since been a tender theme for poets.

In 1814, Silvio Pellico wrote an Italian play on the subject, seen in Milan in 1815, which gave the fourteen-year-old Adelaide Ristori her first great role; the play became a classic. In 1820, it was used as the basis of an Italian opera; in 1882 it was fashioned into a French opera by Ambroise Thomas. D'Annunzio's tragedy on the theme, much more emotional, was written for Eleonora Duse in 1901. George Henry Boker (American, 1823-1890) wrote a blank verse tragedy, *Francesca da Rimini*, 1855, which was revived in 1882 as rewritten by William Winter. In another play on the same story, 1902, by Marion Crawford (American, 1854-1909), Sarah Bernhardt starred. In England, when Stephen Phillips' poems (1897) induced the actor-manager Sir George Alexander to commission a poetic drama, Phillips (English, 1868-1915) wrote *Francesca da Rimini* in 1899. The play was produced in 1902, by Herbert Beerbohm Tree. Phillips wrote several lesser poetic dramas.

When the play was first produced in New York as *Paolo and Francesca* the hand of fate was felt to be too heavy on the lovers. The *New York Dramatic Mirror* (October 13, 1916) quoted blind Agatha's prophetic words in the play—"His kiss was on her lips ere she was born"—and added: "Thus is the drama from the start shadowed, like a Greek tragedy, with an impending doom . . . There is nothing commanding in Paolo, and but little that is appealing in Francesca."

On its revivals, the play was better received. It won praise, too, for the character Phillips added to the story, a widowed and childless cousin of Giovanni's, Lucrezia, who out of her own bitter emptiness envies and spies on the lovers. She it is that betrays them to Giovanni. In a touching scene, the troubled Francesca turns to Lucrezia for help, and the aching need of love in Lucrezia responds, too late.

Paolo and Francesca was revived in New York on December 2, 1924. The *Times* said that it "held the interest beyond expectation . . . A certain high quality emerged and an atmosphere more beautiful than in any other play in town . . . the best role, that of Lucrezia, the most original and most powerful motive in the play, that of the barren woman with her jealousy and thwarted nature." On April 1, 1929 the play again opened in New York, with Philip Merivale and Jane Cowl. Brooks Atkinson said that "if this luscious sort of drama—'not pretty, but beautiful, and passing sad'—has fallen out of favor, it is because the proper actors are lacking to make it alluring." The present company, he added, "have brought off this verse tragedy with deep-shadowed beauty."

The poetry of Phillips is rhetorical, with some lush coloring. But the play is neatly built and the emotions are both natural and profound. The recurrent conflict between loyalty and love has no tenderer telling than in Phillips' dramatic capture of the story of these two star- crossed children.

SWEET LAVENDER   *Arthur Wing Pinero*

One of the most tender of the plays of Arthur Wing Pinero (English, 1855-1934), *Sweet Lavender,* 1888, marks the transition from the spectacular and passion-torn melodrama of the mid-nineteenth century to the psychological social drama of the century's end. It shows, as Allardyce Nicoll has said, "the new style at an early period in its career. With a sure sense of the theatre the author has told a story . . . which did much to accustom audiences to a better dramatic technique. The crude world of melodrama disappears in face of the spirit of this play."

Sweet Lavender is well named in the drama; she is the freshly gentle daughter of Ruth Holt, housekeeper and laundress in the London Temple. Among the lawyers chambered there is Dick Phenyl, a rough old barrister who drinks. With him rooms the student Clement Hale, ward of the banker Geoffrey Wedderburn and in love with Lavender. Geoffrey, disapproving this love, is about to cut Clement out of his will when he discovers that Ruth is his own early sweetheart, Lavender his natural daughter. Ruth comes to nurse Geoffrey through an illness; his love is reawakened, and three marriages shine at the end of the play.

Sweet Lavender opened in London March 21, 1888, and ran for 684 performances. In New York it opened November 13, 1888, for a run of 128 performances. In both cities it has had a half dozen revivals, and it is a popular play in college theatres. The London *Piccadilly* (October 2, 1890) called it "as fresh as the sweet bloom after which it was named." The *New York Herald* (January 7, 1923) said "Sir Arthur's humor and pathos and sentiment are so firmly based on changeless complexes of human nature that the play is moving throughout. Sweet Lavender herself is believable even to a generation accustomed to flappers."

The play's chief distinction rises from the care and the color with

which the characters are drawn. Several critics have placed them—
especially old Dick Phenyl—in the gallery with Dickens' and Thackeray's. The *Boston Transcript* (November 15, 1888) said that Phenyl
"serves to introduce an element for which Anglo-Saxon and Celtic
audiences have always evinced a profound and touching sympathy, no
matter how administered, and this is *Rum.*" The colorful characters and
tender conflicts of *Sweet Lavender* make it good material for the current vogue of turning plays into musicals. In quite different mood, and
with the sexes reversed, it tells much the same story as Oscar Wilde's
A Woman of No Importance*. It lifted the author from his Pinerotic
trifling to solid worth.

As the *London Graphic* (December 30, 1922) remarked, *Sweet Lavender* "is old-fashioned but not out of date." Some may feel that Lavender herself is a bit too sweet and that her lover was picked from the
top layer of a chocolate box, but sentiment is no outworn commodity
in the theatre. The story of the play is well-constructed and moving,
the Temple background is excellently caught, and the characters are not
only limned with sympathy but limbed with truth. *Sweet Lavender,*
combining the emotion and sentiment of melodrama with the character
drawing of latter-day realistic plays, is not merely an interesting tran-
sitional drama, but in itself a pleasant and still moving play.

THE SECOND MRS TANQUERAY   *Arthur Wing Pinero*

Beginning his long career with farces in the liveliest Victorian cur-
tain-raiser mood, Arthur Wing Pinero later turned the course of English
drama toward a serious examination of social problems, then lived to
be surpassed by richer talents along the path he pointed. At the height
of his career Pinero wrote a drama that broke through the politeness and
Victorian reticences of the day to expose a burning social situation, the
problem of a woman with a past—*The Second Mrs. Tanqueray.*

The story is stark. The widower Aubrey Tanqueray marries Paula,
thinking that this respectable action will cloak her past. She is, however, not accepted by society. Aubrey's daughter Ellean goes off to
Paris; when she returns, engaged to Captain Ardale, Paula feels it her
duty to the girl to inform Aubrey that the Captain is one of her former
lovers. Ellean, thus prevented from marrying the Captain, bursts out
against Paula; and, despite Aubrey's offer to start life over with her
away from England, Paula kills herself. Too late, Ellean wishes she had
been more understanding.

When the play was offered, the leading actresses of the time refused
to assume the part of Paula. It was finally given to an unripe girl from
the provinces, who later wrote in her memoirs, "During the first act,
I was simply paralyzed with fear, and I am afraid did but scant justice
to my work." Pinero, walking in the Embankment Gardens—he had not
dared enter the theatre nearby—was told after that first act, that the
performance was a fiasco. He rushed to the actress' dressing room,
clasped her damp and trembling hands, and exclaimed: "Magnificent,
dear Lady! Magnificent! Only play the next three acts as you have played
the first, and we are made!" The actress went back, and made history
for Pinero and for herself. She was Mrs. Pat Campbell.

The play took London by storm. Said the *Star* (May 29, 1893):

"The dialogue is wonderfully telling; the situation nakedly true . . .
This is a really fine play . . . We are filled with an abiding compassion
for the poor woman: we feel as we should feel in tragedy, not the horror,
but 'the pity of it'." The *Times* called it "decidedly a play *à thèse* . . .
The purpose of Mr. Pinero's latest play is to exhibit the hopelessness of
the attempt to raise the profligate woman to the position of the honoured
and happy wife." The *Standard,* however, although it called the drama
"one of the most powerful and absorbing plays the modern stage has
produced," rejected the *Times'* point of view: "An idea has prevailed
that *The Second Mrs. Tanqueray* is an example of that most unpleasant
thing, a play with a purpose, that it was written to enforce a moral,
that Mr. Pinero was bent on departing from the true purpose of the stage
by expounding a social problem. He is far too able a dramatist to do
anything of the sort . . . He furnishes themes which suggest, and, indeed,
enforce reflection; but his main purpose . . . was . . . to write a drama
which should awaken and sustain interest and not to preach a sermon
in the guise of a play . . . Primarily the drama is a study of character and
of a character so complex that the lucidity with which the author has
carried out his design is especially notable."

Accepted by most that saw it as a searching study of a sore problem—
Mrs. Pat Campbell's superb performance helped give the illusion of universality—the play really presents a very special situation, as was
recognized by the *London Illustrated Sporting and Dramatic News* (June
10, 1893): "If we must have productions which some of us would not
wish our womankind to see, let them at least help the world forward.
There is no such justification for *The Second Mrs. Tanqueray.* Mr. Pinero
raises an unpleasant question, and then lays it down; he tells us of the
life, and brings about the death, of an exceedingly improper young person, and there we are left . . . It is no use saying that this is life; it is not
life; it is, bad as we are, one of life's rare exceptions . . . the tragedy of
the finale appears to me more a matter of momentary impulse than the
natural outcome of the play . . ."

Bernard Shaw put his finger on another major flaw in the play when
he observed that Pinero was no profound student of human nature, but
"an adroit describer of people as the ordinary man sees and judges
them." The "ordinary man" of today has tasted so much of Freud, even
though in diluted pourings, that the surface attitudes of the turn of the
century seem outmoded and thin. Pinero, lacking profundity and universality, does not survive as a living playwright. But his dramatic
structure is excellent, building naturally and powerfully from simple
opening to gripping climax; and his theme burst upon the contemporary
public like a social atom-bomb. James Agate, in *At Half-Past Eight*
(1923) said it "began like a bombshell and endures as a landmark. With
it English drama emerged from the . . . nursery, and took for the first
time since the eighteenth century a man's look at the world."

Bernard Shaw, regardless of the fact that Pinero blazed the path he
himself followed, mercilessly averred that Pinero never wrote a line that
might reveal him as a contemporary of Ibsen, and that even his acclaimed stagecraft is feeble. In *The Second Mrs. Tanqueray,* for instance,
Shaw declared, two whole actors are wasted on "sham parts" in the
exposition, while the hero has to rise from his own dinner party and go
out "to write some letters", so that something can be said behind his

back. "What most of our critics mean by mastery of stagecraft is recklessness in the substitution of dead machinery and lay figures for vital action and real characters." Still, Shaw grants that Pinero is "a writer of effective stage plays for the modern commercial theatre". In truth, he was an innovator as well as a success.

In both England and America, the play has had a long, successful career, serving as a vehicle for such famous thespians as Mr. and Mrs. Kendal, Olga Nethersole, Mrs. Pat Campbell, Mrs. Leslie Carter, Gladys Cooper, and Ethel Barrymore. There have been many productions around the United States; Tallulah Bankhead essayed Paula in the summer theatres of 1940. London was still deeply moved by a revival which opened August 29, 1950, for 206 performances.

In 1893, the New York critics were cold to the play. The *New York Dramatic Mirror* declared that "Mr. Pinero's play makes a false start and leads to a false conclusion. It is unreal from first to last, and such skill as it exhibits is purely theatrical and technical." The same paper, on May 22, 1905, said of the play: "Emotions are by no means wanting, but rather etched in with steel-point cunning by that master of technique, A. W. Pinero." And on February 3, 1913, the same paper reflected: "How times do change! . . . Today our women with pasts become the wives of our presidents . . . the neat cleverness of the dialogue and the firm vigor of construction still win our admiration."

The play was still admired in the Arthur Hopkins revival with Ethel Barrymore. Percy Hammond (October 28, 1925) said: "The old tragedy has stamina and stubbornness; it tells the story of the unfortunate Paula as skillfully as any playwright of today could do it." And Alexander Woollcott called it "still engrossing . . . a play that you all must see".

Paula affords an acting part that will lure a star, in a play so well constructed that its climax remains intense. *The Second Mrs. Tanqueray,* though it no longer seems deeply searching, is a powerful presentation of a story that, in its day, woke the theatre to a concern with social themes, and paved the English stage for Ibsen and for Shaw.

THE TREASURE   *David Pinski*

One of the masterpieces of the Yiddish drama, *The Treasure* first brought David Pinski (b. 1872) international attention. In its ironic portrait of human greed, the play depicts the family of Chone the gravedigger, who lives in contented poverty until Judke, his feeble-minded son, goes out to bury a dog and returns with a few gold coins. The family blossoms. Judke's sister Tille, a sharp-witted, sharp-tongued girl, mean, worldly, and ambitious, decks herself in finery, condescends to the neighbors, and sets about securing a fit husband. A host of assorted parasites crowd around: marriage brokers, charity collectors, rabbis, "schnorrers" of every sort, as the village fumes with envy, fawning, vanity, and greed. Chone is most evasive as to the treasure; the truth is the half-wit Judke has forgotten where he found the coins. At night, the villagers swarm upon the cemetery, regardless of whose grave they are defiling — until Judke remembers; and they find four more pieces of gold.

There are many swift serio-comic sketches of the greed-struck villagers in the play. It works with vivid realism to the close, when, as the

Boston Transcript (June 6, 1928) observed, "the night wind blows across the graves; upon it, some hear the plaint of the dead at the cupidity of the living." Following a pattern used later for other ends in *Our Town**, *The Treasure* closes with a conversation of the dead, pressing home the point of the play—that it is not money, but the love of money, that is the root of all evil. Some good, however, has come of the village flurry. Chone returns content to his job; and Tille is happier since even her new mite of a dowry may bring a worthy husband.

The play was produced by Reinhardt in Berlin in 1910, by the Theatre Guild in New York, October 4, 1920.

What chiefly distinguishes *The Treasure*, apart from the universality of the drive of human greed and the humor that softens the sharpness of the satire, is the deft etching of the various portraits, the many aspects of avariciousness in the realized characters that give the play the essence of vivid truth.

SIX CHARACTERS IN SEARCH OF AN AUTHOR   *Luigi Pirandello*

Although the Frenchman Benjamin Crémieux and the Irishman James Joyce had earlier called attention to Luigi Pirandello (Italian, 1867-1936), it was with the production of his *Six Characters in Search of an Author*, 1916, that an awareness of his genius flashed through the theatrical capitals of the world. Fame came late to this brilliant Italian, who began his career as a writer of short stories (writing over 300, many of which he later turned into plays) and who taught literature in Rome from 1897 to 1922, while supporting his insane wife. In 1925 he organized a theatrical troupe which presented his plays in Europe and America. His fame, however, preceded his trip to the United States; his *Six Characters in Search of an Author* had opened in New York on October 30, 1922, with Moffatt Johnston, Margaret Wycherly, Florence Eldridge, and Ernest Cossart. The germ of the play was a short story, *The Tragedy of a Character*, in which a "character" complains about the role given him in a book Pirandello has read.

The play passes so adroitly from the unreal world to the real that the two are fused—indeed, the created characters seem to have more reality than the actual persons beside them. The audience is watching a director rehearsing a play by Pirandello, for which there is not much enthusiasm, when it is interrupted by six lugubrious figures who announce themselves as characters of a play abandoned by their author. They pulse with the life started in them and plead with the director to let them play it through. Unwilling at first, the director grudgingly consents; they go off to arrange a scenario. (The curtain remains up; but this is the end of Act I.)

The characters return with their story ready. When the actors take over their roles, the characters watch, at first with amusement, then with astonishment and disgust, as the actors transmogrify their passions. Finally, they protest: "Of my nausea," cries the stepdaughter, "of all the reasons, one crueler and viler than the other, that have made this of me, you want to make a sentimental, romantic concoction." The daughter turns to the mother: "Shout, mother! shout as you shouted then!" and the mother cries out in genuine anguish. "Good!" says the director. "The curtain can fall right there." A listening stagehand by mistake lets down the curtain, and we have the second intermission. In the last act, the characters work through their dreary doom. The director will have none of them and their story, shrugs over his wasted day and turns back to his own rehearsal as the final curtain falls.

The pattern of the play permits a close examination of the relationship of art and life. A playwright's usual quest of verisimilitude is derided as a covering for the lack of true creative power. The artist foolishly seeks the verisimilar, when "life is full of infinite absurdities." Is not Hamlet more real, better and more fully known, more rounded and actual a person, than most of your neighbors? "When a character is born," says Pirandello, "he acquires immediately such an independence of his author that we can all imagine him in situations in which the author never thought of placing him, and he assumes of his own initiative a significance that his author never dreamt of lending him." This independence is symbolized by the plight of the six characters who have been abandoned midway of their story.

A sordid and a gloomy story comes through Pirandello's theorizing with undiminished power and poignancy. The father, an intellectual, after sending his son to a farm to be reared like a healthy peasant, turns over his simple, domestic wife to his secretary, by whom she has three more children. Years later, in a fashionable establishment that sells expensive garments and expansive girls, the Father is being embraced by a sly young wanton when the Mother, now a seamstress and a pander, cries out "She is my child!" (This scene reaches almost unendurable poignancy as the stepdaughter insists on the truth: "I went there, you see, and with fingers that faltered with shame and repugnance, I undid my dress, my corset." It is here, on the Mother's shouting, that the curtain falls.)

The Father takes back the family, but their tangled relationships breed only torment. They live in a seething stew of hatred, rebellion, and remorse, until the four-year-old girl is drowned in the garden pool, and the adolescent son, gazing after her, shoots himself.

The *Christian Science Monitor* (March 21, 1922) called the play "one of the freshest and most original productions seen for a long time past," a verdict it was accorded everywhere. The play was revived in New York in 1931, with Walter Connolly and Flora Robson; and again in 1933, 1939, 1947, and (Phoenix) 1955. London saw a private performance in February, 1922, but the play was not licensed there until 1928. It was revived in London in 1932, when the *London Times* (February 19, 1932) said: "Repetition cannot dull the brilliance of the play's attack on theatrical shams; it cannot stale the tragedy which we receive in fragments and yet perceive as a whole; but it does persuade us that the Pirandellian parlour-game for metaphysicians is a rather tiresome contrivance . . ." A brilliant production of the play was given in London opening November 21, 1950, with Karel Stepanek as the father, *Theatre World* (January, 1951) reported, "striving with every fibre of his being to explain and justify his equivocal life." Analysis of Pirandello's intention came from the *Boston Transcript* (January 23, 1922): "It is as if the stage has become the teeming brain of Professor Pirandello, and the audience, by some strange psychic license, has been permitted to look right into the throbbing mechanism of a dramatist's mind at work." Some critics discerned Pirandello's frequent method of covering with ludicrous externals a tragic soul. Gilbert W. Gabriel (April 16, 1931) called it "Pirandello's most amazing play. Certainly his most amusing one." And the *London Telegraph* (February 28, 1922) considered it "a comedy in which the humorous element springs from, and is wholly dependent on, a theme of the utmost gravity."

The subtitle of *Six Characters in Search of an Author* is "A Play Yet to be Written", but in it Pirandello presented not only a gripping and a piteous tale, but one of the most searching questionings of the drama.

THE PLEASURE OF HONESTY   *Luigi Pirandello*

This drama, written in 1917, has been attacked as a play of idea, but when one seeks the idea expressed by Pirandello, one discovers that he presses the very point that abstract ideas are useless, if not fantastic; the worth of an idea, of a principle, lies in its practice.

Baldovino, when we first see him, is a queer sort of fellow, detached from the normal world of material things. He has ruled "the heart" out of his existence; hence he can contemplate his unhappy past calmly, with pure intellect. With smiling irony he endures his poverty, although the business men call him dishonest and the shopkeepers refuse him credit because he has never paid some paltry debts. Then, of a sudden, Baldovino is called upon to put the cloak of honesty over a growing shame; he is asked, by an emissary of the rich Marchese Fabio Colli, who is separated from his profligate wife, to marry the pregnant mistress of the Marchese, Agata Renni, and give the child an honest name. The irony of the situation wins his consent, but he insists that, from then on, all their relationships be honest. Baldovino recognizes that the Marchese and Agata's mother plan to get rid of him as soon as the child is born, but consideration for the child's good name bids Baldovino stay. His probity wins Agata's respect; when he senses this, and his own feelings begin to be roused, Baldovino makes up his mind to leave. Agata declares she'll go with him; the recognition of their love keeps the two at home.

Thus the man that has lived in a world of the intellect and abstract idea is brought back to the warmer world of human feeling. Through Baldovino, moreover, Agata discovers the value of thought. She had yielded to the Marchese through sentiment, but, as she watches the sureness with which Baldovino handles the family concerns and the affairs of the banking firm of which the Marchese has made him manager, and as she thinks of the years ahead for her infant son, honesty takes on a specific meaning for her and becomes a vital frame for her days.

After its Italian success, the play was a hit in Paris in 1920. This subtly satirical and metaphysical piece had its American premiere in Los Angeles in 1927, and was performed in New York, in Italian, in 1929.

The drama fuses two drives. It is, and can be accepted as, a psychological story of a curious triangle, of a woman who, loving one man, marries another to keep clean her name and the name of her expected child, and comes to love the man who has lent himself to her protection. Pirandello presents the story with vigor and emotional force; but behind the triangular tribulations is a cogent presentation of a mutual growth from opposite extremes to common ground. The man moves from an artificial intellectual world to temper his ideals and forms with feeling; the woman moves from a world of impulse and sentiment to govern her acts with thought-out principle. And the spectator recognizes, through a rich and probing drama of human ways, that neither wilful abstraction nor total immersion gives proper course in the turbulent sea of life.

RIGHT YOU ARE (IF YOU THINK YOU ARE)   *Luigi Pirandello*

The problem of illusion and truth, in the spell of Pirandello's dramatic weaving, grows tense with the anguish of truly realized persons in this play, written in 1917.

Its action is motivated by the curiosity of gossips in a provincial town, who thrust themselves into what seems a mystery and insist upon learning the truth. To that town has come Signor Ponza as secretary to the Prefect. He and his wife live on the top floor of a building in which his mother-in-law, Signora Frola, occupies the ground floor. Although Ponza is most considerate of, even tender toward, his mother-in-law, he never permits her to visit his wife. The two women shout greetings to one another or exchange messages in a hoisted basket. The gossips break in upon the family to find out what this is all about. Ponza tells them that his first wife, Lina, died four years ago, and that her mother's affliction was so great that when he took Giulia to wife, the mother found comfort in the delusion that the wife was still her daughter Lina. Then Signora Frola tells her side of the story—*i.e.*, that Ponza was so stricken when Lina went to a sanitarium that on her return he thought she was another woman, whom he called Giulia. To appease him, they had even held a second marriage ceremony. A genuine sad vein of humanity runs through the concern of each to keep the other happy. So thoughtful of each other are Ponza and his mother-in-law that the neighbors do not know which to believe. One kindly but amused observer, Lamberto Landisi, bids them accept both stories. Instead they turn to the wife herself. Veiled, vague, almost blurred, she comes to them. She tells them she is Ponza's second wife, and Signora Frola's daughter, and, to herself, no one. In her compassion she has drowned her personality in the truth of their desires.

The play is, of course, a purely symbolic fable. Yet, "with no more substance than this fable to go upon," said Brooks Atkinson (February 24, 1927), "Pirandello manages to work up a passionate, comical rigamarole with a thousand penetrating intimations ... Approaching philosophy in a light fantastic mood, Pirandello has written a thoroughly delightful metaphysical melodrama."

The American premiere of the play was at Cornell University, with Franchot Tone among the student players. Atkinson's remarks were made after the first of a series of New York matinees opening February 23, 1927, with Edward G. Robinson and Morris Carnovsky. On July 22, 1942, in Cleveland, Marta Abba (Italian star in most of his plays) made her first American appearance in a Pirandello play as Signora Frola. After the New York opening, John Anderson called the play "fresh and provocative drama ... deft and engaging foolery, cloaking with silken delights of comedy some suavely savage stuff of human illusion and absolute truth." *Commonweal* (May 11, 1927) added: "There are certain scenes of rare dramatic poignancy and others of highly strung suspense."

Those that consider Pirandello as caught in abstruse intellectual concerns should weigh the title of this drama. He is psychological in his symbols and methods, but he sees danger in the cold intellect; he is almost anti-intellectual in his idea. He declares that, instead of abandoning himself to the warm flow of instinct, man thinks; man sets up theories about himself and about life. Other creatures simply live, but man watches himself live, with the aid of an infernal machine called logic. Hence we begin to classify persons: he is unjust; she is immoral; he is serious; she is a prude. Reality rebels at these clear-cut classifications. Reality is manysided; reality is fluid, warm. Hence there is a clash between intellect and instinct. Reality cannot always be revealed, hence the dilemma within *Right You Are (If You Think You Are)*. The play leaves the townsfolk, and the audience, in doubt as to the "absolute" identity of the wife of Signor Ponza. The usually cautious Mr. Atkinson wagered "one pistareen on the husband's insanity." What, asked jesting Pilate, is truth? The point is that there is no single answer. Pirandello shapes and sharpens that point into a vivid play.

HENRY IV   *Luigi Pirandello*

One of the most popular plays by Pirandello, *Henry IV*, 1922, was performed all over Europe, notably by Georges Pitoeff in Paris in 1925. In England it was shown at Cambridge in 1924 with sets and costumes by Cecil Beaton; in London in 1938 and 1940. New York saw it as *The Living Mask* (Pirandello attended the opening) on January 22, 1924, and again (Equity Library) in 1947. Paris saw another production in 1950.

The play opens in the majestic throne room of the Holy Roman Emperor Henry IV (1050-1106), with courtiers talking of intrigue and Pope Gregory. When one of the courtiers wants to light a pipe, and when another arrives in the costume of the court of Henry IV of France, which dates some five hundred years later, we know that we are beholding a masquerade. We learn that twenty years before, when his beloved Matilda, in a masque and pageant, dressed as Countess Matilda, her suitor Henry matched the costume by dressing as Henry IV. But a rival, Baron Belcredi, pricked Henry's horse, so that he was thrown; when he regained consciousness, he believed himself the actual Emperor. His wealthy sister provided a castle and other means for him to live in that delusion. Now, twenty years later, Matilda, widow, and mistress of the dominating, cynical Belcredi, comes with her daughter Frida and her lover to the castle. A psychiatrist has suggested that if mother and daughter both appear, with the daughter in the costume of the Countess, the shock may restore Henry's mind. It happens, however, that for eight years Henry has been sane, but has preferred the splendor of the eleventh century to the cold shock of return to the modern world. The sight of beautiful Frida dressed as the Countess rouses him; her warm vitality sweeps through the coldness of his "lucid insanity"; he embraces her madly: "She's mine!" Belcredi steps forward; Henry kills him—and recognizes that now he must wear his mask of madness forever.

This "satirical comedy", as Pirandello has called it, works upon the interplay of rationality and irrationality in our lives. Thus Alexander Woollcott could call the work (January 23, 1924) "a psychopathic play of the retreat from reality—a mad flight along a road which a good many

of your neighbors travel for a little distance every day of their lives."
George Freedley (December 12, 1947) declared it "one of the most brilliant plays of the modern theatre."

This absorbing drama probes the troubled depth of human consciousness. For all the masquerade that is built around Henry, his problem is
a poignant and modern one. "When the Emperor Henry IV disappears,"
as Domenico Vittorino has noted, "and the man looms in all the agony
that tortures him, his humanity is as complex and deep as the figure of
the Emperor was stately." Is his enforced madness any less a "lucid
insanity" than that which impels this atomic age toward a third World
War? *Henry IV* is a profound philosophical fantasy on the plight of the
human personality in a complicated and unchosen world.

NAKED   *Luigi Pirandello*

A deft probing into the human soul—with its tangled skein of motives, intentions, designs, and desires beyond our powers of judgment—
gives significance to Pirandello's *Vestire gli ignudi,* 1924 (*Clothe the
naked*), which has been translated as *Naked.* Centered upon the suicide
of young Ersilia Drei, the play also reveals the minds of the three men
that helped to shape her days.

Ersilia had longed for only a modest sort of beauty, such as even a
commonplace person might hope to achieve. A nursemaid in the home
of the Italian Consul in Smyrna, she was engaged to an Italian naval
officer, Franco. When he left her, the baby in her care fell from a
terrace and was killed. Returning to Italy, Ersilia found Franco engaged to another girl, and took poison. The play begins when that first
attempt at suicide fails, and a novelist, Ludovico Nota, attracted by her
story, invites her to his home.

But the story was hers to die with; living, she feels only revulsion
against the men who have given her ugly days. When Franco, contrite,
wishes to marry her, she will have none of him; when he had left her,
she had given herself to the first passerby. In a grueling scene, the
Consul and Ersilia accuse one another: he had wanted only to be as a
father to her; it was the light in her eyes (kindled for Franco!) that had
inflamed him. And we learn that it was while they were making love
that the Consul's baby fell to its death.

Thus all the passion that in Ersilia's death-tale seemed tenderly and
sorrowfully romantic becomes sordid, and wormy with disgust. Nor are
the motives any cleaner than the acts. Ersilia wished to die, not for
love, but because life was too grim a burden. The novelist takes her in,
not out of compassion, but as good material for a romance. Franco returns because, on reading Ersilia's story, his new fiancée casts him aside.
Nevertheless, these men, and the Consul, all turn in anger and scorn upon
the wretched girl, as they learn her story. Why—they cannot understand
—why did she lie?

Naked has stirred audiences deeply wherever it has been played. It
was a sensation throughout Europe. It opened in London, March 18,
1927, with Charles Laughton. New York saw it in French, with Mme.
Simone, in 1924; in English with Augustin Duncan, opening November 8,
1926 for 32 performances. Its poignance was again revealed in a Studio

' production off-Broadway, opening September 6, 1950. The *New York Sun* (October 29, 1924) spoke of "the same old metaphysical shell game," but Gilbert W. Gabriel considered it better than *Six Characters in Search of an Author**.

London emphasized Pirandello's usual concern, *Stage* (March 24, 1927) insisting that he "harped again on his one and only theme, that the unreal is more real than the real, that what is imagined is more actual than the actual." Life put a vivid illustration of this thesis before Pirandello one evening while he was watching a performance of Maurice Rostand's *General Boulanger*. After the suicide onstage, a man in the audience rose and cried: "You don't die only for love; you can also die from eternal persecution." There was a slight crack, as of clapping hands. "See!" said Pirandello to Saul Colin, "the fiction is in the audience; the reality is on the stage." And the unperturbed audience watched the rest of the show—to learn next morning that there had been a suicide in their midst.

Naked, however, presses the problem of reality and irreality to the realm of motives and intentions. Ersilia's impulses, not her deeds, were imagined; the lie was about not her action, but its cause. And her lie, as the *New York Post* (November 9, 1926) pointed out, "attains glorious heights in the literary imagination of her benefactor, acquires essential vitality in her relations with a former lover, dwindles to pathetic cheapness in the reality which leaves her naked, becomes mystically significant in her own neurotic imagination." Yet that lie, around which the others fang and tear at her spirit, gives pathos, gives dignity, to the wretched nursemaid. It is her pitiful grasp at beauty, the one step she can take to give semblance of decent human meaning to the life she is too miserable to hold. Caught unawares by life, she seeks to assume a better pose for dying. When this fails, she goes indeed naked from the world—but, as Vittorino remarked, "Pirandello has clothed her with his sympathy, and with the beauty of his art." Ersilia, however, is not the only one stripped naked, left quivering and raw, by Pirandello's play. The three men in the drama—and uncounted audiences—can hardly cast the first stone.

MAN, BEAST, AND VIRTUE   *Luigi Pirandello*

In this play, written in 1925, Pirandello indulges in an ironic gambol over the relationship of reason, instinct, and morality. Far from having to be taught virtue, he seems to say, we travel toward it by instinct. The same instincts may, it is true, lead us along other paths; then reason has to harness the "beast" in us, so that it may haul us back to virtue.

The thought is presented as a tragedy drowned in a farce. If the play is accepted purely for its surface value, it is a bawdy, risqué skit, with titillating situations. It was offered in New York at "milkman's matinees"—midnight performances for "the tired business man too tired to go home"—opening December 3, 1926, with Osgood Perkins, who, said Gilbert W. Gabriel, performed like a "Yankee at King Boccaccio's Court." The situations of this "boulevard farce," said Brooks Atkinson (December 6, 1926), "are conventionally ribald, and easy to understand once you have caught the salty meaning . . ." Long-stemmed flowers were given to the opening night audience with a tip to the English title, *Say it With Flowers.*

The story is simple. Captain Perrella, on his journeys home, always stops to see his mistress in the next port; his wife receives none of his attentions. She notifies Professor Paolino that he has consoled her so successfully that her good name depends upon her husband's immediate and intimate interest. Paolino takes charge. The Captain laughs boisterously when his wife comes to dinner powdered and painted, and in a low-cut gown. Hopes fall, but rise again when the Captain eats a large portion of the cake that has been liberally dosed with an aphrodisiac. Signora Perrella is to signal Paolino next morning by placing a flower pot on her balcony. Watching early, he rejoices at length to see her — but what is this? — it is with strangely mixed feelings that he watches her setting out not one flower pot but five.

Man, Beast and Virtue, said the *New York Telegraph* (December 6, 1926), is "a highly amusing combination of banter and burlesque . . . a frisky and risqué story now and then is relished by the most philosophical of playwrights . . . The moral, if any, is that you *can* eat your cake and have it too." Dancing on the surface of a triangle of sex, Pirandello shows how Man may summon the Beast to attain Virtue.

Exposed passions seem ridiculous, the play declares. Instinct is honest; reason, hypocritical. Virtue is the name given to the successful mask.

TONIGHT WE IMPROVISE   *Luigi Pirandello*

The oppositions that tear upon art and life, as each strives to be the other, are pressed in *Tonight We Improvise,* 1929. In *Six Characters in Search of an Author*,* Pirandello abandoned his persons midway of their tale; in the present drama, he turns them over to Dr. Hinkfuss (Lamefoot), the director, who boasts that he will bring the author's work to life on the stage. After two acts of Hinkfuss's theatrical calculations, the persons of the story throw the director out, and move with all their living blood and anguish to their destined doom.

The story presents a dominating woman, Signora Ignazia Palmiro, who comes with her four daughters and her meek husband from gay Naples to sober Sicily. Her daughters have a lively time entertaining officers of the Flying Corps. They are all "very beautiful, plump, sentimental, vivacious, and passionate." Mommina, the eldest, sings excellently. One aviator does not join the gaiety. He watches jealously, quarrels, and asks Mommina's hand. Married, he imprisons her, fiercely jealous of her past, the pleasure of which he imagines and fancies her always remembering. Mommina grows old before her time, secluded from all society; but when her sister Totina comes to town on a singing tour, Mommina's thoughts are so strong that they summon her mother and sister. Totina sings the *Trovatore* aria; Mommina joins her in a great burst of song, and with it her heart bursts, too.

Until the last scene, the movement of the story is variously interrupted on three levels of concern. There are the fussy endeavors of the director to extract dramatic values; when the Father is brought home from the cabaret dying, the director protests there is no drama in the entrance, only blank, soggy death. Then there are the efforts of the actors to fit into their parts; they resent the director's using their off-stage names and are already beginning to live the persons assigned them, even in actions not set down in the script. Finally, there is the Palmiro family, with its entourage of lively aviators. The latter are seated in the orchestra with the audience. They watch a motion picture, along with us, and make loud comments while we are politely dumb. The quarrel they start in their seats is continued onstage and takes fire again in the lobby during intermission.

"The play runs smoothly for a time," said the *London Times* (January 29, 1935), "and then, with no warning, a confusion of human temperaments overwhelms it . . . Nonsense and tragedy, ugliness and beauty, vulgarity and fastidiousness, all here are mixed." Complicated in the telling, *Tonight We Improvise* gains power in the performance. Much of its meaning and most of the poignancy of the story come through.

Pirandello was at the opening of his play not only in Italy, but also at the Pitoeff Paris production on January 17, 1935. An Italian company presented the play at the Vienna Drama Festival of 1936 and toured Switzerland and Italy in 1939. The Berlin reception of the play in 1930 was tempestuous; opponents of Pirandello's ideas and methods thronged the theatre; some say that a Reinhardt clique arranged the attack. When the characters in the audience began to quarrel, others in the audience proceeded to throw vegetables. A riot ensued; the play did not reopen.

The American premiere of *Tonight We Improvise* was at Vassar College, December 20, 1936. In New York, Erwin Piscator presented the play at his Dramatic Workshop in 1943 and again in 1946 and 1948. The drama offers no easy anodyne, but probingly examines the bases of human action and sets a provocative pattern along that lightning-lit, that dark but intriguing and intricate region where life blends with art.

AS YOU DESIRE ME   *Luigi Pirandello*

The basic plot of *As You Desire Me*, 1930, was taken from an actual situation in Italy: Brunelli, a professor of Greek at Verona, was reported missing at the front; some years later, Signora Brunelli, in Turin, saw a man who called himself Canella; she insisted that he was her husband, that his denial must be the result of amnesia. The force of her faith convinced the man that he was Brunelli. Pirandello switched the sexes of the chief characters and the result, as Robert Garland (January 29, 1931) said, was "shot with the Italian's metallic and entirely mental sense of comedy . . . a sort of metaphysical mystery melodrama combining most that is worthwhile in Signor Pirandello with most that is worthwhile in Mr. Samuel Shipman . . ." The woman, he added, "plays with fact and fancy as a cat plays with a mouse; saves her soul and loses her body. On paper, it sounds complicated and dull; onstage it is uncomplicated and exciting. From curtain rise to curtain fall, Signor Pirandello's story grips you."

In Pirandello's story, the Unknown One, as the woman is called, is found by the artist Boffi, who had once painted Lucia Pieri's portrait. He is sure that she is Lucia. The woman, a singer in a Berlin cabaret, is the coarse and debauched mistress of the novelist Carl Salter; the latter is a Kraft-Ebbing super-sensualist whose life is a tumult of depravity and violence. Salter shoots himself, and the Unknown One goes off with Boffi. At Bruno Pieri's home she is welcomed as Lucia returned from the dead. Kindness and faith restore her nobility, ravaged as it has been by the horrors of the war. But there are doubts: Bruno does not find on her body a mark that Lucia bore, and the woman wonders whether Bruno welcomes her spirit, or her body, or indeed the estate that her uncle now deeds back to her from her sister. Then Salter, recovered from his wound, brings from a Vienna sanitarium the Demented One, whose mangled body bears a likeness to Bruno's Lucia. Which is the real wife?

The Unknown One scorns the need of proof. If she has the loveliness and bloom of Lucia, if she has all the husband desires of his long-missing wife, is she not more truly his wife than the walking cadaver dragged from the asylum? But seeing that in Bruno and his relatives faith hangs upon the weight of physical proof, the Unknown One goes off with Carl Salter. Pirandello does not disclose which body is the wife's. Plagued with the question, Pirandello once responded: "That is not the point. Even if she was Cia, she is now another person." Life keeps us always changing. It is not in the cold constructions of reason, but in the surety of faith, that human integrity and unity abide.

Onstage, said Robert Garland, *As You Desire Me* is "a straightforward and arresting tale . . . a play among plays," but Brooks Atkinson, after seeing the same performance, on January 28, 1931, with Judith Anderson, was at first more reserved: "The trouble seems to be that the design of the play does not arouse your loyalty for the heroine—which is essential." By the last act, however, all was well: "You instinctively take sides yourself, and you want to believe, which is the essence of Pirandello's doctrine." More detached than the reviewer, Pirandello asks you, not to believe, but to observe the effects of belief and disbelief. According to the expectations and the belief in her, the Unknown One—"a drunken, baleful slattern," as Atkinson described her, "living in sin with a German brute"—becomes gracious, kindly, noble, dignified, until, when doubt smudges the woman she has become, once again there rises the scornful slut, contemptuous of mean-spirited folk; and from their meanness with a satanic nobility she walks away.

"The Strange Lady of Pirandello's metaphysical drama remains a fascinating person." There is rich truth in these words of the London *Stage* (January 22, 1948) on a revival of the play with Mary Morris. "The play itself seems melodramatic in the first act, when the vices of post-Great-War Berlin are the feature; but as soon as we are at the villa, the conflicts and doubts concerning the Lady clearly appear, gathering in strangeness and intensity. Then the play becomes real, and absorbing. Pirandello's stage craft is magnificent. Few modern dramatists have known as well as he how to write effective dialogue and work out a situation so brilliantly. Even for those that do not care for the speculations on human life and understanding, there is an evening of first rate 'theatre', full of excitement, surprise, and character interest." *As You Desire Me*, in addition to being a superb dramatic statement of the problem of reality and the power of faith, is one of Pirandello's best plays.

TO FIND ONESELF   *Luigi Pirandello*

The problem of the interrelationship of life and art is again posed in
Pirandello's *Trovarsi*, 1932, (*To Find Oneself*; also translated as *She
Wanted to Find Herself*). The central figure is modeled upon Piran-
dello's discovery and protégée, Marta Abba, the star of most of his plays.
Like all of Pirandello's plays, *Trovarsi* has been played frequently in
Italy and all over Europe. It has not yet had professional performance
in the United States.

The play opens with a group of modern folk at a Riviera villa awaiting the arrival of the great actress Donata Genzi. Two writers are presenting opposite views of life. The realistic Volpe declares that he must
first experience in order to know. The romantic Salò states that he experiences only what he has previously imagined. Donata agrees with
Salò and laughingly admits that were she to fall in love, she'd probably
copy her acted love scenes. Her thought soon becomes no laughing matter. She goes for a sail with young Elj Nielsen; a storm sweeps over their
boat and sweeps them into ecstatic love. Donata, who has been content
to have no personality save that of each of her roles, is now enanguished
to be a person, to fulfill herself as a vital human with her lover. Elj
watches her onstage; he sees there the woman he has known in intimate
hours. During the performance, Donata feels that she has found herself,
has discovered fullness as an artist together with fullness as a woman.
She hurries to Elj's room—but he has gone. Donata is left with her art,
to live forever in her heroines; to be no person, but to bring to life many
great roles. At the end of the play her bedroom alcove dimly becomes
the setting of a stage; the audience discerns heads upon the curtain there,
and faintly hears the echo of applause.

In the life of Donata Genzi, as in the life of every public figure and
every artist, there are two high seas: the sea of the storm where life
and love sweep on and the sea of faces and eyes where the storms of
abuse and applause await the figure destined to that colder and lonelier
journeying. Again, in this drama, Pirandello opposes the fluidity of
life and the fixity of art. Art may have many patterns, but always it
prepares a mold; life fears lest any mold too soon grow moldy. Yet the
very fluidity of life makes it formless and therefore lacking in the significance art can achieve. Either choice brings its anguish. And what
sounds like an abstract aesthetical consideration works to heartbreak in
the very human figures, wrought with tenderness, understanding and
beauty, of *She Wanted To Find Herself*.

WHEN SOMEONE IS SOMEBODY   *Luigi Pirandello*

Although it was after he had met Bernard Shaw in 1933 that Pirandello wrote this tragicomedy or cosmic farce of what life does to its leading figures, and although some of the chief figure's characteristics bring
Mark Twain to mind, the author could easily have plucked the story from
his own days. For every noted man is condemned to be the image the
public have formed of him. "They make a statue of you," protests the
poet in the play, a figure always dressed in white, his long flowing hair
swept back from the majestic brow, a "public property, like the face
on a coin." So completely has fame stripped away the poet's personal

identity that he is indicated in the drama by no name: three asterisks show that he is a fixed figure, but of stellar luminance.

The play presents ***, just turning fifty. His wife, Giovanna, has the grim, devoted face of a custodian of glory. Their daughter, Valentina, lives in a withdrawn atmosphere, as though she lacked true existence. Their young son, Tito, sums up his world in the constant word "Pappa! Pappa!" Then, at his nephew Pietro's villa, *** finds—in Pietro's sister-in-law Veroccia, who has come to Italy from Russia by way of the United States—a renewed intensity, a fresh vitality, truly the breath of new youth, of a new world. Veroccia cuts ***'s hair short, has him put on sports clothes, and, under the name Delago, his volume of love poems in a new style wins acclaim. Giovanna the wife arrives—the world for too long has missed the light of ***'s glory—and as she strokes the poet's head his hair grows again into its familiar lines. The public figure reassumes its public guise. A second volume reveals that Delago is ***; the public laughs and dismisses the name as an amusing hoax. In the heart of *** this is a bitter tragedy; his own life, his reasserting youth, have been denied him. The image of the great one has been restored; the idol crushes the man. At the fiftieth birthday of ***, he is created a count; the State gives him a palace for his remaining days, after which it will in his name become an orphanage. The speech on this occasion might well be his funeral oration. Indeed, Veroccia, who had given hope to his renewal of youth, exclaims "He is dead." A group of children come to *** as he sits on a bench beside the garden wall. He speaks to them, and after they are gone, as he muses alone, his last words to them light up, like a golden inscription, on the wall behind. And as *** sits in the twilight, the bench moves up and back, the wall with its inscription makes a pedestal: the great man has become his own statue.

Saul Colin, who was with Pirandello when he met Bernard Shaw, has told me that Shaw remarked: "If only you had written in English, you'd have been even more famous than I." In 1934 Pirandello received the Nobel Prize. Throughout Europe he was constantly pestered by gaping admirers. Like Shaw's, his image was taking its mold. In the play *When Someone Is Somebody*, the great writers on the wall of the poet's study, Dante, Ariosto, and the rest, come down and gesticulate, silently arguing the problems of art and of the world, each in the too-familiar way, the frozen attitude fame has assigned him. The drama builds into an ironic and deeply moving story of a great and famous man, a vision of the lonely pedestal upon which every public figure is doomed to become his own statue.

ONE DOESN'T KNOW HOW   *Luigi Pirandello*

Perhaps the most lyrical, the most directly poignant and deeply tragic of Pirandello's dramas is *One Doesn't Know How*, 1933. Searching deeply through the lives of its characters and into the core of human responsibility and choice, it bares the anguish that tears at the heart of the intelligent sensitive man in the drive of life.

The action takes place in the villa of Giorgio Vanzi, where Giorgio and his wife Ginevra live happily near their good friends, Count Romeo Daddi and his wife Bice. The story itself is very simple. One intoxicating day, Romeo and Ginevra succumb to a moment of passion; Romeo confesses to Giorgio, and Giorgio shoots him. The drama of the play lies, not in these outward circumstances, but in the conflict within Count Romeo. To what extent is a man responsible for his acts? Things happen, one does not know how; then one is faced with the finality of a deed. Seldom, if ever, is one wholly conscious, wholly deliberate, in what one does; often one acts by impulse or instinct. But the instinctive act, which is right because it is natural, becomes wrong in the logic of a man-made world and places sin upon one's conscience. The motor of human instinct does not respond to the steering-wheel of convention, and one is wrecked upon life's rocky road.

The degree to which the control of reason slips away was impressed upon Romeo by a boyhood tragedy. In his early teens, upon seeing a peasant lad torture and kill a lizard, Romeo had leapt upon the lad and in the ensuing fight had killed him. That action, beyond any conscious control or deliberate intent, lay within Romeo's spirit, a torment and a reminder. In the present circumstances, its memory brings new torture. If he was able to keep that sin a secret for a third of a century, what secrets might not other faces hide! His beautiful wife, his seemingly devoted and virtuous wife, Bice, what does she conceal? Romeo plagues her until she admits that once, yes, once in a dream she had fancied herself with Giorgio. Can one control, or be responsible for, one's dreams?

On the question of responsibility, the persons of the play are neatly divided. The two women, like most of Pirandello's women, are closer to the instinctive. Carried away for the moment, what can one do, but never mention it! Giorgio, like the average practical man, has adjusted himself to life. He accepts conventional codes; he knows that to lapse from them is to sin; but weakness is human. If one sins, one can at least conform by silence. Another character of the play, Count Respi, is even more civilized. He is a man whose instincts are well harnessed, who calculates his every act; he does not "let himself go", but observes the terrain and makes his path. He is most fully adjusted to human living.

It is that very matter of "human living" which *One Doesn't Know How* challenges. Romeo's last words, after Giorgio has shot him, are "That was done in the human way." For Respi and Giorgio have found a satisfactory way of life—on a physical, sensual plane. But a man that rises beyond that plane to a deeper sensibility demands more searching thought of reality, and of his share in its making. Reality involves more than its own existence; it is colored, and therefore partly created, by our feelings. Feelings drive us to actions of which we are fully aware only when they are irrevocably performed. Here is the dilemma, of responsibility, of sin and guilt, that rives the heart of a noble, earnest man.

One Doesn't Know How derives in part from two of Pirandello's short stories, *Cinci* and *In the Whirlwind*. The play has been widely performed all over Europe; the German translation was made by Stefan Zweig. The great actor Moissi, planning a world tour in 1935, was rehearsing the play in Italian, German, and English when pneumonia drew down his final curtain. America has yet to see a production of this intense and beautiful, probing and poignant tragedy.

SWEENEY TODD   *George Dibdin Pitt*

The story of Sweeney Todd, the demon barber of Fleet Street, has long been popular. Mr. Todd's shop has a chair that can suddenly be dropped through a trap-door into the cellar; the occupant disappears and the next day there is a fresh supply of veal pies. The sailor Mark Ingestrie tempts the fate of the chair by showing the barber his string of fine pearls; down he thumps. "Every trick in the whole calendar of melodrama," as the *New York World* (July 19, 1924) put it, is played before the barber can be trapped and taken to his doom.

The story of Sweeney Todd is not in the Newgate Calendar of London crimes, but his shop on Fleet Street is still pointed out. There is reference in *The Life of the Late Earl of Barrymore* by Anthony Pasquin (John Williams, 1761-1818) to a pastrycook play in 1793, in which the joint of a child's finger is found in a Senator's pie. The story originated in Venice, with sliding trap-door and underground vault; the barber was added in Paris; and it came to England, via the periodical *The Tell Tale*, in 1824. For twenty-five years the story circulated in "penny dreadfuls," and on March 8, 1847, there was produced the play *The String of Pearls; or The Fiend of Fleet Street*, by George Dibdin Pitt (English, 1799-1855). Charles Dickens in the London *Morning Chronicle* exclaimed, "No one should miss seeing Sweeney Todd!" The play remained popular until Frederick Hazleton's version, *Sweeney Todd, The Demon Barber of Fleet Street*, appeared in 1862. Pitt's version ends in the court room at the trial of Sweeney Todd, when the escaped sailor Mark appears; Todd thinks he's a ghost, and confesses. In the Hazleton version, the still free Todd is shown drawing a razor across the bakerwoman's throat to kill off betrayal, when the trap gives way and he plunges into the blazing bake-house.

Later versions include one by Matt Wilkinson, shown from 1870 to 1928; one by Andrew Melville, 1927 and 1932. Most recent productions return to the Pitt version and exhibit the crude melodrama for the superior amusement of our sophisticate age.

When Queen Victoria saw the play—her first command performance— she found it thrilling. Even today, laugh as we may at its exaggerated and obvious horror, there is a measure of uneasiness beneath our amusement. In 1924 the *New York Tribune* (July 18) called it "full of thrills," and the *World* (same date) declared that "it lacks some of the modern gloss of the trade, but the core of it is identical with the hair-raising hokum of all crook plays, detective dramas, and murder trials seen in these parts for eighty years." Less rousingly active and less pathetic than such plays as *The Streets of London**, but with more horror in its theme and as much suspense in its unfolding, *Sweeney Todd* is the epitome of the grisly melodrama.

THE DOG OF MONTARGIS   *René Charles Guilbert Pixerécourt*

The father of melodrama is René Charles Guilbert de Pixerécourt (French, 1773-1844). Showing, as M. W. Disher pointed out in *Blood and Thunder* (1949) "the fall of vice from her sovereign sway in pleasantly lurid forms", Pixerécourt took both the sentimental and the blood-

and-thunder drama, enriched their possibilities of emotional rouse, and gave them the theatrical devices that have ever after accompanied the forms, both in the theatre and on the screen. In his studies of the genre, Pixerécourt indeed first used the word *melodrama* in its current sense.

The most widely produced of his plays, *The Dog of Montargis; or The Forest of Bondy*, 1814, often played as *Aubrey de Montdidier's Dog*, is a dramatization of a fourteenth century tale. Aubry de Montdidier was killed in the forest near Montargis in the year 1371. His dog so persistently barked after a certain Macaire that suspicions centered upon him; Macaire confessed the murder and was hanged. In the play, the dog jumps a gate, rings the bell, takes a lantern in his teeth, and lures the murderer forth.

The Dog of Montargis was widely popular. There were riots for a fortnight in Dublin in 1814, while the company was substituting other plays because the trained dog refused to perform. In 1817 a poodle was touring Germany and Austria as the star; the Duke of Weimar wanted to see the play and Goethe*, since 1791 director of the Court Theatre there, in high dudgeon resigned. The play has been presented with the villain on horseback and the dog leaping high to bring him down. Dickens satirically mentioned a white mouse that once played Montdidier's dog. For his rousing of such emotions—even the brute beast that mutely cries for vengeance!—and for his establishing the distinctive features of modern melodrama, Pixerécourt has been called the Shakespeare of the boulevards.

THE FAIR ONE WITH THE GOLDEN LOCKS *James Robinson Planché*

James Robinson Planché (English, 1796-1880) was a busy man in the English theatre from about 1820 for some thirty years. As a designer, he provided Charles Kemble's revival of *King John** in 1823 with the first authentic costumes in English historical drama. He also wrote many pantomimes and burlesques. His only memorable play, however, is the fairy spectacle *The Fair One with the Golden Locks; or, Harlequinade and Davy Jones's Locker*, 1843.

This play, revived frequently for some forty years, is an outstanding example of the popular blending of song, satire, travesty, fairy tale and spectacle, with the inevitable mid-nineteenth century "transformation scene". The story, upon which extravagant scenes and ballets are hung like Chinese lanterns, is of a haughty Princess, whose golden locks are not only on her head but on her money box, who sets three difficult tasks for the Aged King who wants her hand. He must fetch a ring from the bottom of a swift stream, kill a fierce ogre, and bring her the water of beauty from a dragon-guarded fount. The King, fortunately, was a pre-charter member of the Society for the Prevention of Cruelty to Animals, therefore the fish fetch him the ring, a crow de-oculates the ogre, and an owl brings him the water. But the Princess doesn't like her new husband; he therefore drinks the wrong potion, leaving her free to marry the handsome young champion, Prince Hyacinth.

Comic antics alternate with beautiful scenes and elaborate ballets, springing from this fairy tale with its slightly cynical ending. A clown does a pas de deux with an animated mop; dwarfish figures in a dance

turn suddenly giant. One scene is laid in Davy Jones's Locker along the
bed of the Atlantic Cable (completed in 1865); the sub-oceanic scene is
transformed into a shimmering spectacle of "Refulgent Temples of
Bright Waters, Neptune's Homage to Britannia." In a ballet in the
"Golden Grove of Laburnums and Garden of Sweet Scents", a great
field of variegated flowers becomes a bevy of dancing maids.

Such devices and transformations paved the way to the swift changes
and elaborately gorgeous spectacles characteristic of modern musical
comedies and revues.

THE MENAECHMI   *Titus Maccius Plautus*

The most vigorous and robust of the Roman comic writers, Titus
Maccius Plautus (c. 254 - c. 184 B. C.) probably began his career as an
actor. His name Maccius is derived from Maccus, the clown of ancient
farce. His plays are all based on Greek originals now lost. He wrote
exclusively the *fabula palliata,* or comedy in Greek dress (from *pallium,*
the mantle worn by Greek male citizens). The exact dates of most of
his surviving pays (twenty out of a hundred) are not known; certain
references make it seem likely that *The Menaechmi* (also translated as
The Twin Menaechmi) was written about 215 B.C.; if so, it is Plautus'
earliest extant comedy.

Plautus' best comedy of mistaken identity, the play is, in the words
of J. W. Duff, "a triumph of fun without challenge". Menaechmus of
Syracuse, seeking his long-lost twin brother, comes to Epidamnus,
where he is mistaken for his brother by a cook, a parasite (Peniculus,
"Sponge"), and by the mistress, the wife, and the father-in-law of his
brother, until his slave Messenio recognizes the error and the twins
come together. The comedy, of course, rises from the misunderstandings
onstage; Plautus is very careful to have the audience well aware which
brother they are beholding. He is also very skillful in building up
reasons why the visiting Menaechmus does not understand the mistake
all these folk are making.

The two Menaechmi, being the figures through whom the situations
unroll, are less fully developed than some of the other characters. The
money-seeking courtesan Eratium ("Lovely"); the shrewish wife; the
self-important doctor—apparently a stock figure, but here first surviving—with his countless irrelevant questions, his technical jargon, his
absurd diagnosis and, of course, the most expensive prescription: these
are all richly comic figures, swept along by the story at a pace that
never flags. The play is one of the most popular of the comedies of
Plautus, most frequently revived in schools.

The Menaechmi was the first ancient comedy to be acted in a modern translation. An Italian version by Niccolo da Correggio was performed for the Duke of Ferrara in 1486; an adaptation of this, in Italian
prose, called *Calandria,* ("calandro" means "booby"), by Bernardo
Dovici, Cardinal Bibbiena, was presented at Lyons in 1548 for Henry II
of France and Catherine de' Medici. Others that have adapted the play,
or used its theme, are Trissino, 1547; Sachs, 1548; Firenzuola, 1549;
Cecchi, 1585; Rotrou, 1636; Regnard, 1705, and Shakespeare, in *The
Comedy of Errors.**

Shakespeare's play perhaps added some fun to the plot, but lessened its plausibility, by matching the twin masters with twin slaves. Shakespeare also gave the story a romantic note, ending with the reunion, not only of the twins, but of their parents. Shakespeare, according to Hardin Craig, "loved to play with edged tools. Somebody's life or somebody's happiness is at stake even in his comedies." In *The Comedy of Errors,* the visiting twin will lose his life if identified, whereas in *The Menaechmi* he is in danger of losing only his fortune. Plautus, Craig has also pointed out, "in his realistic world begins with truth and then involves his characters in error; Shakespeare in the mad world of Ephesus begins his episodes with error and enlightens them with flashes of truth." Plautus maintains the cooler, cynical spirit of his comedy to the very end, where the Epidamnian Menaechmus, planning to return to Syracuse with his brother, offers all his property, including his wife, at auction. Shakespeare's play, says George E. Duckworth in the *Complete Roman Drama* (1942), is "usually considered inferior to its Latin original." In eighteenth century London *The Theatrical Inquisitor* declared that Shakespeare's "ignorant modernization of its senile manners is peculiarly unpalatable," but Craig found the Shakespearean version, though "in dramatic manipulation not superior" to the Roman's, "of far greater general significance." Plautus' characters, however, are perennial types.

Plautus apparently introduced into the Roman drama songs and dances that break up the dialogue. These, in *The Menaechmi,* with the pacing of the farcical situations, make Plautus rather than Shakespeare the spirit behind Broadway's hit musical *The Boys From Syracuse* (1938). In its basic value as entertainment, Plautus' comedy retains more than merely historical interest.

THE MERCHANT   *Titus Maccius Plautus*

While lacking the exuberance and also the lyrical song and dance of Plautus' later plays, *Mercator (The Merchant),* 214 ? B.C., has a direct drive of plot and sustained interest. Based upon a Greek comedy of the same name by Philemon, the play presents a familiar theme of ancient comedy, the father contesting against and being outwitted by the son.

Home from a business trip, Charinus has brought a pretty slave girl, Pasicompsa (Altogether Charming), supposedly to serve his mother. Charinus' father, Demipho, covets the girl; father and son quarrel as to her disposition and finally agree to sell her. Using his neighbor as proxy, Demipho outwits his son by purchasing Pasicompsa. But the neighbor's wife thinks that her husband has taken a mistress, and through the neighbor's son the girl is returned to Charinus.

The stage upon which Roman drama was presented was a long and narrow wooden stand, set up temporarily on the occasions of the Roman games (ludi), which took place about ten times a year in Plautus' day, perhaps forty times a year in the days of the Caesars. The long stage represented a street in Rome, with houses behind it; in *The Merchant,* the homes of Demipho and his neighbor Lysimachus. Off stage to the left, by convention, was the harbor; to the right, the Forum and the heart of the city. It was sometimes difficult to keep all the action out of doors; events that had to occur indoors were reported.

Gilbert Norwood has said that *The Merchant* "comes near perfection in its own class . . . sparkling, sophisticated, immoral, light comedy. . . . It is buoyant, rapid, clear, sparkling in plot, dialogue, and situations." In two places, the play parodies frequent episodes of the tragic drama: first, in the dream of Demipho, a tangled absurdity of a nanny-goat and a monkey, which foreshadows the outcome of the play; secondly, in the farewell of Charinus, just before the end of the play when, thinking he has lost the girl, he plans to leave home—a parody of the departure of the mad hero in Euripides' *Heracles** which Norwood had called "a marvelous blend of beauty, pathos, and absurdity."

The play is notable for its attack on the double standard of morality. The slave Syra declares: "It's a harsh law that women live by. . . . If a man secretly takes a harlot, and his wife finds it out, the man goes unpunished. But if a wife even goes out of the house without her husband's knowledge, the man has grounds for divorce, and she's driven out. There ought to be the same law for husbands as for wives."

Without irrelevant buffoonery, *The Merchant* is an excellent example of direct comic drive, with a vivid portrait of an old man made ridiculous by love. It rings with a surprisingly modern tone.

THE COMEDY OF ASSES   *Titus Maccius Plautus*

Plautus' clever and swift-paced *Asinaria* (*The Comedy of Asses*) 213 ? B.C., is based, so the Prologue informs us, on a Greek comedy *The Ass Driver,* by Demophilus. It is a simple comedy, driving its plot directly through natural complications to the usual ending of the satisfied son and the discomfited father.

In this play, however, the father helps the son to win his sweetheart, although he hopes to share her favors. Argyrippus, in love with Philaenium, daughter of the procuress Cleareta, hopes to buy the girl. For this purpose, his father's slaves give him money derived from the sale of some asses (hence, the play's name). Diabolus, a neighbor in love with the girl, also wants to buy her and offers Cleareta a contract for a year's use of her, a contract that is a parody of many such in the ancient serious drama. In spite of him, Argyrippus and Philaenium are joined. Argyrippus' father, Demaenetus, treats them to a feast, at which he makes advances to the girl and she teasingly leads him on. Demaenetus' wife, for a time, from her hiding-place watches the old man's gallantries; then she bursts in upon the feast, with the ironic "Get up, lover; come on home!" that makes a superb comic moment. The Epilogue suggests that Demaenetus has done no more than many watching the play would have been glad to do.

Many critics deem *The Comedy of Asses* one of Plautus' freshest and most happy comedies; Paul Lejay has called it "a play of youth, love, and joy." The frank discussion of a courtesan's life by Cleareta, and the lively tricks of the two slaves, together with the superb comedy of the banquet scene, give distinction and delight to the play.

THE BRAGGART WARRIOR   *Titus Maccius Plautus*

This play, written about 205 B.C., is the best ancient representation of that frequent butt of humor, the soldier who deems himself a cham-

pion in battle and in love. Nothing but the title is known of the Greek
drama, *The Braggart,* on which Plautus' play is based, but the type it
inaugurated has been a favorite in the drama from ancient Greek days
to our own.

For Plautus the story is rather complicated. The soldier Pyrgopolynices has carried off to his home in Ephesus both the slave and the
sweetheart of the young Athenian Pleusicles. Notified by the slave,
Palaestrio, the young Athenian comes to live next door and meets his
beloved by means of a connecting passageway. Finally, through a courtesan disguised as a neighbor's wife, Palaestrio seduces the soldier and
tricks him into sending himself and the kidnapped girl away. The girl
is restored to her lover and the soldier is flogged as an adulterer. While
intrigues are kept clear in the minds of the audience, suspense is not
sacrificed. At one moment, suspicion begins to breed in the soldier's
breast; but quickly Palaestrio recovers control, switches his tactics,
and proceeds deftly to regain the confidence of the conceited soldier,
whose vainglory leads him to the disastrous end.

In this lively but rude farce, the characters are vividly portrayed,
and the braggart soldier is a full-blown caricature. Amusing, too, is
the old bachelor—an unusual figure in Roman comedy—who has little
part in the main action but who comments keenly on the affectations
of society and the blessings of a bachelor's life. There is also effective
contrast between the two courtesans, the faithful sweetheart of Pleusicles and the hussy hired to deceive the braggart soldier, the *miles gloriosus.*

The very names of the characters are comic; Pyrgopolynices means
"conqueror of many towered cities"; Artotrogus (the parasite), "bread-
chewer"; Acroteleutium, "tip-top"; Philocomasium, "lover of drinking
bouts"; Palaestrio, "trickster".

Of all Plautus' plays, this has been the most popular. The Roman
games of 205 B.C. were held for seven extra days, probably to lengthen
the run of the play's performance there. While there are boastful soldiers in other ancient plays, it is from *The Braggart* that later variations stem. Among these may be mentioned Captain Matamore in Corneille's *The Comic Illusion,* 1636; in England, *Ralph Roister Doister*;*
Falstaff and Pistol in Shakespeare; Captain Bobadill in Jonson's *Every
Man In His Humour*.* More recent variants include Rostand's *Cyrano*;*
and the type is recognizable in such comedies as George Kelly's *The
Show-Off*,* as well as in figures of any war play (*Mr. Roberts*,* 1948;
At War With The Army, 1949; the musical *South Pacific,* 1949) or motion picture. Pyrgopolynices, in Plautus' play, declares that his progeny
will live "for a thousand years, from one age to the next"; they have
in truth more than doubled the span of the soldier's boast.

THE CASKET   *Titus Maccius Plautus*

The most sentimental and the least comic of Plautus' plays is
Cistellaria (The Casket), 202 B.C. The young Alcesimarchus and the
courtesan Selenium are his nearest approach to a romantic couple.
Genuinely in love, the young man is violent in grief or anger; when
he is separated from the girl, he threatens to thrice kill the woman

responsible, then to slay himself. The play has not been well preserved, several hundred lines are missing, in whole or part, but the outlines of the story are clear. Alcesimarchus' father insists that his son marry a daughter of Demipho, which breaks the heart of the two lovers, until it is discovered that Selenium is really Demipho's lost daughter by his second marriage. The "casket" contains the trinkets by which the identification is effected. Such recognition scenes abound in plays from Shakespeare to shoddiest melodrama.

Based on a lost play of Menander's, *The Women Who Dine Together*, *The Casket*, in its movement of apparent frustration averted by recognized identity, follows the usual pattern of Menander more closely than was Plautus' wont with his sources. Unusual, too, is the emphasis on feminine figures, who outnumber the men and are more fully developed. The opening scene is an effective contrast of the courtesan Selenium, faithful to her one love Alcesimarchus, and the two women she has just had to dine with her, the tipsy and greedy old procuress, and that bawd's obedient daughter, who supports her mother by "marrying" a new man every night. Demipho's wife and her maid Halisca are also well-drawn figures.

After the opening scene, and an expository monologue by the procuress, Plautus gives us his Prologue (such an interior prologue is found also in *The Braggart Warrior** and often in Menander), spoken by a god. This device permits opening the play with a dramatic movement. Comic scenes might have been among those now lost, but the mood of the play is sentimental rather than humorous. Thereafter the playwright moved to more boisterous moods.

STICHUS   *Titus Maccius Plautus*

Quite different from the other plays of Plautus is his *Stichus*, 200 B.C. It is really a romp in three parts, increasingly broad in comic pattern. In the first part, in an almost tense dramatic mood, old Antipho rebukes his daughters for remaining faithful to their absent husbands, two impoverished brothers who have been long abroad. The women refuse to consider the idea of divorce. There follows a more farcical movement in which the two brothers return, now wealthy. They win over the old man, who wheedles the gift of a slave girl, and they tease, then dismiss, the parasite that has been trying to prey upon the family. Finally the two reunited couples celebrate at a feast. This dinner takes place indoors; onstage is a burlesque of the masters' meal, as their two slaves get tipsy and carouse with their mutual sweetheart, in an ending that recalls the komos and mating revel that closed the old Greek comedy.

The two faithful wives, in their conversation and in their argument with their father, present an interesting picture of Roman social life. The parasite is perhaps more fully drawn, with deft satiric brush and neat dismissal, than in the other comedies. Effective play is made, too, of the messenger, who hurries in with the good tidings of the husbands' return, then in typical comedy fashion takes endless time before he delivers his news. Also frequent in Plautus' comedy is the breaking of the dramatic illusion, the stepping out from the frame of the play, as in a sudden appeal to the audience or, here, as when the tipsy slave

Stichus leans across and gives the musician some wine. This sort of trick has been a source of laughter from Roman days to our own time.

This is the only one of Plautus' plays of which the *didascalia,* the official notice of production, is preserved. From it we learn that the play was produced "at the Plebeian Games in the Plebeian aedileship of Gnaeus Boebius and Gaius Terentius, by Titus Publilius Pellio. Music, on Tyrian flutes throughout, by the slave of Marcus Oppius. Presented in the consulship of Gaius Sulpicius and Gaius Aurelius." This sets it in November, 200 B.C. The play was based on *The Brothers* by Menander (a different play from the source of Terence's *The Brothers**).

Rather a succession of pictures, or skits, than a coherent drama, *Stichus* contains vivid portraits, sharp satire, and broad burlesque. The final convivial scene is comedy that has not lost its humor in constant repetition and variation down the years.

THE HAUNTED HOUSE   *Titus Maccius Plautus*

One of the liveliest of Plautus' comedies, *Mostellaria (The Haunted House),* 196? B.C., depends for its fun less on plot than on amusing situations and the contrasted characters involved in them. Still playing with the stock figures of Roman comedy—a spendthrift young man, his shrewd and tricky slave, and the gulled father—Plautus here makes them more natural, therefore also more humorous; and he attains one of the high spots of ancient comedy in this work, based on the Greek play *Phasma (The Ghost),* probably by Philemon.

While his father, Theopropides, is away, young Philolaches buys and frees his sweetheart and lives a gay life that leaves little of his father's wealth untouched. The slave Tranio comes upon Theopropides, unexpectedly returned; to keep the old man from his son's wild party until all signs of the carousal can be cleared away, Tranio embarks upon a desperate series of lies. He begins by saying they've abandoned the house because it has become haunted. In its place, he continues, they've bought the house next door, and in a cleverly balanced comic scene Tranio tricks the old neighbor into letting the father inspect that house, keeping both men equally deluded. Finally, Theopropides learns of his slave's deceptions and his son's misdemeanors, but, at the intercession of a friend, he forgives his son for having sown his wild oats.

In the play are some of Plautus' most elaborate lyrics; the play probably came fairly close in actual production to a modern musical comedy. Like the musical form, too, is the movement of plot that lapses into a succession of comic situations, to be straightened out at the end by a *deus ex machina* friend. The friend, Callidamates, arrives at Philolaches' party already drunk, giving instructions to his slaves to call for him later. It is his drunken dallying that prevents the quick breaking-up of the party when the old man returns; it is the chatter of his slaves, come to fetch him, that betrays to the old man the fact of his son's misbehavior; and finally, it is he that makes the old man recognize that Philolaches has done no worse than other sons, and is now ashamed and therefore to be forgiven. Such interlocking of a minor character with the plot movement manifests neat construction.

The characters are set off in pairs; contrasting, they illuminate one another. The shrewd and rascally Tranio is counterpoised by his honest fellow-slave Grumio. Philematium, the mistress of Philolaches, is in her naive and faithful simplicity balanced against her cynical and unscrupulous maid, Scapha, who suggests that Philematium seek a variety of lovers; the scene between these two, as Philematium adorns herself while her unseen lover watches and overhears, is superbly amusing. The personal touches given Callidamates make his carousal more than the routine low comedy drunken scene, just as the old Theopropides, balanced against his neighbor Simo, becomes more than the stock comic old butt and buffoon.

The Haunted House was enacted in Latin at Harvard University in April, 1936; at Bryn Mawr College, Pennsylvania, in October, 1936; at Wilson College, Pennsylvania, in December, 1937. The Harvard production used masks and otherwise attempted to reproduce the ancient staging methods. Even for our day, there is much in this comedy to enjoy.

THE PERSIAN   *Titus Maccius Plautus*

This play, written about 195 B.C., is Plautus' nearest approach to an opera-parody of Roman low life. It is a sort of *Beggar's Opera** of ancient Rome. With its lyrical passages, its detailed dances, its several passages of balanced comments and retorts in lively double-entendre repartee, with considerable buffoonery for its own sake, and a final revel (komos) to which even the dupe of the drama is invited, the play provides a lively farcical picture of slaves and seamy citizens.

The plot is not unfamiliar, though it must be observed that the same basic situations permitted innumerable variations; there is little repetition in Plautus. Here we have a slave imitating the usual young citizen. With his master away, the slave Toxilus puts on the airs of a gentleman; he acquires a parasite and covets a courtesan. Borrowing money another slave has been given to buy oxen, Toxilus purchases Lemniselenis from the pimp Dordalus, and frees her. To get back the money, Toxilus persuades his parasite, Saturio, to dress up his daughter as a captive from Persia and sell her to the pimp. Once the transaction is concluded the girl's identity is revealed; since she and her father are citizens, she of course cannot be sold. The deluded Dordalus is further mocked in the final revelry.

The dialogue, in keeping with its characters, is ruder and coarser than usual even in the exuberant and unrestrained Plautus. The slaves meet and lengthily, good-naturedly exchange billingsgate abuse, ranging from the coarse epithets flung between Toxilus and the pimp to the lighter banter tossed between the maid of Lemniselenis and young Paegnium.

Most interesting, and among Plautus' most effective creations, is the daughter of the parasite Saturio. There is amusing irony in the manner in which this child of the slums takes her father to task for his lack of dignity, his dishonesty, and his heedlessness of reputation. For the deception of Dordalus, Toxilus presents the pimp with a letter, supposedly from his master in Persia, which tells of the capture of "Goldtown" in Arabia and of the taking of a high-born maiden now sent home for sale. The pimp is tempted, but afraid to buy the girl without a guaranteed title; he and Toxilus stand aside as the girl and her dealer approach. The girl is in the midst of an intelligent discussion of the sins that beset the city. When Dordalus questions her, she answers with complete truth, yet so cleverly that he is led along unsuspecting, until he is eagerly bargaining for the girl.

Incidentally, when the pimp asks the "Persian slave-dealer" (Toxilus' friend and fellow-slave, Sagaristio) his name, the latter replies with a three-line "contortuplicated" cognomen freely rendered (by Charles T. Murphy) as Blabberodorus Maidvendorovich Lightchatterson Cash-screweroutstein Ibn Saidwhatyoudeserve MacTrifle McBlarney What-onceyougetyourhandson Neverpartwithitski. This is the most ponderous piece of fun in the lively frolic.

THE POT OF GOLD   *Titus Maccius Plautus*

One of the best known of Plautus' comedies is *Aulularia (The Pot of Gold)*, 194? B.C. While there is much incidental comedy in the play, the interest is centered on the character of the miser Euclio, who worries over his pot of gold. Euclio's concern is tangled with his family's story. A wealthy old neighbor, Megadorus, urged by his sister to take a wife, speculates upon the extravagances of a wife who comes with a dowry, and therefore asks Euclio for the hand of his daughter Phaedria. To prepare for the wedding feast, Megadorus provides food and sends cooks to the "poor" Euclio; their presence so worries the miser that he takes out his pot of gold for safer hiding. He is noticed, then spied upon, by the slave of Lyconides, a young man who has seduced and who loves Phaedria. The slave steals the pot of gold and gives it to his master. Although the end of the play has been lost, we know from the Prologue, and from the acrostic "argument" prefixed to Roman comedies, that Lyconides returns the gold to Euclio and in exchange marries the miser's daughter.

Among the neat turns of movement in the play, two are especially clever. Just after Euclio misses his gold, Lyconides comes to confess his seduction of Euclio's daughter; and for some time, while the young man is talking of the girl, the miser thinks he is referring to the gold. Even trickier is the effort of Lyconides' slave, once he perceives that his young master will, honestly, return the gold to Euclio, to retract his story that he has stolen it. Throughout the play, the suspicions of Euclio, his apprehension that everybody knows about his treasure, his constant scurrying to make sure that it is safe—until his very fear of losing it leads to its loss—maintain a high pitch of comic interest.

Among plays that have used the theme of *The Pot of Gold* are Gelli's *The Basket,* 1543 and Jonson's *The Case Is Altered,* 1597. Two plays called *The Miser,* by Shadwell, 1672, and Fielding, 1732, are more directy taken from the most famous descendant of Plautus' play, Molière's *L'Avare (The Miser)*, which was produced in Paris September 9, 1668.

Among other sharp contrasts, the miser of Molière's play is the very incarnation of avarice; Plautus' Euclio is a human being, once poor, to whom the coming of wealth brought also the tormenting fear of its loss. At the end of *The Pot of Gold* (a fragment of the conclusion is extant to tell), when Euclio has given away his daughter and with her his gold, there is pathos as well as comedy in his final words, "Now I shall sleep." Molière's savage satire more thoroughly castigates the avaricious type; Plautus brings us laughter, but also a tinge of sympathy for one who has, gigantic, a fault we all feel nursling in ourselves.

THE ROPE   *Titus Maccius Plautus*

Many critics hail *Rudens* (*The Rope*), 194 ? B.C. as the masterpiece
of Roman comedy. It is not comedy in the sense of broadly humorous
farce, but rather like the romantic comedies of Shakespeare. Its mood
and opening movement remind one of *The Tempest**, and its heroine
comes into the action by being cast ashore after shipwreck, as in *Twelfth
Night**. Her lyric of lament and the song of the fishermen that follows
are among the most beautiful in Plautus. And the swift movement
of its romantic tale, a tender story pricked through with sardonic
humor, with emotional depths plumbed, villainy exposed, and virtue
rewarded, justifies the comparison.

Based on a Greek comedy by Diphilus, the play begins with a characteristically long prologue. (We are told that when Diphilus complimented the hetaera Gnathaena on the coldness of her well water, she
replied that she kept it cold by throwing his prologues into it.) Plautus'
Prologue, spoken by the god Arcturus, explains that the basic coincidence in the action is produced by the will of the god to mete out
justice.

The unique setting instead of a city street represents a stretch of
the African coast backed by a temple of Venus, with hard by the cottage of Daemones, an old man from Athens. To that temple the procurer Labrax has bid young Plesidippus go, and Labrax has sailed
away with Palaestra, a slave girl he was supposed to deliver to the
young man. Wrecked by Arcturus on that selfsame shore, Palaestra
and another girl held by Labrax take shelter in the temple. Labrax
seeks to drag them forth and Daemones, acting as judge in the dispute,
discovers—the proof is in a casket which the fisherman Gripus has
roped in the sea, salvage of the wreck—that Palaestra is his own long-
lost daughter. Palaestra and Plesidippus thus are free to wed.

While the play moves on its course with a well-knit and tender
plot, many of the successive scenes are gems of satire or humor. The
second young woman rescued from the waves is a lively vixen; when
she comes from the temple to Daemones' house for water, there is a
sprightly and pointed conversation between her and Sceparnio, the
slave. When Labrax and Charmides, the man who had advised him to
ship to Sicily, haul their bedraggled bodies to shore, their shivering
and wailing (Labrax even has a vomiting spell) and their growly word-
play make a vivid scene. Labrax, for all his villainy, is a courageous
fellow; he stands up boldly for his claims until Daemones' overseers
bear him down; then, losing the girls, he tries to trick Gripus out of
the treasure Gripus has fished from the sea. Trachalio, the slave of
Plesidippus, has several amusing scenes: one gives the play its name,
when he discovers Gripus with his "hamper-fish" and they begin a
verbal and physical tug-of-war for its possession. Throughout, the
quick dialogue is enlivened by puns and other word-play, not all trans-
latable. Between scenes of low comedy the romantic movement of the
plot drives to its happy close.

Plautus' drama, according to W. Y. Sellar, "entirely enlists both
the moral and the humane sympathies." It is one of the most original

and most effective of Plautus' plays; in quality of the lyric passages, in surge of spirited dialogue, in variety and interest of character-portrayal, it is the most modern in tone of the ancient Roman comedies.

CURCULIO   *Titus Maccius Plautus*

The amusing *Curculio*, 193 ? B.C., one of the shortest of Plautus' plays, is packed with interest. Its plot combines the two most frequent devices of ancient comedy: guileful deception and mistaken identity. The characters that move through it, however, though they are the usual comedy figures, are individualized and made human. Curculio ("Weevil"), the parasite, is also a messenger; he, instead of the usual shrewd slave, slowly relates the news and cleverly carries through the deceits played on the pimp and the captain; he pours abuse, neatly satiric of conditions in Rome, equally upon pimp and banker; and he adds considerably to the lightness and speed of the comedy.

The action is set in Epidaurus, where the pimp Cappadox is spending the night at the temple of the god of healing, Aesculapius. The young Phaedromus sends Curculio to raise money to buy, from Cappadox, the girl Planesium. Curculio, however, steals the ring of Captain Therapontigonus, who also loves the girl and who has deposited money for her purchase with a banker. Using the ring as a seal, Curculio brings the banker a letter, supposedly from the Captain, so that the money is paid and the girl delivered to her lover, Phaedromus. When the Captain discovers the fraud, his seal identifies the girl as his own sister, who was separated from her nurse when the seats at a festival collapsed during a storm; he joins Phaedromus at the wedding feast; and the pimp, having no claim upon a free-born girl, has to return the money.

The play is rich in all sorts of word-play, and perhaps has more obscenity than is usual with Plautus; but the obscenity is counterbalanced by the fact that Planesium has preserved her chastity, a fact that was essential to the Roman audience since she turns out to be free born. Phaedromus is so enamored of the girl that he sings a *paraclausithyron*, i.e., a serenade to his sweetheart's door—the first in Latin literature of what was to become a frequent form of love poetry. The meetings of the lovers have a tenderness underlaid with respect.

The Captain, also deftly drawn by Plautus, is a "braggart warrior" in his speeches, but by his actions is brought down to human size. At the end, though still truculent with the pimp, he is a friendly companion to the man that is to marry his sister. There is a neat passage in the play, when the banker, receiving the letter with the Captain's seal, asks suspiciously why the Captain himself hasn't come. The disguised Curculio answers that a gold statue is being erected to him in Caria, "because the Persians, Paphlagonians, Sinopians, Arabs, Carians, Cretans, Syrians, Rhodes and Lycia, Eatonia and Tipplearia, Centaurfightiglia and Onenipplehostania, all the coast of Libyia, all Winepressbacchanalia, half the nations on earth, were all conquered by him single-handed in less than twenty days." "Damned if you don't come from him," the banker declares, "you jabber such nonsense!" and he proceeds to pay the pimp to release the girl.

A unique feature of *Curculio* is an address to the audience by the property man. Immediately after the scene in which Curculio hoodwinks the banker, the property man comes forth and wonders whether, with such a sharper around, he'll get back the costumes at the end of the play. He then gives a miniature guide to Rome, telling in which quarters what sorts of person can be found. He then departs and the play goes on. His speech is the only vocal appearance of the property man in Roman drama.

In these several respects, *Curculio* is of unusual interest. Despite its brevity, it carries through a typical Roman plot with realistically conceived and humorously developed characters, and it presents an unusually vivid picture of Roman ways.

PSEUDOLUS   *Titus Maccius Plautus*

One of the liveliest of Plautus' comedies, *Pseudolus*, 191 B.C., evidently was a favorite in ancient times. In his essay *On Old Age* Cicero tells us that Plautus rejoiced in the play in his last years. In the first century B.C. the famous actor Roscius played the part of Ballio.

The opening situation is not unusual: a young man needs money to buy his sweetheart from a pimp who has already taken a deposit on the girl from a rival. But the rest of the play is more novel. The Prologue, for instance, instead of containing the usual exposition, consists of but one warning sentence: "You'd better stand up and stretch your legs; a long play by Plautus is about to be staged." The exposition, which follows in the first scene, is given in a highly amusing letter from the girl to her sweetheart Calidorus, in which she laments her imminent departure when the balance of the rival's payment is made.

After the exposition, Calidorus' slave Pseudolus sets his ingenuity a test. He admits the situation to Calidorus' angry father, Simo, and wagers that he'll not only secure the girl, but get the money for her from Simo himself. Later, the pimp, Ballio, is warned that he will be tricked and, though on his guard, he is amusingly cozened; he delivers the girl to the false messenger; when the real messenger comes for her, he thinks him a pretender and pokes fun at him for a time before he learns the truth. Thus the girl is turned over to her sweetheart, and Pseudolus collects his wager and a round bellyful of wine.

Ballio and Pseudolus are both well developed figures. The pimp is the most rapacious and scoundrelly in Roman comedy. He summons forth his covey of courtesans, upbraids them each by name, demanding that they extort from their lovers great gifts for his birthday, or off they'll go to the common brothel. Pseudolus, however, is one of the jolliest of slaves, enjoying every one of his sly devices, faithful to the interests of his young master, but not afraid to match wits and bandy words with the citizens. His final drunken moments are not the conventional carousal, but continue the comic characterization, until his old master goes off with him to drink away the wager.

It is worth noting that, except when the courtesans appear, to take Ballio's abuse, and when Calidorus' sweetheart steals from Ballio's house (none of them saying a word), there are no women in the comedy. With the informal, free and easy tone of the play and the sprightly dialogue, full of quips and contemporary references and verbal play, Plautus enjoys himself as he entertains the audience. When Calidorus wants to know something, his slave nonchalantly but directly answers: "We're acting this play for the benefit of the spectators here. They know; I'll tell you later." The audience is amused, and the action goes on. With the fun enjoyed both on the stage and off, with light and lively action, *Pseudolus* is a gem of Roman comedy.

EPIDICUS   *Titus Maccius Plaudus*

With *Curculio** the shortest of ancient comedies, *Epidicus*, 191 ? B.C., is one of the most complicated in intrigue. There is less incidental buffoonery than is usual in Plautus; interest in the play is maintained by involved trickery and the device of surprise recognition. The play has no prologue; all the essential preliminary information is given by a protatic character, i.e., one that appears only at the beginning of the play, just for the purpose.

The usual story of the young man and his sweetheart is here complicated by two circumstances: (1) young Stratippocles returns from war with a virtuous girl, who has replaced the first one in his favor; (2) the slave Epidicus has meanwhile installed the first girl in the young man's home, making the father believe she is the lost daughter he has been seeking. The situation grows more involved through Epidicus' efforts to disentangle it. The slave fools the father, who delightedly thinks he is helping deceive a neighbor; then the slave himself seems hanged by the rope he throws his young master, until the girl brought home from the war turns out to be the old man's daughter and Stratippocles' half-sister. Epidicus so turns this final situation to his own advantage that his master sets him free.

Plautus puts little stress upon the young man's love; nor does he make clear the situation at the close of the play. Some scholars feel that in the lost Greek original Stratippocles married his half-sister. To the Roman audience this would be incest; Plautus, by not involving the young man deeply, leaves him free to return to his old sweetheart who is still in the house.

In any event, the chief emphasis throughout is upon the activity of the slave, who is a well-drawn and distinctive character. Chock-full of confidence, he brazens his way through difficulties, shows no shame in admitting his wrong-doings, and at the end succeeds in making his old master apologize to him. The character of Epidicus may have suggested, at least has given features to, such later-day rascally servants as Molière's Scapin, and devices of the play may be found in Cieco's *Emilia*, 1579; Cailhava's *The Interrupted Wedding*, 1769, and Lemercier's *Plautus*, 1808. Short and swift-moving, *Epidicus* is a well-managed comedy of intrigue.

THE BACCHIDES   *Titus Maccius Plautus*

Also called *The Two Bacchides*, 189 ? B.C., this play is one of Plautus' livelier comedies. With two young men in love with twin courtesans, both named Bacchis, the play develops many situations of farcical misunderstanding, until at the end the courtesans captivate not only the two young men but also their fathers.

The basic plot is the usual story of the young man's having to raise money—that is, of his slave's having to raise money—to buy the girl before a rival gets her. The existence of the twins makes one young man think for a time that his friend is double-crossing him. Although the audience is kept in suspense as to the slave's devices, these turn out to be of less importance than the emotional complications of the characters themselves.

The characters are presented in contrasting pairs that lend effective distinctness to their natures. One of the courtesans is comparatively simple and honest; the other is a tricky though fetching little vixen. One of the old men is rather easy-going, and quick to forgive his son's youthful indiscretions; the other is a crusty curmudgeon who finally succumbs only to the wily courtesan. Even the conniving slave is counterbalanced by a strait-laced fellow, tutor to one of the young men, who bemoans the lax discipline of the education of his day.

Several contemporary references in the play are still recognizable. The name of the courtesans, Bacchis, was doubtless chosen to permit several references to the licentious bacchanals, which, introduced into Rome not long before, had become so dissolutely orgiastic that in 186 B.C. they were made illegal. At one point in the play Plautus airs a personal quarrel, having a character exclaim: "I can't endure even my favorite play, Epidicus*, if Pellio's acting it." (Pellio had also performed in Plautus' Stichus*.) Wordplay is frequent and lively in The Bacchides, and the lyrics are among Plautus' most varied and best. Based upon Manander's The Double Deceiver, the play richly captures the usual elements of Roman comedy in a knotty intrigue, with natural and effectively contrasted characters.

THE CAPTIVES   *Titus Maccius Plautus*

One of the finest comedies of ancient times, The Captives, 188 ? B.C., deserves the name comedy only because it has a happy ending. While there is considerable quiet humor in the play, fundamentally it has a lofty theme and an inspiring tone, far removed from the usual bawdy Roman farce. Plautus, indeed, in his Prologue deemed it necessary to warn the audience that "there are here no filthy verses that one can't repeat; no perjured pimp appears today, no infamous abandoned courtesan, no braggart warrior;" and in the Epilogue he added that "few comedies of this sort will you find, where those already good may learn to be better. . . . Who vote for modesty, applaud our play."

Set in Aetolia, the play pictures the sorrow of old Hegio, who has lost two sons, one kidnapped long ago, the other recently taken captive in battle and held at Elea. Hegio hopes to regain the second son by an exchange of prisoners. The Elean citizen Philocrates, a prisoner of war in Aetolia, seeks to protect himself by changing places with his slave Tyndarus. Hence Philocrates (who the Aetolians think is the slave) is sent to negotiate the exchange of prisoners, while the slave Tyndarus (supposedly the citizen) is held as hostage. But, despite Tyndarus' fears, Philocrates makes the exchange, and comes back with Hegio's son. Then Tyndarus himself turns out to be the long-lost other son of Hegio.

The exchange of places by Tyndarus and Philocrates is made clear to the audience by the device, which occurs only this once in Roman comedy, of having both characters appear in the Prologue, to be pointed out while the situation that is to come in the play is explained. The audience also knows (as the characters within the play do not) that Tyndarus is Hegio's lost son; this gives frequent dramatic irony to the situations, and lightens with an overtone of humor the old man's grieving at his loss.

The one stock figure, Ergasilus the parasite, is well employed as a foil to Hegio. When the father is hopeful at the prospect of recovering his son, the parasite appears in the deepest dumps; when the father is depressed, when even the lyric measures of the play shift to a tragic pathos, the parasite enters in a state of the highest elation. In addition, through the parasite the play maintains some measure of the low comedy the Romans enjoyed.

The characters possess a dignity and an integrity that give a noble tone to the drama. Master and slave evince mutual loyalty, if not always mutual trust; Hegio (whose name means "leading citizen") is the most self-respecting and venerable old man in Plautus. There is comic irony in the names of the three youths—Philocrates, "lover of conquest"; Aristophontes, "best slayer"; Philopolemus, "lover of conflict"—when all three have been taken prisoner in battle; but they are sober and decent young men. The quality of its persons, and the exalted tone of its theme, led Lessing to call this of all comedies "the finest piece ever put on the stage."

It is interesting to note, during present days of high costs in the theatre, that finances bothered the Romans too. The two sons of Hegio are never onstage at the same time; in all probability, to save expense, one actor doubled in the roles. It may also be noted—though not as a matter of economy, since men played all parts—that there are no female characters in the play.

Among plays that are based on The Captives are Ariosta's I Suppositi, 1502?, which Gascoigne adapted as The Supposes*; Jonson's The Case Is Altered, 1597; Massinger's A New Way To Pay Old Debts*; and Rotrou's The Captives, 1638. With individualized characters, natural though noble, decent without sentimentality, and with a serious theme borne along through swift-flowing incidents in lively lyric patterns, The Captives is one of the richest comedies of ancient times.

THREE-PENNY DAY   *Titus Maccius Plautus*

With its action drawn from the usual basic comedy situation, *Trinummus* (*Three-Penny Day*), 187 ? B.C., has a moral tone almost on a level with The Captives*; Lessing ranked it second among Plautus' comedies. A serious study of a Roman social problem, it contains many reflections upon the life of the day.

When the play opens, we find Luxury, speaking the Prologue, sending her child, Poverty, into Lesbonicus' house. For the young Lesbonicus, during his father's absence, having squandered the family fortune in riotous living, is planning to sell the family home. Here, however, the resemblance to the usual Roman farce ceases. Lesbonicus' sister (there are no women actually in the play) should have a dowry, or the family's social position will drop; it is to secure money for this dowry that Lesbonicus and his slave bend their wits. The old neighbor, meanwhile, has been watchful; asked to keep an eye on Lesbonicus, he it is that buys the house. He also provides a dowry, for three pennies hiring a swindler to pretend to bring it from the absent father. The returning father comes upon the swindler, with amusing misunderstandings which resolve themselves as Lesbonicus promises to reform and both the children prepare to wed.

The direct and comparatively simple movement permits concentration on the characters. While modern taste would provide young women in a story of this sort, only respectable women are called for in the action, and Roman custom would keep these off the stage. The men, however, are diversified and natural. Contrasted with frivolous and spendthrift young Lesbonicus is his serious-minded friend, whose father suggests the Polonius of Shakespeare's *Hamlet*, not merely in the general aspect of his prosy moralizing but also in the details of his observations; his warning to his son against lending is directly echoed in Polonius' admonition to his son. The son in Plautus differs from Laertes in that he takes his father's moral sermons so literally that he takes his father aback: he wants to marry Lesbonicus' sister even without a dowry. His early song against loose loving, incidentally, has considerable lyrical beauty and great charm.

While the dialogue of the drama is not enlivened with spicy or suggestive wit, it is fresh and figurative, as when the slave characterizes the sharpers: "Any one of them could steal the sole of a shoe right off a runner at top speed."

Three-Penny Day has been consistently considered one of Plautus' best works. Its theme recurs in Cecchi's *The Dowry*, 1550; Destouches' *The Hidden Treasure*, c. 1730, in whose sentimental comedy the two young women take a considerable part; Lessing's *The Treasure*, 1750; Colman's *The Man of Business*, 1774. With its simple situation and its shadowing forth of typical problems of Roman life, natural characters are soundly built into an effective play.

TRUCULENTUS   *Titus Maccius Plautus*

The tight hold that a loose love may exercise upon a man has been no more sardonically portrayed than in *Truculentus*, 186 B.C. There are few complications in the plot of this play, which is, rather, a picture of how a courtesan, most fair and most unfair, can squeeze the last coins out of her eager victims.

Four men whose lives are ruined by the courtesan Phonesium are balanced one against the other; the courtesan teases them to vie in extravagance for her favors. The soldier gives her all the trophies of his wars; the countryman lavishes upon her the produce and the profits of his farm; the young citizen, Diniarchus, having already ruined himself for her, continues to scrape up sums for the scraps of her favors; and the "truculent" slave is tantalized by the lust of the others into sloughing his rudeness and bringing forth his savings, to taste of the courtesan's joys.

The intrigue of the play rises from the courtesan's insatiable greed. To gain more gifts from the soldier, she pretends to have had a child by him and hires a child born out of wedlock. Diniarchus turns out to be the child's real father; but even when he goes off to marry its mother, he promises to drop in on the courtesan every now and again. He is so entangled in her snares, indeed, that he lets her keep his child a few days, as bait for the soldier. The yokel and the soldier recognize that they will have to share the courtesan; each wants more frequent hours of her bounty, and the play ends, as her maid sums it up, with "a fool and a madman competing for their own ruin."

Truculentus is a portrait of a courtesan etched in vitriol. Diniarchus starts the play by remarking that "An entire lifetime isn't really long enough for a lover to learn how many roads there are to destruction. If only," he continues, "we could pass on to our descendants the wisdom of the past, then, I'd guarantee, there'd be no more pimps and harlots, and there'd be a lot fewer spendthrifts."

The characters in *Truculentus,* while they are the usual ones, are turned from their usual development to fit the purpose of the author. The soldier on his first appearance notifies the audience that he is no braggart warrior. The slave Truculentus begins as a moral blusterer, worried about his country master cozened by the city courtesan, but instead of devising tricks to extricate his master or to further his master's desires, Truculentus himself turns lecherous. Phronesium is, throughout, more barefaced in her iniquity than Plautus' other courtesans.

Along with *Pseudolus**, *Truculentus* was the author's favorite play. Some moralists among critics have objected to the tone of the drama. Others, like Paul Lejay, deem it Plautus' most satiric comedy, one that evokes not heedless laughter but pertinent thought, as do the more serious dramas of Molière*. This realistic study, in dramatic terms, of a frequent evil in Roman society is a powerful play, not without pertinence to our own times.

AMPHITRYON   *Titus Maccius Plautus*

The most popular of Plautus' plays, *Amphitruo* (*Amphitryon*), 186 ? B.C., is also the only extant Roman comedy that presents a travesty of gods and heroes. With exuberance and gay horseplay matched only in the work of Aristophanes, it romps with delightful abandon over the ancient legend of the birth of Hercules.

In a night made extra long by the god, Jupiter comes to Alcmena disguised as her husband Amphitryon, who is away at war. Mercury, disguised as Amphitryon's servant Sosia, is on guard outside when the real Sosia returns just ahead of his master. The fun of the play is made up of the bewilderment and discomfiture of the mortals, the increasing anger of Amphitryon, and the mischievous amusement of the gods. Finally, we are told of the birth of twins to Alcmena, and the exploit of one of them in killing two snakes that attack the cradle. In a crack of thunder, Jupiter reveals himself as father of the strong babe, Hercules, and Amphitryon decides, for his love's sake, that yielding to a god is being faithful. In a long jesting Prologue, Mercury states that since gods are in the play it cannot be a comedy; since a slave is in the play it cannot be a tragedy; hence he will make it a tragicomedy. The rest is farce. Sosia enters, delivers another Prologue; then Mercury, the false Sosia, beats away the real one, and completes his Prologue.

The only character not developed solely for the fun is Alcmena, whom

J. W. Duff calls Plautus' sweetest and purest woman. "She is a devoted and faithful wife to Amphitryon; his reproaches, when he thinks her unfaithful, bewilder and grieve her." Her character, indeed, gives a dignity and loftiness to the play, for all its boisterous fooling. Arthur Palmer called it "the most simple, dignified, and tender of all the plays of Plautus." It was a great favorite in ancient times, always performed in Rome by public authority when the state was threatened with pestilence, famine, or other calamity, on the theory that showing the god enjoying amorous exploits would please the god and win his favors.

Many later plays have told Amphitryon's story: *The Sosias,* by Rotrou, 1638; *Amphitryon* by Molière, 1668; by Dryden, 1690; by von Kleist, 1807. Roughly estimating the number before him, Jean Giraudoux called his 1936 version *Amphitryon 38.*

There are several differences in detail, in the later versions. Molière introduces Sosia's wife, an ill-favored, ill-natured scold, completely without a sense of humor, as a feminine foil to her witty husband. Dryden, in addition, has a maid for Alcmena, a selfish creature who garners gifts from the gods. In Plautus, there is a pilot who refuses to arbitrate between the two Amphitryons. In Dryden there is a Judge Gripus, through whom the playwright lashes at his time (thinking of Judge Jeffries when the judge in the play is abused): "Thou seller of other people, thou weathercock of government: that, when the wind blows for the subject pointest to privilege, and when it changes to sovereignty, veerest to prerogative."

More basic are the differences in tone. Plautus maintains the high ideals of Roman life; the home is sacred and the woman honored therein; all the abounding humor, even to the pail of slops dumped on Amphitryon, sets no strain upon the social structure. Molière trifles more along the feminine lines, as one might expect at the court of Louis XIV, but he, too, is basically earnest. Dryden, for all his polished wit, reflects the lower tone of the cynical court of Charles II and seems today to exceed the limits of good taste. Sir Walter Scott sums up the French and the English attitude: "Dryden is coarse and vulgar where Molière is witty, and where the Frenchman ventures upon a double meaning, the Englishman always contrives to make it a single one." The coarseness broadened into a leer in the musical comedy *Out of This World* which, with book by Deems Taylor and Reginald Lawrence and music by Cole Porter, opened in New York November 30, 1950, and clumsily set the god's descent in our own times.

Giraudoux is subtler in his humor, turning it also on the gods. His play opens with a delightful scene of Jupiter and Mercury perched on a cloud, looking at earth below, and revealing that, in some respects, the gods are only human. Later, this impression increases; where Plautus has the disguised Jupiter telling Alcmena of his exploits in battle, Giraudoux has him complacently speak of his exploits that long night in bed, and Alcmena innocently reminds him of other, livelier, more enjoyable nights, thus exalting human love above even divine imitation.

Giraudoux' *Amphitryon 38,* adapted by S. N. Behrman, with Alfred Lunt, Lynn Fontanne, and Richard Whorf, was a great success in both America and England. It is interesting to compare the reactions to the play in New York and in London. To New York reviewers, the play was no more than a bedroom farce. John Mason Brown said (November 1, 1937) that it "attempts to approach Bulfinch with a bedside manner;" and Brooks Atkinson elaborated the point: The play "may wear the robes of the time of Greek fables and talk of the gods of Olympus, but it is bedroom farce and only human. It is also the most distinguished piece of theatre the Guild has had the pleasure of presenting to the subscribers in some time. . . . Although the bedroom joke is more durable than most, it is still only one joke for the space of three acts, and it stumbles through a monotonous stretch in the middle of the evening. In several of the scenes, particularly in the sententious prologue, the authors have scribbled some coruscatingly witty dialogues between Jupiter and Mercury, contemplating from on high the strange love customs of the mortals. There is also one colloquy of vibrant irony when Alcmena belittles Jupiter's genius and politely cries down the story of creation. But *Amphitryon 38* does not dazzle the bedroom joke with inexhaustible brilliance, playing all the changes that might be gayly rung on a god's night out among the gullible mortals." Only Richard Lockridge, and he without analysis, felt a richer quality, when Jupiter, facing Alcmena as a god, "grants forgetfulness with a kiss and climbs back to his cloud in radiance. But a little of that radiance is left over for the human couple, lighting their little island of fidelity."

In contrast with these comments, and with George Jean Nathan's dismissal—"The play itself is slight stuff, but it provides a sufficient share of agreeable and witty boulevard entertainment"—were the discerning observations in the *London Times* (May 18, 1938), of the same production and play: Here, the dramatist Giraudoux "is, in the theatre, that increasingly rare specimen, a civilized man who speaks but does not shout and who, having something to say, dares to say it not with bludgeons but with wit, entertainingly, remembering the stage, eschewing the solemn and abominable tub. . . . Here, if you please, is an essay on the disadvantages of being a god and so, by implication, on the delights of mortality. Alcmena is offered immortality and refuses it. It would bore her to be a star and shine endlessly. She possesses, what the gods have not and our own Elizabethans had supremely as a quickener of all their poetry, the joy of transience, the delight of instants, the blissful necessity, of which Olympians can know nothing, to taste the cup, to be a connoisseur of time, before both are snatched away. This is the nature of M. Giraudoux' 'civilization': he preaches not greed but selectiveness and that connoisseurship of life by which the Anglo-Saxons are still a little shocked but which forms a link between Paris and Athens. 'Preaches!' It is the wrong word. As there is no tub, so there is no pulpit, and whoever will may lean back in his stall and enjoy the legend only, the delicious absurdity of Jupiter and his messenger chatting on a cloud, their feet (and more) in the air, or the dashing gaiety of Alcmena, who, with the help of Miss Lynn Fontanne, gives to all truth the aspect of high comedy." Enduring in its wit, timely in its thought, and comic in its staged misunderstandings—knowledge of which sets the audience on a par with the gods—Plautus' *Amphitryon* is a joyous play in its own right, as well as a fruitful stimulus to playwrights.

CASINA   *Titus Maccius Plautus*

Originally known as *Sortientes* (*The Men Who Drew Lots*), 185 B. C., and based on a Greek comedy of that name by Diphilus, this popular play of Plautus' was revived in antiquity as *Casina,* the name of the heroine who never appears in it. It is a lively farce, much of which is sung; the basic indecency, to our standards, of its final situation makes it no less amusing.

Old Lysidamus and his son both covet the fair young slave girl, Casina. Each tries to arrange to have a slave marry the girl, as a cloak for his own gratification. Lysidamus sends his son out of town, but his mother, suspecting her husband's intentions, continues arguing for her son's slave. The two slaves, in an amusing, quarrelsome scene, draw lots; the old man's proxy wins. The wedding is held, but Lysidamus' wife substitutes a disguised male slave for Casina, and out of the bridal chamber tumble first the bridegroom and then the old master, completely duped and shamed.

The comedy flows along with quick repartee and gay lyric movement, and was probably set to sparkling tunes. Its usual theme of the old man tricked was given a new variation that must have tickled the Roman fancy. As in many of the more exuberant farces, there is occasional breaking of the dramatic illusion by talk or reference to the audience, as when the wife, after enjoying her husband's exposure and discomfiture, says that she'll forgive him, "less reluctantly, so as not to make a long play still longer." Neither Casina nor the son appears in the play; the Prologue tells us not to expect the young man: "Plautus did not wish him to come, and broke down the bridge that was on his route."

It is noticeable that the later plays of Plautus have a greater lyrical element, as though the playwright grew fonder, or found his audience fonder, of music. The taste of the audience probably accounts for the increase of exuberant vulgarity in the later plays, though among these are also Plautus' chief satires on vice. Some influence of the early (pre-Roman) Atellan farces, with their frank sex play, may leer in these later comedies. *Casina,* the last of Plautus' surviving plays, is the most care-free and the bawdiest in its plot, as well as one of the liveliest in its movement.

BORIS GODUNOV   *Alexander S. Pushkin*

The Russian poet Alexander Sergeievich Pushkin (1799-1837) was a great admirer of Shakespeare, whom he imitated, as he himself said, "in the free and wide portrayal of characters and in the careless and simple composition of types", when he created his masterpiece, the historical drama *Boris Godunov,* 1825.

The play deals with the reign of Boris Godunov, Regent after the death of Ivan the Terrible. Boris, although suspected of the murder of the Czarevich, Dmitri, arranges for a public acclamation and then, in feigned reluctance like Julius Caesar's, accepts the crown. Meanwhile, a young monastery novice, Gregory, decides to impersonate the missing Dmitri. The rule of Boris, growing harsher and more repressive, drives adherents to the young, handsome, and open-hearted Pretender.

The forces of Boris are defeated; Boris dies. Boris' son Theodore and his sister are murdered; and although the crowd are exhorted, commanded, to cheer, they remain dumb with horror at the piling crimes as the false Dmitri takes the throne.

While incidental scenes of *Boris Godunov* have frequently been played, not only the ban of Czar Nicholas I but, as the *New York Times* (February 27, 1925) stated, "its immense technical difficulties prevented its performance even in Russia." With twenty-four scenes and thirty-five speaking characters, the play calls for the simplicity of Elizabethan staging or the ingenuity of modern revolving-stage techniques, neither of which the nineteenth century provided. The play had its world premiere in Birmingham, England, February 26, 1925, a hundred years after it was written. It was played in Leningrad in 1936, then elsewhere in Russia; but in the meantime, despite the superb power of its poetry and the panoramic surge of its action, the play had been superseded for stage purposes by the opera into which it was turned.

The music for *Boris Godunov* was written by Modest Petrovich Musorgski (1835-1881), and the opera had its premiere in St. Petersburg, January 24, 1874. The plot was changed in a few particulars. Marina, an adventuress whom Gregory in the play casts aside after she has teased his secret from him in the opera is genuinely beloved. And the musical version ends with Boris crying "Behold your Czar!" and pointing to his son Feodor as he falls dead. The operatic version by Musorgski was revised and shortened (1896) by his friend Nikolai Andreievich Rimski-Korsakov (1844-1908). Of the new version, Olin Downes said in the *New York Times* (June 7, 1941): "The simpler design of the blatant contrast of the coronation with its noise and its pomp, and the inner drama of Boris' soul is not only equally efficacious psychology but better theatre." The opera was first sung at the New York Metropolitan November 19, 1913; Czar Boris was a favorite role of Feodor Chaliapin's; Paul Robeson (1941) and Ezio Pinza (1943) have also sung the part.

Pushkin's play, for all its formless progression, is a master work, "a giant among pigmies", said the Russian critic Belinsky. The *Times* called it "a great tragedy that moves from the first line to the last with the inevitability of Greek drama." The *Boston Transcript* (March 18, 1925) said: "There is no mistaking its power." The *Moscow Daily News* (December 20, 1936) claimed that the play "ranks with *Hamlet*" and added: "No wonder that, 'firmly convinced of the necessity of reforming the antiquated forms of our theatre', the father of modern literature and friend of the Decembrists found the plot of his drama in the period of the first great revolt of the Russian peasantry, which 'patriotic' historians labeled 'the troubled time'." While Pushkin was in disfavor after his *Ode to Liberty,* 1820, and was for a time dismissed from public service, there is no sign of any peasant uprising in the play, either in the carefully instigated cries that mark Boris's accession to the throne or in the shocked revulsion that greets Gregory's. But *Boris Godunov,* in poetry and wide canvas and rouse of swift emotions, is a landmark in the growth of Russian drama and a major work of world literature.

BRITANNICUS   *Jean Baptiste Racine*

When *Britannicus* was produced in 1669, Pierre Corneille, aged 63, reproached the 30 year old Jean Baptiste Racine (French, 1639-1699), with having made Britannicus live two more years than history accorded him. Racine retorted that Corneille had allowed the Emperor Heraclius to reign twenty years when history accorded him eight.

When Floridor produced *Britannicus* in December 1669, Corneille sat almost alone at the premiere; the crowd was off watching the beheading of the Huguenot Marquis de Courboyer. The few who saw the play did not once grant it their favor. Boileau, however, expressed the view that *Britannicus* has "the most finished and the most sententious" poetry of Racine's plays. King Louis XIV joined in its praises and its success was assured—though Racine later declared that *Britannicus* won both more applause and more censure than any other of his dramas.

Britannicus presents the climactic moments in the rivalry between Nero and his stepbrother, Britannicus, whose beloved Junie Nero covets. Britannicus is killed, but Junie saves herself by becoming one of the Vestal Virgins. There is little dramatic movement in the play, but intense analysis of the emotions of the characters. Saint-Evremond (striking a blow for Corneille) declared: "There once was a time when one had to choose good subjects, and to handle them well; now all one needs is characters." Racine's interest lay in character rather than theme; but the counterbalance and the analysis of his characters itself grows intense and exciting.

Boileau wrote of the premiere: *Britannicus* "touched me so deeply that the happiness he was apparently soon to enjoy having made me laugh, the story they came to tell of his death made me weep; and I know nothing more pleasant than to have at any given moment a fund of joy or of sadness at the very humble service of M. Racine . . . Others who, for the thirty sols they'd given at the door, thought they had the right to say what they thought, found the novelty of the catastrophe so astonishing, and were so touched to see Junie, after the poisoning of Britannicus, go to become a religious of the order of Vesta, that they would have called the work a Christian tragedy, if they had not been assured that Vesta was not Christian."

Though not so frequently revived in France as Racine's *Phèdre* and *Andromaque*, *Britannicus* has remained popular. It is worth noting that Nero is reproached in the play for having performed before his courtiers; after the premiere of *Britannicus*, Louis XIV never again danced in public. In England, the play proved fairly popular. Thomas Gray, we are told in Norton Nicholls' *Memoirs*, "admired Racine, particularly the *Britannicus*." The play was warmly received by English romantics in general—though Sir Brooks Boothby, who translated it in 1803, wondered whether there was place for "so simple and chaste a tragedy on a stage where even Shakespeare must make way for ballets of action. . . . The characteristic of Racine is purity of taste. He seldom attempts to create, but is content to imitate, and this he always does with great force and infinite propriety of art. His versification is generally agreed to have reached the summit of perfection, in a language the least of all formed either for melody or for figurative expression; and when it is remembered that he has restrained himself to the difficult unities of time and place, suited to the regular and simple construction of his plays, the best performances of Racine will always be considered as masterpieces of dramatic art."

Racine is primarily a musician. His exactness, of both psychology and versification, has led the French to prefer his plays to those with Corneille's "noble fire". His verse, as Laurie Magnus observed in the *Dictionary of European Literature* (1926), is, "at its height, incomparable for its passion, restraint, majesty, and music." These very qualities —passion *and* restraint—however, suggest the reason for the lack of full appreciation of Racine outside of France. Thus F. Y. Eccles in *Racine in England* (1922), states: "His rarest virtue of expression is not exactness, nor propriety, but an ardor robed in discretion, which most foreigners perhaps—and some of his own countrymen—do not distinguish from frigidity and rhetoric." Both a poet and an analyst of characters torn by the opposite claims of devotion and duty, Racine in his chosen range is without a peer.

THE WINSLOW BOY   *Terence Rattigan*

It is through the implications behind its story that *The Winslow Boy*, by Terence Rattigan (English, b. 1912) takes on significance. The audience is told in advance that the play is based on an actual case, the fight of a middle-class family against the British Empire; although the author warned us, in *Theatre Arts* (April, 1947), that "the facts, as stated in the play, are wildly inaccurate and the characters bear no relationship whatever (unless by accident) to the Archer-Shee family and Lord Carson." The play itself (aided by deft direction and sensitive acting) gathers a sense of universality through the quiet persistence of Mr. Winslow until, as Richard Watts emphasized, "in the end you feel that the Winslow victory has really been a triumph for human rights." In days of totalitarian pressure and the subordination of the individual to the state, it is heartening to watch (in life and in the theatre) the plucky and successful fight of a plain citizen to maintain the family integrity—to find an empire on the brink of war pause in its widespread, epochal concerns, to lean down over a personal problem and repeat the traditional but tremendous formula with which Parliament grants review of a government action: "Let right be done."

Terence Rattigan's history did not prepare us for the American success of *The Winslow Boy*. In England, his earlier plays had been popular, two of them having run for over 1000 performances, but all of these plays found Broadway unreceptive. The American theatre was setting Terence Rattigan down as a journeyman whose products had a merit limited to his own land. Then *The Winslow Boy*, which won the Ellen Terry award in England, with a London run from May 23, 1946 to September 6, 1947, came on October 29, 1947 to the Empire Theatre. It ran for 215 performances, and the New York Drama Critics' Circle voted it the best foreign play of the year. On tour through the United States, the play achieved a total of 899 performances, terminating with a condensed television performance by the stage cast, back in New York.

The play is a dramatized version of the story of George Archer-Shee, dismissed for petty theft from the Royal Naval Academy, and of his father's long fight for the right to reopen the case and establish the boy's innocence. "A small boy and the Magna Carta", said John Mason Brown, "suddenly and somehow found themselves fused." Alexander Woollcott wrote lengthily about the case; and Brown's review of the play gave details of a fight against discrimination in the United States.

This "challenging and memorable piece of theatre", as Barnes called it, succeeds through the earnestness and honesty of its cause, and through the very natural, recognizable reactions of the various members of the family to the situation thrust upon them when the expelled boy shrinks home, ashamed of his position yet proudly staunch in his innocence. These early scenes, said Atkinson, "are heart-breaking in their simplicity and directness."

If the wider implications fail to reach across the footlights, the play may seem, as it did to John Chapman, "frightfuly genteel and more than faintly tedious." For if you strip the story bare, as George Jean Nathan pointed out, it is the familiar tale of a person wrongly accused who, "after more vicissitudes than an audience can shake a stick at", is declared innocent and reunited with his family. Usually the climax of such a play is a courtroom scene; here, the noted barrister grills the boy with grueling questions before accepting the case, and the actual trial occurs offstage—told in a neatly humorous variation of the messenger's report, as old as the drama of ancient Greece. To strengthen these familiar situations, Louis Kronenberger felt, the play "falls back more and more on hokum and muted heroics."

For most persons, however, the play successfully carried over the broader implications and the surge of human justice. There is something pitiful as well as heroic in Arthur Winslow's perseverance, while his ordinary wife completely fails to see the significance of his fight and wishes he would drop the matter, for the neighbors are beginning to think them queer. Young Ronnie Winslow himself loses interest; while the trial is coming to its end, Ronnie is out enjoying a motion picture. Equally natural are the reactions of Ronnie's older brother Dick and sister Kate, the boy pluckily urging his father on, even though the mounting expenses of the case mean that he must drop out of college; the girl taking the cause as her own, though therefor she must break with her over-conventional fiancé. And the play neatly avoids the sentimental in merely allowing us to surmise that the barrister—whom Kronenberger called "the icy lawyer with the heart of an oven"—may choose, after the trial is over, to ripen his acquaintance with Catherine Winslow.

The Winslow Boy is an intense and roundly developed drama. With the bright fire of a fine fight for justice illuminating the play, Terence Rattigan made of it a drama of rich significance, a stirring presentation in theatrical terms of the eternal vigilance and the dogged tenacity of purpose that are the price of individual integrity and freedom.

ON TRIAL   *Elmer Rice*

When *On Trial,* by Elmer Rice (American, b. 1892) opened in New York August 19, 1914, Broadway "experienced one of those thrills for which it lives," according to the *New York World.* Shrouded in secrecy until the opening, the play captured audiences not only with the power of its melodramatic story but with the novelty of its technique.

On Trial was the first play to convey its story through a movement akin to what is called "the flash-back" in motion pictures. The idea was suggested to him, Rice told me, by an article of Clayton Hamilton's in the *Bookman,* which suggested a play with scenes in inverse sequence; Rice hit upon the more dramatic movement of going back in order to go forward. The scene of his play is a courtroom during a trial; as the trial advances, new witnesses are called. As the witness begins his story, the stage darkens, then changes—and we watch the story in action. Thus, as we behold the past scenes, our interest is always in the present; we are balancing this episode among the others for its effect upon the jury and as it shapes our own attitude toward the defendant.

The story itself is really less important than the method of presentation. Originally the play was all about a Kentucky feud. By the time it was sold—through Arthur Hopkins, to Cohan and Harris—it told the story of a murder in New York. Mr. Strickland, catching his wife in a lie, and on its trail discovering that she has been visiting his best friend, Mr. Trask, himself pays a visit to this gentleman and shoots him. The play opens with Strickland on trial for murder. The evidence discloses, however, that Mrs. Strickland was not unfaithful: that Trask had compromised her years ago, when she was an unwitting girl of seventeen, and that now he's been ruthlessly blackmailing her. If Strickland knew this, his crime was clearly not immediate impulsive killing but coldly deliberated murder. Strickland claims that he had no knowledge of these facts; indeed, in good faith he had just paid his friend Trask $10,000; but there is no trace of the money. We watch the jury in its vigorous debating of the case. One point is not clear; they wish to recall a witness. And in a last moment surprise, the trap is sprung: Trask's secretary, tangled in his own words, confesses he has stolen the $10,000—and Strickland is freed.

The play's reception was enthusiastic. The audience rose in its seats and cheered. The play, said Acton Davies in the *Tribune,* "made an instant appeal not alone by the compelling power of its story and the big human note which throbbed through all its acts, but by the unique manner in which its scenes were presented. . . . Elmer Reizenstein has not only dared to take his dramatic bull by the horns but has, to carry the animal simile further, actually put his cart before the horse with immense success." The play, said the *World,* "grips with the tenacity of a well spun detective yarn."

Outstanding in memory is the craftsmanship of the play itself. Technique, said Rice, is "not merely the framework of art, but almost its very essence. . . . For it is craftsmanship that channels the tumultuous flow of fantasy and gives body and form to the nebulous stuff that dreams are made of." That craftsmanship is one of Rice's firmest gifts. It is manifest in his first play, *On Trial,* not only in the new stage device of stepping back to leap forward, but in the tenseness of the witness scenes themselves, in the neatly incidental way in which the husband learns of his wife's past—an excellent playing upon his emotions, and those of the audience—and in the climactic suprise when the case seems over, upon the jury's request that the secretary be recalled.

The young lawyer author was freed by the play's success to devote himself to the theatre. In many ways—as one of the organizers of the Federal Theatre, as a president of the Dramatists' Guild, as an astute director as well as a warm-hearted, social-minded playwright—he has worked for the good of the theatre. In his plays, along with an uncanny capture of natural dialogue, he manifests a superb plot sense, an unerring sense of construction—which gave power, and significance in the history of the American theatre, to *On Trial.*

THE ADDING MACHINE   *Elmer Rice*

This is the best American play in the expressionist mode. The Theatre Guild produced it in New York, March 19, 1923, with Dudley Digges and Edward G. Robinson. It was almost immediately produced in London by the Independent Labor Party, and in 1928 by Barry Jackson, and it has had countless revivals in England and throughout the English-speaking world. Foreign language productions have been given in Argentina, Austria, France (by Gaston Baty), Germany, Holland, Hungary, Japan, Mexico, Norway. The play continues to be a challenge to community and college theatre directors.

With tenderness and tragic irony the play pictures the regimentation of middle-class life in a money-bound world. The characters are identified by labels, not names—Mr. Zero; Mrs. Zero; their friends, Mr. and Mrs. One to Seven; the Boss—except for the delightful heaven-sent dream-companion, Daisy Diana Dorothea Devore. Mr. Zero, the patient bookkeeper, expecting praise and a raise after twenty-five years of devoted service, is told by his boss that an adding machine will supplant him—he is fired. Fired by these words, Mr. Zero snatches up a filing spike and stabs the boss. Condemned to death, he reawakens in the next world. There he wanders in a flowery field with Daisy Diana, who had been his office assistant, the secret object of his unsatisfied love; but when nobody seems to care that they are together, Mr. Zero's shocked conventionality sends him away. He then finds himself more at home (which is heaven, which hell?) as he stalks about on a gigantic adding machine, stepping from key to key; until he is reassigned to the old routine on earth, sentenced once more to be alive. The drudgery round, being the creation of a commonplace mind, is dreadfully and endlessly renewed.

The structure of the play roused considerable controversy. The New York *Freeman,* (May 2, 1923) attacked it violently, as "a concoction of strident modernity that would be difficult to explain on any more charitable basis than that it is a clever exploitation of expressionism . . . there is no direct plagiarism—only a complete and audacious surrender to modern forms that is disagreeable in proportion to its calculated hope of succeeding." Contrariwise, the London *Spectator* (March 22, 1924) said "It is in Mr. Rice's bold and novel presentation that the play's force resides;" and the *Boston Transcript* (December 14, 1926) called the play's production America's "emergence into theatrical day."

The *New York Times* (March 20, 1923) upheld expressionism as "the form of dramatic expression best conveying the illusion of reality in the presence of the obviously unreal." It came to Rice, despite the

Freeman, as the natural form for his subject; for, as Rice told me: "I had never seen or read any expressionistic plays when I wrote *The Adding Machine.* In fact, the writing of that play was about the most extraordinary experience I have ever had. I was working on another play and suddenly *The Adding Machine* came to me, practically complete—characters, story, situations, and even some of the dialogue. I began writing it eight hours after the idea hit me and finished it in eighteen days."

The superb structural sense of Elmer Rice and his subtle handling of dialogue are in evidence throughout the play. The opening scene shows Mr. Zero in bed; his wife, combing her hair, delivers herself of a monologue of inconsequential gossip interspersed with spurts of nagging at her recumbent husband, which admirably sets the tone of the play. At the office, Daisy reads the figures with dullest monotony as Mr. Zero books them. But between the numbers their thoughts, dreams of their unavowed romance, drift into audibility. "The thought sequences," the *Spectator* noted, "wander like arabesques, sometimes converging till they almost touch, sometimes interrupted by irritable outbursts between the two thinkers. The dialogue, apparently desultory, fills out the intimate characters of the speakers, and gives their present and past relations to one another in a masterly fashion. It is a skilful and beautiful piece of writing." At the Zeros' party, the friends appear in mechanical reduplication. "They make," the *Spectator* continued, "one after another like a peal of bells, remarks of an inconceivable and desolating banality. The effect is not only comical but terrible; and it is entirely appropriate, for by illustrating symbolically the mechanical monotony of Zero's life and his everlasting concern with sums and figures, it lights up and intensifies the *motif* of the play."

There is similarly effective use of robot responses in the courtroom, with the puppet-like jury automatic in its attention, its whispered deliberations, its unanimous raising of the right arm to point the "Guilty!" But here is the play's most pathetic moment, when Mr. Zero, perhaps dimly discerning the truth that to understand all is to pardon all, tries to make the jury understand his action, and in his inarticulate groping can achieve only a continued mechanical repetition of incoherent phrases. This is at once a true stroke of psychological insight and a pressing of the play's point: so far has mechanization proceeded that it has infected the very soul. This insight continues in the next world, where Mr. Zero dallies with Daisy, and, as the *Freeman* observed, "his prosaic conventional soul asserts itself against the passionate glow of life, which he could endure only by labeling it immoral."

Of the specifically expressionistic devices of the play, that marking the moment when Mr. Zero loses his job is typical. Galsworthy*, in a satirical comment that struck home, characterized expressionism as revealing the inside of a situation without showing the outside. When one receives sudden and shocking news, one grows dizzy, the world seems to spin. Mr. Zero is told that he is fired. And at once the part of the stage on which he stands begins rapidly turning, spinning him around and around. Out of this dizzying whirl, he grasps the fatal spike and kills the Boss.

"Examine this play scene by scene, symbol by symbol," said Ludwig Lewisohn in the *Nation* (April 14, 1923). "The structure stands. There are no holes in its roof. It gives you the pleasure of both poetry and science, the warm beauty of life and love, the icy delight of mathematics . . . Here is an American drama with no loose ends or ragged edges or silly last-act compromises, retractions, reconciliations. The work, on its own ground, in its own mood, is honest, finished, sound."

Striking in its production methods, vivid in its moving scenes, strong in its indictment of the deadening effects of routine working and routine thinking, *The Adding Machine* is a symbolic expressionistic drama that strikes home.

COCK ROBIN   *Elmer Rice*

Cock Robin, 1927, is as deft, and as unexcited, a mystery thriller as one might find in a blue moon of theatrical murders. Opening in New York January 12, 1928, for a hundred performances, it was a critics' joy and ever since has been the amateurs' delight. Hard-boiled *Variety,* commenting on its "absence of thrills", added "it will go nicely for small stock". The more urbane *Boston Transcript* (December 27, 1927) called it "a smooth play, a mystery play for gentlefolk, possibly the first of the kind."

Elmer Rice is modest about the melodrama. He wrote me: *"Cock Robin* was cooked up by P. L. Barry and myself, in the course of a voyage to Europe. We were both hard up and thought it would be a good idea to write a play that contained all the sure-fire ingredients of success. (Maybe that is why it did not do so well.) Anyhow, we worked out the plot on the boat, separated at Le Havre and never saw each other again until six months later when the play went into rehearsal. The collaborating was done entirely by correspondence, with Phil sitting in Cannes and me moving around through Italy, Austria, Germany, Belgium, France, and God knows where."

The structure of *Cock Robin,* as with most Rice plays, is superb. The play opens in an eighteenth century English grog-shop where, while an anguished wench is held in check, two gentlemen fight a pistol duel. One drops. There are shouts "The Guard!" They start to dash away—and the Landlord stops the proceedings. At this point, we discover that these are amateur theatricals: The Cape Valley Dramatic Society is in dress rehearsal. The "Landlord" is the professional director the group has engaged. During the discussion of the rehearsal, we learn that most of the Cape Valley folk dislike Hancock Robinson ("Cock Robin"), and with reason. Indeed, he has, though married, persuaded young Carlotta Maxwell to sail to Paris with him the day after the performance.

Act Two we watch from behind the scenes. The duel goes on again— and Robinson remains lying on the floor, dead. The remainder of the play carries through the investigation until the revelation of the killer, with a number of neat and novel turns. After twisting and twining to discover how the loaded shell got into the revolver, the cast move the body—and find that Robinson was killed by a knife thrust in the back. The cast itself carries on the inquiry, without the usual smart-aleck or brow-beating detective or buffoon officer of the police. Maria, the assistant director, despite her thick glasses has a "kodak eye"; it is through her observation of seemingly insignificant details that the criminal is finally pinned. But all the company recognize that this has been, if ever, justifiable homicide. No one knows anything. The summoned police knock. Maria says "I didn't see a thing! How could I, with *my* eyes?" She polishes her glasses, as the door is opened, and the curtain falls.

Audience emotions, while watching *Cock Robin,* are divided between amusement and excitement. The high point of amusement is the speech of welcome by Chairlady Mrs. Montgomery to those that have come to see the Cape Valley players performing for the benefit of the General Hospital. That speech is a comic gem, an uproarious burlesque of the amateur theatricals chairlady. Said Leonard Hall: "Seldom have I heard anything funnier, and seldom have these old ears listened to such howling and bellowing in a playhouse." Percy Hammond recorded that Robert Benchley laughed so heartily those around thought he must be a claque, and added: "Nothing more quietly cheerful in the way of minor satire is on sale in the Times Square canteens."

Smiles soon give way to shivers as death strikes and suspicion stalks from the wings. The development, however, is a deftly woven argument, progressing through the pressing of logical points, not gun points, with frequent surprise. A program note requested that no one reveal the actual criminal; recent re-reading, however, showed that the play is tense even when the ending is known. As the *London Times* observed (February 25, 1933), "The game is played fairly and with a quite brilliant sense of the theatrical possibilities that lie in the reconstruction of a crime."

Neither Rice nor Barry has often written with a collaborator. This collaboration, born of the accident of an ocean voyage together, produced one of our suavest and most amusing mystery plays.

STREET SCENE   *Elmer Rice*

Broadway producers were initially quite indifferent to the lure of this play. "It was peddled around for over a year," Rice wrote me, "and was turned down by practically every New York producer. . . Nobody had any confidence in the play. A number of actors turned down parts because they thought it had no chance of success. George Cukor, the only first-class director who could be interested in the play, walked out on it in the middle of casting, so I had to take over the direction myself, though I had never directed a play before. Even after an enthusiastic opening and rave notices, the ticket agencies refused for some time to buy, believing the play had no popular appeal. Brady himself thought the play's appeal was confined to New York, and it took me a whole year to persuade him to send a company to Chicago. He was so skeptical about England that he let the English rights lapse, enabling me to do the play there myself."

The play opened in New York on January 10, 1929; it ran for 601 performances and won the 1929 Pulitzer Prize. It has been played wherever English is spoken; also in Argentina, Denmark, France, Germany, Greece, Holland, Hungary, Japan, Mexico, Norway, Palestine, Poland, Spain, and Sweden. While it is a difficult play for a small theatre to present, it is widely popular as the fullest dramatic capture of the teeming life of the tenement folk of a great city. As the *Montreal Herald* declared (October 28, 1930): "Last night we saw the soul of a city, and its body too; felt its mad, despairing lusts, its ruthlessness, its dumb good-heartedness; its gentle hypocrisies and, withal, its inherent dignity . . . life raw and unlovely, without illusion, pretense, or convention. Realism and force there are to this work of Elmer Rice, and a muscularity of Gargantuan proportions."

The scene of the play is the front of a cheap apartment house, its windows wide open, for the action occurs on a hot night and day in June. The plot is simple and melodramatic: Frank Maurrant discovers his wife in the arms of the milkman; he kills them both, runs away, and is caught by the police. Interest, however, lies less in this than in the swarming folk around, whose diverse characters and interests jostle and intertwine up the stairs and on the flagstones of the city. Again and again in reviews recur the words "a slice of life"; "the sidewalks of New York". The *New York Post* (January 19, 1929) admiringly exclaimed: "Along comes a man who merely sits on a New York front stoop for a few hours and tells us about it." The *World* (January 14) declared: "With your first shadowy glimpse he gives you the sights and noises of a shabby New York thoroughfare in mid-summer, dominated by a chipped and dusty brownstone dwelling, still bearing the remnants of a sturdy dignity through the pathos of the better days it has known." Suggested by an actual house on New York's 65th Street, wherein dwell Swedes, English, Italians, Negroes, and Germans, all is authentic, even to the garbage can on the stone sidewalk outside the basement rail.

There is more than the street, however, to the play. Brooks Atkinson probed: "What distinguishes *Street Scene* from a host of synthetic forerunners is Mr. Rice's remarkable sense of character. Here are not merely the automatons of the giddy city streets but the people—the intellectual Jew who runs on endlessly about the capitalistic classes, the Italian musician who dreams of the flowery land from which he came, the office girl who wants to move out to Queens, the pleasant woman who is quietly sacrificing her life to a sick mother, the ruffian taxi driver, the flirt, the school-teacher, all brought into focus with telling stories of character portrayal. . . . Mr. Rice's flowing, somewhat sprawling drama catches the primitive facts of child-birth on the third story, the chicken for soup, the petting after dark, the common hatred of the Jew—race prejudices, class morality, jolly, broad humor, sympathies, jealousies. Again, he expresses no point of view about the matters. For those who are interested, it is sufficient that he has done his portrait with remarkable artistic integrity." Maurrant tells Kaplan to go back where he came from. "Listen," said the *Boston Transcript* (May 6, 1929), "to Maurrant and Jones pummeling everything outside their experience of life and their own courses of conduct as so much Bolshevism, while Maurrant's implement of rectitude is a smoking pistol and the Jones children go cheerfully to the devil in their own way." Out of these many vignettes of city life, the wistful love of young Sam Kaplan and Rose Maurrant as well as the more desperate clutch after happiness of Rose's mother, the play gathers its power.

In 1929 Deems Taylor wanted Rice to write the book for an opera based on *Street Scene;* Rice refused, thinking the play might make a musical almost without change. It did, coming to the stage January 9, 1947, with music by Kurt Weil and lyrics by Langston Hughes. For the musical, the composer felt that *Street Scene* was admirably constructed, "very much like Greek tragedy, with tight unity of time and space, and the inescapability of fate." *Time* (January 20, 1947) called the new version "more folk opera than musical"; *PM* called it "Broadway's first real opera." There are spoken dialogue, recitative at tense moments, and song—solo, duet, quartet, wide chorus. The songs are not just dragged in by the chorus, as in many musicals; they are integrated with the story. The musical nevertheless throws more emphasis upon the melodrama, less fully captures the spirit of the street or reveals the characters of those that walk it through their destiny. The original remains the better play and the finest dramatic capture of the dust and dreams, the degradation and the dignity, the sham and shame and striving honesty and urging simple nobility of the many folk whose ways make up the street scene of the city.

COUNSELLOR-AT-LAW   *Elmer Rice*

With a superb characterization by Paul Muni, Elmer Rice's *Counsellor-at-Law* opened in New York November 6, 1931, for a run of 400 performances. This was followed by six months in Chicago. The West Coast also saw the play in 1932, with Otto Kruger. In Boston, the oaths were deleted. In Philadelphia, the censor said the word "virgin" was taboo. London saw the play in 1934. It has been presented in Austria, Hungary, Italy, Sweden, and Switzerland. Its German production was one of the many things stifled by Hitler. The Prague production (pictured in *Theatre Arts*, November, 1938) had magnificent sets, particularly of the lawyer's outer office, adorned according to European ideas of American lavish display. A little theatre favorite, the play was shown again with Paul Muni on Broadway, opening November 24, 1942; the revival ran for 258 performances and was called by the *Post* (November 25, 1942), a "steadily engrossing play."

As in *Street Scene**, the melodramatic plot of the play is adorned with revealing character sketches, of the folk in trouble that enter the daily routine of the office of a busy city lawyer. There is the poor person, with old family ties, seeking help without a fee—and her Communist son, who refuses aid from a lawyer who is a "dirty traitor" to the cause. There is the visit, annoying in spite of his love, from the lawyer's mother—an old-fashioned Jewess, she; for George Simon came over in the steerage, and worked himself up to Fifth Avenue and prominence by the long, hard—and not always clean—pathway. There are other clients, and clerks. Rice himself was once a practicing lawyer, and knows, as Brooks Atkinson observed, (November 7, 1931), "how actively a lawyer's office illuminates the whole fabric of city life."

One of the smudged episodes of his early legal days creeps back on George and provides the plot of the drama. George has married a society lady who condescends toward him and his past. Her friends, society lawyers, have no liking for George Simon, who, to tell the truth, could be ruthless at times; when one of these men unearths an early shady trick, George's days at the bar seem over. Mrs. Simon turns from him in distaste. But George is not licked; hunting desperately, he finds the flaw in the opponent's armor and forces him to drop the fight.

Richer and wiser, but much sadder, George is left triumphant and love-less—save for the unending devotion of his Jewish secretary.

It may be that beneath this opposition of the society-bred and the spawn of the slums, there is a suggestion of Christian versus Jew. It is true that Rice sets caricatures against the rounded portrait of George Simon; so much so, that the *Outlook* (November 25, 1931) declared: "He has no idea how to depict a lady or a gentleman . . . they are only ridiculous without being in any way true to any conceivable sort of life." The "lady" and the "gentleman"—two characters out of the twenty-eight figures in the play—are pictured as self-centered snobs. Rice is honest in his presentation of the counsellor himself; Burns Mantle noted how, when George is threatened, he reverts to type, he "curses freely, coarsens perceptibly, then exults humanly." In essence, this is a picture of the rise of a slum boy—his profession is incidental—to more pleasant surroundings and circumstances. The struggle has made him shrewd and polished; it has also made him unscrupulous and, when necessary, cruel. He has always had forcefulness; he has learned control. He has followed to its end a path many in the "land of opportunity" have started along; hence he is a figure many eagerly, almost enviously, watch. George Simon is a searching example of the "self-made man," drawn in a consummately developing portrait.

The dialogue, said Atkinson, "glows with life; it is pithy, comic, and a deep revelation of character." The plot itself, with more substance than that of *Street Scene,* makes the play, as Richard Lockridge said, "whip across the stage, missing never a trick, with craftsmanship which is a delight to watch . . . at once portraiture and melodrama, in both categories animating." The drive and reality of the story, the revelation and reality of the character, give power and penetration and lasting value to *Counsellor-at-Law.*

FLIGHT TO THE WEST   *Elmer Rice*

In *Flight To The West,* 1940, Elmer Rice again examined in vividly dramatic terms the basic opposition of our time. Like his *Between Two Worlds* and other dramas of the World War II period, it is chiefly concerned with the totalitarian invasion of democracy, with an invasion not of armed might but of mental attitudes and insidious propaganda. *Flight To The West* bears a double meaning in its title. All the action takes place inside a Clipper plane, from Lisbon via Bermuda to the United States. But on the plane are refugees, and the daughter of an American diplomat, Hope Nathan, returning with her husband from the Hitler threat.

Also on board, besides the crew, are a Nazi envoy to the United States, a millionaire oil man of Fascist potentialities, a slick woman journalist, and a confused liberal. As the airplane speeds along, the many points of view lead to clashes that grow more intense. The young Hope has scarcely given thought to the fact that her husband is a Jew, until the Nazi envoy insults him; then Hope listens with wonder and dismay to the plea of the elderly Jewish woman refugee that she should not bring another Jew into the world. The liberal watches with growing confusion; in the name of individual liberty, it seems to him he must defend the Nazi's right to his own point of view. Feeling grows still more intense when, thanks to some quick work on the journalist's part, a Nazi spy is unmasked and disembarked at Bermuda. Just before the final landing a Belgian refugee shoots at the Nazi envoy; Nathan tries to stop him, and himself receives the shot. The liberal asks the German whether this courageous and generous deed has not softened his heart. The Nazi laughs scornfully, and replies: "His action was entirely un-motivated—it was nothing more than a muscular reflex. If he had had a moment for thought, he would have taken good care not to interfere." These words light up the whole world situation for the liberal. Against the "reason" of the Nazis, he declares his faith in a political system which aims at such things as goodness, truth, kindness, and brotherhood.

In 1939, Rice flew home to the United States on a Clipper plane. Mrs. Ogden Reid of the *New York Herald Tribune* and Paul Patterson of the *Baltimore Sun,* who were fellow passengers, suggested that he ought to get a play out of the trip. Rice agreed that perhaps he would. He wrote his play for the sake of the last scene. Discerning this, John Mason Brown felt it was "less a play than a discussion (more accurately, a ventilation) of issues and dilemmas, tragedies and hopes now-adays known to us all." This being so, it is important to note that the conclusion of the discussion—the liberal's awakening—goes astray. In spite of the plausible plea for love and kindness, these are the obverse of the coins of cruelty and hate—too easily we toss them heads or tails! The liberal's error lies in accepting the totalitarian's estimate of him-self as a thoroughly rational being. The cleverest ruse of the devil is to persuade us he doesn't exist; the shrewdest play of emotion is to strut in reason's garb. By his liberal's confusion, however, Rice the more truly, and the more warningly, illustrates the dangers that lurk, as well as those that strut, in this divided world.

Combining rousing drama with its arousal of thought, the play opened in Princeton December 13, 1940; in New York December 30. Brooks Atkinson praised its "vigor, honesty, and high-mindedness . . . remarkable for the keenness of its portrait of a Nazi diplomat." John Anderson pointed out that the airplane serves as more than a novel background. It is also a reminder of the smallness of the world—and a germ carrier! "The ills of the world" are among the passengers.

Betty Field (Mrs. Rice) acted as Hope Nathan in *Flight To The West,* about the earnestness of which there is no question. The elderly Jewish refugee rises to a particularly poignant moment in her cry, out of her aching sorrow, that no more Jews be born; the horror of the concen-tration camp lies deep within her utterance. The dramatic incidents of the play give added emphasis to its thought, that the best way to fight totalitarianism is by becoming more aware, in living consciousness and daily practice, of the positive values of democracy. This thought Elmer Rice has conveyed in a gripping play.

GREEN GROW THE LILACS   *Lynn Riggs*

One of the liveliest of American folk plays is *Green Grow the Lilacs,* 1930, by Lynn Riggs (American, b. 1899), a tale of Indian Territory in 1900, seven years before it became the State of Oklahoma. The play is, said the *New York Times* (March 1, 1931), "a gusty gambol of the great open spaces . . . with a contingent of hell-for-leather cowboys, who would just as soon shoot you as look at you."

In the midst of all the gaiety and lusty youthfulness coils a picture of repressed perversion. Curley McClain, a care-free bronco-buster and sweet-singing cowboy, loves Aunt Ella Murphey's lovely niece Laurey Williams. To tease Curley, Laura encourages the farm-hand Jeeter Fry, who hides his lust in his room in the Williams' smoke house. Laura lets Jeeter take her to the dance at Old Man Peck's, but Curley takes her away and marries her. At the shivaree (serenading and rough-house of the wedding party), Curley and Laurey are gaily taken by the revelers and pitched on top of a haystack. The brooding and jealous Fry sets fire to the haystack. When this attempt is foiled, he rushes upon Curley; in the ensuing fight, Fry falls upon his own knife and is killed. Cowboy Curley decides to become a farmer and do his share in the growth of the land.

Riggs called his play "a ballad in dramatic form", and song has a part in it—the strumming of a guitar with folk songs and border ballads. The title itself is from a frontier folk song. The play opened in Boston December 8, 1930, and in New York, January 26, 1931, with Helen West-ley, June Walker, and Franchot Tone in his first outstanding part. England saw the play in 1935. It has been popular throughout the United States; Burgess Meredith played in it in the summer of 1939.

The press accepted the drama's authentic folk capture. Brooks Atkinson found it "full of sunshine and the tingle of the open air . . . life drips from every fibre of its narrative." John Mason Brown said that it "gives, as few of our plays have succeeded in doing, a refreshing and authentic sense of having sprung from the earth and belonging to it." It is at once real and quaint, the revivification of a vanished epoch of American growth. Thus the *Cleveland Press* (December 4, 1941) called the play "a series of old-fashioned stereopticon views, animated." Animated is a good word for the colorful exuberance of the play.

In large theatrical centers, *Green Grow The Lilacs* is best known in its musical transformation into *Oklahoma!*, book and lyrics by Oscar Hammerstein II, music by Richard Rodgers, and dances by Agnes de Mille. *Oklahoma!* delays the story seven years so that it can end with Indian Territory's becoming the state.

The chief attraction of *Oklahoma!*, however, is its use of song and dance, by which it simply and beautifully captures the surge and youth-fulness and joy of growing America. Instead of the conventional opening chorus, the play begins with Aunt Ella alone on the stage, while Curley, approaching from the distance, sings "Oh what a beautiful morning!" The choral dances, instead of swinging and swaying hips in the conventional musical comedy style, surge and romp in gay folk rhythms—the modern dance fused with the folk dance in vivid theatrical patterns—and a new era in musical comedy was born.

The story behind the production of *Oklahoma!* shows that, in the theatre, Anguish Avenue abuts on Ecstasy Street. The Theatre Guild, after a series of failures, had found itself forced to lease its fine Guild Theatre for radio. Oscar Hammerstein II had had no success in a dozen years; Richard Rodgers had just separated from his successful lyricist Lorenz Hart. Because of such conditions, the musical version of *Green Grow The Lilacs* had trouble finding backers. It opened (as *Away We*

Go) in New Haven, then moved to Boston; on March 31, 1945, it came to New York as *Oklahoma!* and stayed for 2,248 performances. This broke by ten performances the London record of *Chu Chin Chow** during World War I; only three non-musicals—*Life With Father**, *Tobacco Road**, and *Abie's Irish Rose**—have had longer unbroken runs.

Oklahoma! was a hit in London, too, opening at Drury Lane on April 30, 1947, for a run of 1,548 performances. It "has shaken London up", said Harold Hobson, "more than anything that has hit it since the first flying bomb. . . . It is almost impossible to imagine anything better in its own particular way than *Oklahoma!*" The success of the play was repeated in many parts of the world; in Johannesburg, South Africa, the annual opera season was canceled, to keep the theatre for *Oklahoma!*

Oklahoma! is a gayer and a livelier play than *Green Grow The Lilacs*, managing to convert even the suggestions of perversity into good-humored fun. As a musical, especially in the fresh form of its opening and the ingenious blend of its dancing forms, *Oklahoma!* has been a challenge to later musical comedies. For college and community theatres, however, *Green Grow The Lilacs* remains a sparkling and stimulating folk drama of western frontier days.

THE BAT   *Mary Roberts Rinehart*

From her novel *The Circular Staircase*, 1908, Mary Roberts Rinehart (American, b. 1876) wrote, with Avery Hopwood*, this classic of American mystery thrillers. The play carries over to the stage the tradition of the blood-curdling Gothic novel, with a shiver along every corridor, a shudder at every slowly opened door, and a family skeleton if not a fresh corpse in every closet. Lights fail at crucial moments; muffled shapes slip suddenly out of sight; a gleaming, detached "eye" walks in the darkness.

The story is simple. A rich widow of sixty, Cornelia Van Gorder, has rented the summer home of a banker reported killed in Colorado. Money is missing at the bank; it is hunted in the house by the bank cashier—engaged to Cornelia's niece, Miss Dale, and under suspicion in regard to the missing funds—by a detective, a doctor friend, and a thief, "the bat." A late visitor is mysteriously shot. The doctor discovers the way to a secret room in the house, where they await, and discover, the criminal.

Opening in New York on August 23, 1920, the play ran for 867 performances. In 1922, seven companies were playing it on the road. In London, with premiere January 23, 1922, the play ran for 327 performances. It was revived, in London with Michael Redgrave, and in New York, in 1937. It remains, in little theatre and amateur productions, the most popular mystery thriller.

The mainspring of the play's action is Mrs. Van Gorder. Warned to leave the banker's home, she hires a detective instead. She rallies her friends through the grisly, tense hunt; she presses the tempo of the play. *The Bat* speeds swiftly indeed, and keeps the audience tensely expectant; the identity of the criminal, logical enough when revealed, cannot be guessed before the climactic exposure. The play established the flexible formula of the mystery crime melodrama: Act I, Nobody Suspected; Act II, Everybody Suspected; Act III, The Criminal Caught.

The drama's gripping qualities caught the reviewers' pens. The *New York Globe* said that the play "has never been equalled for wild and delirious thrills." The *London Times* noted that there is "hardly a moment without a thrill." Fourteen years later the *Los Angeles Times* (June 28, 1936) declared that no play since "has ever been able to achieve quite the same 'thrilling and chilling' effects as the original production." The quoted words may remind one of Edgar Allan Poe's "chilling and killing"—and indeed something of the macabre quality of our greatest writer of horror tales flows through this most popular and most shiverful of our murder mystery dramas.

CASTE   *Thomas William Robertson*

Eldest of the 22 children of an English actor (whose youngest daughter became the actress Dame Madge Kendal), Thomas William Robertson (1829-1871) was a pioneer in the growth of the modern realistic drama. In a succession of plays produced by the actor-manager Squire Bancroft at the Prince of Wales Theatre in London, Robertson established the cup-and-saucer drama: plays of a conventional social code, with natural dialogue and ordinary folk in domestic settings. Within the comedy, these folk are faced with a serious situation, as in the later, more radical, social problem play. In particular, as the *Baltimore Sun* (July 7, 1932) expressed the widely recognized fact, "the original ancestors of a good many present-day characters and culminations" are contained in *Caste*.

In the play, despite the objection of his haughty mother, the Marquise de Saint-Maur, the Honorable George D'Alroy marries the ballet-girl Esther Eccles. George, a Dragoon, is sent to India to help quell the Mutiny; rumor of his death widens the chasm between his wife and his mother; but he returns to Esther and their child, and Esther's pluck and firm dignity and persisting love at length win her mother-in-law's affections.

There is considerable humor in the play, rising especially from the contrast between George's haughty friends and family and Esther's frowzy relations. Her sister Polly, engaged to a journeyman gas-fitter, is, as Charles Darnton (April 27, 1910) called her, "a vulgar, good-hearted, lively little creature", while the shabby old fraud their father, a loud, tipsy fellow, searching deep in his pockets in the hope that some one will offer him tobacco, "fills his pipe with comedy". The *New York Dramatic Mirror* (April 29, 1910) indeed, went so far as to say that, "next to Falstaff, old Eccles is probably the most humorous character in English comedy." The *New York Times* earlier (January 24, 1897) remarked that *Caste* is a model of construction: "It could be acted intelligently from beginning to end without a spoken word."

Produced in London in April 1867, the play was announced in New York, by Lester Wallack, for September 2 of the same year. To his surprise, the play opened at the Broadway Theatre on August 5, with Mr. and Mrs. William J. Florence as George and Polly. Wallack opened in Brooklyn and went to court, to discover that Florence had memorized the whole play from the London production, without making a single note, and could not be restrained by law.

The play has had many revivals. Often produced in London before the end of the nineteenth century, in 1867, 1871, 1879, 1889, it attained a hundred or more performances. It was revived at the Old Vic in 1929. The New York revival of 1910 starred Marie Tempest and Elsie Ferguson. Bit by bit, however, the reviews grew less enthusiastic, until in London in 1925 the *New Statesman* (August 8) declared: "*Caste* has no body to it. It has neither psychology nor wit, the humor is crude, the sentiment obvious, the language stilted and platitudinous. . . . Yet Robertson was the best English playwright of his age." *Caste* had suffered the fate of all pioneers: later comers had traveled farther along the trail it blazed. It remains as a landmark, and the earliest of the realistic dramas that still can hold the stage.

CELESTINA   *Fernando de Rojas*

Spanish forerunner both of the novel and of the classical drama is the dramatic romance *The Tragicomedy of Calisto and Melibea,* better known as *Celestina.* An early version may have been composed by Rodrigo Coba of Toledo in 1480; it is known from the two versions by Fernando de Rojas (Spanish, c. 1473 - c. 1537): published in sixteen acts at Burgos in 1499; in twenty-one acts at Seville in 1502. The play, the first act of which is very long, was not produced in its original form, but was widely influential. Acting versions were made of it, or large elements of its story were incorporated in other dramas, for several centuries, as in Cepeda's *Sylvan Comedy,* 1582, and Vaz de Velasco's *Jealous Man,* 1602.

The basic story is that of the love of the noble Calisto for the highborn Melibea; reciprocating his affection, Melibea meets him, in church and in her father's garden. The lovers are overseen; Calisto is set upon and killed, and Melibea follows him to the grave. There is tender romance in the meetings and the fate of these two lovers, truly noble and gentle. Balanced against them is the more earthly love of their two servants, honest but coarse man and willing maid; but especially vivid is the portrait of the go-between Celestina, a shrewd, scheming, realistic bawd, who keeps the story from soaring into too flowery realms of love, and in the garden of romance sows the seeds of the great Spanish realistic and picaresque fiction.

Written in a swift and easy style, with occasional flashes of brilliance, *Celestina* was translated into Latin, as well as into the other Renaissance vernacular tongues. It was widely read, by scholars, by the educated public, and by reformers who used its franker passages for pious lessons, and was the most influential drama of the early Renaissance.

In an adaptation in two acts and eight scenes by Paul Achard, *Celestina* was produced in Paris, December 11, 1946. Set in Toledo, this version showed Celestina entering the maiden's house in the guise of a beggar. She is, however, presented as an attractive trollop and most successful bawd—so much so that, in the confusion after Calisto (in the French 1946 version called Jean Carcante) is killed, his servants murder Celestina for her jewels. The basic story of the play, transferred to modern circumstances, still has power. The original is a milestone in the history of the drama.

DANTON   *Romain Rolland*

Less episodic, less tumultuous, than Büchner's *Danton's Death** on
the same theme, *Danton,* by Romain Rolland (French, 1866-1944), drives
with direct and concentrated force through the days of the French
Revolution in March and April, 1794.

The play has been a great success whenever played; as directed by
Max Reinhardt in Berlin, March 1920, with a cast of a thousand, a
succès fou. Paris saw the play December 29, 1900; England (first at
Leeds, November 14), 1927. Reinhardt, said the *Boston Transcript*
(April 1, 1920) "has made the public take part in the Revolution, lose
its natural equilibrium, and cheer."

There are minor illuminating episodes and figures in the drama:
Lucille, the frantic wife of Camille Desmoulins; Eleonore, the platonic
admirer of Robespierre; the Widow Duplay, Robespierre's matter-of-
fact landlady, who complains of matters again recently pertinent, the
lack of coal and butter, the standing long in line to receive—two eggs.
But the tremendous movement of the play comes in the last act, the
trial of the men whom Robespierre has doomed. On the one hand,
said the *Transcript,* "is Robespierre, the man of duty and of virtue, who
speaks of revolutionary discipline just as Kerensky spoke of it and as
the moderate leaders in Germany have spoken of it, who demands the
personal sacrifice of every one for the good of all, of personal liberty
for the freedom of the people; and on the other, Danton, the passionate
partisan, the all-too-human, live-and-let-live friend of the people, the
untamed lion, hard to rouse but terrible in his wrath. The conflict
between these two makes the drama. Then there are Desmoulins the
literary agitator, weak, spoiled, and effeminate, but of a poisonous
tongue and pen; St.-Just, the fanatical avenging angel of the Revolution; the blustering General Westermann, and the cynical Hérault de
Séchelles, a charming remnant of the *ancien regime,* who sees more
clearly than all."

At the trial, after Desmoulins' outburst, Danton, rising to the charge
that he has conspired against liberty, cries "Liberty is here!" and strikes
his heart. He demands that his accusers face him; and the President
of the Tribunal grows alarmed as the people side with Danton and
shout in his favor. "The thunder of the populace outside", said the
New York Post (July 15, 1920), "the hurly-burly, threats, and breaking
of furniture within, the whole popular hysteria, with the stentorian
voice of Danton above it, shake one's very marrow." The presiding
judge sends Danton's demand to the Convention.

The mob has quieted. The Convention refuses the demand; the judge
orders the noisy prisoners removed before the trial proceeds. The resurgent mob is checked by the guards, the timely arrival of the formidable St.-Just, and the welcome announcement that a distribution
of wood and flour is being made at the docks. The howling Desmoulins
is dragged out; Danton walks calmly to his doom. Rolland makes explicit his thoughts at the play's close through the words of Robespierre's
friends, left in the courtroom, triumphant—till their turn shall come.

The psychology not only of the French Revolution but of revolution—
the various motives that animate the leaders, the fickle surge and baying
of the mob—quickens with surging power the dramatic drive of *Danton,*

to the inevitable doom of death out of which new and—we can hope—
better living will rise.

THE WOLVES   *Romain Rolland*

Imbued with a fervent faith in the people and a deep love of his
country, Rolland embodied these emotions in a cycle of ten Revolutionary dramas. However, *The Wolves* (originally called *Morituri*, and published as by "St.-Just"), in its story parallels the notorious Dreyfus
case; it was enacted in Paris in March 1898, just after the really guilty
man in that case, Esterhazy, had been acquitted (January 1898) by the
military tribunal and Zola had blasted the case open with his pamphlet
J'accuse!

Rolland's play pictures the French Army in difficulties, in 1793.
The Jacobin firebrand Verrat, once a butcher, has the aristocrat d'Oryon
convicted on the evidence of a letter from the German commander
which Verrat knows to be forged. Intervening for a new trial is
d'Oryon's opponent, but lover of justice, Teulier. At this trial, Verrat
passionately displays his wounds, won "in defense of the fatherland."
Amidst popular hysteria d'Oryon is condemned. He declares, "We are
all wolves, and we sharpen our teeth upon the weakest among us."
But in his death d'Oryon holds high the torch of truth, of human dignity
and honor.

The surge of the play is powerful and it rings with emotion; it is
simple, direct, rapidly driving toward its doom. While Rolland had
faith in reason and the ultimate worth of the people, he recognized the
danger of the mob, of both "the beast with a thousand heads, and the
beast-tamers." In addition to the basic question of truth and justice,
Rolland, through the person of Teulier, probes the tangential problem
of a man's first duty: to his conscience, or to his country? With no
women in the play, and a steady, relentless drive, the historical drama
through the past presses to present issues.

The play has been very popular in Europe and its first American
production was an outstanding success of the Yiddish Art Theatre,
January 6, 1922, with Maurice Schwartz. Schwartz played it in English
in 1932 in the version by Barrett Clark (published 1918; in revised
form, 1937).

The Wolves was called by the *New York Times* (December 31, 1922)
"a dramatic version of the most celebrated scandal of republican France,
adorned with fancy trimmings of Rolland pacifism. . . . It moves swiftly,
and its goal is inevitable." Flaming as a blast against a particular injustice, the drama remains a vivid picture of the basic conflicts of
individual freedom versus social discipline, of individual conscience
versus conformity with group desire.

DR. KNOCK   *Jules Romains*

Jules Romains (Louis Farigoule, French, b. 1885) has written in
two distinct veins. As a serious artist, he inaugurated the school of
unanimism, which states that the unifying elements in men, in social
groups, and in nature, are more basic than the individual diversities.
Quite distinct from the unanimist works are the several satiric

farces, beginning with *Knock; or The Triumph of Medicine,* 1923 (translated by Granville Barker*, 1925, as *Dr. Knock*) that made Romains the outstanding comic playwright of the period. This most penetrating of his studies of human frailty and human folly, is the liveliest and most widely known of Romains' plays.

The first scene shows the dilapidated automobile of old Dr. Paraplaid, who is leaving the small town of St. Maurice because it is too healthy. His successor, Dr. Knock, proceeds like a sort of inverted Coué to build up disease. Setting up ominous charts and maps of the human system, he offers the bait of free consultation; and those that crowd in, hale and hearty, droop out with every type of symptom and complaint. The local hotel is converted into a hospital; sanatoriums crop up on every corner; and the once tiny village grows into a vast health resort.

The figure of Dr. Knock is an imposing one. He marches through the play, said the *Boston Transcript* (May 3, 1928) "in wider and wider swath. He is the anxious and advising friend; the discovering and urgent physician; the prince and prophet of medicine's new triumph up and down St. Maurice. He pervades the play and yet crowds not one of the others into the corner. There they are—crier, school-master, chemist, townsfolk and countryfolk, none too far from human semblance and the workings of human nature, yet each in place in the scheme of satrical extravaganza . . . Finally, observe in the little world a microcosm of the larger world beyond—ready to believe what it is told to believe; taking every missioner, political, social, artistic, scientific, commercial, at his own value, so long as he is urgent enough; catching at everything proffered to its ignorance, dread, credulity, or faith. The pity of it—as it is easy to say—but also the humor of it!"

Several reviewers, as the *London Era* (May 19, 1926), called Dr. Knock "a magnificent charlatan . . ." Yet Dr. Knock is more than a charlatan. He is a man with a mission: to convince men of their ailments. His motto is: The healthy are those that do not know they are ill.

At the close of the play, providing an amusing finish, Dr. Paraplaid, returning for his first quarterly check, himself falls victim to Dr. Knock's calm suggestion, and with a bottle of tablets quakes over an imaginary complaint. To his predecessor, Dr. Knock points out the advantages—not to himself, but to the community—of his devices and methods. Not only does it do folk no harm to stay in bed for a time, but they actually relish it. Amid the paraphernalia, the thrice-a-day thermometers, night lights, cautionary lectures, the townsfolk are for the first time really enjoying themselves, and living intensely. Not only is the doctor the most popular man (and one of the richest) around, but the whole countryside is thriving as never before. He is their benefactor, their prophet, their saviour. They kiss the hand that coddles them.

Produced in France by Louis Jouvet, the play ran for four years. It was presented in London April 27, 1926; again December 6, 1928. New York saw it opening February 23, 1928. It was tried again, at Westport, Connecticut, in 1936, in a romanticized version by Laurence Langner and Armina Marshall. In this, the nurse becomes enamoured of the doctor, is repelled when she comes to the conclusion that he is a quack, and returns to his embraces when she recognizes how much well-being (and how much wealth) he has produced. "These are bold and spinning scenes of delicious satire," said the *New York Times* (July 14, 1936), "mixed neatly with a sauce of running humor that keeps the play in a lilting vein." The whole is, said Robert Garland, "a neatly nasty nose-thumbing at the ultramodern medico, his diets, his lamps, his paying inability to let well enough alone." The 1936 version also Americanized the locale and the townsfolk, with, as Garland listed them, "a motley and amusing parade of New York caricatures: an under-taker, a druggist, a miser, a manufacturer, a spinster, a widow, and a couple of local roughnecks."

Dr. Knock is an amusing lesson in the fine art of creating something out of nothing but human faiths and human fears. Psychology and satire romp through this superb dramatic picture of a master salesman, and the credulous folk who succumb to his double-edged sales talk.

ME AND MY GIRL   *L. Arthur Rose*

There is something perennially amusing in the good-natured misfit, in the worthy but unpolished person shown amidst formal surroundings. Humor and satire may flow side by side from such a situation. The audience is left with the comforting if sentimental reflection that kind hearts are more than coronets. An American comedy on this theme is *Peg O' My Heart;* an English musical comedy, *Me and My Girl,* by L. Arthur Rose (English, b. 1887) and Douglas Furber (b. 1885), with music by Noel Gay. Opening in London on December 16, 1937, with Lupino Lane as the Cockney interloper from Lambeth and George Graves as a somewhat downsliding aristocrat, it ran for 1,646 per-formances. The June 25, 1941, revival ran for 208 performances; the August 6, 1945, for 304; the December 12, 1949, for 75 performances.

The play presents Snibson, a Cockney bookmaker's tout, arriving to claim an aristocratic seat as Lord Hareford's heir. He brings his girl along; there are contrasted choruses of Cockneys and aristocrats, and in spite of one pernickety "old baronial bean," as the *London Observer* (December 19, 1937) sedately observed, "the clash of class is satisfactor-ily solved."

Me and My Girl won universal praise. The *Tatler* (August 17, 1938) called it "one of the best musical low comedies ever invented. . . . The book is naive but comic and full-bodied; the gags are vulgar but funny; and the tunes are as catching as the common cold." "Only a very super-ior person indeed," said the *London Times* (December 19, 1937) "could survey this bold spectacle without quickly thawing into a smile. It is the theatrical equivalent of those picture postcards which, when in the holiday mood, we send from the seaside to disturb our sedate acquaint-ances. The story is the perennially entertaining one of the urchin who suddenly finds himself among hoity-toity relations, and it is zestfully unfolded amid scenes loaded with the insignia of aristocracy."

The two main roles receive equal acclaim. "Mr. Graves", declared the *Sketch* (January 29, 1937) "endears us to the blood that runs blue, though the nose is red. He may be said in this piece to represent the aristocracy on its mellower side. There are severer faces. There are those who would tame Mr. Snibson and improve his manners. They gloriously fail." As the Cockney Snibson, Lupino Lane tumbles and somersaults downstairs in velvet and ermine. He sucks a Countess's cocktail through a straw. Asked "Will you help the Old Ladies Home?" Snibson inquires: "Have they got far to go?" He is continually putting his foot in his mouth. "Fortunately, bless the human heart" said James Agate in the *Times* (August 19, 1945) "there are some 'incongruities and fantastications' which are, so to speak, born funny."

The music made some of the critics praise Sullivan. Among the sprightly numbers is a Sextette for Servants. The songs include "You'll Find Us All", and the very popular "Doin' the Lambeth Walk", which gave birth to a new dance. The basic idea of *Me and My Girl* is old but sure-fire; it has been woven into a merry madcap musical, especially appealing to the English love of fun poked at the upper class.

CYRANO DE BERGERAC   *Edmond Rostand*

In the heart of the naturalistic movement in France, Edmond Rostand (French, 1868-1918) returned to the romantic verse drama. In 1897, after Sarah Bernhardt had starred in several of his plays, Rostand reached his peak when Coquelin the elder (Benoit Constant Coquelin; with his son Jean playing Rageneau) took the title part in the poetic drama that won the most enthusiastic popular reception in dramatic history: *Cyrano de Bergerac*.

The story of the play is based very loosely on the life of an actual French poet and soldier (1619-1655), a free-thinker, author of a few plays and of the satires *The States and Empires of the Moon* and—*of the Sun*. In the play, Cyrano is a long-nosed daredevil who, thinking himself too ugly for Roxane whom he loves, aids the inarticulate Christian to woo her. Cyrano writes Christian's love letters, and, in a superb balcony scene, whispers from the dark the poetic phrases that gain Christian entrance to Roxane's heart and to her chamber—while Cyrano below keeps off a noble rival. Christian dies in the wars. Many years later Roxane in her convent discovers, as Cyrano is dying, that he was the author of the letters, that his was the spirit she had always loved. Roxane sighs: "I loved but once, yet twice I lose my love." Cyrano's sense of inferiority he bends to his glory; his love leads to his sacrifice. Yet the final moment of ecstasy atones for a barren life-time. This is the acme of romance.

The story is presented in a style that recaptures both the swagger and the preciosity of the seventeenth century. Its verse mingles bombast and grandiloquence, the flourish and gallantry of D'Artagnan with the sadness and devotion of Don Quixote. The lightness of the period is caught in pastry-cook Rageneau, patron of poets. Its recklessness gleams on the clashing swords, as Cyrano composes a ballade while fighting a duel. The play is a colorful and consummate tapestry of Romance, beneath its care-free bravado playing a quiet undertone of sacrifice and sadness. (This undertone is to be noted also in Rostand's later plays, *L'Aiglon** and *Chantecler**.)

Opening in Paris on December 28, 1897, the play ran for 200 nights to great public and critical acclaim. The usually severe Francisque Sarcey called it "an admirable work, a work of marvelous poetry, but

especially and before all a masterpiece of the theatre." *Le Théâtre*
(January 1898) said that Rostand "has the triple merit of being remarkably witty, thoroughly dramatic, and entirely clear."

Within the year, there were many productions of *Cyrano* in Europe
and the United States. One in Philadelphia and one in New York opened
on the same night, September 28, 1898: the former in an Augustin Daly
version, with Ada Rehan and Tyrone Power; the latter in a version by
Howard Thayer Kingsbury, with Richard Mansfield and Margaret
Anglin. The *New York Dramatic Mirror* called the Kingsbury adaptation "nothing more than a romantic melodrama abounding in all sorts
of theatrical tricks".

The play was a great success everywhere. Sarah Bernhardt and
Coquelin played it in French in New York, opening December 10, 1900.
Almost a dozen English versions have been produced; the most popular
of these is that of Brian Hooker, in sometimes pedestrian but often
swashbuckling, witty, or tender verse. This version was used by Walter
Hampden, who opened as Cyrano on November 1, 1923, and gave his
thousandth performance of the part on May 18, 1936. The *New York
Times,* after the opening, called Hampden's "a production thoroughly
worthy of his ambition, which is the highest. . . . It would be difficult
to exaggerate its charm for all who love humor and fancy, the thrill
of valiant deeds and the glamour of romantic love, enveloped in an
atmosphere of poetic eloquence and shot through by the lightning flash
of wit". The *Telegram* declared: "Here are romance and heroism,
beauty and poetry. Mr. Hampden has made a production of such beauty
that it easily surpasses Mansfield's and Coquelin's alike." Whatever the
merits of the playing, there is no question of the perennial power of
the play.

Cyrano de Bergerac was made into an opera by Walter Damrosch and
William J. Henderson, performed in Chicago and at the New York
Metropolitan in 1913 and revived at Carnegie Hall, with Pasquale Amato
and Frances Alda, in 1938. It was twice reshaped as a musical comedy,
the better version with music by Victor Herbert, book by Stuart Reed,
lyrics by Harry B. Smith, and Lew Fields as the comic Cyrano.

Of the many later productions of the play, most notable in English
is that with Jose Ferrer, in the Brian Hooker version, which opened
in New York October 8, 1946. The revival was heartily welcomed.
Robert Garland said: "When a great play meets a great performance,
that's good news on Broadway"; Robert Coleman, "For our money,
Cyrano de Bergerac is the greatest theatre piece ever penned"; and
Louis Kronenberger, "Rostand's play offers all those dashing, pathetic,
impossibly romantic things for which the human heart secretly hungers;
offers them in abundance, moreover, and offers them with authority."

After a London production (October 25, 1946) by the Old Vic with
Ralph Richardson, Harold Hobson of the *Sunday Times* contrasted Brian
Hooker's "pedestrian translation" with the original: "Those verses are
swift and delightful, their rhymes are marvels of cleverness, they are
both clever and musical, they entrance with their beauty, and they
make one laugh." Hobson also reminds us that, as the French critic
Lemaitre pointed out, *Cyrano* is full of reminiscences: the tumultuous
opening recalls Gautier; the cake-shop, with Cyrano displaying a heart

as tender as his sword is sharp, is redolent of Hugo; the scene with Roxane at the war-camp might have been drawn by Dumas; the attempted self-sacrifice of Christian—matching Cyrano's great-heartedness—has parallels in Alfred de Musset. "To a French audience, then, *Cyrano* is not only a pleasure in itself, but a means of recalling other pleasures. It is a recollection as well as an experience, and combines a crowded and agreeable past with a most acceptable present." Even to those without these prior associations, *Cyrano* is a continuing delight.

Before World War II, *Le Miroir du Monde,* in Paris, asked its men readers which literary hero they would like most to be; the women, which hero they liked most. The first three choices coincided: the men chose Cyrano by a hundred votes over Jean Valjean, with D'Artagnan a close third; the woman chose Cyrano by a clear 1500. Cyrano would probably be the choice in other lands as well. Rhetoric and rue combine in the madcap part, the gallant, grand-manner picture of the grand century, in what Brooks Atkinson has called "the cloak-and-doggerel vein"—in what, next to Hamlet, is the theatre's most popular part: the romantic hero that gives his name to *Cyrano de Bergerac.*

L' AIGLON   *Edmond Rostand*

The battle of Wagram against the Austrians (1809) was the bloodiest of all Napoleon's battles, with a loss of some 25,000 men on each side. As part of the consequent treaty of Schoenbrun, Napoleon married Maria Louisa, daughter of Emperor Francis of Austria. The son of this union, the Duke of Reichstadt, was raised at the court of Francis, and kept without education by Metternich who, before a mirror, used to show the Duke that he had inherited, not the strength of Napoleon, but the indecision and impotence of the Hapsburgs. Followers of Napoleon, disguised as servants, sought to fledge the eaglet *(l' aiglon)* in his father's memory. Edmond Rostand's play, *L' Aiglon,* pictures these scenes and the flight of the Duke toward France, his night on the Wagram battlefield—where he ponders the cost of ambition in blood and tears, as Napoleon's dead forces arise in the princeling's vision—his capture, and his pining death at the gay and trivial court.

When the play opened in Paris March 15, 1900, with Sarah Bernhardt in the title role, Anatole France, Victorien Sardou, Jules Lemaitre, and the elder Coquelin were in the audience. Also in the audience were Dreyfusards, Nationalists, Monarchists, and many that cherished the memory of "the little corporal", each group ready to shout its partisan feelings.

The Duke of Reichstadt was twenty years old, Sarah Bernhardt, fifty-six. It was an opening fraught with more than the usual terrors. The Englishman Maurice Baring reported: "I have never witnessed a more authentic triumph on the stage. I never saw before or since an audience which was prepared to be hostile so suddenly and completely vanquished. . . . It was one of the greatest feats that has ever been achieved in the history of the stage".

In America, Maude Adams opened as "the eaglet" in Baltimore on October 15, 1900, coming to New York in November just before Sarah Bernhardt and Coquelin (as Flambeau). Bernhardt played the role in New York again in 1906 and 1910. Other revivals include one in 1927, with Michael Strange (Mrs. John Barrymore); 1929, with Alexander Kirkland; 1934, Eva Le Gallienne as L' Aiglon, and Ethel Barrymore as the Duchess of Parma; and 1946 (Equity Library). Adaptations have been made by Louis N. Parker, Basil Davenport, and Clemence Dane; the last, used in 1934, considerably shortens the role of the old Napoleonic soldier Flambeau, omitting a poignant scene, Flambeau's attempt to teach the young Duke the art of war, with wooden soldiers.

There is a natural pathos in the story of the wistful, thoughtful young man who regretted at once the devastation his father had spread and the loss of his father's glory. Partly, perhaps, for its political implications, for the patriotic fervor it roused through its presentation of the many nations' pact against Napoleon, French critics have deemed L' Aiglon superior to Cyrano de Bergerac*, in poetically imaginative construction and dialogue, in subtlety of character portrayal, in theatrical effectiveness. Outside of France, Cyrano is generally considered Rostand's greatest play; but L' Aiglon is recognized as rich in beauty, powerful, and poignant.

In London, the Times pointed out (June 14, 1901) that Rostand sought "to make an epoch of history live again, not only on its psychological but also on its visible side. . . . Quite half of the drama is devoted to the pictorial side of the tragedy. The immense number of characters and accessories serve to heighten the effect rather by their appeal to the eye than by their appeal to the brain." In New York, Town Topics, looking back over 100 years, called the play "the most beautiful drama of the century".

In 1934, the play still held its power. The New York American (November 4, 1934) averred: "Time cannot wither it, nor slapdash adaptations turn its hair too grey. It is still one of the world's plays magnificent." Robert Garland called it "a masterpiece in the red plush of its period." Brooks Atkinson felt that the play seemed clothed in "the fustian garments of an earlier period of theatricals." John Mason Brown saw in it an "easy pathos and somewhat tarnished grandeur", but felt its strong appeal as "a thing of big, old-fashioned scenes that hit shamelessly below the belt, of canvas and of greasepaint, of Sardoodledum set to song, of melodious verse and creaking melodramatics, of tall rhetoric and full blown romanticism."

With a sad sweet savoring of nostalgia, most in the audience can readily enter into that dream of a glorious past, shining overbrightly against a dull and imprisoning present. Yet the Duke himself is weighted with more complex feelings, as he longs for a renewal of the glory but emotionally shrinks from the bloodshed involved, and morally lacks the strength of will required to re-establish the broad empire and wide spread of love his father had won. This half-deliberate, half-driven acquiescence in his doom gives to the final moments of the play not the lift of tragic grandeur but the drift of pathos, as the Duke, dying hopeless in Vienna, has read to him the description of his bright christening in Paris. We find pity in the spectacle of a man not risen to the measure of his days. Yet in that uncertain balance of mind and heart and will, L' Aiglon has measured a basic problem of mankind, showing through the eaglet how—and how high—we all may hope to soar, but also the cost and value of our dreams.

CHANTECLER   *Edmond Rostand*

When ill health sent Edmond Rostand to the Basque countryside, in 1899, there came to him the idea of using the birds of the farm to capture something of mankind, "to express my own dreams and to make live, before my eyes, a little of myself." Illness intervened again and again. He told the idea to Coquelin in 1905; the play was ready for rehearsal in 1909, when Coquelin suddenly died. *Chantecler* finally opened in Paris, with Lucien Guitry in the title part, on February 7, 1910, to one of the most brilliant—and most expectant—audiences in the history of the theatre. In New York, despite the eagerness of Sarah Bernhardt and Olga Nethersole, both friends of Rostand, Charles Frohman gave the role of Chantecler to Maude Adams.

In both countries the production was a disappointment. The reason was well put in the *New York Tribune* (January 25, 1911): "The piece loses immensely in the playing. The actors, masked and hampered by their feathers and beaks and claws—only the principals show their faces, and gesturing is of course impossible—are neither one thing nor the other. Comparatively few of their lines get across as they should, and much of the play's poetry and dramatic quality is untranslatable into the visual terms required by the stage." To dwarf the humans to bird size, they are shown against gigantic properties and sets; but something of the play's seriousness and profundity seems also dwarfed thereby.

When read, the play reveals a brilliance that no production has yet captured; a witty satire of mankind, and a proud tribute to humanity withal. A special *Chantecler* number of *Le Théâtre* (No. 268, February 12, 1910) looked beneath the feathers for the heart of the story. The cock, who knows that his crowing wakes the sun, who recaptures his faith even after the hen-pheasant has made him over-sleep the dawn: he is "the Gallic cock", the embodiment of the French love of order. Said Nozière: "He wants to protect the brains of his countrymen from obscurity, and from bad taste. He wants to set society beyond reach of disorder. Never has a more nationalistic piece been written. Yet M. Rostand belongs to no party. There is in his work no bitterness nor hate. His allegorical hero is as resigned to the ingratitude of the many as is Jesus. . . . The play is a hymn to enthusiasm, nature, tradition, work. . . . *Chantecler* defends the French tradition against the foreign and the foreigner. . . . Never has he found accents more human than in this play devoted to the beasts."

Coquelin had seen Chantecler as a creature of gaiety; vain, but buoyant; inventive, a resourceful observer. Guitry interpreted Chantecler as a believer in work, as a thinker, a creature of gravity, a lover of beauty. Maude Adams tried to combine these interpretations, but essentially to show that one must "do one's work, though it cost one's love and one's life." Max Beerbohm felt that Guitry was too steadily grave: "For Chantecler is a dual part. The cock is at once a great figure and a figure of fun." When the sun rises without his summons, "Chantecler, though troubled, is undismayed. The sun, he reassures himself, has risen in answer to the still resounding echoes of some previous day's song. There is grandeur in the thought, as in all the thoughts of Chantecler; but the grandeur of Chantecler is the measure of his grotesqueness."

That grotesqueness, but also that grandeur, gleam in the spirit of man. There is the rivalry of the sexes in the play: the quiet victory of the female; and the complacent self-assurance of the male that turns defeat into a greater triumph. There is a satiric picture of the French people. But beyond these—through the Gallic sense of order that shadows man's attempt to cope with the mysteries of the universe; through the vanity that cloaks man's erection of his powers against nature's driving force—*Chantecler* is a wise and witty, a smiling and searching, a tender and revealing drama of the human spirit in search of beauty and truth.

ABRAHAM   *Roswitha*

The Benedictine nun Roswitha (also Hrotsvitha, a German of the tenth century), was moved to write Christian dramas in Latin in order "to glorify, within the limits of my poor talent, the laudable chastity of Christian virgins in that self-same form of composition which had been used to describe the shameless acts of licentious women." Her plays must have startled the sober men—not to mention her fellow-nuns —of the Middle Ages. To her contemporaries she explained: "I have been compelled through the nature of this work to apply my mind and my pen to depicting the dreadful frenzy of those possessed by unlawful love, and the insidious sweetness of passion—things that should not even be named among us. Yet if from modesty I had refrained from treating these subjects, I should never have been able to attain my object—to the best of my ability to glorify the innocent. For the more seductive the blandishments of lovers, the more wonderful the divine succor and the greater the merit of those that resist, especially when it is fragile woman that is victorious, and strong man that is routed with confusion." With this pious intent, Roswitha wrote six plays, about the year 980.

In her *Paphnutius,* with vivacious dialogue, is one of the earliest tellings of the Thais story, wrought into a novel by Anatole France. It was played in London in 1914, and published in English translation in 1923. Three of Roswitha's plays were produced in New York March 28, 1926: *Callimachus, Dulcitius* and *Abraham. Abraham* was shown in New York again in the edifice of the Church of St. Ignatius Loyola in 1934.

This drama is the story of the redemption of an erring Mary, who has run away and lived a life of sin for two years. The holy father Abraham, whose ward she has been, enters the brothel disguised as a soldier, and brings her forth again, repentant, to a holy life.

The play is written in simple, unstilted, very effective Latin, with truly dramatic scenes. "A thousand years have robbed her of her strength," said John Mason Brown in the *New York Post* (December 17, 1934). "But they have not robbed her of her charm, her intensity, her simplicity, or her desperate earnestness." The plays of Roswitha were modeled upon those of Terence, which were read in the Middle Ages, but not performed. *Abraham* is the most vivid and the most touching of her works, which are the one dramatic product of the millennium between the classical theatre and the mystery and miracle plays that heralded the new drama of the Renaissance.

THE FAIR PENITENT   *Nicholas Rowe*

Nicholas Rowe (English, 1674-1718) was an important influence in the English theatre. His 1709 edition of Shakespeare's plays was the first to divide them into acts and scenes, and to provide stage directions. He also wrote eight plays; *Jane Shore**, and *The Fair Penitent*, 1703, are remembered. They give Mrs. Siddons two of her best acting parts.

The Fair Penitent was constantly revived until well into the nineteenth century. Garrick's first benefit marked his first appearance in the play, as Lothario, which became one of his favorite roles. New York first saw the play at the Nassau Street Theatre, December 31, 1750. The play is memorable not only for its contemporary popularity but because of four more lasting characteristics. This tragedy in blank verse turned from the fate of kings and queens and—in the words of Nicholas Rowe, who quite knowingly initiated the change—presented "a melancholy tale of private woes." Secondly, the play is an early specimen of what we might call the lachrymose drama, inducing not the dry-eyed emotional deeps of great tragedy, but torrents of tears from audiences that indulged in an emotional debauch with "soft, complaining Rowe." In the third place, it presents a character study of a heartless libertine who is nonetheless alluring, that has given a term to the language, the haughty, gallant, "gay Lothario". Finally, *The Fair Penitent* is a landmark in the dramatic presentation of women's rights; in the championing of the equality of the sexes it is almost the only play in two thousand years, passing the torch on from *Medea** to *A Doll's House**.

The story is taken from *The Fatal Dowry*, 1632, by Massinger and Fields, with changes of names and some details of action. In Rowe's play, Sciolto bestows his daughter Calista upon Altamont. She has already fallen in love with Lothario, who pursues his advances. Altamont, surprising the guilty pair, kills Lothario in a duel. Sciolto condemns Calista, but when Altamont kills her, upbraids him for showing no mercy. Altamont is tried for his actions; acquitted, he is killed by a friend of Lothario.

In its century of production the play received highest praise. Samuel Johnson declared: "There is scarcely any work of any poet at once so interesting by the fable, and so delightful by the language." The *London Public Advertiser* (November 10, 1788) felt "that breast must be hard indeed which can resist the griefs of the unhappy fair one." Earlier, however, the same paper (April 13, 1785) had other thoughts of the "fair penitent": "Calista gives a name to the play that does not properly belong to herself; for she shows rather shame than penitence, and does not seem to feel pain because she has been guilty, but because she has been detected." Johnson shared this callous opinion of Calista's conscience. That earlier issue of the *Public Advertiser* thought well of the play as a whole: ". . . perhaps one of the most pleasing tragedies of the English stage. The incidents in general are natural and credible; the story is domestic, and therefore interesting; and the language is judiciously varied according to the situations, but everywhere exquisitely harmonious."

The gay Lothario, whom some think presented "more pleasingly than a villain ever should be drawn", boasts of his success with the fair Calista. Even in his death, Lothario is light-hearted; the grave has no victory. In Calista's defense, it must be remembered that she was in love with her suitor Lothario when her father snatched her away to bestow her upon Altamont. She laments a woman's early years, subject to a father's discipline, and her later years, victim of a husband's tyranny; and she cries out for independence. Here, after *Medea*, is the first swinging of the doll's house door that Nora closed.

As one of the most popular dramas of its time, as a pioneer play in its tearful type and in its women's rights theme, and for its creation of a character whose name is now the general term for such a man, *The Fair Penitent* has fair claim to distinction.

JANE SHORE   *Nicholas Rowe*

The beautiful and witty Jane Shore (died 1527)—wife of a London goldsmith, mistress of Edward IV, accused of witchcraft and forced to public penance in 1483—has been the subject of several literary works. Chief among these is Nicholas Rowe's tragedy, which opened in London on February 2, 1714, and remained a favorite for almost two hundred years. New York saw it first at the new Nassau Street Theatre, March 4, 1754. W. G. Wills made a version of the drama that ran in London, opening September 30, 1876, for 116 performances and, in revival November 24, 1877, for 162 more. The play was popular enough in 1894 to evoke the burlesque *Jaunty Jane Shore,* by Richard Henry (Richard Butler and H. Chance Newton). Among those that have acted in the play are David Garrick and Mrs. Cibber, 1758; Mrs. Siddons, 1789; William Macready and Helen Faucit, 1837; Junius Brutus Booth, and Charles Kemble. Mrs. Siddons declared that the most effective line she ever uttered was Jane's exclamation: " 'Twas he! 'Twas Hastings!''

The play complicates the action through the passing love of Hastings for the Lady Alicia who, when his desires turn from her to Jane Shore, denounces both to the suspicious ears of Gloucester. Jane has repulsed Hastings, but jealousy plagues Alicia on. Hastings is ordered killed, and Alicia goes mad. Jane is condemned to walk the streets clad only in a sheet, with death the penalty for giving her shelter or food. Her husband—who, disguised as Dumont, has been serving Jane throughout her prosperity—comes in his own guise to succor her; he is arrested, and Jane dies in his forgiving arms. Hastings and Alicia, said the *London Chronicle* (November 7-9, 1758) "are pillars which while they add to the beauty, are absolutely necessary to the support, of the fable, and not like those little abominable Gothick nothings which we, nowadays, see foisted into the structure of every dramatic poem, without being either ornamental or useful."

The chief interest in the play is the character of Jane Shore, in the picture of whom the poet improves on the historian. She is a sympathetic figure. As Samuel Johnson says, "the wife is forgiven because she repents, and the husband is honored because he forgives." "There was a plaintive sweetness in her early scenes", the *London Theatrical Observer* (January 3, 1837) said of Helen Faucit as Jane, "exactly in accordance with the poet's portraiture of the repentant fair one; her vindication of the rights of the children of her royal paramour was finely impassioned, and her death scene was uncommonly effective: it affected the imagination without shocking the senses." Jane is made still more appealing in an adaptation of Rowe's play by Mrs. Vance Thompson and Lena R. Smith, which came to New York March 27, 1905; for this pictured her not as King Edward's willing mistress, but forced into submission to his lust. Thus the *Sun* saw her as a "tender woman who has repented of a compulsory sin, and who afterward, because of her steadfast fidelity to duty, is persecuted, starved, exposed to the rigors of wintry weather, and slowly and cruelly driven to the final agony of heartbreak and death. The component attitudes of the character are simplicity, gentleness, innate goodness, and the capability of heroic endurance."

In simple blank verse that, while rarely exalted, is seldom bombastic, *Jane Shore* combines the surging qualities of a chroncle play with searching and sympathetic character portrayal.

THE TRUTH SUSPECTED   *Ruiz de Alarcón*

The hunchback Mexican Juan Ruiz de Alarcón y Mendoza (1581?-1639) had a difficult time indeed in early seventeenth century Spain. Educated in Salamanca, Alarcón went back to Mexico to practice law; then came as a "suitor to the court" in Madrid. Failing to find favor there, he supported himself as a playwright.

In the 1620's, when King Philip IV was an active patron of the theatre, the plays of the time were the periodicals of the people— their news, their editorials, their comics. Dramas were composed by the hundreds, and pirated by "memorizers" at a single performance.

Ruiz de Alarcón worked more slowly, but also more soundly, than most of his fellow dramatists. In a decade, he wrote twenty plays (eight were published in 1628 and twelve in 1634); then he was given a post as reporter for the Council of the Indies; and he wrote no more plays. But during that crowded decade his plays were widely stolen— "some", he remarked, "have become the feathers of other crows".

Cruelly reviled by his rival contemporaries, this Mexican hunchback nevertheless created the comedy of manners in Spain. He turned from the artificial and far-fetched to the natural and human, which he presented simply, naturally, and always with dramatic effectiveness. "His dialogue rises to pinnacles of unrivalled perfection", Alfonso Reyes has observed, "his characters . . . are men of the world; their feet are planted on the solid earth".

The Truth Suspected, published 1634, was among the plays of Ruiz de Alarcón pirated and printed as by other authors. It treats of a young man, Don Garcia, brought back from his student days in Salamanca to his father's house. But he has "too much of the milk of Salamanca on his lips"; the young man is an inveterate liar. He lies himself into a duel, then out of it. He lies when he falls in love with a passing fair lady, Jacinta. Trying to learn her name, he is given the name of her friend, Lucrezia; when the ladies discover his extravagant stories, they permit the confusion of names to continue. Don Garcia's father, Don Beltran, wants to arrange a match between Jacinta and his son. But the boy lies to his father also; and his falsehoods so entangle the situation that Jacinta is betrothed to Don Garcia's friend Don Juan, and Don Garcia—his final efforts to tell the truth coming too late—is forced to take second best with Lucrezia. The last words of the play press home the point: "in the mouth of an habitual liar, one finds the truth suspected".

The character of Don Garcia is clearly and cleverly drawn. Save for his incorrigible preference for a tall tale over an unadorned exactitude, he is a worthy young man. After lying himself out of the duel, he starts to fight it, for his honor. His love itself is sincere; the initial confusion of women was not his, although his fabrications tightened the tangle. The other characters, too, are natural. The two girls are deftly distinguished; as are Lucrezia's father and Don Garcia's. Jacinta catches the spirit of love in a gentle but searching comment—quite refreshing in a woman of those formal days. When Don Garcia asks if he may address his love to her, she responds "The heart loves without permission".

Corneille's best comedy, The Liar, 1643, was based on Alarcón's play. Steele based his comedy The Lying Lover, 1703, on Corneille's, and Molière told his friend Boileau that without The Liar he would never have written The Misanthrope*.

The Truth Suspected was published in the American quarterly Poet-Lore (Winter, 1927) in a translation by Julio del Toro and Robert W. Finney. It still holds its amusing qualities, lightly pressing its lesson as does life itself in its more pleasant moods, allowing us to be thoughtful with a smile.

CHANGE FOR THE BETTER   *Ruiz de Alarcón*

This fresh comedy about the deceiver deceived, published in 1634, is replete with effective scenes, lively repartee, tender dialogue, and felicity of expression.

The play pictures Leonor, a piquant flower of Seville, come to the guardianship of her young widowed aunt Dona Clara, in Madrid. It is their hope that Leonor, who has birth and beauty but no funds to match, will win a happy marriage. But city men have other designs on fresh young country girls. Don Garcia, whom Clara loves but has kept dangling, is caught by the new sparkling eyes of Leonor. When the maid reproaches him for turning from her aunt, Garcia answers that he is merely making a change for the better. For a time Leonor is held by Garcia's protestations of love; the two even invent a sign language (akin to the device in Calderon's later El Secreta à voces: The Open Secret) by which to communicate in Clara's presence. Soon, however, Leonor sees through Garcia; and she uses him to make a marquis, who also is seeking to seduce her, propose marriage instead. When Garcia reproaches her for fickleness, she replies that she is merely making a change for the better.

Alarcón naturally made use of the devices of the theatre of the day. Among these was the aside to the audience, as in the maid's last words: "She's paying him in his own coin." But Alarcón had a greater care for verisimilitude than his contemporaries, and wrapped his ideas in a warm cloak of human nature. He was preoccupied with ethical concerns; but these never turned his better dramas into sermons, while they did give them a richer basis and a stronger theme. Thus, observed Antonio Gil de Zarate, it is the consensus of Spanish critics that Ruiz de Alarcón is "not so fertile as Lope* nor so poetic as Calderon*, but has more depth, more taste, and finer moral standards." The popularity of Alarcón's plays drew the envy and attacks of his fellow-playwrights, but *Change For the Better* continued to draw the public for many years.

No other Spanish dramatist has such elegant and such concise language, so effectively wrought in dramatic dialogue that is vivacious, pungent, provocative, and pleasing. These qualities of dialogue, with freshness and ingenuity of character portrayal, are eminent in *Change For the Better*.

NIGHTS OF WRATH   *Armand Salacrou*

Those familiar with the early plays of Armand Salacrou (French, b. 1900) would not have expected—without the transforming ordeal of war—such a tense drama as *Nights of Wrath*. Known first in literature as a surrealist poet, Salacrou suggested: "Since order is bankrupt, let us try disorder . . . It will lead us to the great secret, perhaps". Following this surrealist trail, Salacrou developed the manner that has been called fantastic realism. A Fourth-of-July pin-wheel shoots out sparks, symbols, monsters, dreamers—flaming tangents of images, ideas, events; always in the center is the whirling core of reality.

Salacrou emerged from World War II declaring that "one must write with one's guts". His subsequent work has been highly realistic; though it does not avoid the use of the supernatural, it probes more directly the serious problems of the day. So grim is Salacrou's approach, indeed, that he has been called "the dramatist of dread". Most searching of his plays is *Nights of Wrath,* 1946, in which Jean Louis Barrault starred in Paris, and which was given a stirring production in New York by the Dramatic Workshop, Maria Piscator directing, opening November 30, 1947.

The play begins with some dead men coming to life. They are members of the French underground, with one *attentiste* (not a collaborator, but one that lifts a finger neither way, waiting to discover how the evils will end). These awakened dead challenge one another and the living to defend their course of action. The play is their story. Bernard Bazire has given shelter to a life-long friend, who stumbles in wounded, after having blown up a German supply train near Chartres. Bazire's wife, sent for a doctor, comes back with a collaborationist; in his train come the Gestapo, and death.

As this story is unfolded, we follow the motives of each person, and see—and see through—the various attempts at self-justification. The author exposes; he does not condemn. And through the drama the troubling question of personal responsibility, of human integrity and human guilt, is sharply posed. The New York production made the movement vivid with a two level setting; at first this is the living room and the upstairs hall of Bazire's house; then, the ground and the railway trestle over which the supply train is to pass; in final transformation, a prison cell.

After this production, Arthur Pollock called Salacrou "a shrewd playwright and a knowing man". Brooks Atkinson stated that the play "relives some of the physical and spiritual tortures of the French underground resistance in 1944 and draws a scornful line between those who risked their lives and those who tried to preserve a safe private neu-

trality. . . . His topic is real, his characters vigorous and his attitude
valid; and the improvised form of his story is absorbing and illuminating". *Nights of Wrath* through the tense story of war-torn individuals,
probes basic and universal problems of human conduct and the constant challenge life flings to the spirit of man.

A SCRAP OF PAPER   *Victorien Sardou*

The plays of Victorien Sardou (French, 1831-1908) are among the
most skilfuly constructed. His persons are not deeply probed; they inhabit an imaginary land of constant intrigue that Shaw scornfully called
Sardoodledum; but they move swiftly through plots dexterously pointed
to an exciting climax; and they hold the audience. The situations Sardou
developed in his stories have been watered down through several generations of lesser plays and motion pictures, until his dramas themselves
come upon us as a gathered store of echoes. Despite this, Sardou's "well-
made" plays will, like old houses, outlast many imitations of the new
commercial breed.

Best of Sardou's comedies of love and intrigue is *Les Pattes de
Mouche*, 1860 (*Fly-Tracks; The Scrawl*), best known in English as *A
Scrap of Paper*. It presents the complications that follow the return of
Prosper Block from a round-the-world trip to forget Clarisse, who has
married a Dutch millionaire, Van Hoven. For Prosper learns that
Clarisse had written a letter offering to elope with him—and the letter
still exists. The remainder of the play depicts the efforts of Suzanne
to recover the letter for her friend Clarisse and the jealousy of Van
Hoven, which link an amusing chain of events until finally Van Hoven
himself, thinking that he is saving a friend, burns the compromising
letter, and Prosper and Suzanne recognize that they are in love.

Although *A Scrap of Paper* provides its opening exposition through
the pre-Ibsenic device of servants chatting as they dust the furniture
(as plays today might use the telephone), it moves with unerring directness through amusing vicissitudes too intricate for detailing. "It is
still alive", said *Vogue* (June 15, 1914) "because it was well made; and
this excellence of craftsmanship has triumphed over its inherent emptiness of content, and preserved it for the entertainment of the public of
today. . . . It may be that ideas change (as human bodies are said to do)
every seven years or so; but artistry endures even through countless
generations." The "emptiness" of which the critic complained (on the
brink of a World War) is a lack of "social significance"; most of the
vases in the great museums are empty. *A Scrap of Paper*, if you wish
it, has a moral: Never make love through an ink-well. Its people are
natural; if not fully rounded, humans: granted the initial situation,
they react with natural feelings; and they are borne on a swift current
of action that carries the audience in equal expectant flow.

A success in Paris, *A Scrap of Paper* repeated its triumph in London,
opening April 22, 1861; the revivals of March 11, 1876 and December 20,
1883 both attained 120 performances; and there were many others up to
1914. In New York, Lester Wallack played *A Scrap of Paper* in 1879,
again in 1884; Mr. and Mrs. Kendal had it in their repertory from 1889
to 1902. In 1905, Henrietta Crosman appeared in a play *Mary, Mary,
Quite Contrary*, by Eugene W. Presbery, which was *A Scrap of Paper*

transferred to an American setting. As the *Boston Transcript* (October 17, 1906) pointed out: "The two plays are identical in plot, incidents, characters, and dialogue." The *Transcript* spoke of the effective manner in which Sardou snares the audience in the emotions of the play, and his skilful construction and rapidly moving story: "These qualities are sufficient to make the play—even Mr. Presbery's play—satisfy the most exacting audience."

Such copies, and even more frequent imitations, and the borrowing of devices such as those Sardou fashioned for the letter hide-and-seek, have made *A Scrap of Paper* so familiar that in a motion picture report in 1930, Bertram Bloch called the play "old-fashioned in its plot ramifications"—but he added "there is still a suspenseful story in the play."

Sardou's comedy *A Scrap of Paper* is his supreme example of the drama of love intrigue, which at times reaches to genuine depths of emotion, but for most of its entertaining course plays, with artifice and carefully devised tensions, laughingly along the never-smooth runways of true love.

DORA   *Victorien Sardou*

There are few plays that for sweep of action cleverly contrived, in commingled political and amatory intrigue, can match Sardou's *Dora,* 1877. Its tangle of spies in double-dealing twist of innocence was timely in two countries; for France was still aquiver with passion and suspicion after the German 1870 seizure of Alsace-Lorraine; and in England there was sharp division of opinion in the quarrel between Turkey and Russia, with eastern politics in every issue of the papers, and intrigue buzzing in every conversation. Sardou's play, then, as *Dora* in France and as *Diplomacy* in England, had both circumstance and construction in its favor. Its power has long outlasted the immediate events.

The play pictures Dora, beautiful daughter of the Marquise de Rio Zares, newly married to Captain Julian Beauclerc, who soon comes to suspect that the two women are Russian spies. Unwilling at first to believe, Julian is indignant, excited, then—convinced by the evidence —mortified, crushed. He reproaches Dora, but promises to forgive her if she will confess; Dora, in a grief that rises toward hysteria as she beats upon the locked door, protests her innocence. Through the neat work of Julian's diplomat brother Henry, and the trail of a woman's perfume, Dora's innocence is established. The guilty one is the Countess Zicka, who is not only a spy but a passionate woman; she too had desired Julian, and in jealous revenge was seeking to destroy Dora. With the Countess and the Russian agent, Count Stein, foiled, Julian and Dora resume their honeymoon.

The movement of the plot is indicated by the quotations that precede the four acts of the English version. I: "Man's love is of man's life a thing apart, 'Tis woman's whole existence" (Byron)—as Dora is absorbed in her love, but Julian is occupied also with international affairs: II: "Mark, now, how a plain tale shall put you down" (Shakespeare)—as the wiles of the Countess convince Julian of Dora's spying. III: "But hither shall I never come again; Never lie by thy side; see thee no more." (Tennyson)—as Julian breaks with the bewildered Dora. IV:

"What do you call the play? The Mousetrap? Marry, how?" (Shakespeare)—as the Countess is caught, and all is happily adjusted.

Dora is not only a turbulent and swiftly moving play; it offers superb acting opportunities. Clement Scott went to Paris to see it, then with B. C. Stephenson wrote the English version, *Diplomacy,* which opened in London, January 12, 1878, with Mr. and Mrs. Kendal and Mr. and Mrs. Bancroft (the producers) for a run of 329 performances. Among London revivals are those of November 8, 1884; February 18, 1893, for 175 performances; March 26, 1915, with Gerald du Maurier, Lady Tree, and Gladys Cooper, for 455 performances; March 8, 1924, with Gladys Cooper again, 365 performances; May 28, 1933, with Gerald du Maurier, Basil Rathbone, and Margaret Bannerman as Dora in a dress noted for its tremendous train. Coming to New York, April 1, 1878, with Lester Wallack and Rose Coghlan, *Diplomacy* won an equally brilliant series of revivals. These included one of 1894, with Maxine Elliott; April 15, 1901, with Guy Standing, William Faversham, Charles Rickman, Margaret Anglin, and Mrs. Thomas Whiffen; 1910 with Faversham, Anglin, and Chrystal Herne; October 20, 1914, with Blanche Bates (Countess Zicka) and William Gillette; and a fiftieth anniversary 1928 production with Faversham, Anglin, Frances Starr, Cecilia Loftus, Jacob Ben-Ami, Helen Cahagan, Rollo Peters, Tyrone Power, and Charles Coburn. *Diplomacy* continues to be frequently performed in stock.

The power of *Diplomacy* was at once recognized. After the London premiere, the *Athenaeum* compared the English version with the original: "Three changes of importance are made. The first is an omission. A scene in which the heroine receives dishonoring proposals from a certain Stramir is described in narrative instead of in action. The man to whom the discovery of the true criminal is ascribable is the brother of the hero, instead of being a friend. He is also presented as a much more serious character. In the concluding scenes, some sympathy is elicited for the woman whose disloyal and nefarious action is the cause of the catastrophe. These alterations are but a portion of those that are made. They are, however, typical. The first is regrettable, but indispensable, if the play is to be reduced into four acts; the second strengthens the morale of the piece, as well as its interest; the third is wrong, and is a concession to English weakness." In general, the five-act *Dora* (although presented in German in New York in 1897-98, and occasionally revived in French), has been supplanted by the more compact *Diplomacy.*

In New York, William Winter wrote on April 2, 1878, that "the originality is in the web of the intrigue. The form . . . is more admirable than its substance." In 1901, save for his words of the cast, Winter reprinted his review of twenty-three years before. Glancing across the years, we may select three other typical comments. The *London Telegraph* (February 8, 1878) declared: "This clever Sardou drama of ruse and subterfuge, of wit versus wit, and tangle versus tangle, seems strangely delightful." More analytically, the *London Times* (May 29, 1933) commented: "It is a genuine pleasure to see a play that fully and frankly uses the stage. Whether we are in the Monte Carlo hotel or in Beauclerc's Paris flat or in his room at the Embassy, almost every commonplace object in front of our eyes is at one time or another called in to aid illusion. A heap of visiting cards and a photograph help to clarify the exposition; a souvenir that the bride receives and a formal letter that she dashes off on the eve of her honeymoon are the evidence that convicts her of treachery; the papers on a desk and the trail of scent that clings to them bring about her vindication; and even out of a harmless, necessary door Sardou hammers out one of the scenes that are by tradition 'great' and in revival are immensely effective still. Modern dramatists have come closer to the reality of things than this extraordinarily clever workman ever tried to come, but they, even when their need is greatest, can seldom make story and stage so much one and the same thing as they are in *Diplomacy*. . . . This typical Sardou piece proved itself quite capable of absorbing a modern audience in its entanglements and its glamorous intensification of character and passion." There is little character analysis in the play; but a surging emotional power, through tensely wrought situations that tangle personal concerns with international affairs, and a swift undeviant movement toward its neatly accomplished close, make *Dora—Diplomacy*—a play long glamorous and still effective in the theatre.

Sardon re-used so many of his successful situations that Shaw referred to his work as *Toscadora*. The many epistles in his plays—handwriting, postmark, paper, perfume, each aiding the plot—mark his best claim to being a man of letters. He was a competent man of the theatre.

LA TOSCA   *Victorien Sardou*

The most successful plays of Sardou were the surging historical dramas of flaming passions and swift violence. With vivid stage effects, often wild stir of crowds, and always a touch of comedy, he built widely successful melodramas, often written for a particular star: Pauline Virginie Déjazet, Sarah Bernhardt, Henry Irving. One of the most gripping of such dramas, written for Bernhardt, is *La Tosca*, 1887.

The action of the play takes place in Rome about 1800, during the alarm and high feeling there after Napoleon's victory at Marengo. Mario Cavaradossi is painting the chapel of Sant' Andrea when the escaped prisoner Cesare Angelotti, disguised in his sister's clothes, appeals for help. Mario hides him; but Mario's sweetheart, the opera singer Tosca, arrives in time to glimpse the petticoats, and to put out the fire of her jealousy Mario tells whom he is sheltering. The police arrive. When their chief, Baron Scarpia, threatens to torture Mario, Tosca reveals the hiding-place of Cesare—who kills himself rather than yield. But Scarpia has become enamoured of Tosca, and only if she grants him her favors will he free Mario. The agreement is reached— then Tosca stabs Scarpia. He, however, with parallel treachery has ordered Mario slain. When Tosca beholds her beloved Mario dead, she leaps from the battlements into the deep waters of the Tiber.

This melodramatic story on the edge of history, with its crescendo of passion, provided an acting part of tremendous fire. Sarah Bernhardt played it in Paris in 1887 and—although Fanny Davenport played Tosca in New York in 1888, and London saw the play in English in 1889 and 1920—it was on the French actress's tours that *La Tosca* revealed its full intensity. The *Illustrated London News* (December 17, 1887, reporting from Paris) declared that Sardou "has applied his great talent, with unrestricted *abandon,* to the concoction of a plot abounding in horror, which gives enormous scope to the histrionic powers of Sarah Bernhardt." The *New York World* (December 21, 1905) declared: "Its ferocious, tigerish heroine fits Bernhardt like a glove—horror piled on horror against a background of lust."

La Tosca, with book by Illica and Giacosa, was transformed from Sardou's play into an opera, with music by Puccini. This was played in Rome and London in 1900; in New York, at the Metropolitan, February 4, 1901. In 1905 Caruso sang Mario; Scotti, Scarpia; Emma Eames, Tosca. Later (1909, 1911) Geraldine Farrar took over the title role— as indeed the opera has supplanted Sardou's drama. The *New York Evening Mail* (March 5, 1888) suggested that Sardou had been turning all his skill and knowledge of the theatre toward parts Sarah Bernhardt might storm through, and that in doing so "he has been reaching deeper and deeper into the cesspool of ignoble motives and foul passions, and if he has not touched bottom now, he certainly cannot be very far from it." The unrelieved rush of treachery and base desire in *La Tosca,* while it gives the play unquestioned power, is likely to remove it beyond the audience's sympathy, if not beyond its credence. The mellowing strains of the music are required, to soften the play to the range of our sensitivities. Even in operatic form, *La Tosca* is a somber drive of fierce and unremitting passions.

MADAME SANS-GENE   *Victorien Sardou*

A vivid historical play, and one of Sardou's most immediate and most lasting successes, is *Madame Sans-Gêne* (Madame Free-and-Easy), 1893. Written with Emile Moreau, the play gave Gabrielle Réjane her first great popularity. She brought it to the United States in 1895 and it has been popular in stock ever since. Henry Irving and Ellen Terry opened in the play in London on April 10, 1897, then toured England and the United States. Mme. Simone played it, in French, in New York, in 1924; Gloria Swanson made a film of it the next year. Cornelia Otis Skinner played it in the summer of 1938. Nina Marshall was in a Spanish film version in 1945. A condensed version, *Madame Devil-May-Care,* with Sarah Churchill, was on television in 1951. This story of Napoleon put in his place by a laundress is a continuously popular blend of historical rouse and amorous entanglement, with brilliant dialogue.

Madame Sans-Gêne is Catherine, who in August of 1792 is laundress to a company of soldiers, which includes Lefebvre, who marries her, Fouché, a shrewd, unfeeling fellow, and a certain Napoleon Bonaparte, a jolly corporal who cannot always pay for his laundry. This much is in the Prologue; the play opens in the year 1811, when Lefebvre is Marshal of France. His wife, who is taking lessons in deportment, is scorned by Napoleon's sisters, who suppress their mutual jealousy to crush the light-hearted and naive Catherine, and have her discarded. Through a succession of palace plots and political intrigues, Catherine, innocent but sharp-witted, works her way. She softens the angry Emperor, then presents a long overdue laundry bill; as they laugh together, she reconciles Napoleon with the out-of-favor Fouché; and the Emperor is happy to have her remain with her husband, Lefebvre.

The major points of Sardou's drama are historical. François Joseph Lefebvre (1755-1820) married Catherine Hubscher, his company's laundress, who retained throughout her husband's rise, under Napoleon and Louis XVIII, the outspoken frankness and quick tongue of a woman of the people. She was, as Sardou pictures her, a vivandière during the early fighting of the Revolution. In the play, the constant simplicity of Catherine's ways, contrasting with the increasing finery and formality of the Emperor's entourage, gives effective character portrayal behind the political intrigue of Sardou's story.

Madame Sans-Gêne retains its power. As the *New York Times* declared (November 4, 1924), the play "remains one of the delightful and blooming pieces of the theatre. It has verve and a hearty spirit; it has wits about it, and a breeze of inexhaustible life. The jolly craft abounding throughout has plenty of style upon it, and its story rattles along with a good French vivacity and tang." The deft construction of Sardou's well-made play drives home the neatly turned situations; the characters have more breath of life than is usual with Sardou, as the historical canvas reveals traits that are common to Catherine, the Emperor's Lady, and the woman next door. These are caught into delightful action in *Madame Sans-Gêne*.

MY HEART'S IN THE HIGHLANDS   *William Saroyan*

After having attracted considerable attention with some short stories, William Saroyan (American, b. 1908) turned to the theatre. *My Heart's in the Highlands* was first printed in *The One-Act Play Magazine;* it was lengthened and produced in New York on April 13, 1939, first by the Group Theatre, then taken over by the Theatre Guild, and achieving 43 performances. It brought a fresh, or a long disused, note into the American theatre: a simple love of man, an acceptance of the worth of humble people and the joy of simple living.

There is hardly any story to the play. An unpublished poet, with his adoring son and a few friendly mice, lives in a shack near Fresno, California. A kindly, frustrated storekeeper, himself on the brink of bankruptcy, gives them credit. They shelter an old Shakespearean actor, out of a home for the aged, who plays the trumpet—evoking nostalgic moods in the neighbors, who come to listen, bearing little gifts. The actor dies. The poet and the boy are evicted. The shopkeeper sees his store failing. The curtain falls.

Pervading all this straitened sequence is a quiet dignity, a self-respecting, non-complaining acceptance of one's lot, a love of living that makes defeat an endurable episode in a journey toward a bright horizon. The nearest the play offers to complaint, to propaganda, is the final remark of the poet's son, a chip off the old happy-go-lucky block: "I'm not mentioning any names, Pa, but something's wrong somewhere."

Like most works of fresh quality, *My Heart's in the Highlands* divided the reviewers. Those that disliked the play, Saroyan answered. Thus the *New York World-Telegram* (April 14, 1939) said "You will search in vain for any trace of truth, beauty, or moral in it." And in that paper, the next day, Saroyan declared of his play: "It's wonderful, in the very truest sense of that dead word. It is full of wonder from the rise of the curtain to the fall of it. . . . The message of the play is the simplest and earliest message of man to man: For the love of God, be alive; be grateful for the miracle of possessing substance, of being able to draw energy from the great source of energy, and for the instinct to approach danger and death with pride, humor, and humbleness. . . . As for the moral of the play, it is the very simplest: It is better to be poor and alive than to be rich and dead. In short, it is better to be a good human being than a bad one. P.S. The idea is not original with me. It is simply that it got misplaced two or three years ago." The *New Yorker* (April 22) observed: "The singular hodge-podge of geometrical scenery, trumpet playing, crepe hair and tangled prose on exhibition in 52d Street conveys no rational message to anybody. . . . I think we'd better forget all about it as soon as possible." Saroyan had anticipated this, in the *New York Journal American* (April 19): "I'm sure it is going to live because it is alive. . . . Of its kind it is a classic." In the Preface to the printed play, Saroyan elaborated: "A classic is simply a first work, the beginning of a tradition, and an entry into a fresh realm of human experience, understanding, and expression. I believe *My Heart's in the Highlands* is a classic."

Although no "tradition" along the play's lines is yet manifest, its lyric quality, and its love of and faith in people, give it continuing values. These were not unrecognized by the reviewers. Arthur Pollock (April 30) remarked that the play is "written with the grace of a hummingbird. . . . It is very important. . . . His heart is in the right place. His heart is in the high lands." And more fully Richard Watts (April 23) declared that the play "is evocative rather than explicit, and its quality perhaps resembles that of music in its intangibility and its appeal to suggestion. . . . He is attempting to create in the manner of a dreamy recollection of childhood a picture of the artistic life of those that have the gift to feel the meaning of beauty but not to put it in words." In a "rag bag of bright scraps—Mr. Saroyan never bothers his head much about continuity, logic, or transition"—said Brooks Atkinson (May 7), "he has created a group of lovable characters who live with each other in amusing or pathetic harmony and give a sunny impression of natural kindness in the midst of a hard, grim, fatally wrong-headed world."

It is not to the head but to the heart that Saroyan's characters look for guidance. The song the old actor trumpets, that gives its name to the play, is a symbol of the high-hearted buoyancy that gives these little figures—and the play—a high significance.

THE TIME OF YOUR LIFE   *William Saroyan*

Saroyan's easy affability, his unreflecting joy in life, his casual use of the drama as a meeting place for important nobodies—important because they are human beings engaged in occupying a soul—swept the New York reviewers and public into an enthusiasm for *The Time of Your Life* that made it the first play to win both the Critics' Circle Award and the Pulitzer Prize. It was initially performed by the Theatre Guild on the road and brought to New York by Eddie Dowling on October 25, 1939, with Dowling and Julie Haydon, for 185 performances. London saw the play February 14, 1946.

The action of the play occurs in "Nick's Saloon and Entertainment Palace" on the San Francisco waterfront. The chief figure is a guy named Joe, who drinks champagne because it gives him interesting thoughts, and who makes a dancing doll to help Kitty, a sort of ethereal prostitute, keep her thoughts from her profession. Kitty is quitting her profession, for the fellow she loves has finally taken a job, so that they can marry. Also in the saloon are the usual hangers about. There's Willy, the pin-ball maniac, forever at the machine. Harry is a lively tap dancer; there's an Arab with a harmonica; and a Negro comes in and plays the piano so well that he's given a job. Old Kit Carson tells tall tales of the west, none of which the habitués believe; some of his stories start and never finish, like his hopeful beginning: "I don't suppose you ever fell in love with a midget weighing 39 pounds."

Into this company comes a group of society slummers. They are paid scant attention by the rest; but a sudden irruption breaks: Blick, the head of the Vice Squad, enters on an angry prowl. His abusive language sets the slummers fleeing; he intends to arrest Kitty, but first— in savage scorn and sadistic pleasure—he orders her to dance a strip tease. As the bewildered Kitty stands hesitant, the braggart Kit Carson pulls out his gun and shoots Blick. The pin-ball machine hits the jack-pot; to the shower of coins the machine lights up the words *American Destiny*.

This comedy, which Saroyan says he wrote in six days, shows no signs of careful construction. It is casual; it does not make efficient use of the theatre; some of its movements seem merely injected vaudeville turns. It does not bother with questions of verisimilitude; there is no indication, for instance, of the source of Joe's freely spent money. The play has, instead of these dramatic qualities, a buoyant love of life and of the living.

Saroyan has, said Walter Prichard Eaton, reviewing the printed play in the *New York Herald Tribune* (January 14, 1940) "a genuine love for all underdogs, and a deep understanding of the essential dignity of each individual spirit, however lowly; and this understanding is not clouded with any materialistic political propaganda." While *The Time of Your Life* is refreshingly free from propaganda, it does at times attempt phil-osophy, and then, commented Brooks Atkinson—but what can we expect of saloon drifters?—"when Saroyan permits himself to discuss ideas he can write some of the worst nonsense that ever clattered out of a type-writer." When, however, Saroyan contents himself with displaying, in tender understanding and respect, persons that do not let life's barren-ness parch their soul, then, Atkinson declared, "some of the warmest and heartiest comedy in the modern drama comes bubbling up through Mr. Saroyan's pungent dialogue, and although it is not realism it is real." "Its compassion is as irresistible", said John Mason Brown, "as its humor is gay. . . . The characters have blood in their veins, real air in their lungs, and joy in their hearts."

Sometimes a novelist like Dickens may be sentimental, almost sac-charine, except for his ink-black villains—may ignore the formal ele-ments of construction in seeming haphazard spread of life, yet by the very exuberance of that life and his love of living infuse into his char-acters a pulsing vitality that makes them moving, makes us consider them, not as book folk, but as neighbors, as persons on our block. Simi-larly Saroyan, in *The Time of Your Life,* in seemingly casual construction gives warmth and dignity and human stature to the persons that have found harbor in Nick's waterfront saloon.

LOVE'S OLD SWEET SONG   *William Saroyan*

Saroyan does not put plot in his plays. When he has but a few characters, as in *My Heart's in the Highlands**, they drift for a while before us. In a more crowded play, like *Love's Old Sweet Song,* 1940, the characters drift by or stay awhile, natural, everywhere at home. Then we, not they, depart—exhausted and exhilarated by our visit.

Such plot as *Love's Old Sweet Song* possesses is summarized by the *Christian Science Monitor* (May 6, 1940): "A postal telegraph boy innocently delivers a fake telegram from a non-existent Barnaby Gaul to a 'beautiful unmarried small town woman', named Ann Hamilton. Jim the pitchman happens along at the moment, and allows himself to be mistaken for Barnaby. Jim tries to go away, but eventually he and Ann are brought together in the home of Stylianos Americanos, a Greek-American wrestler." The small town is Bakersfield, California, where Jim has arrived to put down his suitcase labeled "Dr. Greatheart", to hold a bottle of cure-all in one hand and a deck of cards in the other. Also arriving is a family of Okies (itinerant laborers from Oklahoma), the parents and fourteen children. They settle on Ann's lawn, too tired (from resting) to accept the offer of jobs, the father perturbed at the fact that his eldest daughters have become women, and blaming it on the movies. It is because the Okies stay that Jim wants to leave; but in their persistent pottering the Okies set Ann's house on fire, and after its destruction they have no reason for lingering on her lawn. Before that, other visitors have come: a subscription agent for *Time* magazine (who delivers a rousing oration by merely reciting the names of the paper's staff); a sociological novelist studying the itinerant worker; a photographer from *Life;* two city slickers; a boy on a bicycle; and doubtless several others unnoticed in the crush. Relax, and amid the circus crowd and confusion you will hear love's old sweet song.

Love's Old Sweet Song opened in New York on May 2, 1940, with Jessie Royce Landis, and Walter Huston wistfully gay as the pitchman Barnaby Gaul. The play itself, said the *Christian Science Monitor,* is "part vaudeville show, part musical comedy, part autumn romance, part wrestling match, part three-alarm fire. . . . They do a number of strange and—depending on the viewpoint—wonderful things. Just why they are doing them remains a mystery, even for a Saroyan play. . . . It's fun to be fooled, says Mr. Saroyan. That's why we are fascinated by the tricks of pitchmen. That's why we like pretty clothes, new bicycles, movies, and plays like this."

Saroyan has, in *Love's Old Sweet Song,* as Brooks Atkinson said, "spun some more of his most beguiling improvisations." From the kaleidoscopic shake-up of the play, however, there emerges more of an individual character-portrayal than is usual with Saroyan, and less of his abounding love for all however erring men. His satire of the Okies, for example, is on the level of the unfortunately frequent hill-billy cartoons. His picture of Dr. Greatheart Jim Barnaby Gaul, however, is warm with sentiment, quite unrealistic—no such traveling faker has ever peddled snake-bite cure and bottled happiness—but intimately and pleasantly familiar: human nature ingratiating and brought home. Saroyan, as the *New Yorker* observed (May 11, 1940, changing its mind from *My Heart's in the Highlands** days), has "one of the richest and most fantastic imaginations in the theatre"; and this imagination, lighting many aspects of human character, coruscates in the crowded action of *Love's Old Sweet Song*.

THE FLIES   *Jean-Paul Sartre*

Most vivid of the modern retellings of the Orestes story is *The Flies*, 1944, by Jean-Paul Sartre (French, b. 1905). The account of Orestes' slaying of his mother Clytemnestra and her paramour and consort Aegisthus, after they had killed his father and usurped the throne of Argos, was a favorite among the ancient Greek dramatists. It is presented with emotional intensity in the *Choephori** of Aeschylus. Sartre endows the story with a modern psychological complexity. Although *The Flies* was presented unmolested in Paris during the Nazi occupation, it is a bold defense of freedom against the dictator. It is also the fullest dramatic development of Sartre's philosophy of existentialism.

The new play introduced some variations into the olden story. It pictures Argos as a pestilence-ridden city, plagued by the flies, symbols of the guilt and the remorse of the citizens who, in accepting Aegisthus as their king, share in his crime. The king himself, out of his sense of guilt, has established an annual Day of the Dead, when the citizens wallow in remorse, the graves are opened, and the spirits of their dead torment the living.

On such a day Electra, courageous with Orestes' homecoming, defies her mother and the king. Zeus, watching Orestes with a mixture of cynicism and amusement, expects to plant in the young man the seeds of fear, guilt, and pious reverence. But Orestes calmly dispenses justice in dealing death to his mother and King Aegisthus. He knows neither fear nor remorse.

The flies now cluster like Furies around Orestes and Electra. The citizens of Argos assail the temple where they rest. Orestes tells the crowd: "Aegisthus you did not fear; you read in his eyes that he was of your kind, he had not the courage of his crimes. . . . My crime is wholly mine." Orestes by his deed has taken the guilt from the citizens; they no longer have their old king's murderer as their king. And Orestes, having dealt justice, feels no guilt. The flies, therefore, are powerless over him; and Zeus, baffled by a human who feels no guilt nor remorse, fears for his own reign.

The weaker Electra sinks in remorse before the flies; but Orestes freely goes on his way. The citizens of Argos, without the burden of guilt, must now, he declares, work out the pattern of their days.

The doctrine of existentialism may be traced through the actions of Orestes. He comes to his native city, with no intention of seeking revenge, merely as a curious passerby. Then he learns that to live is to be engaged in life; one may choose one's action, but one must act. One must act, despite the seeming hopelessness of every course of action: "human living begins on the far side of despair". Hence there is anguish involved in any action; also, the burden of responsibility, because whatever one does helps shape the world around. Thus Orestes' killing of

Aegisthus frees the citizens of remorse. They wish Orestes, son of their
rightful king, to stay and rule them. But he will not. For (as it was
put by Simone de Beauvoir, Sartre's associate): "You can help people
to be in the position to be free, but you can't be free for them: they
must find freedom in their own hearts." Each for himself must freely
choose, then create, his own life pattern.

This philosophy underlies the moving drama of The Flies. As Simone
de Beauvoir said to me, "Zeus is the philosophic exponent, Aegisthus
the unthinking expression, of authority, conventional morality, established religion, political power—Petain!—trying to oppress and mystifi-
cate the people." The Flies is also a stirring drama of strong emotions
and stark action, thoroughly effective on the story level. Given vivid
presentation by Erwin Piscator in New York, 1947, and revived at his
Dramatic Workshop in 1948 and 1949, The Flies commanded close attention and deep feeling. Richard Watts (April 18, 1947) spoke of its "several levels of provocative interest" and called it (May 3) "one of the
few genuinely distinguished dramas of the post-war world theatre."
Esquire (November, 1947) pointed out (Piscator's being a non-professional group) that "the most exciting play on Broadway this season is
not, as it happens, on Broadway at all."

Several of the scenes in the play are truly gripping. Most impressive,
perhaps, is that of the hilltop temple and cave of the dead: the rock
rolled from the entrance stops before Electra, who is defiant, exhorting
the abased citizens to rouse from their submissive and piteous remorse—
"a mass scene of terror", said Thomas R. Dash (October 20, 1947) "that
is orchestrated superbly into a ballet of lament and misery", as the
swaying throng falls back into its subjection and fear.

The Flies was enacted in London (University College) and in the
United States at Vassar and Western Reserve. In February 1948, a production by the German director Jürgen Fehling, in the United States
sector of Berlin, was widely hailed—except by the Communist press.
Since the play advocates the freedom of the individual, since Orestes
refuses to guide, direct, or rule the citizens: let them work out their
own way of living, and since the Communists for such reasons were
already opposed to existentialism, the press of the Soviet sector sneered
at The Flies as "Heidigger with a shot of effervescing inanities from the
Café de Flore." All other comments paid tribute to its philosophy and
its power.

The Greeks, though they did not discover all the answers, knew the
basic questions of man's life and the course of human action. Religion;
individual freedom; individual responsibility; fear as enslavement; the
necessity of choice for wholesome living: these problems are all imbedded in Orestes' ancient story, and illuminated for modern pondering
in the tense dramatic action of The Flies.

NO EXIT   Jean-Paul Sartre

Huis Clos (Dead End) in the French original, No Exit was the first
Sartre play produced in America—in New York at the Biltmore Theatre,
November 26, 1946. He was then the chief French exponent of existentialism. Trying to find depths in a simple melodrama, the public overstrained; the play closed after thirty-one performances.

The play pictures the manner in which one's own nature afflicts one, even after death. A bell-boy ushers a man into what we learn is a room in hell. While the man awaits his torment, a woman joins him, then another. They are told that they are to spend eternity together, in that single room. And gradually they discover that their conflicting natures and their thwarted urges create their hell. The devil is a canny gentleman; he lets the dead do their own job of torture.

The dailies' reviewers were manifestly puzzled and disturbed by *No Exit*. George Freedley praised the "decor which was hell in itself, one of the best pieces of interpretative designing I have ever seen." The play he deemed "somewhat cloudy, but head and shoulders above most plays I have seen in recent years". Richard Watts called the play "a taut and absorbing narrative" and in the next breath "static, talkative, and limited in its action". To Louis Kronenberger it lacked "both dramatic impact and intellectual intensity". Before Howard Barnes "a baleful fantasy unfolds with unrelieved ferocity. It clangs like a gong on the stage. Like a gong it has a tendency to grow monotonous." At the end of the season, we critics voted it the best foreign play of the year.

Existentialism, of the Sartre type, begins with no assumptions prior to man's—each man's—being. Each man must therefore make his own world. What he finds around him may seem wretched and hopeless; all the more must each one decide what for him is the human way, and engage himself in life. He must do this, knowing that all his acts help also to shape the world for others.

The three persons in *No Exit* are thus tangled in their own decisions. Having evaded action, Cradeau again and again questions himself and asks the two women to assure him he was not a coward. Estelle can find nothing to do throughout eternity save exercise her charms on Cradeau—precisely the action that quickens the bitterness and rebellion in the Lesbian Inez. "Hell is other people".

There is nothing original, of course, in the existentialist philosophy, though it did give at least a reason for decent action to the youth of Europe hammered cynical by the War. Nor is there much original in Sartre's tense technique; George Jean Nathan (quick with the quip) called the work *Sartre Resartus,* a retailoring of Wedekind and Strindberg. He compared the play to a Montmartre side-show, and declared that its fascination rises from "the human weakness for self-deception which sees the Sultan's favorite nautch dancer in some poor little French provincial tart with an agitating colic". Both the sex and the setting, however, are too grim for any aphrodisiac hold. The audience leaves the play with the sobering thought that from one's own mind there is indeed no exit.

SOILED HANDS   *Jean-Paul Sartre*

Most entangled in controversy of all Sartre's plays is *Les Mains Sales (Soiled Hands).* A hit in Paris in the Spring of 1948, it was promptly produced in London, with Michael Gough and Joyce Redman, as *Crime Passionel.* There too, and in Zurich, December, 1948, the first German production, it won eager audiences, and was violently attacked by the

Communists. The production in Finland was closed by the Helsinki government after Soviet protest. Sartre himself protested the American production. He sued his agent for having approved the American adaptation (somewhat oddly called *Red Gloves*) which, it was claimed, turned his play into "a vulgar, common melodrama with an anti-Communist bias."

The American production, opening in Baltimore, November 15, 1948, then in Boston, New Haven, and New York, roused adventitious interest because it was the vehicle chosen by the motion picture star Charles Boyer for his American stage debut. Defending Dan Taradash's adaptation, Boyer declared: "Everything political and philosophical has been translated word for word. . . . It is a play about power politics, not about Communism."

The press in general praised Boyer's acting; but discussion of the play grew tangled in controversy. George Jean Nathan (December 20) called the play, especially in the emphasis of the direction, definitely pro-Communist. John Chapman (December 5) remarked: "I couldn't find any propaganda or philosophy in it, one way or the other—nor could I find in it much of a play." Robert Garland agreed, calling it "merely a makeshift melodrama". Brooks Atkinson said the play was no more than "a tedious discussion of abstract arguments by cardboard characters". John Lardner, in the *Star* (December 6), called *Red Gloves* "a stimulating and satisfactory show in M. Sartre's tastiest style of philosophical melodrama". This discord among the reviewers hardly drew audiences to the play. Its theme, furthermore, seemed disappointingly remote to those in this country that expected a knock-down political battle in the drama.

The body of the play pictures the young son of a bourgeois, Hugo, who seeks a chance to exercise his devotion to the totalitarian party of the mid-European State of "Illyria". He is sent to assassinate Hoederer, a party leader that has fallen from favor. Assigned as Hoederer's secretary, Hugo comes to like the man; and he tries to argue with the leader —who believes in compromising, in working with other parties, in amoeba-like shifting with events—to win him back into the rigid absolutist fold. As Hoederer meets representatives of other parties, Hugo still argues with him, and with his own conscience; he hesitates to shoot. It is only after Hugo's wife also comes to admire Hoederer, and after Hugo, seeing the two together, misinterprets the situation, that he kills the leader. The court, ignorant of Hugo's assignment to assassination, knowing only the sex story, sentences him to imprisonment for two years.

Surrounding this story are a Prologue and Epilogue. In the Prologue, Hugo, just released from jail, has been summoned by the woman leader of his totalitarian party "cell", to present a full and true account of his mission. The play is his story. In the Epilogue, Hugo discovers that, in the two years of his imprisonment, the Party policy has shifted: Hoederer's 1942 heresy is 1944 orthodoxy; Hoederer is exalted as a martyr, and Hugo himself is to be "liquidated". The cell boss, having once loved Hugo, gives him a chance to change his identity, and be spared; but the cosmic irony of the situation captures Hugo. He at least will not change his position, will not become a compromiser; he goes forth to his death.

In the swift drive of *Soiled Hands* the audience too, in several ironic ways, is neatly entangled. Our sympathies, in the first instance, are engaged in the hesitancy of Hugo. Fascinated, as the *New York Times* (April 18, 1948) reported the Paris production: "Fascinated, the audience struggles with the young man until the catharsis when he finally fires the gun. Half the horror of this moment is the spectator's sudden realization that all evening he has been rooting for action in the form of murder."

Secondly, observe the Communist concern. The play is neither for nor against Communism, one might say. It deals with a dispute *within* the totalitarian party, with the question of conciliating and using one's opponents or holding to intransigent extremism. But from this arises the fact that, no matter which side the spectator finds gaining his sympathies, he is sympathizing with a totalitarian point of view. He is deciding in favor of one form or another of totalitarian tactics. He is thinking out Communist problems, like a Communist.—Not quite. Because he is doing the thinking himself, instead of accepting party procedure, with good party discipline. For this, like Hugo, he must pay the penalty. That is why the Communists attacked the play. Not that Sartre takes sides. "But the very fact of posing these problems", as the *Revue de la Pensée Française* (June, 1948) declared, "of affirming that they exist, is in itself taking a stand." There must be no division of opinion, no discussion, in the ranks.

There are, indeed, a number of problems that the play does pose. The idealist, Hamlet-like, hesitates before the act, especially as all government (indeed, all action) demands that one "soil one's hands" in compromises and expedients. This is the existentalist core of the play, as the *Times* emphasized it, "the problem of individual action, and the protagonist's faltering concern with the meaning of his own freedom. In Sartre's terms, freedom is equivalent to action." But other problems crowd in. There is the problem of a man tangled in circumstances not of his making; specifically, can one who is bourgeois born and bred really fit into the proletarian world? (In Europe recently, this question has often been mooted to men's death.) There is the ever insistent question of means and end: to what degree should one compromise principles to gain one's goal? Does not the very shift, the compromise, alter both the seeker and the goal? Set into this are two subordinate matters: the adjustment of individual conscience to party commitments and orders; and—even when one intellectually deems the deed (here, murder) justified—the pressure of ingrained tradition and habit against the urgent act.

All of these questions are a background of searching thought behind a compelling story, which, as *Variety* noted (April 21, 1948), "moves at a fast clip and is full of extremely strong scenes". There are flaws in the structure: Sartre shows in the body of the play (which, remember, is Hugo's story) matters that Hugo could not possibly know, such as the dramatic argument between his wife and Hoederer when the two were alone. (Hoederer dies, and Hugo explicitly states that his wife never spoke to him again.) But most persons overlook such details in the swift drive of the action, and the surge of insistent concerns.

Sartre is an accomplished hand at melodrama, as he proved in *The Respectful Prostitute,* (1947), which opened in New York February 9,

1948. This caricature of Southern ways in the United States, while, as Nathan said, "a cut-and-dried lynch melodrama" and a grotesque travesty of actual conditions, still has power on the stage. But *Soiled Hands,* with all its intensity of action and emotional power, is considerably more than melodrama. It probes deeply; it provokes to considerate thought. And in its final moment, when Hugo looks squarely at the world—when, as the *Boston Post* (November 23, 1948) put it, "the truth penetrates to his mind, the young man laughs and laughs as a madman might, and the echo of his laughter is still ringing eerily in the theatre when some of his comrades lead him out; for he, too, must be killed now"—in its final moment *Soiled Hands* rises to genuinely tragic stature, as it shows a flash of nobility refusing to soil hands in the farce-tragedy that plays upon our world today.

THE LION-TAMER   *Alfred Savoir*

The Lion-Tamer; or, English As It Is Eaten (Le Dompteur, 1925) is the best example of a type of drama in which Alfred Savoir (French, 1883-1934) excelled: the farce of ideas. With a sprightly plot, much in the mood of the nineteenth century French vaudeville, Savoir intertwines a play of fancy and a play of thought, by comic devices and situations presenting, as in a distorting mirror, his serious theme. He might be called the satirist of *Savoir faire.*

The playwright reached this form by a roundabout path. Coming from his native Poland (where his name was Posymanski), Savoir first wrote serious, bitter dramas, such as *Baptism,* 1908. From this mood, he turned to sparkling comedies of sex, of which the best-known is a hilarious picture of husband-taming, *Bluebeard's Eighth Wife,* 1921. This delighted New York audiences—the New Haven try-out was stopped by the authorities—in 1921, with Ina Claire and Edmund Breese, in adaptation by Charlton Andrews.

Delightful farce, but considerably more, is *The Lion-Tamer,* which was an instant hit both in French and in English: (1925 in Paris, with Spinelli; October 8, 1926 in New York, with Dorothy Sands, Ian Maclaren and Albert Carroll). The play presents Lord Lonsdale carrying on the family tradition. For many generations, the Lonsdales have fought and died for the oppressed; the last frail remnant of the great family can do no less. But he can do no more than travel with a country circus, hating the cruel lion-tamer, hoping, with the incorrigible hopefulness of the idealist, that some day the lions will eat the trainer. The trainer rules his beasts and his wife through fear; Lonsdale tries to soften the trainer by making love to his wife—but at last it is Lonsdale that the lions eat.

The Lion-Tamer has meat beyond the surface story. Beneath its lightly-handled plot runs the opposition of mastery over idea and mastery over man, a symbolic conflict of idealism and absolutism. It is the idealist that is swallowed up. But not so simply. For, as Savoir pointed out, justice and beauty bear with them the inevitable counterpart of beautiful things: revolt, heresy, anarchy. And if the lion-tamer represents power, brutal reality, cruelty, vulgarity, he also stands for order, civilization, law, and the harmony of the universe. "Evil brings forth good, and good, evil. . . . They are at once two aspects of the same phenomenon."

Some of the reviewers of the American version did not reach out to the play's symbolism. The *New York World* asserted: "The scene in which arrangements are duly made for encompassing the wife's infidelity is one of the naughtiest and at times one of the most amusing episodes now on view in this much indulged city", but added (October 28) that the play "is full of bell-boys' wisdom, pseudo-philosophy, cheap boudoir wit, fiddlings with sex as disgusting and deathly as the dreams of an impotent old flaneur." On the other hand, the *Telegraph* averred: "Mr. Savoir recognizes one cosmic truth that most men never discover: that the intimate relations between man and woman, over which murders are done, high and low crimes committed and many heart-breaks and tears wasted, are, in essence, comic." Alexander Woollcott called *The Lion-Tamer* "a highly meaningful, excessively roguish, and distinctly entertaining fable." Barrett H. Clark in the *New York Sun* (November 13, 1926) spoke of the play's superb structure: "It has not a superfluous comma" and said that "it stems from Racine* . . . the analyst of love, the delicate commentator on the erotic ailments of unfortunate women and the sexual tempests of heroic men." The *Telegram* remarked: "Savoir is mocking the public as well as the mad design of the universe, but it would be a dour public that did not enjoy being mocked in such a manner." In *The Lion-Tamer,* sex becomes a vehicle for satire, farce the conveyor of fertile thought.

THE ROBBERS   *Johann Christoph Schiller*

The challenge to the existing order in *The Robbers* came red-hot from the author's life. The frail Johann Christoph Friedrich von Schiller (German, 1759-1805) hated the strict discipline at his regimental school. He later declared: "Of men, the actual men in the world below, I knew absolutely nothing at the time I composed my *Robbers.* Four hundred human beings, it is true, were my fellow-prisoners in this abode; but they were mere tautologies and repetitions of the self-same mechanical creature, like so many plaster casts of one statue. Thus situated, of necessity I failed. In making the attempt, my chisel brought forth a monster, of which (fortunately!) the world had no type or resemblance to show." Thomas DeQuincey called this work of the nineteen-year-old Schiller "beyond doubt the most tempestuous, the most volcanic, of all juvenile creations anywhere recorded . . . has never failed to convulse the heart of young readers." *The Robbers* bears as motto the passage from Hippocrates: "What herbs cannot cure, iron cures; what iron cannot cure, fire cures." Here is, bluntly, the appeal to fire and sword!

Further events of Schiller's life sprang from *The Robbers,* which was published at his own expense in 1781. In January, 1782, Schiller, by then Regimental Surgeon for the Duke of Württenburg, left without leave, to see the production of the play at Mannheim. All the youth of Germany boiled with unparalleled enthusiasm; the conservatives were proportionately shocked. When the Grisons complained to the Duke because the play called their city "the thief's Athens", the Duke ordered Schiller to confine his future writings to medical treatises. The next year, Schiller fled the Duchy, and travelled about Germany for a decade.

The Robbers, in romantic spirit, breathing defiance of law in the name of a noble freedom, pictures Karl von Moor abandoning the evils of his father's court for the free forests of Bohemia, where he lives like a German Robin Hood. Karl's brother, Franz, at the conventional court, is a coarse, scheming villain, holding in his power Karl's beloved Amelia, until—"Only by Moor's hand shall Moor's beloved die"—Karl himself puts an end to Amelia's sufferings. Through the play extravagant incidents sweep with wild passion; strong patriotism—the famous *Lebt Wohl* song; virile and intense love of action; as horror heaps on violent death and enthusiasms outleap order. We are told that, after seeing the play, one German noble abandoned his estate and took to the woods like Karl von Moor. Another German princeling, however, stated: "If I had been God at the moment of Creation and had foreseen that *The Robbers* would be written, I would have left the world unmade."

The Germans of the Storm and Stress period, who soared with the "untamed hope of wild and noble self-expression" of *The Robbers,* were outmatched by the young English romantics. Coleridge, in a letter to Southey, in 1794, exclaimed: "I had read, chill and trembling, when I came to the part where the Moor fixes a pistol over the robbers who are asleep. I could read no more. My god, Southey, who is this Schiller, this convulser of the heart? Did he write his tragedy amid the yelling of fiends?" Later, Coleridge added: "Schiller introduces no supernatural beings; yet his human beings agitate and astonish more than all the goblin rout—even of Shakespeare." Wordsworth borrowed freely from *The Robbers* for his *The Borderers.*

Later in the century, the Schiller cult rose in Bulwer Lytton almost to worship. Thackeray, in the German town of Erfurt, saw Devrient, "the Kean of Germany", as Franz von Moor, and cried: "I think I never saw anything so terrible. There is a prayer which Franz makes while his castle is being attacked, which has the most awful effect which can well be fancied: 'I am no common murderer, mein Herr Gott'." Most fully, in his *Life of Schiller,* Carlyle discussed *The Robbers:* "A rude simplicity, combined with a gloomy and overpowering force, are its chief characteristics; they remind us of the defective cultivation, as well as of the fervid and harassed feelings of its author . . . The tragic interest of *The Robbers* is deep throughout, so deep that frequently it borders upon horror. A grim inexpiable Fate is made the ruling principle; it envelops and overshadows the whole; and under its louring influence, the fiercest efforts of human will appear but like flashes that illuminate the wild scene with a brief and terrible splendor, and are lost forever in the darkness. The unsearchable abysses of man's destiny are laid open before us, black and profound, and appalling."

Carlyle recognized the personal impetus behind the play, which gives such impassioned strength, for instance, to the fiery soliloquy on life and death, yet makes its chief personages more figments of the poet's wild fancy than mortal men. Karl von Moor, said Carlyle, "had expected heroes, and he finds mean men; friends, and he finds smiling traitors to tempt him aside, to profit by his aberrations, and lead him onward to destruction: he had dreamed of magnanimity and every generous principle, he finds that prudence is the only virtue sure of its reward . . . Amelia, the only female in the piece, is a beautiful creation; but as imaginary as her persecutor Franz. Still and exalted in her warm enthusiasm, devoted in her love to Moor, she moves before us as the inhabitant of a higher and simpler world than ours . . . She is a fair vision, the *beau idéal* of a poet's first mistress; but has few mortal lineaments."

In England, even more than in Germany, those hostile to this exuberant rush of unrestrained emotion also spoke forth. In the *Anti-Jacobin* of June, 1798, for example, there appeared a satiric play, *The Rovers,* the joint work of Canning, Frère, and Ellis. Its barbs were directed partly against Goethe's *Stella,* but mainly against Schiller's *The Robbers* and *Intrigue and Love.* The Preface sardonically stated that *The Rovers* aims to instill "a wild desire of undefinable latitude and extravagance," and referred to the German play "in which robbery is put in so fascinating a light that the whole of a German University went upon the highway in consequence of it"—a statement that won wide credence in England.

The first English translation of *The Robbers* was banned by the censor; after being tamed it was produced in London in 1799 under the title *The Red Cross Knights,* with the robbers transformed into knights-errant, and the good brother living happily at the end.

Of the early dramas of Schiller, all in prose, *The Robbers* is by far the most vigorous, fiery, and dramatically intense. The characters and the diction are flush with the extremes of passion, bold in the black-and-white vision of the world that often appears to idealistic youth. But it is the youth of a genius that created *The Robbers;* in it surge the power and the majesty that make Schiller the greatest of all German playwrights.

WALLENSTEIN   *Johann Christoph Schiller*

In Weimar, Schiller came in contact with Goethe*, whose influence added depth to Schiller's vision. Subsequently the study of Kant in large degree tempered his early violence; he grew more steady, more objective, nonetheless a hater of wrongs, but less sure, if not of what is right, at least of how to achieve it.

For seven years at Weimar and during his stay at Jena as Professor of History (a post Goethe reportedly secured for Schiller to get rid of him) Schiller worked on a historical drama which appeared in 1799 as the trilogy *Wallenstein.* In this great drama there is a balance of Hellenic form and Romantic fervor; in it, Schiller came closest to his goal of "wisdom for noble ends, and beauty without softness." Although Laurie Magnus in the *Dictionary of European Literature* aptly remarked that *"Faust* is world poetry, *Wallenstein* is national drama", it is the greatest of German national dramas, "the greatest dramatic work", Carlyle averred, "of the eighteenth century"; of all other plays, said DeQuincey, "nearest in point of excellence to the dramas of Shakespeare."

Wallenstin tells the story of the great general of the German Emperor Ferdinand II, Count Albrecht Wenzel Eusebius von Wallenstein, Duke of Friedland (1583-1634), who crushed the Protestant states, and drove back the invading Swedes under Gustavus Adolphus; then, to strengthen his own power and to guard against intrigues at court, negotiated with the Swedes, and through the connivance of the Emperor was assassinated.

The first part of the trilogy, in one surging scene, is *Wallenstein's Camp*. In irregular rhyming verse the stir of a bivouacked army is conveyed, "all the wild lawless spirits of Europe", said Carlyle, "assembled within the circuit of a single trench." *The Piccolomini*, in five acts of blank verse, develops the treasonous negotiations of Wallenstein with the Swedes and his relations with his officers, especially the two Piccolomini, father and son, who—though the son, Max, is engaged to Wallenstein's daughter, Thekla—remain loyal to the Emperor. *Wallenstein's Death*, also five acts of iambic pentameter, shows Wallenstein in active rebellion. Max Piccolomini is killed in battle against the Swedes; Thekla refuses to survive him. Wallenstein is murdered by Irish and Scotch officers of the Emperor; his sister-in-law, Countess Tertzky, who had urged him to rebellion, takes poison; and Octavio Piccolomini regretfully takes command.

This climactic sweep of history is gathered into unity by the superb dramaturgy of Schiller. Into the play he gathers the surge of the tumultuous times, the clash not only of arms but of opinions and ideals: the problem of freedom and necessity; the antagonism of the actual and the ideal. "Masterly in style and impressive in conception," said Freedley and Reeves in *A History of the Theatre*, 1941, "the huge canvas unfolds graphically to reveal idealism at a time of horrible civil and religious war."

Coleridge's version, 1800, of the last two parts of *Wallenstein* is one of the masterpieces of translation, said by some English critics to surpass the original. However, the entire work has not often been played in English, although *Wallenstein's Camp* should be a temptation and a challenge to a director. In German, *Wallenstein* was played in 1934 at New York's Irving Place Theatre. Its broad canvas has nearest analogy in such a novel as Tolstoi's *War and Peace;* but beyond this it pulses with the dynamic power of living drama as through its vivid chapter of history it widens our outlook and deepens our understanding. In beauty of expression, in structural organization binding many impulsions and many persons into a single emotional drive, in truth of character-portrayal, in wisdom and nobility of impulse and thought, *Wallenstein* is among the great masterpieces of the drama.

WILHELM TELL   *Johann Christoph Schiller*

Though named after a man, this play, written in 1804, is the drama of a great people. It pictures the citizens of a Swiss canton, in 1308, gathering in a crescendo of indignation at their mistreatment by the Governor, impelled by their sturdy self-reliance to strike for liberty, and to establish the oldest democracy in Europe. Somewhat as in the Shakespearean history-play, we behold all classes of society: the nobles, conservatively inclined, by their privileges bound to the Emperor, yet in the crisis taking stand for freedom; the solid citizens, burghers attentive to their rights; and the common people, hunters, farmers, shepherds, whose Swiss cantons instill deep breath of freedom with the mountain air. Binding these pictures together is the legendary story of the Swiss archer, Wilhelm Tell, ordered by the tyrant Gessler to shoot an apple from his own son's head, but with a second arrow beneath his cloak for Gessler's heart, if the first had missed its mark. Arrested for this, Tell escapes and kills Gessler, thus giving start to the struggle that ends Austria's domination, sets Switzerland free.

Schiller's *Wilhelm Tell,* said Carlyle, "exhibits some of the highest triumphs which his genius, combined with his art, ever realized. The first descent of Freedom to our modern world, the first unfurling of her standard on that rocky pinnacle of Europe, is here celebrated in the style which it deserves. There is no false tinsel decoration about *Tell,* no sickly refinement, no declamatory sentimentality. All is downright, simple, and agreeable to Nature; yet all is adorned and purified and rendered beautiful, without losing its resemblance . . . The feelings it inculcates and appeals to are those of universal human nature, and presented in their purest, most unpretending form . . . It is delightful and salutory to the heart to wander among the scenes of *Tell;* all is lovely, yet all is real. Physical and moral grandeur are united; yet both are the unadorned grandeur of Nature. There are the lakes and green valleys beside us, the Schreckhorn, the Jungfrau, and their sister peaks, with their avalanches and their palaces of ice, all glowing in the southern sun; and dwelling among them are a race of manly husbandmen, heroic without ceasing to be homely, poetical without ceasing to be genuine."

Wilhelm Tell was played in Philadelphia by Joseph Jefferson in 1812. It was frequently played in England in the nineteenth century. In Paris, the play was supplanted by the opera based upon it in 1829, with book by Hippolyte Bis and Etienne Jouy, and music by Gioacchino Antonio Rossini; this closes with the rousing hymn to liberty and to the woods and mountains where freedom was bred: "I boschi, I monti!" This popular opera was first played in New York in 1857 and later produced at the Metropolitan Opera House in the 1888-1889 season.

A recent American production of *Wilhelm Tell* opened in Hollywood on May 25, 1939; it was played by a group of refugees and directed by Leopold Jessner. The latter had produced the play successfully in Europe on a cubistic set with platforms, runways, and steps. His presentation did not please the American audience, though *Variety* (May 31, 1939) reported that "distinctly in its favor is the timeliness of its theme, the deadly parallel to despotic rule in European countries at this time."

In a Schiller centennial address in 1859, William Cullen Bryant declared: "Wherever there are generous hearts, wherever there are men who hold in reverence the rights of their fellow-men, wherever the love of country and the love of mankind coexist, Schiller's drama of *Wilhelm Tell* stirs the blood like the sound of a trumpet." Its stirring rouse for freedom makes *Wilhelm Tell* a valid and vigorous drama as long as the need to rouse for freedom makes a prison of some part of earth.

ANATOL   *Arthur Schnitzler*

In considering the plays of Arthur Schnitzler (Austrian, 1862-1931), it must be kept in mind that he was a physician, the author of papers on hypnotism and psychotherapy, and a contemporary of Freud. His plays are explorations of "the vast domain" of the soul. After 1895, when Schnitzler turned almost entirely to literary work (novels and short stories, as well as plays), he helped form the "Young Vienna" group, opposed to the naturalism then triumphant in Berlin. Beyond the individual soul-studies of his dramas spread the various levels of Viennese society, even in his comedies finding overtones of melancholy in the declining Austrian culture. Schnitzler, Sol Liptzin has said, "caught in his gentle hand the last golden flow of Vienna's setting glory, and converted it to art." He seems to be saying, "Eat, drink, and be wistfully merry, for tomorrow civilization will die."

By far the most popular of Schnitzler's plays is *Anatol*. Perhaps Anatol is in some measure Schnitzler himself; for under the pseudonym "Anatol" he issued his earliest works. In the play, Anatol talks of his experiences to his friend Max, with a wit and irony constantly turned upon himself, and with a wistfulness that sends him to his wedding, at the end, sophisticate and almost cynical, but fluttery, nervous and hopeful as any young bride. Of the seven short episodes in the play, most amusing is that in which Anatol prepares to tell Mimi all is over between them—then is caught in surprise and chagrin when Mimi beats him to the break with word of her own new love.

Beneath the frivolity of Anatol, however, one can sense the yearning for an association more firmly tied by understanding, wherein love is not a game one side must lose, but a way of life two folk may walk together. A way unfound, yet ever to be seeking. It is this underlying wistful sense of search—as well as the deft craftsmanship and the witty, charming dialogue—that has won such success for *Anatol*. A life-long flitting from love to love would be a bitter emptiness, as Schnitzler himself indicated in a later playlet, *Anatol's Megalomania,* produced in 1932, which shows Anatol as a shuffling old pantaloon.

Several scenes from *Anatol* were enacted at Ischl, Austria, in 1893; the whole group was not produced until 1910 in Vienna and Berlin. The translation of *Anatol* by Granville Barker, *The Affairs of Anatol,* was presented in London in 1911; in New York, in 1912 with John Barrymore. It was revived in New York in 1931 with Joseph Schildkraut, Walter Connolly, Patricia Collinge, and Miriam Hopkins. Barrymore presented five and Schildkhaut six of the original seven episodes. Various episodes have been frequently presented by college and little theatre groups. Equity Library revived *Anatol* in New York in 1946, directed by Mady Christians (who had played in it under Reinhardt in 1924), with Tonio Selwart and Carmen Matthews.

When *Anatol* was first produced in America, the theme of the play disturbed some reviewers. The *New York Dramatic Mirror* (October 16, 1912) declared: "Anatol is the polygamous animal in which Herbert Spencer once summed up all mankind. But the lovely thing about him is his geniality and utter detestation of hypocrisy. He runs the whole gamut of possible 'affairs' without once besmirching his honor . . . He sins as a perfect gentleman should, if he should sin at all." In Chicago, where the "gentleman" is apparently not so important, the *Record Herald* (December 18, 1912) complained: "The skit is about a gull and his girls . . . As these triumphs are merely the carryings-on of a green youth who flops about like a belated Byronic derelict; no interest attaches to them as experiences in life . . . The mawkishness of the composition occasionally is assuaged by its deft mockery . . . The intention of the thing is deplorable, its effect is tedious and insipid."

The public taste seemed to mellow with revivals. Gilbert W. Gabriel
(January 17, 1931) called *Anatol* "still a treasurable, immensely actable,
delightful little roundelay of sentiment and cynicisms, of farce-lined wit
and charming heart-break . . . Here, in many ways and many smiles,
is the most inviting revival New York has been granted in your day and
mine." Vernon Rice (June 5, 1946) found in the play "variety, contrast,
and consuming interest". Anatol is a lasting figure, for he moves in
smiling earnest on an eternal quest.

Anatol is the most popular picture of the eternal playboy, dwelling in
a wish-world. What gives depth to the character, and the play, is that
beneath the frivolous desires that live in the moment, beneath the urges
that spend themselves on the present joy, stirs a basic yearning—almost
too urgent, too unrealizable, for utterance—for a more stable life of love
and understanding that somehow will endure.

PROFESSOR BERNHARDI   *Arthur Schnitzler*

The most complex of Schnitzler's studies of human nature is *Professor Bernhardi*. In this intense drama, the conflict of ethical and religious standards flares from a Vienna hospital and widely and deeply
tries men's souls.

Acted in 1912 in Berlin, then all over Europe, by Fritz Kortner,
Professor Bernhardi everywhere aroused a storm of discussion. The
play was banned in Germany in the 1930's. New York saw it in German
in 1914 and 1918. It was presented by the Jewish Drama League in
London in 1927. It was acted again in London in 1931, translated by
Hetty Landstone, directed by Heinrich Schnitzler, the author's son, and
in 1936, translated by Louis Borell and Ronald Adam; both times, with
Abraham Sofaer as Dr. Bernhardi.

Freedly and Reeves in *A History of the Theatre*, 1941, called *Professor
Bernhardi* "a far from faultless play about anti-Semitism, which is
robbed of much of its force because its author began it with a situation
which was insufficient to explain the forces released, and because the
conclusion of the play seems ineffectual." The play is more rewardingly
captured, however, when the view is taken that anti-Semitism is not a
basic drive but a hatred roused when desires are thwarted. In a situation
where one cannot have one's way, what easier diversion than to snarl
upon the Jew!

It is a simple humanitarian act, so it seems to Professor Bernhardi,
that brings the storm upon him. A charity patient, in the hospital that
he heads, is unaware that she is dying. The priest, Father Reder, wishes
to see her, to save her immortal soul; the doctor forbids the priest's
going to her, so that her last living hours may be happy. An officious
Catholic nurse, Sister Ludmilla (the only woman we see in the play)
informs the girl that the priest is waiting; the shock kills her. Personal
enmities, then political and religious motives, gather force from this
incident to bring about the Jewish Professor Bernhardi's resignation,
then his imprisonment. Such animosities are aroused that Sister Ludmilla testifies falsely at the trial, making it seem that Professor Bernhardi has denied religious consolation to one seeking it. The priest,
for testifying that in his opinion Bernhardi was honestly doing what
he thought best for the patient, is transferred to a dreary Polish parish.

When Bernhardi, released because Prince Constantin needs the best medical attention, learns these facts, he is urged to apply for a re-opening of his case—and he refuses. He has done what he considers right; let each examine his own conscience.

Professor Bernhardi shows Schnitzler's character-drawing at its best. Each of the dozen doctors at the hospital, Jewish and Christian, is deftly differentiated, his ideas and his prejudices humorously yet honestly caught. There is a superb scene at the end between Bernhardi and the priest, Father Reder, wherein the latter admits the potency of Bern-hardi's attitude, but declares he could not say anything that might be so construed as to harm the Church. The fine balance maintained in this scene may be observed through two concurrent interpretations of it, after the London 1927 presentation. Said the *Era* (February 14): "One of the finest things in the play is the beautifully written scene at the end in which the Jewish doctor and the priest, both idealists serving their idea of right, come to an understanding and shake hands." The *Stage* (February 14), stating that the play strikes "the human note in the final colloquy with Reder, come ostensibly to confess that Bernhardi had been in the right, but really to safeguard his own position", ended its comments with the remark that the Jewish doctor and the Catholic priest "shake hands across the chasm, without looking down into it."

As a matter of fact, the two men do understand and respect one another. Their points of view are on opposite sides of a chasm, it may be, a chasm too deep to fill; but across it understanding and mutual respect may build a bridge. *Professor Bernhardi* is a genuine dramatic contribution to such understanding. "Its enduring power", said the *London Times* (June 16, 1936) "is as a discussion, first, of two opposed systems of thought, and, secondly, of two differing sets of moral values." In fuller detail, Charles Morgan observed this "genuine study of differ-ing sets of values. Bernhardi himself is by no means exempt from criticism; his stubborn refusal to compromise in little things, his fanatical lack of proportion, his special variety of spiritual pride, are set side by side with the excessive desire of priest and politicians to excuse their immediate failures or weaknesses by saying that it is often necessary to subordinate the means to the end. Schnitzler is not impartial; he has his own prejudice and he does not conceal it; but his satire is by no means undistributed. The result is a play of rare balance and subtlety and one that rewards every perceptive delicacy of the players."

The anti-Semitism in *Professor Bernhardi*, thus, is no more than summoned ammunition in several intertangled wars. We see the opposi-tion of the scientific and the religious spirit; more precisely, of the sceptical and the mystical temperament. And beyond this opposition of the scientific humanitarian concern for the immediate welfare and the Catholic concern for the eternal soul, there presses still another basic issue, that of integrity of spirit, of harmony between end and means, of honesty in the advancement of one's own cause. Both of these problems—what one believes, the immediate versus the ultimate values; and how to move toward one's objectives: does even the shiniest goal excuse a tarnished striving?—remain basic in our post-war world. And both of them, naturally fused in the drama of living, are searchingly and sharply revealed in *Professor Bernhardi*.

A GLASS OF WATER   *Augustin Eugène Scribe*

Augustin Eugène Scribe (French, 1791-1861) wrote all or part of some 400 plays, most of them very successfully appealing to the nineteenth century French playgoer. He was the chief manufacturer of the "well-made play", in which the effects are wrought by the well-timed use of theatrical devices, with firmly-knit construction of an often complicated plot leading to a powerful climax. For the most part, the persons of Scribe's plays do not seem real inhabitants of earth, but dwell in what Brander Matthews labeled "the pleasant land of Scribia". Reading several of Scribe's plays in succession does indeed give one an uneasy sense of scribbledeedee; but taken one at a time, many of them are workmanlike models of dramaturgy, truly effective theatre pieces.

One of Scribe's best plays, still in the repertoire of the Comédie Française, is *A Glass of Water*, 1840. It was performed in New York in 1930, in Pasadena in 1936. London saw a fresh adaptation by Ashley Dukes in 1950. The play pictures how great events may spring from little causes; the history of England is altered because a favorite spills a glass of water on a Queen.

From 1702 to 1711 the Duke of Marlborough was virtually the Regent of England, through the influence of his wife, as Mistress of the Robes, Keeper of the Privy Purse, and trusted though imperious companion of Queen Anne. The play shows the Queen as an amiable, good-natured, but weak and over-romantic woman, more interested in the state of her affairs than in the affairs of her state. She and the Duchess of Marlborough are both in love with a gentleman of the court, who prefers the charming but baser born daughter of the Queen's jeweler. Spun along with this quadrangular romance are the swirl and intrigue of national politics, as the Tory Bolingbroke seeks to oust Marlborough and the Whigs. The destinies of the state hang upon the caprices of the court; and Scribe lifts the play to a strong climax when the Duchess' spilling of a glass of water on the Queen's dress floods out the Queen's long-dammed resentment, and sweeps the Duchess to disgrace and Marlborough to his ruin.

There is an effective battle of wits between Bolingbroke and the Duchess as Scribe deftly handles the intertangled themes of politics and sex. The dialogue is undistinguished, but apt and lively. The play, tightly woven and economically built, alternates amusing and dramatic moments, until the two drives, of men's concerns and women's, concenter their forces in the climax.

Plays of this sort, "well-made", mechanically deft but with characters undeveloped while situations are strongly played, may grow a bit dated, with sophisticated audiences. Outside of theatrical centers, *A Glass of Water* is still sure-fire material. It has been frequently played, and was a favorite in Russia until the Revolution.

When *A Glass of Water* had its first American production in English, Robert Garland (March 6, 1930) found it "lovely to look at, arty to listen to, and more than a wee bit tiresome." John Mason Brown insisted this *Glass of Water* was "hard to swallow", but the *New York Herald Tribune* deemed it "still good theatrical stuff". The French encyclopedia *Larousse Universel*, 1922, called it "one of Scribe's most delightful comedies."

In his plays, Scribe reduced great passions and historic events to the level of the plain citizen of the middle class. He was so deft at rousing curiosity and sustaining suspense, at resolving intricate entanglements, at combining the amusing and the moving, that during the performance his characters move with semblance of life, with that illusion of reality which is the secret of great drama. Scribe's works—among the best of which is *A Glass of Water*—carry to the peak of its potentialities the well-made play.

ADRIENNE LECOUVREUR   *Augustin Eugène Scribe*

Few plays in the repertoire of the French theatre have been more tempting to the actress than *Adrienne Lecouvreur*, written in 1849 by Eugène Scribe and (Gabriel Jean Baptiste) Wilfred Legouvé (French, 1807-1903). Played frequently for some sixty years all over Europe and America, the story was known to every playgoer. It is a tenderly pathetic tale of an actress who loved a nobleman, thinking him one of his own retainers, and who at the door of death learned who he was and that he loved her truly. Among those who starred in the play were Rachel, Sarah Bernhardt, Marie Nieman-Seebach, Helena Modjeska, and Olga Nethersole. There have been four adaptations of the play into English.

Adrienne, star of the Comédie Française in 1730, had as rival in love the powerful Princesse de Bouillon. Theatergoers knew her devotion to her dramatic art and its masters. "They know," said the New York *Spirit of the Times* (October 29, 1870), "the strength, tenderness, and endurance of her love for the great Marechal Maurice de Saxe, even while believing him to be only a poor lieutenant attending that famous officer; they know her magnanimity when protecting and saving her avowed, menacing rival; the courage with which, in that rival's own princely salon, she overwhelms her and terrifies her guests by the recitation from *Phèdre**; they have seen her mourning over the 'poor flowers' which she had given to Maurice who, on his knee, prayed for them but who now, as she believes, has sent them back to her as the sign of eternal farewell; have seen her ecstatic joy as Maurice enters, and she knows herself his only love, his wife that is to be, and him her sworn husband; has seen her strength fail as the poison kissed from those 'poor flowers' does its work; have seen her heart-rending delirium, heard her touching prayers for life now that *he* loves her wholly and to live is such happiness, life with him so beautiful, so sweet, his own wife too; and wept as she expired before them, sighing as they slowly turned away and left the theatre, 'Poor Adrienne!' But never have they seen all this more tenderly, touchingly, largely, grandly portrayed than by Mme. Seebach."

Here is praise indeed! Concerning Bernhardt's performance in America in 1896, the *New York Times* said: "Every moment was exquisitely done; love, passion, every variety of emotion touched as keenly, as precisely, as human nature itself. Her death scene, excellent in climactic force, did not thrill one through and through at the moment of Adrienne's recognition of Maurice, as Rachel is said to have done, yet we are willing to miss a momentary thrill in order to reach the perfection of the whole scene." And again in 1905: "Madame Bernhardt was as her best all through, and beyond that praise can hardly go."

The "sometimes repulsive work" of Olga Nethersole—as Alan Dale called it—is another thing. Her 1908 performance, he pointed out, was hailed by a host of women. "They saw Adrienne played as though she were a courtesan, rather than an actress of the sober Comédie Française. They saw 'Morees' de Saxe, the 'hero', kissed in fifty-seven varieties of kiss. They noted that Miss Nethersole can kiss longitudinally, latitudinally, and on the bias. They gleaned that when 'Morees' had lines to speak, and consequently needed his lips to speak them with, Adrienne was just as pleased to kiss his nose. They heard the kiss that reverberated, and the kiss that was silent. . . . Once or twice Miss Nethersole forgot Miss Nethersole, and the effect was delightful. . . . No play could furnish a better foothold for stilt and stereotype than *Adrienne Lecouvreur*. It is a wicked old play, with its stagey types, its absurd soliloquies and its antique situations. The realism that disfigures Miss Nethersole's work has never had a place in Sarah's lexicon."

Most fully, however, *Adrienne Lecouvreur* has been associated with the career of Helena Modjeska. As a young actress in Cracow, she was invited in 1868 to play the title role at the Imperial Theatre in Warsaw. She was warned not to reveal her stage business in the rehearsals; but the jealous company sought to make her performance anti-climactic by putting on the play with their own star, three nights before Modjeska's debut. The debut was, nevertheless, a triumph; and in 1869 Modjeska returned to Warsaw as leading lady. In 1876 she came to America for her health; financial pressure forced her from retirement, and on September 20, 1877, unknown and speaking a new language, she opened in California in *Adrienne Lecouvreur*—and in triumph. The same play brought her to success in New York. However, the *Times* critic preferred her as Rosalind, Mary Stuart, or Camille. He said (January 12, 1886) that Modjeska "is by no means seen at her best as Scribe and Legouvé's morbid heroine. . . . The play is skillfully constructed, and there is a great deal of wit and showy sarcasm in the text. . . . The poetic beauty and elusive charm of Modjeska's acting do not compensate for the absence in the great climaxes of the fire and magnetism of the two great French actresses (Rachel; Bernhardt)".

"Considered in its own school," said the *New York Times* in 1896, "*Adrienne Lecouvreur* is a masterpiece . . . the art of playwriting reduced to its lowest formal terms; the construction of the play, the interweaving of the incidents, is everything. Character and intellectuality are everywhere subordinate to the action." In spite of a plot so often copied, down into Grade B films, that today's sophisticates would call it 'corny', the play's range of emotions, its swift and exciting action, its challenge to a star, make *Adrienne Lecouvreur* one of the truly lustrous works of the theatre.

ATSUMORI   *Seami Motokiyo*

This is one of the No plays, which constitute the classical drama of Japan. These plays, lasting about an hour apiece, but usually presented in groups of five with farcical interludes (*kyogen*), were the chief theatrical entertainment of the aristocratic Japanese for almost 600 years. The No drama is an outgrowth of several earlier forms of entertainment. There were ballad-singers and wandering reciters of popular poetry. There was the masquerade *(sarugaku)* that enlivened the Shinto ceremonies. By the tenth century, the countryside juggling and acrobatics *(dengaku)* had been given shape in a sort of opera with recitative and dance. The Chinese pantomimic dance had been introduced at the Japanese court. This courtly dance *(kagura)*, in delicate and formalized patterns of movement, was blended with elements of these other forms by Kwanami Kiyotsugu (1333-1384), thus creating the No. About 1375 Kwanami, priest of a temple near Nara, was taken under the protection of the shogun Yoshimitsu, a patron of the arts. Kwanami's son, Seami Motokiyo, 1363-1443, further fashioned the form and brought it to its highest peak.

The No drama, acted entirely by masked and elaborately costumed men, is architectonically constructed as a movement of music and dance. The walking about the stage, and the posing during the dialogue, are formalized; in addition, there are wordless dances, such as the many battle scenes and duels, the special dances of the various gods, and a characteristic slow dance *(mai)* mimicking the crane. In most of the plays, the characters are either gods, or ghosts reliving an earthly experience. This device of having an olden story re-enacted by the wraiths of those involved imparts a "distancing" to the events that softens the emotions. The ghosts are wistful wisps of a remembered past; thus the No dramas deal in reticences, in understatement, in delicacy of mood and of diction. Often something lies beneath the surface *(yugen)*; this is symbolized by a white bird with a flower in its beak. The dialogue is reinforced with familiar passages from well-known poems *(tanka)* from the classical anthologies; and the pattern of growth of the drama is advanced by pivot-words: puns, words of two meanings that as they approach bear one significance and as they recede take on another. The chief moods of the No plays, beyond the dances of gods, flower spirits, and other supernatural beings, are praise of the gods; the rouse and especially the pathos of battle; revenge; and grief.

Seami has written plays in all these moods. Most representative of his No dramas is *Atsumori*, written about 1400. It is the story of Kumagai, who in 1184 killed Atsumori in battle, and gave to his own son a flute he found beside the fallen warrior. The play shows Kumagai, who regrets his action (for in an earlier incarnation Atsumori had done him a kindness) now become a priest under the name of Rensei. As he laments, reapers appear and sing the responses. One of the reapers, a flute player, lingers, and reveals that he is the ghost of Atsumori. They re-enact the fatal fight; save that, this time, Atsumori lifts his sword over Kumagai.

In recent years Japan has developed a drama fashioned after that of the western world, but the No plays proffer gentle patterns of quiet and beauty in a noisy world.

THYESTES   *Lucius Annaeus Seneca*

The complicated events of Roman history during the lifetime of Lucius Annaeus Seneca (Roman, 4? B.C.-65 A.D.) made literary references to current happenings inadvisable. As an official in Rome, Seneca incurred the dislike of Emperor Caligula, who aptly characterized Seneca's style as "all sand and no mortar." Caligula was murdered, 41 A.D. In the same year Messalina, third wife of the new emperor, Claudius, had Seneca banished—on moral charges but political grounds. Messalina was killed by Claudius in 48. The next year, Claudius' fourth wife, his niece Agrippina, recalled Seneca, and made him tutor of Nero, her son by an earlier marriage. Agrippina poisoned Claudius in 54, establishing Nero on the throne. To ensure his own safety Nero poisoned his step-brother, Britannicus (see Racine's *Britannicus**) in 55. When Agrippina tried to dominate her son Nero, he killed her, 59 A.D. Despite these murders, the early years of Nero's reign, guided largely by Seneca, were comparatively moderate. About the year 63, however, Seneca found himself thrust out of the Emperor's councils. A conspiracy of Piso, in 65 A.D., was held to involve Seneca, who by imperial order committed suicide.

Seneca, the most influential writer of Latin prose after Cicero, wrote many essays in philosophy. He was interested in science, geography, and natural history and wrote the influential *Natural Questions*. As a playwright, he wrote nine tragedies, all based on Greek dramas, all drawn from Greek mythology.

These olden legends, however, far away though they may seem, ring the changes on thoughts and actions in the Rome of Seneca's day. The long rhetorical speeches, as well as the pointed epigrammatic turns, reflect the oratory of the day. The emphasis, much more than in the original Greek, is on the violent emotions, the outrageous crimes. The sensational, the horrible—with the raising of ghosts, for deeds so abominable the very ghosts do blench—accord with the turbulence of Messalina's and Nero's Rome. From the stories, an alert audience might well draw the immediate allusion. The tyrant is a frequent figure in the plays. The stepmother recurs. And constantly the stories drive home the lesson that crime leads to further crime in endless repetition. The Roman citizen saw the truth of this all around him.

Although there are records of nine Greek plays and eight Roman plays named *Thyestes,* the only one extant is that by Seneca. *Thyestes* is the most gruesome of ancient tragedies. Throughout, it is marked by an atmosphere of gloom, and driven by the spirit of hatred and revenge. The play opens with one of the Furies calling forth the ghost of Tantalus, who shrinks from the dire deeds ahead. For Atreus has, on a pretense of peace, called back his brother Thyestes, who has seduced Atreus' wife. Thyestes returns, although mistrustfully, and asks for his sons. Atreus responds: "I'll restore them to you: and never more shall you be parted from them." There is a banquet of reconciliation. At the end of the feast, the heads of Thyestes' sons are brought in, and Atreus tells him he has fed upon their bodies.

Something of the Stoic fortitude with which Seneca himself ended his life is manifest in his characterization of Thystes. There is dramatic tension, too, in the politeness and restraint—hatred boiling under the kettle's hood—of the brothers' meetings. But the power of the play lies, first, in the overhanging sense of dread, and then, in the burst of horror with the foul revenge. Sharply it observes the tyrant, so cruel a man that "death is a longed-for favor in my realm."

(The sons of Atreus are Agamemnon and Menelaus, so that in the generations ahead Thyestes is avenged, with the doom of the House of Atreus reaching through four generations.)

Thyestes, the most influential of Seneca's tragedies, gave birth to the Elizabethan blood-and-thunder play, the tragedy of revenge, as in Shakespeare*, Kyd*, Marston*, and Chapman*. A line of Seneca's *Agamemnon,* "The only path that's safe for crime is crime," which is the motif of *Thyestes,* is quoted in Latin in *The Spanish Tragedy**, and in *The Malcontent,* by Marston; it is paraphrased in six other Elizabethan dramas. Even Seneca's tricks of style, his neat epigrams, his stichomythia, his closing ethical tags, were copied by the eager Elizabethans.

Two lines of the play—"For whom the morning saw so great and high Thus low and little 'fore the eve doth die"—are quoted in Marlowe's *Edward II** and form the final couplet of Jonson's *Sejanus.*

Scholars for a long time, because of their many rhetorical passages, believed that the plays of Seneca were intended for recitation only; current opinion has it that they were performed. Although the tragedies have many sensational scenes and supernatural apparitions (not gods so much as ghosts), they bring their legendary characters nearer to human proportions than do their Greek originals. The demigods have been reduced to the human level, with human motivations. However extreme, Atreus still is human in his hatred and in his lust for vengeance. That human life, furthermore, as in *Thyestes* at the bitter end, retains its dignity. Man is viewed as acting of his own free will; descending, perhaps, into blackest villainy, but capable also of Stoic fortitude, of clean integrity despite the disintegrating forces of the world. Man may stand erect, proudly human, in the face of disaster.

At the same time, man moves in a world of brutality and crime, the excesses of which were all around Seneca, who put them full and stark into his dramas. His pattern has been the most influential on all tragedy since.

LOVE'S LABOR'S LOST   *William Shakespeare*

Played in 1598 before Queen Elizabeth, *Love's Labor's Lost,* 1590(?), first of the Shakespearean plays, satirizes the dainty devices of the courtiers of the Virgin Queen. Their extravagant fashions and elaborate manners were matched by their highly adorned speech, especially after the success of Lyly's prose romance *Euphues,* 1579: the Italianate gloves and feathers; the smirk and bow of the Spanish grandee; the words fetched from the ink-horn, piled in pedantic periods, heaped in high hyperbole. In the play, hearing the curate and the schoolmaster, Moth observes: "They have been at a great feast of language, and have stolen the scraps." But William Shakespeare (English, 1564-1616) seems to enjoy, as well as satirize, extravagant language.

The play's substance concerns the trifling of four sets of lovers. The King of Navarre and his three courtiers have sworn to eschew feminine company and to devote themselves to study. They must, however, grant audience to the Princess of France, who comes with three of her ladies. The inevitable does not delay; and the movement of the play arises from the manner in which each of the men discovers that the others are also in love. With the spring cuckoo song—'When daisies pied and violets blue'—hinting woman's infidelity, and the winter owl song—'When icicles hang by the wall'—suggesting domestic toil, the play lilts with laughter to its close. In the words of the German critic and translator of Shakespeare, Schlegel: "The sparks of wit fly about in such profusion that they form complete fireworks, and the dialogue for the most part resembles the bustling collision and banter of passing masks at a carnival." The many-colored light verbal banter remains delightful.

Less bantering times found the play less pleasing. When Queen Anne, the wife of James I, saw a performance, she could well have echoed the contemporary criticism: "This play no play but plague was unto me." Jeremy Collier in 1699 said "the whole play is a very silly one". In 1740, a version of *As You Like It* borrowed the Spring Song; in 1762 an adaptation called *The Students* was published but apparently never performed. Until the Romantics, indeed, *Love's Labor's Lost* was quite neglected.

Coleridge saw the play as foreshadowing Shakespeare's greater comedies, "as in a portrait taken of him in his boyhood. I can never sufficiently admire the wonderful activity of thought throughout the whole of the first scene, rendered natural, as it is, by the choice of the characters, and the whimsical determination on which the drama is founded." Swinburne goes a step further: "During certain scenes we seem almost to stand again at the cradle of newborn comedy, and hear the first lisping and laughing accents run over from her baby lips in bubbling rhyme; but when the note changes we recognize the speech of gods. For the first time in our literature the higher key of poetic or romantic comedy is finely touched to a fine issue."

Beneath the romantic dalliance of love, however, Shakespeare presents a deeper thought. "What is the end of study?" Biron asks in the opening scene. The play gives answer. Benjamin Franklin caught the point in a *bon mot:* "A single man . . . is an incomplete animal. He resembles the odd half of a pair of scissors." From Biron's great speech on the education that shines within a woman's eyes, to the final songs with the bird of careless love and the bird of barren wisdom, the play presses home the thought that neither wisdom nor love, neither man nor woman, is whole without the other.

Much has been said of the artificial devices and dialogue of this play. They are attacked by Johnson: "A quibble is to Shakespeare what luminous vapours are to the traveller! He follows it at all adventures; it is sure to lead him out of his way. . . . A quibble was to him the fatal Cleopatra for which he lost the world, and was content to lose it." They are defended by Pater: "Below the many artifices of Biron's amorous speeches we may trace sometimes the 'unutterable longing', and the lines in which Katharine describes the blighting through love of her younger sister are one of the most touching things in older literature." This early play sets the battle—ornate, sumptuous diction versus simple, direct statement—that Shakespeare fights until his writings end. From beginning to end, however, he is sparing in the use of the common copulative (*is*), giving us a great variety of vivid transitive verbs, that carry on the action.

The travesty of *The Nine Worthies,* enacted by the common folk in the play for the Princess, is one of the earliest burlesques in the English theatre.

The first New York performance of the play was on February 21, 1874, at the Fifth Avenue Theatre; it was produced again at Daly's in 1891. More recently in England, Stratford saw the play in 1934; London, at the Old Vic, in 1936. All Shakespeare's plays are performed in series by London's Old Vic: 1914-1923; 1953-1958. New York saw this play again in 1953.

After the 1874 New York production, the *Spirit of the Times* declared the play "undobutedly one of Shakespeare's weakest in point of construction. . . . Whatever attraction the play possesses is not in its incidents or plot, but in the beauty and poetry of its lines."

An age in which the art of conversation, and even the sense of leisureliness that is prerequisite to that art, have been hurried away in the gallop of time, finds diminishing returns from this early frolic of Shakespeare's. However, those in whom a love of language persists, who joy in balanced syllables and fair matched phrases, as well as in the roundabout indirections by which love romps at last home, will still enjoy their feat display in *Love's Labor's Lost*.

KING HENRY VI   *William Shakespeare*

The three parts of *King Henry VI* are separate plays. Scholars believe that Part Two was written first, about 1590. They follow chronologically the history of the king and the Wars of the Roses, with a fidelity to fact no other dramatist has maintained. In fact, arranged in historical sequence, *Richard II**, *Henry IV**, *Henry V**, *Henry VI*, *Richard III**, and *Henry VIII** present a three-century panorama of English history, tracing its course to the birth of Henry VIII's daughter Elizabeth, patron of the playwright. The plays were presented in such sequence at Stratford-on-Avon in 1905 and at Antioch College, Ohio, in 1952. The German critic Schlegel declared that they constitute "a national epic". The plays, teeming with armies embattled against the French, against uprisings of the people or pretenders to the throne, offer vivid portraits of the English kings and emphasize the importance of a strong hereditary line to maintain due order in Britain. They helped contribute to the patriotic spirit of the time; it is said that after Shakespeare's speech of Henry V at Harfleur, the recruiting sergeant had no difficulty in filling his company. The story is drawn from Raphael Holinshed's *Chronicles* (1578). References by Nash, Greene, and others indicate the play's success. However, jealous Ben Jonson sneered at playwrights who used such material.

Part One opens with the dead march for the funeral of Henry V. The successor is an infant and intrigues begin. The adherents of York pluck white roses, the followers of Lancaster pluck red. In France, Joan La Pucelle (Joan of Arc; pictured as in league with the Devil) hurls back the English. The play shows the horrid consequences of rivalry among the nobles, common also while Shakespeare was writing.

Part Two begins with Suffolk, who as procurator for the King had married Margaret in France, delivering his charge to Henry in England. He does not relinquish her wholly, however; and Margaret (O tiger's heart wrapp'd in a woman's hide!) and Suffolk plot the overthrow of the Duke of Gloster, Protector during Henry's minority. The villainy rebounds upon Suffolk. A rebellion of the Kentish commoner Jack Cade is fomented by the Duke of York. This insurrection is travestied in the play, though several of the commoners' remarks are given pungency, referring to the humble origin of all men, the wretched lot of the people, and the lack of redress for wrongs. Jack Cade himself is killed by a Kentish gentleman. York now sweeps into open rebellion against the weakling Henry, and at St. Alban's field defeats the King's forces.

Part Three shows the Duke of York entering London in triumph, despite Henry's earlier boast: "Thrice is he armed that hath his quarrel just!" The forces of Henry then rally, led by the forceful Queen Margaret; York is captured, taunted, and slain. Spurred on by the Earl of Warwick, the sons of the murdered York—Edward; George, Duke of Clarence; and Richard, Duke of Gloster—scour the fields. Henry is imprisoned in the Tower; there, the bloodthirsty Gloster (later to be Richard III) kills him. Edward IV is established on the throne.

Although the March, 1592 performance of *Henry VI* took in the largest sum reported in Henslowe's *Diary* of receipts, the three parts of *Henry VI* are rarely performed. Some of the lines in Part Three were once well known through Colley Cibber's incorporation of them into his popular adaptation of *Richard III**. The three plays have sometimes been compressed into a single play, as by Edmund Kean in 1817, and in the earlier version of John Crowne, 1680, shaped to emphasize the antipapal feeling of his day. John Barrymore acted in a revival in 1920; Parts Two and Three were produced in Pasadena in 1935.

Some critics, deeming the *Henry VI* plays unworthy of Shakespeare, have declared that they are not his. Thus Tennyson ventured: "I am certain that *Henry VI* is in the main not Shakespeare's, though here and there he may have put in a touch." But Samuel Johnson insisted: "The diction, the versification, and the figures, are Shakespeare's." Most critics today agree with Johnson, surely for Parts Two and Three.

In Elizabethan days, the people had their attitudes shaped at least in part by the theatre. *Henry VI* was an instrument toward this end. "It is," said Hardin Craig, "as if Shakespeare had taken England for his hero." Certainly he was setting before the people a clear and searching examination of government, of a ruler's problems and ways. He pressed sharply home the still needed warning against civil dissension. Sharply, too, he stressed the chaos that follows the conqueror. Henry V is scarcely buried when a sentence comparing him to Julius Caesar is interrupted with word of the crumbling of his newly won empire in France.

Henry VI recognizes that the aggressive man is far from the best ruler; he makes the point about his hero-father. It is here to be noted that Henry VI is the only one of Shakespeare's English kings to possess all the "king-becoming graces" listed by Malcolm in *Macbeth**. Thus the play balances the odds of power and virtue.

THE COMEDY OF ERRORS   *William Shakespeare*

This play literally began with a riot. To the first recorded performance, at Gray's Inn on Holy Innocents' Day, December 28, 1594, the members of the Inner Temple were invited. Even standing room was lacking, but they pushed in, and the comedy was delayed by the disturbance. It has been played to crowded houses ever since.

The play, the shortest of Shakespeare's, is also his most artificial, with balanced speeches, occasionally in alternate rhyming, with puns, quibbles, and doggerel verse. Coleridge felt that "Shakespeare has in this piece presented us with a legitimate farce in exactest consonance with the philosophical principles and character of farce". Perhaps this is due to his close following of his source, the comedy *The Menaechmi**, by the Roman Plautus. Shakespeare, however, doubles the Roman twinship by providing the master twins with a pair of twin servants. Early separated, one Antipholus (with his Dromio) has grown to prominence in Ephesus; the other Antipholus (with his Dromio) comes there from Syracuse. The wife Adriana, the mistress, and sundry other citizens mix up the pairs, who confuse their own servants and are tangled in odd situations and threats of jail—until the meeting of the identical twins resolves the confusion. The deeper human sentiment rising from the presence and the reunion of the Antipholus' parents, Aegeon and Aemilia, is another contribution of Shakespeare's. The playwright's removal of the locale to Ephesus may have been influenced by the evil reputation of that city, its inhospitality to strangers, that helped produce Paul's *Epistle to the Ephesians,* in the *Bible.*

The Comedy of Errors has been highly popular; there have been frequent adaptations in Germany, France, Rumania, and other lands. One German version, by Hans Rothe—from Shakespeare from Plautus from a lost Greek original—was re-Englished by Ashley Dukes and performed in London in 1936; the *Times* said "the result of this geminiculture is a cheerful little charade", although this version omits Aegeon, and "with Aegeon goes the scene that touches the Shakespearean comedy with beauty".

Shakespeare deepened the play's mood, not only with the twins' parents, but with the serious notes of jealousy and shrewishness in Adriana, which some scholars deem a reflection of Shakespeare's own home life.

American performances include one by the Ethiopian Art Theatre in 1923. Heywood Broun called this "tiresome . . . but we cannot imagine its being very funny under the most favorable circumstances. It seemed the mustiest foolery possible". Others liked the performance, which was staged on a central platform. John Corbin felt that "the play is frank farce and can be run off successfully only at a heightened tempo and with the action at times running riot in the grotesque". The play was presented at the Century of Progress in Chicago in 1934 and at the World's Fair in New York in 1938. In 1938 and 1939, indeed, it was produced at Columbia, Yale, Northwestern, New York, and Louisiana Universities, at Cleveland, and at Stratford-on-Avon.

In 1938 Richard Watts, Jr. declared: "If you have been wondering all these years just what was wrong with *The Comedy of Errors,* it is now possible to tell you. It has been waiting for a score by Rodgers and Hart, and direction by George Abbott." The musical comedy *The Boys from Syracuse,* with pantomimist Jimmy Savo as Dromio of Syracuse, had come to town in time for Thanksgiving. The critics gave thanks. Brooks Atkinson called it "an exuberant musical comedy . . . giving Shakespeare a commendable assist in the modern vernacular. . . . Let us pass over their bawdries with decorous reserve, pausing only to remark that they are vastly enjoyable, and let us praise them extravagantly for such a romantic song as 'This Can't Be Love' and such gracious mischief as the 'Sing For Your Supper' trio". Sidney B. Whipple was even more emphatic: "I believe it will be regarded as the greatest comedy of its time." John Mason Brown, however, thought it not "really funny", dragging with long waits between the laughs, and too many twin confusions; but he was willing to put the blame for these on Shakespeare: "Mr. Abbott has made a valiant effort to get the great William out of academic hock. . . . With the exception of two or three lines, Mr. Abbott has tossed Shakespeare's dialogue out the window. Even when he follows its content, he does not hesitate to rephrase it in an idiom which is sometimes lusty and always contemporary. . . . One leaves *The Boys from Syracuse* congratulating Mr. Abbott for what he has done and almost—I say, almost—forgiving Shakespeare for his youthful indiscretion."

This 'youthful indiscretion', *The Comedy of Errors,* has been a vehicle for the transfer of laughter from the ancient Greek theatre to stages of every land and recent time.

THE TWO GENTLEMEN OF VERONA   *William Shakespeare*

It is the wandering heart that Shakespeare pictures in *The Two Gentlemen of Verona,* 1592(?), though the mood is romantic comedy. Two of the most popular medieval and Renaissance themes are joined in the play—the pursuit of a wayward lover by a maiden disguised as a page and a man's wooing of the lady-love of his sworn bosom friend. Valentine, at the court of Milan, falls in love with the Duke's daughter, Silvia. Following Valentine from Vienna, his dear friend Proteus, forgetting his own sweetheart Julia, also becomes enamored of the irresistible Silvia. The lonely Julia disguises herself as a man, the first of a long line of similarly disguised women in Shakespeare; she follows Proteus and discovers his infidelity. The usual complications end with the usual readjustment and pairing of the two sets of lovers.

Ideas for the play were drawn from several earlier works, especially the Portuguese Jorge de Montemayor's *Diana Enamorada,* 1542. Hazlitt, indeed, called the play "little more than the first outline of a comedy loosely sketched in". Aspects of it are more fully bodied forth in Shakespeare's later comedies. Thus Julia's disguise as a servitor, bringing messages from the man she loves to his new inamorata, foreshadows the role of Viola in *Twelfth Night**. The philosophical words of Valentine, banished to the forest, look forward to the thoughts of the banished Duke and of Jaques, in the Forest of Arden in *As You Like It**. The matching of wits between the servants, Speed and Launce, however, is amusing in its own right. Indeed, in the version Garrick used in 1762, two extra scenes were added for the antics of Launce and Speed.

The Two Gentlemen of Verona was transformed into an opera in 1820. In 1938 the play was enacted at Stratford as though by boys and girls; this seemed to smooth over one difficulty. There had been considerable critical objection, when Proteus and Valentine are reconciled, to the latter's volunteering to give up his beloved to his friend: "All that was mine in Silva I give thee." One critic declared that this shows "there is no longer even *one* gentleman of Verona!" Playing in the mood of youthful frolic, the *London Times* pointed out, takes the sting from this otherwise difficult line. To the Elizabethan gentleman, however, that declaration of Valentine was natural and proper, for the Renaissance held friendship more binding than love. A quite different interpretation of the play by Harold C. Goddard sees the ending as part of the irony underlying the story, in that the "gentlemen" of Verona are portrayed as far from gentlemanly or gentle. Launce accurately calls Proteus "a kind of knave" and Valentine "a most notable lubber"; and Launce's treatment of his dog is a Quixotic burlesque of gentlemanly behavior. This suggestion gathers worth from Shakespeare's satiric portrayal of gentlemen in other comedies.

Recent American performances include one in 1916 at the University of Wisconsin; 1927, at Pasadena; 1935, at the University of Oklahoma; 1939, with Whitford Kane, at Ann Arbor, Michigan. Of the first American production, by the Keans, at the Park Theatre, New York, October 1846, the *Spirit of the Times* stated: "It was admirably put upon the stage, and . . . we can truly say it was entirely successful throughout." Noting that some believe parts of the play may not be Shakespeare's, the 1846 critic claimed the whole work for the bard. The Bristol Old Vic company produced the play in London in 1952.

In production, the comic elements are usually emphasized; thus Bernard Shaw (heading his review "Poor Shakespeare!") called Augustin Daly's 1895 adaptation "a pleasant vaudeville". But the shafts of laughter strike the bull's eye in human nature with an aim eternally true.

KING RICHARD III   *William Shakespeare*

This play, evidently written in 1593, offers magnificent acting opportunities in the role of "Crouchback" Richard, fierce, ruthless, valiant, every inch a King—save that his mind, like his body, is crooked. So popular was the play in Shakespeare's time that between 1594 and 1620 a dozen other plays quoted or parodied the famous line: "A horse! a horse! my kingdom for a horse!" The image of the horse prominent in this play is closely related to its fierce drive of energy. (Harold C. Goddard called it "a sort of biography of force".) From Pegasus through medieval nightmares and proverbial spurring beggars to Freudian dreams, the horse has been the symbol of the unconscious energy that gallops beneath and often runs away with our conscious selves. *Richard III* is the most rapid in action, the most concentrated in energy, of Shakespeare's plays.

The role of Richard is especially luring in the adaptation made by Colley Cibber in 1699, which converted Shakespeare's drama into a one-man play. Although Sir Henry Irving, in 1896, attempted to restore the Shakespearean scope, later productions (even John Barrymore's in 1920) have preferred to cut nearer the Cibber concentration on the villainous Richard. The Cibber version added bits from others of Shakespeare's history plays; it put the last scene of *King Henry VI** at the beginning, and thus opened with Duke Richard stabbing Henry. David Garrick made his London debut, October 19, 1741, as Richard in the Cibber adaptation, and established himself as the outstanding actor of the day. Garrick was a "natural" performer; in 1746 he challenged the rhetorical, violent James Quin, and they appeared as Richard on successive nights: the public preferred Garrick.

This was the first of Shakespeare's plays to be performed in America; Thomas Kean played the Cibber version at the New York Nassau Street Theatre, March 5, 1750.

The story is drawn from Holinshed's *Chronicles*. As Shakespeare's play opens, Richard, then but Duke of Gloster, brother of King Edward IV, is discontentedly pondering his fortunes. Intrigues follow in quick succession. His brother Clarence is brought to the Tower, there to be murdered at Gloster's command. When King Edward IV dies (oddly for the times, at peace in bed), Gloster has the two young sons of his brother Clarence smothered to death; even the murderers weep at their frail innocence. With the aid of the Duke of Buckingham, Gloster has himself declared King Richard III. Margaret, widow of Henry VI, weeps with Elizabeth, widow of Edward IV, and with the Duchess of York (mother of Edward, Clarence, and Richard) over the orgy of murder that steeps the land. Buckingham, recoiling from the course of wholesale murder, joins with Henry, Earl of Richmond, against the relentless Richard. The armies meet and Buckingham is killed; but in furious combat Richard is overpowered and slain by Richmond, who becomes Henry VII and starts the Tudor line.

Swinburne, after praising *Richard III*, sets it in the tradition of the mighty line of Marlowe: "It is as fiery in passion, as single in purpose, as rhetorical often though never so inflated in expression, as *Tamburlaine** itself." The play makes excellent use of stichomythia with sharp thrust of repartee like the rapid play of sword on sword in fencing.

Bernard Shaw has called the drama the best version of *Punch and Judy*—even to the hump: "Shakespeare revels in it with just the sort of artistic unconscionableness that fits the theme. Richard is the prince of Punches; he delights Man by provoking God, and dies unrepentant and game to the last." There is typical hyperbole in his cry on the battlefield, "My kingdom for a horse!", when he wants the horse in order to preserve his kingdom. There is frank cynicism in his appeal to the nobles at Bosworth Field. The truculence of Richard, indeed, leaves few interpreters of the role mindful of the observation of Henry James, that this part can "best dispense with declamation". Indeed, James feels that the play should never be performed. "The attempt to make real," he argues, "or even plausible a loose, violent, straddling romance like *Richard III*—a chronicle for the market-place, a portrait for the house wall—only emphasizes what is coarse in such a hurly-burly and does nothing for what is fine. It gives no further lift to the poetry and adds a mortal heaviness to the prose."

The swashbuckling performer is nonetheless drawn to Richard. With his wit, adroitness, mordant humor, and unflinching courage, he wields a fascination within his villainy. The final fight of the furious monarch is always a fierce duel, as attested by those that saw David Garrick, Barry Sullivan, Edwin Booth, or Edmund Kean. Coleridge said that watching Kean play Richard was like "reading Shakespeare by flashes of lightning." *Blackwood's Edinburgh Magazine* (January, 1820) pictured Macready, who, "after the mortal wound, lifts himself to more than his natural height and comes pouring down upon his adversary till he reaches him, and then falls at his feet like a spent thunderbolt." The *London Times* (November 16, 1951) quotes a critic of the 1890's as declaring: "Absolutely Henry Irving's Richard is the most Satanic creature I have ever seen on the stage." Yet somehow in New York there was in the mid-nineteenth century a rash of performances by women and children (one Ellen Bateman, aged 4) as Richard, such as that of Charlotte Crampton with a troop of trained horses for the battle scene. The streamlined version of Richard Whorf (first played for the Army's Biarritz-American University in December, 1945, and brought to Broadway on February 8, 1949) oddly omits the final duel of Richard and Richmond, substituting a stylized ballet-battle of the armies—an ineffectual close to an ill-conceived production.

An opportunity for imaginative revelation of Richard's character comes while Richard awaits the result of Buckingham's plea to the Mayor and citizens of London that Richard be crowned. Richard accepts Buckingham's suggestion that he be seen by the Londoners "between two churchmen", with a prayerbook in his hand. Richard Mansfield, playing the part, when the others onstage were not looking righted the prayerbook, which he had been carrying upside down. And when Richard accedes with seeming reluctance to the Mayor's plea that he accept the burden of the Crown, and the Mayor leaves to prepare for the Coronation—Mansfield exultantly flung the prayerbook high in the air. Fit gesture for a spirit that feared not heaven or hell.

Although Shakespeare provides a wide historical canvas, with many figures of all ranks and stations, the play is one great thrust of energy, a single drive of the quest for power finding inevitable doom, as humanity recoils from the arbitrary actions, tyranny, cruelty, and crime. Set in England from 1471 to 1485, *King Richard III* is a horrid picture of emotions and ambitions such as are still loose in the shaken world.

TITUS ANDRONICUS   *William Shakespeare*

Shakespeare's earliest tragedy, *Titus Andronicus*, 1592 (?), is also his most gory. The Roman Titus Andronicus, returning victorious over the Goths with their Queen Tamora and her three sons captive, makes Saturninus Emperor. Thereupon Saturninus spurns Titus' daughter Lavinia, to marry Tamora. Meanwhile Titus' sons, to avenge their brothers slain in the war, have killed Tamora's eldest son. Tamora and her paramour, the Moor Aaron, begin her vengeance by killing Bassianus, the Emperor's brother, in such a way that suspicion falls on Titus' sons Quintus and Martius; the Queen's sons ravish Lavinia, then cut off her hands and her tongue. Aaron promises to send Titus his imprisoned sons if he will cut off his hand as ransom; his hand is returned to him, with their heads. The maimed Lavinia manages to communicate her despoilers' identity. Lucius, Titus' surviving son, seeks the aid of the Goths; they capture Aaron and his new-born son by Tamora. A parley is held at Titus' home. There Titus, after serving Tamora a pie made of the flesh of her sons, kills her and Lavinia. Saturninus kills Titus and is killed by Lucius, who, condemning Aaron to be buried breast-deep and left to die, takes over the Empire to set its days in order.

The spurt of blood across the stage of *Titus Andronicus* has shocked many scholars, some to the extent of protest that the play cannot be Shakespeare's, some—who face the evidence—to the suggestion, made among others by J. Dover Wilson and Richard Watts, Jr., that Shakespeare was burlesquing the tragedy-of-revenge tradition. Actually the play was seriously received and popular; its first recorded performance, January 23, 1594, filled the house, and it had frequent revivals for thirty years.

The play is in the tradition of Kyd's *The Spanish Tragedy**; its horrors echo from Seneca's *Thyestes** and the legend of Philomel in Ovid's *Metamorphoses*. Shakespeare, as Lucius' closing words make clear, uses the dismemberment of the human body to symbolize the disruption of the body politic.

A version of the play by Edward Ravenscroft, enacted at Drury Lane in 1678, ended with Aaron perishing in flames onstage; but as the public display of atrocities grew less appealing, *Titus Andronicus* lapsed from favor. The role of Aaron was a favorite of James Quin's in the 1740's, though the 1860 playbills of Ira Aldridge as Aaron bore the words "not acted for 200 years". There was an Old Vic production in 1923, one at Cambridge, England, in 1953, and a well-received one, the first at Stratford-upon-Avon, with Laurence Olivier as Titus, Vivien Leigh as Lavinia, and Anthony Quayle as Aaron, opening August 16, 1955. *Punch* (March 25, 1953) observed that, in the face of our tabloid sensations, gangster films, and horror comics, "to wrinkle our noses at the gruesomeness of Titus Andronicus only labels us as hypocrites". Harold Hobson, after the Stratford production, called *Titus* "in some important respects, a remarkably contemporary play". We still commit atrocities, we shrink only from displaying them onstage.

Aaron vies with Iago in *Othello** as Shakespeare's closest approach to an unmitigated, unmotivated villain; like Iago, he glories in his evil and goes defiant to his death. Note that in *Titus Andronicus* the source of corruption is in the aliens in power; in Shakespeare's later Roman plays, the corruption springs from the Romans themselves. G. B. Harrison calls the characters inconsistent, but their drive is more direct than Hamlet's. The play makes fierce emotional impact. Its horrors call for careful handling, lest today's finical audiences indeed treat them as burlesque. Properly presented, *Titus Andronicus* shows young Shakespeare testing his varied powers.

KING JOHN   *William Shakespeare*

In no history play does Shakespeare press the lesson to be drawn from earlier events more closely home than in *King John*, 1594(?). After the death of his brother, Richard the Lion-Hearted, John has seized the throne; he must maintain himself by force. Against the French Dauphin, against young Arthur of Bretagne whom Richard has named as heir, against English lords enraged when the imprisoned Arthur is killed, and against the power of the Pope, John must defend his throne. When John dies, poisoned, the Dauphin withdraws, and peace comes to the land as John's son mounts the throne as Henry III. Troubled by the consequences of his own deeds, King John knows no peace; only with the approach of death can he say "now my soul hath elbow-room."

There is a scene of tender pathos, unmatched elsewhere in the history plays, when Prince Arthur wins over the King's chamberlain Hubert, come to burn out the young Prince's eyes. The part of Constance, too, Arthur's mother, has attracted actresses because of the deep maternal affection and the heart-rending sorrow she displays. But the major movement of the play is an illustration of King John's words "There is no sure foundation set on blood, No certain life achieved by others' death."

Two elements of Shakespeare's style first became prominent in *King John*. Here first his images progress, a metaphor once uttered suggesting further development. This associative rise of the image develops in the plays until, as Charles Lamb observed, "Shakespeare mingles everything, he runs line into line, embarrasses sentences and metaphors; before one idea has burst its shell, another is hatched and clamorous for disclosure." The second element of Shakespeare's style, present in *Richard III* but richer here, is the driving home of an abstract idea with a concrete metaphor, as in *cloud of dignity* or *dust of old oblivion*. Metaphors have largely replaced similes, supplanting the looseness of comparison with the tight hold of identity; increasingly, in Shakespeare's plays hereafter, a metaphor grows to a leitmotif. The power of the images is thereby increased and sustained.

The earliest form of this play bears the title *The Troublesome Raigne of John, King of England*. Its events are related in Holinshed's *Chronicles*. Infrequently produced, the play is a succession of alarums, excursions, and tableaux, rather than a unified drive of dramatic action. From the time the theatres were closed in 1642, it was not seen until 1737, and then and lengthily thereafter in a version by Colley Cibber, which minimized the role of the Bastard Faulconbridge and gave great prominence to Constance. Shakespeare's emphasis, reversed by Cibber, is definitely on Faulconbridge, the illegitimate son of King Richard I, whom Shakespeare depicts as an upright and proud Plantagenet, counterbalancing the tyrannical John. In the history plays, Shakespeare usually gives the final words to the person of highest rank; in *King John* not only the final words, but the last words in four of the five acts, are spoken by Faulconbridge.

With Faulconbridge's lines extensively cut, Samuel Johnson, in 1768, observed that the play lacked "the happy force of some other of his tragedies, nor can be said much to affect the passions, or enlarge the understanding." Tennyson, however, in 1883, highly esteemed its poetry: "As far as I am aware, no one has noticed what great Aeschylean lines there are in Shakespeare, particularly in *King John*." The *New York Dramatic Mirror* questioned, in 1915, "what curious turn of courage or whimsicality prompted Mr. Mantell to open his season of repertoire with *King John*? It is by far the least interesting of Shakespeare's historical tragedies. Most of its action depends on parades of pageants, and ensembles; and its central character is so uncertainly drawn that it commands neither respect nor admiration."

It is, indeed, less on the men in the drama than on Constance that actors' efforts and critical attention have centered. Garrick himself was astonished at Mrs. Cibber's performance in the part, and the audience was "electrified, when she threw herself upon the ground in agony." Of the same moment in another production, the moment when Constance learns of her son Arthur's death, Leigh Hunt declared: "All who remember Mrs. Siddons must remember its electrical effect, and how marvelously she reconciled the mad impulse of it with habitual dignity. Miss Kemble (Mrs. Siddons' niece) was almost stationary in her grief. Mrs. Siddons used to pace up and down, as the eddying gust of her impatience drove her." Julia Neilson is among the others that have essayed Constance's role.

King John was produced in 1935 in Pasadena; in 1938, in New York. What time permits to remain, of even the greatest men, is summed up in King John's self-estimate: "I am a scribbled form, drawn with a pen Upon a parchment." The play takes life and continuing significance because that pen was Shakespeare's.

A MIDSUMMER NIGHT'S DREAM   *William Shakespeare*

At the court of Athens, and in the woods nearby, moves *A Midsummer Night's Dream,* 1594(?), a charming idyllic illustration of the remark made in the play: "The course of true love never did run smooth." Without scenery, the Elizabethan dramatist showers us with magic of description in verse. The desire for elaborate decoration overdressed the play and it fell from popularity. Samuel Pepys in 1662 could not endure it; it became an opera, *The Fairy Queen,* in 1692; Garrick also made an opera of it, *The Fairies,* in 1775. It was seen only in adaptations until 1840, when Charles James Mathews and his wife, Lucia Vestris, brought the original version to Covent Garden. All this substitution emphasizes Puck's comment: "Lord, what fools these mortals be!"

The framework of the play (told earlier in Chaucer's *Knight's Tale*) is provided by the wedding of Theseus, Duke of Athens, and Hippolyta, Queen of the Amazons. Probably written for a court wedding, the play seems to some scholars a hint that Queen Elizabeth herself ought to accept the golden chains of wedlock.

The royal nuptials within the play are watched over by the fairy King, Oberon, and his Queen, Titania, with whom Oberon has quarreled. Temporarily bemused by a love elixir Puck spreads at Oberon's command, Titania falls in love with weaver Bottom, temporarily topped as an ass. (E. A. Robinson begins his poem *Ben Jonson Entertains a Man from Stratford* with the comment that Shakespeare "alone of us Would put an ass's head in fairyland.") The lovers Demetrius and Helena, Lysander and Hermia, are intertangled, then properly paired by elfin Puck. Bottom, released from his transmogrification into an ass, is free, along with his fellows—Quince, Snug, Flute, Snout, and Starveling—to present, at the royal wedding feast, "the most lamentable comedy, and most cruel death of Pyramus and Thisbe." After their performance, all go off to bed. The Master of the Revels urged Theseus not to hear these horny-handed sons of toil, for it would be cruel to laugh at their earnest efforts, but Theseus is more tolerant and defends all players. Remarks of this sort, scattered through his plays, show that Shakespeare pondered deeply the problems of actors.

Even in the formal and "classical" eighteenth century, the romantic qualities of the play were appreciated, though Samuel Johnson seems almost grudging of his praise: "Wild and fantastical as this play is, all the parts in their various modes are well written, and give the kind of pleasure which the author designed. Fairies in his time were much in fashion; common tradition had made them familiar, and Spenser's poem had made them great. . . ." A century later, Swinburne was more unreserved: "Here each kind of excellence is equal throughout; there are here no purple patches on a gown of serge, but one seamless and imperial robe of a single dye."

The different characters in the play use as different speech. Royalty —including Oberon for official dicta—uses blank verse. The lovers talk mainly in rhymed couplets. The fairies lilt in a lyrical measure (trochaic tetrameter). *Pyramus and Thisbe* is presented in a parody of the ballad meter. The meaning of the *Pyramus* Prologue is reversed by pauses after the wrong phrases—a humorous device used earlier in *Ralph Roister Doister**. The "rude mechanics" speak prose. Thus the patterns of sound accord with their utterers.

The play itself, as well as Bottom, was "transmogrified" by the earlier Tyrone Power in 1836, as *O'Flannigan and the Fairies;* and 103 years later in a Negro version, *Swinging the Dream;* as a motion picture in 1909 and 1935. A colorful production of the play in its own shape was presented by the Old Vic company in London in December, 1951. Recent American productions include Whitford Kane's in 1934; one at New York University in 1937; one outdoors in 1937 by the Caravan Theatre; one in 1940 at Schenectady; one in 1942 at the University of Washington in Seattle, and one in New York at the Dramatic Workshop in 1952. The Caravan production did not appeal to Burns Mantle, who felt the play's "value as entertainment is largely dependent upon the personality and popularity of its leading players." Brooks Atkinson enjoyed it more; he stated: "*A Midsummer Night's Dream* is make-believe, which is a virtue, for it appeals to the imagination; and there were imaginations ready to be moved last evening. . . . The plot is a subtle weaving of the imagination, none too easy to grasp in the best of circumstances. As befits an outdoor showing, the Federal Theatre actors gave it a rough-and-ready performance at a lively physical pace."

The motion picture version of 1935, by Max Reinhardt and William Dieterle, was a pretentious, rococo, overdone filming, with fairies dancing through heavy mist in shimmering streamers of cellophane; but with one or two good movements, especially the rehearsal of Bottom (James Cagney) and Peter Quince (Joe E. Brown) as Pyramus and Thisbe, just before Bottom acquires the head of an ass; and the chasing through the forest night of the lovers misguided by Puck (little Mickey Rooney whisking to fame in an excellently acted but atrociously conceived role). The picture, furthermore, omits much fine material.

There has been a tendency in productions to emphasize mechanical devices. It is a neat touch, when Bottom awakes after his asinine love-making with Titania, to have him find hay in his pouch. But to have Puck pop out of an opening flower, or (as when Ellen Terry played Puck for Henry Irving in 1859) rise seated on a mushroom that sprouts miraculously from bare ground; or at the words "I'll put a girdle round about the earth in forty minutes" to let Puck slip behind a tree while a dummy flies far into the clouds—and once Ellen Terry had to return before a guffawing audience and carry off the dummy, which had plummeted thudding back onto the stage:—these more questionably follow the play's spirit of make-believe. Augustin Daly, bringing American science to England, in 1895 equipped his fairies with individual electric lights which, commented Bernard Shaw, "they switch on and off from time to time, like children with a new toy."

Not earthy Bottom and his mechanics, however, nor all the obtrusive mechanical devices, can dim the magic of the play itself, in the eternally springtide music of its verse and the spell of its poetry.

THE MERCHANT OF VENICE   *William Shakespeare*

Two popular Renaissance themes—the nature of true love, and the relative power of love and friendship—are here dramatized. They are presented through four movements: the bond story; the ring story (these two are found together in the Italian tale *Il Pecorone,* about 1379, by G. Fiorentine, called Ser Giovanni); the choosing of a casket (in Boccaccio's *Decameron,* 1353); and the opposition of Christian and Jew, culminating in the final order that Shylock become a Christian.

In friendship, Antonio lends Bassanio money wherewith to equip himself to woo Portia—though Antonio must himself first borrow the 3,000 ducats from the Jew Shylock, "in merry jest" assigning as forfeit a pound of flesh nearest his heart. Of three caskets, gold, silver, and lead, among which Portia's suitors must choose, Bassanio picks the leaden casket, finding therein Portia's picture, which means her hand. Shylock's daughter Jessica meanwhile deepens her father's sense of wrong by eloping with Lorenzo, a Christian, and when Antonio's ships are delayed, Shylock in dead earnest demands his forfeit. Then in her love Portia, disguised as a lawyer, with a verbal trick saves Antonio: Shylock may have his pound of flesh, but not one drop of blood. As her reward for saving Antonio, Portia (unrecognized) demands the ring she herself has given Bassanio, and which he has sworn never to relinquish while he loves her. Back home, Portia asks Bassanio where the ring is; his explanation seems feeble, until she shows him the ring in the recognition scene that ends the comedy.

It is in recognition of Portia's quality that Henry James, in 1880, condemned the work of Ellen Terry: "Miss Terry has too much nature, and we should like a little more art. . . . The mistress of Belmont was a great lady, as well as a tender and clever woman; but this side of the part quite eludes the actress, whose deportment is not such as we should expect in the splendid spinster who has princes for wooers."

In 1788 Horace Walpole declared: "With all my enthusiasm for Shakespeare, it is one of his plays that I like the least. The story of the caskets is silly." Hazlitt also disapproved: "Portia has a certain degree of affectation and pedantry about her, which is very unusual in Shakespeare's women. The speech about Mercy is all very well, but there are a thousand finer ones in Shakespeare. We should like Jessica better if she had not deceived and robbed her father, and Lorenzo, if he had not married a Jewess, though he thinks he has a right to wrong a Jew."

Hazlitt's reservations regarding Portia accord with the interpretation of Harold C. Goddard, who points out that the casket, the bond, and the ring episodes all involve a contrast between the outer seeming and the inner reality. Likewise there is a contrast between the flashy exterior of the "golden" world of wealth in the play and the plain exterior of the "leaden" world of worth these gentlefolk do not attain. Their society sparkles; but underneath, it is empty and dull. The first words of Antonio: "In sooth I know not why I am so sad", of Portia: "By my troth, Nerissa, my little body is aweary of this great world", of Bassanio, and of Jessica all indicate their boredom.

Portia herself, of radiant outward beauty, is at the most charitable estimate completely self-satisfied. She is wholly content to be adored. She plans to go to the trial with more attention to the fun of her disguise than to her serious purpose, the hope that her quick woman's wits may save Antonio. She is made somewhat more pleasant if the actress so plays the part as to make it seem that the trick by which she extricates him flashes into her mind at the last moment—if when she asks Shylock to have a surgeon at hand lest Antonio bleed to death and he replies "Is it so nominated in the bond? . . . I cannot find it; 'tis not in the bond", *then* Portia recognizes that the bond contains no mention at all of blood. Otherwise, Portia most cruelly tortures her husband whom she loves, and permits Antonio even to make his last farewells, while all the while she keeps her secret, just to tease on the Jew. Her speech on mercy does seem genuine; but Portia reveals herself, in a few minutes, completely devoid of that quality of mercy, and even interferes when the Duke seems ready to be merciful. Her coaxing of the ring from her grateful husband is lightly intended, but the jest jars. Of all Shakespeare's fair-seeming heroines, Portia of Belmont, "richly left", is poorest in character, complacent, vulgar, unfeeling. The play is indeed Shakespeare's subtlest contrast of reality and seeming. Even in Shylock, as we shall note, there is the outer villain or buffoon and the inner man by nature kindly but by neighbors wronged.

In like contrast, Launcelot Gobbo's play at being torn between his conscience and the fiend is an echo, if not a burlesque, of the conflict between the virtues and the vices that was a stock subject of the medieval debates and the morality plays.

A new use of images is developed in *The Merchant of Venice*. The metaphors at times are premonitory. Thus, even in the conversation on love (Act II, Scene 6), Gratiano employs the figure of ships tempest-tossed; in the next act, we learn that Antonio's ships have been lost in a tempest. This device of the premonitory image is subtly effective; Shakespeare employed it increasingly in the tragedies.

Emphasis on the comedy and the romance was manifest in Fritz Leiber's 1930 production of the play. Thus the *New York Times* called his Shylock "often moving, but never venomous. He is the butt of jest, but not of savagery, and what comes out of the play is rather the charm of a love story than the dread of a fierce forfeit." Of the same production the *Boston Transcript* said: "The play becomes what any lad can see is a 'tight little comedy'. If some of the poetry seems lost, none of the glamour is missing. What if the courtroom scene lends a sinister note? Through it runs the amusing grimace of Portia and her maid over the lost rings. Who cares about Shylock and his shekels, if the laugh comes

last? . . . For once the lads and their girls roaming the Venetian streets
prove convincing. Real mandolins, real guitars, are strummed. . . .
Plainly, Shylock notwithstanding, *The Merchant of Venice* may be taken
lightly and enjoyed in this year of 1930."

Shylock, said Louis Kronenberger in 1947, "is too big for *The Merchant of Venice*—that mere sewing together of a couple of unreal borrowed plots—and yet not big enough for Shakespeare". What happened
was a break in the tradition, and a change in the English heart. The
play was not performed for much of the seventeenth century. An adaptation by Granville in 1701 was called *The Jew of Venice;* the famous
clown Thomas Dogget played the title role. Forty years later, the emphasis shifted; the comedy of tested and responding friendship and love,
with a Shylock buffoon, became the tragedy of a wronged individual
and a persecuted race. In 1741 Charles Macklin—walking through rehearsals, lest the manager prohibit the new interpretation—startled and
conquered the audience with a serious and sympathetic, deeply wronged
Shylock. Pope exclaimed, with more fervor than knowledge: "This is
the Jew that Shakespeare knew!" Shylock, at first a buffoon, then a
villain, became more and more a dignified individual, who thrusts back
at last against unbearable infamies, intolerable wrongs. He became the
symbol of his oppressed people. For fear of offending, the New York
City Board of Education recently withdrew the play from the high
school list of required reading. "When Shylock is played as a man of
dignity and character", said Brooks Atkinson, "his experience is more
than a tabloid sensation, it is a tragedy. In the twentieth century, perhaps we know better than Shakespeare did how painful a tragedy it is."

In this more serious mood, for the 150 years before Hitler, the Germans adopted *The Merchant of Venice*. One of their versions calls
itself "vergrössert and verbessert"—enlarged and improved. The Jews,
a bit later, took hold of the play as essentialy theirs. David Warfield
essayed the role in an elaborate Belasco production in 1923; unsuccessful, he retired from the stage. Stars of the Yiddish theatre have variously
interpreted the part: Jacob Adler's Shylock was dignified and haughty
as an Oriental potentate, Rudolph Schildkraut's was an almost ragged
miser, Maurice Schwartz's was pious, proud of his Jewishness. [In 1948
Schwartz produced a play, *Shylock's Daughter* (based on the novel
Jessica, My Daughter, by Ari Ibn-Zahav), to show, under the circumstances of Shakespeare's plot, the dignity and honor and restraint with
which a pious Jew would really have behaved].

It should thus be clear that there is a wide range for interpretation
of Shylock and for feeling about him. Early critics speak of Cooke's
"savage and determined method of whetting his knife on the floor, and
the fiend-like look that accompanied it." The *London Morning Post and
Daily Advertiser* of November 9, 1781, speaking of Charles Macklin's
"coming down to the footlights and twisting up his face like the horribly
tragic heads of Japanese sculpture", reports that, fronted by such a
spectacle, "a young man in the pit fainted away." Charles Kean—whose
production with Ellen Tree, on December 28, 1848, was Queen Victoria's
first command performance—also sharpened his knife on the floor;
Edwin Booth, as many after him, stropped the blade on the sole of his
shoe. Of Edmund Kean's Shylock, earlier in the century, George Henry

Lewes declared: "From the first moment that he appeared and leaned upon his stick to listen gravely while moneys are being requested of him, he impressed the audience like a chapter of Genesis." (Kean's Shylock stick brought five guineas at the posthumous sale of his effects.)

In the same grim tradition was the performance of Henry Irving, to which the *New York Dramatic Mirror* (December 10, 1887) objected: "We take liberty to think that Mr. Irving chooses the absolutely lowest possible side from which to paint the Jew of Venice . . . It is possible to give the Jew a fine dignity, an intellectual loftiness, and a tragic, fateful intensity of which Mr. Irving has apparently but faint conception. The ideal Shylock is a gentleman—a wicked one, if you choose, but a man of mental training, clear ideas, and fixed purpose which make the good-natured, gullible Antonio and the selfish egotist Bassanio seem vulgar by comparison. Mr. Irving's Shylock is a wolf."

Henry Irving enacted the role as late as 1905 (with Edith Wynne Matthison); but the "ideal" Shylock prevailed. Later American productions include one in French, with Firmin Gemier, in 1924; one in 1925, with Walter Hampden and Ethel Barrymore; in 1928, George Arliss and Peggy Wood; 1930, Maurice Moscovitch; 1931, Otis Skinner and Maude Adams; 1931, Fritz Leiber, Tyrone Power, Helen Menken, Viola Roache, William Faversham, and Pedro de Cordoba; 1935, Ian Keith and Estelle Winwood; 1935 also in modern dress; 1937, Blanche Yurka; 1937 (at Ann Arbor), Peggy Wood, Rex Ingram, Gareth Hughes, and Albert Carroll; 1947, Donald Wolfit and Rosalind Iden. During March 1953 it was seen at the New York City Center.

There were two good off-Broadway productions in 1955, one excellently conceived, the other marked by the understanding performance of Clarence Derwent, with a superb moment as his look abashes the mocking Gratiano after the trial.

By creating a less sympathetic Shylock, two productions roused critical controversy. Of the 1924 Gemier production, J. Ranken Towse declared: "The notable feature of his Shylock is its consistency. It is minutely and beautifully executed, but it shows no gleam of inspiration. It is a striking figure in a spectacular romance, but it is not Shakespeare." Gilbert W. Gabriel countered with the thought that "We are so used, here in America, to oversentimentalized, pro-Jewish Shylocks, that M. Gemier's must seem to many of us an inhuman fiend, a monument to Hate, a constrictor writhing in the net. Whereas, as a matter of fact, M. Gemier's Shylock is probably as close an approach as the modern mixture of audiences will permit to Shakespeare's writing." Similarly, Mr. Wolfit's 1947 performance provoked disagreement. Brooks Atkinson said that it "lacks stature." Louis Kronenberger said his Shylock was "both a hammy and a not too happily conceived one . . . more heartless than drained of heart, more bloodthirsty than bitter—a man, for example, who during the trial scene coldly whets his knife against his shoe." This time, George Freedley took up the cudgels. Admitting that Wolfit is "given perhaps too much to hurling himself physically on the floor with a thud that could be distinctly heard in Row M," Freedley continued: "He plays Shylock uncompromisingly enough to satisfy the most ardent anti-sentimentalist . . . closer to the part that Shakespeare wrote. Beginning with David Warfield, we have been invited to sob over the injustice dealt to Shylock, with little or no thought of honest and generous Antonio. For this service, at least, Mr. Wolfit cannot be praised too highly."

As Gentile guilt and Jewish self-consciousness fade, the irony and beauty of this rich comedy may again be found.

ROMEO AND JULIET   *William Shakespeare*

Shakespeare's tragedy of "the ardours and errors of impetuous youth", of the star-crossed lovers Romeo and Juliet, has fair claim to be called the world's best-loved play. Certainly this struggle of love for happiness despite family feuds has been one of the world's most frequently performed dramas.

The story of *Romeo and Juliet* 1594(?), was first told in a novello (1554) by the Italian Matteo Bandello, dramatized in *Adriana,* 1578, by Luigi Groto (Italian, 1541-1595) and put into English poetry in 1562 by Arthur Broke, whose nine months for its events are compressed by Shakespeare into five days. In Verona Romeo, a Montagu, and Juliet, a Capulet, fall in love; the enmity between their families leads them to marry in secret. Romeo tries to stop a brawl in the families' feud, but his friend Mercutio is killed, whereupon Romeo kills the fiery Tybalt and flees to Mantua. The Capulets wish to marry Juliet to Paris; on the advice of Friar Laurence, she takes a sleeping potion and seems to die. Word of this device is delayed, and does not reach Romeo; at Juliet's tomb he kills first Paris then himself. The waking Juliet, seeing her beloved dead, takes her own life. In the shock of the tragedy the feuding houses are reconciled.

A summary gives scant idea of either the excitement of action or the rouse of beauty that the drama holds. The poetry of young love is ardent throughout, as in the balcony scene, where Juliet ponders and Romeo climbs to claim the first admissive kiss; and the lovers learn, when the lark succeeds the nightingale, that "parting is such sweet sorrow". Their ardor, however, drives them to swift doom, leaving others to sip "adversity's sweet milk, philosophy". In many situations since, of futile quarrels, men have echoed the words of the dying Mercutio: "A plague o' both your houses!"

The emotions, tossed on tempests of love and hate, cannot be continuously sustained. In his tragedies, Shakespeare has often set what is called "comic relief". This does shift the emotional response, relaxing the tension; but usually by its theme (as the porter's talk of eternal damnation in *Macbeth**) it reenforces the major mood. Occasionally Shakespeare goes farther, introducing even burlesque. Thus, when the Capulets mourn Juliet, the audience knows she has but taken a sleeping potion. Shakespeare therefore gives voice to the family grief in exaggerated tones of wailing and follows by the irreverent tomfoolery of the hired musicians. Thus are the audience's emotions preserved for the play's drive to the abyss of doom.

Popular as it may be in its lure to actors, the play has not always been well received. Pepys, in 1662, seeing the first performance after the reopening of the theatres (closed for twenty years by the Puritans) declared "It is a play of itself the worst that ever I heard in my life." Pepys saw a version by James Howard, in which a happy ending and the tragic ending were presented on alternate nights. Thomas Otway's version (*Caius Marius*, 1679), which supplanted the original until 1744, had Juliet awaken before Romeo died. This variation was used by Colley Cibber and by David Garrick, was retained until the mid-nineteenth century, and survives today in Gounod's opera.

Dryden, in 1672, noted that: "Shakespeare showed the best of his skill in his Mercutio, and he said himself that he was forced to kill him in the third act, to prevent being killed by him. But, for my part, I cannot find he was so dangerous a person: I see nothing in him but what was so exceeding harmless that he might have lived to the end of the play, and died in his bed, without offense to any man." In 1818 Coleridge paused in his praise of the play to express an opposite opinion: "All congenial qualities, melting into the common *copula* of them all, the man of rank and the gentleman, with all its excellences and all its weaknesses, constitute the character of Mercutio!"

A number of critics have felt that having the closing deaths come through the accident of Friar John's failure to reach Romeo with word that Juliet had drunk a potion—"the mere mischance of an undelivered letter"—lessens the stature of the play. Thus Hazleton Spencer called it "more pathetic than powerful", and George Pierce Baker labeled it a melodrama rather than a tragedy. The play is, however, by this device (which Shakespeare took from his source) rendered more lifelike; given Romeo's impetuous nature and the need for concealment, the tragic end is inevitable, but (as in *Hamlet**) the instant and the avenue of doom are seemingly haphazard. A different approach is taken by Bertrand Evans in *The Brevity of Friar Laurence,* in *PMLA* (September, 1950). Picturing the play as a tragedy of unawareness, Evans points out that it is less Friar John's failure to reach Romeo than Balthasar's bringing him the false news of Juliet's death that precipitates the fatal end. All five of the young folk—Tybalt, Mercutio, Paris, Romeo, and Juliet—die ignorant of the facts that would have saved them. And at the close, Friar Laurence has to explain to the two families what twisted fate has linked them.

A further analysis of the theme was ingeniously made by G. M. Matthews, in *Essays in Criticism* (April, 1952); he declared that the moving idea in *Romeo and Juliet* is its flouting of contemporary convention in that the marriage contract with Paris is broken by Romeo's intrusion. *The Merchant of Venice**, however, ("In Belmont is a lady richly left") and more emphatically *The Taming of the Shrew** ("I've come to wive it wealthily in Padua") start with the thought of a convenient marriage which more conventionally ripens into love.

This is the first of Shakespeare's plays to dwell upon the relation between the generations, which recurs in *Lear** and *The Tempest**, and which dominated the ancient drama. It also contains Shakespeare's frequent linkage of violence and lust, which are conjoined in Mercutio. Romeo moves toward bodily death when he falls spiritually by lunging from love and peace to bloody vengeance. Juliet moves toward bodily death but triumphs spiritually when she spurns the lust of her nurse's urging that she wed Paris, and consents to the agonizing simulacrum of death to hold steadfast in love to her husband. Romeo's violence companions him to the tomb; there, it mingles with Juliet's love as he exclaims "Thus with a kiss I die!"

A famous theatrical war was waged through the play. In 1750, Garrick's prestige as star and manager was being disputed. Actors Spranger Barry and Mrs. (Susannah) Cibber left Garrick and Drury Lane to work with John Rich at Covent Garden. When they were announced to open the season (September 28, 1750) in *Romeo and Juliet,* Garrick at once announced himself as Romeo, with Miss (George Anne) Bellamy as Juliet. After twelve nights of simultaneous performances, Mrs. Cibber withdrew, and Garrick triumphantly played one night more. For years the merits of the rival Romeos were disputed; but Margaret Barton, in *Garrick* (1949), stated that "either presentation of the play was almost certainly better than any other of which we have records".

Romeo and Juliet was filmed in 1908 and 1911, and in 1936 with Norma Shearer and Leslie Howard; also 1955. American productions of the drama include one with Rollo Peters and Jane Cowl, in 1923, for 157 performances; one in 1934 with Katharine Cornell and Basil Rathbone, Brian Aherne the Mercutio, Edith Evans the earthy Nurse, and Orson Welles the Tybalt; in 1935, Katharine Cornell and Maurice Evans, Florence Reed the Nurse, and Ralph Richardson the Mercutio; in 1940, Vivian Leigh and Laurence Olivier. The record run of 186 performances was achieved by the London production of 1935-6, with Peggy Ashcroft as Juliet and John Gielgud and Laurence Olivier alternating as Romeo and Mercutio. Olivia de Havilland opened as Juliet in New York, March 10, 1951, like a bobby-sox gushling. Earlier productions include one with Charlotte Cushman as Romeo; and Juliet has been played by many a star: Mrs. Patrick Campbell, Julia Marlowe, Olga Nethersole, Modjeska, Ellen Terry, and Ellen Tree. The Germans have tried to claim Shakespeare as their close kin; Goethe's adaptation of *Romeo and Juliet* was played at Weimar in 1812. The play (as also *Macbeth, Hamlet, Othello,* and *Julius Caesar*) had some thirty French versions in the nineteenth century; and in the past fifteen years five complete translations of Shakespeare into French have been finished or gotten well under way.

Productions have not met with as favorable a critical reception as the play itself, though Bernard Shaw warned that "the parts are made almost impossible, except to actors of positive genius, skilled to the last degree in metrical declamation, by the way in which the poetry, magnificent as it is, is interlarded by the miserable rhetoric and silly logical conceits which were the foible of the Elizabethans." Katharine Cornell's production won the most praise in recent years—"realizing brilliantly", said Howard Barnes, "the pageantry, violence, poetry, and passion of the classic." John Mason Brown stated that "seldom has a production of such a drama mellowed and matured as magnificently as Katharine Cornell's revival." Of the Laurence Olivier-Vivian Leigh production, however, Brown declared that the play, "so hot in its impulses, so youthful in its spirit, so tumultuous in its fatuous action, becomes a dead march from the rise of the first curtain." Brooks Atkinson began his review: "Much scenery: no play." Earlier productions were no better received. Of the 1895 revival Bernard Shaw declared: "Mrs. Patrick Campbell's dresses, says the program, 'have been carried out by Mrs. Mason, of New Burlington Street.' I wish they had been carried out and buried." And Mr. Forbes-Robertson's Romeo, Shaw continued, "was a gentleman to the last. He laid out Paris after killing him as care-

fully as if he were folding up his best suit of clothes. One remembers
Irving, a dim figure dragging a horrible burden down through the gloom
'into the rotten jaws of death'." How well "one remembers" Irving
may be judged from Henry James' comment on Irving's work: "It is
the last word of stage-carpentering. . . . The play is not acted, it is
costumed; the immortal lovers of Verona become subordinate and ineffectual figures. I had never thought of *Romeo and Juliet* as a dull
drama; but Mr. Irving has succeeded in making it so."—Irving's opening scene, of the city square of Verona, had children romping, donkeys
passing through laden with wares, and housewives craning from windows as the Montagu-Capulet retainers began their quarrel.

It may be suspected that the audience liked some of these productions more than the critics. For the play itself is as eternal as spring.
It summons the youth within us all to the savoring of one of the
world's best-known and best-beloved love stories—a savoring that loses
none of its tear-pearled pleasure when renewed.

THE TAMING OF THE SHREW   *William Shakespeare*

This rollicking farce sets a man's mastery against a woman's will and
leaves the man comfortably assured that he is the victor—while the
audience notes that the woman still has means to have her way. Its
popularity led to an answer, *The Woman's Prize; or, The Tamer Tamed,*
by John Fletcher, about 1624, in which a shrewd Maria tames the widower Petruchio. *The Taming of the Shrew* was written about 1594.

Petruchio of Verona, come "to wive it wealthily in Padua", finds the
lovers of "gentle" Bianca in dismay because she may not marry until
her elder sister, the shrewish Katharina, has been wed. In a very whirlwind, Petruchio woos wild Kate. He and her father Baptista arrange
the wedding; Petruchio comes late, dressed like a madman; he boxes
the priest's ears and drags Kate off before the wedding feast. Countering her every wish, snatching fine food from her lips as burnt, tearing
rich gowns as rags, he bends her to complete submission: if he say so,
then is the sun the moon. Bianca is won by young Lucentio, whose
tricks enliven the play and outwit his rivals. At the close, Katherina
makes a speech that wins Petruchio the wager as to who has the most
obedient wife. But when Kate (Julia Marlowe) at two o'clock agrees
with Petruchio that it is seven, behind his back she holds two fingers
to the audience to let us know her concurrence is but policy. And when
Kate (Lynn Fontanne) lectures the other wives on the virtue of obedience, her twinkle tells us that she is but exploiting a pleasanter way to
get what she desires. The "shrew" is tamed, but nowise daunted. In
truth, Petruchio is no cruel wife-beater, as in the popular ballad that
earlier told the story. In his excesses he is parodying Kate's faults; she
—being truly less shrew than shrewd—ultimately recognizes this, helps
play the joke, and is cured. Throughout he calls her his "sweet and
lovely Kate", and she becomes so. Her "gentle" sister Bianca, outwardly
sweetly obedient, is finally revealed as a spoiled and pettish girl.

The play has gained in popularity down the years. Samuel Pepys
noted in his *Diary* (1667) that it "hath some very good pieces in it,
but generally is a mean play; and the best part, 'Sawny', done by Lacy,
hath not half its life, by reason of the words, I suppose, not being under-

stood, at least by me." What Pepys saw was John Lacy's adaptation, *Sauny the Scot*, 1667, which transported the characters to England, enlarged the role of Petruchio's clownish servant, here called Sauny, and supplanted Shakespeare's play until the mid-eighteenth century. Garrick in 1736 made a shorter version, *Catherine and Petruchio*, which was very popular. Among those that have played in this version are Kitty Clive, 1736; J. P. Kemble and Mrs. Siddons, 1788; Helen Faucit and Ellen Tree, 1836; Barry Sullivan, 1855; and Henry Irving and Ellen Terry, 1867. The full play, including the *Induction*, was not seen after Tudor times until 1887, when Augustin Daly, in New York and in London, revived it for Ada Rehan. More recently, the play was performed in New York: in 1920 by E. H. Sothern and Julia Marlowe; in 1921 by both Walter Hampden and Fritz Leiber; in 1924 by the visiting French company of Firmin Gemier; in 1927 by Basil Sydney and Mary Ellis in modern dress (as also, the same year, at Harvard University and in Birmingham, England); in 1935 by Alfred Lunt and Lynn Fontanne in a slapdash performance with Richard Whorf as Christopher Sly; in 1936 with Rollo Peters and Peggy Wood; in 1939 at the Old Globe Theatre at the New York World's Fair; in 1940 again by the Lunts, to aid the Finns. In 1948 the play was revived in Chicago, and by Margo Jones in Dallas, Texas. A Margaret Webster production toured the United States in 1949-1950, and in New York Clare Luce opened in a City Center production April 25, 1951.

Many theatrical folk today have lost sight of the purpose of Shakespeare in the *Induction* to the play. This is a shrewd instance of the way in which the playwright appropriated to dramatic use the theatrical conventions of his day—as he employed the upper and the inner stage; as the enacting of female parts by men invited him often to disguise his heroine as a male. One feature of the Elizabethan theatre —humorously detailed in the chapter "How a Gallant Should Behave Himself in a Playhouse", in *The Gull's Horn Book*, 1609, by Thomas Dekker*—was the practice of the gay young blades to sit on the stage itself, and to make loud comments on the actors, their carriage, their clothes, their reading, and their lines. The playwrights of the time must have itched for a way to counter or control these gadflies; with his *Induction*, which leads to the play-within-the-play, Shakespeare neatly turned the trick. (*See* also *The Knight of the Burning Pestle**.)

The *Induction* shows a lord and his retainers, homing in gay mood from a hunt, come upon a drunken village tinker, Christopher Sly. As a lark, they carry him to the manor; when he awakes, he is addressed as Your Honor, and told that he is the Lord of the Manor, now recovered from a fifteen years' nightmare. In his hangover, the befuddled Sly is all confused—until a page enters, dressed as a Lady and announced as his loving wife. Sly is then ready to believe and to act accordingly. Then word comes that players have arrived: in honor of milord's recovery, they will put on a play.

The play they present is *The Taming of the Shrew*. After one more reference, Sly is not mentioned by Shakespeare. He with his "hangover", the tipsy page his "wife", and the others, sat on the stage amid the gallants who had paid an extra sixpence for the privilege. But there is no doubt that the company's most quick-tongued wits were cast as Sly and the Page, and that their *ad lib* comments on the play they watched, and their shafts of repartee exchanged with the gallants onstage, convulsed the delighted groundlings.

Soon after Shakespeare's time, the bloods were transferred from the stage to boxes; and the function of Christopher Sly, protagonist of the *Induction,* became obscured. Ben Webster and Samuel Phelps had Sly fall asleep; Daly did not bring him back after the first act. Later, the *Induction* was often omitted altogether. Alexander Woollcott, indeed, said it was not played from Daly's time until the Basil Sydney production of 1927; he overlooked the Gemier *Shrew* of 1924. The *New York Times* called the Gemier production "loud and boisterous, merry and broad, even bawdy at times, with the dash and swing of a college burlesque. . . . Except for one brief scene some moments later, Shakespeare forgot the roistering Christopher and left him to fall into a broken slumber. Not so Mr. Gemier." M. Gemier was wiser than that critic. So were the Lunts, in whose production Sly stood and stared reproachfuly while embarrassed latecomers hurried to their seats, and otherwise created diversion that made Gilbert W. Gabriel remark "It puts a madcap on the old *commedia dell' arte.* It walks in beauty like a nightmare. . . . The yellow sun which seems to pour so much light down on these pranks and spanks must have the fat, shining face of an all-lovable clown."

Of the 1935 performance by Alfred Lunt and Lynn Fontanne, Brooks Atkinson exclaimed: "The Lunts have stuffed it with all the horseplay their barn loft holds." On their return in 1940, however, he added: "For this theatregoer's personal enjoyment they have painted the lily a trifle too gaudily . . . it begins to lack spontaneity." But they could hardly have been more obstreperous than Cécile Sorel in her 1920 performance at the Comédie Française, in Paris; one night, she tumbled from the stage into the orchestra pit!

The production of Basil Sydney and Mary Ellis went wildly modern, with Petruchio in plus fours tearing up Katherine's wedding gown of latest twentieth century style; with movie cameras to "shoot" the bride; radio sets; and a return to Padua in a tumbledown automobile. (This, incidentally, was equipped with three motors: one to turn the wheels, one to make the sound of a driving engine, and one to blow the actors' clothes as though they were whirling along in an open car.) Alexander Woollcott thought that this production "succeeded in making a pretty good show out of that usually somewhat trying relic"—the play, not the auto—but the *Times* observed that "these little sundries furnish momentary pictorial amusement, but are likely to arouse an expectation greater than they can fulfill. The joke is soon over, but must necessarily be prolonged for the duration of the scene."

A somewhat different, but delightful arousal came to New York on December 30, 1948, when the musical comedy *Kiss Me Kate* took the town with music and lyrics by Cole Porter, book by Bella and Samuel Spewack, choreography by Hanya Holm, sets and costumes by Lemuel Ayers, and a deft cast headed by Alfred Drake, Patricia Morison, Harold Lang, and Lisa Kirk. *Kiss Me Kate* is the tempestuous story of two theatrical folk, akin to Petruchio and Katherine, in a company engaged in playing *The Taming of the Shrew.* The production is somewhat slowly paced and a few of the lyrics are quite irrelevant, but the *Shrew*

scenes are delightfully colorful satire, and some of the lyrics are both
appropriate and highly amusing. A travesty and a treat is whipped out
of Shakespeare in *Kiss Me Kate*. The musical attained 1077 performances in New York, returning after a long tour, with a different but
equally effective cast on January 8, 1952. It has played in Europe and
Australia, and for 501 performances in London, where it opened March 8,
1951. Despite its hilarious and its graceful moments, however, the musical's two movements, of actors living and actors acting, are not wholly
integrated; the experienced theatregoer will still prefer Shakespeare's
The Taming of the Shrew.

Some scholars think that not all of the play is Shakespeare's; others
contend he revised an earlier play. "I can think of no other Shakespearean play that has so little essential Shakespeare in it", said Harold
Hobson in the *London Sunday Times* after a November 4, 1947, revival.
Swinburne earlier put the matter in more complimentary form: "The
refined instinct, artistic judgment, and consummate taste of Shakespeare
were never perhaps so wonderfully shown . . . All the force and humor
alike of character and situation belong to Shakespeare's eclipsed and
forlorn precursor; he has added nothing; he has tempered and enriched
everything." The likelihood is that the "earlier play" is a pirated version of Shakespeare's own comedy, set down from a player's memory.
In any event, Shakespeare in *The Taming of the Shrew* has spangled
with sequins of delightful observation rich cloth of human nature.

KING RICHARD II   *William Shakespeare*

Among the portraits of English kings in Shakespeare's history plays,
perhaps none searches more deeply into a monarch's soul than that of
Richard II. To rule effectively, a king must have authority of will and
power of both mind and hand. Not only are these lacking in Richard,
but he knows their lack, and can but watch himself slump to his downfall. His "unstaid youth" rejects the wise admonitions of his uncle, John
of Gaunt. He seeks to compensate for his lack of drive with wild expenditures. The handsome lad lends ear to every flatterer, but also
breaks into sudden impetuous acts. One of these acts, his seizing the
wealth of John of Gaunt and John's banished son Bolingbroke, as soon
as Gaunt has died, costs him his throne. Henry Bolingbroke comes back
from France; Richard is forced to abdicate; and, soon after Bolingbroke mounts the throne as Henry IV, in response to the new king's
desire Richard is slain. Such a stark opposition of two chief figures—
here, Richard and Bolingbroke—was new in the English drama.

The essential events of the play are drawn from Holinshed's *Chronicles* and Stowe's *Annals*. It was early involved in English politics. Although the play, written about 1594, was first published in 1597, the
scene of Richard's abdication was not printed until 1608 for fear of
offending Queen Elizabeth, who more than once compared herself to
the gentle Richard. On the other hand, it was enacted on February 7,
1601, the day before Essex' rebellion, in order to encourage the plotters
against Elizabeth. For general patriotic purposes, however, no more
ringing words can be found than Gaunt's praise of England, before he
dies. The entire speech was often heard on the British radio during
World War II. More philosophical is Richard's soliloquy upon the

death of kings, which, said William Bliss in *The Real Shakespeare*
(1949), "is almost the most perfect thing Shakespeare ever wrote".
The play has not been frequently revived. Nahum Tate's version of
1680, *The Sicilian Usurper*, with references to the current Popish Plot,
was suppressed after the second performance. Lewis Theobald's version
of 1719, obeying the three dramatic unities, was little more successful.
The play was produced but twice in the eighteenth century. In the
nineteenth, Richard was played by Edmund Kean and his son Charles;
by Edwin Booth; and by Sir Frank Benson at Stratford in 1896 and 1899.
There were productions in London in 1905, with Herbert Beerbohm
Tree and his daughter Viola; in 1916 at Fordham University, New York;
in 1917 at the Old Vic in London; in London by Henry Boynton in 1925;
again in 1934 at the Old Vic. In New York the play was not professionally produced from Edwin Booth's appearance at Daly's Fifth Avenue
Theatre in 1875 until Maurice Evans played in it in 1937, when it
achieved the record run of 171 performances. In the same year, John
Gielgud enacted the doomed Richard in London. The play was performed in 1948 in Germany, Italy, and France. Evans revived it in New
York in 1940 and for another fortnight opening January 24, 1951; and
later in the year Michael Redgrave acted Richard at Stratford-on-Avon.

In 1937 the vitality of the play took the New York critics by storm.
Brooks Atkinson called it "one of the most thorough, illuminating, and
vivid productions of Shakespeare we have had in recent memory. Although Richard II was no hero, now we know that the anguish of his
soul is heroic and has the power to make our hearts stand still . . . It
is the distinction of Richard that his mind grows keener with destruction before his enemies; although he lacks the power to rule, he has the
courage to be his own confessor, and he is most kingly when the crown
has been snatched from his head." Gilbert W. Gabriel was more emphatic still: "No other play of the bard's has so many lines in it of
ringing steel and patriotic bronze." And John Anderson went so far as
to declare that "our theatre has no scene to put beside this Richard's
abdication." When Evans brought *Richard II* back in 1940, Atkinson
said that it "seemed again one of the most absorbing of Shakespeare's
plays." Richard Watts, Jr. praised "its rich and glowing eloquence . . .
one of the most brilliant amalgamations of the poetry and the drama of
Shakespeare that the American stage has known . . . so beautiful a play
that it is strange to note how rarely it has been done in the past. Its
tragic hero is assuredly one of the most moving of Shakespeare's characters."

The king gives a new sort of unity, of tone and feeling, to the play;
Walter Pater compared it to a musical symphony. Yet Richard turns
constantly from action to talk; such words as *tongue, mouth, speech,
word* are frequent in the play. For full appreciation, *Richard II* should
be viewed as the first play of a tetralogy, followed by the two parts of
Henry IV and by *Henry V*. This view, taken by E. K. Chambers in *Shakespeare: A Survey* (1925), sees Henry V as "the ideal king, the divinely
chosen representative and embodiment of the spirit of England . . . He
holds the tetralogy together, from the first mention of his frolic boyhood
at the end of Richard II, through the riot and the budding valours of
Henry IV, until he takes his kinghood on and blazes forth, 'his vanities
forespent', in the glittering careers of Agincourt." Both Henry V and

Richard II spent an "unstaid youth", but the great monarch of action stands as a counterweight to the feeble monarch of words. That kings are but actors on a larger scale is implied in these four plays, by repeated comparison of state and stage.

King Richard recognizes that his life is like a performance. Yet, reflecting on his betrayal and recalling the betrayal of Jesus—the King being God's deputy—the actor becomes a man, and while remaining a symbol of ineffectual divinity rises to human dignity.

Early in the nineteenth century, Hazlitt observed: "*Richard II* is a play little known, compared with *Richard III* . . . yet we confess that we prefer the nature and feeling of the one to the noise and bustle of the other". There was, nevertheless, but a single revival of the former —by the little known Jones Finch—in London, from 1858 to 1900; it required our age's interest in introspection to make the play popular again. Hazlitt found the appeal of *Richard* II in the fact that "the sufferings of the man make us forget that he ever was a king". In appraising a 1947 revival, Harold Hobson of the *London Sunday Times* found the secret of the play's popularity in Richard's self-pity: "He creates, out of the artistic fecundity of his mind, the image of a king who *has* been royal . . . Self-pity: lamentation: hysteria . . . The world today darts hither and thither directionless. It grieves over the hardness of its fate, as Richard did. Of all Shakespeare's kings, he is its prime spokesman. And, if not with spirit, if not with courage, he speaks beautifully, with words that twine about the heart." Too close to ourselves for comfort, *Richard* II is a sympathetic but a warning picture of a well-meaning king too weak to rule.

KING HENRY IV   *William Shakespeare*

The popularity of the two parts of *Henry IV*, 1597(?) featuring history and Falstaff, has been continuous with good reason. As Samuel Johnson stated in 1768: "Perhaps no author has ever in two plays afforded so much delight. The great events are interesting, for the fate of kingdoms depends upon them; the slighter occurrences are diverting and, except for one or two, sufficiently probable; the incidents are multiplied with wonderful facility of invention, and the characters diversified with the utmost nicety of discernment, and the profoundest skill in the nature of man." The play is generally esteemed as the best of Shakespeare's histories.

Part One, drawing its history from Holinshed's *Chronicles,* presents Hotspur's rebellion, and his death at the hands of Prince Hal. In Part Two, the serious historical concern is less; the comic scenes are more varied and especially lively with Doll Tearsheet at Boar's Head Tavern. Yet there is a sound talk between Henry IV and his wild son; much indication of the evils of rebellion; and the significant incident in which Prince Hal tries on the crown while his ailing royal father is still alive. Originally Falstaff was called Oldcastle, and pictured as a Lollard hypocrite misleading the young Prince; presumably the Earl of Cobham, a descendant of Oldcastle, objected, for the name was changed and an apology was inserted in the Epilogue to Part Two, where it is promised that "Falstaff shall die of a sweat, unless already 'e be killed with your hard opinions; for Oldcastle died a martyr, and this is not the man."

Falstaff knew his own limitations, as he shows, sighing "There live not three good men unhanged in England, and one of them is fat and grows old." Maurice Morgann (in 1777), denying that Falstaff, like earlier clowns, was a "mere stage mechanism compounded of rogue and gull", described him as "a man at once young and old, enterprising and fat, a dupe and a wit, harmless and wicked, weak in principle and resolute by constitution, cowardly in appearance and brave in reality, a knave without malice, a liar without deceit, and a knight, a gentleman, and a soldier, without either dignity, decency, or honour." Hazlitt, about a century later, called him "perhaps the most substantial comic character that was ever invented . . ." From these, Bernard Shaw's is a dissenting opinion: "Falstaff, the most human person in the play, but none the less a besotted and disgusting old wretch." Audiences can enjoy Falstaff, though he is not only humorous but also objectionable; the Victorians ignored or resented this conjunction, wishing to laugh only where they felt morally sound. Harold C. Goddard, who also pointed out, in *The Meaning of Shakespeare,* 1951, that the immoral Falstaff and the immortal Falstaff exist in one body, called the robustious knight a "symbol of the supremacy of imagination over fact."

Many Freudian commentators have rushed in on Shakespeare. Perhaps most effective was Dr. Franz Alexander; in his study he shows the parallel between the development of Prince Hal and the typical Freudian picture of the ego's struggle for adjustment: (1) rebellion against the father; (2) conquest of the super-ego (Hotspur, glory rigidly conceived); (3) conquest of the id (Falstaff, anarchic self-indulgence); (4) identification with the father (putting on the crown while the king still lives); (5) assumption of mature responsibility. The last of these comes suddenly, but the sequence is natural.

In 1804 Stephen Kemble—the *big* not the *great* Kemble—played Falstaff without stuffing; in 1895 Julia Marlowe played Prince Hal. Notable, more recently in New York, are the all-star revival in 1926— Otis Skinner as Falstaff; Philip Merivale as Hotspur; Basil Sydney, Peggy Wood, and Blanche Ring, with the *Prologue* spoken by John Drew; the production of Part One by Margaret Webster, starring Maurice Evans, in 1939; and the coming of the Old Vic Company in May 1946. Stratford-on-Avon saw the play in 1951 with Michael Redgrave as Hotspur and Anthony Quayle as Falstaff.

Of the Evans production, January 30, 1939, John Anderson declared: "It was the first time that I can remember a Shakespearean play at which the audience laughed at a clown as loudly as it would at Ed Wynn, without worrying about Divine William at all." Regarding the Old Vic production of Part One, Robert Garland recorded: "Slowly, but surely, a feeling of disappointment began to take possession of the audience. What might have been an integrated projection of a second-string historical play began to be a disintegrated vehicle for the showy actorial portraiture of Laurence Olivier as Hotspur and Ralph Richardson as Falstaff." Robert Coleman, who had found Evans' work "a gorgeous performance of a rousing and risible play", called Olivier's "definitely inferior to many Shakespearean revivals that have been given here with half the fanfare." As Hotspur Olivier seemed a minor Evans. With Part Two, however, opinions abruptly veered. George Freedley wondered why Part One had been played the more often. John Chapman also failed to understand "why this play has not been produced here in almost eighty years . . . a glowing, vigorous work whose drama is relieved by superbly lusty, delightfully lewd comedy."

There is drama as well as history in the vivid portraits of the king and his son, and in the sudden sweep of Falstaff to bewildered pathos at the close. Whether to play the fat knight with exaggerate swagger or more realistically roistering, has divided performers. Falstaff's carrying off of Hotspur, for instance, may be troublesome: a critic remarked that Quin "had little or no difficulty in perching Garrick upon his shoulders, who looked like a dwarf on the back of a giant.—But oh! how he tugged and toiled to raise Barry from the ground . . . It was thought best, for the future, that some of Falstaff's ragamuffins should bear off the dead body." Arthur Colby Sprague urged moderation: "If, too, a good deal of the business was stuffy and uninspired, it might at least serve as a check on such extravagances as we have to put up with, at times, today. Mr. Orson Welles, as Falstaff, in the Play Scene in *Henry IV*, chose to wear a saucepan on his head as a crown. Surely, the cushion which Falstaff names and tradition might once have dictated is quite as funny—and Shakespearean, as well." As a reminder of the more serious portions of the play, there is Leigh Hunt's comment on the 1830 production at Drury Lane: "Mr. Cooper's costume as Henry IV was a real historical picture. We saw the King himself before us, with his draperied head; and the performer, as he rose from his chair, and remained lecturing his son with his foot planted on the royal stool, displayed the monarch well—his ermined robe, stretched out by his elbow, making a background to the portrait."

The plays themselves are a portrait of a period, and of a richly comic life-loving man.

KING HENRY V   *William Shakespeare*

Although frequently shown, this play, Shakespeare's most rousing patriotic pageant, always worries the producers for the reasons set down by Henry James after an 1875 performance: "The play could be presented only as a kind of animated panorama, for it offers but the slenderest opportunities for acting . . . Illusion, as such an enterprise proposes to produce it, is absolutely beyond the compass of the stage . . . To assent to this you have only to look at the grotesqueness of the hobby-horses on the field of Agincourt and at the uncovered rear of King Harry's troops, when they have occasion to retire under range of your opera-glass. We approve by all means of scenic splendors, but we would draw the line at invading armies." Shakespeare himself felt the limitations of the stage for such a play as this, as the *Prologue* shows. It was written about 1598.

Read the play and you have an entirely different impression, as recorded by Ruskin: "That battle of Agincourt strikes me as one of the most perfect things, in its sort, we have anywhere of Shakespeare's. The description of the two hosts: the worn-out, jaded, English; the dread hour, big with destiny, when the battle shall begin; and then the deathless valour: 'Ye good yeomen, whose limbs were made in England!' A true English heart breathes, calm and strong, through the whole business; not boisterous, protrusive; all the better for that. There is a sound in it like the ring of steel." So too, E. K. Chambers in *Shakespeare: A Survey* (1925) speaks of "The unfailing imagery, the abundant eloquence, the swelling phrase . . . the martial ring and hard brilliance of so much of the verse of the play, in which Shakespeare's style reaches its zenith of objectivity and rhetoric."

The story of the play is drawn mainly from Holinshed's *Chronicles*. Prince Hal, now Henry V and a truly royal monarch, after the French Dauphin has sent him a tun of tennis balls as a scornful inauguration gift, invades France. After a stirring appeal leading his men through the breached walls of Harfleur, watching with quiet prayer through the night before Agincourt, Henry triumphs over the more numerous French forces and wins peace with marriage to Katherine of France. With Falstaff dead, his erstwhile comrades Pistol, Nym, and Bardolph are, as William Hazlitt says, "satellites without a sun"; but England's new sense of national unity is suggested, and the humor sustained, through portraits of sturdy Britishers: English Gower, Irish Macmorris, Scots Jamy, Welsh Fluellen with his leek for St. Davy's Day—which the fierce coward Pistol must eat (though of course the stage "leek" has a slice of apple inside!).

Productions have varied in splendor, with Sir Henry Irving's in the 1870's perhaps most scenically elaborate. John Ranken Towne compared Richard Mansfield's, in New York 1899, to Irving's, but added: "the driving force to give animation and dramatic vitality to all the elaborate preparation was wanting." Charles Kean (1830) and after him Macready (1839) had King Henry, in France, pray before Agincourt in a fashion to which *John Bull* objected: "the actor literally kneels down with his soldiery, and the curtain falls to the solemn strains of an organ, brought from England we suppose for the purpose." Few today question music to match a play's mood. In his quest of realism Charles Calvert in Manchester in 1872 raised scaling ladders before Harfleur, with volleys of arrows. His wife's *Memoirs* record that "the supers rose each night to such a pitch of excitement that as he rushed up the eminence, followed by the shouting soldiery, the moment he was out of sight of the audience, he had to jump down and get underneath the platform, or he would, most assuredly, have been mowed down by his own men."

Produced in Pasadena in 1935, in London by Laurence Olivier in 1937 and Ivor Novello in 1938, at Stratford-on-Avon in 1943, and by the London Old Vic opening January 30, 1951, *Henry V* was seen in New York in 1924 with Irene Bordoni and Philip Merivale, in 1925 and 1928 with Walter Hampden, and again in 1931. Percy Hammond called the Hampden production "a substantial and earnest endeavor to bring one of the most cadaverous of Shakespeare's plays back to life," although again the battlefield settings seemed troublesome.

The difficulties of staging, revolving as they do around spectacle and charge, make the play a likely one for motion pictures; and the best film version of a Shakespearean play is the Laurence Olivier *Henry V*, widely shown in this country in 1946. Pictorially superb, with rousing battle scenes, it does not overlook the other values of the play (though it gilds the lily by adding a line from Marlowe). For through the drama comes a feeling that kings are, after all, men; that they have responsibilities as well as—nay, rather than—rights. This most imaginative and stirring of Shakespeare's histories is a surface show of a high-spirited ruler riding to national glory.

Below the surface of the play are more somber depths. Richly, as Harold C. Goddard observed, there is a continuance of Shakespeare's subtle irony, hinting the difference between seeming or saying and being. Georg Brandes objected that the playwright "manifests no disapproval where the king sinks far below the ideal, as when he orders the frightful massacre of all the French prisoners taken at Agincourt. Shakespeare tries to pass the deed off as a measure of necessity." It is, of course, not Shakespeare but Henry that argues necessity as the excuse for slaughter. While the Chorus praises Henry as "the mirror of all Christian kings", the mirror of the play itself shows a conceited and unscrupulous conqueror. As abruptly as he has discarded Falstaff, Henry orders Bardolph executed for robbing a church, whenas his own French campaign is being financed by a church bribe. In disguise at camp, he gives a glove to soldier Williams, pledging his honor to match it man to man; then, as king, his first fobs the challenge off on Fluellen, then tries to pay Williams off; the soldier, more manly than his king, cries "I will none of your money!" As for fighting, King Henry takes as little part in the Battle of Agincourt as Prince Hal in the Gadshill robbery—and, as Goddard remarked, there is scarce any higher ethics in the royal plundering. Almost the first words of Shakespeare's *Henry VI* indicate the crumbling of the power Henry V had gained. Under the bright panoply and gilt costumes of power, Shakespeare lets peep the soiled undergarments of violence, greed, and pride.

THE MERRY WIVES OF WINDSOR   *William Shakespeare*

One of the most successful of Shakespeare's comedies, with a long history of revivals all over the world, is *The Merry Wives of Windsor,* 1598(?), which, legend tells us, he wrote in a fortnight, on Queen Elizabeth's mention that she would like to see Falstaff in love. Hartley Coleridge commented on this idea in 1948 with Victorian emphasis: "That Queen Bess should have desired to see Falstaff making love proves her to have been, as she was, a gross-minded old baggage. Shakespeare has evaded the difficulty with great skill. He knew that Falstaff could not be in love; and has mixed but a little, a very little, *pruritus* with his fortune-hunting courtship. But the Falstaff of *The Merry Wives* is not the Falstaff of *Henry IV**. It is a big-bellied impostor, assuming his name and style, or, at best, it is Falstaff in dotage." Saintsbury, fifty years later, counters this notion: "It is mistaken affection which thinks him degraded, or 'translated' Bottom-fashion. He is even as elsewhere, though under an unluckier star." The Falstaff of *Henry IV*, however, is always resourceful; the Falstaff here is always helpless, and an easy butt.

John Dennis, in 1702, altered the play into *The Comical Gallant;* but this time the original drove the vulgar perversion from the stage. Opinions of the comedy have varied little over the centuries. Thus Samuel Johnson said in 1768: "The conduct of this drama is deficient; the action ends often before the conclusion, and the different parts might change places without inconvenience; but its general power, that power by which all works of genius shall finally be tried, is such, that perhaps it never yet had reader or spectator, who did not think it too soon at end."

And Hardin Craig called it, in 1948, "one of the liveliest comedies in dramatic literature. It has greatness in dramatic situations; and situations, rather than wit, are the basis of English comedy. There is a wealth of incidents, all presented in a breathless bustle."

Shakespeare has ingeniously mixed the ingredients of this English trifle. Some of the material came from the Italian tales of Ser Giovanni Fiorentino; but *The Merry Wives of Windsor* is Shakespeare's only comedy with a setting in contemporary England, and his only play almost all in prose. There are comically exaggerated pictures of ordinary English citizens, Mistress Ford and Mistress Page, their husbands, and the country-folk around, including Justice Shallow and his cousin Slender, a mere puff-ball of foolish froth made immortal. There is Pistol, who cries "The World's mine oyster, which I with sword will open"— and who informs the husbands of Falstaff's rendezvous with their wives. The wives, too, have mischief in their heads; so that first we see Falstaff, hidden in a laundry basket, dumped with the dirty wash into a ditch; then we watch him, disguised as a woman, belabored and beswitched as a polecat, a runyon, a witch; and finally we behold him in the forest at night, wearing horns he'd have loved to plant on the husbands, plagued and burned and pinched by the company disguised as a satyr and fairies, in a burlesque of the May Day stag-mummers' hunt, popular in England from pagan times. It is during this frolic in the forest darkness that the love-story steals off for its climax. For Shakespeare has intertwined with all this rioting and horseplay (indeed, Beerbohm Tree as Falstaff, in 1902, came in on a white horse) the threads of a tender romance. Sweet Ann Page—whom Hartley Coleridge called "a pretty little creature one would like to take on one's knee"—is ripe for a lucky man's picking. Her father would marry her to Slender, with his wide lands and heavy beeves; her mother's eyes are turned to the fashionable and imposing Frenchman, Dr. Caius. Ann's heart belongs to Fenton, whose oats are mainly wild, but who has gentlemanly birth and is full of promise. Three disguised couples steal away during the forest frolic: Dr. Caius and Slender each finds himself with a boy; and the Pages reconcile themselves to Fenton's marriage with Ann.

Productions have tended to stress the foolery or the grotesque extravagances of Falstaff. Thus Oscar Asche in the role devoured an entire fowl at each performance, tearing it asunder with his fingers and pitching the drumsticks at Bardolph. Beerbohm Tree tangled in the dress he put on to try to escape the irate husband, tripped and crawled along the floor while Ford belabored him on the buttocks. Vegetables tumbled from the bag he carried, with which Mistress Page (Ellen Terry) pelted him as he made his way out.

Among recent American performances was one in 1927 with Mrs. Fiske and Otis Skinner, of which John Mason Brown observed that "Mrs. Fiske romped through the farce, adding to the gaiety of a script which, in spite of its riotous moments, is none too hilarious at best. They created happy memories." The play was also produced by Mr. and Mrs. Coburn, in 1935; by the Federal Theatre in Los Angeles, in 1938; and in a "swing version" at Hollywood in 1940. It was revived at the Old Vic in London, opening May 31, 1951, with Peggy Ashcroft as Mistress Page and Roger Livesey as Falstaff.

In New York an April 1938 production was damned by the critics and ran for but four performances. Brooks Atkinson declared: "Although Queen Elizabeth asked to see Falstaff in love she did not require him to woo in a straw hat nightmare . . . Taking advantage of Shakespeare's death, Robert Henderson has dumped old tub o' guts into a frantic production like an experiment in practical joking . . . Queen Bess would have marched Shakespeare off to the hangman if *The Merry Wives* had looked like that in her decisive day." Despite such critical words—which in sober truth the production deserved—those that saw the play seemed to enjoy it; and the *Journal-American* said there is "good solid entertainment in Shakespeare neat at the Empire." Even a bad performance, however critics cavil, cannot destroy all the fun of the audiences watching *The Merry Wives*. The child in us all will laugh at Falstaff's discomfiture; the youth in us all will rejoice in love's winning with sweet Ann Page. More maturely, we shall smile at the all-too-human weaknesses of the earnest husbands and the merry wives.

JULIUS CAESAR   *William Shakespeare*

Based upon North's translation (1579) of Plutarch's *Lives, Julius Caesar*, possibly written in 1598, tells the story of the assassination of the great Roman and the death of the conspirators against him. Partly history, partly tragedy, the drama shows how the idealist may be misled by the practical man, and the practical man doomed by the idealist. For the honest Brutus, once ensnared, overrides the crafty Cassius. During the conspiracy he insists that they take no oaths, that they do not draw Cicero in, and that only Caesar and not Antony be killed; and after the assassination he insists that Antony be allowed to speak and that the foe be met without delay at Philippi. In all these decisions Brutus was honest, pigheaded, and unwise. When craft and honesty seek to work together, both succumb.

Julius Caesar is studded with gems of rhetoric. Working upon his upright friend, Cassius remarks: "The fault, dear Brutus, is not in our stars, but in ourselves, that we are underlings." After the soothsayer bids him "Beware the Ides of March!", Caesar scoffs at fear: "Cowards die many times before their deaths; The valiant never taste of death but once." He goes to the Capitol, is stricken by the conspirators, and falls dead. There is superb contrast in the funeral orations of Brutus and Antony. Brutus is straightforward and reasonable, but utterly unconvincing. Antony, after a disarming start, with shrewd persuasiveness whips the populace to a destroying frenzy against the "honourable men" that have killed Caesar.

The quarrel between Brutus and Cassius before the battle of Philippi is also noteworthy. Brutus is intolerant of Cassius' "itching palm"; but Cassius' shrewdness and Brutus' weight of grief at news of his wife's death effect a reconciliation. Coleridge declared: "I know no part of Shakespeare that more impresses on me the belief of his genius' being superhuman, than this scene between Brutus and Cassius." Bernard Shaw loosed a blast at this bardolatry: "A conceited poet bursts into the tent of Brutus and Cassius and exhorts them not to quarrel with one another. If Shakespeare had been able to present his play to the ghost of the great Julius, he probably would have had much the same reception. He certainly would have deserved it."

Shakespeare's ability to develop characters under the strain of circumstance is shrewdly shown in the presentation of Brutus. Brutus, the only member of the conspiracy with disinterested motives, must convince himself that his honorable intentions justify questionable deeds. He therefore pictures the murder of Caesar as a ritual—"Let's carve him as a dish fit for the gods . . . Let's be sacrificers, not butchers" —but the performance of this "ritual" demands deceit. Thus the initial two scenes of the play—with Shakespeare's frequent device of reiterative imagery—give stress to rituals and ceremonies first performed then desecrated or mocked. The symbolism of ceremony, and the irony, continue through the play as, in Brutus, dedication slumps to policy, then draggles in petty moods. We see the end evoked to give dignity to the means, which then proceed to debase and befoul the course of living. Brutus is an "honourable man" whose very honesty, on an ignoble course, forces self-deception and widens the doom. For Brutus, though honorable at the play's start, is coarsened by the dilemma life has set him. He scorns to secure money by such means as Cassius employs, yet rails at Cassius for not sending him any. His toploftiness in the quarrel—"For I am armed so strong in honesty . . ."—echoes Caesar's vainglory—"But I am constant as the northern star"—and shows that one grows to be the thing one hates.

Ben Jonson (see *Every Man Out of His Humour**) took a fling at a few passages in the play. However, a line he called ridiculous seems really the epitome of a tyrant's self-justification: "Caesar did never wrong but with just cause." Though changed in later editions, these words ensnare the spirit of any man with power. It has been charged that Shakespeare, in his treatment of the common people in this play and elsewhere, shows himself opposed to democracy. This is much like accusing a caveman of not reading newspapers. In Shakespeare's day, the problem was for England to achieve unity and maintain peace under a strong, wise head. Examination of many of Shakespeare's plays shows that although the mob is referred to as a foul many-headed beast, individuals are esteemed according to their worth, not their rank. The sturdy, solid, manly commoners in the plays, indeed, are outnumbered only by the stupid or villainous gentlemen. It may be this charge, nevertheless, that led Bernard Shaw to attack the spirit of *Julius Caesar*. Declaring that it is the craftiest stage job ever done and praising Shakespeare's full organ tones, Shaw protested in 1898 that the portrait of Caesar is a travesty, that not a statement of his is worthy of even "an average Tammany boss. Brutus is nothing but a familiar type of English suburban preacher . . . Cassius is a vehemently assertive nonentity." Shaw's indignation, however, died at thought of Antony: with him "we find Shakespeare in his depth; and in his depth, of course, he is superlative."

Superlative, too, thought briefly seen, are the wife and the servant boy of Brutus. Portia stands staunchly by her husband; she divines, and insists on sharing, his concerns. She, and the innocent boy Lucius, whom Brutus is always rousing from his slumbers, partake of the nobility and slumbering innocence of the misled leader. Lucius, who has fallen asleep over his musical instrument in Brutus' tent, catches in his half-waking words the way his master has been played upon: "The strings, my lord, are false." Once embarked, Brutus urged the conspirators to put on a false face, and the train of violence, falsehood, and greed was started on its repetitive journey.

Productions of this drama have usually been simple, though one in 1875 ended with a great tableau of Brutus' funeral pyre. Junius Brutus Booth found a fit gesture when as Cassius he strode unconcernedly over the fallen Caesar. There was less propriety when, in an Edwin Booth production, the First Citizen and the Second Citizen, each weighing well over 200 pounds, stepped conspicuously forward as Julius Caesar exclaimed "Let me have men about me that are fat!"

Outstanding American productions have included Edwin Booth and Lawrence Barrett (1871), Robert Mantell (1906), William Faversham and Tyrone Power (1912). In 1940 the play was presented in Cleveland Heights, Dallas, and (in modern dress) Kalamazoo, Michigan. The most exciting recent version was the one, condensed to ninety minutes without intermission, of the Mercury Theatre in New York in 1936, with Orson Welles as Brutus, against the brick wall of the theatre, with modern uniforms. A company from Amherst College presented the play at the Folger Shakespeare Museum in Washington in 1949. An arena production, with Basil Rathbone as Cassius and Horace Braham as Caesar, opened in New York on June 20, 1950.

Of the Mercury production, Brooks Atkinson said: "It is revolution taken out of the hands of men and driven by immortal destiny . . . Caesar's resemblance to Mussolini in appearance and manner defines the play so exactly that the dialogue sounds curiously restrained, as though the author could not speak the words he needs for so ominous an occasion . . . When *Julius Caesar* is presented as a play of action, Shakespeare sounds like a Fascist." Richard Watts, Jr. urged the timely associations: "It is amazing how happily and logically the drama fits into its modern framework . . . You cannot escape the feeling that, with the clairvoyance of genius, he was predicting for us the cauldron of modern Europe." John Anderson felt that the production succeeded "enough to blow the hinges off the dictionary". John Mason Brown concurred: "I come to praise *Caesar,* not to bury it . . . the heart of the drama beats more vigorously in this production than it has in years." Burns Mantle, however, detailed his objections to the "lyrics by William Shakespeare and musical voice by Orson Welles and his associates . . . A two-hour recital out of which pop many remembered speeches but no remembered Romans, friends, or countrymen. A *Caesar* in overcoats and felt hats. A *Caesar* that, with a text by Clifford Odets, would likely have been called *Waiting for Julius.* But never the *Julius Caesar* that Shakespeare wrote, nor the Elizabethans nor any of their successors ever staged . . . The conspirators . . . look for all the world like a committee from a taxi-drivers' union. The lean and hungry Cassius is short and round; the envious Casca wears his hat with a rakish tilt; the good Trebonius, the Ligarius, the Decius Brutus are like worried C I O pickets without their shields."

Few productions of the play, however bad, have been able to destroy its vigor. It continues its challenge as—in Bernard Shaw's relenting words—"the most splendidly written political melodrama we possess". Even more, it is a dramatic picture of calculation failing, and dragging down nobility in its ruins. In *Julius Caesar* Shakespeare, writing for the first time under the double influence of the Roman Seneca and the Greek Plutarch, reaches out toward new heights of tragic power.

MUCH ADO ABOUT NOTHING   *William Shakespeare*

Borrowing the serious story of *Much Ado About Nothing*, 1598(?), mainly from Bandello's *Novelle*, 1554, Shakespeare added all that gives the play its sparkle and its life. The virtuous heroine made, by a villain's plot, to seem wanton, so that her lover denies her—as Claudio at the church casts off the innocent Hero—was a widespread medieval motif. Widespread too was the device of having her then play dead so as to effect a final happy restoration. But the absurd constable Dogberry and his Watch, who stumble upon and disclose the villainy, are a unique Shakespearean creation. And Shakespeare brought into the play the love-game played upon Beatrice, "the sauciest, most piquant, madcap girl that ever Shakespeare drew", and Benedick, who swore to remain a bachelor, but whose name is now the byword for a married man. The way in which the two are enticed into a courtship—their friends arranging to have Benedick overhear them say that Beatrice loves him; and Beatrice, that Benedick loves her—leads to some of Shakespeare's merriest trifling. As Coleridge in 1818 summed it up: "Take away all that is not indispensable to the plot . . . take away Benedick, Beatrice, Dogberry and the reaction of the former on the character of Hero—and what will remain?" Swinburne felt that the borrowed and the original parts were admirably fused by Shakespeare: "For absolute power of composition, for faultless balance and blameless rectitude of design, there is unquestionably no creation of his hand that will bear comparison with *Much Ado About Nothing*."

One of the most popular of Shakespeare's comedies, the play was performed at court in 1613 as part of the wedding celebration of the daughter of James I. In 1649 Leonard Digges, in doggerel verse, attested to its unfailing popularity. In 1662 Davenant's *The Law Against Lovers*, a version combining the Beatrice-Benedick plot with that of *Measure for Measure**, supplanted Shakespeare's play; the original was not acted again until 1721. It was popular in Garrick's repertory around 1750; but gradually the play came to be chosen by women stars attracted to the role of Beatrice: Helen Faucit, Ellen Terry, Ada Rehan, and Modjeska. Peggy Ashcroft and John Gielgud acted the play at Stratford, opening June 6, 1950.

The first American performance of the play was in New York at the John Street Theatre, March 17, 1787. More recently, it was produced here by Sothern and Marlowe in 1904, and by the Stratford-on-Avon Festival Company in 1930. It is very popular in college and community theatre revivals. Gielgud played it again in London, opening January 11, 1952. Claire Luce was in a New York production opening May 1, 1952, that lasted for only four performances. The New York production with Ellen Terry and Henry Irving, in November 1884, was an elaborate one. Said the *Times:* "The wit, the tenderness, the playful satire, and the

humanity . . . charmed an audience that filled every part of the Star
Theatre . . . There have been in our day more comely and less ungainly
Benedicts than Mr. Irving . . . But surely there has never been a better
Beatrice than Ellen Terry . . . Infused with the spirit of all that is pure
and lovable in womanhood, sparkling with merriment that does not
hide the tenderness of her heart . . . certainly one of the best dramatic
achievements of its time". Viewing the play again in March, 1885, the
Times reconsidered: "Mr. Irving's Benedict improves on acquaintance
. . . He still seems crusty and odd, but his surliness disappears, and we
find him a good-humored, fair-minded, warm-hearted, brave gentleman,
not so young as he was, but all the better for having seen the world
and learned wisdom by experience. He is still a bit fantastic too, and
overfond of dress and jewelry; but how well the hues of his raiment
harmonize with the colors of the scenes through which he strolls! . . . a
delightful glimpse of the sunny land of romance."

To the chorus of praise of the play, Bernard Shaw set a countering
solo: "The main pretension in *Much Ado* is that Benedick and Beatrice
are exquisitely witty and amusing persons. They are, of course, nothing
of the sort. Benedick's pleasantries might pass at a sing-song in a public
house parlor; but a gentleman rash enough to venture on them in even
the very mildest £52-a-year suburban imitation of polite society today
would assuredly never be invited again. From his first joke . . . to his
last, he is not a wit, but a blackguard . . . Precisely the same thing, in
the tenderer degree of her sex, is true of Beatrice. In her character of
professed wit she has only one subject, and that is the subject which a
really witty woman never jests about, because it is too serious a matter
to be made light of without indelicacy. Beatrice jests about it for the
sake of the indelicacy."—Surely this was the moment for someone to
quote, against Shaw, from the play itself: "Speak, cousin, or, if you cannot, stop his mouth with a kiss!"

A more serious moment in the play is that in which Benedick first
asks Beatrice what he can do to show his love for her. Beatrice, full of
resentment against Claudio for his having spurned Hero at the altar's
foot, cries out "Kill Claudio!" Harold Hobson of the *London Sunday
Times* contrasted the weakness of the Robert Donat revival at the Aldwych Theatre (October 16, 1946) in this scene, with the varied strength
of two other performances, of this "climax and crisis of the play. When
Marie Ney played Beatrice on the radio, in the church scene she spoke
her two tremendous words "Kill Claudio!" in a voice as sharp, as clear,
as cold as an icicle. I froze in my chair as I listened. When Mr. D. A.
Clarke-Smith was Benedick in another production, he sprang back three
paces on his horrified reply, "Not for the wide world!" In the first performance, I have forgotten the Benedick; in the second, the Beatrice. In
this scene at the Aldwych I shall forget both." With such keen observation are the details of Shakespearean performance watched! E. K.
Chambers, in *Shakespeare: A Survey* (1925), also indicated the significance of this moment in the play. He called Beatrice: "High-spirited,
witty, honest, shrewd of apprehension, capable of tenderness: all this
we had seen or guessed her earlier in the play; but for the dialogue with
Benedick in the church we should never have known her inmost soul
is wrought of forged steel and gold." Chambers, however, felt that the
genuine depth of Beatrice's emotion clashes with the predominant moods

of the plot. Claudio and Hero are acceptable, he declared, only on the plane of melodrama, not on the more realistic plane of comedy to which the Beatrice and Benedick episodes in the main shift them. In answer to this, it should be noted that both couples are set in opposition to the romantic idea of love. There is a humdrum realism in the businesslike joining of hands in Claudio and Hero's marriage of convenience. And the other couple join in despising, not love, but the artificial jargon that often masks it; they slough the romantic make-believe and find true love.

The title of the play, as Harold C. Goddard has pointed out, calls for further pondering. There may be an immediate verbal play, for the Elizabethans pronounced "nothing" like "noting", and noting (eavesdropping) starts the action moving. But there are deeper divinings. For "nothing" is what the poet gives a local habitation and a name. "Nothing", said Timon of Athens, "brings me all things." And "nothing", what Cordelia had for Lear, is the choicest human giving. In a sense, the play grows out of nothing, out of things that do not exist. The two bases of the main plot—Don John's statement that Hero was untrue to Claudio; Friar Francis' statement that Hero is dead—have nothing of substance. Here imagination works toward disaster. Out of nothing also rises the underplot: Beatrice and Benedick each hears talk of the other's non-existent love. Here imagination works upon nothing to create something good, as faith in the love helps it into their hearts. A mighty deal may thus burgeon from nothing! One need not be surprised that a later poet, William Butler Yeats, declared "Where there is nothing there is God." Out of nothing, here, beckons the god of love.

Some of Shakespeare's neatest verbal play adorns *Much Ado About Nothing*, as the lovers polish the language, and Dogberry polishes it off. There is neat implication when the Sexton says, of the conspirators against Hero, "Let these men be bound" and Constable Dogberry emphasizes: "Let them be opinioned." The constable's tongue tied the play's theme: "to be opinioned is to be bound"; on the free imagination, one may soar. Here Shakespeare's fancy soars, as he shoots "the paper bullets of the brain" with expert marksmanship. With Dogberry's malaprop phrases, and the blunderings of the Watch that save the situation, the playwright has built some of his best low comedy scenes. In Beatrice and Benedick, he has smilingly satirized human nature while weaving a romped romance. And the feast is further spiced with homely and sound reflections; in a superb play, bountiful in excitement, wit, and beauty.

ALL'S WELL THAT ENDS WELL   *William Shakespeare*

Among the six comedies by Shakespeare mentioned in *Wit's Treasury*, 1598, is *Love's Labour's Won;* this is in all likelihood the play now known as *All's Well That Ends Well*. Some scholars, indeed, trace two styles in the comedy, and aver that the rhymed couplets, the lyrical dialogue, the many puns and conceits, are relics of the early version, while the run-on lines of blank verse with feminine (unaccented syllable) endings, are signs of the revision. The play apparently called for revision, for it was not popular. We have no record of its performance before 1741. It was produced perhaps once a decade, usually in an expurgated version by Kemble, from 1763 to 1900. It was played in Birmingham, Alabama, in modern dress in 1927; in San Diego, 1935; Pasadena, 1937; and Richmond, Virginia, 1938.

The plot of the play—borrowed, via William Paynter's *Palace of Pleasure*, 1566, from Boccaccio—seems a bit far-fetched to have wide appeal to modern audiences. Bertram, Count of Rousillon, ordered by the King of France to marry Helena, decides that "a young man married is a man that's marred." Influenced by his boon companion, the rascally Parolles, he goes through the ceremony, then leaves for the wars, declaring that when Helena presents him with his own seal ring and his own begotten son, he will acknowledge her as his wife. Helena in disguise follows Bertram; substituting for the pretty Diana at an assignation, she secures Bertram's ring, and in due time fulfills the second condition.

The value of the play lies, then, less in the story than in the characters. The play stands out artistically, said Bernard Shaw, by the sovereign charm of the young Helena and the old Countess of Rousillon, and intellectually by the experiment, repeated nearly three hundred years later in *A Doll's House**, of making the hero "a perfectly ordinary young man, whose unimaginative prejudices and selfish conventionality make him cut a very mean figure in the atmosphere created by the nobler nature of his wife." Among the minor figures, the old Lafeu and the adventure-dreading, adventure-boasting coward Parolles are especially neatly drawn. And, as Hardin Craig well put it: "Helena is beautifully attended and vouched for, largely by elderly people. Nothing graces youth more than the friendship of the old. The wise, kindly, clear-eyed Countess of Rousillon loves her as a daughter and knows her heart." A quite different interpretation was advanced by E. K. Chambers, in *Shakespeare: A Survey* (1925). He saw the play as a picture of the way in which love blinds and betrays a noble woman into a poor choice and into demeaning herself to win and hold him, "not Helena's triumph but Helena's degradation . . . It is a poor prize for which she has trailed her honour in the dust." This evaluation, however, smacks more of the doctrinaire twentieth century than of the sentimental sixteenth.

Although it has not been a stage favorite, the play rewards the reader. Hazlitt considers it "one of the most pleasing of our author's comedies. The interest is, however, more of a serious than of a comic nature. The character of Helena is one of great sweetness and delicacy. She is placed in circumstances of the most critical kind, and has to court her husband both as a virgin and as a wife, yet the most scrupulous nicety of female modesty is not once violated. There is not one thought or action that ought to bring a blush into her cheeks, or that for a moment lessens her in our esteem." The men are of quite different nature. In some productions, the play was cut so as to make the scoundrel Parolles the central figure; King Charles I, in his copy of the Second Folio edition of Shakespeare's dramas, wrote as title for this play, *Monsieur Parolles*. Bertram is a cad, to whom Samuel Johnson could not reconcile his heart: "a man noble without generosity, and young without truth; who marries Helena as a coward, and leaves her as a profligate; when she is dead by his unkindness, sneaks home to a second marriage, is accused by a woman whom he has wronged, defends himself by falsehood, and is dismissed to happiness." These portraits are so tinged that Harold C. Goddard has suggested that there is an irony in this picture of two gentlemen of France similar to that in *Two Gentlemen of Verona*,* with their polished exteriors and their putrid core. At the end, there is only a hope that Helena and awakened love will change Bertram, but the King closes the play with an optimistic couplet.

An important element in the drama is the dialogue itself, prose and poetry. The ear is the sure clue to Shakespeare. Whether it be pure tone of beauty or sly twinkle of fun, the words in sound and echo fit the mood. The more important events of the play may seem far-fetched, but the motives and emotions are natural, are in us all. Combined with the character studies are enough poetry and comedy to make the reader find enjoyment still in thinking "all's well that ends well."

AS YOU LIKE IT   *William Shakespeare*

Based upon the prose romance of *Rosalynde,* written in 1590 by Thomas Lodge, William Shakespeare's smiling artificial comedy *As You Like It,* 1599 (?) is "the play most ideal of any of this author's plays" in the opinion of Hazlitt. It captures the mood of courtship in a forest filled with sunshine.

Rosalind, daughter of the banished Duke, watching Orlando wrestle at court, falls in love with Orlando, who with his old servant Adam flies from his brother Oliver's jealous treachery, to the Forest of Arden. Rosalind, herself banished, flees with Celia, the present Duke's daughter and her dearest friend, to the same forest. There, disguised as a boy, she promises to cure Orlando of his love; and a mock courtship carries the days lightsomely along, with the shepherd and court Fool and forest philosopher, until the bad brother and the bad Duke repent, and Rosalind's lifting of the disguise brings on four weddings.

For the Elizabethan gentlefolk, the play deftly balanced the advantages of the town and the country, the court and the forest. For those that fell out of royal favor (and frequent were the occasions and many the persons, with Elizabeth's short temper and shifting politics!), there is proffered consolation. The play burlesques three things: the pastoral vogue in literature; country life itself, though that is also lovingly drawn; and the courtiers that sigh for the country but hurry back to town. The audience is not expected to take the emotions in the play seriously; the very verse grows artificial to weaken the impact on the feelings, as, for instance, when starving Orlando breaks in upon the Duke's company, and the Duke echoes Orlando's words. This artificiality is, at one place, pointed out by Shakespeare himself: When Orlando greets his beloved, "Good day and happiness, Dear Rosalind!", Jaques takes his leave, exclaiming: "Nay, then God be wi' you, an you talk in blank verse." The melancholy Jaques is the first in the long series of observing commentators in the English drama, and Touchstone, a Fool at court, is a philosopher in the forest. (About 1598, the comic actor Will Kemp left the Lord Chamberlain's Company and was succeeded by Robert Armin, a quite different type of comic. This may help to account for the fact that such figures as Bottom and Falstaff were followed by such others as Touchstone and the Fool in *King Lear*.)

Charles Johnson's version, *Love in a Forest,* 1723, with rapiers instead of the wrestling, with Oliver committing suicide, with passages added from *A Midsummer Night's Dream**, was short-lived; by 1741 Shakespeare's own play again commanded the boards. Among the actresses whom Rosalind has lured are Fanny Davenport, Helena Modjeska, Julia Marlowe, Maude Adams, and Marjorie Rambeau (in 1923, the first production of the American National Theatre). The comic scenes and the wrestling match have frequently been stressed in productions. (Wrestling always provides entertaining stage action; *see The Apple Cart**.) In a production offered at the University of Washington, then brought to New York, in 1945, the French fop became a woman: Madame Le Beau. In this "modern" production, as *Variety* put it, Rosalind and her companions were garbed "in the loveliest Basque shirts and pastel shorts this side the Abercrombie and Fitch windows."

Further comedy has always been sought in the scenes where Rosalind is disguised as a boy. *Blackwood's Magazine,* in the mid-Victorian year of 1890, protested: "What can Miss Ada Rehan mean by pulling down her doublet . . . as though she would accomplish the impossible feat of hiding her legs under it—an indelicacy of suggestion at which one can only shudder!" The magazine contrasted with this the decorum of Lily Langtry who gave no sign of embarrassment when in her disguise she encountered Orlando, and "carefully avoided all vulgar clowning in passages referring to her male attire, but when she spoke the line—'Here, on the skirts of the forest, like a fringe on a petticoat'—she put out her hand with a perfectly natural gesture to pick up her own petticoat, and finding none, paused awkwardly for half a second." Rosalind's charm is almost actor-proof. "Who ever failed, or could fail, as Rosalind?" asked Bernard Shaw. "Rosalind is not a complete human being: she is simply an extension into five acts of the most affectionate, fortunate, delightful five minutes in the life of a charming woman." Her pleasant fellowship contrasts sharply with the snobbish wit of Touchstone.

Bernard Shaw disapproved of much of the play after the 1896 London production. Yet he declared that "it has the overwhelming advantage of being written for the most part in prose instead of blank verse, which any fool can write. And such prose! The first scene alone, with its energy of exposition, each phrase driving its meaning and feeling in up to the head at one brief, sure stroke, is worth ten acts of the ordinary Elizabethan sing-song." Part of that exposition, however, is presented without concealment, as though Shakespeare were indifferent to this minor problem of dramaturgy: "What's the new news at the new court?" "There's no news at the court, sir, but the old news"—whereupon we hear what both onstage know but the audience must be told. Sheridan poked fun at such direct recital, in Act II Scene ii of *The Critic.**

The Park Theatre, in New York, opened on January 29, 1798, with *As You Like It*. More recently, the play was performed in New York in 1937; at the World's Fair in 1939; with Helen Craig in 1941; with Donald Wolfit as Touchstone in 1947; and with Katherine Hepburn opening January 26, 1950. There was a production in Rome in 1948, with surrealist scenery and costumes by Salvador Dali; it was presented at the Stratford Festival in 1952. Elizabeth Bergner was Rosalind in the screen version. Of the 1937 production, Richard Watts, Jr. stated "It isn't an academic secret that *As You Like It* is one of the dullest plays ever written . . . There are moments of lyric loveliness and gentle gracefulness in this sylvan narrative, but they are more than counter-balanced by the dull comedy, the antic coyness, and the strenuous high spirits that make the play hopeless dramatically." Recent productions have won scant critical praise—George Freedely thinks the best was "an eighteenth century rendering" by Hilpert at the Deutsches Theater, in Berlin in 1934—but the play itself, even though it is required reading in schools, still has a strong hold on popular favor.

The song "Under the greenwood tree Who loves to lie with me" well illustrates Shakespeare's use of music. In addition to breaking the audience's tension (as does comic relief in the tragedies), this song states the theme of the play, helps establish the forest setting, fills time for the preparation of the Duke's banquet, and by contrast with gay Amiens builds the character of the "melancholy" Jaques.

Orlando's brother, Jaques de Boys, mentioned in the first scene of the play, does not appear until the last, when he speaks the sixteen lines that wind up the plot. This was called "the shilling speech" in the old Shakespearean companies: if the actor was word-perfect, he was given a shilling—which was rarely won. The speech makes Shakespeare's least effective denouement, of the "old religious man" that converts the usurping Duke Frederick, who returns the dukedom to his brother.

It is interesting to note that Shakespeare himself was not wholly be-mused in the merry romp of the enchanted courtship. As foils to Rosa-lind and Orlando, he sets three other pairs. Touchstone takes up with Audrey about as one decides to wear old shoes to an outing. To this casual cohabitation is added another doomed match when the disguised Rosalind tricks young Phebe into marrying the doddering Silvius, whom she detests. Finally, Oliver repents, Celia is nearby and unattached: let's mate them! These cynical counter-currents in the stream of happy love add to the reflective mood that underlies the comedy, as we consider that indeed "all the world's a stage . . . and each man in his time plays many parts."

In its surface sunshine of romance, however, we echo the line in the play Shakespeare borrowed from Marlowe: "Who ever loved that loved not at first sight?"

TWELFTH NIGHT   *William Shakespeare*

"A silly play, and not at all related to the name or day," Samuel Pepys wrote in his *Diary* in 1663, after seeing a performance of Shake-speare's *Twelfth Night; or, What You Will,* 1599(?). During the formal times of Pope and Johnson the play was seldom performed. A version by William Burnaby, called *Love Betrayed; or, The Agreeable Disap-pointment,* had mediocre success in 1703. The original comedy was re-vived in 1741; but it did not become popular until the nineteenth cen-tury. Its presentation at Daly's Theatre in London in 1894 saved that theatre after the disastrous failure, the season before, of Tennyson's *The Foresters.* More recent productions, in New York, include that of Sothern and Marlowe in 1919; Fritz Leiber in 1930; Jane Cowl and Leon Quartermaine in the same year; The Federal Theatre in 1939; Helen Hayes and Maurice Evans in 1940; the Dramatic Workshop, with Marlon Brando, in 1944. There were two effective productions of the play in the United States in 1949, one with Betty Field, one with Frances Reid.

Several outstanding French directors have produced the play; Jacques Copeau (in 1914 and 1919), Gaston Baty, Georges Pitoeff, and Firmin Gemier. In London, the Granville-Barker production of 1912 broke the long tradition of elaborate sets and came, as the *Tatler* said, like "a breath of fresh air over a world super-stuffy with the theatrical conventions of centuries". This simple and charming production was the success of the season and unmatched until the Old Vic 1950 production opening November 4 with Peggy Ashcroft as Viola, which led W. A. Darlington to declare, in the *New York Times* (December 3, 1950) that "to many people, myself most emphatically included, Twelfth Night is the nearest thing to a perfect comedy yet composed in English". The deft New York production in 1955, by the Shakespearewrights, would not incline you to disagree.

Twelfth Night, the feast of Epiphany (the visit of the Magi to the infant Jesus), was traditionally a time of jollity and merry-making. The title thus indicates the mood of the play, as does Sir Toby Belch's query to the sour steward Malvolio: "Dost thou think, because thou art virtuous, there shall be no more cakes and ale?" Hazlitt, in the nineteenth century, showed how far opinion had shifted from Pepys' day: "This is justly considered as one of the most delightful of Shakespeare's comedies. It is full of sweetness and pleasantry." "Structurally it is a joy", Hardin Craig says of *Twelfth Night;* and the play neatly interweaves the stories and the levels of action. For the nobles, it combines two frequent Renaissance themes: identical twins and the consequent confusions; and the maid disguised as page to the man she loves. Thus Viola, as page to Orsino, duke of Illyria, bears his love-messages to Olivia—who falls in love with the page. Orsino also finds himself attracted to the page; so that the complications are agreeably smoothed when Viola's twin brother Sebastian marries Olivia, and Viola, revealed as a maiden, marries the Duke.

Linking this romantic realm with the more humorous everyday world is Olivia's turbulent toss-pot uncle, Sir Toby Belch, who with his timid bean-pole friend, Sir Andrew Aguecheek, and Olivia's maid Maria, wages war upon the steward Malvolio. Malvolio was a figure quickly recognized in Shakespeare's day, being frequent and well-hated: the upper servant that bullies those below him in station. Thus there is much amusing frolic in the tricks played on Malvolio, especially with the letter supposedly from his mistress Olivia—"Some are born great, some achieve greatness, and some have greatness thrust upon them"— that tempts him to come before her cross-gartered, in antic disposition, so that the others gleefully incarcerate him as insane. Malvolio's misadventures, however, must be handled with deft lightness. Thus Beerbohm Tree—who as Malvolio was attended by four tiny pages aping him in dress and deportment—majestically descending the great staircase, slipped to a "crash landing", but, as Bernard Shaw reported: "Tree, without betraying the smallest discomfiture, raised his eyeglass and surveyed the landscape as if he had sat down on purpose." Hardin Craig complains that great actors, playing Malvolio, have been inclined to make his final threat of vengeance too emphatic. The *New York Dramatic Mirror,* in 1920, made this charge specific: "We of the present day cannot laugh at madness, and when Malvolio is tormented with the belief that he is mad, we are tormented also . . . Mr. Sothern elects to play it seriously. The result is that his audience pities him, weeps for him perhaps, and is deeply moved, but feels under its skin that some extraneous mood has crept into the theatre."

There are abundant opportunities for comic business in the play. The drunken bout of Sir Toby and Sir Andrew in Olivia's kitchen is the first such scene in English comedy; it has been almost invariably successful in countless plays since. The many opportunities for comic byplay, indeed, are so tempting as sometimes to lead to excess. Mme. Modjeska, in the duel between the disguised Viola and the cowardly Aguecheek, refrained from hitting her timorous adversary; Julia Arthur first beat him with her sword and then spanked him as he dodged about. In 1820 Aguecheeck tried to get out of the way by climbing the proscenium of the stage; in 1825, he scurried up a handy rope-ladder; later, he clambered up a tree. In 1901, Julia Marlowe protested: "We cannot go far wrong if we let the lines have the center of the stage and allow them to show the poet's meaning. We cannot aid him by a multitude of gestures or by creating intricate business." But still, in 1940, Brooks Atkinson had to exclaim that "the beauty of the current *Twelfth Night* is overladen with a desire to be funny at any cost." Of the same production, Richard Watts, Jr. observed: "Although *Twelfth Night* contains some of the worst features of Elizabethan comedy, it has charm, grace, and loveliness, and these saving qualities are captured in abundance in this handsome and skillful new production."

In addition to the romance and the comedy, the play affords us the lilt of delightful poetry. From its opening words—"If music be the food of love, play on"—to the Clown's song that closes the play—"with hey, ho, the wind and the rain"—as Viola says of Olivia, " 'tis beauty truly blent." *Twelfth Night* is perhaps Shakespeare's most effective commingling of love and lyrical beauty and rowdy laughter . . . and something more. For here, as often in his comedies, Shakespeare plants, for the discerning, guideposts to further thoughts. These were developed by Harold C. Goddard in *The Meaning of Shakespeare* (1951), who noted that the figures in Illyrian society are all marked by excess of various sorts. Sentimentality and sensuality blind their days. It is a seventeenth century version of *Heartbreak House**, Goddard declared, "with the difference that whereas Bernard Shaw depicts his heartbreaking society with blasts of satire and on top of that writes a blistering preface that nobody may miss his point, Shakespeare just holds up what is essentially the same world and allows it to amuse us or break our hearts as we choose. *What You Will.*" There is hope at the end that Viola and Sebastian, rescued from the sea (across which in legends the deliverers come) may bring those drowning in the ocean of sentimentality back to friendly earth, and through love reawaken the spirit.

HAMLET   *William Shakespeare*

The longest of Shakespeare's plays, *Hamlet,* 1600(?), is the most widely discussed of all dramas. Despite the melodramatic vicissitudes of the Prince, many persons find much within themselves like "the melancholy Dane", hesitant before the deed. William Hazlitt went so far as to declare in 1817: "It is *we* who are Hamlet." One reason for the pervasive power of the play is that it closely follows the pattern of the nature-myth of the seasonal death and resurrection of the fruitful world, which lies deep within our human ways.

Among famous discussions of the play in literature are those in Goethe's *Wilhelm Meister's Apprenticeship* and Joyce's *Ulysses*. Voltaire, after his stay in England (1726-1729), sang the praises of Shakespeare's plays, but in 1748 he recanted, setting down a scornful summary of *Hamlet,* which begins, "It is a coarse and barbarous piece that would not be tolerated by the lowest riff-raff of France or Italy," and ends, "Such a work seems the product of a drunken savage."

Constantly thought turns upon the Prince himself, a pale man in black clothes, the lonelier because companioned by doubt and dread, a man, as C. S. Lewis saw him, "from whose hands, as from our own, we feel the richness of heaven and earth and the comfort of human affection slipping away."

The story of Hamlet (Amleth) comes down from the twelfth century *History of the Danes* of Saxo Grammaticus. In the play, returning home for King Hamlet's funeral, Prince Hamlet finds his mother Gertrude remarried and her new husband, the late King's brother Claudius, on the throne. Informed by his father's ghost that the death was not natural, but murder by Claudius, Hamlet plans retribution. To make sure the ghost is not a deceiving fiend, and to expose Claudius' guilt to the court of Denmark, Hamlet arranges for visiting players to enact a similar crime: "The play's the thing Wherein I'll catch the conscience of the King." The King's councillor Polonius thinks Hamlet mad for love of his daughter Ophelia, whom he and Claudius try to use as a decoy to discover Hamlet's thoughts. After the players' acting reveals Claudius' guilt, Hamlet wrings his mother's heart with his reproaches, until, hearing a noise behind the arras, he stabs through it and kills the listening Polonius. Ophelia, broken by the strain, goes mad and drowns herself. Polonius' son Laertes, returning to avenge these deaths, is turned by King Claudius against Hamlet, and persuaded to engage him in a "friendly" duel, with Laertes' foil unbuttoned and poison-tipped. For double assurance, Claudius prepares a poisoned drink for the Prince. As a consequence the Queen, Laertes. the King, and Hamlet, all die. The strong arms of Fortinbras, King of Norway, bring promise of peace to the land.

In addition to containing some of the greatest of all poetry, such as the well-known soliloquy beginning "To be or not to be", *Hamlet* is a superbly constructed drama. The very reticences of the playwright mark his genius. One of the most important moments of the play is a scene unseen, reported by Ophelia to her father. After wandering all night, broken with the dreadful story of his father's ghost, Hamlet comes for comfort to the woman he loves. Instead of springing to help him, Ophelia draws back, scared out of her wits; she runs to her father—"O, my lord, I have been so affrighted!"—and Hamlet recognizes he can put no trust in her.

The weakness of Ophelia, which leads to her later madness, gives the clue to Hamlet's emotional state, left with no one to share his awful burden. His first words in the play, two answers to the King, are twisted, bitter puns. His later distracted manner has led critics, up to our own generation, to argue as to whether Hamlet is mad or merely feigning. Charles Kemble acted Hamlet as mad: his brother John Philip Kemble cut the wilder parts and made him feigning. Samuel Johnson is emphatic: "Of the feigned madness there appears no adequate cause, for he does nothing which he might not have done with the reputation of sanity." Modern psychology enables us to understand his conduct. Pressed with an excessive emotional burden, Hamlet could not suppress, but could direct, his outbursts. Thus to Polonius he speaks of Ophelia; to Rosencrantz and Guildenstern, the King's spies, of his discontent with the narrow confines of his position in Denmark. In the original Amleth story, the madness is feigned, as indeed in other hero tales, such as those of Greek Odysseus and Jewish David. Hamlet's attitude toward Ophelia has troubled many critics. He came to her from the ghost, William Bliss remarked in *The Real Shakespeare* (1949), not only for consolation but also for renunciation. Dedicated to revenge, he could not ask the child Ophelia to share his lonely destiny. This notion was earlier put forward by Lamb to explain "the asperity which he puts on in his interview with Ophelia . . . a profound artifice of love to alienate Ophelia by affected discourtesies, so to prepare her mind for the breaking off of that loving intercourse which can no longer find a place amidst business so serious as that which he had to do." Productions usually, after Hamlet has come upon Ophelia at her prayers, supply some ground, most obviously the king's peeping from behind a curtain, for the sudden suspicion that turns Hamlet's tongue to bitter words. Many critics have complained of Hamlet's procrastination, of his habit of thinking too much on the event. Thus Coleridge called the drama a "tragedy of weakness of will". Other critics have gone so far as to say that the delays arose from Shakespeare's clumsy joining of two earlier versions of the story. Still others, trying to look upon Hamlet with Elizabethan eyes, consider that he has broken from the medieval Christian view of a world dependent upon God's grace, but is unable to decide between the two Renaissance attitudes—the one that finds an essential dignity in man, and the other (Calvin; Montaigne) that sees man as base. Hamlet's wavering actions are then the result of his wavering thoughts. Psychologically, however, the delay is the natural struggle of a sensitive, peace-loving soul against violence. The mind orders an action against which the spirit rebels. When we consider the Prince's task, furthermore, we recognize that the entire action flows in a smooth continuity. For first Hamlet (within the beliefs of Shakespeare's day) must make sure that the apparition of his father is not a fiend tempting him to his own damnation. Then he must fulfill the conditions of a fit revenge: the guilty one must know he is being dealt just punishment; the public (the court) must know this is not murder but revenge; and the punishment must fit the crime, i.e., Claudius, who killed King Hamlet with all his sins upon him, must not be dispatched to heaven while at prayers. Once the prior conditions are met, that is, after the play scene, the drama speeds to its tragic conclusion.

A neat reticence of the author is in regard to the Queen's share of guilt. Knowing that his mother was unfaithful to his father, Hamlet naturally wonders whether she was party to the murder. He flings his suspicion at her in contemptuous words, and the only idea the audience is given as to the Queen's share in the murder must come from the actress' answer: from whether she replies like one confounded in her guilt, or like an innocent one dumbfounded by the accusation. Most actresses seek sympathy by taking the latter tone; and indeed, after Hamlet's reproaches, Gertrude's love of him and her remorse lead her to shelter him against the King. John Barrymore followed Freud's comments and played the scene in Hamlet's mother's room with a suggestion of incestuous love. In the Quarto, Gertrude denies her guilt.

The drama is prominently mentioned by those that indicate in the Elizabethan plays the practice of "episodic intensification," building the immediate scene for its own effect and fullest power, without regard to its value in the scheme of the play as a whole. Sometimes, even, items drawn into the play are hard to account for logically. Critics are still arguing for, instance, as to whether the King sees the pantomime that precedes, and shows the same story as, the play that "catches" his conscience. And, if Ophelia drowns near enough for somebody to give the Queen a graphic description of her last moments, why didn't that somebody save the lorn princess?

The movement is speedy. There is, for all Hamlet's seeming irresolution, a constant bustle of action in the play. In addition to the traveling players, *Hamlet* stirs with the mad scene, with a restless ghost, a wrestling match in a new-dug grave, and a duel with swords flying. Thus the play is "much more a variety show than the later tragedies," avers S. L. Bethell in *Shakespeare and The Popular Dramatic Tradition* (1944). "Its greater popularity on the stage is due to sheer 'entertainment value'; and it is a favorite with the critics because its imperfections leave more room for discussion, and the peculiar character of its hero provides a fascinating subject for every variety of armchair quackery." Viewed within the story's scope, however, as we have seen, Hamlet is so far from peculiar as to be universal; and it is less the play's "imperfections" than its many-sidedness that continually rouses discussion. Note, for instance, the deft but apparently casual contrast of three sons that have lost their fathers by violent death. The sensitive yet impetuous Hamlet and the hotheaded Laertes both unwittingly bring on their own doom; the cool-headed Fortinbras comes in at the end and takes control.

Also notable is the artistry of what T. S. Eliot* in *Poetry and Drama* (1951) called "as well constructed an opening scene as that of any play ever written." Eliot praised the subtle variations in the verse which urge their emotional effects unnoticed, the economy and harmony of the diction—"The first twenty-two lines are built of the simplest words in the most homely idiom"—and the manner in which the poetry promotes the dramatic purpose of the scene.

The play is a masterpiece of irony. Double meanings abound. Hamlet is often acting a part, as the play's reiterative imagery reminds us. In addition to such outstanding instances as the advice to the players and the play to catch the king, images drawn from the theatre carry overtones of this idea. The last three speeches of the play contain puns on theatrical terms (*audience, performed, stage*). The frequent puns themselves, of course, add further force of irony, being understood one way by the listeners on stage, and another by the listeners off. This sense of double meaning is also fostered by the looking-glass image that runs through the play. Art, says Hamlet to the Players, holds a mirror up to nature, and the play within the play mirrors the king's murder. Hamlet tells his mother he will hold up a glass to her—yet the faults Hamlet attacks in others he exhibits in himself. He urges the Players to temperance, and their play rouses him to rage. He kills Polonius on the moment's impulse, than lectures his mother on self-control. The man that holds a mirror up to others sees not himself. Even more dominant in the play is the image of an ulcer, a "worm in the bud". The murder of Hamlet's father, his mother's incestuous marriage (as it was deemed by Shakespeare's England), the usurpation of the throne, all mark a corruption, "something rotten in the state", that the imagery presses home.

Various aspects of the drama are in the tradition that grew from Seneca*, whose complete works had been translated into English by 1571. Thus the gloomy, introspective, self-dramatizing hero, the ghosts urging revenge, the various treacherous horrors and rearing violence, are all in Seneca. Nashe, in the Preface to Greene's *Menaphon* (1589), sneered at writers who copied, from "Seneca read by candlelight . . . whole *Hamlets*, I should say handfuls, of tragical speeches." It need hardly be said that, though Shakespeare borrowed freely, he transmuted the old material into new gold.

The play has been performed continually, since Shakespeare's day. There were performances on the East India Company's ship *Dragon* in 1607 and 1608. The seventeenth century was varied in its reaction to the play, as notes of two diarists attest. John Evelyn set down, on November 26, 1661: "I saw *Hamlet, Prince of Denmark* played, but now the old plays do begin to disgust this refined age." Samuel Pepys, however, noted on August 31, seven years later, that he was "mightily pleased with it, but above all with Betterton: the best part, I believe, that man ever acted." Its first New York performance was at the Chapel Street Theatre, November 26, 1761.

To name the men that have acted Hamlet (women too, e.g., Charlotte Cushman; in a translation by Alexandre Dumas, Sarah Bernhardt) would be to list the most famous players of many lands. Children also have essayed the role; in the 1804-5 season, the English House of Commons, on motion of Pitt the Younger, adjourned to see the fourteen year old William Betty play Hamlet. Legend says that Shakespeare played the Ghost, at the Blackfriars' Theatre, in 1603. Most Hamlets have presented the Prince in an elocutionary, rhetorical, almost grandiloquent manner, even approaching the style that Hamlet, in his advice to the players, tells them to avoid. Thus David Garrick (1742) achieved a truly sepulchral melancholy; so violent was his starting at the entrance of the ghost as to rouse critical attack. Garrick's friend Boswell, defending him, asked Samuel Johnson: "Would you not start, as Garrick does, if you saw a ghost?"—to which Johnson replied: "I hope not. If I did, I should frighten the ghost!" The actor Edwin Forrest hissed William Macready's Hamlet in a rivalry that led to twenty-two deaths; for details, *see Richelieu**. Edwin Booth, after his early exuberance in the role, adopted (1864) a more natural, but still intense and gloomy Hamlet that continued the tradition. This persisted in the interpretation of John Barrymore, best of our time in this vein. Of Barrymore's work Alan Dale cruelly said: "Every actor should play Hamlet at least once —more often if the public permit and eggs are scarce." John Mason Brown, while he felt that Barrymore "excels all others we have known in grace, fire, wit, and clarity", felt also that "he does not sustain all the emotional values of the play. Only in a few fugitive moments did we feel sorry for Hamlet." This rhetorical tradition may still be observed in the more mannered performance of Maurice Evans. Of Evans' work in *Hamlet* (in the uncut play in 1938 and 1939; in a speeded up and simplified "G.I. version", shown widely to the armies and for 131 performances on Broadway opening December 13, 1945) Brooks Atkinson said: "a wild and whirling play of exalted sound and tragic grandeur, and Mr. Evans acts it as though it were a new text that had not been clapper-clawed by generations of actors." Evans' was not the first uncut *Hamlet* of our time. Benson presented the complete play in London in 1900; the uncut *Hamlet* at the Old Vic, annually in the 1920's, was the most crowded event of the season; and Tyrone Guthrie presented it in 1937.

A more natural tone was sought in the Hamlet of Edmund Kean (1814), as in that of Sir Henry Irving, who in 1874 established the record run of 200 performances . This natural quality is also marked in the Hamlet of John Gielgud, who enacted the play in 1939 at Elsinore Castle, Denmark, and in New York in 1936 with Lillian Gish as Ophelia and Judith Anderson as Gertrude, and again for 132 performances in 1944-45, and—although some prefer the performance of Paul Scofield at Stratford-on-Avon in 1948—is perhaps the best Hamlet of our generation. Jean-Louis Barrault played Hamlet in Paris in 1947 in a translation by André Gide. Donald Wolfit enacted the prince on his American tour in 1947. In London, Michael Redgrave was hailed as Hamlet in an Old Vic production opening February 2, 1950. Alec Guinness starred there in 1951 as Hamlet with a beard, but public opinion quickly shaved him. Charles Albert Fechter, in London in 1865, in New York in 1870, was much more successful as an active Nordic Hamlet, with flowing blond hair.

In 1925, at the Birmingham Repertory Theatre, Sir Barry Jackson's production in modern clothes touched off a round of similar productions, including those by Basil Sydney and Orson Welles. The American premiere of the motion picture version, with Sir Laurence Olivier as Hamlet, was completely sold out, in Boston (August 18, 1948), despite picketing by a "Boycott Britain" group, a century after the anti-British riots at the Astor Place Opera House in New York. Olivier, by the way, says that Sir Johnston Forbes-Robertson, who played Hamlet frequently from 1897 to 1913, was "by all accounts the finest Hamlet of the present century." An American company of actors, headed by Robert Breen, presented the drama in the summer of 1949 at Elsinore Castle, Denmark, the historical scene of the story. A tetralogy in verse by Percy Mackaye, *The Mystery of Hamlet, King of Denmark,* was produced in Pasadena in 1949; the first play ends with Prince Hamlet's birth, while the other three present events of his father's reign up to the murder. André Gide's French version of *Hamlet* was the first production of the Renaud-Barrault Company in Paris in October 1946. A rather flat prose version, it was given a superb production and it achieved over 300 performances in Europe before opening in New York on December 1, 1952. In his passionate yet intelligent interpretation of Hamlet in this version of the play Jean-Louis Barrault leaped to the front ranks of truly great actors. We see Hamlet as a man who must dramatize his life, but who, though he becomes a spectator, remains the sufferer.

Whatever the style of the production, the audience is rewarded with

644   SHAKESPEARE

an intense dramatic character study, in richest poetry, relentless in its
drive toward the inevitable doom, although, as in life, the immediately
fatal circumstances seem almost accidental. *Hamlet* is one of the greatest plays, and unquestionably the most continuingly popular play, of
all time.

TROILUS AND CRESSIDA   *William Shakespeare*

Many have declared that this is Shakespeare's wisest and least
pleasing play. Its unheroic picture of Greek legend has long puzzled
critics. Some have seen in the play a symbolic parallel to the battle of
the theatres—of boys' companies and adult actors—of Shakespeare's time.
Some have even suggested that Shakespeare is burlesquing the Greek
heroes out of jealousy of Chapman's translation of Homer; this notion is
taken for granted in a scholar's letter to the *London Times* of February
2, 1951. In all probability Shakespeare is simply telling the story, as
was often done in the middle ages, from the Trojan point of view. In
any event, the drama's origin is so complex that Gilbert Highet calls it
"a dramatization of part of a translation into English of a French translation of a Latin imitation of an old French expansion of a Latin epitome
of a Greek romance." It may have been written by 1598.

Pointing out that none of Shakespeare's plays is harder to characterize, Coleridge observed: "I am half inclined to believe that Shakespeare's main object, or shall I say his ruling impulse, was to translate
the poetic heroes of paganism into the not less rude, but more intellectually vigorous, and more *featurely*, warriors of Christian chivalry—
and to substantiate the distinct and graceful profiles or outlines of the
Homeric epic into the flesh and blood of the romantic drama." Dryden
sought to improve the play. In the Preface (1679) to his revision he
explained: "The tongue in general is so much refined since Shakespeare's
time, that many of his words, and more of his phrases, are scarce intelligible. And of those which we understand, some are ungrammatical,
others coarse; and his whole style is so pestered with figurative expressions, that it is as affected as it is obscure . . . The author seems to
have begun it with some fire; the characters of Pandarus and Thersites
are promising enough; but as if he grew weary of his task, after an
entrance or two he lets them fall; and the latter part of the tragedy is
nothing but a confusion of drums and trumpets, excursions and alarms.
Yet, after all, because the play was Shakespeare's, and that there appeared in some places of it the admirable genius of the author, I under-
took to remove that heap of rubbish under which many excellent
thoughts lay wholly buried."

From the point of view of frequency of performance, the play may
well be referred to as Shakespeare's only failure. Goethe, however, saw
it as Shakespeare at his most original: "Would you see his mind unfettered," said Goethe in his *Conversations with Eckermann*, "read
Troilus and Cressida."

The two movements of this comedy of disillusion are not well knit
together. On the Trojan side is the love story, with Pandarus (whose
name gives us the word *pander*) furthering Troilus' desire for Cressida.
Cressida swears eternal love to Troilus—then, sent in an exchange to the
Greek camp, at once is free of her lips to the generals, and makes a

rendezvous with Diomedes. Cressida is not mentioned nor seen throughout Act Two, which carries along the miitalry aspect of the drama. Ajax,
while Achilles sulks, is sent to fight Hector; their single combat ends with
their shaking hands. Then Achilles, spurred by the death of his friend
Patroclus, takes the field, and comes upon Hector unarmed. The play,
like the *Iliad*, ends with the death of the Trojan hero Hector.

There have been several important productions in recent years: 1916,
at Yale University; 1932, the Players' annual revival in New York (the
first professional production of the play in America; it included Otis
Skinner as Thersites, Eugene Powers as Pandarus, Charles Coburn as
Ajax, Edith Barrett as Cressida, and Blanche Yurka as Helen of Troy);
1938 in modern dress in London; by the Marlowe Society in London in
1948. A 1948 production at Harvard University afforded a delightful
instance of serendipity (happy accident, frequent in the theatre); wire
shapes were used for makeshift helmets — leaving faces and expressions
completely visible — when the ordered helmets failed to arrive.

This is the most explicitly philosophical of Shakespeare's dramas.
Through its two courses of lechery and war — two scenes of the last act
end with a railing upon "lechery: wars and lechery" — the play pictures
the passions corrupting their human victims, until all is "fair without and
foul within". The central theme of violence with its two faces of war
and lust, both with resplendent surface and "putrified core", is embodied
in Helen, in Cressida, in the war itself—in all war, with the pumped glory
and the blood-soaked sod. The same thought runs through many of the
works of Shakespeare. Here is pressed home the final thought that those
engaged in war and lust end in their own destruction.

Also in this play is Shakespeare's most explicit political thinking.
His belief in the value and social need of an hierarchical order, evident
in several of his plays, finds fullest expression in Ulysses' famous speech
on degree and the consequences of establishing a false equality. However, the conduct of Ulysses, in ironic contrast to his words, should warn
us against assuming that he speaks the playwright's own opinions.

Beyond these basic considerations, the incidental wisdom of the play
reveals itself in such lines as "To be wise, and love, exceeds man's
might", "A plague of opinion! a man may wear it on both sides, like a
leather jerkin", and "One touch of nature makes the whole world kin".
Harold C. Goddard has expressed the view that the play includes "a
hundred-odd of the most wonderful lines in Shakespeare." Though
seldom seen, *Troilus and Cressida* continues to be read for its swift
action and its often bitter but always searching reflections on human
nature.

MEASURE FOR MEASURE   *William Shakespeare*

The essential plot of this play originally appeared in Whetstone's
unproduced tragedy *Promos and Cassandra* (1578), based on the Italian
Giraldi Cinthio's *Hecatommithi* (1565). Like *All's Well That Ends Well**,
it resolves its complications by the Boccaccionian bed-trick of the substituted woman. Its theme, however, is more serious, and perennial, being
(as the *New York World* said, at a 1929 production) a "startlingly familiar study of the hypocritical reformer . . . of the agonized conflict in
those creatures that spend their days in enforcing laws and their nights

in breaking them. Shakespeare makes him a sick and tormented soul who would delight the modern psychiatrist."

Vincentio of Vienna, leaving his Dukedom in charge of Angelo, watches in disguise. Angelo presses heavily upon evil-doers; he condemns Claudio to death for his pre-marital relations with Juliet. Then Angelo promises to spare Claudio if Claudio's sister Isabella will yield to his desire—but secretly he orders Claudio killed nonetheless. The disguised Duke arranges that the assignation with Angelo is kept, not by Isabella, but by Angelo's affianced, then discarded, sweetheart Mariana. The next day, revealing himself, the Duke weds Isabella, orders Claudio to marry Juliet, and spares Angelo when he accepts Mariana as his wife. The Duke does, however, mete punishment to Lucio, who has lied and has slandered the Duke's name—such civil sins being less tolerable.

The play was presented by the King's players, December 26, 1604.

In versions by William Davenant in 1662 and Charles Gildon about 1690, *Measure For Measure* did not win popularity. Revived in 1720, the play held interest throughout the eighteenth century. The Romantics neglected the work, although it contains some of Shakespeare's richest dramatic poetry, and Isabella is one of his noblest characters. Later in the nineteenth century it grew popular again, with Adelaide Neilson, Helena Modjeska, and Sarah Kemble Siddons in the role of Isabella. Swinburne, disliking the play, felt that it could not be all Shakespeare's; he insisted it was "very far from thoroughly worthy of the wisest and mightiest mind that was ever informed with the spirit or genius of creative poetry". On the other hand, Pater states that as "the poetry of this play is full of the peculiarities of Shakespeare's poetry, so in its ethics is it an epitome of Shakespeare's moral judgments . . ."

The actions of the Duke, as well as biblical references and other allusions, show him serving as a sort of pastor tending his people. Some of the play's underworld figures—the condemned murderer Barnardine, for instance—are uncommonly interesting. With tolerance and lack of pretension, Shakespeare reminds you to judge not, that ye be not judged.

The play is, in essence, a study of the effect of power on character; it demonstrates that those in authority are often caught in the foul dilemma of having to employ falsehood or force. This is most sharply shown in the scene between Isabella and Angelo, the sheer theatrical effectiveness of which, as Harold C. Goddard said in *The Meaning of Shakespeare* (1951) "can easily blind us to the tangle of moral ironies and boomerangs it involves."

To a post-Elizabethan there may seem certain confusions in the play. E. K. Chambers, indeed, in *Shakespeare: A Survey* (1925), asserts that "many honest readers of Shakespeare quite frankly resent the very existence of *Measure for Measure* . . . Here are the forms of comedy, the byplay of jest and the ending of reconciliation. But the limits of comedy, which may be serious but must be suave, are sorely strained. There is a cruel hint in the laughter, and the engineer of the reconciliation is surely a cynic." It may seem as though tragic material has been forced into the mould of comedy. There are moral ambiguities in the Duke's intriguing and in Isabella's self-righteousness, not to mention inconsistent details in the story. Because of these confusions, some scholars maintain that much of the play is the work of an inferior hand. It may clarify the play's movement, however, to suggest that Shakespeare was writing a politico-moral thesis play; the title is from the *Bible: St. Luke* VI 38, and all Chapter Six of *St. Luke* comes to mind beneath this dramatic examination of the Elizabethan concept of justice and mercy. The difficulty E. K. Chambers feels may arise from the fact that the play combines elements of the sunny romantic comedy with elements of the caustic comedy of humours Jonson* had just made popular. With understanding of these contemporary concerns, the play gathers into an effective pattern.

In 1929 New York was offered a modern version, *The Novice and the Duke*, by Olga Katzin, with Leo G. Carroll. The Stratford Players presented the play on their American tour in the 1930's, and it was performed at Stratford-on-Avon, with John Gielgud as Angelo, opening March 19, 1950. In 1929, Wilella Waldorf called the play "alarmingly up to date. What Shakespeare has to say . . . is uncommonly interesting, too, or would be were it not so completely tangled up in a plot of decidedly uneven quality, interspersed with doubtful comedy which strikes a particularly sour note when played in modern surroundings." Without the modern clothing, in its own atmosphere, *Measure for Measure* may be accepted as an olden plot that continues to have present validity in its pointing of a permanent truth.

OTHELLO   *William Shakespeare*

Its story taken largely from the Italian Cinthio's *Hecatommithi* (1565), *Othello* (1604) is by many deemed Shakespeare's greatest play. It is often referred to as a tragedy of jealousy. Young Macaulay seems to have regarded it so: "*Othello* is perhaps the greatest work in the world. From what does it derive its power? From the clouds? From the ocean? From the mountains? Or from love as strong as death, and jealousy cruel as the grave?" Samuel Johnson saw the drama as driving home a lesson: "We learn from *Othello* this very useful moral, not to make an unequal match . . . I think *Othello* has almost more moral than any other play." The Romantics analyzed the play more aptly. Lamb, in 1834, remarked: "Othello's fault was credulity." Coleridge, a dozen years earlier, plumbed to the heart of the matter: "Jealousy does not strike me as the point in his passion; I take it rather to be an agony that the creature whom he had believed angelic, with whom he had garnered up his heart, and whom he could not help still loving, should be proved impure and worthless . . . It was a moral indignation and regret that virtue should so fall . . . In addition to this, his honor was concerned." In truth, once Othello was persuaded of Desdemona's guilt, he took, regretfully, the sole course that his honor allowed. For Shakespeare's picture of jealousy, note Leontes in *The Winter's Tale*.

As Coleridge analyzed it: "*Lear* is the most tremendous effort of Shakespeare as a poet; *Hamlet*, as a philosopher or meditator; and *Othello* is the union of the two. There is something gigantic and unformed in the former two; but in the latter, everything assumes its due place and proportion, and the whole mature powers of his mind are displayed in admirable equilibrium." Even Bernard Shaw conceded the play's greatness: "When the worst has been said of *Othello* that can be provoked by its superficiality and stageyness, it remains magnificent by the volume of its passion and the splendor of its word-music, which sweep the scenes up to a plane on which sense is drowned in sound . . . Tested by the brain, it is ridiculous; tested by the ear, it is sublime."

The story moves with simple directness. Desdemona, won by the Moor Othello's nature and his stories of his battles for Venice, defies her father to marry him, and goes to Cyprus where Othello is to govern. Iago, Othello's "ancient", invaluable in the battlefield, finding he is of less use in civil affairs, feels slighted; he seeks to turn Othello against his wife, and by stealing a handkerchief Othello has given Desdemona, convinces the Moor of her unfaithfulness. Still loving Desdemona, Othello finds no course open save to kill her. After smothering her, he discovers his error and stabs himself, while the still gloating Iago is led to punishment.

The drama is permeated with irony. In the first act, Othello is called to justify his love before the City Councillors. He does; and, as G. G. Sedgwick points out in *Of Irony* (1949): "At the very moment the speech ends an extraordinary irony, prepared for by a previous order, is enacted before our eyes, baldly suggested by a stage direction, 'Enter Desdemona, Iago, and attendants'. Just as Othello has scored his great and only triumph, his sworn enemy appears as the trusted guard of his wife. There can be no more effective entrance in the range of drama."

It is the honesty in Othello's heart that makes him easy victim; it is the deep love in Desdemona's heart that makes her vulnerable. She has taken out her handkerchief, when Othello says his head aches, to bind his forehead. Already tainted with the suspicion Iago has implanted, Othello brushes her away: "Let it alone." If Desdemona had loved Othello less—Harold C. Goddard pointed out, in *The Meaning of Shakespeare* (1951), the subtle psychology of this critical moment—"she would naturally have noticed the fall of the handkerchief and would, however unconsciously, have stooped and picked it up. But every fiber of her soul and body, conscious and unconscious, is so totally devoted to Othello that the handkerchief for the moment ceases to exist. The slightest deflection of her eye in its direction as it dropped would have been a subtraction from the infinity of her love — just as the movement of Othello's hand when he pushed her hand away measured his distrust of that love, gave the villain his unique opportunity, and sealed his own doom forever. Is there anything in all the drama of the world, I wonder, to equal this in its kind?" The full measure of Desdemona's love is in her dying words when, asked by Emilia "Who hath done this deed?" she responds, "Nobody; I myself. Farewell!" Again, in this play, Shakespeare pits violence against love; the bodies succumb to violence, but love is undismayed, and the spirit exalted.

Othello is one of Shakespeare's most popular dramas. Many stars, among them Booth and Irving, have alternately enacted Othello and Iago. Almost every noted actor has essayed the title part: Quin, Garrick (though Garrick's rival Spranger Barry was more favored in the role), Macready, Forrest (deemed over-violent), Fechter, Kemble. Hazlitt declared that Edmund Kean's Othello was not only the greatest of Kean's roles, but the highest effort of genius on the stage. The Negro Ira Aldridge made his debut, in London in 1826, as Othello; on tour (in Belfast) his Iago was Charles Kean — who played the same role to his father Edmund's Othello on March 25, 1833, when Edmund collapsed on the stage in his final illness. The Italian Ernesto Rossi played Othello in

Rome (1873) and in Paris (1876); Henry James deemed him excelling in the moods of violent passion: when Iago seeks to rouse Othello against Desdemona, Rossi as Othello "seized Iago's head, whacked it half a dozen times on the floor, then flung him twenty yards away". Alexandre Dumas, in 1868, protested against such intensity; but to little avail. The performances of Tommaso Salvini were also noted for the ferocity of the playing, as he toured England and the United States in the 1870's and 1880's—he speaking in Italian, while the rest of the company (Edwin Booth was once his Iago) used the English lines. More than once, in various productions, when Othello has taken Iago by the throat, shouts have come from the audience: "Choke him!" The power of the drama leaps the footlights.

The popularity of the play led to much discussion, even to disputes over the rendering of lines. In Henry Fielding's *A Journey From This World to the Next* (1743) Shakespeare, asked how to deliver the line "Put out the light, and then put out the light", scolds his questioners for petty arguing. In Eliza Haywood's novel *The Husband* (1756) a quarrel over the same line leads to a duel and two deaths.

The smothering of Desdemona was a controversial point, protested by critics in 1717, 1766, 1770, and later. *Town and Country* magazine for April, 1773, declared that "We carry our enthusiasm so far, that we entirely suspend our senses toward his absurdities . . . devoutly view Desdemona stifled to death, then so perfectly restored to life as to speak two or three sentences, then die again, without another oppressive stroke from the pillow". The critic Rymer retorted: "A woman never loses her tongue, even after she is stifled"; but for over a century a dagger was also used; until Salvini put his knee on the actress' breast to speed Desdemona's end. Fanny Kemble, in 1848, objected: "The Desdemonas that I have seen, on the English stage, have always appeared to me to acquiesce with wonderful equanimity in their assassination. On the Italian stage they run for their lives." Something is to be said for Desdemona's acceptance of her fate; but Macready as her Othello eased Fanny Kemble's apprehension by letting down the bed curtains before the despatch. Ira Aldridge, as late as 1865, pulled Madge Kendal as Desdemona out of bed by her hair and dragged her around the stage before he smothered her. The audience hissed; but later performers (as Rossi in 1881) have strangled Desdemona with her own hair; or have struggled with her in the center of the stage and then carried her to the bed for the final disposal. Partly because of this treatment, Desdemona's part has not been sought by actresses, although the first performance ever given by a woman on the English professional stage was that of Margaret Hughes as Desdemona, on December 8, 1660. (There had been a French company with women players in London in the 1630's, and women had long performed in private masques, especially noble ladies in their own homes.) The role of Desdemona demands a star, yet she is quite subordinate to Othello. Nor, indeed, is Desdemona always admired. James Agate in 1939 exclaimed: "Desdemona? I have never been able to see how any actress could make anything out of this extraordinary hybrid. Before the curtain rises she puts up a display of social daring which Ibsen's Hilda Wangel and Mr. Shaw's Ann Whitefield couldn't have come anything near. After which she shows herself to have fewer brains even than Cordelia, and stands next to that immortal gumph in

Ruskin's list of Shakespeare's perfect women." Ruskin, however, comes closer to the general estimate of Desdemona, who loved perhaps not wisely, but certainly well.

In the French theatre, the struggle between the classicists and the Romantics, which burst out over the production of Hugo's *Hernani** in 1830, erupted in a riot the year before when in a production of *Othello* the word *handkerchief, mouchoir,* was spoken: the word was deemed by the classicists too vulgar for dignified drama. (In 1907, the Dublin riots over *The Playboy of the Western World** similarly broke out at the word *shift.*) Alfred de Vigny is among the half hundred that have translated the play into French. The Spanish playwright Manuel Tamayo y Baus in 1867 wrote *A New Drama,* which presents *Othello* as a play within a play, arguing the problem of jealousy. Similarly the motion picture *A Double Life* (1948, with Ronald Colman) shows a man so caught into the role of Othello that he goes forth and finds a "Desdemona" to kill.

There have been a number of recent performances of the drama in New York and on tour: in 1926, 1933, and 1934, Walter Hampden; in 1935, Philip Merivale and Gladys Cooper; 1936-1937, Walter Huston and Brian Aherne; 1940, in modern dress; 1943, the Negro Paul Robeson and José Ferrer; 1944, the Negro Canada Lee at Erwin Piscator's Dramatic Work- shop; 1945, the Robeson company, back from its tour, at the New York City Center. London saw a gripping production in 1947, with Frederick Valk as Othello and Donald Wolfit as Iago. In October 1951 Orson Welles and Douglas Campbell opened in separate London productions. In an off-Broadway production of 1953, Earle Hyman was a striking Othello; William Marshall was effective in a Brattle Players production at the New York City Center opening September 7, 1955. The play was made into a silent motion picture in 1922, with Emil Jennings and Werner Krauss, less successfully into a sound film with Orson Welles in 1955.

Of the 1935 New York performance, general opinion was reflected by Arthur Pollock: "When the plot begins to thicken, and excite the interest of the audience, as it always does, when the actors grow more and more animated, you can hardly notice the playing, you are so wrapped up in the play." It was, declared John Mason Brown, "as perfect an example of scenes drained of their emotions, of fast-moving dialogue and exciting plotting as the whole history of the theatre boasts." The work of Robeson was another thing. There were ten curtain calls for the Negro Othello at the opening; director Margaret Webster and Howard Barnes were favorably impressed, but others were sharply critical. To Wilella Waldorf Robeson was "definitely disappointing" and John Chapman found himself "wishing now and then that he would stop intoning and do something else with speech." George Freedley, a year later, raised another issue: "I find it difficult to accept the idea of Othello's being played by a Negro when Shakespeare so clearly states that this noble general is a dis- tinguished Moor, which is quite another thing. Granted the premises, however, Canada Lee makes a creditable showing in the part . . . He seems to feel and act the part with more conviction than does Paul Robeson, whose very sonority is his most tragic weakness." George Jean Nathan said bluntly: "Black or white, the whole question rests on whether the actor can act the role. Robeson acts it poorly." The pro- duction with Robeson, nevertheless, achieved the play's record run of 280 performances, and showed that it retains its tremendous tragic power.

Some critics have called Iago Shakespeare's one real villain, acting from "motiveless malignity"; but he has at least as strong a motive for his treachery as Benedict Arnold had for his treason—a gnawing sense of merit unrewarded. Shakespeare balances Iago against Othello in many ways. Up to the handkerchief episode, Act III Scene iii, Othello speaks 240 lines; Iago, 574. Othello's words, however, make the poetry of the play; Iago's the machinery and, through the foul figures that he uses, the foreboding.

The drama's conclusion is one of the rare instances of Shakespeare's use of surprise. When the Moor has learned the truth, that he has slain an innocent woman whom he most dearly loves, he tells his tale, and catches the others onstage unawares as he stabs himself, "one that loved not wisely but too well". Othello's lack was less in his love than in his judgment; being honest himself, he could not conceive that another could lie to such cruel ends. *Othello* is not a drama of jealousy, but—here intensified and fiercely lighted by contrasting stations, strong natures, and deep love—a tragedy, oft recurrent in the world, of wily deceit ensnaring simple honesty, and — less common but more exalting — of love holding steadfast against despair.

MACBETH   *William Shakespeare*

This tragedy moves with a fiercer drive than any other of Shakespeare's dramas. It is, as Harold Hobson of the *London Sunday Times* remarked, after a December 18, 1947 revival, "the shortest, most energetic, concentrated, and vehement" of all his tragedies. And A. W. Schlegel said, in his *Lectures on Dramatic Art* (1809-1811), "Nothing can equal this picture in its power to excite terror . . . otherwise the tragic muse might exchange her mask for the head of Medusa."

From the moment that the three weird sisters meet the Scottish generals Macbeth and Banquo returning victorious from battle, and prophesy that Macbeth will be king (succeeded by Banquo's sons), we feel the ominous march of doom. When Lady Macbeth learns of the prophecy and hears that King Duncan is coming to spend the night in Macbeth's castle of Dunsinane, she resolves that he will never thereafter step forth. The death of the King and the piled horrors are inevitable train. After the murder, Macbeth feels fear, which leads him to more murders; Lady Macbeth feels remorse, which leads her to suicide. When Lady Macbeth, after her sleep-walking revelation of her guilt, succumbs and dies, Macbeth voices his sense of futility. Thereafter the witches' prophecies are wrily fulfilled. They have assured Macbeth that he is quite safe until Birnam Wood comes to Dunsinane. Now a guard breaks in upon Macbeth with news that the Wood is nearing: the troops carry branches before them, to camouflage their force. They have told Macbeth that no man born of woman can do him harm. And, facing Macbeth, his fiercest foe reveals: "Macduff was from his mother's womb untimely ript." False assurance swept away, Macbeth summons his manhood: "Lay on Macduff, And damn'd be him that first cries 'Hold, enough!' " Macduff lays Macbeth's head before Malcolm, hailing the new king.

Here Shakespeare faced his most difficult dramatic problem. For he took as his protagonist, not a wronged man (Hamlet), a man imposed upon (Othello), or a noble man weakened by age (Lear), but a vigorous champion at the peak of his power and the height of his honors, turning to fourfold sin. Macbeth is a friend that violates the trust of his friend and benefactor, a soldier that turns upon his commander, a subject that betrays his king, a host — and for this Dante holds the deepest circle of hell — that uses the cloak of hospitality to murder his guest. In Holinshed's *Chronicles* (1577), Shakepseare's source, Macbeth is an open enemy of Duncan; the dramatist sought fuller measure of evil by adding the treachery, which Holinshed has in the story of Macdonwald. While the audience understand Macbeth's temptation—in our lesser fields, which of us has not been assailed?—we watch his acts with gathering horror; yet Shakespeare must so enwrap us in the mood that we follow also with sympathy, that is, with emotional involvement in the flow of Macbeth's feelings. Hence the tragic exaltation of the close, when Macbeth accepting his doom reasserts his human stature, and in his dying struggle is defying the witches, the Fates, as much as Macduff.

Indeed (and this is a measure of Shakespeare's mastery), we feel from the first that the conflict is no mere battle for a crown (save as in this we see the Crown of Heaven) but a gathered onslaught of the forces of evil upon the goodness of the world. With many Biblical parallels, the play drives home thoughts of man's eternal striving; "the murder of Duncan and its consequences", said Roy Walker in *The Time Is Free* (1949), "are profoundly impregnated with the central tragedy of the Christian myth." The witches, as Schlegel said, "are ignoble and vulgar instruments of Hell." Hecate (who may have stood silent in Shakespeare's play; many scholars feel that her speeches are interpolations; her songs appear also in Middleton's play *The Witch*), Hecate is the spirit of evil presiding over the witches' brew at which Macbeth is the sole human figure—contrasted with the feast of the living, from which Macbeth is barred by Banquo's silent ghost, the sole supernatural figure and portent of the defeat of evil. The Porter, who comes when there is knocking at the door after the King is murdered, tipsily muses: "If a man were porter of hell-gate, he should have old turning the key." "Ay, my good fellow," A. C. Quiller-Couch commented in his *Cambridge Lectures* (1943), porter of hell-gate: *"that is precisely what you are!"* The "third murderer" at Banquo's death is in all likelihood the hovering spirit of Macbeth. The play is a specific manifestation of naked evil.

Adding to this general effect of supernatural forces engaged in grim conflict is the atmosphere in which Shakespeare enshrouds the play: darkness, and blood. The first creatures we behold are the witches, who cry: "Fair is foul and foul is fair." The first human we behold is a man bathed in blood. Macbeth's first words are "So foul and fair a day I have not seen." All continues in blood and in darkness. "Stars, hide your fires!" Macbeth cries. Lady Macbeth makes black summons: "Come thick night, And pall thee in the dunnest smoke of hell . . ." Of the play's twenty-six scenes, twenty-two are in darkness or gloom; the four bright scenes are all in the last act, as the forest advances, bringing the forces of righteousness to their triumph. Throughout the play, as Caroline Spurgeon showed in *Leading Motives in the Imagery of Shakespeare's Tragedies* (1930), the figures of speech are clotted with images of blood. These blood-soaked stimuli strike at all the senses. Lady Macbeth in her sleep-walking smells blood on her hands. Macbeth sees a bloody dagger; he hears a voice crying "Sleep no more, Macbeth does murder sleep"; he feels his victims' clotted blood on his hands; and as he cries "I have supped full with horrors!" there is the taste of blood on shriveling palates. The three weird sisters stirred their pot about the time of the publication of King James' book on *Demonology*, which led to the passing of more stringent laws against witchcraft and had eerie echoes in the American colonies. The play thus had a fascination for its time we can but dimly recognize. If, as Henry N. Paul documented in *The Royal Play of Macbeth* (1950), its first performance was at Hampton Court on August 7, 1606, before King James I and his brother-in-law King Christian of Denmark, it came to a London still clouded with the effects of the Gunpowder Pot of Guy Fawkes (November 5, 1605) and the exceptionally severe equinoctial storms at the end of March, 1606.

Later, and for almost two hundred years, *Macbeth* was played in an adaptation by Sir William Davenant (1663?). This omitted the Porter's scene and ended the play with a fight between Macduff and Macbeth. David Garrick in 1743 wrote a dying speech for Macbeth. Samuel Phelps in 1847 tried to restore the original ending, which has the duel offstage, with Macduff bringing back the head of Macbeth. The public's love of a good fight, however, made this unpopular, and productions vied with one another in the closing battle. From eighteenth century Charles Macklin, through Henry Irving in 1888 to Michael Redgrave in 1948, soldiers have dashed across the stage in wild conflict, with echoing clashes beyond; Macduff and Macbeth have fought with sword and dagger to the fatal end. Otis Skinner as Macduff with a downswing of his broadsword once narrowly missed cleaving the skull of Edwin Booth. Irving's Macbeth, losing his sword, fought on with dagger until his weakening fingers clawed the empty air. Redgrave's Macbeth, in a knockabout duel that might have roused the envy of Douglas Fairbanks, finally fell upon his own dagger, snatched by his enemy's hand. Shakespeare's ending was used in the 1951 Dramatic Workshop revival directed by Erwin Piscator, which excellently conveyed the brooding darkness of the drama.

Macbeth (1601 ? 1606) was perhaps first conceived not, as some have thought, to honor the new Stuart King, James I, who was one of the line of Banquo's sons, but by showing the violence of the northern reigns to help justify Queen Elizabeth's execution of Mary Queen of Scots. Today the play is sought, by both actresses and actors, as a vehicle to test their powers. One of its greatest performances was doubtless that at Drury Lane in 1785, with John Philip Kemble and his sister, Mrs. Sarah K. Siddons, who also enacted Lady Macbeth on her farewell appearance in 1812. Since Helena Modjeska's performance in 1888, the sexual tie between Macbeth and his Lady has been emphasized: Lily Langtry in 1889 snuggled amorously in Macbeth's arms while tempting him to the assassination; Lillah McCarthy in 1909 dominated him like an Elizabethan courtesan.

Also variously stimulating the imagination has been the appearance of the three weird sisters. From the Restoration until 1833 their roles were commonly enacted by company comedians playing primarily for the laughter of the gallery. The flying "machines" used by the witches in the Davenant version led to the earliest travesty of a Shakespearean play, *A New Fancy, After the Old and Most Surprising Way of "Macbeth"*, 1675, by Thomas Duffett. In this burlesque witches sing in mid-air and devise lightning before the eyes of the audience with "mustard-pot and salt-peter." Another travesty was written by Francis Talfourd

in 1850. In some productions the witches have been invisible spirits,
but most have shown them fully embodied. The German Schiller, in his
adaptation of *Macbeth*, played at Weimar in 1800, practically denatured
the witches by endowing them with philosophy. His countryman
Schlegel knew better: "Shakespeare's picture of the witches is truly
magical: in their short scenes, he has created for them a language of
their own, which, although composed of the usual elements, still seems
to be a faggoting of formulas of incantation."

In an 1860 production, during the murder of Duncan, the three witches
exulted within a transparency, high in the castle wall. Their platform
collapsed and one of the witches, proving mortal, was killed by the fall.

The manner in which the two murderers reveal their guilt is noteworthy. Macbeth is startled at the hallucination in the banquet scene,
when he sees the dead Banquo take his place at the table. This is
presented in elaborate, ornate verse. Lady Macbeth makes her guilt
known through the troubled words of her sleep-walking. These are of
the utmost simplicity: of 170 words, all but twelve are of one syllable.
Throughout the play, Shakespeare shows full command and rich variety
of poetic expression.

In many ways, *Macbeth* is a counterpiece to *Hamlet*. The one opens
with the ghost, as the other with the witches, to set the mood of the
drama. In each play — with superb craftsmanship — we have twice seen
the supernatural figures before they meet their main objective; hence,
when the man comes, we can concentrate not on them but on the human
reaction. What matters is how their message is received. Against these
structural similarities the two protagonists move from opposite sides in
a spiritual pilgrimage: Hamlet must plunge into sin to achieve salvation;
Macbeth must chastise (make chaste) the world through the fires of sin.
As Roy Walker has observed, Hamlet is noble despite his world; the
world is noble despite Macbeth. Macbeth, in his final rebellion, is man
again, is mortal, and attuned to die: evil has died, and "the time is free."
Goodness and peace once more may walk abroad.

It is also noteworthy how the witches make use of the three types of
dramatic prophecy. Simplest is the prophecy that the prophet (the playwright) makes come true. Thus, in *Julius Caesar**, "Beware the Ides of
March!"; in *Macbeth*, the witches' word that Banquo's sons will rule
(made true in the vision). Subtler is the prophecy that comes wrily
true; it has a literally true outcome but twists unexpectedly, as when
"Birnam Wood" comes to Dunsinane, and a man "not born of woman"
slays Macbeth. Most difficult is the prophecy that makes itself come
true: once the kingship is in the minds of Lady Macbeth and Macbeth,
granted their natures, nothing could stop them in their wild course
towards its securing. The wrily true prophecies are but one form of the
Delphic effects in the play, words or deeds capable of a dual interpretation, of which *Macbeth* contains more than any other of Shakespeare's
dramas. These help to build the impression that behind the material
world of lustful action there boils a deeper world of supernal forces, the
well-springs of human energy and desire.

The play is so short that some have suggested we possess but an
acting version of a longer drama. This might explain the swift rush of
time. With specific chronology, Shakespeare is careless; but of the sense
of time—in amble or gallop—he holds command. He is, however, care-

less also with anachronism, as in the jokes of the Porter, who in the year 1055 turns his humor upon Elizabethan London. The knocking at the gate, on which DeQuincey wrote a most discerning essay, has been the subject of considerable discussion. The Romantics tended to consider the Porter's role a blot on the play. Schiller, in his adaptation, substituted a Watchman with a charming song to the rising sun. Coleridge let loose a notorious heresy: "This low soliloquy of the Porter and his few speeches afterwards, I believe to have been written for the mob by some other hand." DeQuincey's essay thrusts aside these genteel scruples; today this moment is recognized as the turning-point of the play, the annunciation. "What hand is on the hammer? Whose step is on the threshold?" asked Quiller-Couch: "It is, if we will, God. It is, if we will, the Moral Order. It is, whatever our religion, that which holds humankind together by law of sanity and righteousness. It is all that this man and woman have outraged . . . From this moment the moral order reasserts itself to roll back the crime to its last expiation." The Porter thus does not merely bring comic relief between two moments of high tension — the thrust of evil, and the returning thrust of good. He serves also, by the matter-of-fact contrast, to emphasize the blackness of the night and of the appalling deed. And also, as with the grave-digger in *Hamlet** and the farmer that brings the asp in *Antony and Cleopatra**, by the impact of his unwitting appearance — this simple man, unaware of the great events that overhang — he sets a moment of normality with which we may take bearings in the tragic dark.

There have been several recent revivals of *Macbeth*. One in 1927 with Fritz Leiber. In 1928, with Florence Reed (later, Margaret Anglin), and William Farnum, with sets by Gordon Craig. Richard Watts, Jr. found this "more than a little disappointing", and John Hutchens (in the *New York Post*) declared it "gleaming with pictorial excitement, and steadily done almost to death by its players". In 1934, with Walter Hampden. In 1935, with Gladys Cooper and Philip Merivale. In a Cleveland Heights modern version, Macbeth made his first entrance in an armored car. *Macbeth* was played at the Stratford Festival in 1952. In 1936 the Negro unit of the Federal Theatre presented a Haitian version arranged by Orson Welles. This was hailed by Brooks Atkinson, who called the witches' scene "a triumph of theatre art." John Mason Brown dissented on the grounds that Welles' version "bastardizes the Bard but it does not establish him in the jungle . . . very bad, very dull, and almost tone-deaf . . . not only wastes an exciting idea but murders an exciting play."

Macbeth has long appealed on both sides of the footlights. Thus Goethe, who knew the theatre from both sides, declared in his *Conversations with Eckermann*: "*Macbeth*, I consider Shakespeare's best acting play, the one in which he shows most understanding of the stage." Thomas Campbell in 1834 and Henry Hallam in 1854 are among the many that have said, with Abraham Lincoln, "I think nothing equals *Macbeth*."

The 1948 revival by Michael Redgrave and Flora Robson dragged the murky melodrama from its Scottish lair and flung it into the teeth of the audience. Atkinson again gave praise: "A superb *Macbeth* has come to town. No one else in the contemporary theatre has drawn so much horror and ferocity out of it . . ." But to Watts it was "lacking in stature and distinction". Whatever the success of the particular performance, the play continues its challenge to the greatest players, for in no other of Shakespeare's tragedies is such sustained power of poetry combined with such surging of emotion and such unremitting force of action.

KING LEAR   *William Shakespeare*

Drawn from the *Chronicles* of Holinshed, *King Lear* (1605) tells a well-known story; Shakespeare was the first to give it an unhappy ending. His play is his richest study of the relation between the generations, the favorite theme of the ancient dramatists, here pointed in Lear's exclamation: "How sharper than a serpent's tooth it is to have a thankless child!" Henry V heeds his father's wish that he take up arms against France. Hamlet hesitates to obey his father and is lost. Desdemona rebels against her father's will. Cordelia alone maintains both full filial love and spiritual freedom. Like Desdemona's, her words before she dies breathe understanding love, save that Desdemona thinks of her husband Othello, while Cordelia cries to her father Lear that he has "no cause, no cause" for self-blame. In Shakespeare's plays of parent and child other than *King Lear*, however, the emphasis, as their titles show, is on the younger generation. We watch in Prince Hal's growth the way by which a man becomes a king. Cordelia is briefly, though brightly, shown; we watch in Lear the way in which a king becomes a man.

Through Lear's actions, more deeply, the play presses the problem of authority, the maintenance of one's personal standards and proper place. As through the man Hamlet we see into the inner life of all men, so through Lear we see a man's life in relation to all. And since Lear is a king, the whole range of order in the universe hangs on his right rule: with his relinquishment, the family is disrupted, then the kingdom, then civilization (decency), then the soul (sanity itself). Caught into this whirl is the problem of human responsibility, of a man's obligation to assume and maintain the order and the station to which he is called. Man's passage along his years is a growth to mature tasks, mature responsibilities, until, the new seeds scattered, the plant falls. And the safety of all hangs upon each man's assumption of his proper tasks.

Lines of the play contrast two basic attitudes toward responsibility: "As flies to wanton boys are we to the gods: They kill us for their sport" —and the sobering thought: "The gods are just, and of our pleasant vices make instruments to plague us". The second is hammered home in the mocking words: "An admirable evasion of whoremaster man, to lay his goatish disposition to the charge of a star!"

Lear moves, as S. L. Bethell emphasized in *Shakespeare and the Popular Dramatic Tradition* (1944), to a "gradual enlightenment of spiritual blindness". And "as Lear unbuttons and casts off his lendings, so Shakespeare strips him of the accidents of personality, so that only universal humanity remains." Sight is a symbol running through the drama. Goneril declares that she loves her father "dearer than eyesight". When Lear disinherits Cordelia and banishes Kent, that worthy noble cries "See better, Lear!" Gloster, who with his good son Edgar and his villainous bastard Edmund piteously parallels Lear's own more tragic case, is physically blinded—"Pluck out his eyes!" orders Goneril—even as Lear is spiritually blind. The play is a study in spiritual darkness and light. Behind this growth to enlightenment spreads an even more general opposition. Nature is strong in the play: wild nature in the stress of the storm on the heath; animal nature in the vivid imagery of the speech; and pagan nature fronting the Christian attitude toward the world. Religion appears in many forms, from Kent's superstition to Gloster's piety; its teachings grow manifest in Poor Tom, whom the Elizabethans would have recognized as "o' Bedlam", as they watched "the mystery of suffering laid bare to an ancient king by the contemporary village lunatic." From this point of view, Cordelia takes her place as the Christian good: she echoes Christ's words — "O dear father, it is thy business that I go about" (Act IV, iv, 23; see St. Luke II, 49) —and she stands as the goal of Lear's purgatorial struggle. Only through suffering come true understanding, deep love, and lasting peace. The play, however, eschews Christian terminology; it is set in a pagan environment, and heaven is invoked as a pagan deity, or referred to as a part of nature. The play is rooted in nature, its piety is natural. King Lear is a play of maturity, moving toward death; no person in it is parent of a young child; no allusion nor reference brings childhood to the mind. The weight and the woe of age lie on the drama.

The title role has lured the greatest actors, containing a variety of moods that serves as a high challenge. The fond pride of the aged king— succumbing to the flattery of his daughters Goneril and Regan, so that he divides the kingdom between them, rejecting the true love of his youngest daughter Cordelia when she scorns to play the sycophant—must journey through humiliation as the daughters drive him forth, through the dignity yet heart-rending pathos of his mad movements with the Fool on the wild heath, to a final recapture of sanity that breaks, and breaks the heart, with the simple tenderness and poignancy of the death of Cordelia and of Lear. Through the play, said Swinburne, "we look upward and downward, and in vain, into the deepest things of nature, into the highest things of Providence; to the roots of life, and to the stars; from the roots that no God waters to the stars that give no man light; over a world full of death and life without resting-place or guidance . . . Here is no need of the Eumenides, children of Night everlasting; for here is very Night herself." Hazlitt said Lear "is the best of all Shakespeare's plays"; Shelley called it "the most perfect specimen of the dramatic art existing in the world." C. E. M. Joad in Decadence (1949) suggested that "King Lear is superior as a play to Hamlet, precisely because in Lear a cosmic theme, man in revolt against the moral law of the universe and incurring the wrath of the angry gods, is substituted for the rather squalid drama of purely human relations." Basic moral law, and the conflict of the generations, are of course present in Hamlet as well; the difference is that Hamlet has his problems thrust upon him; Lear's own nature creates his problems for himself.

So tremendous is the burden that the play puts upon actor and audience alike, that many have felt King Lear cannot be fitly acted. James Agate has listed the qualities a Lear must convey: "First, majesty. Second, that quality which Blake would have recognized as moral grandeur. Third, mind. Fourth, he must be a man and, what is more, a king, in ruins. There must be enough voice to dominate the thunder, and yet it must be a spent voice." Lamb, in 1810, was blunt: "To see Lear acted, to see an old man tottering about the stage with a walking stick, turned out of doors by his daughters in a raining night, has nothing in it but what is painful and disgusting." Henry James in 1883 reiterated this position: *"Lear"* is a great and terrible poem—the most sublime, possibly, of all dramatic poems; but it is not, to my conception, a play, in the sense in which a play is a production that gains from being presented to our senses . . . I cannot speak of a representation of *King Lear* without protesting primarily against the play's being acted at all."

Nevertheless the play has been frequently performed. It was shown to James I, at court, on St. Stephen's day in 1606. In 1681 Nahum Tate wrote a version with love scenes between Edgar and Cordelia, with the Fool omitted, the language Tatified, and Lear restored to his throne. Most eighteenth century productions continued the happy ending, which was occasionally used by David Garrick. Edmund Kean, about 1815, restored the tragic close, but after three performances had to revert to the happy ending. It was not until 1838 that the original play was revived, by William Macready. The Macready production at Drury Lane achieved startling effects, with the first use of limelight in the theatre. The title role has been essayed also by Phelps, Wallack, Kemble, Irving, Salvini, the Booths, the younger Keans, and Forrest. In 1892 Jacob Gordin wrote a *Jewish King Lear* in Yiddish, transposing the theme from a king's court to the home of a rabbi. In 1930 Fritz Leiber presented Shakespeare's play in New York. It was presented in London and at Stratford in 1936. In New York in 1940 Erwin Piscator made an "epic theatre" production, strengthening the play's lesson for our time with inserted words of World War II refugees, and a final speech borrowed from *Troilus and Cressida**. In 1947, Donald Wolfit opened his New York season with *King Lear,* and Louis Calhern played Lear in New York in 1950. London saw it again, at the Old Vic, in 1952.

More than with any other of Shakespeare's plays except *Hamlet,* details of performance in *King Lear* have drawn critical attention. Bernard Shaw objected to Irving's waste of time over "the trumpery business" of Kent's tripping the steward. In the midst of the wild storm on the heath, Wallack had Kent place his cloak upon Lear's shoulders; Salvini as Lear put his own cloak upon the shivering Fool. Oscar Wilde praised the sensitivity of Salvini's conceptions, especially when, to test the dying Cordelia's condition, he took from Kent's cap the feather he put to Cordelia's lips: "This feather stirs; she lives!"

Critical opinions as to performances have differed greatly. Brooks Atkinson objected to Leiber's 1930 arrangement because it "lops off the story recklessly. *King Lear* is as finely wrought as a piece of architecture in terms of emotions, and you cannot omit the flying buttresses without letting the structure sag." Howard Barnes, however, declared that Leiber "has succeeded brilliantly, in his arrangement, in loosening the sombre tragedy from the dry rot of textbooks and traditional productions." Of Donald Wolfit's work, in London and in New York, opinions differed even more widely. Atkinson called the evening "a carnival of bombast and attitudinizing." However, James Agate declared in the *London Times:* "I say deliberately that his performance was the greatest piece of Shakespearean acting I have seen." Harold Hobson, Agate's successor on the *Times,* after the Old Vic revival of September 24, 1946, recalled Irving's entrance—"Coming down a flight of stairs, he leaned on a huge scabbarded sword which he raised with a wild cry in answer to the shouted greeting of the guards"—then spoke with even greater praise of Laurence Olivier as Lear, referring to his performance as "among the greatest things ever accomplished upon the English stage." Even a poor performance cannot disguise the grandeur, the gloomy magnificence, that strikes to the heart of human nature, and to the hearts of the audience, with *King Lear*.

TIMON OF ATHENS   *William Shakespeare*

Based upon North's version of *Plutarch's Lives*, this play, possibly written in 1605, is the tragedy of the honest, trusting man who looks for equal honesty and generosity in his fair-weather friends. Having lavished his fortune on his friends, Timon turns bitter when they desert him. He then invites his former guests to a last banquet at which he scornfully serves them warm water — and goes to live in seclusion in the woods. Word that he has found gold draws visitors again, but the dying Timon curses all the Athenians—while young Alcibiades breathes hope of better days in the city.

In 1678 Thomas Shadwell added love interest to the story, declaring in his Preface, "I can truly say I have made it into a play." More interesting are the thoughts implicit in the story or given cogent expression in the verse. Samuel Johnson observed that "the catastrophe affords a very powerful warning against that ostentatious liberty which sanctions bounty, but confers no benefits, and buys flattery but not friendship." Johnson possibly had in mind his own experiences; his letter to the Earl of Chesterfield helped destroy the old system of literary patronage. *Timon of Athens* reached the height of its popularity in this age of patrons, with its theme of the patron betrayed.

In the nineteenth century, the play was used mainly as a vehicle for such stars as Kean, Phelps, and Macready, but the twentieth century finds present pertinence in the bitter attack on materialism in Timon's arraignment of Athens; in the program of the 1940 production (in modern dress) at Yale University, Allardyce Nicoll stated that "among Shakespeare's plays, *Timon* addresses our own age as directly as any." The play has also been performed, recently, at Stratford in 1928; in London in 1935; in Pasadena in 1936. The satire rather than the tragedy of the play was emphasized in a production, vividly directed by Tyrone Guthrie, that opened at London's Old Vic in May 1952.

Timon is one of the few plays, according to Hazlitt, in which Shakespeare "seems in earnest throughout, never to trifle nor go out of his way. He does not relax in his efforts, nor lose sight of the unity of his design. It is the only play of our author in which spleen is the predominant feeling of the mind. It is as much a satire as a play: and contains some of the finest pieces of invective possible to be conceived, both in the snarling, captious answers of the cynic Apemantus, and in the impassioned and terrible imprecations of Timon." On the level of history instead of poetry, *Timon* is even more vehement against ingratitude than *King Lear**. The two plays are alike in the condemnation of flattery, the frequent curses, and the animal imagery, as when Timon addresses his fair-weather friends. They both press the thought that misery leads to enlightenment and (like most of Shakespeare's and the Greek tragedies, but unlike those of Ibsen*) they end with the promise of peace. Throughout *Timon*, however, there is irony (as when Timon's bitter sincerity makes the thieves talk of reform) and there is deep intensity.

Indeed the play is usually enacted with bursts of passion. Of Edmund Kean's performance, in 1816, at the words "Tear me, take all, and the gods fall upon you!", the *Theatrical Inquisitor* declared, "Mr. Kean gazed at the bloodhounds who were preying upon his existence, tore open his vest to enforce the offer he had urged, and at length broke from the clamours his distraction could not silence, with an imprecation of tremendous horror on the throng that assailed him". The *Examiner* stressed the brighter vision at the close: "While the squalid misanthrope still maintains his posture and keeps his back to the strangers, in steps the young and splendid Alcibiades in the flush of victorious expectation. It is the encounter of hope with despair". On "life's uncertain voyage", the journey of Timon is one whose vicissitudes we today well may ponder.

ANTONY AND CLEOPATRA   *William Shakespeare*

Although "nothing much greater than *Antony and Cleopatra* has ever been written", as Louis Kronenberger has asserted, this play has not been generally popular. Dryden's version of the story, *All For Love; or, The World Well Lost*, 1678, the one valid play among all the attempts to improve Shakespeare, took its place for almost a century and a half. In 1818, Coleridge tried to restore the values: "Of all Shakespeare's historical plays, *Antony and Cleopatra* is by far the most wonderful. There is not one in which he has followed history more minutely, and yet there are few in which he impresses the notion of angelic strength so much . . . This is greatly owing to the manner in which the fiery force is sustained throughout, and to the numerous momentary flashes of nature counteracting the historical abstraction . . . And if you would feel the judgment as well as the genius of Shakespeare in your heart's core, compare this astonishing drama with Dryden's *All For Love*." Even after this, the play had but occasional revivals. When it was produced in 1897, with Louis Calvert and Janet Achurch, Bernard Shaw said: Strip any passage "of that beauty of sound, by prosaic paraphrase, and you have nothing left but a platitude that even an American professor of ethics would blush to offer to his disciples."

Shaw wrote to me that in his battle against bardolatry he deliberately overstressed his case. There is, in truth, a tremendous conflict in this drama, pointed by imagery of a colossal scale. On the surface the opposition is Egypt and Rome, empire and love: Antony has to choose. But within Cleopatra shine the Egyptian traits; from Octavius Caesar the Roman values frown. They present opposed attitudes toward the universe: love versus duty; generosity versus prudence; indulgence versus restraint; emotion versus reason; impracticality versus worldly wisdom; spontaneous impulse versus common sense. In Cleopatra burn the hidden energies of life; her qualities affirm, those of Rome deny. The good life, even in some measure the Christian good life, is built upon her values. Antony chooses her path, returning to her "from the world's great snare uncaught". Theirs is the right choice — save that they sin through very excess of virtue. Excess, exclusiveness, of love becomes self-love. Hence comes their defeat on earth — but heavenly triumph; for through defeat they lose their weight of self. Shakespeare accepts suicide only in his Roman plays; in them, it is the fullest sacrifice of self. Through this final deed, Roman fortitude blends with Egyptian sensitivity and love. And Antony, who had made "his will Lord of his reason", becomes a full man in his decisive choice.

The facts of the play (1607?) are drawn from North's *Plutarch's Lives*. Several critics have deemed it loosely constructed; thus Samuel Johnson declared it "without any art of connection or care of disposition". Viewed in the light of its major conflict, however, the play, as S. L. Bethell stated in *Shakespeare and the Popular Dramatic Tradition* (1944), is "seen to be a careful pattern of interwoven and contrasting episodes, all duly subordinate to the main design." That design takes glowing shape in the amorous queen. There is naturally much appealing to an actress in this story of the Queen of the Nile whose love so held a Roman that he idled away the Empire in her arms. Wooed back to Rome and wed to Octavius Caesar's sister, Antony still found the silken chains of love too strong. He went again to Egypt and Cleopatra; there, defeated by the Romans, he killed himself. Rather than march a slave in Caesar's triumph, Cleopatra—here at last a resolute monarch—gave suck to an asp and died. The woman's role in the play is as important as the man's. This is true, among Shakespeare's tragedies, only of his love dramas, which mark the equality in their titles. Lady Macbeth, save for the sleep-walking scene that precedes her death, drops from *Macbeth** after the third act; Antony dies in the fourth act, leaving the final act wholly to the Queen.

Of the 42 scenes in the play, many are vividly dramatic. Among these is the meeting of Pompey and the triumvirate, Antony, Lepidus, and Octavius Caesar, on Pompey's galley off Misenum, a bitter mockery of temporal power, as we watch the three drunken men that rule the world. All three, in truth, are more deeply drunken—Lepidus with self-importance, Octavius with lust for power, Antony with infatuation—until sober resolution in extremity clears the mind and illuminates the spirit.

Antony's gentle dealing with his friend Enobarbus, who deserted him after the defeat at Actium, and Enobarbus' consequent remorse and suicide, give further touch of nobility to the decay. The drama is a rich tapestry of magnificence luxuriating to its ruin. There is wide opportunity for scenic splendor; but, most of all, for variety of mood and surging passion in Cleopatra's part. Emotional actresses have therefore been especially drawn to the role. When Lily Langtry essayed the part in 1890, the *Saturday Review* attacked her break with tradition, in that Cleopatra did not lie on a couch for her death scene, as Enobarbus pictures her on the barge when she first met Antony. The *Athenaeum*, however, deemed it a sound innovation to have her seated on the throne: "The aspect of the queen, motionless and erect in her robes, with her handmaids prostrate and dying before her, is superb." In a nineteenth century French production, elaborately staged, a mechanical asp was introduced, which before biting Cleopatra raised its head and hissed. The critic Francisque Sarcey commented: "I agree with the asp."

The final scenes of the play, whatever the vicissitudes of production, are a proud surge of beauty. The earliest meeting of Antony and Cleopatra, as described by Enobarbus, was a magnificent display, a triumph of the senses: "The barge she sat in, like a burnisht throne, Burnt on the water; the poop was beaten gold."

The final meeting of the two lovers, and the movement toward Cleopatra's death, show the triumph of the spirit. The Egyptian sensuality, the pride and passion, in the face of disaster have deepened to steadfast love. Cleopatra faints when Antony dies; her first words on recovering reveal that the vainglorious queen has become "no more but e'en a woman"; yet her resolution is manifest when the dying Antony admonishes her to seek of Caesar her honor with her safety. "They do not go together," she replies, and all her words and actions thereafter prove that Cleopatra has moved through humility to humanity, and to the nobler resources of the spirit. The whole movement, as Harold C. Goddard summed it up in *The Meaning of Shakespeare* (1951), is "one of the supreme things in Shakespeare. The atmosphere of sunset—which Charmian's single phrase, "O eastern star!" turns into sunrise—the universal character of every image and symbol, and above all perhaps the sublimity of the verse, conspire with the action itself to produce this alchemic effect. Here, if ever, is the harmony that mitigates tragedy, the harmony, better say, that creates it."

Little wonder that actresses have been eager to play the part! Or that the reviewers have disagreed, over almost every performance: Helen Modjeska in 1889; Sothern and Marlowe, 1909; Jane Cowl and Rollo Peters, 1924; Tallulah Bankhead and Conway Tearle, with music by Virgil Thompson, 1937; Katharine Cornell and Godfrey Tearle, 1947. Jane Cowl was most favored. John Corbin praised her capture of "the infinite variety of this marvel of courtesans, this mistress of all that is mentally intoxicating, all that is spiritually baleful in feminine allure." Heywood Broun declared that "nothing could be better for the tired business man." The performance was really better than the reviewers, and caught the deeper values of the play. Tallulah Bankhead fared the worst. John Mason Brown led off with the caustic remark: "Tallulah Bankhead as Cleopatra barged down the Nile last night — and sank." John Anderson averred that her "hootchy-kootchy posturings cannot hope to take the place of Shakespeare's words, though they are easier to understand." Brooks Atkinson thought it "difficult to find anything except her courage to praise." Robert Coleman widened the attack to include the drama itself: "If you have any doubts that *Antony and Cleopatra* is the dullest of all Shakespeare's plays" this production "should settle the matter conclusively." Yet Burns Mantle headed his review "Tallulah a Radiant Queen" and the Brooklyn Eagle declared: "Tallulah took the old script and went to town with it . . . She lifts a rather doll-like character out of a wallow of sentiment and makes her a vital, passionate woman." Katharine Cornell's less tumultuous Cleopatra was less violently received. Robert Coleman called it "superlative . . . the only satisfactory production we've seen in our time," but George Freedley felt that "neither Guthrie McClintic nor Katharine Cornell has breathed the life into it which might have made it memorable." Brooks Atkinson observed: "Apart from being a queen, Cleopatra is also the world's most celebrated coquette, sensual as well as capricious. As a poet Shakespeare admires her, but as a man he knows she is a royal slut. The qualities of character we esteem in Miss Cornell are not those of 'the Egyptian dish' that has drugged Marc Antony's will to action. That is the basic weakness of this beautifully caparisoned performance." Opening in London, May 11, 1951, Laurence Olivier and Vivien Leigh presented *Anthony and Cleopatra* on alternate nights with Shaw's *Caesar and Cleopatra;** they brought the two plays to New York on December 12, 1951, the Shakespeare play receiving its most distinguished production of our generation.

Cleopatra will continue to lure great actresses to this drama of the conflict between love and empire. The struggle the play presents on its kingly height is far from unfamiliar on the level of homely hearths. But in *Antony and Cleopatra* the conflict between duty and desire glows with the radiance of the setting sun, through the passionate spirits of a man that might have ruled the world, and of a queen that learned to be a steadfast woman.

CORIOLANUS   *William Shakespeare*

The tragic satire of *Coriolanus*, 1607(?), based on North's *Plutarch's Lives*, presents Shakespeare's most advanced political thinking. The Renaissance was marked by an increasing assertion of the importance of the individual; more and more the "common man" was thrusting himself into public affairs, demanding that his needs and his desires be taken into account. It was natural that such an urge be pictured in the drama; and there was apt parallel to the current trend in the power of the tribunes of the people, and the custom of the candidates for consul to submit themselves to the plebs, in ancient Rome. Thus the Roman general Caius Marcius—for his victory at Corioli surnamed Coriolanus— when selected as consul by the Senate, has to come before the plebs. The people resent his pride and, incited by the tribunes, effect his banishment. In his rage Coriolanus cries "I banish you!" He allies himself with the Volscians, headed by Tullus Aufidius, and they march triumphantly against Rome. Outside that city, his family's pleas move Coriolanus to relinquish the war and, as he expects, he falls by the swords of Aufidius' followers.

The play moves at a swift pace; it was written with fierce rapidities of speech, especially as Coriolanus pours forth his scorn upon the people. Some critics have read from this play a similar scorn on the part of the author. Thus Hardin Craig, thinking that he was defending Shakespeare, said that he "did not hate the common people, but he did apparently think them unfit to rule the state." This puts Coriolanus' conception of the people into Shakespeare's heart — overlooking that the point of the play is that Coriolanus is at fault. Successful in the field as he may be, and well-meaning in the peaceful state, he has a stiff-necked pride that refuses even to try to understand the people among whom he must dwell, and for whom as consul he proposes to rule. The pride of the aristocrat must learn humility. At first, Coriolanus' mother, Volumnia, prods him on the warlike way; later, she, and especially his wife Virgilia, help him to a final acceptance of the spiritual path—an end approached in others of the later plays of Shakespeare, *Antony and Cleopatra** and *King Lear**, but not in *Hamlet**. Coriolanus turns from vengeance, knowing that his choice leads to death.

The political attitude is analyzed by Hazlitt: "The arguments for and against aristocracy or democracy, on the privilege of the few and the claims of the many, on liberty and slavery, power and the abuse of it, peace and war, are here very ably handled, with the spirit of a poet and the acuteness of a philosopher." Where did Shakespeare stand? "The

language of poetry naturally falls in with the language of power . . .
The principle of poetry is an anti-leveling principle. It aims at effect, it
exists by contrast. It admits of no medium. It is everything by excess
. . . It puts the individual for the species, the one above the infinite many,
might before right . . . We feel some concern for the poor citizens of
Rome when they meet together to compare their wants and grievances,
till Coriolanus comes in and with blows and big words drives this set of
'poor rats', this rascal scum, to their homes and beggary before him . . .
Our admiration of his prowess is immediately converted into contempt
for their pusillanimity. The love of power in ourselves and the admiration of it in others are both natural to man: the one makes him a tyrant;
the other, a slave . . . Coriolanus complains of the fickleness of the
people; yet, the instant he cannot gratify his pride and obstinacy at their
expense, he turns his arms against his country . . . He scoffs at their
tribunes for maintaining their rights and franchises: 'Mark you his absolute *shall?*' not marking his own absolute *will* to take everything from
them — his impatience at the slightest opposition to his own pretensions
being in proportion to their arrogance and absurdity." Thus, though he
may seem to attack the people, Shakespeare makes even stronger case
against their would-be master. While there is considerable railing
against the mob in Shakespeare's plays, they abound, as Harold C. Goddard remarked in *The Meaning of Shakespeare* (1951), in "little touches
that reveal an almost Wordsworthian faith in the existence of nobility
and wisdom in obscurity." Shakespeare does not stress these, but leaves
them incidental, as in life itself. In his plays, the number of upright and
independent commoners is exceeded only by the number of rascally or
ridiculous gentlemen. But value lies in the individual, not in the mass.

After the close of the theatres in 1642, London did not see the play
for forty years. Versions by Nahum Tate, 1681, and John Dennis, 1719,
were not popular. James Thomson in 1749 wrote a stately rhetorical
version that was fused with Shakespeare's until the nineteenth century,
as by John Philip Kemble in 1789, 1806, and 1811. Shakespeare's play
was performed in London, and in Philadelphia by Jefferson, in 1813; and
from the time of Macready (1819) it has been fairly popular. Recent
British performances include two in 1901, one with F. R. Benson, and one
"of grand spectacular display" with Henry Irving and Ellen Terry, which
Irving had been promising since 1879; one in 1916 at the Stratford tercentenary; in 1936 and 1939 again at Stratford; in 1938, the Old Vic in
London with Laurence Olivier and Sybil Thorndike; and again at Stratford, opening March 13, 1952, with Anthony Quayle and Mary Ellis. The
London Times reviewer (April 20, 1938) did not like the play, declaring
"There is only one thing to do: keep up the pace and beat the drums."

The first New York performance of the drama was in 1799. Salvini
acted the title part in America in 1885. Coriolanus was the best remembered role of Thomas Sowerby Hamblin, about 1850; one of the best
roles of Edwin Forrest, in the 1860's. A French production at the
Comédie Française in 1934 played to especially crowded houses because,
after the February sixth riots, the French drew a parallel between the
play and their own times. In 1937, a condensation by Arthur Hopkins
was presented by the Federal Theatre at Roslyn, Long Island, with the
mob rushing up aisles from all parts of the house. Favorable criticism
brought this to New York in February 1938. Richard Watts commented:

"The author expresses with considerable enthusiasm his (sic) distaste for the common people, assailing them for their manners, their odors, their language, and their habiliments, until there are moments when you are inclined to believe that he must have called in Mr. Lucius Beebe as collaborator . . . The poetry of the play seldom rises to the greatest Shakespearean heights, but the drama remains a work of unquestioned force and power, and was most decidedly worth reviving."

The power of great acting may be seen even in silent moments, as in the performance of Mrs. Siddons as Volumnia. The actor Charles Mayne Young has pictured it: "I remember her coming down the stage in the triumphal entry of her son, Coriolanus, when her dumb-show drew plaudits that shook the building. She came, alone, marching and beating time to the music; rolling from side to side, swelling with the triumph of her son. Such was the intoxication of joy which flashed from her eye and lit up her whole face, that the effect was irresistible." There are, thus, varied production opportunities in *Coriolanus*: mob scenes, individual moments of intensity; and closing spectacle. Forrest, for instance, in 1863, ended with an imposing funeral pyre for the body of Coriolanus. In the 1838 Macready production, warriors raised the dead body of the conqueror on their shields, draped over it the colorful trophies of war and, trailing their steel pikes in mournful memory, marched slowly up the stage to doleful music. Such an ending, up an inclined road into the distance, was utilized at Fordham University, in a striking 1949 production. Supposedly taking place in the year 2048 (in the "costumes of the time", including atomic rapid-fire guns), this began with the death of Coriolanus. A lecturer explained the play's current pertinence; then we watched the movements of the conflict between the insistent people and the unbending leader, until the common soldiers bore away the corpse of the general. The play seemed equally timely when presented over television, June 11, 1951, with Richard Greene and Judith Evelyn.

"The beast with many heads butts me away", says Coriolanus on his banishment. Today, in many lands, the prowling of this beast gives sharp significance to *Coriolanus*.

PERICLES   *William Shakespeare*

The movement of *Pericles*, 1607(?), differs so greatly from that of Shakespeare's other plays as to suggest that it is only in part his work. Some critics put a specific point to his hand's entry: the storm scene in the third act, which opens with Pericles' cry: "Thou god of this great vast, rebuke these surges!" The early portion of the play some scholars attribute to George Wilkins, who did write a prose paraphrase of the story. But in the very first scene of the play Pericles, beholding King Antiochus' daughter, exclaims: "See where she comes, apparell'd like the spring" — and Wilkins was no second Shakespeare, to have written such a line! A more probable suggestion is that, as preserved, the first two acts are from the hand of a poor reporter. There are, incidentally, some 3,500 obvious misprints in the First Folio edition (1623) of Shakespeare's works.

Throughout the play shine noble passages of rich beauty or sound sentiment attuned to the purpose. Instead of tense dramatic conflict there is unfolded on the stage the long course of an adventure tale, in the vein of the popular late Greek and medieval romances. The English poet John Gower told the story in his *Confessio Amantis* (1390); and in *Pericles* Gower speaks the Prologue to each act, and the Epilogue.

Our thoughts travel through many lands and years. First Pericles, Prince of Tyre, discovers that Antiochus' daughter, whom he would wed, is living incestuously with her father. Leaving them, he brings aid to Cleon and his wife Dionyza, rulers of famine-stricken Tarsus. Shipwrecked, Pericles comes to Pentapolis, where in a tourney he wins Thaisa, the lovely daughter of King Simonides. At sea, Thaisa gives birth to a girl they name Marina; but Thaisa remains unconscious, is thought dead, and in a wooden casket is buried at sea. The unhappy Pericles leaves Marina at his friend Cleon's palace. As Marina grows in loveliness, Dionyza in jealousy for her own daughter would have the girl slain; at the brink of death she is snatched by pirates, who sell her to a brothel-bawd in Mytilene. To Pericles, Cleon reports that Marina is dead. But the purity of the girl, as resistant as her beauty is alluring, beats off the attempts upon her chastity in the brothel; she leaves it and lives honestly but humbly until Pericles, passing by, hears her story and recognizes his daughter. Then, in a vision, the goddess Diana bids him visit her temple at Ephesus; in the priestess there he discovers his long-lost wife, Thaisa—who had been rescued from the chest and recovered from her coma—and the marriage of Marina is happily arranged. The movement of these episodes is enlivened by dumb-show and dancing. The situations vary from the gallant assemblies of aristocrats, and the households of honest citizens, to the seashore toil of humble fishermen, and the earthy grubbing of the brothel pander and the bawd. At the play's close, Gower points the moral of the enacted story.

To those troubled by the far-fetched story, it has been suggested that in his last plays Shakespeare subordinates the plot to the dramatic meaning as a whole. They are to be judged not by the credibility of the (often supernatural) events but by the genuineness of the emotions and the significance of the theme. Thus Derek Traversi in *Shakespeare: The Last Phase* (1953) states that in *Pericles* plot exists "as a function of imagery, and imagery, in turn, is directed to the elaboration of a kind of dream in the course of which normal human qualities, detached from their customary attributes and elevated above their usual status, undergo a process of poetic sublimation to become symbols of a moral rebirth." In *King Lear** this awakening comes too late; in the last four comedies. the family division is healed—in every case through a daughter, symbolically named: Marina, Fidele (Imogen), Perdita, Miranda. And the reconciliation companions restoration and moral regeneration. Pericles says of his daughter, "Thou that beget'st him that did thee beget", recognizing the rebirth. In *Cymbeline**, *The Winter's Tale**, and *The Tempest**—out of storm and tempest the new life is born—the moral redemption is likewise manifest, marking the concern of Shakespeare, in his last comedies as well as his great tragedies, with basic problems of harmony and human worth.

Printed in 1609, 1611, 1619, and 1630, the play was a popular stage piece during the Stuart reigns. Thereafter, it was not performed until Samuel Phelps revived it at Sadler's Wells in 1854, in a spectacular production using seven miles of canvas for rolling billows and moving panoramas as the ship glides along the coast toward the temple of Diana at Ephesus. The play was performed at Pasadena in 1936.

In the reading the play gathers power; seeming at first a sort of mythological adventure tale, it grows more intense because it grows more human. The unusual incidents are accompanied by universal emotions; the passions, more closely involved, make the dangers seem more real; and the motives touch closely to the core of human nature — until, without echoing, we can understand the rapturous tones of Swinburne: "What shall I say that may not be too pitifully unworthy of the glories and the beauties, the unsurpassable pathos and sublimity inwoven with the imperial texture of this play? . . . what, above all, shall be said of that storm above all storms ever raised in poetry? . . . Nothing but this, perhaps, that it stands—or rather let me say that it blows and sounds and shines and rings and thunders and lightens as far ahead of all others as the burlesque sea-storm of Rabelais beyond all possible storms of comedy." The roused passions and personal dangers of *Pericles* make perenially pathetic this medieval romance put into poetry and dramatic form.

CYMBELINE   *William Shakespeare*

The mood of this play is like the air of an Indian summer, with a low morning haze that lifts over clear, crisp beauty. The play, 1609 (?), with its challenging incidents, its ringing lines, and its lovely songs was an instant and long-continuing favorite. We are told that, on New Year's day, 1634, it was "well liked by the King". Tom D'Urfey in 1682 rewrote the play as *The Injured Princess; or, The Fatal Wager,* a pathetic version that held the boards until 1720. Other versions were tried in 1755 and 1759. Garrick appeared as Posthumus in 1761 for the then unusual run of sixteen nights. J. P. Kemble in 1785, Charles Kean, Macready in 1818, and Irving in 1896 have also played that part. (When young, Irving appeared as Pisanio; and John Drew as Cloten.) Still more appealing to players has been the role of fair Imogen, acted by Mrs. Siddons in 1787; in New York by Adelaide Neilson in 1880; by Helena Modjeska in 1888 and again in 1892 with Otis Skinner; by Ellen Terry, with Irving in 1896, a "gorgeous production" with sets by Lawrence Alma-Tadema; by Margaret Mather also in the 1890's; Viola Allen in 1906; Julia Marlowe in 1923 with E. H. Sothern. In 1936 the play was enacted in Pasadena.

The story, drawn from Holinshed's *Chronicles* and from Boccaccio, complicated in the telling, is unfolded on the stage with neat simplicity. Cymbeline, King of Britain, wishes his daughter Imogen to marry his stepson Cloten. Posthumus Leonatus, who is already secretly married to Imogen, flees to Italy—where Iachimo ("little Iago") wagers he will succeed in seducing Imogen. Held off by her purity, by a trick he convinces Posthumus that Imogen has yielded, whereupon Posthumus arranges to have her killed. Imogen, warned by servant Pisanio, flees in disguise. After many adventures — meeting her two brothers, who had been stolen and supposedly killed in infancy; drugged in a cave to awaken beside the headless body of Cloten dressed in the clothes of Posthumus, so that she thinks her husband dead; serving as a page to the Roman commander come to collect tribute, who is routing the defiant British when "a narrow lane, an old man, and two boys" turn the tide of battle—Imogen is brought among the Roman prisoners to Cymbeline's

court. In the play's final scene, twenty-three separate steps of revelation unravel the tangled threads, restore his children to Cymbeline, and
reunite Posthumus and Imogen. Beneath the events of the play we can
discern that the battle between lust and purity, and the battle between
tyranny and freedom, are basically one conflict.

Thoughts on other phases of life may be found in the drama. When
Posthumus, thinking he has killed Imogen, doffs his Italian finery for a
British peasant's garb, we may see in symbol the best impulse of the
Reformation sloughing the excesses of the Renaissance. And with the
two young princes — repeated with Perdita in *The Winter's Tale** and
with Miranda in *The Tempest** — we find a prime pattern for education:
good blood, unaware of its heritage, brought close to nature but reared
in love by a person of civilized wisdom.

Despite its poetry and its thought, *Cymbeline* has been attacked.
Samuel Johnson prosaically declared: "To remark the folly of the fiction,
the absurdity of the conduct . . . and the impossibility of the events in
any system of life, were to waste criticism upon unresisting imbecility,
upon faults too evident for detection, and too gross for exaggeration."
And now at last, said John Corbin in 1923 (October 2) "they have produced a really bad play by Shakespeare. *Cymbeline* was written at the
height of his powers . . . but it was written in a new style then lately
popularized by Beaumont and Fletcher, the tragicomedy of marvelous
adventure and romance—of which Shakespeare at first grasped only the
monstrous absurdities." Most critics, however, have continued to like
the drama. In 1923, Heywood Broun declared that "*Cymbeline* is better
Shakespeare than one or two of his plays much more frequently performed." Alan Dale stated: "There is no other heroine in the Shakespearean repertoire as charming and as rational as Imogen, and it is
difficult to understand why we seem to prefer the lunacy of Juliet, the
imbecility of Ophelia, the farcicality of Katherine, the heroics of Lady
Macbeth, the flippancy of Beatrice, or the moonshine of Rosalind. Imogen
is infinitely superior." Hazlitt countered Johnson's dogmatic characterization with a discerning analysis: "*Cymbeline* is one of the most delightful of Shakespeare's historical plays . . . The most straggling and
seemingly casual incidents are contrived in such a manner as to lead
at last to the most complete development of the catastrophe . . . The
pathos in *Cymbeline* is not violent or tragical, but of the most pleasing
and amiable kind . . . its greatest charm is the character of Imogen . . .
We have almost as great an affection for Imogen as she had for Posthumus; and she deserves it better. Of all Shakespeare's women she is
perhaps the most tender and the most artless . . ."

Even Bernard Shaw succumbed to Imogen. "Pray understand that
I do not defend *Cymbeline*. It is for the most part stagey trash of the
lowest melodramatic order . . . But I am bound to add that I pity the
man who cannot enjoy Shakespeare . . . the Imogen of his genius, an
enchanting person of the most delicate sensitiveness . . ." Shaw, in
correspondence with Ellen Terry, suggested the device of having blood
on the flowers that are strewn over Cloten's body beside the waking
Imogen; but he stressed Imogen's horror at finding this headless man,
rather than her agony a moment later when she recognizes on the body
the clothing of her own husband, which Cloten had donned in his scheme
to ravish her. Shaw, in fact, declaring that "*Cymbeline* though one of

the finest of Shakespeare's later plays now on the stage, goes to pieces in the last act", himself joined the long line of would-be improvers of Shakespeare by writing a new fifth act for the play, which was presented in London in 1937. Shaw's post-Ibsenic conclusion makes the two sons of Cymbeline refuse the new royal life offered them, in favor of their country simplicity, and makes Imogen resent the supposedly "happy ending" that restores her to her husband who had wanted to kill her. In spite of Shaw's claim that he stands "in the same relation to Shakespeare as Mozart to Handel, or Wagner to Beethoven", his re-arrangement — setting twentieth century attitudes on a sixteenth century mood — tumbles him awkwardly from Shakespeare's shoulders. In the fifth act of the original play, after the vision of his ancestors that Posthumus has in gaol (which Shaw omits), with Jupiter mounted on an eagle descending in thunder and lightning to foretell the happy end, Shakespeare at once provides contrast in the gaolers gloating over the condemned Posthumus; and by swiftly succeeding shifts of fortune he holds interest in the fate of the characters. Although the story may have lost flavor of reality since Boccaccio told it, the characters move truly and are truly moving. Those that think they have improved on Shakespeare are usually mistaken.

The sense of gentle sadness, of calm autumnal movement toward the Reaper's scythe, behind which is a harbor of grace abounding, rests as a peaceful cloud over the turbulent stir of *Cymbeline*.

THE WINTER'S TALE *William Shakespeare*

Time has triumphed over Greene's novel *Pandosto; or, The Triumph of Time* (1588), but its story lives on in Shakespeare's *The Winter's Tale*, 1610(?). Despite the unreasoning and unjust jealousy of Leontes, King of Sicilia, and little Mamillius' remark "A sad tale's best for winter", the movement of the story, after its first severities, is kindly and mellow, with country gaiety and revel. King Leontes interprets his queen Hermione's courtesy to their guest, Polixenes, King of Bohemia, as sign of love, and—despite the oracle's declaration that she is pure—he drives her forth. The Queen is given up for dead; her son Mamillius dies of grief; but to the sea-coast of Bohemia ("where there is no sea by near a hundred miles", Ben Jonson chided; but the error is in *Pandosto*) her child the new-born Perdita is brought by old Antigonus. Antigonus is chased away by a bear; a shepherd rescues and rears Perdita. Sixteen years later the charming maid is loved by Florizel, son of King Polixenes, who naturally resents his son's fondness for a shepherd's daughter. Florizel and Perdita therefore flee to Sicilia, where the identity of Perdita is discovered. She is thus restored to her father, Leontes — who, come to view a new-made "statue" of his long-lost wife, finds that the statue breathes, and is indeed Hermione.

Tangled in the story is the light-fingered pedlar and thief Autolycus, a rogue without malice, "a snapper-up of unconsidered trifles", who with his easy ways and merry songs is one of Shakespeare's deftest creations. The plot itself would tax credulity if such things were intended to be believed; but the play's charm lies in its background, its verse, and its pictures of human nature. "For sheer joy in life and breath at the present moment", said Harold C. Goddard in *The Meaning of Shake-*

speare (1951), "the fourth act of *The Winter's Tale* is one of Shakespeare's pinnacles . . . a very superfluity of comic and romantic riches." The close, the reappearance of Hermione stepping off the statue pedestal, is one of Shakespeare's few uses of dramatic surprise. (See *Othello**.)

The wide range of *The Winter's Tale*, in mood, in manner, and in time, has drawn critical objection. Most flagrantly it violates the three dramatic unities (just before *The Tempest**, which most closely observes them). But this gadding about builds into a unity, as the initial scenes in Sicilia, of friendship breaking through jealousy to violence, pass through the pastoral paradise of Bohemia to the final realization of exalting love on earth.

The play has been quite popular, being performed at court in 1611, 1612, 1624, and 1634. In 1751 Macnamara Morgan wrote a pastoral version, *Florizel and Perdita*, which five years later Garrick revised and in which "foolish, lovely Mary 'Perdita' Robinson was adored". For fifty years this version was frequently performed; then in 1802 John Philip Kemble played Leontes in the Shakespeare play, to his sister Mrs. Siddons' Hermione. Charles Kean in 1856 made a lavish and almost archaeological production of the play, opening with Leontes and his guests reclining on couches "after the manner of the ancient Greeks"; the boy Mamillius (played by the young Ellen Terry) had a toy cart modeled after a terra-cotta cart in the British Museum; and—said *Punch* —the bear that chased Antigonus "was an archaeological copy from the original bear of Noah's ark." In the almost equally lavish production of Herbert Beerbohm Tree in 1906, Ellen Terry played Hermione. Some actresses, for instance Mary Anderson, have doubled in the roles of Hermione and Perdita. The *New York Dramatic Mirror* (Nov. 13, 1888) disliked Mary Anderson's English company, calling the setting of the piece beautiful and the whole representation highly picturesque and interesting, but objecting that the performers "all talk in the thick, choky guttural distinctive of the Cockney second-rate actor . . . They all murder their lines with a serene insensibility to taste and meaning . . . Their manner of pronouncing *knowledge no ledge*, for instance, will always seem apocryphal to an orthoepist not trained in an English *co lege*." Evidently London was sending New York as poor a supporting cast as New York for many years sent with its stars to the rest of the United States!

The English production by Granville-Barker in 1912 helped set a simpler fashion for Shakespearean plays. Though the *London Times* mocked a bit: "The costumes are after Beardsley, and still more after Bakst . . . the bizarre smocks and fal-lals of the merry-makers at the sheep-shearing come from the Chelsea Arts Club Ball", it concluded its judgment: "It is very startling and provocative and audacious, and on the whole we like it." The public liked it even more; and the vogue of artful simplicity of production was launched. Recent American revivals include a tour in 1910; a New York production in 1921; the Stratford Company tour in 1931; productions in Pasadena and Chicago in 1937; New York in 1938; Ann Arbor in 1940; and the Theatre Guild production of 1945 with Henry Daniell, Romney Brent, and Florence Reed. George Jean Nathan stated: "Just why the Theatre Guild, in its conceivably somewhat less spacious than infinite wisdom, elected to launch what it has announced as a Shakespearean program with *The Winter's*

Tale jilts the critical faculties . . . The exhibit itself has persisted in being a potential masterpiece hopefully starting on a doomed climb to a slippery mountain peak and ending as a crippled theatrical occasion." Lewis Nichols conversely declared that "on the whole, the trip is successful." Burton Rascoe went further: "In spite of three hundred years of criticism that it is a minor tour de force which doesn't quite come off, this Theatre Guild production of *The Winter's Tale* shows me that it is one of the Bard's great theatrical masterpieces, poignant, lively, entertaining, and beautiful." John Gielgud revived the play in London, opening June 27, 1951; a French production opened in the same month in Paris. The *Christian Science Monitor* of July 14 called the English production "a profound aesthetic experience; Gielgud as Leontes gave the best performance of his distinguished career."

The boy Mamillius, snatched from us while beginning to tell his mother a tale of sprites and goblins — "There was a man dwelt by a churchyard" — lingers in the mind. Swinburne cannot rid himself of thoughts of him: "Even in her daughter's embrace it seems hard if his mother should have utterly forgotten the little voice that had only time to tell her just eight words of that ghost story which neither she nor we were ever to hear ended." As vividly comes Autolycus, crying his "lawn as white as driven snow", traversing the countryside with cheerful song, leading us into a land where heartsease grows, and "daffodils that come before the swallow dares, and take the winds of March with beauty." There is a haunting, perduring beauty in *The Winter's Tale*.

KING HENRY VIII   *William Shakespeare*

The most immediately political of William Shakespeare's plays, bringing the story of England up to the birth of Elizabeth, *King Henry VIII*, 1610(?), may have been written in part by John Fletcher; probably, it was dashed off quickly, for a theatrical or political emergency. The Prologue states that this is "no merry bawdy play", but a tale of greatness tumbled from its high estate, as "mightiness meets misery". That Fletcher wrote part of the play (perhaps his was the later revision) is maintained by A. C. Partridge, in *The Problem of "Henry VIII" Reopened* (1949). By the frequency of typical words, grammatical constructions, and abbreviations—Fletcher would use *'em* and *ye*; Shakespeare, more often, *them* and *you* — Partridge attributes specific parts of the play to each writer, *e.g.*, Act III, ii, the first 203 lines to Shakespeare, the remaining 257 lines to Fletcher. In addition to these lines, there is general agreement that Shakespeare wrote Act I, i and ii; Act II, iii and iv; and Act V, i. Samuel Johnson remarked that Shakespeare's genius, if not his pen, comes in and goes out with Katherine.

Opening with a description of the Field of the Cloth of Gold (1520) *Henry VIII* progresses, faithfully following Holinshed's *Chronicles*, to the christening of Anne Bullen's daughter, the infant Elizabeth, in 1533. Within that period we watch the ruin of the Duke of Buckingham, the annulment of the marriage of Queen Katherine, and the downfall of Cardinal Wolsey. In Wolsey's place we watch the rise of the "good and great" Thomas Cranmer, Archbishop of Canterbury, author of the *Book of Common Prayer*. Elevated by Henry VIII, Cranmer was the forerunner of Bishop Parker and Lord Burghley; he paved the way for

Elizabeth's greatness as in the play, at her baptism, he heralds it. The Tudor rose, planted in conflict and grown through bloody war, came to full blossom in Elizabeth.

The play thus had present pertinence to its first audiences, showing the rise of England's national independence and picturing the fight against the papacy, which was still claiming victims. Productions of the drama were marked by splendor then unusual — set forth, Sir Henry Wotton complained, "with many extraordinary circumstances of pomp and majesty . . . sufficient in truth to make greatness very familiar, if not ridiculous." Wotton's account is of a performance at the Globe Theatre on June 29, 1613, on which occasion the theatre, "filled with people to behold the play", took fire when ordnance ignited the thatched roof, and burned to the ground, though fortunately "nothing did perish but wood and straw." It was rebuilt in 1614 at a cost of £1400.

Henry VIII has had a fairly steady popularity. Samuel Pepys was of two minds about it. In his *Diary* for 1664, he set down: "Saw the so much cried-up play of *Henry VIII*; which, though I went with resolution to like it, is so simple a thing made up of a great many patches, that, besides the shows and procession in it, there is nothing in the world good, or well done." Four years later, however, an entry reads: "to the Duke's Playhouse, and there did see *King Henry VIII*, and was mightily pleased, better than I ever expected, with the history and the shows of it." The acting tradition of the play is continuous; we are told that when Betterton, in 1663, played the king, he was "instructed in it by Sir William (Davenant) who had it from old Mr. Lowen, that had his instructions from Mr. Shakespeare himself." There were over a dozen revivals of the play in the eighteenth century; a production at Drury Lane in 1727 spent the then enormous sum of £1,000 to decorate and costume the procession for the Coronation of Anne Bullen as Queen. In the nineteenth century the play continued popular; Kemble, Kean, Macready, Edwin Booth, Otis Skinner, all put it on; in 1892-1893, to Henry Irving's Wolsey, Ellen Terry was Katherine and Forbes-Robertson was Buckingham. More recently, Beerbohm Tree made an exciting and sumptuous production in New York in 1916, which he considered the greatest success of his career. There was one at Pasadena in 1932; Ann Arbor, 1937; Stratford, 1938; and one with Walter Hampden as Wolsey and Eva Le Gallienne as Katherine, the first production of the American Repertory Theatre, running thirty-nine performances in New York in 1946-1947. This production used two Narrators to speed the action and clarify the history to a modern audience.

Actresses are especially drawn to the part of Queen Katherine, whose demeanor throughout her trial is a noble combination of submissive gentleness and high pride and queenliness; she may be cast off, but cannot be cast down. In the play (though in history she did not die until 1536) she sends her dying blessing to the King. Mrs. Siddons told Samuel Johnson she deemed Katherine the most pleasing of Shakespeare's heroines; and he concurred. Charlotte Cushman, Helena Modjeska, and Fanny Kemble also played the part. The role of Wolsey, in turn, appeals to the actors: Wolsey who worked so faithfully for England, though he raised himself with royal pride to almost kingly state— and strove so zealously for Henry, though his intriguings failed with the Pope's refusal to divorce Katherine, and Wolsey fell. There is a dignity in the Cardinal's behavior as he faces ruin that recaptures the audience's sympathy, as it animates his farewell words. As a neat detail in the production, Charles Kean and Beerbohm Tree, as Wolsey, carried an orange. This marked the Cardinal's fastidious nature; for in Tudor times the segments of the fruit were removed and the skin "filled up again with the part of a sponge, wherein was vinegar and other confections against the pestilent airs", when the Cardinal walked abroad amid the crowd.

Of the two main figures, in the 1946 revival, George Freedley said: "As the ill-treated Queen Katherine, Eva Le Gallienne gives the finest performance of a distinguished career. She is beautiful as well as touchingly tender, majestic, and extremely forceful . . . Walter Hampden's Wolsey is a revelation of simplicity, restraint and malevolence in a role that could be and frequently has been overplayed." The production, Freedley considered "the handsomest Shakespearean revival in the memory of the oldest inhabitant." "Out of an indifferent play," declared Brooks Atkinson, "the A R T has fashioned a memorable performance and a notable production." Louis Kronenberger said: "Actually, *Henry VIII* is a certain amount of history eked out with a certain amount of pageantry, injecting drama where it can, invoking rhetoric where it chooses, and topping the whole thing off with the tinsel about Elizabeth." George Jean Nathan saw it as appealing only to "resolute students of classical curiosae (sic)"; but surely there are many that still find the past pregnant with the future. To these, there is more than splendid pageantry in *King Henry VIII*; there is the spectacle of over-vaulting ambition tumbled to the dust, of perennial passions and plottings, of pride too arrogant and pride in self-respect — human dignity sustained against disaster's tide — caught into rich poetry and vivid drama.

THE TEMPEST   *William Shakespeare*

Many critics consider Shakespeare's last play, *The Tempest*, 1611(?), a symbolic autobiography. All sorts of allegories have been found in its lines. "It shows us," says Richard Garnett, "more than anything else, what the discipline of life had made of Shakespeare at fifty—a fruit too fully matured to hang much longer on the tree." More than anything else, the drama presents a probing of human nature in loveliest poetry.

Samuel Johnson dismissed the play as a mere rippling of the author's fancy: "Of these trifles enough".

Prospero, Duke of Milan, whose "library was dukedom large enough", with his daughter Miranda takes refuge from his brother Antonio's treachery on an island where they live with the help of the air-sprite Ariel and the earthy slave Caliban. When Miranda is a young lady, Prospero uses his book-learned magic powers to summon a tempest (Shakespeare's favorite symbol of tragic conflict) to wreck upon the island Alonso, King of Naples, with his son Ferdinand, Antonio, and others who had connived in the deposing of Prospero. Ariel annoys and perplexes the shipwrecked gentlemen, while Caliban grows drunken with the jester and the butler, Trinculo and Stephano, and plots rebellion against Prospero. Ferdinand, falling in love with Miranda, makes himself her servant. After further exercise of Prospero's magic — in a banquet placed before the newcomers which, even as they reach for the viands, vanishes; and in a wedding pageant and dance of Iris, Juno, Ceres, and nymphs and reapers—Prospero has all the people on the island come together; he reveals his identity, forgives the contrite nobles, and lays his blessing upon his daughter and the prince. "How many goodly creatures are there here!" exclaims Miranda in glad wonder. "O brave new world, That has such people in it!"

The Tempest has been one of the more popular plays of Shakespeare. Dryden and Davenant wrote a version of it in 1667, with numerous new features. This made Prospero guardian of a youth, Hippolyto, who has never seen a maiden, thus balancing Miranda, who has never seen a youth. Miranda has a sweet sister, Dorinda; Caliban has a lecherous sister, Sycorax; and Ariel has a companion spirit, Milcha, for his love. This version was shaped into an opera in 1674 by Thomas Shadwell, and Hippolyto remained on the stage until William Macready brought back Shakespeare's play in 1838. The original play was performed in New York as early as 1773, at the John Street Theatre. It has had frequent revivals throughout the country.

The nineteenth century produced the comedy with magical tricks and spectacular devices. Frank R. Benson, as Caliban, hung head down from the trees with a fish in his mouth. Beerbohm Tree also used the fish. Macready had his Ariel fly about the stage; Charles Kean had Ariel borne on a large bat; at the end of the play, he had a spectacle of the ship's departure, with Ariel watching. Tree used a similar spectacle, but with Caliban looking on "in mute despair". In a Boston production of 1856, Prospero waved his wand: a tree trunk fell, and opened into an armchair for him and Miranda. At another wave of Prospero's wand — with Arnold Daly, in 1897 — a sapling shot up, upon which the magician nonchalantly hung his robe. In 1897, Bernard Shaw attacked these stage effects: "The poetry of The Tempest is so magical that it would make the scenery of a modern theatre ridiculous." The extravagance, nevertheless, has persisted; George Jean Nathan quoted Shaw and reiterated the point after the New York production of 1945.

In 1928, the play was presented in New York with John Barrymore and Louis Wolheim; in 1941 at the University of Washington; in 1942 at the University of California; in 1944 at Vassar College. The 1945-1946 New York production showed Arnold Moss as an imposing Prospero, the Czech comedians Jan Werich and George Voskovec overacting as Stephano and Trinculo, the dancer Vera Zorina miscast as Ariel, and the Negro Canada Lee overly uncouth as Caliban. The Stratford production, opening March 25, 1952, with Ralph Richardson and Margaret Leighton, was more accordant with the play's beauties. In its first season (1955) the playhouse at Stratford, Connecticut, ventured a production of the play.

The 1945 production, despite its inept casting and direction, was cleverly set, according to a plan of Eva Le Gallienne. A central elevation, which we first behold as the deck of the storm-tossed vessel, for the rest of the play is used as the top of a high rock, on which, and around its base as it revolves, the remainder of the action occurs. Several of the critics liked even the acting; but Nathan said that it is "strongly recommended as a valuable education in what, at least partly, a production of The Tempest should not be." Louis Kronenberger condoned its faults, calling the play "perhaps the hardest to project corporeally" of all of Shakespeare's: "Its beguiling side, its air of poetry and enchantment, almost eludes human presentation; while its baser side, its plot twists and comedy scenes, almost exhausts human patience." Yet he must add that "Zorina is not an effective Ariel, nor Canada Lee an effective Caliban." Robert Garland declared that "Canada Lee, camouflaged as the hideous and unhappy Caliban, looks more like a bush walking than anything else I can think of." The 1916 New York production, with Fania Marinoff as Ariel and Walter Hampden as Caliban, was handled with much more delicacy and deftness of touch. With the text uncut, with an Elizabethan simplicity in the staging, this was a delight to all beholders, and won almost unanimous critical praise. The *Tribune* prophesied that it would undoubtedly be forty years "before theatregoers are again enabled to witness as competent a performance as is that now on view." These words still hold true; but even the over-elaborate production of 1945, with its too posturing Ariel and its too growling and groveling Caliban, found a receptive audience, establishing, indeed, a record run of 100 performances.

Ariel and Caliban have drawn considerable attention, as Shakespeare's fullest non-human figures. Ariel—compounded of the two finer elements, fire and air — fulfils his tasks and finds joy in their doing, but would nevertheless be free of them. Caliban—compounded of the two coarser elements, water and earth — must serve, but hates his labors. Men are made of the four elements and a soul; they can rise higher, and sink lower, than these spirits. The play pictures, in the humans, liberty, love, and wonder, but also their opposites, tyranny and license, hatred and lust, and banality and prodigies. As Ariel shows no human signs of affection or personal loyalty and leaves Prospero without regret or any sense of friendly ties, so Caliban lacks the depravity, the lechery or the greed of the degenerate drunken humans. Hazlitt, who calls Caliban one of Shakespeare's masterpieces, says that his character "grows out of the soil where it is rooted, uncontrolled, uncouth and wild, uncramped by any of the meannesses of custom."

Some of Shakespeare's most delightful songs are in this play—"Come unto these yellow sands"; "Full fathom five thy father lies"; "Where the bee sucks, there suck I" — nor is there any better phrased reflection on mortality than Prospero's words after the goddesses' pageant (which were held, in the 1945 production, until the end of the play): "We are such stuff As dreams are made on, and our little life Is rounded with a sleep."

The symbolism of the pageant scene is multiplex, as humans enact persons watching other humans enact spirits that vanish with their play. It seems, said S. L. Bethell in *Shakespeare and the Popular Dramatic Tradition* (1944), "as if Shakespeare had deliberately crowded into a few moments of his last play all that can suggest the manifold mystery of experience." Taking August Strindberg's characterization of the play as "a Buddhist dream", Paul Arnold (editor of *La Revue Théâtrale*) declared that it is a wish-fulfilment dream and the first forerunner of symbolism, Freud, and surrealism on the stage. The characters reveal "so completely and so directly their subconscious tendencies, that they seem to be more like X-rays of the soul than studies of human types." Consequently, M. Arnold continued, *"The Tempest* is like a new table of laws . . . The poet has endowed all art and especially dramatic art with a means of expression of immeasurable power, and has given to the dramatist, by a representation quite like a dream, access to our subconscious life." It is unfortunate that only the post-Freudians can recognize the new "laws" Shakespeare is here said to have set down; and that, in the eerie land to which M. Arnold pointed, the dream is too often a nightmare. It seems, however, that more than man's fate is involved in the play's action; the primal elements are also ranged in battle. Shakespeare here is still the consummate playwright; he provides a varied and a moving action; within this, he snares us into thought of the various levels of reality and bids us contemplate the bases of human existence.

The play drives its creatures on a nameless island in Never-Never Land. No source has been traced for the plot. At Yale University in 1953 the play was produced as science-fiction: a space-ship was wrecked; Prospero watched by television the scenes away from his cell. As often in art, strangeness in one aspect is counterbalanced by tradition in another: Bernard Knox in *English Stage Comedy* (1955) has detailed the resemblances between the characters in *The Tempest* and the stock figures in the comedies of Plautus*. In particular, master and slave—the master helped in his intrigues by the shrewd slave who thus earns his freedom; and everyone save Prospero is in some way at some time enslaved. At the end, however, not only freedom and property are restored, but human worth.

Caliban's meeting with Stephano and Trinculo parallels on its level that of Miranda with Ferdinand, the traditional and continuing low take-off of the high folks' doings. Caliban uses, as Dryden pointed out, "language as hobgoblin as his person." The only touch of low sexual humor in *The Tempest,* Knox continues, "is Caliban's unrepentant laughter when reminded of his attempt on Miranda's virtue; but that one laugh is enough to remind us that he has an ancestry reaching back through scurrilous Plautine slaves and Aristophanic comic actors wearing a leather *phallos* to the ithyphallic satyrs of the Greek vase paintings."

In a sense, *The Tempest* is a memory play. The catastrophe occurs at the start. The images are not premonitory but reminiscent, the sea and the storm constantly recurring in figures. The images, furthermore, appeal to all our senses, sight and hearing fortified by touch, taste, smell. Thus the supernatural in the play is given solid ground of concrete reality, as the characters look back at their earlier days, and we look back upon nature budding into man. Misery, says Trinculo, as he stumbles upon Caliban in the thundery dark, "acquaints a man with strange bedfellows"; but there is lovely as well as odd companionship, and food for thought, throughout the play.

A French attempt at a sequel, *Caliban Set Free,* by Gonzague de Reynold, was produced in Geneva, Switzerland, in 1948. Picturing Caliban, recognizing the baseness of his drunken companions, reformed and made ruler of the island, the play offers an allegory of man's present state. The critic Georges Bonnard called it "a good instance of the profound influence exerted by Shakespeare on modern minds anxious for the future of the values to which he has given shape and form for all times." In addition to the values inherent in the characters and in the symbolism of Shakespeare's play, Prospero makes the closing statement: "The rarer action is In virtue than in vengeance. They being penitent, The sole drift of my purpose doth extend Not a frown further." Here is the judgment on all violent acts. These values, in *The Tempest,* are spun by richest poetry in our souls.

MRS. WARREN'S PROFESSION   *George Bernard Shaw*

In his earliest plays, which George Bernard Shaw (Irish, 1856-1950) called "unpleasant", the thesis drives with a vehemence that precludes the sparkle of wit. The same intensity, however, and perhaps the censorial necessity of conveying some of his meaning in hints, rendered the dialogue unusually pregnant and compressed. Critics who have disliked the subject matter of these plays, in perhaps unconscious self-exculpation, have attacked their artistic quality. As the plays' themes were rooted in current attitudes, they have lost some of their timely significance, but they remain vivid comments on social evils.

The first of the "unpleasant" plays was *Widowers' Houses*, 1892, which began as a collaboration between Shaw and William Archer; the collaboration ended because Archer was aghast at Shaw's battering of the "well-made play" formula. Subsequently Shaw developed the two acts of the attempted collaboration into what he called "a grotesque realistic exposure of slum landlordism." *The Philanderer*, 1893, the second "unpleasant" play, is a satire on sexual attitudes and relations—based perhaps on Shaw's own early experiences.

In the third "unpleasant" play, *Mrs. Warren's Profession*, 1894, Shaw returned to his stark presentation of social evils with a picture of prostitution as the result not of sinfulness but of poverty. The play shows Mrs. Warren as the prosperous proprietress of a chain of brothels across Europe. One of her half-sisters died of drudgery; and rather than "let other people trade in our good looks by employing us as shopgirls, or barmaids, or waitresses," Mrs. Warren systematically traded, first in her own advantages, then in those of an increasing number of impoverished or adventuresome young women. Her daughter Vivie has grown in respectable ignorance of her mother's means of livelihood, and when the play opens she is a very practical young person, of high attainment at Cambridge, looking forward to a professional career as mathematician and engaged to the rather inconsequential Frank Gardner, son of a clergyman. Mrs. Warren arrives with two of her gentleman friends. Vivie keenly questions her mother, breaks through the woman's surprised defenses, and discovers her mother's "profession". In anguish, the mother pictures her early days, and Vivie understands, sympathizes, accepts, and kisses her mother good night. One of Mrs. Warren's friends, Sir George Crofts, a partner in the business, falls in love with Vivie and proposes marriage — even though there's a chance that he is her father. When Crofts, who has invested in the brothels not out of need, but for the high rate of profit, is made the butt of Vivie's scorn, he retaliates by revealing that the Rev. Gardner may be her father—her fiancé Frank, her half-brother. Despite her mother's plea, Vivie rejects the ease and wealth she might enjoy, and turns from her mother, whom she despises as a "conventional woman at heart", living one life and believing another. Vivie has determined to make her own honest living, as a modern woman should. Vivie's rejected Frank dallies with the idea of following Mrs. Warren to Vienna.

Forbidden the stage by the Queen's reader of plays, the drama was published in 1898 with a preface vehemently attacking censorship. It was given "private performance" by the London Stage Society in 1902. In 1905, despite Shaw's warnings, Arnold Daly presented it in the United

States. It was banned in New Haven, but opened October 30 in New York, with 2500 persons turned away, and Police Commissioner McAdoo offering $30 for a seat. In his curtain speech—after the uproar had somewhat subsided—Arnold Daly declared: "I do not think Mr. Shaw's play appeals to the lewd minded, but should be taken as it is — as a strong moral lesson on a phase of society that some might not care to see portrayed." The police disagreed and closed the play; when the courts acquitted the company, public interest had waned. The critics, in general, sided with the police. The *New York American* (October 31, 1905) quoted the Rev. Thomas B. Gregory: "From beginning to end the play — if play it may be called — is a veritable abyss of the vile and the infamous." The *Times* gave a column and a half to discussion of the excitement, half a column to the play: "Mr. Shaw takes a subject, decaying and reeking, and analyzes it for the edification of those whose unhealthy tastes find satisfaction in morbid suggestion . . . it is not only of vicious tendency in its exposition, but it is also depressingly stupid." Echoing the attacks on Ibsen came the *Herald*: "You cannot have a clean pig stye", and the *Sun*: "It is a dramatized stench." The *Post* shrewdly struck at Mrs. Warren's attempted justification of her means of livelihood: "There is nothing so offensive to the normal, clean, and healthy mind as the affectation of a lofty motive in the commission of a mean and dirty action." The practical *World*, on opening night, gave slips to those entering the theatre, asking them to mark their opinion of the play: *Fit* or *Unfit* for the American stage. It collected these after the performance; the next day on the first page, under the heading "*Mrs. Warren's Profession* Is An Offence", the *World* italicized its findings: "The verdict of the majority of those present at the first performance was that Mr. Shaw's play was unfit for presentation on any stage"—and on an inner page revealed the figures: "*Fit*—304; *Unfit*—272; *Not Voting*—424"!

Shaw's Preface suggests in part the cause of these reactions: "The play's dramatic power is used to force the spectator to face unpleasant facts. No doubt all plays which deal sincerely with humanity must wound the monstrous conceit which it is the business of romance to flatter." When the British ban ended in 1924 (with performances opening October 3, 1925 and again March 2, 1926), the attacks were renewed. After a 1935 performance in modern dress, W. A. Darlington, in the *London Telegraph* (July 23) dismissed the play: "Its value, as a tract for the time, has disappeared. Its value as a work of art never existed." The later American reception was more favorable. After a performance by Mary Shaw (who presented the play in 1917 and frequently through the decade thereafter) the *New York World* (April 12, 1918) called it "one of the strongest plays of the modern theatre". Although it has had wide production in Europe, the play was stopped after the first rehearsal in Budapest in 1936 as offensive to morality. The theme is not conducive to frequent amateur performance; but undeniably its presentation is powerful, as New York saw again in the off-Broadway production that opened October 25, 1950. The scene in which Vivie discovers her mother's profession, and her mother defends it, is pitiless and poignant; William Irvine, in *The Universe of G.B.S.* (1949), calls it "perhaps the most powerful situation in any of his plays." It is a crowning irony that the most conventional person in the play is Mrs. Warren; her standards, her indignation at the lack of filial sense of duty, of recognition of her maternal prerogatives, even her attitude toward the brothels whence her income flows: all these mark her as basically a commonplace Victorian. The character of her daughter is also unsparingly limned; her mother's sentimentality is countered by an equally reprehensible hardness in Vivie. As in *The Philanderer*, Shaw condones neither excess. The characters in *Mrs. Warren's Profession*, however, despite the somewhat exceptional source of Mrs. Warren's wealth, come close to such persons as we may still see about. Within the frame of its particular thesis, the play sets universal characteristics.

To some extent, in truth, the characters are not so much persons as living arguments, but the play has been acclaimed as "a masterpiece of realism". The facts are real; the points are potently pressed; the persons are given enough life to color the contention and infuse it with human warmth. Three interlocking ideas are pressed in the play. Shaw makes a moving defense of the woman that turns to prostitution. With equal fervor and sharper pen, he castigates the society that perpetuates and exploits that institution. And beyond this, in the conflict between Vivie Warren and her mother, he puts into human terms the basic struggle between decency and corruption. Shaw is aware that his play probes fundamental questions. It is no accident that, at the final meeting of the two women, he speaks in Biblical terms that recall, and reverse, the relationship of Ruth and Naomi. Bidding her mother farewell, Vivie says, "Your work is not my work, and your ways are not my ways."

In its treatment of Mrs. Warren's profession, the play flings the Marxian economic challenge into the theatre. The prostitute of French novels and plays (a French story had been suggested to Shaw by the actress Janet Achurch, as possible play material) has become the self-analyzing vehicle of a social argument, maintaining that all society shares in any guilt of Mrs. Warren. Indeed, said Shaw in his Preface, "Rich men without conviction are more dangerous in modern society than poor women without chastity." He added, on the 1926 program to *Mrs. Warren's Profession*: "I have only to point to the amount of the dole to remind you that we still are willing to do everything for the virtue of British womanhood except pay for it." Other countries, in the after-years of another war, show that the play's point is continuously timely.

ARMS AND THE MAN   *George Bernard Shaw*

First of what Shaw called his "pleasant" plays, *Arms and The Man*, after a cool reception on its London opening, April 21, 1894, grew to be one of the most popular of the playwright's comedies. It was an immediate hit in New York, opening September 17, 1894 with Richard Mansfield and Lillah McCarthy. London saw the play again in 1906 with Arnold Daly—"a success", said the *Telegraph* (April 17, 1906) "in spite of the Daly handicap"; in 1908; and on the return of the Old Vic Company after the War, October 1944, with Laurence Olivier and Ralph Richardson. Daly played it in New York in 1916; Lynn Fontanne and Alfred Lunt in 1925. Throughout the United States amateur and little theatre productions appear almost every year. New York saw it again, opening October 19, 1950 at the Arena Theatre. Both the amusing dalliance with the romantic attitude in the very act of satirizing it and the constant shafts of thought-provoking dialogue have kept the play entertaining and stimulating.

The play opens in Bulgaria in 1885, in the bedchamber of Raina Petkoff, whose fiancé, Sergius Saranoff, has just been hero of a victory over the Servians. Into that bedroom comes a fleeing Servian captain. Raina, after her first alarm, remembers that the Petkoffs are a family of wealth and refinement; she has seen *Ernani* and, like the host in that opera, will not betray her guest. The prosaic Captain Bluntschli, a Swiss mercenary, completely fagged out, is glad to be rescued but takes it as a matter of course. The chocolate he carries instead of cartridges is all gone; scornfully, Raina offers him a box of bonbons. He falls asleep on Raina's bed. Sometime later, the war over, Bluntschli returns. With swift and amusing tangle and double-barbed banter, he takes Raina for his own. The pompous "hero" Sergius is ensnared by the haughty maid-servant Louka. The servant Nicola, engaged to Louka, relinquishes her as a bride, preferring her as a wealthy patron of the shop he plans to open.

The irreverent and bouncing wit of Shaw, his machine-gun fire of challenging ideas, did not at first appeal to London. In spite of the rapid and constant action, the play has really little story. Even Shaw's good friend William Archer at first could see in the play no more than promise: "I begin positively to believe that he may one day write a serious and even an artistic play, if only he will repress his irrelevant whimsicality, try to clothe his character-conceptions in flesh and blood and realize the difference between knowingness and knowledge." But after some years had passed the English public grew more attuned to the Shavian method. Thus Max Beerbohm, in the *Saturday Review* (January 4, 1908) declared: "I have come to see that much of this seeming fantasy and flippancy was a mere striving after sober reality, and that the reason why it appeared fantastic was that it did not conform with certain conventions of the theatre which the majority of playgoers took as a necessary part of truth to life . . . Fourteen years ago he was not so far ahead in form, as he was in matter, of the average playwright. In form, indeed, he was merely abreast of the time."

The matter or substance of the drama is its realistic, common-sense attitude toward militarism and war, which in the theatre before Shaw had worn the cloak of glory. The title of the play is drawn, sardonically, from the first lines of Vergil's *Aeneid*: "Arms and the man I sing." When the play was produced in Vienna on June 16, 1921, a protest of the Bulgarian Legation and threats of Bulgarian students there closed it after the first performance; but, as the *Boston Transcript* (April 21, 1897) had earlier remarked, "although its scenes were laid in Bulgaria for the sake of giving a fantastic and picturesque atmosphere, the play proved to be a keen and pungent satire on modern English life." Indeed it has been suggested that Shaw's soldiers had actual English models; for glamorous Saranoff, the aristocratic traveler Cunninghame Graham; for efficient Bluntschli, the economist (and a founder of Shaw's Fabian Society) Sidney Webb.

We are shown that war is humdrum, that it has become middle-class. Shaw seems in truth to object less to war than to the romantic allure spun around it. He knows that the most important man in the army is the supply-man. His final thrust of satire in the play comes through the servant Nicola, who has kept out of the army and who at the end willingly gives up a wife to get a customer. Here (as with the flower-girl in *Pygmalion**) Shaw has written a success story of the working class: hotel-owner's son makes good. The playwright might wish the audience to believe that, in succumbing to matrimony, Bluntschli has suffered defeat; but Raina Petkoff will keep her husband secure in the sense of his triumph.

This play, says George Jean Nathan in the *Theatre Book of the Year 1946-1947*, "is after all essentially a libretto with dashes of malapropos satiric wit and, when these are reduced to a minimum, it is as naturally suited to the operatic form as almost anything of Gilbert's." The Germans recognized this quality of the work; Rudolph Bernauer and L. Jacobson fashioned a libretto, with music by Oscar Straus (1909) superbly done and — in English by Stanislaus Stange, as *The Chocolate Soldier* — one of the most successful of recent comic operas. Opening in New York on September 13, 1909, it ran for 296 performances, with New York revivals in 1921, 1930, 1934, 1937, 1942, 1947, and frequent production around the country. In London, the 1910 production ran for 500 performances; the musical has had several revivals. *The Chocolate Soldier*, said the *Musical Courier* (January 15, 1910) is "filled with melody of a distinctly superior quality." Several of the songs have both charm and vitality; "My Hero", "The Chocolate Soldier", and "Falling in Love" are widely remembered and sung. The libretto, too, is continuously effective; it leaves out the sting of Shaw's satire, and manages to make even the practical Bumerli(Captain Bluntschli has become Lieutenant Bumerli) a romantic figure.

The parent play combines with humor and charm a laugh-provoking satire on the stir and contagion and muddle-headedness of war. It quite decapitates the militarist in each of us while leaving us complacently and thoroughly amused. *Arms and the Man* deftly substitutes feminine for military arms.

CANDIDA   *George Bernard Shaw*

Shaw's most frequently presented play, *Candida*, 1894, was written with Ellen Terry in mind, but was first performed by Janet Achurch, March 30, 1895. It has since attracted many stars. There was an amateur production in Chicago, in April, 1899. New York saw the play with Arnold Daly, December 8, 1903; it was also presented in 1905 and 1906; in 1915 again with Arnold Daly; in 1924, 1937, 1942, and 1946 with Katharine Cornell; in 1932 with Blanche Yurka; in 1933 with Peggy Wood. In 1937 in London the play presented Ann Harding, who had played Candida at the Hedgerow Theatre outside Philadelphia in 1924. New York saw it again in 1939 with Cornelia Otis Skinner; Jane Cowl was Candida in the summer of 1942; Elissa Landi in 1943; Congresswoman Clare Booth Luce essayed the role in the summer of 1945. The play has also been constantly performed by college and community theatres, including a "modern dress" revival in Detroit in May, 1948.

More than any other of Shaw's plays, *Candida* presents a personal problem. Candida, wife of the somewhat pompous and complacent Reverend James Morell, is drawn toward the young poet, Marchbanks, who falls flamingly in love with her. The sensitive and keen-witted poet scorns Morell, "moralist and windbag". Morell tells Candida she is free to choose between them; he offers her his strength; Marchbanks offers his weakness. Morell tells Candida he trusts her goodness and her purity; she tells him he'd be wiser to put his trust in her love. And Candida shrewdly knows which of the two is the weaker, needs her the more; she stays with her husband—knowing also that the poet's desolation will ripen and enrich his maturing spirit.

"Mr. Shaw has never written a better speech," said Harold Hobson of the *London Sunday Times*, after the revival opening March 27, 1947, "than that in which Candida talks of those little, nameless, unremembered acts by which a self-sufficient man's wife or mother enables him to burgeon and to glory before an admiring world." Something of the tenderness of the Barrie that wrote *What Every Woman Knows** is here compounded with the wit of the usually more caustic Shaw. In truth, there is no genuine conflict between Marchbanks and Morell. The poet is purposely given but 18 years. He merely precipitates the clarification of the relationship between the Reverend James and Candida Morell. Through his irruption into their lives, they achieve frankness and understanding. Their attitudes toward one another, as G. K. Chesterton pointed out in *George Bernard Shaw* (1909), are harmoniously parallel: "She regards him in some strange fashion at once as a warrior who must make his way and as an infant who is sure to lose his way. The man has emotions which exactly correspond; sometimes looking down at his wife, and sometimes up at her; for marriage is like a splendid game of see-saw."

Some see in the plot elements of Shaw's relations with May Morris, daughter of the poet William Morris. One aspect of the drama—the fate of genius in the world—was earlier treated in Shaw's novel, *Love Among the Artists* (1881). The play may also be viewed as Ibsen's *A Doll's House** reversed: here, the wife sees her husband as he is; she treats him like a doll; and the result is happiness. From any point of view, the play is one of Shaw's least likely to give offense; while it searchingly examines and sharply attacks the conventional views of marriage, the institution of marriage moves on triumphant at the end.

The universal implications, thrusts at conventional morality, revealments of the relations between men and women, rich observation of life, are integrated with the story: here are no long Shavian lectures; this is a full-blooded and moving play. To its story the minor figures—the naive curate, "Lexy" Mill; Burgess, whom Shaw describes as "a vulgar, ignorant, guzzling man, offensive, and contemptuous to people whose labor is cheap, respectful to wealth and rank, and quite sincere and without rancor or envy in both attitudes"; Morell's typist, the abrupt but sensitive Proserpine ("Prossy") Garnett, who Marchbanks at once observes is in love with Morell (and the thought that a woman *can* love Morell terrifies the poet)—all make rich contribution, caught in the author's keen insight and amused outlook. The various minor figures therefore call for careful casting; Mildred Natwick has made a living person out of Prossy; and for Katharine Cornell's 1946 production Burton Rascoe (April 4) headed his review with words of businessman Burgess: "Hardwicke Steals the Show." Shaw emphasized in his Preface that he entered sympathetically into the point of view of every person in the play.

In the play are embodied, as Arthur H. Nethercot reminds us in *P M L A* (September, 1949), the three types of person listed in 1891 in Shaw's *The Quintessence of Ibsenism*. Of every thousand persons, classified according to their attitude toward marriage and the family, Shaw declared, there are 700 philistines, 299 idealists, and one realist. Candida, basically content with the current system of matrimony, is a philistine. Her husband, recognizing but unable to face the flaws in the system, hence building elaborate defense of it, is an idealist. The realist, with courage to face the truth, is the poet Marchbanks. Shaw instanced the poet Shelley as a realist, and in the early productions young Marchbanks was made up to bring to mind the young Shelley, "femininely hectic", Archibald Henderson described him, "and timid and fierce."

The commingling of salvation and sex is a frequent Victorian theme, travestied in the pale young curate of the Gilbert* operettas. But Shaw was enough of a socialist for his early plays to move as "dialectic", from thesis to antithesis to synthesis, showing—as he put it in his words on *Candida*—the ideal's "own revolt against itself as it develops into something higher".

Candida herself is one of the most appealing figures in the modern theatre. As the *New York Dramatic Mirror* said (May 26, 1915): "So wholesomely moral is Candida in her immorality and so captivatingly immoral in her morality that she is one of the most fascinating exhibits in the entire Shaw museum . . ." Opinions of Candida and her "morality" have nevertheless varied widely. Shaw himself, in a 1904 letter to James G. Huneker, unmercifully dissected the sweet wife: "Don't ask me conundrums about that very immoral female, Candida . . . Candida is as unscrupulous as Siegfried: Morell himself sees that 'no law will bind her'. She seduces Eugene just exactly as far as it is worth her while to seduce him. She is a woman without 'character' in the conventional sense. Without brains and strength of mind she would be a wretched slattern and voluptuary. She is straight for natural reasons, not for conventional ethical ones. Nothing could be more coldbloodedly reasonable than her farewell to Eugene: 'All very well, my lad, but I don't quite see myself at 50 with a husband of 35.' It is just this freedom from emotional slop that makes her so completely mistress of the situation." Again one must beware, as Shaw himself warns, of taking Shaw at his face value. Candida may be a Shavian philistine, in that she embraces an attitude that Shaw deems petty and petty bourgeois; but in her conduct within the framework of that system, she is both a realist and a woman of astuteness and command. Candida is, said Eric Bentley, "the sweeter for not being all sugar." She is Shaw's most provocative woman of modern times.

The play has found few detractors. John Mason Brown called it "the wisest, tenderest, and most perceptive of all the realistic plays that have come from Shaw's active pen." In April 1946, Kronenberger felt that "the play itself shows its age and ailments", but most agreed with Barnes: "The plain fact is that *Candida* has the power to withstand the seasons." This is still true.

YOU NEVER CAN TELL   *George Bernard Shaw*

Shaw's first attempt at popular, commercial drama resulted in what Freedley and Reeves call "one of his least characteristic plays" — *You Never Can Tell*, 1896; but you can always tell that a surprise will come with Shaw. This play has the first dramatic use of the legal separation of man and wife and the first stage exhibition of a dentist making an extraction.

Shaw's attempt to write a "well-made play", to suit his drama to contemporary taste, was, John Mason Brown remarked in the *Saturday Review* (April 24, 1948), like putting on a hobble skirt: "Nowadays, it seems as absurd as a hobble skirt would. It is the confinements of its pattern that got in the way of Shaw . . . By his own admission, *You Never Can Tell* found Shaw stooping to conquer. Fortunately Shaw was never meant to be a stooper. All of us are the better off because he has led rather than followed us. Leading is his life work." It is wise, however, not to take Shaw at "his own admission"; if he stooped, it was to put a firecracker beneath the audience's complacency. The play is indeed, as William Irvine says in *The Universe of G. B. S.* (1949), not a copy of but "a satirical compromise with fashionable comedy . . . The total result suggests the Pickwick Club at the height of election excitement."

Shaw for a time seemed mistaken, however, in thinking he had struck the popular vein. Cyril Maude took the play for his company to produce at the Haymarket; but the actors themselves were so confused by the script that Shaw withdrew it. The New Stage Society made it the first of their private ventures, opening November 26, 1899. In 1900 it was shown for a fortnight of matinees in London. Chicago saw an amateur production in February 1903. But it was not until January 9, 1905, in New York, that the public welcomed it for a run of 150 performances with Arnold Daly and Mabel Taliaferro. It had been offered to Richard Mansfield, who refused it, saying that one couldn't popularize a dentist in America. In London, later the same year, H. Granville-Barker produced the play with Nigel Playfair. Since then there have been scores of revivals, one in New York opening on March 16, 1948, with Patricia Kirkland, Frieda Inescourt, and Leo G. Carroll.

The play tells us of Mrs. Clandon, a "modern" woman and authoress, who carried her son Philip and her two daughters, Dolly and Gloria, to Madeira to keep them from the middle-class influence of their father. After eighteen years—when the play opens—they are back at "a watering place" on the coast of England. Here a "five-shilling dentist", Dr. Valentine, falls in love with Gloria—though his joy is mixed with dismay when in twelve short hours she sweeps him into matrimony; and the family is reunited with the father. The idea that a man is reluctant to embrace matrimony, whereas a woman seeks always to snare him into that state, becomes less playful in Shaw's later treatment; here, as Irvine said, it is "an elaborate joke in the process of becoming an elaborate dogma." The suggestion has been put forward that the play is to some extent autobiographical, picturing as Gloria Miss Charlotte Payne-Townshend, whom Shaw — after many delays and hesitancies — eventually married.

The wit of the Shavian dialogue, the crisp, character-catching repartee, cannot be gathered into bouquets for brief savoring. When the play was first produced in New York, the *Dramatic Mirror* called it "the most enjoyable of all Shaw's plays, pleasant or unpleasant, to read to one's self or aloud . . . It is so full of whimsical turns and odd half-lights on human nature that it is brainy champagne with all the sparkle left in. With this clever Irishman there is nothing holy in love; it is only a chemical reaction, or more, perhaps, like a game of chess, where the cleverer party advances her pawns boldly until she can cry 'checkmate' to her fleeing victim, man." However, few critics of 1905 were ready to look upon Shaw as a serious commentator on life.

The play grew to be tremendously popular throughout the world, but when it was revived in New York in 1948 it received mixed notices. Brooks Atkinson tried to defend it: "Let's say this much . . . no other comedy of that period (early 1900's) would be even tolerable . . . It was directed in a key that would make an ordinary farce unbearable." John Chapman remarked, "Somebody said it was the coldest audience he ever saw . . . I wasn't cold—just sleepy." Others spoke more praisefully. George Jean Nathan contended that the play "still retains a deal of its original amusement." George Freedley hailed it as "one of Shaw's most delightful and graceful comedies." Quotations from these mixed reviews were used by the producers, the Theatre Guild, in a *New York Times* (March 18, 1948) advertisement headed "Shavians Arise! Heresy! Sabotage! Treason!". The Shavians rallied enough to give the play a run of five weeks.

In retrospect, the English critic W. A. Darlington has declared: "I have always thought Shaw's chance of becoming a classic rests chiefly on two plays, *St. Joan** and *You Never Can Tell.*" With more of a plot and with less lengthy speeches than many of Shaw's other plays, the latter remains a delightful picture of the "new" woman succumbing to the old emotion—then, like the eternal feminine, taking command. The Shavian woman, who as the instrument of the Life Force subdues the male, first flutters and flowers in *You Never Can Tell.*

THE DEVIL'S DISCIPLE   *George Bernard Shaw*

The first of Bernard Shaw's "Three Plays for Puritans", *The Devil's Disciple*, 1897, is also a play about Puritans. Mrs. Dudgeon, the mother of Dick, "the devil's disciple", is a strict Puritan; she is also an old harridan; she hated her late husband; she bears with "intensely recalcitrant resignation" the blows the Lord has let fall upon her head. It is in revolt against her harsh piety and the sanctimonious hypocrisy he sees around, that Dick Dudgeon has declared himself a diabolonian, and has been content to be an outcast from these over-righteous townsfolk. Dick hates the rigid religiosity that makes children weep and old women nags or witches. When his father's will makes Dick master of the house, old Mrs. Dudgeon is mortally stricken; all the members of the family turn from him, except the "irregular child" of Dick's Uncle Peter, Essie, whom Dick alone has treated with respect. More urgent events sweep on; for this is Westerbridge, New Hampshire, in 1777; and the British, driving through the state, as an example and warning are hanging a leading citizen in every town. Nearby, they have hanged Dick's Uncle Peter; in Westerbridge they come for Parson Anderson. But the Parson is out and, to his wife Judith's distaste, Dick Dudgeon is there. He has taken off his coat because it is wet with rain; he does not disclose his identity and the soldiers carry him off in mistake for the Parson, to be condemned to hang next day at noon. Parson Anderson gallops off to safety. The sentimental Judith—doubtless romantic at heart beneath her drab Puritan garb—swings from hatred of Dick to deep concern and love. To the severe English Major Swindon comes the suave General, "Gentlemanly Johnny" Burgoyne, who chats amicably with the prisoner, especially when Judith frantically cries out that he is not her husband. Identified, Dick is still to be hanged; but in the nick of time, the American officer who the night before drove back the British arrives with a safe-conduct to discuss the terms of their evacuating Westerbridge. Dick is saved. The American officer is Parson Anderson. Judith is ashamed at having thought her husband a coward, and relieved at Dick's promise of silence; the British march off, with the village band playing Yankee Doodle behind them.

This tomfoolery and satire is peppered with wit and wisdom. The plot is swift-moving; beneath it flows an inner action. Parson Anderson is superbly drawn; his tolerant calm in the face of Dick's insults wins Dick's respect and our own. His wife Judith is a superbly satiric capture of the moony, romantic dreamer within the seemingly sober and solid pious woman. Most interesting is the contrast between Dick Dudgeon and his mother. Shaw dwelt on this in his Preface (1900) to the play, comparing Mrs. Dudgeon to Mrs. Clenman in Dickens' *Little Dorrit*. The critics, said Shaw, "took Mrs. Dudgeon at her own valuation as a religious woman because she was detestably disagreeable. And they took Dick as a blackguard, on her authority, because he was neither detestable nor disagreeable." Shaw neglects to observe that the other characters in the play also accept that evaluation. Not quite for the reasons Shaw gives; but it takes a revolution to upset the Puritan values. Opposed to Mrs. Dudgeon's almost vindictive self-sacrifice is Dick's unintended heroism. "On the stage, it appears, people do things for reasons," remarked Shaw. "Off the stage they don't: that is why your penny-in-the-slot heroes, who only work when you drop a motive into them, are so oppressively automatic and uninteresting."

This is not the remark of a cynic; rather, as the portrait of Dick Dudgeon shows, it is the reflection of one who has faith in the essential goodness and dignity of human nature. William Irvine, however, in *The Universe of G. B. S.* (1949), points out that such an assertion of human dignity usually springs in a stable moral climate, from a basic moral tradition and self-discipline—which Dudgeon rejects. "In glorifying the product while deprecating the cause, Shaw is close to moral melodrama." Rather, Shaw is placing in 1777 an early instance of his man-to-be, whose impulses are so ordered that he will do as he pleases, and do right. Shaw complained in his Preface that a critic and the actors rewrote the play, destroying its point by giving Dudgeon a secret love for Judith Anderson. "Dick Dudgeon every night confirmed the critic by stealing behind Judith, and mutely attesting his passion by surreptitiously imprinting a heart-broken kiss on a stray lock of her hair whilst he uttered the barren denial." Shaw took so firm a hand in the productions of his plays that this acting trick was probably never performed, but invented for the satiric effect of the telling—though a motiveless good deed may indeed be, to some persons, inexplicable.

Shaw wrote *The Devil's Disciple* after three years of reviewing bad plays—to show that there were better ones available. He made his point; the play was well received. It had its world premiere in Albany, October 1, 1897, and moved to New York on October 4, with Richard Mansfield. Some of the critics called the play "original"; Shaw laughed at them, pointing out that he used many of the hackneyed devices of the current theatre. What most critics praised was the play's paradoxical twists of thought, its barbed shafts of wit.

Much of the wit strikes sparks that fly between Dick Dudgeon and General Burgoyne. The latter has no essential part in the play; he seems onstage mainly because Shaw—who devoted a long prefatory note to him —was attracted to the man. (John Burgoyne was not only a general, but also a playwright. His *Blockade of Boston* was being performed in Boston in 1776 when an attack on the city interrupted it—as the hanging of Dick is interrupted in *The Devil's Disciple*.)

Perhaps because it shows a defeat of the English, the drama has been always one of the most popular of Shaw's plays in Dublin; the *Irish Times* commented (April 10, 1940): "written as a melodrama, it became, and it remains, something that is a great deal more." Its English premiere was on September 26, 1899. It has been popular in England as in America. The American company of 1923 included Basil Sydney as Dick and Roland Young as Burgoyne. Percy Hammond said (April 23, 1923): "This humorous old nick-o-timer caused many of us to sit on the edge of our chairs last night and grow quite feverish over its beefsteak pudding incidents, as Mr. Shaw called them." The London *Stage* (August 1) in 1940 found the play still a "rollicking bit of realism and odd mixture of picturesque melodrama and ironic farce." The New York production opening January 25, 1950, at the City Center was so well received that it moved over to Broadway for 111 performances; it balanced Maurice Evans as Dudgeon and Dennis King as Burgoyne in a superb display of wit and fine acting. The play's clever use of the appeals of melodrama while it mocks the devices it is using, its sharp and witty attacks upon militarism, its topsy-turvy turns of accustomed attitudes, and its neat exposure of the difference between the religiose and the decent human being, keep *The Devil's Disciple* lively, timely, and fresh.

CAESAR AND CLEOPATRA   *George Bernard Shaw*

Most challenging of "Three Plays for Puritans" is *Caesar and Cleopatra*, 1898, which was written by Shaw not, as some say, to show how Shakespeare should have composed a play, but to set straight the earlier playwright's values. After Shakespeare has pictured Antony as "the soldier broken down by debauchery" and Cleopatra as "the typical wanton in whose arms such men perish", Shaw averred, "Shakespeare finally strains all his huge command of rhetoric and stage pathos to give a theatrical sublimity to the wretched end of the business, and to persuade foolish spectators that the world was well lost by the twain." Shaw felt, moreover, that "sexual infatuation" is dramatically effective only in the comic vein. "To ask us to subject our souls to its ruinous glamor, to worship it, deify it, and imply that it alone makes our life worth living, is nothing but folly gone mad erotically." In Shaw's play the Roman conqueror merely dallies with the Egyptian queen in his moments of relaxation. When war comes he brushes her aside. When he sets out for home, only her calling to him reminds him of her existence. Love, which Shakespeare presents as felling potentates, Shaw sets as a byplay in the recess-time of a busy life.

In the character of Caesar, Shaw likewise differs from Shakespeare; here, Shaw specifically declared that he had improved upon the earlier picture. In the first place, "It cost Shakespeare no pang to write Caesar down for the merely technical purpose of writing Brutus up." In the second place, Shaw "saw the old facts in a new light." Shakespeare presented the Romans—and this is what many fail to see—not as ancient Romans really were, but as persons he might have known, "according to his own essentially knightly conception". The characters in *Julius Caesar** and in *Antony and Cleopatra** talk Shakespearean, and think Elizabethan ideas and values. The characters in *Caesar and Cleopatra* talk Shavian and think twentieth century "advanced" thoughts. Cleopatra, of course, is a mere child of sixteen; but Shaw is careful to explain that such childishness as hers — coquettish, malicious, and supremely selfish — "may be observed in our own climate at the present day in many women of fifty." All of Shaw's persons are essentially of the present day. "They had not the telephone", commented the London *Saturday Review* (November 30, 1907) critic, "and we don't torture our domestics, at least physically. Barring these trifles, I agree with Mr. Shaw that the difference between Julius Caesar and Cecil Rhodes, or Cicero and Mr. Balfour, is one of costume and slang." Take off the trappings, and Caesar — history's, or Shakespeare's, or Shaw's — is a human being even as you and I. Hailed as a novelty, Shaw's treating historical figures as contemporaries really continued the great tradition. He assumed that the Greek warriors of Plato's day had no less of native wit, not to speak of valor, than the soldiers of our own time. The Egyptians of Caesar's time enjoyed a comparatively high culture.

In Shaw's play we meet a Caesar somewhat like Shaw in a toga. Perhaps the character is mellow because, though romantic love is brushed aside, Shaw wrote the play on his honeymoon (he was married in 1898). The portrait is, however, a marked step in Shaw's efforts to find a cure for the ills of society: a definite turn from socialism to the superman. This prospect is given further treatment in *The Apple Cart**, and fullest development in *Back to Methusaleh.** "Caesar", said Sir Cedric Hardwicke in the *New York Times* (December 18, 1949), "is of course Shaw". Hardwicke then quoted Shaw's words of 1918 to his biographer, Hesketh Pearson: "It is what Shakespeare called a history; that is, a chronicle play; and I took the chronicle without alteration from Mommsen. I read a lot of other stuff, from Plutarch, who hated Caesar, to Warde-Fowler; but I found that Mommsen had conceived Caesar as I wished to present him, and that he told the story of the visit to Egypt like a man who believed in it, which many historians don't . . . Although I was forty-four or thereabouts when I wrote the play, I now think I was a trifle too young for the job; but it was not bad for a juvenile effort."

In the play, we come upon Caesar amid his later triumphs, when he is already fifty-four. After the opening alarm of the Egyptians as the conquering Roman cohorts come near, we watch a situation in which ironic comedy deftly blends with tenderness. "Shaw's portrait of an elderly gentleman coaching a girlish queen in the etiquette of ruling", as the *New York Times* observed (August 22, 1935), "is full of admiration and sympathy." The frightened Cleopatra, huddling for shelter between the paws of a Sphinx, takes counsel of an elderly man apostrophizing there. He tells her she is safe from Caesar only if she faces him like a queen. As they walk back to the palace, we watch her drawing assurance and courage from his easy confidence; assuming authority and, when it works, lashing out like a tyrant; fighting for self-control as her slaves drape the royal robes upon her trembling form; recognizing that it is "bitter to be a queen"; and, as she stands desperately proud while the Romans troop noisily in, discovering that the elderly man who has soothed her and strengthened her and brought her back to face the Roman terror — is the man to whom the soldiers lift their swords and shout "Hail, Caesar!" Cleopatra's feline disposition prevents her emulating Caesar's politic clemency. She has her nurse Ftatateeta kill the ambitious eunuch Pothinus for carrying tales to Caesar; and for fear lest the nurse give suck to further treachery, Caesar's blunt bodyguard Rufio passes his word through her throat. Meanwhile the roused Egyptians have fired the city; the great Alexandrian library is consumed in the flames; and Caesar takes precarious post at the Pharos lighthouse. Into the tumult of this surging history, Shaw sets both comedy and beauty. Apollodorus, patrician dealer in aphorisms and art, brings rugs for Cleopatra: "My calling is to choose beautiful things for beautiful queens. My motto is Art for Art's sake." The prosaic sentinel objects: "That is not the password." Cleopatra, who wants to join Caesar at the Pharos, has herself wrapped in a rug and, thus concealed, rowed to the lighthouse station. There she is hoisted on a crane to Caesar; and when the Egyptians advance and Caesar dives to swim to his nearing vessels, Rufio at his call pitches Cleopatra after him. When timely reinforcements cement Caesar's conquest, he sets out for Rome, leaving Cleopatra the consolation that he will send her the captain she once saw and coveted, a dashing young Roman named Mark Antony.

This mingling of ancient history and modern thoughts and perennial humans is a merry frolic garnished with provocative ideas. Its main flow of satire springs from the contrasted and neatly drawn characters, especially the "unadulterated Briton . . . ancestor of Mr. Podsnap", the dignified prude, the literal-minded, the humorless, honest, devoted and brave Britannus. All through the play, ideas and action interflow in a swift coursing. Between Caesar and young Cleopatra the teacher-pupil relationship, frequent in Shaw's plays, may be observed: a realistic and somewhat cynical person awakening and quickening toward fulfilment a younger person not yet deeply aware.

The play was given an amateur production in Chicago, in May 1901. Its professional premiere came in New York October 30, 1906, with Sir Johnston Forbes-Robertson, and was coolly received. The *Tribune* said: "The purpose of it is the deliverance of satirical jibes from behind a stalking horse of farcical history. It seems to be the conviction of this author that everything existent, including human nature, is wrong, and that all things ought to be made over and newly fashioned, according to Shaw." There were similar comments after the London opening, as in the *Illustrated Sporting and Dramatic News* (December 7, 1907): "*Caesar and Cleopatra* made me sleepy at the Savoy . . . The pleasantest moments to myself during the performance were—to put it Irishly, which Mr. Shaw should not mind—the waits while the performance was suspended . . . It is not a history, it is not a tragedy, it is not a comedy, it is not a farce, it is not a burlesque—it is not anything that I can name; it is four acts of mixed negations, not one of which is strong enough to dwell upon." Comparison with Shakespeare was inevitable. The London *Saturday Review* (November 3, 1907) favored its contemporary: "Mr.

Shaw has more learning, and a great deal more wit and humor, than Shakespeare, though he lacks the pathos of the latter." A quarter of a century later, Brooks Atkinson (August 30, 1935) similarly declared: "*Caesar and Cleopatra* is superior to *Julius Caesar* and *Antony and Cleopatra* in thinking and form, being inferior only in passion, which is perhaps the whole thing."

Forbes-Robertson played the role again in 1913, adding the rug-and-swimming act, which he had omitted in the earlier production. Helen Hayes and Lionel Atwill opened the new Guild Theatre in New York with the play on April 13, 1925; Helen Hayes acted in it again ten years later. In 1925, in London, Sir Cedric Hardwicke played Caesar; he returned to the role in New York in December 1949, with Lilli Palmer, for 151 performances. In the summer of 1950 Paulette Goddard acted in the play. London saw it again in 1951 with Laurence Olivier and Vivien Leigh, opening May 10, and alternating with Shakespeare's *Antony and Cleopatra**. This production came to New York on December 19, 1951, Olivier playing Caesar as a world-weary, wise old man. In 1944, in the most expensive film ever made in England, Vivien Leigh played Cleopatra to Claude Rains' Caesar. For this filming, Shaw wrote a brief bath scene intended to bring the Queen's childishness to the level at which Shaw pictured the movie audience. For his theatre audience he employed the usual tricks of the trade while keeping a vivvid story swiftly flowing to bear his ideas along. Thus there are few that will not find harvest of entertainment and thought in this play.

CAPTAIN BRASSBOUND'S CONVERSION   *George Bernard Shaw*

The central figure of this play, written in 1899, is Lady Cicely Waynflete; she produces the change noted in the play's title. Although Richard Watts, Jr. calls her "chiefly a sort of middle-aged Candida", Lady Cicely has youth and charm enough to wind around her little finger all the men she meets. With her to Morocco has come her brother-in-law, the English judge Sir Howard Hallam; among the others in the small town there, are a Scotch missionary, a Cockney hooligan, and a desperately serious brigand. The brigand, Black Paquito—less romantically, Captain Brassbound—has a score to settle with Judge Hallam, who happens to be his uncle, and the instrument of his mother's having been sent to prison. Brassbound arranges to have the judge taken into slavery by a Mohammedan sheik; but in a scene of superb comedy, Lady Cicely, with feminine matter-of-fact, explodes Brassbound's romantic notions of revenge. This, however, empties his life of its meaning. Meanwhile a United States gunboat, getting word of the brigands, has sent out an expedition; the captured Brassbound is held by the gunboat's Captain Kearney. Before him Lady Cicely, always in complete command of herself and any situation, tells the truth and nothing but the truth—when Judge Hallam reminds her that "the English law requires a witness to tell the *whole* truth", she retorts: "What nonsense! As if anybody ever knew the whole truth about anything!"—and she manipulates the hearing with such apparently innocent astuteness that Brassbound is exonerated. With Brassbound free and his life's purpose gone, there seems nothing left but for Lady Cicely to marry him. She is holding out her hand to him when a broadside from his pirate ship breaks the spell; Brassbound dashes off.

Explaining the play's publication as one of the "Three Plays for Puritans", Shaw said: "I have, I think, always been a Puritan in my attitude toward art . . . The nineteenth century has crowned the idolatry of Art with the deification of Love . . . the pleasure of the senses I can sympathize with and share; but the substitution of sensuous ecstasy for intellectual activity and honesty is the very devil". It is the delight arising from intellectual activity that one feels here, for, as Desmond McCarthy said, since Swift "no such insistent preacher has so leavened his lesson with laughter".

Lady Cicely is a superb creation, at once imbued with romantic charm and equipped with such deftly managed store of woman's wiles as makes a mockery of romance. She balances with her common-sense the romantic notions the men hold of revenge as justice; and by her motherliness and her encouragement of the right course (and her artful assumption of candor) she smooths away the masculine villainy and ill-will.

The play was produced in London by the Stage Society in December, 1900. A revival opened on March 20, 1906, with Ellen Terry, for whom the part was conceived, as Lady Cicely. She played it again, opening January 28, 1907, with James Carew (whom she married) as Captain Brassbound. The *London Telegram* (January 29, 1907) conceded that Miss Terry "easily made Lady Cicely charming," but insisted that the play "is pretty tiresome." Subsequent opinion has been more favorable. Grace George appeared in the play in New York in 1916; Gladys Cooper, during the summer of 1939; Jane Cowl, in 1940. Then, Robert Coleman (July 13, 1940) declared it "gorgeous burlesque; an excellent example of what super-fun can be whacked from a slapstick in the hands of such artists as Shaw, Cowl, and company." In 1937 the play was produced in Warsaw under the title *The Pirate and a Lady*. Six years later Dame Sybil Thorndike enacted Lady Cicely in Dublin. In this role, Edna Best showed, at the New York City Center opening December 27, 1950, that the play is still amusing and provocative, with shrewd character study. London felt the same about the revival at the Old Vic, with Roger Livesey and Uursula Jeans, opening April 17, 1951.

The nature of things peeps out, in deft revelation and humorous concern, from beneath the romantic color and adventure and brilliant dialogue of *Captain Brassbound's Conversion*.

MAN AND SUPERMAN   *George Bernard Shaw*

With *Man and Superman*, 1901-1903, Shaw moved for the first time in the full grip of the "life force". For his panacea for the ills of the world he turns from socialism to the superman who was to come into being through "creative evolution".

A. B. Walkley, the critic, had asked Shaw for a Don Juan play. The usual treatment, Shaw felt, had been fully exploited by Molière* and Mozart; hence his use of the storied figures is concentrated into the seldom played third act presenting a dream of hell with Don Juan and the Statue and the Devil in long arguments that end with Don Juan going up to heaven to live in contemplation, while the Statue decides there's more fun to be had by staying in the other place. In Shaw's irony hell is a place where one may have all one desires—save intensity of thought and feeling. The Devil himself is suspiciously like a Congressman. One

of Shaw's most biting speeches is Don Juan's long description of the
Devil's "friends", a piece of rhetoric perhaps intended to outvie Shaw's
hated-beloved master, Shakespeare, who uses such patterns of word play,
as in the curate's characterizations in *Love's Labor's Lost*.

In the play proper, Don Juan is represented by the Englishman John
Tanner and Donna Ana by Ann Whitefield. "Instead of presenting a
diabolonian scoffer who horrified respectable believers by his skepti-
cism," as William Irvine states in *The Universe of G. B. S.* (1949), "Shaw
must present a fanatical revolutionary who horrifies respectable skeptics
by his faith. Instead of depicting a libertine who pursues women, he
must depict a Puritan who is pursued by them." John Tanner, gentleman by birth, wealthy by class, revolutionary by theory, bachelor by
luck, is annoyed at having been made guardian of the sweetly feminine
Ann Whitefield. When friends, including his practical chauffeur, open
John's eyes to Ann's designs upon him, he flees to Spain. There, in the
hands of the bandit Mendoza (formerly a London waiter, fled in despairing love of the chauffeur's sister), in the Sierra Nevada Don John Tanner
dreams his magnificent dream-dialogue in hell. But even to the mountain fastness, Ann follows him. She says that her mother insists on her
marrying John; her mother denies it. Tanner rejects her; she announces
publicly that she has accepted him, and "swoons" at his feet. Ann spins
her feather boa around her neck; for she is the serpent the Life Force
has sent to wrap John in her toils, for the movement of mankind toward
the superman. Her feminine frailty is the velvet over the steel of her
undeviant purpose.

Tanner is somewhat like Sidney Trefusis in Shaw's novel *An Unsocial
Socialist* (1883). There is also Shaw's early sketch *Don Giovanni Explains* (1887), in which the man is the pursued. H. M. Hyndman has
been mentioned as model for Tanner, but in many ways the latter resembles Shaw himself. He pours forth Shaw's ideas and, like Shaw's,
his ideas are met with rejection and ridicule; and he is swept willy-nilly
into matrimony. John Tanner wrote a *Revolutionist's Handbook*, which
is printed as a postscript to the play. It sears with the full bitterness of
Shaw's disappointment in democracy and Fabian socialism; its dicta
reflect the opinions of the poet Blake and suggest those of Ambrose
Bierce's *The Cynic's Word Book* (1906). "Revolutions have never lightened the burden of tyranny," says John Tanner-Shaw; "they have only
shifted it to another shoulder . . . We must eliminate the Yahoo, or his
vote will wreck the commonwealth . . . The art of government is the
organization of idolatry . . . Positive: mistaken at the top of one's voice
. . . Marriage is popular because it combines the maximum of temptation
with the maximum of opportunity . . . Learning: the kind of ignorance
distinguishing the studious . . . Applause: the echo of a platitude . . .
He who can, does. He who cannot, teaches," declared the most didactic
of modern playwrights. (*Positive, learning, applause* are from Bierce.)
Tanner's handbook is in the cynical fashion of his time. Shaw was a
Victorian, not as inverted as he liked to seem; his major characters are
aristocratic.

The play, opening in London May 25, 1905, with the dialogue in hell
left out, was better received by the public than by critics. Granville-
Barker played Tanner in a red beard, to resemble Shaw. The play was
revived in London in 1905 and 1906; opening September 28, 1911 for 191

performances; in 1912, 1927, twice in 1930, 1931, by the Old Vic in 1938 and 1951. The hell scene was first played in London on June 4, 1907, with Robert Loraine. London saw the full play in 1925, 1928, 1935, 1951. It was performed complete in Germany in 1906. The American premiere (without hell but with Robert Loraine) was on September 5, 1905; the play ran for 192 performances. Maurice Evans, opening in New York in the abridged version on October 8, 1947, ran for 295 performances.

In 1947, Shaw had three plays on Broadway: Evans in *Man and Superman*; *John Bull's Other Island** with the Dublin Gate Company; and Gielgud in *You Never Can Tell**. *Don Juan in Hell*, as the dream episode is called, was presented by Charles Boyer, Charles Laughton, Cedric Hardwicke and Agnes Moorehead — without scenery, on a two-year tour, in New York at Carnegie Hall October 22, 1951, and for runs on Broadway in the winter and spring of 1951-1952.

After the London premiere of the dream of hell, Max Beerbohm declared in the *Saturday Review* (June 8, 1907): "Mr. Shaw has never contrived so good an expression of his genius as *Don Juan in Hell*. In no other work of his is one so struck by the force and agility of his brain, by the spontaneity of his humor, and by the certainty of his wit." Quite different were the reviews of the entire play. In the *London Times* (November 27, 1938), James Agate declared that "the characters are doubly dead for the good reason that they never were alive." To lend emphasis, Agate then quoted Max Beerbohm on the main figures of the play: "We can no more be charmed by them than we can believe in them. Ann Whitefield is a minx. John Tanner is a prig. Prig versus Minx, with the gloves off, and Prig floored in every round—there you have Mr. Shaw's customary formula for drama. The main difference between this play and the others is that the prig and the minx are conscious not merely of their intellects but of the 'life force'. Of this they regard themselves, with comparative modesty, as the automatic instruments. They are wrong. The life force could find no use for them. They are not human enough, not alive enough."

Across the ocean, the *New York Telegram* (September 6, 1905), took the playwright to task for stating in the Preface that his point of view is akin to that of Shelley, Ibsen, and Nietzsche: "Save the mark! Shelley, whose sense of beauty was his all, and Mr. Shaw has absolutely none; Ibsen, whose moral force moved the mountains of Norway, and Mr. Shaw confesses he is a wobbler; Nietzsche, whose gigantic sincerity is even painful, and Mr. Shaw doesn't even know what it means." In supplementing these comments George Jean Nathan remarked that though *Man and Superman* is "beautifully written", time has a way of turning saucy platters into platitudes. In truth, there seems in this drama a considerable pother of talk for the simple story. Shaw's inability or unwillingness to curb his characters' conversation, and his refusal to let producers cut his lines, explain why Mrs. Pat Campbell (whom Shaw called "perilously bewitching") was moved to protest, in 1912: "It's too late to do anything but accept you and love you — but when you were quite a little boy somebody ought to have said 'Hush!' just once."

Despite these objections, the play is adroitly attuned to its purpose. The characters may not be humanly real, but they have gusto. Ann Whitefield may not be any particular woman, but she is Everywoman (Shaw conceived her, indeed, after seeing a performance of *Everyman**).

The development of the play is, if delayed, richly adorned, by the trenchant wit, and the dialogue is at the peak of Shavian coruscation. Shaw's most characteristic ideas are presented in sharpest focus. And if, as E. Strauss suggests, in *Bernard Shaw: Art and Socialism* (1942), the love story in Shaw's plays reflects their thought, then the acquisitive woman represents capitalism; and Tanner's succumbing to Ann well captures the modern man's predicament, snared inextricably in the capitalistic mesh and mess, condemned to enjoy its advantages while decrying its deficiencies—until man has been supplanted by superman. But, Shaw admonishes us, beware the Yahoo, whose scion will be Superman of the comics! This danger Shaw does not see how to avert, save by more desperate endeavors of the Life Force, intellect and will joining instinct in the course of creative evolution. Meanwhile the intellect finds wholesome, tasty food in *Man and Superman*.

JOHN BULL'S OTHER ISLAND   *George Bernard Shaw*

Written at the request of William Butler Yeats for the Abbey Theatre of Dublin, *John Bull's Other Island*, 1904, proved beyond the company's resources. It was first produced in London, November 1, 1904, with considerable success. It did not repeat this success on its presentation in New York with Arnold Daly, opening October 10, 1905, and it was not revived in New York until the Dublin Gate Theatre included the play in its repertory, January 10, 1948, on its American visit.

In the play, the Englishman Thomas Broadbent and his Irish partner, Larry Doyle, visit the latter's native town in Rosscullen just before election time. Though Doyle has not been there in 18 years, it is suggested that he run for Parliament; but after his clearheaded and frank analysis of the country's condition and needs, he is brushed aside. Meanwhile the practical Englishman, efficiently clever in his stupidity, amuses the natives; although his motorcar comes to grief against an Irish pig, he carries the election. On his first day in Ireland, Broadbent proposes to Larry's old sweetheart, Nora, who had been awaiting Larry's return all these years. She calls the Englishman drunk—but he persists until she marries him. Thus, on all fronts, the muddling English come out on top of the sensitive, understanding Irish.

Included among the characters are Larry's uncle, a caricature of the stage Irishman, his speech rolling with "a broth of a bye" and the other stock brogue phrases; and an unfrocked priest, Keegan, who, viewing the world with clear unsentimental eyes, is considered slightly crazy. The English enjoyed these pictures of irresponsible, get-nowhere Irish, overlooking the subtler drubbing they receive at the playwright's hands. The play, however, is a presentation less of persons than of Shaw's ideas on various political problems involving the two islands—free trade, separatism and home rule, the disestablished church, unionists, absentee ownership, etc. The relations between Ireland and England are widely explored. As Shaw was in favor of continuing the union between England and Ireland, Prime Minister Arthur Balfour went to see the play four times, taking with him the Opposition leaders.

Although the London public enjoyed it, the critical reception of the play was less than wholehearted. Said the *London Express* (November 2, 1904): "Shaw is, as is his custom, very largely the hero of his new play . . . The play—if this witty, formless, three-hour satire can be called a play—is a brilliant if pessimistic picture of the relations between the two peoples, geographically so near, temperamentally so far apart." The *Leader* felt otherwise: "Jests should not be too long drawn out; no one was surprised to learn at the finish, when the author was called for, that so eminently sane and sensible a person was no longer in the house." American critics were even less enthusiastic in 1905. The *New York Dramatic Mirror* (October 21) declared: "The amorphous mass of hashed epigrams and peppery phrases dragged along for three and a half weary hours . . . The so-called play began nowhere and ended in the same place." Alan Dale concluded: "nor is it likely that such a strenuous tax on the endurance of lighthearted playgoers will ever be applied again." It was still a tax to Robert Garland 43 years later; for he said (February 11, 1948): "The slight triangular story . . . is not enough to carry *John Bull's Other Island* over the long lean stretches where the wit is on the wane and the dialogue is dated." However, Louis Kronenberger recommended the drama: "The Master's only Irish play ranks in certain respects among his most interesting and significant ones . . . There is more than paradox and fireworks . . . it is sound quite as often as it is scintillating." When the Dublin Gate Theatre presented the play in London (December 4, 1947) it won general critical praise.

   John Bull's Other Island, as Desmond McCarthy pointed out, "is a play with hardly any story, with no climax, without the vestige of a plot, and without anything like an ending, in fact without one of the qualities of the 'well-constructed' play; yet it is nevertheless an absolute success." There is little conflict of action or of thought, or even of emotion—the Irishman feels no jealousy when his old sweetheart turns to the Englishman — in the play; but there is sharp contrast of national characteristics, and keen discussion of topics that the movement of history has not dimmed, still sparking in the brightest wit of the theatre of our day.

MAJOR BARBARA   *George Bernard Shaw*

   In *Major Barbara*, 1905, which Shaw disarmingly labels not a drama but "a discussion", he created one of his most fully realized women, Barbara Undershaft—and gave his usual social satire an unusual turn. For the millionaire munitions manufacturer, Barbara's father, Andrew, preaches that poverty is the vilest sin of man and society: "It is our first duty not to be poor." And Barbara, whom social ills have so deeply wrung that she has joined the Salvation Army, learns that the capitalism she detests maintains the charities on which she pins her faith; she sees that the workers in her father's plant are well-off and contented; and, if she does not come wholly to agree with her father about the futility of helping the poor, at least she comes close to feeling that social evils rise out of the degradation that comes with poverty. These ideas Shaw bandies back and forth, mainly in the last act, with much physical action around the Salvation Army, in which Barbara is a major. The unregenerate Bill Walker "bashes the face" of the harmless little salvationist, Jenny Hill—which, said the London *Truth* (December 7, 1905) "is a disgusting spectacle, and sickens the soul of every decent man and woman in the theatre." Barbara, with not meek but militant Christianity, tumbles Bill from his defiance. Greek professor Adolphus Cusins has joined the Army in love of Barbara; Undershaft comes to her shelter —and plays the trombone in the Army band—on condition that Barbara visit his factory and his workers' homes. There, amid busy and happy surroundings, Cusins shifts jobs from Army to munitions plant; Barbara still will marry him. Social work can do less for the shiftless than hard workers can do for themselves.

At the London premiere on November 28, 1905, Prime Minister Balfour was highly amused, but the critics were divided. The *London Graphic* was enthusiastic, calling the play "bewildering, vastly amusing . . . So witty is the dialogue, and so shrewd, that we do not care to miss a line of all the lengthy speeches. There is not an ounce of padding in the play and there is enough material to supply half a dozen dramatists with half a dozen plays." The *Times* most cogently advanced adverse charges—charges to which Shaw more than once pleaded "Guilty, and I don't care." Said the *Times*: "Mr. Shaw has no dramatic skill, has apparently no dramatic instinct, but he is a thinker who from first to last deals with things worth thinking about. And so we turn with relief, nay, with positive joy, from the intellectual commonplaces of the average English playwright to the intellectual eccentricity of Mr. Shaw. We do it against our better judgment. We feel that the dramatic medium is being wasted and misused. We sorrowfully recognize that Mr. Shaw will never recognize what Pater called the responsibility of the artist to his material. But then the other people, who do possess this sense of responsibility, are so mediocre! And Mr. Shaw is so amusing! A dramatist he is not, but he is a splendid pleasure monger. That is why he has become the fashion in a pleasure seeking world. But we venture to address to him one word of warning. He must not abuse his vogue. Amusing as he is, he is not amusing for quite so long as he supposes. The truth is, he doesn't know when to stop. He lapses into longueurs. Before the end of *Major Barbara* was reached, we caught ourselves yawning."

The play has nevertheless been very popular. New York saw it on December 9, 1915 with a scintillant cast including Grace George and Conway Tearle. On November 19, 1928 New York saw it again with Dudley Digges and Helen Westley. *Variety* (November 21) reported that "*Barbara* isn't dated like some of the other pieces." A London production the next year, the *Era* (March 13, 1929) called "splendidly alive . . . the second act is as good as anything in modern drama . . . the long last act touches, despite its extravagances and humors, profundities that make the subjects of most other pieces appear as soap bubbles . . ."

Barbara stands beside Candida as Shaw's most appealing woman. There is broad humor in his treatment of her; she leans over the big bass drum for a tender kiss. There is practical common-sense behind her social rebellion. There is a staunch and vigorous will behind her devout religion. And her various qualities blend to form a rounded and charming creature. "There is a vein of poetry in Mr. Shaw, amongst all else that he is or chooses to be," said the *Boston Transcript* (December 31, 1929); "in *Major Barbara*, it touches Barbara herself with beauty."

Despite its vivid portraits and its well-directed shafts of satire, the play has been called the most widely misunderstood of all Shaw's dramas —probably because Shaw in his prefatory "First Aid to Critics" explained his purpose and thus roused the critics' suspicions. This is clearly his most Marxian play; in it, as William Irvine stated in *The Universe of G. B. S.* (1949), he "impatiently sweeps away meditation and ideas as totally incapable of influencing the world of action, and finds in the violent clash of materialistic egotisms themselves the promise of a Marxist millenium." Looking upon the wretchedness of the world around him, Shaw was seeking a cure. In *Man and Superman** he concluded that it is thought, in the long run, the intellect dictating to the will, that shapes history. In *Major Barbara*, dismissing ideas as impotent, he declared that the pressure of events will forge a Marxian utopia. Barbara compromises with capitalism; but Cusins, while going over to Undershaft's factory, works with the dream of a revolution. In *Androcles and the Lion**, Shaw saw salvation in faith, in the individual sense of moral values. Barbara is saved by compromise; Lavinia (in *Androcles and the Lion*) does not compromise but is saved by a deus ex machina, the Emperor; Joan of Arc (in *Saint Joan**) refuses to compromise, and moves to martyrdom. Barbara and Cusins are dreamers; representing the Christian morality that most folks preach, they embrace the gunpowder morality that most folks practice—telling each other they will make gunpowder work for Christian ends. But Shaw gives little comfort to this optimism of force.

The drama's ideas have to squeeze through incidents and surface drives that keep the stage lively and the audience amused. Among recent productions was one in "modern dress", opening in London March 5, 1935, with Maurice Evans as Cusins. Community theatres constantly revive the play. It was turned into a film in 1941, with Wendy Hiller and Rex Harrison. *Variety* observed: "One more crack about this Shaw guy. He'd make a hot Hollywood gag man." The evidence: when the guard reminds old Undershaft he mustn't take anything combustible near the plant, his wife exclaims: "Sir, I hope you're not referring to me!" W. S. Gilbert before Shaw observed that for public consumption one must always gild the philosophic pill. Shaw—who always proclaimed that his chief concern was with the gilders—in *Major Barbara* makes delightful mixture of merriment and meaning. We laugh as our prejudices bark their shins against the stumbling blocks of common-sense alternately set in our path by practical Andrew Undershaft and romantic Major Barbara.

THE DOCTOR'S DILEMMA   *George Bernard Shaw*

Shaw calls *The Doctor's Dilemma*, 1906, a comedy about death, a tragedy because "its theme—that of a man of genius who is not also a man of honor—is the most tragic theme to people who can understand its importance." In the Preface to the play he states: "Even the comedy which runs concurrently with it: the comedy of the medical profession as at present organized in England, is a tragic comedy, with death conducting the orchestra. Yet the play is funnier than most farces. The tragedy of Dubedat is not his death but his life; nevertheless his death, a purely poetic one, would once have seemed wholly incompatible with laughter."

Behind the play are several actual incidents. Shaw had heard one of his medical friends, Sir Almroth Wright, once ask if a patient was worth saving. William Archer in the *London Tribune* (July 14, 1906), in praising the tragedies of Ibsen*, commented on the fact that Shaw's characters never die: "It is not the glory, but the limitation, of Mr. Shaw's theatre, that it is peopled by immortals." And that summer, Granville-Barker came to Shaw in search of a play. Out of such impulsions Shaw wrote *The Doctor's Dilemma*, which Granville-Barker, acting Dubedat, produced in London on November 20, 1906, with Lillah McCarthy as Jennifer. The play was successful from the very first.

Of several doctors in the play, one, old Sir Patrick, has no faith in physicians whatsoever. Each of the others has his pet nostrum or treatment. "Stimulate the phagocytes." Dr. Walpole diagnoses every case as blood poison; his prescription: remove the nuciform sac. Sir Ralph Bloomfield Bonington ("B.B.") cures all by vaccination, though Sir Colenso Ridgeon warns him: Inoculate in the positive phase and you cure; inoculate in the negative phase and you kill. But B.B. has cured little Prince Henry with Ridgeon's new discovery, opsonin; hence Ridgeon's knighthood and eminence. It is the scant supply of opsonin (which "butters the disease germs so the white corpuscles eat them") that creates the doctor's dilemma. Jennifer Dubedat beseeches Ridgeon to save her husband, a brilliant but amoral artist. Dr. Blenkinsop, less successful than the other physicians, also needs the treatment. Ridgeon can take but one—which? He invites Dubedat to a dinner with his colleagues, after which he will decide. At the dinner, Dubedat borrows money from all the doctors he can separately "touch", including Blenkinsop. When he leaves, the maid discloses that she is Dubedat's wife — Jennifer is living with him without benefit of clergy. Partly for these reasons, partly because he himself is in love with Jennifer, Ridgeon takes as his patient Blenkinsop, leaving Dubedat to B.B. Dubedat dies; Blenkinsop lives to no good purpose. At the posthumous showing of Dubedat's paintings, Ridgeon meets Jennifer, who is writing "The Story of a King of Men. By His Wife". Jennifer is happy; and Ridgeon is aghast to discover that she dislikes him intensely, that she looks upon him as an old fogy, and that, in accord with Dubedat's wishes, she has already remarried. Then, murmurs Ridgeon, "I have committed a purely disinterested murder."

In the conversation of the doctors, Shaw satirizes the stupidity and the cupidity of the medical profession. Balanced against the doctors, who deem themselves men of science, is the man of art, Dubedat. He is not always granted the better argument. Thus — in a passage omitted from the 1921 Boston production — when Dubedat declares "I don't belive there's such a thing as sin," Sir Patrick retorts: "Well, sir, there are people who don't believe there's such a thing as disease, either. They call themselves Christian Scientists, I believe. They'll just suit your complaint. We can do nothing for you." At his death, however, Dubedat has, if not the last word, the most challenging. The "exquisite beauty of his deathbed statement of the artist's creed", as John Mason Brown called it (March 15, 1941), presses a genuine tenderness into the caustic satire of the drama. Hence Gilbert Gabriel (November 22, 1927) declared that the play "manages, for all its Molieresque maunderings against the medical men, its wordy clash of travesties on the inoculators, the vivisectionists, and the fashionable quacks, to lash itself into a loveliness of romantic foolery. Such a smile is on it as even the shadow of the tombstone cannot darken . . . He has made high comedy of death. Pitifully, terribly, before your eyes a rascally young genius dies—and Shaw gives you grace to laugh at it." In truth, the scene is touched with irony, for Dubedat overhears the doctors say that he is putting on a performance and he agrees with them. His "performance" is impeccable, as a last performance should be. A rascal in his living, he proves himself an artist in his dying.

The play had its New York premiere March 26, 1915, with Granville-Barker and Lillah McCarthy. Among New York revivals are that of 1927 by the Theatre Guild with Alfred Lunt and Lynn Fontanne; and that of 1941 with Katharine Cornell and Raymond Massey, which ran for 254 performances. There were London revivals in 1923, 1926, 1939, and 1942. The play continues popular, partly because the layman's awe of doctors makes him ready to laugh at them, partly because of more intrinsic merits. After the 1942 opening, the London *Stage* (March 12) exclaimed: "After nearly forty years it has still the power continuously to compel attention by the sheer interest of its story, the coherence of its argument, the cut-and-thrust dialogue, the sharply defined characterization, and the stinging wit with which Shaw pricks the medical profession." The New York City Center production, opening January 11, 1955, was equally well received.

The conscienceless artist, we are told, is drawn from an actual person, Edward Aveling, with whom Karl Marx' youngest daughter lived much like Jennifer—even to the episode with the maid. The value to society of such a genius-scamp is moot. Indeed, in the play "we are never certain", *Stage* continued, "whether the doctor sacrifices Dubedat on strictly ethical grounds . . . or because he hopes to marry the widow. This obscurity or, it may be, this dual motive, is a flaw in the play." On the same grounds, Desmond MacCarthy objected that "Ridgeon does not do justice to his own motives; he did not decide against Dubedat entirely because he coveted his wife, or because he wished to save her from disillusionment; so this admission on his part confuses the audience's recollection of what has gone before." Rather, it may quicken an alert audience to note that there is no inevitable correspondence between word and deed; not only deliberate liars may say one thing and act another. Life is quite likely to leave a man not fully aware of the comparative weights of the mixed elements in his motives; and — especially when a fate we all must meet is involved — it is good theatre to let the audience exercise its own judgment. There is intellectual exercise aplenty in *The Doctor's Dilemma*.

FANNY'S FIRST PLAY   *George Bernard Shaw*

One of the less earnest of Shaw's pieces, this play, written in 1911 as "a potboiler", combines satire of middle-class society with humorous prodding of the drama critics of the day. It remains a delightful trifle, and a trifle more. As the *London Times* (August 1, 1935) remarked after a revival, the play "has become a costume piece living on its wit. It has enough wit to live on very well."

The play contrasts Count O'Dowda and his daughter Fanny. The Count is a "Count of the Holy Roman Empire"; in the twentieth century, he shuts the nineteenth carefully beyond his doors, and dwells by choice in the costumes and the manners of the eighteenth. His daughter, a bright young lass out of Cambridge, has written a play and the pleased papa is producing it, anonymously, with four London critics as his guests. Fanny's first play turns out to be something quite other than the eighteenth century pastoral masque the Count her father expects. It is a modern picture of middle-class life, with Bobby Gilbey and Margaret Knox—children of two shopkeeper partners—both on separate frolicking parties landing in jail. Bobby, held in check at home by his respectable parents, has been seeking a checkered career with "Darling Dora" Delaney. Margaret, guarded by her pious folks, felt freed by an evening's prayer at a Salvation Festival, went to a dance hall and in a fracas knocked out two teeth of a policeman. The children, back from a fortnight in jail, break the engagement their parents had pressed them into; Bobby teams up with Darling Dora; and Margaret finds a mate in the footman, Juggins—who turns out to be the brother of a duke, led by his social conscience to take a job.

After this play, the four critics invited by the Count discuss, not its merits, but who the author might be. (The fact that *Fanny's First Play* itself was presented anonymously added further spice to this discussion. A program note read: "The epigram in the second act is by Bernard Shaw"). Suggested as authors of Fanny's piece are Granville-Barker and Shaw, who thus come in for analysis. The critic Flawner Bannal, a composite caricature, is asked by the Count whether it is a good play. He responds: "If it's by a good author, it's a good play, naturally. That stands to reason. Who *is* the author? Tell me that; and I'll place the play for you to a hair's breadth." The rather broad caricatures of the critics are thinly disguised exaggerations of actual writers; one of them, Shaw said, assisted in the make-up with which the actor simulated his appearance. The critics whom Shaw did not introduce, he impishly reported in the Preface, "were somewhat hurt." ("Trotter", in the play, is the critic Walkley, "Vaughan" is Baughan, and "Gunn" is Cannan.)

Subordinate to the critical spoofing, yet present and pressed, is the social satire. The eighteenth century Count protests that he would not have minded "what people call an immoral play. Love beautifies every romance and justifies every audacity." What the Count does object to is the lack of respect the children show to their parents, to the general frankness, to the way they "tear down the veils". One critic—in the play —detects, "beneath all the assumed levity of that poor waif and stray", Darling Dora, a note of genuine passion and compassion. Another critic protests: "What does it all come to? An attempt to expose the supposed hypocrisy of the Puritan middle class of England: people just as good as the author anyhow." Another critic, Charles Darnton—outside the play, after the New York opening—declared: "*Fanny's First Play* is really a three-ring circus, with a human menagerie containing the only collection of trained drama critics . . . Not only does complacent Respectability get an awful biff in the eye, but frilled Romance is knocked clean over the ropes." Shaw's Fabian friends thought he was treating his subjects too lightly. Beatrice Webb wrote to Lillah McCarthy: "I wish you could persuade G. B. S. to do a piece of serious work, and not pursue this somewhat barren tilting at the family."

The first London production was on April 19, 1911, by and with Lillah McCarthy. It ran for 622 performances. New York saw it on September 16, 1912. It has been widely and frequently played since, especially in colleges; for its social satire pricks gently for the freedom of youth, and satire of critical pretension—though really the play buffets men of straw —always pleases young folk interested in art. Shaw's neatly delivered blows feel to each person like a pat on the back; it's his neighbor gets the drubbing! The multiplex smile of the master gleams in *Fanny's First Play.*

ANDROCLES AND THE LION   *George Bernard Shaw*

In this play Shaw retells the old tale of the Christian wanderer who plucks a thorn from the paw of an anguished lion and later, "flung to the lions" in a Roman arena, is recognized and fawned upon by the beast he has befriended. The story occurs in the *Attic Nights* of Aulus Gellius, about 150 A.D. Shaw extracts all the circus fun out of the situation, showing Caesar scared to death of the beast, then taking credit for taming it. At odd moments somehow he lifts the play from low comedy to simple yet high assumption of human dignity. Throughout, there is constant probing of basic religious problems.

Accompanying Androcles on the march to the arena are several other Christians. The fierce and brawny Ferrovius is capable of breaking the neck of their Roman guard. And there is the beauteous and aristocratic Lavinia, whom the Roman Captain is perplexed to find dooming herself to the arena. They are all Christians; yet, by a Shavian turn, each holds a separate, individual creed in time of crisis. Thus, as Shaw points out in the Preface, "Androcles is a humanitarian naturalist, whose views surprise everyone. Lavinia, a clever and fearless freethinker, shocks the Pauline Ferrovius, who is comparatively stupid and conscience-ridden." Ferrovius is an early Puritan, wrung with suppressed desires. Caesar, taken with the lion's meek behavior, lionlike spares the martyrs.

The world premiere of the play was in Berlin, November 25, 1912. London saw it on September 1, 1913, with O. P. Heggie and Lillah McCarthy; the same two enacted the play in New York on January 27, 1915; the *Commercial Advertiser* reported that the play was "irresistible even to the gentry who are irritated by the Shavian satire and dialectic." In December 1925, the New York Theatre Guild presented the play, with an eerie forest, painted by Miguel Covarrubias, in which Androcles in fear and the lion in agony crawl toward one another. A Negro Federal Theatre group had a run of over 50 performances in 1939. In the spring of 1946 Ernest Truex played Androcles; on December 19 of that year he came to New York in the play, sponsored by the American Repertory Theatre. While George Jean Nathan disliked the production, he declared that the play's "propulsive wisdom and wit have not materially dimmed." It is still a delightful romp, with a lift for the mind and the spirit. It opened the new playhouse in Cleveland, December 12, 1949. The deft dialogue between the Christian maid and the pagan Captain recalls that in Wilson Barrett's novel *The Sign of the Cross* (1895), in which the Roman prefect walks hand in hand with the maid into the arena.

In a note for the London premiere, Shaw stated: "There is nothing incredible in the story except the theatrical coincidence of the meeting of the two in the arena. Such coincidences are privileged on the stage, and are the special delight of this particular author." For the American production, he added: "None of the characters are monsters: they are just such people as may be found in the United States today, placed in the monstrous circumstances created by the Roman Empire." We can, in truth, recognize such figures in the world today. More searchingly, we find still insistent in our lives the questions moot in the play. Most happily, *Androcles and the Lion* not only provides excellent entertainment but also that exhilarant sense of human worth, that exaltation of the spirit, which is the noblest puissance of the drama.

PYGMALION   *George Bernard Shaw*

Annoyed at the English reception of his earlier plays, Irishman Shaw arranged for a continental premiere of *Pygmalion*. It opened in Vienna on October 16, 1913, and was produced in Berlin a fortnight later. Mrs. Patrick Campbell and Herbert Beerbohm Tree appeared in the play in London on April 11, 1914. At curtain call on opening night, Beerbohm Tree apologized that "the author had been so upset by the loud and frequent applause that he could not stand it any longer and fled in disgust." Shaw sought the notoriety that sprang from insulting the public. Part of the excitement rose from the fact that Mrs. Pat Campbell as Eliza first used the exclamatory word *bloody* on the London stage.

It was a series of such antics, in his life and in his plays, that long kept Shaw's measure from being properly taken. In *Pygmalion* the story is artificial, pleasantly comic; the social implications reside in minor characters and behind the tale. The tale itself is a modern parallel of the story of Pygmalion, legendary sculptor and King of Cyprus, who fell in love with his own statute of Aphrodite. At his prayer, Aphrodite brought the statue to life as Galatea, and Pygmalion married her. Shaw's "Pygmalion" is Henry Higgins, Professor of phonetics, who, come upon a cockney flower-girl in a rainstorm, wagers that in three months he can so transform her as to pass her off for a lady. To Higgins, this is but a task that he accomplishes, a wager that he wins; but in Eliza Doolittle, the flower girl, a new personality has been created. With the manners and speech of a lady, she cannot fall back into her old life, and with those ways has come an asserting will, which selects Henry Higgins, her "creator", as her mate. To Higgins' dismay, he finds that his "laboratory case" has surged into all his life, with emotional entanglements he had not anticipated. "Driven to extreme exasperation," as Brooks Atkinson put the play's ending, Higgins "proceeds to wring Eliza's infernally beautiful neck; and the light of victory instantly gleams in her eyes." Higgins has won his wager, but Eliza has won her man.

Beneath the comedy lies a satire on the superficiality of class distinctions. This is made explicit in the character of Eliza's father, Doolittle, who calls himself one of "the undeserving poor" and is one of Shaw's richest comedy creations.

The story of Pygmalion and Galatea occurs in Ovid's *Metamorphoses*, about 15 A.D. It was dramatized in English by John Marston*, as the *Metamorphosis of Pygmalion's Image*, 1598. W. S. Gilbert* used the story for his comedy (without music) *Pygmalion and Galatea*, 1871, which makes the sculptor a married man; under the fire of the wife Cynisca's jealousy, Galatea decides that her original state was happier, and turns back into a statue. Shaw has combined a modern transformation of the Pygmalion story with that of a Cinderella girl, in one of his liveliest comedies.

Shaw said of the play: "I delight in throwing it at the heads of the wiseacres who repeat the parrot cry that art should never be didactic. It goes to prove my contention that great art can never be anything else." Aristotle earlier observed that all art is didactic—to the adolescent mind.

Mrs. Patrick Campbell brought the play to New York on October 12, 1914, with Philip Merivale replacing Beerbohm Tree, after a German production at the New York Irving Place Theatre. The play is one of Shaw's most popular, with revivals every season or two all around the country. New York saw it in 1926 in Spanish, with Catalina Barcena, and in a Theatre Guild production with Lynn Fontanne. In 1931 Frieda Inescourt and Tom Powers played the leading roles; in 1940, Ruth Chatterton enacted Eliza. The revival on December 26, 1945, with Gertrude Lawrence, Raymond Massey, and Melville Cooper was, as Robert Coleman remarked, "one of the nicest holiday gifts." Wendy Hiller and Leslie Howard acted in the filmed version made in 1938.

Of the play, in the Theatre Guild production, Brooks Atkinson (November 16, 1926) declared: "What remains most vividly is what Mr. Shaw understands more shrewdly than anyone else: the jumble of human relations." Gertrude Lawrence's performance in 1945 was charming but sentimentalized.

Pygmalion continues the Shavian thesis, first seen in *You Never Can Tell**, most fully developed in *Man and Superman**, that the woman is the pursuer in the struggle of the sexes, while the man too tardily wakens to his fate. The popularity of *Pygmalion*—in addition to the continuing sparks the steel of Shaw's wit strikes from the flint of the alert mind—rises from its amalgamation of the social satire and the story and (granting the initial artificiality of the wager) from the engaging conflict of contrasted personalities that not merely reveal themselves but grow through the development of the tale. Eliza grows more aware; Higgins grows more human. The audience grows in discernment and delight.

HEARTBREAK HOUSE   *George Bernard Shaw*

The upheavals of the first World War shook Shaw's thinking into distinctly pessimistic channels. Influenced by Chekhov, especially *The Cherry Orchard**, he worked for several years upon "a fantasia in the Russian manner on English themes" which developed into *Heartbreak House* in 1919. However, he would not permit its public reading or presentation amid the escapist frivolities of the current theatre in a land where his attempted objectivity was being labeled pro-German. The play was printed in 1919, and given its world premiere—on Shaw's insistence being held until after the presidential election—by the Theatre Guild in New York on November 12, 1920.

In the long Preface to *Heartbreak House* Shaw envisaged but one generation before another war, with Germany and Russia, defeated in World War I, again great powers in the world. In his Preface, Shaw explains that "*Heartbreak House* is cultured, leisured Europe before the war", where futile culture and talk spread through an economic, political, and moral vacuum. In England, the alternative to Heartbreak House was Horseback Hall, where the same vacuum was filled with futile talk and hunting. In the play, we watch a group of futile humans, in the Sussex home of old Captain Shotover, endlessly talking of culture and politics and one another, flirting, maneuvering for power or security, laying their souls bare.

Among those gathered in the home of the 88-year-old sea captain are his daughter Mrs. Hesione Hushabye and her philandering husband, Hector; his other daughter, Lady Ariadne Utterwood, just back after years in the Colonies her husband governs; Ellie Dunn, a young thing who loves Hector, woos the Captain, and for a time wants to wed Boss Mangan for his money; Ellie's father, Mazzini Dunn, "a born soldier of freedom" who wrote pamphlets and watched the world and saw that nothing ever really changes; Mangan, who mistakes Hesione's effusion for invitation; and a burglar who deliberately gets himself caught, so that he can pour out a sob story and take a collection. These folk discuss all possible subjects, including the world and its movement toward self-destruction. The burglar and the business man scorn the others' talk, talk, talk, but do not hesitate to seek advantage from their impracticality. When enemy bombs begin to break nearby, the practical burglar and the business man Mangan run out to the cave in the gravel pit — which is where a bomb strikes, sparing the aimless talkers in the house. Yet these are held in the grim prophecy of the Captain, of the ship they voyage in, "the soul's prison we call England . . . She will strike and sink and split. Do you think the laws of God will be suspended in favor of England because you were born in it?" Staunchly against that prophecy England still battles today.

Both Chekhov's *The Cherry Orchard* and Shaw's play show the decomposition of society through a group gathered in a country house; but, as William Irvine pointed out in *The Universe of G. B. S.* (1949), the characters in Shaw's play are allegorical; in Chekhov's typical. Thus we find the Captain standing here as stalwart old England. "His house, built like a ship, somehow symbolizes the sea-trading out of which English wealth and commerce grew. The selling of his soul to the devil in youth and his marriage with a black witch in Zanzibar signify the ruthless colonial exploitation and the savage insistence on prestige inseparable from imperial power . . . When he looks into the past he is Sir Francis Drake — and Bernard Shaw when he looks into the future. He is noticeably Bernard Shaw, for he is fond of macaroni and generally regarded as mad." The other characters likewise symbolize aspects of English life. Lady Utterwood is the Empire; Hesione Hushabye, the British home. Mazzini Dunn is the Victorian liberal — still a lingering form: sentimental and therefore ineffectual. His daughter Ellie is the modern girl, who joins with the Captain as youth and "Old England" must unite. From these symbolical figures, as contrasted with Chekhov's types, it follows that "*The Cherry Orchard* is prophetic as a slide beneath a microscope is prophetic; *Heartbreak House*, as the interpretation of a formula or the demonstration of a theorem." The warning stands, that, without our most careful bolstering, civilization will fall.

This brilliant though pessimistic satire was given a superb production by the Theatre Guild, with Helen Westley and Dudley Digges. When the Guild expressed a desire to cut the play, Shaw cabled "Abandon play. Cancel contract." By mail he explained: "I knew that the cutting of a single syllable would mean failure, as I had myself cut the play down to the bone, as I always do, before printing it . . . Nothing would induce me to consent to the omission of one word of the text, or the curtailment of one minute of the time . . ." The play was produced verbatim; and although it ran for 129 performances, the critics felt there was too much of it. The *New York Sun* called it "a conversational debauch"; Heywood Broun said "we like the needle, but we could dispense with the haystack." The *New York Times* considered the play "a rehash of all his often reiterated scoldings and complaints against everything in English domestic and political life with which he happens to disagree." The play opened in London October 18, 1921; Birmingham saw it in 1923 and 1930; London again in 1932 with Cedric Hardwicke and Edith Evans, and in 1936-1937. New York saw a revival by the Mercury Theatre in 1938 with Orson Welles. On-Stage presented the play in 1950, off Broadway.

The *London Times* (April 26, 1932) sought to analyze the play: "The first act of *Heartbreak House* is exceptional in Mr. Shaw's theatre, for the pleasure it gives is predominantly aesthetic. It has form as well as substance . . . Somewhere about the middle of the second act one ceases to believe in the stable existence of any of the people on any one imaginative plane . . . feeling is dead, and form is broken." There is general agreement that this is one of Shaw's greatest plays, but that the exuberance of the drama detracts from its form and therefore from its power. Brooks Atkinson said (April 30, 1938): "It is the play of a clown and a prophet, full of caustic insight—but O Lord, how long!" Richard Watts felt that "most of it is so shrewd, so wise, so brilliant and so prophetic that the flaws seem of little importance." John Mason Brown was a bit more reserved: "Although genius sails proudly upon the wind-tossed oceans of its speech, it sails on a vessel which is covered with barnacles, burdened with a poorly packed cargo, steered in a haphazard manner, and manned by an unruly crew." Similarly divided was the English critic Ivor Brown, in the London *Observer* (March 14, 1937): "Captain Shotover is one of the greatest of Shavian creations: half fire and air, half rum and realism, he is archangel, inventor, master-mariner, and tough old critic of the social scene. His memory is a morass, yet his mind is sharp as a sword. But he trumpets his verities under handicap. His delivery of judgment on the world is not prolix in itself, but is spoiled by the prolixity of others. Mr. Shaw is rarely guilty of creating a bore, but Mr. and Mrs. Hushabye come as near to it as any of his creatures, and Randall Utterwood is little better . . . *Heartbreak House* has the quality of a masterpiece, though here and there the quantity be swollen and the matter over-ripe."

It is, nevertheless, the conversation in *Heartbreak House* that burgens to searching and searing criticism of the well-meaning, esteemed, and apparently estimable people that help to ruin the world. Some works, like *Moby Dick*, like Rabelais', achieve virtue through their very excess. In refusing to allow his drama to be cut, Shaw showed that a dramatist may be wiser than his critics. They may have the last word on first nights; but his words continue their challenge beyond the footlights.

BACK TO METHUSALEH   *George Bernard Shaw*

Shaw's ponderings about the sorry state of the world led him to the conclusion that only if men live long enough to grow really mature and wise (say 300 years), can civilization be saved. His theory of creative evolution, partly suggested by Samuel Butler's *Life and Habit* (1877), is developed in the Preface, and illustrated in the five parts of Shaw's longest play, the "metabiological pentateuch", *Back to Methusaleh*, 1918-20. The preface has some 30,000 words; the play, 90,000.

Part I, "In the Beginning," opens in the Garden of Eden, where Lilith tears herself asunder to create Adam and Eve, and where the Serpent reveals to Eve the secret of continuance. Eve has been asking "Why? Why?"; the Serpent starts evolution on its way by asking "Why not?" A few centuries later, we see Adam, the digger, waiting for death; Cain, the killer, grasping power and thereby hastening death; and Eve, hoping for something that will make life worthwhile.

Part II, "The Gospel of the Brothers Barnabas," is a satire of society, especially of politics, at the time of the writing. Joyce Burge and Lubin are thinly disguised portraits of Lloyd George and Asquith. The idea of longevity is introduced by Professor Barnabas, and the politicians, thinking he has an elixir, want to decide which persons are to be allowed to use it. When they discover that Barnabas has only a biological theory based upon the human will, Burge plans to use it as a plank in his election campaign.

Part III, "The Thing Happens," set in the year 2150, presents Burge-Lubin, President of the British Isles, conferring with Barnabas about an American invention of a method of breathing under water, which may upset their tables of life-expectancy (according to which all persons work only between the ages of 13 and 43. The country is well-governed, because the public services are manned by Chinese: "Justice is impartiality. Only strangers are impartial.") Motion pictures, shown by the American inventor, of well-known persons that have drowned, reveal that the Archbishop has survived the generations. We knew him as the Reverend Bill Haslam of Part II; he is now 283 years old. The Domestic Minister, Mrs. Lutestring, has lived for 274 years. The two determine to perpetuate the race of long-livers, as the Chinese Chief Secretary points out (with double-edged satire) that the English are still children at sixty and seventy, hence "are potentially the most highly developed race on earth, and would actually be the greatest if you could live long enough to attain to maturity."

Part IV, "Tragedy of an Elderly Gentleman," is set in 3000 A.D., when the "normal" (long-lived) people have taken control, and the short-lived are attended by nurses. The capital of the British Empire is now Baghdad. A short-lived elderly gentleman has come with the Prime Minister to Ireland, center of the normal, to consult the Oracle. She bids the Minister "Go home, poor fool!"; but the elderly gentleman begs permission to stay, and by her compassionate glance the Oracle kills him.

Part V, "As Far As Thought Can Reach," shows children, in 31,920 A.D., hatched from eggs, born adolescent, living some four years in love and play, in artistic creation and procreation—then transmuted to "Ancients". The Ancients live endlessly, until an accident fells them; they spend their centuries without need of nourishment or sleep, in profound and almost wordless meditation. One of the youngsters, a sculptor (Pygmalion; Shaw again uses the name), creates two living dolls that call themselves Ozymandias, king of kings, and Cleopatra-Semiramis, whose human misdemeanors and petty emotions disgust the young ones, until an Ancient wills them to die. The youngsters are briefly bored until the Ancients leave; then briefly bewildered as one of their own group goes off: it is his time to become an Ancient. As night falls, the ghosts of the first living creatures appear from the distance of 4004 B.C., and weigh the centuries. The serpent says "I am justified. For I chose wisdom and the knowledge of good and evil; and now there is no evil; and wisdom and good are one." Lilith, who had given Eve "the greatest of gifts: curiosity", bids the ages dread, of all things, stagnation; she looks forward to "the whirlpool in pure intelligence that, when the world began, was a whirlpool in pure force," and to the day when life shall fill and shall master the myriad starry mansions to their uttermost confines.

Shaw declared, in the *Candid Friend* (May 11, 1901): "I exhausted romanticism before I was ten years old." He has been creating his own brand ever since; *Back To Methusaleh* is its fullest flowering. However, the play lacks the mellowness that the theme deserves; it is embittered by Shaw's disillusionment and rage at the hideous folly of World War I. Thus, in what many think the most vigorous of the parts, "The Gospel of the Brothers Barnabas," he lashes savagely at his political butts, although for his buffetings he has fashioned hardly more than men of straw. In "The Thing Happens," his successful candidate for the House of Commons "was released from the County Lunatic Asylum a fortnight ago. Not mad enough for the lethal chamber: not sane enough for any place but the division lobby." A sharpness has taken the place of the often more even-toned wit; but Shaw is waging the most serious war of his dramatic struggles. *Back to Methusaleh* — more intense than *Man and Superman**, more wide-ranging than *Heartbreak House** — shows long conflict and the ultimate triumph of hope over despair. It is a wry and dry faith that conquers.

Back To Methusaleh undoubtedly represents Shaw's fullest and most deeply pondered study of the problems of mankind. It is, however, scintillant and searching, satiric and expository, rather than dramatic: a thesis in the theatre. The basic problem man faces, as Shaw presents it, is to grow strong enough to surmount the destructive forces that man's own development has loosed within the world. He can achieve this through the creative evolution of the self-conscious mind, achieving indefinite longevity. This leaves him free for the ecstatic contemplation of the free intelligence, which Shaw, in a measure, equates with God.

The play, searching thus widely down the centuries, is far too long for an evening's presentation. In its world premiere (opening February 27, 1922), the New York Theatre Guild divided it into three parts, showing each for a week in turn, to a total of 25 complete performances; in England, under Sir Barry Jackson in Birmingham beginning October 9, 1923, and in London beginning February 18, 1924, the parts were played on successive evenings and matinees. The play was presented in Berlin in 1925; in public readings in New York in 1933; again in London in 1935; in Pasadena in 1938.

After a London revival that spread the various parts over several evenings of February and March 1947, Harold Hobson of the *Sunday Times* was condescending. When "The Tragedy of an Elderly Gentleman" was reached, he declared (February 25) that the play "seems to be approaching the anecdotal instead of the apocalyptic." His shrewdest remarks (March 18) came for "the last and best of the Methusaleh plays: "To argue the hind leg off a dog isn't quite the same thing as to convince him. The dog may lose his leg and retain his opinion. In fact, in *As Far As Thought Can Reach*, Mr. Shaw, the master of paradox, gives the impression of being paradox-trapped. What is he trying to prove? That the emotions are a discarded foolishness; that art, which appeals to them, is useless. How does he try to prove it? By the resources of his art . . . declaring in cadences of undying loveliness that nowhere in life is there any loveliness at all. Every argument Mr. Shaw brings forward is contradicted by the overtones of the phrases in which he expresses it." By this time, however, *Back To Methuselah* had been widely accepted on the stage, and even more widely read.

The critics that saw the premieres were on the whole unimpressed. The *New York Sun* (March 14, 1922) called it "not merely undramatic; it is antidramatic." Heywood Broun declared Shaw "so passionately sincere in this play that it is embarrassing. And after embarrassment has begun to wear off, it is boring." Kenneth MacGowan was annoyed at Shaw's classifying artistic creation as adolescent play, "using art to foreswear art . . ." In England, J. T. Grein declared in the *Illustrated London News* (March 8, 1924) "The play is a magnificent jest—the greatest literary jest ever attempted by a great man, who, conscious that he could do with his public as he pleases, pulled it by the leg and — pulled both off, leg, as well as jest."

A condensed version of the play, arranged by Ellis St. Joseph, was effectively presented by Valerie Bettis, Bramwell Fletcher, Arnold Moss, and Blanche Yurka at New York University, December 11, 1952.

A shrewd criticism of Shaw's ultimate concept was advanced in the *London Times* of January 18, 1952: "Mr. Shaw's Utopia, in which everyone lives to the age of Methuselah and dies at last by accident, is a kind of composite photograph of all the more serious heresies, dominated by the supreme intellectual heresy that the Divine life consists of contemplation . . . Once again we have a religion that is not good enough because it is the expression of a nausea for actual things, of a mere desire for release . . . This barren climax has come to religious thought again and again, so long as it has been thought about religion mistaking itself for religion."

Whatever its shortcomings, *Back To Methuselah* gave timely expression to far-searching thoughts on an insistent problem. Its length may cause it to remain largely a reader's drama; but it remains a delightful experience for the mind in quest of maturity. The play both indicates and illustrates that quest.

SAINT JOAN   *George Bernard Shaw*

Unquestionably the most dramatic treatment of the martyred Maid's story is Shaw's *Saint Joan*. Written out of no social or socialist urge, it is probably his greatest play. Archibald Henderson has expressed the view that it is "the greatest play in English since Shakespeare."

It was not to be expected that Shaw would present the mere story of the Maid. While he followed with great accuracy the details of her trial for witchcraft, he increased Joan's understanding of her religious role. He saw her as the first Protestant, the first to stand steadfast for freedom of conscience against the dictates of the Church. The play presents the episodes of Joan's betrayal, the trial, a touching Inquisition

scene, Joan's disavowal of the voices, then her retraction and assertion
of her own judgment, her own belief in the authenticity of the voices —
which means her death. Shrewdly cynical pictures are given of the
French prelates and the generals who for various political reasons desire
that Joan shall be discredited and removed. In a dream of the year
1455, King Charles, whom Joan had crowned, rejoices that she has been
cleared of the charge of witchcraft. An Epilogue dated 1920—the year of
the Maid's canonization—permits Shaw to examine the meaning of her
story to the world today. The ghosts of those that condemned her come,
each to sing her praise but, on the very grounds of his praising, to urge
that she come not again to the world today. Joan, anguished, cries: "Oh
God, when will the world be ready to receive Thy saints?"

The world premiere took place on December 28, 1923, in the New
York Theatre Guild production with Winifred Lenihan. Dame Sybil
Thorndike enacted Joan in London in 1924, where the Old Vic revived
the play in 1934 with Mary Newcomb and Maurice Evans. Evans came
to New York to act in a 1936 production, opening March 9, with Katharine
Cornell. Elisabeth Bergner enacted Joan in Berlin. Luise Rainer played
in a Piscator production in Washington, D. C. in 1940; Uta Hagen, in a
New York revival, opening October 4, 1951.

Although in March 1924 the French Minister gave Winifred Lenihan
the "Gold Medal of Jeanne d'Arc", the play was roundly attacked in
Paris. In September 1936 "Catholic Action", by publishing a list of
changes it felt should be made, broke off the project for filming Shaw's
play; the story of the Maid was next screened after the stage success of
Anderson's *Joan of Lorraine*. The best screening of the story remains
The Passion of Joan of Arc, 1929, with Mme. Falconetti as Joan; in this,
a series of close-ups of the faces of Joan, her judges, and her prosecutors,
creates a tensely dramatic mood.

Shaw, interested in presenting Joan as taking the first steps of individualism, failed to make a theological distinction drawn by the Church,
between the claim to private judgment regarding the teachings of the
Church in faith or morals, and the claim to private inspiration. The first
claim, always disallowed, produces the heretics, as Wyclif and Luther.
The second claim, when allowed, manifests the mystics, including Joan.
Shaw's oversight of this distinction was probably deliberate, intended to
press his thesis that Joan was a pioneer of the Reformation. How Shaw's
own pressing of distinctions may be overlooked was shown in the comments of Percy Hammond (December 30, 1923): "just another example of
Mr. Shaw's gift for interminable rag-chewing . . . some of this surplus
conversation is none too good. Thus 'Are you an Englishman?' 'No, I'm
a gentleman.'" In his review of the 1936 revival, Percy Hammond repeated this quotation, and added: "George Kaufman might get away with
a crack like that, but Howard Dietz or Moss Hart would be ashamed of
it." Percy was less percipient than Shaw, for the dramatist meant the
remark to help carry a basic point: Joan was both "protestant" and
French; not only the sense of individual integrity but the spirit of nationalism was being born in those days. The yeomen were developing
a national consciousness, but the more conservative "gentleman" of the
day still felt no sense of a nation, but held himself as in the feudal
system. Joan thought of "God and I" without the Church intervening;
this pointed to protestantism. She thought "the King and I" without
the peerage intervening; this pointed to nationalism.

Opinions as to the play in 1923 were mixed. John Corbin, though he said the play "grows mightily in memory", found "many backwater eddies in which the drama was lost in monotonously whirling words." Alexander Woollcott found the play "beautiful, engrossing, and at times exalting". As to the men that convicted Joan, he said Shaw knew they were "just such a baffled, legalistic, dogmatic set of dunderheads as the play *Saint Joan* is likely to find out front in any chance theatre where it may be playing." One of Shaw's secrets, in truth, is the contemporaneousness with which he endows his characters. These figures of past ages are our neighbors, and ourselves.

In this play, Shaw had less need than elsewhere to inject his ideas; they flow naturally from the situation, they issue inevitably from the lips of prelate and protesting Maid. As a consequence, as Luigi Pirandello* said, in the *New York Times* (January 13, 1924): "in no other of Shaw's works have considerations of art been so thoroughly respected as in *Saint Joan*." Shaw's consideration for ideas is equally noteworthy, making Harold Hobson, of the *London Sunday Times*, exclaim of a December 3, 1947 revival: "I wish I had space to praise not only the skill and suppleness of Mr. Shaw's mind in this play, but also its generosity . . . Mr. Shaw believes in Joan; but he knows, not only that her enemies may have been good men, but that their ideas were not necessarily either foolish or wicked. One leaves the theatre in a mood of reconciliation, which is better than that of indignation, however righteous." The artist for once restrained the controversialist; at worst, Shaw had other fish to fry. He pictured a conflict of moral systems, a new good to supersede the old good, with honest intentions on both sides.

And Joan, his protagonist, is doomed by her own pride. "The old Greek tragedy is rising among us," the Archbishop foretells; "it is the chastisement of *hubris*." In a superbly constructed play, with swift scenes capped by miracles picturing Joan's rise, Shaw shows her at the peak of her power already set apart for denial and destruction. First the General, then the King, then the Archbishop, repudiate the Maid. "Her allies oppose her for little reasons, as her enemies, for big", William Irvine pointed out in *The Universe of G. B. S.* (1949). "Then, deserted, denied, and doomed in the midst of her triumph, she rises abruptly from despair to the full height of her lonely pride and inspiration. She will follow God and her voices to the end. The trial scene is a magnificent and beautiful irony on human politics. Never were reasons of state more eloquent, more lofty, more imperious, yet never did they lead to greater catastrophe." The deeper tragedy springs not from evil balanced against good, but from good intentions that tortuously pave the road to hell.

The Epilogue, bringing the play into our own time, was most vigorously challenged. Some critics felt that it was unnecessary, that the audience might have been trusted to make the application to today. "With regard to the play itself," said Irvine, "the epilogue is an anticlimax, a vulgarization, and a lengthy elucidation of the obvious. Even so, it is too irresistible to lose its place on the stage." Defending the Epilogue, Pirandello declared that in this final part of the play "we may gather almost explicitly the reason why Shaw wrote it. This world, he seems to say, is not made for saints to live in. We must take the people who live in it for what they are, since it is not vouchsafed them to be anything else." Shaw might agree that we must take people for what they are; but he would hardly accept the implication that we should take them and keep them, be content with those to whom "it is not vouchsafed" to be better. The play rings challenge to authority, assertion of individual independence and integrity—demand that the better strive, in the hope that they will ultimately prevail.

The 1936 revival found the play accepted as a masterpiece, "increasing in popular stature", said Atkinson, "ever since it was first acted"—but left the Epilogue still in dispute. John Anderson (March 10, 1936) protested: "The point is not whether the play should have an epilogue showing Joan's final triumph, but whether this epilogue is the sort of epilogue *Saint Joan* needs. There are moments when it descends from the high veneration of sainthood to the brassy informality of showing the Girl Who Made Good, a sort of: P.S. She got the job." John Mason Brown, however, felt that "its epilogue, which was widely condemned when the Guild first produced the play back in 1923, now seems to be a further demonstration of Shaw's wisdom . . . It succeeds in giving a sad point and a great glory to this story of the Maid."

Brilliant as Shaw's talk may be, it was protracted beyond the concentration point of many hearers. A revised version (sent to America too late for the 1923 premiere) somewhat shortened the play; but even in 1936 Robert Garland enlisted himself among those "who, along with the Dauphin who is soon to be Charles VII, wish that Joan would keep quiet or go on home." After Shaw's insistence that his plays be uncut has died, they may be handled as freely as Shakespeare's. But remember that the uncut *Hamlet** still proves the most moving. *Saint Joan*, as it now stands, is a vivid portrait gallery in a drama that does not merely preach but lives a battle cry of personal freedom.

THE APPLE CART   *George Bernard Shaw*

In 1929, four years after Shaw received the Nobel Prize, another honor came to him—the creation by Sir Barry Jackson of the annual Malvern Festival for the presentation of Shaw's plays. The first of his works to be performed there, on August 19, 1929, was his new "political extravaganza", *The Apple Cart*. The play delighted the conservatives and shocked the laborites. The latter saw in it a glorification of monarchy, although, as the play itself emphasizes, the monarch holds his power only by threatening to resort to the democratic polls.

The Apple Cart is loosely constructed; it consists of two dramatized political discussions separated by a frolic of the monarch and his "platonic concubine", which ends in a wrestling match because she wants him to stay and he wants to get home in time for dinner with his wife.

The monarch of the play is King Magnus of Great Britain, ruler in the 1960's. His wife is the prosaic and patient Jemima; his recreational lady, the romantic and effervescent Orinthia. Involved in the political discussion are various folk. There is the American Ambassador, whose suggestion that the United States seek readmission into the British Empire is received with considerable concern, since England would thus become a mere appendage to the United States. There are two women in the Cabinet: Amanda, with little education but sterling character, and a sense of humor that at most embarrassing moments pricks her colleagues' pretentiousness; and Lysistrata, a high-strung intellectual, with the best

brain in the government but no sense of humor, and likely if hard pressed
to take refuge in hysterics. Boanerges, the complacent "self-made" labor
leader, is on hand. Such plot as the play has centers upon the efforts of
Prime Minister Proteus to reduce the King's power and to wipe out the
royal veto; and the King's countermove: "rather than be a cipher" (as
Shaw put it in the Preface) "he will abandon his throne and take his
obviously very rosy chance of being a popularly elected Prime Minister
himself." In dismay at this proposal, the Cabinet yields.

The "apple cart" that seems to have been upset is democracy, which
comes in for a thorough walloping in the play. On the one hand, government by the people, we are told, means government by those that can
persuade the run-of-the-mill, low-level populace. On the other hand
looms the tremendous monopolistic trust, Breakages, (un)Limited, which
suppresses inventions and produces perishable objects, thus ensuring
plenty of work, and profit. Lysistrata points out to the King that "it is
not the most ignorant national crowd that will come out on top, but the
best power station; for you can't do without power stations, and you can't
run them on patriotic songs and hatred of the foreigner, and guff and
bugaboo, though you can run nationalism on nothing else." Neither
monarchy nor democracy is the danger, but big business.

The world premiere of the play, under the title *Vanity Fair*, was in
Warsaw, June 14, 1929; it was the seventeenth Shaw play translated into
Polish by Sobieniowski; his theatre had bid for the premiere of *Saint
Joan*, but Shaw, having promised that to the Theatre Guild, gave Warsaw *The Apple Cart*. The play was banned in Dresden in 1930 as reactionary; in the same year Reinhardt produced it in Berlin as *The Emperor
(Kaiser) of America*. *Der Abend* remarked: "Shaw can still put all other
wits into his pocket." The Theatre Guild produced the play on February
24, 1930 with Claude Rains. Richard Lockridge said that Shaw was returning to political themes "as a steam-roller might return to a daisy
patch."

Politics, if not daisied, is indeed a patchwork. Henry Nevinson, in
England, called the drama "a maliciously manufactured contrast between
democracy and royalty to the disadvantage of the former." Shaw, in his
Preface (1930), answered this by saying that there is no longer any battle
between democracy and aristocracy: both have been bought by plutoc-
racy. Indeed, "Democracy is no longer bought; it is bilked. Ministers
who are Socialists to the backbone are as helpless in the grip of Breakages Limited as its acknowledged henchmen . . . I am going to ask you
to begin our study of Democracy," he went on, "by considering it first
as a big balloon, filled with gas or hot air, and sent up so that you shall
be kept looking up at the sky whilst other people are picking your
pockets." Those that are responsible to all—Shaw repeats the old argument—are responsible to none; hence he makes "a desperate bid for dictatorship", for sane and commanding leadership in an else doomed world.
It was inevitable that such a demand would find sharp attack, as
in Henry Hazlitt's words in the New York *Nation* (April 22, 1931):
"Wouldn't it be lovely, the play says in effect, if final political power
were in the hands of a man of charming manners, who would pay no
attention to what the people wanted or demanded but would know in-
fallibly what was good for them, and would provide it; who, though a
member of a hereditary upper class, would appreciate fully the feelings

and needs of workers and slum dwellers; who would never be subject to popular recall yet would never abuse his power; who—We need hardly go on. That is not a solution but a self-contradictory day dream." Even in the specific struggle of King Magnus and Prime Minister Proteus, Hazlitt found Shaw misdirected, "for democratic politicians are strong precisely where *The Apple Cart* makes them appear weak. A successful politician, especially a prime minister, may be a thundering ass so far as his knowledge of economics or his grasp of any abstract or complicated question whatever is concerned; but there is one direction in which he is extremely unlikely to be an ass, and that is in his ability to handle men, to flatter, impress, charm, cajole, bargain, negotiate, outwit." The continuing timeliness of such questions—the value and defects of democracy; the extent to which "benevolent despot" is a contradiction in terms — gives present interest to *The Apple Cart*.

Shaw's defense of the play, though less concernedly, carried over to the looseness of its form, specifically, to the playful interlude with the "romantically beautiful" Orinthia. Why may not he, Shaw queried, like a composer of music, introduce a slow second movement? The boudoir episode, he suggested, provides comic relief; and "Shakespeare understood what I understand; if you put humor into a play, it must be cheap humor." The Interlude, however, has a serious significance: "It completes the portrait of the King, who in the middle of the crisis is seen, not merely as a statesman, but as a human being with a domestic life." Shaw recognized that political discussions, especially onstage, must come in temperate doses; between them, he inserted the trifling of sex, which culminates, like a burlesque of the Greek *gamos*, in a roughhouse tumble of the man and woman on the floor. After this, one can take some more politics! There is, perhaps, a still deeper meaning to be found in the Interlude. Setting aside the autobiographical identification of Orinthia as Mrs. Patrick Campbell and Jemima as Mrs. Shaw—with Proteus poking at Ramsay MacDonald—one may see in the romantic lady the symbol of beauty and art. Shaw (or the King) amuses himself with these; he finds use for them; but he is not deeply tempted; society, the general good, the simple everyday person, come first. Thus, out of debate balanced with banter, Shaw maintains liveliness as through parable and paradox he pummels our minds and challenges our souls. If the cart be tumbling, here are at least tart apples to digest.

IN GOOD KING CHARLES'S GOLDEN DAYS   *George Bernard Shaw*

A "true history that never happened," Shaw called *In Good King Charles's Golden Days*, 1939, an intellectual frolic set in the Restoration days of 1680. From the point of view of the theatre, the play consists of one long act of conversation in which a monarch, a scientist, a religious leader, and an artist cross verbal swords to the bywords of a trio of the king's mistresses, and a much shorter, wholly disconnected act of tender, understanding, though still intellectualized talk between the king and his wife. The two acts together present some of Shaw's finest foolery and some of his most challenging thought.

The main scene is the library of Isaac Newton. To the literal-minded but clear-headed philosopher come George Fox, founder of the Society of Friends, and Mr. Rowley—who is King Charles II in his incognito moments. On the monarch's trail arrive three lovely but possessive and quarrelsome vixens. Nell Gwynne, come for her king, is attracted by the Quaker Fox in his leather breeches. Lady Castlemaine bursts upon them in a rage; she has time to cool somewhat while Newton demonstrates mathematically that Charles could not possibly have been unfaithful to her, as she protests he has, a hundred thousand times.

The Duchess of Portsmouth, go-between for Charles and the French Louis XIV, the Sun King, comes to get a love potion from "Mr. Newton, the alchemist". Save for the darts of these women at one another, when jealousy bares the nails, almost the only physical action in the play is a wrestling match beween Isaac Newton and the King's brother when, on James' refusal to leave, Isaac (whose "home is his castle") tries to throw him out of the window. (A wrestling match is always good theatre, especially when, as Shaw manages to make them— see The Apple Cart*—the opponents are of different rank or sex.) Newton has, in fact, at one time or another asked them all to leave. In spite of his formally restrained impatience, the conversation ranges widely through the issues of the day, with men who are worthy of the Shavian wit. Charles and James argue the theory of modern kingship as opposed to the older ideas; when James proposes the restoration of absolute rule, Charles drily observes: "This is a deuced fogggy country for sun kings." And Charles, with the scientist, the pastor, and the painter, combs out the case for Protestantism and the case for the Pope; science and art fight their battle. Shaw would have liked to use Hogarth as the artist, but the dates don't fit; he therefore brings in the painter Godfrey Kneller. The women make a gay, uncomprehending, but consciously delightful chatter all about.

Newton was right in resenting these intruders. For, if the play can be said to have any conflict, it springs accidentally out of the undirected conversation, as first a remark of the Quaker, and then a remark of the painter, upset two of Newton's basic conceptions, and the idle interruption of a day threatens to spoil the labors of a lifetime. Newton is working on a chronology of the world, based on its creation four thousand and four years before the birth of Jesus; Fox laughs him into the idea that God is not such a niggard of time. And Newton has been building his theory of gravitation on the concept that the universe is, "in principle", rectilinear; whereas Kneller, taking the ladies to witness, assures him that the basic drive — of beauty, and of space — is not a straight line but a curve. We leave the perturbed scientist, to watch King Charles in gentler but still wise talk with Queen Catherine. Some critics have lamented Shaw's picture of Charles the tender and loving husband as a distortion of history. In his Preface, Shaw upholds Charles as "the best of husbands": he used Louise to get money from Louis XIV of France; and "historians who confuse Charles's feelings for his wife with his appetite for Barbara Villiers do not know chalk from cheese biologically." Whatever the facts of history, in this scene between Charles and Catherine the playwright realized some of his tenderest moments. As the London Times (August 14, 1939) put it, "Mr. Shaw does not often achieve and sustain beauty so quiet." Even the matter-of-fact New York Variety (August 23, 1939) called the scene "a touching and fine piece of writing."

The various characters of the play, indeed, are deftly drawn and neatly differentiated. Richard Watts (December 13, 1942) comments on Shaw's handling of the women: "The simple earthiness of Nell Gwynne, the feminine guile of the French Duchess of Portsmouth, the heavy jealousy of the amorous Duchess of Cleveland, the motherly understanding of Queen Catherine—all are managed with humor and dexterity." Outstanding, however, is King Charles, seen more subtly by Shaw than by most writers. As the *London Observer* (May 12, 1940) noted, we watch "the pathos of a wry but very real talent for life which has been warped by historical accident. The potentially sage, and often sad, sovereign has been deflected by destiny into wearing the title of Merry Monarch." Throughout, it is a wise—wise more than witty, though not without wit—and a wistful king that we behold.

The play is not well constructed. It begins as a play about Newton. Then, for a long spell, it is a conversation piece wholly without plot or advancing action. "Mr. Shaw knows well enough," said the *Observer*, "that plays must have movement, but believes that an argument hurtling through the air is as good a form of motion for an intelligent audience as the flash of a sword." In the second act, it becomes a play about Charles, whose picture, Watts adds, is "one of the most winning in all the playwright's portrait gallery." Whatever his theme, through these vital personages Shaw argues with a liveliness and brilliance that hold keen and delighted attention.

The title of the play is itself doubly satiric. The play *The Dame of Honor*, by Thomas D'Urfey, 1706, used seriously, in a song, the refrain "In Good Queen Bess's golden days." A bit later (1734) an anonymous religious and political satire, the poem *The Vicar of Bray*, picturing a time-serving and turncoat minister, used with satiric intent the refrain "In good King Charles's golden days". Shaw took the refrain as a title, and twisted the satiric intent by picturing a short but truly golden mean between the extremes of two revolutions. While the manners in the play have the intertangled roughness and politeness, bluntness and formality, of revolution-enclosed Restoration times, the ideas are sharply drawn to present pertinence. Reading the play is a joy and exhilaration. Seeing the drama is also a rich experience. Shaw wrote the play for the Malvern Festival, at which it had its world premiere on August 12, 1939. James Agate wrote in the *London Times:* "The body and bulk of it is the best warp and woof that has come from the Shavian loom since *Back to Methusaleh**." After seeing a performance in Dublin, Watts wrote (Dec. 13, 1942): "Here once more the master is in his best vein. Here is Shaw at his mellowest and most charming. His lucid writing style has never seemed more winning and attractive." "The critics unite," said Harold Hobson in the *Christian Science Monitor* (September 9, 1939), "in praising the play's intellectual brilliance, its flashing eloquence, its inexhaustible vitality."

Shaw himself said in his Preface: "Anyone who considers a hundred and fiftieth edition of *Sweet Nell of Old Drury* more attractive than Isaac Newton had better avoid my plays: they are not meant for such. And anyone who is more interested in Lady Castlemaine's hips than in Fox's foundation of the great Cult of Friendship should keep away from theatre and frequent worse places." Yet he gives us the ladies as a sauce to the intellectual speculations.

BURY THE DEAD   *Irwin Shaw*

Based partly on Chlumberg's drama *Miracle at Verdun** and sprung
from the same war, this long one-act play, written by Irwin Shaw
(American, b. 1913), has considerable power. The author called it "a
play about the war that is to begin tomorrow". First published in the
April 1936 issue of the *New Theatre* magazine, it was produced in New
York on March 14, 1936. It was given many productions in England
and America by groups opposed (until Russia was attacked) to the
Second World War; the *Daily Worker* of July 30, 1940, estimated that it
had had over fifty productions in the previous six months.

The play pictures six men, just laid in their graves by their war-
weary comrades, who rise, refusing to be buried. The glutted earth
ejects them; the dead will not submit to death. In vain their mothers,
their wives, their sweethearts, beg them to lie down and be forgotten.
A general orders his soldiers to machine-gun the corpses; they refuse.
The corpses begin to advance. The General empties his gun at them;
untroubled, they march right over his slumping form. The live soldiers
follow; the last of them, "deliberately, but without malice", flicks his
cigarette butt at the fallen General.

Shaw's rebellion of the corpses struck home. Most New York reviewers were carried away by their sympathy with the play's plea for peace.
John Anderson called it "brilliant and terrifying and uncanny"; John
Mason Brown considered it "the most eloquent and moving diatribe
against the inanities of war which our theatre yet has known." Gilbert
W. Gabriel said: "It is a long time since I have seen a large audience
so moved, so hotly convulsed, so deeply shaken . . . Here is not only a
strong and beautiful plea, but also a stunning and beautiful play . . .
Shaw is a great poet in a rage."

An effective touch is the complaint of the six soldiers whose lives are
part payment for "the real estate operations" of Generals. Five of them
want living time to see, to hear, to feel the beauties, wonders, mysteries,
terrors of the world. The sixth has a vision of a better world he would
live to help make true.

The play, however, was submerged by the cataclysm of a second
world conflict, against which its desperate appeal for peace is puny.
When one considers the play objectively, it becomes clear that the
judgment of Joseph Wood Krutch, in the *Nation* (May 6, 1936) was
valid: "The writing goes steadily downhill as the symbol is developed in
more and more obvious directions. Shaw grows more prosaic, more
explicit, more vociferous, as he proceeds. The lesson — surely clear
enough — is explained and reiterated in progressively shriller terms
until the play ends in one of those near-riots to which the imagination
of so many peace lovers seems habitually to lead." *Bury The Dead*
might persuade the more emotional to march on City Hall or buy
passage on a Ford Peace Ship; it was less likely than *Miracle at Verdun*
— until a worse war backwashed upon them both — to bring out of the
disordered and futile deaths of human conflict the deeply emotional
yet reflective urge of art.

THE CENCI   *Percy Bysshe Shelley*

While in Rome in 1819, the English poet Percy Bysshe Shelley (1792-
1822) came upon the story of the barbarous Count Francesco Cenci who,
in 1599, in order to dominate his family completely, raped his own
daughter Beatrice. This gentle, amiable girl, driven to desperation,
conspired with her brother and her stepmother to kill the Count; for
this deed, they were condemned to death by the Count's friend the Pope.
Shelley and his wife saw portraits of Beatrice; Mrs. Shelley reports that
"her beauty cast the reflection of her own grace over her appalling
story." Shelley finished in two months one of the masterpieces of the
English drama, *The Cenci*.

Shelley saw his play as preeminently a work for the theatre. He
would have liked Kean to play the Count; and Eliza O'Neil, Beatrice.
Since Shelley was in Rome and in disgrace in England, his friend Thomas
Love Peacock offered the play anonymously to Covent Garden. The
manager was so horrified at the theme he refused even to show it to
Miss O'Neil. The play was printed; Mrs. Shelley reports that "universal
approbation soon stamped *The Cenci* as the best tragedy of modern
times." Macready would have returned to the stage to play it, but
the censor forbade performances. It was not until May 7, 1886, that the
play was presented in a private performance by The Shelley Society.
"The blameless pages of the Press of those days," the London *Stage*
declared on November 16, 1922, "suggested terrible things by their very
reticence. To have attended the performance was almost an act of
rebellion if not of potential immorality."

Translated into French in 1884 and 1934, the play was presented in
Paris in 1891 and 1935; the 1891 production was directed by the poet
Paul Fort, who also played Cardinal Camillo. The play was finally
produced in London in 1922, and again in 1926 and 1933 with Sybil
Thorndike and Robert Farquharson. The first New York production was
by the Lenox Hill Players, opening May 19, 1926. The Bellingham
Theatre Guild of Washington mistakenly called its March 6, 1940, pro-
duction the American premiere. *The Cenci* was presented by "Theatre
Classics" off Broadway in 1950. At every performance, the play proved
a profound and stirring tragedy.

Shelley has told of his own endeavors in writing the play. He felt
that he had treated the incest with enough delicacy to permit the play's
presentation. He tried to be realistic and "attended simply to the impartial development of the characters as it is probable the persons
represented really were." Combining Elizabethan horror with Romantic
sensibility, Shelley created a work of beauty and power.

George Moore stated that at its best the play equals anything of
Shakespeare's. Swinburne called it "the greatest tragedy that has been
written in any language for upward of two centuries." In the London
Observer (November 19, 1922), St. John Ervine declared that Shelley
"had a surer sense of form than Shakespeare, who, throughout his
career, remained careless about the shape of his work . . . We lost
Shakespeare's greatest rival when Shelley was wrecked on his return
from Leghorn."

The character of Beatrice, universally admired, has been variously
interpreted. Praising Sybil Thorndike, Charles Morgan said: "to play

her for the pathos of young beauty in distress would ruin the play; through all her scheming and determination she is supple, fiery, hot-blooded — a girl whose imagination has its roots in her sensuality." Evelyn Keller, on the other hand—the *New York Daily News* (May 22, 1926) said this actress "suffuses her role with a glowing eloquence" — played less like a tiger-lily than like a diamond: beautiful, many-faceted, clear, but cold and hard: all the gentleness and tender hopefulness of youth compressed as by subterranean forces into the crystal adamant of her revenge.

A deep social feeling shines through Shelley's play, as Lewis Casson viewed it, in a producer's note to the 1922 presentation: "Just as Beatrice, the symbol of Truth, Purity, and Innocence, was driven by the extreme symbol of Wrong and Oppression to the violence of Parricide that she might free the world of Tyranny, so Shelley, tortured by the misunderstanding and injustice that surrounded him, chose this weapon of violence and horror to deliver, once for all, his passionate cry for Youth, for Freedom, for Revolution if you will. And just as Authority and Organized Religion turned in revenge on Beatrice and crushed her, so, after this play, the tyranny he was attacking turned and crushed him. Worse than the crime of Parricide it were, to tear the mask of Respectability from Cenci's face, to tell the generation that was driving its children into the mines and factories, and herding its fathers and daughters into slums, that Cenci's 'spirit still lives in all that breathe, and still works the same ruin, scorn, despair'." The play, James Agate declared in *At Half-Past Eight* (1923), is less specifically symbolic but no less personal, "part of the passionate propaganda of a noble mind, which swells the theatre of its presentation to the scope and dimension of a cathedral . . . *The Cenci* is written on three planes — a ground-floor of normal significance, a middle story of spiritual meaning, and an attic wherein the idea streams out of window, the emanation of a philosophy." Yet Agate saw the same symbol in Beatrice herself: "First she had been an individual victim, then a symbol of maiden virtue rudely strumpeted, and now she rose to the embodiment of a pure philosophic idea—the idea of Rebellion. This was what Shelley, whose ruling passion was revolt, was after."

The sheer poetic power of the play, the sensitive study of diverse characters, the gripping story unfolded with remarkable theatrical craftsmanship, the objectively awakened challenge to our moral code, the call to rebel against all enchainment, the underlying earnestness and nobility of the author's spirit, combine to make *The Cenci* an enduring masterpiece of the drama.

THE RIVALS   *Richard Brinsley Sheridan*

Richard Brinsley Sheridan (1751-1816) is the only Englishman that has had a distinguished career as both playwright and politician. His fame as a playwright is based upon three comedies, written within a period of four years. As a young law student, Sheridan married the beautiful Elizabeth Linley of Bath and took her off the concert stage, thus leaving the couple without funds. The theatre always seems a get-rich-quick pathway; Sheridan tried it. His play *The Rivals; or, A*

Trip to Bath, 1774, was accepted by Mr. Harris, manager of Covent Garden. Sheridan wrote to his father-in-law that Harris "and some of his friends also, who have heard it, assure me in the most flattering terms that there is not a doubt of its success. It will be very well played, and Harris assures me that the least shilling I shall get (if it succeeds) is £600 . . . I shall make no secret of it toward the time of representation, that it may not lose any support my friends can give it. I had not written a line of it two months ago, except a scene or two which I believe you have seen in a little farce." But the play opened January 17, 1775, was a failure the first two nights and was withdrawn. Blame has been placed upon the actor John Lee, the "boring player" who enacted Sir Lucius O'Trigger. The truth is that Sir Lucius was a boring part. The play was drastically cut and rewritten. It opened again on January 28, with Laurence Clinch as Sir Lucius, to instant and enduring success. The author won much more than his £600, and fame to boot.

The Preface to the printed play admits that *The Rivals* was withdrawn to "remove those imperfections in the first representation which were too obvious to escape reprehension, and too numerous to admit of a hasty correction." Contemporary judgment is recorded in the *London Evening Post*. The Prologue spoke of the unnamed author as a law student who, "finding Coke, Littleton, Blackstone, etc., to afford but dull amusement, hath commenced poet, to grace his brow with a sprig of bay from Mount Parnassus." The *Post* (January 18, 1775) withheld that sprig of bay: "It [the play] requires much castigation, and the pruning hand of judgment, before ever it can pass on the town as even a tolerable piece. In language it is defective to an extreme; in plot outré, and one of the characters is an absolute exotic in the wilds of nature. Time will not permit a thorough investigation of this Comedy, but if *The Rivals* rests its claim to public favor solely on the basis of merit, the hisses of the Auditors on the first night of representation give reason to suspect a most fatal disappointment . . . the dulness of *The Rivals* lulled several of the middle gallery spectators into a profound sleep."

After corrections and cuts, the play became a favorite on the stage. Thus the *London Gazetteer and New Daily Advertiser* (January 17, 1777) observed: "This piece has a considerable share of merit . . . The plot is interesting and ingenious, the characters natural and new, the sentiments noble and refined; there is a good deal of sterling wit and real humor in several scenes, without ever bordering on obscenities, or the mean subterfuge of a double-entendre, which we think reflects the highest honor on the Author. The whole play last night was received with the strongest marks of approbation by a very numerous and splendid audience." Down the years through the nineteenth and the twentieth century, *The Rivals* has continued to hold. A list of those who have played in it would include almost every star of the English and American stages. In The Players' revival in New York, opening June 6, 1922, were Tyrone Power, Pedro de Cordoba, and Francis Wilson. In the Equity Players' production, opening in New York May 7, 1923, were Sidney Blackmer and Eva Le Gallienne. Later New York revivals came in 1936, 1941, and 1942. The last of these, with Mary Boland, Walter Hampden and Bobby Clark, had lyrics by Arthur Guiterman and music by Macklin Morrow. There was a musical version in London in 1935, with music and lyrics by J. R. Monsell and others, which W. A. Darlington, in the *London Telegraph* (September 17), called "a very bright and attractive show, excellently produced and sung."

The story is quite subordinate to the fascinating gallery of portraits drawn in the play. The plot is, nevertheless, a swiftly moving and continuously interesting tangle around the love of Captain Absolute and Lydia Languish, niece of Mrs. Malaprop. To win the romantic Lydia, the rich Absolute has pretended to be a poor ensign; his friend Bob Acres becomes his unwitting rival; Mrs. Malaprop will not consent to the match. Duels and elopements hang upon the event, until the lovely Lydia resigns herself to wealth and happiness. But how each character stands separately and clearly forth! Sir Anthony Absolute, though the angry father of whom he is a pattern may be traced to the old Roman comedy, is superbly drawn. Indeed, said J. Ranken Towse (June 7, 1922), "Sir Anthony must always be the dominant figure. If a trifle overdrawn, he is an extraordinary and consistent study." Sir Lucius O'Trigger is a furious fire-eater, a combination of the Roman braggart soldier and the Englishman quick with the challenge. Mrs. Malaprop has been called "a Dogberry in petticoats", but her "nice derangements of epitaphs" have given her enduring fame. Bob Acres is the most popular of comic good-natured simpletons. Lydia Languish is an absurd yet delightful, vapory flutter of romance and sweet simple daisy.

Mrs. Malaprop has a direct ancestor in Mrs. Slipslop of Fielding's *Joseph Andrews*, with predecessors in several of Shakespeare's plays. It is to be noted that Mrs. Malaprop is not a fool. She is, on the contrary, quite a shrewd woman; but her desire to speak learnedly catches her often just short of the proper term. It is on the tip of her tongue, but, being a woman, she cannot wait, and a neighbor word (always with the same accent and number of syllables) darts out. "He is the very pine-apple of politeness." "Illiterate him, I say, quite from your memory." But the absurd inconsequencies of Mrs. Malaprop, the comic satire and amusing picture of life, are not all that one may find here. Thus Heywood Broun observed (May 8, 1923) that "the scene between Bob Acres and David just before the duel is as telling and as modern a plea for pacifism as anything Mr. Shaw will write the day after tomorrow." The *New York Journal*, a year earlier (June 7, 1922) had summed up the play's values: "The fine wit, the exaggerated sentiment, and the true humor and faithful characterization of this famous piece, embodied in a well-nigh perfect production, afford an evening of pure delight." Dickens, after Chaucer, comes nearest to giving us another such gallery of British characters, slightly overdrawn for our amusement but real enough for our insight, as Sheridan offers in *The Rivals*.

THE SCHOOL FOR SCANDAL   *Richard Brinsley Sheridan*

After the success of *The Rivals**, Richard Brinsley Sheridan led a busy life. In the same year, 1775, his comic opera *The Duenna* was produced, with music by his father-in-law, Thomas Linley. In 1776, Sheridan took over from Garrick the management of the Theatre of Drury Lane. "In you, Sir," said one of the staff to Garrick, "we have lost the Atlas of the stage." "Well, Sir," responded Garrick, "I have left you a young Hercules to supply my place." The first play presented under Sheridan's management justified the remark. It was Sheridan's own comedy, *A Trip to Scarborough*, 1777, which, in the days before copyright limitations, is a rewriting of *The Relapse; or, Virtue in Danger*, 1697, by John Vanbrugh*. Shortly after the success of *A Trip to Scarborough*, Sheridan presented at Drury Lane, on May 8, 1777, his most successful play, esteemed by many as the greatest English comedy, *The School for Scandal*. It was long in the writing; parts were handed the actors piecemeal, as they were rehearsing. Sheridan supervised the production himself; to prevent poor productions elsewhere, he withheld the play from print. Nevertheless, many pirated versions appeared. For example, the actor John Bernard, who had played in the authorized production, in seven days, for ten shillings a week increase in salary, copied out a version that ran for a season at the Exeter Theatre. The first authentic text of the play — which was printed in twenty-three editions from 1780 to 1799 — was issued in America in 1786, from the copy given by Sheridan to John Henry. (Henry played Sir Peter Teazle in New York in 1786.) The next authentic edition was issued in Dublin, in 1799.

Before its opening, the play had to hurdle obstacles. Moses, the money-lender in the play, was thought too close a portrait of one Hopkins, candidate for City Chamberlain of London; the censor refused the play a license because it reflected "seditious opposition to a court candidate". Through Sheridan's personal friendship with Lord Hertford, the Lord Chamberlain, the license was granted on the very day of the premiere. Thenceforward all was success. The Prologue was by Garrick, then at the height of his popularity. The journalist Reynolds, passing the theatre that evening, recorded that he heard such a noise and vibration that he ran for his life, lest the building fall: it was the applause at the final curtain. All London went to see the play.

Hazlitt has called *The School For Scandal* "the most finished and faultless comedy we have." "No other comedy in the language," said J. Ranken Towse, "contains so long an array of important and vividly contrasted characters."

In the play, Charles Surface is heedless, happy-go-lucky, but honest; his brother Joseph is a scheming hypocrite. The ward of Sir Peter Teazle, Maria, and Charles are in love; Joseph woos Maria for her fortune while also courting the young Lady Teazle. Lady Teazle is tempted to Joseph's room, where the arrival of Sir Peter forces her to hide behind a screen while the men converse — until the screen is thrown down and the Lady exposed. Meanwhile, Oliver Surface, the wealthy uncle of Charles and Joseph, unexpectedly returning from India, resolves, while still unrecognized, to test the character of his nephews. The hypocrisy of Joseph is made clear to all; Sir Peter gives Maria to Charles, and forgives Lady Teazle.

The first reviews of the comedy show as favorable a reception from the critics as from the public. Thus the London *Observer* (May, 1777) declared: "The chief satire of this piece is pointed against hypocrisy and scandal, in which the author displays great genius, wit, and observation. His characters are finely drawn with a masterly pencil, and have strong marks of originality." The *Lady's Magazine* (same date) called the play "an additional proof of that gentleman's great abilities as a dramatic writer . . . The characters are drawn with a bold pencil, and colored with warmth and spirit . . . The dialogue of this comedy is easy and witty. It abounds with strokes of pointed satire, and a rich vein of humor pervades the whole, rendering it equally interesting and entertaining."

Down the years, a list of great players attests the popularity of the play; its one drawback for staging is that it deserves a galaxy of stars for the many important parts. Among those that have played in it may be mentioned Charles Kemble; Ada Rehan and John Drew, in Daly's production in 1891; Junius Brutus Booth in 1892; Ben Greet and Edith Wynne Matthison in 1899. In 1923, in New York, The Players' revival used John Drew, Robert Mantell, Walter Hampden, Ethel Barrymore, and Violet Kemble-Cooper. Ethel Barrymore—whose mother and grandmother had also played the part—acted Lady Teazle in 1931 and frequently for a decade thereafter. John Gielgud revived the play in London in 1937. An adaptation called *Lady Teazle* opened December 30, 1881, with Fanny Davenport. A musical version, also called *Lady Teazle*, with Lillian Russell in the title part, opened December 24, 1904, with book by John Kendrick Bangs, lyrics by Roderick C. Penfield, and music by A. Baldwin Sloane. This was hailed as the best musical comedy of the season; it followed Sheridan closely and added a number of lively songs.

If any scenes may be selected as outstanding in a play so consistently entertaining, there are: for sentiment, that in which Charles, selling the family portraits to his uncle in disguise, refuses to let go the portrait of "the ill-looking little fellow over the settee" who is his uncle; for satire, the gathering of the scandal-mongers, Sir Benjamin Backbite, Lady Sneerwell, and Mrs. Candor, who "strike a character dead at every word"; and for dramatic intensity, perhaps the most famous scene in English comedy, the exposure of Lady Teazle behind the screen.

Praise of the play has not been universal. On November 24, 1789, when President Washington in New York took the State's governor, the foreign ministers, and some Senators to see the play, one of the latter characterized it as "an indecent representation before ladies of character and virtue." Washington was with the majority who have enjoyed it. Among the dissenters has been Henry James, who reviewed a Boston production in the *Atlantic Monthly* (December, 1874): "In sentiment, what a singularly meagre affair it seemed! Its ideas, in so far as it has any, are coarse and prosaic, and its moral atmosphere uncomfortably thin . . . The distinctly amusing scenes . . . are those in which Lady Sneerwell's guests assemble to pull their acquaintances to pieces . . . To measure the difference between small art and great, one should compare the talk of Sheridan's scandal-mongers with that scene in Molière's *Misanthrope** in which the circle at Célimène's house hit off the portraits of their absent friends. In the one case one feels almost ashamed to be listening; in the other it is good society still, even though it be good society in a heartless mood." James allows, however, that the play wins popularity through wit that everyone can understand and think himself clever; as well as through "its robustness and smoothness of structure, and its extreme felicity and finish of style."

Many players have been singled out for their performance in this comedy. Horace Walpole praised Mrs. Fanny Abington (a former flower girl, the original Lady Teazle; Sir Joshua Reynolds selected her to sit for his painting of "The Comic Muse". For "The Tragic Muse", he chose Mrs. Sarah Kemble Siddons.) Charles Lamb sang the praises of Palmer as Joseph Surface; in Lamb's opinion, this actor "stole the play." The London *Examiner* (October 15, 1815) called Charles Kemble "the best Charles Surface we have ever seen"—and added, "Why can we not always be young, and seeing *The School For Scandal?*" Brooks Atkinson (January 11, 1931) gave garlands to Ethel Barrymore: "Few episodes in the British drama have greater prestige than the screen scene . . . Miss Barrymore has shown us why." The vitality of the play was attested (January 11, 1931) by John Mason Brown: "Not only does its fun still belong to it as they perform it, but it comes bubbling out so contagiously that an audience cannot resist it . . . still comes down the centuries as an irresistible comedy." Good fun, and smiling satire at the hypocrisy that we prefer to see in our neighbors, and at the vanity in ourselves that makes us its easy victims; a superb gallery of comic yet recognizable figures; and a dramatic story superbly told, sustain the freshness of *The School For Scandal.*

THE CRITIC   *Richard Brinsley Sheridan*

Originally presented on October 30, 1779 as an afterpiece, *The Critic* is the most successful play in the tradition of the dramatic burlesque. It satirizes not only the sentimental tragedy of Sheridan's day, but the supercilious and often malignant criticism of the time. Dangle and Sneer are the two critics; their easy vicitim is Sir Fretful Plagiary (a caricature of the dramatist Richard Cumberland, who had sneered at *The School for Scandal**). When Plagiary complains that the Drury Lane manager has stolen bits from his manuscript, Sneer suggests that Plagiary take a cruel revenge by declaring the manager the author of the whole piece! But the most amusing figure is Puff, "a Practitioner in Panegyric or a Professor of the Art of Puffing," whose analysis of the varieties of what we call ballyhoo and blurb is as fresh, as searching, and as pertinent today as when it was first spoken. Puff has written a tragedy, "The Spanish Armada"; he takes Sneer and Dangle to a rehearsal. This tragedy is an absurd burlesque, mingling actual historical figures at the time of the Spanish Armada — Sir Walter Raleigh, Sir Christopher Hatton, Lord Burleigh — with burlesque creations: Tilburina, daughter of the Governor of Tilbury Fort; and Don Ferolo Whiskerandos, a Spanish prisoner whom Tilburina loves. Among the characters are an Italian family with a French interpreter—all unintelligible. Dangle and Sneer tear the tragedy to tatters as we watch a spectacle of the English and Spanish fleets in fierce battle; the triumph; and a final procession and choral dance of English river gods.

When the play opened, the *London Gazeteer and New Daily Advertiser* (November 1, 1779) observed: "The audience were informed . . . that an affectation of sentiment and scrupulous virtue had destroyed the true spirit of comedy; and that modern tragedies were so very moral, pious, and dull, that they put the actors almost, and the audience quite, to sleep — that trick and situation were introduced instead of the wit and humor of comedy, and of natural feeling and genuine pathos in tragedy. To expose these errors was therefore become the proper subject of satire in the present day . . . The purpose aimed at is effected by a kind of burlesque parody, of which there are several thousand lines extended through the greater part of two acts. These must have been a very tedious, laborious, and disgusting task; and the effect of this kind of ridicule is so very strong, that it soon grows tiresome and disagreeable. The public opinion of modern tragedy is already so very low . . . that the game is hardly worth the pursuit." The reviewer discerned some passages that seemed aimed at older playwrights; indeed, "some which seemed more applicable to Shakespeare than to any other writer." The play does, in truth, parody the obvious method of conveying information to the audience that Shakespeare employed in As You Like It* and The Tempest*.

Several reviewers found a different reason for objection. It was the practice, at that time, for persons in need to advertise their poverty and plead for assistance in the public press. Puff announces that he has supported himself for several months by advertising fictitious distresses. The Spectator at once cried that this satire was "too severe, and may be of dangerous tendency, in preventing the hand of benevolence being extended to real objects of distress. There are impostors of every class — but charity is already too cold to require further chill upon it." The Universal magazine of August 1781 brought up the point again, mentioning that the audience "expressed some displeasure at Puff's boast," and adding: "Nobody could suspect that the Author, in the Wantonness of Wit, could wish to divert the humane Attentions of the Benevolent from the real Objects of Charity; and Mr. King (who played Puff) converted their Displeasure into Marks of Approbation, by seizing a lucky Moment to assure Sneer that he did not mean to deaden his Feelings, or lessen his Humanity, but merely to awaken his Prudence."

A parody of contemporary foibles, such as The Critic, is likely soon to seem out of date; revivals continually interpolated jokes to keep the humor fresh; and Jack Bannister (the original Whiskerandos) told Charles Mathews (who played Puff for over thirty years) how Sheridan himself laughed at the new lines: "The style of tragedy it ridicules has passed away, probably elbowed out of existence mainly by the force of this very satire; and it is only by the plentiful interpolation of jokes referring to the present that the public is now entertained . . . Even the swallowing of the moustache by Whiskerandos, which has often been denounced as 'too broad', was taken from an accident which really happened, on the first night of Leigh Hunt's play of A Legend of Florence, to a Mr. Moore, who played the principal character, and who was obliged to leave the stage for some minutes, being totally unable to proceed with his part . . . I can safely assert that there is not one 'gag' introduced that I cannot, from my own experience, cap with an actual one even exceeding it in absurdity." The Critic survives, however, because most of what Sheridan caught on his comic barbs is lastingly rooted in human nature.

The play has been frequently revived. The New York Times (December 25, 1938) reported that a Harvard University production dressed Dangle and Sneer to resemble Alexander Woollcott and George Jean Nathan. A revival by the Old Vic company was brought to New York on May 20, 1946, with Laurence Olivier as Puff and Ralph Richardson as Lord Burleigh. All the reviewers felt the freshness and vigor of the piece; John Chapman called it "as wise to show business as tomorrow's drama page or next week's tradesheet. Wiser. It deflates the conceit of everybody connected with the stage. It hands the audience many laughs about critics — and then quite deftly deflates the audience. Its comments on playwrights cannot be bettered . . . And, as the company romps with abandon through the performance, it is a definite and utterly delightful example of dreadful acting. The play within the play is just bad enough to mirror all the sins of Actors' Equity and British Equity combined."

The Critic has scarcely anything in the way of plot, of situations, even of form; it achieves its uproarious effects through romping fancy and verbal ingenuity. It remains the freshest satire of the foibles and excesses of critics, playwrights, actors, and audiences, as it laughs at the ways of the theatre that it loves.

JOURNEY'S END   *Robert Cedric Sheriff*

Undoubtedly the most successful, and in many minds the best, play about the first World War is *Journey's* End, by Robert Cedric Sheriff (English, b. 1896). It made its debut in London, January 21, 1929. On March 22, 1929, it opened in New York City for a run of 99 performances; in June it was revived. By March, 1930, it was being played by 56 companies in 22 languages. Between the two wars it was frequently revived; in Calcutta in 1931; at the University of Washington in 1937, and many places and times between. In 1941 it was performed by the 165th Infantry while in training in Georgia. It was shown again in London, opening October 5, 1950.

The play pictures the last four days in the lives of some dozen soldiers holding a short sector of the British front near St. Quentin against the German advance of March, 1918. Among the tense soldiers a few stand out. Stanhope, though a mere youngster, has had four years of the war; only constant drinking keeps his taut nerves from the break. Lt. Osborne, affectionately called "Uncle", walls himself against the strain with talk of flowers and good old *Alice in Wonderland*. Hibbert is on the edge of hysterical terror—saved from utter funk when Stanhope unveils his own agony of mind. The cockney Lt. Trotter is more fortunate, being gifted with a lack of imagination that leaves him comparatively calm. Raleigh is a rooky just up from training school. We watch this assorted group of soldiers through the nerve-crumbling monotony of standing guard, and through their routine hours. Occasionally a simple action attains swift poignancy—as when Raleigh writes home; or when they quickly don gas masks at Trotter's call, and what he smells turns out to be "a blinking May tree." Poignant, too, in the unspoken expectancy of doom, are the preparations for the daylight raid of Osborne and Raleigh. Raleigh returns with a prisoner — and horror. Stanhope, whom Osborne had been sustaining, breaks. But the next morning, when orders come to hold at all costs against the German advance, they pull together again. A shell sends Raleigh to die in Stanhope's arms. A second shell blasts the dugout. The group have come to their journey's end.

R. C. Sheriff had had more experience as a soldier than as a playwright, before setting hand to his play. He had written a few amateur plays for production by friends. Letters to the family during the war, which Sheriff tried to shape as a novel, grew into this play. It was rejected by most London managers. Bernard Shaw, reading it, was not especially enthusiastic; but a Stage Society production ensued with Laurence Olivier. Then Maurice Browne, who had done considerable work with little theatres in America, took the drama for his first London production. In it were Melville Cooper, Colin Clive, and Maurice Evans. Before bringing the play to the United States, Gilbert Miller opened the American company for a week in London. Both houses were sold out. In the American production were Leon Quartermaine and Colin Keith-Johnston, who also played in a 1939 New York revival.

The British Secretary of War, Sir Laming Worthington-Evans, called Journey's End "the finest play I have ever seen." The Prince of Wales (later Duke of Windsor) said it was "the most impressive play I have seen in all my life." In America the reviewers were equally stirred. Richard Lockridge called it "the finest play that tragic conflict has produced. Pity catches at your throat. Gallantry sends chills along your spine." Alexander Woollcott, in the Ladies' Home Journal (September, 1935) linked Journey's End with The Green Pastures as "the two finest plays evolved in the English-speaking theatre during the post-war era." R. Dana Skinner, in Commonweal (April 10, 1929) sought to explain the source of the play's power, as a revelation of men's souls on the brink of eternity. Contributing was the "awesome silence which pervades so much of it—a broken silence which fairly throbs, like the murmur of the earth itself before dawn. . . . But whether at the mists of dawn, or in the amber of an afternoon sun, or in the candle-lit gloom of night, there is always the feeling of last hours, of nature hushed before the summons of God, and of men bidding brave, unhurried good-byes to the only existence which they have known." Breaks in the gloom and the stillness help to establish the mood; the characters themselves are revealed through constant action. There is no single drive of plot; but the incidents of the play, insignificant in themselves, are given meaning through the lens they form by which we see the various men, and are given depth by the imminence of doom we feel in ourselves and sense in them, the unspoken recognition, with each routine movement or simple act, that this may be the last time. What Price Glory?* pictures the rowdy devil-may-care of the soldier away from the front; Journey's End faithfully and poignantly conveys the fears and the devotion, the breaking yet controlled anguish, of steadfast service unto death.

IDIOT'S DELIGHT

Robert E. Sherwood

"The world is playing Idiot's Delight. It is a game that never means anything and never ends." Such is the feeling, in Idiot's Delight, of Harry Van, once a "shill" with a carnival show, now a "hoofer" leading a group of American chorus girls seeking to enliven Europe with their dancing act. They are caught in a hotel in the south Tyrol, on the border of four countries, at Zero Hour in the next World War. We watch while a French Communist, a German scientist, and an English artist slip the cloaks of their ideals to become cogs in the war machine. More

objective stands the munitions magnate, who "had the honor of pro-
moting" the war; he moves off to safety, leaving behind his Russian
mistress, Irene. Harry Van (who is sure, despite her evasion, that she
is a girl he slept with in 1925 back in Omaha) gives up his chance to
cross the border in order to stay and help Irene. Despite his apparent
flippancy and his antic ways, Harry is basically serious, an earnest if
somewhat superficial observer of human nature.

The play, by Robert E. Sherwood (American, 1896-1955), was
warmly received. It opened in New York on March 24, 1936, running
for 121 performances with Lynn Fontanne and Alfred Lunt, the latter
especially amusing in his song and dance act with his blonde chorus
girls. It was revived August 31, 1936, and ran for 179 performances
more. In London, with Raymond Massey and Tamara Geva, it opened
on March 22, 1938 for a run of 230 performances. Lenore Ulric has
played it in the summer theatre; Clark Gable in 1939 starred in the film
version. The play proved equally pert and pertinent when it opened,
May 23, 1951, at New York's City Center, with Lee Tracy, Ruth Chatterton, and amusingly caricatured chorines.

The American reviewers hailed the comedy: "Idiot's Delight," said
Gilbert Gabriel (March 25, 1936), "and yours and mine." "It causes you
to shake with laughter and with fear," said Robert Garland, "to remain
around and cry 'Bravo!'." It is, said the *Literary Digest* (March 28,
1936), "a thundering, contemptuous blast at nations that make war, men
who make bullets, and the inarticulate, sheep-like humanity that allows
itself to be in peonage to war." In Melbourne, Australia, the *Argus*
(February 6, 1939) declared the play "touched off an explosion in the
theatre . . . a farce with tragic cross-currents, a melodrama with a
biting lesson, a tragedy with even a dash of musical comedy." In this
play Sherwood most fully heeds the W. S. Gilbert* injunction that one
must always gild the philosophic pill. The reviewers in England, though
they liked the play, more soberly questioned its implications. *"Idiot's
Delight* is not a masterpiece of argument," said James Agate in the
London Times (March 27, 1938). "It is very nearly a masterpiece of
light theatre with a core of thought." Even that core was challenged
by Charles Morgan, writing from London for the *New York Times* (April
10, 1938): "To speak of war as an idiot's delight and to rail at mankind
as fools because they suffer it, is a terrible arrogance. War is no one's
delight; and men who are prepared to suffer for an idea are not idiots.
. . . Because it fails to recognize this, Mr. Sherwood's piece, though a
splendid piece of rhetoric, remains unsatisfying because it seems to have
missed its aim as a criticism of contemporary life."

The English felt the wings of war too close to be content with the
shallow optimism of Harry Van and the surface satire of Robert E.
Sherwood; yet *Idiot's Delight* drives home, with laughter over wells of
emotion, a basic sense of human decency and faith in the survival of
human values.

ABE LINCOLN IN ILLINOIS   *Robert E. Sherwood*

Dealing with what have been called the undramatic years of the
Great Emancipator's life, *Abe Lincoln in Illinois*, 1938, richly reveals
their spiritual seeding for the later harvest. The play shows the change

in Lincoln from the hobbledehoy, shrewd but unambitious "artful dodger" whose chief desire was to be left alone, to the earnest man aroused for humanity, the vigorous embattled champion of human rights. Leaning heavily on Carl Sandburg's *Life of Lincoln*, the play takes us from the early days in Salem of 1830, when the six-foot-four Lincoln was a shy but determined lad of twenty-one, through the days of his love for Ann Rutledge, of his work as an attorney in Springfield, of his courting, dodging, and being courted by, Mary Todd — whose fanatical ambition was a whip to Abe's flagging will — on to that summer of 1858 when Lincoln stood up to Stephen Douglas on the planks of a country debating platform. The play ends as we watch the rear of a train on which the new president has embarked for the White House.

This drama was the first production of the new Playwright's Company, organized by dramatists Anderson*, Berman*, Howard*, Rice*, and Sherwood. After a premiere in Washington, October 3, 1938, with Raymond Massey, it opened in New York on October 15 for a run of 472 performances, to the highest critical acclaim. It won the 1939 Pulitzer Prize and has been widely performed throughout the country. Paris saw the play in 1948, called *Si je vis* (*If I Live*).

The importance of the theme of democracy to the present day did not escape, and indeed may have lent enthusiasm to, the critics. Thus Richard Watts declared (October 30, 1938): "Here is not only one of the finest and most stirring of American plays but one of the most glorious achievements of all that is best in the national spirit . . . shows us something of the soul and the genius of our best-beloved national hero, brings to us a sense of the greatness of the true democratic spirit, and makes the fierce struggle of the most ominous period in our history a burning contemporary issue. . . . Magnificently played by Raymond Massey in one of the finest performances of the modern theatre, *Abe Lincoln in Illinois* is the greatest of our patriotic dramas." *Stage* (November 1939) found the play equally pregnant: ". . . one of the memorable events of our time — of all time . . . makes no concessions to streamlined playgoing. It is not, in the popular sense, good theatre. There is no pull for pace, climax, theatric persuasiveness. Here is simply great drama, greatly conceived, greatly played. Here is one of those rare occasions when the gifts of a playwright and an actor join to kindle a blaze which illumines a dark moment of history. In a time when what is happening in the world today cannot — apparently — be interpreted on the stage in terms of valid theatre, the overtone and implication of this play come like a searchlight beam cutting through a fog."

Like most plays that seek to cover a stretch of years, the drama depends upon chosen episodes to give the effect of continuous growth. This task *Time* (October 24, 1938) felt that it accomplished "not altogether convincingly." The play is best in its evocation of mood, the aroused mood of democracy upsurging, and in its psychological study of Lincoln's mind. His love for Ann Rutledge, for instance, is deep and devoted "because he's happened to fasten on her his own romantic ideal of what's beautiful and unattainable. Let him ever attain her, and she'd break his heart." It is by his losing her, in her death, that she holds him forever. Equally understanding, though more stormy, is the picture of Lincoln's ways with Mary Todd — though it might be more appropriate to speak of her ways with him. The tender memory of one woman's love, and the persistent prick of another woman's urge that he take part in life, helped shape in Abraham Lincoln the understanding devotion and the resolve that gave course to our country's history and added decency to democracy. This clarion call for human decency, for democracy based on fellow-love, rings through *Abe Lincoln in Illinois*.

THERE SHALL BE NO NIGHT   *Robert E. Sherwood*

This drama about Finland's courageous stand against Soviet aggression sprang of a broadcast from Finnish trenches on Christmas of 1939.

Its story centers upon the reaction of a Finnish family to the Soviet invasion: the Nobel Prize winning neurologist Kaarlo Valkonen, his American-born wife Miranda, his son Erik, and Erik's fiancée Kaatri. As the play opens the neurologist is broadcasting to America, questioning the value of the elimination of pain: will not people then become pampered and stupid; do not pain and trouble quicken the mind? Their national problem intrudes upon the household. Kaarlo feels that the Russian people do not want to fight; Erik has faith in the Mannerheim line. Both prove wrong. Erik is killed on ski patrol; Kaarlo, rejecting a chance to leave the country, feels he must fight against a gathering world insanity. In a schoolroom near Viipuri Bay, Kaarlo and his comrades await the order to march to certain death. His wife prepares to burn their home; there shall be no surrender.

There shall be no night because men no longer talk of the glory of war; they accept it as a task that must be done. But individuals are awakening; more and more will ask "*Why* must it be done?" Then are the war-mongers and the tyrants doomed. This is the argument of the play, but the history of the play shows how far down the years fulfilment of such hopes must lie. After a premiere in Providence on March 29, 1940, the drama opened in New York on April 29 with Alfred Lunt and Lynn Fontanne, for a run of 115 performances and the Pulitzer Prize. The Lunts toured in the play as a benefit for the brave but overwhelmed Finns. Then Hitler invaded Soviet Russia — and the program notes for the 1941 road tour were carefully worded: "In this development of Hitler's murderous career, the Finns have been compelled to fight and die on his side . . . Since this play first opened, no important line of its text has been changed . . . The purpose of this play was to set forth the tragedy of every civilized home in every civilized but unprepared free country which happened to lie in the path of the international assassins. It was and is obvious that this play, written by an American for Americans, was and is intended to say that this same tragedy may come upon us." That tragedy came with Pearl Harbor, after which, the *New York Post* reported (December 15, 1941) Mr. Sherwood decided that "the best interests of this country" would be served by closing the production. Two years later the play opened in London and ran for 220 performances—with the characters and situations altered to apply to the Italian invasion of Greece!

Despite — or because of — the failure of reality to match its ideals, the play struck a deep chord in many hearts. Most reviewers looked upon it as a dramatized sermon rather than as a drama. "I don't think *There Shall Be No Night* can be taken," said Wolcott Gibbs (May 11, 1940) "as much less than a plea for our immediate and total entry on the Allied side — only because he [Sherwood] knows no other way to preserve the kind of life that self-respecting men and women can live . . . Too often the message, in the form of nearly interminable monologues by Mr. Lunt, brings the action to a standstill, and much too often Mr. Sherwood's deep feeling betrays him into the kind of prose that sets a Hearst editorial apart from any other writing in the world." That the intended message is correctly expressed by Mr. Gibbs may be seen from Sherwood's Preface: "There could be only one reason for America's reluctance to give any help to the Finns, and that was abject fear. And if we were in a state of abject fear, then we had already been conquered by the masters of the slave States, and we must surrender our birthright. So I decided to raise my voice in protest against the hysterical escapism, the Pontius Pilate retreat from decision, which dominated American thinking and, despite all the warnings of the President of the United States and the Secretary of State, pointed our foreign policy toward suicidal isolationism." This intention of the play, pressed by the author's earnestness, divides its power to the disadvantage of the other face of the play's coin — the ultimate hope of a rebellion for peace.

In London of 1943 reviewers were more wholehearted and more nearly unanimous in the play's praise. The *New Statesman and Nation* (December 25, 1943) gave it a Christmas gift of superlative: "the most moving war tragedy yet seen upon a London stage . . . It is conceived in the spirit of that old Anglo-Saxon ballad of defeat, celebrating the Battle of Maldon, 991; also the spirit of Winston Churchill's speeches in our darkest hour." Adding to such comments more purely dramatic criticism, James Agate in the *London Times* (December 19, 1943) praised the skill and naturalness of the drama.

The idea behind *There Shall Be No Night* may today seem a trite thought in an insecure world, but the personal drama that embodies the thought remains vivid, poignant, and true.

THE LITTLE CLAY CART   *King Shudraka*

This charming play is attributed to the renowned Hindu king Shudraka of the fifth and sixth century, but it may have been the work of the court poet Dandin. The same story seems to have been told about 350 A.D. in a drama by Bhasa, *The Poor Charudatta*, of which four acts are extant. Shudraka's play, in ten acts, is one of the few classical Hindu plays that deal largely with common people. This social type of Sanskrit drama is called Prakarana.

The story of *The Little Clay Cart* intertangles love and political intrigue. Charudatta, a bankrupt prince, and Vasantasena, a lovely and upright courtesan, are in love; she gives his little son, who has only a little clay cart to play with, the wherewithal for a gold one. She is to ride in Charudatta's bullock cart to meet him, but instead lets Aryaka, claimant to the throne, escape in it. In another cart, Vasantasena is intercepted by Samsthanaka, the vain and villainous brother-in-law of the king; when she rejects his advances, he strangles her and accuses Charudatta of the crime. A Buddhist monk (formerly a shampooer, a gambler whose debts Vasantasena had paid) comes upon her, revives her, and brings her to court just in time to save Charudatta. Aryaka, now king, honors Charudatta (who begs mercy for his accuser); Vasantasena is freed from her status as courtesan and becomes Charudatta's wife.

Although the story was told in Goethe's poem *The God and the Bayadere* and used in a ballet popular about 1830, the beauty, tenderness, and humor of the play were first brought from the Orient in a nineteenth century French translation by Gerard de Nerval (1808-1855) and Joseph Mery (1798-1865). Arthur William Ryder translated the play into English in 1905, but it was not until after Irene Lewisohn saw it in Bombay that the Neighborhood Playhouse of New York produced the play on December 5, 1924. The *Evening World* (December 18, 1924) said the play (some 1400 years old) showed "no trace of age whatever . . . it filled an evening with interest and delight." The *Sun* (November 5, 1926) felt it possesses "the loveliness and timelessness of idyllic drama . . . a Hindu holiday of utter grace, romance, wit, beguilement." There was a pleasantly staged production in New York in 1953.

In addition to its charm and tenderness, its frequent wit and occasional irony, the play draws neat fun from a number of minor figures, excellently, realistically drawn. The shampooer who lost at gambling and turned monk has already been mentioned. There is also Sharvilaka, the scientific burglar; before he breaches a wall he calculates whether to make an ovoid, rhomboid, or merely rectangular opening. The hole that he does make helps the plot by permitting him to discover the villain at work. Each minor character, neatly and humorously drawn, is thus caught into the main movement. In its course the play not only presents its romantic story, but displays the intrigues of politics, the corruption of justice, the character of the wicked, and the workings of fate. The action is effectively spread over a colorful background: the city of Avanti and its environs, streets, gardens, market place, and court. In its wide survey of men and their ways, said V. Raghavan in the *Encyclopedia of Literature* (1946), "such rich and varied material has gone into the *Mrichhakatika* that one might say no other play holds up the mirror to life so widely as does this one. Shudraka's composition is full of action but at the same time rich in poetry: now romantic, in the love of the hero and the heroine; now hilarious, with the wit and fun of the gamblers and the solecisms of Samsthanaka; now charming, in the descriptions of rain and music; now thrilling, in the poetical developments; now reaching heights of moral dignity, in the characters, not only of the important figures but of such lowly persons as the cart-driver; now touching, in the title incident of little Rosahena and the clay cart, and the incident of the Brahman hero, on the eve of his execution, bequeathing to his little son the sacred thread, Yajñopavita, 'the ornament of the Brahmans, gemless and goldless though it is'. The drama is full of varied emotional appeal, and is undoubtedly the most stageworthy of Sanskrit dramas."

In translation, too, the language is deft and pleasantly flowing, being, as Gilbert W. Gabriel said (December 8, 1924), "extraordinarily graceful English, brimful with iridescent couplets and quatrains, quips and images." Coming across the centuries, the charming drama *The Little*

Clay Cart shows us that in all times and climes politicans will intrigue
for power and place, love will exert its gentle but insistent force — and
poets will write great plays.

EYVIND OF THE HILLS   *Jóhann Sigurjónsson*

Based on an eighteenth century Icelandic folk legend of sheep thieves,
this violent tragedy was written in 1911 by Jóhann Sigurjónsson (1880-
1919), the first Icelandic author to write plays in Danish and the first
playwright of distinction to draw upon the colorful Icelandic life for
a setting.

The chief figure in the play is not the sheep-stealing Eyvind, but
Halla, the fierce woman who pits the brawny Eyvind against Bjorn, her
betrothed, then follows the outlaw Eyvind to a lonely life in the hills.
There, the threat of the law that seeks them out, but even more the
elemental forces of cold and hunger, destroy first their children, then
their love, then their very existence. In the early scenes especially,
before the tragic loom has grown relentless, there are vivid moments
of local color, some touched with irony. The wrestling match (a favorite
not only in melodrama, from which the motion pictures have borrowed
its tumultuous appeal, but also in dramas as different as *As You Like
It** and *The Apple Cart**) is here used to show Halla's delight in power,
as she teases her suitor Bjorn to try a fall with Eyvind. But there are
greater forces than man's, to beat down the outlaw.

Produced in Iceland December 25, 1911, in Copenhagen May 20, 1912,
the drama won instant acclaim and a permanent place in the Scandinavian theatre. Produced in New York February 1, 1921 with Margaret
Wycherly and Edward G. Robinson, it was hailed as a masterpiece. The
Post called it "imaginative, powerful, pessimistic . . . of genuine tragic
calibre." It gathers pace slowly, with emphasis on local color; but the
last two acts are crowded with tragic incident, swept along with dialogue
of beauty and power, swirling with a wild rhetoric until it drops to a
bitter and ominous calm for the fatal close.

The play, as the *New York Call* said (February 3, 1921), "is epic
in quality with the wild magnificence of the sagas. With its broad,
sweeping spaces and the limitless years passing over the two who defied
the world and fate, it paints the eternal tragedy of man and woman.
Its theme, for all its primitive freshness of manner, is one of sad sophistication, for it proves again that eternal truth, 'Love is not enough!'
The brave passion of youth disintegrating with the years, with suffering
and with loneliness, until it becomes perverted into bitterness and
hatred — that is the essential tragedy of Halla and Eyvind of the Hills."
The review in the *New York Globe* said the play manifests "unques-
tionable vision, elevation of spirit, beauty, and emotion." In the
creation of Halla, declared the *Tribune*, "Margaret Wycherly held her
audience in half terrified but rapt attention, carrying them into the
heart of tremendous emotions." Too grim for the entertainment seekers
on Broadway, too difficult for most little-theatre groups, *Eyvind of the
Hills* reawakens in the spirit the storms and the passions, but also the
indomitable will, of bleak and battered Iceland and elemental man.

THE RUSSIAN PEOPLE   *Konstantin Mikhailovich Simonov*

No play shown outside "the iron curtain" more fully represents the vigorous propaganda theatre of the Soviets than *The Russian People*, by Konstantin Mikhailovich Simonov (b. 1915). Produced in Moscow and serialized in *Pravda* in 1942, the play was shown in Washington, D. C. in an adaptation by Clifford Odets, opening December 14 of the same year. Eleonora Mendelssohn and Luther Adler were in the cast; Soviet Ambassador Litvinoff was in the audience. In the *Information Bulletin* of the Embassy of the U.S.S.R. (December 12, 1942), the play's director, V. Stanitsyn, explained: "We regard Simonov's play as the portrayal not of an isolated episode but of the war as a whole." And the author declared: "If my play is acted in such a way that the audience does not call for revenge, then it is not serving its purpose."

In nine episodic scenes, we see a Soviet village partly occupied, partly besieged, by the German Army. The two parts are separated by a river, which the Soviet lass Valya, an Army chauffeur, swims with messages. The situation of the beleaguered Russians is presented simply, realistically, much as it doubtless frequently occurred. There is the active guerrilla leader, young and ardent. His second in command, old Vasin, is a veteran of three wars — whose nephew is a spy. Among the waiting men is Globa, a colorful, lighthearted Lothario, who infuriates the earnest Valya with his notion that women should concern themselves with adorning men's lives, but who when the call comes is staunch to do his duty. The Quisling mayor is tortured by the Nazi commanding officer; his loyal wife poisons the Nazi's tea. In the midst of the daring and the dying, these folk remain simple. They compare photographs from home. Above all, they wait with a simple, unshakable faith in victory. They are surrounded; they have no water and no food — but also no despair. Many may die; each is ready; victory will come.

The reaction of Soviet audiences to the play is shown in the words, quoted in the Theatre Guild playbill, of the critic K. Borisov: "The hearts of the spectators beat faster, and no one is ashamed of his tears . . . We are not only touched, but intent; we are not only shaken, but filled with hatred of the enemy . . . 'The motherland demands it' — this is the root of all the emotions, deeds, and actions of these people. 'The motherland demands it' — this is the law to which their lives, thoughts, and feelings are subordinated." The American response to the play was not so enthusiastic, although *Variety* (December 16, 1924) dubbed the play "good red melodrama and rousing theatre. It pulls no punches in its propaganda preachment." The *Washington Times-Herald* said that "the adjective that best describes it is 'naive'."

The Russian People is marked by the two cardinal attributes of the propaganda play: it presents its plot and its theme in elementary, unmistakable, black-and-white fashion; and it appeals to a deep, almost religious faith in the audience. However natural the story and shrewd the dramatic presentation, such a play will certainly seem naive to those that do not share its ideals and faith, and will leave them cold, if not repelled. For those that accept its assumptions and aspire to its goals, this is one of the strongest and most moving of Soviet dramas.

THE MURDER IN THE OLD RED BARN   *Montague Slater*

Perhaps the best known title in all melodrama is *The Murder in the Old Red Barn*, also called after the victim, *Maria Marten*. Truly truth is stranger than fiction, for this play, based upon the true life story of Maria Marten and William Corder, is almost too fantastic to set upon the stage. Maria, a farm girl of Suffolk, England, had a child by Thomas Corder that died, then one by Peter Matthews, who sent her a few pounds from time to time. When she became pregnant by William Corder, Thomas' elder brother, Maria thought it time to sanctify these births by wedlock. Corder promised to marry her, asked her to meet him, and—she disappeared. Corder, a bit later, advertised for a wife; over fifty women answered. He married Mary Moore and with her money opened a school for girls. Then Maria Marten's stepmother had a dream, following which Maria's father went to Corder's red barn and dug up Maria's body. Clutched in the skeleton fingers was the fob of Corder's watch. The trial, opening February 7, 1828, was attended by women who wept for gentle Corder; his hanging was witnessed by over 10,000 persons, including fifty coach-loads of the aristocracy.

The rope that ended Corder's days was sold by the hangman at a guinea an inch. The editor of the *Newgate Calendar*, J. Curtis, wrote a book on the murder and the trial one copy of which, still preserved in the public library of Bury St. Edmonds, is bound with the tanned skin of William Corder. The night of his hanging, *Macbeth** was playing at Drury Lane; when Duncan asked: "Was execution done on Cawdor?" a voice from the gallery stopped the show with the cry: "Yes! I saw him hanged this morning!"

While Corder was still on trial, two plays based on his story were produced. The more successful of these, *Maria Marten*, by Montague Slater, revised by John Latimer in 1840, sent Maria to her doom disguised as a boy, and gave her an honest gypsy suitor, Carlos, upon whom Squire Corder threw suspicion of the deed. A 1935 motion picture version gave Carlos the final thrill of hanging the guilty Corder. In some versions Corder's child is born, then poisoned by its father. A version widely played at the turn of the century, *The Red Barn; or, How London Lives*, made the man that unearths the crime the murderer's brother.

No record can be checked of the performances of this hardy perennial of melodrama. During the 1920's and 1930's, it was still evoking appropriate horror in rural regions while London and New York, and in their trail college theatres everywhere, were presenting it for the laughter of post-Freudian playgoers. In London of 1924 it ran for five months. At the American Music Hall in New York, opening February 1, 1936, it reached over a hundred performances.

The Board of Education Co-operative Theatre presented it in London in 1937. In Baltimore, Maryland, it was produced by the Play-Arts Guild in 1934; survivors of that company played it in a barn at Catonsville, Maryland, on September 15, 1951—on a stage platform that rested on eighty-four bales of hay, with the backdrops on large window blinds rolled up or down for changing.

The essential story of this play is not greatly different from that of *An American Tragedy* by Theodore Dreiser. It is the treatment — with speed of exciting incidents in total disregard of psychological searching or even character portrayal—that explains why the play has provided over a century of thrills.

THE DRUNKARD   *William Henry Sedley Smith*

A "domestic temperance drama by W. H. Smith and a gentleman", *The Drunkard; or, The Fallen Saved* was presented in Boston in 1843 by P. T. Barnum as an "illustrated sermon" on the evils of drink. Many respectable people shunned the theatre in Barnum's day, but at his Museum the "sermon" attained 144 performances. Written by William Henry Sedley Smith (American, 1807-1872) in four facts, the melodrama was played constantly for a score of years; in New York, opening June 17, 1850, it ran for 198 performances. At the Boston performances, we are told, "it was no uncommon sight to see scores of men and women weeping like children". Toward the end of the century productions dwindled. With the twentieth century advent of Prohibition in the United States, the fortunes of *The Drunkard* underwent a decided shift. It became a nostalgic drama: through its fifteen scenes the audiences hissed the villain, reassured the heroine, and cheered the hero, while thumping mugs of "near beer" on the tables. Later the liquor grew stronger but the amusement no less. The play is nowadays presented without sets in front of painted drops; between the acts there are vaude-ville skits, songs and dances, singing waiters, and acrobats. Presented at the Provinectown Theatre, New York, December 30, 1929, during Prohibition, the play proved a persistent piece; on March 10, 1934 it reopened for 277 performances. London tried it in 1934 and 1942. In Los Angeles, "the longest run in the history of the legitimate theatre" began on July 6, 1933, and every night since—for a total to date of over 7,000 performances—the Theatre Mart has presented it. Mary Pickford spent at the play "one of the gayest evenings I ever remember". The comedian W. C. Fields, who saw it some two-score times, called it "the greatest show on earth". In 1939 the play was presented in Sydney, Australia. In 1944 it was banned by Boston; Chairman Mary Driscoll of the Licensing Board declared: "The Board does not approve of the production of the play in connection with a place licensed to sell alcoholic beverages."

The story grows out of the machinations of the evil lawyer Cribbs, playing and preying upon Edward Middleton, a fine, honest fellow, but with an unfailing failing for drink. The play opens with an old-fashioned wedding in a cottage as Edward marries Mary. It moves deviously down the husband's drinking course—there is the famous saloon scene in which his innocent child, Julia, sings "Father, dear Father, come home with me now." As Edward, under the lawyer's plying, grows more besotted, "Be revenged on the world!" Cribbs cries, and seeks to induce Edward to forge the name of the philanthropist Adam Rencelaw on a check. Edward refuses, Cribbs himself signs Rencelaw's name. Meanwhile, Cribbs seeks to seduce Edward's wife Mary who is starving in an attic; this failing, he forges a will, forecloses their home, and blames all their misfortunes on weak Edward. "Mother, do not cry!" Julia pleads. Mary's prayers are answered when Adam Rencelaw succeeds in foiling the plots of lawyer Cribbs and reunites with his family the repentant Edward, who has sworn off forever. Tangled in the plot are such persons as battling Farmer Stevens and wandering mad Margaret, and such happenings as a bottle's being handed to the drunkard by an arm reaching out of a hollow tree-trunk.

"When the West was new *The Drunkard* was old," said the *Los Angeles Times* (July 5, 1936); but it was to such audiences as the miners who crowded the West that the play made serious appeal. It belongs, like *East Lynne**, to a less sophisticated theatre age than that of Broadway, out beyond the towns touched by the touring companies. As sophomores gibe at the lowly freshmen, so those recently advanced beyond this play in theatrical sophistication find fun and complacent superiority in laughing at the husband who "came to swig and stayed to swoon". Other levels draw other diversion from the play. "Shakespeareans," said Ivor Brown (in the *London Observer;* December 2, 1934) "will observe that the author thought Ophelia worth stealing, and other scholars will welcome the Latinity with which the sinful lawyer can stiffen his plots and plans. Simpler folk will enjoy the persistence with which vice attacks and the punctuality with which virtue pops up to the defence."

The recent popularity of the play is a reminder of one value of the theatre unique among the public arts — the added emotional drive that rises from an audience's undergoing an experience together. There would be the thin lip of scorn pressed against *The Drunkard* by the few that might peruse it in the library; in the theatre, there is the open mouth of laughter, the shared gusto of the audience and the players. The villain leers defiance at those that hiss him; the heroine thanks them for taking her side. The spectators join the between-the-acts singing and now and again a star in the audience is persuaded to make her table the stage. The theatre comes into its own, fully though on the level of just good fun, as a home of shared experience. And one may question whether *The Drunkard* could be successful, even as a butt, if it did not have—beneath its crudity and simple sermonizing, its ink-well villain and white-wash heroine, its hustlings and poundings and heroics — a basic core of vitality and an upward surge of the spirit as with a Salvation hymn.

AJAX   *Sophocles*

During the youth of Sophocles (Greek, 497-405 B.C.), the theatre was dominated by Aeschylus*. Rivalry between the two playwrights soon developed as each quickly took advantage of the innovations of the other. Sophocles, who had a weak voice, discontinued the practice of having the dramatist perform his own plays. He added a third actor to the company. Aristotle states that Sophocles introduced scene painting. He increased the number and variety of stage properties. In his later works, he did not follow a single theme through a trilogy, but presented three plays on different subjects. Of some 123 plays that he wrote, seven survive, the earliest, *Ajax*, written when he was fifty.

Sophocles was very popular in his day and a devoted son of Athens.

In the dramatic contests he won the first prize twenty-four times; all his other entries won second place. When first Sophocles and Aeschylus presented opposing plays in the dramatic contest in 468 B.C., public feeling ran high. To satisfy everyone of the impartiality of the ten judges, the archon did not select them by lot as usual. When the ten generals entered the theatre to make the opening libations to the gods, he named them judges; they gave the victory to Sophocles.

Ajax (*The Whip-Bearing Ajax*), 447(?) B.C., presents an episode of the ancient legends that falls between the *Iliad* and the *Odyssey*. When Achilles died, Ajax and Odysseus both desired the dead hero's armor. It was awarded to Odysseus; Ajax in his pride felt that he had been slighted, and resolved to kill the Greek leaders. At this point the play opens. The program of a New York production (March 24, 1904) sums it up: "Self-glory and scorn of the gods are punished by madness, during which Ajax commits acts unworthy of himself; acts which on the recovery of his sanity so overwhelm him with shame that he escapes only by death; acts which are so dreadful in the eyes of the Greeks that they are unwilling to give his body decent burial until Odysseus, who has learned humility and justice from Athena, intercedes in behalf of the dead hero and perusades Agamemnon to allow the sacred rites to take place."

Sophocles' style has a sweetness that earned him the nickname, "the Attic bee". His chief advance beyond Aeschylus is in his concern for character. In Aeschylus it is an external fate, a "curse", that works upon the mortals of the story; in Sophocles, there is a heroic attitude toward life, within the character, that drives him to his doom. Even the minor figures are carefully drawn. Tecmessa, the loyal concubine of Ajax, is one of the most appealing women in the Greek drama. Odysseus is no stock hero; he has natural, human traits: alarm when the madman Ajax is about to come from his tent; but magnanimity at the close, when his words win proper burial for his fallen rival. Only Menelaus the Spartan—Sparta was the foe of Athens, in Sophocles' day— is shown as consistently base. A further neat touch in several of Sophocles' plays is the introduction of silent characters, usually children—here, the young son of Ajax and Tecmessa—whose silent helplessness and bewildered sorrow add considerably to the emotional power of the drama. Euripides also uses such children, as in the *Medea**.

The chief character, Ajax, is most carefully drawn. His excessive pride (hybris) has set the madness upon him, so that he wreaks havoc upon the Greek flocks and scourges a ram he takes to be Odysseus. Yet he must be rehabilitated—perhaps, indeed, that was the basic reason for Sophocles' writing the play—because the most famous Athenians, Miltiades, hero of Marathon, Thucydides, and Alcibiades, claimed descent from Ajax, King of Salamis. With care and consummate skill Sophocles follows the mental anguish of Ajax from the time he recovers his reason and discovers his mad actions through the shame and the heroic resolve that lead to his suicide and "peace".

In the *Ajax*, as in Sophocles' plays thereafter, the gods are less external forces than symbols of the hero's own impulses. The temple of Zeus at Olympia showed a figure of Heracles straining every muscle to uphold the heavens, while the goddess Athena with one relaxed arm makes the deed possible. This interaction of the human and the divine becomes in Sophocles a manifestation of the divine within the human. The *theos*, the outer god, has become the *ethos*, the inner spirit. Ajax holds to his standards. His nobility leads to, but triumphs in, his death. In two other important aspects the drama marks a growth in theatrical art. There is first a conscious increase in the use of dramatic irony, which raises the audience as it were to Mount Olympus, contemplating, with such prevision as the gods possess, the imminent plight of the unwitting mortals. When Ajax, for example, speaks of "peace" to come, the chorus sings a song of joy at his recovery; but allusions that the chorus fails to catch let the audience know that Ajax himself is looking forward to the peace of death. The second change is the bringing of direct, even violent, action onto the stage. Before *Ajax*, combats, murders, and other desperate deeds occurred out of sight, and were reported by messenger. Here, when Ajax is ready to die, he plunges on his sword in full view of the audience. This revolutionary change was not adopted for all subsequent Greek plays; but it is basic in the shift from a primarily lyric to a truly dramatic theatre.

Frequently produced in ancient Greece, the drama was enacted at Cambridge, England, in 1883. During rehearsals for a 1903 production by the Greeks in Chicago, the Athenian and the Spartan Greeks quarreled over the parts; all the Spartans stayed away from one rehearsal, and an Athenian remarked, "I guess the Peloponnesian War will never end." The first New York production, also in Greek, was in 1904.

"A day can humble all humans, and a day can lift them up." With beauty, dignity, and power Sophocles' *Ajax*, showing the hero fallen because he refuses to live with shame, lays bare for our beholding the deep impulses of human nature and the consequences our natures bring upon ourselves.

ANTIGONE   *Sophocles*

Sophocles' thirty-second play, *Antigone*, written in 442 B.C., was in ancient times considered his best work. Its theme is the still insistent conflict of the individual and the state, the question of the right of a person to reject a human edict that in his judgment violates a higher law. Its story is told nowhere else in ancient writings and may be Sophocles' invention.

As told in Aeschylus' *Seven Against Thebes**, the two sons of Oedipus have slain each other. In *Antigone*, King Creon orders Eteocles, the son that had defended Thebes, to be buried; but he denies to Polyneices, the son that had attacked the city, the funeral rites that were of final import to the Greeks. Antigone resolves that her brother shall be decently buried. In the opposition of wills that follows, Antigone is led to death; Creon's son Haemon, who loves her, kills himself; his mother then does the same in grief for him; and Creon is left to mourn the results of his obstinate pride.

The drama abounds in splendid passages and choral lyrics. Early in the play is a splendid eulogy of man; later, a rousing ode to love. Sophocles' contemporaries, in addition to the beauty and the forcefulness of the drama, may have discerned in some of Creon's specious arguments satiric shafts against the sophists, then becoming prominent in Athens. As a result of the play's success, tradition reports, Sophocles was appointed in 440 B.C. (along with Pericles) as one of the generals to conduct the Samian War.

The play has continued successful. In the nineteenth century, it was presented frequently in London. In 1846 it was done with music by Mendelssohn. Six years later Miss Vandenhoff made a tremendous impression as Antigone. The *Lady's Newspaper* (April 10, 1852) quotes the *London Times* as saying she "produced an effect perfectly electrical, and totally unlike anything else that we have seen," and the *Observer* as declaring her work "one of the most perfect impersonations on the English stage, or, it may be, in the whole compass of the English drama." From Covent Garden, London, a production of 1844 was brought the next year to New York. There the *Spirit of the Times* (April 12, 1845) commented that "*Antigone*, the concluding section of the Oedipus story, is the simplest, least mechanical, most sublime . . . The language is assuredly sublime; the words of the chorus, in places light and graceful, at times measured and affecting." Within a week, however, in the vogue of the day, a burlesque of the play appeared.

In more recent years the drama has been reshaped to various purposes. Jean Cocteau wrote a version, with music by Arthur Honegger, which, translated by Francis Fergusson, was presented in New York by the American Laboratory Theatre, opening April 24, 1930. Cocteau declared that if one "photographs Greece from an airplane one sees it in quite a new light. It is in this way that I wished to translate *Antigone*. From a bird's eye view great beauties are lost; others emerge for the first time: new relationships, blocks, shadows, angles and reliefs are discovered." The critics recognized that in the Cocteau version great beauties were lost; his triumph, said John Mason Brown, "consists of robbing the original of both its dignity and its beauty and putting nothing in their place." Cocteau here failed as aviator, photographer, and playwright.

Political use has also been made of the play. Walter Hasenclever rewrote it in 1916 as a protest against World War I: "*Antigone* was for me the bearer of the ideal of emancipation and of human brotherhood in the desert of murder and violence." Creon and his marshal, in this version, resemble Kaiser Wilhelm II and Ludendorff. Hasenclever's version was adapted for Soviet Russia in 1929 by Gorodetzky; the director Tairov stated: "In our transcription of the play, *Antigone* is the tragedy of the insufficiently organized and therefore until now unsuccessful attempt of the European nations to cast off the yoke of imperialist Absolutism or Fascism, which reared its throne on the corpses of the fighters for a new life."

Such contemporary twistings and limitations of an eternal thought seem bound to make the play banal. We have had recent evidence that they do; for Jean Anouilh rewrote it in Paris during World War II, and his modernized version, translated by Lewis Galantiere, was brought to New York on February 18, 1946, with Cedric Hardwicke as Creon and Katharine Cornell as Antigone. Although superb acting kept the play onstage for 64 performances, Anouilh, seeking both to placate the Germans who occupied Paris and to rouse the French, succeeded merely in boring Americans. He presented Creon not as a harsh tyrant, but as a calm worker for law and order, which are to him more important than any individual code of morals. When his son and his wife commit suicide Creon sighs and goes to a Cabinet meeting. Anouihl's product, said the generous George Jean Nathan, proved "less Sophocles than sophomore." In addition to these stage versions and perversions, the play has been translated by R. C. Jebb; by R. C. Trevelyan; by Dudley Fitts and Robert Fitzgerald — whose translation, said the *New York Times* (March 5, 1939), "brings the play measurably nearer to us than most"—and by Shaemas O'Sheel. The Fitts-Fitzgerald version was movingly directed by N. Bryllion Fagin at the Johns Hopkins theatre in Baltimore in 1949.

The superb and sensitive character-drawing of Sophocles is manifest in the play. The frail and feminine Ismene is effectively contrasted with her resolute and calm sister Antigone; yet for all her weakness Ismene is ready to die for those she loves—an emotional quality that is met with scorn by the deliberate and reasoning Antigone, sure both of her rectitude and her pathway. Without compromise or regard for consequences, she does what she feels is right, knowing it will bring on her doom. Creon, on the other hand, recognizes his error as he mourns over his son's body. Both were unalterable; he with the obstinacy of a tyrant; she with the firmness of a hero.

Among the technical devices that mark Sophocles' skill, two may be mentioned. He introduces comic relief into the tragedy (as later, Shakespeare*), making the guard over Polyneices' body a bit of a wag, with pity for Antigone as he arrests her, but not so much pity as he'd have had for himself if she had slipped by. And he makes effective use of silence to add to the dramatic intensity, as when, on hearing of her son's suicide, Creon's wife Eurydice steals wordlessly away to end her own life.

The beauty and the vibrant force of *Antigone* press through the well-knit drama. Its basic conflict of the individual judgment and will against the mandate of the state is as recurrent as its final thought is true: "Great words of prideful men are ever punished with great blows and, in old age, teach the chastened to be wise."

THE TRACHINIAE   *Sophocles*

The influence of Euripides is especially marked in *The Trachiniae* (*The Women of Trachis*), 437 B.C.(?). Here, more than in any other of Sophocles' works, the prologue follows the Euripidean pattern; and the chorus, as regularly with the younger man, plays hardly any part in the tragedy, being reduced to little more than lyrical interludes. The poisoned robe of this play recurs in Euripides' *Medea**, 431 B.C.; Sophocles in line 1101 seems to quote from Euripides' *Mad Heracles** (line 1353); but the question of indebtedness is still a scholars' dispute.

Heracles, bringing home his bride Dejaneira, with a poisoned arrow slew the centaur Nessus who tried to ravish her. The dying centaur told Dejaneira that the clotted blood around his wound, if used as a charm, would keep Heracles from loving any other woman more than he loved her. The drama opens with Dejaneira awaiting Heracles' homecoming; the last of his labors and the last of the penalties the gods have laid on him are over. It is prophesied that if he reaches home safely, Heracles will live happily forever. Word of Heracles' approach rejoices Dejaneira. She hears, also, that Heracles is enamored of his slave Iole;

therefore Dejaneira rubs the Nessus charm on a cloak and sends it with
her welcome to Heracles. The hero, donning the cloak, finds his body
caught into sudden fire. Learning of Nessus' cunning and fatally decep-
tive truth, Dejaneira kills hereslf. The anguished Heracles orders his
son Hyllus to build his funeral pyre on Mount Oeta and then to
marry Iole.

The German critic A. W. Schlegel thought the play not good enough
to be Sophocles', but others have felt that it will bear comparison with
his greatest tragedies. Its devices are typically Sophoclean: the introduction of the tortured Heracles on the stage, the silent departure of
Dejaneira to her self-inflicted death, the economy of means with which
the entire play is constructed. The emphasis on character, too, is Sophoclean. Heracles in his torment kills his herald and rails upon his wife;
he is an unchained fury. But Dejaneira is outstanding among the
women of the Greek drama, probably, said Cedric H. Whitman in
Sophocles (1951) "the only completely dignified picture of a passionately
devoted woman extant in Greek tragedy": gentle, affectionate, loving
but worried about her husband, and with sympathy even for her supposed rival, the captive Iole; yet she employs little tricks, as when she
worms out of the herald word of Heracles' feeling for Iole, and she lacks
foresight to see through Nessus' scheme for wreaking vengeance.

The uncertainty of human knowledge, indeed, is emphasized throughout the drama. It glints through the double-meaning in the words of the
centaur Nessus, and in the prophecy about Heracles. It is pressed home
by the chorus, which responds, when Dejaneira asks its advice about
rubbing the charm on the cloak: "You must do it to find out." "Why is
knowledge terrible?" Dejaneira wonders. The Sophoclean answer is
that it comes too late.

Gilbert Murray's translation of the drama, which he called The Wife
of Heracles, was reviewed with favor in the London Times of September
6, 1947. The play presents a not widely known episode of classical
myth; and, although it has universal overtones, the legend itself does
not deeply enough stir modern sympathies to win modern performance.
The Trachiniae remains an appealing character study, with ironic shadings, of the inglorious though unflinching end of a proud hero, and the
destructive power of a jealous love.

OEDIPUS THE KING   Sophocles

Most students of the drama consider this play the masterpiece of the
ancient stage. Aristotle mentions it more than any other play and calls
it a model in the treatment of its plot. It is truly a superbly constructed play. Two important aspects of Greek and of much modern
tragedy — the "recognition" scene and the peripeteia or reversal of fortune — are so deftly developed that they come together: Oedipus' awareness of his identity is also Oedipus' doom.

The play begins with Theban citizens pleading with their king, Oedipus, for relief from the pestilence that is devouring the city. Creon returns from the oracle with word that first the city must cleanse itself of
the defilement within, and must avenge the murder of its former king,
Laius, who has been killed in a roadside brawl. Step by step — with a
skill unsurpassed in the neatest detective story of today — as Oedipus

seeks the source of the pollution, we learn the fatal facts. It had been prophesied that the son of King Laius and Jocasta would kill his father and marry his mother; the infant, therefore, had been given to a shepherd to leave to die. Laius' widow, Jocasta, has married the hero Oedipus, who has saved Thebes by solving the riddle of the Sphinx. With gathering horror, as the inquiry goes on, Jocasta suspects the truth and tries to stop the investigation. Teiresias, the blind seer, bids Oedipus seek no further. But Oedipus, blinder than the seer, forces the inquiry on. Jocasta rushes away and hangs herself. Though the light begins to dawn in him, Oedipus takes the only honorable part, insisting that the inquiry proceed. In an awful moment, he wakens to the knowledge that he himself is that son of Laius, that the prophecy has been horribly fulfilled. Oedipus blinds himself and goes forth a wanderer, leaving Creon to guide the recovery of Thebes. Silently Antigone and Ismene, the two little daughters of the incestuous union, stand watching and by their presence deepen the tragic grief.

The characters are developed with a skill that matches that of the play's structure. Creon is a temperate man; his response to Oedipus' charges that he is stirring trouble is restrained; his reasons for not wishing to be a ruler are measured, and pertinent today; his gentle firmness with the broken Oedipus makes him most sympathetic (quite unlike the side he reveals in the *Antigone**). Jocasta is a warm-hearted woman whose love does not blind her; she tries to calm Oedipus, to mediate between him and her brother Creon; she grows into a richly developed tragic figure. Oedipus himself is the criterion of tragic heroes, a great man doomed not through depravity but through the very excess of some good quality in him. It is his firmness on the proper path, in the quest of his people's good, that brings him doom. The play ends with the maxim that opens *The Trachiniae*: "Count no man happy until he has crossed life's border free from pain."

Athens was devastated by a great plague from 430 to 427 B.C. Most scholars believe that the play was written at this time. Others, pointing out that the dramatist Phrynichus had earlier been fined for a play reminding the Athenians of misfortunes, believe that Sophocles produced his drama before the plague. The story was, indeed, most popular among the playwrights. All three of the great tragedians and at least ten minor ones wrote plays of Oedipus. Julius Caesar wrote one. Seneca's version, of about 60 A.D., survives. In modern times Sophocles' play continued popular. Racine called it "the ideal tragedy." Corneille wrote *Oedipe* in 1657; in his version, Oedipus is not a noble figure, but suspicious, designing, not heedful of his people's well-being but eager to keep his crown. The version by Dryden in 1679 introduces much new material, including a daughter of Laius and Jocasta for whom Creon incestuously hungers; it is ranting and bloody. Voltaire's version, in 1718, makes the most vigorous use of the story in modern times; it introduces Philoctetes (*see* Sophocles' play by that name) as another suitor for Jocasta and emphasizes the cruelty of the gods. Voltaire's play was popular because of certain scandals in court circles of his day; similarly, Shelley's *Oedipus Tyrannus, or Swellfoot the Tyrant*, 1820, was a satire on the matrimonial affairs of George IV. (Oedipus means swollen-foot: when the infant was exposed, it was hung to a tree by a twig passed through its feet.)

The drama has been frequently revived. Oedipus was the greatest role of the French actor Mounet-Sully, around 1880; he played it in New York in 1894. The first American production was at Harvard University in 1881, in Greek, with a cast of a hundred and nineteen. In 1882 George Riddle produced the play in New York, Oedipus speaking Greek, the others English. The first wholly English performance was with John E. Kellard in 1911. *Oedipus* was played in New York in German with Rudolph Christians in 1914. In 1931 an elaborate production of Jean Cocteau's French version, with music by Stravinsky and Stokowski conducting the Philadelphia Orchestra, was given at the Metropolitan Opera House with Paul Althouse as Oedipus and Margarete Matzenauer as Jocasta. In May 1948 the Habima Players presented the drama in New York in Hebrew. It was played in Delphi, Greece, in 1951. A French version by André Gide was enacted by Jean-Louis Barrault in Paris and in London in 1951. The modern Greek version of the Greek National Theatre, with superb use of the chorus, was shown in New York opening November 24, 1952.

Several recent productions in English are memorable. In 1915 Augustin Duncan presented Margaret Wycherly as Jocasta, with the Chorus sung and danced by Isadora Duncan and her group. In 1923 Sir John Martin-Harvey brought to the United States a production that Max Reinhardt had supervised, in the vigorous Gilbert Murray translation. The *New York Times* (October 26, 1923) declared that *"Oedipus Rex* came to life last night in its true Hellenic quality, as few modern productions of Greek tragedy have ever done." Of a later Reinhardt production in London, James Agate, in the *London Times* (October 4, 1936), observed: "The final exit through the audience is one of those colossal mistakes of which only your highbrow producer is capable." In Dublin in 1933 the Abbey Theatre produced a version by William Butler Yeats, a fiery poetic translation of the vivid Greek. This version was brought to New York by the Old Vic Company in 1946, with Laurence Oliver giving his best performance of the tour, as Oedipus. The presentation was grimly realistic, with the blood from the blinded Oedipus smearing the cheeks of his little weeping daughters. The production unfolded, said Howard Barnes (May 21, 1946) "with soaring imagination and artistry." Two recent versions in France call for attention. Both include the legend of Oedipus and the Sphinx. In the short and shocking play by André Gide (1931), all the characters are proud and corrupt; the sons of Oedipus' incest seduce their sisters. Gide makes his play banal with trivial puns and images, as he makes it perverse with added horrors; but he presses home the thought that sin is infectious. Jean Cocteau's *The Infernal Machine* (1934) rises to eloquence in the dialogue and is effectively imaginative in many moments. But in sum, where Gide made the story more horrid, Cocteau made it more sentimental. Even in its incestuous horror, the Greek original holds the chastity of art.

One reason for the perennial hold of *Oedipus* lies in the fact that its legend of the king that kills his own father follows the pattern of the primordial drama, the nature myth and ritual slaying of the Old Year by the New Year, which then marries the wife-mother Nature. This primordial pattern of incest, at once abhorrent and essential for the primitive renewal of a people's strength, still lurks in the fixations and the complexes—including the Oedipus complex—that modern psychology finds lurking within us all. However, the play needs no reenforcement from modern psychology; rather, it gives forcefulness of illustration to a basic human drive.

Through the ages the drama has lived, to deepen in our hearts and minds the sense of human suffering; of human dignity in the grip of great misfortune; of human power to bear. And out of such tragedy, through its truth and its beauty, wells an exaltation, a reaffirmation of human onward effort and human worth.

ELECTRA   *Sophocles*

The story of Electra survives in plays of all three of the great Greek tragic dramatists: the *Choephori** of Aeschylus, the *Electra*, 413 B.C., of Euripides, and the *Electra*, 414(?) B.C., of Sophocles. In all three, the basic plot is the same: Orestes, grown to manhood, returns to Mycenae, where his sister Electra has been awaiting him, and kills his mother Clytemnestra and her lover Aegisthus, the murderers of his father. The minor variations in the plays show the different natures and purposes of the dramatists.

When Sophocles wrote his drama Aeschylus had been dead for forty years and his drama was a monument, the public's love of which Sophocles had to weigh and counterbalance to win approval of his different emphasis. Sophocles presents to the intellect a character-study of a woman pressed upon by grievous circumstance. He develops skillfully the high-spirited Electra, by contrast with her mother and with her weaker sister, driving with resolute sense of duty to the desperate deed as she "defends the right, and shows to godless men how the gods vindicate impiety." To strengthen this feeling, Sophocles neglects Clytemnestra's more legitimate motive for killing her husband, his sacrifice of their daughter Iphigenia, and emphasizes her lust for her lover Aegisthus. Electra urges her brother to the deed; when Clytemnestra shrieks inside the palace, Electra cries out "Strike again!" The play ends with a note of triumph, and the chorus concludes that the curse has fallen from the house of Atreus, "crowned with good by this day's enterprise". Sophocles alone has Clytemnestra die before Aegisthus; this order also keeps prominent the earlier crime and the justice of the present deed. But this is Electra's play, not Orestes'; its theme is endurance and the choice of adversity because of the soul's demands upon itself.

Euripides' *Electra,* which may be an answer to Sophocles,' tones down the horror and seeks to humanize the deed. It thus makes Electra a more sympathetic figure, and has proved the most appealing of the three dramas. Plutarch tells us that in 404 B.C., at the end of the Peloponnesian War, when Lysander was pondering whether to wipe the fallen Athens from the earth, a citizen of Phocis sang the opening chorus of Euripides' *Electra*, "O Agamemnon's child, Electra, to thy humble cot I come": a gust of pity swept the assembled leaders, and Athens was spared.

Recent American productions of Euripides' play include many by Mr. and Mrs. Coburn in the 1910's; one by Actors Equity in New York **in**

1924; at Carnegie Tech, Pennsylvania, in 1932; off-Broadway in 1951. But most recent revivals, like that of London's Old Vic on March 13, 1951, have used the starker *Electra* of Sophocles. The Greek National Theatre brought its modern Greek version to New York with Katina Paxinou in 1952. (For various adaptations of *Electra,* see Aeschylus' *Oresteia**.)

The role of Electra has lured many great stars. Mrs. Pat Campbell opened in New York on February 11, 1908, with Mrs. Beerbohm Tree as Clytemnestra, in a version translated by Arthur Symons from the 1904 German adaptation of Hugo von Hofmannsthal. This mixture of potent Greek and perfervid Freud produced, said the *New York World* "a performance true in every detail to a well wrought conception, plastic, picturesque, and horrid, with a now smothered, now outbursting lust of revenge, a kind of craze of blood . . . curious, sensually cruel—and fascinating." Margaret Anglin, beginning with an open-air performance in Berkeley, California, in 1915, returned to the role of Electra frequently. In 1918, in New York, she alternated the roles of Electra and Medea (for a comparison, see Euripides' *Medea**). John Corbin (February 17, 1918) observed: "It does take some little detachment of mind to enter into the mood of a heroine who rejoices in matricide as a religious duty. The greater credit, then, to Sophocles and to Margaret Anglin that the performance stood out in such glowing colors, had power to move us so deeply." Nine years later Brooks Atkinson (May 4, 1927) said that her performance held "all the majesty of Greek tragedy at its best . . . full austerity and frigid beauty . . . She is an instrument rather than a personality; she is a sublimation of justice purging the house of Atreus." Margaret Anglin used the E. H. Plumptre translation; a less effective version by J. T. Sheppard was used in the 1932 production, with Blanche Yurka as Electra and Mrs. Pat Campbell this time as Clytemnestra. The *New York Herald-Tribune* (January 9, 1932) felt that the "treatment was marked by a Shakespearean robustness rather than that marble-like austerity commonly associated with the classic Greek."

No more recent American productions can match the work of Margaret Anglin, especially in the 1918 performances at Carnegie Hall, including music by Walter Damrosch. There was a production in Greek at Randolph-Macon College in 1943. Katina Paxinou, who with the Royal Theatre Company of Greece gave a Greek production at Cambridge, England, in 1939, with, said the *London Times* (June 19, 1939), "an effect not only of its natural power but of an extraordinary freshness", gave English readings of the play in New York in 1942. In French, Jean Giraudoux produced a version in Paris (June 17, 1937), which began with Electra unaware of her mother's misdeeds, and which slowed the action by many comments of the modern dramatist. Concentration of the action around the long steps and the central door helped give simple beauty and austere power to a production, in the translation of Francis Fergusson, in April 1948 by the Johns Hopkins Playshop in Baltimore. The best productions, indeed, have been made with vigorous translations, not modernized adaptations. "Euripides still appears to us," said Clayton Hamilton in *Vogue* (April, 1918), "as he seemed, long ago, to Aristotle, 'the most tragic of the poets', but Sophocles is more august and monumental in the architecture of his plays." That "architecture" rears, in the story of Electra, a lofty tragic figure, still made most vivid and most touching in the telling of the ancient Greeks.

PHILOCTETES   *Sophocles*

Written when Sophocles was 87 years old, his *Philoctetes* won first prize in the contest of 409 B.C. It is the best presentation of a moral problem in the Greek drama.

The play is based upon an episode in the Trojan War. Long before the point at which Sophocles' drama opens, young Philoctetes, for having lighted Heracles' funeral pyre, was by that dying hero given his bow and arrows. When the Greeks set out against Troy, they had to stop to sacrifice at a shrine; Philoctetes, who guided them, was bitten by a serpent and afflicted with a loathsome, unhealing sore and stench. The Greek commanders thereupon ordered Odysseus to maroon Philoctetes on the uninhabited island of Lemnos. Now, after nine years of vain siege of Troy, it is prophesied that if Achilles' son Neoptolemus come to Troy, and if Philoctetes willingly bring Heracles' bow and arrows, the besieged city will fall. The play opens with Odysseus and Neoptolemus come to Lemnos for the arms. Odysseus remains the same throughout, the shrewd schemer with no moral qualms, justifying the means when the end is the glory of Greece. But each of the other two main figures works through a human problem. Neoptolemus, a noble, patriotic youth, is persuaded by Odysseus, whom Philoctetes would have recognized and spurned, to use guile to secure the bow and arrows essential to their victory. The youth's repugnance, then his yielding for his country's sake, are admirably shown. After winning Philoctetes' friendship and the weapons, however, Neoptolemus in honest revulsion finds the deceit too mean; he frankly tells Philoctetes who they are and what their needs and returns the bow and arrows. Philoctetes, the young man says, should freely accompany them to Troy. Now the moral conflict shifts to the breast of the older man. It is harder for him to be generous. Through long years on the lonely island he has nursed his hatred with his injury: what has his country done for him, that he should now strike for her? Neoptolemus recognizes the validity of the objection and agrees to go with Philoctetes back to Greece. This friendship wakens a responsive chord in Philoctetes. Then Heracles, who had given Philoctetes the bow and arrows, comes down onto the stage and bids him go to Troy. After he has held firm against guile, force, even friendly persuasion and the promise that his sores will be healed, then freely the will of Philoctetes himself (as Cedric H. Whitman views it, in *Sophocles,* 1951), makes the fit choice, as a noble man must. Philoctetes beholds Heracles, and "suddenly his victory appears to him. There are few moments in drama more breath-taking than this one." The god makes manifest the divinity within the man. The "god from the machine" has become the voice of the spirit.

The story of Philoctetes was very popular; six lesser dramatists used it, as well as the great three. Only Sophocles' version remains; but the critic Dion Chrysostomus, of the first century A.D., has left us a comparison of the versions of Aeschylus, Sophocles, and Euripides. (Euripides' was presented in 431 B.C. along with the extant *Medea*.*) According to Dion, Aeschylus' version was marked by simplicity, greatness of soul, power of thought and language; Euripides' by keen rhetoric and choral exhortations to noble deeds; Sophocles' — as we, too, can attest — by dignity and naturalness, truth to human nature. The farewell of Philoctetes to Lemnos, where he has long dwelt in fortitude, makes a rare and exalted close to the drama.

Philoctetes is without female characters. Its men are among the most complex in ancient drama, shrewdly studied, clearly portrayed. Their problems of the practical versus the decent action, of concern for one's own interests versus concern for the good of the state, of the endurance of injustice and many woes with unquenched nobility, are fundamental in every time and have had few more searching presentations in the drama.

OEDIPUS AT COLONUS   *Sophocles*

The longest extant Greek tragedy (1,779 lines), *Oedipus at Colonus*, possibly written in 406 B.C., is by many acclaimed as Sophocles' best. The last play of the aged dramatist, it was produced posthumously in 401 B.C. by his grandson, Sophocles the younger, and won the first prize. The work was highly esteemed throughout antiquity; Longinus, a critic of the third Christian century, remarked: "Magnificent are the images that Sophocles has conceived of the death of Oedipus, who makes ready his burial amid the portents of the sky."

We see here the last hours of Oedipus, twenty years after he has blinded himself. He has come, a beggar in rags, to Colonus in Attica, but still a figure of majesty and of portent. For it has been prophesied that the city where he is buried will have a future of peace and glory. Creon, King of Thebes, therefore comes to take Oedipus back to that city; he refuses to go and is protected by Theseus, King of Athens. Oedipus walks — as though sight had returned to him, or a god were his guide — to the place where he has to die and, in an awe-filled silence, disappears.

This is the only known play on the theme of Oedipus' final hours. Sophocles saw the dramatic possibilities in the subject; but also, Sophocles was born at Colonus, where Oedipus died, and the playwright was moved by a deep devotion to his native land. Colonus was a division of Attica just north of Athens; Sophocles' choral lyric (lines 668-719) in praise of the city, along with that in Euripides' *Medea** (lines 824-845), is the noblest tribute to Athens in the Greek drama. When Sophocles' son charged the nonegenarian playwright with incompetence, Sophocles' only defense was to recite in court this lyric, which he had just composed: he was at once acquitted. The poetry throughout the play is unsurpassed in Sophocles; another great speech is Oedipus' comment (lines 607-623) on the changes wrought by time. The conception of Oedipus in this play is richer and nobler than in Sophocles' earlier *Oedipus Rex**. Beggar in body, the blind man is noble in spirit, He walks with his daughter as guide yet bears himself assured by an inner power. Time has dimmed the horror of his deeds, his killing his father and marrying his mother, and, as he has acted innocently, he is burdened with no sense of guilt. There still is vigor in the man, as shown in the vehemence with which he curses his undutiful sons, who for their own ends would have him return to Thebes. Oedipus rebukes them for their persistence

SOUTHERNE

on an ignoble way; but he himself has moved toward tranquility and peace, to the final calm that, all passion spent, marks the noble end of a great man.

Perhaps for some contemporary purpose that we cannot guess, Sophocles makes Polyneices (see *Seven Against Thebes**) not the younger but the elder son of Oedipus. King Creon of Thebes, Sophocles presents as an unscrupulous schemer who comes in guile and leaves in violence. King Theseus of Athens he shows as a just and beloved ruler and protector of the weak. Like a man of lofty character, Theseus has a democratic spirit; he welcomes the exiled and beggared Oedipus. As the Athenians had defeated a Theban detachment near Colonus in 407 B.C., the year before the play was written, it is obvious that Sophocles' deep love of his country and his desire to cheer it in the present crisis contributed to the power of the play. Athens was in desperate straits, her leaders incompetent, her armies crumbling, her citizens unfed; yet Sophocles speaks of Athens as inviolable. Time goes on, but remains the same; fortitude and knowledge, enduring, grow. The fortitude of Athens is embodied in Oedipus.

Recent productions include one in Berlin in 1929, another at the Greek Theatre of Syracuse, Sicily, in 1936. There are several English translations of the play: a rather literal one by R. C. Jebb: a poetic one by Yeats; one by R. C. Trevelyan. Reviewing the last-mentioned version, the *London Times* (June 22, 1946) declared that it "conveys, more certainly than any other Greek play, the sense of ultimate serenity." The play was performed in New York, off-Broadway, in 1955.

Certainly there is no easy optimism in this last play of the great dramatist, written in his nineteenth year, when a long war was moving toward disaster for his beloved city. Yet the final words are of courage and fair pride, for the chorus calls: "Come, cease lamentation, lift it up no more; for verily these things stand fast." Here, against the triumph of death, Sophocles erects the dignity and the will of man in one of the most beautiful and most exalting of all dramas.

OROONOKO   *Thomas Southerne*

Come to London, Irish-born Thomas Southerne (1660-1746), became a friend of Dryden, for some of whose plays he wrote prologues or epilogues. After writing several comedies which were as risqué as their titles indicate and the times encouraged, he turned to more serious efforts and wrote *The Fatal Marriage; or, The Innocent Adultery*, 1694, based on Mrs. Aphra Behn's novel *The Nun; or, The Perjur'd Beauty*; and *Oroonoko; or, The Royal Slave*, 1695, based on Mrs. Behn's novel of the same name (about 1678). These two tragedies of Southerne were great successes; their influence on the eighteenth century tragic playwrights, and thus in the shaping of nineteenth century melodrama, was greater than Shakespeare's.

Oroonoko is the first picture of "the noble savage" mistreated, debased, and enslaved by the heedless and avaricious European; it opens the trail to the works of Rousseau and the other Romantics. The play presents the sad life of the Negro prince Oroonoko and his beloved Imoinda, as slaves in Surinam in the West Indies. Imoinda, daughter of an African general, was sold into slavery when the king, enamored of her, discovered that she was in love with his heir, Oroonoko. Later, Oroonoko is himself captured by an English slave-ship; he is reunited with Imoinda in Surinam. There, he heads a slave rebellion which is checked by the promises of deputy-governor Byam. However, the promises are false; the slaves are turned over to the cruel and vengeful slave-drivers. Imoinda is especially reserved for the deputy's lust; rather than submit, she kills herself. Oroonoko kills the false Byam, then takes his own life. The passion of the white deputy-governor for Imoinda, added to Mrs. Behn's story by Southerne, made an important impelling force in the dramatic drive.

The play was first performed in London, December 1695. It moved almost an entire century to tears. Its climax, said the *Dramatic Historiographer* (1735), is "a catastrophe truly mournful in itself, but much more so as it is heightened by the most tender and affecting language, and set off with all the embellishments of poetry which a dramatick piece will admit, without going beyond nature." Through the eighteenth century London saw at least fifteen revivals. The New York premiere was at the John Street Theatre, October 18, 1783. The play lapsed from favor during the nineteenth century. Ralph Richardson played Oroonoko in a Malvern Festival revival, August 1932. The *London Times* (August 4, 1932) said: "A big situation is constantly being deflated by rant, and psychological insight shattered by the contrivance of the next situation or the under-plot. On the other hand, though the poetry is cold the sentiment is warm, and the play has the vitality which belongs to a tract for the times . . . *Oroonoko* has the essential elements of tragedy — conflict of loyalties, and catastrophe (in this, a suicide pact); but there is too much base action to 'purge' us by terror, although there is pity enough."

There are majesty, and dignity too, in the characters; and the "fatal flaw" that tragedy requires, in the excessive passions of Oroonoko. There are also, despite the rhetorical ranting and the only occasionally happy phrase — the play is the source of the expression "Pity's akin to love" — a grandiose range of emotion, and an exalted spirit that sets honor and freedom as more precious than life itself. These still hold power, and raise *Oroonoko* to a more than merely historical place among tragic melodramas.

GAMMER GURTON'S NEEDLE *William Stevenson*

Acted at Christ's College, Cambridge, for several years after 1553 and published in 1575, *Gammer Gurton's Needle,* by William Stevenson (died in 1575), is the first English comedy with a wholly native theme. _Ralph Roister Doister*, which preceded it by a decade, draws upon Roman themes and types, though it sets them in England; *Gammer Gurton's Needle* is native from the first stitch in the Prologue to the final prick. It is, furthermore, a folk play; the characters are not only English, but close to the English soil.

The story is scarcely more than a dramatized incident. Gammer Gurton loses her precious needle, supposes that it is stolen, and sets the village in an uproar on the hunt for it. "The crazy Diccon", as Allardyce Nicoll has described it, "the dull-witted Hodge, Dame Chatte the gossip, Doctor Rat the curate, and Master Baylye are all dragged into the storm, and just as its height seems nearing, the needle is found in the most unexpected of places. The comedy, perhaps, is a trifle rough; the scenes occasionally take on the coloring of mere horseplay; but there is a genuine breath of fresh air, a healthy breeziness, in situations and in dialogue, which mark out *Gammer Gurton's Needle* as a play not to be forgotten." Others might think that the place where the needle is found is quite the expected spot, but the play works up to it deviously, so that the discovery comes — as is proper in the theatre — with surprise followed by instant acceptance as natural. The long rhyming lines of the play carry a lively vernacular; much of it consists of the characters' mutual abuse.

There have been a number of recent revivals of the play, especially by college theatres. Brooklyn, New York, saw it in 1933; Westchester, New York, in 1937; Oxford, Ohio, 1939; New York University, and Alabama College, 1940. Recent performances in England include one at the Malvern Festival of 1937 and one in London in 1940. Back in 1564, it was played before Queen Elizabeth on her visit to Cambridge.

The various incidents of the hunt for Gammer (Grandmother) Gurton's needle enliven the movement of the play while they enlighten us as to the mood and spirit of early English village life. Many of the characters are well caught, especially the simple Hodge with his long-drawn explanations—in one case twenty-four lines all ending "see now . . . see now?" — that never explain. The humor is no less English and no less vigorous and fresh today for being rough-house and plain-spoken in the frank countryside way of calling a spade a dirty spade. This earliest English comedy has a new-mown-hay-and-manure savor of folk drama found in few plays since its time.

The needle is found when Diccon smacks Hodge hard on the buttock.

THE FATHER   *August Strindberg*

Perhaps the most widely read and performed of all the plays by (Johan) August Strindberg (Swedish, 1849-1912), *The Father* pictures the relentless struggle between a fairly intellectual man and a determined woman, with "a woman's intuitive unconscious dishonesty."

At first the disagreement between Cavalry Captain Adolph and his wife Laura seems not ominously important: they have different ideas as to the education of their daughter Bertha. Neither will yield, however; and the struggle grows into a fight for mastery. Laura intimates that perhaps Adolph has no right to speak, perhaps he is not Bertha's father. Adolph grows increasingly baffled, increasingly violent; Laura seizes upon a letter in which he says he thinks he's going mad as a pretext for locking him a straitjacket; and in a fit of apoplexy Adolph dies.

The violence of the play, its almost naturalistic realism and over-whelming surge of unloosed passion, brought attacks from some critics, upon whom Strindberg promptly showered a counterblast. The play won wide attention throughout Europe. Zola, the father of naturalism, praised it highly; and in the next six years Strindberg wrote fourteen naturalistic dramas, almost all of them on the same central theme. It should be noted that Strindberg does not, as many wrongly suppose, blame the woman. He indicates that she is usually the more unscrupulous, the shrewder, therefore the more often successful, in the battle of the sexes; but the battle itself he sees as inevitably rooted in nature's ways.

In its juxtaposition of violence and sentiment, this drama bears resemblances to Shakespeare. In the drive of its action, the play observes the Greek unities of time and place. Yet in its sharp, bitter dialogue, ranging from quiet hate to apoplectic fury, and in its naturalistic presentation of human character and motives, the play is thoroughly modern and distinctively Strindberg's own. There is no more harrowing scene in the drama since King Lear's wandering in the storm, than the piercingly ironic moment in which the Captain's old nurse, believing she is acting for his good, croons childhood memories to him while, without his recognizing what she is doing, she slips on him and ties tight a straitjacket.

The American premiere in New York on April 9, 1912, won mixed reviews. The *New York Dramatic Mirror* (April 17) stated that "dramatically, the play abounds in striking characters and effective scenes", but added: "The trouble with introspective thinkers like Strindberg is that they question human minds and motives so much that either they don't know what they do believe, or they make themselves believe any fantastic things they wish." Along this line, the *World* (April 10) declared that the play is "teeming with morbid and unnatural situations." In 1928 Robert Whittier acted Captain Adolph in New York, in his own adaptation of the play, ill received. In London meanwhile (1927) a company including Robert Loraine played in it successfully, continuing in London and on tour for four years and bringing the play to New York on October 8, 1931. Robert Garland said that in comparison, "the depression seems bright and cheerful". John Anderson called the play "one of the most unpleasant and most fascinating of the modern classics, a cruel, obsessed, almost maniacal tirade aimed, from the top of its screech, at the conspiracy of women against men."

The play found vivid revival by the Studio-7 group in New York in 1949; less happily, with Raymond Massey on Broadway; but Munich the same year saw a production with Fritz Kortner which Ellis St. Joseph found "supremely alive, and charged with contemporary importance." Kortner gave the play a fresh and challenging interpretation, making its essence the overwhelming of high intelligence by the forces of stupidity. The Captain is an inquiring and accomplished scientist; he naturally desires to give his daughter the opportunity of free intellectual growth, away from the superstitious women now encompassing her. The play starts as high comedy; the Captain's wife is a beautiful woman using her sex to wheedle her way with him; only gradually, out of stupid determination not conscious will to power, does this complacently bourgeois woman rally to her aid the professional stupidities of the doctor, the minister, and the soldier, to break the spirit of the man that moves with conscious mind. The drive of the play intensifies ominously until the Captain is torn to fury and madness. Then the high intelligence, forced to recognize the power of stupidity in the world, accepts defeat; and calm in the straitjacket as a toga'd Senator, the Captain looks death in the face and passes judgment on his conquerors. His body, even his will, is broken; but at the final thrust he is again the captain of his soul.

Here is the supreme tragedy of the play—as of the world today: creative intelligence doomed by blind stupidity, powerless save to know its own worth even as it dies. It was inevitable that the forces of reaction should seek to close Kortner's production; and it is a hopeful sign that it continued to run well into 1950.

This interpretation does not lessen, but sets a richer glow upon, the battle of the sexes in the play. Brooks Atkinson (October 9, 1928), calling it "one of the great works of modern drama", noted that "Strindberg writes like a demon possessed. There is nothing quite so cruel, pathetic, and remorseless as this living portrait of a man of intellect succumbing bit by bit to the cold fury of a voracious virago. All that he is becomes his undoing. The superiority of his intelligence is his vulnerable spot in this conflict with a woman. Although the father is the victim and the mother the treacherous aggressor, Strindberg takes pains to show that the strife is instinct in the nature of things. Being a genius, he turns his drama into a hurricane of the furies. It is a dance of death of the evil forces in the world." "No finer play has been written for a century," said Gilbert W. Gabriel; "no stronger, and no dismaller." "What raises the play to greatness," said Alan Harris, in the Introduction to *Eight Famous Plays by Strindberg* (1949), "is those moments where Strindberg rises for an instant above his own frantic rancor and sums up the whole tragedy of life in a few words of sublime fairness." *The Father* is the clearest and most powerful of Strindberg's dramatic presentations of the universal need of adjustment between the sexes, of the time-long war in which some happy couples find truce, but which others wage unto their mutual destruction.

MISS JULIE   *August Strindberg*

After *The Father**, Strindberg drove his dramas for a time more directly on naturalistic lines. Encouraged by a letter from Emile Zola, he wrote the two-act *Miss Julie* (also translated as *Countess Julia*), 1888, which Alrick Gustafson in *A History of the Modern Drama* (1947) calls "probably the best frankly naturalistic play ever written."

The story is simple. On Midsummer Eve Julie flirts with, then gives herself to, Jean, the valet of the Count her father. The valet then tries to assert himself as cock of the walk. Julie recognizes the essential vulgarity of the situation. When the Count returns and rings for his valet, Jean too feels that the situation is impossible. He hands Julie a razor, and she takes her life.

Beneath these surface events the dramatist examines the elements of heredity and environment that have made these two what they are. The static picture of many naturalistic plays—a "slice of life" that lies on a slab for our examination—Strindberg replaces with a dynamic growth of understanding and emotional intensity. The contrasted natures of the two vividly reveal them both: the conventional Jean, who builds the evening episode into plans for a permanent union; the aristocratic, bored Julie, who toys with the idea of going away with Jean, but cannot leave her bird behind—whereupon Jean chops off its head before her eyes. And her eyes open to the coarseness of the man, to see that simple human decency demands that the vulgar situation come to an end.

In his printed preface to what he declared was "the Swedish drama's first naturalistic tragedy", Strindberg suggested production devices that were startling novelties at the time, but have since become commonplace technique for realistic drama. He proposed side spotlights instead of footlights; very little make-up, and a simple, natural tone of speech and performance. Antoine distributed copies of this Preface to the Paris audience at the French premiere in January 1893. The play has been a favorite in repertory on the Continent. It was shown in New York for special matinees in 1913, and became popular with little theatre groups. London saw it in 1929; in 1933 in French, with Pitöeff; and in 1939. A recent American revival opened in Philadelphia January 20, 1947 with Elisabeth Bergner, who had played Julie in Berlin, Vienna, and Paris.

The drama rose partly from Strindberg's marriage in 1877 with Siri von Essen, which grew increasingly stormy until their divorce in 1891. But it had other springs as well. One of the continuous conflicts within the troubled Strindberg was the question of class. Son of an aristocratic father and a socially inferior mother, he never adjusted himself to any social stratum. His play, as Alan Harris said in the introduction to *Eight Famous Plays* (1949), "is saturated with class feeling, and Strindberg certainly saw himself in the valet, the coming gentleman, by virtue of his energy and ability, as against the 'degenerate' aristocrat." The Swedish working-class audience cheered when the valet triumphed.

Received by the public with combined repulsion and fascination, the play was called by the *London Era* (October 2, 1929) " a startling, almost a terrifying, experience. . . . a midsummer nightmare. But although its theme is peculiarly repellent and concerns itself almost exclusively with human weaknesses and the baser side of man's nature, the technical skill with which the piece is constructed forces us to follow, with closest attention, the working out of the tragedy. Here is a masterpiece of playwriting; the sense of reality with which it is imbued is so strong that we feel inclined at times to turn our eyes away from a spectacle which seems so painful and so personal. . . . Decidedly this play is only for those who are able to do without illusions." The *London Times* (February 14, 1933) even more clearly pictured at least the Anglo-Saxon unwillingness to submit to the play's mood: "It has a fierce intensity peculiar to Strindberg's genius which has the effect, for many spectators, of carrying the action so far beyond their interpretation of nature that they defend themselves intuitively from its attack by attacking in return with an accusation of insanity. It is the play's quality of abnormal imaginative pressure, the core of its greatness, that stands in its way." *Variety* (January 29, 1947), reporting the Philadelphia production of the play, against its will accords it high praise: ". . . as current Broadway fare—definitely thumbs down . . . The tone is definitely tragic, and in the hands of a less capable actress would probably elicit laughter from audiences definitely not as 'class-conscious' as those of half a century ago. Thanks, however, to Miss Bergner's glowing performance and the indisputably poetic fire and fluency of Strindberg's prose, *Miss Julie* does still possess an enthralling power."

There is rich development of the figures in *Miss Julie,* which is a searing study of character, to be set beside Ibsen's *Hedda Gabler**, of boredom seeking distraction, yet preferring death to the dictatorship of

754 STRINGBERG

vulgarity. Deep within its depressing drive, there is thus held clean the urge for decency within the human soul.

THE DANCE OF DEATH August Strindberg

In the most hopeless and heavy-hearted of all his dramas, the two parts of The Dance of Death, 1901, Strindberg made his most pessimistic presentation of the endless war of man and woman. In the drama, after twenty-five years of marriage, a deep, ingrown hate has festered in the lives of Artillery Captain Edgar, of an island garrison, and his wife Alice. Edgar is a self-centered domestic tyrant, but Alice is strengthened by the power of her loathing. When their friend Curt, Alice's cousin, comes for a visit, each tries to use him as a weapon against the other. Alice for a time seems the victor, because she throws her body into the fight; but after her yielding, Curt flies from the witches' cauldron of seething hate. By superhuman will, Edgar pulls himself together after a heart attack; he will not accord Alice the satisfaction of his dying. Their fate is a drear continuance of horrid hate, in loathsome union. The second part of the drama carries on the dreary struggle to the dregs of Edgar's doom. It contains, however, a tender and hopeful episode of love between Allan, Curt's son, and Judith, Edgar's daughter, which, as Alan Harris remarks in the introduction to Eight Famous Plays (1949), "almost succeeds in transfiguring it by its poignancy and beauty."

Though gripping in performance, the play is too depressing to be often presented. In New York, it was shown May 9, 1922, in a special performance by the Theatre Guild, in a condensed version—the two parts together—by Henry Stillman, that piled on the horrors almost too horrendous. Yet it displayed, said the New York Dramatic Mirror (May 22, 1922), Strindberg's "uncanny gift of gripping dialogue." The picture of Edgar was especially impressive. The New York Stage (Midsummer issue, 1922) called his portrait "a supreme study in selfishness, demonstrating the devastating effect of a strong-willed egomaniac in his society, which terminates only with his death. It is, of course, all told in a minor key mordantly bitter, almost cynically repulsive, and yet so convincing in the telling that one's interest is perfectly sustained. His will for evil is as potent as the disasters wrought by the fates in the old Greek tragedies." New York also saw the play (Part I) in German, with Irene Triesch, opening December 16, 1923. The two parts were played in London in November and December 1925. The London Stage (November 27, 1925) said: "The two characters are intensely interesting, and the grip of the author all-powerful in spite of what appears to be an indifferent translation." Revived in Vienna in 1925, the play was hailed as Strindberg's "most famous work." It was shown again in London, in 1928, with Robert Loraine. The New York Times (February 5, 1928), reporting the London production, said that the play "has a spiritual power that makes all its structural weaknesses seem unimportant." These "weaknesses", indeed, are imperceptible in the fierce psychological drive of the drama.

This play differs from Strindberg's other works on the theme of the sex war in that here the man is the more active agent of evil. During his stroke the Captain has a vision of hope which leads him to seek a reconciliation; thus Strindberg presses the double irony of an illusion based on an illusion. This play, declared the *New York Herald* (December 17, 1923), is "the full sized canvas of a picture for which his more familiar *Miss Julie, Creditors* and *The Father* were merely preliminary sketches. If ideas rather than morals could ever excite the censors of the theatre, this play would undoubtedly be banished from every stage in Christendom, for it is a savage warning versus the holy state of matrimony, undermining the whole structure of family life. Ibsen's rebellious Nora, once so horrible an example of revolutionary ideas, is an amiable Pollyanna creature beside Strindberg's Alice."

[Strindberg's *The Dance of Death* is not to be confused with a play of the same name by the English poet W. H. Auden, staged in 1936 by Alfred Kreymborg in the New York Federal Theatre. This is a drama of the English middle class.]

The naturalistic presentation of the tortures of embattled souls can go no further than in Strindberg's play. He looks into the awful depths of "that yawning abyss which is called the human heart", and lifts for our beholding the monsters of the deep. "It is the normally suppressed, but not abnormal, life of thought breaking out into speech", said Alan Harris, "that gives *The Father** and *The Dance of Death* their peculiar horror, and, incidentally, makes the conventions of polite society, so easily assailable from many sides, suddenly seem infinitely precious." Infinitely precious, too, to Strindberg's tortured spirit, were thoughts of happy domesticity and peace; and Harris finds a personal yearning in remarks that dot the dramas. But the strains of his life did not relax. Continued pressure means explosion, the bursting of the bonds of reason into the distorted realm of phantasmagoria, nightmare, and the mad. This leap Strindberg took in *The Dream Play** and *The Spook Sonata**. Thus *The Dance of Death* is his last, and his most powerful, lucid and logical drama of human lives.

THE DREAM PLAY   *August Strindberg*

With *The Dream Play*, 1902, Strindberg moved wholly into the irrational land of fantasy. With some half-hundred persons, through fifteen scenes, there flows a timeless spectacle of the miseries and evils of human life and the human spirit. There is no single story of embattled urgencies or hates, but a pageant of the agonies of humanity, the absurdities of human attempts at justice, the mockery of human endeavors to find the meaning of life or to imbue it with meaning. There is no objective analysis of a situation or of a character, but a threnody with the reiterate refrain: "Life is evil! Men are to be pitied!" And yet the whole arrives at the hopefulness of beauty.

In the vision of the Poet, the daughter of Indra comes to earth to see what life is like. With the incongruities, inconsequentialities, irrationalities, and sudden juxtapositions of a dream, she is exposed to the sufferings and the cruelties of mankind. She wishes to see with the eyes of a man, to hear with the ears of a man, to think with those curious convolutions that are the human brain. The grotto of one scene has the shape of the human ear. "The characters," said Strindberg, "split, double, multiply, vanish, solidify, blur, grow clear. But one consciousness reigns above them all — that of the dreamer; and before it there are no secrets, no incongruities, no scruples, no laws. There is neither judgment nor exoneration, merely narration. And as the dream is for the most part painful, rarely pleasant, a note of melancholy and of pity for all living things runs all through the wobbly tale. Sleep, the liberator, often plays a dismal part; but when the pain is at its worst, the awakening comes and reconciles the sufferer to reality, which, however distressful it may be, seems nevertheless happy in comparison with the torments of the dream." The daughter of Indra, in this phantasmagoria, meets the Officer (who may represent the body), the Lawyer (the mind), the Glazier, the Coal-heaver, and other human aggressors or victims; everyone is either an oppressor or oppressed; only the Poet (the heart) wins some measure of freedom from life's enslaving toils.

The play, which some critics have said will act best in the mind, was presented in Berlin in 1916 by Rudolph Bernauer, with Irene Triesch; even more successfully there in 1919 by Max Reinhardt. In 1919 in Vienna, Joseph Schildkraut played the Officer. *The Dream Play* was presented in New York, opening January 20, 1926, at the Provincetown Playhouse. London saw it in 1933 with Donald Wolfit. There was a very successful revival in Stockholm in 1935, with further symbolic touches: the Poet was made up to resemble the bust of Strindberg; the Officer, the portraits of Strindberg in his youth.

The critics in New York were, on the whole, baffled by the play. Thus John Anderson (January 21, 1926) protested: "Nothing is so palpably unreal as bogus unreality . . . There are, nevertheless, some startlingly beautiful moments in it." In the *Montreal Daily Star* the next week, Clifford Baker was moved to comment on the New York reaction: "The production of Strindberg's play by the Provincetown group was the signal for an avalanche of ridicule and invective . . . It was a simple thing for the local wise men to accuse Strindberg of dire and distasteful pessimism. It never occurred to one of them that Strindberg was more optimist than pessimist, that not once did he miss an opportunity of pressing home the fact that the ills of humanity are humanity's own. A mind not devoid of imagination might deduce from this that humanity has the power of curing them." Indeed, out of these later, unrealistic plays of Strindberg there does rise the shimmering of human hope. The *London Times* (April 3, 1933) remarked that the play has "unity less in action than in thought, and less in thought than in spiritual impulse." The compassion in the daughter of Indra must find fruition in deeds, through the gathered wisdom of man; but the hopelessness that shrouds man's lot breaks with a faint glimmer as through a rift. The play is, despite the wretchedness it depicts, decidedly not sordid; much of it is tender, and it is full of lyric beauty. In setting, too, a production of *The Dream Play* lilts with beauty, opening with a glory of giant hollyhocks, behind which stands a castle crowned with a bud, which at the play's end blossoms as a great chrysanthemum. Certain features persist in various guises, like the door with the clover-leaf opening, like the linden tree that becomes a hat-stand in an office, a candelabrum in a church. Music as well plays a harmonious part in gathering the many dream symbols into a rich pattern of beauty.

The thought of the play similarly sifts through the crowded inco-
herencies of its telling, "richly interesting and alive," said the *New York
Daily News* (January 21, 1926), "as viewed in the jumbled vision of the
dreamer." "There are passages," said Gilbert W. Gabriel, "that hammer
at your heart until they have battered it completely out of human shape
or ordinary usefulness." Without the wilder eccentricities of *The Spook
Sonata**, *The Dream Play* imposes its mood upon the audience, as for
some years it imposed its technique upon the experimenters in the
world theatre.

THE SPOOK SONATA   *August Strindberg*

In 1907, Strindberg and director August Falck opened the Intimate
Theatre in Stockholm. This was a "chamber theatre" seating fewer than
200 persons, dedicated to the plays of Strindberg, which were becoming
too difficult for the wider public. The best of Strindberg's plays written
during the four years of this theatre is *The Spook Sonata*, 1907.
Looking at the same world as in *The Dream Play**, Strindberg is in
more savage mood. There is no pity here. With a great flail of mockery
and satire, he strikes forth in all directions. The nightmare Life-in-
Death gallops through the drama in the wildest conglomeration of evil,
of decrepit, distorted creatures, who live in agony or madness or spring
from beyond the grave. Most evil of the play's creatures is the vampirish
octogenarian Hummel, who from his wheel-hair or his crutches pours
grief and confusion upon the rest. He says he has saved the girl he
killed—we see her wraith in Act I; finally he is strangled by the Mummy.
The Mummy is a woman who lives in a cabinet sealed away from daylight, under a marble memorial to her own spent beauty; she dresses
like a parrot, and when brought forth squeaks and squawks in parrot
tones. She has a delicate daughter, a girl who cannot live without hya-
cinths. There is also a crippled and self-deified student who returns to
claim the girl's child as his, only to be driven away. There are elaborate
meals, yet everybody is starving; for the cook squeezes all the nourishment from the food before she serves. The decayed remains of a de-
ceased milkmaid pass to and fro. Phantasmagorias multiply, a symbolic
array of the greeds and lusts that prey upon the world; until at the end,
when the girl dies, the student turns and warns those across the footlights that their sins, too, will find them out.
In a swirl of weird colors, masks, and bizarre stage effects, the drama
was presented at the Provincetown Playhouse in New York, opening
January 5, 1924, with Clare Eames and Walter Abel. Alexander Woollcott (January 7) called it "a sedulously eccentric, elliptical, and singularly baffling play", but added that it "holds the attention taut". Percy
Hammond stated: "Strindberg again comes to the gloomy conclusion that
the earth is a morgue and a madhouse . . . After attending *The Spook
Sonata* I began to suspect that Strindberg's pessimism is not so terrible
as is his manner of presenting it." The *Telegram* saw in the play "sudden flashes of that great light which the Illuminated Ones of all ages
have cast on reality . . . close to the danger line where sheer inspiration
lapses into sheer insanity." The *Drama Calendar* (January 14) more
trenchantly declared that the play's mood is "so powerfully imagined and

so poignantly expressed, it can hardly fail to exhilarate and grip an audience which looks for more than a pleasant time. The thrusts pierce with unerring skill, and the imagery is richly fantastic."

In Europe, where the drama was promptly and widely played, it came in the van of the "modern" modes, the successors to naturalism in the theatre. Thus by the time the play came to New York, Eugene O'Neill could say, in a program note for the Provincetown Playhouse: "Strindberg was the precursor of all modernity in our present theatre, just as Ibsen, a lesser man as he himself surmised, was the father of the modernity of twenty years or so ago . . . Strindberg is the greatest interpreter in the theatre of the characteristic spiritual conflicts which constitute the drama—the blood of our lives today . . . All that is enduring in what we loosely call 'Expressionism'—all that is artistically valid and sound theatre—can be clearly traced back through Wedekind to Strindberg's *The Dream Play, There Are Crimes and Crimes, The Spook Sonata*." But the play found many of the New York critics unprepared for its nightmarish technique, unwilling to accord Strindberg the place O'Neill and Ibsen gave him. Thus Gilbert W. Gabriel (January 7, 1924) blandly surmised that Ibsen's remark "may have been a soft answer to turn away Strindberg's wrath, or simply the pleasant gesture of one who knew the world would safely contradict him . . ." Americans, Gabriel went on to confess, "seem always to react to Strindberg with that antagonism which neurotics exhibit in the presence of the downright insane." It was not until its comment on the Stockholm revival of the play that the *New York Times* (December 8, 1935) hailed Strindberg as "the one blazing, flaming genius in the whole of Swedish literature."

In the whole of world drama, there are few playwrights whose hatred of the evil of life pours with such a black bile and vitriolic power. Certainly there is no other play so eerily compelling, in its maggoty, chimeric compounding of nightmare dreads, so Dantesque in its lightning-sear over human ills and human evils, as Strindberg's drama macabre. Such works as this mark Strindberg as exponent of an attitude caught in a character's words, that life is "horrible beyond all description"; mark him, as Alan Harris put it, in the introduction to *Eight Famous Plays* (1949), as "a name of power to the Western world, the representative man of an attitude toward life which will never be outdated so long as the human predicament remains." It should not be overlooked, however, that the playwright's bitterness rises from a hatred of the evils in the world; behind this there is an equally burning desire for human betterment. Gorki has compared Strindberg to the hero of a Danubian legend, who tore out his own heart and set it on fire to light his fellow-men on the way to freedom. *The Spook Sonata*, by its shimmering over the baleful aspects of mortality, gives dramatic urgency to man's most horrid battle, the grim struggle against the forces of destruction within himself.

MAGDA   *Hermann Sudermann*

A novelist before turning to the theatre, Hermann Sudermann (German, 1857-1932) brought to the stage a mixture that the public heartily welcomed—a presentation of social problems in the spirit of naturalism and a development of those problems in the technique of "the well-made play", with rousing devices of the theatre and neatly prepared climactic situations. In his early dramas, however, there is a measure of artificiality in the production of effects. The motivation of the characters seems of less concern than the striking situation. *Heimat*, 1893 (in English, *Magda*, 1894), strikes more surely home, with a modern problem. Magda, who has left her strict army-officer father to escape an unwelcome marriage after an affair, returns home years later a famous opera star. Learning that the man who had wronged her is Keller, now local councillor, the father insists on their marriage. Keller is agreeable; Magda, though she has outgrown the seedy conventionality of the little town, consents also—until she learns that to protect Keller's reputation she must leave their child behind. When she refuses, her furious father is foiled in his attempt to kill her by a fatal apoplectic stroke. The theatricality of this final escape does not weaken the power of the play; and its basic situation and development are essentially true.

The role of Magda provides superb acting opportunities. "What a grand sweep the part of Magda has!" exclaimed Brooks Atkinson (January 26, 1926). "No wonder emotional actresses have pounced upon it savagely." Among these actresses have been Helena Modjeska (New York, 1894); Sarah Bernhardt (London, 1895; New York, 1896 and 1905); Eleonora Duse (London, 1895; New York, 1896 and 1902). Within a year, London saw the play in German, French, Italian, and English. In *Magda*, Mrs. Patrick Campbell made her New York debut, January 30, 1902. In the same year John Barrymore made his debut as Lieutenant Max to Nance O'Neil's robustious Magda. Others that have played Magda include Mrs. Fiske (New York, 1899), Olga Nethersole (New York, 1906), Bertha Kalich (often in Yiddish; in English, New York, 1926). The original Magda (Berlin, November 1893) was Rosa Popa. The *London Times* observed in 1923 that "not a season passes in which two or three actresses do not seek as Magda to challenge comparison with almost innumerable predecessors." Most notably, Sarah Bernhardt played Magda in London the night after the Italian Eleonora Duse; the critics averred that "the tremendous acting of Duse exposed the false heroics and the tricks" of her French rival. Bernard Shaw, in particular, ranked Duse superbly first, with Mrs. Pat Campbell, the next season, a halting third. Duse was liked in the part in New York, too. The *New York Dramatic Mirror* (March 7, 1896) declared of her, in her first contemporary role in New York: "Everyone left the Fifth Avenue Theatre last night in a glow of enthusiasm. . . . In Magda perhaps more than in any of Duse's other performances, she excites one intellectually and emotionally."

When Bertha Kalich revived the play in 1926, the *New York Sun* (January 27) already referred to it as "that classical masterpiece, *Magda*." The *World* called it "a moving and absorbing experience in the theatre . . . the play still marches, sometimes through shrewd theatrical claptrap, sometimes through profound and undated wisdom." If some critics feel that it has not worn well, it is in part, at least, because many plays since have essayed its technique with a similar story. (A strikingly similar theme preceded *Magda*, in the Russian Aleksandr Ostrovski's *Guilty Without Guilt*, 1884. Sudermann probably was unacquainted with this play.) Burns Mantle reminded such carping critics (January 27, 1926) that "none of the many writers who have aped him in the last thirty years has bettered the pattern he gave them."

Two struggles combine to give the play power: the battle of wills between father and daughter; and the conflict of standards between the conventional and the freer ways of life. The opportune death of Magda's father may seem contrived; yet the *Boston Transcript*, on the occasion of Nance O'Neil's tour, called the play "a high example of that form of pure drama in which the characters and situations are the logical outcome of events and are moved utterly by the inexorable logic of fate." As a starring vehicle, as a rousing dramatic clash, and as a vivid contrast of attitudes and conventions, *Magda* still makes a powerful appeal.

THE JOY OF LIVING   *Hermann Sudermann*

Among the many plays that poured from Sudermann's pen, the most rousing and the most controversial is *The Joy of Living*. Presented in Berlin in 1901 (*Es Lebe das Leben*), the play was adapted by Edith Wharton and brought to New York with Mrs. Pat Campbell on October 23, 1902. Sudermann tends to try variations on his own themes; this play, on a higher social plane, reviews some of the problems of *Magda*. Long before the play opens, Countess Beata and Baron Richard were lovers. Now Richard is a close friend of Beata's husband, who, urged by his wife, relinquishes his own political power to advance the more brilliant Richard. Richard's political opponent unearths the old affair; but scandal must be avoided. There can be no duel. Richard's own son unwittingly sentences his father, when he declares: "A man of honor would be more eager to give his life than the husband would be to take it." To save Richard from suicide, Beata takes an overdose of her heart medicine, leaving the men to their careers without scandal.

A New York opening has seldom found reviewers so divided. *Theatre* (December, 1902) tried to brush the play aside: "A large proportion of the five acts is occupied with conversations of psychological facts and socialistic tendencies, and those who hail such a conglomeration as a superb play, and pronounce its author one of the greatest dramatists of all time, are to be compassionated when they are not laughed at." The *Brooklyn Eagle* granted that Sudermann "knows how to supervise realism by art"—but continued: "We respect the resolute courage of a woman who greets death to save her lover from the consequence of their common guilt. But we can discover no moral strength in the character of a woman willing to use her husband as a cat's paw to advance the political interests of her paramour." The *World* pretended to be judicial: "Generally speaking, the drama falls within the limits of the frank discussions of social corruption which have no right in the interests of public decency to be exploited on the stage and no claim on the ground of the moral deductions to be drawn from them, to be performed before the mixed audiences in places that are essentially for public entertainment. It is a disheartening clinic of morbid emotions, in which there is not one gleam of light, not one ray of pleasure, and not one moment of relaxation." The *Journal* plumped solidly against the play, under the heading "*Joy of Living* is Climax of Modern Morbid Licentiousness". When the play's tour reached San Francisco, the *Examiner* there (April

7, 1903) declared that Sudermann "has taken the slop hopper and dumped it on the front lawn."

After the 1902 opening, the *New York Times* called it "the high-water mark of the intellectual drama . . . a remarkable, an extraordinary, a triumphant effort of the dramatist's skill . . . No actress of modern times, save perhaps Duse, could equal its eloquence of sorrow, culminating in splendor of tragedy." The *Herald* said that the play "worked up to the final climax with tremendous passion and power, with psychological truth, and with great ingenuity of construction." The *Boston Transcript* felt the play an improvement over Sudermann's earlier work: "Moralize he must, prose even, now and then; but he has learned to make his reflections spring close from the progress of the play and to work them into his texture. Above all, the ethical standard of these reflections in *The Joy of Living* is a long and high advance over that of *Die Ehre* (*Honor*) and of *Heimat*.*"

Looking back the next Sunday, the *Times* surveyed these reviews: "Only one paper, the *Evening Post*, showed the least comprehension of what it is really about—of the vast moral and social implications . . . the critic of this paper chose to judge the play, not in a spirit of intellectual hospitality, but according to those very standards of conventional morality against which it aimed. . . . Herr Sudermann's whole purpose was to show that the existing social conventions sometimes cramp the spirit and deaden the soul . . . To anyone who is willing to take Beata for what Sudermann intends, she can scarcely fail to seem the most thoroughly studied, the most complexly organized, and the most quiveringly vital woman in the modern drama."

An excellent picture of German upper-class attitudes and problems of its day, the play is a searching study of a woman's soul, of the complex problems of a liberated but loving and noble spirit. It reaches into questionings of conventions and values rooted in our society. These aspects of the play, some of the critics appreciated. But its deeper irony they missed. In the sardonic movement of a love that works its own destruction, an idealism that batters down its own goal, we grow aware that Beata's entire spirit, her deep impulses and her basic outlook on life, are diametrically opposed to the conventional and opportunist political creed she is actually furthering, through the advancement of her beloved Richard. Beata, in her love and devotion, never comes to a realization of this fact. Her self-sacrifice, however, awakens Richard to the sterility of his aims; it is not only because his life has been emptied of his beloved Beata, it is because he now knows his life-work is empty, that Richard declares: "I live on because I am dead." Beata, in her toast to the joy of living, when she drinks the fatal draught, queries "Which of us really dares to live?" The meaning of true living, of the effort and end of integrity and sound striving, is searchingly probed, through a tense dramatic story, in Sudermann's *The Joy of Living*.

THE PLAYBOY OF THE WESTERN WORLD   *John M. Synge*

Sardonic humor, the most frequent mood of John Millington Synge (Irish, 1871-1909) is especially keen in his most famous work, *The Playboy of the Western World*, 1907.

This attack on the ignorance and crass hero-worship — really, bully-worship — of the Irish common folk pictures Christie Mahon, after slicing open the head of his tyrant father, accepted as a hero in a village far away. Pegeen, romantic daughter of the public-house owner, gives up her timorous Shawn Keogh for Christie boy; and the Widow Quinn angles for his favors. Suddenly the "slain" father appears. As the village folk turn against Christie, in desperation he tries to kill his father; but this is no far-off legendary slaying, this is near at hand, and murder. When the horrified villagers want to deliver Christie to the police, his father joins the boy in the fight to keep him free; and they set out for home again on equal terms. Christie has found his manhood and self-confidence. Pegeen alone is left lamenting the loss of the only Playboy of the Western World.

The chief target of Synge's satire is the habit of accepting appearances for reality, of taking things at their face value. Ironically, that is just how his play (like the earlier Irishman Swift's *Modest Proposal*) was taken. There were riots at its opening at the Abbey Theatre, Dublin, on January 26, 1907. There were even more boisterous riots among Irish-Americans when it was first played in New York, Philadelphia, and Boston. The *New York Dramatic Mirror* (November 29, 1911) reported the disturbance under the headlines: "Synge Play Greeted As No Other Play Has Ever Been Received in New York—100 Police Quell the Disturbance." The attack began, appropriately, with the hurling of an Irish potato. Among those arrested for creating the disorder were Barney Kelly, Patrick O'Connor, and Shean O'Callaghan. Attorney Spellisy, himself Irish, declared at the trial: "The sketch was the nastiest, vilest, most scurrilous and obscene thing I have ever seen. I don't blame them for hooting." A niece of the Irish patriot Robert Emmet testified she had seen O'Callaghan throw four eggs. He was fined $10.00. The excitement approaches that when riots in Paris greeted the mention of *handkerchief* in *Othello** and more lengthily Hugo's *Hernani**. Many of the protesting Irish were especially indignant at the author's picture of Pegeen; for, they said, no good Irish girl ever mentions her shift. As late as 1933, several Irish-American organizations petitioned the Irish Consul-General to have the Irish Free State cancel the subsidy of the Abbey Theatre because it continued to present the play, with its "filthy language, drunkenness, and prostitution", and its maligning of the Irish people.

After a time, however, convinced by others that they should be proud of the play, more of the Irish took it to their hearts. At the 1930 New York production Brooks Atkinson could say: "Out of the balcony, whence the vegetables and abuse came in 1911, chuckles and titters kept up a steady commentary on the play, and proved that the gallery gods, like many of the monarchs of the orchestra, knew the play by heart and needed only a suggestion or two from the stage." Later, Atkinson remarked (October 30, 1932) that "talk that 'kicks the stars', like the prancing mule in Synge's own play, restores the theatre to its highest uses." John Mason Brown called the play "one of the richest, most imageful, and full blown of all modern comedies." The play is a mixture of the comic, the sardonic, and the tender. The first two qualities are linked in Maxim Gorki's remark: "In it, the comical side passes quite naturally into the terrible, while the terrible just as easily becomes comic." The tender mood of the drama was best described by James Agate, in the *London Times* (October 29, 1939): "The scene after Christy's victory at the sports contains the best love-making since *Romeo and Juliet* . . . In fact though it be heresy to say so, there are ways in which the Synge is better than the Shakespeare." With dramatic deftness, this romantic spell is broken — saved from sentimentality — by the arrival of Christy's bandaged father, furious to break his braggart son's bones. Nor, indeed, are the persons themselves in any sense romantic: Christy, as Agate said, "badly wants what the Army used to call delousing", and Pegeen is a girl "wi' the stink o' stale poteen".

The underlying bitterness and sadness were emphasized by Edward Shanks in the London *Outlook* (August 13, 1921), who felt that "the play is extraordinarily bitter; it is perhaps the most bitter work of art that exists . . . Synge's laughter is sad and his satire holds no liveliness . . . His poetry is as depressing as it is impressive." Not one of the characters in the play, Shanks observed, is an upright, decent person.

Not merely the notoriety of its early productions, but its intrinsic qualities have made the play a favorite little theatre work. A recent professional New York performance opened October 26, 1946 with J. M. Kerrigan and Burgess Meredith. John Chapman said that "Synge's bubbling yet deep-thrusting comedy of a thin-witted exhibitionist is the perfect vehicle for its cast." George Freedley declared that "few plays in modern dramatic literature are as satisfying."

The dialect of the play calls for notice. Originally dialect in the drama was limited (as in Shakespeare's *Henry V**) to a character or a group for purposes of contrast, usually comic. In Synge's drama, we find what Allardyce Nicoll has called "the triumph of the new conception, where dialect (expressing a certain sphere of life removed by certain peculiarities from 'normal' city existence) is used, not to form a contrast with something else, but in and for itself."

The Playboy of the Western World demands pondering. Its rapid movement of comedy and satiric drama will otherwise speed one past its deeper riches, of tenderness and sadness, of pithy human joy, coarse human weakness, but earthiness touched with grandeur and with grace.

DEIRDRE OF THE SORROWS   *John M. Synge*

"Till an Irish poet has killed his Deirdre," said the *Boston Transcript* (May 4, 1910), "he is like a brave who has not yet killed his man." The story of the doomed Deirdre has been told by Yeats* (presented in London, 1908, with Mrs. Pat Campbell); by Lady Gregory* (*Cuchulain of Muirthemne*, a telling of the whole cycle of legends); by James Stephens (London, 1923, a very sensitive dramatic recapture); by A. E. (George William Russell, 1929). The drama of Synge, all but complete when he died, is, said Allardyce Nicoll, "the most powerful of all the many efforts made to dramatize that most poignant of all Irish legends." Synge's play was performed at the Abbey Theatre in Dublin, January 13, 1910; in London, May 30, 1910; in New York, September 27, 1920. On the Canadian radio it was accorded a three-hour production in 1946 in opera form, with libretto by John Coulter and music by H. Willan.

New York saw the Synge play again on September 5, 1936 with Jean Forbes-Robertson and Michael MacLiammoir.

The legend of Deirdre is in the Red Knights' Branch of the Ulster Cycle of Irish tales. Deirdre is a beautiful foundling raised by the Druids, who set a curse upon any that might marry her. Beloved of Conchubor, the aging king of Ulster, Deirdre flees with the young hero Naisi (also Naise, Naoise). They live in happiness until they are lured to return; Naisi is stabbed by Conchubor's men and Deirdre kills herself beside his grave.

It is a simple and familiar story, but it carries a widespread sadness, the grief that rises from the imbalance of youth and age, when power and love flash within different hearts. The pattern of the play follows the legend. Except for this simple structure, however, as the *Manchester Guardian* (quoted in the *Boston Transcript,* May 4, 1919), pointed out: "everything in Synge's play is wholly original. It is written in a prose . . . close to speech, and as musical, austere, and melancholy as natural sounds like the crying of curlews or the whistle of blown grasses, rhythmic plaintiveness which in this last play has more changes of melody than it ever had, thinning to a whine for the crazed spy Owen ('It's a poor thing to be so lonesome you'd squeeze kisses on a cur dog's nose') or swelling to a noble stateliness in Deirdre's dying descant on her own fate in life and in story . . . In this last play, Synge not merely got back to his own balance; he perfected it, and was able, while keeping as fiercely clear of sentimentalism as ever, to achieve a tenderness and radiancy of beauty that he had not before reached. The ecstasy of the two lovers over their life together in exile, 'waking with the smell of June in the tops of the grasses', has this quality, and so has the whole expression of their mood of surrender to the general consignment of lovers to death . . . The impression left by the passages of exaltation was of a loveliness quite unembittered . . . All that was Synge is expressed in this play, the sure ear, the instinct for idiom, the brooding joy in hard, strong lines of character, the disdain for artistic compromise, the energy of tragic imagination—as well as a new serenity of beauty."

A word more might be said of the language of the play. Deceptively simple, as peasants might speak—Owen says, of a girl he once had loved, "now she'd scare a raven from a carcass on the hills"—the accustomed words build into apt and vivid images, like country hands that cup the poetry of clear spring water, and the spring ripples on in many-shaded rhythm. Fragile but well nigh flawless, *Deirdre of the Sorrows* combines closeness to the Irish soil and tender telling of an olden legend into a drama of poignant loveliness and beauty.

CHITRA   *Rabindranath Tagore*

Best known of the short poetic dramas by Rabindranath Tagore (or Thakur; 1861-1941) is *Chitra*, 1913, written in the year in which this distinguished Hindu writer was awarded the Nobel Prize. His quiet charm, mystical appeal, and evocative poetic qualities led Tagore's countrymen to call him Vakpati, Lord of Speech.

Chitra is a tender one-act poetic drama, picturing the love of the princess Chitra and the young hero Arjuna. Descendant of a long line of warriors, Chitra has been brought up as a man. When she sees Arjuna, however, she prays; and the God of Love answers her prayer, granting her supreme beauty for a year. So happy are she and Arjuna that even a god, when the year is over, would lack the immortal indifference, or the human cruelty, to break that mutual spell.

During the second and third decades of this century, *Chitra* was played in little theatres all over the world. At a Boston production, the *Herald* (February 9, 1915) called it "a charming example of the poetic drama. The dialogue is flowery, picturesque, rhapsodic. Rare poetic expressions are put into the mouths of the lovers. The scenes are idyllic, tender, passionate." The *Globe* stressed "the farseeing vision, the transforming spiritual beauty, the epic daring, the triumphant humanity of Tagore's immortal play . . . a thing of yesterday, today, and forever."

Written in a colorful but languorous poetic prose, *Chitra* comes upon us like a beautiful legend which, although its figures are faraway heroes, awakens emotions that nestle in every heart.

BUSHIDO   *Takeda Izumo*

In the years when the Theatre Guild was still cocooned within the Washington Square Players, the greatest success this group achieved was the one-act tragedy of sacrifice, *Bushido*, by Takeda Izumo (Japanese, 1688-1756). Directed by Michio Ito, the play opened in New York November 13, 1916, with Katharine Cornell, Glenn Hunter, and Jose Ruben. It has since established itself as a classic of the little theatre.

The story of *Bushido*, written in Japanese in 1746, is an episode from the long tragedy of Sugawara, a Japanese ruler of the ninth century. Chancellor Sugawara had been godfather to three brothers, Plum, Cherry, and Pine (Matsuo). The first two died defending Sugawara; Matsuo aided the successful usurper Tokuhara. The episode presented in *Bushido* ("Bushido" means fealty to the liege lord) is known in Japanese as *Terakoya* (*The Village School*) or *Matsuo*; it shows the return in Matsuo of a sense of loyalty, and his supreme sacrifice.

The Chancellor's son, Shoozigh, hunted by the usurper, has been located in Gango's village school; his head is demanded. The usurper's chamberlain arrives with Matsuo to identify the child; and he is slain. But the slain child is Matsuo's. Knowing that no peasant boy will fool the chamberlain, Matsuo has dedicated his own son, Kotaro, for the sacrifice; "of his own free will he came, a fragile child of scarce eight years, yet fearless, like a bold, undaunted hero." The anxiety of the schoolmaster, the quiet grief of the mother, the futile anguish of Shoozigh, who would not have permitted the sacrifice, are minor tones of somber feeling in a well-wrought, economically developed, and emotionally gripping play.

From the atonement of Matsuo, and especially from the self-sacrifice of his son, rise a truly tragic exaltation, with dignity and honor reaffirmed. *Bushido* effects this exaltation with simple means, with undertones of suggested feeling welling to high dramatic power.

OUR AMERICAN COUSIN   *Tom Taylor*

Trenchard Manor, England, is the scene of this famous play by Tom Taylor (English, 1817-1880). The wealthy estate has fallen upon evil days, for Sir Edward Trenchard has been tied up in mortgages and cast down by his tricky agent, Mr. Coyle, who will relent only if Trenchard's daughter Florence will marry him. Despite the family troubles, all are shaken with laughter at the odd speech and odder ways of their cousin Asa, just over from America. Asa is beneficiary, to the extent of $400,000, under old Mark Trenchard's will; Mrs. Mountchessington therefore casts her cap at him, but Asa falls in love with pretty Mary Meredith, the milkmaid. When Asa discovers that Mary is the natural linear heir of Mark Trenchard, he lights his cigar with the will. Meanwhile, with the aid of Coyle's clerk, Abel Murcott (who had proposed to Florence when he was her tutor and, rejected, had taken to drink), Asa finds a flaw in Coyle's mortgage. Florence is freed to marry her sailor, Harry Vernon; Asa is hitched to his Mary; and sundry other couples are fitly joined.

When *Our American Cousin* was first written, in 1858, among the minor characters was a frail miss, Georgina, who fell in a Victorian faint on the filmiest breath of a provocation. Also present — given only forty-seven lines in the original version — was a literal-minded Lord Dundreary with side whiskers and a habit of pronouncing "w" for "r". This comic role was entrusted to E. A. Sothern (1826-1881). In his entrance on opening night, Sothern stumbled over a tear in the carpet, recovered himself with a skip and a hop, and was greeted with howls of laughter. That skip and a hop, repeated nightly as the character's natural gait, his inane appearance, his literal interpretation of every remark, and his robust love-making with the delicate Georgina, made the part so popular that it grew until it became the most important in the play; and E. A. Sothern became one of the most famous figures on the American stage. Some productions of the play have been called *Lord Dundreary*, and the long side-whiskers Sothern wore in the part became known as dundrearies.

In the premiere production of *Our American Cousin*, the part of Asa Trenchard was played by Joseph Jefferson (1829-1905), seven years before his debut in Boucicault's *Rip Van Winkle**. *Our American Cousin* was first presented by Laura Keene (1826?-1873) at her own New York theatre; she played the part of Florence Trenchard. Influence of the play has been visible in the English theatre for some time, as in *The Silver King*, by Henry Arthur Jones* and Henry Herman (1882).

Our American Cousin established new long-run records on both sides of the Atlantic. Opening in New York October 15, 1858, it ran for 138 performances. The *Spirit of the Times* (October 8, 1859) was moved to comment: "Miss Laura Keene, with a perverseness that can be accounted for only on the grounds of sex and profession, has the most provoking way of always setting at naught the prognostications and wise auguries of the critics, as well as her own speculative anticipations, failing where success seems certain, and gaining triumphs from experiments that bode little but disaster. Look at *Our American Cousin*, tried almost as a desperate chance, when first-class pieces, cast better than they ever had before, under her management, wouldn't pay expenses. Miss Keene herself never expected it would go, and the critics, to a man, pooh-poohed the idea of its running through a week. Yet it brought her crowded houses nearly all the season." At a time when theatre was taboo in many respectable homes, the *Century* magazine (March 5, 1859) declared: "Parents may take their children to see it and they will be richly compensated by the amusement, without danger to their morals."

In Washington, D. C., *Our American Cousin* opened on January 31, 1861, for a record run of 35 nights. In London, at the Haymarket, the play reached 36 performances after its premiere, September 12, 1860; it played again in 1861; it opened January 27, 1862, for a record run of 314 performances; and it achieved almost a score more of revivals along the century. In New York City, Sothern's son, E. H. Sothern, played Lord Dundready in 1907 and after. In American life, the play became linked with a deeply tragic occasion. Laura Keene, who had played Florence Trenchard over 1,000 times, was giving a benefit performance, her last appearance in the role, at Ford's Theatre in Washington, on April 14, 1865. The play was interrupted by the assassination, in his theatre box, of President Abraham Lincoln. The *London Illustrated Times* (May 6, 1865) tells how Laura Keene, "the leading lady of the stage . . . proceeded to the box and endeavored in vain to restore consciousness to the dying President. It was a strange spectacle—the head of the ruler of thirty millions of people lying insensible in the lap of an actress, the mingled brain and blood oozing out and staining her gaudy robe. In a few minutes Mr. Lincoln's unconscious form was removed to a house across the street, and here the soul of the President took its final departure."

Lord Dundreary has become almost a legend in the theatre. There is joy in watching the gradual gathering, then the bursting of an idea, as reflected in his urbane and inane countenance. The *Boston Transcript* (January 15, 1908) shrewdly observed: "Dundreary stumbles, but at bottom he is never stupid. Rather he takes everything with a wholly simple and innocent literalness and so finds what is really a new point of view. Such humor lasts because it is rooted in genuine human traits, which it exaggerates and travesties." The *New York Times* (January 10, 1908) called Dundreary "such a delightfully sincere idiot that we cannot but love him."

More sense, but just as amusing characterization, may be observed in Asa Trenchard. Said the *Times*: "The climax of the second act, which shows the wild and woolly American 'shooting up' the family armor just to see if his hand is 'still in', is absolutely far funnier than anything in the comedy line that our modern stage can offer."

In these days of the conversion of plays into musicals, it is surprising that no one has yet transformed *Our American Cousin*, which is not only one of the most famous and successful comedies of the last hundred years, but still a vigorous and highly amusing play, with a lively story swept along by engaging characters.

THE TICKET-OF-LEAVE MAN   *Tom Taylor*

If for no other reason, *The Ticket-of-Leave Man*, 1863, will be remembered because of the figure who, pulling off his disguise, exclaims "Who am I? Hawkshaw, the Detective!" Its main personalities, Bob Brierly and Hawkshaw, said the *London Times* (September 21, 1946) "have made *The Ticket-of-Leave Man* immortal . . . By any standard other than that of the 'reformers' it is the outstanding play of the Victorian drama." Its facile author, Tom Taylor, wrote more than 100 plays.

The play centers around Bob Brierly, saved from a drunkard's grave by the power of love; then framed and sent to jail for forgery. His sentence served, Bob loses job after job as a jailbird, until the criminals, headed by "The Tiger", James Dalton, think they have forced him into working with them. Using the boy Sam Willoughby as their unwitting tool, the criminals, who have made their plans in a tea-garden, and slipped away during a public-house brawl, are now waiting in the churchyard near the office they intend to rob. Bob, whom they think they have forced to their purpose, reveals his honest intentions. The criminals close upon him, but before Jack Dalton can wreak his foul revenge, Hawkshaw the Detective steps forth, and gets his man. Bob in the meantime has won the heart of May Edwards, the fair heroine.

The Ticket-of-Leave Man continues to win high praise. Allardyce Nicoll, in *A History of Late Nineteenth Century Drama* (1946) stated that it "is one of the first melodramas to deal with the criminal life of London, to take as a hero a man who had suffered imprisonment for association with criminals, to introduce a detective on the stage, and to break away from the familiar domestic interior sets in an attempt (as in the restaurant scene) to treat of the teeming world of contemporary social life." The *Times* (date above) adduces earlier examples: a hero who had suffered through criminal associations, in *The Heart of London; or, The Sharper's Progress*, by William Thomas Moncrieff (1794-1857); the teeming life of the day, in *The Bohemians of Paris*. The plot—which Taylor took largely from *The Return of Melun*, by Edward Brisebarre and Eugène Nus—was borrowed soon again, for Hazlewood's *The Detective; or, The Ticket-of-Leave's Career*, 1870. The *Times* agrees, nonetheless, that "when Professor Nicoll says that *The Ticket-of-Leave Man* 'has a quality of its own which must induce us to rate Taylor as one of the more noteworthy dramatic authors of the century,' the statement cannot be doubted." "To this day," said the *New York Herald-Tribune* on July 16, 1933, "Hawkshaw the Detective retains a vitality altogether thrilling to the gods of the gallery."

Opening in London May 27, 1863, *The Ticket-of-Leave Man* achieved the then remarkable run of 407 performances; in New York, November 30, 1863, it began a run of 102. The play was most popular throughout the century; W. J. Florence played Bob Brierly over 1500 times. *The Ticket-of-Leave Man* was presented in Provincetown, Mass., in 1933, with Richard Whorf as Dalton, and Kate Mayhew—who in 1869 had played the boy Sam Willoughby—playing Sam's grandmother.

A Victorian homily was read on October 13, 1863, when the *London Globe* reported: "It is to be feared, says Sheridan, 'that people go to the theatre chiefly to amuse themselves'; and it may be feared that such was the chief object of a certain absconding clerk in going to a theatre with £2,500 of his employers' money in his pocket, with which, 'in the ease of his heart', as Wordsworth says, he had taken himself off from Liverpool. But the ease of his heart could not stand the pressure of Mr. Tom

Taylor's play. *The Ticket-of-Leave Man* awakened three-fifths of a conscience in the clerk's breast—he was so affected that he went out of the theatre, got three envelopes, and sent £1,500 back to his employers. This clerk took his place in the theatre, if not a hardened, yet certainly an unsoftened and unchastened offender against social law and right. He went out of the theatre a striking example of instantaneous conversion from the error of his ways." If this be not the shrewd strike of an early press agent, it shows something of the effect produced by the dramatically rousing scenes, especially the sudden swoop of Hawkshaw.

The *London Illustrated Sporting and Dramatic News* (April 26, 1884) called *The Ticket-of-Leave Man* "a most welcome bill of fare." Early in an age of swift and spectacular melodramas, it held its own even against such ripsnorters as *Under the Gaslight* and thrilled generations of audiences such as now wait for "The Shadow" and other mystery shockers on the air.

BECKET   *Alfred, Lord Tennyson*

In the year in which Alfred Tennyson was made a peer, his tragedy *Becket*, 1884, was published. Although it was not intended for the stage, Henry Irving saw theatrical possibilities in the drama and won Tennyson's approval for a production, though the poet died before his play was enacted. It opened in London on February 6, 1893, with Irving, and Ellen Terry as Rosamund, for a run of 112 performances. Irving, who scored a personal triumph in the role of Thomas à Becket, frequently revived the play, and acted in it on the night of his death in 1905. (Alfred, Lord Tennyson, English, 1809-1892.)

In the nineteenth century, *Becket* was occasionally presented at the homes of the nobility, as in 1886 at Wimbledon. It has been professionally revived several times, and was played regularly at the Canterbury Festival until 1935, when it was supplanted by T. S. Eliot's drama on the same subject, *Murder in the Cathedral**.

Tennyson's play is based upon the life of St. Thomas à Becket (1118?-1170), intimate friend of King Henry II of England until he reluctantly accepted appointment by Henry, in 1162, as Archbishop of Canterbury. Thereafter, Becket felt obliged to oppose the King's measures against Church privileges. He spent seven years in exile. On his return, the disputes broke out again; and the King in passion spoke words that led four of his knights to Canterbury, where in the Cathedral they slew the Archbishop, on December 29, 1170. King Henry did penance there; and Becket's shrine became the most famous in Christendom. The poet Chaucer's *Canterbury Tales* presents a group on pilgrimage to Becket's shrine.

Tennyson added to the story of Becket himself the tale of his protecting fair Rosamund de Clifford, Henry's beloved, from the wrath of Henry's Queen, Eleanor of Aquitaine. The play begins dramatically and symbolically with a game of chess between Becket and Henry, in which the bishop mates the king, whereupon the impetuous King kicks over the chessboard. In these opening moments, Henry reveals his dissatisfaction at the independence of the clergy, particularly in regard to its holdings; he gives voice to his fears that Queen Eleanor may seek the life of

Rosamund, for whom he has provided a secluded "bower" and now seeks Becket's protection, even though Becket disapproves of the amour; and he appoints Becket Archbishop of Canterbury. Later, Eleanor meets Rosamund's little son Geoffrey, and makes him innocently lead her to Rosamund's bower. Here, Eleanor and her henchman Fitzurse would kill Rosamund, but Becket arrives to save her. Fitzurse remembers the Archbishop's scorn; and, at the end, it is Fitzurse that strikes the first blow, before he, De Brito, De Tracy, and De Morville dash from the Cathedral while lightning flashes light the interior and reveal Rosamund kneeling beside Becket's body.

Henry Irving's acting version of *Becket* was well received in the United States. The *New York Tribune* (November 19, 1893) reported: "It has some moments in it that are divine, and it has also something of the mystery that many poets and playwrights fail to grasp . . . The scene in the last act approaches the nearest to a passion play that has been done in our time. All through are a great nobility and a great purity." "Particularly effective," said the *London Times* (June 6, 1933) in reporting a performance at Canterbury, "were the scenes between Eleanor and Rosamund, the feeding of the beggars by Becket, and the murder scene, after which Becket's body was borne through the audience by the monks." Clement Scott remarked, in the *Illustrated London News* (July 28, 1894), "It stands out as a very fine and bold piece of workmanship, interesting, dramatic. . . . There are no dull or unnecessary moments in it. . . . *Becket*, in every respect, is a play of which English art can be justly proud."

Becket is written in prose and blank verse, with a few pleasant lyrics —a troubadour love song of Eleanor of Aquitaine; a pleasant love duet in Rosamund's bower. In Tennyson's version, without the Irving dramatic intensification, *Becket* is rather static until toward the end, with many passages of eloquent rhetoric; but it is vibrant with a deep integrity, and it possesses considerable strength and beauty. Setting loyalty to one's heavenly and to one's earthly king in stark opposition, *Becket* keeps a stirring theme pulsingly alive.

THE WOMAN OF ANDROS   *Terence*

Born in Carthage, the slave Terence (Publius Terentius Afer; Roman, c. 195-159 B.C.) was educated and freed by the Roman senator Terentius Lucanus, whose name he took. He became a member of the learned circle of the time; some scholars think Scipio may have helped write his plays. Since all his comedies are adaptations (four of the six, from Menander*), they might have less prominent place if we possessed the originals. It is known, however, from various sources — including Terence's own Prologues, which he used not to tell the play's story, as was the ancient custom, but to defend his own dramatic practices — that Terence combined and otherwise altered the Greek dramas he drew upon.

The earliest of Terence's plays is *Andria* (*The Woman of Andros*), produced at the Megalensian Games in April, 166 B.C. by the actor-manager Lucius Ambivius Turpio and set to music by the slave Flaccus, "for flutes of equal size, right- and left-handed." These two men produced and composed the music for all six of Terence's plays. Five of these (*The Mother-in-Law* is even shorter) are of about 1,000 lines; but their many scenes — they average twenty-five — indicate that Terence relied largely on stage action.

Terence invariably used a double pot; in this, his first play, rather simply. *The Woman of Andros* presents the usual New Comedy story of a young man, in love with a courtesan, whose father wants him to marry a citizen's daughter. Terence complicated the situation by having young Pamphilus promise to marry both his sweetheart (by whom he has had a child) and the citizen's daughter. Also, the playwright provided a second young man, in love with the second girl. The play moves to its happy solution when, after the usual number of complications, it is revealed that the supposed courtesan is a second daughter of the citizen.

This familiar plot Terence sparkles with a number of novel features. The father, instead of being the butt of the clever slave, himself plans the intrigue in the play, trying to catch his son by a pretended wedding; and it is by his being told the truth and refusing to believe it because he expects a lie, that the old man is self-deluded. While not telling the story of the play in the Prologue sacrifices some dramatic irony, it adds considerably to the suspense. And, while mention of the possibility that Pamphilus' sweetheart may be a citizen prepares the audience — despite the slave's rejection of the idea as nonsense — for such an outcome, the fact that she is the other girl's sister comes as a complete surprise. Finally, all those in the play are of good character, well drawn and effectively distinguished, likable persons.

Several remarks in the play became proverbial; especially the cautionary Nequid nimis, Nothing too much.

The style of *The Woman of Andros* marked Terence at once as a master. Replacing monologues with dialogue, he speeded up the movement of the drama. Disdaining the spirited and rude, at times crude, colloquial speech of Plautus*, he achieved naturalness without sacrificing grace. He used fewer lyrical meters than Plautus, and a simpler metrical construction. He used interjections and other devices of speech deftly; and (unlike Plautus) might open a scene in the middle of a metrical line, with a naturalness as though life were breaking in. Like all ancient writers of comedy, Terence uses the aside; but he has added a humorous effect, in using it as an interjection of the thoughts of one person while another is speaking. The breaking of dramatic illusion, however, by having a character step out of his part to address the audience — a frequent device in broad comedy — Terence does not employ; and, after *The Woman of Andros*, it is not an actor but the musician that at the close of the play requests the audience's applause.

Among plays that are based on *The Woman of Andros* are Steele's *The Conscious Lover*, 1722, and Bellamy's *The Perjured Devotee*, 1739. The novel by Thornton Wilder, *The Woman of Andros*, 1930, is a romantic handling of the theme.

The two lovers of the sub-plot, in Terence' play, present the first instance in comedy of a respectable young man wooing a respectable young woman of good family. *The Woman of Andros*, as a whole, within its comic framework of error, self-deception and intrigue, is the first instance of a friendly play about friendly people, entangled — as what good folk may not be? — in complications that can be ironed out with patience, good-will, and the gentle hand of the goddess of good luck. This is the only sense in which the gods come into the dramas of Terence. *The Woman of Andros* is an amiable, sympathetic picture of upper middle class society, simply and perennially human.

THE MOTHER-IN-LAW   *Terence*

Terence's *Hecyra* (*The Mother-in-Law*) is a sober problem play, a study of the difficulties of married life in ancient times, of the situations that may arise to produce estrangement among even the best-intentioned of families, and — with the help of the goddess good luck — the final reconciliation. Based on a Greek play of Apollodorus that was drawn from Menander's *The Arbitration**, *The Mother-in-Law*, unlike most comedies, begins with the couple already married, and ends when they are reunited.

The story is the familiar one of a woman assaulted before marriage; her suitor (in this case, her husband) rejects her when the child is born, and accepts her when the child ultimately turns out to be his. Terence' treatment of this motif wholly lacks the usual dramatic irony; instead of watching, amused, with full knowledge of the end, the audience shares all the ignorance, misunderstanding, and confusion of the characters until the final surprise. Pamphilus, although he sends his wife away, loves her; he therefore does not reveal her shame. At first, the mother-in-law is blamed for the girl's departure; then it is supposed that Pamphilus has cast off his wife for a courtesan. Thus, when all is readjusted, the neighbors need never know the family complications that for a time threatened to disrupt the happy home.

The Mother-in-Law, possibly because of its serious intent, is the only play of Terence without a double plot. It contains comparatively little humor; M. S. Dimsdale has declared that it is "hardly a comedy at all." The slave, the usual source of considerable humor, is time and again thrust off the stage. Terence, indeed, poked fun at some of the usual stage tricks and conventional devices. He refused to let the various characters know, "as is done in the stage plays", more than they need. Not only the neighbors but Pamphilus' own father remains ignorant of the reason for the conciliation; and the very slave that brings the good news that establishes the husband as father of the child, doesn't know the significance of his tidings. The closing words of the play are the slave's bewildered remark: "I've done more good unwittingly today than ever I did knowingly before."

While the men in the play are well contrasted, the women are especially carefully drawn. The young wife herself does not appear in the drama; but the mother-in-law and the courtesan are two of Terence's most effective figures. Each belies her type. The mother-in-law is a sympathetic soul, bewildered when her husband reproaches her for her daughter-in-law's departure, ready to sacrifice herself for the children's happiness. And Bacchis, as George E. Duckworth has said, is "the most attractive courtesan in Roman comedy." Her profession does not cause her to lose her dignity, nor her sense of human values; she is truly happy when, through the ring Pamphilus has given her (which he had snatched from the finger of the girl he raped), the couple are reunited. The careful and sympathetic portraiture of these women, and the understanding picture of the loving and sympathetic husband, give *The Mother-in-Law* its more serious purpose, and its special value.

Presented in 165 B.C., and in the spring and the fall of 160 B.C., *The Mother-in-Law* was not well received until the third occasion. We are told that, at the first two performances, livelier sports lured the audience — at the play's premiere, a rope-dancer drew away the crowd; but Philip Whaley Harsh rather harshly decided that these first failures were "primarily the fault of the author and not of the audiences." Duckworth, on the other hand, praising Terence' ability "to rise far above the conventional technique of his day and to write more serious drama with vigour and originality", suggested that the Roman audience, attuned to farces, was unprepared for so serious a handling of the usual comic theme. Gilbert Norwood went so far as to call *The Mother-in-Law* "the purest and most perfect example of classical high comedy, strictly so called, which dramatic literature can offer from any age or any nation." The play is indeed a rich conversion of a farce motif into a serious dramatic study.

THE SELF-TORMENTOR   *Terence*

In *Heautontimorumenos* (*The Self-Tormentor*), 163 B.C., Terence again proves his dramatic ingenuity by combining two familiar stories in a novel way. The play presents two young men who seek to deceive their fathers, for one needs money for a courtesan, and the other wishes to marry a poor girl to whom his father objects. Terence livens these trite motifs by concentrating attention on the two old men.

Menedemus, whose severity has sent his son off to the wars, has repented of his harshness, and is punishing himself by drudgery work on his farm. He is a conscious self-tormentor. His friend Chremes, a good-natured busybody, full of sound saws, is constantly giving out good advice that he does not follow, and tangling himself in the very difficulties he counsels others to avoid. He is an unconscious self-tormentor. Which of us is not one of the two?

While the two fathers provide the chief interest in the drama, several other aspects of the play are worthy of note. The usual surprise ending has in this play been moved into the body of the drama; the recognition that the girl Menedemus' son loves is his neighbor's daughter does not solve, but further complicates, the problem of the story. Once again Terence, but this time with the slave conscious of the trickery, used the device of having the slave deceive the old men by telling them a truth that they do not believe.

The Self-Tormentor is one of the few ancient plays in which the "unity of time" is violated: a night intervenes between Act II and Act III. The play also begins with a novelty, in that characters are in the midst of activity onstage at the start: Menedemus is working his farm as Chremes comes out to speak with him.

One of the most famous remarks of classical antiquity, frequently quoted in all ages since, is made by Chremes in this drama: Homo sum; humani nil a me alienum puto: "I am a human being; I consider nothing human foreign to me." This universality is embodied in the play itself. With a trickily complicated intrigue of interwoven plots, Terence has achieved searching and sound character study, of individuals through whom we all may see ourselves, in *The Self-Tormentor.*

PHORMIO   *Terence*

In *Phormio,* one of the two plays of Terence based indirectly, by way of *The Claimant* of Apollodorus, on a comedy of Menander's, the skill of the playwright continues to improve. He develops the intrigue of his double plot—on the stock situations, one young man requiring money for his mistress; the other seeking parental recognition of his marriage with a dowryless girl — with increasing novelty of device and detail. The sparkle of his dialogue, the brilliance of his interweaving construction of the story, enliven the episodes and quicken the drive of the play. With not quite the searching characterization and psychological depth of his masterpiece, *The Brothers**, *Phormio* is the most humorous and exuberant of Terence' tightly-woven plays. It has, deservedly, been the most popular for school production, from the Renaissance to our own day.

In some degree the pattern of *Phormio* approaches that of the plays of Plautus*. The title character is a parasite; one of the characters is a procurer. Neither of the young girls actually appears in the play, the only females being a wife of one of the old men and the Nurse through whom the final recognition is effected. But the parasite is no stock figure; he combines with the greed of his type the shrewdness of the scheming slave, and it is through him that the intrigues move. Thus, after he has learned of changing circumstances, as the *London Times* (December 18, 1933) observed after a performance at Westminster, Phormio "promptly changes his scheme in order to have the parents finance their own undoing. There is no motive for this but sheer pride of technique."

The intricate story is neatly intertwined. Two elderly brothers, Chremes and Demipho, have sons. Chremes' son, Phaedria, loves a music girl; Demipho's son, Antipho, loves a poor but respectable girl whose mother is dead. While Antipho's father is away, the parasite Phormio arranges a trick: acting for the second girl, he brings suit to establish that Antipho is the girl's nearest of kin and therefore, by Roman law, should marry her. Antipho deliberately loses the suit, and they are wed.

There is no revelatory Prologue; every episode is built with suspense and hangs upon surprise. Chremes and his brother have arranged to have Antipho marry Chremes' daughter. Chremes, in truth, has not yet seen his own daughter; she is the offspring of an earlier (bigamous) marriage, now coming to live with him because that first wife has died. If she marries outside the family, there'll have to be a revelation, a scandal, a divorce — and Chremes' still living wife has all the money! So the two old men plot to get rid of Antipho's bride. Phormio offers to take her away — for the very sum the other young man needs to purchase his mistress. Then Chremes discovers that the bride is this very daughter of his whom he is seeking. Naturally, now, Chremes wants the marriage to hold; and his efforts to tell his brother the truth, without having his wife learn of his earlier bigamy, form one of the high points in the comedy. Phormio, also learning the facts, uses them so that Chremes' son gets his music girl. With neat dramaturgy, each of the two plots thus works upon the other. And the recognition, which usually closes the comedy, here adds another complication before the happy end.

While *Phormio* does not especially deal with the virtue of courage, it gives us a familiar adage in that regard; from the play comes the saying "Fortune favors the brave."

Among the characters of *Phormio*, Terence has Demipho consult three lawyers. The hedging circumlocution of their replies and the circular counsel they offer, so that after all three have advised Demipho he is precisely where he started, make excellent caricature. But more than character, in *Phormio* it is the rapidly changing situations that liven the play, and the shifting emotions to which these circumstances give rise. Unfounded pessimism leaps to unfounded hope; comic fear soars into ecstasy, as one character after another finds his aims frustrated, then apparently fulfilled — on the brink of the goal to be brushed aside once more. Phormio, who engineers these shifts of fortune, is as rascally a fellow, and as attractive a rascal, as ancient comedy affords.

Among the plays influenced by *Phormio* are Colman's *The Man of Business*, 1774, and Molière's *The Escapades of Scapin*, which itself was utilized for Otway's *The Cheats of Scapin*, 1677, and for Ravenscroft's *Scaramouch a Philosopher*, 1677. Cardinal Newman, adapting *Phormio* for Westminster production in 1881, changed the procurer into a cruel stepmother.

Phormio, in neatness of intricate construction and liveliness of witty dialogue and comic drive, is one of the most effective of ancient comedies.

THE EUNUCH   *Terence*

The most popular in ancient times of Terence's plays, performed twice on a single day, *The Eunuch*, 161 B.C., is his nearest approach to farce. Woven into the double intrigue are two stock figures, a boastful soldier and a parasite, who, along with the intriguing slave, add more horseplay and broad humor than usual in Terence.

The plot involves two brothers, one of whom is the soldier's rival for the affections of a courtesan. The younger brother, loving a supposed sister of the courtesan, disguises himself as a eunuch to gain access to her, and rapes her. When this girl is disclosed as a citizen, he marries her. And his elder brother, convinced that the courtesan prefers him, consents to let the soldier, while making a major contribution to her support, have a minor portion of her favors.

Terence is not content, however, to let the usual situations develop without novel variations. Many neatly turned details explain the play's great popularity. More basic are the character portrayals, some novel, all masterly. The boastful soldier, in *The Eunuch*, is prouder of word than of sword; it is his wit that he esteems — and his lack of wits that makes him easy mark. The parasite laughs at those he gulls into feeding him; readily and expertly he turns over his old host, the soldier, to the untender mercies of the two brothers, his hosts-to-be. The younger brother, Cherea, is especially well drawn. His youthful overbubbling excitement in love; the ardor with which he pursues his beloved; the self-satisfaction over his conquest, with which he is so transported that he must pour out his story — and that story of his ravishing the maiden after her bath is a gem of delicate restraint and pictured enjoyment: all these establish one of the most successful portraits in ancient comedy. The courtesan herself is quite a pleasant young woman, as fair to the young man she favors as her profession allows; as agreeable as charming. There is no vulgarity in the play, but even in its broadest moments a basic decency.

Episodes of farce are equally well handled, as the siege of the courtesan's house by the aggrieved soldier. Neatly farcical, too, are the rapidly moving last scenes of the play, with their swift alternations of feeling, from joy to sadness, from hope to despair, before the final reconciliation and general delight.

The style of *The Eunuch* is graceful, a bit more lively and exuberant than that of Terence's other comedies. Colorful figures of speech abound, as in the slave's opening reflections on love, which, knowing no reason, cannot be managed by rule; and as in the later exclamation: "Ruined like a rat, betrayed by my own squeak!", or the comment since adapted as motto by many a learned restaurateur: *animus est in patinis*, "my spirit's in my pans." Attracted by these features, but repelled by the broader and more farcical aspects of the play, Gilbert Norwood has called *The Eunuch* "a strange medley of qualities. Dull and brilliant, immoral and edifying, abjectly Plautine and splendidly Terentian—it is all these by turns." Within its basic decency, it is Terence' liveliest and bawdiest farce.

Among later plays influenced by *The Eunuch* are Udall's *Ralph Roister Doister**, Jean de Baif's *L'Eunuque*, 1568; Aristo's *The Supposes**, also Gascoigne's; Pierre Larivey's *The Jealous Ones*, 1580; Wycherly's *The Country Wife**; and Sedley's *Bellamira*, 1687. Cardinal Newman adapted *The Eunuch* for a performance at Westminster in 1880.

More farcical than Terence' other plays, *The Eunuch* nevertheless maintains his high standards, both of human dignity and of deft dramaturgy, and provides a lively picture of Roman exuberance and Roman commonsense, neat capture of the society of the day, in the frame of an amusing story.

THE BROTHERS   *Terence*

Adelphoi (*The Brothers*), 160 B.C., is Terence' last play and his masterpiece. Again he takes the two most common motifs in the New Comedy — a young man who needs money for his mistress, and a young man hiding his involvement with a poor but respectable girl — joins these in an intricately but neatly woven plot, and out of the usual material makes an unusual play. In *The Brothers*, Terence' chief concern is the contrast between two elderly brothers, and particularly their different ideas on the bringing up of youth. With these characters and the consequent happenings, Terence built the shrewdest social problem play of ancient times.

Demea, a strict and stern parent, has brought up his son Ctesipho most rigidly. His son Aeschinus, he has left to his easy-going bachelor brother, Micio, who believes in kindness and trust. Both boys deceive their mentors. In the end, after numerous complications, each boy gets his girl. But the progress of their loves is wholly subordinate to the conflicting mental attitudes of the two elder men. The interest, M. S. Dimsdale has said, "is educational and ethical as much as dramatic"; but this is the dictum of a library scholar. *The Brothers* drives ahead as drama; the opposed educational theories are made manifest, in the young men and their old mentors, as impelling forces to living action.

Neatly, Terence holds the balance between the two educational points of view. The forbearing Micio shrewdly observes to his brother: "There are many signs in people's characters whereby you may easily guess, when two persons are doing the same thing, how it will affect them; so that you can often say: 'It will do this one no harm; it will harm that one' — not because what they are doing is different, but because their characters are different." The two boys are all right, Micio continues; let them have scope. And if they seem a bit extravagant, remember that as we grow older we grow wiser, except that we become "keener after money-making than we ought to be. Time will make them sharp enough at that."

The friendly, hospitable, beneficent ways of Micio seem to work out, and Demea decides to adopt them. Indeed, he reminds Micio that an old man should fight that money-loving impulse, should not merely preach but practice generosity. Micio is thus pressed into a reluctant marriage with the bride's mother; he is plagued until he gives away a farm, frees and establishes his slave — and recognizes that even along his gentle path of generous geniality, one may go to extremes. The turnabout of Demea, called by J. W. Duff "the drollest thing in Terence," paves the way for Micio's discomfiture, in a superb scene that is, as Gilbert Norwood put it, "the legitimate fruit of the whole play, the perfectly sound result of that collision between Micio and Demea which has created and sustained the whole wonderful drama." Demea has learned that severity must be tempered with tolerant understanding; Micio, that discipline must reenforce forbearance. The doctrine of the golden mean, "nothing too much", has been pressed delightfully home. And the two old men ruefully ponder the idea that Menander set down (preserved in a fragment of the original of *The Self-Tormentor**): "Every father is a fool."

All the men in *The Brothers* are excellently drawn and shrewdly contrasted. Micio, the easy-going city dweller, fond of ease, is guardian of the solid, responsible Aeschinus, who can make decisions: Aeschinus is firm in his desire to marry a poor girl; and, to shield his brother, he is ready to shelter his brother's music girl. And Demea, hardworking country fellow, has raised Ctesipho, who seeks the luxuries and extravagant pleasures of the city. The interplay of these four persons, on two age levels of contrasting natures and ideas, makes thought-provoking comedy. Behind them, even the two slaves are differentiated, the one scrupulous, the other dissolute. The sympathies of the author, despite his even-handed balancing of the concerns, perhaps were drawn toward the mild Micio. It is only in Micio, S. C. Sen Gupta observed, in *Shakespearian Comedy* (1950), "in the whole range of Latin drama, that we have a character who has not been dwarfed by the plot." "Micio's tolerance and wisdom," said George E. Duckworth, "his understanding of human nature, make him Terence's most attractive male character." *The Brothers* is the New Comedy's most attractive play.

After the success of *The Brothers*, Terence took a trip to Greece; there, with the manuscripts of further plays, he died the following year.

The Brothers has influenced many later playwrights. Terence was so popular in the tenth century that the nun Hrotswitha* wrote six plays, with the pious intention of "moralizing" Terence. To us, his integrity, dignity, and moral earnestness are clear, and give his dramas a noble fervor.

Later works using situations from *The Brothers* include Giovanni Cecci's *The Unlike*, about 1580; Marston's *The Parasitaster*, 1606; Beaumont and Fletcher's *The Scornful Lady*, about 1609; Molière's *The School for Husbands**, 1661; Steele's *The Tender Husband*, 1705; Diderot's *The Head of the Family*, 1758; Colman's *The Jealous Wife*, 1761; Cumberland's *The Choleric Man*, 1774; and Fielding's *The Fathers*, 1778.

With its well-knit plot, lifting the usual farce motifs into a high comedy of character, and with searching analysis of the eternal problem of the education of youth, *The Brothers* combines intrigue with intellectual interest, and is the most richly stimulating of the Roman comedies.

THE WITCHING HOUR   *Augustus Thomas*

The prolific playwright Augustus Thomas (American, 1857-1934) made his name in the theatre as a sound craftsman and vivid colorist, fashioning melodramas that flamed with action and captured something of the recklessness, confusion, and tumultuous growth of our pioneer days.

After the turn of the century, while American audiences were still hostile to Ibsen and other new European playwrights, Thomas began to provide more thought-provoking dramatic fare which in some degree prepared a proper attitude for the social drama just ahead. The theatre, he declared, "is a place for the visualizing of ideas." Utilizing his rich dramaturgic powers, he wove into successive melodramas problems of the day; without sacrificing the vigorous drive of the story, he added the enrichment of thought.

The best of Thomas' plays is *The Witching Hour*, which opened in New York on November 18, 1907, for a run of 212 performances. Its complex, well-knit plot centers upon the question of telepathy, of the power of mind over mind. This becomes a factor in the killing of a man by Clay Whipple, at the home of the professional gambler Jack Brookfield, with whose daughter Viola both Clay and the district attorney, Frank Hardmuth, are in love. At the trial, Brookfield tries to bring the entire psychic will power of the community to bear upon the jury; acquittal follows.

Various theatrical devices, including a cat's-eye—a United States Supreme Court Justice had fought a duel with Clay's father over a cat's-eye (this scene was originally performed as a playlet at a Lambs' Gambol, and probably suggested the fuller drama)—lend melodramatic power to the play. The idea of telepathy doubtless grew in Thomas' mind during his seasons as advance agent for a noted mind-reader, Washington Irving Bishop. Credibility for this basic idea of the play is secured in ingenious ways; among these, Brookfield's giving up gambling when he recognizes that he's been winning not through card skill but through his telepathic powers.

Of this quality, after the premiere, the *New York Dramatic Mirror* (November 30, 1907) reported: "To those who have followed, even slightly, the last decade's investigations in psychology, this presentment of the theory of the force of mind will not lack plausibility. The seeker after entertainment will undoubtedly be impelled to consider the idea while enjoying the story and the acting." Augustus Thomas himself, in his curtain speech on opening night, stated that there are two ideas in the play: first, that a thought is a dynamic force; secondly, and as a consequence of this, that it behooves everyone to be extremely careful as to the nature of his thoughts.

Some of the critics seemed not quite sure how serious Thomas was in his presentation of the power of the mind. Thus *Theatre* magazine (January, 1908), while paying tribute to his skill, wavers over the theme: "Mr. Thomas always exhibits in his work qualities that place him far in advance of the ordinary playwright. He has individuality, virility, spiritual insight, independence of thought, humor, sincerity, a charming facility of apt and incisive expression, and an artistic infallibility in the writing of scenes. *The Witching Hour* is fascinatingly interesting in many of its details, but on the whole the play proves nothing and is without substance of truth . . . We do not undertake to sweep aside, with a single sentence, the mysteries of the human soul in its communication with the living and the dead . . . One of the incidental causes in the action is a cat's-eye, a most baneful stone. It is flashed in the face of an innocent young man by a completely obnoxious young man, who immediately suffers the more or less proper penalty for his temerity and half-drunken brutality. The innocent young man becomes a murderer by the swift use of a heavy ivory paper-cutter. The impression that is left is that this is a trivial matter. The important thing is the telepathy that it gives occasion to."

Others accorded *The Witching Hour* the highest praise. The *New York Post* stated: "There are passages of sentiment in the play, which, for loveliness of feeling, have not been surpassed in the modern drama." William Winter called it "the most interesting drama in years . . . the play of the century."

If the theme of *The Witching Hour* today seems somewhat superficially handled, it is in large measure because this play was a trailblazer along what is now the drama's most traffic-laden road. It still has power as sheer melodrama, and its theme remains a significant and unsolved problem.

CHARLEY'S AUNT   *Brandon Thomas*

Although he wrote two other plays, actor Brandon Thomas (English, 1856-1914) is remembered only for *Charley's Aunt*, one of the funniest farces of several generations. Its first run, opening in London on December 21, 1892, was for 1,466 performances. It was revived in London almost once a year from 1901 to 1938. In New York, the original run, opening October 2, 1893, was for 205 performances; among revivals, that of October 17, 1940, with Jose Ferrer, reached 233 performances. For a quarter of a century there were always one or more companies on tour with the play in England. *Charley's Aunt* has been performed in twenty-two languages, including Esperanto. Samuel French, play publishers, report that among 125,000 American amateur theatrical groups, *Charley's Aunt* is the most popular play. Lewis Funke, in the *New York Times* (October 10, 1948) recorded that the estate of Brandon Thomas was still doing $100,000 a year business, over the world, with *Charley's Aunt*. It proved still popular in the summer theatres of 1952, alongside the film version of *Where's Charley?* with Ray Bolger.

Charley's aunt is Donna Lucia d'Alvadorez, a widow, left a fortune by her husband in Brazil. She is about to visit Charles Wykeham, at St. Olde's College, Oxford — just in time, Charley figures, to be chaperon for the visit of his sweetheart, Amy Spettigue, and of Amy's friend Kitty Verdun, sweetheart of Charley's friend Jack Chesney. Jack's father, Colonel Sir Francis Chesney, pops up from India with a load of debts; Jack suggests that his widower father marry Charley's wealthy aunt. Then Charley's aunt wires that she's been delayed. Refusing to be without the girls, Charley persuades Babbs—Lord Fancourt Babbersly—who arrives dressed up for some theatricals as a Victorian old lady, to impersonate the missing aunt. Suspicious old Spettigue — Amy's uncle and Kitty's guardian — arrives; when he learns that the chaperon is the fabulously rich widow, he becomes an ardent suitor.

There is considerable comic confusion. "Aunt Lucia" kisses the two girls. The two boys try to get them away, so that each can propose to his sweetheart. The two men manoeuvre to be alone with the aunt, to snag her fortune—though Colonel Chesney is considerably relieved when the old hag rejects him. Further complications develop: Charley's actual aunt, Donna Lucia, arrives, a comely widow of forty, with a quick wit and a sense of humor; and a girl, Ela Delahay, also appears, who is the dream girl Babbs had once too briefly seen. Sensing something askew, Donna Lucia introduces herself as Mrs. Beverly-Smythe, to discover what plots are under way. Sir Francis prefers "the poor Mrs. Beverly-Smythe" to the millionaire aunt, and wins her. Meanwhile, Spettigue under the spell of his engagement to "the wealthy widow" has given permission for the girls to marry the boys. Charley, unwilling to accept happiness through fraud, reveals the deception; but the real Donna Lucia, taking the letter Spettigue addressed to her, reveals her identity, and four couples are made happy as the curtain falls.

Charley's Aunt requires deftly artificial playing. Then, the response is wholehearted. A typical comment is that, after a production in Polish, of the *Warsaw Weekly* (July 17, 1937): The play is "already classical in style, situations, and characterization; the humorous power is great and it excites laughter in the most earnest people, even when the stupidity or improbability of the situation is quite evident." It should be noted that criticism of melodrama or farce on the score of improbability shoots at the wrong target. These plays are not meant to be believed; the audience grants what Coleridge said art always requires, "the willing suspension of disbelief". No more did Elizabethan audiences believe the disguises and coincidences of their comedies; these were accepted because, without disturbing the mood of the play, they added to the audience's pleasure.

Babbs introduces himself to the girls as "Charley's aunt from Brazil, where the nuts come from"; the words have become a sort of trademark for the play. ("Nut", to Victorian England, was slang, not for a lunatic, but for an outlandish dresser.) As in most good farce, the fun in *Charley's Aunt* is in the main not verbal, but sprung out of the situations, which follow mistake with understanding in swift and errant succession. There is always a hearty burst of laughter, for instance, when that particular and prudish Victorian lady, "Charley's Aunt" — Babbs in a supposedly unseen moment — is discovered smoking a cigar!

In 1948 *Charley's Aunt* was converted into a musical, *Where's Charley?*, with book by George Abbott and music by Frank Loesser. The superb acting of that "cross of string bean and jumping bean", Ray Bolger, made this an effervescent delight. Opening in Philadelphia September 13, *Where's Charley?* came to New York October 11, 1948, for a run of 792 performances, with another six weeks starting January 29, 1951. The musical complicates the fun by eliminating Babbs and having Charley himself impersonate his aunt.

When Ray Bolger is not romping about the stage, the interest in the musical version slackens. *Charley's Aunt*, however, being free of any "timely" concern, and sufficiently artificial to make its Victorian concepts of chaperon and guardian's consent part of the frolic, continues to be a lively and a very entertaining farce of impersonation and the fun that rises from confused identity.

THE OLD HOMESTEAD   *Denman Thompson*

The prime example of rural melodrama is unquestionably *The Old Homestead*. It is a "family drama" at which one can laugh and cry by turns, recognize one's neighbors on the stage, and never take offense. It established new records in theatre history. The play, like its main character, Josh Whitcomb, remains "spry as a kitten."

Denman Thompson (American, 1833-1911) in 1875 built a vaudeville sketch for himself, fashioning out of two friends in his home town of Swanzey, New Hampshire — *Joshua* Holbrook and Otis *Whitcomb* — a comic picture of the countryman visiting the big city. In 1877, he expanded this sketch to a three-act melodrama, which was reshaped in 1885 as *The Old Homestead*. The latter, with the author playing Josh Whitcomb, opened in Boston, April 5, 1886. In its travels, it reached New York on August 30, 1888 — and stayed for 200 weeks, setting a record unbroken until 1926, with *Abie's Irish Rose**. It ran over 100 weeks in Philadelphia, 75 in Chicago, 50 in San Francisco, and 25 in several other theatre cities. It has been constantly played all over the country. Produced in Keene, New Hampshire, in 1933, to mark Thompson's hundredth anniversary, the play has been enacted every July since in his home town of Swanzey. The farm at Swanzey, said H. I. Brock in the *New York Times* (August 13, 1933), was the "homely scene from which were drawn the rustic characters and the rural backgrounds of a stage piece that became so familiar to millions of Americans from the Atlantic to the Pacific that it took on the aspect of a minor national institution."

Nor have recent productions been given to draw laughs at the old-time melodrama. The *Boston Transcript* (November 25, 1924) explained: "The audience did not view *The Old Homestead* as a dramatic curiosity by any means. The audience, and it was not in the least a commonplace one, kept step with the play and extracted huge and genuine enjoyment from it." At the close of the play, Joshua Whitcomb, "when on his knees in prayer, gravely suspended his orisons, threw the drunken husband out of the window and resumed his devotions. It had the essence of 'good theatre', for the contrast between the act itself and the entirely serious way in which it was accomplished, instantly shot over the footlights . . . It is not fair to call this an old-fashioned play. It was never dramatically in fashion . . . yet there was something in *The Old Homestead* which gave it an honest appeal and which carried it to spectators of cultural and theatrical taste."

The story of *The Old Homestead* is a simple one. Suspected of theft, Reuben Whitcomb leaves the old farm. When he is cleared, his father Joshua comes to New York, hoping the boy has not been ruined by the lures and luxuries of the big city. And, at Christmastide, the wandering Reuben returns home. It is manifestly not the plot that won so many audiences. Chiefly, it was the homespun good nature and shrewd sense of Josh Whitcomb (with a credit to the author's acting: "Joshua Whitcomb is Denman Thompson dramatized". Thompson played the part over 1500 times; his successor, Henry Horton, over 2,000). The local color added considerably to the interest; but, said the *New York Times* (August 31, 1888) of the first act: "The live oxen and the real load of hay, the well of sparkling cold water, and the weather-stained farmhouse built solidly on the stage . . . do not dwarf the natural humor and simple pathos of the piece." The New York scenes present a realistic view of Grace Church, at Broadway and Tenth Street, whither many a person that had seen the show made a pilgrimage; and a palatial city home that overawed Joshua, as he hopped over the expensive rugs, suspiciously tugged back his carpet bag from the butler, circled around the circular divan, and covered his eyes against the marble Venus. "Best of all," thought the *Times*, "is the scene of homely New Year's festivities in the last act, when the logs are blazing in the kitchen fireplace, the prodigal returns, and the feast is set forth . . . a delightful transcript of real New England life."

Colorful New England characters surround Joshua; among them, little Rickety Ann, spinster Aunt Matilda of the keen and caustic tongue, Seth Perkins who never grows old, and Cy Prime, nigh on to eighty, who boasts of being the biggest liar in Cheshire County. These are amusing foils to the central figure. "It was the reality of the character of the old farmer," said the *New York Herald* (September 6, 1902), "that moved the audience and increased the warmth of his reception as the play went on. The old man makes one merry with his quaint wit and his comical blunders, but he makes one think, too, and there is about the play a wholesomeness that is good." Wholesomeness is the heart of *The Old Homestead*, as humor kicks its heels.

"A minor national institution" the play remains; though far from the sophisticated lights of the big cities, it is still out of time's catching, still simple, still heartwarming. We might apply to the play's continuing life Joshua's dry remark of a pesky neighbor's dying: "No complaint —everybody satisfied."

MAN AND THE MASSES   *Ernst Toller*

For his part in revolutionary activities, as a leader of the short-lived Bavarian Soviet Republic, Ernst Toller (German, 1893-1939) in 1919 was sentenced to five years in prison. During his confinement, he wrote plays that stirred the world. The first of these is *Masse-Mensch*, 1920, translated by Louis Untermeyer as *Man and the Masses*; it is a tragedy of the social revolution. "It literally broke out of me," said Toller, "and was put on paper in two days and a half. The two nights that my imprisonment forced me to spend in a dark cell were abysses of torment. My mind was tortured with visions of faces, demonic faces, faces tumbling over one another in grotesque somersaults. In the mornings, shivering with fever, I sat down to write and did not stop until my fingers, clammy and trembling, refused to serve me."

Although Toller was a Communist, the dramatist in him rose beyond the politician. He stated that he did not believe in proletarian art save as it merges into the universally human. And *Masse-Mensch* indicates that the Moloch of rebellion is no better than the Moloch of state.

There are no individualized characters in *Masse-Mensch*, though three persons stand out of the surging mass. The Man represents the bourgeois state. The Nameless One represents the lust of the mob for release and revenge. The Woman is the spirit of fair-dealing in the world. Married to the Man, she becomes a comrade of the revolutionary, but pleading all the while for passive resistance, not for blood. The Woman wants a peaceful strike; the masses want War! Revolution! "I will not have fresh murder!" at first the Woman cries; then reluctantly she acquiesces: "You are the masses. You are right." She finds that the masses are fully as unfeeling, as cruel, even toward their own, as ever the capitalist. When the bloody rebellion is beaten down, the Woman, by a twisted irony, is condemned to death as a leader of the fighters. With shoulders squared, eyes troubled but unafraid, she goes to her doom, wondering at what long last true brotherhood will come. For when violence enters, the means corrupts the end; the many that leap forth with noble purpose surge on with ignoble lust.

Masse-Mensch was presented in Berlin in 1921 (directed by Jürgen Fehling, with Maria—later known as Marlene—Dietrich as the Woman) in a swirling production that swept the audience as a whirlwind. Tumultuous performances followed all over Europe. The expressionistic staging, shrouded in darkness with spots of brilliant light, the few scenes of actuality—the Woman leaving her husband; the Woman appealing to the other man not to use force — these were puny moments beside the wild phantasmagorias, such as the Stock Exchange scene where bloated profiteers gorged themselves with human carrion, and grotesque forms leapt in an obscene dance around a stock ticker while war consumed mankind. And constantly there was the loom and threat of the masses, now drawing ominously near, now wavering, now shrinking back, but never dispersed, always watching, fanged, ready to encircle and to strike. There is a final tremendous spectacle of the condemned Woman when, as the *Boston Transcript* (April 28, 1924) described it, "enchained, drooping, silhouetted against a cerulean sky which throws into relief great looming shadows, frantic ghoulish reflections of her out-tossed arms and clanking manacles, she holds debate over her soul, over the burden of many murders and endless suffering, and comes to heap invectives upon God Himself that He should allow such wrongs to be."

The surge and ebb and renewed flow of the masses is caught in the rhythmic dialogue of the play, where a single voice, outcrying, may be interrupted or joined by two more; then a quartet of protest, a single voice, a full chorus, until the diapason of revolt roars forth.

Man and the Masses was presented by the Theatre Guild in New York, April 14, 1924, with Blanche Yurka, Ullrich Haupt, and Jacob Ben-Ami as the spirit of the masses. London saw it a month later with Sybil Thorndike. The *Manchester Guardian* (May 23, 1924) called the play "a symphony of distress: individualism and pacifism, typified by the Woman, proclaim the strophe; mass-violence, typified by the Nameless One, returns the antistrophe. Reason is muffled in the awful music of frustration . . . a kind of ecstatic battering against the closed doors of eternal problems which Toller does not seek to answer but restates from the abysses of his own despair." Yet, in her death-cell, when the Priest says that "Mankind is evil from the first," the Woman responds: "Mankind is groping toward the good." *Masse-Mensch*, in its picture of revolution, reveals the fierce futility of force. Grim and grisly in its stage effects, it is a violent and despairing plea for human brotherhood.

THE MACHINE WRECKERS   *Ernst Toller*

Like *Man and the Masses*, *The Machine Wreckers*, 1922, was written while Ernst Toller was in prison. Unlike the earlier play, it seeks to cast light upon contemporary urgencies through a torch held up to the past. It pictures the vain revolt of the English weavers in Nottingham, 1811. The Prologue quotes Lord Byron's maiden speech in the House of Lords, a defense of the weavers.

The workers of England, at the beginning of "the industrial revolution", were consumed by a double fear: that the machines would deprive them of their jobs and leave them reft of livelihood; that tending the machines would reduce them to mechanical serfs and leave them reft of humanity. In the play, they confuse the owners of the machines, as their oppressors, with the machines being forced upon them. The question is whether to rise in violence and destroy both oppressors and machines, or whether to band together in organized and peaceful protest. Fear and roused anger sweep the workers into violence, until they bring death upon their leader, and defeat upon their cause. Dimly there is a clouded hope that, some day, the machine may be, not the workers' master, but a true servant of all mankind.

In structure, *The Machine Wreckers* is the best of Toller's plays, moving through its ten scenes with the tensely dramatic drive of a well-knit story. Around the individual workers and employers Toller, with his usual skill in handling crowds, swirls a swarm of striking workers. But the chief figures of the drama, while representing opposed points of view, are also felt as real persons, engaged emotionally in a personal struggle for what they think is just and right. The employers are dyed a bit too heavily as villains, but the degradation and the wretched poverty of the workers are given not merely mass presentation in looming symbol, but actual embodiment in humans with whose plight we are concerned.

After Reinhardt's production in Berlin, *The Machine Wreckers* was quickly shown all over Europe. The United States saw it more tardily: at Carnegie Technical Institute in Pittsburgh in 1926; the first professional production, in Boston October 24, 1927, in a translation by Ashley Dukes; the New York premiere at the Henry Street Settlement, April, 1937. The *Boston Transcript* did not like the play: "There is a reasonable enough kernel . . . but the nut around it is worm-ridden and sour." The *Boston Globe* saw it in a better light, with "scenes tremendously forceful in their dramatic and emotional appeal. There is not a little sardonic humor, and considerable poetic symbolism, but for the most part the drama is sheer tragedy."

Comparable to Hauptmann's *The Weavers** as a drama of workers' revolt, *The Machine Wreckers* is limited in interest by its subject and its bias; but within the field of labor relations it is a vivid dramatic presentation of Toller's constant theme: the futility of force, and humanity's one hope, the truly felt and truly operating brotherhood of man.

HOOPLA!   *Ernst Toller*

After his release from prison, Toller found himself in a world that left him dismayed. He set his impressions, sardonically, into the tragic drama *Hoppla, wir leben* (*Whoops, we're alive!*), 1927, which was presented in England in 1928 as *Hoopla!* It has not yet had professional production in the United States.

Hoopla! is the story of Karl Thomas, a Communist agitator who, after the commutation of his death sentence, is confined in a mad-house. Released after ten years, he blunders about in a new world. His former comrade, Kilman, now a powerful Socialist minister with reactionary leanings, tries to brush him aside with platitudes. Thomas attends a party election, where all seems craven and fruitless. He gets a job as a waiter in a hotel; mankind seems contemptible, vile. Thomas goes to shoot Kilman, but when he sees him again deems him too petty to be worth the powder. A Nationalist, however, does flash by and shoot Kilman; Thomas is arrested for the crime. Just before the news that the assassin has confessed, Thomas hangs himself in his cell.

In Toller's plays there seems a despair beyond which the playwright could not rise. It was a disillusionment rooted in weakness, without that summoned proud human strength which can look at hopeless evil and yet survive. In one drama, *Pastor Hall*, 1939, based on the experience of Pastor Martin Niemöller, Toller did picture a man who, despite persecution, holds steadfast to his faith. But in the same year, in New York, Toller committed suicide.

Hoopla! as produced in Berlin by Erwin Piscator, seemed a revelation in the theatre, a promise and at once a fulfillment of the effectiveness of the new technique. Between the acts of the play, motion pictures — newsreel shots of actual history — linked the personal events of the drama with world affairs around. The stage itself showed five rooms on various levels. As C. Hooper Trask described the production in the *New York Times* (December 11, 1927), "The backing of each of these sections is a white screen, on which is thrown from behind either a stereopticon picture or a film. Also, a good part of the time, a transparent scrim is let down over the front of the stage, and movies and captions are projected on this from another concealed machine. In the first scene in the prison, the figure of a sentry appears at the back, comes terrifyingly near, and fades away. As the prisoners attempt to break out of their cell, motion pictures of soldiers shooting are thrown on both sides of the scrim at the front. During the voting scene in the restaurant, moving pictures of election riots are thrown on several of the screens, while in the center photographed ballots come floating down in a never-ending chain. In the final scene the various prisoners are communicating with each other by telegraphic raps and their messages are flashed word by word on the scrim opposite their respective cells." The vividness of the presentation, and the sense of integration, widening the story of the one man to a capitulation of the era, constituted "a complete triumph of modern technique."

The documentary presentations of the American Federal Theatre, *The Living Newspaper*, are adaptations of the technique here developed by Piscator. The best of *The Living Newspaper* "editions", *One Third of a Nation*, gave protesting vividness and vehemence of illustration to President Roosevelt's concern over "one-third of a nation ill-clothed, ill-fed, ill-housed." Mingling actors and motion pictures, placarded processions, harangues, and snatches of drama, *The Living Newspaper* sought to use the theatre to present burning issues of the day. More deeply, but no less urgently, *Hoopla!* makes vivid the state of the Germany of its day, with the death of morale and the dearth of values that made empty and desperate spirits ready for a dictator's call.

THE POWER OF DARKNESS   *Leo Nikolayevich Tolstoi*

The novelist and moral philosopher Leo Nikolayevich Tolstoi (Russian, 1828-1910), rather late in life, after his conversion to a personal pacifist Christianity, wrote several dramas that are starkly powerful and widely influential. The first of these, *The Power of Darkness*, 1866, is a grim picture of peasant depravity, lightened only by a final impulse toward atonement.

The Power of Darkness was preceded, and some think excelled, by a simple peasant play of the Russian Alexsi F. Pisemski (1820-1881), *Bitter Fate*, 1859. The story of Tolstoi's play is more complicated. A young farm woman, egged on by her mother, poisons her old husband so as to be free to gratify her lust for her farm hand, Nikita, who himself has seduced then killed an orphan girl. Married to the farm woman, Nikita seduces her half-wit stepdaughter. This girl gives birth to a child —which Nikita—after the two older women have baptized the babe— kills so that the girl can marry a complaisant neighbor. Haunted by the child's cries, Nikita drinks; then, under the spell of the mellowly drunken old soldier Mitrich, Nikita gathers courage and decency and at the girl's wedding confesses his crimes.

Forbidden in Russia, *The Power of Darkness* had its world premiere at the new Théâtre Libre in Paris, 1888; in Germany, it was played the next year at the new Freie Bühne in Berlin. Russia permitted it in 1902, with Stanislavski as Mitrich. The premiere in English was the New York Theatre Guild production, January 19, 1920, with Frank Reicher,

Helen Westley, and Henry Travers. An adaptation by Abram Hill, produced in New York in 1948, transferred the locale and characters to a Negro farmhouse in the Southern United States. (Similar transformations have been made of *The Lower Depths** and *The Cherry Orchard**.) It has everywhere been recognized that *The Power of Darkness* is, as H. W. L. Dana has called it, a "tremendous and appalling" drama.

Tolstoi surrounds the grisly details of his story with minutiae of everyday peasant life that lend reality to the picture, and sharpen the intensity of these events by the feeling that they are less exceptional than commonplace, wherever men are driven to toil like beasts of the field. The nearness of sin presses upon us out of the play, said Kenneth Macgowan (January 21, 1920): "Its horror walks by day and fills a theatre with the dread of sin . . . Yet the light of God is in it. It is no stained-glass radiance. It flickers and flashes from the brain of a poor old stammering peasant who cleans cesspools. At the end it blazes forth as his son makes public confession of sin upon sin and crime upon crime, in a scene of the utmost tragic power."

What Tolstoi builds toward (as also in *The Living Corpse**) and what matters, is not the long array of horrid crimes, but the final awakening, atonement, and redemption. "The point of the play," as the *Christian Science Monitor* said (May 14, 1949), "lies in its climax, when the laborer . . . recognizes that he cannot escape punishment by hanging himself, but falls on his knees in repentance and begs pardon of God." It is of this scene that Bernard Shaw said "I remember nothing in the whole range of drama that fascinated me more"—and Zola cried in the theatre: "Don't change a single word!" *The Power of Darkness*, out of its horror, in almost unbearable intensity drives to a final blinding calm.

THE LIVING CORPSE   *Leo Nikolayevich Tolstoi*

The most popular of Tolstoi's dramas is *The Living Corpse*, 1900. In it he pictures, on a higher social level, deterioration and crime, lighted by the same final courage of atonement as marks *The Power of Darkness**.

Tolstoi died before *The Living Corpse* was finished. His daughter gave it to the Moscow Art Theatre, where it had its premiere in September, 1911, directed by Stanislavski. It was so popular that soon it was running simultaneously at two theatres in Moscow and one in St. Petersburg. Reinhardt produced it in Berlin in 1913, with Moissi as Fedya; Moissi played this—his greatest role—in New York in 1929. New York had already seen the play: in German with Jacob Adler, opening November 3, 1911, and again in 1916; in English, opening October 3, 1918, with John Barrymore (under the title *Redemption*; Fedya became Fedor). Many deem this, and not his Hamlet, Barrymore's greatest role. In 1929, New York saw it (after the Moissi German performance) in English with Jacob Ben-Ami and Eva Le Gallienne. *The Living Corpse* continues, in repertory and community groups, to show its intense power.

The story of the play comes from an actual case told Tolstoi by his friend Judge N. Davydov, in which the couple went to jail. In the play, the attractive, dissolute weakling Fedya, loving his wife, wishes to free her so that she can make a happier marriage. Lacking courage to commit suicide, he simulates it; and Lisa marries Victor. Fedya himself leads a happier wastrel life until, in a café, he tipsily tells his story. A blackmailer overhears him, and ultimately Victor, Fedya, and Lisa are brought to trial for collusion and bigamy. And at last Fedya finds the courage to free Lisa by making his suicide real.

Although the entire story is graphic, with stinging dialogue, the character of Fedya stands out as one of the great creations of the modern drama. His gradual degeneration is a masterpiece of development. We see him first pale and poignantly beautiful, dissolute, yet full of sensitive feeling, half passional, half spiritual: an aristocrat through and through. He remains dandified for a while even in the garish bloom of the sordid café where, drinking amid the gypsies, he accepts his filthy surroundings until he acquires a filthy self. His maudlin scene with the gypsies — does he love the flaming Masha, who makes him forget for a while? — is followed by hectic flares of passion, as his finer nature rouses impulses of rebellion still, and as his frame is racked by want and dissipation. One volcanic outburst sears across life, love, hatred, and death, as he turns upon the magistrate who in the name of justice pries off the lids of souls. The intensity of his life increases as its end nears — until the upsurge of his latent decency spreads like a sunset calm, and his final moment of self-sacrifice is almost a consecration.

The Living Corpse comes with powerful impact upon the audience. "It is graphic, varied, and hectic", said *Theatre* magazine (November, 1918), "and psychologically introspective in its study of the lack of will . . . It is impressive in its simplicity and exploited by suggestion." With its eleven somewhat episodic scenes, the play impressed the *New York Times* (October 4, 1918) as having an effect "curiously similar to that of an Elizabethan chronicle history . . . it is richly atmospheric, and abounds in character sketches as masterly as they are brief." It is, as Gilbert Seldes summed it up in the *New York Graphic* (December 7, 1929), "one of the great creative works of our time."

Although Tolstoi satirizes the absurdity of indissoluble marital ties, and the stupidity of the judiciary class, the essence of the play is the character of Fedya, and his winning through to the final act of redemption. "The man is a constant storm of conflict", said the *New York Telegraph* (December 9, 1929), "a struggle between a desire to pity himself and the almost resistless impulse to dramatize himself." Psychoanalysts might find a merging of these urges, even in Fedya's final, decent act; but which of us will cast the first stone? While Fedya's circumstances may be particular, his nature is universal; we have in ourselves, as of Hamlet, something too of Fedya. In *The Living Corpse*, Tolstoi has, with more power and more discretion than his pictured magistrate, lifted the lid that guards the human soul.

THE REVENGER'S TRAGEDY   *Cyril Tourneur*

Long neglected on the stage, though constantly praised by critics in the reading, *The Revenger's Tragedy*, 1607, by Cyril Tourneur (English, c. 1575-1626) is a richly colored drama in which violent emotions course to equally violent ends. Couched in tempestuous broken blank verse, with occasional rhyming couplets and some prose, the play, as John Addington Symonds said in the Preface to the Mermaid Edition, "is an entangled web of lust, incest, fratricide, rape, adultery, mutual suspicion, hate, and bloodshed, through which runs, like a thread of glittering copper, the vengeance of a cynical plague-fretted spirit. Vendice emerges from the tainted crew of Duke and Duchess, Lussurioso, Spurio and Junior, Ambitioso and Supervacuo, with a kind of blasted splendour. They are curling and engendering, a brood of flat-headed asps, in the slime of their filthy appetites and gross ambitions. He treads and tramples on them all. But he bears on his own forehead the brands of Lucifer, the rebel, and of Cain, the assassin. The social corruption that transformed them into reptiles, has made him a fiend incarnate. Penetrated to the core with evil, conscious of sin far more than they are, he towers above them by his satanic force of purpose." Vendice, properly executed at the drama's close for his own deeds, shows the unending pattern in which crime breeds crime.

The play's events justify Vendice's perturbation almost to frenzy. Knowing that the Duke's son Lussurioso covets their sister, Castizia, Vendice and Hippolito, disguised as his messengers, test their mother, Gratiana; and she seeks to persuade her daughter to the amorous meeting. The scene in which the two brothers reveal their identity and reproach their mother, who repents, is fraught with passion. "The reality and life of this dialogue," said Charles Lamb, "passes any scenical illusion I ever felt. I never read it but my ears tingle, and I feel a hot flush spread my cheeks, as if I were presently about to 'proclaim' some such 'malefactions' of myself, as the brothers here rebuke in their unnatural parent; in words more keen and dagger-like than those which Hamlet speaks to his mother. Such power has the passion of shame truly personated, not only to 'strike guilty creatures unto the soul', but to 'appal' even those that are 'free'." Lussurioso is killed for his passionate endeavors.

The Duke himself desired Gloriana, the beloved of Vendice, and when she repelled him had her poisoned. The play opens with Vendice, holding Gloriana's skull, watching the Duke go by. Later, Vendice puts clothes beneath that skull, in a darkened room, smears deadly poison on the grisly face, and entices the lecherous Duke to come for a kiss and die.

Played in London March 8, 1937, for the first time since Tourneur's day, *The Revenger's Tragedy* proved powerful indeed. The *Times* wondered whether the public of today could accept the "shameless intensity" of its passions, for now "appeal is rarely made, and response is usually wary, to what is histrionically appalling, prodigious, and extreme." Nevertheless, the *Times* praised the part of Vendice, "the largeness and . . . tormented grandeur of the half-insane figure who sees in the tainted ducal family the epitome of humanity and works upon it with abominable ingenuity a kind of rough justice"; and praised also "the forcible directness, the persistent urgency, and the fine gravity of the dialogue." The *Telegraph*, expressing the hope that the play will be more frequently performed, said that "the tremendous passion which inspires both theme and writing calls for dramatic expression", and found in Vendice a figure "that offers great possibilities for a really fine actor." The horrid circumstances of the play do not mitigate its present emotional power.

The story of *The Revenger's Tragedy* sounds like a fragment of Italian history, but there is no known source for Tourneur's plot. There is equal violence, save for a happy ending, in Tourneur's other play, *The Atheist's Tragedy*, 1611. He has, however, created no character more interesting than Vendice, who is one of the outstanding figures of our early drama.

Vendice is true to his sense of honor and of duty; yet he is cruel even to outrage in his revenge. This tempest of righteousness wreaking evil gives the grandeur of a stormy sunset to *The Revenger's Tragedy*, one of the most vivid, swirling revenge plays of Elizabethan times.

A MONTH IN THE COUNTRY   *Ivan Turgenev*

The one memorable play by the Russian novelist Ivan Turgenev (1818-1883), built, as Stanislavski said, "on the most delicate curves of love experience," is *A Month in the Country*, 1850. "For the lover of fine shades, of subtle approaches," the play—anticipating Chekhov* and Jean-Jacques Bernard's "drama of the unexpressed"—is a touching comedy of boredom reaching out for love and closing fingers on frustration.

On the isolated estate of the practical Islaev, his wife Natalia (Natasha) Petrovna regrets her more glamorous past, and is fearfully conscious of her waning charms. Bored by the languid and polite attentions of her husband's friend Mikhail Rakitin, Natasha is roused to fresh love when the zestful young Aleksei Belaev arrives as tutor for her son. Aleksei is equally ready to flirt either with the twenty-nine-year-old Natasha or with her seventeen-year-old ward Vera (Veroshka); but Natasha's jealousy and ardor drive him back to Moscow. Rakitin, despite Islaev's pleading, also leaves. The observant and cynical Dr. Ignati Spigelski, the only one who has been getting what he wants, teaches the clumsy old neighboring landowner Bolshintsov how to propose, and thrusts the now bitter and lonely Vera, who had bloomed beneath the tutor's attentions, into the old man's arms. Natasha is left frustrate, more lonely and more bored than before.

A Month in the Country was at once recognized as a masterpiece. It has had frequent performance in many lands. In London it was first seen on July 5, 1926; again in 1936; in an adaptation by Emlyn Williams, February 11, 1943, with Michael Redgrave as Rakitin, for 313 performances; and at the Old Vic opening November 30, 1949. In New York, the Theatre Guild presented the play, borrowing much from Stanislavsky's Moscow productions of 1909 and after, on March 17, 1930, with Alla Nazimova, Dudley Digges as the doctor, Henry Travers, and Alexander Kirkland. Ruth Gordon was in the Williams adaptation in Westport, Connecticut, August 2, 1949.

The half-tones of *A Month in the Country*, its soft regrets, pale passions, and inexpressive sighs, are, said the London *Stage* (July 8, 1926), "infinitely less depressing than the dull, if more closely analytical, dramas of the ever boosted Chekhov". It is, as the *Chicago Journal* (August 19, 1926) declared, "a beautiful play all through; but its second act seems one of the most beautiful things in modern drama." It is hard to realize that this delicate drama, its effects wrought by suggestion and understatement, was written, as John Mason Brown pointed out (March 18, 1930), "when Turgenev himself, as a resident of Paris, was sitting nightly before the dramas of Scribe* and Musset*; in fact, when the playgoers of England and America were still patronizing the claptrap of such ardent claptrappers as Sheridan Knowles and Dion Boucicault*."

The portrait of Natalia Petrovna is superb. On the isolated Islaev estate she still holds the stage, but with no significant lines to speak, no situation to command, no attitude to strike. She feels herself, as N. Bryllion Fagin put it in the *Hopkins Review* (Fall, 1949), drooping toward a settled age.

William Archer has compared Chekhov's plays to opera librettos: the performance fills in the music. This is even more true of *A Month in the Country*, wherein, as the *London Times* (October 1, 1936) stated, "the passions are implied, and actors are left a thousand eloquent omissions through which, if their insight and skill be equal to the extraordinarily difficult task, the heat of the invisible flames may be conveyed. There, to those that admire conscious art, the play offers exquisite pleasure." These reticences, however, in no wise lessen the sense of reality. The play is, indeed, the *Times* continued (October 4, 1936), "full of an astounding actuality, which persuades us that the actors when they have completed one scene retire not to their dressing-rooms but to some other part of the house to resume a life from which they have been momentarily snatched. Any scene presented to the audience is only a section of the stage, those sections out of view seething with life though we do not see it."

The picture of life in *A Month in the Country* is as rounded as reality. Pathetic it is, in Natasha's weak-winged and foredoomed flight from futility, and in the environing waste and misdirection. Yet always the touch of life's comedy comes as a timely leaven: just when the subtlety threatens to sink into flatness, the cynical observations of the doctor lift the mixture again, with wit and understanding that quicken the mind to companion the flow of the emotions. Turgenev has, with a mellowness unknown to Chekhov, written a masterly drama of waning lives.

THE CONTRAST   *Royall Tyler*

A member of the Harvard Class of 1776 that graduated into the Revolution, Royall Tyler (American, 1757-1826) left Boston for New York with an unfinished play that became *The Contrast; or, The Son of American Liberty* — the first timely and enduring American drama. It opened at the John Street Theatre, in New York, April 16, 1787, while Congress was in session there. When the play was printed in 1790 George Washington headed the list of subscribers. *The Contrast* not only declared the independence of the American spirit, but in Jonathan— too proudly free to be the "servant", he was the "waiter" of Colonel Manly — also presented, in all his handiness and ready shrewdness, the first stage Yankee.

The "contrast" in the play is, of course, between the old world and the new. Colonel Manly is a gallant officer, come (like the author) from Boston to New York. Dimple, who has been abroad "to rub off a little of the patroon rust", is a rake and a spendthrift; he seeks the hand of Maria Van Rough, because of her father's possessions, while secretly he is paying court to the wealthy Letitia. Dimple's ways have imposed themselves upon old Van Rough, but young Maria's heart goes out to Manly. With the help of his "waiter" Jonathan, who can mend even a battered love situation, the Colonel wins his lady.

The contrast between the masters is repeated in their men. Dimple's servant, Jessamy, assumes English airs; he quotes Lord Chesterfield at second hand. Jonathan is the simple Yankee, since familiar on our stage, whom others at their peril may take for a simpleton.

In the course of *The Contrast*, Maria sang the ballad *Alknomook*, which was popular for many years; and Jonathan sang *Yankee Doodle* for the first time on the stage.

The Contrast was soon played in Philadelphia, Boston, and Baltimore. Charleston, South Carolina, saw it in 1793, also in 1940. The play has had some dozen revivals, around the country, in the past decade.

Interesting chiefly because of its historical position, as the first dramatic assertion of American manhood against the effete, false culture carried from the Old World, and as the first stage appearance of the characteristic Yankee, *The Contrast* has also an intrinsic dramatic spark that catches emotional fire in presentation today.

RALPH ROISTER DOISTER   *Nicholas Udall*

The first English comedy, *Ralph Roister Doister*, was written about 1540 by a scholar familiar with the Latin comedies of Terence* and Plautus*. Nicholas Udall (1505-1556) was headmaster of Eton; later, of Westminster School. Good Roman structure and good English figures and fun are fused; there are, said Allardyce Nicoll, "a series of excellent stage tricks, and a dialect which is moderately easy in spite of the fettering rime."

The Four P's of Heywood had sown the seed of English comedy. To combine a skilfully constructed fable with Heywood's character delineation, John Addington Symonds suggested, was all that comedy required to bring it to maturity. This union Nicholas Udall effected in his *Ralph Roister Doister*.

The character of Ralph is that of the *miles gloriosus*, the boastful warrior, which springs from Plautus' play of that name. Ralph is a boaster and a coward; he has money, but spends it foolishly. He is vain of his appearance, imagining himself what his fellows of later times would call a "masher" or a "lady-killer". Ralph is, at the moment of the play, drawn toward Widow Custance, and in the absence of her fiancé, the merchant Gawyn Goodluck, Ralph seeks to win her. He is about equally helped and hampered by his boon companion, the parasite Merygreek, who flatters and bullies and bosses Ralph. The winsome widow, unable to get rid of the pair, determines to get what fun she can out of them. Gawyn, returning, is jealous; but an old friend, and Ralph's cowardly confession, clear the window and the situation.

Although the intrigue of the play is typical of Roman comedy, the figures in *Ralph Roister Doister* are genuinely English. Ralph, for all the lengthy dramatic background of his type, speaks and acts like those in the audience around, fringed with the frank exaggeration of satire. Merygreek, Gawyn Goodluck, and the rest are native stock. The dialogue, too, is vernacular, and lively; with the movement of the play, it creates an atmosphere of urbanity, a merry mood of life among the comfortable middle class of old England. The play was long popular for performance in English schools. The essential elements of comedy as we know it today are all present: characters ridiculous and serious (some the more ridiculous for taking themselves seriously), incidents laughable in themselves, temporary misunderstandings that rise to a climax of bewilderment, and more.

The merriment of the play remains delightful entertainment. "Definitely farce," said the *London Times* (August 2, 1932) when it was produced at the Malvern Festival. Allowing for the change in mode of expression, there are still robust humor and amusing incident in *Ralph Roister Doister*.

THE PROVOK'D WIFE   *Sir John Vanbrugh*

In one year, 1697, Sir John Vanbrugh (English, 1664-1726) saw onstage his two greatest successes, *The Relapse* (see *The School for Scandal**) and *The Provok'd Wife*. The latter continued popular throughout the eighteenth century. Betterton and Mrs. Barry were in the original cast; others who have played in the comedy include Colley Cibber, Nance Oldfield, Peg Woffington, and David Garrick. There were London revivals in 1919 and 1936.

The play opens with Sir John Brute—a scold and a coward—regretting his marriage. Matrimony confines him, bores him, chafes him. His wife, naturally, seeks solace elsewhere. At Spring Garden, she is frolicking with Constant — whose friend Heartfree is there with Mrs. Brute's niece, his beloved Belinda—and Lady Brute is on the brink of yielding to Constant when jealous Lady Fancyfull arrives. The men and the ladies repair to Lady Brute's, but Sir John comes home unexpectedly. He had been arrested, while disguised in a parson's gown, for engaging in a street brawl, and been lectured and dismissed by the magistrate. Although Sir John finds the men concealed, he accepts the explanation that they are there because of Heartfree's hopes of Belinda. At the same time, his jealousy has been sufficiently aroused for him to find more value in his wife and to treat her with more attention and respect thereafter.

Vanbrugh was the most spontaneous, in creation, of the playwrights of his time, and *The Provok'd Wife* is written much as he might have talked. The result is that the dialogue remains surprisingly fresh and lively; and the characters, though put through situations similar to those in dozens of the dramas of the day, seem natural and hearty, quite humanly endowed with impulses and feelings. It is this quality that explains the complaint of the critic of the *London Chronicle* (October 7, 1758): "It is amazing to me that Mr. Garrick will attempt the part of Sir John Brute . . . in which he is absolutely prejudicial to the morals of his countrymen."

There were other complaints about the play's morals. As one small bow to these, the parson's gown in which Sir John Brute disguises himself was changed to a lady's dress. (A deeper obeisance was Vanbrugh's writing of *The Provok'd Husband**.) But the bluntness of the portrayals has helped keep them alive. Thus W. A. Darlington in the *London Telegraph* (October 6, 1936) found *The Provok'd Wife* "a gay and lively piece." And the *Times* (same date) felt that Vanbrugh wrote "fashionably, grossly, and amusingly . . . The comedy smilingly insists that laughter is not (whatever French psychologists say) incompatible with some degree of emotion." *The Provok'd Wife* remains one of the most alive of the seventeenth century comedies.

THE PROVOK'D HUSBAND   *Sir John Vanbrugh*

Begun by Sir John Vanbrugh, completed by Colley Cibber (1671-1757) and produced in 1728, *The Provok'd Husband; or, A Journey to London* pretends to be an apology for *The Provok'd Wife**. The printed preface says of Vanbrugh: "It was as a full atonement for the licentiousness of *The Provoked Wife*, that he conceived and began *The Provoked Husband*." The probability is, however, that Vanbrugh was taking advantage of the publicity attendant upon the controversy over his earlier comedy. To be sure, there is no figure in the new play as disagreeable as Sir John Brute and (probably because of Cibber's handiwork) the main characters are more morally upright, or at least more quickly penitent; but the intrigue of the subplot (which was later used in *The Belle's Stratagem*, 1780, by Mrs. Hannah Crowley) is typically Restoration in its pranked flirtations and attempted seductions. As a consequence of the veneer of apology and respectableness, however, the history of the two plays has been different. *The Provok'd Wife* was virtually unproduced throughout the nineteenth century, but has proved vigorous and entertaining in the twentieth; *The Provok'd Husband*, played constantly until 1860, has been without professional production since.

Among those that have played in *The Provok'd Husband* are Nance Oldfield, Garrick, Peg Woffington, John Philip Charles, Fanny Kemble, Ellen Tree, Macready, Helen Faucit, and Charlotte Cushman. America saw the play at the Nassau Street Theatre, New York, January 6, 1752.

The "provoked" husband, Lord Townly, begins precisely as does the provoking husband of the earlier play, with the question: "Why did I marry?" Lord Townly is plagued with a wife whose one thought is for society, for cards, for gilded dalliance, for all the trumpery frills of a "profligate course of pleasures." Her reputation is still clear, but how soon ill-fame may splash upon it, Lord Townly shudders to think. He decides to leave her and make his reasons known. Through this resolve — and the friendly urging of Lord Townly's friend Manly, who loves Townly's sweet sister, Grace — Lady Townly is won back to proper concern for her conduct and her name. The subplot of the play brings to London the solid and stupid country gentleman, Sir Francis Wronghead, with his wife, his son Richard, and his daughter Jenny. Lady Wronghead, made giddy by the London whirl, is easy prey for the fortune-hunting Count Basset, who woos the mother while trying to win the daughter, and to pacify his mistress with the son. The whole Wronghead family is saved, in the nick of time, by gallant Manly.

Criticism estimated *The Provok'd Husband* rather on moral than on dramatic grounds. Thus the London *Monthly Mirror* (1804) called the play "perhaps, on the whole, the best comedy in the English language . . . it is calculated to expose licentiousness and folly, and would do honor to any stage." A more objective note of criticism crept into the comments of the London *Lady's Newspaper* (November 20, 1847): "a very amusing comedy, full of life, bustle and variety, throwing us a

little into the past, yet without any of the rust of antiquity about it."
Popular as *The Provok'd Husband* used to be, it is heavily burdened with
the respectability that Cibber, if not Vanbrugh, added to its moral tone,
and is unlikely often now to grace our stage.

THE STAR OF SEVILLE   *Lope Felix de Vega Carpio*

Lively in life as in writing, Lope Felix de Vega Carpio (1562-1635)
was the first great influence in the Spanish drama to ripple widely
through the theatrical world. He has been called "the incarnation of
Spain", and his plays — some 1800 of all sorts and sizes, of which about
470 survive — touch upon every aspect of Spanish life and interest.
While this "prodigy of nature", as Cervantes called him, was mainly a
national glory, his popularity widened the influence of theatrical art
throughout Europe; ideas from his plots and aspects of his technique
were extensively borrowed. He created the comedy of gallant manners.
He renewed the ancient classical figure of the *gracioso*, the humorous
confidential servant. In many of his plays, he made the woman the
center of dramatic interest. In his metrical address, *The New Art of
Writing Plays in these Times*, 1608, he admitted the validity of the
classical rules, but declared that he broke them in order to please the
unlearned spectators. Despite the spontaneous ease of his writing,
Lope's plays are dexterously constructed, usually in three acts, with
colorful dialogue that is often romantically emotional and sometimes
reaches ornate grandiloquence. Usually it presses his points so shrewdly
home that his name, as in the expressions "a Lope woman", "a Lope
diamond", came to signify the highest excellence.

Perhaps most representative, and best known of Lope's plays outside
of Spain, is his historical drama *The Star of Seville*. In this, the cloak
and sword atmosphere is at its most brilliant, as the *pundonor* (point of
honor), which became a basic force in the Spanish drama, presses the
lovers to unhappiness. The King, desirous of Stella (the Star of
Seville), orders his knight Don Sancho Ortiz to kill Stella's brother,
Bustos Tabera, who is protecting her. The King then delivers Don
Sancho to Stella, but she renounces vengeance, whereupon Don Sancho,
equally honorable, surrenders himself to the authorities. The King, his
conscience touched, admits he had set Don Sancho upon Stella's brother;
he now proposes that Stella and Don Sancho wed. They love one another, but because of her brother's death at Don Sancho's hands, their
union is impossible. Such — the play ends — "Such are the people of
Seville. And now Lope consecrates to you this tragedy, giving eternal
fame to the Star of Seville, whose marvelous history is writ on tablets
of bronze."

There was a new English translation of the play, by Elizabeth C.
Hullihen, in 1955.

In Don Sancho's agony over killing his beloved's brother, he has a
vision of hell in which he mocks at the knightly code of honor. This
may be a feeling of the playwright's as well. In his many social dramas,
while he idealizes the King, Lope pictures him chastising the hidalgos for
their cruelty toward the common people, with whom his feelings flow.
In *The King the Greatest Justice* (which brings to mind Calderon's *The*

Mayor of Zalamea*), for example, the King condemns to death a noble
who has ravished a peasant's bride. Lope's best play in this mood is
Fuente Ovejuna (The Sheep Well), which twentieth century Spain
again found vivid and pertinent. It pictures an episode of the war for
the Spanish crown between Alonso of Portugal and Ferdinand of Aragon
in 1476. A cruel commander, seeking to rape the peasant girl Laurencia,
is driven off; Laurencia and her bridegroom Frondoso rouse the village
of Fuente Ovejuna to revolt and kill the commander. The peasants
are tortured, but when asked the names of the guilty, all answer only
"Fuente Ovejuna". Ferdinand, learning the story, pardons the village.
In addition to such social dramas, and his lighter comedies of cloak and
sword, Lope wrote about 400 *autos sacramentales*, short religious dramas
performed in the open on the feast of Corpus Christi.

"No play of Lope's," said Brander Matthews in *Chief European Dramatists* (1916), "is more characteristic of his method than *The Star of
Seville*. It is a typical example of the comedy of cloak and sword, with
its high-strung hero, its high-strung heroine, its traditional comic servant, allowed to comment at will on the story as it unrolls itself. There
is a swift succession of situations, always effective, in spite of the occasional artificiality by which they are brought about—situations effective
because they have been artfully prepared for, skilfully led up to, and
powerfully handled when at last they are presented. The dialogue is
sometimes stiff with rhetorical embroidery, but in general it is easy with
the freedom almost of improvisation. Throughout the play we cannot
fail to perceive the facility and the felicity of the born playwright, joying in his task, carrying on his story with a light hand and yet holding
it with a firm grasp."

Lope first made popular this type of drama, which reached a later
peak in the plays of Hugo*. *The Star of Seville* captures the surging
spirit of the Renaissance in Spain, the period of the world's bounty outpouring theatrical gold.

THE CLOISTER   *Emile Verhaeren*

There is an almost grim power beneath the lyric quality of the dramas
of Emile Verhaeren (1855-1916), outstanding poet of the "Young Belgium" group whose motto was "Let us be ourselves." His most successful play in Belgium is the comparatively peaceful *The Dawns*, 1898,
which makes appeal to universal brotherhood. Outside Belgium, however, he is known by two plays of more violent mood, in which passion
swells to intense power: *Helen of Sparta*, 1912, and *The Cloister*, 1900.

Within the monastery of *The Cloister* there is a quiet struggle between the patrician monks that have been its traditional directors and
the sturdy, intelligent, ambitious sons of the people that have more
recently found home within the cloistered halls. This conflict is taking
shape in the rivalry between the patrician Dom Balthazar and the more
blunt Father Thomas to succeed the old Prior, when Balthazar is moved
to confess that, years before entering the Order, he had killed his father
in a drunken surge and had allowed a wayfarer to be punished for the
crime. The brotherhood set a penance for Balthazar; but on the advice
of his friend Dom Mark, and, as the Prior puts it, "drunk with humility",

Balthazar interrupts a public service to confess his crime to the whole village. The monks have no alternative; they expel Balthazar, to face the penalties of civil justice; and, during the troubled moments, Thomas gains the Prior's promise of the succession.

The play makes clear that it is not true penitence — which, after the monks' hearing, would have held Balthazar silent with his God — but, rather, a perverse pride that drove him to the public declaration of his guilt. This all-male company (save for the worshipping townsfolk at the close) mirrors within the cloister the frets and ambitions of society outside; its ways are sequestered, but its passions are no less intense for being controlled than those that lay folk feel: no less demanding, and no different.

The Cloister was presented in New York, June 5, 1921, by the Theatre Guild, with Frank Reicher as Father Thomas. The *Globe* praised "the elevation of mood throughout, the poetic handling of the subject . . . excellence of the verse." The *Post* felt that it is "a work of simplicity, admirable proportion, and a deal of the power that restraint can give." Politics, personal ambition, overweening pride, work to a play of power, within the lyric beauty and the outwardly calm movement that rises to a vivid climax in *The Cloister*.

THE ESTRELLA RANGE   *Gil Vicente*

The "Portuguese Shakespeare", Gil Vicente (c. 1465-1536), was the first outstanding dramatist of the Renaissance. Goldsmith, musician, and actor in his own early plays, Vicente was court poet to King Manuel of Portugal, whose sister Lianor was his patron, and to Manuel's son and successor, King John III. Of his forty-four surviving plays, eleven — mainly the early ones — are in Castilian Spanish, seventeen are in Portuguese, and the others use both languages.

Most dramatic of all Vicente's plays is the pastoral tragicomedy *The Estrella Range* (the Serra da Estrella, in the province of Beira, is the highest mountain range in Portugal), played before John III at the birth of the Infanta Dona Maria, 1527. Opening with a song of joy by the spirit of the mountains, the play develops the intertangled amours of a group of shepherds and shepherdesses. Gonzalo loves Madalena, but is pledged by his father to Catalina, who loves Ferdinand who sighs for Felipa whom Rodrigo loves. A hermit has them draw lots; the tangles are undone; the Mountain Spirit promises happiness and plenty to all. Two players from Castille arrive and challenge the dancers of the Serra, and the play ends with a general song and dance. The characters of the shepherd folk are well drawn. Although in this early stage of the modern drama there are many long monologues, Vicente breaks often into natural, even sprightly, dialogue.

Just before the writing of *The Estrella Range*, Sá de Miranda had returned from Italy, bringing the new and polished meters of the Renaissance into fashion, and scorning the ruder octosyllabic verse; but Gil Vicente continued the lively if rougher measures he had learned to use, and in them gave Portugal its finest lyrics. Interwoven in the talk are many proverbs, in a manner that continued in the Portuguese and Spanish drama and novel and is noted in *Don Quixote*. The people of the time are caught in wide variety.

Vicente's dramas were printed in a collected edition in 1562. They were popular not only in Portugal and Spain but also in the Lowlands. The clergy, however, sharply attacked them for their satire. From the edition of 1586 nine plays were removed and the remainder were expurgated. Changing dramatic styles have kept the plays in the library, although no other Portuguese playwright of his stature has appeared; but in the past seventy-five years there has been increasing attention to his work. F. Bouterwek, in a German study in 1805, remarked on "the wonderful simplicity and sense of truth" in the plays, and Aubrey F. G. Bell in *Gil Vicente* (1921) emphasized the individuality of his work. The plays are still enjoyable reading, with their gay or earnest freshness, their pleasant or satiric portraits, and their lyrics of beauty and charm. Vicente is the first dramatic genius on the road to Calderón, Shakespeare, and the further flowering of the Renaissance.

S.S. TENACITY   *Charles Vildrac*

Le Paquebot Tenacity (*S.S. Tenacity*), by Charles Vildrac (French, b. 1882), is a simple play. Its lack of rousing action is counterbalanced by the deftly drawn portraits of its characters: Mme. Cordier, owner of the cheap seaport restaurant; Therese, her waitress; the garrulous and hard-drinking but kindly observer of life, Hidoux; and the two main figures, Bastien and Segard, printers and friends on their way from Paris to try their fortunes in far-off Canada.

Segard is a simple, stay-put sort of fellow; he is there because he has been swept along by the decisive Bastien, who prides himself on his firm will. The two men are attracted to the pleasant waitress; but while the dreamer Segard merely loves Therese, the practical Bastien takes her. Therese and Bastien go off together, leaving Segard alone to continue the trip to Canada—where he never wanted to go in the first place. The name of the ship bears cargo of irony.

Played at Jacques Copeau's Theatre in Paris in 1920, *Le Paquebot Tenacity* was a warm success. London saw *S.S. Tenacity* June 15, 1920, with Basil Sydney; New York, January 2, 1922. Its gentle quality gave the play no lengthy run in English; but it was welcomed by the critics. "One of the most delicately written plays we have seen in a long time," the London *Era* called it. "The story is but the thread to string together three or four exquisitely conceived character studies. The whole thing is quite slight, and perfectly blended." In New York, Alexander Woollcott praised the "telling and convincing seduction scene." The *Evening World* commented: "Steering clear of theatrical claptrap, *S.S. Tenacity* is as staunch and true a play as has come to this port from France or any other country in many a day . . . Seldom do we get a play that touches life so closely . . . the life of workaday people who have little more than they put on their back, yet take their lot uncomplainingly and get along as best they can." Segard is bewildered and buffeted by life, but moves humbly yet with innate dignity along the path life allows him. One cannot say that he is pushed along; others may spin him and point him, but he goes forward of his own motor force.

The simple yet searching study of human nature, of common folk moving through more or less ordinary days, involved in actions calling for no heroic resolution or tumultuous roar of passion — the motivation and the deed done, even as you and I—give the play quiet distinction.

ZAIRE   *Voltaire*

The spirit of reform that marks the other work of François Marie Arouet (French, 1694-1778), who took the name of Voltaire, also characterizes his activity in the theatre.

In addition to writing some fifty plays, he carried through a number of stage reforms. He was responsible for having spectators removed from the stage itself, clearing the way for the spectacular scenes he delighted in. In various other ways, he strove to improve working conditions in the theatre. In England from 1726 to 1729, he saw the actors and actresses highly respected. In the year of his return to France, the great French actress Adrienne Lecouvreur was denied the right of Christian burial; whereas the English actress Mrs. Anne Oldfield was accorded a funeral in state at Westminster Abbey. Voltaire wrote a scathing poem on *The Death of Mlle. Lecouvreur, Noted Actress*; circulated in manuscript, it fell into the hands of the Church party, and brought their wrath upon him. In safety, outside France, Voltaire sought to regain favor with the tragedy *Eriphyle*, which, incidentally, brought back ghosts into French tragic drama. *Eriphyle* failed. Undeterred, Voltaire wrote *Zaïre* in eighteen days and on August 13, 1732, it opened to loud acclaim. As with others of his plays, Voltaire turned over his share of the profits to the actors.

Zaïre, an heroic romance half in prose and half in verse, combines elements of the *Othello** theme with elements of Racine's *Mithridate*. Written rapidly, it was amended throughout rehearsals until Dufresne, playing Orosmane, refused to learn the new lines. Anonymously Voltaire sent him a partridge pie; in the beak of each bird was a set of corrected verses. Dufresne ate the pie and learned the lines. The play, Voltaire's favorite, also became the public's. The opening run was for nine nights; later the same year, beginning November 12, it ran for twenty-one performances, and has been frequently revived.

Within the classical limits, Voltaire introduced several novelties in *Zaïre*. For the first time in heroic romance, the characters are French. In the conflict between love and religion, love—for the first time in the French drama—proves the more powerful. And, also for the first time in French classical drama, a high-born person kills out of jealousy.

The story of the play centers around *Zaïre,* captured daughter of a French nobleman. She has been brought up from infancy at the court of Orosmane, Sultan of Jerusalem, toward whom she is drawn and who wishes to marry her. Her father and her brother, a fanatical Christian, wish her to return to France and the Christian faith. The Sultan, discovering Zaïre's rendezvous with one Nerestan, in a jealous fury stabs her. Learning that Nerestan is Zaïre's brother, he sets the Christians free and stabs himself. This action converts the fanatic Nerestan to a deeper and more tolerant faith.

Contemporary critics, on the side of the Church, were waiting to attack *Zaïre*. Thus J. B. Rousseau protested that the play teaches that "all the efforts of grace have no power over the passions." Voltaire was charged with raising passion above pity, and above the claims of religion. Two parodies of *Zaïre* appeared almost at once: *Harlequin on Parnassus,* by the Abbé Nadal; and *The Foundlings,* by Romagnesi and

Ricconini. The public took sides by flocking to Voltaire's play and letting the parodies languish.

Zaïre is rhythmed almost like the libretto of an opera. Despite its use of a love motif balanced against religion, more attention is given to the psychological preparation than to the actual deed. The result is a certain restraint, a certain static quality; yet, as Georg Brandes has pointed out, "The weaknesses of Zaïre are common to all French trage-dies." The emphasis of the play, Brandes continued, is not so much on the actions, or even the persons of the drama, as "on the cadence and polish of each couplet; on careful balance within each couplet, and in the structure of the tragedy as a whole, with its symmetrical contrasts produced by the variation and synthesis of emotional tempo in the different scenes." Zaïre's pondering of the play's problem, it may be noted, her speech balancing her love against the faith of her fathers, is a paraphrase of Dryden.

In his form as in his ideals, Voltaire was against extremes. Zaïre thus sets a cultivated civilization, the Sultan's, against fanaticism, and a benevolent royalism against mob rule. The play points toward Vol-taire's own goal of civilized tolerance. It teaches us, said Brandes, "that Paganism has its virtues, the same virtues as are usually called Chris-tian; it teaches furthermore that even the best Christians may destroy normal happiness by regarding the demands of their fanaticism as sacred obligations." The right Church folk of Voltaire's day would hardly welcome this lesson!

Zaïre moved fairly quickly across the Channel. Aaron Hill (1685-1750) adapted it as Zara, calling the Sultan Osman. Zara opened in January, 1736, and ran for fourteen performances. As Zara, Mrs. (Susannah Maria) Cibber made her debut; the part was her favorite for revivals. Charles Didbin called Zara "Hill's best play." In Voltaire's Zaïre, Lombardi and Salvini also played. An opera was made of it in 1890. It still has a place on the French stage, and in the reading it is a vivid, intense, and noble drama, in admirably balanced verse.

MEROPE   *Voltaire*

In 1738 Voltaire wrote to his old teacher, Father Tournemine: "Most reverend Father, is it true that my Mérope has pleased you?" The theme of his play, for once, held nothing at which the Church found oppor-tunity to cavil.

The story of Mérope is from Greek myth: Polyphontes, having mur-dered Cresphontes, King of Messenia, takes both the throne and the widow, Mérope. Aepytus, son of Cresphontes and Mérope, comes in disguise, claiming the reward for having killed their son (himself)—and kills Polyphontes. Mérope stabs Aepytus; then, in a touching scene, rec-ognizes the dying youth as her own son.

Without any attack on the Church, Mérope has all Voltaire's sensi-bility, all his humanitarian earnestness and tolerant stand. Voltaire stated that in Mérope he was returning to the Greek tragic mode; by this he meant, apparently, that the play has no love story.

Mérope has no love story; for this reason, the actors refused the play. The Abbé Voisenon, enthusiastic over the drama, used his influence, and on February 20, 1743, *Mérope* was presented with Mlle. Dumesnil in the title role. The enthusiasm was so great that the author himself was summoned to the stage—a novel practice at the time. As Lessing told of it, "*Mérope* called forth the wildest applause, and the parterre gave the poet such an ovation as had never before been recorded . . . Henceforth a new play was seldom performed without its author's being asked to perform also."

The story of Merope had been dramatized in Italy in 1713 by Scipione Maffei, to whom Voltaire's play was dedicated, and by George Jeffrey in England in 1731. Voltaire poked fun at Jeffrey's version. In England, Aaron Hill and Voltaire, after the success of *Zara*, had been great friends. But when Hill's adaptation of *Alzire* failed, and also his *Roman Revenge* (from Voltaire's *The Death of Caesar*), Voltaire had no more friendly words for Hill. Now, bitterly, Hill defended Jeffrey, and said he would adapt Voltaire's *Mérope* to free it from the ineptitudes of the Frenchman. The English version opened in 1749; Garrick "looked and acted like an angel." In 1750, by command of the Prince of Wales, there were three performances for the benefit of Hill, who died (February 8), "in the very minute of the earthquake," the day before the first performance. Hill's *Mérope* was popular on the English stage for almost seventy years.

Voltaire's *Mérope* still holds its place in the French theatre. The critics, however, have differed as to its merits. Fontenelle stated: "The performance of *Mérope* did great honor to Voltaire; on reading the play, one is forced to conclude that it did still greater honor to Mlle. Dumesnil." And Lytton Strachey more recently and more directly declared: "His heroines go mad in epigrams, while his villains commit murder in inversions." This remark, however, would condemn the entire body of French tragedy. Carlyle, in the London *Foreign Review* (1829), more discriminatingly observed: "Inferior in what we may call general poetic temperament to Racine; greatly inferior, in some points of it, to Corneille, Voltaire has an intellectual vivacity, a quickness both of sight and of invention, which belongs to neither of these two. We believe that, among foreign nations, his tragedies are considerably the most esteemed of this school."

Bruntière summed up the concern of Voltaire, seeing beyond his culture and tolerance to its basis in respect for the dignity and integrity of the individual: "The hidden soul of the tragedy of Voltaire is the importance he gives to, the price he puts on, human life: so considerable that, while passion may sometimes excuse, nothing in the world can ever justify, its violent suppression."

On Voltaire's return to Paris from Switzerland, he was accompanied by an enthusiastic throng to the theatre, to see a performance (March 30, 1778) of two of his plays: *Nanine*, and his last tragedy, *Irene*. All the royal family were present, save King Louis XIV himself, still hostile to Voltaire. Between the plays, Voltaire, beside his laurel-crowned bust, was crowned with a laurel wreath. The excitement of the occasion—the most enthusiastic acclamation ever accorded a French dramatist—was too much for the aged Voltaire; he fell ill, and two months later (May 30), he died. The Church refused him Christian burial.

Voltaire's plays are a rich product of the neo-classical spirit. Restrained in emotion, balanced in structure, dignified in tone, they present dramatic situations that drive home the evils of excess — even, nay especially, excess in a good cause — and make a moving plea for reason, tolerance, and truth.

THE ORPHAN OF CHINA   *Voltaire*

The free-thinking, free-loving Ninon de Lanclos, dying at the age of eighty-four in 1705, left the precocious eleven-year-old François Arouet 2,000 francs, to buy books. Perhaps among these was a translation of *The Orphan of Chao* (*The Dual Self-Sacrifice*), by Chi Tien-Hsiang, which half a century later Voltaire adapted as *Tchao Chi Kow Eul; ou, l'Orphelin de la Chine* (*The Orphan of China*).

Chi was one of the scholars and aristocrats that, after the Mongol Kublai Khan conquered China in 1277, refused to serve the Emperors of the new Yuan dynasty. These men expressed their patriotism through novels and dramas, writing over 500 plays in a period of fifty years. *The Orphan of Chao* (about 1350) was one of the hundred that became Chinese classics.

The play pictures the devotion of two followers of Chao Su, who was slain by the usurper Tu An Ku, about 600 A.D. To protect the newborn son of their dead leader, Chen Ying substitutes his own son (a common device, used later in the Japanese *Bushido**). To prevent the usurper from suspecting the subterfuge, Chen Ying gives his son to his comrade Kung Sun; then, as they have arranged, he goes to Tu An Ku as an informer, declaring that Kung Sun is harboring the slain ruler's heir. Kung Sun and the infant are slain; as a reward, Chen Ying's "son" —the heir to the throne, thus saved—is taken into the palace of Tu An Ku and raised as the usurper's child. In this manner, the tyrant rears the avenger who one day will fall upon him.

Voltaire softened this tragic story, using the power of a woman's love to effect a happy ending. He set the events in the reign of Genghis Khan (Kublai's grandfather). When Zam-Ti wishes to sacrifice their son, his wife Idamé, to save the child, informs Genghis Khan of the substitution. Genghis, in love with Idamé, wishes to carry her off; she, as faithful a wife as she is a devoted mother, tells her husband, and suggests that he kill her and himself. The Khan, breaking in upon this scene, is moved by Idamé's virtue to spare the child and to take Zam-Ti as his councillor.

Voltaire's *The Orphan of China* was the first French play to turn from Greek and Roman antiquity to the Orient. An audience of 1300, with some 200 seated onstage, assembled at 5:30 p.m. on August 20, 1755 and hailed Mlle. Clairon, who at this premiere first broke the tradition of wearing contemporary gowns (the hoopskirt) and dressed for the period of the play. She also inaugurated the trend toward simpler and more realistic acting. For these various reasons, the play was widely discussed. It remained long popular in the French theatre.

In the Chinese theatre, *The Dual Self-Sacrifice* has lasted more continuously. At a production in New York (Columbia University, April 16, 1955) it was enlightening to observe how the Chinese audience, keenly alert throughout, responded to shades of expression and turns of delivery in the well-known drama. The two chief characters, secretly comrades, must outwardly manifest hatred and scorn, as the "informer" is forced, for fear that their scheme will fall through, to taunt and to torture his friend — until, hiding his anguish under his guile, he brings about the death of his son and his friend, thus ensuring the royal heir's safety. There are loyalty and irony in this drama, and intensity of emotion, that transcend the limitations of language.

THE WESTERN CHAMBER   *Wang Shih Fu*

After China's conquest by the Mongols during the Yuan Dynasty (1280-1368), the scholars, excluded from government posts, found expression in the drama. Some 550 plays were written in about fifty years. Outstanding among these is *Hsi Hsiang Chi (The Romance of The Western Chamber)*, by Wang Shih Fu, which, according to Younghill Kang in the *New York Times* (August 15, 1937), is "considered by Oriental critics the best specimen of Mongol drama." *The Western Chamber* drew its plot from a play written in the vernacular about 800 A.D.

The play shows the young scholar Chang stopping at a Buddhist monastery while on his way to the capital to take the examinations. He encounters Lady Cheng, the widow of a minister, her daughter Ying-Ying, expert in embroidery and the classics, and their alert and intelligent maid, Hung Niang. Chang promptly falls in love with Ying-Ying. However, Ying-Ying is also desired by Flying Tiger, the leader of a bandit host. Lady Cheng promises her daughter to whoever drives off the bandits. Chang, with the help of "the General on the White Horse," accomplishes this; but the young couple learn that Ying-Ying's father had already betrothed her to another. They exchange love poems and vows; a friendly monk helps them; and finally their love seems so intense and so desperate that Lady Cheng feels forced to unite them.

Long popular in China, *The Western Chamber* was given its first performance in English, translated by Henry H. Hart, at Sacramento Junior College, March 10, 1938. A version by S. I. Hsiung was acted in London, in 1938-39.

The play has many beautiful lyric passages, and the characters are drawn with considerable charm, against the mild Spring background of the monastery in the hills. It lacks the swift pace of western drama, but flows with the almost untroubled tranquility of a gentle stream on a quiet evening. The pleasant country folk are well caught; there is a touch of mischief in the nimble-witted maid; and the fragrant breath of eternal romance keeps the two lovers fresh across the centuries.

THE WHITE DEVIL   *John Webster*

John Webster (English, 1580?-1625?) began his theatrical career by collaborating with other playwrights (Marston and Dekker), then in two great works established himself as the outstanding creator of the tragedy of blood. The preface, 1612, to *The White Devil* indicates the difference between Webster and most of his contemporaries; he compares his aims to those of Euripides*, declares that he writes slowly and carefully, and hopes for the judgment not merely of his time but of posterity.

The White Devil; or, The Tragedy of Paulo Giordano Ursini, Duke of Brachiano, With the Life and Death of Vittoria Corombona, the Famous

Venetian Courtesan, based upon actual events in Italy from 1581 to 1585, was acted by the Queen's servants about 1608; it was revived in 1635, 1665, and 1672. A version by Nahum Tate, called *Injured Love; or, The Cruel Husband*, was produced in 1707. The play thereafter was largely confined to the library; but after Charles Lamb called attention to it, it became one of the best known of Elizabethan tragedies. A revival at Cambridge, England, in 1937 went on a widely successful Scandinavian tour. There were productions in London in 1935 and 1947; one in New York, by Equity Library, in 1947. The London *Theatre World* (May 1947) called the production "a notable theatrical event"; the New York *Variety* said it was "a remarkable theatrical experience." The drama still holds great power in the playing, as was shown even in the modern dress, sweater-girl production of the New York Phoenix Theatre in March 1955.

Webster was concerned with the problem of evil in the world, more specifically, of sin; for he believed in free will and deliberate choice. He believed, also, that evil is predominant in the present life.

The characters of Webster fall into three general groups. There are the creatures of a single ruling passion, regardless of all others and all else in its fierce drive. Such are Vittoria and Brachiano in *The White Devil*. Then there are the cynics, who see all mankind as fools or knaves, amid whom they coldly calculate their own way to power. Such a one is Flamineo, Vittoria's brother. Finally there are the good, like Brachiano's wife Isabella and Vittoria's and Flamineo's mother Cornelia: noble, pitiful, courageous—and passive victims of evil passions not their own. In Webster's plays, the good folk are destroyed in body, but steadfast in soul; the evil-doer also is destroyed, recognizing that he is a sinner. Flamineo has "felt the maze of conscience" in his breast. And the hope of a new period of moral order closes the tragedy.

In *The White Devil*, Flamineo, to promote his own fortunes, lays his eager sister Vittoria open to the adulterous passion of Brachiano, by effecting the murders of Brachiano's wife and Vittoria's husband. When his brother Marcello is horrified, Flamineo kills him; their mother Cornelia goes mad with grief. After a trial, Vittoria is imprisoned, but runs away and marries Brachiano. Avengers finally kill Brachiano, Vittoria, and Flamineo.

The power of Webster's play rises not from the succession of melodramatic incidents, but from the deep sense of human nobility that animates the author, despite his dark vision of human life. "Webster is a true tragic poet," said David Cecil in *Poets and Story-Tellers* (1948): "one who, facing the most dreadful and baffling facts of human experience in all their unmitigated horror, yet transmutes them by the depth and grandeur of his vision into a thing of glory." "No poet," said Swinburne, "is morally nobler than Webster."

There is, in *The White Devil*, not so much a direct progression of plot as a succession of dramatic moments: a poignant, then a passionate, then a delicate situation. "Each part," said John Addington Symonds in the preface to the *Mermaid Edition*, "is sketched with equal effort after luminous effect upon a murky background; and the whole play is a mosaic of these parts." Tableaux and processions, pageantry and related fantastic or symbolic dreams, irrelevant though they may sometimes seem to the progression of the plot, are nonetheless essential to Webster's

purpose. They bring before us, in multicolored life, the crowding temptations and the devilish drives that press men into devious ways of evil.
We watch, in dumb show, the death of Isabella, by kissing a poisoned
picture of her husband Brachiano. In dumb show, too, we watch
Flamineo's murder of Vittoria's husband, Camillo. Such scenes stir the
emotions deeply as the words. Even grimmer is the scene in which
Brachiano's enemies, disguised as monks come to comfort him when sick,
proceed to strangle him. "This is a true love-knot, sent from the Duke
of Florence," smiles one of them, as he slips the noose around Brachiano's
neck. Here irony tightens horror.

The Webster colors this dramatic flow with a dark beauty of language —
a diction at once poetic and struck deep with the diseases Webster sees
in life. Through his language we feel, as Clayton Hamilton has said,
"flashes of poetic insight into the elemental emotions which throb in the
heart of man, passages of awful grandeur which stir to the very core,
touches of delicate tenderness relieving the gloom that hovers over a
tale of human ruin." Webster's figures press his oppositions, as when
Brachiano exclaims "Woman to man Is either a god or a wolf." Even
speaking of ordinary things, the metaphors seem a lightning flash that
briefly illuminates the nether darkness: "You speak as if a man Should
know what fowl is *coffined* in a baked meat Afore you cut it open"; and
in more homely fashion, "They that sleep with dogs will rise with fleas."
The most frequent motifs are of poison, which kills from concealment,
and infection, which corrupts before 'tis seen.

The character of Vittoria Corombona is superbly drawn. She suggests the murders of her husband and Brachiano's wife, through a dream
she tells of a yew-tree. By conceiving his scene thus, David Cecil has
pointed out, Webster "turns an ugly episode of lust and treachery and
assassination into a thing of sinister magnificence. The strangely precise
images set the fancy mysteriously and sublimely astir: the ear thrills to
the subtle muted music of the versification. Yet though he beautifies the
horror of his scene, he does not soften it." At her trial, Vittoria stands
splendid in intellect and courage, brazening it out like virtue itself, indignant. "This White Devil of Italy," declared Lamb, "sets off a bad
cause so speciously, and pleads with such an innocence-resembling boldness, that we seem to see that matchless beauty of her face which inspires such gay confidence into her, and are ready to expect, when she
has done her pleadings, that her very judges, her accusers, the grave
ambassadors who sit as spectators, and all the court, will rise and make
proffer to defend her, in spite of the utmost conviction of her guilt."
This "diversivolent woman"—"fair as the leprosy," Hazlitt called her,
"dazzling as the lightning" — is a true figure of tragedy.

The deftness and delicacy of Webster's language enable him to move
from the arousal of horror to the evocation of tenderness and pity. The
madness of Cornelia spills forth in a song that suggests the mad Ophelia's:
"Call unto his funeral dole The ant, the field mouse, and the mole" — of
which Lamb said: "I never saw anything like this Dirge, except the Ditty
that reminds Ferdinand of his (supposedly) drowned father in *The
Tempest**. As that is of the water, watery, so this is of the earth,
earthy. Both have that intenseness of feeling, which seems to resolve
itself into the element which it contemplates."

This power over language, this nobility of soul, enabled Webster, "Shakespeare's greatest pupil in the art of tragedy," Symonds called him, to carry the tragedy of blood — begun by Kyd, developed by Tourneur, transformed in *Hamlet** — to its ultimate perfection. With Webster's death, the species died — though its ghosts roam through the realm of gory melodrama. In *The White Devil,* we see the tragedy of blood at its noblest and best.

THE DUCHESS OF MALFI   *John Webster*

The second of Webster's great tragic studies of the consequences of sin in the world, *The Duchess of Malfi,* 1613?, is based upon a story in Bandello's Italian *Novelle,* retold in Painter's *Palace of Pleasure,* 1566. The play was published in 1623, 1640, and 1678. A Spanish play based on the story was written in 1618 by Lope de Vega*.

The Duchess of Malfi was revived in London in 1707; it was adapted as *The Fatal Secret* in 1735 by Lewis Theobald (emendator of Shakespeare, and victim of Pope's *Dunciad*). Webster's play was produced again in 1850, 1859, 1864, 1869, and 1892; again in 1935; 1939; and in 1945 with John Gielgud; it was brought to New York in a modern version by W. H. Auden, opening October 15, 1946, with Elisabeth Bergner as the Duchess, John Carradine as the Cardinal, and Canada Lee as Bosola.

In the play, Bosola, servant of the Duchess, seeks advancement by betraying her to her brothers, Duke Ferdinand and the Cardinal. She is secretly married to her steward, Antonio; her brothers, desiring her duchy, have warned her not to remarry; at their instigation Bosola tortures and murders the Duchess and two of her children. Bosola has been corrupted by the evil world; he has followed its unscrupulous pattern. Now he repents, and warns Antonio. But by a bitter irony, seeking to kill the Cardinal, Bosola accidentally kills his new friend. Then Bosola attacks the Cardinal; Duke Ferdinand, now gone mad, interferes; and all three die.

Some of the current reviewers found little merit in the revival of *The Duchess of Malfi.* Howard Barnes (October 16, 1946) bluntly called it "archaic nonsense." Brooks Atkinson said it "might be described as Shakespeare without the magnificence"—whatever that leaves. George Freedley dubbed it "fustian." More, however, praised the play. John Gassner described it as "a timeless nightmare in which human beings are writhing grubs in darkness." And Louis Kronenberger praised "the high voltage, the fierce shock, of the story." Perhaps the play was blamed when the fault was the performers'; Canada Lee, the Negro actor, "in white-face", was disappointing; and the coy Miss Bergner made the heroine a very—though not veritable—arch duchess.

Few Elizabethan dramas outside of Shakespeare's have been more highly praised than *The Duchess of Malfi.* Newspaper comments of the nineteenth century include that in the London *Lady's Newspaper* (November 23, 1850): "The plot of this play is simple to the last degree, but the author has filled it with horror, mental and physical, to its extreme complement." The *London Times* (April 14, 1868) declared: *"The Duchess of Malfi* is most admirably placed on the stage . . . It is impossible to speak too highly of this magnificent production."

The use of devices of horror is greater in *The Duchess of Malfi* than in *The White Devil**: around the imprisoned Duchess rings the clamour of lunatics; the effigy of her murdered husband is displayed to her; the ingenious and perverse cruelty of her torturer summons before her on earth the hell to which, hereafter, not all their devilish will can make her fall. This scene rings with horrendous grandeur in Webster, and in the description of Charles Lamb: "All the several parts of the dreadful apparatus with which the duchess's death is ushered in are not more remote from the conceptions of ordinary vengeance than the strange character of suffering which they seem to bring upon their victim is beyond the imagination of ordinary poets. As they are not like inflictions of this life, so her language seems not of this world. She has lived among horrors till she is become 'native and endowed unto that element.' She speaks the dialect of despair; her tongue has a snatch of Tartarus and the souls in bale. What are 'Luke's iron crown,' the brazen bull of Phalaris, Procrustes' bed, to the waxen images which counterfeit death, to the wild masque of madmen, the tombmaker, the bellman, the living person's dirge, the mortification by degrees? To move a horror skilfully, to touch a soul to the quick, to lay upon fire as much as it can bear, to wean and weary a life till it is ready to drop, and then step in with more instruments to take its last forfeit — this only a Webster can do. Writers of an inferior genius may 'upon horror's head horrors accumulate,' but they cannot do this. They mistake quantity for quality, they 'terrify babes with painted devils,' but they know not how a soul is capable of being moved; their terrors want dignity, their affrightments are without decorum." This, agreed Hazlitt, "is not the bandying of idle words and rhetorical commonplaces, but the writhing and conflict, and the supreme colloquy, of man's nature with itself."

Clayton Hamilton went still further in his praise: "In sudden sallies of penetrating genius, in flashes of insight into the mainsprings of human action and the subtle emotions which lie deep-seated in the human heart — in short, in those very excellences which move us in the greatest tragedies of all time—he stands all but preeminent, and admits of no peer but Shakespeare himself . . . Bosola is the typical 'melancholy, discontented courtier' . . . but he is soon to display an underlying humanity of character which places him far above all other rogues of the Elizabethan tragedy of blood . . . Nothing could be more natural and more truly womanly than the way in which the reserve of the unsuspecting Duchess is melted away by the hypocritical sympathy of Bosola. This subtle expedient is entirely new in the annals of roguery, and clearly demonstrates Webster's preference for resorting to psychological rather than to purely theatrical motives to carry on his plot." After the Duchess is arrested, Hamilton continued, "there follows that magnificent symphony of terror which constitutes what, with the single exception of the third act of *Othello*, is the greatest *single act* in the English language."

The Duchess of Malfi is a supreme example of the tragedy of blood. In fact, "considered *solely as a tragedy of blood*," said Clayton Hamilton, "the mechanism of *The Duchess of Malfi* is superior to that of *Hamlet*. While Shakespeare clung to the clumsy figure of the ghost crying out for revenge, Webster wisely discarded an expedient so essentially mechanical. While Shakespeare relinquished the stock villain, who had always been one of the most interesting characters in the tragedy of blood, Webster applied his genius to creating creatures of flesh and blood to replace the one-sided figures of his predecessors, and gave us such admirable studies as the contrasted Machiavellians, Ferdinand and the Cardinal, and the heroic rogue, Bosola. The action of Webster's play is simpler and more concentrated than that of the Shakespearean tragedy, and the climactic development of the revenge and the counter-vengeance is magnificently handled."

The simple and tender touch of Shakespeare is matched in Ferdinand's words as he looks on the body of his twin sister: "Cover her face; my eyes dazzle; she died young."

The Duchess and "the white devil" of Webster's other play are both figures of intense dramatic power; as Swinburne aptly calls them, Webster's "two sovereign types of feminine daring and womanly endurance, the heroine of suffering and the heroine of sin." Although the Duchess (like Caesar in Shakespeare's *Julius Caesar**) is the early center of sympathy, Bosola (like Brutus) is the chief driving force in the play. Through the fierce course of Bosola's sinning, and the belated ills of his repentance, as well as through the Duchess's courage and faith, the noble moral fervor of Webster combines with his poetic and dramatic power, to vivify and enrich, as lightning over a stormy landscape, the passion-torn pattern of *The Duchess of Malfi*.

The plays of Webster, as the poet H. D. suggested in *By Avon River* (1949), give us, "in a Renaissance setting, parables that represented unbearable actuality." His was a tortured England, and his works "are outstanding examples of the black wave of terror and despair that swept over the island as a result of the dissolution of the monasteries, and the seven years spent by Mary in trying to restore them. Following the fires of martyrdom and the reeking stench of the unburied was an aftermath or after-birth of Hell." If England then, what with plagues and persecutions, took on the fetid air of a shambles, Webster's plays, for all their dark thunder, are a stand of nobility amid the ruin.

THE AWAKENING OF SPRING   *Frank Wedekind*

Beginning as a German journalist, then a novelist and playwright, Frank Wedekind (1864-1918) organized a theatrical company and toured his native country. He acted in many of his own plays. As a dramatist, he was opposed to the naturalism of his time, "a mere copy of life"; his plays move with an intensified imagination, eerie and at times spectral, that makes him a forerunner of expressionism.

Two themes give force to Wedekind's dramas. Most pervasive is his picture of the sexual impulse as the driving force of life. Man refuses, as Wedekind sees it, to admit this fact, and with various forms of hypocrisy seeks to hide this basic urge. Civilization itself, indeed, seems to the playwright little more than the gloss men have set over the natural impulse of sex. The second theme is the inherent conflict he sees in man's striving for both integrity and happiness.

The most noted of Wedekind's dramas is *The Awakening of Spring*, 1891 (not produced until 1905, when Reinhardt's production ran for 325 performances). This drama pictures the sexual urge as it becomes manifest at puberty, and shows how the conventional educational methods may wreak havoc in the adolescent mind. In poetic, but quite natural and frank presentation, *The Awakening of Spring* carries us through fifteen scenes, that bring the inquiring minds and urging bodies of three children to disastrous consequences. Moritz, a serious, thoughful lad, full of wonder about life, failing in his school examinations, commits suicide. Meanwhile, the mother of Wendla, one of the school girls, avoids Wendla's questions about the sister's new baby; and when a storm drives young Melchior and Wendla to seek shelter in a hay-loft, they discover for themselves the facts of life. Wendla dies in an attempted abortion. Melchior, escaping from the reformatory to which he is sent, comes upon Wendla's tombstone. Here, the spirit of Moritz and a masked man representing Life struggle for Melchior, who finally decides it is his obligation to live.

For all its frankness, *The Awakening of Spring* is a tender and deeply touching drama. The scene in the hay-loft is delicate and moving; it is played in darkness, faintly broken by lightning flashes. There is masterly irony in the faculty meeting scene, with the hide-bound teachers arguing more insistently over whether or not to open the window than over Melchior's behavior. There is a gruesome scene in the reform school to which Melchior is sent, that most hopefully misnamed of institutions! Building its power—in a technique the expressionists borrowed—through a succession of rapid scenes, *The Awakening of Spring* drives relentlessly home its picture of the effect of hypocrisy, of sex evasion, upon these adolescents. The play is, indeed, as the *New York Dramatic Mirror* said when it was presented here in German (March 22, 1912) "an intense and absorbing work."

The Awakening of Spring was presented in English in New York on March 30, 1917, with Fania Marinoff as Wendla, as a "membership" production under the auspices of the *Medical Review of Reviews*. License Commissioner Bell saw a rehearsal at noon, and forbade the play, but a court injunction enabled the matinee to begin at four o'clock. The reviews ranged from deepest moral indignation to high artistic praise.

Burns Mantle led the chorus of protest, calling the play "a purposeful but profitless drama that does not act . . . All that it reveals to Anglo-Saxon minds, and particularly to Anglo-Saxon youth, is at once suggestive of hidden nastiness and a thoroughly unhealthy adolescence . . . We naturally resent the assumption that we now stand in serious need of help from the outside . . . We resent it particularly at this time and from this source, when a bloody war is each day proving that however materially efficient Mr. Wedekind's frankly-spoken and seriously philosophical people may have become, they still stand sadly in need of a spiritual rebirth to put them on so much as even terms with the civilized peoples of the earth. We resent it again when we note that practically every vice report that is published, and every degenerate tendency or crime that is traced to its source, is found rooted in minds and muck that are not native to this country. The task of clearing the scum from the melting pot is ours, for we are all in it; but we have a fixed notion that both the method and the manner in which the task shall finally be accomplished should also be ours . . . As propaganda they like it in Berlin. Its creation there would indicate that they need it in Berlin. We are quite content that they should keep it in Berlin."

Without dragging in the World War to damn Wedekind, the *Times* also objected to the play: "Adolescent sexual perversions are discussed and acted in this drama with coarse freedom. That they are common enough in the United States to warrant the exploitation of such cases in the theatre is certainly open to question . . . Scenes like the one showing flagellation among children cannot be anything but degrading unless before an audience of physicians and alienists." The *Globe* (April 3, 1917), on the other hand, expressed regret that this "powerful, masterly play" had to be seen under such untoward auspices: "No other work in literature so sympathetically interprets the storm and stress of youth at the age when it is torn between its desires and the dread of the unknown . . . Instead of being invited to see it as a work of art by a distinguished author we were asked to submit our dull heads to instruction and homily. How Frank Wedekind would have grinned if he could have seen Henrietta Rodman informing us in tragic tones that this was an historical event second in importance only to the Russian Revolution — a piece of innocent blatherumskite to which we listened in respectful stupefaction not unmixed with explosive titters." The *World* thought the play limited in its appeal: "Indeed this is a play primarily for parents, and poor little pregnant Wendla, grown wise too late, strikes the keynote when she exclaims, 'Oh, Mother, why didn't you tell me everything?'" The *Sun* felt that Wedekind had seen beyond the immediate situation: "He takes the fact, known to every parent in the world, that adolescence is beset with sexual difficulties, and builds on it a heart-breaking, sinister, and capricious tragedy."

The play proved still touching in an off-Broadway production opening October 9, 1955.

In numerous plays, Wedekind has dramatized the urgency and primacy of the sexual impulse. Other playwrights who have shown the moon calf, the early flush of new-found love, have, as George Jean Nathan compared them to Wedekind, taken us to Wedekindergarten. Seldom has there been a more tender, discerning, and poignant dramatic picture of the early rouse of sexual impulse and wonder in groping childhood than in the tragic movement of *The Awakening of Spring*.

GOAT SONG   *Franz Werfel*

The tragic *Bockgesang* (*Goat Song*), 1920, of Franz Werfel (Austrian, 1890-1945) probably roused more controversy than any other modern play since the dramas of Ibsen*. Not even those of Pirandello* are open to so many interpretations as this greatest play of the Austrian poet, dramatist and novelist—best known in America for his novel and motion picture, *The Song of Bernadette*, 1941.

The surface story of *Goat Song* is an eerie one. In a Serbian village, about 1790, there escapes from its secret prison a monster, half-human, half-goat, which its farmer-parents had been hiding for many years. The sight of its awful shadow across the sky bloodies the world, as peasants, gypsies, and Jews revolt against the landowners. Ikons and relics are smashed; the countryside is devastated. Stanja, betrothed to the monster's normal brother, Mirko, but led by the student Juvan to join the revolt, goes as a living sacrifice to the monster. The Turkish soldiers come and crush the revolt. Mirko and Juvan are killed; the monster's carcass is exhibited by the scavenger, a penny a peep. Despite the burning of their farmstead, for the first time the monster's parents, Stevan and his wife, discover peace. And beneath the breast of Stanja the child of the monster is coming to be.

Goat Song excited audiences all over Europe. In New York, The Theatre Guild gave it elaborate production (January 25, 1926), directed by Jacob Ben-Ami, with Edward G. Robinson, Albert Bruning, Blanche Yurka, George Gaul, Lynn Fontanne, Helen Westley, Alfred Lunt, and Herbert Yost, with a great cyclorama for the ominous signs in the heavens, above the background of the Serbian hills. Discussion meetings were held, to elucidate the drama's meaning.

Bockgesang, goat song, is a literal translation of the Greek word *tragoedia*, which means, and gives us the word, tragedy. The early Greek tragedy may have sprung from rituals of the goat-god — perhaps linked with the meaning observed in the Biblical story of the scapegoat. Thus there is a literal binding of the monster, in Werfel's play, with the release of passions that, by their very explosion, leads to a release from passion, to a calm and peacefulness — within which the seeds of the next revolution brood. Thus the goat-monster represents the spirit of revolution, which through oppression bursts to violence, by that very violence defeats its ends, and slumps to weary acquiescence in which the cycle is renewed. But beyond these general meanings, the details of symbolic reference multiply, until, as the *New Yorker* (February 6, 1926) declared: "every hen and loiterer, housewife or gypsy, stands for a whole class, a nation at large, some force or foolishness in the human race." And beyond the political significancies, out of the apprehensions of the parents that led them to hide away their monster-son (as with the monster of Calderon's *Life Is A Dream,* in the world of symbols, and with the horned human of Crommelynck's *The Magnificent Cuckold**) rises the lesson that what we dread, we create: our greatest evils are the figments of our fears, which become the realities we have to face. The world today should take heed.

The atmosphere of *Goat Song* is given ghoulish intensity, through the media of expressionism, of which mode Werfel was a pioneer. His reworking of Euripides' *The Trojan Women**, Wolfgang Paulsen in the *Columbia Dictionary of Modern European Literature* (1947) hailed as "a milestone in the history of the expressionist theatre." In *Goat Song* scenes drunk with excitement reel in and out amid scenes of tenderness and loving promise — the wild pagan orgy in the despoiled church, the deathlike quiet among the charred ruins of the farm, where the monster's parents discover peace. The goat-man itself is, as Alexander Woollcott stressed, "unseen save for one monstrous shadow thrown athwart the sun, unheard save for one dreadful cry out of the shadows (when the woman comes in to him), as mighty and as destroying a sound as ever I heard issue from a human throat." *Goat Song* is, Woollcott continued, in the pamphlet *Second Thoughts on First Nights,* "a timeless, untethered play, of the stature, say of *Peer Gynt*.*"

Neatly the development of the play draws us into its symbols. The whole of the first act is on the realistic level; we may suspect, but we need not seek, further heights of meaning. Werfel, said the *Boston Tran-*

script (February 16, 1926): "evokes the concentrating and intensifying word, the impinging image, the sustained speech, that are trait and emotion caught out of the moment, the personage — the impulses and deeds of humanity thick and deep behind . . . A veracious realist might not better achieve the scene of the outcasts and the elders in petition and repulse. A poetic playwright might not better snare the supernatural promptings and stirrings through the vagabonds and visionaries of the inn." Thus out of the action wells the vision, in a tangled growth of beauty and horror like the flaming passage of mankind.

Werfel's other plays move out of the expressionist technique. Still using some of its devices is the "magic trilogy" *Mirror Man*, 1920, a fantastic drama of man's conquest over his evil self, as Thamal at last beats back the temptations of the "mirror man", who seeks to lead him into sin. *Juarez and Maximilian*, 1923, produced in New York in 1926, is in the form of a realistic historical play, but is rather a psychological study of the Austrian Archduke Maximilian, Emperor of Mexico, 1864-1867, who is presented as a true humanitarian, refusing all recourse to violence, who goes to his death gladly, rather than relinquish his ideals. *Paul Among the Jews*, 1926, picturing the moment of the breaking of Christianity from Judaism, and *The Kingdom of God in Bohemia*, 1930, a drama of the breakdown of ideals with the acquisition of power among the fifteenth century Hussites, and the disillusionment of their leader, Prokop, renew Werfel's earlier interest in religion. *The Eternal Road*, 1935, is less a drama than a great spectacle, a succession of episodes from the harried history of the Jews, in another dark hour of persecution. Indeed, all of Werfel's plays focus upon the deeper values of life. Most vivid and most searching of them is *Goat Song*, showing how both fear and oppression breed violence and how futile violence is. The eerie plot and bizarre effects of production make one feel as though one's mind were heaving in an atom-burst; but dimly, on restoring foot to earth, one glimpses stars.

DIAMOND LIL   *Mae West*

As actress and author, Mae West (b. 1892) occupies in the American theatre a special niche that she has carved for herself. She swaggers in it superbly, the tired business man's bosom friend. To establish herself as prime exponent of one aspect of our life, she had not only to develop her special type of performance, but also to write the plays to which that performance adds body and form. No picture of the American theatre would be complete without Mae West.

In the United States, women are the dominant sex. They own most of the property; they shape most of the mores. In the traditional eye, women fall into two categories: mistress or mother — sinner or saint. From this division flows man's attitude toward sex: it does not exist (saint), or (sinner) it must be hidden. It peeps through, for a wink or a leer, in "off-color" stories, in musical comedy skits and girlie shows. These are but flicks and flashes; in America, sex must hide.

Mae West, as actress and author, flaunts sex in bold bedizenment. She gives release to the greatest American inhibition. Yet — despite Comstockian protests and puritanical raids — we are not shocked, but delighted. For — and this is her subtlety and her success — Mae West adds just the touch of paraded effrontery that makes her marketing of her wares a superb self-parody; and sex becomes sexless. So caught are we in the touching-up of the performance, that the lass is no longer lascivious. Mae West alone, said Ellis St. Joseph, has made saltpeter glamorous. "Sexcess" is the secret of her success. Mae West alone has made us laugh at sex.

Of the three or four plays in which Mae West has bosomed herself to America, the best is *Diamond Lil*. I say three *or* four advisedly, because *The Pleasure Man*, which opened in New York October 1, 1928, seems to be a variation of *The Drag*, which, after various encounters with the censors and the police, closed before reaching Broadway. In both plays, the big scene is a wild party of homosexual carousing, but the "pleasure man" himself is abnormal only in the extent, not in the direction, of his desires.

Before this play, Mae West wrote under the pseudonym Jane Mast, and on April 26, 1926, opened in New York in a play called *Sex*, for which she spent ten days in jail. *Sex* is the story of Margie La Mont, a gay girl of a disorderly house, whose exploits carry her from Montreal to Trinidad, with one torrid love scene and with her introduction, seemingly a sweet society girl, as the fiancée of a young man of high society. It is after Margie recognizes this young man's mother as a woman who had come to the Montreal dive on a joy party, that Margie gives up the social whirl for her less complicated joys with a sailor. *Sex*, said the Telegraph (April 28, 1926) hits "the speed limit of suggestiveness'; the *American* declared that "a more flaming, palpitating play has not been seen here-abouts for some time." But the *New Yorker* critic averred that Mae West's pretending to be an innocent girl of wealth and refinement "I shall always cherish as one of my fondest memories in the theatre."

On April 9, 1928, *Diamond Lil*, the best of the Mae Westerns, came to New York for a run of 176 performances. The story of New York's Bowery in the 1890's was "suggested by Jack Linder," but the flavor of the dialogue and the overtone that gives the events their tang are wholly Mae West's. The play established the author-star in her unique and unassailable position in the American theatre. London was less hos-pitable in 1932; but in 1948 *Diamond Lil* ran there for ten months. Again in New York, opening February 5, 1949, it continued for 181 perform-ances. *Cue* (February 12, 1949) hailed the return of "an indestructible American institution named Mae West . . . She could read the budget and make it sound erotic." After a long tour, the play came back to New York on September 14, 1951, but now with an overemphasis on its physical aspects, crystallized in the fact that on opening night detectives lurked about while Mae West wore over a million dollars worth of diamonds. Then they were safely carted back to storage, where it is perhaps time that the play joined them.

Diamond Lil is set in the Bowery saloon of Gus Jordan, district boss and runner of white slaves to Rio de Janeiro. Flashiest of the fancy girls is his mistress Diamond Lil, who wears impossibly fabulous costumes, honey-colored ostrich plumes, and more diamonds than the Metropolitan horse-shoe, and sleeps in a pink bed shaped like Leda's swan. Among the other men who look, with equal ardor but varying degrees of impetuousness and possessiveness, upon the luscious and lickerish Lil are a powerfully sexed Latin, a Bowery politician who is double-crossing Gus Jordan, an escaped convict—who comes dramatically into Lil's bedroom during a violent storm—and a Salvation Army Captain. Lil always loved a uniform. And neatly Lil plays upon these men so that one gets rid of another—except for the Salvation Army man, who turns out to be no other than "the Hawk", of the Secret Service. He arrests Gus Jordan, and salvages Diamond Lil for himself. The curtain falls on their embrace. Her last words are: "I always knew you could be had."

Through the scenes of this "lurid and frequently rousing melodrama" walk shoplifters and stagger drunks. In the saloon, we watch a floor show, with singing waiters, ancient yet agile acrobats, and Diamond Lil flaunting her charms in songs of the 1890's and a lively version of *Frankie and Johnny*. One scene sends genuine shivers along delighted spines. Rita, the procuress from Rio, jealous for her Latin lover, takes a stiletto from her stocking and steals upon Lil; watching in the mirror, Lil turns and pins her assailant to the couch—only to discover that the dagger has pierced Rita's back and killed her. (In the 1951 production, Lil viciously stabbed the dame.) A knock at the door; it's a policeman. And as the officer warns Lil that her convict lover has broken jail and may be expected to visit her, she combs the long tresses of the dead woman, and talks to her as though to a resting friend, until the policeman shuts the door and she is safe alone.

Diamond Lil is a woman of no uncertain pathway. When one of the girls exclaims: "Goodness, what beautiful diamonds!" her instant response flicks: "Goodness had nothing to do with it, dearie." While she may seem only a peahen in a gilded cage, she is really a shrewd and thoroughly competent woman, decent, too, by the dingy lights of the Bowery. When the Salvation Army Captain remarks that the cold gleam of her diamonds reflects the emptiness of her soul, Lil's thoughts for a spell turn to self-examination; and you may believe—if you are the sort of playgoer that looks beyond the final curtain—that the Captain's ethical teaching (combined with his lusty love) will keep Lil faithful to him. It is to the Captain that she speaks the line that has become Mae West's trade-mark: "Come up 'n' see me some time!"

Diamond Lil, like a knife in a poison-bite that cuts deeper than the snake fangs, so digs into sex that it makes sex clean. The play is, said the *New York Times*, "amply if somewhat embarrassingly entertaining;" but the embarrassment is rather at our usual shamefast attitude than at its present purging. The story and color of the play, as the *New Yorker* on February 2, 1949, quoted its own review of 1928, capture "a certain flash brashiness that reached a climax in the underworld of New York in the 1890's, as few subtler playwrights could have done it." But *Diamond Lil* survives, not for its colorful background and eventful story, but for its unique and superbly extravagant presentation, at once exposure and exposé, of sex.

HÄNSEL AND GRETEL   *Adelheid Wette*

Hänsel and Gretel, by Adelheid Wette (German, 1858-1916), with music by Englebert Humperdinck, is the formal German operatic counterpart of the free and easy British pantomime *Babes in the Wood**. The story is retold from the tales of the brothers Grimm. Hänsel and Gretel, dancing about their cottage, are driven out by their mother Gertrude, to pick berries in the wood. Their father Peter, a broom-maker, comes home; Gertrude remembers that the Crunch Witch lives in the forest, and the parents are alarmed. Meanwhile, the children have been put to sleep by the Sand Man; in their slumbers a guard of angels descends from Heaven to watch over them. They awaken, nevertheless, to find themselves beside the Gingerbread Hut of the Crunch Witch; and when in their hunger they nibble at the house, the Witch seizes them. She decides to fatten Hänsel for her table; but Gretel is a plump enough morsel to enjoy at once. The Witch makes the children help her start the fire. When she wants Gretel to get into the oven, they ask her how; as she shows them, they shove her in and slam the door. Hänsel in joy sings out the Witch's charm; this brings to life the gingerbread figures beside the house; they are children the Witch has charmed. Just as the Witch is burned to a crisp, Peter and Gertrude arrive, overjoyed to find their children alive and safe.

In some productions, the oven with the witch inside explodes. The forest scene, especially the golden stairway of the Angels and the ginger-bread hut of the witch, afford opportunity for colorful decoration. At the close come general festivity and a lively dance. *Hänsel and Gretel* is indeed a Grimm tale made gay.

Produced at Weimar December 23, 1893, and at Munich December 30, within two years *Hänsel and Gretel* was heard in England, Italy, Holland, Belgium, and America. New York saw the opera in English for a run opening October 8, 1895; also, in German, at the Metropolitan Opera House. In many cities it has become a traditional Christmas revival. It was presented over television in 1949, and has often been produced with puppets.

The music of *Hänsel and Gretel* is pleasantly accordant with the lighter aspects of the story. As H. E. Krehbiel has analyzed it: "Humper-dinck has built up the musical structure of *Hänsel and Gretel* in the Wagnerian manner, but with so much fluency and deftness that a musical layman might listen to it from beginning to end without suspecting the fact . . . The little work is replete with melodies which, though original, bear a strong family resemblance to two little songs which the children sing at the beginning of the first and second acts, and which are veritable nursery songs in Germany . . . The prelude is built out of a few themes which are associated with some of the most significant elements of the play . . . They stand for dramatic ideas and agencies; and when these are passed in review, it will be found that not the sinister but the amiable features of the story have been chosen for celebration in the overture." Among the more effective moments are the "Brother, come dance with me," the Sand Man's song "I send the children happy dreams," the Prayer theme that heralds the angels; the Witch's song, and the music of the final rousing celebration. There is the pleasure of childhood memories of fairy tale and wintry evenings, mingled with the pleasure of charming and surging music, in the fairy opera *Hänsel and Gretel*.

SALOME   *Oscar Wilde*

With his aesthetic eccentricities and his bland admission of his superior tastes and talents, Oscar Fingall O'Flahertie Wills Wilde (Irish, 1856-1900) caught public attention early. Coming to America for a lecture tour, in 1882, he announced at the Customs House: "I have nothing to declare but my genius."

In 1891 Wilde wrote his first important drama, the one-act *Salomé*. The story of Salomé is succinctly told in the *Bible* (Matthew 14; Mark 6). Salomé's mother, Herodiade, divorces Herod Philip to marry his brother, Herod Antipater, Governor of Judea. This marriage is denounced by John the Baptist (Iakanaan), whom Herod imprisons. Salomé dances ("the dance of the seven veils") before Herod, when he promises her whatever she wishes, even to half his kingdom. At her mother's bidding, she asks for the head of John the Baptist on a silver charger.

The story of Herodiade was amplified during the Middle Ages, with the suggestion that Herodiade was in love with John. The subject attracted the late nineteenth century French. H.-L. Lévy made a painting, 1872, of Salomé presenting the head to her mother. Mallarmé's poem *Herodiade* probes the psychological complexities of the young woman. Massenet's opera *Herodiade*, 1881, adds the notion that Salomé also is infatuated with John the Baptist, who spurns her advances and castigates her lust. Flaubert's tale *Herodias, The Story of Salomé*, 1887, sets the dance and its reward at a feast Herod is giving for his Roman guests. Borrowing features of the last three, Oscar Wilde wrote his *Salomé* in French, producing, Archibald Henderson has said, his "one dramatic achievement of real genius, an individual and unique literary creation." His play ends with Salomé's kissing the lips of the severed head; and while she is in this ecstasy of lustful revenge, Herod nods and his soldiers beat her to death beneath their shields.

Salomé tempted the actress Sarah Bernhardt; she had the play in rehearsal in London in June 1892, when the Lord Chamberlain refused to license it on the ground that it introduced Biblical characters. Its world premiere was in Paris, with Lugné-Poë playing Herod, at the Théâtre de l'Oeuvre, October 28, 1895. It was played "privately" in London May 10, 1905; in 1906, 1911, 1918, and the spring and fall of 1931. The London ban was removed in 1932.

In New York, *Salomé* has undergone many vicissitudes. It was played in 1906 by Sothern and Marlowe; Julia Marlowe called Salomé her favorite role. Mimi Aguglia presented the play there in Italian, December 22, 1913. The *Sun* declared that "the scene with the head of the prophet on the charger was the most startling thing that has been done here in a long time. No detail of physical abandon was spared." The *Tribune* added that the actress showed "the naturalness of an ordinary little live tigress rather than the hideous creepiness of Wilde's decadent nightmare." The Washington Square Players, with Helen Westley, Rollo Peters, and Walter Hampden (as John) gave a more balanced presentation of *Salomé*, April 22, 1918. On May 23, 1922, a flapper Salomé came to town with bobbed red hair; this "disgustingly stupid wiggler," said the *New York Commercial Advertiser*, "went through an interminable series of lewd contortions to the accompaniment of Hawaiian strains."

There were two productions in 1924. Of one, the *Telegraph* (July 19) reflected: "It is hard to conceive of Wilde's Salomé as a thinking creature. She is a pagan, not a Hellenist. When he wrote this sensual drama, Wilde attempted to show just how powerless we are in the face of our instinct. He makes us but children in the hands of whim and impulse." The other 1924 production had an all-Negro cast, with a male Salomé. In 1950, *Salomé* was presented at the College of the City of New York.

The "dance of the seven veils" has been performed separately many times, for artistic or sensational purposes. Lili Marberg in Munich (1905-7) danced in the play. At the International Festival of the Dance in Warsaw, 1933, Ruth Sorel won first prize with *Salomé*. The Croatian Mia Slovenska danced it in 1936. In its less aesthetic aspects, the dance was performed on the Midway at the New York World's Fair in 1940.

In 1897 Sudermann* wrote *The Fires of St. John* on the Salomé story. Richard Strauss, with a libretto based on Wilde's play, composed the opera *Salomé*. Briefly banned by the Kaiser, this had its premiere at Dresden, December 9, 1905 (with one woman to sing and another to dance Salomé). In New York, Olive Fremstad sang it in German, January 22, 1907; Mary Garden, in French, in 1909 — at the Manhattan Opera House; the Metropolitan banned it until 1934. In motion pictures, *Salomé* was filmed with Theda Bara, 1918, and with Nazimova; Hedy Lamarr wanted to act it onstage in 1939, but was restrained by court order because of her film contract.

Oscar Wilde, to the grisly complexities of the story of Salomé, added further lustful details. The Captain, Narraboth, who leads her to Iakanaan, is in love with Salomé; when he finds her wholly unconcerned, he kills himself; she pays no heed to the fallen body as she tries to seduce the prophet. Herod, too, is quick with desire for his niece and stepdaughter Salomé; so that his final act of execution is sprung at once of justice, jealousy, and revenge. As Wilde truly said in *De Profundis*, "I took the drama, the most objective form known to art, and made of it as personal a mode of expression as the lyric and the sonnet; at the same time, I widened its range and enriched its characterization."

In stagecraft as well, *Salomé* has theatrical power. The dance itself has shocked and delighted all audiences. Then Salomé's audacious demand stills the theatre. When Herod, jealous of Salomé, annoyed at Herodiade, fearful of a popular revolt, reluctantly at last gives command, the Executioner descends into a pit in the midst of the frozen guests; there are sounds below, then silence — then slowly the head of the prophet appears, upraised on a platter rising from the pit. It is a gruesome moment, exceeded only by the cruel joy with which Salomé seizes the head and kisses the stilled lips — and the savage clamor as she is crushed beneath the soldiers' shields. The play climbs the topmost rungs of climax.

Salomé is indeed, as Archibald Henderson described it in *European Dramatists* (1913), "a fevered dream, a poignant picture . . . The characters stand forth in chiseled completeness from the rich Galilean background like the embossed figures upon a Grecian urn . . . Jokanaan is a wonderfully realized figure — the incarnation of a primitive, intolerant prophet, the voice crying in the wilderness — commanding rapt atten-

tion far less by what he says than by what he is . . ." As for Salomé,
"The world swims in a scarlet haze before her eyes . . . lust, scorn, revenge, and death meet in that terrible kiss of a woman scorned . . . With
all its verbal jewelry, the dialogue is at times momentously laconic."
Decadent lust, with the fires of desire scorching into hate, finds dramatic
expression of gripping power and ripe beauty in *Salomé*.

LADY WINDERMERE'S FAN   *Oscar Wilde*

At once, with *Lady Windermere's Fan*, 1891, Oscar Wilde took London
with delighted surprise. Many critics still think the play his most
brilliant social comedy. With a vividly dramatic plot, brilliantly satirized characters, and dialogue that scintillates with bon mot and paradox,
Lady Windermere's Fan bred a swarm of imitators and excelled them.

The play presents Lady Windermere on the eve of her twenty-first
birthday ball, learning that her husband has been most attentive to a
Mrs. Erlynne. When Lord Windermere asks his wife to invite Mrs.
Erlynne, she indignantly refuses; on his insistence, Lady Windermere
declares that she will break her fan across Mrs. Erlynne's face should she
be bold enough to come. Mrs. Erlynne, it happens, is really Lady
Windermere's divorced mother, long away; Lord Windermere, who alone
knows her identity, is trying to help her back into society.

When Mrs. Erlynne attends the ball, Lady Windermere in exasperation goes to the rooms of her admirer, Lord Darlington. Mrs. Erlynne
follows her, and has persuaded her to go home — when the men, including Lord Windermere, arrive. The women hide, but Lady Windermere's
fan is noticed; to avert scandal from her daughter, Mrs. Erlynne steps
out, and Lady Windermere slips away unseen. She changes her opinion.
about Mrs. Erlynne — who once more beats retreat from England, but
this time with her daughter's esteem.

Announced as *A Good Woman*—its real title kept secret until the eve
of the opening — *Lady Windermere's Fan* came to London February 20,
1892, for 156 performances. Marion Terry played Mrs. Erlynne; and
again in 1904. There were London revivals in 1911 and 1930, and one
opening August 21, 1945, with John Gielgud and Isabel Jeans, for 602
performances. In New York, the play ran for eight months in 1893;
it was shown again in 1904; 1914; 1918, with Margaret Anglin; opening
October 14, 1946, with Cornelia Otis Skinner, Estelle Winwood, Henry
Daniell, Penelope Ward, and Cecil Beaton (who also designed the colorful costumes and the sets); and in 1948 at the Provincetown Playhouse.
The play has been frequently produced in community theatres.

At the London premiere, the cordial reception prompted Wilde to say:
"I have enjoyed the evening immensely. The actors have given us a
charming rendering of a delightful play, and your appreciation has been
most intelligent. I congratulate you on the great success of your performance, which persuades me that you think almost as highly of the
play as I do myself."

The plot of *Lady Windermere's Fan* took strong hold on the early
audiences. For the first two nights, there was no relationship established
between Lady Windermere and Mrs. Erlynne. Then they were revealed
to the audience as mother and daughter, in the last act; but very soon
this revelation was shifted to Act I. This is, of course, its most powerful

presentation; when Lady Windermere threatens to strike with her fan the woman we know is her mother, the audience stiffens with tense expectancy. Brander Matthews exclaimed: "You couldn't have pried me out of my seat with a crowbar!"

Later, however, the hold of the story weakened. Thus on November 21, 1904, the *London Telegraph* stated: "The play is perhaps not quite so great as we thought it. It is very clever, very bright, very ingenious, a lightly-told comedy which affords an excellent entertainment, a brief story which is throughout interesting and at one moment positively absorbing. But its figures do not always strike one as psychologically true or observed from the life; its second act is not very effective—we do evening parties better on the stage nowadays; there is never enough motive for the sudden lapse of the heroine from the strict code of morals in which she has hitherto brought herself up. . . . Despite all criticism, just or unjust, real or imaginary, it is still quite clear that *Lady Windermere's Fan* is a brilliant piece of work. Its dialogue is admirable in point and subtlety; the interest in the last two acts is sustained to the very end; the third act positively grips one by its vivid dramatic power. On Saturday night, when revived at the St. James's Theatre, the play came out as fresh, or almost as fresh, and entrancing as ever. The verbal fireworks had all their old scintillation . . . We have rarely sat through a premiere in which the verdict of the audience was more unanimous and more overwhelmingly favourable." Another two score years, and we find John Mason Brown (November 9, 1946) turning Wilde's superior laugh back on the playwright: " 'One must have a heart of stone to read the death of Little Nell without laughing' was Oscar Wilde's comment on *The Old Curiosity Shop*. Much the same kind of heart is needed nowadays not to laugh at the passages in *Lady Windermere's Fan* which Oscar intended us to take with the utmost gravity. These graver melodramatic interludes are among the funniest in the play. Indeed, among the many paradoxes in which *Lady Windermere's Fan* abounds, perhaps the final one is that all we can now take seriously in the text is its gaiety. If this is so, it is because what Wilde's people say remains wonderfully witty, whereas what they do has become patently absurd . . . Yet surely there never was a more diverting bad play than *Lady Windermere's Fan*. Or one that has more shimmering virtues." The adverse comment is invariably qualified; and in truth, despite changing social conventions, the story still holds power. "It's true that it has aged," said the New York *Billboard* (February 6, 1932), "but not because of the years since it was written; merely because of the copies that have been made of it since. These copies have made stale and flat and profitless a plot that isn't nearly so bad as it may now seem."

It has also been pointed out that most of Wilde's characters utter Wildean epigrams, that they are artificial, unreal. Thus James Agate in the *Masque* (No. 3, 1947), while pointing out that Mrs. Erlynne is "very nearly the first example on the modern stage of the courtesan, or something of that sort, being treated sympathetically," added: "Mrs. Erlynne is redeemed by her wit, for if a character is witty enough nobody cares whether it is true to life or not. Whereas Lady Windermere is the complete goose." Agate, too, made amends, speaking in the *London Times* (August 26, 1954) of the play's wit: "This is superb throughout, and inferior—may one think?—to Congreve and Sheridan only in this, that it does not grow out of the character, but is sprinkled indifferently over fool and fop, like a gross feeder with the pepper-pot."

Wilde's epigrams are often but inversions of a truism, and beneath the epigram lurks melodrama; but there is enough of both to keep the audience waiting for more.

A WOMAN OF NO IMPORTANCE   *Oscar Wilde*

The wit of Wilde continues to sparkle in his dramatic examination of the "double standard," *A Woman of No Importance*. The play presents Lord Illingworth, meeting and liking young Gerald Arbuthnot, offering Gerald a post as his secretary. Gerald's mother insists that he refuse the post, without, however, giving her reason — Illingworth, who turned her away years ago, as "a woman of no importance," is Gerald's father; and she fears the playboy influence Lord Illingworth may have upon her son. Illingworth's nature pops out in his advances to Gerald's fiancée; Gerald is about to beat him, when the mother confesses their relationship. Lord Illingworth, repentant, proposes to marry her; now Mrs. Arbuthnot dismisses him as a man of no importance.

A Woman of No Importance opened in London, April 19, 1893, with Fanny (Mrs. Bernard) Beere, Julia Neilson, and Fred Terry; it ran for 113 performances. The play was revived there in 1907 and 1915. New York saw it on May 26, 1893, with Rose Coghlan and Maurice Barrymore; again in 1916, with Margaret Anglin and Holbrook Blinn. Despite its brilliance, the subject is not conducive to frequent revival, especially in conservative small towns. On its production in New York, the *Illustrated American* (May 27, 1893) declared: "The theme of *le fils naturel*, though long ago seized upon by the dramatic sociologists of France and Germany, is new to the modern English stage. Mr. Wilde has dealt with it daintily, gracefully, and refreshingly, but not masterfully. He has produced an hors-d'oeuvre, not a chef-d'oeuvre." To the charge that Wilde inserts epigrams anywhere, the critic continued: "Mr. Wilde's seemingly adscititious employment of brilliant dialogue, his constant recourse to epigram and aphorism, is not nearly so reprehensible as the circumstance that all of his wit, humor, and repartee have to do with but one subject —woman."

There is, however, more than wit in *A Woman of No Importance*. The play embodies an attack upon the conventional attitude that there is one law for men and another for women. James Agate, indeed, in the *Masque* (No. 3, 1947), stated that this point is too heavily pressed: "Not all the wit in Mayfair can sweeten that little tract called *A Woman of No Importance*." It was judged otherwise in performance. Charles Darnton (April 26, 1916) declared: "Stupid people who imagine themselves to be intelligent when they say merely that Oscar Wilde's plays are 'brilliant' have something to learn from Margaret Anglin, who makes *A Woman of No Importance* so human that clever, superficial tricks of speech leave no more lasting impression than a rainbow." The *New York Dramatic Mirror* (April 29) felt that "this story — of a woman who, betrayed and deserted twenty years before, fights to shield her illegitimate son from the influence of his father — effectively withstands the passing of the years. Its flashing wit still bites, its epigrams still strike home, it is still a keen-edged satire upon society." More probingly, the *Christian Science Monitor* (April 27) pointed out: "After a whole evening of assertion that the conventional right is always wrong, the right triumphs. The woman of no importance becomes of the greatest importance. The man of greatest importance, the man of mighty inverted truths, is revealed as of no importance whatever; his little house of epigrams tumbles about his head. And off toward the sunlit garden, one arm around the son who has chosen her in preference to his father, the other around the girl he has chosen for his wife, walks the woman who has thrilled her audience with a deeper understanding of mother love. Wilde dabbles in the mud till he is tired of it; then he picks a flower. Most of us forget the mud in remembering the fragrance of the flower."

Lord Illingworth, who has lived according to the principle that "nothing succeeds like excess," says of Society: "To be in it is merely a bore. But to be out of it is simply a tragedy." This flippancy — though many have thought it characteristic of Wilde himself — is flayed in this play of Wilde's. Wilde, indeed, can be both caustic and kind. To the critics that had declared *Lady Windermere's Fan* has too little action, he recommended the first act of *A Woman of No Importance*: "There is absolutely no action at all. It is a perfect act." The actress Mrs. Beere, in the London *Sketch* (April 26, 1893), testified: "Mr. Oscar Wilde is a delightful author. Most dramatists are very touchy about their work; but he seemed quite anxious to alter and cut down his play to suit stage purposes." The man must not be mistaken for his characters. Oscar Wilde is, nevertheless, neatly characterized through a remark of Flaubert, who said that a writer should be like God in His universe: present everywhere but visible nowhere. Wilde is visible — manifest — in all his creatures, in all his works.

Judged on the basis of his plays, Wilde is a moralist as well as a wit. Changing social conditions may render less urgent and less timely the theme of *A Woman of No Importance*; the basically tough moral fibre, and the surface of scintillant wit, endure.

AN IDEAL HUSBAND   *Oscar Wilde*

The many persons that accept Wilde as a trivial spinner of superficial wit, a mere polisher of epigrams, should more thoughtfully look beyond these at the core of his dramas. *An Ideal Husband*, 1894, strikes deep into the conventional codes, as Bernard Shaw pointed out in *Dramatic Opinions and Essays*, "in Sir Robert Chiltern's assertion of the individuality and courage of his wrongdoing as against the idealism of his stupidly good wife, and in his bitter criticism of a love that is only the reward of merit." But when the surface dazzles, few discern the depths.

Lord and Lady Chiltern, as the play opens, are holding a soirée. To this comes Mrs. Chevely, "a genius in the daytime and a beauty at night"; Lady Chiltern recognizes her as a schoolmate expelled for theft. Lord Chiltern, Under-Secretary of Foreign Affairs, discovers that Mrs. Chevely still holds a letter incriminating him in the giving of advance information on State policy, a score of years ago. With this, she attempts to force his hand in the current issue of an Argentine Canal. He wavers, then—when his wife protests his changing point of view—refuses. Mrs. Chevely reveals Chiltern's early act to his wife. Lord Goring, who had loved Lady Chiltern, and who once knew Mrs. Chevely "so little" that he got engaged to her, has in the meantime pinned a bracelet theft on Mrs. Chevely, and traded that secret for Lord Chiltern's incriminating letter. Goring, whom Chiltern's sister Mabel has promised to marry, helps Lady Chiltern to readjust her values; and Lord Chiltern moves on, with her richer love, to a post in the Cabinet.

The serious purpose of Wilde, hidden beneath his wit, did not escape all his critics—despite Shaw's prophecy: "The English critic, always protesting that the drama should not be didactic, and yet always complaining if the dramatist does not find sermons in stones and good in everything, will be conscious of a subtle and pervading levity in An Ideal Husband." The London Press (March 17, 1895) analyzed more deeply: "So far as we may estimate the peculiar excellence of this unconventional author, it would seem that Oscar Wilde derives his power from naturalism. He has an Ibsenistic quality . . . Wilde holds the mirror up to the smart people in England as cleverly as Ibsen depicts the peasant folk of Norway. That, it seems to me, is the reason why his plays are enjoyable. They are bits of nature painted with masterly technique, with quick intuition, with local atmosphere, and with exact naturalness. An Ideal Husband, divested of its extravagant passages, which are put in to catch the general public and are irritating to those who know the real people and the real object of Oscar Wilde's study, is a very true picture of life in modern English society. Wilde's distinctive gift in comedy is naturalism." And in New York, the Sun (September 7, 1918) declared this "Wilde's most satisfactory play, as it has not only the wit and polish of high comedy, but also a solid substratum of good sense. Indeed, it has a sincerity that Wilde seldom allowed himself to express." The Globe remarked that "the scintillant flashes of humor, the playful gambolings with words, are beyond mere persiflage and repartee. They have a surer foundation in the keenest observation of men and manners."

The opposite tendency, to mock at Wilde as a man of ideas while hailing his wit, continued. It appeared in the New York Times (September 17, 1918): "Wilde's wit was never more luminous . . . it is possible his philosophy was never more profound . . . The business of the play is to show the degrees by which the husband rises to the point where honor seems fairer than his career and reputation, and by which his lady realizes that it is better to be the wife of a real human being than to burn incense before an ideal. Nothing could be sounder than the 'message' of the piece. Mrs. Humphrey Ward could not do better. But it is hardly the forte of Wilde to act as messenger boy." Later, Ivor Brown in the London Observer (November 21, 1943), smiled at "this curious museum-piece whose bones had been dug out of the overworked goldfields of Sardoodledum by Fingal O'Flahertie Wills while the great Oscar Wilde titivated the corpse with the jewels of his wit . . . The plot, it may be explained, discharges a lurid stream of compromising letters, ladies in bachelors' premises, stolen jewels, Cabinet secrets betrayed, and the faithful hearts of a Rising Liberal and his noble young

consort, hearts beating as one until nearly riven asunder by la Femme
Fatale." And James Agate, in the *Masque* (No. 3, 1947), declared that
he would have great "difficulty in thinking that this wittiest of playwrights took the slightest interest in what emotions Lord X was feeling
between paradoxes, or what Lady Y was meditating between *bêtises*."

Wilde himself felt that the critics had missed the point of the play,
had lost "its entire psychology," he said in an interview reported in the
Cleveland Plain Dealer (February 3, 1895) "—the difference in the way
in which a man loves a woman from that in which a woman loves a man;
the passion that women have for making ideals (which is their weakness) and the weakness of a man who dares not show his imperfections
to the thing he loves . . . The critics really thought it was a play about
a bracelet." The jewels of Wilde's wit make a sparkling cluster; but
they are set in solid thought.

An Ideal Husband, opening in London, January 3, 1895, ran for 119
performances. Its revival of November 16, 1943, with Dame Irene Vanbrugh, Martita Hunt, and Esme Percy, ran for 266 performances. In
New York, it played for five weeks at the Lyceum Theatre, opening
March 12, 1895, with Herbert Kelcey, Isabel Irving, and Mrs. Thomas
Whiffen — although the September 16, 1918 production with Norman
Trevor, Constance Collier, Merle Maddern, and Julian L'Estrange called
itself the New York premiere. This production announced itself as
"modernized by George Alexander," which led Louis Sherwin to exclaim "Who in the name of greasepaint is Alexander, to presume to cut
and edit the work of his betters?" Sherwin might, appositely, have
quoted Lady Markby in the play itself: "You are remarkably modern,
Mable. A little too modern, perhaps. Nothing is so dangerous as being
too modern. One is apt to grow old-fashioned quite suddenly."—It is the
modern attitude toward morality in *An Ideal Husband* that now seems,
to some, "old hat" and trite. The surface is as glittering as ever, but we
have made many soundings in its depths. Those depths of thought, however, though better known, remain sound.

THE IMPORTANCE OF BEING EARNEST   *Oscar Wilde*

In *The Importance of Being Earnest*, 1894, Oscar Wilde is, for the first
time in his dramas, completely playful. There is no underlying thesis in
this play; its social satire plays lightly over the characters as — with integrity of taste and cultured poise, however absurd in conduct and paradoxical in speech — they breeze through the deft and rapid movements
of a farce. In *The Importance of Being Earnest*, said James Agate in the
Masque, Wilde has written "the wittiest light comedy in the language."

The Importance of Being Earnest opened in London, February 14,
1895, with Irene Vanbrugh. It was revived there in 1902; in 1909, opening November 30, it attained 324 performances; more recent revivals include one July 7, 1930, for 104 performances; an "Old Vic" production in
1934; John Gielgud and Edith Evans, January 31, 1939; another in August,
another in December, 1929; and one in 1942. New York saw the play in
1902, with Margaret Anglin and William Courtenay; in 1921; 1939, with
Estelle Winwood, Clifton Webb, and Hope Williams; with John Gielgud
in 1947, "giving Wilde's finest play," said *Time* (March 17) "a wonder-

fully high-styled production . . . often farce at its most absurd. But it is also farce at its most elegant — as insolently monocled in manner and as killingly high-toned in language as mischievous tomfollery can make it." "There couldn't be anything in the theatre," said Richard Watts (March 4, 1947), "much more delightful than John Gielgud's enchanting production of Oscar Wide's masterpiece . . . if only for its zestful creation of that wonderful Wildean world of wit, beauty, charm, and grace, where every man is debonair and epigrammatic and every woman lovely — save the dowagers, who are witty and greatly enjoy their own paradoxes." There has been little save praise for *The Importance of Being Earnest*.

There has been, however, some analysis as well. Max Beerbohm, in the London *Saturday Review* (December 11, 1909), observed: "In *The Importance of Being Earnest* there is a perfect fusion of manners and form. It would be truer to say that the form is swallowed up in the manner . . . The bare scenario is of the tritest fashion in the farce-writing of the period. Jack pretends to his niece, as an excuse for going to London, that he has a wicked brother whom he has to look after. Algernon, as an excuse for seeing the niece, impersonates the wicked brother. Jack, as he is going to marry and has no further need of a brother, arrives with the news of his brother's death; and so forth. Just this sort of thing had served as the staple for innumerable farces in the sixties and seventies and eighties—and would still be serving so if farce had not now been practically snuffed out by musical comedy. This very ordinary clod the magician picked up, turning it over in his hands—and presto! a dazzling prism for us. How was the trick done? Part of the play's fun, doubtless, is in the unerring sense of beauty that informs the actual writing of it. The absurdity of the situations is made doubly absurd by the contrasted grace and dignity of everyone's utterance. The play abounds, too, in perfectly chiselled apothegms—witticisms unrelated to action or character; but so good in themselves as to have the quality of dramatic surprise . . . But, of course, what keeps the play so amazingly fresh is not the inlaid wit, but the humour, the ever-fanciful and inventive humour, irradiating every scene. Out of a really funny situation, Oscar Wilde would get dramatically the last drop of fun, and then would get as much fun again out of the correlative notions aroused in him by that situation."

The situations referred to by Beerbohm far from exhaust the absurdities of the play. Just as John (Jack) Worthing has invented a brother named Ernest as an excuse for going to London, so Algernon Moncrieff has invented an invalid named Bunbury as an excuse for going to the country. Jack is engaged to be married to Gwendolen Fairfax, daughter of Augusta, Lady Bracknell. Jack is also the guardian of Cecily Cardew, who is being wooed by Lady Bracknell's nephew, Algernon. Algernon gains admission to Jack's country house by pretending to be Jack's brother, Ernest. The deceit is uncovered; but so is Jack's past. Jack was the baby left in the hand-bag of Miss Prism at the Victoria Station, London; this means that he is really Algernon's long-lost elder brother—named Ernest. Miss Prism is relieved enough to accept the hand of the Rev. Canon Chasuble; Jack embraces Gwendolen; Algernon embraces Cecily; and Wilde embraces the opportunity for a final pun that gives the play its name.

In *The Importance of Being Earnest* Wilde maintains complete unity of cultured banter and farcical play. "Even in a jocular play," said Allan Monkhouse, in the *London Times* (February 5, 1939), "we expect the dramatist to steady himself occasionally and say something about the Union Jack or the sanctity of home, and in Wilde this austerity of art that never trifles with morals or realities, except in the sense that it is all trifling, is disturbing to respectable citizens. . . . The day may come when this country has deserted the Union Jack for a pair of crossed broomsticks and the sanctity of the home is held for an intolerable thing. And if it does, how will Wilde be concerned? Not at all. His masterpiece belongs to no time and no place."

Subtitled "a trivial comedy for serious people," *The Importance of Being Earnest* sends its ripples afar. Appreciation of its range and power came from so polished a stylist as Walter Pater: "His genial, laughter-loving sense of life and its enjoyable intercourse goes far to obviate any crudity that may be in the paradox, with which, as with the bright and shining truth that often underlies it, Mr. Wilde startling his countrymen carries on, more perhaps than any other, the brilliant critical work of Matthew Arnold." Catching the savour of a society in its rippling flow, *The Importance of Being Earnest* is a joy to all that appreciate the theatre as art.

OUR TOWN   *Thornton Wilder*

Beginning his literary career as a writer of novels—*The Bridge of San Luis Rey* won the 1927 Pulitzer Prize for fiction—Thornton Niven Wilder (American, b. 1897) turned also to dramatic adaptations (Obey's *Lucrece** in 1932 for Katharine Cornell; Ibsen's *A Doll's House** in 1937 for Ruth Gordon; Nestroy's *Life Is a Joke to Him** as *The Merchant of Yonkers* in 1938) and to original plays. *The Merchant of Yonkers*, rewritten as *The Matchmaker*, was presented in London, then New York, in 1955, with Ruth Gordon in her liveliest comic role.

The most popular of Wilder's dramas and one of the most effective evocations of the spirit of American small town life is *Our Town*. Opening in New York February 4, 1938, with Frank Craven, it ran for 336 performances and won the Pulitzer Prize. London saw the play April 30, 1946. *Our Town* has been played constantly in various parts of the United States; it has already found a place in text-book anthologies of American literature. It was shown on television in 1950. Thornton Wilder himself has more than once (*e.g.*, Summer, 1950) enacted the stage manager in the play.

Suggested by the poem *Lucinda Matlock* (one of the pioneer group in Edgar Lee Masters' *Spoon River Anthology*), which the play quotes, *Our Town* presents life and death in Grover's Corners, New Hampshire. It moves by the simplest means, with no set scenery, just a few props. A "stage manager" saunters in and introduces the town and the people. He gives facts, statistics, shrewd observations, in a dry, matter-of-fact way that cuts to the heart of the topic, hence touches the audience's heart. Among those that we meet are Dr. and Mrs. Gibbs, with their children George and Rebecca, and their neighbors, the local editor Mr. Webb and his wife, with their children Emily and Wally. We watch the awakening of the town—the rouse of the milkman, the slink of the town drunkard—the chores of the day; and the drift toward evening, with the children's homework and the neighbors' chat. Three years later (in Act II), George is giving up his thoughts of college to marry Emily and settle on a farm. We watch the homey bustle before the wedding, the interchange of the family's chatting, the paternal talk to the son before his new responsibilities: all simple, natural, familiar yet touchingly roused to real emotion. Nine years later (in Act III), we watch the dead in the cemetery of Grover's Corners: they are sitting in chairs above the graves, commenting on the ignorant ways of life. Emily, who has died in childbirth, has just joined them; their lack of interest in the living folk perplexes her; she grieves when George throws himself on her grave; she wants to go back. Allowed to pick a day, Emily returns to the happy time of her twelfth birthday — to recognize how limited is the scope of living life, how hurried, how unseeing, are the folks on earth. Reconciled to her eternal future, Emily rejoins the dead; and life and death continue their pattern at Grover's Corners.

"Grovers Corners"—one of the children receives a letter addressed—"Sultan County, New Hampshire, United States of America, Continent of North America, Western Hemisphere, the Earth, the Solar System, the Universe, the Mind of God." The children are overawed; but Thornton Wilder is suggesting that the simple, kindly folk of Grover's Corners might indeed be moving along a line of hope for the destiny of mankind. The play speaks to the years ahead: "Well, people a thousand years from now, this is the way we were — in our growing-up, in our marrying, in our doctoring, in our living and our dying." Here is the humble, staunch backbone of the American way of life; here is democracy's cradle, and democracy's growth.

"In all my days as a theatregoer," said Alexander Woollcott, "no other play has ever moved me so deeply." "It captures the mind and the spirit of this country," said Robert Coleman, "as have few plays of our time." It is, said Brooks Atkinson, "one of the finest achievements of the current stage." It presents, said the *New York Sun*, "not the isolated experience of the day but the whole pattern of life from the ancient past into the depths of the future."

So simply is the story of *Our Town* presented, with the "stage-manager" Narrator, with plain folk in ordinary talk on the almost bare stage, that there seems nothing unusual in the gathering of the dead in the last act, their calm aloofness setting the face of the future against the ephemeral grief of the mourners. Though it shows the living as incapable of fully realizing life's gifts, *Our Town*, in the simplest dramatic form, is a moving reaffirmation of the values of living.

THE SKIN OF OUR TEETH   *Thornton Wilder*

This combination of slapstick and fantasy, of seemingly grab-bag and helter-skelter gathering and commingling from all times upon the earth, presents a picture of man's man-long struggle for survival and his wonderment as to why it is worth that trouble to survive. The picture of Mr. Antrobus (the name is from a Greek word meaning *man*) battling the forces of nature and of fellow-men, seeking to increase his understanding and improve his lot, striving to wrest a corner of contentment and peace from his troubled days, grows ironically yet tenderly through Thornton Wilder's kaleidoscopic play.

The audience is drawn into the play's action, as a military band marches, playing, down the aisles; newsreels and colored slides entertain the gathering crowd. There is a meeting of the Ancient and Honorable Order of Mammals, Human Division. A pretty girl, Sabina, repeats the cue lines and behaves like a burlesque of a maid in a parlor drama. In the first act, the world is being almost overwhelmed by the Ice Age. George Antrobus, of Excelsior, New Jersey, who has just invented the alphabet and the wheel, sends a singing telegram as a dinosaur and a baby mammoth shiver. He broadcasts a message to all mammals. Many of the audience laughingly agree when the maid Sabina looks across the footlights to say to them: "I hate this play, and I don't understand a word of it!" In the second act, which is a great convention—wide sideshows and fortune tellers and merry drinking and noise—Antrobus picks the blossoming Sabina as Miss Atlantic City, and Sabina (the eternal Lilith) picks Antrobus as her future mate. The more matter-of-fact Mrs. Antrobus (the eternal Eve) goes calmly on maintaining the family home. Indeed, after the great world conflict (it is now Act III), Mrs. Antrobus bustles everybody back to the business of home-building: "There's nothing to get emotional about. The war's over." Her son Henry returns from the War with the mark of Cain and a burning hatred. George Antrobus, who had sworn to kill the boy, merely makes him douse his head in cold water. Gladys Antrobus comes up from the cellar shelter with her baby. Sabina gives George the beef-cubes she has been hoarding—keeping one to pay her admission fee to the movies. She can stand this "crazy old world" if now and again she sees a movie. And the crazy old world goes on.

All of this time-leaping action occurs in settings as fantastic as the events. The scenery disappears when Sabina dusts it. After the war's devastation, Mrs. Antrobus pulls up the walls of their home again. As the ice moves nearer, we are told they are burning pianos in Hartford; Antrobus picks up some of the theatre seats to feed the fire. The telescoping of time—Ice Age and radios; dinosaurs and bathing beauties; refugees that include Homer, Moses and "the Muse sisters"—adds to the whirligig spin of the human span. The play's wide pattern was defended by the author in the *New York Times* (February 13, 1938): "The theatre longs to represent the symbol of things, not the things themselves. The theatre asks for as many conventions as possible. A convention is an agreed upon falsehood, an accepted untruth. When the theatre pretends to give the real thing in canvas and metal and wood, it loses something of the realer thing which is its true business." The true business of *The Skin of Our Teeth* is through man's unending struggle to ring a clear note of faith in man—in Eve's simple, clear-headed hold on essentials, in Adam's more roundabout, sometimes more pig-headed, but undaunted constant rebuilding. And an eye for the surplusage beyond living's need, of beauty, of peace, and of art.

Opening in New York, November 18, 1942, with Tallulah Bankhead and Fredric March, *The Skin of Our Teeth* ran for 356 performances, and won the 1943 Pulitzer Prize. It came to London May 16, 1945, with Vivien Leigh; again September 11, 1946, for 108 performances. Betty

Field was in a summer production in 1948, at Westport. The play found the reviewers sharply divided. The *Baltimore Sun* (October 15, 1943) referred to the "stubborn groups of New York critics who mistook Mr. Wilder's sophomoric display of mental confusion for something arty;" but there were resignations from the Critics' Circle when the play did not receive the critics' award (no award was made, that year). The *New York Post* (November 21, 1942) said that Wilder "is now using the theatre chiefly as a medium to distract attention from the fact that he has nothing left to say of any particular significance. *The Skin of Our Teeth* is one of the emptiest dramas any modern philosopher ever turned out; but as a comic extravaganza, it has its points." *Variety* (February 24, 1943) estimated that "between ten and fifteen patrons" walked out of every performance. Balanced against these opinions are such comments as that of the *Herald Tribune* (November 22, 1942): "A play of cosmic and cockeyed proportions has come to town;" and Alexander Woollcott's hail: "Thornton Wilder's dauntless and heartening comedy stands head and shoulders above anything else ever written for our stage."

The controversy as to the value of *The Skin of Our Teeth* grew complicated when Henry Morton Robinson (poet, and senior editor of the *Readers' Digest*), Professor Joseph Campbell of Sarah Lawrence College, and others, attacked the play as "a bold and unacknowledged appropriation of a dead man's work", charging that its characters, philosophy, situations, and language are thinly disguised borrowings from James Joyce's *Finnegan's Wake*. The tendency toward a combined simplicity and stylization, however, and blent symbolism and fantasy, is evident in Wilder's earlier plays and adaptations. And the theme of mankind's constant survival "by the skin of our teeth" was presented earlier in the drama by, among others, Edouard Dujardin, in *The Eternal Return*, 1932 — Dujardin, from whom James Joyce acknowledged that he appropriated the interior monologue technique of his *Ulysses*. Such cross-currents of influence are less than reprehensible, being inevitable, and often fruitful.

The Skin of Our Teeth, with Helen Hayes and Mary Martin, was one of the two plays presented in Paris for the 1955 "Salute to France". Returning, it toured, then opened on Broadway, August 17. The clever trick of telescoping ages seemed less fresh, and lengthily labored. The breaking of the players from their parts, to discuss themselves or the play, seemed an unnecessary complication if not a confusion. But Atkinson called the production "perfect".

The mixed merits of *The Skin of Our Teeth* were well caught by Ivor Brown, in the *London Observer* (September 15, 1946), who called the play a "clever-clever charade and sermon for all." Plays such as *The Skin of Our Teeth* remind us that out of the "proud and angry dust" may somehow be fashioned a shining star.

THE CORN IS GREEN   *Emlyn Williams*

The Welsh actor Emlyn Williams (b. 1905) had already won attention by several plays, especially the two melodramas *A Murder Has Been Arranged*, 1930, and *Night Must Fall*, 1935 (a hit in London and in little theatres, though less heartily welcomed on Broadway) when his play *The Corn Is Green* established him as a considerable playwright. It was played superbly by Dame Sybil Thorndike and the author in London, in 1938. In New York Ethel Barrymore made it one of her best roles. Opening on November 26, 1940, with her and Richard Waring, Thelma Schnee, Sayre Crowley and Rhys Williams, it ran for over a year, then toured the country until it returned for another New York run, on May 3, 1943. It was presented in 1946, with Cherry Hardy, by Equity-Library. A film was made of it in 1945. The title is from an old English proverbial warning used in Kyd's *The Spanish Tragedy**: You count your harvest when the corn is green.

The action of the play lies in an almost illiterate mining district of Wales, where the middle-aged English spinster Miss Moffat founds a village school, discovers a boy of genius, fosters his talent, and enlists the help of the at first hostile gentry to enter the boy for an Oxford scholarship. The boy, Morgan Evans, passes the examination. But earlier, in a discouraged moment, he could not pass the tempting Bessie Watty; and now, in the moment of his triumph, Bessie returns with the demand that he support their baby. Miss Moffat saves him from disaster by adopting his illegitimate child, and sends him forth to enrich the world.

When the play opened in London, the *Times* (September 21, 1938) warned aspiring dramatists from venturing on such a theme, but admitted having had "an uncommonly well rewarded evening, to which the Welsh songs are a genuine and moving contribution . . . The outstanding quality of Williams' work is its moderation . . . All his play's background —the village school, the Welsh and the English, the rare feeling of humanity with which he endows his stage—is a recommendation of his central narrative so strong as to cloak its minor improbabilities."

Granted the boy's genius, the "improbabilities" are minor indeed; but it has been argued that the melodramatic episodes of the slut Bessie and her baby are extraneous to the main drive of the drama. Sex, however, does rear its head even in Welsh mining towns; and the final sacrifice of Miss Moffat is not only natural to her but integral to the play's movement. Miss Moffat, while she is a deftly differentiated individual, is also a born teacher: by faith, resolution, and self-denial, she passes the flame of enlightenment and beauty to a soul that will bear it farther.

Several of the scenes in the play are especially effective. Kronenberger (May 4, 1943) declared that "the most dramatic and exciting moment of the play is still the moment when Morgan Evans sits down to take his examination for Oxford." There is a tenderness even more moving in the scene where, on his first return from the University, Morgan sits by Miss Moffat and tells her of his thoughts as he walked up Oxford's High Street, how the subjects he'd been cramming then took pattern in his mind, and the world gathered beauty and meaning.

The assemblage of Welsh figures in the drama won Brooks Atkinson's praise (November 27, 1940): "His characters are glowing members of the human race — some of them comic, one of them supercilious, one of them slatternly, another dour but aspiring. Representing all sorts of pride, vanity, rebellion, coarseness, stubbornness, and good-will, they make an uncommonly attractive lot, and Mr. Williams keeps moving them in and out of his drama with intimate understanding."

The Corn Is Green is a superb theatre play. It has a heart-warming role for the star, and several excellent parts for other players. Its theme, of the teacher's, of the older generation's, sacrifice for the enrichment of those to come, is widely appealing. Its background is unusual and colorful.

All in all, *The Corn Is Green* has enough melodrama and sex to keep it exciting, enough devotion and struggle for good ends to keep it exalted. *Theatre,* 1941, called the play "tenderly tragic," but in 1947 Freedley, in *A History of Modern Drama,* called it "a tender comedy." It mingles tears and smiles as life itself, and—keeping its sentiment within the range of truth — presents some hardworking and humble persons of whom humanity may be proud.

A STREETCAR NAMED DESIRE   *Tennessee Williams*

Broken spirits of the once fair South seem to be the specialty of Thomas Lanier "Tennessee" Williams (American, b. 1914), both in his one-act and in his full-length plays. His first produced full-length play, *Battle of the Angels,* was accepted by the Theatre Guild, presented in Boston, 1943, and then withdrawn. *The Glass Menagerie,* 1943, was almost withdrawn in Chicago, but favorable criticism turned the tide and it went on to win the Critics' Circle Award as the best play of 1945.

The promise of Tennessee Williams came nearer to fulfillment when on December 2, 1947, *A Streetcar Named Desire* won acclaim, and later gave Tennessee Williams the Pulitzer Prize, as well as his second Critics' Circle award. It ran in New York for 855 performances, then toured the country, returning to New York May 23, 1950, for two weeks at the City Center. Again the play was favored with a superb production: the squalid living-room-bedroom-kitchen, with street and stairs to the left, had a rear wall of scrim so that lighting could make visible the street behind. Staged by Elia Kazan, the play showed Jessica Tandy, later Uta Hagen, as Blanche DuBois, Kim Hunter as her sister Stella Kowalski, and Marlon Brando as Stanley Kowalski, in their best roles.

In the play, Blanche du Bois, with the old family mansion overburdened with debts, has had to work for a living, teaching in the town school. She seeks to sustain her gentility by flaunting it, and thereby makes clear that it has gone. She seeks to preserve the vitality she no longer feels pulsing within her by pulsing in semblance of passion with every man. Become too notorious a harlot, she is told to leave town. *A Streetcar Named Desire* opens with her attempt to escape her past, at her sister's shabby home in New Orleans. But however far a bird may fly, it takes its tail along—and Blanche's is gaudy but faded plumage. Her sister Stella welcomes her; but Stella's coarse, rough-neck husband, Stanley Kowalski, sees right through Blanche's preening. He breaks up her attempt to lure his friend Harold into marrying her. When Stella goes to the hospital to have her baby, Stanley goes to bed with Blanche. Stella, on her return, sizes up the situation, but refuses to admit the truth. The only way to make her relations with Stanley endurable is to have Blanche taken away to an insane asylum.

The picture that carries Blanche from the forced gaiety of her arrival to her final enforced confinement, spares no details. Its very thoroughgoing detail won *A Streetcar Named Desire* mixed reviews. Richard Watts, for example, pointed out that "her downfall is studied with almost loving detail. The result is that the play has a painful, rather pitiful quality about it." John Chapman, on the other hand, called it "throbbingly alive, compassionate, heart-warmingly human." George Jean Nathan said that the author "seems to labor under the misapprehension that strong emotions are best to be expressed strongly only through what may be delicately termed strong language . . . that theatrical sensationalism and dramatic substantiality are much the same thing." Whereas Brooks Atkinson declared that "although Blanche cannot face the truth, Mr. Williams does . . . Out of poetic imagination and ordinary compassion he has spun a poignant and luminous story."

Only a few would disagree with Louis Kronenberger's opinion, that *A Streetcar Named Desire* marks "an enormous advance over that minor-keyed and too wet-eyed work, *The Glass Menagerie*." Yet, in two ways, the end of the play is disappointing. In the first place, the emphasis is shifted at the close. The play is concerned with the "harlot's progress," with the downward troubles of Blanche DuBois—but bearing her off to the asylum solves her sister's problem, not her own. Secondly, the exaltation of truly tragic art is replaced by a sniffling pity. Howard Barnes said of the final scenes: "They are truly touching, but they lack some of the nobility that defines high tragedy. These are minor defects." It is, rather, the play's major failing that it builds to no rouse of spirit at the end. Blanche goes off, not horror-stricken yet her own master, like self-blinded Oedipus; she is a whipped and frightened child. Her world ends not with a bang, but with a whimper. We leave depressed; not exalted, as after tragic surge.

Again the symbolism is left for the audience to develop. (We are told that there was actually, in New Orleans, a streetcar with the destination-sign "Desire"; this is of course immaterial.) Blanche, looking unbelievably at her sister's squalid home, explains: "They told me to take a streetcar named Desire, and then transfer to one called Cemeteries and ride six blocks and then get off at—Elysian Fields." Later on, Blanche confuses desire with life; but her opening words suggest that desire leads to death—if one ride on the car of desire only.

Nathan declared that the play, "making realistically dramatic such elements as sexual abnormality, harlotry, perversion, venality, rape, and lunacy . . . while unpleasant, is not disgusting, yet never rises to be enlightening." To which Ellis St. Joseph (whose astute and urbane observations should more often find print) retorted that when the unpleasant is not enlightening it is disgusting. St. Joseph declared of *Streetcar* that Williams "has insisted on making a tragedy out of a cartoon." The devices and the deeds are, in truth, from the stock-in-trade of the old, murky melodrama. Over in Paris Robert Kemp, quoted in the *New York Times* (October 30, 1949) called the play "a collection of scraps of old melodrama fixed up with sauce *à l'Americaine* and sprinkled over with alcohol. Nothing in it could less resemble what I like." Despite such reactions, *A Streetcar Named Desire* achieves a measure of distinction through the searching study it makes of a blasted soul.

The 1951 motion picture version of the play presents Blanche at the end as obviously insane; indeed, she is usually so presented, now, on the stage. The other interpretation—that she is near the breaking point,

but must go to the asylum because her sister cannot face the truth —
makes the characters more complex and the situation more poignant.
In either case, there is climactic irony in the fact that Kowalski's rape
of Blanche while Stella Kowalski is at the hospital having her child,
the very act that sets the final teeter to the balance of Blanche's sanity,
is the act that Stella must dismiss from the world of reality in order to
live with her husband, and can dismiss by calling Blanche, who proclaims
it, mad. And, however natural, it is a sinking betrayal that the coarse
and ruthless Kowalski, whose one virtue is that he is straightforward,
in this one test of his honesty stands silently by. He that cast the first
stone has added the last straw. And their broken world is patched with
an untold lie.

A Streetcar Named Desire was a hit both in London and in Paris.
Both productions emphasized Blanche's urge of sex. In London, where
it opened October 12, 1949, with Vivian Leigh, and ran for 333 performances, the play was nicknamed "The Bus Called Lust". In Paris, the
play was produced with extra, ironic effects behind the transparent
backdrop. For example, while Stanley is raping Blanche, beyond the
scrim there writhes and pumps a Negress belly-dancer. "The latest sensation in Paris?" wrote Ellis St. Joseph: "A Streetcar Named Desire,
adapted by Jean Cocteau—and directed as if it were Mae West in The
Madwoman of Chaillot*." This tone of melodrama, hushed in the pathos
of Williams' treatment, is nevertheless implicit in his story, which does
not rise to the more universal tones, and the exaltation, of tragedy.

"A Streetcar Named Desire," John Mason Brown stated, "is more than
a work of promise. It is an achievement of unusual and exciting
distinction." Contrariwise, J. C. Trewin in A Play Tonight (1952) says
Williams "has not persuaded us that Blanche's genteel-murky past, muddled present, or dark future, can matter a stick of gum to anybody but
Blanche."

EAST LYNNE   Mrs. Henry Wood

After Uncle Tom's Cabin*, the most popular play in American professional stage history is East Lynne. It was adapted, in several versions, from the novel by Ellen Price (Mrs. Henry) Wood (English, 1814-
1887), which appeared in 1861-1862 in the Baltimore Weekly Sun. Under
the copyright law of the day, Mrs. Wood received never a penny royalty
from a play that continued unendingly through the nineteenth century,
blossomed later into half a dozen films, and, said William Winter, "caused
more tears than the Civil War." Samuel French's catalogue calls the
play "the daddy of all the old-fashioned melodramas, the most talked
of play ever written."

The "sufferin' drama" has no more vivid example than East Lynne.
Its story is simple. Orphaned in her late teens, Lady Isabel Vane sees
her childhood home sold to Archibald Carlyle — who, however, marries
Isabel and brings her from the unhappy quarters where she is being
mistreated, back to East Lynne to live. Sir Francis Levinson, with a
forged note, makes Isabel believe that Carlyle wants to get rid of her,
to marry his old flame, Barbara Hare. Maddened with jealousy, Isabel
runs off with Levinson; her husband swears that she will "never darken
his door again." Sadly wiser, awake to Levinson's villainy, Isabel re-

turns to East Lynne, disguised as a governess for her child, little Willie. In some versions, Carlyle recognizes Isabel and sends her away; in others, her sadness and her love for their dying child soften his forgiving heart. Some versions provide two death-bed scenes, as the forgiven mother follows her child to heaven. Especially heart-rending, in our grandmothers' tender days, was Isabel's anguished cry at the death of her son: "Dead! Dead! And never called me Mother!"

The first play based on Mrs. Wood's story was *East Lynne; or, The Elopement*, an adaptation by Clifton Tayleure, opening in Boston April 21, 1862. Tayleure sold the rights to this for $100, and wrote another, *Lady Isabel of East Lynne*, which opened in Washington February 2, 1864. Meanwhile there was a version by Benjamin C. Woolf called *Edith; or, The Earl's Daughter*, December 9, 1862. New York saw *East Lynne* on March 23, 1863, with Lucille Western, who became famous throughout the United States as Isabel. The first version in England was *The Marriage Bells; or, The Cottage on the Cliffs*, by W. Archer, November 12, 1864. London also saw an adaptation by John Oxenford, February 5, 1866, in which Miss Heath played Isabel over 1500 times; and a version by Alfred Kempe, January 16, 1873. Of an American adaptation by G. L. Stout, the *New York Handbill* (April 13, 1864) declared: "This drama is the truest to nature, the most powerful in intensity of passion ever witnessed in America . . . The audible sobs of women, the tears of strong men, and the thrilled silence! . . . More powerful in its influence for good than the most elegant exhortation of the Poet or the Preacher, the Pulpit or the Press." Modjeska is among the many actresses that have acted the popular role of Isabel. Nance O'Neil appeared in it (February 28, 1898) in an adaptation by McKee Rankin; the *New York Sun* complained: "With her youthfulness and intelligence, she is still a derelict in the pocket-handkerchief epoch" — but admitted that *East Lynne* remained "a most effective tear-producer." It was a maxim, until the first World War upset tradition, that on the English stage a man could not call himself an actor unless, as a child, he had played little Willie.

The last serious presentations of *East Lynne* on Broadway — it still finds many tender hearts across the countryside — were with Blanche Bates and Wilton Lackaye in 1917, and with Mary Blair in 1926. (It was filmed with Lou Tellegen and Alma Rubens in 1925; with Clive Brook, Conrad Nagel, and Ann Harding in 1931). Productions have since been proffered (in New York, 1932, 1935; in London, 1931, 1934) for those that like to sport superior laughter before what moved their fathers —and their mothers, bless them!—when they still were young. But the spell is not so easily cast aside. As the *London Telegraph* (January 25, 1934) grudgingly admitted, of Mrs. Cedric Hardwicke as Isabel, "There was a moment in the final scene when she was quite moving, which is a tribute not only to the actress but to Mrs. Henry Wood." And the *London Times* (September 29, 1931) more freely declared, though they had come to laugh: "Our sympathy with these poor souls was, as the play proceeded, most insidiously aroused . . . The quite mechanical stimulation produced . . . something not unlike the conditioned reaction Mrs. Henry Wood intended." If you are not maturely alert, the elementary but elemental appeal of *East Lynne* will snare you still. So symbolic has the drama become of the traveling companies, that Gladys

Hurlbut chose as title for her trouper's autobiography, 1950, the sign many towns have many a season seen: *Next Week — East Lynne!*

East Lynne, together with its like a hundredfold, has little growth of character, and little portrayal of rounded individuals. Its strength lies in its emotional situations—through long familiarity now called "stock"— which were unusual enough to rouse interest while natural enough to win credence. A person theatre-wise may smile on such a play; but to dismiss it would evince small grasp of theatre history, or of social shift. Through the nineteenth century, especially in England and the United States, the processes of democracy and of public schooling produced a wide population of newly literate, and just literate, folk, with — for the first time for such a class — a bit of leisure, and a bit of money to spend in it. Just as they had begun to learn the rudiments of the three R's, so they must have rudimentary plays when they began to learn the theatre. (A similar process was inevitable with the further widening of spectators when the motion pictures came, and of auditors with radio, and of both with television. All of these forms, indeed, have one foot still in the kindergarten.) Of the emotional dramas appealing to an untrained but eager theatrical taste, among the most touching and tender, as well as the most popular, is *East Lynne*.

THE PLAIN DEALER   *William Wycherley*

Though critically well received when produced in March 1674, *The Plain Dealer*, 1666, was slower in winning popular favor than *The Country Wife**, and has not had so many revivals. It has a story of less immediate application to daily life — even the life of the London gallant — but its wit and its originality, and its character portraits, make it the best of the comedies of William Wycherley (English, 1640-1716).

The "plain dealer" of the play is Captain Manly, who on going to sea entrusts his money to his beloved Olivia and Olivia to his friend Vernish. He has little faith in humanity else; but his faith here is sadly misplaced, for on his return Manly finds the two married, and Olivia unwilling to give back his funds. With the help of his servant Fidelia, with whom Olivia becomes enamoured and makes rendezvous, Manly hopes to expose the perfidious heartless woman. Vernish breaks in upon them; in the scuffle, Fidelia is wounded—and discovered to be a woman, who in love of Manly had disguised herself to be with him. The spell of Olivia broken, Manly gives Fidelia his love.

Other characters add to the satiric picture of the times. The Widow Blackacre is a litigious old woman, who teaches her son to go to court on every occasion and any pretext—until he turns the lesson upon her own estate. Novel and Plausible, two coxcombs of the town with hopes of Olivia's favors, open their eyes when her letters to them are exchanged; save for the name, the contents are identical. When Olivia, with affected prudery, and her cousin Eliza, with the candor of simple honesty, engage with Novel and Plausible in a critique of *The Country Wife* (written after but produced before *The Plain Dealer*, to which this scene is an addition) Wycherley's brilliant antitheses and sparkling fancy reach their height. This scene was suggested by Molière's *Critique of The School for Wives**, as other parts of the play were suggested by his *Misanthrope**; but Wycherley's handling of the situation is as original as his development of them is ingenious. As Voltaire said in the *Letters Concerning the English Nation* (1733), "All Wycherley's strokes are stronger and bolder than those of our *Misanthrope,* but then they are less delicate; and the Rules of Decorum are not so well observed in this play."

Some critics have felt that, while Molière's misanthrope reaches almost tragic intensity in his hatred of human hypocrisy, Wycherley's becomes almost odious in his sense of superiority to the hypocrites around. Molière, in truth, shows that excess of blunt frankness in Alceste, as well as excess of polite pretense in those about him, leads to social evils, whereas Wycherley seems to condone, if not to approve, the rude bluntness of Manly. There may, indeed, be something of the author in the man, for many of the playwright's contemporaries referred to him as "manly Wycherley".

The preface to the 1766 edition of *The Plain Dealer* states that the play "was one of the most celebrated productions of the last century; it acquired him the personal friendship of two of his sovereigns, and the praises of the learned both at home and abroad; and certainly we find in it the happiest combination of wit, humour, character and incident, that can be imagined." At the same time, it was remarked that propriety "could allow no charms in a tainted beauty"—and it was an expurgated version by Isaac Bickerstaffe that David Garrick presented, on December 7, 1765, and this sweeter-scented adaptation held the stage for the next half century. Nineteenth century productions were few. *The Plain Dealer* was shown again in London, November 15, 1925. In plot, the play is far-fetched; in morals, while it presents the laxity of its time, it excoriates the licentious in its satire and its story, and shows faith, love, and honesty triumphant. In fertility of invention, in richness of wit, while later surpassed by Congreve*, it gave him lessons. The dedication of the play to the aging but notorious procuress Mother Bennet is characterized by Steele in the *Spectator* (No. 266): "The ironical commendation to the industry and charity of these antiquated ladies, these directors of Sin after they can no longer commit it, makes up the beauty of the inimitable dedication to *The Plain Dealer,* and is a masterpiece of raillery on this vice." In this dedication, Wycherley remarked that objection had been made, not to the manners in the play, but to his satire of these manners: "'Tis the plain-dealing of the play, not the obscenity; 'tis taking off the ladies' masks, not offering at their petticoats, which offends 'em." *The Plain Dealer* is a deft portrayal of prudery masking prurience, a masterpiece in its satire of Restoration society.

THE COUNTRY WIFE   *William Wycherley*

Popular in his person for a time, upon the Restoration scene, more lengthily popular in his dramas that mirror that licentious age, William Wycherley represents that period at its most typical range of gallantry and polite seduction. His first drama, *Love In a Wood; or, St. James's Park,* acted in 1671, led him into the arms of the King's mistress, the Duchess of Cleveland. His second, *The Gentleman Dancing-Master*,* was less successful, both personally and on the stage. His third to be produced (though written after *The Plain Dealer**), *The Country Wife,*

1672, most extravagantly exploits the manners and attitudes of the time. In this play, Allardyce Nicoll has said, "the Restoration comedy of manners reached the acme of impropriety; yet this play contains some of the most brilliant scenes produced in an age when wit was sharpened upon wit and lightness of touch descended even upon dullards and dunces."

The play catches in its satiric net both excessive jealousy and excessive trust. Mr. Pinchwife brings his artless country wife, Margery, to London, for the marriage of his sister Alithea. Alithea's fiancé, Sparkish, by his credulity, loses her to a rival, Mr. Harcourt. And Pinchwife, by the very tricks and connivings of his jealousy (forcing her for a time to dress as a man; again, to send a disdainful letter to her pursuer) throws his wife into the arms of the libertine Horner, who takes what God sends him and justifies his name. At the end, Horner, who has given scope to a rumor that he is impotent so as to gain scope for his amours, persuades Pinchbeck that his wife is innocent; for the sake of family peace, Pinchbeck pretends to believe, and the play ends with a cuckolds' dance.

The Country Wife swept London with gales of laughter. It was constantly revived until 1766; then David Garrick presented an expurgated version he called *The Country Girl*, which held the stage throughout the nineteenth century. In 1884 there was a production with John Drew, Otis Skinner, and Ada Rehan. Of a later revival with Ada Rehan, the *Boston Transcript* (April 26, 1898) declared: "Even with the comedy in its present shape, *The Country Girl* is a play of abundant wit and sparkling intrigue. Its plot is both complicated and lucid; its turns and twists are made with startling rapidity, but the motives are all as clear as daylight, and the progress of the story is never obscure. The characters are lifelike, their doings are human and sensible, and the entire play is a thing to give infinite pleasure and satisfaction to audiences obliged to put up with our modern substitute for stage humor known as farce comedy." More recently, the expurgated version of *The Country Wife* ran in London, opening March 2, 1934, for 183 performances. The unexpurgated play ran there in 1936, with Edith Evans, Ruth Gordon, and Michael Redgrave; and in 1940. In New York, Ruth Gordon achieved 90 performances, opening November 30, 1936, with the full comedy. *Stage* (February 1937) said that the play, "packed with vivid duplicity, blatant with biological urge, tipsy with Wycherley's effervescent and fermenting dialogue, blunt, brilliant, magnificent, dumps verbal rough diamonds as from a burlap bag." Cambridge, Massachusetts, saw a production of the play for seven weeks in 1950, with Madge Elliott and Cyril Ritchard.

The question of the morality of *The Country Wife* has engaged many critics. Macaulay called the play "a licentious intrigue of the lowest and least sentimental type between an impudent London rake and the idiot wife of a country squire . . . too filthy to handle and too noisome even to approach." This mid-Victorian attitude was countered in advance by Lamb: "They break through no laws or conscientious restraints; they know none. They have got out of Christendom into the land—what shall I call it?—of cuckoldry—the Utopia of gallantry, where pleasure is duty, and the manners, perfect freedom." Steele had earlier, in the *Tatler*

(April 16, 1709), called the play "a good representation of an age when Love and Wenching were the only business of life." Hazlitt felt that Miss Peggy (the "country girl" substituted for Mistress Margery Pinchwife) "is a character that will last forever, I should hope . . . while self-will, curiosity, art, and ignorance are to be found in the same person, it will be just as good and intelligible as ever, because it is built on first principles and brought out in the fullest and broadest manner." The London Times (March 3, 1934) declared that "it is remarkable, considering what a subject Wycherley has to discuss, how little gross his language is; it is not decorous, but neither is it brutal or corrupt." The Telegraph (March 3, 1934) summed it up: The Country Wife is "a brilliant picture of an unsavoury period . . . one of the most amusing comedies in the language."

Although some of the situations in The Country Wife are borrowed from Molière's The School for Wives* and The School for Husbands*, they are handled with originality as well as ingenuity. Among the play's most brilliant scenes is that in which Pinchwife forces his wife to write a letter repelling Horner. Nowhere since Shakespeare, said James Agate in the London Times (October 25, 1936), is there "a more brilliant example of pure comedy than this famous letter-writing scene." "As innocent to behold as a snowdrop," as the London Illustrated News called her (March 1, 1924), "and as wily within as a flower of witching Oriental perfume," Margery is pressed by her husband's own insistence into taking what Alithea calls "the innocent liberty of the town," and actually has Pinchwife lead her (masked and in her sister's gown) to an assignation with her lover. Licentious as Wycherley may be, there is no denying the tart flavor of his dialogue, the bawdy fun in his situations, and the keen satire that shows excess of caution bringing on the very consequences that it feared.

THE LAND OF HEART'S DESIRE   William Butler Yeats

Along with Lady Gregory*, George Moore, and Edward Martyn, William Butler Yeats (1865-1939) gave spur to the literary revival in Ireland. This group opened the Irish Literary Theatre in Dublin on May 8, 1899. One of the plays on the opening bill was The Countess Cathleen, by Yeats. It drew upon Irish legend, to which he returned in the better known Cathleen ni Houlihan, 1902 — a picture of the ageless woman (Ireland herself) for whom the young men leave their brides, to die — as also in Deirdre, 1906, and in other plays. The theme of The Countess Cathleen, the struggle between material gains and spiritual values, also recurs in the plays of Yeats. He is best known as a poet; and his most effective plays are the one-act dramas in verse.

The Land of Heart's Desire, 1894, pictures an humble Irish home with a good-humored father, a bad-tempered mother, and a simple son with his bride, Maire. She is dissatisfied with their stodgy life, and is released by unwittingly fulfilling a fairy law: on May Day eve, she gives to the fairies, at their asking, milk and fire. The atmosphere of the household is in effective contrast with the manners of the fairy folk that tempt, then come for, Maire. When the fairy-child goes off, and Shawn seeks to clasp his bride, he finds himself holding "the bole of an ash-tree changed into her image."

This simple, poetic unfolding of an Irish folk legend gathers a quiet beauty of mood. Written for and acted by Florence Farr in London in 1894, on a bill with Shaw's *Arms and the Man**, it won immediate welcome for its tender, evocative melancholy, and has been continuously popular with little theatre groups. Its first New York production was in 1900; Mabel Taliaferro played it there in 1903; Margaret Wycherly, in 1905. The National Intercollegiate Dramatic Association presented it in Washington, D. C., in 1938.

Of the first New York production the *Sun* (October 28, 1900) declared: "Yeats made a peculiar impression by simple means and with no silly pretentiousness . . . The story was simply told, the lesson of it was clearly taught, and the whole composition was so unassuming that it had the manner of a primer tale. Yet the allegory was too obvious to require any strenuous elucidation, and the weirdness was impressive without recourse to anything confessedly abnormal." Although the *Mirror* (November 3), unappreciative of its poetry, called the play "absolutely lacking in dramatic effect," the *Times* (October 28) was more moved, by what it considered "a psychological fancy in clear language and with dramatic potency." With its poetic evocation of a mood, with the interweaving of local color and legendary tale, there is a tender swell of quiet beauty in *The Land of Heart's Desire*.

THE HOUR GLASS   *William Butler Yeats*

The direct or symbolic contrast of material aims and spiritual values continued in the plays of Yeats, through *The Shadowy Waters*, 1900 (revised in 1904 and 1906) and the one-act morality *The Hour Glass*, 1903 (in prose; rewritten in verse, 1912). Later in his career, influenced by the No plays of Japan, Yeats wrote several abstract plays for dancers. He also translated, in 1933, Sophocles' *Oedipus Rex**, his version being used by the Old Vic in 1945.

There is a direct simplicity in *The Hour Glass* that appeals to the spiritual impulse in us, as the development of the drama appeals to the aesthetic. The play shows a Wise Man, who has followed, with his pupils, the error of the ancients: "There are two living countries, the one visible and the one invisible . . . the learned in old times forgot the invisible country." The Wise Man has so persuasively taken the ancient road that in all the village only Teigne, the Fool, believes in things unseen. The Wise Man gives Teigne four pennies, with which Teigne has his shears sharpened, to cut the nets he says the ungodly have spread in the fields to catch the angels. But one angel comes to the Wise Man, warning him that he will die within the hour and, unless a believer be found, will scorch in hell. Vainly the Wise Man seeks someone with faith. All have learned his lesson; they think he is but testing them. His own children echo his words: "There is no heaven; there is no hell; there is nothing we cannot see." Then Teigne the Fool brings in his childlike faith—which the Wise Man, before he dies, prays that his pupils again may share.

The Hour Glass has been very popular among persons where its lesson may be taken for granted. Played in New York in 1904, and with Margaret Wycherly as the Fool in 1905, the play found sceptics arguing not its dramatic qualities but its theology. Thus the *New York Dramatic Mirror* (April 16, 1904) challenged the play: "It is not likely to interest 1904 audiences in America, for the reason that purgatory and hell-fire have been laughed out of the rational brain by Robert Ingersoll, and the majority of sane men and women believe in a better world than this, and also in a Supreme Being. In countries like Spain, Italy, Ireland, and France it ought to go well, but not with the critics, who are not likely to be convinced that an Irish Voltaire can in a few minutes relinquish the convictions of years on the visits of an angel, which are very few and far between." Such a review makes nonsense in the last sentence; for even one visit from an angel would carry the utmost conviction. More subtly, in its first sentence the reviewer overlooks the fact that the audience he pictures, and indeed he himself, are precisely as the Wise Man in the drama. It is these persons that need the lesson of *The Hour Glass*. The cleverest ruse of the devil is to persuade us he doesn't exist. Those that accept the existence of hell know also that God gave His Son to keep man from its torments. Others may look through the story at the general thought that life requires faith as well as reason. They can therefore accept *The Hour Glass*, as it should be accepted, for the simple drive of its dramatic beauty.

THE MELTING POT   *Israel Zangwill*

From early humorous writings Israel Zangwill (English, 1864-1926) turned in 1892 to a study of Jewish conditions in the novel *Children of the Ghetto*. This was dramatized in 1899, and with its wide popularity did much to improve the status of the Jew. Zangwill followed *Children of the Ghetto* with other novels and plays of Jewish life. The most successful and influential of these is a picture of the Jewish immigrant in America, *The Melting Pot*, 1908. The play received on the whole very favorable criticism. By many critics it was hailed as the drama that most fully captured the meaning of our expanding democracy; and the title of the play, until the First World War, was often used as a synonym for the United States.

The story of *The Melting Pot* entangles European memories with American hopes. David, a young Jewish composer, the only member of his family to survive the Kishinev massacre of 1903, has come to New York, where he falls in love with Vera Revendal, also from Russia but a non-Jew. The millionaire Quincy Davenport wants to divorce his wife and marry Vera; he brings Vera's father from Russia to prevent her marrying a Jew. David sees, in Baron Revendal, the leader of the Kishinev pogrom, and he turns from Vera. Then, on the Fourth of July, David's symphony "America" is played to an immigrant audience; David's faith in the melting pot of democracy returns, and he and Vera face the future together, as true Americans.

The Melting Pot had its premiere in Washington, October 5, 1908; it went to Chicago on the 21st, it reached New York September 17, 1909. Everywhere it kindled great excitement. In the play, David rails upon the millionaire, Quincy Davenport, as a blight upon America; from his box on opening night President Theodore Roosevelt exclaimed: "You're right; I've been warning the people against these Quincy Davenports." The President, however, objected to the immigrant's words, in the play, referring to the millionaire's desire for a divorce: "We are not native-born Americans; we hold our troth eternal." Zangwill declared that the President was no Czar and had no control over art, but he changed the line to "Not being members of the Four Hundred, we hold even our troth sacred." And, back in England (November 21), Zangwill wrote: "I am convinced that, in regard to the great mass of the American people, the married life is stabler and better than that of the English in many respects."

President Roosevelt called *The Melting Pot* "one of the best plays I've ever seen." Whereupon A. B. Walkley, in the *London Times*, exclaimed: "What a stupendous naiveté there is in such a statement as that! For, after all, what is this glorification of the amalgamated immigrants, this exaggerated freshness of the New World and staleness of the Old, this rhapsodizing over music and crucibles and statues of Liberty, but romantic claptrap?" To this, the American playwright Augustus Thomas* made rejoinder: "Having gone to the theatre with a constant enthusiasm for the last forty years, and having been professionally associated with the institution for twenty-five years, I am inclined to agree with Mr. Roosevelt."

The lawyer Clarence S. Darrow said "This drama should mark a period in our upward ascent as a nation." The financier and philanthropist Jacob H. Schiff called it "a great play—a great human canvas—a feat of genius." The drama reviewer Burns Mantle declared: "The play's message should be driven deep into the heart of every foreign-born person in the country." The *Washington Times* said in an editorial (October 10, 1908): "Has it waited for a foreigner to write a great American play? *The Melting Pot* would indicate so. For in it finds expression the very genius of our national life." The *New York Telegraph* (September 19, 1909) called it "the most powerful and splendid play of modern times."

There were dissenters. Thus, after the New York opening, Alan Dale protested: "The Jewish 'tendency of mind' is impudently idiotic." The *New York Times* more objectively objected: "It is awkward in structure, clumsy in workmanship, and deficient as literature." But the play was even more provocative, in its day, than in recent seasons have been such motion pictures as *Gentleman's Agreement* and plays that have won awards and that have roused protests like a recent one, similar to Alan Dale's, from a drama reviewer who referred to himself as a "pale-faced Protestant." (Alan Dale was the pen-name of Alfred J. Cohen.)

The *Chicago Daily News* (October 21, 1908) came nearest to the basic fault of the drama, pointing out that Zangwill "has swamped a magnificent theory in rhetorical excess, framed some vivid and tragic tableaux of Kishinev in anguish too torturing to be endured, and by his own luxurious genius for Yiddish hysteria, picturesque but ineffectual, he has nearly written a long Niagara of the woes and faults of Judea, instead of a startling American drama . . . He does not clear the air of shocking reminders, nor does he put the young tempestuous Jew into the American melting pot with his Irish, Dutch, French, and English emigrant strugglers, but leaves him still the victim of the haunting face which ordered the butchering of the Jews that fatal Easter morning."

The original draft of *The Melting Pot* did not have the description of the Kishinev massacre. Walker Whiteside, who starred in the play, had read the manuscript and thought it would fail; George Tyler, the producer, felt that it would be a hit, but that it needed the picture of Kishinev to justify David's turning from Vera. Zangwill refused to make any change; Whiteside visited him in England, read the play aloud; and Zangwill added the emphasis on the massacre. This increased the pathos but lessened the universality of the drama.

The Melting Pot remains, nevertheless, despite its over-emotional presentation of the theme, the first and still the best dramatic plea for interracial understanding and picture of the United States as a crucible where people of all the earth are being fused into that new form, the democratic American. As the *Baltimore World* (October 13, 1908) declared, "*The Melting Pot* is a prophecy—a prophecy of life that may come, that has long been dreamed of, but has never been realized." Social conditions have in many respects changed since 1908, but the vision of *The Melting Pot* remains valid, and—unfortunately—remains a dream.

THERESE RAQUIN   *Emile Zola*

The novelist Emile Zola (French, 1840-1902), founder and chief of the naturalistic school of fiction, made several efforts to write for the theatre. His first venture, at the height of the naturalistic furore, was his one lasting success. This was the dramatization of his novel *Thérèse Raquin*, 1867 (also called *Thérèse*).

The story is one of crime wreaking its own revenge: murder will out. Thérèse Raquin has come to loathe her shiftless, consumptive nincompoop of a husband, Camille, and his doting mother. She eggs on her lover, the artist Laurent, until one day they drown Camille, but their story makes his old mother thank them for trying to save him. After a year, Camille's mother herself suggests that they marry. In the bridal chamber hangs a painting of Camille by Laurent. And beneath it the couple, soul-sick with gathered horror at their crime, reproach one another. Camille's mother overhears — and is stricken with paralysis. Only her eyes are alive; but they burn with scorn and fever for revenge. Thérèse and Laurent grow more and more unable to endure their burden, until they find release in a double suicide.

The production of *Thérèse Raquin* in Paris on July 11, 1873 divided the city. The champions of naturalism hailed the play as the first tragedy in the genre. The opponents admitted the play's power, but attacked its theme and its presentation of only mean folk in sordid situations. They asked why a "slice of life" must always slice through the viscera. When London saw the play, opening October 10, 1891, in an adaptation by George Moore, at J. T. Grein's Independent Theatre, its forcefulness was equally felt. The *Graphic* declared: "The play is one of great power, and produces a deep impression by apparently simple means. The characters seem very human, the dialogue is very natural, and the atmosphere of horror is wonderfully created. By simple, subtle touches one is caused to feel the coming horror and to understand and sympathize with the soul-quakings of the guilty pair . . . As for morality, I can only say that the naturalists are the most desperately moral of all the schools." Basically, Zola in *Thérèse Raquin* presents the searching moral idea that crime brings its own punishment.

What shocked th   sensitive, in *Thérèse Raquin*, was not the
moral to be extract   the story, but the lack of moral fervor, of
moral fibre, in th   s, their loathly level of ethical unconcern;
and certain det   tion. Thus Boston audiences in 1892 were
shocked when th   bride, beneath the slain man's portrait, un-
dresses to receive   erer lover-turned-husband.

Against such   e *New York American* (December 31, 1892)
launched strong a   We are a nation of boys and virgins. It would
shame our shrin   tity, suffuse our lily-white natures with the
pink of pudicity i   ight to discover in *Thérèse Raquin* something
besides the frank   y of Zola's theme, such as the unflinching
methods of its trea   he masterly development of effective details,
the unswerving pu   f the rational, inevitable end . . . We see in
Thérèse Raquin on   cture of lust, and bourgeois lust at that . . .
When, a twelve-mo   ter the murder of the drivelling, snarling invalid Camille, Thérè   l her lover meet in the intimacy sanctioned by
marriage, we crane c   ks to miss no part of a scene concerning which
rumor has aroused c   vliest anticipations. To acknowledge to our
selves that these are t e touches of an artist giving life, color, movement, atmosphere, the ter to impress upon us his meaning — not his
craft—would be to con ourselves of an appreciation, an admiration of
what we know in our s e simplicity to be unseemly, indecent . . . To
him who views the mu   blamed play of M. Zola in a spirit free from
the hyperaesthesia of rity that afflicts the national temper, *Thérèse
Raquin* cannot fail to pi sent many of the characteristics of the mighty
tragedies which embod d the lofty scheme of Greek morals. It lifts
guilt above the fallible dgment of man, and submits its punishment to
the unerring wisdom of eity. That is the acme of human tragedy, and
that is the acme to whi t the tragic lesson of *Thérèse Raquin* ascends."

After a 1934 London roduction, Charles Morgan also emphasized the power of the play, as iewed in the eyes of the mother: "Zola saw Madame Raquin as a m ror of conscience, a personification of avenging fate . . . The audience is battered by horror and suffering. The analysis of character is elaborate and thorough. The dialogue has economy and spring."

Such qualities, combining in an onslaught upon audience emotions, have brought *Thérèse Raquin* frequent revival. London saw it in 1923, and in 1928 with Emlyn Williams as Camille. The 1934 London version was called *Thou Shalt not* ——. A powerful New York production opened October 9, 1945, with Eva Le Gallienne, and with Dame May Whitty eerily vivid as the old mother. This version ended with the mother recovering from her paralysis sufficiently to start a message informing on the couple; she does not complete her story, but they confess to the police.

Zola, in his naturalistic zeal, wanted his characters not to be played but to "live" before the public. "I wanted," he said, "to make a purely human study, free from all extraneous interest, going straight to its goal: the action lying not in any story whatsoever but in the internal conflicts of the characters; there was no longer a logic of facts, but a logic of sensations and feelings; and the dénouement became a mathematical consequence of the given problem."

Lauded as *Thérèse Raquin* has been, and powerful as it still is, the

play nonetheless lacks the exaltation of t   The reason for this
lack was set down by James Agate, in At H   Eight (1923): "Conceiving it his duty to protest against the R   ith their glorified
stories of changelings, their windy nursery   nd their *grands
mots bêtes* — the protestor went too far fo   ense and not far
enough for high tragedy. What Zola's play la   lity. But nobility
to this realist was *vieux jeux*, the worn-o   of Aeschylus and
Shakespeare, Racine, le père Hugo, the whole   tic crowd. Igno-
bility was his theme, the bee in a very cleve   *Thérèse Raquin*
tramples powerfully in the mud; it holds us   picture of the bespattered souls sinking deeper, until they   nerged. The play
stamps us with their story. But, being in th   it cannot reflect the
stars. It remains a grim picture of a passi   ed couple, torn by
their own emotions as the play tears at ours   *se Raquin*, the best
naturalistic drama by the leading figure in   vement, thus illustrates at once naturalism's limitations and its   t force.

DON JUAN TENORIO   *José Zorrilla y Moral*

One of the most familiar figures in wor   iterature is Don Juan,
whose name has become the label of the rec   ss rake and triumphant
libertine. There was, apparently, a Don Mig   l Mañara in fourteenth
century Seville, who seduced a trusting maid   then killed her father,
and spent his later days doing penance in a m   astery. Out of his story
grew the play *El Burlador de Seville* (*The Se   cer of Seville*) by Tirso
de Molina (pseudonym of the Spanish monk   briel Tellez, 1570-1648),
the first dramatization of the Don Juan tale.   this telling, the statue
comes into action. After Don Juan has seduc   Dona Anna, he kills the
Commandant Don Pedro, her father, who has   ome seeking vengeance.
In the graveyard, the statue of Don Pedro w   rns Don Juan to repent
and change his ways. Don Juan laughs, and in mockery invites the
statue to a banquet—at which the statue plung   Don Juan down to hell.
"Tirso de Molina did not invent the story of the Statue," declared the
London Times (September 23, 1949), "nobody invented it. It is a symbol
of the dominion exercised over the living by the dead, a dominion present
in the human imagination since the earliest times. When Don Juan
mocks the Statue he outrages a great taboo. In his amorous intrigues,
he is a sinner at odds with society; in his dealings with the Statue he
calls down on himself the wrath of God." This deep-rooted horror at
the knight's blasphemy combines with the fascination of his conquests to
give strong and wide appeal to the Don Juan story.

Just how Don Juan achieves his dominion over women, Molière* is
the only dramatist to indicate. In his *Don Juan, ou Le Festin de Pierre*
(. . . *or The Stone Feast*), 1665, there is a superb scene in which Don
Juan, caught between two women with whom he has been dallying,
makes each believe she is his only love. After Molière, many other playwrights retold the story: Thomas Corneille, in French, in 1673; Thomas
Shadwell, as *The Libertine*, in English, in 1676. With music by Mozart,
and libretto by Lorenzo da Ponte, Molière's play was turned into the
opera *Don Giovanni, or, The Marble Guest*. This, the most popular of
all versions of the story, had its premiere in Prague, October 29, 1787.
Its American premiere was in 1824. At the Metropolitan Opera House,

New York, it marked the debut of Antonio Scotti in 1899; in Dallas, Texas, of Ezio Pinza in 1929. A Metropolitan performance, January 23, 1908, enlisted Scotti, Feodor Chaliapin (as Don Juan's servant, Leporello), Emma Eames, Johanna Gadski, and Marcella Sembrich, with Gustav Mahler as conductor. In the opera, Leporello, an impudent rascal and poltroon, sings to Dona Elvira a list of Don Juan's conquests — in Spain, 1,003; in Turkey, 91—to a total of 2,670 women fallen to his charms.

In addition to poems and stories (Byron, Merimée, Tolstoi) plays about the fabulous libertine continued. There was a burlesque of *Don Giovanni* by T. Dibdin (English, 1771-1814) played in New York in 1819. The German Christian Grabbe combined two great symbols of man's questing in his *Don Juan and Faust*, 1829. In 1830 the Russian Pushkin* followed Molière, in his "dramatic scene" *The Stone Guest*, but by making Don Juan sincere pointed toward the admiration of Baudelaire. The French Alexandre Dumas père in 1836 wrote *Don Juan de Mañara; or, The Fall of an Angel*. This has five acts, but in mood is like a medieval mystery, with good and bad angels accompanying Don Juan throughout the play, and struggling for his soul. It contains duels and deaths by the half-dozen, seductions, suicides, elopements, murders by sword and by poison, ghosts, and spectral visions. Thackeray, in his *Paris Sketch Book*, protested against Dumas' play as immoral, indecent in its effect. About fifty years later, Edmond Haraucourt made a four-act verse play of the Dumas version, and in 1937 *Don Juan de Mañara* became an opera, with English book by Arnold Bennett and music by Eugene Goossens. In the Dumas version and its followers, Don Juan repents and ends his years in a monastery.

Perhaps heeding Thackeray—at any rate, for Victorian taste—Richard Mansfield, on May 17, 1891, appeared in *Don Juan, The Sad Adventures of a Youth*, which, he declared, "avoided every incident or allusion that might be thought indelicate." He changed the reckless rake into a little Lord Fauntleroy gone wrong. More searchingly, the Spanish playwright Echegaray*, in *The Son of Don Juan*, 1892, showed the sins of the father visited upon the son: Don Juan stands by as his child Lazarus, dying, cries (like a ghost of Ibsen's *Ghosts**) "The sun—mother—give me the sun." Bernard Shaw, in his *Dramatic Opinions and Essays* (Vol. I, 81-89) quoted a long speech of Don Juan's from Echegaray's drama, concluding that Spain had produced "a genius of a stamp that crosses frontiers." Shaw's own *Don Juan in Hell* [the vision of John Tanner (named from Don Juan Tenario) in the third act of *Man and Superman**] marks a second step in the libertine's reclamation. The first step was taken by the superb poet of French decadence, Charles Baudelaire (1821-1867), in his dramatic poem *Don Juan*, in which a Byronic gentleman, leaning on his rapier in Charon's barge crossing the Styx, disdains to take notice of the pageant of his years translated into an infernal spectacle. Baudelaire's poem was enacted in Paris in 1948; the *London Times* (September 23, 1949) declared: "The impious libertine of a Counter-Reformation Seville became a martyr, one of the greatest saints in the romantic canon . . . Damnation became apotheosis . . . The arch-Romantic, Mr. Bernard Shaw, took matters to their logical extreme in *Man and Superman* by harrowing hell and sending Don Juan heavenward after Rembrandt and Mozart."

Recent years have seen no stay in the flood of Don Juan plays. Carl Sternheim wrote one in German, 1910; James Elroy Flecker, in English verse, 1911. Three French versions are noteworthy. Henri Bataille's *The Man With the Rose,* presented in New York, with Lou Tellegen, September 5, 1921, is a modernized version, sophisticated and cynical. Edmond Rostand's *The Last Night of Don Juan,* 1922, adapted by Sidney Howard and presented in New York in 1925, on the other hand, exalts the ideals of spiritual love and womanly virtue. André Obey's *Don Juan* (played by Pierre Fresnay in Paris; likewise in London opening February 26, 1934, in French) is written as a medieval morality. Don Juan in this play represents sinning, suffering humanity, struggling, blundering, groping for happiness in a life that leads to death. Don Juan hides from his fear of death by making love to women; conquest gives him a momentary sense of power, of security. When he is about to be condemned for his rape of Anna, Elvira—who has always loved him—seeks to save him by marrying him. Don Juan thanks her, puts a dagger to his breast, and by embracing a prostitute he had set on the downward path, presses the blade into his repentant heart.

The most widely popular of the dramatic retellings of the Don Juan story is *Don Juan Tenorio,* 1844, by José Zorrilla y Moral (Spanish, 1817-1893). This was the favorite play of Emperor Maximilian, who during Zorrilla's stay in Mexico (1855-1866) had the author direct private performances at Chapultepec Castle. In many Catholic cities and towns of Spain and Spanish America, after the visits to the cemetery on All Souls' Day (November 2), Zorrilla's play is presented every year, as a sort of horrible example and dramatic catharsis. Don Juan is really bad, the *New York Herald-Tribune* (November 3, 1929) reported after such a production. "He teaches a lesson, though, in the grand manner, and in beholding — for six or seven hours — his magnificent strut, his swordplay-and-satin wickedness, you can almost have your sin and abjure it too." Zorilla's poetry is potent, the reviewer continued: "It soothes the ear, this stately verse, with its sonorous climaxes of rage, consternation, the very best *amor,* exaltation, and damnation." It is a richly surging drama, recapturing the power of the olden story.

The figure of Don Juan lends itself to many meanings. It has been viewed as embodying the constant impulse of man's body, as Faust represents the tireless impulse of man's mind. It has been viewed as showing the attempt of man to hide from his fears. It is best presented when the dramatist, like Zorrilla, presses no single symbol of his own, but shows within Don Juan qualities and urges that in lesser measure every man can recognize within himself, so that the universal human figure takes the unique and individual aspect of each one. Thus Don Juan Tenorio becomes another, a less Puritan and more catholic Pilgrim, on blundering, destructive, yearning, pathetic progress toward a goal he can only dream.

THE CAPTAIN OF KOPENICK   *Karl Zuckmayer*

An amusing and sharply pointed satire on unquestioning subservience, on the instant obedience a uniform commands, swept all of Europe with laughter in *The Captain of Köpenick,* by Karl Zuckmayer (German, b. 1896). Based on an actual incident, the play depicts the plight of an old cobbler who cannot get a passport. (In much of Europe passports are required of every citizen, even within his own town).

As a young man, cobbler Voigt was sent to prison for petty larceny, and for the rest of his life he finds himself a marked man. Unable to get a decent job, or to provide himself with a "clean" passport, he struggles more and more hopelessly until his fifty-seventh year. Then he steps forth. For he has noticed what unquestioning obedience is given a man in uniform; indeed, says the dealer in second-hand clothes: "If this uniform went for a walk without anyone in it, every soldier would salute it, it's so genuine!" In the railway station washroom of the town of Köpenick, the cobbler dons the captain's uniform. He then commandeers a troop of soldiers, marches them to the Town Hall, arrests the Mayor and sends him to Berlin, demands an accounting of the Treasurer, and accepts the town's current funds. Unfortunately, the suburban town does not have a passport office.

Voigt goes back to the Berlin slums; the hoax becomes a headline sensation. When everyone is seeking the impostor, Voigt walks into headquarters and says that, if they promise him a clean passport, he'll reveal the false captain's whereabouts. They do, and he does. The officials' mirth is so great that we are led to believe Voigt will be let off lightly. When one of them tells Voigt he was lucky, the old man retorts: "Luck is the first requirement in a commander, Napoleon said." They want to see the cobbler in the uniform and posture of command, and the play ends as Voigt gets a look at himself in a mirror and cries the notorious two words: "Im—possible!"

The Captain of Köpenick develops its story in a succession of rapid scenes. Some are soberly moving, touched with a bitter view of life, as when Voigt's brother-in-law welcomes him to stay and try to make a fresh start, though his sister fears that he may become a burden; and Voigt watches over the death-bed of their child. Most of the scenes are humorous, though even then with sober undertones, as in the attempt, in a cheap café, to bargain with a tart, who protests: "You can't ride me as though I'm a ten cent bus!" Voigt can't get work unless he is registered, and the police won't register him until he has a job. Out of his lifelong quandary Voigt emerges by a process of self-hypnosis: "I put on the uniform and then I gave myself an order, and then I went and carried it out." He acts on the principle that "a man is looked upon as he makes himself look."

The Captain of Köpenick had its premiere in Berlin in 1928, with Werner Krauss. The play, and the motion picture made of it in 1931, were banned in Germany in 1933. The story was refilmed in America in 1941, with Albert Bassermann, and has come to the stage again since the War. Its capture of the human weakness of unquestioning obedience to an outer form combines with lively movement, with natural characters and dialogue, to give the play a continuing sober significance beneath its rollicking laughter.

PLAYS BY UNKNOWN AUTHORS

THE BOOK OF JOB

"A philosophic religious dramatic dialogue of great intensity," as Leo Auerbach described it in the *Encyclopedia of Literature* (1946), *Job* has increasingly been presented in dramatic form. Some scholars believe that this book of the *Bible* was written about 400 B.C. by an Alexandrian Jew sufficiently Hellenized to be aware of the classical Greek theatre. As Richard Green Moulton showed by his arrangement in 1907, no changes in the text are needed—only in the format—to convert the poem into a great drama of Job's temptation and steadfastness under trial. "With great boldness," said the *New York Times* (March 8, 1918), "and with a frankness remarkable in the fifth or sixth century before Christ, it copes with the problem of the origin of evil and its persistent flourishing in this world . . . The final appeal is to God, who speaks in answer from the whirlwind, and bids men trust and revere His wisdom, though it passes understanding."

In an arrangement by Horace Kallen, *The Book of Job* was presented at Harvard University, May 8, 1916. It was presented in New York, March 7, 1918 with George Gaul as Job and Walter Hampden as Elihu; again in New York in 1922; in Los Angeles in 1932. Of the New York premiere, the *Times* stated: "What most deeply impressed yesterday's audience was not the profundity of the thought; it was the intense drama, the vivid struggle of wills, that underlies the poem. If the philosophic speculations of this Job lacked clarity and constructive development it was because he was one quivering agony of soul-suffering, and could only cry out to his friends and to his God to be consoled. His 'comforters' were likewise less remarkable as disquisitionists than as dramatis personae—saliently, if quite simply, characterized as pharisaical exponents of ancient wisdom that rides roughshod over present suffering. Even the Voice from the Whirlwind did not greatly impress one as accounting for evil and human woe; but it came as a stunning climax. Let those who can, enjoy *The Book of Job* as philosophy. To yesterday's audience it was high poetic drama."

We are told that the devil can cite Scripture for his purpose. In 1934, under the auspices of the German Ministry of Enlightenment and Propaganda, a production was given in Cologne of *The Play of Job the German*. This began, as does the *Bible* drama, with Satan's declaring that Job is devoted to God only because all is well with him, and God flinging His fateful challenge: on Job's response to Satan will hang the salvation of the world. But among Job's afflictions is an enemy's advance; his sons gird for war; and Job exclaims: "That is good! When the youth of a land ceases to be warlike and lusty in fighting, it lets its country go to ruin. Who will not fight shall not possess." And when, at the close, discomfited Satan retreats, the Choir sings: "Praised be the victory of the German."

The Book of Job, without such transmogrification, is a majestic and passionate dramatic poem, as Job, outside his village in the land of Uz, lifts up his voice in protest, in bewilderment, in wonder, and in joyous praise of his God. In the face of all his wretchedness, against the crude arguments of his harsh comforters, Job's exultant cry "I know that my Redeemer liveth" rings with dramatic triumph, with inner truth and shining beauty.

OCTAVIA

Preserved with the tragedies of Seneca, and sometimes attributed to him, but probably written by another in the Senecan style, *Octavia*, c. 70 A.D., is the only extant *fabula praetexta*, or classical play of Roman history.

The Roman Emperor Nero, declared a public enemy by the Senate, committed suicide in 68 A.D.; hatred of him was still intense when *Octavia* was written. The play is a sympathetic picture of his stepsister and wife, Octavia, whom Nero put aside for Poppaea. An uprising of the people in protest was summarily put down; the play ends with the lamentation of Octavia as she is being led to her death.

The play is essentially a succession of diverse scenes — of mournfulness; of vengeance; of Agrippina's ghost prophesying Nero's doom — rather than a well-knit drama. There is an effective speech by Seneca when, on his first entrance, he laments that fortune has set him high, thus preparing him for a fall; obscurity would have assured him of safety and freedom.

There are, in the play, several effective examples of stichomythia, especially the sharp exchange between Seneca and Nero. The author, with brilliant satire, makes Nero's first words an order for the death of two prominent citizens. Seneca suggests moderation; Nero defends his action. Nero is presented as a villain, and justifies himself mainly on the ground that a monarch can do what he will, and is a fool to do otherwise. Yet there is a suggestion of excuse in one phrase of the tyrant's: "Let him be just whose heart is free from fear." Any moment of the Emperor's life might be his last; his safety seemed to demand his cruelty; his cruelty brought on his death. "Crime perpetuates crime." This is the most frequent thought of ancient serious drama.

Thoroughly Senecan in its attitude, in its summoning of ghosts, in its quicker moments of dialogue, *Octavia* reveals the hand of the disciple only in its feebler construction and in the metrical simplicity of its choral odes. The play is Senecan even in its underlying dignity and faith in man. As C. L. Thompson observed: "The vitalising theme of the play is justice, the right of individuals and of the people to a square deal. It is not given them in the play; the tragic denial of it to the chief character, and the dismal failure of the people to make their protest heard, make the appeal of the play carry as no successful consummation could."

Octavia has many moments both of beauty and of power. It is especially significant as the sole surviving ancient historical drama.

QUEROLUS

Of the dramatic production, whatever it may have been, of the nine hundred years from the first to the tenth century, only one play survives, *Querolus; or, The Pot of Gold*, c. 420 A.D. Its author is unknown.

Querolus is a sequel to *The Pot of Gold** by Plautus. The Plautus play pictures the alarms and excursions of the miser Euclio, who has buried a pot of gold that is eventually brought to proper use. The later play deals with Querolus, the son of Euclio. The old man, dying, left gold of which the son knew nothing. The secret of the treasure was given to the parasite Mandrogerus. Mandrogerus, instead of telling Querolus about it, as he has promised, worms his way into the house, and by religious and astrological hocuspocus carries off the treasure-urn. It contains ashes. The chagrined Mandrogerus hurls the urn back through the window—whereupon it breaks, and reveals the gold. "We present here," says the Prologue, "a fortunate man saved by his destiny, and a trickster cheated by his own trickery."

The comedy has many lively moments, in sprightly dialogue with undercurrents of thought. Particularly effective is the first act, a long conversation between Querolus (the Complainer) and his household god, in which the god makes the point that Querolus had better bend his wishes to reality. Sober reflections flavor the piece: Everybody must pay for his fun . . . Match your desires to your powers . . . Recognize that Titus has a treasure-box, but also Titus has the gout . . . When well off, don't complain that others fare better.

Beyond these turns of thought, there are ingenious turns of plot. At the end, Mandrogerus, whom Euclio had made heir of half the estate, tries to claim the gold he thinks Querolus has recovered, but Querolus belabors him with charges of impiety for having stolen the family ashes, until the parasite begs for mercy.

While the household god presents the idea of an unchangeable fate, in that good fortune must come to Querolus, several passages in the play, such as the remarks that the most righteous are the most miserable, suggest the impact of Christianity. Man needs the help of God. Base deeds and desires are everywhere; God may work through them to good. The story of the play is a dramatic illustration of this thesis.

Some of the conditions of the time may be learned from the drama. The Prologue was addressed to a patron who provided the author "with a noble leisure which I can devote to the writing of plays." There are long dialogue discussions of philosophical, religious, social, and legal questions. Cicero was still a popular and influential figure; the audience was evidently expected to recognize Mandrogerus' pompously tragical use of Cicero's exclamation "O tempora! O mores!" (O times! O customs!). There is mild satire in the play, but (just as today, for commercial reasons, works declare that "any resemblance to actual persons is purely coincidental") then, for the author's safety, the Prologue declared: "No one should find a resemblance to reality, for we are making up the whole story."

Coming as a ray of light out of what we, in our ignorance of them, call the dark ages, *Querolus* reveals that, though manners and accidents of outward manipulation of nature may change, the essential spirit of man faces the same problems, with the same qualities and the same alternatives of action, in every age. The play is a mild but mellow comedy, its neatly rounded thoughts pressed home through a neatly rounded story.

THE CIRCLE OF CHALK

Out of a cycle of one hundred plays of the Yuan dynasty (1259-1368) in China, by way of a nineteenth century prose and verse French translation of Stanislaus Julien, *Hoei-Lan-Kin* (*The Circle of Chalk*) was adapted in 1924 in German by Klabund (pseudonym of Alfred Henchke, 1891-1928). Reinhardt's 1925 production, with Elisabeth Bergner, was a hit. The English version by James Laver, opening in London January 22, 1931, with Anna May Wong and Laurence Olivier, ran for over a year. New York, in 1933, saw a version by I. S. Richter. Erwin Piscator presented the play at his Dramatic Workshop, with Dolly Haas, in 1941 and in revivals through the next decade. From Klabund, Bertolt Brecht* drew his German *Caucasian Chalk Circle,* translated into English by Eric and Maja Bentley in 1947.

The circle is a symbol of personal integrity; and in *The Circle of Chalk* the steadfast heroine Hai Tang, subjected to many trials, sustains her integrity through all her suffering and her final elevation to the Imperial throne. When her father, oppressed by taxes, kills himself, the young Hai Tang is sold to a House of Joy. Thence, despite the bidding of Prince Po, she is bought by Ma, the tax official. Ma's first wife, the childness crone Yu Pi, poisons Ma, and declares that Hai Tang has not only committed the murder, but also stolen Yu Pi's baby, claiming it as her own. Through bribery and corruption Yu Pi presses hard upon Hai Tang. But at court the judge, disreputable and cynical drunkard though he is, subjects the two women to the traditional test of the chalk circle: the child is put within the circle and released to the two women; only the true mother can lead him out. Yu Pi tugs hard at the child; Hai Tang does not touch it. And with the wisdom of Solomon, the judge decides that Hai Tang, who would rather lose than hurt the child, is the true mother. Prince Po adds the crowning happiness when he admits that he is the father of Hai Tang's child.

When *The Circle of Chalk* was presented in Vienna, in 1925, its charm made "an impression to which the critical faculty readily surrenders". The London 1931 production showed girls in gilded cages in a House of Joy, guarded by a hideous unsexed headsman. In 1945, with more simplicity of décor, the play seemed "a pleasing piece of willow-waly." In New York the *Post* (March 26, 1941) praised its "quaintness and delicacy"; the *Christian Science Monitor* (March 27) found it "full of emotion, beauty, and vitality."

The Circle of Chalk is remarkable for the naturalness of the many characters, who seem to grow from the earthy movement of the story. There is a homely healthiness, too, in the comments of many of the figures, especially of the corruptible judge who unexpectedly (to Western minds; the Chinese knew that this style of play must have a happy ending) restores the child to its mother. There is also considerable humor in the play: sometimes this is just good fun, as when the palanquins (hobby-horse poles with a head on top) justle for place on the Peking road; sometimes it is caustic against abuses of the times, abuses still found in many lands.

There is lyrical verse of considerable beauty in *The Circle of Chalk*. Brecht's version is also poetically rich, but in its two acts the Story-teller Brecht employs seems almost to be presenting two stories, first the long-suffering woman's experiences, then the vicissitudes of the judge. It is only at the end, in the test of the circle, that he makes the stories join.

Part folk-tale, part realistic revelation of men and women urging toward good through all their weakness and evil, *The Circle of Chalk* brings simple beauty and friendly laughter and basic truths out of a far land and distant century. It is further evidence of the changing roots of human nature, and of the timelessness of art.

THE PASSION PLAY

Two themes of the medieval mystery play survive, in various modifications of the original forms, in current and widely played religious drama. One of these is in *The Passion Play*, the drama of the passion (suffering) of Jesus Christ. This presents episodes, varying from play to play, of the last days of Jesus. The play is enacted, in some communities, in annual remembrance of the lifting of a plague or other local disaster; or as a pious offering at Easter time or at the Feast of Corpus Christi. The other major surviving theme is in *The Shepherds' Play**, or some other enactment of the Nativity, the birth of Jesus, presented as part of the Christmas festival. (See *Everyman**.)

The best known drama of the passion of Christ is that which is enacted once every ten years at Oberammergau, Bavaria. This dramatic representation of the last days, the crucifixion and the resurrection of Jesus has been given by the villagers, interrupted only by the Franco-Prussian and the two World Wars, since 1634, to keep a vow made during an epidemic of the Black Death. In the early nineteenth century, miracle plays were banned in Bavaria, having become worldly, coarse, even immoral. *The Passion Play* of Oberammergau was then rewritten by Father Ottmer Weiss, of nearby Ettal Abbey, with music by Schoolmaster Rochus Dedler. Approved by the authorities, it became so popular that in 1870 the Oberammergau Burgomaster protested: "We do not wish the spectacle of our Lord's Passion, now represented here for 230 years, to be made a scheme for money-making by foreign speculators, and I enter an indignant protest against such a profanation of the intention of our play, which, descending to us as a solemn vow from our ancestors, aims at purifying the feelings from worldly thoughts." The attitude of the community has changed. The open-air theatre at Oberammergau now seats 4,000; and in 1934, at the 300th anniversary of the cessation of the plague, some 400,000 spectators attended *The Passion Play*. Performances were revived in 1950.

While the Oberammergau presentation is the best known, it is by no means the oldest of the many productions. The one at Freiburg was begun in 1264 and claims to have been shown without interruption since 1600. At Barzio, Italy, with a rather primitive text by a Genoese priest, *The Passion Play* has been presented since the early seventeenth century. A very interesting production, and perhaps the oldest continuous one, is that of the almost inaccessible town of Roquebrune, on the French Riviera. The scene in the Garden of Olives is performed under real olive trees; the company moves in solemn procession to the Stations of the Cross—and has done so annually, it is claimed, without missing a single year, since the great plague of 1467. Other quite old productions are those at Benediktbeurn, Bavaria, and St. Gall, Switzerland. Other European cities have had annual performances for many years.

With variant details, and different degrees of elaboration — *The True Mystery of the Passion*, re-enacted in Paris in 1936, was a 34,000-line play in 1582 and took six days to perform — the passion plays follow the same general pattern. Most of them begin after Judas's betrayal, presenting the Agony in the Garden, Christ before Pilate, the Condemnation, the Carrying of the Cross — at Oberammergau the most famous Christus,

Anton Lang (who acted the role 1900-1930) carried a hundred pound cross, and was suspended upon it for twenty-two minutes — the Crucifixion, the Descent from the Cross, the Resurrection, and the Ascension. The whole is a sort of Divine Comedy; its theme is mankind's redemption. The dialogue is simple, devoted; it is often crude, and usually without literary distinction. The quality of the play rises from the earnest devotion of the performers and from the simple faith of the spectators, which makes them one with the soul-story enacted before their eyes.

The law of England now prohibits representations of Jesus in any place licensed for public performance. Almost every other land with numerous Catholics has its passion plays, varying according to the spirit and customs of the country. The most elaborate in the New World is probably that given in the village of Chinantis, Guatemala, every Good Friday for some 300 years. Judas is chased by the crowds, as he shakes his bag of silver; sometimes the actor has been given really rough treatment.

The United States also has its passion plays at the Easter season. The Black Hills *Passion Play* is an old one; others seem more sporadic. Two in the east were presented over thirty years. *Veronica's Veil* was enacted beginning 1915 at Union City, New Jersey — Veronica, wife of Caiaphas, wiped the blood from the face of Jesus as He carried the Cross: the veil thus used became miracle-working. And in Brooklyn, New York, from early in this century until 1942, the Redemptorist Fathers sponsored annual productions of *Pilate's Daughter*.

Simple or elaborate, but essentially of the folk, these passion plays throughout Christendom perpetuate not only the spirit and faith they exemplify, but the essential drama of the Christ story, and the eternal spirit of the theatre—the bodying forth of things unseen, the challenge to man's powers, the surge of man's resolve and exaltation—that took its birth in the church.

THE SHEPHERDS' PLAY

Second only in popular interest to *The Passion Play** is the drama of the Nativity of Jesus. This was always well represented among the mystery plays of the tenth to the fourteenth centuries. And it is in the joyous celebration of the coming of the infant Jesus that humor seems first to have entered modern drama. "The hilarity of *The Second Shepherds' Play*," as Freedley and Reeves remarked in *A History of the Theatre* (1941), "is still funny." A production of this play of the English Wakefield cycle, of the fourteenth century, was given with marionettes at New York University, in 1938. Into the manger, where a cradle is awaiting the expected babe, comes a shepherd who has stolen a lamb. Fearful of pursuit, he looks for a place to hide it, and tucks it, covered all save the nose, into the cradle. The searchers, and others, come; all admire the new-born babe until, in the midst of the chorus of praise, it opens its mouth and says "Baa!"

Variations of *The Shepherds' Play* are still presented in many Catholic regions. In Mexico, at Christmastide, *Los Pastorales* (*The Pastoral Plays*) are enacted in the Sunday Schools, in a form tradition says was used by St. Francis in Umbria, in 1223. In the backyards, meanwhile, or in the village square, there is presented a play, *Los Pastores* (*The Shepherds*) passed down by word of mouth. Manuscripts of this do exist, some, it is claimed, set down in eleventh century Toledo; but in hundreds of Spanish-speaking towns and villages, daily for the twenty-four days from "the good night" (Christmas Eve) to Candlemas, the play is performed as in the oral tradition.

Hence there are many local variations on the basic biblical theme. Some details are widespread, such as the famous remark of the Shepherd who objects to following the Star of Bethlehem: "If Heaven wants to see me, let Heaven come to me!" This folk play contains further elements of humor, which the sober Passion Play lacks. The Devil tries to keep the angels and the shepherds from Jesus's crib. At the end, with the Devil sent howling to Hell—his tail perhaps popping with firecrackers —the shepherds raise the infant Jesus and sing a lullaby; then the cast begs the Holy Babe for His blessing.

Often the productions of these plays were decorated like the naive religious folk paintings, and as piously regarded. One in Spain was described in the London *Pictorial World* of May 22, 1880: "After the Magi had presented their gifts to Mary, who was seated beside a pasteboard manger, surrounded by pasteboard oxen, with a great deal of genuine straw about, at the tinkle of a little bell ballet girls in short skirts and pink tights darted from the side scenes and, pirouetting around the group, finally struck an attitude with their hands over the cradle and their elevated toes pointing to the audience . . . It was deeply religious to the people, and many women wept." The mingled sobriety and fun, the jollity and reverence, of these occasions, draw the fullest audience participation, and are a rich continuance of folk dramatic art. (See *Everyman**.)

The spirit of such dramas still stirs in contemporary authors. There is tenderness and true simplicity in Claudel's *The Tidings brought to Mary**. The *Bethlehem*, 1902, of Laurence Housman* is a Nativity favorite; it has been produced annually at Kinosha, Wisconsin, for the past twenty years. Henri Ghéon (French, 1875-1944) and Henri Brochet (French, b. 1898) have given us such modern Nativity plays as Ghéon's *Christmas on the Square*, 1937 (translated by Sister Marie Thomas, O.P.), and Brochet's *Noel dans le hameau perdu*, translated by M. S. and O. R. Goldman as *Christmas at the Crossroads*. Mrs. Goldman has written such plays in America. These are intended for production by amateur religious groups and are presented in various parts of this country and Canada, as well as France, every Christmastide. They are deftly as well as reverently written, by intelligent, sensitive, and skilful hands; and they show that the basic drives of the theatre—its first, its fundamental and its highest appeal, that lifts the soul in exaltation—still gather power wherever the drama takes form.

EVERYMAN

In the Middle Ages, when the church official with his poking-stick could not keep the peasants awake through the long sermons in Latin, some wise old priest decided to let the people, in their own language, know what was going on. And outside the church, one Sunday, was a sort of float, with a man holding a boy over a butcher-block; in the vernacular, the gaping crowd was told the story of Abraham about to sacrifice his son Isaac to the Lord. In this manner, the mystery play was born, with—as a modern press-agent might put it—"God's mysteries made manifest."

At first, only Bible stories were shown. Later, episodes in the lives of saints and holy martyrs were pictured; some scholars call these miracle plays. The earliest known in England is the play of St. Katherine, performed about 1100 by the schoolboys of Dunstable. Such plays were popular for some 400 years. Many sections of England developed series of mystery and miracle plays; among the few of these extant are the York, the Wakefield, and the Chester cycles, of the thirteenth and fourteenth centuries. Dramatically effective episodes abound in them. In the Wakefield play of *The Crucifixion*, for example, there is a superb touch of heroic dignity in the complete silence of Jesus through the long dialogue of his four torturers.

The Church drew upon the assistance of the various guilds to present these plays; after a while, the guilds took them over. The Bakers' Guild, accustomed to roasting and boiling, put on *The Harrowing of Hell*; the Carpenters' Guild put on *Noah's Ark*. The York Cycle was probably developed by three poets with the aid of forty-eight guilds. Its plays run from Creation to Doomsday, including Adam's fall, the Passion, Resurrection, and Ascension, the fall of Lucifer, and Christ's harrowing of Hell. In an abridged and modernized form, the York Cycle was presented in 1951 at the Festival of Britain, its first performance since 1570.

There were often considerable tenderness and pathos, with occasional subtle character sketches, in the mystery plays. Thus, when little Isaac becomes aware that his father is preparing to sacrifice him to the Lord, he is overcome by fear; his pleadings that he be spared are pitiful; but gradually he senses his father's own struggle and anguish, until, mastering his fear of death, the boy not only accepts the situation but seeks to assuage his parents' grief.

As soon as the Guilds relieved the sober churchmen of the burden of presenting the mysteries, the introduction of another note was inevitable. Youth everywhere is irrepressible; with the entrance of the apprentices came horseplay and humor. Noah's wife, for instance, refuses to enter the ark without her neighbor gossips, and must be hauled aboard, kicking and squealing. While the empty cradle waits in the stable, for the soon-to-be-born Jesus, a boy hurries in with a lamb he has stolen. Shepherds are in quick pursuit; he tucks it into the cradle, and persons coming in bend over to admire the beautiful baby, until it bleats at them. Out of such episodes in the miracle and the mystery play, native comedy —as in the English *Gammer Gurton's Needle**—came to birth. (For further discussion, see *The Passion Play** and *The Shepherds' Play**.)

In the fifteenth century, another form of drama came into being. As the miracle and the mystery presented a religious story, the morality presented an ethical lesson, by means of an allegory in dialogue. The characters were such figures as Death, The World, Justice, Peace; most popular was Vice, played either as a devil or as a fool. These moralities were very popular in the reign of Edward IV of the house of York, of the white rose (king 1461-70, 1471-83) when England was torn asunder by the Wars of the Roses (1455-1485), with the Princes killed in the

Tower, with intriguing, and fighting in France, with the introduction into England of printing and the silk industry—a turbulent, disorderly time, when a man might well think to his soul. And at the market-fairs, everyone eagerly awaited the covered wagon, atop which a platform was adorned with "stations", from Heaven's Gate at the left to Hell's Mouth gaping at the far right, through which the damned would be dumped to Hell (in the dressing room below). Between Heaven and Hell were the earthly stopping-places, church, home, tavern, of mankind's journey.

Far and away the best of these dramatized allegories is the English *Everyman*, c. 1450. It is probably from an earlier Dutch version; the pattern is that of a Buddhist parable told in *Barlaam and Jehoshaphat*, perhaps by John of Damascus, who died in 1090.

Left in the libraries for a couple of centuries, *Everyman* was revived in 1901 by William Poel, whose simple, moving production was joined in 1902 by Ben Greet, with Edith Wynne Matthison as Everyman. The latter gave the play its first American performance, in New York, October 13, 1902, and it is impossible to count the revivals since. *Theatre* magazine (November 1902) declared that the "naive allegory is rendered with simple reverence and strangely moving effect . . . its sombre morality far outweighs the occasional suggestions of pensive poetic charm . . . Its fundamental lesson is effective now and always, since, with Death's inevitable summons awaiting us, 'this memory all men may have in mind'."

The *London Times*, in 1939, exclaimed: "Curious how much better the play acts than it reads!" A little thought, however, makes this less strange. An abstract quality, on a printed page, may seem to have no more life than a wooden signpost moved mechanically. But on the stage, how present Slovenry, save like the town drab? How Drunkenness, save like the tavern toss-pot, with personal touches the watching villagers will recognize? On the stage, Death looms with a fearful actuality, and Greed and Friendship and the Five Wits come to life indeed. The morality play is thus the beginning of the satirical picture of everyday life in the drama.

Ben Greet continued his production of *Everyman* in England and America for some thirty-five years. It has also been played by college and community groups every year; for instance, in 1936, it was presented by the Barter Theatre, and by the WPA in special performances in churches on Sunday. After a 1929 performance at Columbia University, New York, Montrose J. Moses, in the *Columbia Institute Magazine* (November), praised its "permanence of human characterization, with clearness and definiteness of allegory . . . by far the best knit, the most closely wrought morality of all time . . . in such a morality as this, we see the artist-playwright dominant over the ecclesiastic." Of an earlier New York performance, with Charles Rann Kennedy, Edith Wynne Matthison, Constance Bennett, and Pedro de Cordoba, the *New York Dramatic Mirror* (January 26, 1918) declared that "the vitality of this old play still endures." In 1955 it went on tour with college casts in California and in New England.

In the German town of Salzburg, in the open square before the cathedral, the lavish director Max Reinhardt, on June 11, 1913, gave a performance of a German version of *Everyman — Jedermann*, by Hugo von Hofmannsthal. The enthusiastic reception of this adaptation led to the holding of an annual festival at Salzburg, and to productions far and wide. An English adaptation of the German version, by Sir John Martin-Harvey, called *Via Crucis*, was presented at Stratford-on-Avon, December 15, 1922, and in London and New York in 1923. This was also played at the Hollywood Bowl, California, in 1936, with Ian Keith (and, later, Lionel Atwood) as Everyman, with Peggy Wood and Lionel Braham. In the meantime, the Reinhardt production itself came to the Century Theatre, New York, in 1927, with a German cast including Alexander Moissi as Everyman, Vladimir Sokoloff as Death, Arnold Korff, Maria Solveg, Harold Kreutzberg, Dagny Servaes, Lili Darvas, Hermann Thimig, and Hans Thimig.

The German *Jedermann* makes Everyman a wealthy burgher; Death interrupts him during a lavish banquet for his *belle amie*. The setting and the spectacular mode of presentation were on the grand Reinhardt scale that set the pace for Hollywood's most "stupendous" productions. They were far from the quiet earnestness and ominous sobriety of the English morality play. *Jedermann*, said Samuel Chotzinoff at Salzburg, August 22, 1936, "has everything but simplicity"—but it achieved, on its prodigal scale, a powerful and lasting effect. Brooks Atkinson, indeed, after a New York production by refugee actors, wondered (May 9, 1941) whether *Jedermann* doesn't go too far: "Taken out of its period, *Everyman* seems to modern ears uncomfortably like an immorality play. For Everyman manages to have a lot of cake and eat it, too. He is rich and sinful; he . . . holds iniquitous wassail with his mistress and revellers. Although an eleventh hour conversion gets him into heaven with enviable alacrity, it takes a keener eye than this theatregoer has to detect any improvement in his moral character."

About the Reinhardt production, however, there were few dissenting opinions, although Alexander Woollcott found himself "smouldering with resentment over the great wealth of the protagonist." There is, indeed, a change of emphasis, of values, from the English *Everyman* to the German *Jedermann*; instead of you or me receiving an awful summons, we watch the less immediately self-involving spectacle of a rich man trying to get into heaven. But, on its own terms, *Jedermann*, as Gilbert Gabriel said (December 8, 1927), "is crammed with splendors for the eye, largesse of bells and uplifting voices for the ear — when God the Invisible spoke out of the unplumbed blackness of the opening scene, it was as if He had torn a Vesuvius from the forehead of the earth, and were using it for a megaphone. And Death answered Him in cruel, feverish staccatos, his words splintering as jaggedly as bleached bones." Brooks Atkinson also found this production imposing: "Dr. Reinhardt's command of all the instruments of the theatre achieves two or three effects that are nothing short of miraculous. For instance, after the orchestra has sounded the opening bars of Einar Nilson's score, antiphonal choirs, dimly lighted, sing from opposite boxes just under the dome of the theatre. And nothing else anywhere in the performance communicates the supernatural mood of the legend as forcefully as the spirit cries of 'Jedermann!' 'Jedermann!' 'Jedermann!', some far off, some frightfully close at hand, while Everyman at his banquet table listens as though to the voice of Doom. They are dying words; they summon Everyman to the judgment of his Maker. Dr. Reinhardt has timed them and varied them with the stygian grimness of Death itself."

That the play is most effective when produced simply was evident in

a Poel production in the open air, with Everyman at the end going down
into an actually dug grave, while sparrows were twittering by.

Jedermann is a tremendous and a moving spectacle; *Everyman* is a
tremendously moving play. Its very simplicity gives it a deeper impact,
a wider import. The morality plays, said W. H. Haddon Squire in the
Christian Science Monitor (September 18, 1943), "are as eloquent of
those who made them, acted them, and listened to them, as are the
cathedrals that gave them birth — Gothic was first and foremost a folk
art." *Everyman*, he continued, holds its strength through the "vividness
of its metaphor and imagery and the clean, square-cut vigor of its
English." There is a quiet dignity in Everyman, as he finds his earth-
bound qualities (his companions) slipping from him, that marks man's
noblest response to the one summons all men must heed. The journey
of Everyman, simply told in dramatic form, bears a spell of beauty, and
a challenge of conduct, for us all.

MASTER PIERRE PATELIN

The farce of *Master Pierre Pathelin* (later printed as *Patelin*) is the
earliest extant comedy of the modern theatre. It was probably written
by a lawyer about 1464. Produced in 1469, it was published at Lyons in
1485. The farce has been played again and again, and altered down the
ages. A lively New York production opened March 20, 1916, with Helen
Westley, Roland Young, Glenn Hunter, and Edward J. Ballantyne of the
Washington Square Players, which became the Theatre Guild. John
Masefield directed the play in London in 1926. The play may be by
Antoine de la Salle (c. 1398-1461); the original is in eight-syllable
verses. The most frequently used French version is that of Brueys
(1640-1725) and Palaprat (1659-1721), called *Lawyer Pathelin*. The
most frequently used adaptation in America is that of Moritz Jagendorf,
in Federal Theatre productions of 1938, and in many little theatres since.

The play consists of two bits of amusing trickery, cleverly intertwined. Lawyer Patelin, after long bargaining with a draper, marches
off with a roll of cloth, the draper to follow for payment. Come to
Patelin's house, the draper finds Patelin in bed. Then follows a scene of
which, said Henry James in the *Galaxy* (April, 1887), "the liveliest description must be ineffective. Patelin pretends to be out of his head, to
be overtaken by a mysterious malady which has made him delirious, not
to know the draper from Adam, never to have heard of the dozen ells of
cloth, and to be altogether an impossible person to collect a debt from.
To carry out this character, he indulges in a series of indescribable antics,
out-Bedlams Bedlam, frolics over the room dressed out in the bed
clothes and chanting the wildest gibberish, bewilders the poor draper
to within an inch of his own sanity, and finally puts him utterly to rout."
Patelin then dances triumphantly with his wife.

To lawyer Patelin comes a shepherd, accused of stealing a sheep.
Patelin bids the fellow, no matter what is asked him, answer only "Baa!"
Before the judge, Patelin argues that the shepherd has lived so long with
his flock that he has become as simple and as innocent as the sheep themselves; he could not possibly have stolen one of them. But the owner
of the sheep is the very draper Patelin has outwitted, and the lawyer is

wearing a suit made of the draper's cloth. On seeing him, the draper begins to cry out for his cloth or his money. The judge tries vainly to keep the draper to the question of the stolen sheep, until in exasperation he dismisses the case, bidding the shepherd never again come before him.

Alone with his client, Patelin rubs his complacent hands. Congratulating himself on the cleverness with which he has saved his client, Patelin asks for his fee. The shepherd looks at him, and says "Baa!"

These intertwined anecdotes unite in an uproarious comedy. In current playing, directors usually shorten the scene of Patlein's pretended delirium, in which, railing in several dialects, he chases the draper as though trying to drive out the devil. The delight with which we see the cheater cheated makes us completely overlook the sorry state of the draper, who has been doubly duped.

The judge, confused by the draper's demanding his cloth, several times exclaims: "Revenons à ces moutons!" (Let's get back to these sheep!) This expression (reproduced by Rabelais as "Retournons à nos moutons") has become a proverbial reminder when someone slips away from the subject. *Master Pierre Patelin* is a vivid reminder of the escapades and trickeries of the middle ages. While it does have a bedroom scene, it is not only the first French farce, but almost the only one without emphasis on sex.

ARDEN OF FEVERSHAM

Arden of Feversham, 1579?, like *Machinal* of recent years, draws its plot from a notorious murder. This one, recorded by Holinshed, took place in February, 1550-1. Since the characters are commoners, the play has been called the first middle-class tragedy. George Lillo, who later wrote the domestic tragedy *The London Merchant**, also wrote a play based on the Arden story.

Mistress Arden and her lover Mosbie—an emotional, quarreling couple, with Mosbie always softening to Alice Arden's allure — hire two ruffians, Black Will and Shakebag, to murder Arden. As Arden, with his friend Franklin, is returning home, he is attacked and killed. The plot being discovered, mainly through the detective work of Franklin, the guilty pair are put to death.

Published in 1592 by Edward White, who also issued unauthorized printings of Shakespeare's plays, *Arden of Feversham* is probably a revised version of *The History of Murderous Mychaell*, listed in the Revels Office as performed in 1579 at Whitehall by the Lord Chamberleyne's servants. Some have thought that *The Tragedy of Mr. Arden of Feversham* — to give the play its full title as printed — is an early work of Shakespeare. Its verse is of uneven quality, with some lines that give substance to such attribution.

Especially effective is the dramatic irony with which the play moves toward the murder. On the road, Franklin is telling Arden a story of a faithless wife, confronted with and trying to outface the clear evidence of her guilt. Franklin has a sick spell; his breath grows short, he cannot go on with the tale, which Arden is eager to have him continue—until, in a moment, the murderers put Arden beyond all further hearing.

Few plays of Tudor times deal with other folk than kings and nobles. The drama that finds importance in the lives of ordinary folk, through

Lillo and Ibsen* to the domestic dramas of today, Tennessee Williams'* and such popular probing as *The Death of a Salesman**, has an early forceful forerunner in the tragedy of *Arden of Feversham.*

BABES IN THE WOOD

Like Topsy, the British Christmas spectacle that is still called a pantomime "just growed" in the late nineteenth and early twentieth century. In part fairy tale, in part burlesque of current events and personalities, the pantomime employs dance and song, spectacular theatrical effects and tricky devices, comic lines and funny situations, pageantry, elaborate or fantastic costumes, characters drawn from the Bible, from British history, from continental folktale and legend—and mixes a madcap merry potpourri for the holiday season. A frequently revived pantomime is *The Forty Thieves,* and another favorite is the lovely pantomime based on the fairy tale of *Cinderella,* which, presented annually at the Christmas season, remained for more than a hundred performances in 1883, 1893, 1895, 1905, 1922, 1925, 1931, 1934, 1936, 1939, 1942, 1943, 1945. Drawn from a widespread folk story retold by Grimm, which was fashioned also into the opera *Hänsel and Gretel**, the most popular of these Christmas pantomimes is *Babes in the Wood.*

In Allardyce Nicoll's *Appendix B*: Catalogue of plays from 1850 to 1900, in his *History of Late 19th Century Drama,* there are two pages listing licensed plays called *Babes in the Wood,* as the Christmas pantomime was altered from year to year. The *Babes in the Wood* pantomimes were in blossom by 1875. Among the most popular of these annual extravaganzas have been the one opening December 26, 1888, which ran for 176 performances; that opening December 27, 1897, for 135; December 26, 1907, for 116; December 26, 1920, for 108; December 24, 1941, for 114; December 23, 1942, for 113. The 1938 production at Drury Lane had over 200 in the cast.

The two "babes" are usually Dorothy and Norman, or Marjorie Daw and Jack Daw. Their wicked and childless uncle (The Duke; Baron Hardup; Baron Bluster) sends them into the woods, with two ruffians who are to kill them. These ruffians (Tuff and Duff; Ta-ra-ra and Boom-de-ay) fight one another, and the children run off. The wood is Sherwood Forest; hence Robin Hood and Maid Marian appear. (Some versions use the title *The Babes in the Wood and Bold Robin Hood.*) With less excuse, Noah and the creatures of the ark parade; or a living alphabet; or the mantel-piece porcelains come to life in eighteenth century costumes. The Court of the Snow Queen spreads forth like a three-dimension Valentine, a gorgeous spectacle, with fairies flying in the snow; or Neptune's Grotto glitters in shimmering green, with mermaids and undersea sprites. Demons, fairies, gnomes, abound in elfin dances; and ever and anon a clown, or an ass-headed oaf, or a mischievous spirit, sings a patter-song or a satirical topical lyric. At some late hour, the lost boy blows his horn, Robin Hood comes to the rescue of the Babes, and Fairy Goodwill brings the bad Baron to proper repentance.

Dozens of authors, song writers, composers, and comic concocters of quips and cranks and wanton wiles have through the years had fingers in these Christmas puddings. Augustus Harris was responsible for productions of the 1890's. The 1905 version was mainly by A. A. Milne*. Horace Lennard wrote the 1940 book. Many of the comedians have supplied their own material. Some of the songs remain for successive versions; others are sung for a season, and replaced. There is constant freshness and variety, over a basic pattern that runs on through the years.

A wholly satiric travesty of *Babes in the Wood* was presented in London as a subscription production (thus avoiding the censor), in 1939, by Unity Theatre. The Queen said to King Useless the Useless: "All right, be huffy and abdicate." The wicked uncle carried an umbrella, looked like Chamberlain, and gave the Babes to the ruffians Hitler and Mussolini. The Fairy Wish-Fulfilment waved her wand. Lady Astor and the Cliveden set sang "England is made safe for our class"; but Robin Hood—the spirit of old England—arrived in time to save the Babes and their land. This political burlesque traded upon the popularity, but could effect no permanent distortion, of the Christmas pantomime. Fresh and in honest delight and love of living, the pattern is an ever popular one; for the 1950 Christmas season, the British on their tight little isle produced 150 pantomimes, with 20,000 performers.

Babes in the Wood is the most varied, the most spectacular, the most popular, and the most delightful, of the recurrent Christmas pantomimes. And the Christmas pantomime is a colorful and happy capture of the hopeful and ever resurgent free spirit of England, romping in the theatre to celebrate the eternal upward rouse of men of good will.

INDEX

Listed below in Roman type are those plays which are given detailed treatment in this book under the titles cited. Alternate titles, in English or other languages, and titles of plays discussed within an article, are in italics.